THE OXFORD HAN[

EDMUND SPENSER

THE OXFORD HANDBOOK OF

EDMUND SPENSER

Edited by

RICHARD A. McCABE

OXFORD
UNIVERSITY PRESS

OXFORD
UNIVERSITY PRESS

Great Clarendon Street, Oxford, OX2 6DP,
United Kingdom

Oxford University Press is a department of the University of Oxford.
It furthers the University's objective of excellence in research, scholarship,
and education by publishing worldwide. Oxford is a registered trade mark of
Oxford University Press in the UK and in certain other countries

Published in the United States of America by Oxford University Press
198 Madison Avenue, New York, NY 10016, United States of America

British Library Cataloguing in Publication Data
Data available

Library of Congress Cataloging in Publication Data
Library of Congress Control Number 2010930300

ISBN 978–0–19–922736–5 (Hbk)
ISBN 978–0–19–870967–1 (Pbk)

In memory of
Jenny McCabe (1928–2008)
'But yet the end is not'

PREFACE

THE forty-two essays that compose this *Handbook* attempt to examine the entire canon of Spenser's work in the light of current critical concerns and the imminent publication of a new OUP edition of the *Complete Works* to replace the Johns Hopkins *Variorum* (1932–57). The five sections into which they are arranged are intended to be neither discrete nor exclusive, as frequent cross-referencing across the volume indicates. Part I, 'Contexts', seeks to elucidate the circumstances in which the poetry and prose were written, and suggests some of the major political, social, and professional issues with which Spenser's writing engages. Part II, 'Works', presents a series of new readings of the canon informed by the most recent scholarship. Part III, 'Poetic Craft', provides a detailed analysis of what Spenser termed the poet's 'cunning', the linguistic, rhetorical, and stylistic skills that distinguish his writing. Part IV, 'Sources and Influences', examines a wide range of subtexts, intertexts, and analogues that locate the works within the literary conventions, traditions, and genres upon which Spenser draws—and not infrequently subverts. Part V, 'Reception', grapples with the huge issue of Spenser's effect on succeeding generations of editors, writers, painters, and book-illustrators, while also attempting to identify the most salient and influential strands in the critical tradition. No such *Handbook* can hope to be exhaustive, let alone definitive. The aim is to contribute to an ongoing process of analysis, appreciation, and response by providing contemporary readers with an informed and provocative basis for further study. No 'agreed' view of Spenser emerges from this work. The contributors approach the texts from a variety of viewpoints and employ diverse methods of critical interpretation. The *Handbook*, like the canon it examines, invites plurality of response.

In designing the layout and content I am indebted to suggestions from many scholars and contributors, in particular to Patrick Cheney, Tom MacFaul, Bart Van Es, and the very generous and constructive scholars who read the proposal for the Press. They helped to bring clarity to the enterprise; such things of darkness as remain I acknowledge mine. Especial thanks are also due to Andrew McNeillie and Jacqueline Baker of OUP, and to the staff of the Bodleian Library. I am grateful also to many of my colleagues at Merton College, Oxford, for fielding a wide range of enquiries of an historical, classical, philosophical, and bibliographical nature, and to the Fellow Librarian Julia Walworth. Finally I am grateful to the forty-three other contributors who collaborated with me and one another to bring this project to fruition.

Richard McCabe

Merton College, Oxford

CONTENTS

....

List of Illustrations   xi
List of Abbreviations   xiv
List of Contributors   xvii

Introduction   1
RICHARD A. MCCABE

PART I. CONTEXTS

1. Spenser's Life   13
   WILLY MALEY

2. Spenser and Religion   30
   CLAIRE MCEACHERN

3. Spenser and Politics   48
   DAVID J. BAKER

4. Spenser's Secretarial Career   65
   CHRISTOPHER BURLINSON AND ANDREW ZURCHER

5. Spenser, Plantation, and Government Policy   86
   CIARAN BRADY

6. Spenser's Patrons and Publishers   106
   WAYNE ERICKSON

7. Spenser's Biographers   125
   PAUL D. STEGNER

PART II. WORKS

8. *A Theatre for Worldlings* (1569)
    TOM MACFAUL   149

9. *The Shepheardes Calender* (1579)
    CLARE R. KINNEY   160

10. *Letters* (1580)
    JOSEPH CAMPANA   178

11. *The Faerie Queene* (1590)
    LINDA GREGERSON   198

12. *Complaints* and *Daphnaïda* (1591)
    MARK DAVID RASMUSSEN   218

13. *Colin Clouts Come Home Againe, Astrophel,* and
    The Doleful Lay of Clorinda (1595)
    PATRICK CHENEY   237

14. *Amoretti* and *Epithalamion* (1595)
    ROLAND GREENE   256

15. *The Faerie Queene* (1596)
    ELIZABETH JANE BELLAMY   271

16. *Fowre Hymnes* and *Prothalamion* (1596)
    DAVID LEE MILLER   293

17. *A Vewe of the Presente State of Ireland* (1596, 1633)
    ELIZABETH FOWLER   314

18. *Two Cantos of Mutabilitie* (1609)
    GORDON TESKEY   333

19. 'Lost Works', Suppositious Pieces, and Continuations
    JOSEPH L. BLACK AND LISA CELOVSKY   349

PART III.   POETIC CRAFT

20.   Spenser's Language(s): Linguistic Theory and Poetic Diction   367
       DOROTHY STEPHENS

21.   Spenser's Metrics   385
       JEFF DOLVEN

22.   Spenser's Genres   403
       COLIN BURROW

23.   Spenser and Rhetoric   420
       PETER MACK

24.   Allegory, Emblem, and Symbol   437
       KENNETH BORRIS

25.   Authorial Self-Presentation   462
       RICHARD A. MCCABE

PART IV.   SOURCES AND INFLUENCES

26.   Spenser and the Bible   485
       CAROL V. KASKE

27.   Spenser and Classical Literature   503
       SYRITHE PUGH

28.   Spenser and Classical Philosophy   520
       ANDREW ESCOBEDO

29.   Spenser and History   538
       BART VAN ES

30.   Spenser, Chaucer, and Medieval Romance   553
       ANDREW KING

31.   Spenser and Neo-Latin Literature   573
       LEE PIEPHO

32.   Spenser and Sixteenth-Century Poetics   586
       ELIZABETH HEALE

33. Spenser and Italian Literature   602
    JASON LAWRENCE

34. Spenser and French Literature   620
    ANNE LAKE PRESCOTT

PART V.   RECEPTION

35. Spenser's Textual History   637
    JOSEPH LOEWENSTEIN

36. Spenser's Literary Influence   664
    MICHELLE O'CALLAGHAN

37. Spenser and the Visual Arts   684
    CLAIRE PRESTON

38. The Formalist Tradition   718
    DAVID SCOTT WILSON-OKAMURA

39. The Historicist Tradition in Spenser Studies   733
    JOHN D. STAINES

40. Spenser and Gender Studies   757
    THERESA KRIER

41. Psychoanalytical Criticism   775
    ELIZABETH D. HARVEY

42. Postcolonial Spenser   792
    ANDREW HADFIELD

Index   807

List of Illustrations

Chapter 9 (Kinney)

9.1.   *The Shepheardes Calender* (1579). Title page.
       [Bodleian Library: 4 F 2 (11) Art. BS.]   161

9.2.   *The Shepheardes Calender* (1579). *Aprill.*
       [Bodleian Library: 4 F 2 (11) Art. BS.]   164

Chapter 24 (Borris)

24.1.   *Be Moderate, Not Credulous,* from Andrea Alciato, *Emblemata*
        (Lyons: Guillaume Rouille, 1551), 22.
        Courtesy of the Thomas Fisher Rare Books Library,
        University of Toronto.   439

24.2.   Author's Impresa, *With Body on Earth and Mind in the Heavens,*
        from Gabriele Simeoni, *Le imprese heroiche et morali,* title page;
        in Paolo Giovio, *Dialogo dell'imprese militari et amorose*
        (Lyons: Guillaume Rouille, 1574).
        Courtesy of the Thomas Fisher Rare Books Library,
        University of Toronto.   441

24.3.   Title page, from Piero Valeriano, *Hieroglyphica* (Lyons:
        Thomas Soubron, 1595).
        Courtesy of the Centre for Reformation and Renaissance
        Studies, Toronto.   443

Chapter 37 (Preston)

37.1.   Epigram 5 (anonymous woodcut), (Jan Van der Noot, *A Theatre for
        Voluptuous Worldlings* (1569)). Reproduced by kind permission
        of the Syndics of Cambridge University Library.   692

37.2.   *August* eclogue (anonymous woodcut), (Edmund Spenser, *The
        Shepheardes Calender* (1579)). Reproduced by kind permission
        of the Syndics of Cambridge University Library.   693

37.3.   *November* eclogue (anonymous woodcut), (Edmund Spenser,
        The Shepheardes Calender (1579)). Reproduced by kind permission
        of the Syndics of Cambridge University Library.   694

37.4.   William Kent (engraving), the old woman's house (Edmund
        Spenser, *The Faerie Queene* (1751)). Reproduced by kind permission
        of the Syndics of Cambridge University Library.   696

37.5.   William Kent (engraving), the House of Pride (Edmund Spenser,
        The Faerie Queene (1751)). Reproduced by kind permission
        of the Syndics of Cambridge University Library.   697

37.6.   William Kent (engraving), Britomart and Merlin (Edmund
        Spenser, *The Faerie Queene* (1751)). Reproduced by kind permission
        of the Syndics of Cambridge University Library.   698

37.7.   William Kent (engraving), Arthur and Merlin (Edmund Spenser,
        The Faerie Queene (1751)). Reproduced by kind permission
        of the Syndics of Cambridge University Library.   699

37.8.   Louis Fairfax-Muckley (woodcut), Cambel and the Mond brothers
        (Edmund Spenser, *The Faerie Queene* (1897)). Reproduced by
        kind permission of the Syndics of Cambridge University Library.   700

37.9.   Louis Fairfax-Muckley (woodcut), Geryoneo (Edmund Spenser,
        The Faerie Queene (1897)). Reproduced by kind permission
        of the Syndics of Cambridge University Library.   701

37.10. Arthur J. Gaskin (woodcut), *Januarie* eclogue (Edmund Spenser,
        The Shepheardes Calender (1896)). Reproduced by kind permission
        of the Syndics of Cambridge University Library.   702

37.11. Walter Crane (woodcut), *Januarie* eclogue (Edmund Spenser,
        The Shepheardes Calender (1898)). Reproduced by kind permission
        of the Syndics of Cambridge University Library.   703

37.12. Walter Crane (woodcut), *August* eclogue (Edmund Spenser,
        The Shepheardes Calender (1898)). Reproduced by kind permission
        of the Syndics of Cambridge University Library.   705

37.13. Walter Crane (woodcut), Britomart and the tapestries of Busirane
        (Edmund Spenser, *The Faerie Queene* (1894–6)). Reproduced by
        kind permission of the Syndics of Cambridge University Library.   706

37.14. Walter Crane (woodcut), Busirane (Edmund Spenser, *The Faerie
        Queene* (1894–6)). Reproduced by kind permission of the Syndics
        of Cambridge University Library.   707

37.15. H. J. Ford (watercolour), the seven-headed serpent (Andrew Lang,
        The Red Romance Book (1905)). Reproduced by kind permission
        of the Syndics of Cambridge University Library.   708

37.16. George Stubbs, *Isabella Saltonstall as Una* (1782), reproduced by kind permission of The Fitzwilliam Museum, Cambridge.   709

37.17. Henry Fuseli, *Prince Arthur's Dream of the Fairy Queen* (c.1785–8), reproduced by permission of the Kunstmuseum, Basel.   710

37.18. John Singleton Copley, *The Red Cross Knight with Fidelia and Speranza* (1793), reproduced by kind permission of the National Gallery, Washington, D.C.   711

37.19. William Blake, *The Characters of The Faerie Queene* (c.1825), reproduced by kind permission of the Syndics of Cambridge University Library.   712

37.20. F. R. Pickersgill, *Amoret, Aemylia, and Prince Arthur in the Cottage of Sclaunder* (1845), reproduced by kind permission of Tate Britain.   713

List of Abbreviations

....

Unless otherwise specified all quotations from Spenser's poetry and prose in this *Handbook* are from the following editions, abbreviated as below:

Spenser 1989   *The Shorter Poems*, ed. W. Oram et al. New Haven, CT: Yale University Press, 1989.
Spenser 1999   *Spenser: The Shorter Poems*, ed. R A. McCabe. Harmondsworth: Penguin Books, 1999.
Spenser 2001   *The Faerie Queene*, ed. A. C. Hamilton. Text ed. H. Yamashita and T. Suzuki. Harrow: Longman Annotated Poets, 2001.
Prose   *Spenser's Prose Works*, ed. R. Gottfried. Johns Hopkins *Variorum Edition*, vol. ix. Baltimore, MD: Johns Hopkins Press, 1949.

Other regularly cited editions of Spenser are abbreviated as follows:

Spenser 1912   *Poetical Works*, ed. J. C. Smith and E. De Sélincourt. Oxford: Oxford University Press.
Spenser 1997   *A View of the Present State of Ireland*, ed. A. Hadfield and W. Maley. Oxford: Blackwell, 1997.
Variorum   *The Works of Edmund Spenser*, ed. E. Greenlaw et al., 11 vols. Baltimore, MD: Johns Hopkins Press, 1932–57.

Regularly cited reference works and databases are abbreviated as follows:

Cal. Car. MSS *Calendar of Carew Manuscripts*
CSPI   *Calendar of State Papers Irish*
CSPD   *Calendar of State Papers Domestic*
CSPS   *Calendar of State Papers Spanish*
CSPF   *Calendar of State Papers Foreign*
Carpenter   F. I. Carpenter, *A Reference Guide to Edmund Spenser*. Chicago: University of Chicago Press, 1923.
Cummings   R. M. Cummings (ed.), *Spenser: The Critical Heritage*. New York: Barnes and Noble, 1971.
EEBO   Early English Books Online
Johnson   F. R. Johnson, *A Critical Bibliography of the Works of Edmund Spenser Printed before 1700*. Baltimore, MD: Johns Hopkins Press, 1933.
Jones   H. S. V. Jones, *A Spenser Handbook*. New York: F. S. Crofts, 1930.
Judson   A. C. Judson, *The Life of Edmund Spenser*. Baltimore, MD: Johns Hopkins Press, 1945.
McNeir   W. F. McNeir and F. Provost, *Edmund Spenser: An Annotated Bibliography 1937–1972*. Pittsburgh: Duquesne University Press, 1975.

NDNB	*New Dictionary of National Biography*
NHI	T. W. Moody, F. X. Martin, and F. J. Byrne (eds), *A New History of Ireland*, 9 vols. Oxford: Clarendon Press, 1976–84.
OED	*Oxford English Dictionary*
SE	A. C. Hamilton (ed.), *The Spenser Encyclopaedia*. Toronto: University of Toronto Press, 1990.
SP	State Papers, Public Record Office (MSS)
Wells	W. Wells (ed.), *Spenser Allusions in the Sixteenth and Seventeenth Centuries*, 2 Pts, *Studies in Philology*, Texts and Studies, 1971–2.

Spenser's works are abbreviated in notes and citations within the text as follows:

Amor	*Amoretti*
Ast	*Astrophel*
CCH	*Colin Clouts Come Home Againe*
Comp	*Complaints*
Daph	*Daphnaïda*
DLC	*The Dolefull Lay of Clorinda*
Epith	*Epithalamion*
FH	*Fowre Hymnes*
FQ	*The Faerie Queene*
HB	*An Hymne in Honour of Beavtie*
HL	*An Hymne in Honour of Loue*
HHL	*An Hymne of Heauenly Loue*
HHB	*An Hymne of Heauenly Beavtie*
Letters	*Three Proper ... Letters. Two ... Commendable Letters*
MHT	*Prosopopoia. Or Mother Hubberds Tale*
Muiop	*Muiopotmos, Or the Fate of the Butterflie*
Prose	*Spenser's Prose Works, Variorum Edition*, ix *(1949)*
Proth	*Prothalamion*
RR	*Ruines of Rome: by Bellay*
RT	*The Ruines of Time*
SC	*The Shepheardes Calender*
TCM	*Two Cantos of Mutabilitie*
TM	*The Teares of the Muses*
TW	*A Theatre for Worldlings*
VB	*The Visions of Bellay*
VG	*Virgil's Gnat*
View	*A Vewe of the Presente State of Irelande*
VP	*The Visions of Petrarch*
VW	*Visions of the Worlds Vanitie*

Scholarly journals are abbreviated as follows:

CL	*Comparative Literature*
CLS	*Comparative Literature Studies*
EA	*Études Anglaises*
EHR	*English Historical Review*

EIC	*Essays in Criticism*
ELH	*English Literary History*
ELN	*English Language Notes*
ELR	*English Literary Renaissance*
ES	*English Studies*
HLQ	*Huntington Library Quarterly*
HJ	*Historical Journal*
IHS	*Irish Historical Studies*
JEGP	*Journal of English and Germanic Philology*
JHI	*Journal of the History of Ideas*
JMRS	*Journal of Medieval and Renaissance Studies*
JWCI	*Journal of the Warburg and Courtauld Institutes*
L&H	*Literature and History*
MLN	*Modern Language Notes*
MLQ	*Modern Language Quarterly*
MLR	*Modern Language Review*
MP	*Modern Philology*
N&Q	*Notes and Queries*
PMLA	*Publications of the Modern Language Association of America*
PQ	*Philological Quarterly*
REL	*Review of English Literature*
RES	*Review of English Studies*
RS	*Renaissance Studies*
SAQ	*South Atlantic Quarterly*
SEL	*Studies in English Literature*
SP	*Studies in Philology*
SQ	*Shakespeare Quarterly*
SpN	*Spenser Newsletter*
SR	*Studies in the Renaissance*
SSt	*Spenser Studies*
TLS	*Times Literary Supplement*
TSLL	*Texas Studies in Language and Literature*
UTQ	*University of Toronto Quarterly*
YES	*Yearbook of English Studies*

LIST OF CONTRIBUTORS

David J. Baker is Peter G. Phialas Professor in the Department of English and Comparative Literature at the University of North Carolina at Chapel Hill. He is the author of *Between Nations: Shakespeare, Spenser, Marvell and the Question of Britain* (1997), and *On Demand: Writing for the Market in Early Modern England* (2010). With Willy Maley he co-edited *British Identities and English Renaissance Literature* (2002).

Elizabeth Jane Bellamy is Professor of English and John C. Hodges Chair of Excellence at the University of Tennessee, Knoxville. She is the author of *Translations of Power: Narcissism and the Unconscious in Epic History* (1992) and *Affective Genealogies: Psychoanalysis, Postmodernism, and the 'Jewish Question' after Auschwitz* (1997). With Patrick Cheney and Michael Schoenfeldt she co-edited *Imagining Death in Spenser and Milton* (2003).

Joseph L. Black is Associate Professor in the Department of English at the University of Massachusetts, Amherst. His publications include *The Martin Marprelate Tracts* (2008) and various articles on Renaissance literature and book history; he was editor of the *Sidney Journal* 2000–5. With Robert Fehrenbach he co-edited *Private Libraries of Renaissance England*, vol. vii (2009); with Anne Lake Prescott, *The Broadview Anthology of British Literature*, vol. ii: *The Renaissance and Early Seventeenth Century* (2006); and with Alan Rudrum and Holly Nelson, *The Broadview Anthology of Seventeenth-Century English Verse and Prose* (2000).

Kenneth Borris is Professor of English Literature at McGill University. A former Canada Research Fellow and winner of the MacCaffrey Award, he has authored *Spenser's Poetics of Prophecy in 'The Faerie Queene' V* (1990) and *Allegory and Epic in Renaissance English Literature: Heroic Form in Spenser, Sidney, and Milton* (2000). He has edited *Same-Sex Desire in the English Renaissance: A Sourcebook of Texts, 1470–1650* (2004). With George Klawitter he co-edited *The Affectionate Shepherd: Celebrating Richard Barnfield* (2001); with George Rousseau, *The Sciences of Homosexuality in Early Modern Europe* (2008); and with Jon Quitslund and Carol Kaske, *Spenser and Platonism, Spenser Studies* XXIV.

Ciaran Brady is a Fellow and Associate Professor of History at Trinity College Dublin. He is the author of *The Chief Governors: The Rise and Fall of Reform Government in Tudor Ireland* (1994) and of a biography of *Shane O'Neill* (1996). He is the editor of (and a contributor to) several collections of essays and the author of several articles in scholarly journals.

Christopher Burlinson is a Fellow in English at Jesus College, Cambridge. His publications include *Allegory, Space, and the Material World in the Writings of Edmund Spenser* (2006) and, with Andrew Zurcher, *Edmund Spenser: Selected Letters and Other Papers* (2009).

Colin Burrow is a Senior Research Fellow at All Souls College, Oxford. He is author of *Epic Romance: Homer to Milton* (1993), and *Edmund Spenser* (1996), and of numerous articles, chiefly on the reception of classical literature in the Renaissance. He has edited *The Complete Sonnets and Poems* for the Oxford Shakespeare (2002), *Metaphysical Poetry* (2006), and the poems for the *Cambridge Edition of the Works of Ben Jonson*.

Joseph Campana is Associate Professor of English at Rice University. He has published essays on Renaissance literature in *PMLA, Modern Philology, Shakespeare,* and elsewhere. He is the author of *The Pain of Reformation: Spenser, Vulnerability, and the Ethics of Masculinity* and two collections of poetry, *The Book of Faces* (2005) and *Natural Selections* (Iowa Poetry Prize, 2012). Currently, he is completing a study of children, sovereignty, and the works of William Shakespeare called *The Child's Two Bodies.*

Lisa Celovsky, Associate Professor of English at Suffolk University, studies Renaissance poetry, epic romance, and gender issues. Her essays on Spenser and on members of the Sidney family have appeared in *English Literary Renaissance*, the *Sidney Journal,* and *Studies in Philology.*

Patrick Cheney is Distinguished Professor of English and Comparative Literature at Penn State University. He is the author of *Spenser's Famous Flight: A Renaissance Idea of a Literary Career* (1993) and *Marlowe's Counterfeit Profession: Ovid, Spenser, Counter-Nationhood* (1997), as well as co-editor of *Worldmaking Spenser* (2000) and *Imagining Death in Spenser and Milton* (2003). A past President of the International Spenser Society, he currently serves on the Editorial Board at *Spenser Studies* and is a General Editor of *The Oxford Edition of the Collected Works of Edmund Spenser* (forthcoming). In 1996 and 2001, he co-directed international Spenser conferences at Yale and Cambridge.

Jeff Dolven teaches Renaissance literature at Princeton University. His first book, *Scenes of Instruction in Renaissance Romance* (2007), considers relations between poetry and pedagogy at the end of the sixteenth century; he has published on Renaissance poets from Wyatt to Milton. He is currently working on a book about literary style in the sixteenth and twentieth centuries, and his own poems have appeared in the *Paris Review, TLS, Yale Review,* and elsewhere.

Wayne Erickson teaches English at Georgia State University. His book *Mapping The Faerie Queene: Quest Structures and the World of the Poem* (1996) outlines the spatial, temporal, and generic geography of *The Faerie Queene.* He has edited a collection of essays on the paratexts of the 1590 *Faerie Queene* (2005), has written brief biographies of Gabriel Harvey and William Ponsonby, and has been thinking and writing about the printing and publishing of Spenser's works for over twenty-five years.

Andrew Escobedo, an Associate Professor at Ohio University, is the author of *Nationalism and Historical Loss in Renaissance England: Foxe, Dee, Spenser, Milton* (2004), which won the 2005 Nancy Dasher Prize awarded by the College English

Association of Ohio. He is currently working on a project about personification as an expression of Renaissance ideas about the will, and was a Fellow at the National Humanities Centre, 2009–10.

Elizabeth Fowler is a General Editor of the forthcoming *The Oxford Edition of the Collected Works of Edmund Spenser* and the author of *Literary Character* (2003). She is an occasional architectural designer and is currently teaching and writing on poetry and the history of the built environment, poetry and disposition, and the premodern vernacular history of constitutional thought. She lives in the Blue Ridge Mountains and is Associate Professor of English at the University of Virginia.

Roland Greene is Professor of English and Comparative Literature at Stanford University. He is the author of *Unrequited Conquests: Love and Empire in the Colonial Americas* (1999) and *Post-Petrarchism: Origins and Innovations of the Western Lyric Sequence* (1991). With Elizabeth Fowler he co-edited *The Project of Prose in Early Modern Europe and the New World* (1997). He is the author of numerous essays on Spenser, Shakespeare, Wyatt, and other figures in Early Modern English and continental literature.

Linda Gregerson is the Caroline Walker Bynum Distinguished University Professor of English Language and Literature at the University of Michigan, where she teaches Early Modern literature and creative writing. She is the author of *The Reformation of the Subject: Spenser, Milton and the English Protestant Epic* (1995) and *Negative Capability: Capability: Contemporary American Poetry* (2001) and editor, with Susan Juster, of *Empires of God: Religious Encounters in the Early Modern Atlantic* (2011). She has also published five volumes of poetry: *Fire in the Conservatory* (1982), *The Woman Who Died in Her Sleep* (1996), *Waterborne* (2002), *Magnetic North* (2007), and *The Selvage* (2012).

Andrew Hadfield is Professor of English at the University of Sussex. He is the author of a number of works on Renaissance literature and culture, including, *Shakespeare and Republicanism* (2005), *Shakespeare, Spenser and the Matter of Britain* (2003), and *Spenser's Irish Experience: Wilde Fruit and Salvage Soil* (1997). He has edited, with Raymond Gillespie, *The Oxford History of the Irish Book*, vol. iii: *The Irish Book in English, 1550–1800* (2006); *The Cambridge Companion to Spenser* (2001); and, with Paul Hammond, *Shakespeare and Europe* (2004). He is the editor of *Renaissance Studies* and a regular contributor to the *TLS*.

Elizabeth D. Harvey is Professor of English at the University of Toronto. She is the author of *Ventriloquized Voices: Feminist Theory and Renaissance Texts* (1992), co-editor with Kathleen Okruhlik of *Women and Reason* (1992); with Katharine Eisaman Maus, *Soliciting Interpretation: Literary Theory and Seventeenth-Century English Poetry* (1990); with Theresa Krier, *Irigaray and Premodern Culture: Thresholds of History* (2004); and editor of *Sensible Flesh: On Touch in Early Modern Culture* (2003).

Elizabeth Heale was a Senior Lecturer in the Department of English at the University of Reading and is now an Honorary Research Fellow. She is the author of *The Faerie Queene: A Reader's Guide* (2nd edition, 1999), *Wyatt, Surrey and Early Tudor Poetry* (1998), and *Autobiography and Authorship in Renaissance Verse: Chronicles of the Self* (2003).

Carol V. Kaske is Professor of English Emerita at Cornell University. She is the author of 24 scholarly essays, mostly on Spenser, and three books: with John R. Clark,

Marsilio Ficino, Three Books on Life, a Critical Edition and Translation with Introduction and Notes (1989); *Spenser and Biblical Poetics* (1999); and *Edmund Spenser: 'The Faerie Queene' Book I*, edited with introduction and notes (2006).

Andrew King is Lecturer in Medieval and Renaissance English at University College Cork. He is the author of *The Faerie Queene and Middle English Romance: The Matter of Just Memory* (2000), as well as articles and book chapters on Spenser, Sidney, Shakespeare, and other medieval and Early Modern topics and authors.

Clare R. Kinney is Associate Professor of English at the University of Virginia. She is the author of *Strategies of Poetic Narrative: Chaucer, Spenser, Milton, Eliot* (1992) and has edited *Ashgate Critical Essays on Women Writers in England, 1550–1700*, vol. iv: *Mary Wroth* (2009). Her published articles include work on the Sidney circle, Spenser, Shakespeare, medieval and Renaissance romance, and the Renaissance reception of Chaucer.

Theresa Krier is Professor of English at Macalester College. She is the author of *Gazing on Secret Sights: Spenser, Classical Imitation, and the Decorums of Vision* (1990), and *Birth Passages: Maternity and Nostalgia, Antiquity to Shakespeare* (2001). She has edited *Refiguring Chaucer in the Renaissance* (1998) and, with Elizabeth D. Harvey, co-edited *Luce Irigaray and Premodern Culture: Thresholds of History* (2004).

Jason Lawrence is a lecturer in English at the University of Hull. He is the author of *'Who the Devil Taught Thee So Much Italian?': Italian Language Learning and Literary Imitation in Early Modern England* (2005), and a co-editor of *The Accession of James I: Historical and Cultural Consequences* (2006). He has published essays on Samuel Daniel, Shakespeare, Spenser, Marston, Tasso, Guarini, Ariosto, and Cinthio, and is currently working on a book entitled *Tasso's Afterlives in England*.

Joseph Loewenstein is Professor of English and Comparative Literature, and directs the Interdisciplinary Project in the Humanities at Washington University, where he has taught since 1981. He is the author of two recent books on the history of intellectual property and the rise of 'possessive authorship'. Currently, he is one of the editors of *The Oxford Edition of the Collected Works of Edmund Spenser*; he is also writing a study of the material props of identity in the English Renaissance tentatively entitled 'Accessorizing Hamlet'.

Peter Mack is Professor of English and Comparative Literature at the University of Warwick. He is the author of *Renaissance Argument: Valla and Agricola in the Traditions of Rhetoric and Dialectic* (1993) and of *Elizabethan Rhetoric: Theory and Practice* (2002). He is editor of *Renaissance Rhetoric* (1994) and co-editor, with Edward Chaney, of *England and the Continental Renaissance: Essays in Honour of J. B. Trapp* (1990). He was editor of the journal *Rhetorica* 1998–2002. He is currently writing a history of Renaissance Rhetoric.

Willy Maley is Professor of Renaissance Studies at the University of Glasgow. He is the author of *A Spenser Chronology* (1994), *Salvaging Spenser: Colonialism, Culture and Identity* (1997), and *Nation, State and Empire in English Renaissance Literature: Shakespeare to Milton* (2003). He is editor, with Andrew Hadfield, of *A View of the Present State of Ireland: From the First Published Edition* (1997). He has also edited five collections of essays: with Brendan Bradshaw and Andrew Hadfield, *Representing Ireland: Literature and the Origins of Conflict, 1534–1660* (1993); with Bart Moore-Gilbert and Gareth Stanton, *Postcolonial Criticism* (1997); with David J. Baker, *British Identities and English Renaissance Literature* (2002); with Andrew Murphy, *Shakespeare and Scotland* (2004); and with Alex Benchimol, *Spheres of Influence: Intellectual and Cultural Publics from Shakespeare to Habermas* (2006).

Richard A. McCabe is Fellow of Merton College, and Professor of English Language and Literature at Oxford University. He was elected FBA in 2007. He is author of *Joseph Hall: A Study in Satire and Meditation* (1982), *The Pillars of Eternity: Time and Providence in 'The Faerie Queene'* (1989), *Incest, Drama, and Nature's Law 1550–1700* (1993), and *Spenser's Monstrous Regiment: Elizabethan Ireland and the Poetics of Difference* (2002/5). He has edited *Edmund Spenser: The Shorter Poems* for Penguin (1999). With Howard Erskine-Hill he co-edited *Presenting Poetry: Composition, Publication, Reception* (1995), and with David Womersley, *Literary Milieux: Essays in Text and Context Presented to Howard Erskine-Hill* (2007).

Claire McEachern is Professor of English Literature at the University of California—Los Angeles. She is the author of *The Poetics of English Nationhood, 1590–1612* (1996); editor (with Debora Shuger) of *Religion and Culture in the English Renaissance* (1997); *The Cambridge Companion to Shakespearean Tragedy* (2003), and a number of Shakespeare's plays, including the Arden 3 edition of *Much Ado About Nothing* (2005).

Tom MacFaul is Lecturer in English at Merton College, University of Oxford. He is the author of *Male Friendship in Shakespeare and His Contemporaries* (2007) and *Poetry and Paternity in Renaissance England: Sidney, Spenser, Shakespeare, Donne and Jonson* (2010).

David Lee Miller is Carolina Distinguished Professor of English and Comparative Literature at the University of South Carolina, where he directs the Centre for Digital Humanities. He is one of the five General Editors of the forthcoming *The Oxford Edition of the Collected Works of Edmund Spenser*. He is the author of *The Poem's Two Bodies: The Poetics of the 1590 'Faerie Queene'* (1988) and *Dreams of the Burning Child: Sacrificial Sons and the Father's Witness* (2003). With Gregory Jay he co-edited *After Strange Texts: The Role of Theory in the Study of Literature* (1985); with Alexander Dunlop, *Approaches to Teaching Spenser's 'Faerie Queene'* (1994); with Sharon O'Dair and Harold Weber, *The Production of English Renaissance Culture* (1994); and with Nina Levine, *A Touch More Rare: Harry Berger, Jr. and the Arts of Interpretation* (2009).

Michelle O'Callaghan is a Reader in the Department of English and American Literature at the University of Reading. She is the author of *The 'Shepheards Nation': Jacobean Spenserians and Early Stuart Political Culture* (2000), *The English Wits: Literature and Sociability in Early Modern England* (2007), and *Thomas Middleton, Renaissance Dramatist* (2009). She is co-editor with Kate Hodgkin and Susan Wiseman of *Reading the Early Modern Dream: The Terrors of the Night* (2007).

Lee Piepho is Shallenberger Brown Research Professor of English Literature at Sweet Briar College. He is the editor and translator of *Mantuan's Adulescentia* (1989) and the author of *Holofernes' Mantuan* (2001), a study of Italian humanism in Early

Modern England. He has articles comparing the organization of Mantuan's eclogues and *The Shepheardes Calender* and on books newly discovered to have been in Spenser's private library. Recently he has been working on international Protestant culture in Britain and continental Europe, and has published 'Paulus Melissus and Jacobus Falckenburgius: Two German Protestant Humanists at the Court of Queen Elizabeth', in *Sixteenth Century Studies*, and 'Making the Impossible Dream: Latin, Print, and the Marriage of Frederick V and the Princess Elizabeth', in *Reformation*.

Anne Lake Prescott is Helen Goodhart Altschul Professor of English at Barnard College and also teaches at Columbia. A past President of the International Spenser Society and recently President of the Sixteenth Century Society (2007–8), she is currently on the board of the Sidney Society and the John Donne Society. She is the author of *French Poets and the English Renaissance* (1978), *Imagining Rabelais in Renaissance England* (1998), and articles on such topics as the poems of Marguerite de Navarre, the English refusal of the Gregorian calendar, John Donne and the songs of David, Elizabeth I, Thomas More's jokes, and Ben Jonson's masques. She is co-editor with Hugh Maclean of the *Norton Critical Edition of Spenser* (1993); with Betty Travitsky of *Female and Male Voices in Early Modern England: A Renaissance Anthology* (2000); and with James Dutcher of *Renaissance Historicisms: Essays in Honour of Arthur F. Kinney* (2008). Her current interests include Early Modern women, almanacs, and the image of David in the Renaissance.

Claire Preston is Fellow and Lecturer in English at Sidney Sussex College, Cambridge. Her books include *Sir Thomas Browne: The World Proposed*, co-edited with Reid Barbour (2008); *Bee* (2006); *Thomas Browne and the Writing of Early Modern Science* (2005); and *Edith Wharton's Social Register* (2000); she is the General Editor of the Oxford *Complete Works of Thomas Browne* (in progress). She received the British Academy's Rose Mary Crawshay Prize in 2005; she was a Guggenheim Fellow (2008–9) and was awarded a British Academy Research Development Award (2008–9). She is currently writing about Early Modern literature and scientific investigation.

Syrithe Pugh is Senior Lecturer in English literature at the University of Aberdeen. She is the author of two monographs, *Spenser and Ovid* (2005) and *Herrick, Fanshawe, and the Politics of Intertextuality: Classical Literature and Seventeenth-Century Royalism* (2010), and has also published various articles on intertextuality in Spenser, Sidney, Gascoigne, Jonson, Herrick, and Fanshawe. She is currently working on Spenser's use of Virgil.

Mark David Rasmussen is Professor of English at Centre College. He has edited a collection of essays, *Renaissance Literature and Its Formal Engagements* (2002), and is currently writing a study of poetic complaint from classical antiquity to the Renaissance.

John D. Staines is Assistant Professor of English Literature at the John Jay College of Criminal Justice in the City University of New York, and he has taught Spenser at the CUNY Graduate Centre. He has also taught at the College of the Holy Cross and Earlham College. He is the author of *The Tragic Histories of Mary Queen of Scots*

1560–1690: Rhetoric, Passions, and Political Literature (2009) and has published articles on Spenser, Milton, Shakespeare, and Early Modern politics.

Paul D. Stegner is an Assistant Professor of English at California Polytechnic, San Luis Obispo. His articles have been published in *Shakespeare Studies*, *Journal of English and Germanic Philology*, and in *Critical Essays on Shakespeare's 'A Lover's Complaint': Suffering Ecstasy*, edited by Shirley Sharon-Visser (2006). He is currently writing a book on the afterlives of sacramental confession in Spenser, Marlowe, Shakespeare, and Donne.

Dorothy Stephens is Professor of English Literature at the University of Arkansas. She is the author of *The Limits of Eroticism in Post-Petrarchan Narrative* (1998) and the editor of *The Faerie Queene: Books Three and Four* (2006). She received the Isabel MacCaffrey Award in 1992 and served as President of the International Spenser Society from 2006 to 2007.

Gordon Teskey, Professor of English at Harvard University, is author of *Allegory and Violence* (1996) and of *Delirious Milton* (2006), which won the Milton Society's Hanford Prize. He is editor of the Norton edition of *Paradise Lost* (2005).

Bart Van Es is a Fellow of St Catherine's College, and Lecturer in English Language and Literature at Oxford University. He is author of *Spenser's Forms of History* (2002) and editor of *A Critical Companion to Spenser Studies* (2006). He has written articles on Spenser, historiography, and classical reception in the early modern period. His current book project is a study of Shakespeare and the acting companies.

David Scott Wilson-Okamura is an Associate Professor of English at East Carolina University. He is the author of *Virgil in the Renaissance* (2010).

Andrew Zurcher is a Fellow and Director of Studies in English at Queens' College, Cambridge. He is the author of *Spenser's Legal Language: Law and Poetry in Early Modern England* (2007), and *Shakespeare and Law* is forthcoming as an Arden Critical Companion. With Christopher Burlinson he has recently edited *Edmund Spenser: Selected Letters and Other Papers* (2009). He is one of the five General Editors of the forthcoming *Oxford Edition of the Collected Works of Edmund Spenser*.

INTRODUCTION

RICHARD A. McCABE

Poetry is a useful art.
—Boccaccio

A poet's ability to generate commentary was commonly regarded in the Renaissance as a hallmark of genius (Kennedy 1995). The verse of Homer and Virgil descended to the Italian Humanists with a wealth of expository scholia and annotation which they duly augmented and transmitted. The advent of printing saw the widespread dissemination of Classical texts 'cum commentariis variorum', the first 'Variorum' editions recording centuries of scholarship, speculation, and critical dispute. By the end of the fifteenth century the texts of Dante and Petrarch competed with the ancients as sites of linguistic and philological concern and as key texts in the wider debate about the nature of literature's role in society. Only when seen in this context can the radical import of Spenser's *Shepheards Calender* be appreciated. No English poet had received the level of critical attention accorded to the ancients or Italians. The 'new poet' was determined to change all that. The first edition of his pastorals came equipped with the sort of paratexts and commentary one might expect from a scholarly edition of Virgil's *Eclogues*, yet the studied incompletion of the gloss, adumbrating areas of covert intent to which the glossator is not 'privy', is clearly designed as an invitation to future editors. The gloss, in other words, is not intended to be definitive—definitive is where critical invention goes to die—but seminal. Not content to be the creator of a new poetic, Spenser launched a new exegetic: his own.

This *Handbook* responds to a call for commentary issued by Spenser himself. By prefacing *Virgils Gnat* with the injunction 'ne further seeke to glose upon the text', he inspired generations of commentators to do just that ('Dedication', 10). Similarly the 'Letter to Ralegh' which accompanied the first instalment of *The Faerie Queene* is better understood as an attempt to generate than to provide exegesis. Its initial assertion of allegorical intent, 'knowing how doubtfully all Allegories may be construed', constitutes an open invitation to a certain kind of hermeneutic. The letter's inconsistencies are consequently as productive as its assertions. Only the poem's 'general intention' is stated 'without expressing of any particular purposes or by-accidents therein occasioned'—they are left to the reader. The verb 'read' is used in a dazzling variety of senses throughout *The Faerie Queene* but its basic meaning, as the *OED* indicates (v. 1), is to consider, interpret, or discern. It is not only books that can be 'read' but emblems, signs, buildings, pictures, and even people, actions, and intentions. All of the poem's protagonists are in this sense also readers, attempting to interpret the world in which they move and involving us in that activity as they do so. Extensive meta-readings are conducted by Arthur and Guyon in the House of Alma (II.x). Britomart repeatedly 'over-reads' the cryptic injunctions of the House of Busirane 'yet could not find what sence it figured' (III.xi.50) and, in what constitutes an allegory of allegory itself, the name 'Bon Font' that 'few could rightly read' is barely distinguished in the 'cyphers strange' of a palimpsest through the partially over-written letters of 'Malfont' which 'was plainely to be red' (V.ix.26). Everything depends on how we take 'rightly': read one way it endorses political censorship, read another it condemns it. It is an issue that goes straight to the heart of Spenser's conflicted mentality. 'I have Redd that in all ages', he has Eudoxus say in *A View of the Present State of Ireland*, 'Poets have bene in speciall reputacion and that me seemes not without great Cause' (*Prose*, 124). But Eudoxus has not 'redd' enough—at least of Spenser. Irenius is arguing for censorship precisely because the Gaelic poets are held in 'speciall reputacion'. The advocate of poetic liberty in England is the proponent of literary censorship in Ireland. The duality that complicates so much of *The Faerie Queene*, shadowing 'virtue' with barely distinguishable vice, is deeply rooted in the author's mindset. Polar opposites have a disturbing habit of converging in his life and work. His texts demand vigilance: over-reading, under-reading, meta-reading.

'Caveat lector'. But this was an attitude that Spenser consciously cultivated. From the outset of his career he courts the active, critical reader and his canonicity rests upon the way in which successive generations of such readers have risen to the challenge. E. K. implies that the way in which readers respond to Spenser reflects on themselves as much as the poet: the construction of his verse is 'learned wythout hardnes, suche indeede as may be perceived of the leaste, understoode of the moste, but iudged onely of the learned' (Spenser 1999: 28). This was an audacious claim to make for a new work, but the depth and variety of subsequent critical engagement with Spenser's texts, examined in Part V of this *Handbook*, is a fair measure of his accomplishment. It is my personal view that the commentary attributed to E. K. is very likely to be the outcome of collaboration between Spenser and Harvey (McCabe 2000), but even if that is not the case the *Calender* labours to create an impression of collaboration between poet and critic. In E. K., the Elizabethan reader is given to understand, the new poet has found a qualified editor. And the message upon which that editor insists is one central to the whole Humanist project, the message that Boccaccio hammered home in the *Genealogia Deorum* when he insisted that poetry is a 'useful' art and therefore worthy of such attention (1930: 36–9).

But how exactly was poetry 'useful'? Boccaccio was drawing upon the Horatian ideal of the 'utile dulce', commonly interpreted in the Middle Ages, particularly through such texts as the *Ovide Moralisé*, as the provision of moral benefit through aesthetic delight. But he also recognized the inherent problem in such an approach, the potential collapse of the useful into the utilitarian. His argument was more broadly based. Poetry was nothing less than a 'science' (rather than a mere 'faculty') requiring a set of remarkable technical skills, including a profound linguistic competence encompassing 'the precepts of grammar and rhetoric' and 'a strong and abundant vocabulary' (40). It required a knowledge of ancient texts, national histories, and topography. It had sufficient power to corrupt or elevate. It might 'arm kings . . . launch whole fleets from their docks . . . stimulate the dull, restrain the rash, subdue the criminal and distinguish excellent men with their proper meed of praise' (39–40). It was, in other words, an active instrument in the life of the mind, a refiner of language, and a peculiarly potent medium for anatomizing desire in all of its many forms.

These arguments serve as the basis for E. K.'s presentation of the *Calender* and his justification for providing it with a 'gloss'. The new poet is to England's 'mother tongue' what Theocritus was to Greek, Virgil to Latin, and Petrarch to Italian. Like them he is engaged in a national project, the refinement of the vernacular and enrichment of its literature. By developing English he develops Englishness, ensuring that his countrymen will not be accounted 'alienes' in their own tongue or country. Linguistic, and consequently literary, nationalism was central to his vision. Deploring the linguistic 'degeneracy' of the Old English in Ireland, Irenius asserts that 'wordes are the Image of the minde So as they procedinge from the minde the minde must be nedes affected with the wordes So that the speache beinge Irishe the harte muste nedes be Irishe for out of the abundance of the harte the tonge speakethe' (*Prose*, 119). By contrast, the new poet has 'laboured to restore, as to theyr rightfull heritage such good and naturall English words, as have been long time out of use and almost cleare disherited' (Spenser 1999: 27). This emphasis on reclaiming one's 'heritage' proffers poetry as an agent of personal and national identity, thereby implying that the new poet fulfils the Horatian ideal of becoming 'utilis urbi' ('useful to the state' [*Epistles* II.i.124]). But the essential point, laboured alike by Horace, Boccaccio, and E. K., is that a poet's utility inheres in his craft. It is not just that he conveys an improving or 'useful' message—others may also do that—but that the medium through which he does so lends any such message a peculiar efficacy. If the poet 'never lies' it is not because he 'never affirms', as Sir Philip Sidney suggests (Alexander 2004: 34), but because he crafts a fiction more compelling than fact, a fiction with the potential to become an affirmative 'vision'. What Spenser cultivated was not the crudely simplistic moral didacticism that does indeed tend to reduce the useful to the utilitarian, but the broader didacticism that recognizes in the literary arts the potential for a deep disquieting of all that is complacent and received. That perception of poetry led commentators such as Servius to recognize in Virgil a critique of the power structures he was supposed to praise, and led E. K. to imply that the burden of even the 'moral' eclogues is a good deal more intricate than the categorization might have suggested. The remarkably enigmatic quality of the 'emblems' appended to the various eclogues perfectly captures the most salient feature of their artistry, and the tendency towards dialogue and debate that pervades so much of the Spenser canon, both poetry and prose, points in the same direction. Later schools of criticism might advance the notion of the equality of 'discourses' but the Renaissance mindset saw things quite differently. At their best the poetic arts were seen to promote an exceptional level of subtlety and sophistication, a heightened quality of communication distinguished by acute verbal discipline and metrical economy that could not be achieved otherwise. Poetry was not just a useful art but a vital one. It offered unique opportunities and the effect was an extraordinary power to 'move', what Sidney termed 'praxis' (Alexander 2004: 22). This is primarily what lies behind the proem to *Faerie Queene* IV. What Spenser is defending is the assertion that the worth of the poem inheres in the very elements to which his antagonist has taken exception.

At the heart of this *Handbook* is the section entitled 'Poetic Craft' and to my mind it provides the justification for having a *Handbook* at all. Without his literary skills Spenser would be indistinguishable from the scores of secretaries, civil servants, and colonists who sought personal advancement on the fringes of empire, living their lives, as one contemporary observer put it, 'among the savage Kernes in sad exile' (Hall 1969: 66). Without his literary skills he could never have produced the works examined in Part II upon which his reputation rests. Spenser's subjects are often drawn from the public sphere, but when he speaks of art it is invariably its transformative power (for good or ill) that he emphasizes: the notion of metamorphosis which recurs so obsessively throughout his poetry constitutes a metaphor for the plasticity of the poetic art. Spenser was Elizabeth's subject, but she was his. She might create a poet laureate, but only he could create Gloriana. She is invited to see herself in the many mirrors of his art (III *Proem*, 5), reflected, refracted, flattered, and distorted. 'This is, and is not, Cressid', says a bewildered Troilus is Shakespeare's play (5.2.145), and the reader's response to Gloriana partakes of the same dilemma: this is, and is not, Elizabeth. The inevitable gap between the ideal and real entails an element of critique in the highest panegyric—in fact the higher the panegyric, the deeper the dichotomy.

Spenser distinguishes between the 'methode' of a poet and an 'historiographer' and not least because of the former's immersion in *literary* history. In devising his work he has 'followed all the antique Poets historicall' and their Renaissance imitators, Arisoto and Tasso. The reader is therefore invited to approach the events of history through the conventions of genre, to watch as the Poet 'thrusteth into the middest, even where it most concerneth him, and there recoursing to the thinges forepaste, and divining of things to come, maketh a pleasing Analysis of all' (Spenser 2001: 716–17). Oddly enough the term 'analysis' is seldom if ever glossed, yet it is crucial. It entails, as the *OED* demonstrates (n. 1), a breaking down of complex phenomena into their component parts for better understanding. The epithet 'pleasing' has often led it to be taken in an anodyne sense, but the 'pleasure' of Spenserian verse is of a tougher nature: 'therfore do you my rimes keep better measure', says the poet sarcastically, 'and seeke to please, that now is counted wise-men's threasure' (VI.xii.41). The emphasis on 'analysis' denotes the cutting edge of Spenserian poetics: just as he writes what has been termed 'hard' pastoral, he also writes 'hard' romance. Fredric Jameson held that historical romance tends 'to resolve the real contradictions of history in imaginative form' (1983: 118), but Spenser more characteristically affords irresolution or at best deferral. His poetry is analytical in the most disturbing sense. We are not reassured by the *Legend of Justice* because the transformation of Elizabethan military might into the inhuman automaton that is Talus was never calculated to have that effect. Although it was once common to seek a key to Spenserian poetics in Spenserian prose the relationship is far more complex. It may well be the poetry that opens the locks of the prose. The image of Talus captures something of the Irish enterprise, and imperial violence in general, that eludes Irenius even at his most graphic. The polyvocality of the verse manages to articulate what is left unspoken in the prose dialogue.

Spenser writes the poetry of engagement not escape. *The Shepheardes Calender* treats dangerous matter and was published anonymously, the *Complaints* were censored in England for attacking Lord Burghley, and the second part of *The Faerie Queene* was banned in Scotland for attacking the memory of Mary Queen of Scots. Ironically the more 'power' that poetry is deemed to have, and the more 'praxis' it is seen to exercise, the more likely are the authorities to regard it as a competing power. Censorship acknowledges the importance of literature by suppressing it. To such disapproving readers as Burghley Spenser states that he does 'not sing at all' (IV Proem, 4). But could he afford to be so exclusive? Burghley was at the centre of government, Spenser at its margins. Boccaccio's theory of poetry, like Philip Sidney's, is cast as a defence. Though powerful in one sense, poetry was feared to be impotent in another. In Virgil's ninth eclogue a defenceless community of pastoral poets attempts to continue singing despite the encroachments of their hostile countrymen and the knowledge that 'amid the weapons of war . . . our songs avail as much as, they say, the doves of Chaonia when the eagle comes' (11–13). It had been rumoured that Menalcas's songs had won them the sort of protection accorded to Tityrus in Eclogue I, but in reality they are all fated to be dispossessed like Tityrus's unfortunate neighbour Meliboeus. Taken together these two eclogues provide much of the subtext for Spenser's various accounts of the literary career from the complaints of the 'October' eclogue, through those of *The Teares of the Muses*, to the dramatic shattering of Colin's vision of the Graces on Mt. Acidale and the final unleashing of the Blattant Beast. But it is precisely this engagement with the social context of literary creativity that ensures that the relentless self-reflexivity of the canon never issues in solipsism. Spenser's determination to cultivate an active readership is symptomatic of this aspect of his work. Calidore errs in reading pastoral as escapist only to learn that it is, quite literally, inscribed in epic conflict, and the sour conclusion to Book VI illustrates the vulnerability of poetic vision to contemporary politics. The essays in the first section of this *Handbook* attempt to elucidate the more urgent issues and circumstances with which Spenser's works engage—social, polit-ical, religious, and professional. They are not intended to be exhaustive or to constitute a biography. Rather, they attempt to sketch the major axes of contextual concern against which Spenser's creative development may be plotted.

Perhaps the most distinctive feature of Spenserian poetics is the extraordinary fusion of allegory and parody that is so perfectly calculated to capture both the glory and futility of empire, the element of Sir Thopas in Prince Arthur, the savage in the chivalrous, the disquieting similarity between grand vision and grand folly. The great foundational metaphor, the concept of 'faerie', condemned as ignorant superstition in the *Calender* (gloss to 'June', 25) but proffered as sublime invention in the epic (I *Proem*, 2–4), hovers uncertainly between the two. There are, of course, precedents in ancient literature—Aeneas carries his vision of Roman destiny from the under-world to the overworld through the gate of false dreams (*Aeneid* VI, 893–8)—but the phenomenon is peculiarly disquieting in Spenser's case because it has its roots not just in the perception of the world's 'vanities', but in the possible 'vanity', or delusiveness, of poetic invention itself. It is, so to speak, the nightmare that haunts the vision, the self-doubt against which the 'defence' of poetry—though overtly directed against the Burghleys of the world—must ultimately be made. In theory, as the argument to the 'October' eclogue claims, poetry is 'a divine gift and heavenly instinct not to be gotten by labour and learning, but adorned with both: and poured into the witte by a certaine *enthusiasmos* and celestial inspiration'. The notion is Platonic, as the gloss indicates, yet Plato was commonly regarded as an enemy to poetry and had identified *enthusiasmos* as a species of insanity. In his dedicatory letter to Gabriel Harvey, E. K. illustrates this ambivalence when he dismisses 'the rakehellye route of our ragged rymers (for so themselves use to hunt the letter) which without learning boste, without iudgement iangle, without reason rage and fome, as if some instinct of Poeticall spirite had newly ravished them above the meanenesse of commen capacitie' (Spenser 1999: 28). The 'instinct' is simultaneously identical and contrary to Spenser's own, just as Colin's vision of the Graces is simultaneously sublime and illusory. The very terms 'art' and 'craft' which denote the poet's 'cunning' ('December', 42) have a range of pejorative connotations that undermine it: the episode of the Bowre of Blisse is, amongst other things, an extended meditation on this problem.

The defence of poetry seeks to create, or 'fashion', a community that will endorse the practice of poetry by granting it a public 'place'—this is, after all, what lies at the heart of the 'October' eclogue: 'O pierlesse Poesye, where is then thy place? (79). Unless the activity is recognized as 'worthy and comendable', the skill, however great or potentially transformative, is doomed to frustration. If only William Alabaster were 'knowne to *Cynthia* as he ought', Colin tells us, 'His *Eliseïs* would be redde anew' (*CCH*, 402–3). It is a very telling, and self-reflexive, phrase: if the queen were to recognize her would-be laureate, people would read his work differently and in so doing they would 'read' of a different, 'new' Eliza. Because Spenser was aware that self-crowned laureates are actually uncrowned laureates, Colin's vision of the Elizabethan court is one of wasted opportunities and squandered talents. It is an unpromising backdrop against which to endeavour epic but it ensured that the poem would respond to the more recalcitrant aspects of Tudor life rather than merely to the dictates of its political dogma. It made the poetry more interesting at the policy's expense. It ensured that Belphoebe would develop as a satire on Gloriana, that Mercilla would show little if any mercy, and that Cynthia would finally be seen in eclipse.

To attempt to project the future course of Spenser studies is to place oneself in the position of Merlin as he tries to predict the course of English history after Elizabeth (III.iii.50). 'Yet the end is not' I can easily agree, but the wizard's 'halfe extatick stoure' is harder to negotiate. But there is good reason to share his optimism. This *Handbook* is merely another stage in a process that will continue with the publication of the forthcoming OUP edition of the *Complete Works* to which it serves as companion and herald. The intention is to replace the Johns Hopkins *Variorum* of the 1930s and 1940s with an edition that is at once more responsive to the textual history of Spenser's career—to the history and ecology of the Spenserian book—and to the collaborative circumstances in which so many of his works, such as the translations of *A Theatre for Worldlings*, the Spenser–Harvey *Letters* (1580), and *Astrophel* (1595), were produced or brought to press (see Chapters 8, 13, 16, and 35 below). By also including such previously unpublished materials as the secretarial letters written on behalf of Lord Grey, documents inscribed but not composed by Spenser, the edition will afford a new insight into the ways in which the poet's personal modes of epistolary authority and political polemic were honed in the services of the state (see Burlinson and Zurcher 2009).

   Though often insufficiently valued, editorial work is crucial to literary study. Generation after generation it is the new editor who revives the new poet. The process of collaborative creativity and critique that Spenser suggests in E. K. is central to literary study generally. New editions necessarily generate new readings because they constitute new readings in themselves. The history of Spenserian reception changed forever when Matthew Lownes added the *Two Cantos of Mutabilitie* to *The Faerie Queene* in 1609, and again when Sir James Ware complemented the first edition of *A View of the Present of Ireland* with a selection of the poems, and profoundly when the editors of the 1679 Folio prefaced the poetic works with extracts from the Spenser–Harvey *Letters* (including Spenser's Latin verse) and appended at the end a full text of *A View* (see Chapter 35 below). But these editors were continuing a tradition begun by Spenser himself. He was the first editor of *The Faerie Queene* and the 'text' was in transition from the outset. Readers of the 1596 *Faerie Queene* must have been astonished to find the original conclusion to Book Three not merely altered but revised so substantially that the outcome of the storyline shifts from lovers joined to lovers parted. Spenser was fully aware of the critical implications of textual variance: 'difference of texts' is credited in *Mother Hubberds Tale* with occasioning religious schism (387). Yet he consciously sets his readers the challenge of 'difference', not only of competing versions and editions but even of identical versions repeated in differing contexts, such as sonnets 35 and 83 of the *Amoretti* (see Chapter 14 below).

   The new OUP edition is heavily informed by the material history of the Book in its respect for contexts and paratexts. If one attempts to read the Spenser–Harvey *Letters* in the Johns Hopkins *Variorum* one finds Spenser's contributions in the main text (albeit in reverse order to that of their original publication) but Harvey's replies (also in reverse order) in an appendix at the back of the volume set in the same point size as the annotations. It is as though Spenser's co-author and collaborator is be regarded as no more than an extended footnote to the poet's work—an impression strengthened by the total absence of annotation for Harvey's writings. Nothing could be further removed from the reading experience of the Elizabethans. The artistic conception of the work as a *correspondence* is wholly lost and Spenser's letters become almost unintelligible (see Chapter 10 below). The work is the victim of a radically interventionist editorial process that, in seeking to extract a purely 'Spenserian' voice from the text, distorts what it attempts to identify by ignoring the collaborative ethos at the heart of the volume's aesthetic. As the title indicates, the whole point of the publication is to offer two voices in dialogue and promote the writers as 'university wits': *Three proper, and wittie, familiar Letters: lately passed betvvene two Vniversitie men.* 'Between' is here a key term and the new edition will restore the original design.

An even more crucial difference between the old *Variorum* and its replacement will consist in the manner in which the latter reflects the course of Spenser's publishing career. By segregating the shorter poems into separate volumes, and consigning them to the status of 'minor' works, the John Hopkins *Variorum* supplies a very disjointed account of Spenser's artistic development. Six years elapsed between the first and second editions of *The Faerie Queene* but in the meantime there appeared the *Complaints, Daphnaïda, Colin Clouts Come Home Againe, Astrophel,* and the *Amoretti & Epithalamion.* Elizabethan readers came to the second edition of the epic through those other works and the effect must have been quite unsettling—particularly in view of what Thomas Warton first identified as Spenser's habit of self-imitation (Warton 1807: II, 1–46). In the *Legend of Temperance* Sir Guyon, a virgin knight, destroys the Bowre of Blisse in the service of Gloriana, but in the *Amoretti* the lady's 'fayre bosom' is identified as the speaker's 'bowre of blisse' (76) and his 'hungry eyes' (83) strongly suggest Acrasian lust (II.xii.78). It is not that these details are wholly irreconcilable but that they function to provoke intergeneric readings that problematize both works even as they unify the canon that contains them. By elucidating the chronological evolution of that canon in all of its variety, the new edition will inevitably demonstrate the inadequacy of Classical templates—such as the Virgilian *rota*—to Spenser's career and suggest more immediate comparisons with Early Modern authors.

By respecting the integrity of the Spenserian texts and making available for the first time a comprehensive survey of variant readings, the new edition will inevitably prompt new interpretations. The question is what form will they take? The history of the Spenserian book is likely to take centre stage for a while and the availability of the new texts in electronic form, combined with materials already available in Word-Hoard and on EEBO, is likely to facilitate much needed reconsiderations of Spenser's language, particularly in comparative contexts. These in turn will undoubtedly feed into new generic and formalist studies leading to reassessments of the development of Spenser's technical skills over the course of his writing life. A major benefit, I would hope, would be a reappraisal of Spenser as a translator and adaptor. The essays gathered in Part IV of this *Handbook* attempt to delineate something of the range and richness of Spenser's sources, subtexts, and intertexts but, as their authors indicate, much remains to be done. What emerges very strongly, however, is just how much of Spenser's canon is inscribed within invisible quotation marks—like the song of the rose in the Bowre of Bliss, or the description of the Goddess of Love in the Temple of Venus. Spenser is in dialogue with a dazzling range of ancient, medieval, and contemporary texts and a wider comparatist approach would certainly prove fruitful.

The contributors to the fifth section of the *Handbook* make it clear that a great deal of work also remains to be done on the reception of Spenser in both literature and the visual arts. Relatively little, for example, is known of the poet's influence outside the English-speaking world, and too little of the various ways in which he has inspired paintings, book illustrations, and music. On a wider canvass, Spenser's peculiar form of 'allegory', of speaking otherness in all its forms—'of forreine lands, of people different' (*MHT*, 765)—continues to provide one of the most significant sites in Early Modern literature for studying the interface between aesthetic and political theory. Taken in conjunction, moments such as Prince Arthur's reading of the 'Briton Moniments' in *Faerie Queene* II (x.1–69), the narrator's personal address to contemporary 'Britons' on the subject of empire in *Faerie Queene* IV (xi.22), and Irenius's assertion that some of the most savage of the Irish descend from the Britons (*Prose*, 170–1), open avenues of approach not just to Spenser's politics but to his poetics that we have yet to explore. It is scarcely surprising that he had such an impact on his contemporaries and upon subsequent generations of readers and writers: he changed the course of literary history, reforming English metrics and initiating a debate about the nature of 'poetic' language; he raised major issues about the relationship of art to commerce and patronage, and about the conflict between artistic liberty and state censorship; he contributed to a still ongoing debate on the aims and ethics of colonialism and the consequences of racial difference; and he examined the role of myth, legend, and literature in the construction of national identities. For decades now his work has been at the centre of interest in the fields of narratology, allegory, historicism, and formalism. If the purpose of education is to inspire independent, critical thought, his canon is 'didactic' in the best possible way. Four centuries after his death he continues to be the subject not only of academic study but of poems, novels, and plays. But most important of all, he continues to be read and enjoyed. A useful art indeed!

BIBLIOGRAPHY

Alexander, G. (ed.) (2004). *Sidney's 'The Defence of Poetry' and Selected Renaissance Literary Criticism*. London: Penguin Books.
Boccaccio, Giovanni (1930). *Boccaccio on Poetry*, ed. and trans. C. G. Osgood. Princeton: Princeton University Press.

Burlinson, C., and A. Zurcher (eds) (2009). *Edmund Spenser: Selected Letters and Other Papers.* Oxford: Oxford University Press.

Hall, Joseph (1969). *The Poems of Joseph Hall*, ed. A. Davenport. Liverpool: Liverpool University Press.

Jameson, F. (1983). *The Political Unconscious: Narrative as a Socially Symbolic Act.* First pub. 1981. London: Methuen.

Kennedy, W. J. (1995). *Authorizing Petrarch.* Ithaca, NY: Cornell University Press.

McCabe, R. A. (2000). 'Annotating Anonymity, or Putting a Gloss on *The Shepheardes Calender*', in J. Bray, M. Handley, and A. C. Henry (eds), *Ma[r]king the Text: The Presentation of Meaning on the Literary Page.* Aldershot: Ashgate, 35–54.

Warton, Thomas (1807). *Observations on 'The Fairy Queen' of Spenser.* First pub. 1754. 2 vols. London.

PART I

CONTEXTS

CHAPTER 1

....

SPENSER'S LIFE

....

WILLY MALEY

SOURCES AND SILENCES

....

The list of Elizabethan Edmund Spensers includes one who fathered a son called Hamlet in 1570 (Eccles 1944: 421; Welply 1932: 129). Probably no relation, though given the uncertainty surrounding the sources for the poet's life, anything's possible. Alas poor Spenser, we do not know him well. Two weddings and a funeral can be confirmed. Much else is speculation. Even the marriages and burial retain question marks. Neither a 1938 search for Spenser's grave in Westminster nor excavations sixty years later at Kilcolman, Spenser's home for the last ten years of his life, yielded significant results, though the 'E. K.' latterly engaged in the Kilcolman project, Eric Klingelhöfer, has given us the lineaments of Spenser's living arrangements (Eagle 1956; Klingelhöfer 2005). Nor does this essay promise to unearth fresh evidence, though it is a dig of sorts that sets out to sift the settled facts of the life. A familiar lament in Spenser studies is the absence of a proper biography. The 1922 Irish Public Record Office fire destroyed a key archive. Fortunately, some scholars had access to that material, which is why we know about Spenser's second wife and son (Welply 1932: 169). Papers allegedly destroyed in the fire at Kilcolman in October 1598 are beyond us.

Rather than bewail what we lack, this essay focuses on existing documentary evidence, following the course of the life, detailing key events and probabilities in a rigorous examination of the extant evidence, with as much by way of conclusion as it will bear. Knowledge of Spenser's life is gleaned from three sources: his Irish letters, his poetry and prose, and the testimony of contemporaries. Douglas Hamer, commenting on Spenser's second marriage before the first was widely known, said of the tendency to seek information in *Amoretti* and *Epithalamion*: 'It is exceedingly dangerous to assume biographical facts from the dates of publication of Spenser's poems' (Hamer 1931: 271).

If extrapolating from the literary work risks becoming too speculative, sticking to the secretarial work is equally fraught, as here the poet is acting as amanuensis rather than author. There has to be more to Spenser's life than his whereabouts in Ireland at a given time. Future work—Burlinson and Zurcher's selection of Spenser's letters, and Brink's researches—will augment our understanding. Andrew Hadfield's claim that 'The more literary may, paradoxically, be the more truthful work', makes his biography even more eagerly anticipated (Hadfield 2008: 72).

If the few 'facts' of Spenser's life are found in his own writings, those of contemporaries, and the Irish state papers, the problem is that the first includes works anonymous, controversial, and disputed, the second consists of backhanded compliments as well as praise, and the third contains the main body of Spenser's handwriting, but in the rather prosaic form of letters dictated by his employers (though with some poetic license). Few writers with such substantial bodies of published work leave so little in the way of surviving literary manuscripts, though the letters he scribed and signed amount to a significant holograph archive. The evidence of the state papers and other documentary material, the evidence of the prose, including prefaces, literary letters, and the *View*, the evidence of the poetry, and the evidence of his peers are all we have.

Through organizing messengers during Grey's deputyship, Spenser gained access to supplies of ink and paper. The fruits of office were self-evident. To be in charge of so much writing material, in a country nicknamed 'the paper state' for its administrative burden and reliance on intelligence, was perfect for any author, especially one engaged in an epic production (Morgan 1993: 17). Although Spenser's status as secretary has been elegantly explored by Richard Rambuss (1993), his role as messenger is arguably less remarked upon. If he was literally made in Ireland, like his greatest work, then this context was long underexplored. Recently, the pendulum has swung from embarrassment to excitement. It is now hard to read Spenser outside of an exhaustive Irish context precisely because the documentary evidence is concentrated in the Irish state papers. This has enriched our understanding, but skewed the life.

MODEST BEGINNINGS

The verse epistle to *The Shepheardes Calender* refers to it as 'child whose parent is unkent'. Its author's origins are equally obscure. His father may have been the John Spenser who moved to London in the 1560s—described as a 'free jorneyman' in the 'arte or mysterie of clothmakinge' in October 1566 (Heffner 1938–9: 83)—and joined the Merchant Taylors Company, since Edmund was schooled at an institution founded by that company. In *Amoretti* 74, Spenser's mother's name is given as Elizabeth. A letter from Harvey suggests Spenser had siblings, including a younger brother. At least one followed him to Ireland. Beyond their possible names—Sarah, and John (or James)—little is known of them.

Here is what we think we know. Spenser was born in London, in 'East Smithfield near the Tower', if we believe one early commentator (Heffner 1938–9: 84). The poet himself tells us only that he was a Londoner by birth: 'mery London, my most kyndly Nurse, | That to me gaue this Lifes first natiue sourse', as he says in *Prothalamion* (127–8). The likeliest date of birth is 1552, based on evidence of activities in 1569. Spenser began his formal education at the new Merchant Taylors' School for boys, founded by the Guild of Merchant Taylors on 20 September 1561, formally constituted four days later. The school was housed in an old mansion called the Manor of the Rose, in the parish of St Lawrence-Pountney. Statutes limited pupils to 250, comprising 100 poor men's sons, making no parental contribution, 50 others at half-fee of 5 shillings a quarter, and 100 'rich or mean men's children'. Spenser entered Merchant Taylors' as a 'poor scholar'. Its headmaster, classical scholar and educational theorist Richard Mulcaster, was an eloquent advocate of the English language who nonetheless recognized the necessity of augmenting it with borrowings from other tongues. Among fellow students were Thomas Kyd, Lancelot Andrewes, and Thomas Lodge. The school day began at 7 a.m. summer and winter, and ended at 5 p.m., with an intermission from 11 a.m. to 1 p.m.

On 16 August 1562, a visitation to Merchant Taylors' involved Edmund Grindal, Alexander Nowell, and Thomas Watts, key figures in Spenser's early years. At eight o'clock on the morning of 13 November 1564, pupils presented themselves before a board of examiners, including Miles Coverdale, renowned for his 1535 translation of the Bible. Spenser may have been amongst those who presented copies of verses and epistles to Bishop Grindal, later praised as 'Algrin' in *The Shepheardes Calender* ('Julye', 213–30). Also present was Alexander Nowell, Dean of St Paul's (Maley 1994: 2). The Dean's brother, Robert Nowell, Attorney of the Court of Wards, established before his death a fund for poor scholars, of which Spenser was beneficiary both at school and on going up to Cambridge. Nowell is reputedly the bridge between Spenser and the Dudleys (Webster 1934). On 12 November 1565 a third visitation was undertaken by Watts. Two other Spensers are associated with the Merchant Taylors' Company in this period, Robert, and Nicholas, elected Warden on 12 July 1568 (Brink 1997: 50).

1569: SENIOR SCHOOLBOY, FIRST-YEAR STUDENT, FOREIGN SERVANT, TRANSLATOR

1569 is the year Spenser first materializes in several guises: pupil at Merchant Taylors', fresher at Cambridge, published translator, and courier in France.

The only official record of Spenser's schooldays dates from his final year, when he was one of six 'poor schollers' gifted a gown and shilling for the funeral of wealthy

London lawyer Robert Nowell, who died on 6 February 1569 and was buried in St Paul's Cathedral. Among the other schoolboys—thirty-one from five London schools—was Richard Hakluyt (1552?–1616) of Westminster School (Hamer 1947: 219–20). Hakluyt was the same age as Spenser, suggesting this was a role performed by senior boys. On 28 April 1569 Spenser next shows up on the radar, receiving ten shillings from the Nowell bequest, 'at his gowinge to penbrocke hall in chambridge' (Eccles 1944: 414). Dean Alexander Nowell was trustee of his brother's estate, and his steward, James Wotton, kept a book of disbursements.

On 20 May Spenser was admitted to Pembroke Hall, one of thirteen 'sizars', poor scholars given servant's duties, from 'size', a portion of bread and ale which the poor student had free. Before matriculating, Spenser embarked on a literary career. His translations of poems by Petrarch and Du Bellay appeared with woodcut illustrations as an introduction to *A Theatre for Worldlings* (1569), entered in the Stationers' Register by Henry Bynneman on 22 July 1569 (see Chapter 8 below). In his work, Spenser is largely silent about the facts of his own early life, besides a brief allusion to 'mother Cambridge' in the description of the river Cam in Book IV of *The Faerie Queene* (IV.xi.34.7). We know he forged a friendship with Fellow of Pembroke and Professor of Rhetoric, Gabriel Harvey (1552–1631), a close contemporary in years, but a senior member of the college during Spenser's time as an undergraduate.

As well as having translations published as he progressed from school to university, and of a type that prefigures *The Shepheardes Calender*—poems with woodcuts, presented anonymously—Spenser seems to have served as a messenger in the pay of the Elizabethan state, foreshadowing his long secretarial service in Ireland. On 18 October 1569, a bill was signed to 'Edmonde Spencer' for bearing letters from Tours, in France, for Sir Henry Norris (c.1525–1601), English ambassador there, to Elizabeth, suggesting Spenser was engaged at an early stage in his career in secretarial work for influential figures:

Payde upon a bill signed by Mr Secretarye dated at Wyndsor xviij° Octobris 1569 To Edmonde Spencer that broughte lres to the Quenes Ma^{tis} from Sir Henrye Norrys knighte her Ma^{ts} Embassador in Fraunce beinge then at Towars in the sayde Realme, for his charges the some of vj^{li}.xiij^s.iiij^d. over and besydes ix^{li}. prested to hym by Sir Henrye Norrys. (Maley 1994: 4)

Spenser's knowledge of French—his translations made him a worldly worldling—rendered him a prime candidate for such an assignment, and lest we think him young at seventeen we must remember the equally youthful Raleigh was in this very month serving with the Huguenots in France (Eccles 1944: 415). Sir Henry Norris arrived in France in 1567 as English ambassador, probably through the influence of the Earl of Leicester, and played a lead role in unsuccessful negotiations over the return of Calais in line with the treaty of Cateau-Cambrésis of 3 April 1559. It would be interesting had Spenser witnessed the end of the English pale in France before settling in the English pale in Ireland.

If the Edmund Spenser who carried letters from France for Sir Henry Norris on 18 October 1569 was the poet this has implications for his date of birth. One cannot conceive of a fifteen-year-old boy being entrusted with sensitive state documents, suggesting an earlier date of birth than 1554, closer to 1552. There would be a neat circularity in Spenser's career as a courier—and he was courier rather than courtier—if he was the bearer of these letters, as his last act on record was carrying correspondence back to London from Cork for the fifth of Sir Henry's six sons, Sir Thomas Norris (1556–99), almost exactly thirty years after fulfilling a similar duty for his father, and for a similar sum.

If Spenser was carrying letters to the Continent as a seventeen year old this chimes with his entrance into Cambridge and first published work. Precocious? Yes, but not overly so. In *Tragicall Tales* (1587) George Turberville (*c.*1543/4–97?) addressed an epistle to his friend 'Spencer' dating from 1569, when Turberville was secretary to the English ambassador to Russia (Turberville 1587: 186). Most critics discount this reference (J. M. B. 1854: 204; Rollins 1918: 533–5)—others ignore it (Sheidley 1990)—while Craik's comment that Turberville, being about thirty, was 'not the age at which men choose boys of sixteen for their friends' strains credulity (Hales 1869: liv). Turberville was as young as twenty-five in 1569, and as a captain in Ireland in 1580 was a contemporary of Spenser's there (Lyne 2004). Is it so far-fetched that a young man—and published poet—entrusted with letters to the English ambassador to France might be the recipient of an epistle from his Russian counterpart? Did foreign service in France mark the beginning of Spenser's career as a secretary?

In November/December of this year a James Spenser was serving as Master of the Ordnance in Ireland, and if he is a relative, this suggests Spenser may have had family connections in that country prior to his official arrival there in 1580 with Lord Grey (Maley 1994: 4, 11). Spenser received further payments from the Nowell bequest over the next two years—six shillings on 7 November 1570, two shillings and sixpence on 24 April 1571. Further evidence of his financial need and the sources of patronage on which he depended? Or does the myth of the 'poor scholar' fail to grasp that this term was a conventional construction that need not imply real poverty (Hamer 1947: 223)? Finally, as part of the warp and woof of this period it's worth noting that another recipient of the Nowell bequest was Pembroke contemporary Edward Kirk, prime candidate for E. K. (Hamer 1941: 221). Kirk matriculated as sizar in November 1571 (Cooper 1860).

In 1571 there is a John Spenser at Merchant Taylors' School, a John Spenser matriculated as sizar at Pembroke in Easter 1575, taking his BA in 1577–8, and a John Spenser installed as Constable of Limerick on 23 November 1579. If these three are one, the parallels with Edmund's career strengthen the conjecture that John was the poet's brother. In 1570 or early 1571, Harvey was involved in a debate at Hill Hall, Theydon Mount, Essex, centre of the Smith family estate. Participants in a discussion of classical precedents for colonial projects included Thomas Smith junior, Sir Humphrey Gilbert, Sir Thomas Smith, Dr Walter Haddon, John Wood, 'and several others of gentle birth'. In *Foure Letters*, 1592, Harvey refers to 'my Cosen, M. Thomas Smith . . . Colonel of the Ards in Ireland' (Jardine 1993: 65; Stern 1979: 65–6). Since the early 1570s are the period of Spenser's closest involvement with Harvey, the Smith debate, recorded by Harvey in Latin marginal notes to his copy of Livy's *Decades*, suggests an early acquaintance with Irish affairs. Spenser mentions Smith and Harvey together in the gloss on 'couthe' in the January eclogue of *The Shepheardes Calender*, where Smith's book of the commonwealth (*De Republica Anglorum*) is name checked ('Januarye', 10 gloss).

At Cambridge, Spenser received five 'aegrotat' (sick) payments: eleven and a half weeks between Lent and Trinity, 1571; six weeks in Midsummer and seven at Michaelmas (September–December), 1572; six weeks in September 1574, and thirteen weeks from that October to Epiphany. One critic wonders whether the 'suspicious frequency' of such payments, if alluding to absences from Cambridge, might suggest Spenser was taking care of business or bearing letters abroad rather than laid up in bed. A year's absence is a considerable period. Does the fact that supplicats for Spenser's degrees contain supposedly standard caveats about fulfilment of requirements point to spells of interrupted study in the service of the state (Millican 1939)? Or does the fact that such payments are common, and the particular periods of absence coincide with spells when the university broke up because of plague, make any suspicions intriguing but unsustainable (Attwater 1936: 48–9)? Richard McCabe makes the telling point that Cambridge would be unlikely to pay its students for service to a patron or the state, and it's worth recalling that the 'Edmonde Spencer' who delivered letters for Henry Norris was paid twice, by Norris and the Crown.

Spenser obtained his BA on 16 January 1573, entitling him to be called a 'gentleman', officially styled 'Dominus', graduating MA on 26 June 1576, sixty-sixth in a list of seventy (Millican 1939: 469). What does a graduate of Cambridge, with some experience as a messenger, do? If Spenser's nurse was London, and his mother Cambridge, then Ireland was his foster mother, and a rough raising it was too. It was in Limerick on 1 July 1577, if we are to accept the alleged eyewitness account of Irenius in the *View* as the poet's own recollection, that Spenser saw a grief-stricken foster mother drink her son's blood rather than let the earth absorb it (*Prose*, 112). This account of the execution of 'A notable Traitour', Murrogh O'Brien, can be read alongside the fact that a messenger named Spenser is recorded delivering letters and a 'cast of falcons' to Robert Dudley, Earl of Leicester, from Sir William Drury (1527–79), Lord President of Munster on 8 July 1577 (Maley 1994: 7). Spenser was possibly serving the then Lord Deputy, Henry Sidney, Leicester's brother-in-law. Philip Sidney's 'Discourse of Irish Affairs', written in September 1577, was presented to the queen in January 1578. On 12 September 1578 Henry Sidney left Ireland for the last time, and two days later Drury was sworn in as Lord Justice. Spenser claims acquaintance with Philip Sidney by 5 October 1579 (*Prose*, 6).

Dr John Young, former Master of Pembroke Hall, became Bishop of Rochester in Kent on 1 April 1578 and Spenser soon became his secretary (Long 1916). For this two pieces of evidence survive, an embarrassment of riches. On 23 November Spenser made out a rental receipt as secretary to Bishop Young, and on 20 December he presented Harvey in London with four 'foolish bookes'—*Howleglas, Scoggin, Skelton,* and *Lazarillo*—telling him he must read them by 1 January or forfeit his four-volume Lucian (Stern 1979: 228). Spenser also presented Harvey with a piece of travel literature, a copy of Jerome Turler's *The Traveiler*, published in 1575, inscribed:

'Gabrielis Harveij'. 'ex dono Spenserii, Episcopi Roffensis Secretarii. 1578' (A gift of
Edmund Spenser, secretary of the Bishop of Rochester) (Stern 1979: 237). Harvey
alludes to Turler's book in the letter to Spenser of 23 October 1579 (*Prose*, 444; Maley
1994: 8).

1579: SHEPHERD, COLIN, IMMERITO

1579 was especially auspicious. The prefatory epistle to *The Shepheardes Calender*,
signed 'E. K.', dated 'from my lodging at London thys 10. of Aprill', mentions lost
works, salvaged as parts of longer poems (one, the 'Courte of Cupide', presumably
reworked as *The Faerie Queene* III.xi–xii), in keeping with Spenser's frugal habits of
revision. *The Shepheardes Calender* was timed to coincide with the publication of the
Spenser–Harvey correspondence containing clues to its authorship. Spenser was back
in London by 10 July, perhaps signalling the end of his Kentish secretaryship. On 5
October he claims to be serving the Earl of Leicester, in a 'composite epistle of three
parts' dated 5, 15, and 16 October 1579, from Leicester House, Westminster, and
Mistress Kirk's, respectively (Welply 1941: 456). Spenser first wrote to Harvey to say
that, having entered the earl's service, he was ready to travel abroad for his new
master. Ten days later he was in 'some use of familiarity' with Philip Sidney and
Edward Dyer, discussing the reform of English poetry (*Prose*, 6). Harvey mentions an
acquaintance with Daniel Rogers, another associate of Sidney's and erstwhile informer of Henry Norris's (*Prose*, 477). The Leicester–Sidney circle had interests in Ireland—on 23 November Leicester was one of a group of privy councilors mandated 'to
consult of the affairs of Ireland'—so Spenser could be seen to be taking up that
service when he went there with Lord Grey the following summer.

On 27 October 1579 Spenser married 'Machabyas Chylde' at St Margaret's Church,
Westminster. Baptized there on 8 September 1560, her parentage is unrecorded
(Eccles 1944: 424). Spenser's first wife is thought to be the daughter of Robert Chylde
and Alice Lorde, married in St Margaret's on October 18, 1556, but no conclusive
evidence exists (Eccles 1944: 424). Edmund and Maccabaeus had one child, Sylvanus,
possibly named after Mulcaster's son 'Silvan' who was christened on 12 March 1564 in
St Lawrence Pountney, parish church of Merchant Taylors', a christening Spenser may
have attended. He may also have been at the boy's untimely funeral on 28 January
1573 (Welply 1941: 57). 'Sylvanus' also appears in Mantuan's eclogues, so behind
Mulcaster was a literary source. We have no date of birth and few details of Sylvanus
Spenser, probably born in 1580. He signed a Marriage Licence Bond to wed Ellin
Nagle, daughter of David Nagle, in 1601 and had entered into his property by that
date (Welply 1941: 438). Spenser's first marriage also produced an 'eldest daughter',
Katherine (Welply 1933: 93). Another significant event of 1579 was Lord Justice
Pelham's proclamation at Limerick on 6 November that every English horseman

under his command should wear red crosses, front and back, 'either of Silke or Cloth'. Coming so close to Spenser's embarking on *The Faerie Queene* this appears fortuitous (McLane 1959; Maley 1994: 10–11; Smith 1955). On 5 December 1579, *The Shepheardes Calender* was entered in the Stationers' Register.

On 6 March 1580, James Spenser carried letters to Limerick from Burleigh to Henry Wallop (McLane 1959: 100). On 2 April Spenser told Harvey he was working on *The Faerie Queene*. Harvey called it '*Hobgoblin* runne away with the Garland from *Apollo*' (*Prose*, 472). 'Hobgoblin' had been used by one of Spenser's circle, Thomas Drant, in *Horace his arte of poetrie, pistles and satyrs englished* (1567: Biii). Spenser and Harvey's *Three Proper, and wittie, familiar Letters*, was entered into the Stationer's Register on 30 June. Harvey's last letter of 24 May mentions 'a goodly Kentishe *Garden* of your old Lords', a reference to Spenser's former service in Rochester (*Prose*, 466). The epistle 'To the Curteous Buyer' is dated 19 June. To these were attached *Two Other, very commendable Letters, of the same mens writing*. On 14 July Sir William Pelham (d. 1587), Lord Justice of Ireland, sues for 'furtherance of his brother Spenser's suits' (Maley 1994: 12). This reference to John Spenser, Pelham's brother-in-law through marriage to Pelham's sister, Mary, coincides almost exactly with Edmund's arrival in Ireland (Welply 1932: 147). On 15 July, Arthur, Lord Grey de Wilton, was appointed Lord Deputy of Ireland. Spenser probably arrived in Chester on 28 July, accompanying Grey aboard *The Handmaid*, arriving in Dublin on 12 August. Letters in his hand appear from 29 August (cf. Chapter 4). Spenser would have attended Grey's investiture in Dublin, on 7 September. James Spenser died this month.

After his second anonymous foray into verse, Spenser, having set himself up as the most promising poet of his generation, failed to publish for the next decade. *Theatre* and *Calender* receded—though the latter went through successive editions and was frequently quoted and imitated—as Ireland became worldly stage and pastoral retreat. Spenser was busy both with the formidable task of writing *The Faerie Queene*, and his various duties as colonist and career civil servant. On 25 August 1580, the English were routed in Glenmalure, Wicklow, by Irish forces led by Feagh McHugh O'Byrne and James Eustace, third Viscount Baltinglass (1530–85). The notorious massacre at the Fort d'Oro (Golden Fort), Smerwick, on the Dingle Peninsula, occurred against this backdrop. From 13 September, a Spanish-led force occupied Smerwick. Grey reached the fort on 31 October. The siege began on 7–8 November. Spenser, through Irenius, claims to have been present on 9 November 1580, when the Lord Deputy and his captains, including Walter Raleigh, put to the sword—after surrender—600 Spanish and Italian troops. In letters to Elizabeth and Burghley, scribed by Spenser, Grey justified his actions on grounds of expediency. Spenser later defended Grey against charges that he was a 'blodye man' (*Prose*, 159). Spenser's descriptions of the execution of Murrogh O'Brien, the Smerwick Massacre, and the Munster Famine are among the most graphic passages in the *View* (*Prose*, 158). These eyewitness accounts, debatable as personal testimony, are the closest we have to autobiography. Irenius, declaring himself an eyewitness—'my selfe beinge then as neare as anye'—tells Eudoxus that when the fort's commander, Sebastiano di San Giuseppi, sued for grace, Grey never guaranteed safe passage (*Prose*, 161–2). Grey died in October 1593, so did not live to see himself defended by his former secretary, a defence perhaps prompted by the death of Spenser's former patron, and the continuing violence in Ireland. He did live, though, to see the dedicatory sonnet appended to *The Faerie Queene* addressed to him in 1590 (Spenser 2001: 731).

Criticism of Grey's Deputyship hinged on his bloody reputation and favouring of followers, including the bestowing of lands taken from 'rebels'. One man's rebellion was another's land-grabbing exercise. Grey's tenure as Lord Deputy ended on 31 August 1582, two years after it had begun. Grey had often asked to be recalled, in angst-ridden letters scribed by Spenser, requests fuelled by bad publicity in England. He remained praiseworthy in the eyes of 'New English' planters, Spenser included, who considered his harshness fitted to the times. It should be emphasized that, given Spenser's eighteen years minimum in Ireland, his secretaryship under Grey (1580–2) is only a small part of his administrative experience. Grey's recall marked the end of Spenser's secretaryship and the beginning of his deputyship, as assistant to Lodowick Bryskett, Clerk for the Council of Munster.

In his *Discourse of Civill Life* (1606), originally intended for dedication to Lord Grey, Bryskett placed Spenser among an elite literary gathering at Bryskett's house near Dublin in 1582, where the poet declines to speak on moral philosophy as he is already covering this topic poetically in *The Faerie Queene* (Pafford 1972: 26–9). Taken together with Harvey's comments in the correspondence this suggests an early starting date for Spenser's epic and a lengthy process of editing and revision. As well as Bryskett and Raleigh, there were new neighbours with reputations as writers, including Geoffrey Fenton, Barnaby Rich, Thomas Churchyard, and Barnaby Googe. Far from being the last resort of the failed and frustrated, Ireland was a testing-ground for those inclined towards experimentation, innovation, and alternatives to established authority.

On 12 May 1583 Spenser is one of twenty-seven men appointed commissioners for musters in County Kildare for two years, expected when called upon 'to summon all the subjects of each barony, and then so mustered in warlike apparel' (Maley 1994: 37–8). It is worth noting here that a James Spenser later served as Master of Musters in Munster, and was five years provincial commissioner of Musters in Ireland with William Jones. Is this the William Jones for whose translation of *Nennio, or a Treatise of Nobility* (1595) Spenser wrote a commendatory sonnet? He would not be the first English translator to find himself in Ireland (others, besides Bryskett, include Fenton, Florio, and Googe). On 6 November 1583, Bryskett, whose various offices Spenser seems to have shadowed as a more junior figure, was officially installed as Clerk of the Council of Munster, and secretary to Sir John Norris, aka 'Black Jack' (*c.*1547–97), President of the Council. Spenser acted as Bryskett's deputy from at least 31 December. His whereabouts in this period can be gauged—or guessed at—from the movements of the new Lord Deputy, Sir John Perrot, from the dates of sessions of the Dublin parliament, and from letters in Spenser's own hand. Assuming that Perrot required secretaries to follow him on tours of duty, Spenser may have accompanied him through Munster and Connaught in July 1584, before heading north to Ulster, returning to Dublin in October.

Raymond Jenkins calls the period 1584–9 'The Uncertain Years', a crucial spell marking Spenser's transition from secretary to settler and archly anonymous author to writer of a major national epic (Jenkins 1938). By 8 December 1585 Spenser secured the Prebendary of Effin, a benefice attached to Limerick Cathedral. A 'prebend' was a pension or plot of land granted to a cathedral to fund a secular priest or regular canon. In the May and July eclogues of *The Shepheardes Calender*, Spenser attacked such lay appropriations as corrupt, and in *Mother Hubberds Tale* a priest conversing with a fox illustrates the careerism implicit in the pursuit of such offices (lines 479–501; see below pp. 40, 41).

As (Deputy) Clerk of the Council of Munster, Spenser likely attended the sessions at the presidency court in Limerick and Cork throughout 1585 and 1586. Plans were drafted to establish a colony of English settlers in the province on property in the region of 630,000 acres confiscated from the Earl of Desmond after the Desmond Rebellion (1579–83). Forfeited lands were surveyed in the autumn of 1584, and the plan for plantation, drawn up in December 1585, passed through the Irish parliament the following year. The plantation was parcelled out as 'seignories' of 12,000 acres. The Articles for the Munster Plantation received royal assent on 27 June 1586. The settlers, or 'undertakers'—undertaking to occupy plots of the plantation—were digging their own graves on land recently witness to the walking dead of war and famine. A curious parallel exists between Spenser's own account of the Munster famine of the early 1580s and 'A Brief Note of Ireland' of 1598, though second time around the 'unhappie Ghostes' are colonists, not natives (*Prose*, 236).

The Munster Plantation seigniories were subdivided into 4,000 acre plots (cf. Chapter 5). Spenser acquired an estate of 3,028 acres in County Cork, connected to the ruined castle of Kilcolman (Irish for 'Colman's Church')—one of the smaller portions granted to English settlers from over half a million acres, surveyed by 16 February 1587 but not occupied until 3 September 1588 at the earliest—described as 'a large castle, old, and dilapidated, which at the present time has no use except to shelter cattle at night' (Maley 1994: 43). Spenser's estate was 1,000 acres shy of his original allocation, the shortfall perhaps in part the subject of his subsequent feud with Lord Roche. Spenser may have inhabited an adjoining house as well as occupying the castle itself. Like Dublin, Cork supplied Spenser with a wide range of colleagues, companions, and contacts, as well as writing time and materials. Munster proved fertile ground for fertile minds, accommodating a respectable group of literary figures. Here was an areopagus, a gathering of shepherd-poets, away from Cambridge, court, and city. As well as Raleigh, who had a vast estate of over 42,000 acres, or three and a half seignories, neighbours included Richard Beacon, Meredith Hanmer, and Sir William Herbert, all authors of treatises on Ireland. Raleigh's visit to Kilcolman is recorded in *Colin Clouts Come Home Againe*. Spenser presumably visited in turn Raleigh's house at Youghal, where the latter served as mayor.

A sonnet to Harvey dated Dublin 18 July 1586, later included in Harvey's *Foure Letters* (1592), suggests Spenser spent time in the Irish capital (Spenser 1999: 500). The evidence of the Irish state papers implies Spenser spent most of the following year in Munster. Some time in 1587 or 1588 Spenser's sister, Sarah, married John Travers, who later served under Essex as Commissary of Victuals at Carrickfergus, and her brother assigned as a wedding gift two plough lands of his Irish estate, subsequently disputed territory (Welply 1932: 149; 1940: 93). Maurice, Lord Roche, Sixth Viscount Roche of Fermoy (d. 1600), a prominent Old English landowner, complained to the Queen's Commissioners that English planters had illegally occupied his land. Thus began a lengthy process of litigation.

1589: KILCOLMAN, *THE FAERIE QUEENE*, COURT, AND *COMPLAINTS*

On 22 May 1589 Spenser secured official possession of Kilcolman. One of the 'undertakings', or conditions, to which he had agreed, entailed establishing a colony of six English households. A key criticism of the Munster plantation after its overthrow in October 1598 was the settlers' failure to fulfil their obligations with regard to peopling the plantation. It was hard to entice families over to that war-torn region. Two documents show Spenser involved in Chancery disputes in Dublin at this time. On 10 June 1589, Richard Roche of Kinsale and Edmund Spenser entered a bond in Chancery between Spenser and Hugh Strawbridge. On 18 June Spenser was entrusted with the delivery of James Shropp to Newgate, Dublin (Gillespie and Hadfield 2001: 250; Welply 1932: 110–14). On 12 October 1589, Lord Roche protested about encroachments upon his property, naming Spenser among the guilty parties. The undertakers in turn alleged that Roche 'has imprisoned men of...Mr. Edmund Spenser and others. He speaks ill of Her Majesty's government and hath uttered words of contempt of Her Majesty's laws, calling them unjust' (Maley 1994: 51–2). Accusation following counter-accusation, and the case haunted Spenser throughout the 1590s, perhaps influencing the debate on jurisdiction and territorial rights in *Two Cantos of Mutabilitie* (Coughlan 1996). Sylvanus Spenser later married the granddaughter of William Roche, a kinsman of Lord Roche (Welply 1932: 202). Intermarriage, against which Spenser inveighed in the *View*, went with the territory, as his own family tree attests (*Prose*, 117, 119–20; Welply 1932).

In October 1589 Spenser left Cork for Court with Raleigh. The first three books of *The Faerie Queene*, entered in the Stationers' Register on 1 December 1589, appeared early in 1590. Spenser's 'Letter to Raleigh' is dated 23 January 1590. On 26 October 1590, Spenser received official confirmation of his estate at Kilcolman in the form of a royal grant. *Complaints* was entered into the Stationer's Register on 29 December 1590. In a preface to the reader, the printer, William Ponsonby says that since his previous publication for Spenser—*The Faerie Queene*—proved so successful, he has 'endeavoured by all good meanes [...] to get into my handes such smale Poemes of the same Authors; as I heard were disperst abroad in sundrie hands, and not easie to bee come by, by himselfe: some of them having bene diuerslie imbeziled and purloyned from him, since his departure ouer Sea' (Spenser 1999: 165).

About this time, Raleigh, fellow recipient of the appropriated Desmond lands, introduced Spenser's poem—and, perhaps less likely, the poet himself—to Elizabeth. On 25 February 1591 the Queen granted the poet a life pension of £50 a year, to be paid in four annual installments: Lady Day (25 March), Nativity of John the Baptist (24 June), Michaelmas (29 September), and Christmas (Berry and Timings 1960: 255). Spenser's life now looked less haphazard, with royal recognition, a permanent foothold in Ireland, and the first part of his epic in print. Things were looking up, but he'd be dead before the decade was out, still only in his late forties. Although he published nothing new in the 1580s, in the dedicatory letter to Raleigh prefixed to *Colin Clouts Come Home Againe*, dated from Kilcolman 27 December 1591, Spenser assured his patron he was 'not alwaies ydle as yee thinke, though not greatly well occupied, nor altogither undutifull, though not precisely officious' (Spenser 1999: 344).

Spenser certainly proved productive in the years that followed. His work is cited with increasing frequency among contemporaries, including Samuel Daniel, John Florio, Abraham Fraunce, Sir John Harington, Christopher Marlowe, Thomas Nashe, Henry Peacham, and George Peele. *Daphnaida* appeared under Ponsonby's imprint early in 1591, with Spenser's dedicatory preface dated from London, 1 January. *Axiochus*, a meditation on mortality between Socrates and an old man, appeared the following year. The modern attribution to Spenser rests on verbal echoes (especially *The Faerie Queene* II.xii.51).

In Ireland, protracted legal wrangling with Lord Roche hampered Spenser's efforts to make his holding appear as permanent as the royal grant had implied ('forever in fee farm'). The year 1593 saw Roche once more complaining bitterly of 'Edmond Spenser, gentleman, a heavy adversary' (Maley 1994: 60). Spenser acted as Queen's Justice for Cork in 1594. We do not know what happened to Spenser's first wife. We do know that on St Barnabas Day, 11 June 1594, Spenser married Elizabeth Boyle, kinswoman of Richard Boyle, who as Earl of Cork became one of Ireland's greatest landowners. Elizabeth was also related to the Spencers of Althorp (Heffner 1938–9; Strathmann 1943). They had one child, Peregrine. Elizabeth, daughter of Stephen—of Bradden, near Towcester, Northamptonshire (Welply 1924: 446)—and Joan Boyle, was one of four children. Her mother remarried after her father's death in 1582, to Ferdinando Freckleton, and this became significant when a suit was brought in the interests of the children of her former marriage (Welply 1924: 446; Strathmann 1943). Elizabeth Spenser remarried twice—to Roger Seckerstone in 1600 and Robert Tynte in 1612/13—bearing each husband a son before her death on 23 August 1622 (Welply 1924: 445; 1932: 63). Spenser's courtship and marriage, depicted in the sonnet sequence *Amoretti* and marriage hymn *Epithalamion*, entered in the Stationers' Register on 19 November 1594, appeared as a single volume in early 1595, 'Written not long since'. The dedicatory note by Ponsonby to Sir Robert Needham, says he assumed responsibility for publishing the poems in their author's absence, describing Spenser as 'that wel-deseruing gentleman' (Spenser 1999: 386). The pastoral satire,

Colin Clouts Come Home Againe, appeared the same year, but its dating 'From my house of Kilcolman' on 27 December 1591 suggests it was prepared four years earlier. Published together with *Colin* was *Astrophel*, the elegy for Philip Sidney, dedicated to his widow, Frances Walsingham, Countess of Essex. Sidney died in 1586, so this is presumably yet another selection from the back catalogue, timed to coincide with the publication of Sidney's *Apology for Poetry* (1595). At this time, Spenser published a commendatory sonnet prefixed to William Jones's translation of *Nennio, or a Treatise of Nobility* (1595). This fragment of Spenser's corpus, outside the orbit of most criticism, exemplifies the faith in merit that endeared him to Milton. The work is recommended to

> Who so wil seeke by right deserts t'attaine
>   vnto the type of true Nobility,
> And not by painted shewes and titles vaine,
>   Deriued farre from famous Auncestrie.   (Spenser 1999: 500)

Ironically, Spenser had attached himself to a house of ancient fame, the Spencers of Althorp, and in a public manner that suggests the claim held water (Spenser 1999: 130).

Spenser may have completed the *View* by summer 1596, before travelling to London to attend the weddings celebrated in *Prothalamion*. The *View* recommends the appointment of a Lord Lieutenant to oversee Irish affairs and refers to 'suche an one I Coulde name uppon whom the ey of all Englande is fixed and our laste hopes now rest' (*Prose*, 228). Commentators suggest Spenser was looking to Essex, who assumed that office on 12 March 1599, within two months of paying for the poet's funeral. Spenser continued his environmentally friendly publishing practice, recycling in the green style, with the appearance of *Fowre Hymnes*, the first two written 'in the greener times of my youth', dated 1 September 1596, dedicated from the court at Greenwich (Spenser 1999: 452). This volume contained the second edition of *Daphnaida*. This year also witnessed the publication of *Prothalamion*, a marriage hymn celebrating the spousals of Lady Elizabeth and Katherine Somerset, daughters of the Earl of Worcester, an associate of Essex. Spenser may have attended the weddings, held at Essex House, London, on 8 November 1596, given his presence in London recorded in the *Fowre Hymnes*. That Essex is lavishly praised in *Prothalamion* lends weight to the earl's identification as Spenser's candidate for Ireland in the *View*.

If Spenser was in London in November 1596 then he may have felt the backdraft from a heated exchange of letters. The second edition of *The Faerie Queene* (1596) fell foul of James VI. One touchy subject depicted allegorically in Book V was the trial of Elizabeth's cousin, Mary, Queen of Scots, mother of the reigning Scottish king, executed on 8 February 1587. Two of Spenser's patrons, Grey and Leicester, were commissioners at the trial ('MS Notes to Spenser's *Faerie Queene*' 1957: 512). Robert Bowes, English ambassador in Scotland, informed Burghley on 1 November 1596 that King James, distressed at the depiction of his mother in V.ix, had ordered copies of the poem destroyed, asking that his English counterpart do likewise. Bowes wrote to Burghley again on 12 November, having persuaded James the poem was not published with royal approval. James insisted the poet 'for his fault may be tried and duly punished' (McCabe 1987; Maley 1994: 67–8). This was a fraught month for Spenser. On 20 November he brought a bill before Chancery, and two days later he is mentioned in a Chancery writ involving Erasmus Dryden, Edward Cope, and John Matthewe (Hamer 1931: 273; Welply 1924). The story unravelled by W. H. Welply is one whereby Spenser and his new wife, Elizabeth, together with her brothers George and Alexander, sued for the legacy they were entitled to on coming to full age or marriage after their mother remarried. Spenser continued to acquire land in Ireland, despite the growing menace of Hugh O'Neill, Earl of Tyrone, whose forces overran English-controlled territory. In 1597 Spenser bought the castle of Renny in south Cork and its surrounding lands for his young son, Peregrine, for £200. Buttevant Abbey also came into his possession. By 7 February 1598, Spenser was in arrears for the rent of this property (Maley 1994: 71).

The *View* was entered in the Stationers' Register on 14 April 1598 but a note in one manuscript (Bodley NS Rawlinson B. 478) reads 'Mr Collinges | pray enter this Copie for mathew Lownes to be printed when he do bringe other authoritie' (Maley 1994: 72). Some critics conclude the text was suppressed, but works entered in the register were sometimes queried because of turf wars between publishers. Matthew Lownes was a printer with piracy in his past (most notably over Sir Philip Sidney's *Astrophil and Stella*), so the *View* may have been caught up in a tug-of-war between rival printers (Hadfield 1994). Around twenty manuscript copies survive including one Essex may have carried during his Irish campaign (cf. Chapter 17).

On 14 August 1598, English forces were routed at the Battle of the Yellow Ford. On 30 September, with the Munster Plantation verging on violent dissolution, the Privy Council appointed Spenser sheriff of Cork. Despite the rebuke from King James and apparent apprehension around publishing the *View*, Spenser still had friends in high places—at least in Ireland. On 4 October 1598, Sir Thomas Norris and others informed London that a force of 2,000 'rebels' was advancing towards them. Limerick fell the next day. Within two weeks the New English settlement was overthrown, Kilcolman sacked and burnt. Spenser's family fled to Cork city where the poet was ensconced on 7 December.

Confusion persists as to when Spenser left Ireland for the last time, although Ray Heffner put forward a clear case many years ago (Heffner 1933: 222). Spenser appears to have left Cork after 13 December bearing two letters from the President of Munster, Sir Thomas Norris, to the Privy Council and Robert Cecil, dated 9 and 13 December respectively, detailing the desperate situation in the province. On 21 December Norris wrote to the Privy Council again mentioning his 'last of the 9th this month, and sent by Mr. Spenser' (but not the letter to Cecil of the 13th). The two letters carried by Spenser arrived with the poet in London on or about the 24 December. Norris's second letter to the Privy Council was received at Whitehall on 29 December. On 30 December Spenser was paid a messenger's fee of £8. It is possible this sum was disbursed among separate messengers, with Spenser not the sole recipient.

1599: PENSION, MONUMENT, WORKS

Spenser died in King Street, Westminster, on 13 January 1599. According to Ben Jonson, 'the Irish, having robbed Spenser's goods and burnt his house and a little child new-born, he and his wife escaped, and after he died for lack of bread in King Street' (Parfitt 1984: 465). No other evidence of the dead child exists and critics consider it unlikely Spenser starved, having been paid £8 for delivering letters and with £25 pension in the offing. In *Tritons' Trumpet* (1621) John Lane repeats in rhyme the report of Spenser's death by starvation. After a two-month siege it is not too far-fetched that a man who had scarce escaped with his life might respond to Essex's offer of twenty crowns with the words 'the medicine comes too late for the pacient!' (Heffner 1933: 223).

Moreover, 'we have no record of the payment of the pension' prior to his death (Heffner 1933: 224). In fact, evidence suggests the pension was not paid till February—to a third party. Selling-on of pensions was common practice, as was borrowing against one's pension, so Spenser could have secured funds quite readily. The first instalment of Spenser's pension, for the month following 26 February 1591, was collected on 25 March by Edward Blount, former apprentice of the printer William Ponsonby, and another Merchant Taylors' son who published Marlowe's *Hero and Leander*, Florio's *Montaigne*, and Shakespeare's first folio (Berry and Timings 1960: 255). Ponsonby collected the next instalment on 24 June, Richard Wilson the Michaelmas 1593 instalment, and on 25 March 1594 Ralph Warde made the collection, after which payments were made half-yearly. George Dryden, brother of Erasmus, collected the Michaelmas 1594 pension, and the next record available shows that Thomas Walker picked up Spenser's £25 on 31 January 1598, and the same sum on 26 August 1598. Henry Vincent—son of Elizabeth Spenser of Northamptonshire, conceivably Edmund's mother by former marriage (Brink 1997: 51)—collected the last instalment of £25 on 28 February 1599, six weeks after Spenser's death. The reason for the late payment was the drain on the treasury caused by the Irish wars, and specifically the overthrow of the Munster Plantation (Berry and Timings 1960: 257–8). Funds usually available from 24 December were not released till 5 February.

Buried in Westminster Abbey, near Chaucer, on 16 January, Camden spoke of Spenser's 'hearse being attended by poets, and mournful elegies and poems, with the pens that wrote them, thrown into the tomb' (Maley 1994: 80; Wells, II, 178–9). Was Hamlet Spenser, then aged twenty-eight or twenty-nine, among the mourners? In 1620, Ann Clifford, Countess of Dorset, to whose mother and aunt *Fowre Hymnes* was dedicated, commissioned Nicholas Stone to erect a monument inscribed: 'Heare lyes (expecting the Second comminge of our Saviour Christ Jesus) the body of Edmond Spencer, the Prince of Poets in his tyme; whose divine spirit needs noe othir witnesse then the works which he left behinde him. He was borne in London in the yeare 1510. And Died in the yeare 1596' (Judson 1945: 207; Maley 1994: 80). Fittingly, this belated epitaph managed to mangle its few facts—recalling Spenser's probabilistic approach to history reliant on 'monimentes of Churches and Tombes' (*Prose*, 85)—but the claim that Spenser's works are his best witnesses still stands. The monument notwithstanding, no grave was found during that 1938 search (Eagle 1956). Welply's harsh judgement of biographical studies of the poet—'This is just blethers' (1941: 56)—is hard to shake off. Without the riches of the work the scraps of the life from schoolboy to sizar to secretary to settler to sheriff would be a vain foraging after straw.

BIBLIOGRAPHY

I thank Andrew Hadfield, Thomas Herron, and Richard McCabe for reading successive drafts and saving me from errors, ghosts, and bad puns.

Attwater, A. (1936). *Pembroke College, Cambridge*. Cambridge: Cambridge University Press.

B., J. M. (1854). 'Queries Concerning Spenser'. *N&Q* SER 1, 10: 204–5.

Berry, H., and E. K. Timings (1960). 'Spenser's Pension'. *RES* NS 11/43: 254–9.

Brink, J. R. (1997). 'Edmund Spenser's Family: Two Notes and a Query'. *N&Q* 44: 49–51.

Cooper, T., and C. H. (1860). 'Edward Kirke, the Commentator on Spenser's *Shepheardes Calender*'. *N&Q* SER 2, 9/212: 42.

Coughlan, P. (1996). 'The Local Context of Mutabilitie's Plea'. *Irish University Review* 26/2: 320–41.

Eagle, R. L. (1956). 'The Search for Spenser's Grave'. *N&Q* 201: 282–3.

Eccles, M. (1944). 'Elizabethan Edmund Spensers'. *MLQ* 5/4: 413–27.

Gillespie, R., and A. Hadfield (2001). 'Two References to Edmund Spenser in Chancery Disputes'. *N&Q* 48/3: 249–51.

Hadfield, A. (2008). 'Secrets and Lies: The Life of Edmund Spenser', in K. Sharpe and S. Zwicker (eds), *Writing Lives: Biography and Textuality, Identity and Representation in Early Modern England*. Oxford: Oxford University Press, 55–73.

Hales, J. W. (1869; 1883). 'Edmund Spenser', in R. Morris (ed.), *Complete Works of Edmund Spenser*. London: Macmillan, xi–lv.

Hamer, D. (1931). 'Spenser's Marriage'. *RES* 7/27: 271–90.

——(1941). 'Some Spenser Problems'. *N&Q* 180: 165–7, 183–4, 206–9, 220–4, 238–41.

——(1947). 'Edmund Spenser's Gown and Shilling'. *RES* 23/91: 218–25.

Heffner, R. (1938–9). 'Edmund Spenser's Family'. *HLQ*, 2/1: 79–84.

Jardine, L. (1993). 'Encountering Ireland: Gabriel Harvey, Edmund Spenser, and English Colonial Ventures', in B. Bradshaw, A. Hadfield, and W. Maley (eds), *Representing Ireland: Literature and the Origins of Conflict, 1534–1660*. Cambridge: Cambridge University Press, 60–75.

Jenkins, R. (1938). 'Spenser: The Uncertain Years 1584–1589'. *PMLA* 53: 350–62.

Judson, A. C. (1945). *The Life of Edmund Spenser*. Baltimore: Johns Hopkins Press.

Klingelhöfer, E. (2005). 'Edmund Spenser at Kilcolman Castle: The Archaeological Evidence'. *Post-Medieval Archaeology* 39/1: 133–54.

Long, Percy W. (1916). 'Spenser and the Bishop of Rochester'. *PMLA* 31/4: 713–35.

Lyne, R. (2004). 'Turbervile, George', *NDNB*.

McCabe, R. (1987). 'The Masks of Duessa: Spenser, Mary Queen of Scots, and James VI'. *ELR* 17/2: 224–42.

McLane, P. E. (1959). 'Was Spenser in Ireland in Early November 1579?' *N&Q* 204: 99–101.

Maley, W. (1994). *A Spenser Chronology*. London: Macmillan.

Millican, C. B. (1939). 'The Supplicats for Spenser's Degrees'. *HLQ* 2/4: 467–70.

Morgan, H. (1993). *Tyrone's Rebellion: The Outbreak of the Nine Years War in Tudor Ireland*. Woodbridge: Boydell and Brewer.

'MS Notes to Spenser's *Faerie Queene*' (1957). *N&Q* 202: 509–15.

'Oliver Cromwell and Spenser's Grandson' (1866). *N&Q* SER 3, 19/215: 113–14.

N., W. L. (1853). 'Spenser's *Fairy Queen*'. *N&Q* SER 1: 8: 367.

Pafford, J. H. P. (ed.) (1972). *Lodowick Bryskett: Literary Works*. Farnborough, Hants: Gregg International.

Parfitt, G. (ed.) (1975; 1984). *Ben Jonson: The Complete Poems*. Harmondsworth: Penguin.

Rambuss, R. (1993). *Spenser's Secret Career*. Cambridge: Cambridge University Press.

Rollins, H. E. (1918). 'New Facts about George Turbervile'. *MP* 15/9: 513–38.

Sheidley, W. E. (1990). 'Turberville, George'. *SE*, 704.

Smith, R. M. (1955). 'Origines Arthurianae: The Two Crosses of Spenser's Red Cross Knight'. *JEGP* 54: 670–83.

Stern, V. F. (1979). *Gabriel Harvey: His Life, Marginalia and Library*. Oxford: Clarendon Press.

Strathmann, E. A. (1943). 'Ferdinando Freckleton and the Spenser Circle'. *MLN* 58/7: 542–4.

Turberville, George (1587). *Tragicall tales translated by Turberuile in time of his troubles, out of sundrie Italians*. London.

Webster, C. M. (1934). 'Robert Nowell'. *N&Q* 167: 116.

Welply, W. H. (1924). 'Edmund Spenser: Some New Discoveries and the Correction of Some Old Errors'. *N&Q* 146: 445–7; 147: 35.

——(1932). 'Edmund Spenser: Being an Account of Some Recent Researches into His Life and Lineage, with Some Notice of His Family and Descendants'. *N&Q* 162: 110–14, 128–32, 146–50, 165–9, 182–7, 202–6, 220–4, 239–42, 256–60.

——(1933). 'More Notes on Edmund Spenser'. *N&Q* 165: 92–4, 111–16.

——(1940). 'Edmund Spenser's Brother-in-law, John Travers'. *N&Q* 179: 70–8, 92–7, 112–15.

——(1941). 'Some Spenser Problems'. *N&Q* 180: 56–9, 74–6, 92–5, 104, 151, 224, 248, 436–9, 454–9.

CHAPTER 2

....

SPENSER AND RELIGION

....

CLAIRE McEACHERN

ONE of the greatest challenges in thinking about the past is trying to imagine a prior moment without remembering 'how it all turned out', with the same degree of suspense and muddle experienced by its original participants. This effort is perhaps especially difficult when imagining Reformation England, a period and place marked by schism and whose partisan consequences include such episodes as the English Revolution, with its lethal conflict between religious sectaries and the established religious and political orders. The religious dimensions of Spenser's poetry are indeed indebted to a contention-ridden—that is, richly dramatic—landscape of Elizabethan religious identities. His poetry can picture this terrain in terms of antithesis, and perhaps as a result readers have often sought to identify him with myriad political and doctrinal positions along the spectrum of Reformation Christianity.[1] But it is important to remember that in the 1570s and 1580s, the years during which Spenser came of age both poetically and politically, many of the divisions and parties teased out by the events of the following seventy years were as yet intertwined. His poetry thus owes as much to the centripetal as the centrifugal tendencies of contemporary confessional persuasions. Its religious aspects are conditioned not only by Spenser's hallmark syncretism, or the 'middle way' of the Elizabethan religious settlement (capacious or compromised, depending on the interpreter), but the nature of the Elizabethan church in its inaugural decades.

Spenser and his national church were nearly of an age. Born in the early 1550s, Spenser was probably six years old by the time Elizabeth I came to the throne in 1558, and thus had already lived through two different regimes and their unique religious foundations. In 1561 he matriculated as one of the first students of the newly established Merchant Taylors' School, a flagship of Elizabethan state educational reform, and his formal religious awareness was shaped by another new institution, that of Elizabeth I's state church. The state-prescribed *Primer* from which he probably learned to read packaged between its covers the ABC, a Latin grammar, the Catechism, and a selection of prayers and psalms cued to the official liturgy.

When Elizabeth I became England's monarch in November of 1558 her *Act of Supremacy* resurrected her father Henry VIII's statutes establishing dominion of the English Crown over ecclesiastical matters, and, for extra legal measure, repealed her half-sister Mary I's act repealing those statutes (Bray 1994: 318). Mary's regime had reassigned ecclesiastical jurisdiction to the papacy when she succeeded her (and Elizabeth's) younger half-brother, Edward VI, in 1553, and in their turn Elizabethan church officials were required to renounce allegiance to foreign authority, i.e. to the 'Bishop of Rome'. A swift seven months later in June 1559 the *Act of Uniformity* (1 Elizabeth I, c. 2) established more particular ground rules for Elizabeth's ministers and their flocks (Bray 1994: 329). The prime focus of this legislation was the decreed use of the *Book of Common Prayer* throughout the kingdom as a means to a nationwide standard of devotional practice: 'where heretofore there hath been great diversity in saying and singing in churches within this realm, some following Salisbury use, some Hereford use, some the use of Bangor, some of York, and some of Lincoln, now from henceforth all the whole realm shall have but one use' (Booty 1976: 16). In theory, henceforth all inhabitants of Elizabeth's dominion could (and should) be praying in unison on any given Sunday, and in English. In an age of few standardized or uniform national institutions, this ideal of a homogeneous national time, space, and tongue was a novel one.

This book's chief function was to direct the dissemination of *the* book. By following its calendar of monthly readings and thirty-year almanac of holy days, a congregation would hear the Old Testament once a year, the New Testament three times, and the Psalter once a month. Material appropriate to holy days was specified, as was the order of ritual for Holy Communion, and for those ceremonies marking life's major passages: Baptism, Confirmation, Matrimony, Thanksgiving after Child-birth, Visitation of the Sick, and Burial. Parishes were required to purchase both the *Book of Common Prayer* and an English Bible, but the preface to the former promised that 'by this order the curates shall need none other books for their public service ... by the means whereof the people shall not be at so great charge for books as in time past they have been' (Booty 1976: 16). Penalties for the failure to adopt the *Book of Common Prayer* ranged from the loss of a year's profit of a benefice for a first offence to life imprisonment for a third; for their part, parishioners were compelled under pain of twelve pence to attend church on Sundays and holy days, and forbidden to 'derogate, deprave, or despise' said book in 'interludes, plays, songs, rhymes, or by other open words' (Bray 1994: 331).

The promise of merely two required texts was not long adhered to: other mandated purchases for every church soon included Erasmus's *Paraphrases* (1517–24) (a commentary on the New Testament) and, for preachers, the *Book of Homilies* (1559) (ready-made and prescribed sermons on fundamental spiritual and practical topics). In time these four books would be joined by John Foxe's *Actes and Monuments of the English Church and People* (1563), a history of the Reformation in England from the 'primitive' Apostolic church through its centuries-long trials in the papal wilderness until the recent martyrdoms under Mary Tudor and its deliverance by Elizabeth I (who in the 1584 edition was herself included among her sister's persecutions). Parishes were directed to secure these books in the sanctuary where all could consult them, albeit 'out of the time of services'—no fact-checking during a sermon (Bray 1994: 337). In addition to these books, with their idealized visions of the time, text, space, and story of the national church, the church in which Spenser grew up was also governed by more practical guidelines for worship. Accompanying the *Act of Uniformity* was a collection of 52 *Injunctions*, a set of operating instructions detailing the practical nature of church comportment for both minister and flock.[2] Preachers were to read these aloud quarterly, and in them we can trace the lineaments of a Protestant practice.

Some of these *Injunctions* marked the new church off from its Roman predecessor quite clearly. Leading off and reiterated throughout was the prohibition against idolatry, and a reminder of the true source of grace—preachers

shall not set forth or extol any images, relics or miracles, . . . nor allure the people by any enticements, to the pilgrimage of any saint or image, but reproving the same . . . shall teach that all goodness, health and grace ought to be both asked and looked for only of God, as of the very author and giver of the same, and of none other. (Bray 1994: 336)

The importance of preaching was stressed: ministers were to read a Homily aloud weekly, and deliver at least one other sermon quarterly, 'wherein they shall purely and sincerely declare the Word of God, and in the same, exhort their hearers to the works of faith, mercy and charity' (Bray 1994: 336). If a preacher was not up to the task of composing a sermon himself, he could resort again to the *Book of Homilies*. A 'comely and honest pulpit' was to be provided in a 'convenient place'; readers were charged to speak 'leisurely, plainly and distinctly' (Bray 1994: 341). For their part parishioners were to be seated in 'quiet attendance' (Bray 1994: 338) during the entire service; bell-ringing during the service was 'utterly forborne', as were processional services (Bray 1994: 340). Attending services in neighboring parishes was discouraged, except in the case of an extraordinary sermon on offer; preachers too were forbidden to wander beyond the districts for which they were licensed to preach. Attendance would be taken.

Much as official narratives of Protestantism sought to configure revolution as retrieval, so too the *Injunctions* minimized the break with the past when possible. If peregrinating services were discontinued, the practice of rogation was permitted annually 'at the time accustomed' (Bray 1994: 340).[3] If the church furniture (and interior domestic decoration) was drastically altered by the removal of visual aids to worship—'shrines, tables, and candlesticks, trundles or rolls of ware, pictures, paintings and all other monuments of feigned miracles'—music, and the beneficed musicians, were to remain, 'for the comforting as such as delight in music' (Bray 1994: 345). As ever, parishioners knelt during times of supplication as 'heretofore hath been accustomed' (Bray 1994: 346). Almsgiving and tithing were to continue, and good works were encouraged, albeit not now as a means but a testament to their author's receipt of grace. For above all, 'foreasmuch as variance and contention is a thing which most displeaseth God,' state powers sought to prevent social unrest: 'discord among the people . . . slanderous words and railings whereby charity, the knot of all Christian society, is loosed' (Bray 1994: 345). The fiftieth Injunction acknowledges that such disturbances can stem from 'all alterations but specially in rites and ceremonies'—in other words, from the kind of changes the *Injunctions* themselves enact (Bray 1994: 345). But perhaps of greater concern was the grist such changes might give to the perennial tensions within and between communities: disputes over precedence (triggered by processional services); boundary contests between neighbors or villages; garden-variety disrespect for authority generally. For instance, those who would shirk harvest work now had a new excuse: to 'superstitiously' claim the Sabbath's prerogative. So Injunction 20 decreed that 'all parsons vicars and curates shall teach and declare unto their parishioners that they may with a safe and quiet conscience . . . save that thing which God hath sent' (Bray 1994: 340), and get the harvest in. Slander, a perennial threat to communal harmony, now had fresh terms of abuse: 'these convicious words: Papist or papistical heretic, schismatic or sacramentary, or any suchlike words of reproach' (Bray 1994: 345).

Doctrinal exhortations are scarce on the ground in these regulations: for instance, while the theology of the Eucharist goes unelaborated, the type of ceremonial bread does not (although the latter may have implied the former) (Bray 1994: 348). This practical emphasis is partially no doubt because theology was considered the proper province of the *Homilies*, rather than of the communal conduct book that was the *Injunctions*. But it is also because the chief function of all official texts was to secure a harmonious, peaceful, and productive community by regulating behavior, and offering frequent reminders that 'the laudable ceremonies of the Church [are] commanded *by public authority* to be observed'.[4] In a similar spirit the Preface to the *Book of Common Prayer* refers any 'doubts' and 'diversity' about its usage to the bishop of a diocese, and from there to the archbishop—a hierarchical chain of command in which the final arbiter was the monarch. There was some recognition that political change could breed social disorder, or at least psychic confusion; tellingly, the one theological point made explicit in the *Injunctions* is that ministers 'shall learn, and have always in a readiness, such comfortable places and sentences of Scripture [that] this vice of damnable despair may be clearly taken away and firm belief and steadfast hope surely conceived of all their parishioners' (Bray 1994: 339). But for the most part the *Injunctions* worked from the outside in, on the premise that social order wrought through the regulation of conduct cultivated spiritual correctness, rather than the other way round.

The speed with which the *Injunctions* and the *Act of Uniformity* appeared in 1559 bespeaks the government's concern to pacify a community roiled not only by regime change but fresh memories of the Marian prosecution of heresy. This alacrity perhaps owed even more to the reign of Edward VI, for both the *Prayer Book* and the *Injunctions* were in fact conceived in the late 1540s and early 1550s, mostly by Thomas

Cranmer, and thus lay waiting ready-made and only gently used for their resurrection by Elizabeth I. It was perhaps the seemingly expedient nature of this recycling effort that led those in favor of yet further reform to hope that these protocols were but a temporary or provisional stopgap meant to undergo yet further reformation once order had been secured and the passage of regime change safely weathered. But while these protocols may have had to await their theorist in Richard Hooker, whose *Ecclesiastical Polity* was published in the 1590s, they were not, as some hoped, merely inaugural. Five years after Elizabeth's accession in 1563, the systematic theological rationale to be known (after their 1571 revision) as the Thirty-Nine Articles appeared, and these too were based on the work of Archbishop Cranmer (the Forty-Two Articles that had been published in June 1553 only to be rescinded a month later at the death of Edward VI have been described as 'the most advanced systematization of Protestant theology then in existence anywhere' (Bray 1994: 284). For all the Protestantism of their doctrinal pitch—justification through faith alone, the sufficiency of scripture, the vanity of purgatory, the memorial nature of the sacrament, predestination—the Articles also reiterated the practical primacy and permanency of the *Book of Homilies* and the *Prayer Book*; in other words, the outward, official, and ceremonial character of common worship had come to stay. This was Spenser's English church.

The details and character of these founding gestures are worth dwelling on, not only because they mark the church that Spenser knew, but also because they were the prime focus of subsequent conflict, conflict which would serve to hone the church, which would continue throughout Spenser's lifetime, and which would provide much of the grist for his poetry. This church was soon assailed from at least two principal directions. At first the intellectual and polemical energies of defending it were, predictably enough, directed toward the Roman Catholic institution from which it sought to distinguish itself. Bishop John Jewel spearheaded this effort, in his Paul's Cross 'Challenge Sermon' of 1560, his *Apology of the English Church* (1563), and his decade-long exchange with Thomas Harding. He was joined not only by like-minded establishment apologists but thinkers of a more radical bent, all of whom considered the attack against Rome a task that could never afford complacency, however much the association of Rome and Antichrist might appear both obvious and commonplace. These latter included men such as William Fulke, Master of Pembroke Hall, Cambridge—Spenser's college—whose 'abstract policy [it was] . . . to leave no Catholic work of controversy unanswered, if he could help it', a mission which kept him publishing regularly throughout the 1570s and 1580s (Milward 1977: 7). Keeping battle on this flank alive throughout the latter half of the sixteenth century were not just challenges conducted in print, but the regular punctuation of events such as the Papal Bull of 1570, declaring Elizabeth I a heretic and absolving her subjects under threat of excommunication of their obedience to her; the founding of the English Catholic seminaries at Douai in 1568 and Rome in 1579 to train a ministry for English Catholics; the fomenting focal point of Elizabeth's cousin and potential heir, Mary Queen of Scots (executed in 1587); the prospect (live until the early 1580s) of Elizabeth's marriage, possibly to a Catholic foreign prince; continental wars of religion and the ongoing campaign to subdue Catholic Ireland; and the advance upon England of the Spanish Armada in 1588, a battle in which the English navy allegedly owed its victory (or at least its narrow escape) to God's providential favor of English Protestantism as evidenced in the inclement conditions of the English Channel.

If events such as these stoked the fires of national antagonism with Roman Catholicism throughout Spenser's adult writing life, the English church was also fighting on another front soon after its establishment. Once it became apparent in the early 1560s that the government had little intention of further altering the protocols of the English church beyond their initial, essentially Edwardine, character, those voices in favor of putting yet more distance between England and Rome grew increasingly restive, in particular with the ceremonial aspects of the official church liturgy. The first shot across the bow came, appropriately enough, with dispute about external forms.[5] The Vestiarian controversy, beginning in 1566 and continuing for about the next five years, took up the issue of the government-prescribed apparel for ministers 'such as cap, gown, tippet' intended to sartorially mark them out from their congregants (Frere and Douglas 1954: 11). Ministers who found this requirement obnoxious and redolent of Rome cited in defense of their antipathy the contrary practices of the primitive church (for them, the mythical institution that was the measure of most things); its defenders, while granting the indifference of special clerical garments to spiritual function, maintained their importance as a mark of deference to temporal hierarchy.

Such Erastianism, or subordination of ecclesiastical to secular power, was of course the rub for those thinkers who hoped that their English church would continue to purge itself of 'popish' practices, and who became increasingly frustrated by Elizabeth's refusal to permit any parliamentary address to ecclesiastical matters. The debate over clothing was just the tippet of the iceberg, and in 1572 reformist hopes and grievances were laid out in an *Admonition to Parliament* (soon followed by a *Second Admonition*) urging the removal of institutional restrictions upon worship such as the prayer book—'an unperfect book, culled and picked out of that popish dunghill, the Masse book full of all abominations' (Frere and Douglas 1954: 21). Some of the objections were to institutional aspects such as the cursory way in which moral infractions such as blasphemy or adultery were 'slightly passed over' by the traditional shame-based penalties of ecclesiastical courts ('With pricking in a blanket, or pinning in a sheet'), in contrast to the severe fines exacted for failure to conform to the 'popish orders and ceremonies' of the *Prayer Book* ('excommunication, suspension, deprivation, . . . banishing, imprisoning, reviling, taunting, and what not' (Frere and Douglas 1954: 17)). Of particular heinousness was the engrossing of multiple livings by allegedly ill-trained individuals (who 'run fysking from place to place . . . [and] covetously join living to living'), and the resulting underemployment of more qualified and deserving ministers (Frere and Douglas 1954: 10). Even worse was the garnishing of livings (and their income) by laymen in whose patronage they sometimes languished. The state-prescribed, mass-produced, and standardizing texts were seen as enabling such practices, in supplanting inspired preaching by rote reading, whereas in the primitive church, 'ministers were not tied to any form of prayers invented by man, but as the spirit moved them, so they powred forth hearty supplications to the Lord.... Reading is not feeding, but it is as evil as playing upon a stage' (Frere and Douglas 1954: 22).

Underwriting the economic and institutional critiques was a notion of worship signally different from the official one. The Presbyterian vision of a preacher in every pot was an argument not only for increased employment opportunities but about the origin and operation of prayer. How best to penetrate the sinful soul, to 'reform the disordered, to bring them to repentance, and to bridle such as would offend'? Was it, as the state's model suggested, by scripting their actions from without, by the imposition of a standardized ritual of harmonious hierarchy? Or was it, as more aggressive Reformers thought, by reaching deep within the self, and penetrating that of another, by means of inspired exegesis of God's word? What in fact was the relationship between actions and inner spiritual states? Which came first, godliness or godly conduct?

The authors of the *Admonition* claimed to share the same goal as the established church, namely, to ensure that by restoring 'Christ into his kingdom, to rule in the same by the scepter of his word, and severe discipline', that 'the Prince may be better obeyed, the realm more flourish in godliness' (Frere and Douglas 1954: 18). Their understanding was that civil obedience came from within, from the affective reformation of the subject's will by means of a penetrating preaching that would 'prick' the conscience and 'pierce the heart' (Frere and Douglas 1954: 115). Root out sin and an obedient subject would result. According to this view, a ritual performance of corporate homogeneity was too generic, predictable, and insufficiently gripping, allowing people to tune out; repetition of gestures or words, far from inscribing social harmony or spiritual welfare, permitted individual deviance to flourish behind the masks of gesture:

One he kneeleth on his knees, and this way he looketh, and another he kneeleth himself asleep, another kneeleth with such devotion, that he is so far in talk, that he forgetteth to arise till his knee ache ... another bringeth a book of his own, and though he sit when they sit, stand when they stand, kneel when they kneel, ... most of all he intendeth his own book. Is this praying? (Frere and Douglas 1954: 24)

As Ramie Targoff has written, 'What to the Establishment represented a successful mechanism for edifying large numbers of people was to the non-conformists a spiritually deadening imposition upon minister and congregation alike' (2001: 37). The Elizabethan regime's attempt in the 1570s to suppress 'prophesyings', exercises in which ministers vied to interpret scripture in public debates as a means to refine their exegetical skills, suggests that official authorities shared the sense that inspired preaching (or the public spectacle of competing interpretations) might well be quite stirring, but not in a good way. Unlike its critics, however, the regime was not willing to bet that the end result of such preaching would be a well-ordered populace. Its optimism lay rather with the power of common prayer, which, far from being cynically considered as a merely superficial means and measure of conformity, was 'a mechanism that successfully mold[ed] the naturally flawed impulses of the worshipper, whose faith can only be stimulated through regulated external forms' (Targoff 2001: 48).[6]

The authors of the *Admonitions* contrast the idealism of their own position with the sordid political practicalities of the established one, but in a way their critique served to point out just how very impractical and utterly ideal the vision of unanimity offered by the official church was. The *Admonition* authors' caricature of the official model of worship as promoting a robotic social order at the expense of the soul's salvation denies the emphasis in both the *Prayer Book* and *Injunctions* on fostering Christian charity, and the belief that the harmony achieved through corporate congruence was not merely gestural but something quite spiritually profound. But if the idea that 'now the whole realm would have but one use' had a certain beauty, in truth the realities of personnel, language, custom, and culture meant that adherence to the established protocols varied by region as well as social strata (a rule of thumb being the further one got from the London–Cambridge axis, the less likely it would be to find parishes formed in the official image; on the other hand, as both sides admitted, it could be just as difficult to find doctrinaire Christians—let alone Protestant ones—even close to the center of the polity).[7] The *Act of Uniformity* might specify penalties for its violation, but in a country with no police force or standing army, where in fact the only government official most people ever encountered was their local preacher, the prospect of their enforcement was a highly theoretical one, dependent on the persuasions (in both senses of the term) of the preacher. Order in the Tudor state, as Patrick Collinson has written, 'was an elusive quarry to be pursued, or a treasure to be jealousy guarded', particularly as the mechanisms of pursuit and possession were chiefly oratorical (1982: 2). Hence the charged locus of the pulpit. For Spenser, writing as of 1580 from Catholic Ireland, the image of this church—filtered through the lenses of nostalgia for his youth, homesickness, or geographical remoteness from the disputes—may have been especially ideal.

This is not to say that he was unaware that this was an ideal contested from within as well as from without. The terms and arguments forged by the *Admonition* controversy became definitive ones. Of this, as of the dispute with Rome, there was much to come, over many decades, and in a variety of rhetorical keys, from the serious to the satirical: replies, and replies to those replies; answers, answers to answers, defenses of answers to answers, and defenses of defenses. The combative polyvocality of Spenser's *Shepherd's Calendar*, in which homely shepherds debate (among other things) models of pastoral function, owes much to this fractious and capping climate of polemical rejoinder (as both *Calendar* and climate do to the rhetorical training of university education). The opening episode of *The Faerie Queene*, in which the snake-woman 'Error' vomits upon the knight of Holiness a substance whose main ingredient is 'bookes and papers', mixed with 'great lumpes of flesh' and 'loathly frogs and toades', was an image no doubt deeply resonant for any Elizabethan pursuivant of religious controversy (I.i.20).

Thus in thinking about these contexts with respect to Spenser, a few caveats come to mind (besides that, of course, of textual vomit). First, many of the debates, whether between Protestants (established) and Catholics, establishment Protestants and more reform-minded ones, or the latter and Catholics (just to choose three possible pairings of disputants), were indeed structured by a binary cast of rhetoric, due to the polemical habit in which the advocate of one position sought to configure his own as the absolutely true one (as in the True Church) and his opponent's as utterly false (i.e., Antichrist). But as the fact of at least three possible parties to the discussion indicates (and there were eventually more), the actual landscape was often more of a spectrum of fine distinctions, some hair-splitting, within a single category: Christian. The fact that one of the best-selling devotional manuals of this period, *A Christian Directory guiding men to eternall salvation* (1584), was a Protestantized edition, by a minister 'conventionally classified as a moderate Puritan', of a text authored by a Spanish Jesuit and midwifed for an English audience by an English one, spoke volumes on this score (literally—sixteen editions in 1585 alone) (Collinson 2002: 397). Complicating the picture further is that some debates were concerned with the practices of worship, and others were more theologically oriented (not, of course, that the one could not imply the latter: discussion over the role of state control involved and invoked assumptions about how souls were best pierced). However, much as criticism of the official church was in the 1570s and 1580s internal to that church rather than directed at it from outside, so too doctrinal differences— between, for instance, a model of salvation with little scope for human collaboration and one with more—had yet to emerge as either starkly discrete or linked to particular ideas of church governance and worship (e.g. hard-line Calvinism with Puritan separatists). Though the initial lineaments of conflict would persist and entrench, it is more a matter at this time of emergent positions formulating and coalescing, of tectonic plates rumbling beneath the surface of official consensus. Spenser's most obvious portrait of religious controversy, figured in the difference between the virgin Una and the whore Duessa in Book I of *The Faerie Queene*, in fact addresses the way in which broad distinctions (and distinct broads) have the habit of turning into strange bedfellows. Clearly partisanal or binary portraits of this terrain, as Spenser well understood, were a kind of wish-fulfillment, more an idealization than a description of Elizabeth I as Gloriana. If only.

Second, a historical gaze tends to accentuate the high relief of the peaks, not merely as opposed to the valleys or sloughs, but at the expense of the entire lumpy terrain: what looks like a crescendo of religious controversies between establishment and reformist forces—the late 1560s Vestiarian and the early 1570s *Admonitions* controversies culminating (for all Spenserian purposes) in the Marprelate tracts of the late 1580s—may not have seemed so purposive or portentous for someone living through them (again, especially if they had left England in 1580). Spenser was in his late teens in the later 1560s; his late twenties when the *Shepherd's Calendar* was published in 1579; and his late thirties when the controversy between the church and its internal critics reached its boiling point. If controversy was a constant, it was an intermittent constant, and while living through these decades may have been an experience of increasing tension, it is equally possible that the more perennial public flare-ups over church discipline were the more unremarkable they became.

Third, while the rhetorical energy and industry of debates over the nature of worship in the 1570s and 1580s—the period most relevant to a consideration of Spenser's work—was indeed extraordinary, satire of clerical hypocrisy and incompetence was an English poetic convention operative as least as far back as Chaucer and as far forward as Trollope (nor is it, á la Moliere, exclusively English).[8] Even in the course of Spenser's poetic career it occurs both early (*Shepherd's Calendar*, 1579) and late (*Mother Hubbard's Tale*, 1591). In the first instance, Spenser praises one 'gentle shepherd Algrind', a thinly disguised figure for Edmund Grindal, Archbishop of Canterbury, who fell out with Elizabeth I in 1577 for his refusal to suppress prophesyings; in the second poem, in 'a plague o' both your houses' move, he satirizes not only an indolent clergyman whose 'care was, his service well to saine, | And to read Homilies upon holidays: When that was done, he might attend his playes' (392–4) but also those who seek preferment by aping a precisionist mien, 'fashion[ing] eke a godly zeale, | Such as no carpers contraryre reveale | ... There thou must walke in sober gravitee ... | Faste much, pray oft, looke lowly on the ground' (*MHT* 493–8). Thus using anticlerical critique to peg Spenser's confessional politics may not yield much (even if such pegs were available in the 1570s or 1580s, and I am suggesting they were not). Public officials have always made broad targets, and clergymen were the only such officials with whom most early modern persons ever had contact. Nor was complaining about incompetent and hypocritical clergy just the habit of those speaking against the practices of the established church. Indeed, bishops, unlike most ardent reformers, were in the institutional position to do some actual reforming, and the energetic ones spent much of their time doing just that (Collinson 1982: 39–91). Furthermore, even a casual observer of this scene could not help but notice how reformist attacks on ecclesiastical abuses could function as an ideological disguise for equally sinister forms of greed: for instance, as a cover for aristocratic engrossment of ecclesiastical property. Allegory was not just the property of literature, and there were several wolves seeking to cloak themselves in the anticlerical sheepskin in this moment.

Spenser's works and life can indicate a variety of 'takes' on the contexts and issues of Elizabethan church reform, as well as on such doctrinal controversies as there were. Scholarly evidence for these hinges on things as various as his renderings of poetic conventions, explicit references to current controversies (or their veiling metonyms—e.g. traditional rural festivities for Catholic superstition), or his deployment of scriptural plots and personae. Spenser's dark political allegory in Book I of *The Faerie Queene* links Duessa's Mary Tudor with Orgoglio's Philip of Spain and portrays both as persecutors of England's patron saint, and suggests that we can at least rule out the possibility of Spenser's affiliation with Catholicism. Many of his villains seem to embody the worst of what Protestants considered a superstitious Catholic reliance on deceptive images. But other material suggests a sympathy for traditional religion: for instance, his malevolent portrait of Kirkrapine, despoiler of church property, or the House of Holiness' model of repentance through good works more commonly associated with Catholicism. On the other hand, Spenser models much of the plot of Book I after that of Foxe's *Actes and Monuments*, and Una's insistence on Redcrosse knight's elect status seems to gesture toward a more Calvinist model of salvation.

The landmarks of Spenser's career bespeak a gallimaufry as well. His first publication, as he reached the end of his time at the Merchant Taylors' grammar school, was a 1569 translation of the sonnet sequences by Petrarch and Du Bellay within the apocalyptic vision of a *Theatre wherein be represented ... the miseries and calamities that follow the voluptuous Wordlings* by the Dutch Reformer Jan Van der Noot, whose Revelation-indebted imagery suggests an energetic protest against traditional religious formations. A decade later, in *The Shepherd's Calendar*, when, as David Norbrook writes, 'issues of ecclesiastical pride and luxury were newly controversial,' 'the rhetoric of the ecclesiastical eclogues is at least superficially similar to the radicals' propaganda, and led many later Puritans to claim him as one of their own'—although Norbrook concludes 'Spenser was clearly more disposed to compromise' (Norbrook 1984: 60–2). In the early 1570s, when the *Admonition* Controversy began, Spenser had a front-row seat, enrolled as he was at Pembroke College, Cambridge, formerly home to John Whitgift, the prime champion of the establishment. In 1576, two years after taking his MA (in effect, a preparation for preaching) Spenser took employment as secretary to the Bishop of Rochester, John Young, who worked to curtail the Presbyterian movement. But one year later he was secretary to the Earl of Leicester, a figure of some renown as a supporter of the reform-minded. In his *View of the State of Ireland* Spenser acknowledges that the island's being in the grip of papistry did not overmuch help its assimilation to English rule, but rather than seeing Ireland as a prime canvas for immediate reformation, he recommends, contrary to his otherwise 'scorched earth' policy, that this religion be left untouched for the time being, as a kind of thing indifferent and maybe even useful in advance of other forms of colonial reform.[9] He even recommends the repair and refurbishing of church buildings on the rather anti-Puritan grounds that an impressive outward show of religion will attract 'rude people to the reverensinge and frequentinge theareof' (*Prose*, 223); he supported the foundation of Trinity College Dublin (1592) as a potential source of native Reformed ministers who could appeal to the populace in their native tongue (*Prose*, 142).[10] Like another ardently Protestant poet, Sir Philip Sidney, Spenser himself, despite his layman's status, received the income from a living in his Irish lands—precisely the kind of abuse the authors of the *Admonition* had in their sights (McClane 1961: 101). Protestants were known for their suspicion of images; Spenser is a painter of glorious word pictures.[11]

In other words, if Spenser's poetry exhibits an awareness of the many possible positions along the ideological spectrum of Tudor Christianity, it may be because he had himself occupied more than a few, or at least had opportunity to observe their variety as he made his way toward both his poetic and political careers. From such varied experience he gained an ability to theorize the problem of religious difference; his poetry, even in Book I of the *Faerie Queene*, can often seem to look with a bird's eye upon these disputes, to address the problem of choosing among the various alternatives, and the way they have of collapsing into each other, rather than weighing in on one side or the other. In his travels across this landscape Spenser also could not have helped but acquire the sense that valuation of a given position along the spectrum was an exercise in relativism rather than absolutes (England was less Protestant than Geneva, but more so than France). No doubt he also was fully aware of how such positions could be mitigated by contexts and timing. Grindal, for instance, a hero of the *Shepherd's Calendar*, might have been a success when stationed in York, when his task consisted of tactfully reining in Northern recusants, but less so when that success promoted him to Archbishop of Canterbury, and he was required by Elizabeth I to exercise the same zeal with respect to the other extreme. Spenser may have been guilty of garnishing a living in Ireland, but it may have been for lack of a suitable occupant, or in order to prevent it from falling to the greater evil of a Catholic priest. The realities of governance require such compromises, whereas the anti-establishment notes and daring topical address of *The Shepherd's Calendar* are—much like its bravura handling of verse forms—a young man's calling card. Staking out an Elizabethan religious identity was (and is) a finicky business. Hypocrisy was a preoccupation of Elizabethan anticlerical satire not merely because the church found itself pondering the relations of actions and insides, but because of the frequent need of Elizabethans to mediate between principles and practical, situational politics. Preaching and practice have always been difficult to align, but maybe nowhere more so than in a culture where the very relation of each to other was under intense scrutiny.

It may be that Spenser's stake in these issues lay less in urging a particular position than with using them as fodder for poetry in a prophetic vein and in a civic register.[12] For an Elizabethan to write about religion, namely *the* arena where relations between the state and the subject were being hammered out at this time, might not necessarily be a declaration of commitment to anything but the public relevance of poetry and poets. No doubt to those in search of a specific and consistent ideological edge for our poet—by which is usually meant reformist-leaning—this can sound prevaricating. There is a certain metonymic irony by which the construction of Spenser as inclined to establishment religious formulations even while he acknowledged the problems raised by reformist voices itself imitates what reformist voices understood as the prevarication of the established church. It does not help that Spenser's most beautiful spiritual expression is a *tour de force* of ritual syncretism, where the personal and the ritual, the domestic and the cosmic, earthly comforts and heavenly priorities all come together in a resoundingly harmonious vision. While intuiting a writer's temperament is no doubt folly, the writer of the *Epithalamium* seems, for that day at least, to have found in ritual something soul-piercing indeed.

What we can say for certain is that Spenser's interest in 'fashioning a gentleman', as he proclaims in his 'Letter to Raleigh' that accompanied the 1590 edition of his epic, is of a piece with the questions raised by these controversies of and over the Elizabethan church. How are the best persons best made: from the molding of the interior subject from without, through the performance of proper behavior, or by letting that behavior be shaped by ideals antecedent to instruction? What *is* an ideal? Which is the best teacher, sermons or experience, doctrine or error? Is a person best fashioned by his own efforts, or is he the creation of another? Can you judge a knight by his armor, a virtuous woman by her clothing, or a person's intentions to the good (or ill) by their conduct? Does the armor make the knight, or the knight the armor?

These questions reverberate at a metacritical level as well: how does a reader read signs, and interpret events? Spenser uses the verb 'to read' and its variants in a dauntingly athletic range of index. Just as debate over the nature and character of the Elizabethan church largely turns on the role of external forms in shaping spiritual identity (collective rituals, clothing, visual vs aural prompts to worship), so the work of reading *The Faerie Queene* is preoccupied with the perils of interpretation: what do surfaces signify, and how far can action go to shape intention (or vice versa)? The poem's stylistic commitment to the personified rendering of psychological states has largely been attributed to Spenser's embrace of medieval literary topoi, of a piece with the archaism of his diction—the psychomachia of the morality play, for instance, which dramatizes an interior landscape through the personification of the components of personhood and the exchanges between them. But it could be argued that such a choice is not an archaism so much as Spenser's attempt, one he participated in with *all* parties to Reformation, to find a language that excavates and exfoliates the human interior, to penetrate the carapace of selfhood in order to render the inside as outside as possible. By far the holiest figure in Book I, 'heauenly Contemplation | Of God and goodnesse was his meditation,' is virtually transparent: 'Each bone might through his body well be red, | And euery sinew seene through his long fast' (I.x.47).

It is primarily the first book of Spenser's epic, the 'Book of Holiness', that has been considered the domain of 'religion', on account most obviously of its titular virtue, its narrative debt to Revelation, the range of topical allusions and their relative point-edness, and above all the dilemma it poses for its hero of distinguishing between, at the very least, two faces of religion. Its hero is Redcrosse knight, who bears the emblem of the cross on his shield, and arrives attempting to champion the virtuous Una ('the one') in her contest against a proverbial dragon, even as he is bewitched and bewildered by her rivals. These include the shape-maker Archimago, his creation the succubus Una, and the villainous Duessa ('doubleness'), herself bearing no casual resemblance to the Whore of Babylon as painted by the Book of Revelation.

The book thematizes the problems of excavation, of getting beyond the surface to the interior. This is a project not only for the protagonist but his reader, although the latter enjoys some of the relative benefits of dramatic irony by which a narrator tips off an audience to a character's mistakes in advance of their making. Redcrosse first appears 'a gentle knight . . . pricking on the plaine', in a much-battered suit of armor, but we soon find out that its dents cannot possibly be evidence of his own experience, for 'armes til that time did he neuer wield' (I.i.1). Events soon prove him singularly inept if well-intentioned, at least to start with—a knight far more on the outside than on the in. He fights a series of antagonists, dispatching them with an increasing degree of physical competence, but what really undoes him are matters of the heart: first, his belief that his lady is wanton, and later, his own capitulation to the persuasions of Despair.

While clearly it is the very human flaws in Redcrosse's inner affective state— his vainglorious zeal, his anger, his impatience—that are partly to blame for the two-steps-forward, one-step-back nature of his quest, the tragic aspects of his plight are also due to the sad fact that virtue's own appearances can mislead. Una herself seems largely exempt from the errors in judgment that bedevil her knight, and certainly her distresses do not rival those of later damsels (such as Florimell, Miss Out-of-the-fire-into-the-frying-pan), but it is nonetheless the desireability of that very appearance, however modestly cloaked, that is largely responsible for her pica-resque adventures among idolatrous satyrs and ravening beasts. It may even be the very cloak that is the problem: Una's seemly veil denotes both her virtue and her inner sadness (I.i.4), especially by contrast with the meretriciously attired and brazenly uncovered Duessa, but it is also what allows the villain Archimago to fabricate a false Una in order to deceive her knight: 'Her all in white he clad, and ouer it | Cast a blacke stole most like to seeme for *Una* fit'. While Archimago perhaps could just as easily have fabricated her face as he does her 'tender partes | So liuely, and so like in all mens sight' (I.i.45), Spenser goes out of his way to emphasize the sartorial media of deception. So too it is not merely Despair's words that seduce Redcrosse to suicide, but his visual aids: first he reiterates the ponderousness of Redcrosse's errors, then, as a clincher, 'He shew'd him painted in a table plaine, | The damned ghosts, that doe in torments waile' (I.ix.49). Perhaps, as some readers would have it, there is some dig here at the media of Catholic (or the Elizabethan Settlement's) protocols of worship. But if Spenser laments the delusional powers of images, he also acknowledges (bleakly? ironically? gleefully?) that we have little alternative. Just as an English church could not disavow institutional protocols and still be a church as it was understood in this moment (people have to perform *some* collective actions, even if it is simply gathering in the same place at the same time), so too Una must in this world wear *something*, even if that costume causes as much trouble as it prevents.[13]

Also troubling is the fact that the clarity promised in the act of revelation proves elusive. The unveiling of Duessa by Prince Arthur reveals a loathly hag indeed, but such revelation also reveals yet another surface in need of decoding, one with a fox's tail, a bear's paw, and an eagle's claw in the place of feet, and in some ways far more enigmatic than a mere Whore of Babylon. Nor does it prevent Duessa from putting her clothes back on to deceive another knight, another day. This wry suggestion of futility also afflicts the construction of virtue: Redcrosse's innocence is the source of his goodness, but also of his weakness. His experiences breed knowledge and competence but also a rap sheet. While he finally achieves the object of this quest—victory over the dragon, and Una as his betrothed—he is not allowed to enjoy it, but needs to continue to ride forth. Goodness urges that we reject evil, but also that, at least in this world, we keep it around as a tutelary foil. There is no escaping the contradictions and double-binds that constitute this vale of tears.

Such imbrications also register in the varied theological resonances of Book I. As Darryl Gless has argued, the theological terrain of the Elizabethan church is as complex and intertwined as the political or institutional in this moment, particularly as regards the respective roles of works and grace. Even Calvinism, with its commit-ment to a predestinarian schema, came close to acknowledging the collaborative nature of human salvation, such that works were not merely indicative of faith: 'On the one hand, Red Cross' salvation is assured; on the other it is impeded because the faithful must cooperatively labor and therefore must sin' (Gless 1994: 157). Clearly Redcrosse despite his elect status needs to make an effort—resting, let alone quitting, is a knight's greatest temptation. Nor does election exempt him from error or from a flirtation with despair; even if he isn't, objectively speaking, among the reprobate, it doesn't mean he can't *feel* like it on occasion; in fact, the elect might be the most vulnerable to despair (Snyder 1965). In fact, the work of Book I, insofar as it is achieved in the House of Holiness, seems to be finding a way to shoulder the burden of one's own inevitable sinfulness such that it doesn't impede either further application (despite its attendant sinfulness) or hope of salvation: 'His mortal life he learned had to frame | In holy righteousness, without rebuke or blame' (I.x.45). This seems a primarily affective, interior project. On the other hand, the rather traditional nature of Redcrosse's penitential regime—fasting, alms, even the revelation of his own saintly status—seems to suggest that good works matter in some way, even if it is not exactly clear how.[14] Is such a theological medley evidence that Spenser was inconsistent or muddled, or that his culture was? Or, to frame it differently, does it merely testify to his sensitivity to the complex, dynamic, and poetically fruitful nature of these religious questions, even as they were being formulated simultaneously in his world? Does the poem unwittingly founder on these contradictions, or is it about them?

The book of Holiness presents the most obvious sight of Spenser's spiritual preoccupations. Its composition during the 1580s places it closest to the period of Spenser's English residence and hence proximity to religious controversy. But the heroes of Spenser's other five books—Temperance, Chastity, Friendship, Justice, and Courtesy—avatars of the overarching supervirtue 'Magnificence' embodied by Prince Arthur, could also be considered to represent ideals of a spiritual life in its both affective and social manifestations. They too are components of gentility, and while Spenser was no doubt concerned with social status, gentility in *The Faerie Queene* is as much a spiritual as a social quantity. In a way, the latter virtues are even more concretely Christian—at least at first glance—than the rather abstract and ethereal 'Holiness' (Gless 1994: 26–8). For instance, when Guyon, the hero of Book II, falls, he is protected by an angel in a passage modeled on the temptation of Christ in the wilderness, and Book VI is preoccupied with issues of 'Grace'. In another way, the subsequent five virtues could be said to be dimensions of Holiness, spin-offs from Redcrosse even as all six virtues comprise aspects of Magnificence himself.

Certainly the problems that bedevil Redcrosse (and his reader) in Book I persist throughout the work: mistakes in reading and judgment; the temptation to rest or even quit an arduous quest; the need to recognize and remedy character flaws in order to fight external villains; the persistent ingenuity of the enemy; and the wearying deferral of the much-sought ethical competence to a heavenly horizon, whose flip side is of course delight and delay. While Spenser's sketch of a twelve-book plan for the poem indicates he did not intend to break off halfway, the incompletion enacts attenuations that beset even the hardest working and best intentioned of his heroes. Guyon, the hero of Book II, is meant to moderate in himself and others 'strong passion, or weake fleshliness' (II.iv.2), but this is a task Redcrosse had to learn as well, leaping before looking into Error's den, 'full of fire and greedy hardiment' (I.i.14), or just as rashly, being 'much enmoued' and 'thoroughly... dismaid' by the speech of Despair (I.ix.48–50). Guyon's destruction of the Bowre of Blisse suggests the victory of restraint over sensual excess, but even as Holiness cannot renounce the world, and just as differentiating between churches means differentiating between women rather than transcending the category, so too temperance is not abstinence so much as moderation and mediation. In a similar vein, Britomart, the protagonist of 'Chastity' in Book III, is an untowardly active and ardent damsel in quest of her husband, making us wrestle with the paradox of the Protestant notion of married chastity, with its attempt to integrate an ethically productive sexuality into the world rather than quarantine it. Justice is perhaps the most 'outward' of Spenser's concerns (even as Book V's topical presence is most intense), but even there we find ourselves confronting differences between absolutes and their moderation, theories and practices. So too Courtesy is potentially misleading, 'not in outward shows, but inward thoughts defynd' (VI *Proem*, 5). In each instance Spenser asks us to interrogate a term we may have thought we understood, and makes us acutely aware of the contingencies entailed in defining it. In this sense, all of Spenser's epic provides a gloss on Elizabethan religions, with their pressing and intense desire for clarity, and the humbling recognition that such is not an earthly possibility.

NOTES

1. For a puritan Spenser see Hume (1984); for an Anglican one (even sympathetic to Catholicism), Whitaker (1950), McClane (1961), and Wall (1988); Gless (1994) discusses the entwined strands of Reformed doctrine in the Elizabethan moment and its registration in Book I of *The Faerie Queene*. King (1990, 2006) investigates Spenser's deep and broad connections to Reformation political and poetic cultures and provides a succinct overview of the reception history of Spenser's religious elements.
2. The *Act of Uniformity* was ratified by Parliament (its passage though the House of Lords helped by the fact that many bishoprics were unfilled); the *Injunctions* were issued in the name of Elizabeth alone after the Parliament went home (she and her chief minister, William Cecil, were responsible for the tinkering with the Edwardine template).
3. Rogation involved the processional recitation of the saint's litanies during the three days prior to Ascension Day (six Sundays after Easter).
4. Phrases in italics are Elizabethan amendments to the Edwardine text.
5. And in fact, doctrinal controversy (e.g. Calvinism vs Arminianism) did not really begin to roil the English church until the beginning of the seventeenth century. Sixteenth-century dispute turned primarily on *how* people should worship.
6. See also Maltby (1998).
7. See, for instance, Green (1996) for the vast array of catechisms in this period. The degree and nature of the English Reformation continue to be matters of critical debate. See, for instance, Dickens (1989), Collinson (1967), Duffy (1993), Haigh (1993, 2007), and Lake (1988).

8. On this point see King (1990).
9. Lewis (1953) states, 'His religious views are elusive and he twice professes his laic igno-rance; but they are certainly not those of a Protestant missionary nor of a bigot. He is sure that popery is not "the pure spring of lyfe" but "nothing doubtes" the salvation of many Papists' (378). Norbrook (1984) argues slightly to the contrary: 'In Ireland he was to advocate repressive measures to stamp out a still more conservative set of rural traditions and effect a Protestant cultural revolution' (71).
10. On this point see McCabe (2002), 117–21.
11. For Spenserian iconoclasm see Greenblatt (1980), Gross (1985), Gilman (1986), Gregerson (1995).
12. Mallette (1997) considers the tactical nature of Spenser's recourse to Elizabethan religious discourses.
13. For a discussion of this dynamic to the poem's religious constitution of national identity and difference see McEachern (1996), Chap. 3.
14. On this point see Cefalu (2004).

Bibliography

Booty, J. (ed.) (1976). *The Book of Common Prayer 1559.* Washington, DC: Folger Library Press.
Bray, G. (1994). *Documents of the English Reformation.* Minneapolis: Fortress Press.
Cefalu, P. (2004). *Moral Identity in Early Modern English Literature.* Cambridge, Cambridge University Press.
Collinson, P. (1967). *The Elizabethan Puritan Movement.* Oxford: Oxford University Press.
—— (1982). *The Religion of Protestants: The Church in English Society, 1559–1625.* Oxford: Oxford University Press.
—— (2002). 'Literature and the Church', in David Loewenstein and Janel Mueller (eds), *The Cambridge History of Early Modern Literature.* Cambridge: Cambridge University Press.
Dickens, A. G. (1989). *The English Reformation.* University Park, PA: University of Pennsylvania Press.
Duffy, E. (1993). *The Stripping of the Altars: Traditional Religion in England 1400–1589.* New Haven, CT: Yale University Press.
Frere, W. H., and C. E. Douglas (1954). *Puritan Manifestoes.* London: S.P.C.K.
Gilman, Ernest B. (1986). *Iconoclasm and Poetry in the English Reformation: Down Went Dagon.* Chicago: Chicago University Press.
Gless, D. J. (1994). *Interpretation and Theology in Spenser.* Cambridge: Cambridge University Press.
Green, I. (1996). *The Christian's ABC: Catechisms and Catechizing in England c. 1530–1740.* Oxford: Oxford University Press.
Greenblatt, S. (1980). *Renaissance Self-Fashioning: From More to Shakespeare.* Chicago: University of Chicago Press.
Gregerson, L. (1995). *The Reformation of the Subject: Spenser, Milton, and the English Protestant Epic.* Cambridge: Cambridge University Press.
Gross, K. (1985). *Spenserian Poetics: Idolatry, Iconoclasm and Magic.* Ithaca: Cornell University Press.
Haigh, C. (1993). *English Reformations: Religion, Society and Politics under the Tudors.* Oxford: Oxford University Press.

—— (2007). *The Plain Man's Pathway to Heaven*. Oxford: Oxford University Press.

Hume, A. (1984). *Edmund Spenser, Protestant Poet*. Cambridge: Cambridge University Press.

King, J. N. (1990). *Spenser's Poetry and the Reformation Tradition*. Princeton, NJ: Princeton University Press.

—— (2006). 'Religion', in Bart Van Es (ed.), *A Critical Companion to Spenser Studies*. London: Palgrave MacMillan.

Lake, P. (1988). *Anglicans and Puritans: Presbyterianism and English Conformist Thought from Whitgift to Hooker*. Cambridge: Cambridge University Press.

Lewis, C. S. (1953). *English Literature of the Sixteenth Century, Excluding Drama*. Oxford: Oxford University Press.

McCabe, R. A. (2002). *Spenser's Monstrous Regiment: Elizabethan Ireland and the Poetics of Difference*. Oxford: Oxford University Press.

McClane, P. (1961). *Spenser's Shepherd's Calendar: A Study in Elizabethan Allegory*. Notre Dame, IN: University of Notre Dame Press.

McEachern, C. (1996). *The Poetics of English Nationhood, 1590–1612*. Cambridge: Cambridge University Press.

Malette, R. (1997). *Spenser and the Discourses of Reformation England*. Lincoln, NE: University of Nebraska Press.

Maltby, J. (1998). *Prayer Book and People in Elizabethan and Early Stuart England*. Cambridge: Cambridge University Press.

Milward, P. (1977). *Religious Controversies of the Elizabethan Age*. London: Scolar Press.

Norbrook, D. G. (1984). *Poetry and Politics in the English Renaissance*. London: Routledge and Kegan Paul.

Snyder, S. (1965). 'The Left Hand of God: Despair in Medieval and Renaissance Tradition'. *SR* 12: 18–54.

Targoff, R. (2001). *Common Prayer: The Language of Public Devotion in Early Modern England*. Chicago: University of Chicago Press.

Wall, J. N. (1988). *Transformations of the Word: Spenser, Herbert, Vaughan*. Athens, GA: University of Georgia Press.

Whitaker, V. K. (1950). *The Religious Basis of Spenser's Thought*. Palo Alto, CA: Stanford University Press.

CHAPTER 3

....

SPENSER AND POLITICS

....

DAVID J. BAKER

AFFILIATIONS, INTERESTS, LOYALTIES
....

'Tyrants that make men subiect to their law, | I will suppresse', threatens a giant in the
fifth book of Edmund Spenser's *The Faerie Queene* (1590/6). '[N]o more' will they
'raine'. The 'Lordings . . . that commons ouer-aw' he will 'curbe' and 'all the wealth of
rich men to the poore will draw' (V.ii.38). But 'righteous *Artegall*' (V.ii.39), the
'Champion of true Iustice' (V.i.3), will have none of it. It is the Allmighty who
'maketh Kings to sit in souerainty', he informs the giant, and 'subiects to their powre
obay' (V.ii.41). His 'counsels depth thou canst not vnderstand' (V.ii.42). Shortly after,
Artegall's iron companion, Talus, shoulders the giant off a cliff and beats away the
'lawlesse multitude' (V.ii.52) that has gathered to hear him.

   What are Spenser's sympathies in this episode? Does his defense of royal prerogative imply that he was a monarchist, and here we have one more protestation of his
loyalty to Elizabeth I, the 'Most High, Mightie And Magnificent Empresse' of his
dedication? When Talus disperses the 'rascall crew' (V.ii.52), is he expressing Spenser's distaste for the mob and any form of government that might allow its participation? Or is it possible that Spenser is 'really on the side of the Giant' (Hadfield 1998:
179)? Might his proposals for redistributive justice suggest an affinity for those
oppressed by 'Tyrants', and might this affinity have led Spenser to consider limits
on royal prerogative? Was he one of those 'dismayed by the growing powers and the
growing ostentation' of monarchy in his kingdom and 'by the corresponding decline
of representative institutions' (Worden 1991: 445), that is to say, a republican?

It seems unlikely that he could have both of these inclinations, but the question persists: what, politically speaking, *was* Edmund Spenser?

In this essay, I will say, not that this question is *mal posée*, but that it doesn't go far enough towards explaining Spenser's works. Put most crudely, the 'was Spenser a ———?' question implies a continuing adherence on Spenser's part to a coherent set of political doctrines, and few would claim to find that in his works. But even the most sophisticated answer to this question suggests that Spenser had an ongoing attachment, no matter how wavering or ambivalent, to some political program, no matter how capaciously defined, while Spenser's own works, I think, suggest just the opposite. Some of the larger outlines of Spenser's commitments are well known. He favored, for instance, patrons who were militant and interventionist in their Protestantism. For all that, attempts to align Spenser's religion with specific Protestant doctrines have come to very little, in part because, as Darryl Gless reminds us, 'sixteenth-century English protestant doctrines are complex and contradictory, subject to variable readings determined by interpreters' subjective differences as well as their differing stations within political, economic, and social structures' (1994: 16). The same holds for Spenser's politics: general tendencies are very hard to link to specific beliefs.

Questions about Spenser's political leanings are usually addressed through a combination of evidence. His acquaintanceship is noted (politics by association, as it were). His poetry is mined for examples. And quotations from political theorists with which he may have salted his prose are brought forward.[1] All this is certainly relevant, but the Spenser we are offered usually comes across as a less evasive and a more definite thinker than the one we know. Of course, Spenser had a politics—a bundle of affiliations, interests, and loyalties—and learning what these might have been is a crucial first step. When we consider further, we usually find that these affiliations, interests, and loyalties are not only multiple, but often contradictory as well. And, of course, Spenser did not somehow float free of the political controversies of his day. As we will see, his works are intimately keyed into those controversies. Often, though, it is the intellectual difficulties that define these controversies that come to be defining for this poet's thought as well. And that in itself tells us something about the style of mind with which Spenser approached the political questions of his time. Spenser can best be understood as a close student (and exemplar) of the problems around which Renaissance political theory organized itself, and not as a steady advocate of any one agenda or doctrine.

FOREIGN POLITIES

In late Elizabethan England, Niccolò Machiavelli loomed as a large and ominous presence. On stage, he came to stand for everything that was devious, Italianate, and wicked. The Devil himself took up Machiavelli's first name and in this period was known as 'Old Nick'. And Machiavelli's thought saturated the political discourse of the time. We can be certain that Spenser had read his works, and not just the more notorious, though neither the *Discourses* (1531) nor *The Prince* (1532) was published in English translation till well after his death. Gabriel Harvey, the friend of Spenser's student days, claimed that among the 'good fellowes' of his acquaintance at Cambridge there were some 'amongst us [who] begin nowe to be prettely well acquaynted with a certayne parlous book callid, as I remember me, Il Principe di Niccolo Macchiavelli, and I can peradventure name you an odd crewe or tooe that ar as cunninge in his Discorsi sopra la prima Deca di Livio' (Harvey 1884: 79).

A strong case can be made for the underlying cohesion of Machiavelli's thought.[2] This theorist believed that the republic was the best form of polity, and that all classes should have a hand in its governance. But republics were unstable to begin with, he thought, and over time they were prone to the decay brought on by the inevitable contentions of men for place and advantage. Countering this tendency required a strong ruler willing to adopt whatever means of governance might prove effective, however immoral these means might seem (or even be). '[T]his must be taken as a general rule,' says Machiavelli in the *Discourses*, offering Rome as his example,

that never or rarely does it happen that a republic or kingdom is organized well from the beginning or is completely reformed apart from its old institutions, unless it is organized by one man alone; or rather, it is necessary for a single man to be the one who gives it shape, and from whose mind any such organization derives.

But 'what he has instituted will not long endure if it rests upon the shoulders of a single man, . . . it endures when it remains a matter of concern to many and when it is the task of many to maintain it.' When they recognize the 'goodness' of the 'republic' inaugurated by its 'prudent founder', 'they will agree not to abandon it' (Machiavelli 1997: 45). In the *Discourses*, Machiavelli also noted how easily the 'many' could be deceived and how quickly they could be goaded into mob action. Still in all, he thought, a people in the mass 'is more prudent, more stable, and of better judgement than a prince' (Machiavelli 1997: 143), at least as regards their own interests. '[M]en fool themselves greatly in general questions but not so much in the particular' (Machiavelli 1997: 119).

It was *The Prince*, however, and not the *Discourses*, that left an indelible imprint on the Renaissance mind. In this treatise, 'written', said one commentator, 'by the hand of Satan' (quoted in Fischer 2006: xxxvi), Machiavelli famously urges the ruler to do whatever he finds necessary to gain and to keep power. If cruelty is required, then it should be 'well committed (if one may use the word "well" of that which is evil)' (Machiavelli 1988: 33). When the ruler first seizes control, he should impose his punishments decisively and all at once, so that such acts can soon cease and the people, who now fear him, do not come to resent him as well. When he governs, he 'should not worry about incurring a reputation for cruelty; for by punishing a very few he will really be more merciful than those who over-indulgently permit disorders to develop, with resultant killings and plunderings' (Machiavelli 1988: 58). If needed, he should also be 'a great feigner and dissembler' (Machiavelli 1988: 62), though he should not allow himself to be perceived as such by the people, lest he lose their respect.

And how should the ruler regard the people in turn? 'For this may be said of men generally: they are ungrateful, fickle, feigners and dissemblers, avoiders of danger, eager for gain' (Machiavelli 1988: 59). What the ruler does is ultimately for their good, but they cannot be expected to see that. Indeed, it has been said that it is just this rejection of any notion of man as a 'political animal endowed with moral and political rationality' able 'to transcend private interest in pursuit of a transcendent common good' (Rahe 2000: 301) that sets Machiavelli off from such classical predecessors as Aristotle and Cicero and makes him the innovative political thinker that he was.

Out of such materials, as Sydney Anglo has shown, early modern thinkers shaped different versions of the Florentine. Some, such as the anonymous French author of *Vindiciae, Contra Tyrannos* (1579), set themselves against the 'evil arts, vicious counsels, and false and pestiferous doctrines of Niccolò Machiavelli'. He held him and his supposed followers responsible for 'disrupting the commonwealth on the basis of the authority of those who rule it' (1994: 8, 9). Prominent among the detractors was Innocent Gentillet, whose *Contre-Machiavel* (1576) was much read and seems to have set the tone for much later vituperation. There, Gentillet purported to demonstrate that 'Nicholas Machiavell, not long agoe a Secretarie of the Florentine commonweale...understood nothing or little in...Politicke science... and that he hath taken Maximes and rules altogether wicked, and hath builded upon them...a Tyrannical science' (quoted in Anglo 2005: 285). Still others, however, took Machiavelli's somewhat guarded approval of the republic as a polity and began to elaborate doctrines of 'republicanism' from him.[3]

Given the seeming discrepancies between the *Discourses* and *The Prince*, it's not surprising that many found the two books hard to reconcile, although they certainly tried, often by taking the first as sincerely meant and the other as duplicitous. About six years after the treatises saw print, Reginald Pole, a visitor to Florence, was being told by Italian informants that their author had purposefully written *The Prince* to trick the Medici into overreaching, thus precipitating their own downfall. Machiavelli himself, supposedly, had claimed this.[4] And, in 1585, Alberico Gentili, later Regius Professor of Civil Law at Oxford, declared that the author of the *Discourses* was a 'very great enemy to tyranny' and that he had written *The Prince* not to 'instruct the tyrant but to expose openly his secret deeds and exhibit him naked and clearly recognizable to the wretched peoples' (quoted in Rahe 2000: 271).

Really, then, there was no one 'Machiavelli' in this period. Indeed, it's questionable how well Gentillet and other polemicists even understood Machiavelli's claims. As Anglo notes, here and there Machiavelli attracted a genuine adherent (Harvey, Spenser's friend, was one), and he achieved great notoriety. For the most part, though, he appears in early modern thought as a stand-in for whatever odious tendencies are the target of the moment—when, that is, he's not being cited as an authority. Eventually, Machiavelli's doctrines and the interpretation of those doctrines became so detached from one another that the Florentine was reduced to a 'mere figure of speech' (Anglo 2005: 573). The writer that Spenser and his contemporaries knew as 'Machiavelli' was contradictory and variable: he was the republican who worked to bring down tyrants, and he was also the amoral pragmatist whose ideal ruler let nothing stand between him and power.

Now, it's quite clear that in Ireland, which has been called a 'laboratory of Renaissance political ideas' (Morgan 1999: 9), Spenser was exposed to Machiavellian thought. A work that emerged from this same laboratory, Richard Beacon's *Solon His Folie* (1594), consistently applies Machiavelli's precepts to the kingdom.[5] But it's not at all clear that, even in Ireland, Spenser was able to achieve a similar coherence. What Spenser seems to have done instead is to use the apparently conflicted Machiavelli as a placeholder for *both* the more republican and the more absolutist tendencies in his own thought. Take, for instance, his reference to Machiavelli near the end of his *A View of the Present State of Ireland*, the only place in his works where he invokes the Florentine. Irenius, one of the discussants in this dialogue, has called for the appointment of a 'lord lieutenant' to oversee the Irish kingdom:

[A]nd this I remember is wortheley obserued by machiavell in his discourse vppon Livie wheare he Comendethe the manner of the Romaines gouernement in givinge absolute power to all theire Consulls and gouernours which if they abused they shoulde afterwardes dearelie Answeare and the Contrarye theareof he reprehendethe in the states of *Venice* of florence and manye other principalities of Italye whoe vsed to limitt theire Chief officers so streightlye as that thereby some times they haue loste suche happie occacions as they coulde neuer come vnto againe. (*Prose*, 229)

Recently, this passage has been read both as a statement of the need for limits on the Crown's powers[6] and as a brief for more power for the Crown's representatives,[7] and that it can be read both ways is, surely, the most significant thing we can notice about it. Spenser commends the granting of 'absolute power' as appropriately Machiavellian, but that power, he says, is delegated and may be withdrawn, although by whom isn't obvious. In the example from the *Discourses* that Spenser uses, the Roman *res publica* would have been the final arbiter. But in the practice Spenser is discussing, it would be the royal government of Elizabeth I. She currently appointed the Lord Deputy for Ireland and would appoint any 'lord lieutenant'. Spenser's lines are nicely balanced between republican and absolutist imperatives. They urge the need for untrammeled authority in the kingdom, but their tenor also works against this advice as Spenser elaborates on the constraints that would curb that authority (constraints which his Machiavelli seems to like when imposed by the Romans after the fact but dislike when imposed concurrently by the Florentines or the Venetians). Presumably, in calling for a 'lord lieutenant' for Ireland, Spenser registers the Machiavellian core belief that true political reform comes only when a vigorous and decisive ruler (re)grounds the polity on a secure foundation. 'Howe then doe ye thinke is the reformacion [of Ireland] . . . to be begonne?', Irenius is asked elsewhere in the *View*. 'Even by the sworde', he answers, 'for all those evills muste firste be Cutt awaie by a stronge hande before anie good Cane be planted' (*Prose*, 147–8). Machiavelli allowed Spenser to imagine a truly radical extirpation of the evils that plagued

Ireland. But, unlike Machiavelli, Spenser was not willing to be clear on what the final source of that cleansing rigor might be. The passage poses questions it does not answer. How, for instance, can power be both 'absolute' and constrained? The 'lord lieutenant' Spenser proposes will in 'particuler thinges ... be restrained thoughe not in the generall gouernement' (*Prose*, 229). But who will sort out the general from the particular? Elizabeth I? Or a 'great ... personage' (*Prose*, 228) who will operate in her name but, like all Machiavellian rulers, work for a larger good barely distinguishable from his own ambition?[8] When Spenser invokes Machiavelli, he locates very precisely the problem of ultimate governance in Ireland, but he does not resolve that problem.

A similar duplicity can be found in Spenser's use of the French political theorist, Jean Bodin. Bodin was known in the Renaissance mostly as the author *Six Books of the Commonwealth* (1576), where he offers a compelling argument for the inherent prerogatives of the absolute sovereign. He points out that, as a matter of logic, 'if the prince can only make law with the consent of a superior he is a subject; if of an equal he shares his sovereignty; if of an inferior, whether it be a council of magnates or the people, it is not he who is sovereign' (Bodin 1955: 43). Ultimate authority, wherever it might reside, is in principle indivisible. And if a ruler is an 'absolute sovereign', Bodin says, then no recourse to 'process of law is possible' against him, 'even though he has committed all the evil, impious, and cruel deeds imaginable'. Such a prince is the originator of the law and its epitome; resistance is treason. Above all, in no way can it be lawful to kill this prince, to try to do so, to urge others to do so, or even to 'wish' or 'consider' doing this. Looking across the Channel to England, Bodin saw an example of such a ruler. There, the king's 'authority is unquestionably [his] own, and not shared with any of [his] subjects in particular' (Bodin 1955: 67).

Bodin's *Six Books* was widely available in French and in Latin translation, and, as the sixteenth century wore on and Elizabeth and her advisors moved to shore up her prerogative, his views were adopted by many at her court. Not only did his absolutist claims answer to the new tenor of political thinking there, but they offered an intellectual counterweight to a worrying line of argument that held princes ultimately accountable to the people. This in itself was not objectionable. Much of English political theory was 'constitutionalist' in that it took as a received premise that the monarch was 'appointed to protect his subjects in their lives, properties and laws; for this very end and purpose he has the delegation of power from the people; and he has no claim to any other power but this' (quoted in Hudson 1942: 116), or so Sir John Fortescue had declared in the fifteenth century. The Tudors found representative institutions useful—up to a point. However absolutist her beliefs, Elizabeth was at least willing to concede a loyal Parliament a role in her deliberations.

Some, however, had begun to draw the conclusion that a monarch who had a mandate from God to protect the people ought also to be answerable to them when he failed to do so. Readers at court would also have been aware of another French theorist, the author of *Vindiciae, Contra Tyrannos*. 'We should always bear this in mind,' he says, that 'kings are created for the benefit of the people; and ... those who are zealous in the interests of the people are considered to be kings, and those who pursue their own are ... really tyrants.' Moreover, 'justice bids us to check tyrants and overthrowers of right and the commonwealth' (1994: 110, 185). (The reign of Eliza-beth's half-sister, Mary, had provoked similar claims from John Ponet in his *Shorte Treatise of Politike Power* (1556), a possible source for the French text.[9]) Against such presumption, Bodin's precepts seemed a useful check.

However, Bodin's thought is also divided against itself, at least in its emphases. For one thing, Bodin is not always so stringent in rejecting any role for the people in a commonwealth. Machiavelli, as we saw, broke with his classical predecessors. For him, a dependable but narrow self-interest was the best that could be expected of the hoi polloi. In an earlier work, *Method for the Easy Comprehension of History* (1566), Bodin rejects Machiavelli's innovation—'he would have written more fully and effectively and with greater regard for truth, if he had combined a knowledge of the writings of ancient philosophers and historians with experience'—as well as his republicanism—'of all states none more unhappy than Florence existed as long as it was democratic' (Bodin 1945: 153, 270). But, in the ideal state as he defines it, the magistrates and laws exert a certain sway on the prince. A kingdom harmoniously unified in and by its God-fearing prince is best for the 'citizen body' (Bodin 1945: 286). Even in the *Six Books*, he reminds the ruler not to impose his prerogative on his subjects in all things, for 'the more one tries to constrain men's wills, the more obstinate they become'. Laws should not be arbitrary, but suited to the 'nature of the people' (Bodin 1955: 142, 146). The analytical rigor of Bodin's absolutism was tem-pered, in his writings, by a certain acknowledgment of the contingencies of actual rule.

As with Machiavelli, we can't be certain what Spenser made of Bodin. He would have read him, surely. (Harvey placed the works of Bodin alongside Machiavelli's on the tables of those 'good fellowes' he knew at Cambridge.) Bodin's prescriptions for an orderly kingdom in France, it has been suggested, may show up in Spenser's schemes for subduing Ireland (Hadfield 1997: 73–7). But nowhere does Spenser cite Bodin in the *View*, and he could have found such prescriptions in many other places. Spenser's response to Machiavelli, we noted, seems to be refracted among the various Machiavellis available to him. Somewhat similarly, his use of Bodin seems divided along the lines of Bodin's own contradictions.

Consider, for example, one place in the *View* where an editor is 'fairly certain' that we find a 'trace of Bodin' (Spenser 1970: 226). In his *Six Books*, Bodin urges that, on the one hand, the sovereign should mandate a 'form of religion' 'since it is the force that at once secures the authority of kings and governors, the execution of laws, the obedience of subjects, reverence for magistrates, [and] fear of ill-doing'. Even discus-sion in matters of religion is 'on no account [to] be admitted', since it leads to 'dispute'. On the other hand, Bodin acknowledges that coercing subjects into adopt-ing one or another religion will not work. Somewhat hopefully, he suggests that the prince lead a virtuous life, 'follow[ing] the true religion without hypocrisy or deceit' (Bodin 1955: 140, 141, 142). Then the people might come to emulate him. Lacking Machiavelli's sense of the ways in which a self-interested populace and an equally self-interested ruler accommodate one another, Bodin slides between premises. Absolute sovereignty is required, except when it will not succeed, and then . . . something else.

In the *View*, Spenser displays just this wavering when it comes to upholding religion in Ireland. Indeed, this is one of the most conspicuously ambiguous passages in his treatise. '[F]for Religion litle haue I to saie my selfe', he confesses,

beinge...not professed thearein, and it selfe beinge but one so as theare is but one waie thearein. ffor that which is trewe onelye is and the rest are not at all. yeat in plantinge of religion thus muche is nedefull to be obserued that it be not soughte forciblie to be impressed into them with terrour and sharpe penalties as now is the mannour, but rather deliuered and intymated with mildenes and gentlenes soe as it maie not be hated before it be vnderstode and theire professours despised and reiected. (*Prose*, 221)

This passage does in fact offer a fairly close parallel to Bodin's *Six Books*, but in its ambivalence, not its argument. There is, as Bodin puts it, only 'one religion, one truth, one divine law' (1955: 141), but Spenser does not have much to say about it, 'beinge... not professed thearein'. Religion must be 'planted' whether the Irish will or no. But not in any forceful way. The same writer who can declare elsewhere in the *View* that, since 'we Cannot now applie Lawes fitt to the [Irish] people...we will applie the people and fitt them to the Lawes' (*Prose*, 199) now tells us to avoid 'terrour and sharpe penalties'. Paraphrasing Bodin allows Spenser to advocate mass conversion in Ireland while at the same time discouraging too much severity. From Bodin, he takes contradictions, which he then refashions into nuanced, somewhat self-subverting prose. The influence of Bodin is clear enough, but what Spenser has absorbed from this French theorist is a hesitancy about key principles, a tacit pragmatism, and not the more rigorous pronouncements for which he is known. This is why, as I have suggested elsewhere, Spenser's debt to Bodin does not come down to specific doctrines or proposals, but to the internal discrepancies that permeated his *oeuvre* (Baker 2001: 55).

SMITH'S REPUBLIC

Later in his life, Spenser moved into the orbit of Robert Devereux, the second Earl of Essex. Today, when critics try to locate Spenser politically, they often point to his association with this nobleman (who is said to have paid, in 1599, for the poet's funeral). Around Essex there gathered a loose coalition of malcontents and idealists: military officers whose careers were blocked, divines of a so-called 'Puritan' persuasion on the outs with the Anglican establishment, frustrated courtiers kept from grace by royal favorites—and thinkers whose imaginations favored alternatives to the 'regocentric' government of Elizabeth I. Some of this faction entertained the claim that resistance to royal tyranny might at times be legitimate. Essex, with his outsize ambitions and openness to anti-absolutist views, drew the disaffected to him. What he held out was himself, a figure in whom all could see the embodiment of their own aspirations and alienation.[10]

Spenser's association with this coterie is important. It suggests that he felt constrained by the dwindling possibilities of Elizabeth's reign, that he was antagonistic to Spanish imperialism and sympathetic to the cause of trans-national Protestantism, and that he found a correlative for these feelings in the charismatic Essex. But can we infer from this association that Spenser grew overtly hostile to Elizabeth late in her reign? Or that he would have understood this or that work of Elizabethan political theory in this or that way? I would say no. The poetry and prose he has left us does not support such claims. In contrast, it usually implies a nuanced engagement with current politics that cannot be reduced to factional alliances.

Let's take as a test case the *De Republica Anglorum* of Thomas Smith. Spenser's association with Essex has led one historian, A. N. McLaren, to say that his reading of this signal work would have been hostile.[11] Spenser, 'like others of the Essex circle, fought a rearguard action against [its] redefinition' of royal prerogative, and he did this 'most obviously in the *Faerie Queene*' (McLaren 1999: 203). *De Republica Anglorum* was published in 1583, and it would be reprinted fifteen times (translated into Latin, it went to four editions). Its larger ideas would have been familiar to any informed Englishman, but it saw print at a specific juncture: England was moving into what has been called the 'second reign' of Elizabeth I, the years from 1585 to 1603. These were marked by 'xenophobia, war-weariness . . . and turmoil', and they saw an answering obsession on the part of the royal government with threats to 'state security', with 'the subversiveness of religious nonconformity', and with 'the threat of "popularity" and social revolt' (Guy 1995: 1)—with everything, in short, of which the Essex faction was suspected.

Smith was at once an accomplished scholar—'the flower of the University of Cambridge' (quoted in Smith 1982: 2), its first Regius Professor of Civil Law in 1540, its Vice Chancellor in 1543, Provost of Eton College in 1547—and a canny political operator. An intimate of Francis Walsingham and William Cecil, he joined the Privy Council in 1571 and ended his career as Principal Secretary of State, serving from 1572 to 1576. *De Republica Anglorum* was written, he tells us, in 'the vij yeare of the raigne and administration thereof by the most vertuous and noble Queene Elizabeth . . . when I was ambassador for her majestie in the court of Fraunce' (Smith 1982: 144). Spenser himself (or whoever provided the tenth 'Glosse' to 'Ianvarye' in his *Shepheardes Calendar* (1579)) took notice of 'the worthy Sir Tho. Smith . . . his book of gouerment', as well as 'other his most graue and excellent wrytings'.

Smith begins his treatise in Aristotelian fashion, distinguishing 'Common wealthes' according to the number of those who govern: 'one alone', monarchy; 'where the smaller number', aristocracy; 'where the multitude doth rule', democracy (Smith 1982: 49). In practice, he warns us, 'seldome or never shall you finde any common wealthe or governement which is absolutely and sincerely made . . . but always mixed with an other' (Smith 1982: 52). In setting forth this political typology, Smith was following the precedent of Thomas Elyot's *The Boke Named the Gouernour* (1531). But Elyot had been adamant that 'where equalitie was of astate amonge the people', that 'monstre with many heedes', 'rancour' and 'confusion'

(Elyot 1967: I, 19, 10) were sure to follow. Smith, by contrast, seems to confine himself to description. A commonwealth properly so called is 'a society or common doing of a multitude of free men collected together and united by common accord and covenauntes among themselves, for the conservation of themselves aswell in peace as in warre' (Smith 1982: 57).

This definition was often quoted in the seventeenth century by republicans looking to restore a measure of self-governance to England's people. Smith himself, though, is chary of attributing the final say to any one 'estate' or personage in the kingdom. England, he demonstrates, is what was called a 'mixed monarchy'. In his polity, authority is shared, and political actors of every sort have their claims to make. Smith grants a prerogative to Parliament. It possesses the 'most high and absolute power of the realme of Englande' (Smith 1982: 78), but only when it works in concert with the Crown. A bill becomes law when, after due consultation among the various orders of the kingdom represented 'in either house', 'the Prince himselfe . . . doeth consent unto and alloweth. That is the Princes and whole realmes deede: whereupon justlie no man can complaine, but must accommodate himselfe to finde it good and obey it' (Smith 1982: 78). Sovereignty results from a joint affirmation that culminates in, but does not entirely consist of, the king's assent. (This was an influential formulation of the 'king-in-Parliament' model of government.) At the same time, Smith grants the Crown an absolute prerogative, absolute, that is, in certain respects. In England, the 'Monarch . . . hath absolutelie in his power the authoritie of warre and peace', 'absolute power in crying and decreeing the monies of the realme', in dispensing with laws 'whereas equitie requireth a moderation to be had', and so on. 'To be short', says Smith, 'the prince is the life, the head, and the authoritie of all thinges that be doone in the realme of England' (Smith 1982: 85, 86, 88).

Still, seventeenth-century republicans were not entirely wrong to find a precursor in Smith. He could imagine a case where a 'good and upright man, and lover of his countrie' might seek to 'dissolve' his 'common wealth' if its ruler was 'evill . . . and unjust', though he concludes that 'meddl[ing] with the chaunging of the lawes and governement' is always 'hasardous' (Smith 1982: 51, 52). And while he declares that the lowest 'classe amongest us', the laboring poor, 'have no voice nor authoritie in our common wealth', he warns that they should not be 'altogether neglected' (Smith 1982: 76). Smith's deepest impulses, it appears, are both inclusive and conservative. He wants to fashion a polity in which no one is left out (entirely), but where most of the power resides at or near the top of the existing hierarchy.

Here, though, is where things start to get complicated. Smith may have wanted to keep authority concentrated among the elite, but, within the elite, there was an inevitable jockeying for power, and it seems that what Smith also wanted was to exclude from *absolute* power one particular member of the governing class: Elizabeth I. The presence of a queen on England's throne presented the political nation with an intractable problem: she was a woman. The 'deeply rooted conviction permeating European society' was that 'women were at least relatively incapable of supreme command' (McLaren 1999: 142), and yet England was ruled by the 'daughter to King *Henrie* the eight' (Smith 1982: 144).

English political theory offered few precedents for this anomaly. In the fifteenth century, Sir John Fortescue had opined that 'no woman ought soveranly or supremely to reygne upon man' (quoted in McLaren 1999: 46). And, during Elizabeth's reign, John Knox outraged the Queen by declaring that to 'promote a woman to bear rule, superiority, dominion or empire above any realm, nation, or city is repugnant to nature [and] contumely to God' (Knox 1985: 42). McLaren argues convincingly that the kingdom's elite responded to this dilemma by erecting a structure of interlocking claims. The monarch who headed up England, they said, held office at God's behest. In her person, her 'body natural', Elizabeth I was a woman, but the 'body politic' which she represented and into which she was incorporated at her coronation was not; it was male. Around the Queen, moreover, were arrayed a body of counselors, godly men who made up for the 'deficiencies of female rule' and served as a 'bulwark of order' (McLaren 1999: 48). Smith, says McLaren, was one of the theorists to advance such claims. In his *De Republica Anglorum*, he made sure that the 'sexe not accustomed (otherwise) to intermeddle with publicke affaires' would 'never . . . lacke the counsell of such grave and discreete men as be able to supplie all other defaultes' (Smith 1982: 65).

Smith's 'mixed monarchy', therefore, is in fact as much prescriptive as it is descriptive. The England that he wants is not the England that the lineage of Henry VIII has bequeathed him, and the polity he designs is meant to accommodate the inconvenient fact of Elizabeth I's womanhood. Not surprisingly, Elizabeth did not like Smith much and only grudgingly admitted him to the Privy Council. In a letter to Cecil in 1563, Smith went so far as to compare queens to children: both can be 'used'. When shown 'a piece of gold or silver, or peradventure, a knife . . . some fair printed paper, or some pretty apple', they let 'fall the one to reach at the other' (quoted in Shrank 2004: 165).

And Spenser's own stance towards his queen? An older Spenser criticism saw *The Faerie Queene* as one long encomium to the monarch 'renowmed for pietie, vertve, and all gratiovs government', as the poet says in his dedication. More recently, readers have been finding a potent mix of devotion and hostility in Spenser's portrayals. Certainly, Spenser was conscious of the problems that Elizabeth's femaleness posed for her subjects, particularly as she aged. In both the second and the third books of *The Faerie Queene*, prophetic visions of a future 'British' line splutter out as they reach the moment when 'shall a royall virgin raine' (III.iii.49). The implication may very well be, as Andrew Hadfield suggests, that 'Elizabeth [is] already past childbearing age'. It was 'all too late anyway' for dynastic hopes; 'the dye had been cast' (Hadfield 2004: 120).

This, however, does not amount to an outright dismissal of the Queen's prerogative, as a look at another key episode in *The Faerie Queene* shows. In Book V of that epic, Spenser personifies Mary Queen of Scots as Duessa, one of the most transparent of his interventions into the politics of the time. As Arthur and Artegall enter the court of Mercilla, a shadowed figure for Elizabeth, they encounter a 'Poet bad' 'whose tongue was for his trespasse vyle | Nayld to a post, adiudged so by law' (V.ix.25). They witness a trial of a 'Ladie of great countenance and place' (V.ix.38) whose guilt is asserted by Zele, Authority, and Justice, though leniency is urged by Pity and others. At the moment of judgment, though, Mercilla,

> whose Princely breast was touched nere
> With piteous ruth of her so wretched plight,
> Though plaine she saw by all, that she did heare,
> That she of death was guiltie found by right,
> Yet would not let iust vengeance on her light;
> But rather let in stead thereof to fall
> Few perling drops from her faire lampes of light;
> The which she couering with her purple pall
> Would haue the passion hid, and vp arose withall.   (V.ix.50)

As every English reader would have understood, the verse referred to the events of 1587, the trial and death of Mary, who had been found guilty of plotting against the Crown, but who had been executed only when Elizabeth's hand was forced by her Privy Council. One Scottish reader understood this too: James VI of Scotland (soon to be James I of England), who in 1596 demanded that Spenser, for his *lese majesty* against his mother, 'may be dewly tryed & punished' (quoted in Goldberg 1983: 1).

Critics have been quick to pick up on the charged ambivalence of this episode. It's written by a poet, and it features a poet, Bonfont—his name 'raced out' and, on a sign above his head, changed to '*Malfont*' (V.ix.26)—forced to curb his tongue (literally) by a monarch who demands praise for her benevolence but orchestrates, or at least allows, the death of a fellow prince. With whom in the poem does Spenser align himself, they ask, those who wish to see Duessa granted a measure of grace or those who wish to see her utterly condemned? And, by implication, with whom do Spenser's political sympathies lie: with those who in the 1590s upheld the Queen's prerogatives, even as she vacillated, or those who had tired of their aging and imperious monarch and were exploring other, more participatory models of royal government? With Elizabeth the querulous absolutist or Essex the disgruntled courtier? What's more likely, I would say, is that Spenser's sympathies lie with Thomas Smith—or better, perhaps, with a certain version of him.

As Elizabeth I grew older, she began to insist more and more on her inviolable prerogatives and final authority. Her Privy Councilors did not hold their offices 'by birth', she insisted. They rendered their services only so long as 'it shall please her Majesty to dispose of the same' (quoted in McLaren 1999: 142). But her Privy Councillors were committed to thinking of their Queen, along Smithian lines, as the embodiment of the 'godly nation' (one who just happened to be female) and of themselves as the 'grave and discreete men' who spoke for the commonwealth. In the 1580s and then into the 1590s, McLaren shows, a 'collusive relationship' developed between Elizabeth and her advisors as all concerned lined up behind a theory of 'mixed monarchy' that left room for *both* of these emphases while dampening down 'levelling propensities in the body politic' (McLaren 1999: 224, 225), a very delicate political symbiosis indeed. This 'collusion' was what allowed Elizabeth's government to operate even though, *au fond*, she and her Privy Council had incompatible understandings of her prerogative. Contending interests and ideologies were thereby accommodated; these included but were not limited to the Queen's own.

Ironically, the publication of Smith's *De Republica Anglorum* in 1583 (six years after his death) helped enable this compromise. The treatise that had once been written to hedge Elizabeth about and constrain her prerogative became an 'official' text of her government. Successive editions, each of them declaring on its title page that it had been 'Seene and allowed', featured interpolations and 'revisions . . . taking Elizabeth's queenship as a given' (McLaren 1999: 221). Its 'authors' now included editors who silently amended the text to conform to the new policy. 'We live in Smith's Republic' (Harvey 1913: 197), Gabriel Harvey wrote in the margin of a book in 1582. By this he meant, no doubt, the polity that Smith (his patron) had conceived in *De Republica Anglorum*. But, by the time he jotted his note, England's government had become something other than the 'mixed monarchy' that Smith had envisioned: it was 'mixed', certainly, but according to an uneasy compromise (supposedly underwritten by Smith) that permitted Elizabeth and her chief advisors to exercise power, and not just despite, but by means of the contradictions they shared.

It is *this* anxious compromise, I think, and not the starker choices offered by Essex that Spenser rehearses in his portrayal of Mary's trial and death. Notice how the trial episode is organized: distinct political views are simultaneously given their due and counterpoised with their opposites (one reason, of course, that critics have come up with divergent readings). The notion that royal Mercy might not be a 'part' of Justice is dismissed as a conceit of 'Clarkes' and their 'deuicefull art' (V.x.1), and the absolute validity of Mercilla's 'doome of right' (V.x.2) is asserted. The final 'iudgement' is hers, and only hers, 'Iustice gainst the thrall' (V.ix.49). At the same time, Duessa is rightfully 'damned by them all' (including Artegall and Arthur), and it is their 'strong constraint' that 'enforce[s]' (V.x.4) the queen's decision. The overzealous councilors are perhaps a little pushy, but they turn out to be right. When Mercilla rises 'vp withall' at the end of Canto ix, she is not escaping from her court and its politics. Rather, this sort of obscurity is the signature style of her court and its politics—a style that Spenser has mastered and is quite willing to adopt as his own. The question of who was finally responsible for the warrant (signed by Elizabeth) that resulted in Mary's death (as demanded by her Privy Council) is exactly the one that nobody at court wants to answer. And neither does Spenser. He aligns himself with a split alignment of power, and, like the Queen and her advisors, positions himself on both sides of such questions. The trial of Duessa presents an incoherent but politically expedient argument for the existing configuration of royal authority.

Spenser's attempts to mime the indeterminacies of Elizabeth's court, it should be said, did not always work out well for him, and neither did this one. The court's realpolitik was often more flexible, and also more punitive, than he was prepared to accommodate. Sometimes he seems to have invited controversy. In *Mother*

Hubberds Tale (1591), he satirized Lord Burghley, the Queen's advisor ('For men of learning little he esteemed'). Unsold copies were confiscated by the censors. Earlier, Spenser had published *The Shepheardes Calendar* anonymously, in part, it seems, because he knew that his treatment of such topics as the Queen's proposed marriage to a Frenchman, the Duke of Anjou, and his defense of Archbishop Grindal ('Algrind'), recently 'sequestered' by Elizabeth, was bound to offend some at court. How closely was he able to gauge such controversy ahead of time, though, and was he always ready to deal with the consequences? That in itself is hard to gauge. In the event, his depiction of Duessa went too far. *The Faerie Queene* was banned in Scotland when it appeared in its entirety in 1596. Once it became clear that Spenser had greatly offended James VI in his handling of his royal mother, Elizabeth's support for the poet evaporated. The English ambassador to Edinburgh could tell James, truthfully, that his fears that the epic had been authorized by the English Crown, 'passed with previledge' (quoted in McCabe 1987: 224), were quite unfounded. As Richard McCabe puts it, by 1596 it was 'clear that Spenser was never to become Elizabeth's Vergil' (McCabe 1987: 242). The expediency and duplicity that he had epitomized in the 'wretched' (V.ix.38) Duessa was, as it emerged, not characteristic of her alone.

What, then, of Spenser's political influences? Can we know what he would have made of Smith's writings, say, and how he would have responded to them? Perhaps it would be better to say that Spenser was influenced by that complex of ideas that came to be associated with Smith and that was (variously) elaborated out of his writings. And, instead of saying that Spenser was either for or against this Smithian discourse, we could say that he and Smith, and many other political thinkers of the day as well, shared a repertoire of problems. Both Smith and Spenser, I would guess, had to negotiate their way around the twin facts of Elizabeth I's femaleness and her power. Their Queen is at once their ruler and their predicament. They must perforce acknowledge her claims for prerogative (overstated as they may be) while finding the means to keep a 'mixed monarchy' properly mixed, acknowledging that other voices (including their own) have their say too.

To separate out each of those voices, though, is no easy matter. Spenser, it's fair to say, had read *De Republica Anglorum*. But which *De Republica Anglorum* did he favor? The work as Smith penned it? (This circulated widely in manuscript and is noted by E. K.) Or the work as it was published under the aegis of the government of Elizabeth I? In his own writings, does he engage with the first or the second—or, in some more subtle way, does he register, respond to, and participate in the politico-editorial process that turns Smith's text from the first into the second? Politics in this period, it has rightly been said, was 'carried on through an extraordinary confusion of tongues, and the history of political thought can be reconstructed only through a serious effort of discrimination, translation, and decipherment' (Kelly 1994: 47). Terms shift slightly, and sometimes drastically, with context. Today's circumstances are framed in yesterday's rhetoric by thinkers who borrow from one another and rearrange tropes and arguments as they do. And what J. G. A. Pocock has said about early modern republicanism—that it was 'a language, not a programme' (quoted in Worden 1991: 446)—is so of many of the interwoven strands of political thought in the period. The relays between theory and practice were often multifarious and unpredictable. Spenser spoke many of these political 'languages'; he was fluent in some of them. But we should not conclude from this that he was committed to one or another of the 'programmes' that could at times be derived from them. Maybe, in some cases, he was.[12] His use of these 'languages' prevents us from finally knowing that, as I suspect it was meant to.

Spenser's work (or Machiavelli's or Bodin's or Smith's) cannot be subsumed under a single, consistent vision. Understanding Spenser's politics does not lead us to establish direct influences upon him or to conscript him into one faction or another, enlisting him under the banner of some early modern 'ism'. It leads us to the place where *The Faerie Queene* begins: with doubtful 'Allegories' and 'darke conceit[s]' 'without expressing of any particular purposes or by-accidents therein occasioned' (Spenser 2001: 714).

Notes

1. Cf. Gless (1994), 2: 'Studies of Spenser's theological contexts incline unselfconsciously to adopt a common strategy: the poet's convictions are inferred from passages in his poems, read in light of what little evidence remains of his political and social affiliations; this inferentially constructed "Spenser" is then considered solid enough to warrant further interpretive inferences'.
2. See Fischer (2000).
3. Scholars differ about whether English 'republicanism' was a distinct and consequential political discourse at the turn of the seventeenth century or whether it became that in the 1650s, and then only briefly as a hedge against 'tyranny'. See Peltonen (1995), Worden (1991, 2002), and Hadfield (2005), 17–53.
4. See Rahe (2000), 271. Pole himself was deeply hostile to Machiavelli. See Anglo (2005), 115–42.
5. See Peltonen (1994), Hadfield (1997), 42–7, and Anglo (2005), 467–76.
6. Hadfield (1998), 172–3; (2003), 284–5.
7. Wilson-Okamura (2003), 258–60.
8. Robert Devereux, the second Earl of Essex, is thought to be Spenser's candidate for the job: 'suche an one I Coulde name vppon whom the ey of all Englande is fixed and our laste hopes now rest' (*Prose*, 228).
9. See Hudson (1942), 199–200.
10. Eventually, Essex's dissatisfaction with Elizabeth's reign drove him to action. In 1600, after returning from a failed Irish campaign the previous year, he led an uprising and marched on the city of London. He did not, however, garner the popular support he had expected and was arrested, tried, and then executed in 1601.
11. I'm indebted to McLaren's superb reading of Elizabethan politics throughout this section.
12. His policy proposals in *The View of the Present State of Ireland*, for instance, were often specific and unequivocal. It is when we try to attach policy to politics, to a larger, coherent theory of government, that we run into trouble.

BIBLIOGRAPHY

Anglo, S. (2005). *Machiavelli—The First Century: Studies in Enthusiasm, Hostility, and Irrelevance*. Oxford: Oxford University Press.

Anon. (1994). *Vindiciae, Contra Tyrannos*, ed. and trans. G. Garnett. Cambridge: Cambridge University Press.

Baker, D. (2001). 'Historical Contexts: Britain and Europe', in A. Hadfield (ed.), *The Cambridge Companion to Spenser*. Cambridge: Cambridge University Press.

Beacon, R. (1996). *Solon His Folie*, ed. C. Carroll and V. Carey. Binghamton: Center for Medieval and Early Renaissance Studies.

Bodin, J. (1945). *Method for the Easy Comprehension of History*, trans. B. Reynolds. New York: Columbia University Press.

Bodin, J. (1955). *Six Books of the Commonwealth*, ed. and trans. M. J. Tooley. Oxford: Basil Blackwell.

Elyot, T. (1967). *The Boke Named the Gouernour*, ed. H. Croft, 2 vols. New York: Burt Franklin.

Fischer, M. (2000). *Well-Ordered License: On the Unity of Machiavelli's Thought*. Lanham: Lexington Books.

—— (2006). 'Prologue: Machiavelli's Rapacious Republicanism', in P. Rahe (ed.), *Machiavelli's Liberal Republican Legacy*. Cambridge: Cambridge University Press.

Gless, D. (1994). *Interpretation and Theology in Spenser*. Cambridge: Cambridge University Press.

Goldberg, J. (1983). *James I and the Politics of Literature: Jonson, Shakespeare, Donne, and Their Contemporaries*. Baltimore: Johns Hopkins University Press.

Guy, J. (1995). 'Introduction, The 1590s: The Second Reign of Elizabeth I?', in J. Guy (ed.), *The Reign of Elizabeth I: Court and Culture in the Last Decade*. Cambridge: Cambridge University Press, 1–19.

Hadfield, A. (1997). *Edmund Spenser's Irish Experience: Wilde Fruit and Salvage Soyl*. Oxford: Clarendon Press.

—— (1998). 'Was Spenser a Republican?' *English* 47: 169–82.

—— (2003). 'Was Spenser Really a Republican After All?: A Response to David Scott Wilson-Okamura'. *Spenser Studies* 47: 275–90.

—— (2004). *Shakespeare, Spenser and the Matter of Britain*. Houndmills: Palgrave MacMillan.

Harvey, G. (1884). *The Letter Book of Gabriel Harvey, 1573–80*, ed. J. L. Scott. London: Camden Society.

—— (1913). *Gabriel Harvey's Marginalia*, ed. G. C. Moore. Stratford: Shakespeare Head Press.

Hudson, W. S. (1942). *John Ponet (1516?–1556): Advocate of Limited Monarchy*. Chicago: University of Chicago Press.

Kelly, D. (1994). 'Elizabethan Political Thought', in J. Pocock, G. Schochet, and L. Schwoerer (eds), *The Varieties of British Political Thought, 1500–1800*. Cambridge: Cambridge University Press.

Knox, J. (1985). *The Political Writings of John Knox*, ed. M. Breslow. Washington, DC: Folger Books.

McCabe, R. A. (1987). 'The Masks of Duessa: Spenser, Mary Queen of Scots, and James VI'. *ELR* 17: 224–42.

Machiavelli, N. (1988). *The Prince*, ed. Q. Skinner and R. Price. Cambridge: Cambridge University Press.

—— (1997). *Discourses on Livy*, trans. J. C. Conway Bondanella and P. Bondanella. Oxford: Oxford University Press.

McLaren, A. (1999). *Political Culture in the Reign of Elizabeth I: Queen and Commonwealth 1558–1585*. Cambridge: Cambridge University Press.

Morgan, H. (1999). 'Beyond Spenser? An Historiographical Introduction to the Study of Political Ideas in Early Modern Ireland', in H. Morgan (ed.), *Political Ideology in Ireland, 1541–1641*. Dublin: Four Courts Press.

Peltonen, M. (1994). 'Classical Republicanism in Tudor England: The Case of Richard Beacon's *Solon his Follie*'. *History of Political Thought* 15: 469–503.

—— (1995). *Classical Humanism and Republicanism in English Political Thought 1570–1640*. Cambridge: Cambridge University Press.

Rahe, P. (2000). 'Situating Machiavelli', in J. Hawkins (ed.), *Renaissance Civic Humanism: Reappraisals and Reflections*. Cambridge: Cambridge University Press.

Shrank, C. (2004). *Writing the Nation in Reformation England 1530–1580*. Oxford: Oxford University Press.

Smith, T. (1982). *De Republic Anglorum*, ed. M. Dewar. Cambridge: Cambridge University Press.

Spenser, Edmund (1970). *A View of the Present State of Ireland*, ed. W. L. Renwick. Oxford: Clarendon Press.

Wilson-Okamura, D. (2003). 'Republicanism, Nostalgia, and the Crowd'. *SSt* 17: 275–90.

Worden, B. (1991). 'English Republicanism', in J. H. Burns (ed.), *The Cambridge History of Political Thought 1450–1700*. Cambridge: Cambridge University Press.

—— (2002). 'Republicanism, Regicide and Republic: The English Experience', in M. Van Gelderen and Q. Skinner (eds), *Republicanism: A Shared European Heritage*, 2 vols. Cambridge: Cambridge University Press.

CHAPTER 4

....

SPENSER'S SECRETARIAL CAREER

....

CHRISTOPHER BURLINSON

ANDREW ZURCHER

Copia Respondet Originali

Spenser's secretarial career, especially during his twenty years in Ireland, has a particular importance for historians as well as for literary critics. The period of his service to Arthur Lord Grey of Wilton, Lord Deputy of Ireland (1580–2), and to the brothers Sir John and Sir Thomas Norris, governors of Munster (c.1582–9), coincided not only with a seismic shift in English literary production, but with a similarly far-reaching revolution in administrative and secretarial practice. These two parallel developments—in different ways consequences of the humanist pedagogical transformations that swept through England in the mid-sixteenth century—were combined in the experience and writing of a number of contemporary secretary-authors, from Thomas Wilson and Lodowick Bryskett to John Donne, but in no one more so than Edmund Spenser. The tensions between secrecy and revelation, trust and betrayal, decorous address and disinterestedness, the diverse materialities of texts and the meanings they import, and even aesthetics and significance—all familiar concerns from Spenser's poetry—are phenomena as much of the secretariat as of the study. In what follows, we will look carefully at published and prescriptive accounts of the office of a secretary in Elizabethan England, as well as the archival evidence of Spenser's practice of secretaryship in Ireland, where the idea of a secretarial career found (for Spenser) its covert, particular, material, and significant expression. From the opposition between these two ways of examining Spenser as a secretary—ideal and particularized, English and Irish—will emerge those ethical and epistemological problems, with their concomitant opportunities, that Spenser seems to have discovered in his epistolary career.

The sixteenth century was a period of rapid change in the theory and practice of the secretarial office. The position of the Principal Secretary of State was in the process of being transformed, by secretary-councillors like William Cecil, Lord Burghley, Sir Francis Walsingham, and Burghley's son, Sir Robert Cecil, into a role of national political influence (Evans 1923; Alford 1998). At the same time, a number of men who worked in or alongside the Queen's Principal Secretariat, such as Robert Cecil, John Herbert, Robert Beale, and Nicholas Faunt, and also professional men of a lower standing and with a different interest in promoting the accomplishments and dignity of the profession, attempted to define afresh the secretary's responsibilities and ambiguous social position. These writers were certainly influenced by the humanist epistolary and rhetorical tradition (Erasmus's *De Conscribendis Epistolis* above all), and by European handbooks such as Francesco Sansovino's *Del Secretario* (1564), but they derived most of their claims from their own experience of a rapidly changing social and professional environment. Faunt emphasizes the indispensability of the secretary, and the variety of his employment, when he writes that 'amoungst all particuler offices and places of charge in this state, there is none of more necessarie vse, nor subiect to more cumber and variablenes; then is the office of principall Secretarie' (Faunt 1905: 499–500). The business of the secretary now entailed a complex set of administrative procedures, and the prescriptive account of the office offered by Beale, as by Faunt, stresses the efficient and faithful discharge of paper duties. When preparing the incoming post, for example, Beale's secretary was to 'abbreviate on the backside of the lettres, or otherwise in a bie paper, the substantiall and most material points which are to be propounded and answered'; similarly, his secretary was to 'have a care that the Clerks of the Councell keepe a perfect booke of the Lords' sittinges' (Beale 1925: 425–6). Faunt's secretary, similarly, should spend his time compiling 'journall[s]' and 'sundrie bookes of paper for the Regestring of all instruccions and lettres of forraine partes into Ireland or vnto the Sea, and the minutes of lettres of further direccions groweing vpon sundrie accidents and newe occasions [. . .] as likewise the answeres and Relacions of their Charges and Commissions' (Faunt 1905: 503–4). Detailed studies of the secretariats of the Cecils (Smith 1968) and Robert Devereux, Earl of Essex (Hammer 1994) have shown them to have been large offices, in which many secretaries worked together and often in rivalry with one another.

And yet, even for so bureaucratically minded a body as Beale, the secretary's effectiveness depended on his ability to judge the mood of his master or mistress as adroitly as any friend or lover: 'Learne before your accesse her Majestie's disposition by some in the Privie Chamber with whom you must keepe credit', he counsels his reader, and 'when her highnes is angrie or not well disposed trouble her not with anie matter which you desire to have done' (Beale 1925: 437–8). Other writers, chief among them Angel Day, recognized the unstable hybridity of an office being pulled apart by conflicting pressures toward a new bureaucracy, on the one hand, and a courtly fashion for humanist rhetoric and friendship, on the other; as Day writes, in his 'function and place . . . being in one condition a *Seruant*, [the secretary] is at the pleasure and appoyntment of another to be commaunded: and being in a second respect as a *friend*, hee is charely [i.e. dearly] to haue in estimate, the state, honour, reputation and being, of him whom he serueth' (Day 1592: 110). The basic problem, as Day noted, was the secretary's 'partaking [. . .] with so many causes of importance, & vndiscouered secrets & counsels' (Day 1592: 119). Indeed, Day goes so far as to suggest that the title of secretary 'was not so much at the beginning appropriate vnto him, whose vse and imploiment consisted soly in habilitie to write well, and in neate and fine forme to set foorth his *Letters*'; but rather an ethical responsibility, 'carying with it selfe a purpose of much weightier effect', and demanding the 'Trust, Regard & Fidelitie' of the service for his master (Day 1592: 108).

The conflicted view of Elizabethan secretaryship that emerges from the writings of Day, Beale, Faunt, and others—was the secretary an officious officer, or burdened with an ethical *officium*?—provides a basis for our understanding of Spenser's role in the Dublin and Munster administrations in the 1580s, but there are some crucial differences. Most importantly, Spenser's position was one neither of private secretary nor of public clerk, but rather an amalgamation of the two: a private secretary working as part of a larger federated secretariat, and assuming duties beyond the remit of personal service. In addition, the conditions of service in Ireland radically distorted many of the fundamental tenets of the private and professional models of secretaryship we have been considering; the skill and trust that Angel Day sees as the principal virtues of the good secretary took unexpected and exaggerated forms in the factional world of Elizabethan Ireland. The loyalty of a secretary in this treacherous and volatile political landscape was paramount, and Grey took pains to secure Spenser's trustworthiness, while Spenser, for his own part, likely took his own pains to prove it. The material record of Spenser's activity as a secretary and clerk in Dublin and in Cork suggests strongly not only that he occupied a position of unusual authority and access within the government administration, but that he developed habits of practice and thought, and was exposed to ideas and arguments, which could have had pronounced effects on his poetry. Social historical readings of early modern secretaryship such as those of Alan Stewart (1995) and Michael McKeon (2005: 228–32) have picked provocatively at the secretary's 'speciall cabinett, whereof he is himselfe to keepe the Keye' (Beale 1925: 428), and have stressed the 'Couertnes, Safety, and Assurance' that Day requires of his secretary's privy 'Closet' (Day 1592: 109); similarly, insofar as the secretary 'is a keeper and *conseruer of secrets*' (Day 1592: 110), Richard Rambuss has argued that, for Spenser's allegory, secrecy is 'the veil that hides (and makes) secrets', and thus functions as 'the tableau for writing' (1993: 3). Spenser managed secrets; but he also dealt in codes and sealing, extensive and circumspect book-keeping, and elaborately complex patronage relationships. His pen exposed him to war, to law, and to commerce. In linguistic, political, theological, financial, and philosophical respects, his secretarial appointments between 1580 and 1589 represent not lost years, but years of indispensable, formative experience.

The manuscript evidence of Spenser's secretarial career turns out to be surprisingly suggestive. (The manuscripts are summarily catalogued in the checklist at the end of this chapter; selected texts are available in Burlinson and Zucher 2009.) At least 120 separate documents demonstrably associated with Spenser's pen survive from the period between 1580 and 1589. Most of these are letters or other official papers written, copied, addressed, or otherwise handled by Spenser in his capacity as private secretary to Lord Grey; they include formal reports to Queen Elizabeth on Irish matters, letters (of different degrees of intimacy) to Sir Francis Walsingham and other politicians in the English court, copies of informations and agreements, examinations and petitions. Some later letters survive from Spenser's period of attendance on Sir John Norris, Lord President of Munster, and his brother, Sir Thomas Norris, Vice President of Munster, and the collection also includes a few papers drafted by Spenser acting in his own affairs. Of these, just over half are written completely in one of Spenser's three hands—a cursive, regular, and elegant secretary; a similarly brisk but again consistent and elegant mixed hand; and a formal or 'set' Italian hand used for dispatches from the Lord Deputy to the Queen (on these hands, see Burlinson and Zurcher 2005: 36–42). The rest of the documents contain paratextual marks—subscriptions, certifications, addresses, or other endorsements—added by Spenser in the preparation and dispatch of the papers from Ireland to London.

One of the clearest conclusions to emerge from an analysis of Spenser's written correspondence is the close personal and material association between the Irish secretary and his masters. His close implication in Grey's affairs, for example, is clear from the manuscript record of his first few months in Ireland. Spenser likely travelled to Ireland on the *Handmaid* in August 1580 with Grey, arriving in Dublin on the 12th. Despite a delay in receiving the sword of state, Grey immediately assumed his viceregal duties, but our first clear sighting of Spenser's secretarial activity is not until the 28th (SP 63/75/73), following Grey's disastrous defeat to Feagh McHugh O'Byrne in the chieftain's Wicklow stronghold, Glenmalure. The first nine extant letters from Spenser's hand (SP 63/75/73, 63/75/75, 63/75/84, 63/76/1, 63/76/5, 63/76/6, 63/76/7, 63/76/9, 63/76/10) are all copies of letters forwarded by Grey to Walsingham, mostly concerning the Ulster lord Turlough Luineach O'Neill and his attempts to have his 'urraghs'—the traditional fealty due the O'Neill by the petty chiefs of Ulster. Spenser must have been attending his master quite closely between late August and mid-September, when he was called upon to make regular and immediate copies of these dispatches. After these, nothing survives of Spenser's writing until Grey's first report to the Queen from the camp at Smerwick on 12 November (SP 63/78/29). The apparent 'silence' of Spenser's pen during this period may, of course, be the result of historical accident—many of the documents issued from the Dublin secretariat during these years have since perished—but it is likely that it arose at least partly from two other, related causes. First, Grey spent most of September in frantic preparation for two major military displays, against O'Neill, and against the Earl of

Desmond and the Spanish and Papal forces allied with him, who had recently landed in Dingle and were occupying James FitzMaurice's old fort at Smerwick. These preparations would have required substantial secretarial work, in the dispatch of letters, directions, commissions, protections, orders for victualling, and so on—none of which would have reached England, and most of which would have been lost during the subsequent field operations. The second cause of Spenser's silence during this period was undoubtedly Grey's own silence, during his march from Dublin to Dingle between 6 October and 4 November. Spenser's regular personal attendance on Grey, which continued throughout his service, is probably the single most important feature of his secretarial career in Ireland: as a servant to Grey in 1580–2, and to other masters in later years, Spenser's time and place were not his own; but, equally, he must have enjoyed almost unparalleled access to the councils, parleys, views of forces, and other key events of the period, with all of the exposure to news, intelligence, and argument that such access necessarily entailed.

The evidence of Spenser's access to the innermost traffic of the Dublin secretariat, with its subtle codes, is unequivocal. Physically present at the Lord Deputy's side during many of the major military and political crises of Grey's deputyship, Spenser controlled the flow of information between Grey and his ministers and captains, and between most Dublin officials and their Irish and English correspondents. It is easy for a modern observer to forget the degree to which early modern political and military activity was governed by epistolary circulation, as well as the dispatch of more formal written instruments; and similarly easy to overlook the ways in which the practical exigencies of so scripted a legal and political community could affect, and often privilege, the men charged with its function. It might reasonably be objected that modern historians perceive a bias towards written communications simply because this is the evidence that survives, but regular evidence from the written record refutes this. The thirst for written news constantly expressed by councillors on both sides of the Irish Sea testifies to the especial importance of written dispatches to the Irish service (see, e.g., Burghley's exasperated demand for news from Lord Deputy Sir Henry Sidney in March 1566, SP 63/16/67). When Grey first incurred the Queen's disfavour in the winter of 1581–2 for extravagant grants of estates to his servitors, auditor Jenyson wrote privately to Burghley in protest, enclosing the copy of a 1568 letter from the Queen to Sir Henry Sidney, concerning the procedures to be followed in the granting of lands (SP 63/87/42 and 63/87/42/1); the care with which Jenyson had husbanded this paper over 13 years, and the faith he had in its instrumentality in this event, point to the substantial status of written materials in this period. Because all ordinary news and intelligence was circulated— even over short distances—by written dispatches that could be verified (both by signature and by seal) and retained, Spenser's secretarial duties as copyist and certifier must necessarily have brought him into direct contact with essentially all of the major policy, military, and financial issues confronting the Irish council between 1580 and 1582. Admittedly, Grey sometimes wrote to Walsingham in his own hand, and sometimes to Walsingham and to others by other secretaries—of the 67 extant letters sent from Grey to Walsingham between August 1580 and August

1582, for example, 29 bear no evidence of Spenser's pen—but even in many of these cases (as will become clear) it appears that Spenser handled and dispatched the documents himself.

If secretarial manuals of the period betrayed anxiety about a private secretary's social status, in Elizabethan Ireland that anxiety was transformed to outright commodity and self-interest. Elizabeth and her Privy Council went to extraordinary lengths to control appointments to comparatively junior offices in Ireland, precisely because such offices enjoyed manipulable powers to copy, certify, and distribute accounts; to issue legal orders; and to control the circulation of information on sensitive matters. Again, it was a regular practice of Grey's—as of Lord Deputies before and after him—to choose his London messengers ('bearers') carefully, especially when the information being sent was sensitive; these bearers required trust precisely because their charge could so easily be corrupted or overstepped. In such an environment, it is not surprising to find people like Lodowick Bryskett, the clerk to the Council in Ireland, offering in April 1581 to act as an intelligencer for Burghley (SP 63/82/19); probably following Burghley's favourable reply, and within only a few weeks, Bryskett wrote again to Burghley to request his support in promoting him to the position of Secretary of State for Ireland (SP 63/82/53) upon the death of the incumbent, John Chaloner; and a few weeks later, again to Burghley, to inform him of the Lord Deputy's support for the appointment (SP 63/83/27). In return for his offer of information—an offer Bryskett undoubtedly kept secret from his Dublin colleagues—this secretary clearly expected patronage. If written communication, then, represented the only currency of politic transaction in contemporary Ireland, it also offered a currency of credit, preferment, and favour. Like Bryskett, Spenser could not have helped but be one of its chief brokers.

Beale writes of the secretary's responsibility for keeping custody of his master's codes and ciphers (Beale 1925: 428), a practice apparently pursued at least some of the time in Westminster, where Walsingham's secretaries prepared transcripts of the elaborate substitution cipher used by Sir Henry Wallop in his private correspondence with Walsingham (see, e.g., SP 63/77/2, 63/77/22, and 63/77/23). In Dublin, however, ciphers seem to have been more carefully kept; Wallop, for example, only used cipher in autograph letters, indicating that he kept the key to himself. Grey, similarly, relied on a simple substitution cipher, along with ciphers for important personages and places, for the more sensitive parts of his communication with Walsingham, which he used almost exclusively in autograph letters (and, in fact, the presence of significant amounts of code in these letters may be part of the reason that they were not given to Spenser for the production of fair copies, but sent instead in the original; see, e.g., SP 63/82/6 and 63/83/6). A distinct and more elaborate cipher appears sparingly in Grey's formal letters to the Queen. This cipher appears only in those letters written in Spenser's Italian hand (i.e., not in those prepared by other secretaries), and in the instances where it appears there are clear signs that Spenser produced the fair copy with blanks ready for Grey's completion (see, e.g., SP 63/82/54, where Grey added a passage in cipher, then a passage in his own approximation at a formal italic hand,

and then more cipher). That Grey kept personal and private custody of his cipher suggests that, though Spenser must necessarily have been privy to Grey's business, he was not given unfettered access.

Grey's use of cipher in his formal and personal letters may point to a slight distance between master and servant, but other evidence in the extant manuscripts suggests unambiguously that Spenser had been given custody of Grey's personal seal, and that he was therefore responsible for folding and sealing, if not always addressing, all of Grey's correspondence (including that produced in consultation or collaboration with the Irish Council). On many of the extant letters in Grey's hand, in the hands of various other scribes, and even occasionally in Spenser's own hand, minuscule notes appear—generally on the recto of the first or, occasionally, the verso of the last page—indicating the identity of the intended recipient. So, for example, we find at the left foot of the first page of SP 63/93/34, a letter of 21 June 1582 from Grey to Walsingham in Grey's autograph italic, a note in Grey's hand reading 'Mr Secret' (i.e., 'Secretary', or Walsingham). These notes indicate to the person folding, sealing, and addressing the letter the identity of the recipient to whom the letter should be addressed; in the case of letters without formal salutation of the recipient by name (in this example, Grey begins with a mere, 'Sir . . .'), such a note was the only guiding indication a secretary would receive on how to complete the address. The importance of these notes lies in the way they demonstrate a necessary gap between the writing and the sealing of the letter—one occasioned by Grey's need, as well as that of his junior secretary or secretaries, to leave documents for Spenser to dispatch them. The summary table of extant addressee notes on p. 72 shows clearly that—with a few explicable exceptions—Grey and his junior secretaries regularly left materials for Spenser to complete, whereas Spenser never left them for anyone else, nor in the normal course of business used addressee notes on his own letters.

The patterns indicated by this table are striking. It is clear that, when leaving letters for Spenser to seal and address, Grey was not especially consistent about folding them first; this indicates a reasonable amount of trust in his secretary. In instances where the addressee note appears on the rear panel of the last verso of the letter, Grey could only have positioned the note correctly once the document had been folded, whereas in other cases he clearly passed the letter back to Spenser with the paper still unfolded—otherwise, Spenser would not have been able to see the note on the front foot of the first page. There may be a slight correlation between the sensitivity of the letter's contents and Grey's care in folding the letter before adding an addressee note, as generally speaking those letters with substantial amounts of code were folded before being annotated; yet in SP 63/83/43, Grey left a coded letter open. Second, other secretaries when writing for Grey left their notes for Spenser's completion but, by contrast, Spenser never affixed an addressee note to a letter that was afterward addressed by anyone but himself. This bespeaks a clear chain of command, and identifies Spenser as the chief of Grey's secretaries and copyists. Finally, Spenser never in the two years of his service to Grey used an addressee note

Document	Grey to:	Text hand	Address hand	Note details
63/80/32	Walsingham	secretary	Spenser	1: left foot of first recto (letter hand); 2: top left corner of final verso (Grey)
63/81/4	Walsingham	Grey	Spenser	left foot of first recto (Grey)
63/81/42	Leicester	Grey	Spenser	left foot of first recto (Grey)
63/82/6	Walsingham	Grey	Spenser	left foot of first recto (Grey)
63/82/16	Walsingham	Grey	Spenser	mid-front panel of verso (Grey)
63/82/48	Walsingham	Grey	Spenser	right foot of last recto (Grey)
63/83/6	Walsingham	Grey	Spenser	top rear panel of verso (Grey)
63/83/43	Walsingham	Grey (code)	Spenser	left foot of first recto (Grey)
63/84/3	Walsingham	Grey	Spenser	mid-rear panel on verso (Grey)
63/84/12	Privy Council	secretary	Spenser	mid-rear panel on verso (Grey)
63/84/26	Walsingham	Grey	Spenser	lower edge of verso (Grey)
63/84/28	Walsingham	Spenser	Spenser	1: left foot of first recto (Spenser); 2: mid-panel rear fold (Spenser)
63/86/53	Walsingham	Grey	Spenser	right lower edge of verso (Grey)
63/88/9	Walsingham	Grey	Spenser	right foot of verso (Grey)
63/88/10	Walsingham	Grey	Spenser	left foot of first recto (Grey)
63/88/15	Walsingham	Grey	Spenser	left foot of first recto (Grey)
63/88/40	Walsingham	Grey	Spenser	rear mid-panel on verso (Grey)
63/91/17	Walsingham	Grey	Spenser	rear mid-panel on verso (Grey)
63/91/52	Burghley	Spenser	Spenser	left foot of first recto (Spenser)
63/91/53	Walsingham	Spenser	Spenser	left foot of first recto (Spenser)
63/92/9	Privy Council	Spenser	Spenser	left foot of first recto (Spenser)
63/92/26	Walsingham	Grey	Spenser	left foot of first recto (Grey)
63/92/52	Walsingham	Grey	Spenser	rear mid-panel on verso (Grey)
63/92/86	Privy Council	Spenser	Spenser	rear mid-panel on verso (Spenser)
63/93/34	Walsingham	Grey	Spenser	left foot of first recto (Grey)
63/93/46	Burghley	secretary	Spenser	left foot of first recto (letter hand)
63/93/64	Walsingham	Spenser	Spenser	left foot of first recto (Spenser)

himself, except in six exceptional cases where it was required by the nature of the letter (commendations being carried by special messengers), or by the extraordinary circumstances of Grey's disfavour and imminent recall (during which period Spenser had to send letters to Grey at Kilmainham for his signature). Spenser had no need for addressee notes, because when he wrote a letter, he also addressed it; so close was his relationship with Grey that, upon bringing him a letter for his signature, he never then had to put it aside, but could immediately fold, seal, and address it. It may be worth noting, in addition, that there is no evidence that Spenser ever used addressee notes in his service to the Norris brothers in Munster, where the small size of the secretariat and its undoubtedly more personal character would have made them redundant.

Two other aspects of the manuscript evidence also point to Spenser's trusted position in the Dublin castle information hierarchy. William Fulwood's *Enimie of*

Idlenesse (1568) prescribes clear rules for the decorous composition of a letter's 'subscription', that parting salutation interposed between the letter's text and the sender's signature: according to Fulwood, the subscription:

> must be don according to the estate of the writer, and the qualitie of the person to whome we write: For to our superiors we must write at the right syde in the nether ende of the paper, saying: By your most humble and obedient sonne, or seruant, &c. And to our equalles we may write towards the midst of the paper saying: By your faithfull frende for euer &c. To our inferiors we may write on high at the left hand saying: By yours &c. (Fulwood 1568: A8^r; cf. Gibson 1997)

The careful deployment of the subscription was essential to the decorum of early modern address, but it also had other functions—most importantly, it physically defined the end of the letter, making it impossible for the sender to add any further text except in a postscript. This did not present a real problem for Grey's personal letters, of course—his postscripts have the same status as the main bodies of his letters—but when a secretary was concluding a letter from the Irish Council, the careful positioning of the subscription was crucial to the corporate legitimation of the letter's contents. Generally speaking, Grey's junior secretaries did not presume to add the subscription when they produced fair copies for his signature, but left it to the Deputy to pen his own carefully worded formula. Spenser occasionally followed the same practice, but in many instances he also produced the subscription, a reflex consistent with what we know of his humanist cultivation in courtesy, and with his similarly effortless ability to observe decorum in the composition of addresses. More importantly, Spenser seems on at least three occasions (SP 63/87/32, 63/89/55, and 63/92/86) to have added the subscription to the fair copy of a letter produced by another secretary, demonstrating conclusively that he carried letters from the secretariat to the Lord Deputy, and suggesting that he was present at the signing. On the first of these occasions, Spenser's addition of the subscription to a corporate letter sent from the Irish Council clearly places him in the Council chamber itself.

This corroboration of Spenser's primacy in the secretariat, and high level of access in the Dublin administration, is also consistent with what we can surmise about the way Grey's letters were sealed. The use of addressee notes indicates that Grey left most of his letters, whether folded or not, for Spenser to seal, address, and dispatch, but further evidence suggests that, even when Grey folded and addressed his own letters, he still left the final process of sealing to his secretary. Generally speaking, the address was added to the letter after the sealing had been completed, as is clear from two letters—SP 63/85/13 and 63/90/23—where the format of Spenser's address clearly indicates that the seal was already in place when it was composed (Burlinson and Zurcher 2005: 62–5). But a third letter, SP 63/92/52, indicates that even when Grey had folded the letter himself, he still left it to Spenser to seal and add the address. In this case, Grey had drafted a letter to Walsingham of a highly sensitive nature, and had folded it and added an addressee note to the back of the packet. He wished to include with the letter an enclosure—a draft warrant for reimbursement of his expenses— which is mentioned in a postscript. Because the affiliation of these two documents would create a packet too thick for the usual folding technique, a more elaborate packeting procedure had to be used, involving paper bands inserted through slits in the outer sheet of the letter, with the points of contact between band and paper sealed and impressed with wax. As in the case of SP 63/85/13, which was also sealed with bands, Spenser wrote the address partly across the band after it had been fixed in place, such that removal of the band upon opening the letter deleted a small part of the address: in SP 63/92/52, the 'W' from Walsingham's name has been lost, immediately adjacent to the still extant slit. Grey clearly felt some sense of risk in preparing this letter for dispatch, for he took the trouble to fold it before leaving it—presumably in a locked cabinet—for Spenser to process, but he was obviously also constrained to rely on his secretary for sealing the letter, for it was the nature of Spenser's position, and authority or trust, to discharge this office.

Nor did Spenser's postal privileges begin and end with Lord Grey. The post bark that sailed regularly between Dublin and Chester doubtless received and delivered letters from and to a wide range of paying customers, in both official and personal capacities. Yet it would be extremely unlikely that official post destined for ministers and others working in Dublin Castle, whose offices called them unpredictably on campaign, or whose personal affairs or health kept them from constant attendance on their duties, was not bundled and routed through a central distributor in the castle. Spenser, as the principal point of contact for the Lord Deputy's dispatches, must regularly have handled and dispatched letters written and sealed by others— and thus have been in a position to keep an eye on who was writing to whom. The surviving accounts of Grey's administration (SP 63/92/20/1) show disbursements to Spenser and a small number of other secretaries (Lodowick Bryskett, clerk to the Council; and Nathaniel Dillon, Bryskett's deputy) for 'rewards to messengers', which reflect their (in some cases possibly notional) responsibilities for receiving and dispatching documents. Grey's junior secretary, Timothy Reynoldes, received an allowance for materials, but was not reimbursed for rewards to messengers; the whole sum (of £160 17s 4d) went to Spenser. And there is another important reason to identify Spenser as the figure through whom correspondence in and out of Dublin may have been channelled. Official dispatches in the Irish service, as well as within England, were denoted as *packets*, and accorded a special priority, such that those responsible for postal traffic were obliged by law to forward them with all possible expedition (Crofts 1967: 73–4). A packet of letters would sometimes be bound in a paper wrapper, but would always be tied together, and a special formula attached to the outermost document, or to the label: 'For her Maiesties speciall affaires', sometimes with a special note to the messenger, reading 'post hast for lyfe' (Crofts 1967: 76–7). Only certain officials were licensed to mark official packets with this distinctive formula: as it happens, one of the few surviving examples from the period of Grey's deputyship occurs adjacent to the address of one of his letters to Walsingham (SP 63/84/14), and in Spenser's italic hand.

Spenser's administrative privilege at the heart of the Dublin secretariat mattered so much precisely because of the factional, divisive, and conspiratorial nature of the New English community in Dublin during this period, and it is by understanding his secretarial career in this context that we can begin to appreciate its importance for our interpretation of his literary writing. Political power among the Old and New English in Ireland during Elizabeth's reign was closely linked to favouritism or factionalism at court. Even a superficial survey of Grey's epistolary career in Ireland makes it clear that he counted Walsingham an 'especiall good frend', and wrote to Burghley both less often and in much more guarded and perfunctory ways. This factionalism—running for most purposes along a Walsingham–Burghley split—operated at medial and lower levels of the administrative hierarchy, too, so that the treasurer Sir Henry Wallop considered himself a friend to Walsingham, but the receiver Edward Waterhouse and auditor Thomas Jenyson wrote candidly to Burghley. A consummate adept of this factionalism was Geoffrey Fenton, who played both sides continuously through the period of Spenser's service to Grey (and prospered by similar means thereafter). Fenton unabashedly encouraged factionalism, as when he wrote in March 1580/1 to the Earl of Leicester (SP 63/81/19), recommending that Leicester put forward a candidate for the vacant office of Chancellor of Ireland, in order to maximize his own commodity. When the Dublin administration was absorbed in its business, such factionalism may have been an irritation to some, but did not represent a threat to order; but when resources became scarce or the Queen's disfavour was aroused—precisely Grey's predicament in the spring of 1582, after he had ill-advisedly used his prerogative of 'howse fynding' (see SP 63/82/48) to lavish exorbitant rewards on his 'men'—then the ideological and factional rivenness of the Council and its underlings could become dangerous. While Henry Wallop had not made one of the small group of councillors (Malby, Fenton, and Loftus) who had written to Burghley on 20 November 1581, advertising to him Grey's excesses and proclaiming their innocence (SP 63/86/71; Fenton's super-subtlety led him to pen a further letter to Burghley, on the same day (63/86/72), urging him to keep their 'device' secret), he was apparently suborned to betrayal by Burghley's importunate letters, and confessed in March 1582 that he knew Grey had done wrong (SP 63/90/56), but was nonetheless reluctant to inform against him.

As it was by means of letters that the Machiavellian factional politics of Fenton were played out, it was the letters—with the secretaries who wrote, sealed, dispatched, received, recorded, and filed them—that Grey and others sought to control. Hugh Brady, Bishop of Meath, for example, complained to Walsingham in December 1581 (SP 63/87/6) that scarcely a letter could pass without being searched, and that if suspicion were aroused by any document's address or bearer, it was forthwith 'suppressed'. Fenton, not to be outdone in counsels clandestine, wrote to Burghley on 1 September 1581 (SP 63/85/31) recommending that the Irish Lord Garrett—at court under suspicion for connivance in the Pale rebellion—be carefully watched and his letters secretly read. Such 'reading' could be every bit as palaeographically analytical as our own exertions: Grey reported in a coded letter to Walsingham of March 1581 (SP 63/81/36), concerning an intercepted treasonous paper he was forwarding (now lost), 'The hande in the Copie is thowght to bee ment by 112 [i.e. is thought the Earl of Ormond's hand; see *OED*, 'mean', *v.* 4] but surely I doe not thynck it is so'—the Dublin government seems to have called in a palaeographer (and who would have recognized his hand so well as the secretary who had copied, and certified copies of, so many of Ormond's letters?). But when the government and its agents could not get at the letters themselves, they sought out the secretaries: auditor Jenyson wrote to Burghley shortly after Grey's revocation in late 1582 (SP/63/95/12), warning him that, because Wallop and Nicholas White, Master of the Rolls, had come under suspicion as intelligencers to Burghley, they had devised a plan to approach one of Burghley's secretaries, to persuade him to divulge the identity of the real informer (naturally, Jenyson himself). It is in this environment of suspicion, distrust, and combination that Spenser was trusted by Grey, and heavily rewarded for his corresponsive faith. Grey had to depend on the fidelity of a secretary who would read his privy as well as his formal reports; copy and certify his intelligence; protect, authenticate, and dispatch his correspondence; and keep in secure notebooks the indispensable records of his service. This secretary would handle his ciphers and keep his seal, and would reward and probably debrief his messengers. In this environment, patronage was not a luxury, but a necessity. The lease Spenser acquired to a manor in Enniscorthy, near Wexford, within a month of Grey's expedition there against the Cavanaghs in May 1581, was the fruit of a relationship on which the success and security of Grey's secretariat, and hence his government, depended.

Between 1580 and 1589 (and possibly thereafter), Spenser served in an office defined by its preoccupation with decorous address, meticulous book-keeping, and constant vigilance over security. While he may or may not have had a partial or even free hand in the actual drafting of Grey's more generic correspondence (e.g., orders, receipts, some letters of commendation or protection), Spenser would certainly have become adept at the nuanced rhetorical codes and distinctions in register necessary to his place. If his poetic skills were at all sharpened by the encounter, his experience of the practical ethics at the centre of the Dublin and Munster governments no doubt tested his moral learning to its limit, and it is no surprise to find that the allegorical ideals of *The Faerie Queene* (1590, 1596) are persistently punctured by their own narrative explication. Espionage, censorship, patronage, conspiracy, war, and council-chamber courtesy dominate the surviving Spenser letters; his role as copyist, certifier, sealer, and dispatcher of these documents, in turn, placed him, as it were, in the window of their traffic: a husbander of secrets, but also a medium of communication.

APPENDIX

Spenser's Letters and Papers: A Checklist of Documents

In closing it will be helpful to survey the preoccupations and features of Spenser's surviving letters and papers, and to comment briefly on the nature of the collections in which they now reside. Spenser's secretarial service in Ireland between his arrival in Dublin in August 1580 and the last extant letter he drafted for Sir Thomas Norris in July 1589 was primarily that of a copyist. The documents he copied were mainly letters, which during his service to Grey concerned the whole range of policy, military, financial, and personal issues upon which Grey and the Norris brothers regularly reported to Walsingham and Burghley. In the early part of Grey's deputyship, these letters typically reported on military and political developments, as well as the routine business of victualling the army, accounting for their expenses, bemoaning the terrible sickness (and weather), and protesting against the lack of financial support from England. Occasional flashes of humanity illuminate Grey's letters, especially to Walsingham, not only in his increasingly laboured pleas to be recalled from his post, but here in his thanks for Walsingham's help in arranging a match for Grey's niece, there in Grey's succinct report that a son had died. As the two years of his service wore on, Grey's dispatches became ever more preoccupied with the charges that began to mount against him as a result of the perceived extravagance of his rewards to allies, clients, and servants, and ever shriller in his demand to be recalled.

Among this abundance of frank reports to Walsingham, and slightly terser dispatches to Burghley, four other kinds of documents appear. Official reports to the Privy Council and to the Queen concerning high events (e.g., the defeat of the Papal and Spanish force at Smerwick, the discovery of the Earl of Kildare's treason) were generally produced in set hands and a more elevated tone: these letters were written with extra care, because they would in a sense become documents of record. Secondly, like many of his fellow councillors in Ireland Grey regularly dispatched letters of commendation for retiring captains, fellow ministers, or upstanding Irish burghers, letters that acted something like a combination between an introduction and a passport. Between these two extremes of the capital and the trivial, Spenser seems to have been kept relentlessly busy with the constant production of copies of documents to be sent on to Westminster. Grey forwarded not only letters, but examinations of prisoners, articles agreed in treaties and ceremonies of submission, as well as more mundane record-keeping, from summaries of accounts to an index of recent correspondence. Finally, at the end of the checklist that we provide below, a scattering of manuscripts represents the only remaining record of Spenser's autograph writing in his own voice: these are the three extant papers Spenser produced in connection with the estate, Hap Hazard, carved out of the Earl of Desmond's escheated lands near Buttevant. These three papers—and particularly the complaint against Viscount Roche of Fermoy—are interesting for what they can tell us about Spenser's links to other undertakers, officials, and farmers around Cork at this time.

While Spenser can be identified palaeographically with only a limited set of manuscripts in the National Archives, the British Library, Hatfield House, and a few other minor collections, students of the Irish historical context in which he worked and wrote will, naturally, want to know much more about the collections as a whole, their history, and their calendars and indices. The most important (and complex) collection of state records is that of the State Papers, Ireland series (SP 63) in the National Archives (Public Record Office). Hans Hamilton, the editor of an early calendar, wrote in 1859 that 'the correspondence in this Department [i.e., of State] relative to the Viceregal Government of Ireland, has ever been preserved in a separate series' (*CSPI 1509–1573*: i); and yet under this word 'ever' coils a heterogeneous set of provenance relations. The Tudor and Stuart 'Paper Office' must have acquired the substantial nucleus of the surviving material from the secretaries to the Privy Council, and indeed the 'Paper Office' itself developed from the archive managed by these secretaries for the use of Sir Francis Walsingham and, after him, Robert Cecil (Guiseppi: I, 1). Walsingham's own papers were likely absorbed into the archive just before or immediately after his death, and seem to be represented almost in their entirety; while Burghley's papers were only partly joined with those of the government departments, the other part subsequently being divided between Hatfield House and the Landsdowne collection in the British Library (Guiseppi: I, 2). The papers of other council members or ministers found their ways into the series at different points, some as late as the mid-nineteenth century (*CSPI 1509–1573*: ii). The accession of discrete bodies of material at different dates means that the collection is anything but comprehensive; and the high volume of materials accessioned during an early period—the bulk of it very likely during the later years of Elizabeth's reign—makes it very possible that documents were selected or withheld for personal or at least practical political purposes. Users must beware incorrect dates and endorsements (many of them apparently the result of Burghley's later-life errors), the occasionally haphazard separation of letters from their enclosures, and the host of physical limitations attending on the reading of the manuscripts, such as the extensive damage suffered over centuries of variable care.

But above all, users of the State Papers, Ireland, must recall what the collection does not contain. In the Four Courts fire of 1922 virtually all of the 'Dublin-side' records perished; users of the National Archives collection should remember that, because nearly all record of the correspondence sent from Westminster to Dublin has been lost, they are always listening to only one side of a complex conversation. (There is one class of important exceptions: drafts, minutes, abstracts, and other partial papers never sent to Ireland survived in the State Paper Office, and give some idea of the material that has been lost.) But the National Archives collection does not contain even a full record of the 'English side' of that conversation, but only those materials successfully gathered by the Paper Office from the Privy Council and Queen, Walsingham, Burghley, and a few others; letters or other materials sent to other contacts at Court, or to contacts outside of court, do not survive in this collection, nor do the National Archives contain a complete record of what these correspondents received from Dublin. A good example of the limits of the collection is afforded by SP 63/91/26, a list in Spenser's hand of letters and documents recently dispatched to Walsingham in April 1582, presumably compiled for security purposes. This document lists nine letters recently copied and forwarded, primarily including documents relating to O'Donnell and to Edward Butler, brother of the Earl of Ormond and Sheriff of Tipperary. Only five of these letters survive—all three from Edward Butler, one from Sir Warham Sentleger to the Lord Deputy, and one from Thomas Arthur, Recorder of Limerick, to Sir Lucas Dillon. The other four, which on the whole were probably more interesting—including the copy of a letter from the Pope to Sir Hugh O'Donnell, and one from the Earl of Desmond—probably disappeared precisely because they were more intensively valued and used. This example admittedly provides only one limited perspective on the overall survival of documents in the collection, and on the kinds of documents to survive, but from this evidence it does seem that survival was at best spotty, and that in some cases, at least, it was the most valuable or topical materials that disappeared from the central collection first.

It only remains to be said that the historical work on Spenser's letters and papers is as incomplete as the archive itself is heterogeneous and permeable. Perhaps the only thing that can be definitively declared is that more Spenserian papers will be found, some very likely of considerable importance. The following checklist must therefore be treated as a view of the present state of Spenser's work in Ireland.

Letters and Papers in the Hand of Edmund Spenser: A Checklist

Document reference	Date	Sender/recipient	Hands
Folger MS X. d. 520	1576–1580?	—	L
University of Kansas, MS uncat North 2C:2:1	23 November 1578	copy of Erhardus Stibarus to Erasmus Neustetter	L
TNA PRO: SP 63/75/73	28 August 1580	rental receipt for the parsonage of Kirtling	A
		Grey to Walsingham (?)	
TNA PRO: SP 63/75/75	29 August 1580	copy, Ormond to Grey	L
		Grey to Walsingham (?)	
TNA PRO: SP 63/75/84	31 August 1580	copy, Hugh Magennis to Grey	L
		Grey to Walsingham (?)	
TNA: PRO SP 63/76/1	2 September 1580	copy, Hugh O'Neill to Grey	L
		Grey to Walsingham (?)	
TNA: PRO SP 63/76/5	3 September 1580	copy, Nicholas Bagenall to Grey	L/A
		Grey to Walsingham (?)	
TNA: PRO SP 63/76/6	3 September 1580	copy, Hugh O'Reilly to Grey	L/A
		Grey to Walsingham (?)	
TNA: PRO SP 63/76/7	4 September 1580	copy, Hugh O'Neill to Grey	L/A
		Grey to Walsingham (?)	
TNA: PRO SP 63/76/9	4 September 1580	copy, Hugh O'Neill to Grey	A
		Grey to Walsingham (?)	
TNA: PRO SP 63/76/10	4 September 1580	copy, Viscount Gormanston to Grey	L
		Grey to Walsingham (?)	
TNA: PRO SP 63/78/29	12 November 1580	copy, John Barnes to Grey	L/A
		Grey to the Queen	
BL Add. MS 33924, ff. 6–7	28 November 1580	Grey to Burghley	L/A
TNA: PRO SP 63/78/68	30 November 1580	Grey to Walsingham	L/A
TNA: PRO SP 63/79/24/1	22 December 1580	Grey to Walsingham	L
		copy, Grey to the Queen	
TNA: PRO SP 63/79/26	23 December 1580	Grey and Council to the Queen	A

(continued)

(Continued)

Document reference	Date	Sender/recipient	Hands
TNA: PRO SP 63/80/32	27 January 1580/1	Grey to Walsingham	A
TNA: PRO SP 63/81/1	1 March 1580/1	Grey to Walsingham	A
TNA: PRO SP 63/81/4	2 March 1580/1	Grey to Walsingham	A
TNA: PRO SP 63/81/15	7 March 1580/1	– copy, articles between Richard Yneren Burke (McWilliam Eighter) and Nicholas Malbie	L
TNA: PRO SP 63/81/20	11 March 1580/1	– copy, Miler Magrath to Lucas Dillon	L/A
TNA: PRO SP 63/81/27	14 March 1580/1	Grey to Burghley	A
TNA: PRO SP 63/81/34	18 March 1580/1	Grey to Walsingham (?)	A/C
		copy, Mayor of Cork to Grey	
TNA: PRO SP 63/81/36/1	13 March 1580/1	Grey to Leicester (?)	L/A
		copy, Ormond to Grey	
TNA: PRO SP 63/81/36/2	20 March 1580/1	Grey to Leicester	A/C
		copy, 'Advertizements from Waterford'	
TNA: PRO SP 63/81/39	March 1580/1	Grey to Walsingham (?)	L
		copy, submission of Richard Yneren Burke (McWilliam Eighter) to Nicholas Malbie	
TNA: PRO SP 63/81/42	23 March 1580/1	Grey to Leicester	A
TNA: PRO SP 63/82/6	6 April 1581	Grey to Walsingham	A
HH Cecil Papers, 11/91/970	6 April 1581	Grey to Burghley	A
TNA: PRO SP 63/82/16	7 April 1581	Grey to Walsingham	A
HH Cecil Papers, 11/94/976	22 April 1581	Grey to Burghley	A
TNA: PRO SP 63/82/48	24 April 1581	Grey to Walsingham	A
TNA: PRO SP 63/82/54	26 April 1581	Grey to the Queen	L/A
TNA: PRO SP 63/83/6	12 May 1581	Grey to Walsingham	A
TNA: PRO SP 63/83/6/1	29 April 1581	Grey to Walsingham	A/C
		copy, Ormond to Grey and others	
TNA: PRO SP 63/83/6/2	n.d.	Grey to Walsingham	A/C
		copy, Countess of Desmond to Ormond	
TNA: PRO SP 63/83/6/3	10 May 1581	Grey to Walsingham	A
		copy, Grey and Council to Ormond	
TNA: PRO SP 63/83/43	9 June 1581	Grey to Walsingham	A

TNA: PRO SP 63/83/45	10 June 1581	Grey to the Privy Council	A
TNA: PRO SP 63/83/47	10 June 1581	Grey to Walsingham	L/A
TNA: PRO SP 63/84/3	5 July 1581	Grey to Walsingham	A
TNA: PRO SP 63/84/12	10 July 1581	Grey to the Privy Council	A
TNA: PRO SP 63/84/13	10 July 1581	Grey to the Privy Council	L/A
TNA: PRO SP 63/84/14	10 July 1581	Grey to Walsingham	L/A
TNA: PRO SP 63/84/26	18 July 1581	Grey to Walsingham	A
TNA: PRO SP 63/84/28	18 July 1581	Grey to Walsingham	L/A
TNA: PRO SP 63/85/5	10 August 1581	Grey to the Queen	L/A
TNA: PRO SP 63/85/6	10 August 1581	Grey to the Queen	A
TNA: PRO SP 63/85/13	12 August 1581	Grey to the Privy Council	A
HH Cecil Papers, 11/113/1026	26 August 1581	Grey to Burghley	A
HH Cecil Papers, 11/114/1029	28 August 1581	Grey to Burghley	A
TNA: PRO SP 63/85/34	2 September 1581	Grey to the Privy Council	A
TNA: PRO SP 63/85/37	12 September 1581	Grey to the Privy Council	A
TNA: PRO SP 63/86/50	6 November 1581	Grey to the Queen	L/A
TNA: PRO SP 63/86/51	6 November 1581	Grey to the Privy Council	A
TNA: PRO SP 63/86/53	6 November 1581	Grey to Walsingham	A
TNA: PRO SP 63/86/53/1	6 November 1581	Grey to Walsingham	A
		copy, *Grey to the Queen*	
HH Cecil Papers, 12/16/1078	28 November 1581	Grey to Burghley	L/A
HH Cecil Papers, 12/19/1081	10 December 1581	Grey to Burghley	L/A
TNA: PRO SP 63/87/29	10 December 1581	Grey to the Queen	A
TNA: PRO SP 63/87/32	10 December 1581	Grey and Council to the Privy Council	S/A
TNA: PRO SP 63/87/64	29 December 1581	Grey to Walsingham	L/A
TNA: PRO SP 63/88/2	3 January 1581/2	Grey to the Privy Council	L/A
TNA: PRO SP 63/88/9	7 January 1581/2	Grey to Walsingham	A
TNA: PRO SP 63/88/10	9 January 1581/2	Grey to Walsingham	A
TNA: PRO SP 63/88/12	12 January 1581/2	Grey to Burghley	L/A
TNA: PRO SP 63/88/15	13 January 1581/2	Grey to Walsingham	A
TNA: PRO SP 63/88/39	25 January 1581/2	Grey to the Queen	L/A
TNA: PRO SP 63/88/40	27 January 1581/2	Grey to Walsingham	A

(*continued*)

(Continued)

Document reference	Date	Sender/recipient	Hands
TNA: PRO SP 63/89/11	4 February 1581/2	Grey and Council to the Privy Council	A
TNA: PRO SP 63/89/18	5 February 1581/2	Grey and Council to the Privy Council	L/A
		copy, *John Nugent's confession*	
TNA: PRO SP 63/89/30	13 February 1581/2	Grey to the Privy Council	L/A
TNA: PRO SP 63/89/35	18 February 1581/2	Grey to the Privy Council	L/A
TNA: PRO SP 63/89/55	February 1581/2	Grey to Walsingham	S/A
TNA: PRO SP 63/90/1	1 March 1581/2	Grey to Walsingham	L/A
TNA: PRO SP 63/90/23	14 March 1581/2	Grey to Walsingham	A
BL Cotton Titus B.xiii fol. 364	23 March 1581/2	—	L/A
		copy, *'Advertizementes sent out of Mounster'*	
TNA: PRO SP 63/90/31	24 March 1581/2	Grey to Walsingham	L/A
		copy, *Edward Butler to Edward Waterhouse*	
TNA: PRO SP 63/90/48	27 March 1582	Grey to the Privy Council	L/A
TNA: PRO SP 63/90/52	28 March 1582	Grey and Council to the Privy Council	L/A
TNA: PRO SP 63/91/11	4 April 1582	Grey to Walsingham	L/A
TNA: PRO SP 63/91/17	8 April 1582	Grey to Walsingham	A
TNA: PRO SP 63/91/17/2	8 April 1582	Grey to Walsingham	A
		copy, *Warham Saintleger to Grey*	
TNA: PRO SP 63/91/22	12 April 1582	Grey to the Privy Council	A
TNA: PRO SP 63/91/26	12 April 1582	Grey to Walsingham	L/A
TNA: PRO SP 63/91/38	19 April 1582	Grey and Council to the Privy Council	L/A
TNA: PRO SP 63/91/52	30 April 1582	Grey to Burghley	L/A
TNA: PRO SP 63/91/53	30 April 1582	Grey to Walsingham	L/A
TNA: PRO SP 63/92/9	7 May 1582	Grey to the Privy Council	L/A
TNA: PRO SP 63/92/10	7 May 1582	Grey to Walsingham	L/A
TNA: PRO SP 63/92/11/1	9 May 1582	Grey to Walsingham	L/A
		copy, *Grey and Council to the Queen*	
TNA: PRO SP 63/92/20	9 May 1582	Grey and Council to the Queen	A
TNA: PRO SP 63/92/26	10 May 1582	Grey to Walsingham	A
TNA: PRO SP 63/92/30	11 May 1582	Grey and Council to the Privy Council	L
TNA: PRO SP 63/92/46	16 May 1582	Grey to Walsingham	L/A

Reference	Date	Description	Hand
TNA: PRO SP 63/92/52	22 May 1582	Grey to Walsingham	A
TNA: PRO SP 63/92/85	28 May 1582	Grey to the Privy Council	L/A
TNA: PRO SP 63/92/86	28 May 1582	Grey to the Privy Council	S/A
TNA: PRO SP 63/93/34	21 June 1582	Grey to Walsingham	A
TNA: PRO SP 63/93/46	22 June 1582	Grey to Burghley	A
TNA: PRO SP 63/93/64	29 June 1582	Grey to Walsingham	L/A
TNA: PRO SP 63/93/64/1	29 June 1582	Grey to Walsingham	L/A/C
		copy, Thomas Meagh to James Meagh [McKedagh O'Moore]	
TNA: PRO SP 63/94/15	10 July 1582	Grey and Council to the Privy Council	A
TNA: PRO SP 63/94/28	16 July 1582	Grey to Walsingham	L/A
TNA: PRO SP 63/94/46	28 July 1582	Grey to Walsingham	L/A
TNA: PRO SP 63/94/47	28 July 1582	Grey to Walsingham	L/A
TNA: PRO SP 63/94/61	31 July 1582	Grey to the Privy Council	L/A
TNA: PRO SP 63/94/62	31 July 1582	Grey to Walsingham	A
TNA: PRO SP 63/94/107	29 August 1582	Grey to [unknown recipient]	C
		copy of High Commissioners to Grey	
TNA: PRO SP 63/115/13	7 March 1584/5	John Norris to the Privy Council	L/A
TNA: PRO SP 63/115/14	7 March 1584/5	John Norris to the Privy Council	L/A
TNA: PRO SP 63/115/15	7 March 1584/5	John Norris to Burghley	L/A
TNA: PRO SP 63/115/16	7 March 1584/5	John Norris to Walsingham	L/A
TNA: PRO SP 63/115/41	31 March 1585	John Norris to Burghley	L/A
TNA: PRO SP 63/115/42	31 March 1585	John Norris to Burghley (?)	L
TNA: PRO SP 63/135/66	1 July 1588	Thomas Norris to Walsingham	L/A
TNA: PRO SP 63/140/37	22 January 1588/9	Thomas Norris to the Privy Council	L/A
TNA: PRO SP 63/144/70	May 1589	Edmund Spenser to the Commissioners	L/A
TNA: PRO SP 63/147/16	12 October 1589	Edmund Spenser and others to Walsingham (?)	L/A
BL Add. MS 19869	ca 1589	Edmund Spenser to [unknown recipient]	L
		Spenser's grant to McHenry	

L, document in Spenser's hand; C, certified by Spenser, with his signature; S, subscription in Spenser's hand; A, address in Spenser's hand; TNA: PRO SP, The National Archives: Public Record Office, State Papers series; BL, British Library; HH, Hatfield House.

BIBLIOGRAPHY

Alford, S. (1998). *The Early Elizabethan Polity: William Cecil and the British Succession Crisis, 1558–1569*. Cambridge: Cambridge University Press.

Beal, P. (ed.) (1980). *Index of English Literary Manuscripts 1450–1625*, 2 vols. London: Mansell.

Beale, Robert (1925). 'A Treatise of the Office of a Councellor and Principall Secretarie to her Majestie' (1592), in C. Read (ed.), *Mr Secretary Walsingham and the Policy of Queen Elizabeth*, vol. 1. Oxford: Clarendon Press, 423–43.

Burlinson, C., and A. Zurcher (2005). '"Secretary to the Lord Grey Lord Deputie Here": Edmund Spenser's Irish Papers'. *The Library* 7th SER 6: 30–69.

—— (eds) (2009). *Edmund Spenser: Selected Letters and Other Papers*. Oxford: Oxford University Press.

Calendar of the State Papers Relating to Ireland, 1509–1670, 24 vols. London: HMSO.

[*Carew* (1867–73).] Brewer, J. S., and W. Bullen (eds). *Calendar of the Carew Manuscripts Preserved in the Archiepiscopal Library at Lambeth*, 6 vols. London: Longmans, Green for HMSO.

Carpenter, F. I. (1923). *A Reference Guide to Edmund Spenser*. Chicago: University of Chicago Press.

Crofts, J. (1967). *Packhorse, Waggon and Post: Land Carriage and Communications under the Tudors and Stuarts*. London: Routledge and Kegan Paul.

Day, Angel (1592). *The English Secretorie*. London: Thomas Orwin for Richard Jones.

Evans, F. M. G. (1923). *The Principal Secretary of State: A Survey of the Office from 1558 to 1680*. Manchester: Manchester University Press.

Faunt, Nicholas (1905). 'Discourse Touching the Office of Principal Secretary of Estate, &c (1592)', ed. Charles Hughes. *EHR* 20: 499–508.

Fulwood, William (1568). *The Enimie of Idlenesse: Teaching the Maner and Stile how to Endite, Compose, and Write All Sorts of Epistles and Letters, as well by Answer as Otherwise*. London: Henry Bynneman for Leonard Maylard.

Gascoigne, George (1573). *A Hundreth Sundrie Flowres*. London: Henry Bynneman for Richard Smith.

Gibson, J. (1997). 'Significant Space in Manuscript Letters'. *The Seventeenth Century* 12: 1–9.

Goldberg, J. (1990). *Writing Matter: From the Hands of the English Renaissance*. Palo Alto, CA: Stanford University Press.

Guiseppi, M. S. (1963–8). *Guide to the Contents of the Public Record Office*, 3 vols. London: HMSO.

Hammer, P. E. J. (1994). 'The Uses of Scholarship: The Secretariat of Robert Devereux, Second Earl of Essex, *c.* 1585–1601'. *EHR* 109: 16–51.

Heffner, Ray (1931). 'Spenser's Acquisition of Kilcolman'. *MLN* 46: 493–8.

Herbert, J. (1894). 'Duties of a Secretary [1600]', in G. W. Prothero (ed.), *Select Statutes and other Constitutional Documents Illustrative of the Reigns of Elizabeth and James I*. Oxford: Clarendon Press.

McCabe, R. A. (2002). *Spenser's Monstrous Regiment: Elizabethan Ireland and the Poetics of Difference*. Oxford: Oxford University Press.

MacCarthy-Morrogh, M. (1986). *The Munster Plantation, 1583–1641*. Oxford: Clarendon Press.

McKeon, M. (2005). *The Secret History of Domesticity: Public, Private, and the Division of Knowledge*. Baltimore: Johns Hopkins University Press.

Maley, W. (1994). *A Spenser Chronology*. Basingstoke: Macmillan.

O'Dowd, M. (ed.) (2000). *Calendar of State Papers, Ireland: Tudor Period, 1571–1575*. Kew: Public Record Office.

—— and R. Dudley Edwards (1985). *Sources for Early Modern Irish History, 1534–1641*. Cambridge: Cambridge University Press.

Petti, A. G. (1977). *English Literary Hands from Chaucer to Dryden*. London: Edward Arnold.

Price, L., and P. Thurschwell (eds) (2005). *Literary Secretaries / Secretarial Culture*. Aldershot: Ashgate.

Rambuss, R. (1993). *Spenser's Secret Career*. Cambridge: Cambridge University Press.

Smith, A. G. R. (1968). 'The Secretariats of the Cecils, circa 1580–1612'. *EHR* 83: 481–504.

Stewart, A. (1995). 'The Early Modern Closet Discovered'. *Representations* 50: 76–100.

—— (2004). 'Instigating Treason: The Life and Death of Henry Cuffe, Secretary', in Erica Sheen and Lorna Hutson (eds), *Literature, Politics, and Law in Renaissance England*. Basingstoke: Palgrave Macmillan, 50–70.

CHAPTER 5

....

SPENSER, PLANTATION, AND GOVERNMENT POLICY

....

CIARAN BRADY

THE plantation which was to play such a fateful role in Spenser's personal and imaginative life has conventionally been seen as a crucially important staging post in a long-term historical process of the English colonization of Ireland; and Spenser's own efforts to comprehend and give expression to his experience in that plantation have likewise been seen as profoundly illuminating documents in the work of uncovering and understanding the forces and impulses underlying that process. Like most interpretative traditions this perspective has much to commend it, and nothing will be attempted here to deny its lasting validity. But the adoption of a long-range perspective which privileges the grand pattern over its individual elements runs the risk not only of misunderstanding the character and role of those elements, but also of misperceiving the complex nature of the pattern itself. It has been conventional, for instance, to treat the plantation established in the 1580s and the settlement which flourished in the early seventeenth century as stages in the same single process of colonization, and to diminish the significance of the rebellions and wars which scorched the province between 1598 and 1603. The degree of continuity is, of course, high. But the significance of that great disruption also deserves recognition, not only because it was the direct result of the multiple contradictions and deficiencies which characterized this first effort at planting in Munster, or because these contradictions were themselves the consequence of the deeply confused character of English governing attitudes toward Ireland in the sixteenth century, but also because it was amidst such confusions that Spenser's profoundly troubled perception of Ireland's place in England's world was conceived.

CONTEXTS

Seen from the longer perspective the plantation attempted in Munster in the mid-1580s appears to form part of the centuries-old process by which England seized Irish land by force, settled it with its own subjects, and proceeded to establish legal claim to this act of dispossession. The English colonization of Ireland had begun in the twelfth century, was gradually brought to a halt in the late thirteenth century, and underwent a phase of recession and contraction in the fifteenth century only to be revived in the second quarter of the sixteenth century. It was this Tudor revival that proved irreversible. Beginning tentatively with the confiscation of the lands of the attainted house of Kildare, gaining in confidence with the first intrusion into the lands of the native Irish dynasties of the midlands, spreading and becoming diffuse through a number of small and independent enterprises in colonization in Ulster and Munster, it gained unprecedented force with the great initiative launched in Munster, following the destruction of the earldom of Desmond in rebellion. The project for plantation in Munster also entailed several innovations which entitled it to be seen as representing an important development in the history of English colonization. It was the first plantation scheme to be based on the attainder of a descendant of the original twelfth-century conquest. It was the first of such projects to see the English government in Whitehall (rather than its representative in Dublin) take direct responsibility for an enterprise that might nowadays be described as a public–private partnership. It was the first to envisage the large-scale migration of people from England to Ireland on a planned and highly structured basis. And with its novel designations of 'adventurers', 'servitors', and 'deserving natives' as recognized groups within the new social settlement, the Munster plantation became the model for future plantations in the seventeenth century, most notably the plantation of Ulster and, the most ambitious colonization scheme of them all, the 'Cromwellian settlement' of the 1650s.

  Such is the view from the longer perspective. But on closer inspection other features assume a greater prominence in a manner which blurs this simple pattern. The first of these novel characteristics listed above is a case in point. Desmond was indeed the first great scion of the English–Irish aristocracy to be attainted; but he was also the exception. Following the collapse of their rebellion an attempt was made to resettle the lands of the Fitzgeralds of Kildare in the 1530s, but it never developed far, and in the early 1550s the house was fully re-established on the return of the exiled 11th earl (Carey 2002; MacNiocaill 1992). Other descendant families of the original conquerors such as the Nugents of Meath and the Eustaces of Kildare were similarly threatened by the tumults of the sixteenth century, but they too either escaped confiscation or achieved a partial restoration within a short time (Maginn 2004; Walshe 1990). In this period the fate of the Fitzgeralds of Desmond and their followers was therefore quite unusual, and the plantation that followed upon it was correspondingly unique. Between the 1550s and the early 1600s it was the Gaelic Irish of Leinster, Ulster, and Connacht (the original targets of the twelfth-century conquest) who suffered far away the greatest number of attempts to dispossess them (Maginn 2005; Morgan 1988; Rapple 2008).

A further irony relating to the exceptional fate of Desmond also complicates our understanding of the character of the plantation which succeeded his fall. From the beginning of the Tudor revival of interest in the governance of Ireland, it was from Desmond's own ethnic group—from the descendants of the old colonial community or 'the English of Irish birth', as they termed themselves—rather than from English statesmen in Whitehall that the most vocal demands for a renewal of war against the native Irish and the further extension of the colony first issued. In the 1520s and 1530s Cardinal Wolsey and Thomas Cromwell were plied with formal and informal proposals issuing from Ireland strongly seeking the support of the Crown for the renewal of colonization, and texts by Sir William Darcy, Thomas Bathe, Robert and Walter Cowley, and above all Patrick Finglas's 'Book of the getting of Ireland and of the decay of the same' all reiterated the urgency of reviving the old colonial enterprise before the confines of the original Anglo-Norman colony shrunk into oblivion (Bradshaw 1979; Quinn 1946–7).

Yet if the political and intellectual elite of the English of Irish birth were to the forefront in making the case for renewed colonization in the middle of the sixteenth century, it cannot be said that their voices exerted any great influence over the policy-makers of Tudor government. This was in part because of a suspicion concerning the promoters' self-interested motives: Thomas Cromwell and Leonard Grey, the Lord Deputy, were as resistant to the Butlers projects of the 1530s as Elizabeth and Secretary Cecil were wary of Sir John of Desmond's thirty years on. But it is also a reflection of the degree to which English policy-makers had developed a more sophisticated alternative to the traditional solution of war, conquest, and dispossession which placed its confidence in the possibilities of re-establishing English rule in Ireland through the mechanisms of political, social, and cultural assimilation.

The origins of this alternative approach to the English governance of Ireland were several. It arose at least in part from a hard-headed recognition that the Tudor regime lacked the resources to re-launch any kind of military conquest which did not entail massive risks of cost, loss of control, and outright failure. It also had origins in the constitutional embarrassments which arose from England's breach with Rome and conflict with the Holy Roman Empire; and doubtless it also had roots in that renewed confidence in the possibility of political, social, and legal reform that historians have identified as 'civic humanism' (Bradshaw 1979; Brady 1994: Chap. 1). But what is of primary relevance here is the fact that, from the later 1530s to the closing years of the sixteenth century, English policy in Ireland was premised on the conviction that the majority of the island's inhabitants—Gaelic Irish and English–Irish—could be made answerable to and respectful of the authority of English governance through diplomacy, education, and the extension of legal and administrative structures throughout the island. Such an outlook was by no means innocent or naïvely benign. It was fully recognized that all of the native Irish would not automatically be converted to the benefits of English civility without resort to the occasional threat and use of coercion in individual cases. And similarly it was envisaged that the superiority of the English way of life would best be demonstrated by practical examples in specific locations. For both these reasons the introduction of colonial settlements was never regarded as an alternative or opposing strategy. In contrast, it was viewed as an important supportive instrument to be employed when the opportunity or the need arose. But it is important to emphasize that it was within this assimilationist programme that the first of the several Tudor exercises in plantation arose (Brady 1994: Chap. 7).

CONTRADICTIONS

Before Munster, experiments in plantation sanctioned by the Crown had taken one of two forms: those instigated by, or with the cooperation of, the English administration in Dublin, and those which were the product of private speculative enterprise. The largest exercise of this first kind was the plantation begun in the midland territories of Laois and Offaly in the mid-1550s by Lord Deputy Sussex after his bloody repression of the O'Mores and the O'Connors who, he believed, had broken the terms of a truce he had negotiated with them (Dunlop 1891; White 1967). As conceived by Sussex, the Laois–Offaly plantation was an amalgam of several earlier models, the military garrison, the private consortium, and, most interestingly, the old colonial model of the English–Irish in which the earls of Kildare and Ormond were both granted substantial holdings. But each was now forged into a kind of unity under the singular authority of the Irish viceroy. In Sussex's eyes the establishment of a plantation under viceregal rule was an important support to, rather than a contradiction of, the larger plans for legal and administrative construction he was proposing for the island as a whole. Whatever his personal vision, however, Sussex's plantation soon deteriorated as his own authority as viceroy declined; and the settlement gradually emerged less as a genuinely new plantation than as an arena of competing fiefdoms, each exercising a feudal power over a large servile class of native tenants, clients, and dependants (Carey 1999a; Fitzsimons 1998).

Though not unprecedented, it was in the late 1560s and early 1570s that the second form of colonial strategy based upon private initiative became more prominent. Among the earliest of such was the adventure launched by Sir Peter Carew in South Leinster in 1568 where, on the basis of escheat, the latter claimed title to the ancient Anglo-Norman barony of Idrone now occupied by a sept of the Gaelic [Irish]

Kavanaghs (Nicholls 1977–81; Prendergast 1859). But there were several others. A private plan for the establishment of a colony in the territory of the Fews in Ulster emerged sometime in 1567, and more significant were a set of proposals from overlapping consortia of private speculators which included Sir Warham St Leger, Jerome Brett, Sir John Fitzgerald, brother of the earl of Desmond, and Humphrey Gilbert for ambitious and wide ranging colonizing schemes in Munster (Piveronus 1979; Quinn 1938: I, 491–7). More important than any of these were two schemes developed for Ulster in the early 1570s.

The first of these was the project of a true Whitehall insider, Sir Thomas Smith, who used his position as Secretary of State to advance his own scheme of establishing a modest and exemplary colonial settlement in the Ards peninsula (in modern Co. Down) which Smith envisaged would be a demonstration of all the benefits which the adoption of English culture could bring immediately to those willing to accept its practices, customs, laws—and its governing authority (Morgan 1985; Quinn 1945). The second of these private projects—the Earl of Essex's 'enterprise of Ulster'—was more ambitious in scope. In return for a temporary grant of total autonomy and the powers to sublet large leaseholds to his chosen followers, Essex proposed to recapture that portion of the ancient earldom of Ulster east of the Bann entirely at his own cost. Though in this sense the project harked back to the original conquest, Essex was also careful to commit himself to the assimilationist aspirations of orthodox policy. His purpose, he claimed, was not to expel the native Irish, but to liberate them from the Scottish invaders who had usurped the English Crown's rightful overlordship, and then to invite them to partake of the benefits of civility once the territory had been cleared and its future secured (Brady 1994: 251–3; Devereux 1853: I, 34–6).

The significance of these precursors to Munster, however, should not be overstated. Of them all only three—Carew's, Smith's, and Essex's—ever took practical shape. And of these three the only one to succeed was hardly a plantation at all: Carew's assumption of feudal rights in Idrone involved no displacement and no new settlement, but was merely the assertion of a protective overlordship over a Gaelic Irish sept, hard pressed by their English–Irish neighbours, the Butlers of Ormond. The other plantation efforts failed miserably. Smith's little colony was quickly overrun and his own son murdered by his Irish servants; while Essex's larger effort foundered in a welter of blood after his murder of Sir Brian MacPhelim O'Neill and his massacre of scores of the MacDonalds on Rathlin Island. Significantly, both promoters laid the blame for the failure of their projects neither on the viability of their plans nor on the resistance of native forces, but on the subtle subversion of the English viceroys in Dublin. And in this they had considerable justification. Sir William Fitzwilliam, lord deputy between 1571 and 1575, was less than subtle in his hostility to both Smith and Essex.[1] But even his predecessor, Sir Henry Sidney, whose enthusiasm for colonization has frequently been exaggerated, was strikingly ambivalent in his approach to individual projects. He was a firm supporter of Carew's anti-Ormond non-plantation; and there is no doubt that he was anxious to advance some of the Munster schemes, notably those of St Leger which envisaged participation of the house of Desmond. But towards plantation proposals concerning Ulster he was distinctly cool. He gave no support either to Smith or to those seeking to establish a colony in the Fews; and he sought subtly to undermine Essex's scheme by arguing that it should either be extended throughout the province (a proposal the cautious Privy Council would never endorse) or abandoned altogether.[2]

Sidney's ambivalence may be accounted for in part by his strong attachment to his own version of the assimilationist programme which he had devised as 'composition' (commuting traditional forms of levy such as coyne and livery or cess into permanent fixed taxes) and in part to issues of personal connection: he was a close associate of St Leger's and not a friend of Essex. Yet the consistently ambiguous attitudes of Dublin Castle towards plantations resided in more than personal considerations. A potential for serious tension and disagreement was always inherent in the relationship between the viceroy in Dublin and the court at Whitehall. Competition for Irish office, for military commissions, religious benefices, for grants of land, trading privileges, and the like was a constant source of tension within the relationship, and became even more serious when, as frequently happened, they became inextricably involved with the initiation and development of a particular policy, whether it be the appointment of a provincial president, or the establishment of a commission of enquiry. But plantation projects, which involved both prospects for personal advancement and questions of policy in very high degree, intensified such tensions immeasurably. In so far as they exercised full control over a project, such as Sussex did in the midlands, they could be regarded happily as integral elements of their own programme of government; and where, as in Sidney's case, the individual promoters were close associates of the governor similar support was forthcoming. But the further the viceroys were from exercising influence over the private adventurers and the more the latter were capable of exercising independent influence over powerful figures at Court, the more hostile the viceroys in Dublin were likely to be (Brady 1986).

The potential of plantations to widen the breach between Dublin and Whitehall was discernible in most of the schemes mooted in the 1560s and the early 1570s, and was contained only through their early failure. But what was to be essayed in Munster in the 1580s was at once far grander in scale, far more promising in its potential gains, more far reaching in its policy implications, and far more favoured at Whitehall than any previous undertaking. And it bore within it, therefore, in a much more concentrated form the structural, political, and constitutional contradictions which lay at the heart of the Tudor involvement in Ireland as a whole.

CONTENTIONS

Though it was in many ways a culmination of the tendencies that had been unfolding in Ireland from mid-century, the scheme for a plantation which was developed for

Munster in the wake of the death of the 14th earl of Desmond in rebellion in November 1583 was also in its peculiar combination of those tendencies quite unique. The Desmond lordship was not the first major territorial entity to be confiscated by means of attainder, but it was the largest and the most extensive. Originally estimated as more than 700,000 acres (by contemporary Irish measurement) and realizing eventually around 300,000 acres, the territory of the Desmond lordship spread throughout the counties of Limerick, Cork, Waterford, and Kerry with small parcels in Tipperary and Clare (Canny 2001; Dunlop 1888; MacCarthy-Morrogh 1986). Within its confines, moreover, lay some of the richest and most cultivated land in Ireland. In contrast to the midlands and to east Ulster, the beneficiaries of confiscated land in Munster could expect to acquire holdings whose profitability was already clearly established and whose developmental potential was immense.

The very characteristics which marked out Munster's potential as an investment were also, however, the source of the most serious challenges which its would-be developers would face. Such an unprecedented supply of potential land had become available only after the most prolonged and most dangerous war which the Tudor regime had yet faced in Ireland, and the threats posed by that war had by no means been resolved upon the death and attainder of the earl of Desmond. During the course of the rebellion Munster had been the objective of three separate foreign expeditions sponsored by the papacy and permitted by Philip II. And while none of them had presented even the slightest danger in themselves, nothing had occurred to suggest the impracticality of a more carefully devised and more powerful plan of invasion. In terms of geopolitics Munster remained as vulnerable to a Spanish assault after the rebellion as it did previously, and in the darkening diplomatic scenario of the mid-1580s there was little reason to presume that such an attempt might not sometime be made (Lyons 2003; Palmer 1994, 1995; Silke 1970). This external threat posed by invasion was supplemented by an even more alarming internal one. Though their numbers had been extensively depleted through killing, starvation, and disease, there remained in the province in 1584 a substantial element among the native population now bitterly alienated from the English Crown and ready to join again in any revolt against its claim to sovereignty that might arise.

Other problems produced by the Desmond war were also left unresolved by its conclusion. In the midst of the rebellion it was the common assumption both among the soldier-adventurers serving in Munster and the English administrators in Dublin that those who had been most actively involved in the suppression of the rebellion should attain the lion's share of the spoils in terms of both land and goods. This, after all, was the practice in the midlands, and in Essex's Ulster adventure. The extension of this principle to Munster would have entailed for some old Munster hands, such as Sir Warham St Leger and Sir Walter Raleigh, a consolidation or in some cases a considerable extension of interests in land and rents which they had already acquired either formally or informally in the course of the rebellion or had enjoyed for several years previously. While for officials, such as the Secretary of State Geoffrey Fenton or the Vice-Treasurer Sir Henry Wallop, it might entail acquiring an estate as a *rentier,* collecting rents and other perquisites through middlemen as the original owners had most likely done.[3]

At the outset there was no reason to assume that such conventional suppositions should be disappointed in Munster. But the manner in which it was to be effected was complicated by two additional and novel influences. The first and most immediate of these were the particular claims of Thomas, 10th Earl of Ormond. It was Ormond, who had taken principal charge of operations when the rebellion unexpectedly revived in ferocity towards the close of 1581 and who, through his deployment of his own forces, his diplomacy, and his sheer reputation, was more than any other figure responsible for its final suppression. He thus presented the Tudor government with a delicate problem. Of his service and his ultimate loyalty there could be no doubt, and the considerable military and diplomatic forces at his disposal (which had been displayed so effectively in the war) might in the future be an inestimable support to the feeble English hold on Ireland in a time of invasion. No distant feudal lord, Ormond was also a courtier who resided for most of the time in England. He was very well connected with other leading courtiers, and as everyone knew, he remained high in the affections of Elizabeth herself. His interest in the reconstruction of post-rebellion Munster was not, therefore, to be denied.

But his past service and future importance could not obscure the extent to which his triumph in Munster had seriously upset the political balance in Ireland. For in destroying his ancient rivals, the house of Desmond, and in consolidating his extensive network of clientage and connection throughout the province, Ormond had established himself as the single most powerful figure in Tudor Ireland, realizing a position of prominence for his dynasty which successive English viceroys from the 1530s on had sought to avoid: a threat not only to the immediate interests of the servitors and others competing for a share of the profits in a Munster plantation but to the very nature of English rule in the island as a whole. In addition to the military and administrative office-holders seeking reward for their service, Ormond represented a powerful competing Irish interest whose claims could neither be fully accepted nor fully ignored.[4]

Even as it was reconfiguring the political balance in Ireland, the Munster rebellion significantly altered the manner in which Ireland featured in Whitehall's political calculations. Though the degree to which factional interests and rivalries shaped the character of Elizabethan court politics has been somewhat overstated in the past, it remains clear that the tensions which had afflicted the court in the 1560s were surfacing once more in the mid-1580s as discontent aroused by the Queen's proposed marriage with the Duc of Anjou deepened amidst the disagreements surrounding Archbishop Whitgift's pursuit of radical clerics, Leicester's campaign for intervention in the Netherlands, demands for the arraignment of Mary Queen of Scots, and the ever-growing fears of Catholic conspiracies and assassination plots (Adams 1991; Alford 2008; Leimon 1981; Worden 1996). Underestimated by more recent historians of the court, Ireland, moreover, had never ceased to be a source of court rivalries throughout the reign—even in the consensual 1570s. But in the 1580s, in particular, the Desmond rebellion, with its combined security threat and the looming prospect of the most lavish increment of confiscated lands since the dissolution of the monasteries, provided a powerful mix for the revival and intensification of the Elizabethan court's inherent potential for alliance and rivalry (Brady 1986; McCormack 2006; Morgan 1995).

The intensification of interest in Ireland in Whitehall, the demands of the soldiers for recompense, and the towering shadow of Ormond all combined to increase pressure on the central organ of government in Ireland conventionally charged with the task of making and enforcing policy, the viceroyalty. In part this challenge to viceregal authority was political and managerial: the office simply did not have the capacity to assert an effective executive independence over all three. But deeper difficulties underlay such frustrations. By its very ferocity, its duration, and its appeal to foreign powers, the Desmond rebellion had constituted a direct challenge to the policy of assimilation through tenurial and legal reform which, in contrast to military confrontation and large-scale dispossession, had been the dominant key in Tudor government in Ireland. In elevating Ireland's position in English constitutional law to the level of a united kingdom, and abrogating the traditional division of the king's English subjects and the king's Irish enemies, the act for the kingly title of 1541 had introduced potentially profound difficulties regarding the constitutional standing of the old English–Irish feudal lordships which were slow to emerge. As late as the 1550s Sussex was able to claim that the Gaelic dynasties of O'Moore and O'Connor, whose lands he proposed to plant, had rejected by rebellion the offers of reconciliation extended to them under the 1541 legislation and so continued in the status of outlaws: no act of attainder was required in their case. And in the 1570s Smith and Essex rested their claims on the old Anglo-Norman earldom of Ulster which was a direct inheritance of the Tudors. They were not confiscating the lands of rebels or enemies, but of invaders from a foreign sovereignty. They were reviving a right long left in desuetude; and those who accepted those claims would be left in peace as tenants of the Crown.[5] In this they in no way differed from Carew's adventure among the Kavanaghs.

Even then, however, the claim to the old earldom of Ulster, whose boundaries remained indeterminate, was subject to some doubt through legislation recently passed in the Irish parliament of 1569 which had been designed to supplement the statute of 1541. Concerned to deny the late Shane O'Neill's claims that as 'The O'Neill', the official head of his clan, he possessed distinctive rights which could not be abrogated under the terms of the treaty signed with his father in 1542, the 'act for the attainder of Shane O'Neill' had essayed an important elaboration of the kingship act of 1541. All of the inhabitants of the island were, it asserted, both from time immemorial and by prescription directly, subjects of the English Crown who needed no intermediary to represent them to their sovereign. In undermining the claims of Gaelic overlords, the act, however, also endangered the claims of Anglo-Norman potentates where their claims to overlordship had not been clearly established on conventional feudal law. This was partly the case in Ulster, and such a realization may have coloured Sidney's less than enthusiastic attitude towards the Ulster projects during the 1570s. But it was even more palpably the case in Munster where the power of the Desmond Fitzgeralds and their Anglo-Norman dependants over the Gaelic Irish lordships of the province was based more on alliances of protection and intimidation than on feudal obligation. The paper schemes of the Munster projectors in the 1560s were devised without the potential embarrassments arising after 1569, and in any case the emphasis of justification in several of their propositions rested on the claim of *dominium vacuum*, the concept that newcomers had a right to seize and acquire title to territories not fully settled or exploited by original natives (Brady 2005; Goebel 1950; Quinn 1938: I, 491–7).

This, however, was a claim that could not be advanced in regard to Desmond in the 1580s, for the bulk of the land covered under the attainder had been fully settled and developed by the Fitzgeralds for centuries. On the other hand the Fitzgerald lordship was honeycombed with territories occupied by native Irish dynasties whose relationship with the Fitzgerald's was in terms of feudal law quite uncertain. Such were the so-called 'chargeable lands', the sometimes substantial tracts which, though held as freehold, were also subject to Desmond's claims of feudal overlordship (MacCarthy-Morrogh 1986: 71–81).

The status of these 'chargeable lands' had always been deeply uncertain because the Fitzgerald claims had for long been disputed by many of the residents of the lands themselves. But in the light of the constitutional legislation of 1541 and 1569 other complexities began to emerge. The feudal claims of the Kildare Fitzgeralds had not proved to be particularly controversial in part because the local English residents of Kildare who disputed them were the very interest whom the government wished to recognize as direct freeholders under the new settlement, and in part because the Gaelic Irish inhabitants over whom such claims were made retained at that time the status of 'the king's Irish enemies' who had no rights of residence in the lordship in any case. In post-rebellion Munster, however, neither of these conditions applied. For in its desire to make as much of Desmond's inheritance available for confiscation and plantation by new settlers, the government was loathe to allow his estate to be reduced and fragmented in such a highly inefficient way; and its determination in this regard was strengthened by the conviction that many of those who now disputed the feudal claims of the Desmonds had themselves been implicated in the rebellion. Yet at the same time the disputants vigorously denied culpability on several grounds from outright assertions of innocence, pleas of coercion, and claims that they had received a full pardon from Ormond in the closing days of the war, down to the troubling assertion that the illegality of their subjection to Desmond was strongly upheld by the legislation of 1541 and 1569.[6] Given the extreme tensions now arising within the components of the Tudor regime at central and local levels and at the mediating level of the Irish viceroyalty, the emergence of deep internal contradictions in the underlying assumptions of Tudor government in Ireland and in the policies that derived from them could hardly have occurred at a worse time. And their ill-effects were to become plain in the earliest days of the Munster plantation.

CONFUSIONS

···

The powerful and contradictory forces shaping the plantation are most obvious in the inconsistent manner in which the government set about initiating the process of confiscation in the first place. At the outset the government determined to proceed through the conventional legal process of escheat administered under the authority of Dublin: juries were impanelled in each of the shires, an inquisition was held to determine and confirm the extent and value of the escheated property, the title was investigated (in most cases found for the Crown), and a surveyor was appointed to draw up detailed accounts of each portion of the confiscated property in preparation for leases to be issued by chancery. This was the standard practice which had been followed in Ireland in regard to attainted and confiscated lands since the 1530s (MacCarthy-Morrogh 1986: 4–19).

But from the beginning in Munster, Whitehall began to make differences. First it interrupted preliminary proceedings, summoning the surveyor, Sir Valentine Browne, home for consultations and further instructions thereby delaying proceedings by almost nine months in 1584 during which time hardly any inquisitions were held. The commissioners then worked hastily but, as they themselves admitted, imperfectly and haphazardly, with the result that their findings were challenged and subjected to a series of provisos and reservations in the Irish parliament in 1585, and continued for decades thereafter to be successfully challenged in the courts. While the traditional mode of survey thus produced a fragmented, scattered, and deeply uncertain royal estate, the council in Whitehall moved to impose an impressively regular but wholly unrealistic schema for the division and allotment of estates into hierarchically layered 'seignories' of 4,000, 6,000, 8,000, and 12,000 acres, and enumeratimg also the number of freeholders, copyholders, tenants-at-will, and cottagers to be included in each seignory. To support this radical plan the Privy Council then issued public offers to would-be investors on the basis of a set of terms and conditions, and established in the summer of 1586 a second commission designed to conduct not a legal survey, but a detailed physical measurement and division of lands into these layered seignories.[7]

Though it had never been actually introduced previously in Ireland, a similar innovation had been anticipated by St Leger and his associates in their 1569 propositions for settlement in Munster (MacCarthy-Morrogh 1986: 33–8). But as that scheme had envisaged wholesale removals, it was, even in the time of rebellion, considered to be too radical by the Privy Council and was shelved. Now, however, the council appeared to be adapting a part of it while denying its prime underlying premise. The St Leger scheme, moreover, was a private enterprise: once the confiscations had been completed, the adventurers expected to be allowed to make their own arrangements. But the Privy Council now assumed the responsibility not only for the recruitment and the negotiation of terms with the new 'undertakers', but also for arbitrating between them and the natives and the office-holders now awaiting their rewards.

The willingness of the council to assume such unprecedented responsibility is partly due to its acute awareness of the imminent security problems presented by Munster. The rapid importation into the province of a substantial English settlement with strictly defined militia responsibilities was an effective way of ensuring that any future invasion would meet with resistance. But it was also due to an equally clear understanding that the investment prospects in the province were too large to be left either to a private consortium or to the discretion of the viceroy in Dublin Castle. And in this regard the motives of the councillors were less than pure. The decision to centralize control of the plantation presented the councillors with unprecedented opportunities for exploiting the potential riches of Ireland for themselves. In the past, questions of Irish patronage had featured to some degree in the calculations of leading courtiers, producing regular tensions at court and between the court and Dublin. But Munster with its unparalleled opportunities for gain was different. For this reason several of the councillors themselves became directly involved in investment in the plantation: Lord Chancellor Hatton and Chief Justice Sir John Popham sought for and secured substantial seignories in the initial scheme; and the relations and clients of others, such as Sir Edward Denny (cousin of Lord Burghley) and Sir Valentine Browne, were heavily committed to investing there. But more importantly the very manner in which the council issued a broad call to the nobility and gentry of the nation to submit tenders for investment in Ireland provided its members with an exceptional opportunity for the exercise of grace and favour. The redistribution of Munster's broad acres, in short, supplied them with the greatest prospect for the stimulation of a court-centred land market that had existed since the confiscation of the monastic lands in the 1530s and all the attendant benefits which it brought to those at its core (MacCarthy-Morrogh 1986: Chap. 2).

On every side, then, the Council found itself faced with choices to be made between both natives and settlers and among the settler groups themselves. But the issues thus presented by such a plethora of choice, it soon appeared, were more than a matter of speculative or strategic calculation. They constituted a set of ideological and ethical confusions which lay at the heart of the Tudor government's attitude toward Ireland.

Most obvious among the difficult choices presented to the council were the competing claims of the 'servitors' and the 'undertakers' within the planter interest. The active recruitment of a large number of investors who were to be granted extensive 'seignories' under strict conditions for their habitation, institutional development, and defence marked an audacious step in the council's strategic thinking regarding plantation. But it was also a serious break with recent practice which recognized that, since it lacked the resources fully to remunerate those who were committed to a long-term career in Ireland, the Crown should permit its officers to sue for such estates as arose from the casual confiscation of ecclesiastical, rebels', or felons' lands. The Privy Council's plan for a full-scale plantation represented something of a shock to these expectations. But its disregard of the traditional garrison interest was not deliberate. Instead the council assumed that some servitors would sue for one of the lesser seignories and that those unable to avail of grants in their own right would be received as valuable and substantial tenants within the estates of the great undertakers. Such optimism was unwarranted, however, for several reasons. Very few of the servitors were in a position to compete for the seignories with the great undertakers. As soldiers who had gone unpaid for years, they regarded themselves as creditors of the Crown and expected remuneration in the form of direct grants of land rather than favour with a superior landlord class. They resented the suggestion that those areas over which they asserted their authority and whose resources they had enjoyed without interference during the war years should now be subsumed into the great seignories. But most importantly of all they realized that the terms laid upon the undertakers for the settlement and development of a model English society in the province were directly inimical to the means by which they had pursued their own interests in the area during the war years, that is by the adoption, extension, and intensification of the methods of informal taxation and extortion and protection through which the Fitzgeralds of Desmond and many of their followers had operated for centuries (Canny 2001: Chap. 1; MacCarthy-Morrogh 1986: 53–6; Rapple 2009).

The Privy Council's subordination of the interests of the servitors to those of the undertakers may be seen as a clear signal that it regarded the most pressing strategic and financial objectives of the project as complementary rather than opposed to the orthodox long-term aim of recreating a version of the English commonwealth in Ireland. But such theoretical consistency was not reflected to any degree in practice. Instead the council's decision to attempt a physical survey of the escheated territories introduced an extended and gravely damaging delay. Though the decision to recruit English undertakers had been made as early as January 1585, the survey of the area was begun only in the summer of 1586 and continued into the following year. The first letters patent to undertakers were not issued until September 1587 and thereafter proceeded slowly: the final ones were not issued until 1595. From this delay several consequences followed. First the interest of undertakers waned. Of the original number of 86 projected in 1585 only 35 identified undertakers retained an interest two years later. Even among those, moreover, second thoughts were arising. Most came to view their allotments only in the summer of 1587, and only a minority stayed for any considerable time (MacCarthy-Morrogh 1986: 67–9). In the meantime, the servitors who had initially feared an invasion of scores of undertakers made the most of the delay, quietly tightening their grip on the territories through their dealings with the native inhabitants while insistently pressing their own claims for reward. As the clarity of the original scheme faded, and as security concerns mounted so the council became increasingly attentive to the complaints and demands of these military men, and increasingly deaf to complaints raised concerning their conduct by both the undertakers and the locals (MacCarthy-Morrogh 1986: 61–9).[8]

The increasingly lawless and extortionate conduct of several of the military figures as constables, sheriffs, and seneschals, and as commissioners of martial law, was to supply the single most disruptive force in the first phase of the plantation, ultimately provoking large numbers of the native inhabitants into revolt, and annihilating the council's initial vision of the plantation (Sheehan 1982).[9] But the more immediate effect of the success of the servitors was felt among the undertakers. To some, such as Sir William Herbert and Sir Thomas Norris, the behaviour of the servitors was repugnant.[10] Other undertakers, however, such as Sir Edward Denny and St Leger, frequently found it useful to employ the support of the garrison men against their fellow settlers and the local lords with whom they found themselves in dispute.[11] And similarly, while many of the local lords were bitterly resentful of the soldiers' extortions, others found their familiar mode of operation far preferable to the threats to their traditional forms of authority presented by a civil plantation (Canny 2001: 154–9; MacCarthy-Morrogh 1986: 81–91, 130–2). The soldiers thus added a further level of complexity to the scheme of plantation which not only contributed to its chronic lack of progress and increasing instability, but also, and more importantly, to profound doubts about the character, viability, and purpose of the project of establishing English civility in Ireland as a whole.

There remained a second and quite opposite manner in which the council's determination not to depart from the conventional assumptions as to how such reform was to be conducted ironically contributed further to fatal delay. From the outset the council's attitude towards the inhabitants of Munster was deeply confused. On the one hand by its decision to proceed by means of individual attainders the council appeared to concede that not all of the inhabitants had been rebels, and that only the servants, tenants, or allies of the rebel Desmond should suffer the consequences of rebellion. And it also appeared willing to honour the extensive pardons which Ormond had issued to actual rebels in his efforts to end the war (MacCarthy-Morrogh 1986: 16–17). On the other hand, the acts of attainder drafted for the Irish parliament of 1586 contained the names of many of those pardoned by Ormond and, more importantly, in its elaborate plan for the organization of seignories from which all natives were to be excluded, and especially in the survey conducted in 1586 on the basis of this scheme, it seemed to envisage the widespread clearance of territories along the lines proposed by the notorious project of 1569.[12] In this the council was encouraged by the discovery of evidence of a secret combination between Desmond and some of the most important provincial lords under which they pledged to aid him in rebellion.[13] And in the early stages of surveying the council remained firm in its resistance to the claims of the occupants of the 'chargeable lands', supporting St Leger in the case of his allotment at Kerricurrihy.[14] A commission established in 1588 to hear and determine native claims for exemption from confiscation was similarly unsympathetic: of a total of seventy-six cases heard, all but one were rejected (MacCarthy-Morrogh 1986: 97–100; Sheehan 1983).

Yet there was soon some slippage within this unyielding position. Pressure in the Irish parliament compelled the Dublin government to agree to the reversal of several of those named in the bill of attainder. A similar softening was discernible in regard to those native plaintiffs claiming to hold mortgages of rebels' lands negotiated by them long before they had gone into rebellion. Though such claims had at first been rejected out of hand, several were upheld on appeal.[15] The government also became increasingly nervous over the case of 'the chargeable lands', and in 1589 it conceded that the residents of such lands should remain unmolested on condition of paying a negotiated 'composition' rent to the Crown based on Desmond's earlier charges (MacCarthy-Morrogh 1986: 73). This was a major concession, all the more so because it increased pressure on the new settlers to contribute to a government tax.

But even more significant was the increasingly sympathetic attitude which the government in Whitehall displayed towards individual plaintiffs who claimed actual innocence of the rebellion. As early as 1587 the government confounded the claims of its own chief surveyor, Sir Valentine Browne, in ordering the exemption from the plantation of all lands within the lordship of MacCarthy–Mór (MacCarthy-Morrogh 1986: 81–3). This was exceptional at that time. But in 1592 a second commission established to determine the continuing claims for exemption proved to be systematically far more sympathetic than its predecessor four years earlier, upholding slightly more than 50% of the claims (Sheehan 1983). The most serious and most ominous concession, however, arose in relation to those native landholders whose independence of the Desmonds and their rebellion was never in doubt. These were the relatively small number of freeholding occupiers of land which, though within the escheated territories, were independent of the Desmond estates. In the council's paper plan of the plantation with its neat divisions of seignories of regulated and uniform extents the existence of such a group was not recognized at all. When the surveyors and measurers arrived in 1586 to do the actual measuring out of the plantation estates the awkward existence of this group holding slivers of freehold which cut up and fragmented the neat blocs of seignories could no longer be ignored. Confronted by this untidiness the undertakers proposed removal and compensation elsewhere. When the freeholders refused, the lord deputy in Dublin attempted persuasion, but, in the now characteristically cool attitude of viceroys towards colonial entrepreneurs, refused to contemplate coercion in accordance with the settlers' wishes (MacCarthy-Morrogh 1986: 79–80). And so they stayed put: a living testimony to the artificiality of the original conception of the plantation and a serious threat to its future development and prosperity. But they also testified to the confused and conflicting influences operating on the most important organ of Tudor government which, for the first time, elected to play a dominant role in the formulation and implementation of English policy in Ireland.

CRITICAL RECONCEPTIONS

It was in reaction to the pressures so relentlessly generated by the richly confused efforts of the Crown to institute a resettlement of Munster in the late 1580s that the great rebellion which overran the plantation (and Spenser's share in it) broke out in the autumn of 1598 (Sheehan 1982). But even before that crisis arrived, it was the gradual comprehension of the profound ideological and ethical contradictions underlying such practical confusions that the great outflow of critical, polemical, and highly original literature, including Spenser's own troubled writing, took shape. The inventive and original character of this remarkable body of material produced in the first years of the Munster plantation has long been the subject of intense scholarly commentary. The purpose, significance, and influence of tracts by Spenser, Richard Beacon, Sir William Herbert, Robert Payne, and several others have been extensively analysed and interpreted (Canny 2001: Chap. 1; Hadfield and Maley 2000; Herron 2007: Chap. 1; Morgan 1999). But this discussion has, not infrequently, taken place within a somewhat artificial context. In some treatments the marked differences between such texts have been suppressed or diminished and they have been fused together as collective evidence of an emerging colonial ideology; and in a slightly more subtle manner their location along this spectrum has been essayed, and the extent to which some rather than others served to set the agenda of future English thought about Ireland assessed.

But this retrospective emphasis on what was to come—rather than on what was actually happening—has seriously distorted both the immediate context in which this body of writing first arose and the distinctive characteristics of its individual components. For though they have subsequently been accorded a profound inter- pretative significance, at the time of their composition they represented only a very small quantity in comparison with the vast body of more official forms of writing that the plantation had generated—state memoranda, private suits, complaints of abuse, and above all the vast corpus of legal proceedings—all of which testify to the continuing conviction that what was being undertaken in Munster could still be comprehended within the normal structures and processes of English law and governance. That such an implicit confidence was becoming increasingly unfounded was steadily being made clear by the interlocking set of contradictions detailed above. But what remained equally clear was the fact that the government in Whitehall, whose actions and inactions had done so much to expose the weakness of the entire English project in Ireland, was either unwilling to recognize or incapable of recogniz- ing the gathering crisis.

For those who actually did recognize the gap between the government's aspirations and the consequences of its attempts to realize them, the impulse to stake out an entirely different perspective, to open a new mode of argument, and to engage a far broader audience arose not merely from literary ambition or intellectual originality, but from urgent necessity. It was this imperative that, at its simplest, gave rise to Robert Payne's pamphlet *A Brief description of Ireland* (1589), a hugely optimistic tract that directed its appeal to a far broader audience than those bring recruited by the council in the hope of generating a far more independent interest in the province. And a similar drive underlay Richard Beacon's far darker *Solon his follie* whose thinly veiled allegory was intended not simply to soften his indictment of recent English policies and practices in Ireland, but to alert a different audience (the book was published in Oxford and addressed to a learned readership) to the more general threat of the decline and corruption of commonwealths which the example of Ireland represented (Beacon 1996; Carey 1999b; Orr 2008; Peltonnen 1994). In his *Croftus: sive de Hibernia* Herbert attempted a more subtle (but no more effective) appeal to a scholarly audience of divines and dons in the hope that his proposal for a state university scheme funded by taxation would cut the Gordian knot of corruption, faction, and administrative neglect which he saw all around him in Munster (Brady 2000; Keaveney and Madden 1992).

And finally it is in the light of all these efforts that Spenser's *View* must also be seen. A manifesto for neither some homogeneous 'New English colonial elite' nor some radical Protestant millenarian movement, Spenser's *View*, though replete with its own incoherencies and unresolved contradictions, nonetheless contained the most profound perception of the nature of the challenge posed to England by its latest adventure in Ireland and the most extreme prescription for its address (McCabe 2002). This was in part because of his own remarkably varied experience of the English presence in Ireland. It was Spenser who as secretary to Lord Grey witnessed at first hand the pressures operating on the viceregal office, and the cost for those who failed to withstand them. It was his experience of the rebellion and of its aftermath that enabled him fully to appreciate the resilience, ambivalence, and ambition of the English–Irish community and of their most powerful representative, Ormond. Similarly it was his roles as undertaker, and later as sheriff of Cork, that enabled Spenser to experience at first hand the recurring conflicts between law and force and between self-interest and political reform that characterized the early days of the plantation. And it was from an embittered familiarity that he understood all too well the dark and self-defeating rivalries of Whitehall. But above all it was the poet of *The Faerie Queene* who more than anyone perceived that what had happened in Munster between the late 1570s and the mid-1590s not only epitomized the appalling perils faced by England in Ireland, but also exposed the even more fundamental menace to the survival of England itself as a united, independent, and reformed commonwealth. Whether the *View* was to become the foundation text of all further English thinking about Ireland is a contention which may not always gather assent; but of its status as a most eloquent and most terrible expression of a late Elizabethan crisis of identity there can be no doubt.

NOTES

1. See, for example, Fitzwilliam to Burghley, 14 March 1572, SP 63/35/32 and the exchange of letters between Smith and Fitzwilliam on 8–9 Nov. 1572, 63/38/30, 31.
2. Sidney's 'Opinion on certain articles by the earl of Essex', May/June 1573, SP 63/40/60; on the context of this document see Brady (1994), 143–5.
3. Among the several petitions for recompense among soldiers and administrators see SP 63/112/78 (Sir John Norris); 63/91/2 (Wallop); 63/91/41–2, 45 (St Leger); 63/106/24 (Richard Speart and others); 63/106/33 (Sir William Stanley); 63/133/7 (Sir George Bouchier); 63/118/75 and enclosure (Fenton); 63/124/12 (Jacques Wingfield et al.).
4. On the fear and resentment of Ormond see, inter alia, the lord justices to Burghley and Wallop to Walsingham 4, 7 Feb 1583, SP 63/49, 56; also Wallop and Browne to Walsingham, 5 Dec 1584, 63/113/16; the ambivalence of Whitehall towards Ormond is well expressed in Walsingham to Wallop, Jan. 1585, 63/114/53.

5. Smith to Sir William Fitzwilliam, 18 May, 2 Nov 1572, *CSPF, 1583 and Addenda*, 489–90; Bodleian Library Carte Mss 57/435; Essex to Burghley 10 Sept. 1573 in Devereux (1853: I, 34–6).
6. *CSPI, 1586–8*, 52–3, 262–3, 384–7; 'Memorial' concerning chargeable lands, 23 Dec. 1589, SP 63/149/53.
7. 'Articles for the re-peopling and inhabiting . . . of Munster', June 1586, *CSPI, 1586–8*, 84–9. 'Note of the profit that may grow . . . by planting in Munster', SP 63/121/62.
8. On the slowness of the surveyors proceedings see *CSPI, 1586–8*, 261–3, 271–5.
9. 'On the causes of rebellion in Ireland' in *CSPI, 1600–1*, 124–5; further evidence for the responsibility of the military in provoking rebellion in 1598 is supplied in Sheehan (1982).
10. Sir William Herbert, a substantial undertaker in his own right, was the most trenchant contemporary critic of the arbitrary and exploitative conduct of the military men. See his 'Tracts' presented to the Privy Council in 1588 in *CSPI, 1586–8*, 527–47; Norris to Privy Council, 21 Jan. 1589, ibid. 110–11.
11. The conduct of some undertakers deprecated by Herbert in his tracts (note 33) are corroborated by the Munster Vice-President: Sir Thomas Norris to Burghley, 21 Jan. 1589, SP 63/140/36.
12. *Irish Statutes* I, 418–19, 422–4; 'Articles for the re-peopling and inhabiting . . . of Munster', June 1586, *CSPI, 1586–8*, 84–9.
13. Fenton to Burghley, 8 May 1586, SP 63/124/7 enclosing the secret enfeoffment.
14. St Leger to Elizabeth, 31 Jan. 1584, SP 63/107/58.
15. 'Orders made before the Commissioners in Munster in 1592', Jan. 1593, SP 63/168/10 enclosure (i).

BIBLIOGRAPHY

Adams, S. (2002). *Leicester and the Court: Essays on Elizabethan Politics*. Manchester: Manchester University Press.

Alford, S. (2008). *Burghley: William Cecil at the Court of Elizabeth*. New Haven, CT: Yale University Press.

Beacon, Richard (1996). *Solon his follie, or a politique discourse touching the reformation of common-weales conquered, declined or corrupted*, ed. C. Carroll and V. Carey. Binghamton, NY: Medieval and Renaissance Texts and Studies.

Bradshaw, B. (1979). *The Irish Constitutional Revolution of the Sixteenth Century*. Cambridge: Cambridge University Press.

Brady, C. (1986). 'Court, Castle and Country: The Framework of Government in Tudor Ireland', in C. Brady and R. Gilespie (eds), *Natives and Newcomers: Essays on the Making of Irish Colonial Society, 1534–1641*. Dublin: Irish Academic Press, 22–49, 217–19.

—— (1994). *The Chief Governors: the Rise and Fall of Reform Government in Tudor Ireland, 1536–1588*. Cambridge: Cambridge University Press.

—— (2000). 'New English Ideology in Ireland and the two Sir William Herberts', in Amanda Piesse (ed.), *Sixteenth Century Identities*. Manchester: Manchester University Press, 75–111.

—— (2005). 'The Attainder of Shane O'Neill, Sir Henry Sidney and the Problems of Tudor State-Building in Ireland', in C. Brady and J. H. Ohlmeyer (eds), *British Interventions in Early Modern Ireland*. Cambridge: Cambridge University Press, 28–48.

Canny, N. (2001). *Making Ireland British, 1580–1650*. Oxford: Oxford University Press.

Carey, V. (1999a). 'John Derricke's *Image of Irelande*, Sir Henry Sidney, and the Massacre at Mullaghmast, 1578'. *IHS* 31: 305–27.

—— (1999b). 'The Irish Face of Machiavelli: Richard Beacon's *Solon his follie* and Republican Ideology in the Conquest of Ireland', in H. Morgan (ed.), *Political Ideology in Ireland, 1541–1641*. Dublin: Four Courts Press, 83–109.

—— (2002). *Surviving the Tudors: The 'Wizard' Earl of Kildare and English Rule in Ireland, 1537–1586*. Dublin: Four Courts Press.

Devereux, W. B. (1853). *Lives and Letters of the Devereux, Earls of Essex, in the Reigns of Elizabeth, James I, and Charles I, 1540–1646*, 2 vols. London.

Dunlop, R. (1888). 'The Plantation of Munster, 1584–1589'. *EHR* 3: 250–69.

—— (1891). 'The Plantation of Leix and Offaly, 1556–1622'. *EHR* 6(1): 61–96.

Fitzsimons, F. (1998). 'The Lordship of O'Conor Faly, 1520–1570', in W. Nolan et al. (eds), *Offaly: History and Society: Interdisciplinary Essays on the History of an Irish County*. Dublin: Geography Publications, 207–42.

Goebel, J. (1950). 'The Matrix of Empire', in J. H. Smith (ed.), *Appeals to the Privy Council from the American Colonies*. New York: Columbia University Press, xii–lxi.

Hadfield, A., and W. Maley (2000). 'A View of the Present State of Spenser Studies', in J. K. Morrison and M. Greenfield (eds), *Edmund Spenser: Essays on Culture and Allegory*. Aldershot: Palgrave Press, 183–96.

Herron, T. (2007). *Spenser's Irish Work: Poetry, Plantation and Colonial Reformation*. Aldershot: Palgrave Press.

Keaveney, A., and J. Madden (eds) (1992). *Croftus Sive de Hibernia Liber*. Dublin: Irish Manuscripts Commission.

Leimon, M. M. (1989). 'Sir Francis Walsingham and the Anjou Marriage Plans, 1574–81'. Unpublished PhD, Cambridge University.

Lyons, M. A. (2003). *Franco–Irish relations 1500–1610: Politics, Migration and Trade*. Royal Historical Society, Studies in History. Woodbridge: Boydell Press.

McCabe, R. A. (2002). *Spenser's Monstrous Regiment: Elizabethan Ireland and the Poetics of Difference*. Oxford: Oxford University Press.

MacCarthy-Morrogh, M. (1986). *The Munster Plantation: English Migration to Southern Ireland, 1583–1641*. Oxford: Clarendon Press.

McCormack, A. M. (2005). *The Earldom of Desmond, 1463–1583: The Decline and Crisis of a Feudal Lordship*. Dublin: Four Courts Press.

MacNiocaill, G. (ed.) (1992). *Crown Surveys of Lands, 1540–1541, with the Kildare Rental Begun in 1518*. Dublin: Irish Manuscripts Commission.

Maginn, C. (2004). 'The Baltinglass Rebellion, 1580 : English Dissent or a Gaelic Uprising?' *HJ* 47(2): 205–32.

—— (2005). '*Civilizing' Gaelic Leinster: The Extension of Tudor Rule in the O'Byrne and O'Toole Lordships*. Dublin: Four Courts Press.

Morgan, H. (1985). 'The Colonial Venture of Sir Thomas Smith in Ulster, 1571–1575'. *HJ* 28(2): 261–78.

—— (1988). 'The End of Gaelic Ulster: A Thematic Interpretation of Events between 1534 and 1610'. *IHS* 26 (101): 8–32.

—— (1995). 'The Fall of Sir John Perrot', in John Guy (ed.), *The Reign of Elizabeth I: Court and Culture in the Last Decade*. Cambridge: Cambridge University Press, 109–25.

—— (ed.) (1999). *Political Ideology in Early Modern Ireland*. Dublin: Four Courts Press.

Nicholls, K. (1977–81). 'The Kavanaghs, 1400–1700'. *Irish Genealogist* 5: 435–77; 6: 573–80, 730–4; 7: 189–203.

Orr, A. D. (2008). 'Inventing the British Republic : Richard Beacon's *Solon His Follie* (1594) and the Rhetoric of Civilization'. *Sixteenth-Century Journal* 38(4): 975–94.

Palmer, W. (1994). *The Problem of Ireland in Tudor Foreign Policy, 1485–1603*. Woodbridge: Boydell Press.

—— (1995). 'Ireland and English Foreign Policy in the 1570s'. *The Historian [Albuquerque, NM etc.]* 58(1): 87–100.

Peltonen, M. (1994). 'Classical Republicanism in Tudor England: The Case of Richard Beacon's *Solon His Follie*'. *History of Political Thought* 15: 469–503.

Piveronus, P. J. (1979). 'Sir Warham St. Leger and the First Munster Plantation'. *Éire-Ireland* 14 (2): 16–36.

Prendergast, J. P. (1859). 'The Plantation of the Barony of Idrone'. *Journal of the Kilkenny and South East Ireland Archaeological Society* 2(2): 400–28.

Quinn, D. B. (ed.) (1938). *The voyages and colonizing expeditions of Sir Humphrey Gilbert*, 2 vols. London: Publications of the Hakluyt Society.

—— (1945). 'Sir Thomas Smith (1513–1577) and the Beginnings of English Colonial Theory'. *Proceedings of the American Philosophical Society* 89.

—— (ed.) (1946–7). 'Edward Walshe's "Conjectures" concerning the State of Ireland, 1552'. *IHS* 5(20): 303–22.

Rapple, R. (2008). 'Taking Up Office in Elizabethan Connacht: The Case of Sir Richard Bingham'. *EHR* 123(501): 277–99.

—— (2009). *Martial Power and Elizabethan Political Culture: Military Men in England and Ireland, 1558–94*. Cambridge: Cambridge University Press.

Sheehan, A. J. (1982). 'The Overthrow of the Plantation of Munster in October 1598'. *Irish Sword* 15: 11–22.

—— (1983). 'Official Reaction to Native Land Claims in the Plantation of Munster'. *IHS* 23: 297–318.

Silke, J. J. (1970). *Kinsale: the Spanish Intervention in Ireland at the End of the Elizabethan Wars*. Liverpool: Liverpool University Press.

Walshe, H. C. (1990). 'The Rebellion of William Nugent, 1581', in R.V. Comerford et al. (eds), *Religion, Conflict and Coexistence in Ireland: Essays presented to Monsignor Patrick Corish*. Dublin: Four Courts Press, 26–52, 297–302.

White, D. G. (1967). 'The Tudor Plantations in Ireland before 1571'. Unpublished PhD, University of Dublin.

....

CHAPTER 6

SPENSER'S PATRONS AND PUBLISHERS

....

WAYNE ERICKSON

THIS essay examines the production of Edmund Spenser's books, that is, the biographical and cultural conditions that led to their being written and, more centrally, the collaborative enterprise among the poet, his patrons, and members of the Stationers' Company that led to the books' being printed and distributed. Spenser wrote, of course, because he was a poet, but he accomplished the writing because he had jobs that afforded him the time and security to do so and, in part, because he had the support and encouragement of friends and patrons. He published his books because he had the ambition necessary to the task and because the book trade afforded him the economic and mechanical means to do so, and he risked publication, including the attendant possibilities of failure, approbation, or disapproval, because he had patrons who he knew or imagined would support and authorize the venture, mitigating criticism and participating in success. According to a common formulation of the time, Spenser, his publishers, and, implicitly, his patrons 'set foorth'[1] his books by setting them in type and by setting them forth for sale into the hands of readers, as ships set forth on perilous but sometimes successful voyages of exploration, acquisition, and conquest. The relevance of the latter metaphor, however, despite its apparently sound resonance, demands drastic qualification within the contexts of Elizabethan patronage and the book trade, for to compare Spenser's publishing ventures to the 'venturous vessell[s] [that] measured | The *Amazons* huge riuer...Or fruitfullest *Virginia*' invites a charge of irresponsible and uninformed exaggeration, as if books had the value of colonies (II *Proem*, 2). On the other hand, setting books forth onto the stormy sea of the marketplace, to be cast about by capricious winds of opinion and judgment, compares fairly accurately, though again less consequentially, with Colin Clout's estimation of the dangers that attend merchant adventurers (or courtly climbers) who set forth on the 'ghastly dreadful' sea of aspiration: 'Bold men presuming life for gain to sell, | Dare tempt the gulf, and in those wandring stremes | Seek waies unknown, waies leading down to hell' (CCH, 208, 209–11; Oram 1990: 347). Despite some risk and small gain, Spenser chose to publish, calling on patrons and stationers to assist.

Despite occasional professions by the author and his narrators of unworthiness, frustration, and neglect, Spenser's speculative ventures into publishing earned him, during his lifetime, the respect and admiration of many and, within twenty years of his death, a monument on his grave that celebrates 'the Prince of Poets in his tyme; whose Divine Spirit needs noe othir witnesse then the works which he left behinde him' (Judson 1945: 207). Nonetheless, for the purposes of this essay, which seeks to situate Spenser as accurately as possible within Elizabethan patronage and publishing, the estimation of the poet's contemporary fame recorded on his monument as a witness to his works demands, as the ship metaphor above, some fairly severe qualification. Spenser published during his life only books of poetry—for lack of a more appropriate term, works of literature—and since literary patronage and literary publication accounted for only a small part of the system of patronage and the trade in books, Spenser remained, despite his relative literary fame, on the fringe of both of these cultural institutions.

Patronage, the engine behind much Elizabethan political and economic power, was dispensed by the Queen or, more frequently, by the Queen's representatives in the aristocracy, the government, and the military. Most often, it yielded cash, offices and positions, titles and honors, grants and leases of land, patents and monopolies, pensions, and wardships; the recipients of these benefits, in turn, accrued the prestige and economic and political power that allowed and obliged them to perform their own duties as patrons. Patronage of artists made up some part of the larger system, patronage of writers in the form of small gifts and minor offices a small and minor part of artistic patronage, and literary patronage a very small and minor part of that. Furthermore, writers, particularly literary authors, would probably receive patronage only as a reward for or in anticipation of loyalty and service of some other, more useful kind, in which case it often becomes difficult to quantify a separate category called literary patronage. An analogous situation governed the production of books: among the books produced in Elizabethan England, a very small percentage were literary works—fiction, poetry, and plays—and most of these, compared with books of other kinds, were issued in relatively small editions. From this broad perspective, literary patronage and literary publication played a relatively insignificant role in the Elizabethan world.

Still, literary writers did receive various kinds of patronage, they did publish their books, and those books had readers who, like the writers, probably thought the books much more valuable than their share of the patronage and publishing market made them appear—indeed, valuable despite their lack of popularity or because of it, witnesses to the world's distorted values. With these readers and patrons in mind, the category of literary patronage probably requires a broad definition, one that includes all those who support and encourage writers in their endeavors, without, at the absurd limit, calling every reader a patron. As a corollary, since the exact nature of patrons' involvement with writers often resists quantification, perhaps, as a broad category that demands qualification, patrons might be thought to include all those to whom writers dedicate their books. These proposals make sense for the study of Spenser's patrons because Spenser's dedications expose more about the poet's relationships with and attitudes towards his patrons than all the contested scraps of biographical documentation combined.

That said, and before turning to Spenser, I offer two final reality checks concerning patrons, dedications, and the value of literary publication. At the conclusion of his *Defence of Poetry*, in his peroration, Philip Sidney reviews in an extended anaphora the various reasons why poets ought to be admired and celebrated, finally insisting that patrons ought to believe poets 'when they tell you they will make you immortal by their verses'. 'Thus doing', he continues, his tongue planted firmly in his cheek, 'your name shall flourish in the printers' shops; thus doing, you shall be of kin to many a poetical preface; thus doing, you shall be most fair, most rich, most wise, most all, you shall dwell upon superlatives' (Sidney 1973: 121). As for what the poet receives for all this, Gabriel Harvey, as usual, has something to say. In his 'Gallant familiar Letter' to Immerito, after quoting from *The Shepheardes Calender* a portion of Cuddie's exasperated complaint about the lack of reward afforded poetry, Harvey admits that Cuddie and Hobbinoll have been remiss in their service to '*Mistresse Poetrie*' but that Colin Clout has lately served her well. With slight envy and much ironic exaggeration, Harvey imagines the rewards accompanying Colin's service to the lady poetry: 'peraduenture, by the meanes of hir special fauour, and some personall priuiledge, [Colin] may happely liue by *dying Pellicanes*, and purchase great landes, and Lordshippes, with the money, which his *Calendar* and *Dreames* haue, and will affourde him' (*Prose*, 471). As fully aware as Sidney and Harvey of poets' persistently unrealistic expectations, Spenser wrote poetry, whatever ancillary responsibilities, rewards, and disappointments conditioned and attended his labor. And he addresses his patrons not only with the required professions of loyalty and respect but also with sincere appreciation, eloquent candor, and, often, a characteristic touch of subtly ironic play; he treats his dedicatees as intelligent people who will enjoy his poems and endorse their publication.

SPENSER'S LIFE IN PATRONAGE

Colin's initial action in *The Shepheardes Calender*, breaking his pipe, though presented as a frustrated reaction to Rosalind's indifference, would have registered most powerfully and suggestively with Spenser's learned readers as a protest against the poet's neglect by patrons, a reading that Kelsey and Peterson's lengthy litany of classical and Renaissance examples and of Spenser's allusions to them convincingly demonstrates (2000). The broken pipe (*calamos*), like the 'afflicted stile' with which the poet attempts to write Elizabeth's glory (I *Proem*, 4), combined with the castration anxiety signaled explicitly by the torn bagpipe in the woodcut to *January* (29), suggests the impotence precipitated by the poet's lack of patrons. Colin's action, like Cuddie's complaints in *October*, proposes that the poet who 'fails to gain support . . . will succeed in fulfilling the "perfecte paterne" of the poet's life like other true poets who preceded him' (Kelsey and Peterson 2000: 237). This portrait of the poet's typically impeded career trajectory is doubly ironic: Colin's refusal to sing paradoxically generates the narrative of *The Shepheardes Calender*, and the fit of pique occurs at the beginning of Spenser's career, before the poet has accomplished anything that merits patronage.

Spenser's ingenious enactment of the poet's predicament introduces a theme voiced by various narrators throughout Spenser's career: reproof of court corruption and, more specifically, dismay over the court's indifference to 'learning' (*RT*, 440) and the consequent lack of support afforded those 'learned Impes' who serve Clio and those who serve Calliope's 'learned skill' (*TM*, 75, 428). While the proverbial figure of the disgruntled poet facing worldly indifference and antagonism is conventional enough to be a cliché, Spenser adds some contemporary force to his complaint by lamenting the deaths of Leicester, Sidney, and Walsingham, whose former influence has been co-opted by Burghley; now, 'learning lies unregarded' (*RT*, 440) at a court in which the 'true wisedome [of] . . . learned forheads' (*TM*, 80–3) has been replaced by the censorious 'rugged forhead' (IV *Proem*, 1) of 'he that now welds all things at his will' (*RT*, 447). According to Spenser and his narrators, Burghley rewards the wrong kind of learning. Although these sentiments, repeated here in *Complaints* and elsewhere throughout Spenser's career, are no doubt sincere expressions of the poet's opinions, Spenser's perennial 'dislike and distrust of the court and courtly life', as noted by C. S. Lewis long ago (1963: 317), suggest a less than enthusiastic desire on Spenser's part to take up life at court.[2] Furthermore, the complaints of Spenser's narrators concerning lack of patronage need not automatically be accorded unmediated biographical relevance; when, for instance, the narrator of *Prothalamion*, who sounds suspiciously like a grown but still dissatisfied Cuddie, bemoans 'my long fruitlesse stay | In Princes Court, and expectation vayne | Of idle hopes, which still doe fly away' (6–8), one might wonder when Spenser accomplished a lengthy residence at court. Be that as it may, the laments of Spenser's narrators should at least be qualified by Spenser's relatively successful life in the world of Elizabethan patronage. Even if his pursuit of patronage never fulfilled his initial aspirations, which themselves may be Colin's and Cuddie's as much as Spenser's own, Spenser succeeded in attracting enough patronage to live fairly comfortably and to write well enough and publish enough to become one of the greatest poets in the English language.

When Spenser was eight or nine, he entered the recently established Merchant Taylors' School as a poor scholar. The school's first headmaster, the influential pedagogue Richard Mulcaster, is probably represented as Wrenock in *The*

Shepheardes Calender, in which case he 'Made [Colin] by arte more cunning in the same' (*December*, 42). Mulcaster may have been Spenser's first patron, for his connections to the Dutch community in London may have led to Spenser's being chosen to compose the translations of poems by Petrarch and Du Bellay included in the English translation of Jan Van der Noot's *Theatre for Worldlings*, published in 1569 with Van der Noot's dedication to Queen Elizabeth. Spenser's translations, according to Van Dorsten, 'mark the almost invisible transition from Tottelian anthology pieces to the late seventies experiments' and thus 'the effective beginning of a new period in English literature' (1970: 63, 75).

Spenser arrived in Cambridge on 28 April 1569 carrying ten shillings from the bequest of the wealthy lawyer Robert Nowell, a gift that must no doubt be considered patronage insofar as it supported the education that enhanced Spenser's poetic abilities; Spenser received two more reported grants from the bequest before he left Cambridge. On 20 May he was admitted as a sizar to Pembroke Hall, and sometime after 3 November 1570 he made the acquaintance of the slightly older Gabriel Harvey, who had been elected fellow of Pembroke after receiving his B.A. from Christ's. The two became intimate friends and doubtless remained so for the rest of Spenser's life. If support, encouragement, and intellectual engagement define one form of patronage, then Harvey, represented as Hobbinol in *The Shepheardes Calender*, must be considered one of the most significant patrons of Spenser's formative years. Broadminded, ambitious, well read, and socially inept, Gabriel Harvey was probably one of the most visible literary personalities of his day. He became an eminent and controversial university teacher and scholar who challenged the orthodoxy of Aristotelian logic, conservative humanist pedagogy, Galenic medicine, and Ptolemaic cosmology by endorsing Ramist, Paracelsian, and Copernican models; he taught Latin rhetoric, Greek, civil law, and medicine. In addition, he was a skilled Latin poet, a prodigious annotator of the books in his vast library, and a proponent of beautiful handwriting, consistent phonetic orthography, and New Style Gregorian dating. He wrote and published letters; university lectures; elegiac, epideictic, and commendatory verse in English and Latin; and an outpouring of defensive invective leveled at Thomas Nashe that is almost as much fun to read as Nashe's endlessly fascinating and scurrilous assault on Harvey.

Since residency was not required while studying for the M.A., Spenser may have left Cambridge any time following his graduation as B.A. in spring 1573 but certainly soon after being granted his M.A. on 26 June 1576. By 1 April 1578, he was employed as secretary to his next patron, John Young, Bishop of Rochester, who had been master of Pembroke during Spenser's time there. Young perhaps knew enough about Spenser to hire him, but Young also seems to have respected Harvey, for he had rescued Harvey from trouble a couple of times in Cambridge. If Harvey helped get Spenser his first position, he performed a genuine act of patronage. As for Young's patronage, the bishop provided entrance into a public career and perhaps time for Spenser to continue work on *The Shepheardes Calender*. Besides room and board, the poet's greatest need is time, and here in Bromley, Kent, Spenser may have had short periods of *otium* (Judson 1945: 49).

Documentary evidence for the next, crucial year of Spenser's life, during which time Spenser's civil and publishing careers took off, is sorely lacking. Some of the brief summary that follows derives from a dubious source, published letters between Spenser and Harvey that span 5 October 1579, when Harvey says Spenser was in London, to 2 (or 10) April 1580, by which time *The Shepheardes Calender* had been published and Spenser apparently served as one of the Earl of Leicester's secretaries, with bigger responsibilities perhaps on the horizon. The time covered by the Spenser–Harvey letters, plus the few months that remained before Spenser arrived with Lord Grey in Ireland by 12 August 1580, furnished Spenser's closest approach to life at court, probably not a very close approach. Similarly, Sidney's implicit or explicit support and encouragement during this time inspired Spenser's poetic aspirations, but the closest Spenser comes to admitting any direct interaction with Sidney is his very subdued statement to Harvey that 'Master *Sidney*, and Master *Dyer*, . . . haue me, I thanke them, in some vse of familiarity' (*Prose*, 6). Still, Spenser probably sought and received approval from Sidney for Immerito's dedication of *The Shepheardes Calender* to him. Characteristically, and oddly, Spenser supplements or even partly displaces the dedication to Sidney with E. K.'s dedicatory epistle to Harvey; furthermore, if E. K. is actually a foil for Harvey and Spenser, which seems likely, then they together make Harvey a secondary patron of the work and, in effect, both patronize it by advertising their own and each other's works, as they do in their published letters.

No one knows what series of events and what people arranged Spenser's appointment as secretary to the new Lord Deputy of Ireland, Arthur Lord Grey de Wilton, and scholarly opinions concerning this crucial event continue to proliferate. Perhaps some offence to Leicester sent Spenser off to Ireland, or perhaps some supporters helped him avoid the fallout from political and religious indiscretions in *The Shepheardes Calender*. More likely, one or more influential persons provided the patronage that led to Spenser's appointment to a very good position. In that case, Spenser accepted the post to pursue his public career, but he may have been motivated in part by either his suspicion of his limited chances for a court career or his inability to see himself as an aspiring courtier. And perhaps Spenser imagined that life in Ireland would afford him what poets traditionally sought from the patrons of their pastoral poems: a small plot of land and a small house in which to write. Eventually, perhaps facilitated in part by Grey's early patronage, Spenser became a landowner in Ireland. His initial appointment as the Lord Deputy's secretary was probably facilitated by Leicester or Sir Henry Sidney, one of the most influential acts of patronage in the history of English literature. No doubt, Spenser would have written had he stayed in England, but much of what he wrote he wrote in Ireland, a fact that partly makes his works what they are.

By the time Spenser returned to England again in 1589, he had a powerful new patron in Walter Ralegh, but in *The Faerie Queene*, published while Spenser was in England, he remembers that when he went to Ireland he left behind Sidney, now dead, the patron who, he tells the Countess of Pembroke in his dedicatory sonnet to her, 'first my Muse did lift out of the flore'; and he remembers that Grey, 'the Patrone of my Muses pupillage', had 'large bountie poured on [him] rife' (Spenser 2001: 734, 731) while he was in Ireland, patronage that may have afforded Spenser some of the security that helped him finish the first three books of his epic. Spenser probably met Ralegh in 1580, when Ralegh served as a captain under Grey, and Spenser and Ralegh perhaps renewed their acquaintance in 1588 when Spenser was in Cork and Ralegh served as mayor in nearby Youghal. If Colin's experiences recounted in *Colin Clouts Come Home Againe* agree 'with the truth in circumstance and matter', as Spenser claims in his dedication of that work to Ralegh (525), then Ralegh (the Shepheard of the Ocean) visited Spenser (Colin Clout) at Kilcolman during the summer or fall of 1589, at which time, if not before, they acquainted each other with their poetic works. According to this scenario, Spenser accompanied Ralegh to England in October of 1589, Ralegh arranged for Spenser's audience with the Queen, at which time Spenser may have read to Elizabeth from his manuscript of *The Faerie Queene*, and, in the next few months, Spenser and his friends orchestrated one of the signal publishing events in English literary history. Spenser's dedication of his epic to the Queen, permission for which may have been provided personally to Spenser or, more likely, arranged by Ralegh, records a mark of patronage that, in Spenser's nearly unique case, was accompanied by a life pension of fifty pounds per annum, granted by the Queen on 25 February 1591 (Berry and Timings 1960). Spenser's pension, apparently an explicit case of cash patronage for a literary work, certainly rewarded the royal praise and patriotic cultural work presumed to be effected in Spenser's national epic, though it is difficult to imagine the pension's being awarded, by tradition over Burghley's objection, in the absence of Spenser's loyal public service to the Crown.

The remainder of Spenser's engagement with the world of patronage in 1590 appears in the complex dedicatory matter appended to the first edition of *The Faerie Queene*: Spenser's 'Letter to Raleigh'; seven commendatory verses, including two by Ralegh and one by Harvey; and seventeen dedicatory sonnets by Spenser to a wide range of powerful Elizabethan figures. In the 'Letter', Spenser defends his poem's epic status while simultaneously apologizing for the fictional subject matter and the allegorical method. In the *Commendatory Verses*, Spenser's friends and fellow poets celebrate the poet's achievement while acknowledging the power of Elizabeth's censure. And in the *Dedicatory Sonnets*, while soliciting both protection and appro- bation and offering gratitude to some, Spenser both disparages his poem and asserts its worth, exploiting the tension between humility and authority to create a signifi- cant poetic work, what Oram calls 'Spenser's brief sonnet sequence' (2008: 115).

Extant copies of the 1590 *Faerie Queene* contain various configurations of the *Dedicatory Sonnets*: some, apparently the first copies to be put up for sale, include ten sonnets; some include seventeen sonnets, a reordered combination of the first eight of the original ten and seven new ones followed by the final two of the original ten; but most copies (over half of those extant) include twenty-five sonnets, the original ten followed by the reordered fifteen (see Brink 2003: 8–9; Johnson 1933: 16). This and a few other anomalies of the edition are vexed bibliographical and biographical issues that have received a variety of critical responses.[3] Spenser arranges his dedi- catees in roughly hierarchical or heraldic order (Brink 2003; Stillman 1985): Sir Christopher Hatton, Lord High Chancellor; William Cecil, Lord Burghley; Edward de Vere, seventeenth Earl of Oxford; Henry Percy, ninth Earl of Northumberland;

George Clifford, third Earl of Cumberland; Robert Devereux, second Earl of Essex; Thomas Butler, tenth Earl of Ormond and Ossery; Charles Howard, Lord High Admiral; Henry Carey, first Lord Hunsdon; Arthur Grey, fourteenth Lord Grey de Wilton; Thomas Sackville, Baron Buckhurst; Sir Francis Walsingham; Captain Sir John Norris; Sir Walter Ralegh; Mary Herbert, Countess of Pembroke; Elizabeth Spencer Carey; and all the ladies of the court. The proliferation of dedications, some, perhaps many, to people Spenser probably never met, certainly makes it difficult to call all these people Spenser's patrons; besides, for many of these dedicatees, Spenser's publishing event was less than a minor blip in their grand and important lives. On the other hand, Spenser addresses them as patrons, and he employs their presence both to assert the importance of his work and to mediate its reception—the primary work of literary patrons. In a sense, Spenser had only two traditional patrons, Grey and Ralegh, unless Sidney should be included; the rest are either friends or people with whom he had only glancing contact.

Spenser probably returned to Ireland early in 1591, no doubt glad to get back to his friends there, one of whom, Lodowick Bryskett, probably deserves mention as one of Spenser's patrons. For one thing, Bryskett probably represented to Spenser a continuing affiliation with Sidney, for Bryskett had been an early friend of Sidney and had accompanied him on his Continental tour. Furthermore, most of the positions Spenser held in Ireland were intimately connected with Bryskett: Spenser replaced Bryskett as clerk of Faculties in the Irish Court of Chancery even before Grey was recalled and served as Bryskett's deputy clerk in the Council of Munster. Finally, Spenser was one of the guests reported to have been present at a gathering at Bryskett's home in 1582, as recorded in Bryskett's *A Discourse of Civil Life*, a composite translation from the Italian of, for the most part, Giambattista Giraldi's *Tre dialoghi della vita civile*; Bryskett replaces the Italian participants in the conversation with his guests, including Spenser, who famously declines to discuss his work in progress, *The Faerie Queene* (Bryskett 1970: 22–3).

From 1591 to 1596, Spenser finished the second installment of *The Faerie Queene*, published it and other works, remained devoted, in his way, to Ralegh, and perhaps sought the patronage of Essex; but the record of his life in the world of literary patronage during this time survives primarily in his appreciative thanks for support printed in the dedications to his works. While Spenser's dedicatory material, in *The Faerie Queene* and in the books that he subsequently published, is thoroughly innovative in its variety and extent, its content, especially in dedications to women, which dominate post-*Faerie Queene* dedications, conforms for the most part to the conventional norms of literary dedication, summarized with grace and concision in Margaret Ascham's 1570 dedication to William Cecil of the posthumous publication of her husband Roger's *Scholemaster*: 'Sondry and reasonable be the causes why learned men haue used to offer and dedicate such workes as they put abrode, to some such personage as they thinke fittest, either in respect of ability of defense, or skill for iugement, or priuite regard of kindenesse and dutie' (Ascham 1970: 173). In a word, Spenser asks his dedicatees to 'vouchsafe' his publications.

Complaints, Spenser's mid-career retrospective anthology, appeared in early 1591, either before or slightly after Spenser returned to Ireland, depending on how one reads a few contemporary accounts concerning the publication. Spenser wrote dedications for five of the nine works included in the volume, all to persons—four of the five women—with whom he probably had some form of minimal personal contact and from whom he claims to have received some kind of support. The first work in the volume, *The Ruines of Time*, Spenser dedicates to Mary Sidney, Countess of Pembroke, whom he thanks for 'manie singular favours and great graces' (Spenser 1989: 231). This dedication, like the one to her in *The Faerie Queene*, expresses Spenser's enormous debt to her brother Philip's support and inspiration, the seed that sprouted but withered with Sidney's death. Three of the works included in the publication offer dedications to three of the daughters of Sir John Spencer of Althorp, with whom Spenser claims kinship in all three dedications. He dedicates *The Teares of the Muses* to Alice Spencer, Lady Strange, wife of Ferdinando Stanley Lord Strange; *Prosopopoia: or Mother Hubberds Tale* to Anne Spencer, Lady Compton and Mounteagle, both of whose husbands—William Stanley, Lord Mounteagle, and Henry, Lord Compton—were dead by 1589; and *Muiopotmos: or The Fate of the Butterflie* to Elizabeth Spencer, Lady Carey, wife of Sir George Carey. The dedications to Lady Strange and Lady Carey mention 'bounties' of which Spenser has been the recipient. The only other dedication in the volume, the only one to a man, and the only one to Leicester during Spenser's career, is the enigmatical sonnet to Elizabeth's former, now dead, favorite that introduces *Virgils Gnat* with a riddling allusion to some 'wrong' suffered by Spenser at Leicester's hand and its apparent allegorization in the poem. In the same year, 1591, appeared the elegy *Daphnaida*, which Spenser dedicates to Helena Snackenborg, Lady Helena Marquesse of Northampton, recently married to Sir Thomas Gorges. Spenser requests her 'honourable favour and protection', but most of the dedication comprises a genealogical outline that praises the dedicatee while justifying the dedication.

In 1595 appeared *Colin Clouts Come Home Againe*, with a dedication to Ralegh dated 27 December 1591, and *Amoretti and Epithalamion*, with a dedication by Spenser's publisher, William Ponsonby, to Sir Robert Needham, whose ship is said to have brought the manuscript to England, and two commendatory poems, probably by Geoffrey Whitney and his son. The dedication to Ralegh continues the complex and enigmatical literary interchange between the two that began in the texts appended to the 1590 *Faerie Queene*; here, amid apparently innocent banter, Spenser thanks Ralegh for 'singular favours and sundrie good turnes' and asks for his protection (526). Spenser was apparently in England sometime during 1596, when the second edition of the first three books of *The Faerie Queene*, published along with the first edition of Books IV through VI, appeared lacking all the original appended texts save Ralegh's and Harvey's commendatory poems. Spenser's final dedication of his life, to two daughters of Francis Russell, Earl of Bedford, prefaces *Fowre Hymnes*, also published in 1596. The dual dedication to Lady Margaret, Countess of Cumberland, wife of George Clifford, and to Lady Anne, Countess of Warwick, wife of Leicester's brother Ambrose Dudley, remarks on the ladies' influence on the composition of the poems, thanks them for 'great graces and honourable favours', and, in what could serve as a summary of all of Spenser's dedications, 'humbly beseech[es them] to vouchsafe the patronage' of Spenser's poems (Spenser 1989: 690). Although *Protha-lamion* (1596), a poem celebrating the betrothal of the two eldest daughters of Edward Somerset, fourth Earl of Worcester, lacks a dedication, its title page, which lists the family members involved in the event, might be thought to serve as a dedication. Spenser may have been seeking the patronage of Worcester or, more likely, he may have been seeking the patronage of the Earl of Essex, who was at the height of his career, is highly praised in the poem, and was at the time Worcester's friend. Although no records indicate that Spenser received patronage from Essex, the earl did pay for Spenser's funeral less than three years later.

SPENSER IN THE BOOK TRADE

Perhaps it is worth reviewing the process that transformed Spenser's manuscripts into books for sale.[4] All of Spenser's books were produced in London by members of the Company of Stationers, and members of the Company were, for the most part, printers, booksellers, or bookbinders or some combination of the three; the word *publisher* did not exist in its modern meaning until the middle of the seventeenth century, but the term is nonetheless helpful to describe the person who arranged for the publication and distribution of a book. For a fairly small number of stationers, such as Spenser's primary publisher William Ponsonby, publishing was a significant aspect of their work in the trade, but for most, publishing was an ancillary activity, 'a form of speculation' (Blayney 1997: 391). Stationers sought out manuscripts to publish, talked authors into publishing their manuscripts, and agreed to publish books by authors seeking publication; since no modern sense of copyright existed, stationers did not need authors' permission to publish manuscripts. If authors were involved, publishers usually paid them small amounts for their manuscripts, which then became the property of the publishers. Few made much money in the sixteenth-century English book trade, least of all the authors, who indeed sometimes paid to have their books published. Once the publisher had a manuscript in hand, he paid a fee for allowance to print to whomever had the authority to grant it, though after the 1586 decree of the Star Chamber, the Stationers' Company took over most of the responsibility for granting authority or allowance to print, despite the fact that government and church authorities remained the official licensers. Thus, the publisher often paid a fee only to the Company for a license, which granted him sole ownership of copy within the Company; the transaction was entered in the Stationers' Register. If the publisher sought extra insurance that his copy would not be infringed upon, he could have the copy registered and entered as his for a further fee to the clerk.

Once the publisher controlled copy, he took the manuscript to a printer, who would, if he took on the job, calculate the amount of paper needed—which would be supplied by the publisher—and the total price for composition, correction, and presswork. Having accepted the printer's price, the publisher purchased paper and delivered it to the printer, who printed the books and delivered them to the publisher in quires or in sheets folded in half, pressed flat in heaps, and tied around a waste sheet; the publisher also received any extra paper and odd printed sheets. The publisher, who was also the wholesaler, sold perhaps fifty percent of the books to Company members for a fifty percent markup and forty percent to retailers for a higher markup since retailers sold for an additional fifty percent markup; the publisher, who was probably also a bookseller, thus saved ten percent for sale in his own shop. He would probably not wholesale any bound copies, though he would probably bind some copies for his shop, especially if he were also a bookbinder, as was Ponsonby. Customers usually bought unbound copies. It is very unclear how many books circulated and how much money anyone made out of all this. In one of his final essays, and with the same informed skepticism displayed in his magisterial *Printers of the Mind*, McKenzie asserts that there is 'still no satisfactory model of the economics of the London trade...during the hand-press period' and goes on to demonstrate that the surviving data can confirm neither the proportion of total output represented by surviving books nor the number printed for most editions (2002: 553, 555–6). Blayney's imaginary publisher of a play in 1600 makes four or five pounds from his eight hundred copies, which Blayney is hard pressed to find worth the effort (1997: 405, 412). Edmund Spenser decided quite early in his life that he would write and publish books, but how much money he made, how many of his books were put up for sale, and how closely he attended personally to the printing and publishing of his books—that is, how much time he spent in St Paul's Church-yard and how well he knew his stationers—remain obscure (for further information on this see Chapter 35 below).

In 1569, Henry Bynneman printed and published in octavo at the sign of the Mermaid on Knightrider Street the English translation of *A Theatre for Worldlings*, including Spenser's translations from Petrarch and Du Bellay; the Dutch and French versions had been printed the previous year by John Day. Among Spenser's works printed during the poet's lifetime, only one other, *Amoretti and Epithalamion*, is an octavo; all the rest are quartos. One of the most important Elizabethan printers, Bynneman received the patronage of Archbishop Parker and Christopher Hatton, and through Leicester and Hatton held the privilege from 1578 to 1580 to print dictionaries, chronicles, and histories. During his career from 1566 to 1583, he printed some two hundred titles in multiple editions, including Holinshed's *Chronicles* in 1577 (2,835 small folio pages) and many classical and Continental writers: Aristotle, Boccaccio, Castiglione, Cicero, Erasmus, Plutarch, and Ovid, among others. In 1580, he printed and published *Three Proper, Wittie, and Familiar Letters*, the Spenser–Harvey letters. His books, according to Clegg, 'epitomize the world of English letters during the English Renaissance' (1996: 40), which suggests for young Edmund Spenser a rather propitious entry into the London book trade.

Spenser's next publication, *The Shepheardes Calender* in 1579, was, along with the 1590 *Faerie Queene*, one of the most typographically significant literary publications of the second half of the sixteenth century, and, at five editions through 1597, one of only three of the poet's works to be reprinted during his lifetime, the other two being *Daphnaida* and the second edition of the first three books of *The Faerie Queene*, both in 1596. Hugh Singleton, bookseller, printer, and bookbinder from 1548 to 1593, printed and published the book at the sign of the Golden Tun in Creede Lane. The book's distinctively innovative typographical design, especially for an English literary publication from this relatively early date, 'deployed typography as part of its meaning in much the same manner' as Bynneman's printing of John Whitgift's *The Defence of the Aunswere to the Admonition* (1574): 'to indicate the different character of the constituent parts; just as scholarly books distinguished between the author's text and commentary, the *Calender* blended argument (italic), eclogue (black-letter), and gloss (roman)', together with the woodcuts, to 'register the polyphony within the text' (Bland 1998: 100).

Additionally, as Heninger points out, 'the typographical layout of *The Shepheardes Calender* follows explicitly the format of an edition of Jacopo Sannazaro's *Arcadia* prepared by Francesco Sansovino and printed by Giovanni Varisco at Venice in 1571' (1988: 35). Heninger argues that the decision concerning the design, which he links to Harvey, was meant 'to flatter Sidney, announce allegiance to him, and secure his good offices' (1988: 42) in anticipation of trouble connected with the hazardous aspects of the book's subject matter, particularly its allusions to religious controversy and the French match. From this perspective, and with Bland's implicit suggestion of an allusion to Whitgift's *Defence* in the design of the *Calender*, Spenser's book revives the memory of events that broke over Cambridge in 1569, Spenser's first year there, and becomes a late addition to the *Admonition* Controversy, implicitly waving Thomas Cartwright's banner in the context of the French match. Singleton, far from an innocent bystander, spent his long career printing mostly protestant religious books, including, most dangerously and in the same year as the *Calender*, John Stubbes's *Gaping Gulf*, for which he, Stubbes, and the publisher William Page were arrested, convicted of conspiracy to incite sedition, and sentenced to have their right hands amputated. Singleton was pardoned, apparently because of his old age but perhaps with the help of Walsingham. It is difficult not to associate the activities in Singleton's printing house in 1579 with Sidney's *Letter . . . to Queen Elizabeth, touching her marriage with Monsieur* (Sidney 1973: 33–7), thus adding another layer of enticing but unsubstantiated relationship between Spenser and Harvey and the Leicester–Sidney circle.

The Stationers' Register records Singleton assigning copy of the *Calender* over to John Harrison, the younger (known to bibliographers as John Harrison II), on 29 October 1580, and Harrison held rights to the copy until his death in 1618, publishing six editions between 1581 and 1617, including those of 1611 and 1617 that became parts of Matthew Lownes's folio editions of Spenser's *Works*. With five editions during Spenser's lifetime, the *Calender* has often been assumed to be Spenser's most popular and best-selling work, and the assumption might be correct, but McKenzie warns against 'drawing inferences about total demand from the number of known editions' (2002: 556). Especially in the case of a literary work, for which demand would be low or unknown, a publisher would, given the high cost of paper, find it profitable to produce a small edition that would be likely to sell out; another edition would be even less expensive to produce because the copy would not have to be licensed or registered again. Four or five editions of the *Calender* may have sold out, but the editions were probably small, especially considering Harrison's reputation as a sly businessman. According to McKerrow, Harrison 'was constantly breaking the rules and orders of the Company and was fined on several occasions for infringing other men's copyrights' (1910: 125–6), including his distribution in London of Waldegrave's pirated edition of Sidney's *Arcadia* (1599). Harrison occupied the same place of business, at the sign of the Golden Anchor in Paternoster Row, for his long career, selling books and publishing a wide range of titles, including, as in the case of the *Calender*, successive editions of Shakespeare's *Lucrece* and *Venus and Adonis*. Thomas East printed the second edition of the *Calender* in 1581, John Wolfe printed the third in 1586, John Windet the fourth in 1591, and Thomas Creede the fifth in 1597.

William Ponsonby (1547?–1604)—bookbinder, bookseller, publisher, and prominent member of the Stationers' Company from 1571 to 1604—caused to be printed and sold a body of work, including most of Spenser's and Sidney's publications, that earned him McKerrow's celebration as 'the most important publisher of the Elizabethan age' (1910: 217). McKerrow's pronouncement probably derives in part from Ponsonby's connection with the works of Sidney and Spenser and may also record the great bibliographer's more general inclination to value literary and historical texts over other types of publications, for the range of subject matter among Ponsonby's books deviates markedly from the norm. Bennett's estimates of the percentages of Elizabethan books in various categories, based on Klotz's subject analysis of 'English printed books' in the Huntington Library's chronological file, provides a rough norm: religion (40%); literature (25%); geography, history, and news (10%); law (10%); arithmetic, astronomy, and popular science (8%); commerce, economics, education, and conduct (5%); and miscellaneous (2%) (Bennett 1965: 269–70; Klotz 1938: 417–18). Since these figures appear to record only books printed in English and take no account of output, they substantially distort total production and probably magnify the percentage in the literature category, which makes the distribution among Ponsonby's publications all the more unusual. Of a total of sixty-six titles, including two published in partnership and excluding nine reprinted editions, Ponsonby published twenty-seven literary volumes (41%); twenty-two volumes on subjects of history, military science, and political philosophy (34%); fourteen volumes on religion (21%); and three volumes on practical science (4%). Bennett's categories and mine do not quite align, but the differences apparent in the categories of literature and religion are quite striking. Although Ponsonby published works on all these subjects throughout his career, religious works marked his early years (1579–89), literature the prolific middle of his career (1590–96), and history and military science his later years (1596–1604). As his success and reputation grew, so did the format size of his books: he started out publishing octavos, graduated to quartos by 1589, and published nine folios near the end of his career.

Apprenticed to William Norton in 1560, Ponsonby took up his freedom in the Company of Stationers on 11 January 1571, opening a shop before 25 March 1577 in large quarters opposite the great north door in St Paul's Churchyard, at the sign of the Bishop's Head. He took on two apprentices—the second of whom, Edward Blount, became one of the partners in publishing Shakespeare's First Folio—and he married Joan Coldock, daughter of Francis Coldock, master of the Stationers' Company in 1591–2 and 1595–6. On 17 June 1577, Ponsonby made his first entry in the Stationers' Register and, in 1579, published John Allday's anthology *The Praise and Dispraise of Women*. This culturally significant book resurrects the memory of *The First Blast of the Trumpet*, John Knox's incendiary diatribe against female rule, in order to appraise the topic and defeat Knox's position with varied and open-minded inquiry. Of the sixteen volumes Ponsonby published between 1577 and 1586, ten endorse resolute but moderate protestant views consistent with those of the Continental reformers favored by Elizabeth and the Earl of Leicester. Among these books, Ponsonby published three translations (from Latin and French) of works by Heinrich Bullinger, the important Zurich reformer whose commentary on Revelation influenced Van der Noot's *Theatre* and whose championing of the Psalms of David as lyric poetry influenced the translations of Sidney and the Countess of Pembroke. Ponsonby's first publishing excursions into imaginative literature included Henry Middleton's beautiful printing of *Sacrosancta bucolica* (1583), Ogerius Bellehachius's Latin pastoral poem in honor of Elizabeth, and the pastoral romance *Gwydonius*, or *Greene's Card of Fancy* (1584), one of the first works by the notorious Robert Greene.

In November 1586, a month after Sidney's death, Ponsonby initiated a series of events with significant consequences for both his career and English literature. Having discovered that a fellow stationer had submitted for licensing a manuscript of what is now known as Sidney's *Old Arcadia*, Ponsonby conveyed this intelligence to Sidney's friend Fulke Greville, who, on the same day, wrote to Walsingham to recount the episode. In the months that followed, Sidney's friends and relations went to work, and by 1588 Ponsonby had permission from Sidney's agents to license the *New Arcadia* to his copy; by 1590, using his contacts with Sidney's agents in concert with the regulatory power of the Stationers' Company, Ponsonby had cornered the market on publications related to Sidney, including those of the Countess of Pembroke and her associates. It is perhaps through these relations that Ponsonby became the publisher of *The Faerie Queene* and the rest of the works Spenser published during his life. Loewenstein suggests the ways in which Ponsonby's actions involving the publication of Sidney's and Spenser's works represented a significant moment in the development of the concept of intellectual property (1996: 100–2). Another influential consequence of Ponsonby's 1590 publications is outlined by Bland: the printing of the 1590 editions of *Arcadia* and *The Faerie Queene* in English roman type helped precipitate a shift in the typography of literary works. Of the five plays printed in London in 1590, all were printed in black letter; of the eighteen plays printed in 1591, seventeen were printed in roman. From that point on, roman type predominated in the printing of literary works. Bland believes that Ponsonby and his Sidney connections made a 'deliberate decision . . . to associate Spenser with Sidney through typography and format', a circumstance made all the more likely given the close association between John Wolfe, who printed the 1590 *Faerie Queene*, and John Windet, who printed the *Arcadia* (Huffman 1988; Bland 1998: 106–10).[5]

Between 1590 and 1596, Ponsonby published all of Spenser's remaining works printed during the poet's lifetime, with the exception of *Axiochus*, a translation from the Greek of a pseudo-Platonic work, which was printed and published by Cuthbert Burbie in 1592 and is probably the work of Spenser. The printers Ponsonby employed to print Spenser's works were the same ones who printed the majority of his other publications until his death in 1604. Thomas Orwin printed *Complaints* and *Daphnaida* in 1591; Peter Short printed *Amoretti and Epithalamion* in 1595, the same year that Thomas Creede printed *Colin Clouts Come Home Againe*; Richard Field, who became Ponsonby's most often employed printer, printed both parts of *The Faerie Queene* and *Fowre Hymnes* in 1596; the printer of *Prothalamion* in 1596 is unknown, but may have been Orwin.

During his last decade and a half, Ponsonby also published Fraunce's *Ivychurch* and *Emanuel* (1591), both dedicated to the Countess of Pembroke; Sidney's 1593 folio *Arcadia* and 1598 folio *Works*; Ralegh's *The Flight of the Revenge* (1591); Chapman's *The Shadow of Night* (1594); the Countess of Pembroke's translations of Garnier's *Antonie* (1595) and de Mornay's *Discourse* (1600); a translation of Machiavelli's *Florentine History* (1595); *A Historie of George Castriot* (1596), with a commendatory sonnet by Spenser; plus several large folios, including Holland's translation of Plutarch's *Moral Works* (1603) and Edmondes's *Observations on Caesar's Commentaries* (1604).

Following Ponsonby's death in 1604, rights to many of his titles, including Spenser's works, were transferred to Simon Waterson, Ponsonby's brother-in-law, who, two months later, turned over to Matthew Lownes the rights to most of these books, including Spenser's. In 1609 Lownes published a folio *Faerie Queene*, including the *Mutabilitie Cantos*, printed, as would be all his Spenser folios, by his brother Humphrey Lownes, the only exception being the 1617 *Shepheardes Calender*, which John Harrison II still held the rights to; apparently, Matthew Lownes made some kind of an agreement with Harrison. The folios of 1611 to 1617 were printed in sections to be sold separately, and in a recent article Galbraith explains the intricacies of these printings as well as pointing out, based on his own calculations, that the folio editions, far from being the lavish editions one might expect, were less costly to produce than quartos like Ponsonby's would have been (2006: 30). Matthew Lownes entered Spenser's *A View of the Present State of Ireland* in the Stationers' Register on 14 April 1598 but apparently never printed it, 'probably because he was unable to obtain the necessary authority' (Johnson 1933: 51). The *View* was finally published in 1633 in Dublin by Sir James Ware in a slightly expurgated version (Spenser 1997: xxi–xxvi).

Although several contemporary manuscript copies of the *View* and of some of Spenser's poems are extant, no holograph manuscripts of any of Spenser's works are known to exist; therefore, those who take pleasure and find profit in the reading of

Spenser's books owe a debt not only to the poet himself and to the patrons who supported and encouraged him but especially to the stationers who produced the books that have facilitated the survival of Spenser's works.

NOTES

1. Spenser (1989), 223, 334. All references to Spenser's shorter poems are to this edition and are cited in the text by line number for poems and by page number, as here, for other texts.
2. For further examples of Spenser's criticism of the court and court patronage, see *MHT*, 892–918, and *CCH*, 660–794. For two complementary views of Spenser's career and courtly aspirations that differ in emphasis from the view expressed here, see Helgerson (1978) and Oram (2005).
3. The paratexts of the 1590 *Faerie Queene* have received some attention, but there is much more to be done. See Brink (2003), Erickson (1992, 1997), Loewenstein (1996), D. L. Miller (1987), Oram (2008), Owens (2002), Teskey (1990), and the eleven essays on the subject in Erickson (2005).
4. My brief outline of the process of book publication in sixteenth-century London derives from Bennett (1965), Bland (1999), Blayney (1997), Gaskell (1971), Johnson (1933), Kastan (2002), McKenzie (1969, 2002), and, of course, McKerrow (1951).
5. The bibliographical description of the printing of Spenser's books, compared, for instance, to that of Shakespeare's plays, remains in its infancy. But much work has been done on the 1590 *Faerie Queene*. See Bland (1998), Brink (2003), Galbraith (2006), Johnson (1933), Suzuki (2005), Yamashita (1993), and Zurcher (2005, 2005–6).

BIBLIOGRAPHY

Ascham, R. (1970). *English Works*, ed. W. A. Wright. Cambridge: Cambridge University Press.

Bates, C. (2002). 'Literature and the Court', in D. Lowenstein and J. Mueller (eds), *The Cambridge History of Early Modern English Literature*. Cambridge: Cambridge University Press, 343–73.

Bennett, H. S. (1965). *English Books and Readers: 1558 to 1603*. Cambridge: Cambridge University Press.

Berry, H., and E. K. Timings (1960). 'Spenser's Pension'. *RES* NS 11/43: 254–9.

Bland, M. (1998). 'The Appearance of the Text in Early Modern England'. *TEXT: An Interdisciplinary Annual of Textual Studies* 11: 91–154.

—— (1999). 'The London Book-Trade in 1600', in D. S. Kastan (ed.), *A Companion to Shakespeare*. Oxford: Blackwell, 450–63.

Blayney, P. W. M. (1997). 'The Publication of Playbooks', in J. D. Cox and D. S. Kastan (eds), *A New History of Early English Drama*. New York: Columbia University Press, 383–422.

Brennan, M. (1983). 'William Ponsonby: Elizabethan Stationer'. *Analytical and Enumerative Bibliography* 7/3: 91–110.

—— (1988). *Literary Patronage in the English Renaissance: The Pembroke Family*. London/New York: Routledge.

Brink, J. R. (1991). 'Who Fashioned Edmund Spenser?: The Textual History of *Complaints*'. *SP* 88/2: 153–68.

—— (1996). '"All his minde on honour fixed": The Preferment of Edmund Spenser', in J. H. Anderson, D. Cheney, and D. A. Richardson (eds), *Spenser's Life and the Subject of Biography*. Amherst, MA: University of Massachusetts Press, 45–64.

—— (2003). 'Materialist History of the Publication of Spenser's *Faerie Queene*'. *RES* NS 54/213: 1–26.

—— (2005). 'Precedence and Patronage: The Ordering of Spenser's Dedicatory Sonnets (1590)', in W. Erickson (ed.), *The 1590* Faerie Queene: *Paratexts and Publishing*. Studies in the Literary Imagination 38(2): 52–72.

Bryskett, Lodowick (1970). *A Discourse of Civill Life*, ed. T. E. White. Northridge, CA: San Fernando Valley State College.

Burlinson, C., and A. Zurcher (2005). '"Secretary to Lord Grey Lord Deputie here": Edmund Spenser's Irish Papers'. *The Library* 7th SER 6(1): 30–75.

Clegg, C. S. (1996). 'Henry Bynneman', in J. K. Bracken and J. Silver (eds), *The British Literary Book Trade, 1475–1700*, Dictionary of Literary Biography 170. Detroit, MI: Gale Research, 37–40.

—— (1997). *Press Censorship in Elizabethan England*. Cambridge: Cambridge University Press.

Duff, E. G. (1948). *A Century of the English Book Trade*. London: The Bibliographical Society.

Erickson, W. (1992). 'Spenser's Letter to Ralegh and the Literary Politics of *The Faerie Queene*'s 1590 Publication'. *SSt* 10: 139–74.

—— (1997). 'Spenser and His Friends Stage a Publishing Event: Praise, Play, and Warning in the Commendatory Verses to the 1590 *Faerie Queene*'. *Renaissance Papers* 13–22.

—— (ed.) (2005). *The 1590* Faerie Queene: *Paratexts and Publishing*. Studies in the Literary Imagination 38(2).

Fox, A. (1995). 'The Complaint of Poetry for the Death of Liberality: The Decline of Literary Patronage in the 1590s', in J. Guy (ed.), *The Reign of Elizabeth I: Court and Culture in the Last Decade*. Cambridge: Cambridge University Press, 229–57.

Galbraith, S. K. (2006). 'Spenser's First Folio: The Do-it-Yourself Edition'. *SSt* 21: 21–49.

Gaskell, P. (1971). *A New Introduction to Bibliography*. New York/Oxford: Oxford University Press.

Geimer, R. A. (1969). 'Spenser's Ryhme or Churchyard's Reason: Evidence of Churchyard's First Pension'. *RES* NS 20(79): 306–9.

Hannay, M. P. (1990). *Philip's Phoenix: Mary Sidney, Countess of Pembroke*. New York/Oxford: Oxford University Press.

Helgerson, R. (1978). 'The New Poet Presents Himself: Spenser and the Idea of a Literary Career'. *PMLA* 93(5): 893–911.

Heninger, S. K., Jr. (1988). 'The Typographical Layout of Spenser's *Shepheardes Calender*', in K. J. Holtgen, P. M. Daly, and W. Lottes (eds), *Word and the Visual Imagination: Studies in the Interaction of English Literature and the Visual Arts*. Erlangen, Germany: Universitie-Bibliothek Erlangen-Nurnberg, 33–71.

Huffman, C. C. (1988). *Elizabethan Impressions: John Wolfe and His Press*. New York: AMS Press.

Johnson, F. R. (1933). *A Critical Bibliography of the Works of Edmund Spenser*. Baltimore: Johns Hopkins University Press.

Judge, C. B. (1934). *Elizabethan Book-Pirates*. Cambridge, MA: Harvard University Press.

Judson, A. C. (1945). *The Life of Edmund Spenser*. Baltimore: Johns Hopkins Press.

Kastan, D. S. (2002). 'Print, Literary Culture, and the Book Trade', in D. Loewenstein and J. Mueller (eds), *The Cambridge History of Early Modern English Literature*. Cambridge: Cambridge University Press, 81–116.

Kelsey, L., and R. S. Peterson (2000). 'Rereading Colin's Broken Pipe: Spenser and the Problem of Patronage'. *SSt* 14: 233–72.

Klotz, E. L. (1938). 'A Subject Analysis of English Imprints for Every Tenth Year from 1480 to 1640'. *HLQ* 1(4): 417–19.

Lamb, M. E. (1982). 'The Countess of Pembroke's Patronage'. *ELR* 12(2): 162–79.

Lewis, C. S. (1963). *The Allegory of Love: A Study in Medieval Tradition*. New York: Oxford University Press.

Loewenstein, J. (1988). 'For a History of Literary Property: John Wolfe's Reformation'. *ELR* 18: 389–412.

—— (1996). 'Spenser's Retrography: Two Episodes in Post-Petrarchan Bibliography', in J. H. Anderson, D. Cheney, and D. A. Richardson (eds), *Spenser's Life and the Subject of Biography*. Amherst, MA: University of Massachusetts Press, 99–130.

McCabe, R. A. (2007). '"Thine owne nations frend | And Patrone": The Rhetoric of Petition in Harvey and Spenser'. *SSt* 22: 47–72.

McKenzie, D. F. (2002). 'Printing and Publishing 1557–1700: Constraints on the London Book Trades', in J. Barnard and D. F. McKenzie (eds), *The Cambridge History of the Book in Britain*. Cambridge: Cambridge University Press, 553–67.

McKerrow, R. B. (ed.) (1910). *A Dictionary of Printers and Booksellers in England, Scotland, and Ireland, and of Foreign Printers of English Books*. London: The Bibliographical Society.

—— (1951). *An Introduction to Bibliography for Literary Students*. Oxford: Clarendon Press.

McKitterick, D. (2003). *Print, Manuscript, and the Search for Order, 1450–1830*. Cambridge: Cambridge University Press.

Miller, D. L. (1987). 'Figuring Hierarchy: The Dedicatory Sonnets to *The Faerie Queene*'. *Renaissance Papers* 1987: 49–59.

Miller, E. H. (1959). *The Professional Writer in Elizabethan England: A Study of Nondramatic Literature*. Cambridge, MA: Harvard University Press.

Oram, W. A. (1990). 'Spenser's Raleghs'. *SP* 87(3): 341–62.

—— (2005). 'Spenser in Search of an Audience: The Kathleen Williams Lecture for 2004'. *SSt* 20: 23–47.

—— (2008). 'Seventeen Ways of Looking at Nobility: Spenser's Shorter Sonnet Sequence', in *Renaissance Historicisms: Essays in Honor of Arthur Kinney*. Wilmington, DE: University of Delaware Press, 103–19.

Owens, J. (2002). *Enabling Engagements: Edmund Spenser and the Poetics of Patronage*. Montreal: McGill-Queens University Press.

Parry, G. (2002). 'Literary Patronage', in D. Loewenstein and J. Mueller (eds), *The Cambridge History of Early Modern English Literature*. Cambridge: Cambridge University Press, 117–40.

Peterson, R. S. (1998). 'Laurel Crown and Ape's Tail: New Light on Spenser's Career from Sir Thomas Tresham'. *SSt* 12: 1–31.

Plant, M. (1965). *The English Book Trade: An Economic History of the Making and Sale of Books*, 2nd edn. London: Allen and Unwin.

Rosenberg, E. (1955). *Leicester, Patron of Letters*. New York: Columbia University Press.

Sidney, P. (1973). *Miscellaneous Prose of Sir Philip Sidney*, ed. K. Duncan-Jones and J. Van Dorsten. Oxford: Clarendon Press.

Stillman, C. A. (1985). 'Politics, Precedence, and the Dedicatory Sonnets in *The Faerie Queene*'. *SSt* 5: 143–8.

Suzuki, T. (2005). 'A Note on the Errata to the 1590 Quarto of *The Faerie Queene*', in W. Erickson (ed.), *The 1590* Faerie Queene: *Paratexts and Publishing. Studies in the Literary Imagination* 38(2): 1–16.

Teskey, G. (1990). 'Positioning Spenser's Letter to Ralegh', in H. B. de Groot and A. Leggatt (eds), *Craft and Tradition: Essays in Honour of William Blissett.* Calgary: University of Alberta Press, 35–46.

Van Dorsten, J. A. (1970). *The Radical Arts: First Decade of an Elizabethan Renaissance.* Leiden: Leiden University Press.

—— (1981). 'Literary Patronage in Elizabethan England: The Early Phase', in G. F. Lytle and S. Orgel (eds), *Patronage in the Renaissance.* Princeton, NJ: Princeton University Press, 191–206.

Williams, F. B., Jr. (1962). *Index of Dedications and Commendatory Verses in English Books before 1641.* London: The Bibliographical Society.

Yamashita, H., et al. (eds) (1993). *A Textual Companion to* The Faerie Queene *1590.* Tokyo: Kenyusha.

Zurcher, A. (2005). 'Getting It Back to Front in 1590: Spenser's Dedications, Nashe's Insinuations, and Ralegh's Equivocations', in W. Erickson (ed.), *The 1590* Faerie Queene: *Paratexts and Publishing. Studies in the Literary Imagination* 38(2): 173–98.

—— (2005–6). 'Printing *The Faerie Queene* in 1590'. *Studies in Bibliography* 57: 115–50.

CHAPTER 7

SPENSER'S BIOGRAPHERS

PAUL D. STEGNER

SPENSER'S tombstone in Westminster Abbey, which was erected by Anne Clifford, Countess of Dorset, in 1620, praises 'the Prince of Poets in his tyme; whose Divine Spirrit needs noe othir Witness, then the Works which he left behind him' (Cummings, 339). This inscription reaffirms Spenser's self-presentation as England's national poet that began with the promise in E. K.'s 'Epistle' to *The Shepheardes Calender* that the 'new Poete' will be 'beloued of all, embraced of the most, and wondred at of the best' (Spenser 1999: 25). The identification of Spenser's works as the principle witness for his life also signals the close connection between biographical interpretations of his writings and the development of his biography. The primary difficulty facing Spenser's biographers has always been the lack of documentary evidence about significant portions of his personal life and literary and secretarial careers. In response, they consistently have turned to his poetry, prose, and correspondence for details about his life and career.

This turn toward Spenser's works for material about his life merely perpetuates the fictions he himself constructs and provides no 'objective' viewpoint. Many biographical accounts of Spenser's 'exile' to Ireland demonstrate this closed system of interpretation. In an analysis of the dedicatory sonnet to Robert Dudley, Earl of Leicester, in *Virgils Gnat*, Edwin Greenlaw, for instance, uses Spenser's ambiguous reference to being '[w]rong'd' by 'you (great Lord) the causer of my care' to fabricate the story about how Leicester 'sacrificed his young admirer' to exile in Ireland (1910: 557). Spenser's biographers have offered a variety of narratives about how he secured his prominent position in the early modern English literary system, and they recently have expanded their focus to consider in detail the relationship between his literary and professional careers. Yet their life narratives regularly confirm and reinforce Spenser's self-presentation in his literary fictions.

Although the biographical tradition consistently reinscribes Spenser's self-representations, it nevertheless continues to refashion his life to reflect changing literary, cultural, and critical expectations. A survey of the biographical tradition demonstrates how the sixteenth- and early seventeenth-century depiction of Spenser as an excellent though impoverished poet gave way in the late seventeenth century to the image of him as a gentleman poet connected to the aristocratic Despencers of Althorp and intimate friends with Sir Philip Sidney and Sir Walter Raleigh. In turn, this image has largely been replaced in the late twentieth and early twenty-first century with the presentation of Spenser as a 'self-crowned laureate' and a 'self-made man' in his literary and professional careers (Helgerson 1983; Rambuss 2001: 16).

Accounts of Spenser's life also correspond to general changes in the writing of biography.[1] In the late sixteenth and early seventeenth centuries, biographers typically compose short notices and 'character-sketches' that offer personal and sometimes intimate details, but often make no effort to construct a larger chronological account (Nicolson 1928: 53).[2] In the late seventeenth century, though, they begin to attend to individual temperament and to produce comprehensive life narratives. Yet it is not until the eighteenth century, due to the influence of Samuel Johnson and James Boswell, that biographers concentrate on 'the personal and the private life, the life of the inner man' (Edel 1984: 37).[3] Spenser's biographers reflect these trends in life writing, frequently describing the poet's overall serenity and happiness, but they lack too many details to create a complete psychological portrait. In the nineteenth and early twentieth centuries, biography generally moves away from psychological analysis and becomes more 'patriotic and exemplary' (Hamilton 2007: 111). Biographies of Spenser that appear during this period similarly highlight Spenser's contributions not only to the English literary tradition, but also to the formation of a national cultural identity. By the mid-twentieth century, biographers challenge this depiction of Spenser as they increasingly situate Spenser's life and career within a variety of historical and cultural contexts. The development of Spenser's biography is in many ways an ongoing process of rearranging and reinterpreting documentary evidence, anecdotes, and critical theories to produce an image of Spenser that fits a particular historical moment.

THE SIXTEENTH AND SEVENTEENTH CENTURIES

Sixteenth- and seventeenth-century accounts of Spenser's life provide important glimpses into Spenser's literary and professional careers. Yet these biographical notices often give little sense of chronology and offer little verifiable documentary evidence. These accounts contain many anecdotes and claims about Spenser's life and works that subsequent biographers have interpreted with suspicion or dismissed outright.[4] Despite their shortcomings, they are significant because they indicate how Spenser's life was recorded and constructed in the first hundred years after his death. These biographical notices help to solidify the reception of Spenser as Elizabeth's laureate poet and, paradoxically, as an impoverished author exiled to Ireland. In the process, they set many of the terms for subsequent biographical and critical studies.

William Camden, an antiquarian and teacher at Westminster School, provides the earliest accounts of Spenser's life in two Latin biographical sketches (1600 and 1615). Camden's description of Spenser's pre-eminence 'among the English poets of our age' indicates that he had achieved the reputation that he claimed and sought during his literary career. Camden reinforces Spenser's literary standing during his life by describing how poets cast 'their dolefull Verses, and Pens too into his graue' at his funeral. In addition, Camden is the first biographer to include two highly significant professional details of Spenser's life. First, he explains that Spenser, 'labouring with the particular destiny of Poets', experienced 'pouerty' (Cummings, 315–16). This description of Spenser's financial difficulties establishes the biographical foundation of critical interpretations of Spenser as an impoverished and disillusioned poet. Spenser's financial hardship re-emerges in almost every subsequent account of Spenser's life, such as Ben Jonson's much disputed account in *Conversations with William Drummond of Hawthornden* (written 1619) that Spenser suffered such poverty after leaving Ireland that 'he died for lake of bread in King Street' (Cummings, 136). Second, Camden records that Spenser was impoverished 'although hee were Secretary to [Arthur] *Grey* Lord Deputy of *Ireland*', and thus offers the first biographical evidence about Spenser's dual professions of poet and secretary (316).

Subsequent seventeenth-century biographical notices expand on the contrast between Spenser's poetic genius and his professional and personal failures. The most famous reason for Spenser's financial difficulties involves the mutual animosity between him and William Cecil, Lord Burghley. Robert Johnston's sketch of Spenser's life (written before 1639, published 1655) offers the allegation that the poet died 'in misery ... because it was believed that in *Mother Hubbards Tale* he had savagely maligned the Chancellor Cecil' (Cummings, 319). Beginning with Thomas Fuller's 1662 account, moreover, the cause of the Spenser–Burghley hostility is elaborated in the so-called 'rhyme-reason' anecdote, an unfounded story that would nevertheless continue to appear in biographies as late as the mid-nineteenth century. According to Fuller, Burghley attempted to withhold Spenser's royal pension because he believed it was too high (Geimer: 1969). After Spenser presented the Queen a short poetic complaint during her progress that he 'receiv'd nor rhyme nor reason' why his pension had not been forthcoming, she demanded that the pension be paid and rebuked Burghley (Cummings, 320). In a 1675 account, Edward Phillips states that Spenser took Burghley's insult 'so much to Heart, that he contracted a deep Melancholy, which soon after brought his life to a Period' (Cummings, 324). For many biographers, then, Burghley had become the villain in Spenser's life and the cause of his exile, poverty, and eventual disillusionment.

Seventeenth-century biographers also begin to use Spenser's historical allegory as an important lens through which to reconstruct his life narrative. According to the anonymous 1679 biography, which was included in the third folio of Spenser's *Works*, Spenser 'continued in Town, a Poet, a Lover, and a man of Business: A Poet indeed, without a Rival, but not so successful a Lover' because the treachery of Menalcas and 'Apostacy of his Mistress' Rosalind 'gave him occasion bitterly to complain' (Cummings, 325). This attempt to uncover the true identity of his allegorical characters would shape biographical and critical interpretations of Spenser, reaching its zenith in the Old Historicism of the late nineteenth and early twentieth centuries.

Interestingly, the relationship of Spenser to his contemporaries is not a prominent feature of biographical accounts until the late seventeenth century. The antiquarian John Aubrey, in *Brief Lives* (1697), is the first to tell the inaccurate story that Spenser failed to gain a fellowship at Pembroke Hall, losing out to Lancelot Andrewes, later Bishop of Winchester (322). More significantly, biographers pass over Spenser's relationship to Sir Philip Sidney and make no mention of the Areopagus, an unsubstantiated literary circle with members that may have included Spenser, Sidney, Gabriel Harvey, Sir Edward Dyer, and Fulke Greville (Gair 1990). This silence is particularly noteworthy given Spenser's enthusiastic claims to having 'some vse of familiarity' with Sidney, and about Sidney's central role in the group's project to reform English verse (*Prose*, 6). By 1675, however, Phillips states that *The Shepheardes Calender* brought Spenser to Sidney's attention and that 'he made him known to Queen Elizabeth, and by that means got him preferr'd to be Secretary' to his father Sir Henry Sidney, brother-in-law to the Earl of Leicester. This account also attributes Spenser's financial hardship not to the animus of Burghley but to the loss of his 'great Friend' Sidney, which caused Spenser to 'f[a]ll into poverty' (Cummings, 323).

Later biographers emphasize Sidney's influence on Spenser's literary career. According to the popular though unverifiable anecdote first recorded in the 1679 life, Spenser met Sidney after going to Leicester House 'furnish't only with a modest confidence, and the Ninth Canto of the First Book of his *Faery Queen*' (325). Sidney was so impressed after reading the twenty-eighth stanza that he ordered his servant to pay the author fifty pounds. After reading each subsequent stanza, Sidney eventually increased the sum until it reached two hundred pounds, but stopped and 'sent an invitation to the Poet' before he would 'hold himself oblig'd to give him more than he had' (325).[5] After meeting Spenser, Sidney became 'not only his Patron, but his friend too', going so far as to secure from the Queen a pension as '*Poet Laureat*' (325). This misidentification in the 1679 life of Spenser as poet laureate, which in fact was not officially instituted until John Dryden was named to the position during the reign of Charles II in 1668, reflects contemporary desire to establish an illustrious ancestry for the post (Broadus 1921: 33–7). By the end of the seventeenth century, Sidney's place in Spenser's career had become so important that Dryden states that the death of Sidney 'depriv'd the Poet, both of Means and Spirit, to accomplish his Design' of *The Faerie Queene* (Garrett 1996: 263). The development of the Spenser–Sidney relationship reinforces the financial and literary connections between poet and patron and establishes the biographical tradition of Sidney's overarching influence in Spenser's professional and literary careers.

Spenser's Irish experience is another significant feature of many sixteenth- and seventeenth-century biographical accounts. As early as Camden's 1615 notice, Ireland is described as a place of exile where Spenser had 'scarse time or leisure to write or pen any thing' and was robbed and forced out of his estate by 'Rebels' (Cummings, 316). Ben Jonson is the first to blame Irish rebels for the death of Spenser's 'little child new born'—a contention that many later biographers would reject (Cummings, 136). In his 'Preface' to *A View of the Present State of Ireland* (1633), Sir James Ware expands on Spenser's life in Ireland, explaining that Queen Elizabeth bestowed upon Spenser 3,000 acres of land in Co. Cork, and introduces the unfounded story that Spenser had finished *The Faerie Queene*, but that it was lost by the 'disorder and abuse of his servant' (Cummings, 317). The most interesting part of Ware's account is his discussion of how the historical context of Ireland may have affected Spenser's polemical treatment of Ireland in *A View*:

> The troubles and miseries of the time when he wrote it, doe partly excuse him, and surely we may conceive that if hee had lived to see these times . . . he would have omitted those passages which may seeme to lay either any particular aspersion upon some families, or generall upon the Nation. (318)

Ware's attempt to rationalize and excuse the harsh policies directed toward the Irish in *A View* indicates how the text was and continues to be a contentious subject in the reception of Spenser's life and writings. Furthermore, the anonymous biographer in the 1679 third folio introduces the first glimpse of Spenser's descendants in Ireland by recounting a story that his great-grandson Hugolin Spenser attempted to reclaim 'so much of the Lands as could be found to have bin his Ancestors' after the Restoration (Cummings, 326). Later biographers develop the account of Spenser's time in Ireland from simply a means 'to forestall poverty' to include the opportunity for him to 'give his energies to Apollo and the Muses in peace and leisure' (Cummings, 319). This image of Ireland as a temporary retreat for Spenser reappears frequently in biographies through the twentieth century.

THE EIGHTEENTH CENTURY

Eighteenth-century biographers of Spenser do not record a considerable amount of new documentary evidence about his life. In the influential biography of 1715, for example, John Hughes admits the paucity of historical material (Cummings, 340).[6] Yet for biographers generally the greatness of Spenser's writings confirms his standing as an author of 'extraordinary . . . Genius' (Birch 1751: viii). The number of editions of Spenser's works during the period attests to his ongoing popularity and prominent place in English literature. Important biographies of Spenser are appended to editions of his works, including Hughes (1715), Thomas Birch (1751), John Upton (1758), and Ralph Church (1758).[7]

Eighteenth-century accounts continue the seventeenth-century project of extrapolating details about Spenser's life from his writings. In the 1715 edition of Spenser's *Works*, Hughes, partly because of the 'obscure and imperfect' accounts of Spenser's life, writes that 'as to many other Men of Wit and Learning' he is 'to be much better known by his Works than by the History of his Life' (Cummings, 334). Developing this relationship further, Upton, in his 1758 edition of *The Faerie Queene*, writes that a reciprocal relationship exists between Spenser and his works: 'As every original work . . . represents, mirrour-like, the sentiments, ideas and opinions, of the writer; so the knowledge of what relates to the life, family, and friendships of such an author, must in many instances illustrate his writings; and his writings again reflect the image of the inward man' (I: v). For Upton, the life and works may be reflected in each other, but the works contain the 'inward man', the essential Spenser. Consequently, Spenser's poetry has so 'much of himself interspersed, that they are a kind of memoirs' (I: x).

One of the primary contributions of eighteenth-century scholarship to the development of Spenser's biography is the 'refreshing skepticism' about the truthfulness of anecdotal evidence recorded in earlier life accounts (Judson 1953: 162). Hughes, for instance, states that he is 'somewhat uncertain' about the anecdote regarding Spenser sending Sidney the ninth canto of *The Faerie Queene* (Cummings, 335). Yet he includes these stories and other doubtful anecdotes, such as his loss of a fellowship to Andrewes and completion of *The Faerie Queene*. Upton, too, rejects the anecdotal account of Spenser and Sidney's first meeting as 'one of those ill-timed stories handed down to us' (1758: I: v). He nevertheless accepts the 'rhyme-reason' story because it 'does not carry with it any inconsistencies of time or place' (I: vii). At limited points, Spenser's biographers also reject anecdotes that had built up around his life and career. In his 1751 biography, for example, Birch refutes the story of Spenser losing a fellowship to Andrewes by citing a seventeenth-century biography of Andrewes in evidence against it (I: iii). On the whole, however, the absence of documentary evidence apart from previous biographical notices about Spenser makes it impossible for eighteenth-century biographers to confirm their doubts about the anecdotes surrounding Spenser's life.

Spenser's connections with aristocratic circles continue to play an important role in eighteenth-century biographies. Hughes notes that Spenser claimed 'Affinity with some Persons of Distinction' in several dedications of his poems, his friend–patron relationship with Sidney, his 'intimate Friendship' with Sir Walter Raleigh, and his acquaintance with Queen Elizabeth (Cummings, 334, 338). Further, Birch begins his account of Spenser's life by praising his excellent writings, 'his Employment in a publick post, and his Friendship with the most illustrious Contemporaries for Rank and Learning' (1751: I: i). He closely aligns Spenser with the Leicester faction at court, stating that Burghley's animosity toward the poet did not stem from 'any personal Prejudice', but rather from Spenser's 'early Attachment to the Earl of *Leicester*, and afterwards to the Earl of *Essex*' (I: xvi). Along the same lines, the anonymous biographer of Church's 1758 edition of Spenser's *Works* emphasizes Spenser's connection with his aristocratic ancestors, speculating that Spenser's father was originally from the North (I: xviii). The extent to which eighteenth-century biographers develop Spenser's closeness to Sidney may be observed in Upton's depiction of Spenser and Sidney's interactions at Penshurst. According to Upton, ''Tis plain likewise from many passages in his Pastorals, that he often visited at Penshurst in Kent. At this delightful place, with the accomplished Sidney, he studied poetry and philosophy, especially the Platonic, which is interwoven in his poems' (1758: I: xv). This utopian intellectual community becomes the milieu in which Spenser composed the *October* and *November* eclogues and Sidney discovered Spenser's 'genius' and 'persuaded' him to advance his literary career from pastoral to epic (I: xv). These accounts suggest that Spenser may have needed the assistance of aristocratic patrons, but that his genius secured him equal footing with them.

During the eighteenth century, Spenser's religion becomes for the first time a subject of biographical interest. Spenser's treatment (and disapproval) of Puritans in *The Faerie Queene* had been advanced by Jonson, who remarked in *Conversations with Drummond*, 'by the Blating Beast the Puritans were understood' (Cummings, 136). Yet eighteenth-century accounts identify Spenser as sympathetic to Puritan factions. Upton, a clergyman in the Church of England, claims that Spenser was unable to find preferment in England because he not only 'had joined himself to the puritanical party, first to Leicester and Sidney, and after their deaths to the Earl of Essex', but also had criticized Bishop Aylmer and praised Archbishop Grindal in *The Shepheardes Calender* (1758: I: xvii). By contrast, the anonymous biographer of Church's edition expands on Jonson's interpretation of the Blatant Beast, concluding that Spenser's anti-Puritanism had 'probably . . . much offended the Puritans' during the English Civil War and speculating that they might have defaced his funeral monument (1758: I: xlvii).

Eighteenth-century biographers also develop Spenser's professional career and literary life in Ireland. Interestingly, they often focus not on Ireland as a place of exile, but rather as a place of professional advancement and literary productivity. Hughes describes Spenser's Irish experience as an escape from a tumultuous life in England where '[h]is Life now seem'd to be free from the Difficulties which had hitherto perplex'd it' (Cummings, 338). Similarly, biographers depict Spenser's estate at Kilcolman as 'a most pleasant and romantic Situation' where Spenser could write *The Faerie Queene* (Birch 1751: I: xviii). Despite this portrait of leisure, they also stress Spenser's suffering at the hands of the Irish during the uprising of Hugh O'Neill, Earl of Tyrone. In so doing, life narratives of Spenser's Irish experience recall his poetic fictions: the secretary-poet's idyllic retreat at Kilcolman is destroyed, just as the world of Pastorella is invaded by marauders in Book VI of *The Faerie Queene*.

THE NINETEENTH CENTURY

The nineteenth century stands as a period of great activity in Spenser's bio-graphical and critical tradition. The number of editions of Spenser's individual and collected works, inclusion of Spenser in American and English collegiate curricula, and founding of the Spenser Society (1867–94) manifest Spenser's general and academic readership (Radcliffe 1996: 104–48). Biographers and critics apply Old Historicist methods to their accounts of Spenser's life and uncover new information, such as evidence against Spenser formally holding the position of poet laureate, his appearance in Lodowick Bryskett's *Discourse of Civil Life* (1606), his attendance at the Merchant Taylors' School, and the identification of Elizabeth Boyle as his second wife.[8] Biographers also renew their efforts to identify Spenser's ancestry in England and descendants in Ire-land.[9] The first free-standing biography of Spenser appears during this period—Richard W. Church's *Spenser* (1879), which is included in the English Men of Letters Series. Significant biographers include Henry Todd (1805), George Craik (1845), John S. Hart (1847), Francis J. Child (1855), John Payne Collier (1862), J. W. Hales (1869), and Alexander B. Grosart (1882–4).

Nineteenth-century biographers continue to praise Spenser as a poetic genius who enjoyed immediate fame and success with the appearance of *The Shepheardes Calender*, which only increased with the publication of the two installments of *The Faerie Queene*. Indeed, Church describes the publication of Spenser's epic as a turning point in English literary history and identifies Spenser as the 'harbinger and announcing sign' of a new era of greatness in English literature (1879: 35). Biographers renewed their efforts to find Spenser's life in his literary works and interpreted his allegorical characters, such as Rosalind, E. K., and the knights in *The Faerie Queene*, as representing historical figures. Expanding the skepticism that defined eighteenth-century biographies, they also rejected many legends and anecdotes that had accrued in earlier life accounts. In particular, Todd's biography 'demolish[es] much of the mythology surrounding Spenser', including stories that Spenser served with Sir Henry Sidney in the 1570s, the 'rhyme-reason' anecdote, and Jonson's account of Spenser's starvation (Radcliffe 1996: 110). Yet many anecdotes, such as Spenser's formal position as poet laureate, had become so entrenched in the biographical tradition that they continued to be repeated (Craik 1845: III: 186).

In addition, biographers recast Spenser as a poet embodying nineteenth-century aesthetic and poetic ideals. They frequently apologize for Spenser's involvement with the 'foolish scheme' of modeling English versification on classical metrics, which is announced as a project advanced by Spenser, Harvey, Dyer, and Sidney in the Spenser–Harvey correspondence (Child 1855: I: xxi). Furthermore, Hales goes so far as to fashion Spenser as a forerunner to the Romantic poets who, like Milton and Wordsworth, possessed 'a certain great self-containedness . . . that he carried his world with him wherever he went' (1869:

I: xxxi). This literary genealogy from Spenser to Milton to the British Romantics indicates the formation of the canon of English literature and would influence critics through the twentieth century.

Nineteenth-century biographers concentrate on Spenser's involvement in prominent aristocratic and literary circles. Every biographer accepts that Spenser descended from the 'ancient and honourable family of Spencer', though at times they admit the poet's precise relationship is not fully known (Todd 1805: I: iii). By the same token, Spenser's affiliation with the Sidney–Leicester circle occupies a central place. Sidney remains a friend and patron of Spenser. Hart describes the progress of this relationship as a meeting of 'warm hearts and kindred tastes' in which 'acquaintance soon ripened into friendship, and friendship into intimacy' (Hart 1847: 32). Biographers credit Sidney with securing Spenser's estate at Kilcolman, introducing him to a 'circle of those friends' which included Leicester and Grey, and acquainting him with the Queen (49). These aristocratic connections and friendships in England and Ireland identify him as a gentleman not through education or professional advancement, but rather by birthright.

By the middle of the nineteenth century, Spenser's biographers often include another member in the poet's circle of literary friends—William Shakespeare. Interpreting 'our pleasant *Willy*' in *Teares of the Muses* (208) and the shepherd Aetion in *Colin Clouts Come Home Againe* (444) as Shakespeare, Collier 'gladly indulge[s] a belief that he and Spenser were intimate friends' (1862: I: xcvii).[10] Subsequent biographers treat this friendship as unquestionable and even attribute Spenser's unhappiness in Ireland to his separation from Shakespeare. Hales explains that 'to be parted from the friendship of Shakespere—surely this was exile' (1869: xxxi). In so doing, biographers seek to present Spenser as a contemporary author who quickly recognized Shakespeare's greatness in the early 1590s and one well connected with the early modern English literary scene.

Spenser's problematic relationship with the Elizabethan court remains an important subject for biographers at this time. They reiterate the eighteenth-century explanation that his difficulties with Burghley were a consequence of 'the poet's early attachment to the Earl of Leicester, and afterwards to the Earl of Essex; who were both successively heads of a party opposite to the lord treasurer' (Todd 1805: I: lxxxvi–lxxxvii). In addition, several biographers use Spenser's political satire of Burghley as evidence of his strength of character, describing him as 'daring' for speaking out 'plainly and courageously' against a 'political Jesuit' (Collier 1862: I: lxxxiv; Grosart 1882: I: 85). On the other hand, some biographers criticize Spenser's positive representations of the Queen. Child indicts Spenser for 'committing . . . the ineffectual simony of selling niches in the Temple of Fame', and Church criticizes him for his 'gross, shameless, lying flattery paid to the Queen' (Child 1855: li; Church 1879: 136). These critiques anticipate Marx's description of Spenser as 'Elizabeth's arse-kissing poet' (Shepherd 1989: 3).

For nineteenth-century biographers, the subject of Spenser's puritan sympathies becomes an even greater point of contention. For those aligned with High Church Anglicanism, such as Church, an Anglican priest and member of the Oxford

Movement, Spenser may have been a conforming Puritan, but his 'puritanism was political and national, rather than religious' because his poetic mind differed from the austerity of the Calvinists (1879: 16).[11] This tension between political Puritanism and traditional Catholic aestheticism reappears in Church's portrait of Spenser as internally divided between a Puritan hatred of Rome and an appreciation of 'the poetical impressiveness of the old ceremonial' (112). By contrast, the Scottish Presbyterian Grosart cites Milton's description of Spenser by arguing that he was an intensely religious 'Puritan of the grave and "sober" ... [and] "solemn" sort' (1882: I: 34). Spenser's Puritanism functions in such cases as a mirror in which his biographers perceived their own religious convictions.

Spenser's Irish experience re-emerges as a subject of striking disagreement for Spenser's nineteenth-century biographers. They describe Ireland as a place of 'dreary exile' for Spenser that caused him to look 'on the scene of the world as a continual battle-field' (Hales 1869: xxx; Church 1879: 149). Yet several are also critical of the English colonial administration and Spenser's support of its policies. Comparing England's relationship to Ireland with France's toward Algeria in the early nineteenth century, Church criticizes England's 'dreadful policy' toward the Irish and Spenser's inability to look at Ireland with anything but 'greedy eyes' in search of professional and financial advancement (66, 68). However, he contends that Spenser reflects the general attitude of English colonists and suggests that he was 'profoundly unconscious' of English cruelty toward the Irish (173). On the other hand, some biographers defend the harsh political policies in *A View*. Todd is the first biographer to speculate that *A View* 'was probably composed at the command of the queen' (1805: I: cxxiii). More polemically, Grosart defends the massacre at Smerwick and laments the failure of the Elizabethan policies in Ireland, claiming, 'Ireland might have been as England' (1882: I: 152). The subtext of some biographies, notably Church's and Grosart's, is the resemblance between Spenser's Irish experience and nineteenth-century English colonial policies in Ireland.

Spenser's biographers also reinforce the depiction of him as disillusioned and melancholy in his literary and poetic careers. Spenser's 'life-long vein of melancholy', writes Grosart, may be detected as early as the Harvey–Spenser correspondence and recurs throughout his life (1882: I: 185). Rather than follow this tradition of presenting Spenser as disillusioned, Child offers the alternative interpretation that the poet was not subject to 'great sorrow' and that his 'atmosphere of mild melancholy' is 'in part an illusion produced on the reader by the habitually pensive attitude of his mind, or by the melody of his verse' (1855: I: liii). The majority of biographers nevertheless present Spenser's later works as filled with disappointment over a lack of advancement. Even though many dismiss Jonson's account of Spenser's misfortunes during the Irish rebellion as a 'popular exaggeration' and 'mythical', many nevertheless interpret his professional and personal misfortunes as informing his poetic fictions (Hales 1869: liv; Grosart 1882: I: 229). This preserves the traditional coupling between Spenser's poetic genius and his disillusionment.

THE TWENTIETH CENTURY TO 1945

The early twentieth century stands as a period of extensive research and development in Spenser's biographical tradition. Numerous periodical articles record discoveries about Spenser's life and career, including evidence verifying his secretaryship under the Bishop of Rochester, the possible name of Spenser's first wife as Maccabaeus Child, and additional information about Spenser's family and descendants; they also cast doubt on established biographical traditions, such as the existence of the Areopagus.[12] Significant life accounts appear in editions of Spenser's works, including those by William Butler Yeats (1906) and Ernest de Sélincourt (1912). In addition, the first book-length study of Spenser's Irish experience, Pauline Henley's *Spenser in Ireland* (1928), is published during this period. The most extensive and only full-length biography of the twentieth century, Alexander Judson's *Life of Spenser* (1945), appeared as part of Johns Hopkins University's *Variorum Edition* of Spenser's works.

Several twentieth-century biographers depart from earlier life narratives by situating Spenser's life within larger historical contexts. Concentrating on the political side of Spenser's life and writings, Henley challenges the perception of Spenser as 'the unpractical weaver of magic fancies' and argues that he 'could become on occasion the ruthless apostle of coercive government' (1928: 7). Her analysis treats the broad social and political conditions in late sixteenth-century Ireland and Spenser's role in the English colonial program, before turning to consider Irish influences on Spenser's writings. Judson likewise attempts to reconstruct 'the atmosphere in which Spenser moved' and, in the process, to identify him as representative of early modern English habits of thought (1945: vii). Judson explains that Spenser's 'attitude toward the Irish, his aristocratic point of view, his acceptance of current scientific and political theories, his belief in the ethical function of poetry, his thirst for fame, his ardent Protestantism, his love of beauty—all these were thoroughly representative of his epoch' (212). This contextual approach in many ways anticipates the move toward New Historicism in late twentieth-century Spenser studies.

Even though new evidence provided biographers with a more complete understanding of Spenser's life, they still lack many important details about his literary and professional careers. As a consequence, they reiterate many conventional life narratives in order to fill in missing details. In his edition of 1912 De Sélincourt admits that '[t]here is no evidence that' Spenser and Sidney's 'relationship became one of close personal intimacy', but contends that 'Spenser's love for Sidney was probably the deepest formative influence upon his life' (xiii). In the same vein, when discussing Spenser's return to England to oversee the publishing of the 1596 installment of *The Faerie Queene*, Judson conjectures that Spenser spent time with a wide circle of friends that included his Cambridge mentor Harvey, his former employer the Bishop of Rochester, and Raleigh, whom Judson believes Spenser was trying to reinstate in the Queen's favor with the publication of *Colin Clouts Come Home Againe* (1945: 184). This depiction of Spenser's network of friends reinforces the image of Spenser as a gentleman whose company reflects his social standing.

Spenser's autobiographical representations in his literary works and the works themselves also remain the most important archive for understanding Spenser's life. De Sélincourt describes Spenser's self-presentation in his pastoral poems as 'his own idealized autobiography' (1912: xiv). Continuing a well-established interpretive tradition, this approach is often grounded on identifying figures in Spenser's poetic fictions as allegorical self-representations. Judson, for example, not only finds the clearest evidence of Spenser's conflict with Burghley in *Mother Hubberds Tale* and *The Faerie Queene*, but also his long-standing sympathy with Puritanism in the religious eclogues of *The Shepheardes Calender* (1945: 153–4, 177, 33).

Spenser's biographers thus use his poetic and prose works as keys to unlock his true identity. What they claim to find in his writings repeats, though sometimes with different emphases, the well-established interpretation of Spenser's 'nature' as filled with internal contradictions (Yeats 1906: 231). According to Emile Legouis, Spenser may support the Puritans and be 'averse to the beliefs of the Middle Ages, which to his eyes were only superstition and idolatry', but 'in poetic feeling Spenser remained Catholic to the core' (1926: 32–3). According to Henley, the contradictions between Book VI of *The Faerie Queene* and *A View* transform Spenser's Irish experience into a psychomachia: 'It was the struggle in him of the poet against the politician' (1928: 143). Similarly, Yeats explains that Spenser may appear to be a moralist in *The Faerie Queene*, but that he is actually guilty of an 'unconscious hypocrisy' because underneath his moral allegory he is 'all the while . . . thinking of nothing but lovers whose bodies are quivering with the memory or the hope of long embraces' (1906: 234). For his early twentieth-century biographers, even those tensions of which Spenser was not fully aware could be deduced from his literary works.

Biographical treatments of Spenser's Irish experience, perhaps more than any other subject, depict Spenser as internally conflicted. In his famous statement on Spenser's obedience to the English colonial project, Yeats describes how Spenser sacrificed poetic identity to political duty: 'When Spenser wrote of Ireland he wrote as an official, and out of the thoughts and emotions that had been organised by the state' (1906: 238). In *The Allegory of Love* (1936), C. S. Lewis extends this line of reasoning when, in reference to Book V of *The Faerie Queene*, he explains that Spenser 'becomes a bad poet because he is, in certain respects, a bad man' (357). By contrast, de Sélincourt minimizes the influence of Spenser's difficulties in Ireland: '[I]t is easy to make too much of these petty worries; for it is clear enough that they did not seriously disturb his happiness and peace of mind' (1912: xxxiv). In his *Life of Spenser*, Judson concludes in the final analysis that 'the total impression made by his life is that of serenity' (1945: 211). This depiction of Spenser's 'serenity' and happiness counters the frequent image of his disillusionment and echoes the biography appended to the 1679 third folio, which concludes with the claim that Spenser 'was, in a word, compleatly happy in every thing that might render him Glorious, and Inimitable to future Ages' (Cummings, 327). From this perspective, Spenser's transcendent poetic vision and personal happiness remained unclouded by pressing concerns and responsibilities in Ireland.

The Late Twentieth Century:
The Rise of Critical Theory

The post-war ascendancy of New Criticism, with its separation of biography from criticism, contributed to the decline of conventional biographical studies of Spenser. As early as 1925, W. L. Renwick argued for this separation: 'The life of Spenser has been written, so far as it is known—that is, in its main events—and the poems have been related to the life . . . Now, we cannot draw near to Spenser through knowledge of external events . . . or through biography' (3–4). Instead of a development of Spenser's life narrative, Patrick Cheney notes that during the late twentieth century '*chronology replaces biography* as the convenient textual staple of the Spenser edition' (2006: 32). The period after the publication of Judson's *Life of Spenser* in 1945 enters what may be described as a post-biographical phase in Spenser studies.

The return to historicism in the late 1970s nevertheless initiated a reconsideration of the connections between Spenser's life and his literary works and career. New Historicist and other theoretically informed critics generally consider biography in order to situate Spenser's 'social identity' as colonial agent, author, and secretary (Knapp 2003: 61). In *Renaissance Self-Fashioning* (1980), Steven Greenblatt connects Spenser's social mobility to his participation in the general cultural project of self-fashioning. Greenblatt contends that, in the case of Spenser, 'in art and in life, his conception of identity . . . is wedded to his conception of power, and after 1580, of colonial power' (185). As opposed to the early image of Spenser as a gentleman poet, Greenblatt seeks to 'demystify' Spenser by revealing his conformity to state authority.

Critical readings of Spenser's Irish experience similarly stress the interplay between his position as a colonial agent and his representations of early modern Ireland. According to Muriel Bradbrook, Spenser was 'buried in a kind of Elizabethan Siberia' in Ireland and his endurance of this 'brazen world' brought out a 'harshly efficient and repressive' side in *A View* (1960: 103, 109). Ciaran Brady likewise contends that Spenser exhibits 'dark and bloody feelings' about Ireland which cause *A View* to be 'nothing short of a sustained exercise in bad faith' (1986: 18, 41). In an attempt to answer the question of 'what went wrong for Spenser' and 'gave rise to this splintering of moral vision which drove him to write in such a tortured and distorted manner', Brady turns to Spenser's biography and connects the development of his political theory to his persistent difficulties with the Irish (41). Developing Lewis's claim to have discovered evidence of moral corruption in the allegory of *The Faerie Queene*, Andrew Hadfield, in *Edmund Spenser's Irish Experience* (1997), explains that the 'poem and its author ceased to be "mere English" when both left England in the 1570s or 1580s and were "corrupted" by their relationship with Ireland' (202). For Hadfield, Spenser's Irish experience indicates that he 'cannot be read—and never should have been read—as a straightforwardly English writer' (11). In addition, Richard McCabe, in *Spenser's Monstrous Regiment* (2002), considers the English and Irish response to *A View* by examining how the poet's grandson William Spenser petitioned Cromwell to restore his landholdings. McCabe connects William's appeal to 'the ancestral Protestantism of the Spensers' and renunciation of Catholicism to Guyon's escape from the Bowre of Bliss and 'the baleful influence of an Irish Catholic mother, the sort of mother repeatedly attacked in *A View*' (285). These critical reinterpretations of Spenser's life challenge the master narrative of Spenser as England's national poet by historicizing his problematic relationship with the English colonial project in Ireland.

In *Self-Crowned Laureates* (1983), which inaugurates career criticism in Spenser studies, Richard Helgerson examines Spenser's laureate ambitions in the context of the historical formation of authorship. This process involves a 'metamorphic loss of identity' through which Spenser 'ceased to be Master Edmund Spenser of Merchant Taylors' School and Pembroke College, Cambridge, and became Immerito, Colin Clout, the New Poet' (10, 63). This transformation prepares Spenser to assume the role as England's laureate poet. For Helgerson, what Spenser returns to at the end of his career, however, is 'the pastoral, the personal, and the amorous', and what he 'repents is not poetry but his engagement with the active world' (97–8). Such an interpretation of Spenser's inability to maintain the equilibrium between shepherd and poet laureate acts as a variation on the image of Spenser's renunciation and disillusionment in his late life and works.

Subsequent career criticism often centers on Spenser's relationship to the Virgilian authorial progression from pastoral to epic (*cursus* or *rota Vergiliani*) and the tensions between the active and contemplative life in the formation and representation of his literary career. David L. Miller identifies in Spenser's career a 'split poetics' between 'vision' and 'persuasion' that ultimately cannot be sustained (1983: 213, 199). According to Miller, Spenser's later writings manifest that the poet '[n]o longer tr[ies] to carry his vision back into the human community' and fashion virtuous readers; rather, 'he waits to be carried once and for all into the community of his vision' (225). By contrast, Cheney, in *Spenser's Famous Flight* (1993), argues that in *Prothalamion* Spenser in fact displays a 'renewed commitment to the goal of fame and glory organizing the New Poet's career.... When we last glimpse him, he is turning from contemplative back to courtly poetry' (229–30). According to Cheney, Spenser 'reopen[s] his literary career' toward the end of his life rather than becoming disillusioned and withdrawing from the world (22).

In addition, career criticism analyses the place of Spenser's sexuality in his self-presentations as an author. Joseph Lowenstein contends that *Epithalamion*, which represents 'as much an occasion within generic *career* as an event in *biography*', seeks to establish a 'unity of career' (1986: 299–300). Further, he posits that Spenser, like Milton, 'maps matters of vocation on his own sexual biography' and consequently experiences a vocational crisis in his second marriage to Elizabeth Boyle (301). Focusing on representations of same-sex desire in the early modern period, Jonathan Goldberg reconsiders Spenser and Harvey's friendship in *The Shepheardes Calender* and their correspondence. He argues that 'the historically specific situation of the apparatuses of a homosocial pedagogy' provides a site from which to launch 'the Spenserian career—in life, in letters' (1992: 80). Examinations of Spenser's career challenge the innate poetic talent and unquestioned recognition of Spenser's literary works that dominated the biographical tradition and instead emphasize how he negotiated, even as he helped to shape, early modern English literary, cultural, and sexual practices.

Interest in Spenser's career also extends beyond his literary ambitions to his profession as a secretary in England and Ireland. Since Camden's early seventeenth-century account, Spenser's biographers were aware of Spenser's secretarial position under Lord Grey and often read his extra-literary careers as an effort to resist impoverishment. Yet his secretarial and administrative careers were treated as unrelated to his literary works. In *Spenser's Secret Career* (1993), Richard Rambuss explores how 'Spenser's vocational aspirations and agendas as a poet are never cordoned off from his professional pursuit as a secretary of office, status, and political influence' (9). Consequently, Rambuss views Spenser's poetic works, beginning with *The Shepheardes Calender*, 'as an advertisement of Spenser's qualifications for secretaryship' (30). In a subsequent essay, Rambuss accentuates the importance of Spenser's multiple careers, arguing, 'Spenser's laureate aspirations were inscribed within an established career track which projected advancement through dual service as poet/bureaucrat, eventually leading to higher offices' (1996: 14). This image of Spenser as both a professional administrator and a poet reconciles earlier accounts of Spenser's conflict between his poetic vocation and economic necessity and points to a long-term strategy in which he directs his literary and secretarial ambitions toward the same goal.

THE LATE TWENTIETH AND EARLY TWENTY-FIRST CENTURY: BIOGRAPHY RECONSIDERED

The late twentieth and early twenty-first century experiences a return to biography in Spenser studies. Several important discoveries are made, including a contemporary letter that verifies the controversy surrounding the publication of *Mother Hubberds Tale* (Peterson 1998), and additional documentary evidence about Spenser's relationship with his Irish neighbors.[13] A number of short biographical accounts are included in reference works and introductions to Spenser, including those by Ruth Mohl (1990), Donald V. Stump (1996), Colin Burrow (1996), William Oram (1997), Richard Rambuss (2001), Andrew Hadfield (2004), and Patrick Cheney (2006). In addition, several book-length studies, including Simon Shepherd's (1989) Marxist interpretation of Spenser's life, Willy Maley's (1994) chronology, and Gary Waller's (1994) literary life, indicate the influence of critical theory and historicism on the biographical tradition. The publication of *Spenser and the Subject of Biography* (1996), edited by Judith H. Anderson, Donald Cheney, and David A. Richardson, further demonstrates the extent to which these trends will shape the next full-length biography of Spenser. More recently, Andrew Hadfield's '"Secrets and Lies": The Life of Edmund Spenser' (2008) suggests what direction Spenser's biographical tradition will take in the future.

In the wake of critical theory, biographers call attention to the historically situated perspectives of earlier life narratives of Spenser. In particular, Judson's biography is described as a 'fantasy version—appropriate for the 1940s—of what "Spenser" ought to be', and other earlier biographers are criticized for 'displac[ing] politics with poetics' and in the process constructing a 'transcendent Spenser' (Shepherd 1989: 21; Rambuss 1996: 8, 15). In response to this critical self-awareness, biographers acknowledge, in varying degrees, that each narrative of Spenser's life 'will therefore be constructed differently by different readers' because they reflect a variety of personal, political, literary, sexual, and religious investments (Waller 1994: 4). In the place of conventional life narratives, many biographers view his life from a variety of critical perspectives, fashioning, as Stump observes, not 'one Spenser but many Spensers' (1996: 259). The recurring image of Spenser as a 'liminal' poet 'sitting on cultural boundaries' and 'speaking from the margins rather than the center' illustrates one type of shift in biographical accounts of his professional and literary lives (Burrow 1996: 10; Oram 1997: 2). Spenser's identity as an outsider, which results from the increased critical and biographical interest in Spenser's Irish experience and manifests the influence of poststructuralist and postcolonial theory, replaces earlier depictions of him as occupying a privileged role in early modern literature and culture.

In addition to the changes in life narratives, recent biographers and critics show an increased skepticism about the connection between Spenser's life and his works. Since the early eighteenth century Spenser's biographers have admitted the incompleteness of their life accounts, but many have recently called attention to the difficulties of extrapolating Spenser's life from his works (Anderson 1996: x). Miller argues that finding Spenser the man in his works will always fall short: 'we are always invited to seek him...everywhere and nowhere, under erasure throughout the massive thesaurus of his work' (1996: 171). This skepticism extends to the Spenser–Harvey correspondence, which biographers describe as presenting a collection of 'facts' that 'are too good to be true', even while recognizing that the letters are 'the only...source for Spenser's biography at this crucial time' in the early 1580s (Burrow 1996: 4; Woudhuysen, *SE*, 435).[14] This emphasis on the disjunction between Spenser's self-representations and verifiable external evidence stands as one of the most striking shifts in the biographical tradition.

Increased scrutiny also extends to the anecdotes and legends surrounding Spenser's life and career. Biographers have increasingly attempted to 'distinguish facts from inferences that have gained credibility through repetition' (Brink 1997: 94). In *A Spenser Chronology*, the most detailed collection of historical information related to Spenser's life, Maley reflects this critical trend and takes an interdisciplinary approach to synthesize 'the literary life of Spenser...and the historical life of Spenser' (1994: xiii). He responds to the criticism of Judson's biography by aiming 'to abjure "inference, surmise, and conjecture"' and limiting his focus to historical evidence related to Spenser's life (xiv–xv). This leads him to accept Harvey as Spenser's '[e]arly friend and mentor', but to pass over unsubstantiated accounts of his friendship with his patrons and superior Irish administrators (97). Likewise, Maley refrains from connecting Spenser's religion to that of his patrons or contemporaries. The move toward documentary evidence displaces the traditional narrative core of many early biographies but raises new questions of interpretation and method.

At the beginning of the twenty-first century, methodology stands as a central issue in writing Spenser's next biography.[15] The challenge confronting Spenser's biographers remains how (or whether it is possible) to write a life narrative without using his autobiographical self-representations in his literary fictions. The question of where Spenser's 'social identities', as encoded in his literary fictions, end and his personal life and thought begin remains an acute problem. Commenting on the 'apparent timidity of would-be biographers of Spenser', Hadfield remarks, 'we are presented with a fundamental dilemma: either take what appears in the literary works as evidence of the poet's life or abandon any quest for that life and declare that it is unwritable' (2008: 60). In response, he states, 'we should be wary of *not* reading Spenser's poetry in terms of his life and opinions' (67). Analysing the merging of the political and personal in *Epithalamion*, Hadfield speculates that Spenser's representation of the consummation of his marriage 'can be read as a more accurate representation of the poet's life than the passages in the Harvey letters and the paratexts in the *Calendar*' because they 'may be mediated by other concerns. The more literary may, paradoxically, be the more truthful work' (71–2). In this sense, Spenser's writings continue to act as his own key witness and to shape the writing of his life narrative. If recent studies of Spenser's life and career are any indication, Spenser's biographical tradition has moved beyond the earlier idealized accounts about his position as the 'prince of poets'.[16] The influence of historicism and theory evinces that the image of Spenser in the next full-length life narrative will certainly balance his engagement with the realities and pressures of early modern England and Ireland with his vision of poetic fame and 'ioyous rest and endlesse blis' (I.x.52).

NOTES

1. For an overview of the history of biography, see Altick (1969), Parke (1996), and Hamilton (2007).
2. On the development of biography in the seventeenth century, see also Stauffer (1930).
3. On the changes in life writing in the eighteenth century, see Longaker (1931).
4. On Spenser's seventeenth-century biographers, see Wurtsbaugh (1936), 11–28 and Judson (1946).
5. For the Spenser–Sidney friendship, see Judson (1945), 57–61; Pask (1996), 83–112.
6. Frushell explains that Spenser was omitted from Samuel Johnson's *Lives of the Poets* because of the publishers' claim that 'they had no room for Spenser' (1996: 123).

7. Many of these eighteenth-century biographies have been compiled by David Hill Radcliffe and are available online at *Spenser and the Tradition: English Poetry 1579–1830* (http://198.82.142.160/spenser/). On Spenser's eighteenth-century biographers, see Judson (1953).

8. On Spenser's poet laureateship, see Malone (1800), I: 84–5. On Spenser in Bryskett's *Discourse of Civil Life*, see Todd (1805), I: lvi. On the Merchant Taylors' School, see Grosart (1877), xiii–xxv. For a discussion of Elizabeth Boyle, see Grosart (1882–4), I: 200–2. For additional nineteenth-century references relating to Spenser's life, see Carpenter (1923).

9. On Spenser's ancestry and family, see Grosart (1882), I: xi–lxiv. On Spenser's descendants, see Craik (1845), III: 243–52.

10. For Willy see *Variorum*, VIII: 317–21, and Hieatt, *SE*, 641.

11. On the admiration of High Church Anglicans for Spenser, see Radcliffe (1996), 108–9.

12. On Spenser's secretaryship, see Gollancz (1907–8). On his first marriage, see Hamer (1931), Eccles (1931), and Welply (1941), 56–8. On Spenser's family and descendants, see Welply (1940), (1941) 57, and (1944). On the Areopagus, see Maynadier (1909). References to early twentieth-century biographical sources are collected in Carpenter (1923), Atkinson (1937), and McNeir and Provost (1975).

13. On Spenser's Irish experience, see Brink (1994, 1996) and Gillespie and Hadfield (2001).

14. On the questionable 'evidentiary value' of the Spenser–Harvey correspondence, see Quitslund (1996).

15. For a recent overview of methodological questions about writing early modern biography, see Sharpe and Zwicker (2008).

16. The number of projects currently underway demonstrates the resurgence of interest in Spenser's biography: Andrew Hadfield is planning a biography of Spenser, and Jean R. Brink is writing a documentary life of Spenser. I thank Professors Hadfield and Brink for their correspondence about their current work on Spenser's biography.

BIBLIOGRAPHY

Altick, R. D. (1969). *Lives and Letters: A History of Literary Biography in England and America.* New York: Knopf.

Anderson, J. H, D. Cheney, and D. A. Richardson (eds) (1996). *Spenser's Life and the Subject of Biography.* Amherst: University of Massachusetts Press.

Atkinson, D. F. (1937). *Edmund Spenser: A Bibliographical Supplement.* Baltimore: Johns Hopkins University Press.

Birch, T. (1751). 'The Life of Mr. Edmund Spenser', in T. Birch (ed.), *The Faerie Queene*, 3 vols. London: Privately printed, 1: i–xxxvii.

Bradbrook, M. (1960). 'No Room at the Top: Spenser's Pursuit of Fame', in J. R. Brown and B. Harris (eds), *Elizabethan Poetry.* London: Edward Arnold, 91–110.

Brady, C. (1986). 'Spenser's Irish Crisis: Humanism and Experience in the 1590s'. *Past and Present* 111: 17–49.

Brink, J. R. (1994). 'Documenting Edmund Spenser: A New Life Record'. *ANQ: A Quarterly Journal of Short Articles, Notes, and Reviews* 7: 201–8.

—— (1996). '"All his minde on honour fixed": Spenser's Irish Preferment', in J. H. Anderson, D. Cheney, and D. A. Richardson (eds), *Spenser's Life and the Subject of Biography.* Amherst: University of Massachusetts Press, 45–64.

—— (1997). 'Appropriating the Author of *The Faerie Queene*: The Attribution of the *View of the Present State of Ireland* and "A Brief Note of Ireland" to Edmund Spenser', in P. E. Medine and J. A. Wittreich (eds), *Soundings of Things Done: Essays in Early Modern Literature in Honor of S.K. Heninger, Jr.* Newark, NJ: University of Delaware Press, 93–137.

Broadus, E. K. (1921). *The Laureateship: A Study of the Office of Poet Laureate in England.* Oxford: Clarendon Press.

Burrow, C. (1996). *Edmund Spenser.* Plymouth: Northcote House.

Cheney, P. (1993). *Spenser's Famous Flight: A Renaissance Idea of a Literary Career.* Toronto: University of Toronto Press.

—— (2006). 'Life', in B. Van Es (ed.), *A Critical Companion to Spenser Studies.* New York: Palgrave, 18–41.

Child, F. J. (1855). 'Memoir of Spenser', in F. J. Child (ed.), *The Poetical Works of Edmund Spenser*, 5 vols. Boston: Little, Brown; rpt. 5 vols. in 3 vols. Boston: Houghton-Mifflin, 1878, I: vii–lxxiii.

Church, R. (ed.) (1758). *The Faerie Queene of Edmund Spenser*, 4 vols. London: William Faden.

Church, R. W. (1879). *Spenser.* New York: Harper and Brothers.

Collier, J. P. (1862). 'The Life of Spenser', in J. P. Collier (ed.), *The Poetical Works of Edmund Spenser*, 5 vols. London: Bell and Daldy; rpt. London: George Bell and Sons, 1891, I: ix–xc.

Craik, G. L. (1845). *Spenser and His Poetry*, 3 vols. London: Charles Knight; rpt. New York: AMS Press, 1971.

Eccles, M. (1931). 'Spenser's First Marriage'. *TLS* 31 December: 1053.

Edel, L. (1984). *Writing Lives: Principia Biographia.* New York: Norton.

Frushell, R. C. (1999). *Edmund Spenser in the Early Eighteenth Century: Education, Imitation, and the Making of a Literary Model.* Pittsburgh: Duquesne University Press.

Gair, R. (1990). 'Areopagus', in *SE*, 55.

Garrett, M. (ed.) (1996). *Philip Sidney: Critical Heritage.* London: Routledge.

Geimer, R. A. (1969). 'Spenser's Rhyme or Churchyard's Reason: Evidence of Churchyard's First Pension'. *RES* 20: 306–9.

Gillespie, R., and A. Hadfield (2001). 'Two References to Edmund Spenser in Chancery Disputes'. *N&Q* 246: 249–51.

Goldberg, J. (1992). *Sodometries: Renaissance Texts, Modern Sensibilities.* Palo Alto, CA: Stanford University Press.

Gollancz, I. (1907–8). 'Spenseriana'. *Proceedings of the British Academy*, 99–105.

Greenblatt, S. (1980). *Renaissance Self-Fashioning: From More to Shakespeare.* Chicago: University of Chicago Press.

Greenlaw, E. A. (1910). 'Spenser and the Earl of Leicester'. *PMLA* 25: 535–61.

Grosart, A. B. (1882–4). 'Life of Spenser', in A. B. Grosart (ed.), *The Complete Works in Verse and Prose of Edmund Spenser*, 8 vols. London: Privately printed, I: xi–253.

—— (ed.) (1877). *The Spending of the Money of Robert Nowell of Reade Hall, Lancashire: Brother of Dean Alexander Nowell.* London: Privately printed.

Hadfield, A. (1997). *Edmund Spenser's Irish Experience: Wilde Fruit and Salvage Soyl.* Oxford: Clarendon Press.

—— (2004). 'Spenser, Edmund (1552?–1599)', in *NDNB*.

—— (2008). '"Secrets and Lies": The Life of Edmund Spenser', in K. Sharpe and S. N. Zwicker (eds), *Writing Lives: Biography and Textuality, Identity and Representation in Early Modern England.* Oxford: Oxford University Press, 56–73.

Hales, J. W. (1869). 'Edmund Spenser', in R. Morris (ed.), *Complete Works of Edmund Spenser.* London: Macmillan; rpt. 1893.

Hamer, D. (1931). 'Spenser's Marriage'. *RES* 7: 271–90.

Hamilton, N. (2007). *Biography: A Brief History*. Cambridge, MA: Harvard University Press.

Hart, J. S. (1847). *An Essay of the Life and Writings of Edmund Spenser*. New York: Wiley and Putnam.

Helgerson, R. (1983). *Self-Crowned Laureates: Spenser, Jonson, Milton, and the Literary System*. Berkeley: University of California Press.

Henley, P. (1928). *Spenser in Ireland*. Cork: Cork University Press; rpt. New York: Russell and Russell, 1969.

Hume, A. (1984). *Edmund Spenser: Protestant Poet*. Cambridge: Cambridge University Press.

Judson, A. C. (1945). *The Life of Edmund Spenser*. Baltimore: Johns Hopkins University Press.

—— (1946). 'The Seventeenth-Century Lives of Edmund Spenser'. *HLQ* 10: 35–48.

—— (1953). 'The Eighteenth-Century Lives of Edmund Spenser'. *HLQ* 16: 161–81.

King, J. N. (1990). *Spenser's Poetry and the Reformation Tradition*. Princeton, NJ: Princeton University Press.

Knapp, J. (2003). 'Spenser the Priest'. *Representations* 81: 61–78.

Lee, S. (1904). *A Life of William Shakespeare*. New York: Macmillan.

Legouis, E. (1926). *Spenser*. London: J. M. Dent.

Lewis, C. S. (1936). *The Allegory of Love: A Study in the Medieval Tradition*. Oxford: Oxford University Press; rpt. 1986.

Loewenstein, J. (1986). 'Echo's Ring: Orpheus and Spenser's Career', *ELR* 16: 287–302.

Longaker, M. (1931). *English Biography in the Eighteenth Century*. Philadelphia: University of Pennsylvania Press.

McCabe, R. A. (2002). *Spenser's Monstrous Regiment: Elizabethan Ireland and the Poetics of Difference*. Oxford: Oxford University Press.

McNeir, W. F., and F. Provost (eds) (1975). *Edmund Spenser an Annotated Bibliography, 1937–1972*. Pittsburgh: Duquesne University Press.

Maley, W. (1994). *A Spenser Chronology*. Houndmills: Macmillan.

Malone, E. (ed.) (1800). *The Critical and Miscellaneous Prose Works of Dryden*, 4 vols. London: H. Baldwin and Son.

Maynadier, H. (1909). 'The Areopagus of Sidney and Spenser'. *MLR* 4: 289–301.

Miller, D. L. (1983). 'Spenser's Vocation, Spenser's Career'. *ELH* 50: 197–231.

—— (1996). 'The Earl of Cork's Lute', in J. H. Anderson, D. Cheney, and D. A. Richardson (eds), *Spenser's Life and the Subject of Biography*. Amherst: University of Massachusetts Press, 146–71.

Mohl, R. (1990). 'Spenser, Edmund', in *SE*, 668–71.

Nicolson, H. (1928). *The Development of English Biography*. London: Hogarth Press.

Oram, W. A. (1997). *Edmund Spenser*. New York: Twayne.

Parke, C. N. (1996). *Biography: Writing Lives*. New York: Twayne.

Pask, K. (1996). *The Emergence of the English Author: Scripting the Life of the Poet in Early Modern England*. Cambridge: Cambridge University Press.

Peterson, R. S. (1998). 'Laurel Crown and Ape's Tail: New Light on Spenser's Career from Sir Thomas Tresham'. *SSt* 12: 1–35.

Quitslund, J. A. (1996). 'Questionable Evidence in the *Letters* of 1580 between Gabriel Harvey and Edmund Spenser', in J. H. Anderson, D. Cheney, and D. A. Richardson (eds), *Spenser's Life and the Subject of Biography*. Amherst: University of Massachusetts Press, 81–98.

Radcliffe, D. H. (1996). *Edmund Spenser: A Reception History*. Columbia, SC: Camden House.

Rambuss, R. (1993). *Spenser's Secret Career*. Cambridge: Cambridge University Press.

—— (1996). 'Spenser's Lives, Spenser's Careers', in J. H. Anderson, D. Cheney, and D. A. Richardson (eds), *Spenser's Life and the Subject of Biography*. Amherst: University of Massachusetts Press, 1–17.

—— (2001). 'Spenser's Life and Career', in A. Hadfield (ed.), *The Cambridge Companion to Spenser*. Cambridge: Cambridge University Press, 13–36.

Renwick, W. L. (1925). *Edmund Spenser: An Essay on Renaissance Poetry*. London: Edward Arnold.

Sharpe, K., and S. N. Zwicker (eds) (2008). *Writing Lives: Biography and Textuality, Identity and Representation in Early Modern England*. Oxford: Oxford University Press.

Shepherd, S. (1989). *Spenser*. New York: Harvester.

Stauffer, D. A. (1930). *English Biography before 1700*. Cambridge, MA: Harvard University Press; rpt. New York: Russell and Russell.

Stump, D. V. (1996). 'Edmund Spenser', in D. A. Richardson (ed.), *Sixteenth-Century British Nondramatic Writers*, 3rd series, *Dictionary of Literary Biography*, vol. 167. Detroit: Gale Research, 228–63.

Todd, H. J. (1805). 'Some Account of the Life of Spenser', in H. J. Todd (ed.), *The Works of Edmund Spenser*, 8 vols. London: F. C. and J. Rivington, I: iii–clxxiii.

Upton, J. (1758). 'Preface', in J. Upton (ed.), *Spenser's Faerie Queene*, 2 vols. London: J. and R. Tonson, I: v–xlii.

Waller, G. (1994). *Edmund Spenser: A Literary Life*. Houndmills: Macmillan.

Welply, W. H. (1940). 'Edmund Spenser's Brother-in-Law, John Travers'. *N&Q* 179: 74–8, 92–6, 112–15.

—— (1941). 'Some Spenser Problems'. *N&Q* 180: 56–9, 74–6, 92–5, 151, 224, 248, 436–9, 454–9.

—— (1944) 'John Travers—A Correction and Some Additions'. *N&Q* 187: 143–4.

Wurtsbaugh, J. (1936). *Two Centuries of Spenserian Scholarship (1609–1805)*. Baltimore: Johns Hopkins University Press.

Yeats, W. B. (1906). 'Introduction', in W. B. Yeats (ed.), *Poems of Spenser*. Edinburgh: T.C. and E.C. Jack, xiii–lxvii; rpt. 'Edmund Spenser', in *Cutting of an Agate*. New York: Macmillan, 1912, 213–55.

PART II

WORKS

CHAPTER 8

....

A THEATRE FOR WORLDLINGS (1569)

....

TOM MacFAUL

A Theatre wherein be represented as wel the miseries and calamities that follow the voluptuous Wordlings, As also the great ioyes and plesures which the faithfull do enioy. An Argument both profitable and delectable, to all that sincerely loue the word of God by John (Jean) Van der Noot was published in 1569,[1] the year before Queen Elizabeth's 'excommunication' by Pope Pius V set England more firmly in opposition to Roman Catholic Europe than had hitherto been the case. It was written at a time of international crisis, when the Protestant cause in Europe seemed close to defeat (Brigden 2000: 231–2). Spenser's contribution of 'Epigrams' and 'Sonets' to this vigorously Protestant volume prefigures his career as the poet of a nation in (mostly beleaguered) opposition to Rome. As Van der Noot's ideas and images are mostly very common for his time (in the Reformed camp at least) one must be careful not to exaggerate his direct influence on Spenser; nor can one assume that his positions would automatically become Spenser's, though the young scholar would obviously have eagerly read the volume which had given him his first public poetic outing. With these caveats in mind, we can still find almost all of Spenser's later preoccupations in embryo in the *Theatre*: it is dedicated to Queen Elizabeth, as *The Faerie Queene* would be; it is the work of an exile, as Spenser would later consider himself (McCabe 1991); it is concerned with the Low Countries, where Spenser's patron and hero Sidney would die; it is apocalyptic, as some sections of *The Faerie Queene* would be; it is anti-prelatical, as *The Shepheardes Calender* would be (if in a more sophisticated way—McLane 1961) and uses woodcuts as that volume does; its ideas of the world's vanities would become central to the *Complaints* volume, and an important aspect of almost all of Spenser's later verse; and finally it inaugurated Spenser's career as a translator which would continue in *Virgils Gnat* and *The Ruines of Rome*. The volume, published nearly simultaneously in Dutch, French, and English, presents itself as at the centre of a great struggle involving Protestants of three nationalities. Even though his work for the volume was anonymous, the teenage Spenser must have felt enormously flattered to be involved in such a public undertaking, and a sense of international involvement through the writing of poetry stayed with him throughout his career. Although the *Theatre* would scarcely receive much comment had Spenser not contributed to it, it deserves attention in its own right before we can situate Spenser's relation to it, and its influence on his poetic and intellectual development.

Van der Noot's Text

The poems Spenser translated for the *Theatre* are not merely decorative prefatory material; they provide the main texts on which Van der Noot's prose is a commentary. The Dutchman comments directly on the poems by Petrarch/Marot and Du Bellay, though rather more loosely on the apocalyptic 'Sonets' which conclude the selection—his commentary there is more on the original source in Revelation itself, which is expounded at great length. Despite Alfred W. Satterthwaite's comment that 'the prose need not concern us because it clearly does not concern Spenser' (Satterthwaite 1960: 25), it is important to examine what Van der Noot actually has to say. J. A. Van Dorsten describes the *Theatre* as 'not a Puritan tract', arguing that 'paradoxically, the militant Van der Noot's ultimate message is one of unity and grace' (Van Dorsten 1970: 77–8); it is, however, dubious to see the tract's eirenic conclusion as cancelling the anti-Catholicism of the whole. Additionally, if puritanism is not an appropriate term for Van der Noot's outlook, it is also inappropriate for virtually anyone's in 1569—the text can still fairly be taken as indicating a position of 'forward protestantism' (Worden 1996). Its protestantism may not be typical of English reformism at the time (King 1990: 233–4), but it is eager to create a sense of common cause.

Van der Noot tells his dedicatee Queen Elizabeth that he has left his native Low Countries 'as well for that I would not beholde the abhominations of the Romyshe Antechrist, as to escape the handes of the bloud-thirsty' (Aiii^r). He delineates the Queen's virtues in ways that would become typical of Spenser: 'your highnesse as a rare *Phœnix* of your time, are singular and peerelesse in honoure and renoune, in princely maiestie, wisedome, skil, beautie, fauour, mildenesse, curtesie and gentlenesse' (Aiiii^r); he calls her an Astraea, but her principal value is as a champion of international Protestantism. His commendation of the Elector Palatine Frederick as 'the floure of all Christian Princes in these dayes' (Avii^r) may therefore be seen as urging Elizabeth to follow his active example. The position of exile gives Van der Noot a certain authority to speak, and lends his voice urgency.

What he voices is vigorous opposition to the papacy and all its supporters, including a certain anti-prelatical aspect that might not have gone down well with the Queen: 'After this sort did the bishops proceede in al kindes of vanitie and idlenesse, to become loytring prelates puffed vp in pride and presumption, wherby veritie and truth was defaced, and quite abolished' (fol. 18ᵛ); these bishops have some resemblance to Spenser's Orgoglio in *The Faerie Queene* (I.vii–viii). Van der Noot attacks Catholics' 'false priesthood vows not to mary, Sodomitish chastitie, auricular confession, or at least the fashion of it, and other more supersitions' (fol. 27ʳ), and deplores the persistence of papist ritual in the Reformed churches. Even the Eucharist is attacked as a kind of grotesque 'Comedie' (fol. 29ᵛ). Despite Rasmussen's argument that Rome is merely a symbol of worldly vanity rather than the enemy per se (Rasmussen 1980: 18), Van der Noot's concluding eirenicism is more hopeful than really optimistic: 'it is possible yet, namely so long as the malice and violence of Sathan and his membres be bridled & tied shorte, so long shall the godly people haue peace & quietnesse, and shal see some yeares of grace' (fol. 93ᵛ). Nonetheless, he urges the godly to put on the whole armour of God—quietness may be preferable, but it may also be necessary to fight. Van der Noot derives from Du Bellay's poems a compendium of charges against Rome that goes well beyond those implied in the verse itself. Although he regretfully confesses his Catholic origins, the vigour of his attack on Catholicism is ironic, given that he would later reconvert; the text's Protestantism is, however, undoubtedly radical. Typical of this is the reading of the Beast of Revelation, which is taken to symbolize devilish Catholicism. Like Spenser's Dragon in *The Faerie Queene* Book I, the Beast itself can do no harm, only its human agents can: 'Wher as he dallieth onely by playe, there do they seriously force and violently compell' (fol. 21ʳ–21ᵛ). This is an important thought for Spenser: after the dragon is killed at the end of *The Faerie Queene* Book I, we might wonder what further ills can be done—but one of the major points of the poem's structure is that human evils persist after the destruction of their supernatural sponsor (McCabe 1989).

Usefully for Spenser, the volume gives a poetic and philosophical genealogy to protestantism. David Norbrook argues that Van der Noot's volume presents Petrarch 'as a visionary poet groping towards a Protestant world-view even though he placed too much importance on worldly things' (Norbrook 2002: 40). In addition to Petrarch, Van der Noot gives an impressive list of supposed proto-reformers, including William of Occam, Dante, and Savonarola, 'Albeit, the light of Gods truthe was not then so perfectly reueled vnto them as it is now a dayes (God be praised) vnto vs' (fol. 56ʳ). The poems may suggest a similar sense of tradition, but they are a rather baroque compendium, written by the Humanist Petrarch (via the sceptical Marot), the Catholic (if critical) Du Bellay, and the Protestant Van der Noot—as such, they offer a journey from near-darkness to Reformed light. The sequence of poems is not meant to be a seamless whole: in fact, given Du Bellay's infamous attacks on Marot (in *Défense et illustration de la langue français*, 1549), the presentation of the works of these two poets side by side in one volume has a considerable tension. Rasmussen argues that Van der Noot's commentary sees lust as central to humanity's illusory apprehension of the world, and the amorous Petrarch is therefore treated with some ironic and critical distance. Van der Noot also omits poems of Du Bellay that allude directly to Revelation: 'by omitting the sonnets which most explicitly suggest this interpretation, Van Der Noot left the Du Bellay persona without scriptural moorings' (Rasmussen 1980: 13). These moorings are supplied by the apocalyptic Sonets and the extensive commentary on them.

SPENSER'S TRANSLATIONS

The translator of Van der Noot's prose says of the Petrarch/Marot 'Epigrams' 'I haue out of the Brabants speache, turned them into the Englishe tongue' (fol. 13^{r-v}), and of the Du Bellay sonnets, 'I haue translated them out of Dutch into English' (fol. 14^v); this may seem to throw doubt on Spenser's authorship of the translations, but the translator of the prose possibly refers to the precis of the poems which immediately follows, given that the French text says at these points that he has put the subjects of the commentary in *here*—'I'ay voulu *icy* inserer' the Petrarch and 'i'ay *icy* inseré' the Du Bellay ([EVII^v], [EVIII^r], my emphasis). There is little real doubt that the Petrarch/Marot and Du Bellay poems (at least) are by Spenser.

As one might expect from a poet who was only fifteen to seventeen years old, the 'epigrams' and 'sonets' are not particularly impressive work. The translations of the apocalyptic 'sonets' are particularly weak, slavishly following the word order of the French (they make no use of the Dutch at all). This fact, along with the higher proportion of mistaken renderings and of end-stopped lines, led Satterthwaite (1960) to question Spenser's responsibility for these four poems. If he is right, we might wonder why—had Spenser *already* translated the Du Bellay and Marot poems? (If so, we must assume that Spenser was an assiduous youthful translator, with a stock of French translations, rather than assuming that he happened to have the needed poems to hand.)

Spenser's work is not entirely unskilful, though: the versions of Marot/Petrarch show an attempt, however unsystematic, to provide unity through repeated rhyme. Spenser may thereby signal his awareness that this is, in its Petrarchan original, one poem. Grosart thought it unlikely that Spenser 'could have caught so much as he has done of the spirit of Petrarch without having been able to read the Italian original' (Grosart 1882: 18); this is probably overstating the case: it is clear that Spenser is primarily translating Marot's French rather than Petrarch's Italian, but some small incidentals of phrasing indicate that he was also consulting Petrarch. Using an intermediate and better known language to get at an original seems to have been one key method of language acquisition in Spenser's time (Lawrence 2005). A couple of examples will suffice: in Epigram 5, Spenser seems to have got his 'straunge' (3) from Petrarch's 'strania' (49), with no equivalent in Marot; in Epigram 6, Spenser describes the lady as forsaking love 'proudely' (4), deriving from Petrarch's 'superba' (64), whereas she is a 'rebelle' against love in Marot.[2] Joseph Loewenstein suggests that the description of 'The Visions of Petrarch' in *Complaints* as 'formerly translated' 'may refer to Marot's labour and not to Spenser's own prior work' (Loewenstein 1996: 117)—given that the Du Bellay poems are not similarly designated; if this is so, Spenser is clearly conscious of the role of the intermediary poet.

Whilst Spenser is mostly a fairly literal translator of Marot's French, there are some touches which would become characteristically Spenserian. In Epigram 2, his double emphasis on seeming and show (4–5) is added: this would become Spenser's favourite way of warning us that appearances deceive and that outward beauty is about to collapse. In Epigram 3, 'celluy plant heureux' is rendered as 'this royal tree' (12), giving us a stronger sense of pride before a fall; when presenting this idea, the later Spenser tends to invoke concepts of royalty. Certain key Spenserian words are also introduced: his favourite word for death, 'vntimely' (Epigram 1, 12) is used of the hind (rendering Marot's 'en brief temps'); he ends the sequence wanting to 'rest' in the earth (Envoy, 4, rendering Marot's 'gesir'), invoking the key concept with which he would conclude the Mutability Cantos.

The Du Bellay 'Sonets' translations are given continuity with the 'Epigrams' by the repetition of the word 'rest' (on which the former sequence concludes) in their first line, and more Spenserian diction pops up throughout the sequence. Sonet 1 is a fine example: he renders 'le souci du jour laborieux' as 'the careful trauailes of the painefull day' (4), and we could be reading mature Spenser: the double meanings of care-full and travail, and the assonance on disyllabic words giving way to a monosyllabic substantive are highly characteristic. The use of 'the worldes vnstedfastnesse' (12, rendering 'la mondaine inconstance') and 'stay' (14, for 'espère') would return in the Mutability Cantos. In Sonet 6, Spenser uses a characteristic portmanteau word, '*lompe* of fire' (10, my emphasis), suggestive of both lump and lamp. In general, some efforts are made to use more homely diction than Du Bellay's: most notably in needlessly translating the Sirens of Sonet 10 into mermaids.

The oddest thing about the Sonets, of course, is their use of blank verse (the omission of some sonnets being Van der Noot's responsibility). This must have been Spenser's own initiative (even the Dutch versions rhyme). Given that Spenser is one of the great rhymers in English, one cannot suggest that haste was the cause; indeed, one can detect a certain *effort* not to rhyme here. It may partly be a matter of 'attempting to produce unrhymed "sonnets" as some sort of vernacular equivalent to the then very fashionable Neo-Latin epigram' (Van Dorsten 1990: 685), but there may be other, more aesthetic causes for Spenser's decision. The lines generally end with impressive monosyllables which could easily be rhymed upon, and there is a sense of absent rhyme, a certain hollowness in the tone: this is a verse of grandeur as it were asking for the correspondence of rhyme and not receiving it; the dead Roman monuments seem to be hoping for some answer in the present and demonstrating only their irrelevance. If this is not a wholly successful technique, it does have some haunting and haunted moments. When there are occasional half-rhymes, we also sense the tiny echo of greater significance, lost and quiet voices speaking across time; the wailing Nymph of Sonet 8, for example, nearly reaches the music of rhymed verse:

> Where is (quod she) this whilome honored face?
> Where is thy glory and the auncient praise,
> Where all the worldes hap was reposed,
> When erst of Gods and man I worshipt was?   (5–8)

The Du Bellay poems work on the ruins of rhyme as well as of Rome, but they end with an impressive full feminine rhyme, perhaps waking us back to a modern (Reformed) world of meaningful relations: 'And seeing her striken fal with clap of thunder | With so great noyse I start in sodaine wonder' (Sonet 11, 13–14).

A truer wonder, then, is supposed to be found in the last four 'apocalyptic' Sonets, also in blank verse, translating sonnets derived from Revelation and probably written by Van der Noot. Sadly, they are the weakest poems in the sequence, perhaps because they are not Spenser's, perhaps because the originals are also weak (at least in the French from which he was working). Despite their dramatic theme, there is something almost comically bathetic about the verse construction:

> Then did I see the beast and Kings also
> Ioinyng their force to slea the faithfull man.
> But this fierce hatefull beast and all hir traine,
> Is pitilesse throwne downe in pit of fire.   (Sonet 14, 11–14)

Only when the biblical cadence itself is preserved does the verse impress: 'A voyce then sayde, beholde the bright abode | Of God and men. For he shall be their God, | And all their teares he shall wipe cleane away' (Sonet 15, 5–7). The half-rhyme here has an effect, but it is mainly the memory of Tyndale's version that gives this its force. Although there are many foreshadowings of Spenser's later verse, then, the real interest of the volume lies in its ideas, and in its influence on Spenser's later poetry.

INFLUENCE ON SPENSER'S LATER WORK

The most striking quality of the *Theatre* volume is its use of emblematic woodcuts. Michael Bath argues convincingly that the images illustrating the Petrarch–Marot poems derive from watercolours in a manuscript of Marot's verse. However, he also argues that it is the woodcuts (used in the English edition, which came after the

Dutch and French versions) that derive from the watercolours, and that the copper-plate images in the Dutch and French texts, probably by Marcus Gheeraerts the elder, were a third stage of image transmission (Bath 1988: 82–7; see pp. 690–1 below). This may seem an odd sequence, but whatever the reasons for it, it had an effect on Spenser: copperplate images were still a rarity in England, and the fact that Spenser's work ended up illustrated by woodcuts points towards their use in *The Shepheardes Calender* ten years later. The crude but iconographically clear style of woodcut imagery may have suited Spenser better than the fine detailing of copper-plates (Bender 1972: 151), but it may have been the accidents of publishing history that led him in this direction.

The *Theatre* translations were not attributed to Spenser in modern times until Grosart (1882), but the first folio of Spenser's *Works* (1611) places the 'Visions of Petrarch' (in their *Complaints* version) at its end, thus neatly closing the poet's *oeuvre* with a version of the poems with which he began; that positioning may also suggest that the poem(s) had real and abiding significance for Spenser. Joseph Loewenstein argues that the *Theatre* poems should be given some prominence in any career model of Spenser's writing: 'That the twenty-two sonnets in *The Theatre for Voluptuous Worldlings* are not identified as Spenser's should not set them securely outside the circle that includes the poems made canonical by Virgilianist criticism, since *The Shepheardes Calender* is similarly anonymous' (Loewenstein 1996: 116). He also contends that the reference to a commentary on dreams in the *November* gloss and dedicatory letter to Harvey may be making a claim on the genre of the *Theatre*—a planned 'proto-*Complaints*' (Loewenstein 1996: 118); whatever the truth of this, Spenser does signal his ambition to be a Petrarchan visionary poet. If Petrarch is a key influence on Spenser, Marot is approached more tentatively. In *The Shepheardes Calender*, 'E. K.'s gloss to *January* argues that Colin is a French name, and gives the authority of 'the French Poete Marot (if he be worthy of the name of a Poete)'; this is hardly flattering to the poet Spenser had translated, and whom he explicitly imitated in *November*. It is ironic that the Catholic (if critical) Du Bellay would have a stronger influence on Spenser than the semi-Protestant Marot, and it is the Sonets section that has the more obvious connections with Spenser's later verse.

Sonet 1's reference to 'flying vanitie' would become a characteristic Spenserian trope, as in *June*'s 'flying fame' (74) in *The Shepheardes Calender*. Beyond such stylistic aspects, the most obvious connections are to the *Complaints* volume, where the poems were revised. In Sonet 3, Bart Van Es calls Spenser's 'With flushe stroke downe this noble monument' 'rather clumsy', and prefers the version in *Visions of Bellay*: 'Which this brave monument with flash did rend' (42) (2002: 28). I am inclined to prefer the earlier version (which was surely meant to read 'flashe', given the later version's use of this word): its effect of suddenness, something that is central to the whole sequence of poems, is more powerful and dislocating, and the ironic persistence of the word 'monument' at the end of the poem perhaps accords better with what Van Es calls Spenser's 'evocatively multivalent' use of the word.

It is not just the revisions of the translations themselves that connect the *Theatre* and *Complaints*. Sonets 12 and 13 and van der Noot's commentary might be glosses on *The Ruines of Time*:

> What nowe is of th' *Assyrian* Lyonesse,
> Of whome no footing now on earth appears?
> What of the *Persian* Beares outragiousnesse,
> Whose memorie is quite worne out with yeares?
> Who of the *Grecian* Libbard now ought heares,
> That ouerran the East with greedie powre,
> And left his whelps their kingdomes to deuoure?
>
> And where is that same great seuen headded beast,
> That made all nations vassals of her pride,
> To fall before her feete at her beheast,
> And in the necke of all the world did ride?
> Where doth she all that wondrous welth nowe hide?
> With her own weight down pressed now shee lies,
> And by her heaps her hugeness testifies.   (64–76)

Spenser here seems to pity the fall of the Beast and Whore of Babylon, however ironically. Indeed, the whole *Complaints* volume, subtitled as '*sundrie small Poemes of the Worlds Vanitie*', may be seen as an updating of the *Theatre*, with the addition of a more continuous verbal artistry, and a stronger sense of pathos.

In *The Faerie Queene*, Spenser makes recourse to *Theatre* material generally when he wishes to undermine heroic achievement and remind us of Last Things. Van der Noot's sentiment, 'Consideryng then the nature and condition of worldly things, whiche if they were not of them selues most miserable, yet is ther not any thing in them that iustly might be called ours, vnlesse it be vaine & ydle' (fol. 4ᵛ–5ʳ), may be compared to Spenser's: 'If any strength we haue, it is to ill, | But all the good is Gods, both powre and eke will' (I.x.1). Clearly, it is hard to disentangle the influence of Van der Noot and the Bible, particularly Revelation, but one can say that it was Van der Noot who first focused Spenser's attention on apocalyptic material and its poetic resonances. Sonet 15 (whether or not it is Spenser's) anticipates the beautiful use of the same passage in Book VI of *The Faerie Queene*:

> Then tooke he vp betwixt his armes twaine
>   The litle babe, sweet relickes of his pray;
>   Whom pitying to heare so sore complaine,
>   From his soft eyes the teares he wypt away,
>   And from his face the filth that did it ray,
>   And euery litle limbe he searcht around,
>   And euery part, that vnder sweathbands lay,
>   Least that the beasts sharpe teeth had any wound
> Made in his tender flesh, but whole them all he found.   (VI.iv.23)

The fourth line clearly echoes Revelation 21: 4: 'And God shall wipe away all tears from their eyes; and there shall be no more death, neither sorrow, neither crying, neither shall there be anymore pain; for the first things are passed' (Geneva Bible); on the other hand, the resonant positioning of 'away' at the line's end is the same as in the *Theatre*: 'And all their teares he shall wipe cleane away' (7). Similarly, Van der Noot's 'They shall strip hir naked, that so many as behold hir, may cry out vpon hir, & detest hir, and finally consume hir flesh' (fol. 49ᵛ) obviously anticipates the stripping of Duessa in *The Faerie Queene* (I.viii.46–9). A key sentiment of the *Theatre* is 'Briefly, the hearts of carnall & voluptuous men are neuer at rest, haue neuer inough, but be driuen by the meanes of concupiscence, which reigneth in them, always to be *careful*, to watche, to toyle and moyle, to wishe, to mistrust, to sue and busily to be occupied' (fol. 1ᵛ–2ʳ, emphasis added). This may be compared to Spenser's presentation of Care in Book IV of *The Faerie Queene* as 'a wretched wearish elfe' sleeplessly working 'to small purpose' (IV.v.34–5). The connection here is not so much a matter of verbal echoes, but in the idea of care as the property of the carnal lover, for it is the agitated Scudamour who encounters this figure.

Perhaps the most subtle linkage between the *Theatre* and *The Faerie Queene* is the following passage: 'Where this tree standeth, whiche neuer is without frute, nor drieth vp, or withereth, which dothe not onely beare twyce a yeare fruite, signifying all the vnspeakable giftes of the holy Ghoste, but rendreth his frutes euery month of the yere, that is, continually, both Sommer and winter' (fol. 89ʳ)—obviously, such an image (which Spenser could have got from any variety of texts) may inspire the tree of life in *The Faerie Queene* Book I, but the phrasing may also have inspired some elements of his presentation of the Garden of Adonis:

> There is continuall Spring, and haruest there
> Continuall, both meeting in one tyme:
> For both the boughes doe laughing blossoms beare,
> And with fresh colours decke the wanton Pryme,
> And eke attonce the heauenly trees they clyme,
> Which seeme to labour vnder their fruites lode.   (III.vi.42)

The connections are subtle, then, and should not be pressed too far, but their sum persists through Spenser's work. The dismissal of Grosart's idea that Van der Noot made an appearance as Diggon Davie in *September*—now generally thought to represent Richard Davies—has also made us dismiss his further idea that Spenser and Van der Noot formed a friendship (Grosart 1882: 25); it is perhaps not so absurd a notion, given Spenser's persistent ability to engage the loyalties of older intellectuals. Some strands of his work may stand as tributes to the author whose work first carried him into print.

Notes

1. The Dutch version is called, in full, *Het theatre oft Toon-neel, waer in ter eender de ongelucken ende elenden die den werelts gesinden ende boosen menschen toecomen: ende op dander syde tgheluck goet ende ruste die de gheloouighe ghenieten, vertoont worden. Niet min profijtelyck dan verheuchelyck voor alle lief hebbers des goddelycken*

woorts, der Poëteryen ende Schilderijen. (London: J. Day, 1568—STC, 18601); the French, *Le theatre anquel sont exposés & monstrés les inconueniens & miseres qui suiuent les mondains & vicieux, ensemble les plaisirs & contentements dont les fideles ioüissent. Matiere non moins profitable, que delectable à tous amateurs de la parolle de Dieu, de la poësie, & de la peinture* (London: J. Day, 1568—STC, 18603)—note that the English title does not try to appeal to lovers of poetry and painting as both the Dutch and the French titles do.

2. References to the *Theatre* and other shorter Spenserian poems are to Spenser (1999).

BIBLIOGRAPHY

Bath, Michael (1988). 'Verse Form and Pictorial Space in Van der Noot's *Theatre for Worldlings*', in *Word and Visual Imagination: Studies in the Interaction of English Literature and the Visual Arts*, ed. Karl Josef Höltgen, Peter M. Daly, and Wolfgang Lottes. Erlangen: Univ. Bibliothek Erlangen-Nürnberg.

Bender, John B. (1972). *Spenser and Literary Pictorialism.* Princeton, NJ: Princeton University Press.

Brigden, Susan (2000). *New Worlds, Lost Worlds: The Rule of the Tudors 1485–1603.* London: Penguin.

Du Bellay, Joachim (1967). *Les Regrets, precédé de Les Antiquités de Rome et suivi de La Défense et Illustration de la Langue Française*, ed. S. de Sacy. Paris: Gallimard.

Grosart, A. B. (1882). *The Complete Works in Verse and Prose of Edmund Spenser*, 9 vols. London. vol. I: *Life of Spenser.*

King, John N. (1990). *Spenser's Poetry and the Reformation Tradition.* Princeton, NJ: Princeton University Press.

Lawrence, Jason (2005). *'Who the devil taught thee so much Italian?': Italian Language Learning and Literary Imitation in Early Modern England.* Manchester: Manchester University Press.

Loewenstein, Joseph (1996). 'Spenser's Retrography: Two Episodes in Post-Petrarchan Bibliography', in Judith H. Anderson, Donald Cheney, and David A. Richardson (eds), *Spenser's Life and the Subject of Biography.* Amherst, MA: University of Massachusetts Press.

McCabe, Richard A. (1989). *The Pillars of Eternity: Time and Providence in* The Faerie Queene. Dublin: Irish Academic Press.

—— (1991). 'Edmund Spenser: Poet of Exile'. *Proceedings of the British Academy* 80: 73–103.

Norbrook, David (2002). *Poetry and Politics in the English Renaissance*, 2nd edn. Oxford: Oxford University Press.

Petrarch, Francisco (1976). *Petrarch's Lyric Poems: The* Rime Sparse *and Other Lyrics*, trans. and ed. Robert M. Durlig. Cambridge, MA: Harvard University Press.

Rasmussen, Carl J. (1980). '"Quietnesse of Minde": *A Theatre for Worldlings* as a Protestant Poetics'. *Spenser Studies* 1: 3–27.

Satterthwaite, Alfred W. (1960). *Spenser, Ronsard and Du Bellay.* Princeton, NJ: Princeton University Press.

Van Dorsten, J. A. (1970). *The Radical Arts: The First Decade of the Elizabethan Renaissance.* Leiden: Leiden University Press.

—— (1990). '*A Theatre for Worldlings*', in *The Spenser Encyclopaedia*, ed. A. C. Hamilton. Toronto: University of Toronto Press.

Van Es, Bart (2002). *Spenser's Forms of History.* Oxford: Oxford University Press.

Worden, Blair (1996). *The Sound of Virtue: Philip Sidney's* Arcadia *and Elizabethan Politics.* New Haven, CT: Yale University Press.

CHAPTER 9

....

THE SHEPHEARDES CALENDER (1579)

....

CLARE R. KINNEY

In 1579 Edmund Spenser publishes his first book of poetry. He does so anonymously: a prefatory lyric 'To His Booke' is simply signed 'Immeritô' (the unworthy one). The book's title page (Figure 9.1) tells us it is *The Shepheardes Calender Conteyning twelve Æglogues proportionable to the twelue monethes*, and a sixteenth-century reader would have received a rather mixed message concerning the genre of what was to follow. The first words suggest something akin to a popular and didactic miscellany, *The Kalender of Shepherdes*, an early modern almanac (based on a French original) which had been reprinted many times since its first publication in 1506. The *Kalender* combines practical advice for herdsmen and husbandmen, tuned to the seasonal cycle, with long passages of moral and spiritual instruction. The title page's supplementary reference to 'Æglogues' would, however, complicate the notion that one was about to peruse a compendium of vernacular pieties: the word immediately evokes a classical source and a very resonant literary precedent. Virgil's *Eclogues* (composed *c.*42–35 BCE) comprise ten poems divided between a wide variety of imagined rural voices; shepherds who sing and speak (and argue) within carefully rendered natural settings. His 'eclogue book' is capacious in theme and tone: a prophetic celebration of the birth of a child who will usher in a new golden age precedes a lamentation for a dead shepherd; cheerful, competitive erotic song-making is juxtaposed with poignant attempts to remember fragmentary, half-lost lyrics; laments for lost or scornful lovers are folded together with testimonies to the much more material losses of dispossessed and exiled pastors whose lands have been given to the returning veterans of an emperor's wars. The eclogues' multiple perspectives suggest an 'associative unity, graspable only in the work as a whole' (Bernard 1989: 51).

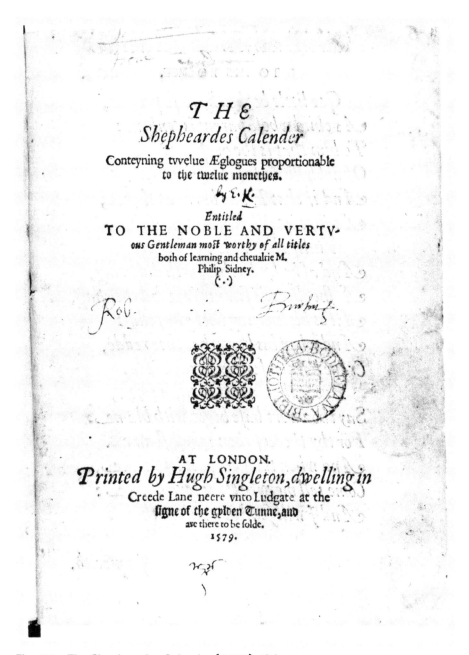

Fig. 9.1. *The Shepheardes Calender* (1579), title page.
[Bodleian Library: 4 F 2 (11) Art. Bs.]

Vernacular tradition collides with humanist learning from the very inception of the Spenserian text; at the same time, an artfully 'low' genre of poetry—and one very hospitable to moral and political agendas as well as to meditations upon love, loss, and mutability—is reshaped to fit the calendrical year. An eclogue is literally a 'selection' (Gk. *eklegein*: to choose); multiple eclogues offer a congeries of pastoral meditations, here bound to a seasonal design that is both cyclical and linear. The reader is teased by a promise of progression complicated by a testimony to stasis. *The Shepheardes Calender* hints that we are to follow the history of its first speaker, the lovelorn Colin Clout, but Colin travels only from a record of his erotic frustration (and the failure of his love lyrics to move his beloved Rosalind) in *Januarye* to an assertion of a kind of artistic death drive in *December*: his return to a failed beginning is emphasized by the fact that, after experimenting with many other verse forms in the intervening poems, his creator recycles the stanzaic form of *Januarye* in the final eclogue. In order to progress (or regress) to *December*, however, the reader of *The Shepheardes Calender* also encounters a community of other speakers, some of whom deplore Colin's love melancholy and circulate different lyrics of his making, others of whom take part in debates on matters which seem quite distinct from Colin's meditations on the pains of love and the perils of poetry.

The Kalender of Shepherds had offered monologic sermonizing; *The Shepheardes Calender* offers eclogues in which multiple speakers, within and across poems, explore matters erotic, political, and aesthetic. Spenser's miscellany also exploits pastoral poetry's ready deployment of ostensibly 'rude' speakers to mask topical references and to offer elevated commentaries on the human condition: the pastoral poet, as Spenser's contemporary George Puttenham writes, may 'under the veil of homely persons, and in rude speeches . . . insinuate and glance at greater matters' (Puttenham 2007: 128). In preceding centuries the convenient pun that makes a pastor a priest as well as a shepherd had already been aggressively exploited by the Italian poets Petrarch and Mantuan in satirizing ecclesiastical abuses; the latter's pastorals had been rather leadenly translated into English by George Turbeville in 1567. The French Protestant poet Clément Marot had similarly appropriated the genre for political and religious purposes. Spenser would also have been familiar with the English pastoral experiments of William Barclay (*c*.1515) and Barnabe Googe (1563). *The Shepheardes Calender* is, however, far more poetically various than any of those native works (Turbeville and Googe write only in monotonous and inflexible four-teeners) and much more thematically multifarious. Indeed Spenser's eclogue book constitutes one of the most ambitious poetic debuts of any poet in any language.

Spenser/Immeritô dedicates his work to the young Philip Sidney, humbly sending his 'unkent' child to find protection from 'Enuie' beneath this prospective patron's wing ('To His Booke', 5–7).[1] Yet the very assumption that the work will provoke envious responses hints that Immeritô's representation of his work as baseborn and unworthy is disingenuous, and a contemporary reader would recognize that *The Shepheardes Calender* had been furnished with a critical apparatus and commentary more usually seen in scholarly editions of the works of respected authors of antiquity. A mysterious figure who signs himself E. K. prefaces its poems with an introductory letter to Spenser's scholarly friend Gabriel Harvey, praising the efforts of the 'new Poete' (25) and associating his project with those of a host of respected classical, Continental, and English precursors. E. K. offers a detailed (albeit often question-begging) explanation of the volume's agendas in his letter, prefaces each month's eclogue with a paragraph purporting to set forth its 'argument', and adds copious notes and glosses to the poems. The elaborate machinery in fact occupies about half of the work (McCabe 2000: 35). Immeritô himself adds a poetic envoi to the cycle of eclogues, written in 'epic' hexameters and describing his accomplishment as if it were already a canonical text: 'Loe I haue made a Calender for every yeare, | That steele in strength, and time in durance shall outweare' ('Envoi', 1–2). *The Shepheardes Calender* was indeed *re*classicized—translated into Latin by one Richard Dove—very shortly after its publication (Norbrook 2002: 61).

E. K. tells Spenser's readers that they are witnessing the first flight of a new poet and reminds them that pastoral projects have long been associated with the beginning of prestigious poetic careers: 'So flew Virgile, as not yet well feeling his winges. So flew Mantuane, as being not full somd. So Petrarque ... Boccace ... Marot ... Sanazarus' (29). The new poet's work is already modestly monumental and, even more importantly, it evokes the Virgilian career trajectory, in which pastoral experiments will eventually lead to the writing of a national epic. Spenser's entry on to the literary scene is at once humble and ambitious, anonymous and self-advertising (the very word 'calendar' derives from *kalein* (Gk.): to announce). It was also successful: the poet's achievement is praised, for example, in Philip Sidney's *Defence of Poesy* (*c.*1580) and William Webbe's *Discourse of English Poetrie* (1586) (Sidney 1989: 242; Cummings: 57–8). *The Shepheardes Calender* would go through five editions in the next eighteen years, and the identity of its author seems to have been an open secret from the start.

The far from unassuming nature of the new poet's debut is emphasized by the elaborate mixed media presentation of the *Calender*, a mediation that extends well beyond E. K.'s commentary. Each month's eclogue is accompanied by an original illustrative woodcut and each one ends with an 'emblem', an aphoristic signature given to each speaker.[2] For example, at the end of the *November* eclogue, in which Colin Clout elegizes the dead shepherdess Dido, he is assigned the emblem 'La mort ny mord': death does not bite (210). The emblems augment the multiple discourses of the *Calender* (they variously offer fragments of Greek, Latin, French, and Italian) and are gnomic enough to require additional glosses from the industrious E. K.

The effect of the paratextual supplementations of Spenser's lyrics can be illustrated by a glance at *England's Helicon* (1600), a popular anthology of Elizabethan pastoral verse. In this collection, one of the *Calender*'s most striking poems, Colin Clout's song celebrating Elizabeth I as 'Elisa, Queene of shepheardes' in the *April* eclogue, is reprinted in isolation, given the misleading title 'Hobbinoll's Dittie in prayse of Eliza Queene of the Sheepheards', and stripped of all editorial commentary. By contrast, the eclogue from which it derives begins with a woodcut illustration which pre-emptively contradicts (or demystifies) the pastoral tribute to 'Elisa' and her attendant Muses, Graces, and shepherdesses by depicting a shepherd playing to a

Aprill.

Ægloga Quarta.

ARGVMENT.

THis Æglogue is purposely intended to the honor and prayse of our most
gracious soureigne, Queene Elizabeth. The speakers herein be Hobbinoll and Thenott, two shepheardes: the which Hobbinoll being before mentioned, greatly to haue loued Colin, is here set forth more largely , complay-
ning him of that boyes great misaduenture in Loue, whereby his mynd was
alienate and with drawen not onely from him, who moste loued him, but also
from all former delightes and studies, aswell in pleasaunt pyping, as conning
ryming and singing, and other his laudable exercises . Whereby he taketh
occasion, for proofe of his more excellencie and skill in poetrie, to recorde a
songe, which the sayd Colin sometime made in honor of her Maiestie, whom
abruptely he termeth Elysa.

Thenot.   Hobbinoll.

TEll me good Hobbinoll, what garres thee greete?
    What? hath some Wolfe thy tender Lambes ptoꝛne?
Oꝛ is thy Bagpyppe bꝛoke, that soundes so sweete?
Oꝛ art thou of thy loued lasse foꝛloꝛne?

Oꝛ bene thine eyes attempred to the yeare,
Quenching the gasping furrowes thirst with rayne?

Like

Fig. 9.2. *The Shepheardes Calender* (1579), *Aprill.*
[Bodleian Library: 4 F 2 (11) Art. Bs.]

group of women in contemporary court dress surrounding their monarch (Figure 9.2). E. K.'s preliminary prose Argument announces that *Aprill* is intended to honour Elizabeth, but also notes that it begins with a conversation between Hobbinoll and Thenot about Colin's poetic errancy, and that the song to Elisa is introduced by Hobbinoll to testify to Colin's previous accomplishments. We then progress to the actual exchange between the two shepherds, in iambic pentameter quatrains, in which we hear not only about the shepherd-poet's alienation from his music but also about the disruption of the friendship between Hobinoll and Colin by Colin's love for the uncaring Rosalind. Only then does the reader finally read Colin's elaborately structured lyric, which Hobbinoll recites at Thenot's request. The eclogue concludes with Hobbinoll and Thenot again lamenting Colin's self-destructive obsession with an unobtainable woman; two emblems assigned to these speakers quote two teasing fragments from Virgil ('O quam te memorem virgo?' 'O dea certe', 162–5) which thus associate Elisa with Venus disguised as a follower of Diana in Book I of the *Aeneid* and celebrate her as both virgin and goddess.[3] The reader must then negotiate several pages of E. K.'s commentary, which include notes on the two speakers' dialect usages, glosses (some of them very rambling) of mythological allusions, speculations about the identity of Rosalind, interpretations of topical and historical references, and an extended paragraph on the significance of the *Aeneid* quotations.

Colin's song to Elisa is thus framed by multiple voices and exfoliating commentaries (with E. K. becoming in effect another voice in the eclogue's conversation); the whole performance is far more complex than the naked lyric which appears in the later anthology under a title that erases the fact that one singer is performing and putting into circulation another poet's song. *The Shepheardes Calender*'s other eclogues similarly combine mixed media and competing voices. Spenser's eclogue book offers us not only polyglossia (and different poetic performances) *within* eclogues but also an embracing assortment of voices and texts that produce a larger polyphony and a potential conversation *between* eclogues. To summarize briefly— and, inevitably, reductively—*Januarye* introduces Colin in the third person: 'A shepheards boye (no better doe him call)'; the poet-swain then offers an extended love complaint, projecting his miseries upon his natural surroundings and concluding his lyric by breaking his pipe. *Februarie* presents a dialogue between cocky young Cuddie and resentful old Thenot which sets youth against age and eventually gives us Thenot's retelling of a fable, ascribed to the dead poet Tityrus, of the upstart Briar and the long-suffering Oak. *March*'s voices are those of two adolescent shepherds, Willye and Thomalin, who recount their first encounters with Cupid's darts. *Aprill* has already been summarized; the debaters of *Maye* are Piers and Palinode (whom E. K. associates with the competing perspectives of Catholic and Protestant ministers); their very different responses to witnessing the month's seasonal folk games turn into a quarrel about 'pastoral care' in a much larger sense, and end with Piers' fable of the Kid who falls to the sleights of the deceiving Fox (a fable whose thrust Palinode appears to misunderstand entirely). In *June*, Colin reappears, bewails the false shepherd Menalcas's appropriation of his Rosalind's affections, and insists to Hobbinoll that he has lost his poetic powers and cannot reconnect with the poetic source represented by the dead poet-shepherd Tityrus. *Julye* returns us to ecclesiastical satire: Thomalin and Morrell project a dispute over the competing claims of humble devotion and elevated aspiration upon the relief map of their world, and Thomalin, in a particularly transparent topical reference to the suspension from office of Elizabeth I's reforming Archbishop Grindal, recounts a tale about the unhappy fate of the good shepherd Algrin. In *August* we have a Virgilian singing match between the lovelorn Perigot and the cheerfully subversive Willye; after the contest is concluded, their judge, Cuddie, repeats an elaborate love complaint, in sestina form, composed by Colin Clout. *September* revisits religious satire as Diggon unfolds to Hobinoll the dire consequences of his desire to journey into foreign parts; he recites the abuses he has seen in Rome, and finishes with an admonitory story about a wolf in sheep's clothing. *October* contains Cuddie and Piers's debate about the place and powers of poetry (and some very trenchant lines about the current dearth of good patrons prepared to support good poets), in the course of which Cuddie insists that the 'famous flight' of the poet of truly 'aspyring wit' could only be achieved by the absent Colin (85–9). Colin himself reappears in *November* where, at Thenot's prompting, he sings a poignant elegy for the dead shepherdess Dido; the eclogue book concludes, in *December*, with Colin's retrospective indictment of his wasted years and talent. He likens winter's withered flowers to his own lost 'flowers' of rhetoric (109–12), and finally hangs up his pipes and bids Rosalind forever adieu as he awaits his death.

Spenser's bravura display of his own talents is emphasized by his command and framing of many voices in collision: *The Shepheardes Calender* is a strikingly dialogic text and its pastoral debates often seem to have no clear winner. E. K. variously classifies the eclogues as 'plaintive', 'recreative', and 'moral' (32), and some scholars have hewed very carefully to his divisions in discussing the work (Hamilton 1956; Johnson 1990). His tripartite taxonomy seems inadequate to the task, however, since several eclogues include more than one of the characteristics he identifies (Willye and Perigot's 'recreative' singing match of *August*, for example, is followed within the same eclogue by Colin's consummately 'plaintive' sestina). The new poet sets forth a very rich sampler of his poetic abilities, which includes his own complicated masking as both Immeritô and Colin Clout—or is it Spenser who masks as Immeritô and Immeritô, as Louis Montrose suggests, who masks as Colin? (1979: 36). Spenser's speakers deploy a wide range of pastoral discourses: there is a world of difference between the voices that lament their estrangement from the poetry of the past and those that criticize the ministers of the present, or between the elegant iambic pentameter of the Petrarchan laments of Colin Clout and the quasi-Chaucerian couplets in iambic-anapestic tetrameter of the satirical eclogues.[4] At times one discursive convention slips into another within the same eclogue: in *Maye*, Piers's critique of Palinode's celebration of actual shepherds at play slides into rather different territory when his use of the word 'pastor' becomes metaphorical, and he turns from criticizing the idle pastimes of the young to indicting more spiritually errant shepherd-priests: 'I muse, what account both these will make, | The one for hire, which he doth take, | And thother for leauing his Lords taske, | When great *Pan* account of shepherdes shall aske' (*Maye*, 51–5).

We are also offered a dazzling range of poetic forms, both within and among the eclogues. *August*, for example, begins with roughly four-beat lines split between two speakers in an ABABCC scheme; its competitive 'roundelay' between Perigot and Willye is a variation on common ballad metre, with each singer taking alternate lines; the lyric that Cuddie recites at the singing game's conclusion offers the first English example in print of the sestina form popularized by Petrarch, substituting an intricately patterned recurrence of six words at line endings for conventional end-rhyme. Elsewhere Spenser gives us an abbreviated form of rhyme royal in *Januarye* and *December*, tetrameter couplets alternating with single trimeters in *March*, a very difficult and flashy variation on ottava rima in *June*, 'fourteeners' in *Julye* (an eclogue with some ties to Mantuan's eighth eclogue, already 'Englished' in that same metre by Turbeville) and elaborate stanzaic forms, reminiscent of the Petrarchan *canzone* and alternating long and short lines to powerful effect, in *Aprill*'s celebration of Elisa and *November*'s lament for Dido. The author's delight in conspicuous multiplicity is also evident at the level of his intertextual borrowings. *Aprill*'s celebration of Elisa/ Elizabeth seems strategically placed to echo Virgil's own 'messianic' fourth eclogue. Mantuan, as I have noted, is alluded to in *Julye* (and is also an important presence in *October*); the Greek poet Bion in *March*; Clément Marot's elegy for Queen Loyse of France and his 'Eglogue au Roy' from exile are glanced at in *November* and *December*, respectively. Spenser, to be sure, enters into his own dialogue with his sources: his acts of imitation are always re-creative.

FATHERING *THE SHEPHEARDES CALENDER*

In his preliminary laying out of the 'generall argument of the whole booke', E. K. defends rather laboriously the author's decision to locate the beginning of his calendar year in January rather than in March, invoking in passing the classical figure of Janus, the ancient guardian of the new year whose two faces look forwards and backwards at once (34). Janus is indeed a fitting presiding deity for a work in which a tyro takes his first flight—and searches for a patron—with his eyes upon the literary history that has preceded and produced him. The new poet's originality is predicated upon and constituted by a very complex unfolding of his own *origins*, and this self-awareness has interesting consequences for his work. Pastoral discourse is far from monolithic—and, as Annabel Patterson has pointed out, it can be highly instrumental: the Virgilian model was reappropriated and reshaped for different poetic and political agendas at different historical moments (Patterson 1987: 7). Spenser's reworking of multiple versions of pastoral creates particularly emphatic tensions between the 'Arcadian' and the 'Mantuanesque' strains within the genre

(Cullen 1970: 2–4). The Arcadian world is idealized and idyllic—but also vulnerable (to time, to the power of eros, to death); the Mantuanesque world is already imperfect, fallen. The green world offers no escape from the sins of the town, the court, the church: in mirroring them, it becomes a satirical instrument in the pastoral poet's hands. No shepherd preaches contentment or celebrates the green world's beauty or peace within the space of *The Shepheardes Calender* without another voice contradicting his words.

The complexity of Spenser's backward glances is emphasized by his work's simultaneous invocation of classical and vernacular father figures. *October* alludes to the 'Romish Tityrus' Virgil, invoking him both as a poet who (unlike the complaining Cuddie) was blessed with a supportive patron and as the precursor and exemplar whose career took him from humble pastoral to national epic (55–60). But Colin Clout in *June* and both speakers in *Februarie* refer to Chaucer under the same name of Tityrus; for Colin, he is the wellspring, the poetic source, from whom he fears he is estranged. The quasi-Chaucerian form of the satirical eclogues also reminds us that sixteenth-century commentators ascribed such anti-ecclesiastical satires as *The Plowman's Tale* and *Jack Upland* to Chaucer's authorship: this version of the predecessor is the proto-Protestant and homely homilist constructed and lauded by John Foxe and other contemporary commentators (King 1990: 26–8).

The fact that Spenser includes an English as well as a Roman Tityrus in his work underscores *The Shepheardes Calender*'s energetic defence of the dignity of the poetic vernacular and its interest in uncovering a more 'original' and authentic English. Spenser's language is consciously archaizing (and also embraces a good scattering of regional dialect words) and E. K. addresses this fact in his prefatory letter, where his justification of the new poet's practice entangles him in some interesting contradictions:

whether he vseth [his 'auncient' words] . . . as thinking them fittest for such rusticall rudenesse of shepheards . . . or els because such olde and obsolete wordes are most vsed of country folke, sure I think . . . that they bring great grace and, as one would say, auctoritie to the verse. (26)

The same strategy that confirms the 'rusticall rudenesse' of the eclogues' speakers also confers 'grace' and 'auctoritie' on the poetry and perhaps becomes another aspect of Immeritô's own self-authorization as he strives to reconnect with a more authentic poetic tongue (see Chapter 32 below). This is paralleled by Colin Clout's desire to have his own work fed by the Chaucerian wellspring. Immeritô's alter ego laments his alienation from the Chaucerian source in *June*, wishing that 'some little drops would flowe, | Of that the spring was in his learned hedde' (93–4). His pessimism is, however, contested within *November*. Thenot, requesting to hear Colin's songs, speaks of his friend as one who has been 'watered at the Muses well' and is himself a source of poetic nourishment for less skilful poets: 'The kindlye dewe drops from the higher tree, | And wets the little plants that lowly dwell' (30–2).

From Thenot's perspective, Colin is already an inspiring father figure who has achieved the 'famous flight' that Cuddie, in *October*, had declared to be better fitted to Colin than to himself. Nevertheless, the Janus-faced *Calender* suggests that Colin must be left behind as Immeritô continues his journey: the first flight of the new poet concludes with Colin relentlessly bearing witness to an abortive poetic career as he hangs up his pipe: 'My spring is spent, my sommer burnt vp quite . . . | Winter is come, that blowes the bitter blaste, | And after Winter dreerie death does hast' (*December*, 128, 143–4). We might also note that even as Immeritô's envoi to his work echoes one classical poetic father—specifically, the final self-apotheosizing lines of Ovid's *Metamorphoses*—to declare that the *Calender* itself will transcend time and continue 'till the worlds dissolution' ('Envoi', 4), it simultaneously insists that it should not try to compete with either its Romish or its English progenitors: 'Dare not to match thy pype with Tityrus hys style, | Nor with the Pilgrim that the Ploughman playde a whyle' ('Envoi', 9–10). The work's teasing combination of humility and aspiration (and its paradoxically 'backward' self promotion) continues to the very last.

Unfolding *The Shepheardes Calender*

How can readers keep in focus the shape-shifting *Shepheardes Calender*, deal at a glance with its bravura display of poetic technique, its vigorous engagement with literary history, its passionate reflections on the poetic vocation, and its devious topicality? One of the challenges facing them is the fact that the eclogues have been pre-edited: the assiduous E. K. is always at hand to nudge them towards an interpretation.[5] E. K.'s commentary is very various: his notes range from quite simplistic glossing (as when he laboriously explains the very well-known iconography of Cupid in his *March* apparatus) to very technical observations ('a pretty Epanorthosis . . . and withall a Paronomasia', cf. gloss to *Januarye*, 61). Sometimes they offer flatfooted and reductive moralization that fails to attend to poetic and thematic nuance; at other times, they are confusing or evasive.[6] Although Hobbinoll appears in several eclogues before *September*, it is only then that he is identified as the author's donnish friend Gabriel Harvey. The headnote to *October* describes Cuddie as the 'perfect paterne of a Poete', but Cuddie's interlocutor, Piers, at times seems to make more compelling points about the poetic vocation and Cuddie himself defers to Colin Clout's superiority as an exemplary artist. In the notes to *Julye*, E. K. simply says that 'Algrin' is 'the name of a shepheard' (gloss to 213), although the anagrammatic reference to Archbishop Grindal is quite transparent. More than one critic has observed that E. K.'s question-begging remarks—his glosses that need glossing—provoke the reader to additional interpretation (Norbrook 2002: 68; Patterson 1987: 127) and that their lack of transparency allows Spenser simultaneously to reveal and conceal his topical thrusts. (The issue of what constitutes appropriate transparency actually becomes a topic of debate within the *Calender* in *September*, when Hobbinoll first asks Diggon not to 'speake so dirke' (102), and then accuses him of speaking 'too plaine' (136) after he lambastes priestly misconduct.) The very typography of *The Shepheardes Calender* fosters a kind of doublespeak:

as McCabe notes, the black letter Gothic typeface of its poems suggests an ancient text, but the 'modern' roman typeface of its commentary suggests topicality and contemporary relevance (McCabe 2000: 37).

It is worth looking more closely at an instance of E. K.'s incomplete glossing. In *Aprill*, Colin's encomium to Elisa lauds her as '*Syrinx* daughter without spotte, | Which *Pan* the shepheards God of her begot' (50–1). E. K. begins his note on line 50 by recapitulating the Ovidian narrative of Syrinx's metamorphosis into reeds to escape Pan's pursuit 'which he seeing, tooke of them, and in remembraunce of his lost love, made him a pype thereof' (67). Our commentator then changes tack to tell his reader that 'by Pan is here meant the most famous and victorious King,' Elizabeth I's father, Henry VIII (68). E. K. does not have anything to say about his interesting implication that Syrinx is thus the politically rather more problematic figure of the executed Anne Boleyn. Even more strikingly, he leaves it to the reader to think through the logic of the surprising Ovidian genealogy: if Elisa is the reed pipe that Pan 'begets' upon Syrinx, she is also a pastoral instrument and, by extension, a poet's pastoral music. Immeritô's encomium of Elisa 'plays' the queen: he makes her his song, appropriating her and reconstructing her in accordance with his own desires for his own self-advancement.

We are invited to be active interpreters, but it is a tricky business to unfold the text. E. K. announces that *The Shepheardes Calender* was composed by its author to 'allay the heate of his passion' and to offer a warning to other young men wandering in the 'Labyrinth of Loue' (29). William Webbe, in *A Discourse of English Poetrie* (1586), echoes E. K.'s emphasis on its admonitions (in the Colin eclogues) against entanglement in 'loue and youthfull vanities', but then proceeds to summarize the moral agendas of several of the other eclogues, insisting upon the text's multifariousness (Cummings: 58). Even at the formal level, this multifariousness offers interpretive challenges. Spenser's eclogue cycle tempts the reader to trace a narrative across the calendrical year (the 'Colin Clout story' being the most popular). But within individual eclogues, different discursive structures compete for the reader's attention. Does Colin Clout's plaintive sestina in *August* retrospectively deflate the less polished love complaints of Perigot (which are themselves subverted by Willye's playful commentary), or is the relentless high seriousness, the formal recycling of woe, and the borderline narcissism of the sestina pre-emptively interrogated by the more playful dialogue that precedes it? Alternatively, do the narrative sections of the satirical eclogues adequately exemplify or conclude the debates that frame them or do these fables, like *Februarie*'s tale of the Oak and the Briar, consistently fail to resolve the problems raised in the preceding dialogues (Cullen 1970: 32)?

Critical discussions of *The Shepheardes Calender* have resulted in various strategies to address its multiplicity. Paul Alpers suggests that since 1950 there have been two distinct trends in scholarly commentary: earlier scholarship, which treats the *Calender* as a 'prototype of *The Faerie Queene*' and emphasizes its 'epic striving, moral vision, and allegorical techniques', gives way, in the late 1970s, to discussions of what the *Calender* reveals about 'the problematics of a poetic career in Elizabethan England' and about 'the way various social pressures and realities make their presence felt in the poem' (Alpers 1988: 163). (It could be argued that there is an even more extended critical cyclicity in play here: in an influential 1956 article, A. C. Hamilton differentiates *his* approach from those of earlier critics over-obsessed with identifying the eclogues' topical allusions (171–2).) One might distinguish, perhaps, between metaphorical and metonymical approaches to the text: the former attempting a totalizing reading and identifying the work's shaping poetic agendas, the latter concentrating upon moments at which historical contingency interrupts or inflects the poetic project, making a single eclogue (or perhaps a group of eclogues) speak for the whole.

Pastoral has always tended to address the loss of innocence, the shattering of Arcadia (by death, by erotic frustration, by the impingements of an already fallen world outside the idyll). *The Shepheardes Calender* certainly speaks to this tradition, but its interest in personal poetic ambition and its explicit allusions to the Virgilian career model also encourage a meliorist and teleological reading, especially if the reader separates what Miller neatly terms the 'negative *bildungsroman*' of Colin Clout from the poetic trajectory of his creator, Immeritô/Spenser (Miller 1979: 233). For Hamilton, *The Shepheardes Calender* is the prologue to the 'heroic' poet's 'truly dedicated life in the world' (Hamilton 1956: 181); for Isabel MacCaffrey, the work anticipates *The Faerie Queene*'s 'discontinuous continuity, multiple reference, analog-ical relationships that point simultaneously to likeness and unlikeness' (MacCaffrey 1969: 89). There are, to be sure, striking divergences within critical meditations on the 'career narrative': while Patrick Cheney asserts that an Orphic and vatic power is already made manifest within the eclogues (Cheney 1993: 23), Helgerson emphasizes that the *Calender* is a record of frustration as well as ambition, in which Colin's failures haunt the aspiring epic poet (Helgerson 1983: 69). Teleological accounts of the *Calender* tend to identify the *November* eclogue as a transformative moment in its unfolding, arguing that although Colin may revert to despair in *December*, the lyrical consolation he offers in the preceding eclogue—the metamorphosis of 'carefull verse' to 'joyfull verse' in its elegiac refrains—models poetry's power to transcend earthly imperfection and loss.

Other critics have focused upon *The Shepheardes Calender*'s intertextuality and its creative reworking of its multiple sources (Cullen 1970; Hoffman 1977; Johnson 1990; Patterson 1997). Bruce Smith argues that the shifting generic allegiances of the poem—most notably its relations with the classical eclogue, the medieval almanac, and the Renaissance pastoral romance—imagine different readers and invite differ-ent reading strategies at different points in the work (Smith 1980: 70–2). Such readings tend to foreground the *discordia concors* of the poem, the larger design that its competing discourses produce; they invite the reader to forego finding synthesis or resolution within any individual eclogue or discrete debate in favour of recognizing the complicated dialogic process of the whole (Cullen 1970; Greene 1987; Shore 1985). Harry Berger's striking analyses emphasize in particular the work's acute awareness of its own belatedness and its intermittently parodic, interrogative, and satirical stance towards the pastoral tradition (Berger 1988: 288). At the very start of his calendrical journey, Colin declares 'Thou barrein ground, whom winters wrath has wasted, | Art made a myrrhour to behold my plight' (*Januarye*, 19–20) and Berger notes that the punning syntax, in which the word 'art' hovers between verb and noun, immediately 'denaturalizes' nature, insists upon the artfulness (and, one might add, the instrumentality) of pastoral (Berger 1988: 332).

Other aspects of that instrumentality are foregrounded in the criticism that addresses Spenser's religious and socio-political agendas. Explorations of the eclogues that offer ecclesiastical satire (*Maye, Julye, September*) have variously offered us a moderate Protestant Spenser who steers clear of extreme polemic (Hoffman 1977) and a Spenser who writes within a much more radical tradition of Protestant reformist or prophetic poetry (King 1990; Norbrook 2002). A rather different historicization of *The Shepheardes Calender* shapes Louis Montrose's influential article on Spenser's 'poetics of courtship', which identifies in his eclogue cycle a 'recurrent attempt to transform language into power' and to make poetic ornament a tool of personal advancement. Montrose proposes that the encomium of Elisa in *Aprill*, Colin's 'amorous courtship' of Rosalind throughout the sequence, and his 'spiritual courtship' of Dido in *November* offer permutations of the same agenda. He also revises previous discussions of the spiritual and poetic transcendence putatively achieved by Colin in his *November* elegy to suggest that Spenser quite consciously makes the consolatory apotheosis of Dido 'the symbolic vehicle of the poet's own aspiration' (Montrose 1979: 35, 51). Berger develops this particular angle on the gender politics of *The Shepheardes Calender* to offer a thoughtful meditation on what he terms the 'Young Men's Pastoral Association' wherein women may be figured as muses, monarchs, beloveds, trophies, or adversaries but are always poetically instrumental rather than persons in their own right (Berger 1988: 359).

The *Aprill* eclogue has been particularly important to the many critics who have addressed the topicality of *The Shepheardes Calender* in the context of 1579's urgent debates over the threat to English national identity and religious allegiance occasioned by the proposed marriage between Elizabeth I and the Catholic Duc d'Alençon (Lane 1993: 17–26; McCabe 1995: 23–7; Norbrook 2002: 73–9). Hugh Singleton, Spenser's publisher, had earlier in that year published a pamphlet strongly criticizing the French marriage (an act which eventually resulted in the prosecution and mutilation of its author, John Stubbs, for seditious writing, and a narrow escape from judicial punishment for Singleton himself). *Aprill*'s rapturous celebration of the emphatically virginal Elisa and its Virgilian emblem ('O quam te memorem virgo?') can in context be seen as prescriptive and interrogative rather than descriptive encomia; the eclogue is in any case a relatively early contribution to the cult of Elizabeth as the 'Virgin Queen' (Norbrook 2002: 76). The larger designs of the eclogue cycle may also be more darkly admonitory. In the *Aeneid*, Virgil's Dido—a female ruler who enters into a doomed liaison with a foreigner—is also called Elissa; if one maps the *Calender*'s Elisa onto the *Calender*'s Dido, the *November* elegy can be read as a counterweight to *Aprill*—a proleptic memorial to an Elisa who will be dead to her Protestant nation if she marries her French suitor (Lane 1993: 25; Patterson 1987: 121).

Alpers identified two distinct strains within scholarship on *The Shepheardes Calender*; more recently, Richard Chamberlain has sought to complicate the 'transcendentalizing interpretations' that ignore the material particularity and historical specificity of Spenser's text and to broaden the political readings that downplay its poetics (Chamberlain 2005: 38). He proposes, instead, a neo-aesthetic perspective that 'refuses to grant absolute sovereignty either to the abstract or the material, the rational or the experiential' (53). He is not, to be sure, the first to imagine such a critical synthesis. Alpers himself suggests we might historicize Spenser's aesthetic practice, arguing that Spenser's idiosyncratic deployment of a very wide range of pastoral performances is itself an emphatically 'historical' event, made manifest in the poet's 'domestication' of competing traditions to create a lyrical and rhetorical 'domain' that can embrace 'imagination and moral awareness, emotional energy and the felt lessons of experience' (Alpers 1988: 174–6). Lynn Staley Johnson offers a somewhat different inclusive approach, declaring that *The Shepheardes Calender* promotes a 'reformation at once broadly national and intensely personal' (1990: 1). In her account of Spenser's multifaceted project of moral, institutional, spiritual, and poetic renewal, formal devices have their own discursive functions and the poet's deployment of experimental 'parodies, truncated forms, false closures' interrogates literary tradition and becomes a vehicle for socio-political critique (6).

BACKWARD GLANCES AND THE RETURN TO PASTORAL

Let us linger for a moment upon the notion that form has its own story to tell in *The Shepheardes Calender*. In Chapter 21 below, Jeff Dolven proposes that the eclogue book records a contest for metrical primacy between the variants on ballad tetrameter we see in (for example) *Februarie*, *March*, *May*, and *September* and the iambic pentameter of *Januarye*, *June*, *October*, the frame to *November*, and *December*—the iambic pentameter that will, of course, emerge as the governing metre of *The Faerie Queene*. In Dolven's account, the battle of the beats underpins the story of Colin's (or Immeritô's?) 'ambition and his nostalgia, his yearning toward epic and his allegiance to the . . . wellspring of his poetic energies' (p. 397 below). That wellspring contains both the popular vernacular ballad and Chaucerian verse (sixteenth-century readers did not sound Chaucer's terminal 'e' and thus tended to resolve his lines into something more like tetrameter). Nevertheless, the backwards 'Chaucerian' pull that appears to challenge—and to be displaced by—a new epic discourse turns out, on closer investigation, to gesture towards an interesting continuity with the epic project to come.

The Chaucerian work most actively invoked in *The Shepheardes Calender* is Chaucer's sophisticated and lengthy romance of the Trojan War, *Troilus and Criseyde* (Kinney 2004). E. K. alludes to the work at the very start of his prefatory 'Epistle' (25) and Immeritô's own very first line (in his dedicatory poem to Sidney), 'Goe little booke: thy selfe present', recalls Chaucer's envoi in the *Troilus*, 'Go, litel bok, go litel myn tragedye' (5.1786), as does his own envoi's instruction: 'Goe lyttle Calender, thou hast a free passeporte' ('Envoi', 7). And Immeritô's final command that his *Calender* the 'high steppes adore' ('Envoi', 11) of nobler writers (including Chaucer himself) revises the Chaucerian narrator's concluding instruction to *his* book: 'kis the steppes where as thow seest pace | Virgile, Ovide, Omer, Lucan, and Stace' (5.1791–2). The envoi's backward glance at this particular poem of Chaucer's is especially interesting, I would suggest, because Immeritô's pursuit of the Virgilian trajectory will very specifically supply what his English Tityrus refused to offer in *Troilus and Criseyde*, namely, a vernacular epic.

In his genre-bending romance, Chaucer takes up the matter of Troy, invokes various Muses and intermittently displays a striking consciousness that he is writing a 'poem historicall' as he meditates upon diachronic language shifts and issues of literary transmission and reception—but he carefully distinguishes his concerns from those of epic. His narrator declares that if he had chosen to write of the deeds of Troilus, he could relate his feats in battle, but 'for that I to writen first bigan | Of his love' (5.1768–9) he is not interested in arms and the man; his readers must seek out other authors if they wish to read of Troilus's heroic prowess (5.1770–1). Immeritô may humble himself before his predecessor, but he is homing in on territory Chaucer edged up to but chose not to colonize. Nevertheless, Spenser will never really stop 'romancing' Chaucer—he will be reinvoked in Book IV of *The Faerie Queene* where Spenser's completion of an unfinished Chaucerian romance, *The Squire's Tale*, will complicate his own admixture of epic and romance. This 'recycling' of Chaucer suggests that nothing is ever left completely behind in the Spenserian *oeuvre* (to put it another way, the Virgilian career trajectory is always recursive). *The Shepheardes Calender* has already shown us how Colin's songs recirculate in Colin's absence even as Colin's author busily remakes the work of Virgil, Mantuan, and Marot and ascribes the fable Thenot recounts in *Februarie* to Tityrus-Chaucer. Nor should we forget that Colin Clout himself—for all his hanging up of his pipes in *December*—will be reincarnated and recirculated within Spenser's *oeuvre*.

Colin Clout first reappears (translated from the English to the Irish countryside) in *Colin Clouts Come Home Againe* (1595). There, as the primary speaker in an extended and eccentric eclogue that records his visit to the English court, and for all his compliments to Elizabeth I and to a much more idealized version of Rosalind, he takes on a role more akin to that of the speakers of *The Shepheardes Calender*'s explicitly satirical eclogues. His celebration of Elizabeth, her ladies, and various contemporary court poets is complicated by his extended attack on courtly dissimu-lation, backbiting, and vanity in a world of flatterers where there is 'no place for any gentle wit' (*CCH*, 707). We have a new version of Cuddie's *October* lament about incompetent readers who cannot prize the poet (not to mention the dearth of noble patrons for the aspiring maker) rehearsed in the more urgent tones of the artist in exile.

Spenser's next revival of Colin is rather different. In Book VI of the 1596 edition of *The Faerie Queene*—a book in which epic-romance has digressed (or regressed) very emphatically into pastoral space—he is the swain whose music sustains the dance of the Graces on Mount Acidale: 'Colin Clout (who knows not Colin Clout?) | He pypt apace, whilest they him daunst about' (VI.x.16). The nonchalant parenthetical question assumes both a continuum within Spenser's *oeuvre* and the already 'monumental' identity of the author's pastoral alter ego; however, the episode teasingly contradicts *December*'s concluding representation of a despairing and moribund artist. The music of this Colin sustains the visionary spectacle of secular grace in action, paying tribute the while to an unnamed Beloved who becomes the fourth Grace at its centre (VI.x.11–16). His moment of triumphant artistry is, however, exquisitely fragile; it is shattered, somewhat ironically, by the arrival of the all too curious patron of Courtesy, Sir Calidore, the questing hero of Book VI, and Colin, breaking his pipes, re-enacts the frustrated self-silencing of *Jaunarye* (VI.x.17–18). Colin then assumes the role of E. K., painstakingly glossing the scene to Calidore, the inadequate reader who can only feed his 'greedy fancy' on the place and its inhabitants (VI.x.21–8; 30). It is difficult to know what to emphasize here: the author's return to the pastoral dynamic of *The Shepheardes Calender* to articulate a visionary epiphany (the naked Graces, lacking all 'false dissemblaunce' (VI.x.24) might seem to reinvoke the primal virtues of the green world) or his pessimism about the possibility of ever communicating such a vision in a world of imperfect readers. What is clear, however, is that Spenser's interest in the problems faced by the practising poet and in the difficulties of *any* act of poetic meditation, so carefully enacted by both the poetry and the paratexts of *The Shepheardes Calender*, is as acute and alive at the end of his career as it is in his artistic debut.

NOTES

1. All quotations from *The Shepheardes Calender* are from Spenser (1999). Parenthetical references offer line numbers in the case of quotations from the poetry, page numbers in the case of quotations from E. K.'s prose paratexts and critical apparatus.
2. Luborsky has discussed at length the illustrations to *The Shepheardes Calender* and emphasizes their uniqueness (the publisher was not simply recycling available images). Not for another two hundred years would depictive woodblocks be 'specially made to accompany new imaginative poetry' (1981: 18). See also Claire Preston's discussion of the woodcuts in Chapter 37 below.
3. Translation: 'How shall I address thee, maiden?' 'Surely a goddess.'
4. For a more detailed discussion of the metrical and formal work of *The Shepheardes Calender* see Jeff Dolven's essay in this volume (Chapter 21) and also Woods (1984), 139–44.
5. The identity of E. K. has always provoked much critical commentary: suggested E. K.'s have included the obscure Edward Kirke, Spenser's friend Gabriel Harvey, and Fulke Greville. Louise Schleiner has offered a particularly trenchant summary of the debates and has

herself made a convincing case that 'Spenser primarily wrote the apparatus, with the initial help and general inspiration of Harvey' (1990: 380).
6. E. K's notes and apparatus were preserved through the first eight editions of *The Shepheardes Calender*; they were erased in subsequent publications, only reappearing in modern scholarly editions.

BIBLIOGRAPHY

Alpers, Paul J. (1988). 'Pastoral and the Domain of Lyric in Spenser's *Shepheardes Calender*', in Stephen Greenblatt (ed.), *Representing the English Renaissance*. Berkeley and Los Angeles: University of California Press, 163–80.

Berger, Harry, Jr. (1988). *Revisionary Play: Studies in the Spenserian Dynamics*. Berkeley and Los Angeles: University of California Press.

Bernard, John D. (1989). *Ceremonies of Innocence: Pastoralism in the Poetry of Edmund Spenser*. Cambridge: Cambridge University Press.

Chamberlain, Richard (2005). *Radical Spenser: Pastoral, Politics and the New Aestheticism*. Edinburgh: Edinburgh University Press.

Chaucer, Geoffrey (1987). *Troilus and Criseyde*, ed. Larry D. Benson et al. *The Riverside Chaucer*, 2nd edn. Boston: Houghton Mifflin.

Cheney, Patrick (1993). *Spenser's Famous Flight: A Renaissance Idea of a Literary Career*. Toronto: University of Toronto Press.

Cullen, Patrick (1970). *Spenser, Marvell, and Renaissance Pastoral*. Cambridge, MA: Harvard University Press.

Greene, Roland (1987). '*The Shepheardes Calender*: Dialogue and Periphrasis'. *SSt* 8: 1–33.

Hamilton, A. C. (1956). 'The Argument of Spenser's *Shepheardes Calender*'. *ELH* 23: 171–82.

Helgerson, Richard (1983). *Self-Crowned Laureates: Spenser, Jonson, Milton and the Literary System*. Berkeley and Los Angeles: University of California Press.

Hoffman, Nancy Jo (1977). *Spenser's Pastorals: The Shepheardes Calender and 'Colin Clout'*. Baltimore: Johns Hopkins University Press.

Johnson, Lynn Staley (1990). *The Shepheardes Calender: An Introduction*. College Park: Pennsylvania State University Press.

King, John N. (1990). *Spenser's Poetry and the Reformation Tradition*. Princeton, NJ: Princeton University Press.

Kinney, Clare R. (2004). 'Marginal Presence, Lyric Resonance, Epic Absence: *Troilus and Criseyde* and/in *The Shepheardes Calender*'. *SSt* 18: 25–39.

Lane, Robert (1993). *Shepheards Devises: Edmund Spenser's* Shepheardes Calender *and the Institutions of Elizabethan Society*. Athens, GA: University of Georgia Press.

Luborsky, Ruth S. (1981). 'The Illustrations to *The Shepheardes Calender*'. *SSt* 2: 3–53.

McCabe, Richard A. (1995). '"Little booke: thy selfe present": The Politics of Presentation in *The Shepheardes Calender*', in Harold Erskine-Hill and Richard A. McCabe (eds), *Presenting Poetry: Composition, Publication, Reception: Essays in Honour of Ian Jack*. Cambridge, Cambridge University Press, 15–40.

—— (2000). 'Annotating Anonymity, or Putting a Gloss on *The Shepheardes Calender*', in Joe Bray, Miriam Handley, Anne C. Henry (eds), *Ma(r)king the Text: The Presentation of Meaning on the Literary Page*. Aldershot: Ashgate, 35–54.

MacCaffrey, Isabel G. (1969). 'Allegory and Pastoral in *The Shepheardes Calender*'. *ELH* 36: 88–109.

Miller, David L. (1979). 'Authorship, Anonymity and *The Shepheardes Calender*'. *MLQ* 40: 219–36.

Montrose, Louis Adrian (1979). '"The perfect paterne of a Poete": The Poetics of Courtship in *The Shepheardes Calender*'. *TSLL* 21: 34–67.

Norbrook, David (2002). *Poetry and Politics in the English Renaissance*, rev edn. Oxford: Oxford University Press.

Patterson, Annabel (1987). *Pastoral and Ideology: Virgil to Valéry*. Berkeley and Los Angeles: University of California Press.

Puttenham, George (2007). *The Art of English Poesy*, ed. Wayne A. Rebhorn and Frank Whigham. Ithaca, NY: Cornell University Press.

Schleiner, Louise (1990). 'Spenser's "E.K." as Edmund Kent (Kenned/of Kent): Kyth (Couth), Kissed, and Kunning-Conning'. *ELR* 20: 374–407.

Shore, David R. (1985). *Spenser and the Poetics of Pastoral: A Study of the World of Colin Clout*. Kingston and Montreal: McGill-Queen's University Press.

Sidney, Sir Philip (1989). *Sir Philip Sidney: The Major Works*, ed. Katherine Duncan-Jones. Oxford: Oxford University Press.

Smith, Bruce R. (1980). 'On Reading *The Shepheardes Calender*'. *SSt* 1: 69–93.

Woods, Susanne (1984). *Natural Emphasis: English Versification from Chaucer to Dryden*. San Marino: Huntingdon Library.

CHAPTER 10

....

LETTERS (1580)

....

JOSEPH CAMPANA

In 1580 five letters exchanged between Gabriel Harvey and Edmund Spenser appeared in a slender quarto volume from the publisher H. Bynneman. The letters, two by Spenser and three by Harvey, were grouped under separate title pages: *Three proper, and wittie familiar letters: lately passed betvveen two Vniversitie Men: touching the Earthquake in Aprill last, and our English reformed Versifying* and *Two Other, very commendable letters, of the same mens writing: both touching the foresaid Artificiall Versifying and Certain other particulars.*[1] For the student of Spenser—and especially for the student of an emerging golden age of Renaissance literature—the letters tease and tantalize with suggestive possibilities.[2] Casual references to works of Spenser (either lost or never written) abound, including the *Dying Pelican, Stemmata Dudleiana, Dreames,* and *Nine Comedies.* Out of the conversational texture of these letters emerges evidence of the composition of *The Faerie Queene,* not only from Harvey's famous derogation of that poem ('Hobgoblin runne away with the garland from Apollo'; *Prose,* 472),[3] but also from Spenser's reference to Ralph Holinshed's *Chronicles of England, Scotland, and Ireland,* which traces the rivers of England and thus proved useful in the composition of the *Legend of Friendship*—though Spenser then imagined his treatment of the marriage of the Thames and Medway to be part of an as-yet unwritten independent poem to be entitled *Epithalamion Thamesis.* For the reader of *The Shepheardes Calender* interested in the identity of E. K., there is material to consider (such as the casually referenced Mistress Kirk) but there are few conclusions to be reached.[4]

Already it is apparent that along with their suggestive content these letters are riddled with ambiguity. The letters do not seem to be published in chronological order, with those in the second section predating those in the first, although the precise dating of these letters may now be impossible and the dates given in the quarto may be arbitrary.[5] Moreover, while Gabriel Harvey signed his letters, and references in the correspondence point to Spenser's identity (including a rare direct reference in Spenser's lengthy Latin verse to Harvey), Spenser did not sign the letters with his own name, refusing the authorizing gesture of the signature for the elusive if, due to the recent publication of *The Shepheardes Calender*, now familiar moniker 'Immeritô'. For a poet toying with anonymity, what might he and Harvey have wanted readers to know? We can assess this partly by virtue of the titles, for while Spenser and Harvey were not necessarily involved in such details of publication, the letters are not without distinct marketing hooks. Clearly, that they were both university men was a distinction important to the allure of the letters. Equally important to the marketing of this little quarto must have been the phrase 'familiar letters', which identified its publication with an epistolary tradition equally rooted in classical antiquity and in early modernity's increasing interest in letters, from published correspondence to rhetorical manuals designed to enhance one's prowess as an author of epistles. Discussions of the future of English verse would have attracted notice, as the literati of early modern England debated prosody, rhyme, and a host of other literary proprieties. And the burgeoning taste for news (satisfied by an ever-growing body of prose tracts and pamphlets) might have been aroused by the promise of commentary on recent events, including a much-noted earthquake of 1579 also described by Arthur Golding, Thomas Churchyard, and others.[6]

To approach the surface of the letters—their mix of strategic anonymity; their attempt to combine the exclusivity of private, elite exchange characteristic of literary coteries with the mass appeal of publication; and their elusive and simultaneous address to both a singular friend and a reading public—is to be faced with contradiction not to mention a certain hybridity.[7] As already suggested, the letters detail private affection, circles of friends, literary debates, news of public events, English hexameters, and Latin verses, to inventory just a few of their features. To read Spenser's *Letters* is to confront the difficulty of reading them. What kind of information comes from these letters and what use might they be to students of Spenser? Do they tell us about Spenser's life, his poetry, or both and in what ratio? How do we understand the highly wrought rhetoric and affect of the early modern letter? How do classical and early modern notions of friendship intersect with emerging formations of sexuality and emerging notions of the literary author? How important, indeed, is Gabriel Harvey to Spenser and to Spenser's emerging poetic sensibility? How are students of Spenser to understand the literary debates within the letters? What do these sorties in the intertwining arenas of letter and friendship tell us about the poet of *The Shepheardes Calender* and his progress as a writer, especially since the poetics of Spenser's letters seem to contradict the poetics of *The Faerie Queene*? Are the poems included within the letter mere exercises or real evidence of larger concerns at this early moment of England's would-be laureate?

Obstacles to the extraction of personal, political, or poetic certainties from the letters are myriad. To begin with a search for what we might learn of Spenser's life is to be put in the traditionally frustrated position of the biographer. As Judith Anderson puts it, although Edmund Spenser is the major nondramatic poet of the Tudor period, less is known about his life than about that of Sir Philip Sidney or even of William Shakespeare, the contemporary artists whose achievements are comparable to his. Few personal documents such as letters written by him survive, and the traces of his life in other kinds of records are meagre and often ambiguous. (Anderson 1996: ix)

The *Letters* are no exception to this problem. To be sure, there seem to be tantalizing references to Spenser's service with the Earl of Leicester, Leicester's navigation of Queen Elizabeth's nuptial negotiations, and a journey abroad Spenser was to take in Leicester's service.[8] However, as Jon A. Quitslund has argued, 'anyone who regards the hyperbole, allusions, postures, and badinage of Immerito's intimacies as husks hiding kernels of true feeling or the facts of life will be disappointed; only the written words remain' (1996: 83). Posture seems an especially appropriate word to describe one of the interpretive tangles of the letters. For while we should not interpret such posturing as pure fiction, it is clear that Spenser and Harvey alike were energetically involved in the project of fashioning public literary identities, implying that they belonged to an emerging establishment and associated with other literary figures, most importantly Sir Philip Sidney. Spenser and Harvey sought to appear to be both the fresh voices in a new wave of English verse *and* writers already central to an understanding of the tradition of English verse. Like one wandering through one of romance's many dark woods—and few are as richly obscure as the dark woods of Spenserian verse—the reader of the *Letters* has the opportunity to consider a series of provocative tangles. What follows here is an attempt to trace, if not untangle, the politics and erotics of epistolarity, friendship, and verse in these pivotal writings, which allow us to consider a Spenser whose first major work, *The Shepheardes Calender*, had just sailed into the world of print and whose defining opus, *The Faerie Queene*, was underway. I attempt to contextualize early modern letters and early modern friendship with reference to the formal properties of the former and the erotic properties of the latter, both of which have garnered much attention from historians of early modern sexuality. Friendship and epistolarity both played a central role not only in the highly public nature of intimacy in early modernity but also in the struggle to articulate the function of literary writing at a moment when what it meant to be English and what it meant to be an author were both hotly contested. This contestation is the primary subject of the letters.

EARLY MODERN LETTERS, EARLY MODERN FRIENDS

Early modernity was the age of the letter. And just as early modern England was the age of the letter, so too was it the age of the friend. Not only are those cultures of epistolarity and friendship nearly unthinkable without one another, but they also trace a lineage back to the classical era while simultaneously serving at the beck and call of modernity. To generalize about letters is to risk reducing their complex singularity to simple correspondence. As Desiderius Erasmus, author of the influential treatise on letter-writing *De Conscribendis Epistolis* averred, 'To expect all letters to conform to a single type, or to teach that they should, as I notice even learned men sometimes do, is in my view at least to impose a narrow and inflexible definition on what is by nature diverse and capable of almost infinite variation' (1985: 12). At the same time, the radical variability of the letter made it an ideal vehicle for the complexities of the age. As Claudio Guillén has argued, the letter was simultaneously 'one of the classical genres that is cultivated again or resurrected during the Renaissance' and a form whose rapid growth in popularity was a consequence of the effort to develop genres capable of grappling with 'the opulent New World recently discovered, beyond the Atlantic, or the humble and endlessly rich regions of inner, individual, daily experience' (1986: 71, 99). Guillén notes a corresponding 'notorious growth of both the social practice of correspondence and the printing of books incorporating the practice as a channel of communication, while also providing models that in turn enrich and stimulate actual letter writing' (1986: 81). Guillén thus describes a fascinating literary-political feedback loop, with the increasingly fictionalized nature of the letter drawing its energy from real correspondence while endowing that correspondence with the urgency and intensity of the elusive rhetoric of epistolary fictionality. The complications of the epistolary tradition that have been elucidated of late by early modern scholars were anticipated by the 'Envois' of Jacques Derrida's *The Post Card*, which are both 'a performance and analysis of the irreducible twists in any sending system, and of the effects of these twists on what is supposedly most private within such a system' (1987: xii).

If the letter was the meeting place of the fictions of rhetoric and the realities of social life, it was also the location of 'a rich mixture of contrivance and intimacy' (Maurer 1982: 184). Lynne Magnusson has argued that 'the Elizabethans enacted their personal relationships with a rhetorical complexity and eloquence' easy to neglect (Magnusson 1999: 1). Moreover, Magnusson reminds us, 'the early modern state transacted its administrative business, for the most part, in personal letters' (1999: 92). Indeed, the personal or familiar letter of the era, however seemingly frank, intimate, and confidential, must give us pause, as Jonathan Goldberg confirms, arguing that 'writing begins with an awareness of the person, not as an individual but rather as a social category' (1990: 252). Of course, the fantasy of epistolarity is an immediacy of communication, however distant the correspondents. Angel Day, author of the widely consulted treatise *The English Secretary*, defines the letter as follows: 'An epistle therefore, is that which usually we in our vulgar, doe tearme a Letter, and for the respectes thereof is called the messenger, or familiar speach of the absent, for that therein is discouered whatsoever the mind wishes in such cases to have delivered' (1967: 1). Or, more simply and intimately, the letter provides 'the familiar and mutuall talke of one absent friend to another'. Of that nearly infinite variety of letters that Erasmus invokes, Day describes the 'familiar letter', which itself may be divided into several types, as one 'wherein we express and declare to those farre from us, the matters or newes presentlie in hand amongst us' (Day 1967: 8). Or, in Jonathan Goldberg's formulation, 'Immediacy is mediated, and the letter stands in the place of the face-to-face communication of the messenger, writing is structured as the familiarity of speech. One man and another function as bordering absences that meet in the letter' (1990: 251). Out of these bordering absences was woven a network of familiar speakers whose separation incited intense affective and erotic valences and whose purportedly private devotions were central to the circuits of social influence. Friendship was the name for that network of homosocial bonds that found its ideal expression through the fictionality and subterfuge of the letter.

Critics have wondered whether it is possible, let alone advantageous, to distinguish between letters familiar and those amatory, that is to say between friendship and desire. To be sure, the familiar letter evokes discourses of desire and, in so doing, perhaps shares the function of the amatory letter. If Day's treatise is characterized by an 'insistence that the relationship of man to woman be termed "love" and that between man and man be safely called "friendship"' (Bergeron 1999: 7), it is also true that early modernity provides ample evidence of erotic epistolary exchange between men. David Bergeron's *King James and Letters of Homoerotic Desire* (1999), an edition tracing the homoerotics of a monarch's letters to his favourite familiars, finds a classical counterpart in Amy Richlin's *Marcus Aurelius in Love* (2006), which collects the letters between Marcus Aurelius and his teacher Marcus Cornelius Fronto. These editors face the same challenge as the reader of the correspondence between Erasmus and Servatius Rogerus. 'What conclusions', Forrest Tyler Stevens asks, 'should we draw from the letters? Was Erasmus a homosexual? Worse still, was he a jilted homosexual pursuing an unwilling, straight acolyte? Were monasteries refuges for those pleasures one dare not name among Christians? . . . But deeper still, the controversy is about the nature of letters and literature as evidence' (Stevens 2004: 125).

The eroticism of early modern letters is not merely an index of identity or desire. Indeed, if we consider friendship a radical social and sexual organization, we might recall what Foucault emphasizes in an interview entitled 'Friendship as a Way of Life'. 'The problem', he suggests, 'is not to discover in oneself the truth of sex but rather to use sexuality henceforth to arrive at a multiplicity of relationships' (Foucault 1989: 204). So while for some the homoeroticism of familiar letters provides more candidates for a who's who in early modern homosexualities, studies of early modern friendship—from the pioneering work of Alan Bray to more recent treatments by Jeffrey Masten, Laurie Shannon, and others—offer a way of considering complex networks of affect and obligation. Masten invokes among friends a radical and 'absolute identicality, indistinguishability, and interchangeability' (2004: 371). No mere personal alter ego, friendship's implications are political. Shannon notes that 'the radical likeness of sex and station that friendship doctrines require singly enable [*sic*] a vision of parity, a virtually civic parity not modelled anywhere else in contemporary social structures' (2002: 2). Such forms of likeness were located in what Goldberg (1992) describes as the open secret of male homosociality evident in homeomorphic structures of mirroring that echo through Spenser and Harvey's letters as well as through *The Shepheardes Calender*. Moreover, as Bergeron and Masten suggest, the intense affectivity of male friendship is fully embodied in what can be described as 'the intertwined relationship of the body and the body of letters' (Bergeron 1999: 5). Conventional descriptors signal this intertwined relationship. 'As a recurrent term in friendship's vocabulary', Masten argues, '*sweet* indicates the fungibility of male friends—not merely the exchangeability and indistinguishability of identities or selves but also the way in which what we have regarded as an identity trope is imagined in this culture as literally embodied' (2004: 376). The language of sweetness suggests the shared pleasures of the mouth (tasting and kissing, to be sure, but also talking and reading aloud), which point equally to both the sharing of erotic experience and the sharing of words.[9] What precisely did Spenser and Harvey share when it came to the subject of words?

SPENSER's LETTERS, SPENSER's FRIENDS

Friendship records the coexistence of embodied networks of affect and fantasies of likeness, parity, and interchangeability, both of which structured male homosocial relationships in early modern England. And as we remember the extent to which friendship, however powerfully and affectively embodied, did not erase the differences (such as sex and station, among other markers of alterity) constitutive of the highly hierarchical culture of early modern England, we begin to see a fundamental conflict between the symmetrical and asymmetrical relationships that structure Spenser's letters with Harvey. To be sure, Spenser addresses his letters to Harvey with customary grandiloquence: 'To the Worshipfull his very singular good friend, maister G. H., Fellow of Trinitie Hall in Cambridge' (*Prose*, 5). Spenser's second letter, more simply, addresses itself 'To my long approued and singular good frende, Master *G. H*' (*Prose*, 15). If the theory of friendship implies interchangeability, the practice of friendship is a continuing negotiation of the differences that interrupt the ideal of the friend as alter ego. Thus Spenser is keen to display his deference to Harvey: 'And that you may perceiue how much your Counsel in al things preuaileth with me, and how altogether I am ruled and ouer-ruled thereby: I am now determined to alter mine owne former purpose, and to subscribe to your aduizement: being notwithstanding resolued stil, to abide your farther resolution' (*Prose*, 5). While it is not entirely clear what the subject of Harvey's advice is—at moments it seems to be about the sending of letters—Spenser's zeal to submit to Harvey only increases in this first letter: 'in all things I attribute so muche to your iudgement, that I am euermore content to adnihilate mine owne determinations in respecte thereof' (*Prose*, 6). How are we to understand Spenser's submissive gestures—mere convention, proof of affection, or evidence of friendship as both a way of life and a social network?

To be sure, while Spenser continues to refer to his 'unfained affection, and zeale towards' Gabriel Harvey (*Prose*, 6), he also imagines himself as enviably moving up in the world of courtly influence and becoming part of a coterie from which Harvey remains distant. He refers to Harvey's 'desire to heare of my late being with hir Maiestie' before regaling him with developments regarding 'the two worthy Gentlemen, Master *Sidney* and Master *Dyer*, they haue me, I thank them, in some vse of familiarity'. As we can see, the word 'familiar' that in the context of letters connotes such intense affect between men also suggests the weave of courtly networks as Spenser sees himself admitted to the company of influential men: Sir Philip Sidney, who needs no introduction, and the courtier and poet Sir Edward Dyer. But the letters also ring with affection for Harvey. Letters and verses are fine tokens of affection, to be sure, and Spenser's second letter opens with a mild rebuke to Harvey, who 'restraineth his Penne' (*Prose*, 15). 'But', Spenser admits, 'I woulde rather I might yet see youre owne good selfe, and receiue a Reciprocall farewell from your owne sweete mouth' (*Prose*, 8). Spenser's longing for embodied communication with Harvey appears not only in that term 'sweete' that Masten exposes as an index of the potent physicality of male friendship discourse, but more importantly, Spenser recalls the shared bed—the bedfellow relationship so important to Bray's early work on sexuality in early modern England—as the scene of his poetic communion with Harvey (Bray 1982). Referring to verses included in the third letter, Spenser inquires, 'Seeme they comparable to those two, which I translated to you *ex tempore* in bed, the last time we lay togither in Westminster?' (*Prose*, 16). And indeed the verses immediately following return to an erotic language of incorporation, moving from the taste of sweetness to the potency of hunger: '*That which I eate, did I ioy, and that which I greedily gorged*' (*Prose*, 16). Arguably, the allure of other men is embodied in early modernity not only in figures of sweetness but in figures of eating and devouring. More important, perhaps, is this breakdown in the language of mirroring (or identification) that Goldberg finds in both these letters and in *The Shepheardes Calender*. As Goldberg argues, 'Spenser slept with Harvey, and it is no secret. Indeed this is the open secret of a *proper* and *familiar* scene' (1992: 79). Of the many things Harvey and Spenser may have done in bed, reading, writing, and translating we can be sure of. The letters aspire not merely to sharing a bed but to sharing with the other in a bodily way, incorporating the friend as the self. Quitslund suggests that 'all efforts to separate Spenser's identity or character from Harvey's involve a mistaken view of the *Letters*' (1996: 82). Thus the fantasy and the eroticism of friendship depend not merely on mirrors and absences but on the notion of a shared body, the corpus being both the shared corporeality of the physical body and the shared identity of an authorial body. It is to the poetics of the letters that we must then turn to see how the idea of a poetic sensibility, shared in the body, develops in the letters.

SPENSER'S *AREOPAGUS*, ENGLAND'S NATION OF VERSE

The era in which Spenser and Harvey exchanged and published their letters witnessed the emergence of a great age of poetry. Thus, in retrospect, it seems already to have been a great wellspring of established and time-honoured literary traditions. A closer examination of the period reveals that it was experienced as a time riddled with anxiety and uncertainty. The question of what English literature should be was the central issue of the day, one evident in the proliferations of literary defences, definitions, and manifestos.[10] Given the diminishing contemporary importance of traditional form in the perennially endangered audience for poetry, such debates can seem overwrought or merely antiquated. When we think of Spenser as the poet whose greatest work codified a hypnotically rhythmic, rhyming stanzaic form of singular power and lasting influence, it may surprise us to recall that in the letters Spenser participated in what may seem one of the historically stranger literary debates of the age. The battle was waged over prosody, and the central question was whether English poetry should follow its own native tradition of rhyming, accentual verse or should imitate the unrhyming, quantitative verse of the ancients (despite its palpable mismatch with the tendencies of the English language). As Derek Attridge remarks of Sidney at the beginning of his survey of early modern English prosody,

Sidney's scrupulous appointment, in his *Apologie for Poetry*, of equal praise to the traditional English manner of writing verse and to the imitation of classical metres in English, strikes the modern reader—as it must have struck most readers from a decade after its publication in 1595 to the present—as astonishingly over-generous to the latter species of verse. (1974: 1)

More pointedly, Attridge asks, 'Why should so many writers, among them poets of such distinction as Sidney, Spenser and Campion, have devoted so much time and effort to an enterprise which held out such slender hopes of success?' (1974: 2).

The idea that the author of *The Faerie Queene* was, even briefly, not only sympathetic to, but an advocate of, the quantitative movement was so thoroughly unacceptable to later literary critics that the 1679 edition of his *Works* 'inserts an "almost" before his statement to Harvey that Sidney and Dyer have "drawn mee to their faction"' (Attridge 1974: 232). To be sure, Spenser locates himself within a coterie of advocates of quantitative versification—Edward Dyer, Thomas Drant, and Sidney among others. Dyer and Sidney, Spenser admits,

haue proclaimed in their ἀρείω πάγω, a generall surceasing and silence of balde Rymers, and also of the verie beste to: in steade whereof, they have by authoritie of their whole Senate, prescribed certaine Lawes and rules of Quantities of English sillables, for English verse: having had thereof already great practice, and drawen mee to their faction. (*Prose*, 6)

It is unclear whether this Areopagus was an actual, concerted movement or a convenient figure to express Spenser's momentary affiliation.[11] We may indeed wonder whether Spenser had merely fallen under the influence of the charismatic

Sidney. But it seems this affiliation was not solely the product of influence, as Spenser further admits to changing his tune, being 'of late, more in loue with my Englishe Versifying, than with Ryming: whyche I should haue done long since, if I would then haue followed your councell' (*Prose*, 6). The extent to which Spenser and Harvey agreed on a common vision of 'English reformed Versifying' remains a question; that subject, along with a finer sense of Spenser's poetic craft, is treated thoroughly by Attridge and in greater detail in Chapter 21 below. It is clear that, despite his zeal for reformed English versifying, Spenser was aware of some difficulties attending the project:

For the onely, or cheifest hardnesse, whych seemeth, is in the Accente: whyche sometime gapeth, and as it were yawneth ilfauouredly, comming shorte of that it should, and sometime exceeding the measure of the Number, as in *Carpenter*, the middle sillable being vsed shorte in speache, when it shall be read long in Verse, seemeth like *a lame Gosling, that draweth one legge after hir:* and *Heauen* being vsed shorte as one sillable, when it is in verse stretched out with a *Diastole*, is like a lame Dogge that holds vp one legge. (*Prose*, 16)

Technically and aesthetically, the new versifying posed its advocates some serious challenges.

But subtending discussions of what we now often consider solely formal issues (such as prosody) was the very notion of what it was to be English and to conceive of a singularly English nation with cultural traditions that not only reflected but also supported what Richard Helgerson has argued was a relatively new sense of the nation. Indeed, we might compare the fervor of debates on meter and rhyme with the English-only movement in the United States, where the declaration of an official language represents, for some, the safeguarding of national identity and the securing of the nation's borders. As Helgerson has argued, Spenser's letters to Harvey help clarify an emerging nationalist project in Elizabethan England developed by writers as various as Spenser, Coke, Camden, Drayton, Shakespeare, and Hooker. Helgerson takes his cue from Spenser's desperate cry to Harvey, 'Why a God's name may not we, as else the Greekes, haue the kingdome of oure owne Language, and measure our accentes, by the sounde, reseruing the Quantitie to the Verse?' (*Prose*, 16). Debates about the merits of accentual versus quantitative meter pertain to the question of what it means to have a kingdom of one's own language, one 'whose boundaries are determined by the language of its inhabitants' and is thus 'no longer a kingdom in the purely dynastic sense' (Helgerson 1992: 2). This newly focused interest in a different sense of England as a nation ('its land, its people, its institutions, and its history') inflected discussions of verse with a 'dramatic expression of ambition, cultural envy, and frustration' (Helgerson 1992: 3). Helgerson construes the project of Elizabethan literature as a consequence of an emerging tension between what is later termed the gothic and the classical, between the particularity of a dark English past and the superior knowledge and tradition of an enlightened classical antiquity. Thus that mixture of ambition and frustration culminates in a single question:

The Greeks had the kingdom of their own language. Why, Spenser asks, can't we? Why must we be consigned to perpetual subjection and inferiority? This pressure, this tension, this conflict of aspiration and insecurity, brings us close to the crisis from which both Elizabethan poetry and the larger project of English self-representation emerged, close to the desperately hopeful sense that, were England to rival the greatness of Greece and Rome, something decisive needed to be done. (Helgerson 1992: 3)

More recently, Carlo Ginzburg finds that the (eventually successful) defense of rhyme was not only part of debates over the virtues of the ancient and the modern but, more importantly, they were part of a debate about England's relationship to the Continent and of the 'long process' of 'the insularization of England' (2000: 42).

   More pointedly, the fractures between Spenser and Harvey emerging from beneath the flowery surfaces of friendship rhetoric reveal significantly different political visions. Attridge finds little practical difference between the two on the subject of quantitative verse, arguing that 'Spenser and Harvey wrote broadly the same kind of quantitative verse' (1974: 189). But to parse the letters with a nationalist project in mind reveals a great rift between the two. As Helgerson notes, Harvey objects to the technical and political properties of Spenser's verse experiments:

Where Spenser had used the language of sovereign power eager to subdue rough words and have the kingdom of them, Harvey responds in terms made familiar by centuries of resistance to royal encroachment. . . . He accuses Spenser of usurpation and tyranny, locates authority not in the king but in 'God and his English people,' proclaims the value of custom and the order of law, supports the peaceful enjoyment of immemorial privileges and liberties. (1992: 28)

For friends, other selves, or absent bedfellows, this would represent a potent disjunction. Thus the rhetoric of friendship in these letters, with their fantasy of a network of friends mutually incorporated in one body and in one nation of verse, begins to take on an elegiac intensity; friendship is increasingly associated with loss and absence, not solely because of the literal physical distance between Spenser and Harvey but, more pointedly, because the literary journeys each were to take increasingly shared neither a common purpose nor a common terminus.

THE POETRY OF FAMILIAR LETTERS

What we may think of as an elegiac tone in this exchange begins to surface in the texture of the epistles and even more powerfully in the poems included within those letters. The letters exchanged between Spenser and Harvey include quantitative exercises, a lengthy Latin poem written by Spenser for Harvey, and an equally lengthy poem written by Harvey for Spenser. It is easy to dismiss these poems as mere exercises or as the minor effusions of a youthful poet and his less talented friend. Attridge maintains that 'the importance of the verse in the Spenser/Harvey letters, apart from our natural interest in the minor writings of a great poet, lies in its direct exemplification of the forces at work behind the movement, untempered by thoroughgoing adherence to the Latin model or by sensitivity to the result as English poetry' (1974: 188). More pointedly, Attridge maintains that 'the quantitative verse of both Spenser and Harvey gives the impression of hasty composition, and judged as poetry, only Spenser's "Iambicum Trimetrum" is of any value' (1974: 190). But the value we assign these poems cannot be strictly limited to their prosodic accuracy or the aesthetics of their composition.

Spenser's 'Iambicum Trimetrum' may or may not satisfy the partisans of quantitative verse, but it does serve as a telling backdrop for the other poems in Spenser's letters. It is perhaps not insignificant that the only verse on the subject of love that features a female beloved is an exercise, accomplished but uninspiring. The level of verse becomes more elevated and more artful as Spenser shifts to Latin, which we might say serves as the preferred idiom of homosociality in Renaissance England, and addresses his affection for Gabriel Harvey. The poem, 'Ad Ornatissimum Virum', appears in translation in the notes to the *Variorum* text of the letters (*Prose*, 256–8), in a prose translation of the poem in Richard McCabe's edition of Spenser's shorter poems (Spenser 1999: 578–9), and in a hitherto unpublished translation by Quitslund that appears for the first time in this volume and to which this essay refers.

Spenser opens with a salutatory grandiloquence familiar from the letters, addressing the poem 'Ad Ornatissimum virum, multis iamdiu nominibus clarissimum, G.H. Immerito sui, mox in Gallias nauigaturi' ('To G[abriel] H[arvey], the most illustrious of men, already distinguished by many titles, from his *Immerito*, about to set off to France and Italy, *Fare Well*'). The deferential opening continues in the first few lines, which construe Spenser as the lowly, younger poet and Harvey as the master: 'Sic malus egregium, sic non inimicus Amicum: | Sicque nouus veterem iubet ipse Poëta Poëtam, | Saluere' (123–4) ('So a rogue, to the honored one; so one not unfriendly, to a friend; | And so the new poet wishes the old one well'). If the poem opens with praise for the elder poet, it also opens with a sense of foreboding, as the vicissitudes of fortune make their appearance. What begins with the wishing of good fortune to Harvey and the anticipation of a sea voyage on the part of Spenser quickly modulates to the metaphorical near-shipwreck of Spenser's affections. Throughout the poem, the journey Spenser describes will shift terrain from Petrarchan to Odyssean before settling in on the often frustrated journey of the young poet seeking his laureate crown in a world of adventitious courtiers. But the first storm the speaker encounters is his own unworthiness on the sea of fortune, as his absence from (apparently) Harvey leaves him in a state of reasonless longing:

> ego solus ineptus.
> Nam mihi nescio quo mens saucia vulnere, dudum
> Fluctuat ancipiti Pelago, dum Navita proram
> Inualidam validus rapit huc Amor, et rapit illuc.
> Consilijs Ratio melioribus usa, decusque
> Immortale leui diffissa Cupidinis Arcu.
> Angimur hoc dubio, et portu vexamur in ipso.   (133–9)

> I alone am unfit.
>
> For my mind, wounded by I know not what blow,
> Has lately been tossing on the perilous ocean, while my captain,
> Powerful Love, jerks the fragile vessel now this way, now that.
> Reason, with her better counsels, and immortal honor
> Are dispersed by Cupid's light bow.
> I am tortured by doubt, and tossed about even in port.

Unlike the tepid 'Iambicum Trimetrum', the pathos of loss feels most intense here where the absent beloved is the friend. Although the discourse of love directs itself to the friend, Harvey appears in the poem as an exemplary stoic, capable of resisting the strong pull of desire. More resilient than Odysseus, who resisted immortal temptations to return to his wife, is Harvey:

> Praeque subumbrata Splendoris Imagine tanti,
> Praeque illo Meritis famosis nomine parto,
> Caetera, quae Vecors, uti Numina, vulgus adorat,
> Praedia, Amicitias, armenta, peculiar, nummos.
> Quaeque placent oculis, formas, spectacular, Amores,
> Quaeque placent ori, quaeque auribus, omnia temnis.   (163–8)

> Compared to such an obscure image of splendor,
> Compared to that name begotten by famous deeds,
> Other things which the giddy rabble adore as idols—
> Farms, friendships, cattle, profits, bags of money,
> Whatever pleases the eye, beauties, spectacles, loves,
> Whatever pleases the palate or the ear—you despise them all.

Of course, Spenser is well aware that Harvey's admirable stoicism, his satirical condemnation of worldly pleasures and other indices of social prominence, may also be his Achilles heel. 'The world', after all, 'is so full of fools' (65). Even poets fall into the trap of trying to please the rabble crowd through popular appeal:

> quisquis placuisse Studet Heroibus altis,
> Desipuisse studet, sic gratia crescit ineptis.
> Denique Laurigeris quisquis sua tempora vittis,
> Insignire volet, Populoque placere fauenti,
> Desipere insanus discit, turpemque pudendae
> Stultitiae laudem quaerit.   (176–81)

> whoever studies how to please great men
> Studies how to play the fool, for favor increases toward the inept man,
> Whoever, therefore, wishes to distinguish his life
> By wearing a laurel crown, and to satisfy by winning favor with the people,
> Learns to pretend madness, and seeks base praise
> For shameful folly.

The dilemma here is cast as Harvey's, but it was, no doubt, already clear—painfully clear, indeed—whose star was to rise faster in the world of English letters. Spenser comes awfully close to admitting this when he claims that Harvey is no poet, though he justifies this remark by explaining that Harvey refuses to play the fool by entering the public world of poetry to please great men and to win favor with the people (184–7).

Spenser not only describes and advises Harvey; he also corrects Harvey, whose admirable stoicism may in fact be too stern. And here, yet again, it seems that Spenser is giving himself advice as he directs Harvey to a more moderate path: 'Nec tu delicias nimis aspernare fluentes, | Nec serò Dominam, venientem in vota, nec Aurum | si sapis' (192–4) ('Nor ought you to spurn flowing delights too severely, | Nor a wife brought at last to the altar, nor (if you are wise) | An offer of gold'). Already the middle way of temperance is in Spenser's mind, as are the potentially deleterious effects of denying all pleasure. Yet Spenser also expresses the quintessential anxiety of the poet who worries that he may violate the Horatian dictum grounding literary value in the balance of pleasure and utility:

> Omne tulit punctum, qui miscuit utile dulci.
> Dij mihi, dulce diu dederant: verùm utile nunquam:
> Utile nunc etiam, ô utinam quoque dulce dedissent.
> Dij mihi, (quippe Dijs aequiualia maxima parvis)
> Ni nimis inuideant mortalibus esse beatis,
> Dulce simul tribuisse queant, simul utile   (202–7)

> He wins the prize who mingles the sweet with the useful.
> The gods long ago gave me sweetness, but never anything useful:
> How I wish even now that they had given me some utility along with sweetness.
> May the gods (for surely to them the greatest are equivalent to the small),
> Unless they envy mortals who are too happy,
> See their way to giving me the sweet and the useful together.

Spenser's momentary crisis of confidence sends him back to a language of arduous journeys, for not only is he 'born under an angry star' but he is also destined to pass through inhospitable landscapes (all poets being 'sociij Vlyssis' or 'comrades of Ulysses') and not unlike Ceres, 'Passibus inde Deam fessis comitabimur aegram, | Nobile cui furtum quaerenti defuit orbis' (214–16) ('the grieving goddess, | From whose searching the earth withheld the renowned theft'). The invocation of Ceres makes it seem that Spenser's poetic anxiety, pleasure without utility, opens up on a deeper fear—the failure to produce:

> Namque sinu pudet in patrio, tenebrisque pudendis
> Non nimis ingenio Iuuenem infoelice, virentes,
> Officijs frustra deperdere vilibus Annos,
> Frugibus et vaucas speratis cernere spicas.   (217–20)

> For one feels ashamed, as a youth not without talents,
> To be wasting the green years uselessly,
> At home with unworthy duties in the shameful shade,
> Picking empty ears out of the hoped-for crops.

Spenser's refrain must feel familiar to us. We might hear the anticipatory echoes of John Milton's 'Lycidas', which portrays the similarly anxious and frustrated sensibility of a poet's 'green years'. The young poet fears he will never find what will enable his talent to be realized—the right project, the right language, the right audience, the right style. For many poets it seems the experience of talented anticipation is filled with shame and the fear of waste. And for all that Spenser lauds Harvey as one capable of marrying the pleasurable and the useful, this example of a failed elder poet must have also been potent and less than comforting.

By the end of the poem, the exuberance of Spenser's affection for Harvey is by no means blunted; the tone of his address is, however, more wistful. Spenser imagines his departure on a long and hard journey towards poetic excellence as Harvey's deprivation: 'Quis dabit interea conditas rore Britanno, | Quis tibi Litterulas? quis Carmen amore petulcum? (223–4) ('Meanwhile', Spenser asks, 'who will send you little letters? | Steeped in Britain's dew? Or a poem impudent with love?') He imagines Harvey as 'quamuis omnibus amicis / Innumeris, geniûmque choro stipatus amaeno' (230–1) ('surrounded by a crowd of friends | Innumerable, and by a pleasant chorus of wits'); Spenser appends after the poem a protestation of love: 'Mi amabilissime Harveie, meo cordi, meorum omnium longè charissime ('my most loveable Harvey, my heart, by far the dearest of all to me'). But the poem closes with a wish for a missing friend; Harvey:

> Immerito tamen unum absentem saepe requiret,
> Optabitque, Utinam meus hîc Edmundus adesset,
> Qui noua scripsisset, nec Amores conticuisset,
> Ipse suos, et saepe animo, verbisque benignis
> Fausta precaretur: Deus illum aliquando reducat. Etc.   (232–6)

> Will often still miss the one absent, Immerito,
> And will wish, 'If only my Edmund were here,
> Who would have written news, nor would he have ceased singing his loves.
> And often in his heart and with the kindest words,
> He would seek favor. May God bring him back once more.' Etc.

The wish for the friend's return is central to the epistle of friendship. After all, letters are predicated on absence. But the mournful tone Spenser adopts as the voice of Harvey bespeaks a larger elegiac cast resulting from a growing sense of fracture between the two. The younger poet may wish to apprentice himself to, and model himself on, the elder poet, but Harvey would prove to be inadequate. Indeed, the friendship may not have flagged, as evident in a 1586 sonnet written by Spenser about Harvey and appended to a collection of Harvey's letters and other writings (Harvey 1592: 75). Although we note a continuity of affections from the 1580 *Letters* and 'Ad Ornatissimum Virum' to the later sonnet, by 1586 Spenser no longer identifies his friend Harvey as the elder poet. In contrast, Harvey appears as the consummate taste maker, who wields his 'critique pen' (3) without regard for the opinions of the high, the mighty, or the foolish: 'For Life, and Death is in thy doomeful writing: | So thy renowme liues euer by endighting' (13–14). This compliment to Harvey could not be more emphatic, yet it also removes him from the shared terrain of an arduous journey in the service of poetry. No matter how singular the friend, Harvey was not to be the poetic alter ego Spenser may once have thought he had. As Richard McCabe puts it,

The impact of *The Shepheardes Calendar* was far greater than that of any of [Harvey's] own publications and the new poet quickly eclipsed the new man. Their shifting status is perceptible even in the Spenser-Harvey *Letters*. As the situation is presented there, it is Immerito who is 'familiar' with the great and the good and who labors to recommend Harvey to them for friendship's sake. (2007: 59)

For McCabe, the invocation of friendship was, for the circles Spenser and Harvey travelled in, tied up with networks of patronage and obligation. In his words, the '"friendly intertextuality"' of poets praising and petitioning one another in print 'turned poet into patron and patron into poet' (2007: 56). But for all that the *Letters* advertise a burgeoning marketplace of potentially profitable literary relationships, in retrospect patronage would not be adequate to describe Spenser's relationship to Harvey. The powerful sense of obligation in the *Letters* comes to be tangled up in an equally powerful sense of failed projects, hopeless ambitions, and worlds of verse never to be.

English Letters

The letters exchanged between Spenser and Harvey tease with a series of lush possibilities never to be realized: the love between Spenser and Harvey, their shared ambition as poets, their own Areopagus at the head of a unified nation of versifiers, their own circle of friends and wits innumerable. This exchange was recorded and published not solely for posterity but for the sake of what must have been imagined as a timely intervention in present affairs, literary and otherwise. But we might most profitably think of these letters as an archive of impossible futures. The quantitative movement was to be as elusive and impermanent as both Harvey's literary prominence and the godlike power Spenser attributes to his critical pronouncements. At the same moment Spenser was reminding Harvey that there was no shame in marriage ('Ad Ornatissimum', 70–1), a grammatical construction in the Latin of Harvey's epistles allowed him to teasingly and affectionately render his beloved Spenser in the feminine gender—'O mea Domina Immerito, mea bellissima Collina Clouta' (*Prose*, 476).[12]

What form of union pertains to Spenser and Harvey? What body did they share in the world of English letters when they no longer shared a bed or, necessarily, literary tastes? Answers to such questions are elusive. But perhaps the most interesting feature of the letters is the fantasy of a corporate literary identity. The inquiries of Roland Barthes and Michel Foucault have long encouraged literary critics to reconsider what exactly we mean when we refer to an author.[13] If Barthes declared the death of the author (to give birth to the reader), Foucault explored the author function and its consequent (and often unspoken) assumptions about literary texts. In the course of historicizing the inquiries of Barthes and Foucault, the case for the thoroughly collaborative nature of early modern drama has been made more visible in recent years, while for authors such as Spenser the idea of the literary career has taken centre stage.[14] Still, these letters tempt us to understand Spenser and Harvey as friends and erotic collaborators, coauthors of some uncertain variety. The mixture of Latin and English poetry and prose held a special allure for this correspondence. It was the place of friendship in as much as it allowed for the maximum public display of literary mastery *and* remained available as a medium for communicating deep intimacies between men. These intimacies include the homosocial or homoerotic tonalities of male friendship, but they also run deeper and were not confined to classical languages. Indeed, as the letters themselves show, English was readily available as a language capable of conveying erotic intimacies between men—actual or imagined. In the *January* eclogue of *The Shepheardes Calender*, E. K. parses the modalities of relation that might govern Colin's relationship with Hobbinol, his 'very speciall and most familiar freend'. E. K. invokes 'pederasticie', 'gynerastice', and 'disorderly love' (or sodomy) the last of which he denounces. Alan Stewart has explored the entanglements of sodomy and humanism in scenes of friendship, patronage, and pedagogy, arguing that in this era 'Texts were commissioned, written, taught, learned, presented, dedicated, accepted, and read within a series of socially acknowledged but socially problematic transactions between men' (1997: xliv).

But what was problematic in the Spenser–Harvey correspondence was not its eroticism, at least not for Spenser. As Lorna Hutson has argued, 'the friendship articulated in literature tends to be, reflexively, *about* literature; that is it tends to articulate itself as arising from the intimacy of shared reading and writing' (1994: 3). These letters, and especially his most eloquent (if elegiac) expression of friendship for Harvey, 'Ad Ornatissimum Virum', allowed Spenser to admit his deepest fears as a poet—that he was inadequate to the task of writing, that the years of apprenticeship stretching behind were likely to result in nothing but shame and waste, and that his vocation would create isolation rather than community, as his rising (and Harvey's sputtering) writerly fortunes would attest. It is no wonder, then, that friendship would become such an important notion for Spenser. The unfulfilled fantasy adumbrated by these letters, the fantasy of a network of authors as friends, was to be articulated only later in the *Legend of Friendship*, where, despite the language of subservience deployed in reference to Chaucer, Spenser parlays subservience into an imagined network of friendship extended to a poetic mentor. That network was made of verse, and it confirms that the deepest intimacies of Spenser's writing, the ones in which he displays the greatest vulnerability, concerned his capacities as a poet. The relationship between Spenser and Harvey proved incapable of sustaining a collaborative identity. But Spenser could at least imagine a literary alter ego, a friend who was a bedfellow and a writing fellow. Perhaps it is no accident then that Spenser already had in mind the image of the great confluence of rivers in England that provides the culminating spectacle of the *Legend of Friendship*. In the idea of friendship and in the landscape of the Renaissance letter, Spenser conjured for himself an imagined (if foreclosed) future in which the fantasy of shared literary identity could assuage the pain, frustration, and fallibility of literary singularity and reassure the youthful poet that his green years were neither a shame nor a waste.

Notes

1. The standard text of the *Letters* provided by the *Variorum* collates six extant quartos (*Prose*, 1). The *Variorum* separates Spenser and Harvey's correspondence, numbers the letters, and reorders them to reflect the likely order of composition. Following the initial title page, a reader of the original quarto, after being greeted by a 'wellwisher' of Spenser and Harvey, would have encountered a letter by Spenser dated April 1580 (III in the *Variorum*) followed by Harvey's lengthy epistle containing his description of the famous earthquake of 1580 and Harvey's responses to Spenser's views on verse (IV and V in the *Variorum*). Following a second title page, the reader would then encounter two letters dated October 1579, the first by Spenser, which included the English verse exercise 'Iambicum Trimetrum' and the Latin poem to Harvey 'Ad Ornatissimum Virum' (I in the *Variorum*), and the second by Harvey (II in the *Variorum*).
2. The constraints of space require an almost exclusive focus on Spenser's letters. Readers more curious about Harvey might consult Harvey (1884) for drafts of letters and other jottings, and Stern (1979) for an account of his life and works.
3. For Harvey's views see Shore (1987) and Thomas (1940).
4. For the identity of E. K., see *Prose*, 486, and Carroll (2005).
5. On the subject of dates see *Prose*, 1; Caldwell (1926); Hewlett (1927).
6. Golding (1580) and Churchyard (1580) describe the same earthquake in pamphlets published in the same year (and, certainly in the case of Golding and possibly in the case of Churchyard, by the same publisher) as the *Letters*. On that earthquake and Harvey's description of it, see Snare (1987) and *Prose*, 477–9.
7. Jon Quitslund, in perhaps the best account of the sheer ambiguity of the letters, argues that they 'are as heterogeneous in style and contents as any postmodern text' (1996: 88).
8. Both the letters and Spenser's Latin verse to Harvey refer to such a journey but, as the editors of the *Variorum* put it, 'No evidence that Spenser made the trip has ever come to light' (*Prose*, 258).
9. Arguably, oral figures of male–male eroticism not only abound in early modern literary works, from Spenser and Nashe to Defoe, but also tend to be occluded by the now limiting invocation of sodomy through a critical overattention to figures of penetrative sex or cross-dressing. For alternative accounts of the queer erotics of orality, see Campana (2007a, b).
10. On early modern literary defenses see Ferguson (1983) and Matz (2000). On Spenser's relationship to such defenses later in his career, see Campana (2005).
11. As we learn from the *Variorum*, 'Discussion of the Areopagus has dealt chiefly with its existence or nonexistence as an organized literary group' even though 'this question doesn't seem to have arisen before 1862' (*Prose*, 479).
12. This may indeed reinforce the sense that Spenser dramatizes, through the characters of Colin Clout, Hobbinol, and Rosalind in the *January* eclogue of *The Shepheardes Calender*, an ever-more erotically distant relationship with Harvey and a turning from homo- to

heteroeroticism. See Goldberg (1992), 63–103. See also related accounts of the ambivalent eroticism of pastoral in Smith (1994) and Guy-Bray (2002).

13. See Barthes (1978) and Foucault (1977).

14. On the erotic, collaborative nature of theatrical writing, see Masten (1997). On Spenser and the idea of a literary career, see Helgerson (1983), Guillory (1983), and Cheney (1993) among others. On the eroticism of poetic influence in the works of Spenser (and in relation to Chaucer), see Guy-Bray (2006).

BIBLIOGRAPHY

Anderson, J. (1996). Foreword to J. Anderson, D. Cheney, and D. Richardson (eds), *Spenser's Life and the Subject of Biography*. Amherst: University of Massachusetts Press, ix–xiv.

Attridge, D. (1974). *Well-Weighed Syllables: Elizabethan Verse in Classical Metres*. Cambridge: Cambridge University Press.

Barthes, R. (1978). *Image, Music, Text*. New York: Hill and Wang.

Bergeron, D. (1999). *King James and Letters of Homoerotic Desire*. Iowa City: University of Iowa Press.

Bray, A. (1982). *Homosexuality in Renaissance England*. London: Gay Men's Press.

Bray, A. (2003). *The Friend*. Chicago: University of Chicago Press.

Caldwell, J. (1926). 'Dating a Spenser-Harvey Letter'. *PMLA* 41(3): 568–74.

Campana, J. (2005). 'On Not Defending Poetry: Spenser, Suffering, and the Energy of Affect'. *PMLA* 120(1): 33–48.

—— (2007a). 'Cruising Crusoe: Diving into the Wreck of Sexuality', in Christopher Mounsey and Caroline Gonda (eds), *Queer People: Negotiations and Expressions of Homosexuality, 1700–1800*. Lewisburg, PA: Bucknell University Press, 159–75.

—— (2007b). 'The State of England's Camp: Courtesans, Curses, and the Violence of Style in *The Unfortunate Traveller*'. *Prose Studies* 29(3): 347–58.

Carroll, D. (2005). 'The Meaning of E.K.'. *SSt* 20: 169–81.

Cheney, P. (1993). *Spenser's Famous Flight: A Renaissance Idea of a Literary Career*. Toronto: University of Toronto Press.

Churchyard, T. (1580). *A warning for the wise*. London: Iohn Allde, and Nicholas Lyng [and Henry Bynneman?].

Day, A. (1967 [1599]). *The English Secretary*. Gainesville, FL: Scholars' Facsimiles and Reprints.

Derrida, J. (1987). *The Post Card*. Chicago: University of Chicago Press.

Erasmus, D. (1985). *De Conscribendis Epistolis Formula* and *De Civilitate Morum Puerilium*, in *Literary and Educational Writings* 3, vol. XXV of *Collected Works of Erasmus*, ed. Craig R. Thompson, J. K. Sowards, and A. H. T. Levi. Toronto: University of Toronto Press.

Ferguson, M. (1983). *Trials of Desire: Renaissance Defences of Poetry*. New Haven, CT: Yale University Press.

Foucault, M. (1977). *Language, Counter-Memory, Practice*. Ithaca, NY: Cornell University Press.

—— (1989). *Foucault Live*. New York: Semiotext(e).

Ginzburg, C. (2000). *No Island is an Island: Four Glances at English Literature in a World Context*. New York: Columbia University Press.

Goldberg, J. (1990). *Writing Matter: From the Hands of the English Renaissance*. Palo Alto, CA: Stanford University Press.

Goldberg, J. (1992). *Sodometries: Renaissance Texts, Modern Sexualities.* Palo Alto, CA: Stanford University Press.

Golding, A. (1580). *A Discourse vpon the Earthquake that hapned throughe this realme of England and other places of Christendom, the sixt of Aprill, 1580, between the hours of five and six in the evening.* London: H. Binneman.

Guillén, C. (1986). 'Notes toward the Study of the Renaissance Letter', in B. Lewalski (ed.), *Renaissance Genres.* Cambridge, MA: Harvard University Press, 70–101.

Guillory, J. (1983). *Poetic Authority: Spenser, Milton, and Literary History.* New York: Columbia University Press.

Guy-Bray, S. (2002). *Homoerotic Space: The Poetics of Loss in Renaissance Literature.* Toronto: University of Toronto Press.

—— (2006). *Loving in Verse: Poetic Influence as Erotic.* Toronto: University of Toronto Press.

Harvey, G. (1592). *Foure letters, and certaine sonnets.* London: John Wolfe.

—— (1884). *The Letter Book of Gabriel Harvey,* A.D. *1573–1580,* ed. Edward John Long Scott. London: Camden Society.

Helgerson, R. (1983). *Self-Crowned Laureates: Spenser, Jonson, Milton and the Literary System.* Berkeley: University of California Press.

—— (1992). *Forms of Nationhood: The Elizabethan Writing of England.* Chicago: University of Chicago Press.

Hewlett, J. (1927). 'Interpreting a Spenser-Harvey Letter'. *PMLA* 42(4): 1060–5.

Hutson, L. (1994). *The Usurer's Daughter: Male Friendship and the Fictions of Women in Sixteenth-Century England.* London: Routledge.

McCabe, R. (2007). '"Thine owne nations frend | And Patrone": The Rhetoric of Petition in Harvey and Spenser'. *SSt* 22: 47–72.

Magnusson, L. (1999). *Shakespeare and Social Dialogue.* Cambridge: Cambridge University Press.

Masten, J. (1997). *Textual Intercourse: Collaboration, Authorship, Sexualities.* Cambridge: Cambridge University Press.

—— (2004). 'Toward a Queer Address: The Taste of Letters and Early Modern Male Friendship'. *GLQ: A of Lesbian and Gay Studies* 10(3): 367–84.

Matz, R. (2000). *Defending Literature in Early Modern England: Renaissance Literary Theory in Social Context.* Cambridge: Cambridge University Press.

Maurer, M. (1982). 'The Poetical Familiarity of John Donne's Letters', in S. Grenblatt (ed.), *The Power of Forms in the English Renaissance.* Norman, OK: Pilgrim Books, 183–202.

Quitslund, J. (1996). 'Questionable Evidence in the *Letters* of 1580 between Gabriel Harvey and Edmund Spenser', in J. Anderon, D. Cheney, and D. Richardson (eds), *Spenser's Life and the Subject of Biography.* Amherst: University of Massachusetts Press, 81–98.

—— (2001). *Spenser's Supreme Fiction: Platonic Natural Philosophy in* The Faerie Queene. Toronto: University of Toronto Press.

Richlin, A. (2006). *Marcus Aurelius in Love.* Chicago: University of Chicago Press.

Shannon, L. (2002). *Sovereign Amity.* Chicago: University of Chicago Press.

Shore, D. (1987). 'Spenser, Gabriel Harvey, and "Hobgoblin Runne Away with the Garland from Apollo"'. *Cahiers Elisabethains* 31: 59–61.

Smith, B. (1994). *Homosexual Desire in Shakespeare's England: A Cultural Poetics.* Chicago: University of Chicago Press.

Snare, G. (1970). 'Satire, Logic, and Rhetoric in Harvey's Earthquake Letter to Spenser'. *Tulane Studies in English* 18: 17–33.

Stern, V. (1979). *Gabriel Harvey: His Life, Letters, and Marginalia.* Oxford: Oxford University Press.

Stevens, F. (2004). 'Erasmus's "Tigress": The Language of Friendship, Pleasure, and the Renaissance Letter', in J. Goldberg (ed.), *Queering the Renaissance*. Durham, NC: Duke University Press, 124–40.

Thomas, S. (1940). 'Hobgoblin Runne Away with the Garland from Apollo'. *MLN* 55(6): 418–22.

CHAPTER 11

....

THE FAERIE QUEENE (1590)

....

LINDA GREGERSON

THE first installment of Spenser's *Faerie Queene* announced itself as a publication of some moment. Boldly dedicated to the Queen of England, embellished with explanatory apparatus, commendatory verses, and a clutch of sonnets addressed to notables of the English court and its colonial administration, the poem was explicit about the laureate trajectory of which it intended to be a part. 'Lo I the man,' the poet declares, in imitation of lines that introduced Renaissance editions of Virgil's *Aeneid*. The Virgilian lineage is anything but pure in the cantos that follow: crossing Ariostan with Arthurian romance, medieval allegory with Petrarchan lyric, fabliau with chronicle and georgic, the poem is hybrid in the extreme. But *The Faerie Queene*, from its first syllables, construes itself as occupying the place of national epic, and it is in this context that its rich hybridity and capaciousness must be understood. Spenser's poem proposes to tell a nation the story of its own consolidating destiny. And more: aspiring to fashion its reader in consummate virtue, which is to say, in consummate fitness for service to a polemically idealized Reformation Faerie Queene, the poem imagines for itself an active role in bringing that destiny about.

OVERVIEW

....

On the title page of the 1590 *Faerie Queene*, the reader is promised a poem '[d]isposed into twelue books', each of them representing one of the twelve moral virtues. Upon opening the volume, however, the reader discovers only three books of the promised complement: *The Faerie Queene* entered the world as a work-in-progress. To be sure, that progress had been formidable, each book comprising a proem and twelve cantos, each canto comprising roughly four dozen stanzas and a brief abstract of the action or 'argument', the whole amounting to more than eighteen thousand lines of verse. Little wonder that the poet/ploughman announces at the end of Book III that his team has 'woxen weary' (III.xii.47) and requires a little rest.

Appended to the back of the 1590 poem was another sort of document, which readers have taken very seriously indeed: a 'Letter of the Authors' (the 'Letter to Ralegh') purporting to expound his 'whole intention in the course of this worke'.[1] Addressed to Sir Walter Ralegh, courtier, adventurer, colonist, patron, and fellow poet, the 'Letter to Ralegh' sets forth a key to the poem's foundational 'Allegory', as well as a general justification of allegorical method, which second component has often been read as a kind of *ars poetica*. Why not deliver your moral lessons plainly, by way of precepts or sermon? Because, says the poet, 'doctrine by ensample' is much more powerful and better absorbed than doctrine 'by rule'. Why not give us everything in proper sequence, conforming to chronology? Because, says the poet, the work of a 'Poet historical' differs from that of an historiographer: the historiographer tells a linear narrative, each thing as it occurred in time, whereas the poet 'thrusteth into the middest', invoking things past and things-to-come in a manner that makes for 'pleasing Analysis'. Pleasure and analysis: here one does especially well to take the poet at his word. The reshuffling of ordinary chronology not only invites the reader to enjoy delightful byways, speedings-up, and slowings-down; it also allows the poet to investigate, and unfold, the deep structure of his materials.

Allegory, in Renaissance rhetoric books, was broadly defined as 'extended metaphor',[2] with all the flexibility and variation the phrase implies. Far from contriving a series of static equivalences, allegory proposes a series of figures 'displaced from normal usage' and sets them in motion. Pictorial allegory, including the immensely popular emblem books of the period, relies upon juxtaposition to achieve semantic mobility: the conjunction of picture and motto, or received symbol and concretizing detail, are intended to prompt rather than to foreclose interpretation. The chief source of motion in a poem like *The Faerie Queene*, of course, is narrative or action-in-time. When Spenser describes the broad outlines of his knights and their adventures in the 'Letter to Ralegh', he distinguishes between the narrative's elaborating '[a]ccidents' ('[a]s the loue of Britomart, the ouerthrow of Marinell, the misery of Florimell . . . and many the like') and its central 'intendments'. But we badly underestimate his poem unless we understand how powerfully the 'accidents' can alter cumulative meaning.

As key to his basic 'intendments', the poet describes to Ralegh events he proposes to narrate in the twelfth and last book of his massive poem. In the hands of an historiographer, he allows, these events would occur in Book I, for they take place at the chronological beginning of the fictive narrative. As we shall discover, they also take place at their topographical and hermeneutic center, when the Queene of Fairies holds her annual feast. This feast extends over the course of twelve days, on each of which the Queene bestows an 'adventure' upon a chosen knight, who then departs from court in order to pursue his quest. Twelve days then, twelve quests, twelve knights, and twelve symbolic virtues, each precipitated by a wrong that must be righted. On the first day of the feast, a fair young lady arrives in court to petition the Queen for relief: her parents are being held hostage by a fierce dragon and their kingdom laid to waste. Though the champion who begs the honor of coming to their rescue is an unlikely figure in rustic dress, he is transformed when he dons the armor of Holinesse, or Redcrosse Knight. On the second day, a Palmer arrives at court with a bloody infant in his arms, the infant's parents having been slain by an enchantress; to redress this wrong, Sir Guyon is sent forth as the Knight of Temperance. On the third day, a knight named Scudamour arrives in distress: his beloved has been taken in thrall by a vile enchanter. Scudamour is duly commissioned to rescue the lady, but we are advised that he will find this quest beyond his powers and will need to be supplanted by a knight called Britomart. About the quests, and patron virtues, that will occupy Books IV through XII, the poet for now has nothing to say.

By withholding these tales of origin from the body of the poem itself (or deferring them until a future culmination that was, in the end, never to be realized), Spenser plunges his readers into narrative action whose organizing source and center can only be inferred. By appending the 'Letter to Ralegh', he can provide some scaffolding for readers while still preserving the poem's powers of incitement-to-speculation. Why then was the 'Letter' dropped from later editions of The Faerie Queene? Why do the 'Letter' and the poem diverge in a number of narrative details? Which part shall we construe as 'accident' and which as 'intendment'? Readers have found these puzzles endlessly fascinating.

Book I, The Legend of Holinesse, begins exactly as the 'Letter' would lead one to expect. We meet the patron knight and his lady Una; we are told the nature of his quest; we follow him through a number of preliminary adventures. But when Una and her champion are separated by their arch enemy Archimago, the narrative divides as well, multiplying its trajectories and personae, complicating its network of purpose and deception, incident and digression. Holinesse tests his strength against the avatars of Error, Lust, Doubt, Pride, Faithlessness, and Despair; Una, who is also a figure for unity of spirit, endures a series of assaults and rescues. But why are so many of the villains associated with the saints and popes, rosaries and elaborate vestments? Because Edmund Spenser, like others of the activist Protestant faction to which he belonged, saw the Roman Catholic Church as a hive of corruption and spiritual coercion. In The Faerie Queene the enemies of Holinesse are also, and more specifically, the enemies of Reformed Christianity and of England, which Spenser saw as the leading national bastion for a universal Reformation. For Spenser, the fate of nation and faith are inextricably entwined: when Redcrosse suffers a critical defeat, he is rescued from imprisonment by Prince Arthur, a key figure in English national mythology; when he nearly succumbs to despair, he is healed in the House of Holinesse and shown a vision of the Heavenly Jerusalem. Restored to spiritual health, Redcrosse appears to fulfill his quest decisively in a triumphant three-day battle with the dragon, but in a pattern that will assume increasing importance through the remainder of *The Faerie Queene*, his marriage to Una is deferred.

Book II, *The Legend of Temperance*, begins mysteriously at odds with the 'Letter to Ralegh'. Continuity is in the keeping of the enemy Archimago, whose machinations incite Guyon to an armed encounter with Redcrosse. When that encounter modulates to friendly recognition, Redcrosse's blessing upon Guyon's as-yet-unspecified adventures serves as proxy for the authorizing power ascribed in the 'Letter' directly to the Faerie Queene. For Guyon and his companion the Palmer appear at the outset to be wandering with no more particular purpose than general knightly 'adventure'. They make no mention of the Faerie Court; their encounter with Amavia and the Bloody Babe, as with a dense succession of impediments and antagonists, appears to be governed by accident. In chivalric romance, of course, narrative 'accident' is merely another word for destiny. Each new encounter further articulates the manifold nature of Guyon's foundational antitype, Intemperance. Each encounter is a clue, or thread, that leads the knight to the entangling web of Acrasia, whose defeat has become the object of his quest. And despite the cultivated air of inadvertance, the narrative reveals a number of significant structural parallels to Book I. Like Redcrosse, and indeed, at the same convergence of cantos, Guyon must endure helplessness and be rescued by Arthur. Like Redcrosse, Guyon's preparation for his culminating struggle includes a visionary revelation of his private and corporate identity: what Redcrosse learns from Contemplation in the House of Holinesse Guyon learns from the chronicle of Faerie Land and Arthur from the chronicles of Britain. Reading over the shoulders of his heroes, Spenser's own readers are meant to discover their deepest alignments with nation and body-of-faith, with past and hoped-for future. And Guyon's quest? Successfully concluded (Acrasia's Bowre is destroyed) but with less than resounding finality (Acrasia herself is merely 'led . . . away' at II.xii.84). Enforcing the sense of more-to-come, a number of figures introduced in Book Two—Braggadochio and Belphoebe in particular—will re-emerge more fully in subsequent parts of the poem.

Book III, *The Legend of Chastity*, and the only book to feature a woman as its eponymous hero, departs more radically from the 'Letter to Ralegh' than anything that has gone before. Not until the eleventh, or penultimate, canto will Scudamour enter the narrative and relate the story of Amoret's abduction. Britomart meets her predecessors, first in opposition, then in friendship, as was the pattern in Book II, but then deliberately misleads them about her purpose. That purpose, revealed to the reader in an interpolated back story, is the search for a knight she has seen in a looking glass, but that knight will make no direct appearance in the 1590 *Faerie Queene*. Furthermore, after the expeditious defeat of a proud challenger on the seashore, Britomart herself will disappear for more than a third of the Book that claims her as its patron. Previous patterning breaks down in other ways as well: Arthur, who has fought for Redcrosse and Guyon when they could not fight for themselves, whose overarching virtue, the poet tells Ralegh, sums up the virtues of all other knights, does not come to Britomart's aid at all but charges off in wild pursuit of Florimell, vaguely 'hoping' that this beautiful damsel turns out to be the Faerie

Queene to whom he has pledged undying fidelity. The shift from storyline to story-line becomes more strenuous: 'It yrkes me, leaue thee in this wofull state,' says the poet to one of his characters (III.viii.43), whom he then proceeds to abandon. The proliferating digression of earlier books appears at times to exceed authorial control: when Arthur learns that Florimell has fled the Faerie Court in search of wounded Marinell (III.v.8–10), the poem seems to have forgotten that the former's flight (III.i.15 ff) precedes the latter's wounding (III.iv.16). Tone broadens to include frank parody: the revelation of personal and racial destiny that would normally enlighten the eponymous hero in Canto Ten is spoken by a knight (Paridell) whose personal behavior debases the very heritage he represents. And the unabsorbed remainder that marked the conclusion of Books I and II (Redcrosse's deferred nuptials, Acrasia's ambiguous fate) enlarges to encompass original purpose: when Britomart fulfills the quest of Chastity by restoring Amoret to the arms of her husband, Scudamour, her original quest, quite unfulfilled, comes back to haunt her. '[H]alfe enuying' the bliss she has secured for others, she longs for the promised husband of her own. But she longs '[i]n vaine' (III.xii.46).

SEQUENCE AND CAUSALITY

'A Gentle Knight was pricking on the plaine,' clothed in a conundrum. His armor is old, bearing the honorable marks of hard and bloody use, but the knight is new, having never borne arms before. The armor is a good fit: the knight's faith is a true match for the red cross he wears on breast and shield, and the quest that constitutes the knight's immediate prehistory and purpose, a quest expeditiously outlined in the earliest stanzas of his eponymous book, bear all the trappings of familiar Christian legend.[3] Memory and futurity have produced a single inscription. The meantime, like the reader and the knight himself, has some catching up to do. It is not until he has slain the dragon Errour that Redcrosse proves himself '[w]ell worthy' (I.i.27) of the armor he wears, or so we are made to understand by the lady who has brought him both armor and quest. As to the initial conveyance of that armor, and the even deeper mysteries of the knight's origin, we must wait for the tutelage of Contemplation in canto x, or must consult a source quite outside the main body of the poem, in order to find them out.

As described in the 'Letter to Ralegh', *The Faerie Queene* takes its structural logic from the analytical divisions of philosophy. Twelve private moral virtues, summed up in the person of Prince Arthur and the comprehensive virtue of magnificence,[4] govern the projected twelve books of the poem, each virtue embodied in the person of a patron knight. But Spenser has little confidence in static systems: his poem takes its method not from logic but from 'historical fiction', its propositions doubly inflected by time. The time is that of action or event (history as narrative) and also that of discovery (history, in the Greek sense, as inquiry).[5] Thinking is a form of motion in *The Faerie Queene*; the intersecting momentums of 'accident' and 'intendment' endow its exemplary figures with the liveliness of experiment.

Having slain the dragon Errour and absorbed, or so one might imagine, a cautionary lesson about unintended byways, Redcrosse asks the very next creature he meets for news of 'straunge aduentures' (I.i.30), for all the world as though he were not already bound to adventure on a grand scale. Never mind that this stranger turns out to be the malignant Archimago in disguise: surely Una's champion, contracted to fight the usurping monster who holds her homeland in thrall, is not altogether at leisure for miscellaneous adventures? But error in *The Faerie Queene* is neither bounded nor purely inimical: it is also the necessary, even the felicitous, path. *Errare*: to wander. So that the dragon Errour and the wandering woods in which it dwells are versions of a single phenomenon. And wandering, which subjects the knight to error, is also at the heart of his vocation: error is the etymological heart of errantry. Wedded to both fate and accident, purpose and inadvertence, focused quest and adventitious fortune, Spenser's narrative mines the fertile cross-purposes of epic and romance to reveal in allegory not a fixed system of equivalences or dicta but a foundation for cognitive method. To say that Redcrosse must be tested is to put the case too weakly: Redcrosse must *become* the Knight of Holinesse, unfolding the nature of his constituent virtue in the (wandering) course of narrative action.

'Cause' in Faerie Land is both a prompting and a goal, redundant in manifestation and recursive in effect. In narrative terms, it takes three tries for Archimago to separate the Redcrosse knight from Una; yet each of his deceptions rings changes on a single obsessive theme: the lady whose integrity or 'oneness' the knight relies upon in order to secure his own is (falsely) revealed to be loose. In the first instance, a false dream prompts Redcrosse to lascivious thoughts of Una as seductress. In the second, waking instance, a false Una dismayingly continues the seduction begun in dream. In the third, the 'guiltie sight' (I.ii.6) of false Una in carnal embrace with a false squire causes Redcrosse at last to flee. The adjectival slippage here is consequential, part of a recurrent Spenserian technique. In Book II, the fiend who follows Guyon through the Cave of Mammon will long to destroy his 'greedy pray' (II.vii.34). In Book III, Malecasta will rise from a 'wearie bed' under cover of 'guilty Night' (III.i.59) and, fainting, will fall to the 'sencelesse grownd' (III.i.63). To ordinary understanding, prey is not greedy, predators are, and weariness is the property of those who sleep in beds and not of beds themselves. But according to the logic of Spenserian allegory, displaced attribution betrays the workings of causal contagion. A thing may be known by the attribute it prompts, or accommodates, in others; a vision may implicate the beholder. And double negatives are intensifiers: the redundancies in Archimago's machinations advance his malignant purpose by furthering his powers of insinuation. As Redcrosse's dream first kindles the knight's own wanton imaginings and only then distills them in a wanton version of Una, so his startled waking is ambiguously prompted by 'vnwonted lust' or 'wonted feare' of trespass (I.i.49). The Una he wakes to, as to a dream outside a dream, can therefore seem to be drawn from within, horrifically bodying forth the knight's own guilty thoughts. And his angry departure from Archimago's hermitage is prompted as much by 'gealous fire' (I.ii.5) as by moral disapprobation. 'Sight' may refer to the bias as well as the object of vision, hence 'guilty'. False spirits and a false dream may bring about a crooked truth: the guilty sight is 'his'.

For another lens on sequence and causality in *The Faerie Queene*, we may consult the looking glass that launches the (chronological) action of Book III. Narratively, the glass is part of a withheld and belated back story: before we learn anything of its precipitating role, we encounter *in medias res* the knight it has made. The Book of Chastity begins, as had the Book of Temperance, with a ceremonial transfer of patron power, Guyon giving place to Britomart as Redcrosse had earlier given place to Guyon. Arthur makes an authorizing appearance of his own, as does the Redcrosse knight, suggesting at the threshold of the poem's third quest that virtues surveyed sequentially are meant to gather cumulative force. But discord has a role to play as well. When the glass is at last disclosed, it tells a tale quite different from the one Britomart has just conveyed to Redcrosse about her upbringing and immediate purpose, different also from the story Spenser tells in the explanatory 'Letter to Ralegh'. According to the 'Letter', the chronological origin and chief 'intendment' of Book III will be Amoret's imprisonment and Scudamor's quest to set her free, but the patron knight of Chastity (who is not Scudamor at all) learns nothing of these matters until a chance encounter in the penultimate canto of her book. Nor has she, as professed to Redcrosse, been driven by the general desire for martial honor: she is seeking a face in a glass.

The looking glass in question has the power to reveal '[w]hat ever . . . to the looker appertaynd', from 'lowest earth' to 'heuens hight' (III.ii.19). Its capacity is not omniscience per se, in other words, but an adaptable bias of vision. Like its false counterpart, the dream of Redcrosse Knight, it simultaneously alters the looker and seems to be compounded of her own innermost thoughts. For Britomart's gaze is not entirely casual: impelled by curiosity about her nuptial destiny, she has seen in the glass a knight who wounds her heart with love. The wound reduces her to suffering; her suffering rallies Glauce to her aid; Glauce leads the way to Merlin, who narrates the future the knight in the glass portends. As is the rule in epic prophecy, this future is also the reader's (collective) past: the chronicle history of Briton from Arthurian antiquity to the rise of the Tudors. What the prophecy has not yet become is knightly quest. But Glauce, ever the pragmatist, forces the question: 'What *meanes* shall she out seeke, or what wayes take?' (III.iii.25; italics mine), or perhaps she needn't act at all, since all is fated? '[T]he fates are firme,' Merlin concedes, 'Yet ought mens good endeuours them confirme.'[6] So the knight in the glass becomes a course of action.

The apparent reversal of accident and intendment in the Book of Chastity follows subtler divergences in the Book of Temperance, but the interchangeable workings, or rather the corroborative function, of chance and destiny had long been a staple of chivalric romance. Nor is my point simply that the real path of writing has put the poet intriguingly at odds with his own precis, as rendered in the 'Letter to Ralegh'. *The Faerie Queene* makes method of its own conspicuous breaking down. No sooner does the poet establish a provisional template for allegory-in-motion than it begins to work its own subversion. What seems straightforward in the Book of Holinesse— an initiating quest, a set of byways that progressively refine the nature of that quest and the champion's fitness for his task, a final struggle in which the afflicted are relieved and the enemy destroyed—is even in the first instance beset by other, competing vistas. The very purification that seals the Redcrosse Knight in worthiness, revealing to him his origins and destiny, also estranges him from his (merely) earthly task. 'O let me not', he asks, with heavenly Jerusalem in sight, 'turne againe | Backe to the world' (I.x.63). The labor that was to be his culmination is transformed before it happens into a lesser, interim achievement. More conspicuous yet is the disjunction between initiating motive and epic achievement in the Book of Chastity. If Britomart successfully rescues Amoret and repairs the breach in lawful espousal, at least until the next installment of the poem appears, that success leaves her an outcast at the close of her own adventure, 'halfe enuying' (III.xii.46) the lovers she has aided and brought not one whit closer to her own amatory conclusion.

Digression and deferral, repetition and recursivity are the narrative manifestations of multiple allegiance. Spenser's project in *The Faerie Queene* is at once an anatomy of the individual soul, the consolidation of national identity, a theorization of moral agency on both private and political planes, a thought experiment in the relationship of history to that which lies beyond it, the 'whole' that gives impetus to holiness. For persons of faith in the era of Calvin, the questions put by Redcrosse to Contemplation and by Glauce to Merlin bore real urgency: what is the relationship between transcendent hope and earthly wandering, between what we shall come to and what we must do? Spenser himself was part of an activist Protestant faction that construed the English nation as a crucial interim vehicle for the Reformation of the universal Christian church: how could that interim, and the violence at its disposal, be kept in proper alignment with its justifying end? The problem for the poem is to keep its multiple temporalities, and its bifurcated construction of 'cause', in play. The genius of Spenser's poetic is its ability to poise one genre-based momentum against another, the orchestrations of epic against the dispersals of romance, the stateliness of chronicle and pageant against the scramble of improvisation, the long arc of history and history's subsumption against the short arc of human passions. That *The Faerie Queene* entered the world of print as the fragment of something larger and yet to come was merely a special instance of poetry's chronic circumstance.

PERSONATION

Redcrosse, Guyon, Britomart; Una, The Palmer, Glauce; Archimago, Acrasia, Busirane: such are the primary units of imagination in Spenser's poem, those his readers

most readily track and easily remember. Bound in fruitful tension between metaphorical and narrative obligations, they differ radically from the dramatic characters
that were at the time evolving in the public theatre of Spenser's English contemporaries and also from the speaking subjects of the English Renaissance lyric. It is not
that the dramatists were more interested in psychology or the lyricists in subjectivity
than was the author of *The Faerie Queene*: the question is one of representational
mapping. Since Wyatt had adapted and profoundly altered Petrarch in the fraught
context of the Henrician court, the English lyric had been captivated by the possibilities of speaking voice as a symptom of personality, the construction of lyric
persona as back formation. The drama was conducting experiments with individuated temperament, motive, and conflict that decisively shaped our later conventions
of psychological 'depth'. Both literary modes had come to imply coincidence
between the contours of psychology and the parameters of literary character.
For the purposes of allegorical epic, by contrast, Spenser wilfully disaggregates
psychology and character.

If we construe literary 'character' in the simplest possible sense, as a fictional
creature endowed with animation, the category comprises a widely differential
population in Faerie Land. Arthur and Ignaro, Belphoebe and Despair, Hellenore
and the Squyre of Dames scarcely seem to inhabit a single plane of being. Some of
them flatter our habits of measuring 'fullness' in terms of aptitude for learning and
change; others seem tethered to purely instrumental roles. But all are subject to
shifting spectra of representational expedience; all occupy the fertile ground between
exemplary and catalytic utility, between the attribute embodied and the attribute
prompted in others. And some metamorphose in the course of the poem and traverse
different representational fields as they do, as illustrated with particular richness by
the character of the jealous miser in *The Legend of Chastity*.

Historically, the psychology of a figure like Malbecco is a kind of prosthetic or
external organ. His coherence, in other words, relies more upon the audience that
invents and judges him than upon the internal psychology and ambiguous semantics
of jealous 'possession'. Malbecco's forebears, the generic blocking figure of New
Comedy, the cuckold of fabliau, and the Pantalone of the Commedia dell'Arte, are
conventionally said to exercise a monopoly on goods, material and sexual, that a
younger generation of males, exemplified by poet and audience, hopes to inherit or
usurp. Decrepit old age, avarice, goatish lust: the conflated and overdetermined vices
that envious heirs assign to a figure like Malbecco themselves constitute the anticipatory figure of youth's revenge. Decrepitude, an introjected and preemptive version
of the impediment so central to the momentum of Petrarchan and courtly love, is
paradoxically understood to fan the flames of concupiscence even as it thwarts erotic
and material ambition, the courtship and courtiership that are Malbecco's particular
inaptitudes. But the concupiscence thus aggravated is not Malbecco's alone. Even
within the fiction, Malbecco's concupiscence infects the lives of others, and the
cuckold, like any common coinage, reveals as much about the community in
which he circulates as about the value with which he has been stamped. As Spenser

sets it in motion, the goatishness attributed to an impotent old man is much like the blindness that conventional iconography assigns to Cupid:

> False loue, why do men say, thou canst not see,
> And in their foolish fancie feigne thee blind,
> That with thy charmes the sharpest sight doest binde,
>
> .   .   .   .
>
> Thou seest all, yet none at all sees thee . . .   (III.x.4)

The poet is explicating here one of the more fluid properties of his own character-ological method—the shifting conference of figures who suffer or exemplify and figures who induce. In the first case, an allegorical figure directly bodies forth the psychic or material condition for which it is named: such figures habitually populate the set-pieces of allegorical pageantry, where Idleness is drowned in sleep and Gluttony drowned in fat (I.iv.19, 21). In the second case, an allegorical figure functions as the precipitating cause or occasion of the condition for which it is named. These functions overlap, for example, in Despair (I.ix) and Furor (II.iv), each of whom suffers the fault of spirit for which he is named even while he induces it in others. A more externalized version of this contagion may be seen in the unregulated belligerence inflicted by Pyrochles on anyone within his reach, as captured in the motto on his shield: '*Burnt I do burne*' (II.iv.38). Even the Squire of Dames (III.vii) is guilty of occasioning the feminine looseness he pretends merely to document, as the narrator makes explicit in an afterword (III.viii.44). But Ignaro (I.viii.30 ff) merely suffers chronic ignorance; he cannot be said to transmit it in any significant way. For the rarest variation of them all, we must wait for a later installment of Spenser's poem, where the Blatant Beast wounds reputation far and wide but remains terrifyingly impervious to the bane it spreads (VI.i.7 ff.).

Malbecco is among those allegorical figures in *The Faerie Queene* whose function is both exemplary and catalytic at once. His own phallic powers are impaired: he is charged, by cruel default, with the goatish disposition implied by an old man's marriage to a young and beautiful woman; he is charged as well with the goatishness produced in others by the spectacle of his misalliance. The old man turns his wife's lustiness into licentiousness by depriving her of kindly joys and closely mewing her up, and though Paridell is admittedly an habitual seducer, Malbecco aggravates temptation by subordinating hospitality to egregious suspicion and by exhibiting in every attendant meanness and inaptitude his conspicuous sexual mismatch. This mismatch serves as incitement, or so the traditional logic goes, to other concupiscent males.

But Malbecco's transformation is more than reiterative confirmation of the conventional proprietary and erotic competitions that lecherous and miserly old men have long been made to signify. Spenser's tale of a cuckold begins in the productive divide between a figure of speech (Mal-becco, the goat) and the corresponding figure of narrative (the impotent old miser who jealously guards a beautiful wife). As long as he effectively blocks the wheels of commerce, both mercantile and connubial, as long as he is possessed of a wife and gold he fears to lose and cannot use, the considerable tensions among the character's source pathologies, between his native and his alienable properties, endow a reservoir of action and prevent his collapse into solitary and static personification. But jealousy contrives to bring about the world it has pictured to itself. When Malbecco loses the wealth and the wife that have maintained him in the frenzy of possession, he also loses his catalytic danger to others. Beginning with a goatish name and becoming a creature of horns and hoofs, Malbecco sees even his allegorical status transformed in the course of Spenser's tale. Collapsing from a figure of plot to a figure of speech, from a fictional 'man', however impaired, to a weightless collection of attributes, he ends his days in ghastly perpetuity as 'Gealosie', pure and simple.

Personation in *The Faerie Queene* comprises a legion of variants. The Palmer belongs to the poem's order of knightly confederates: like Una, he is part guide and part faculty or aptitude; like Glauce he is part enabler and part (fallible) interpreter. Arthur is both summation and narrative surrogate, establishing his claim to each of his constituent virtues by coming to their rescue and fighting in their stead: most straightforward are his labors on behalf of Redcrosse and Guyon; more complex, his labors on behalf of Britomart, which underwrite her own surrogacy for Artegall in Book V. In Timias, the poet contrives a sort of Arthur-in-training, one more vulnerable to wounding and, tellingly, more serviceable to political allegory and topical allusion.[7] In False Florimell, he devises a trenchant critique of Petrarchism and its underlying psychology. In Praysdesire and Shamefastnesse, he subtly inflects a universal template with the contours of individuated predilection. Because their example and their context manifest so well the fluidity of Spenserian personation, they will bear a moment's pause:

In the Castle of Alma, constructed as an elaborate spatial allegory for the human body and its regulation by humors, anatomy, and spiritual discipline, Arthur and Guyon meet, separately, the ladies who mirror their own affective dispositions. Prays-desire bodies forth for Arthur and Shamefastnesse for Guyon the liabilities of even intemperate virtue. So the topos of the body is universal, but the journey through it individualized. And universality itself is a faceted phenomenon. In the turret of Alma's Castle, Arthur and Guyon encounter the three faculties of mind: Phantastes (fancy), Judgment (whom we know by means of attributes though not by name) and Eumnestes (memory). And here the poet makes us understand that these are collective faculties as well as the generic faculties of the individual. Eumnestes recalls Methuselah's infancy; he preserves the memory of the race; in other words, his scope is not merely that of individual mental prowess and cumulative experience, but of human culture writ large.

Which brings us to the reader. It is not Elizabeth alone who is invited to 'behold thy face' in the mirror of the poem (II *Proem*, 4). Personation activates the default motion of readerly identification, the tendency to seek on the page that bigger-than-a-breadbox, smaller-than-a-doorframe something that can be taken to approximate the self. But cognitive repose is antithetical to Spenser's purpose. So his particular methods of personation in *The Faerie Queene* rigorously deny the reader any frictionless attribution of wholeness or unified psychology to individual personae. His characters are fragments, some more so than others, part vehicle for meaning and part receptor site, a site where grace (in Book I) or destiny and national allegiance (in every book) may act upon the understanding. Their shifting alignments, both inside the fiction and off the page, reveal the Queen in the maiden, the chosen reader in the Queen, the nation in the reader, the fugitive outline of wholeness-to-come in every temporality.

DOUBLING AND DIVISION

The first great triumph of *The Faerie Queene's* arch-villain Archimago is to see his guests 'diuided into double parts' (I.ii.9). Divided from Una, Redcrosse is self-divided too, '[s]till flying from his [own] thoughts' (I.ii.12). On one level, this passage illuminates the paradox of felicitous pairing, the two-ness that secures one-ness: Milton will make a similar point when he causes Adam in Paradise to address Eve as '[s]ole partner and sole part of all these joys' (*PL*: IV, 411). More fundamentally, the doubling division illuminates the poet's working theory of self. The unified self makes no appearance in *The Faerie Queene* except in the guise of *process*; the self the poem esteems is grounded in devotion to that which is outside the self and in the action devotion requires. Doubling and division may work oppositionally, testing virtue's constancy. But they also work analytically, unfolding the complex nature of virtue by articulating its constituent parts: they are the poet's tools as well as the tools of his villains.

No sooner has the stuttering progress of false dream and false spirit severed Redcrosse from Una than Spenser plunges his knight into another version of narrative doubletake. Now in dangerous league with Duessa, Redcrosse encounters a man who has undergone an Ovidian metamorphosis into the shape of a tree.[8] Like Redcrosse, Fradubio has been maliciously estranged from his one true love; like Redcrosse, he has been entangled by duplicity in the person of Duessa. The tale he recites is a cautionary instance of the one unfolding before us in the narrative present. Redcrosse fails to recognize himself in the suffering person of Fradubio, but failed warning is part of the path. To re-cognize: to know again. Narrative redundancy has a cognitive role to play.

And Virtue's path is error-strewn. Felicitous alliance is missed at first or miscon-strued; adversaries and false doubles abound. Archimago will range throughout the 1590 *Faerie Queene*, Duessa as far as Book V, but most of virtue's antitypes or mirror inversions are purpose-built: Holinesse (Book I) meets refining opposition in Luci-fera, or Pride, and Despair; Temperance (Book II) in Furor and Mammon, or irascible and appetitive excess; Chastity (Book III) in Malecasta and Malbecco, or sexual looseness and sexual hoarding. When adversarial struggle veers toward psy-chomachia by means of ambiguous pronouns, as when Redcrosse fights the destined dragon or Guyon and Arthur the hoards of Maleger, the poet is simply making more explicit the chronic intimacy of type and antitype. Characters in *The Faerie Queene* are born and propelled according to the double logic of affinity and aversion. Among the false doubles and cognates that proliferate throughout the poem, some are blatant (Archimago disguised as Redcrosse, Duessa disguised as Faith, a spectral automoton that passes for Florimell), others subtle (Phaedria's placations of Guyon and Pyrochles mimic the mediating virtues of temperance), yet others frankly parodic (Braggadocchio's bunglings constitute a veritable textbook on failed knighthood). The poem's characters, of course, unlike its readers, are not privy to the secrets of malicious disguise or false creation; they encounter even the most blatant antitype or simulacrum as a fresh interpretive conundrum. Within the poem, virtue must learn its own nature by navigating the complex terrain of antipathy and alliance. Outside the poem, with a partial, but only a partial, interpretive advantage, the reader is invited to do the same. From either perspective, the image in the mirror is a cumulative composite.

The redundancy and recursivity so prominent in Spenser's narrative sequence find cognates in the figural and rhetorical fabric of the poem. The reader, for example, encounters a kind of echo relationship between one plane of figural representation and another. Ekphrastic description of the Medea carved in ivory on the gates to the Bowre of Bliss (II.xii.44–5) anticipates the fictional Acrasia who presides within the Bowre and, by the way, acknowledges the witch's mythic genealogy. The figure of Verdant, languid in Acrasia's lap (II.xii.72–80), anticipates ekphrastic description of the Adonis woven into Malecasta's tapestries (III.i.34–8); both Temperance (Book II) and Chastity (Book III) have lessons to learn from the sensual supine. More complexly, Venus and Adonis in the Garden of Adonis (III.vi.46) echo both Acrasia/Verdant and the earlier Venus/Adonis in Castle Joyeous (III.i.34–8): we are asked to work through the differences between necrotic predation and the life-in-death of cyclical fecundity. And some of the poet's figural displacements interrogate the very foundation of his art: the perpetual flight that makes Florimell so elusive and so infinitely alluring renders in another key the teasing erotics of veiling in Acrasia's fountain (II.xii.63–8). False Florimell (III.viii.5–9) anthologizes in her material person the very metaphors that constitute the blazon to Belphoebe (II.iii.22–30); the gold and vermeil of the sonneteers become, inside the fiction, the gold and vermeil of a witch's ingenuity.

Rhetorical echo captures the power of the twice-told tale. In an especially rich instance, the figure of Despair marshals all the resources of scriptural and proverbial eloquence to lure the Redcrosse Knight to suicide. His imagery is that of Genesis and Psalms, his precepts cunningly edited versions of those to be found in the sermons of Jesus and the letters of Paul. When Redcrosse ventures, speech for speech, a counter-argument (I.ix.41–2), his words are nearly impossible to distinguish from those of his adversary, so closely has the latter mined the sources Redcrosse knows and trusts. So strongly do Despair's persuasions echo with all they pervert, so masterfully do they augment on the rhetorical level the seductive reprisals of echoing and alliterative sound, that Redcrosse is transfixed, as if with 'inchaunted rimes' (I.ix.48). He hears and believes, believing that what he hears rhymes with what he has heard before.

And though Una recalls him to the proper remembrance of heavenly mercy, the mesmerizing pull of self-annihilation has not yet done with him. Brought to better understanding in the House of Holinesse, Redcrosse so acutely recoils from mortal life and from his own past sins that he desires 'to end his wretched dayes' (I.x.21). The symptoms of his spiritual progress mimic the symptoms of his furthest abjection.

The twice-told tale has a venerable pedigree. In his abduction of Hellenore, Paridell parodically reprises the actions of his namesake Paris, whose abduction of Helen brought so much destruction to Troy. But in his earlier narration at Hellenore's supper table, Paridell reprises the actions of an ancestor yet more distinguished and central to the mythic prehistory of Britain. Aeneas' narration of the fall of Troy at Dido's banquet table in Books II and III of the *Aeneid* is the *locus classicus* of the lethally seductive twice-told tale. Dido already knows the story by heart: she has had it painted on the temple walls of Carthage. Her fate is sealed when she hears it again on the lips of the man whose story it is. Dido goes missing from Paridell's tale—it would scarcely advance his cause to keep her there—but the responsive quickening that defines her role in Virgil is here divided between the characters of Hellenore and the Knight of Chastity herself. It is Hellenore who succumbs erotically, but Britomart succumbs in 'countries cause' (III.ix.40), touched to the quick by what she encounters as a racial memory. 'For noble *Britons* sprong from *Troians* bold' (III.ix.38), she has heard, and from Merlin (III.iii.21–50) she also knows that the story continues in her very person. The legacy is mixed, as Western epic has always acknowledged. From Homer's tale of 'a whore and a cuckold'[9] to Virgil's tale of an abandoned queen to Geoffrey of Monmouth's tale of a nation founded by a fleeing parricide (III.ix.48), empire has built its foundations with the mortar of bad conscience.

And hence the double lineage, a Paridell and a Britomart both: the one a narrative and a genealogical sideline, made to siphon off some of the queasier aspects of inheritance, the other a restorative main branch. Double lineage is one of the great remedial strategies in Spenser's poem, an essential feature of the effort to imagine a world that will at once improve upon and be of consequence to the world that has been given. Redcrosse sets the pattern here: 'sprong out from English race' (I.x.60), he is fostered, veritably cross-bred in Faerie Land; descended from kings, he is trained to conscience and consciousness 'in ploughmans state' (I.x.66). The name he inherits from ploughman's labor (*Georgos*, man of earth) in Faerie Land is the name by which, in destined futurity (which is also prehistory to the poem), the now-canonized knight will be repatriated to England as patron saint, consolidating the nation's aspirations and sense of self.[10] The very branches of his lineage are riddled with doublings and divisions of their own: Redcrosse's ancestors were Saxon, hostile to Britons; their ground was Wales, cradle to Arthur, birthplace of the Tudors, titular realm, since a thirteenth-century *anschluss*, for heirs to the Crown of England, yet always an ingested foreign entity, imperfectly absorbed. Redcrosse learns his ancestry as part of his rededication to a cause—Contemplation calls it 'earthly conquest' (I.x.60)—whose full consequence he begins to apprehend only when he beholds the heavenly goal it requires him to defer; the man of earth is spirit too.

In double lineage and the double dedication it implies, Redcrosse is not alone. Prince Arthur is the cross-bred product of British blood and Faerie tutelage; his nursery and first conscious home was Wales (I.ix.3–4). Artegall is a changeling like Redcrosse (III.iii.26–7), Marinell the son of a sea nymph and a human father (III.iv.19). Belphoebe and Amoret were engendered by a god on a Faerie, adopted and raised by goddesses. Satyrane, born of a human mother (I.vi.22–3), has been raised by the satyr who raped her and, following the broad-minded logic of Ovidian fable, derives from this union not dishonor but a double aptitude, both human and feral: the only bastard named in his biography is 'bastard feare' (I.vi.24), which he is taught to banish. And Britomart's very armor is emblem of a double lineage. Worn by Angela, it was the armor of a Saxon queen, fierce enemy to Britomart's father and to her nation. Worn by Britomart, it enables a quest that is British to its very core: the new-minted female knight will secure her nation's champion and restore him to his homeland, will fight at his side to protect the nation from enemy invaders, will engender with him a race of kings who will restore the British title to their 'auncient Troian blood' (III.iii.22–3). But this transposition is also a consolidation, for Angela is no simple antithesis. She is also part of an exemplary line of female warriors, affording crucial precedent for an inexperienced, and anomalous, martial maid. Enlarging the precedent, Glauce recites an honor role: *Bunduca, Guendolen, Martia, Emmilen* (III.iii.54), all safely British. But a scant ten stanzas later, in one of the poet's own expostulations on behalf of women and their 'Antique glory', the honor role tellingly expands: *Penthesilee, Debora, Camill'* (III. iv.1–2). Political alliance is no longer the connecting thread: Penthesilea was an ally to the Trojans, but Camilla fought against them. Confronted with an historical record censored by 'enuious Men' (III.ii.2), women and the poets who celebrate them must craft a hybrid ancestry.

And hybrid realms. The doubling of most sweeping consequence to Spenser's poem, of course, is the doubling of England and Faerie Land, which some, he fears, will call a 'painted forgery':

> Sith none, that breatheth liuing aire, does know,
> Where is that happy land of Faery,
> Which I so much doe vaunt, yet no where show ...   (II *Proem*, 1)

In defense of his creation, the poet wittily claims his place in the Age of Discovery: Were not Peru, Virginia, and the River Amazon unheard of just a few short generations ago? Might not the future disclose yet other realms? Of all the world 'least part to vs is red' (II *Proem*, 2). In truth, the poet expected his readers to recognize the land of Faerie for what it was, and what poets alone can provide: an imaginative augmentation to a world found lacking. Faerie Land is a corrective, a space for the licensed play of political critique, moral persuasion, social experiment, partisan petition. It is the universal testing ground for knighthood, both elfin and Briton alike, the field where courage, ingenuity, vision may demonstrate their substance, and where ambition can advance its career. In this it is very like the New World as Spenser's countrymen construed it, or like the outposts of colonial Ireland.

POETICS

Sequence and causality, personation, doubling, and division: poetry thinks in formal manifestations. Spenser's foundational formal decision, as he envisioned and composed the 1590 *Faerie Queene*, was to forge an all-but-impossible, fecund contract with the mixed imperatives of epic, allegory, Petrarchan lyric, and romance. These in turn generate the poem's figurative contours. Personation is the chief of them: a flexible bodying forth of abstract distillation, hypertrophic affect, and linguistic convention, all subject to the vicissitudes of narrative time. Spenser's characters traverse a complex representational spectrum, no sooner soliciting the reader's expectations in one direction—that of psychological 'fullness' or stable symbolic meaning—than willfully derailing them by means of another. They are recombinant fragments; their effect is that of distributed consciousness. They ignite and occasion the poem's other methods of figuration, whose contours we can no more than outline here.

The chief of them are four in number. First is the construction and elaboration of allegorical place, of which the House of Pride (Book I), the Cave of Mammon (Book II), and the Garden of Adonis (Book III) are prominent examples. Second is ekphrasis, or the verbal rendering of objects already, within the fiction, the product of human artifice: tapestries, sculpture, paintings, garments and weaponry, masques and processions. These include, for example, the pageant of the Seven Deadly Sins as well as the ivory gate to the Bowre of Bliss and the tapestries and walls of beaten gold in the House of Busirane. Third is blazon, and here I would like to expand the term beyond its strict Petrarchan confines, making it parallel to the categories of ekphrasis and allegorical place. 'Blazon' in this larger sense refers to the extended figural rendering of (fictionally) animate creatures, comprehending therefore the six-stanza description of two naked damsels in Acrasia's fountain (II.xii.63–8) as well as the virtuosic inventory of Belphoebe's beauties in Book II (iii.22–30). Fourth and final is epic simile, the ceremonial dilation of a parallel vista, often a homely one, at a juncture of particular plot intensity. Thus, the poem will augment a scene of combat (I.i.21–4) and scenes of psychological obsession (III.vii.1) or psychological transition (III.iv.13) with analogues from nature and the natural elements. Linking all four figurative devices is their power to alter the pacing of the narrative, to waylay action for the duration of a stanza or a canto, to interpolate a parallel vista or point of view, to puncture time or slow it down.

And timing is the essence of prosody, whose chief manifestation in this poem is the Spenserian stanza, devised especially for *The Faerie Queene*. Its parameters are these: nine iambic lines, eight of them five-footed and the ninth hexameter, rhymed so as to form interlocking quatrains and a final couplet, in the pattern ababbcbcc. Parameters easy to summarize but strenuous to observe, especially in large quantity: for the 1590 *Faerie Queene* alone, Spenser generated more than two thousand such stanzas. One would have thought it a Procrustean bed, inimical to limberness, to the speeding up and slowing down that narrative depends upon, and indeed, the stanza works at odds with other forms of pacing in the poem. But this internal tension contrives to function as an enlivening rather than a deadening constraint and is of a piece with Spenser's other formal propositions, like the allegiance to a hybrid genre. Shot through with competing formal claims, *The Faerie Queene* makes of its own method a model for the discipline of discovery. Multiplied and overdetermined, intentionality breaks its own closed circuit and opens up to surprise.

The poet is also a master of those supple variations that make of accent and syllable, line and stanza both scaffolding and excitation to the living verse. As witness the following syncopation of syntax and meter:

> The woodborne people fall before her flat,
> And worship her as Goddesse of the wood;
> And old *Syluanus* selfe bethinkes not, what
> To thinke of wight so fare, but gazing stood,
> In doubt to deeme her borne of earthly brood ...   (I.vi.16)

The iambs are strict but the cadences remarkably varied, the lines end-paused in four instances out of five but the single exception so deftly managed as to freshen and destabilize the lines before and after. At just the point of enjambment, syntax does a doubletake: the 'what' that glimmers for a moment as grammatical object of 'bethinkes' traverses the line break to become the grammatical object of the infinitive 'to thinke'. Giving purpose to pleasure, moreover, this musical disturbance mimics the disturbance in Sylvanus' mind.

Cantos have a cadence too. Not only are they poised within a layered dynamics of scale (stanza, canto, 'book', and poem) and bound to the rise and fall of narrative action (battle, journey, catalogue, seduction), they are varied with varying modes of address and opacities of speaking voice. Nowhere is this more conspicuous than at the canto's launch. Some cantos move directly to action, *in medias res*; some pause first for reflection or homiletic counsel. Some begin with apostrophes to the Queen, faire ladies, the muse; some mark the transition from night to day. Some submerge the narrative voice in near transparency; others temporarily crystallize the narrative voice into narrative persona, which in turn expostulates, apologizes, professes weariness with the poet's task or suffering on behalf of his suffering heroines. From the frank buffoonery of Braggadocchio to the sibling comedy of Venus and Diana (III.vi.20–4) to the subtler undermining of Arthur's extended complaint against night (III.iv.55–60), the poet plays levity in many keys, and these within the grander sweep of epic vision and ethical high seriousness. So tonal modulations compound and counterpoint rhetorical modulations, and both are scored against the ground rhythms of stanza and narrative quest.

The varieties of formal and cognitive phrasing in Spenser might fill volumes, but a final example—the half-line—will have to do. Twice in the course of the 1590 *Faerie Queene,* the poet violates metrical contract by means of a broken line. The first occurrence marks the very center of the ten-stanza blazon to Belphoebe (at l. 45 of 90) and, tellingly, the very center of the lady's anatomy, at the 'golden fringe' of her short garment (II.iii.26). The effect, as one so expert in the erotics of veiling would have been well aware, is one of mingled delicacy and prurience: the poet contrives to have it both ways. The second occurrence involves a moment of less ambiguous delicacy, when Arthur interrupts Guyon's profusion of thanks (II.viii.55). On five other occasions, Spenser disrupts his line with broken speech or syntax rather than a broken metric. One derailment marks Braggadocchio's botched effort to embrace Belphoebe while she is praising the active life (II.iii.42); two others mark the breakdown of prophecy at the threshold of the present, once in Briton Moniments (II.x.68) and once in the course of Merlin's visionary disquisition to Britomart (III.iii.50).

Two final instances occur in a single scene and nicely illustrate Spenser's cultivation of contrasting tonalities. When Malbecco, pursuing his absconded wife, mistakes Braggadocchio for a possible champion of his cause and offers the latter payment, Braggadocchio feigns the posture of offended dignity, with predictably botched results:

> . . . Thy offers base I greatly loth,
> And eke thy words vncourteous and vnkempt;
> I tread in dust thee and thy money both,
> That, were it not for shame, So turned from him wroth.   (III.x.29)

This mangling of civility in the service of chivalric 'honor' is one of Spenser's broadest comic effects. Four stanzas earlier, however, Malbecco's own speech has broken down not in hypocrisy, as we might have expected, but in distress: 'For I . . . A silly Pilgrim . . . seeke a Lady . . . ' (III.x.25). The very simplicity of the language is part of its surprising power. And when, contrary to literary type, the cuckold forgoes revenge out of concern for his lady's 'safety' (III.x.39), he confirms this odd moment of pathos and further unsettles the predictable satiric formula. The miserly cuckold is a pattern that distills a great deal of cultural hostility and conflict, as we have had occasion to remark, and Spenser will drag Malbecco through the ghastliest humiliations to an intractable allegorical conclusion, but, remarkably, he detours first into a moment one might almost call disarming.

THE READER AND THE NATION

Sir Walter Ralegh was a key patron during Spenser's Irish years, the man who procured the poet's introduction at court when he was in England to oversee publication of the 1590 Faerie Queene, the man he addresses in the explanatory 'Letter' and clearly imagines as one of the poem's primary readers, a man as deeply versed as any in the dense intertwinings of personality and personal ambition that animated Elizabethan statecraft. Ralegh composed two commendatory sonnets to accompany the 1590 quarto and, true to genre, these verses praise the author for surpassing all predecessors. The predecessor singled out above all others is not, however, Virgil or Ariosto or Tasso, as might have been expected. It is the lyric Petrarch: 'Me thought I saw the graue, where *Laura* lay,' writes Ralegh, and sees it covered in oblivion. Praising Gloriana for surpassing Laura, of course, enables Ralegh to promote his own interests with the Queen who served as Spenser's model, but this double expedience merely deepens the purchase of Ralegh's strategic analogy. In Elizabethan England, the vocabularies of political address, in letters, paintings, masques, and royal entrances, were infused with those of the Petrarchan love lyric. Spenser's poem makes literary use, but also and crucially makes literary *trial*, of political rhetoric borrowed from literary prototypes. And in a poem designed to occupy epic space—to imagine and promote and shape a corporate subject—Spenser rehearses again and again the psychic economy defined by lyric. The poet's premise, of course, and his argument, is the reciprocal production of corporate and private, cognitive subject and political subject, nation and faith. The 'priuate morall vertues' described in the 'Letter to Ralegh' are the constituent components of public and collective life.

Which brings us to the reader once again. The two aspects human agency assumes in Spenser's poem, the authorial and the interpretive, correspond to the twin obligations of civic life: we are obliged to act and to understand. Spenser underscores the interdependence of these functions in one of his favorite verbs: to read. His characters are perpetually exhorted to 'read' their tales, which is to say, to relate them, while the poet professes a readerly relation to the narrative before him, as though its momentums preceded his own: 'So oft as I this history record, | My hart doth melt with meere compassion' (III.viii.1). Both tropes are conventional, but the blurring of boundaries is meant to be real. To read is also to see or discern,[11] and the poet of *The Faerie Queene* construes this as a shared project. The poem is built to produce the reader that it, and the nation, require. The redundancy, hiatus, and overdetermination that characterize the narrative, the dizzying dissolve from one representational plane to another, the now-corroborative now-dissonant superimpositions of classical and Christian figuration demand an active reading subject, whose production and refinement is the one true end of Spenser's poem.

Notes

1. Though the 'Letter to Ralegh' has received the great preponderance of critical attention, the volume included other appendages as well, as mentioned above: seven commendatory verses, whose authors are identified by means of initials or pseudonyms; a group of dedicatory sonnets (numbering ten in parts of the print run, fifteen or seventeen in others); a prominent page of dedication to Queen Elizabeth. For recent critical analysis of these 'paratexts', see Erikson (2005).
2. For three modern studies of the subject that have been of particular importance to readers of *The Faerie Queene*, see Fletcher (1964), McCaffrey (1976), and Teskey (1996).
3. The most influential account of St George appears in *Legenda Aurea*, compiled by Jacobus of Voragine, Bishop of Genoa, c.1260–75 and first printed in 1470. *The Golden Legend*, which dominated Western hagiographical literature for centuries, survives in approximately 900 manuscripts and from 1470 to 1530 was the most frequently printed book in Europe. Caxton's English edition was first published in 1483.

4. In the entry 'Virtues' in *SC*, Ronald Horton conveys with admirable concision why the most satisfying account of Spenser's overarching allegorical structure is still that provided by Josephine Waters Bennett and Rosamond Tuve, building upon the earlier work of Thomas Keightley. For a later speculative account of the projected 24-book *Faerie Queene*, see Hieatt (1987).

5. ἱστορία: a learning or knowing by inquiry (*OED*).

6. Faith and works, in other words. In its own practical imperatives *The Faerie Queene* thinks through a key Reformation debate.

7. On Spenser's allegorization of Ralegh in the person of Timias, see Spenser (2001), 344 n and 463 n.

8. For the prototype of this transformation, see Ariosto, *Orlando Furioso* 6.26–53.

9. See Shakespeare, *Troilus and Cressida* II.iii.72–3.

10. Saint George, whose own nationality is obscure and variably reported (Voragine says he was a nobleman of Cappadocia and a tribune in the Roman army), has proved remarkably amenable to national adoption: he is a patron saint of Portugal, Germany, Lithuania, and Malta as well as of England. See Gregerson (2008).

11. As witness lengthy entries in the OED. See especially sense I.4, attributed to Spenser alone.

SELECTED BIBLIOGRAPHY

Berger, H. (1957). *The Allegorical Temper: Vision and Reality in Book II of Spenser's 'Faerie Queene'*. New Haven, CT: Yale University Press.

Erikson, Wayne (ed.) (2005). *The 1590 Faerie Queene: Paratexts and Publishing* (special issue of *Studies in the Literary Imagination* 38(2)).

Fletcher, A. (1964). *Allegory: The Theory of a Symbolic Mode*. Ithaca, NY: Cornell University Press.

Gregerson, L. (1995). *The Reformation of the Subject: Spenser, Milton, and the English Protestant Epic*. Cambridge: Cambridge University Press.

—— (2008). 'Spenser's Georgic'. *SSt* 22: 185–201.

Hieatt, A. K. (1987). 'The Projected Continuation of "The Faerie Queene": Rome Delivered?' *SSt* 8: 335–47

Horton, R. (1990). 'Virtues'. *SE*, 719–21.

MacCaffrey, I. G. (1976). *Spenser's Allegory: The Anatomy of Imagination*. Princeton, NJ: Princeton University Press.

Miller, D. L. (1988). *The Poem's Two Bodies: The Poetics of the 1590 'Faerie Queene'*. Princeton, NJ: Princeton University Press.

Montrose, L. A. (1996). 'The Elizabethan Subject and the Spenserian Text', in P. Parker and D. Quint (eds), *Literary Theory/Renaissance Texts*. Baltimore: Johns Hopkins University Press, 303–40.

Parker, P. (1979). *Inescapable Romance: Studies in the Poetics of a Mode*. Princeton, NJ: Princeton University Press.

Teskey, G. (1996). *Allegory and Violence*. Ithaca, NY: Cornell University Press.

Tuve, R. (1966). *Allegorical Imagery: Some Medieval Books and Their Posterity*. Princeton, NJ: Princeton University Press.

CHAPTER 12

···

COMPLAINTS AND DAPHNAÏDA (1591)

···

MARK DAVID RASMUSSEN

DURING 1591, the year after the first installment of *The Faerie Queene*, the publisher William Ponsonby issued in quick succession two more volumes by Edmund Spenser: the collection of miscellaneous short poems titled *Complaints*, and *Daphnaïda*, a single poem mourning the recent death of the nineteen-year-old Douglas Howard, wife of Spenser's acquaintance Arthur Gorges. Both quarto volumes were prepared for the press during Spenser's visit to England in 1589–91, and both seem designed to capitalize on the recent success of *The Faerie Queene*. And they have at least two other things in common. Both books showcase poetry of unconsoled lamentation, 'complaints and meditations of the worlds vanitie; verie grave and profitable', as Ponsonby put it in his preface to the *Complaints* volume. Throughout most of the time since their publication neither book has been highly regarded by readers of Spenser. Introducing his fully annotated edition of *Complaints*, the great early twentieth-century scholar William Renwick sniffed: 'It is not on these *Complaints* that Spenser's poetic reputation rests. None of his greatest things are here' (Renwick 1923: 179). And the late twentieth-century critic who has written most extensively on *Daphnaïda*, William Oram, has called it (among other things) 'a gloomy, tenacious, obsessive, long-winded poem' (Oram 1981: 141). Yet in recent years readers of Spenser have found new rewards in these old books, with the *Complaints* volume in particular discovering a more receptive audience than at any time since its publication. Some of this fresh interest in *Complaints* may be traced to the publication in 1989 of the Yale edition of Spenser's shorter poems, whose careful introductions and notes encouraged readers to consider the volume 'as an integrated whole' (Spenser 1989: 222). Equally responsible for this shift in appreciation are a number of developments in literary criticism and in Spenser studies since the 1980s, many of which are recorded elsewhere in this *Handbook*. They include an ongoing redefinition of what constitutes literary value; a sustained focus on the social, political, and cultural conditions of authorship in Elizabethan England; a closely related fascination with the dynamics of Spenser's careers, both as a poet and as a public official; a sharper awareness of how this poet enacts his work within what Jonathan Crewe, following Nashe, has called 'the paper stage' of the individual printed volume (Crewe 1986: 100); and perhaps most important, a fuller recognition of the complex possibilities for meaning afforded by the mode of poetic complaint.

FRAMING SPENSER'S *COMPLAINTS*: CRITICAL APPROACHES TO A RECALCITRANT BOOK

Many of the critical developments just mentioned emerged during the major reva-luation of Spenser's 1579 *Shepheardes Calender* that took place in the late 1970s and early 1980s. While readers in previous decades, trained by New Critical principles to admire linguistic complexity and formal coherence, had found little to engage them in Spenser's pastoral sequence, new historicist critics like Richard Helgerson and Louis Montrose brought the volume to life by showing how its poems evoke in intricate detail the tensions of Spenser's own experience as an aspiring poet in the Elizabethan cultural milieu.[1] Moreover, these critics agreed in viewing all elements of the printed book as part of its statement—not just the poems themselves, but the prefatory epistle and glosses by E. K., the woodcut illustrations preceding each eclogue, and even the distribution of typefaces upon the printed page, were all seen to participate in the volume's enactment of a fraught moment in Spenser's poetic career.

Given the success of this career-and-volume-centered approach, it would seem only natural for critics to focus a similar attention on Spenser's *Complaints*. Like the eclogues of *The Shepheardes Calender*, individual *Complaints* can seem less than aesthetically dazzling. May they, too, be read as participating in the tensions of a career enactment? Perhaps; yet it must be said that in many ways the volume resists such scrutiny. One challenge comes from its timing. By publishing the first install-ment of *The Faerie Queene* in 1590, Spenser had arrived at the end point of the Virgilian progression from pastoral to epic. What sense does it make, one year later, for him to release a volume of *Complaints*? To be sure, this question must arise in relation to any volume published after the move into epic; the Virgilian progression leaves no room for a sequel. But 'complaint' seems a distinctly non-laureate, even retrograde, term. Indeed, when Patrick Cheney, with great ambition and aplomb, extends the Virgilian progression into a multigeneric model to cover Spenser's entire poetic output, he simply leaves the *Complaints* volume out of account (Cheney 1993: 3). It is a moment that doesn't quite fit.

Moreover, while *The Shepheardes Calender* presents its readers with an orderly sequence of twelve eclogues, keyed to the months of the year and prefaced by the admiring epistles of E. K., *Complaints* brings together miscellaneous poems written over a twenty-year period, and seems to present them in no particular order. The verso of the volume's title page offers a list of 'the sundrie Poemes' that it contains:

1. *The Ruines of Time.*
2. *The Teares of the Muses.*
3. *Virgils Gnat.*
4. *Prosopopoia, or Mother Hubberds Tale.*
5. *The Ruines of Rome: by Bellay.*
6. *Muiopotmos, or The Tale of the Butterflie.*
7. *Visions of the Worlds vanitie.*
8. *Bellayes visions.*
9. *Petrarches visions.*

The poems listed here include both original works and translations of poems by Virgil, Du Bellay, and Petrarch, on topics ranging from the embittered laments of the city of Verulamium over her lost glories and of the nine Muses over the decline of poetry and patronage, to the satiric beast fable of *Mother Hubberds Tale* and the playful mock epic *Muiopotmos*, which narrates the death of a butterfly. (Insects loom large in *Complaints*.) Included in the mix are sonnets, stanzaic poems in rhyme royal, sixaines, and ottava rima, and one poem, *Mother Hubberds Tale*, in Chaucerian heroic couplets. The earliest written works are the last two sets of *Bellayes visions* and *Petrarches visions*, rewritten versions of the translated sonnets first published in *A Theatre for Voluptuous Worldings* in 1569 (see Chapter 8 above), while portions of *Mother Hubberds Tale* seem to respond directly to the Alençon crisis of 1579, and *Virgils Gnat*, a translation of the pseudo-Virgilian *Culex*, may also have been written at about that time, but in any case well before the death in 1588 of the Earl of Leicester, to whom the poem is dedicated. Another noble death, that of Sir Francis Walsingham in April 1590, provides the latest datable reference within the poems, in the lines of *The Ruines of Time* that mourn his passing. Some poems in the volume, most notably *Virgils Gnat* and *Mother Hubberds Tale*, show signs of different stages of revision, while others, such as *The Teares of the Muses*, *The Ruines of Rome*, *Muiopotmos*, and *Visions of the Worlds Vanitie*, are not easily datable by external or internal criteria.[2] Finally, while all the elements of *The Shepheardes Calender* as a printed book—the texts of the poems, the illustrations, commentary, typefaces, and so on—seem to contribute toward a complex but coherent effect, the most striking bibliographic peculiarity of *Complaints* actually heightens its diffuseness, for the book contains no fewer than four title pages, one for the volume as a whole, and one for each of three poems (*The Teares of the Muses*, *Mother Hubberds Tale*, and *Muiopotmos*) prefaced by dedicatory epistles addressed to the three daughters of John Spencer of Althorp, with whom Spenser claimed affinity. Since *The Ruines of Time* is also prefaced by a dedicatory epistle, addressed to Mary Sidney, the effect is to divide the book into four sections, each beginning with a title page (in the case of *The Ruines of Time*, that of the volume as a whole), and each opening with a poem prefaced by a dedicatory epistle:

1. *The Ruines of Time*
2. *The Teares of the Muses*
   Virgils Gnat
3. *Mother Hubberds Tale*
   The Ruines of Rome
4. *Muiopotmos*
   Visions of the Worlds Vanitie
   Visions of Bellay
   Visions of Petrarch

Each of these four sections ends on the last page of a signature, so each might have been sold, or presented, separately, as well as together with the rest of the volume. That one of the title pages, that for *Muiopotmos*, bears the date of 1590 rather than 1591 only adds to the impression of a book heading in several directions at once.[3]

Even the extent of Spenser's involvement in the production of the volume is unclear. In his preface, Ponsonby draws attention to his own efforts in gathering together and publishing 'such smale Poemes of the same Authors; as I heard were disperst abroad in sundrie hands, and not easie to bee come by, by himselfe'. The apparent implication is that Spenser did not participate in this process, though at least since Renwick and Stein most writers on *Complaints* have viewed Ponsonby's statement as a blind for Spenser's own involvement.[4] Inflammatory passages in certain poems, particularly the thinly veiled attacks upon Elizabeth's chief minister, Lord Burghley, in *Mother Hubberds Tale* and *The Ruines of Time*, may have been reason enough for Spenser to keep his distance. In the event, *Complaints* was 'called in' by official decree shortly after its publication—that is, unsold copies were impounded from booksellers—and *Mother Hubberds Tale* was omitted from the posthumous edition of Spenser's *Works* published in 1611, when Burghley's son Robert Cecil was still alive.[5]

For all these reasons—the timing of the volume, its miscellaneous contents and bibliographic features, its lack of clear-cut authorial direction—*Complaints* poses a peculiar challenge to those who would view it as enacting a specific moment in Spenser's career. Since the 1980s, criticism of *Complaints* has taken two main directions, one primarily historicist and one primarily formalist in its orientation. Historicist critics embrace both the miscellaneous nature of the volume and its non-laureate status, reading *Complaints* as staging a deliberate turn away from the Virgilian model and its reliance on court patronage.[6] By reclaiming his 'disperst' earlier works as his own property, Spenser issues 'a new statement of poetic self-reliance' (Rambuss 1993: 95) that heralds the 'general turning toward the autobiographical and the self-centered' (Crewe 1986: 56) that characterizes his later work.[7] As most fully developed by William Oram, this critical approach hears in the volume 'an explosion of frustration at the court' that 'has a pivotal place in Spenser's work'

(Oram 2005: 26). Such interpretations tend to focus on particular moments within the poems that thematize career issues, such as the passages of anti-court invective in *Mother Hubberds Tale*, *The Teares of the Muses*, and *The Ruines of Time*, or the emblems in *Visions of the Worlds Vanitie* of the destruction of the strong by the weak. However, in a few suggestive pages Judith Owens has proposed that the distinctive features of the printed book offer further support for such a view, arguing that the very diffuseness of the volume's bibliographical characteristics helps to enact 'the larger, centrifugal, anti-court movement which defines the volume as a whole' (Owens 2002: 34).

Given the circumstances both of the volume's 'calling in' and of Spenser's later career, this reading of *Complaints* as enacting a disillusioned turn away from the court seems immediately plausible; it is probably the consensus reading of the volume among Spenserians today. A second group of critics, smaller and less influential than the first, has focused mainly on questions of form, and particularly on Spenser's use of poetic complaint. 'Complaint' in Spenser's day can designate a bewilderingly wide variety of poems, including love-laments, estates satire, and the complaints of fallen monarchs and forsaken women popularized by *The Mirror for Magistrates* and Samuel Daniel's *Complaint of Rosamond*.[8] As John Kerrigan observes, complaint is best understood as a mode rather than as a genre—that is, as a set of attitudes and practices that finds expression in various forms.[9] Given the polymorphous nature of complaint, it seems obviously useful for critics like Hugh Maclean and Linda Vecchi to point out affinities of particular poems in the volume with particular versions of complaint that Spenser would have known.[10] In the first full-length study of *Complaints* since Harold Stein's 1934 monograph, Richard Danson Brown goes further. For Brown, what unites the *Complaints* volume is Spenser's growing desire to use traditional forms of complaint to express new meanings. In the earliest written *Complaints*, the two sets of visions originally translated in 1569 and *Virgils Gnat*, Spenser remains relatively comfortable within the medieval tradition of complaint as a vehicle of moral instruction, but in such later written poems as *Mother Hubberds Tale* and *Muiopotmos* he repeatedly calls that tradition into question. The trajectory of the volume is from traditional complaint to what Brown terms 'innovative complaint', which 'articulates the complexities of the mortal condition, and constructs a mimesis no longer tied to moralistic imperatives' (Brown 1999: 254).

In their different ways, both the historicist and the formalist interpretations of *Complaints* view the volume as a pivotal moment in Spenser's working life, yet each approach has its limitations. Perhaps the most immediately vulnerable to criticism is Brown, who reads the poems carefully but places those readings in the service of a cliché, that of the trail-blazing poet who leaves outmoded traditions behind. Brown's book is simply not in dialogue with the main body of Spenser scholarship over the past few decades, with its intricate contextualizing of Spenser's life and work. The historicist approach to *Complaints* suffers from the opposite defect: it fails to fully engage the poems. At least as it has been developed so far, this reading of *Complaints* tends mainly to highlight representative moments from the volume, moments that are irrefutably 'there', but not necessarily identifiable with the work's full meaning.[11] Such a piecemeal approach may be hard to resist, given the volume's diverse materials. But to adopt it is to fall short of the rich integration of historicist analysis with close reading that made critical work on *The Shepheardes Calender* so compelling.

READING THE *COMPLAINTS*

Is it possible to combine the insights of historicist and formalist practices so as to bring the volume into focus 'as an integrated whole'? I think that it is, and I think that the key to such an approach is a fuller understanding of the paradoxical dynamic of poetic complaint. In all of its many varieties, complaint is poetry of unconsoled grief. Whether its topic is death or erotic frustration or, more broadly, the failure of an ideal, the purpose of complaint is to prolong the experience of loss, reiterating the sheer fact of disaster. In this respect, complaint may usefully be distinguished from elegy. Elegy works upon loss, works upon death, to create something new: Lycidas exalted, *Lycidas* the poem.[12] This is precisely what complaint will not do. Its strength comes from its impassioned refusal to 'get over' the trauma it mourns. Yet this very refusal may seem at once too submissive and too willful, a perverse insistence on suffering. (In a Christian context, it is also theologically wrong.) Stylistically complaint tends toward a literal-minded repetition, as it dwells on the reality of what has vanished. As a form of poetic self-assertion it is at once passive and aggressive: it succeeds by failing.

Throughout his working life as a poet, Spenser is fascinated by the paradoxes of poetic complaint. He is not alone in this: such other canonical poets as Catullus, Virgil, Ovid, Petrarch, Chaucer, and Shakespeare draw quite self-consciously on the antithetical possibilities of the mode at various points in their careers.[13] But no one does so more thoroughly than Spenser in *Complaints*. Poems originally written at various times for various occasions use the paradoxes of complaint to probe issues central to Spenser's own poetic practice. Whether or not the collection was designed with this end in mind, the effect of gathering its poems is to generate an internal dialogue about the circumstances of Spenser's career and his activity as a poet. By tracing the main lines of this dialogue as it transpires within the pages of *Complaints*, we should be able to experience the volume more fully, as both a formal and a historical/cultural event.

So, the opening poem of the collection, *The Ruines of Time*, stages an encounter between an unnamed narrator and the plaintive female figure of Verlame, genius of the destroyed Roman-British city of Verulamium, whom he observes weeping on the banks of the Thames. Verlame's extended lament, occupying 448 of the poem's 686 lines, or 64 rhyme royal stanzas, falls into three roughly equal parts. Tearing her hair and clutching a broken rod, Verlame first bewails at length her own fall and that of

Rome (ll. 22–174), and then rather surprisingly turns to mourn the recent deaths of great Elizabethans, beginning with Spenser's former employer, the Earl of Leicester, and concluding with Sir Philip Sidney (175–343). Thoughts of Sidney and his verse prompt Verlame to extol at length the power of poetry to immortalize its subjects (344–448), but these lofty thoughts eventually subside, as she recalls the lowly status of poetry in the present day, when the Muses are scorned by those in power. (Lines 451–5, like 216–17 earlier, are transparent attacks on Burghley.) Verlame concludes by returning to her own ruined state, before vanishing 'With dolefull shrikes' (471) and leaving the narrator behind.

As an iconic figure of female grief, weeping at the water's edge, Verlame is cross-bred out of classical and biblical traditions that include the Ariadnes of Catullus and Ovid and the Babylonian exiles of the 137th Psalm; her most immediate precursor is the weeping personification of Rome, tuning 'hir plaint to falling rivers sound' in the tenth poem of Du Bellay's *Songe*, first translated by Spenser for the 1569 *Theatre*. The florid rhetoric of her complaint inevitably recalls that of *The Mirror for Magistrates*, whose speakers often distill their grief into rhyme royal stanzas. Above all, though, as Carl Rasmussen has shown, Verlame's thinking and motives are flawed (C. Rasmussen 1981). In a Protestant context, not only is she tainted by her Roman associations, but her excessive contempt for the world veils excessive attachment. Even Verlame's vaunting claims for poetry—that it can shatter the 'seven fold yron gates of grislie Hell' (372) and bring dead souls 'to eternall day' (376)—only manifest 'her insatiable egocentricity' (C. Rasmussen 1981: 170).[14] In her grief and in her bragging she embodies the paradoxical energies of the plaintive will, the urge to exert oneself upon the world through the process of lament.

The chief work of the poem is to dissociate Spenser himself from Verlame's perspective. This is accomplished in the poem's concluding section, which establishes a sharp distinction between the speaker of the poem and its author. After Verlame vanishes, the sympathetic narrator remains behind, 'Renewing her complaint' in his mind, 'wounded' with anguish and 'frosen' with horror (479–83). Sympathy for her woe has paralyzed his thought. And now, unbidden, two sets of visions appear, 'by demonstration me to teach' (488). First come six emblems of the transitory nature of worldly things, much like those in the translated poems in *A Theatre*: a collapsed altar, a fallen tower, and the like. The narrator weeps uncontrollably at these images that mirror his and Verlame's shared sorrow, but a loud voice bids him to turn away from these images of 'vanitie and griefe of minde' (583) toward 'hope of heaven' (585). A second set of six images now depicts the apotheosis of Sir Philip Sidney, dead in 1586 but here memorialized by the ascent into the sky of a swan, a harp, a coffer, a bridal bed, a knight on a winged horse, and a golden ark. As these images become constellations, they celebrate Sidney's transcendence of death and offer a new model of poetic disinterestedness. Each image is a discrete 'signe' (601, 615) that may easily be 'red' (633), irrespective of the will of its creator. As elegiac substitutions, they constitute the true 'eternizing' of Sidney promised in the poem's dedication. Yet so identified is the narrator with Verlame's suffering that he fails to recognize any difference between this second set of emblems and the first, and the poem proper ends with him unconsoled, 'for dole . . . almost like to die' (672).

Only in the poem's 'Envoy' do we hear the voice of Spenser himself, as he addresses first Sidney's spirit and then Mary Sidney, the poem's dedicatee:

> Immortal spirite of *Philisides*,
> Which now art made the heavens ornament,
> That whilome wast the worlds chiefst riches;
> Give leave to him that lov'de thee to lament
> His losse, by lack of thee to heaven hent,
> And with last duties of this broken verse,
> Broken with sighes, to decke thy sable Herse.

> And ye fair Ladie th'honor of your daies,
> And glorie of the world, your high thoughts scorne;
> Vouchsafe this moniment of his last praise,
> With some few silver dropping teares t'adorne:
> And as ye be of heavenlie off spring borne,
> So unto heaven let your high minde aspire,
> And loath this drosse of sinfull worlds desire.   (673–86)

In the exquisite poise of these lines, Spenser acknowledges his own investment in what he writes: the broken verses voice his own broken sighs. Unlike the second set of emblems, the poem openly expresses the concerns of its maker. But this expressiveness is not plaintive: neither self-aggrandizing nor sheerly disinterested, the poem is an indirect rendering of the author's desires, carefully modulated and controlled, made on another's behalf. When Spenser asks Mary Sidney to grace his lines with 'some few silver dropping teares', he echoes the reference in the poem's second line to 'silver streaming *Thamesis*', and when he speaks of his work as a 'moniment' to Sidney he recalls the reference in line 5 to the lack of a contemporary 'moniment' to Verlame's former glory. Both echoes are also reversals. Mary Sidney's 'few' tears contrast with Verlame's unstoppable abundance, and Spenser's 'moniment' evokes the transcendence of worldly things rather than bookmarking their past existence. The final injunction to 'loath this drosse' sounds like a relapse into the rhetoric of complaint, but what is to be loathed turns out not to be the world itself, as Verlame seems to loathe it, but excessive *desire* for the world; like the rest of the 'Envoy', the line seeks and finds a balance.[15]

The Ruines of Time, then, opens *Complaints* by staging an exorcism of complaint, a purging of the self-assertive energies of the plaintive will. The poem is also a self-reflection. As Margaret Ferguson observes, Verlame's emblematically broken scepter recalls the breaking of Colin's pipes in the *January* eclogue as a figure for Spenser's 'own sense of poetic impotence' (Ferguson 1984: 34). If, as has often been suggested, Verlame's complaint is itself a pastiche of passages from Spenser's earlier works, then specimens of Spenser's earlier work are literally implicated in her willful self-assertion.[16] In the 'Envoy', Spenser finds an independent poetic voice that is neither egotistical nor self-effacing. In comparison, the volume's second poem, *The Teares of the Muses*, must feel like a regression. The nine Muses who lament in sequence in this poem are, like Verlame, incarnations of feminine woe, expatiating on their griefs in sixaines that recall the plaintive *January* and *December* eclogues. But here there is no alternative, elegiac or otherwise, to complaint. At the poem's end, the Muses break their instruments, and the poem subsides into silence: 'The rest untold no loving tongue can speake' (600).

Perhaps because the Muses' laments strike readers as so repetitive in substance and tone, *The Teares of the Muses* has been among the least commented-upon of Spenser's shorter works. Yet as I have shown elsewhere (Rasmussen 1999), the poem is far more complicated, and far more interesting, than it initially appears. While its ostensible aim is to expose the circumstances that thwart poetry-making in Elizabethan England, in fact the poem works ironically to implicate the Muses themselves in the conditions of their own demise. Over the course of the poem several different narratives of the Muses' fall emerge and reflect upon one another. As told in the laments of Euterpe, Terpsichore, and Erato, the poem's central myth relates the overthrow of the Muses, '[l]ike Virgin Queenes with laurell garlands cround' (309), by the 'base-borne brood' (392) of Ignorance. This overthrow is depicted in the linked class and gender terms of Elizabethan rule, with the recreative Muses attacked by obscenely prolific male figures who stain their 'chast bowers' with 'brutishnesse and beastlie filth' (269–70), but as these sections of the poem develop it becomes clear that the Muses rely on this very defeat to quicken their song, a ceaseless 'pouring forth' (4, 230, 415, 595) of tears and lamentation that mimics the masculine copiousness of their foes. Other narratives of the Muses' fall place their laments in a similarly equivocal light, revealing the Muses' desires for ascent, Astraean flight, or the possession of an authorizing secret as mirroring the competitive energies of their antagonists—as dissembled expressions, that is, of the plaintive will. Throughout, we see the paradoxical condition of passivity and aggression, of self-effacement and self-assertion, that characterizes the working of complaint.

Spenser's Muses obey the rhythms of what Harry Berger, Jr., writing on *The Shepheardes Calender*, has called 'the recreative/plaintive dynamic' of 'the paradise principle', that is, 'an obsessively repeated alternation between paradisal expectations and bitterness, or . . . a "fall" from the first to the second followed by an effort to return' (Berger 1988: 278).[17] For Berger, plaintive anger and recreative delight are mutually reinforcing aspects of a single urge, a self-assertive refusal to accept the world as it is found. In enacting this refusal, both the plaintive protest and the recreative withdrawal into the bower represent equally willful initiatives. In *Teares*, the two alternatives are given a social coding, as the opposed urges of a non-aristocratic poet operating within the Elizabethan cultural milieu, torn between the passive reproduction of aristocratic fictions and a self-consciously transgressive assertion of 'base' authorial will. Both alternatives hold a powerful appeal for Spenser, who is at once 'Elizabeth's arse-kissing poet' (Prawer 362), in the notorious phrase of Karl Marx, and a writer whose 'peculiar stubbornness' (Oram 2005: 43) compels him to speak truth to power. What was presented in *The Ruines of Time* as a more abstract dilemma about poetic agency—how may an author avoid the extremes of self-interest and self-effacement?—is here reframed as a conflict whose terms derive from the specific circumstances of Spenser's historical moment. But in *Teares* no third alternative is offered, no access to an independent poetic voice, no way out of the recreative/plaintive impasse.

If *Teares* looks back to *The Ruines of Time*, reinterpreting aesthetic dilemmas as culturally produced, it also looks forward to the subsequent poems. By revaluing the mutually reinforcing passive and aggressive urges of complaint as aristocratic disinterestedness and non-aristocratic anger and spite, and by giving those alternatives full imagistic development, *Teares* establishes a thematic of complaint that operates throughout the remainder of the volume, even in poems that are not generically plaintive. So, the next poem, *Virgils Gnat*, centers on the opposition between a recreative shepherd, asleep in the pleasant shade of the bower, and the plaintive gnat whose sting warns him of a serpent's attack. The gnat is swatted for his pains, and that night he appears to the shepherd in a dream, complaining that he is trapped in the underworld, prevented from reaching the Elysian fields until his good deeds on earth are acknowledged. Upon waking, the shepherd fashions a tomb-mound for the gnat, covered with flowers and bearing a grateful epitaph.

The poem translates a Latin work, *Culex*, that in Spenser's day was attributed to Virgil. While Spenser's ottava rima translation stays relatively close to the Latin original, such expansions as he does make, including a moralizing stanza on the gnat's lament on 'fortunes mutabilitie' (560), tend to heighten the poem's plaintive coloring. But Spenser's most significant alteration comes not from the details of his translation but from his framing of the poem by a dedicatory sonnet addressed to the Earl of Leicester, 'late deceased'. This sonnet links the 'Gnatts complaint' (14) to an unspecified grievance of Spenser's own against his former employer—'In clowdie teares my case I thus complaine' (3)—and thus recasts the Latin poem as an allegory of the relations between a poet and his patron. Within the terms that we have seen established in *Teares*, the shepherd, 'the flocks great Captaine' (268) and 'Lord of himselfe' (113), embodies recreative leisure as an aristocratic self-delight, while the gnat, 'His little needle ... infixing deep' (287), expresses the *ressentiment* of mingled service and spite that characterizes the plaintive condition. (The gnat's sting also looks forward to the emblems in *Visions of the Worlds Vanitie* of the destruction of the great by the small; five of the emblems in that sonnet sequence feature insects.) The polarity between the two alternatives is further sustained by a remarkable string of references to 'care' and 'carelessness' occurring over the course of the poem, a semantic cluster that associates the shepherd with the recreative condition of carelessness and the gnat with the plaintive burden of care.[18] But while *Teares* represented these alternatives as mutually reinforcing and self-canceling, Spenser in *Virgils Gnat* shows a way out. At the poem's conclusion the shepherd wakes from the 'carelessnesse' (323) of his slumbers and adopts the gnat's 'intollerable cares' (632) as his own: 'Now ... | ... wondrous cares | His inly grieved minde full sore opprest' (642). Unlike the narrator of *The Ruines of Time*, however, the shepherd is not disabled by his sympathy for the woes of another. Instead, his construction of a monument to the gnat is described as if it were a literary composition, the plotting and fashioning of a 'worke' that realizes the poet's 'thought' (650–6).

The conclusion of *Virgils Gnat*, then, recalls exactly the balance achieved in the 'Envoy' to *The Ruines of Time*, as the shepherd acquires the ability to shape his work on another's behalf. The shepherd's monument beautifully avoids the liabilities of both plaintive spite and recreative disinterestedness. Here, though, the resolution is achieved by a character within the poem rather than by its author. For the dedicatory sonnet to Leicester puts the plaintive frame back into place. Not only does the sonnet identify Spenser with the plaintive gnat, but it presents him as still resenting his 'late deceased' patron as 'the causer of my care' (2). If the poem itself points a way out of the recreative/plaintive cycle, the sonnet presents that solution as beyond Spenser's grasp, at the moment he writes.

Plaintiveness in *Mother Hubberds Tale*, the next poem in the volume, is most closely associated with the condition of the narrator, who retells Mother Hubbard's fable of the fox and the ape, as they seek their fortunes by successively adopting the roles of shepherd, priest, courtier, and, finally, monarch and chief minister. As Kent Van den Berg has shown in impressively thorough detail, the poem is filtered through the melancholy consciousness of its teller (Van den Berg 1978). Like the 'righteous Maide' Astraea, mentioned in the poem's opening lines, who leaves the earth 'for disdaine of sinfull worlds upbraide' (1–2), the narrator is an all-or-nothing absolutist who rejects the impurity of the fallen world. His attitude arises from personal frustration, as we learn in his long, barely controlled outburst on the evils of serving at court (892–914). The corrective to the narrator's moral absolutism, and its lack of engagement with the world, is found in the digression describing the ideal courtier (717–93), who uses the recreative withdrawal (760) into the pleasant delights of music, love, and verse to rekindle his mind for action in 'his Princes service' (768–73). Yet this figure has no impact whatsoever on the events of the poem. As Van den Berg aptly notes, Spenser 'could have brought the courtier into the action by making him the one to expose and banish the Fox and Ape, but he does not. The portrait is included not for the story's sake but for the narrator's; the courtier is an ideal counter-type to the prevailing corruption' (Van den Berg 1978: 93). Within the generic context of estates satire, Chaucer offers a relevant contrast. As described in 'The General Prologue' to *The Canterbury Tales*, Chaucer's Knight and Parson, like the gentle courtier, represent estates ideals, but each intervenes meaningfully on the road to Canterbury. From the narrator's perspective, any such engagement with the conditions of the world runs the risk of contamination. And yet the resolution to the tale's plot comes from just such an engagement, as in the final episode Jupiter refrains from a vengeful destruction of the two rascals, sending instead Mercury, god of thieves, as his highly equivocal envoy to set matters straight. In so bringing matters to a close, the poem leaves the consciousness of its plaintive narrator behind.

Both *Virgils Gnat* and *Mother Hubberds Tale*, then, offer alternatives to the recreative/plaintive dynamic, in the abilities of the shepherd and the ideal courtier to move beyond the two poles of the plaintive condition, but these alternatives are represented as beyond the reach of Spenser himself, in the dedicatory sonnet to *Virgils Gnat*, and of the narrator who retells the fable of Mother Hubbard. *Muiopotmos* returns to the impasse depicted in *Teares*. Here, the recreative/plaintive dynamic reappears as the conflict between the 'careles' (375) butterfly Clarion, fluttering about the flower beds, and his antagonist, the spider Aragnoll, the 'bondslave of spight' (245).[19] The spider's grudge against the butterfly derives from a weaving contest between Aragnoll's mother, Arachne, and the goddess Minerva, and Spenser's retelling of this competition, drawn from the sixth book of Ovid's *Metamorphoses*, is the interpretive center of the poem. Arachne's tapestry depicts the rape of Europa by Jove, a scene enlivened by Arachne's imaginative sympathy for Europa's plight: 'But (Lord) how she in everie member shooke' (285). By contrast, Minerva's tapestry is dispassionate, though far from disinterested. It depicts a story in which Minerva herself appears, her debate with Neptune for the patronage of Athens, but the scene is presented as objectively true and legible without reference to the creator's desires. Each of the gods depicted is easily recognizable ('Eathe to be knowen', 311), including both Neptune by the 'signe' of his 'warlike steed' (316–17) and Minerva by her spear and helmet. In the margins Minerva depicts a butterfly, 'Fluttring among the Olives wantonly' (331), and it is this lively image that causes Arachne to pine away with the 'poysonous rancor' that transforms her into a spider. (In Ovid it is Minerva who accomplishes this change.)

The weaving contest associates the conflict between Aragnoll and Clarion with two aesthetic approaches, each defined by opposite poles of the plaintive dynamic. Aragnoll's 'Enfestered grudge' (354) and 'secrete joy' (393) at Clarion's approach reflect a cankered version of Arachne's emotional investment in the topics of her art, which now becomes a vengefully plaintive spite. Clarion's carelessness is similarly associated with the bad faith of Minerva's depiction of the butterfly at the margins of her tapestry, a depiction that seeks to disguise images of divine power as sheer aesthetic play. The inset myth of the butterfly Astery, told in lines 113–44 and Spenser's own invention, reinforces this identification of the butterfly's carelessness with the vengefulness of those in power, as it connects the beauty of the butterfly's wings to the anger of Venus at the industriousness of one of her handmaidens, whom she transforms into a butterfly. The beauty of Clarion's wings recalls the memory of Astery's 'pretended crime, though crime none were' (143): it is a sign of the arbitrary working of power. The conflict between Minervan and Arachnean alternatives, between recreative aristocratic fictions and plaintive self-investment, is replayed in the combat between Aragnoll and Clarion, which ends with the death of the butterfly, his corpse left 'the spectacle of care' (440). If the poem's conclusion seems to present the 'base' side of the plaintive condition as victorious, that is only because carelessness has always dissembled its own pursuit of care, its own engagement in destructive spite. As with the gentle Muses and the brood of Ignorance, the plaintive cycle is endlessly repeatable, and always comes to the same woeful end.

I have saved for last the four sonnet sequences included in *Complaints*: *Ruines of Rome*, which comes between *Mother Hubberds Tale* and *Muiopotmos*, and the three sets of visionary sonnets that close the volume, *Visions of the Worlds Vanitie*, *The Visions of Bellay*, and *The Visions of Petrarch*. The relations of these four groups of poems to one another and to Spenser's earlier work in Van der Noot's *Theatre* are extraordinarily complex. *Ruines of Rome* is Spenser's translation of Joachim Du Bellay's sonnet sequence *Les Antiquitez de Rome* (1558), thirty-two sonnets contemplating the fallen remnants of the imperial city. Du Bellay's 1558 sequence was followed by a set of fifteen visionary sonnets, *Songe*, presenting a series of emblematic images of Rome's fall. Spenser had translated eleven of these sonnets into blank verse as part of his contribution to Van der Noot's *Theatre*; in *The Visions of Bellay* these blank verse translations are revised as English sonnets, and the four sonnets from *Songe* left out of *A Theatre* are now included.[20] This sequence is preceded in *Complaints* by *Visions of the Worlds Vanitie*, the only original rather than translated sequence of sonnets in the volume, and the volume concludes with *The Visions of Petrarch*, revisions of Spenser's rhymed versions in *A Theatre* of Petrarch's *Rime Sparse* 323, presenting six allegorical images of the death of Laura, Petrarch's beloved.[21] Of particular interest here is the way that the reordering in *Complaints* of poems from the 1569 *Theatre* reframes, and significantly changes, their meaning. The sequence in the earlier volume began with the six translated poems from Petrarch (via Marot), collectively titled *Epigrams* and each accompanied by a woodcut of its visionary image. This section was followed by a sequence of *Sonets*, also illustrated by woodcuts, and including the eleven translated visions from Du Bellay's *Songe*, followed by a set of four blank verse sonnets, probably translations of poems by Van der Noot, relating visionary moments from the biblical Book of Revelation. The effect is of a coherent progression, from Petrarch's plaintive lingering over Laura's loss to the more carefully guided sequence of visions from Du Bellay and the Bible, leading the reader to the consolation of Christian hope. The reordering of the poems and inclusion of new material in *Complaints* undoes this progression from complaint to consolation. Spenser's original sonnet sequence, *Visions of the Worlds Vanitie*, thoroughly demystifies the two sections of revised translations that follow it. While *The Visions of Bellay* and *The Visions of Petrarch* present visions that come unbidden to the poems' narrator, the first set of visions is presented as an externalized image of the speaker's own melancholy reflections on the debasement of his age, 'Picturing that, which I in mind embraced' (11). The emblems of the undoing of the mighty by the meek are presented by a narrator who clearly identifies with the vindication of the powerless and in the final sonnet acquires a new authority through this identification; what is evoked are the actual interests motivating the visionary moment. And while in the 1569 *Theatre* access to a higher truth was granted by the four visionary sonnets from Revelation, in *Complaints* these sonnets are omitted, and rather than ending with them the volume concludes in the plaintive mode of Petrarch with which the earlier work had begun. The contrast between the elegiac 'Envoy' to *Ruines* and the final sonnet of *The Visions of Petrarch* is especially strong, as the collection closes with a relapse into plaintiveness: 'And though ye be the fairest of Gods creatures, | Yet thinke, that death shall spoyle your goodly features' (97–8).

This has been a whirlwind tour of a fascinating book of poems. Perhaps inevitably the works least well served have been the two richest aesthetically, *Mother Hubberds Tale* and *Muiopotmos*, about which much more might be said in support of my approach. (The same is true of *Ruines of Rome*, which I have left entirely undiscussed.) But I hope the preceding remarks have at least shown that Spenser's collection is not most comprehensively defined by its isolated moments of criticism of the court and Elizabeth's chief minister, as powerful as these moments are. Such readings take the stance of the angry complainer as paradigmatic for the volume as a whole, ignoring how systematically the poems themselves call that stance into question. What more broadly unifies the volume is Spenser's ongoing engagement with the mode of complaint as he works through issues relating to his own poetic practice within the Elizabethan milieu. Does the volume present a coherent statement about these issues? Is it a turning point? As so often with Spenser, much depends on perspective. Viewed from the vantage point of the 'Envoy' to *The Ruines of Time*, the volume may seem to showcase issues that by 1591, after the publication of the first installment of *The Faerie Queene*, have already been confronted and resolved. In so representing his past failures, Spenser affirms his present success.[22] But if *Complaints* is read as a linear sequence a second possibility emerges, one familiar to readers of *The Faerie Queene*: an initial solution of a dilemma, like Redcrosse's slaying of Errour, is presented as premature and incomplete, as underestimating the difficulty of the conflicts that remain. As we will see in the next section, the tenacious presence of complaint within Spenser's work may speak in favor of this second possibility.

DAPHNAÏDA AND THE ENDURANCE
OF COMPLAINT

That the dilemmas of complaint remain unresolved for Spenser is one inference that may be drawn from the publication of *Daphnaïda* in the same year as *Complaints*. As the most recent bibliographical study (Weiss 1999) has shown, the two volumes must have been printed virtually simultaneously—both from a single job-lot of paper—and it is impossible to say which appeared first, though the usual critical approach is the one followed here, of reading *Daphnaïda* as a kind of coda to Spenser's collection. At least one contemporary reader apparently adopted the same approach, since of the three extant copies of *Daphnaïda* (as contrasted with forty-four of *Complaints*), one is bound together with a copy of *Complaints*, making the poem look very much like a final section of the anthology, opening with a new title page. Still, given the date of the poem's dedication, January 1, 1591 (almost certainly 'new style'), it is entirely possible that *Daphnaïda* appeared before *Complaints*, which must have been published at some time between its entry in the Stationers' Register of December 29, 1590 and March 19, 1591, when the date of purchase was inscribed in one of the surviving copies of the book.

The title page of *Daphnaïda* describes the poem as 'An Elegie upon the death of the noble and vertuous Douglas Howard', the nineteen-year-old wife of Sir Arthur Gorges, a close friend of Sir Walter Ralegh and at least an acquaintance of Spenser's: in his dedicatory epistle Spenser speaks of 'the particular goodwill' he bears toward him. Spenser's poem transposes into the genre of pastoral eclogue the characters and situation of Chaucer's first major poem, *The Book of the Duchess*, whose occasion was the death of Blanche of Castille, the wife of John of Gaunt. In both works, an unnamed narrator engages in dialogue with a sorrowing figure dressed in black, but while the trajectory of Chaucer's poem seems to be toward a kind of therapeutic healing for the Man in Black, an acceptance of the hard fact that his beloved White is dead, in *Daphnaïda* the grieving figure, Alcyon, remains willfully unconsoled, refusing the narrator's offer of a night's hospitality 'till he were better eased' (559), instead rushing out of the poem 'With staggering pace and dismall looks dismay' (564).[23] Perhaps the most influential interpretation of the poem to date has been that of William Oram, who reads it as a portrait of an obsessive mourner who remains stuck in his grief, unable to achieve any higher understanding of his loss (Oram 1981). For Oram, the poem bears a message for Arthur Gorges, urging him not to follow the example of his fictional counterpart by losing himself in grief. This reading of *Daphnaïda* has much to recommend it. Alcyon's extended complaint, in seven sections of seven seven-lined stanzas each, is numerically ordered in a way that contrasts diametrically with the unsettled quality of his mind; even when, in the middle section of his lament, Alcyon recognizes that his Daphne has been transported by death to 'a better place' (366), he only reiterates his desire to 'willfully increase my paine' (378). To be sure, such doleful rhetoric is normal in pastoral elegy, but usually such poems as Theocritus' first Idyll, Virgil's fifth Eclogue, Spenser's own *November*, and Milton's *Lycidas* build toward a moment of acceptance and consolation. In *Daphnaïda* that moment never comes.

Other critics, though, have offered an alternative to the ironic reading of Alcyon's lament, suggesting that his plaintive accents need to be taken more seriously. For Ellen Martin the poem asserts 'the poetic value of melancholia, withdrawal, intensity, and distraction' (Martin 1987: 108), while for Glenn Steinberg it expresses apocalyptic longings (Steinberg 1998) and for Patrick Cheney an unillusioned early modern engagement with death (Cheney 2003). These revisionist approaches to the poem remind us that when Spenser writes complaints he engages with issues that have a real power and allure. While in the *Complaints* volume Spenser mainly uses the paradoxes of complaint to reflect upon his own poetic practices, plaintive moments in *The Faerie Queene*, such as the laments of Britomart, Florimell, Arthur, and Amavia (to name only a few), employ the mode far less equivocally, as a vehicle 'to communicate the painful vitality of lived experience' that Joseph Campana sees as the defining aim of Spenser as a poet (Campana 2005: 38).

In conclusion, two late retrospective moments seem especially worth noting. Spenser's poem celebrating his own wedding, *Epithalamion* (1595), begins by invoking the Muses and recalling their laments in *The Teares of the Muses*, when 'ye list your owne mishaps to mourne' (7). Now Spenser asks the 'learned sisters' (1) to 'lay those sorrowfull complaints aside' (12); as Joseph Loewenstein well observes, the command to celebrate overrides not just the Muses' past plaintiveness, but also the force of complaint itself as characterizing a prior stage in Spenser's development (Loewenstein 1986: 299–300). Similarly, *Prothalamion* (1596) opens with a narrator who, depressed by 'sullein care | Through discontent of my long fruitlesse stay | In

Princes Court' (5–7), seeks to relieve his feelings by walking along the banks of 'silver streaming *Themmes*' (11), an echo of the opening of *The Ruines of Time*. Again celebration is expressed against the felt weight both of the present urge to lapse into sorrow and of complaint as an earlier moment in Spenser's publication history. As these moments in Spenser's epithalamia suggest, the *Complaints* volume becomes in retrospect a watershed moment in Spenser's career, a continually available point of reference. The final lines of Spenser's published works, the two stanzas of the eighth of the *Mutabilitie Cantos*, are similarly retrospective. Pondering the complaint of Mutabilitie in the previous canto, the narrator adopts the rhetoric of *The Ruines of Time* and Spenser's vision poems, speaking of his loathing of 'this state of life so tickle', before turning to anticipation of 'that same time when no more *Change* shall be | But stedfast rest'. Spenser's final poetic wish for vision, the wish to be granted 'that Sabaoths sight', is made against the backwards pull of complaint.

NOTES

1. For more on this body of critical work, see Chapter 39 below.
2. For what is still the most thorough survey of the problems of chronology, see Stein (1934), 27–72, as well as *Variorum* 8: 521–627, *passim*, though many questions of dating and revision remain unsettled.
3. See Weiss (1999) for the most recent bibliographical analysis of the volume, supplementing and on some points supplanting Johnson (1933) and Stein (1934).
4. See Renwick (1928), 179–80, and Stein (1934), 12–20, followed by, e.g., Spenser (1989), 217 and Spenser (1999), 580–1. Brink (1990) offers a vigorous dissent.
5. For a full account of the volume's calling in, see Peterson (1998), who includes the text of a gossipy contemporary letter discussing the scandal, previously known only from later and less direct allusions in Harvey, Nashe, and others.
6. This reading of *Complaints*, most fully developed by Rambuss (1993), 78–95, and Oram (2005), was partly anticipated by Crewe (1986), 55–6, and Bernard (1989), 111–22.
7. This shift toward the personal in Spenser's later work, long a critical commonplace, is linked by Montrose (1996) to Spenser's new status as a property-holder in Ireland.
8. For surveys of some of the varieties of poetic complaint in the period, see especially Smith (1952), 19–23, 103–26; Peter (1956); Maclean (1990); Schmitz (1990); Kerrigan (1991); and Brown (2004), 178–223.
9. Kerrigan (1991), 52, following Fowler (1982), esp. 106–11.
10. See Maclean (1990) and Vecchi (1984).
11. For this characteristic weakness of much historicist reading, see Rasmussen (2002).
12. See Sacks (1985) for a now-classic study of elegy as a process of psychological and aesthetic substitution. Especially pertinent to complaint are the discussions of anti-elegiac mourning in Ramazani (1994) and Spargo (2004).
13. See Patterson (1992) and Dubrow (1986) for the self-reflexive uses of complaint in Chaucer and Shakespeare.
14. See Brown (1999), 120–5, on the extremity of Verlame's claims.
15. My reading of the final line follows C. Rasmussen (1981), 177, though he does not distinguish between the poem's narrator and author.

16. Renwick (1928), 188–90, first proposed that *Ruines* was built from fragments of earlier poems, a proposal partly endorsed by the editors of Spenser (1989, 1999), among others. This might explain why at lines 253–9 and 306–16 Verlame speaks as a poet rather than in her own voice.

17. Berger's detailed analysis of the interaction of recreative and plaintive attitudes underlies much of my own thinking about *Complaints*; see Berger (1988), 277–94, as well as 49–50, on the 'willed passivity' of Spenser's Muses.

18. Of the seventeen uses of 'care', 'careles', and their derivatives in the poem, seven translate an analogous word (some variant of *cura*) in the Latin text (ll. 29, 94, 136, 137, 243, 426, 632), while ten are original to Spenser (31, 97, 107, 145, 153, 246, 323, 336, 632, 642).

19. Exponentially more criticism has been written on *Muiopotmos* than on any of the other poems in *Complaints*; the poem has been read as encoding topical references, as an ethical, theological, or aesthetic allegory, or simply as a *jeu d'esprit*. A complete critical history is impractical here, but see Ramachandra (2005), 80 for a deft summary of the main approaches. Herron (2006) offers a topical 'Irish' reading.

20. See *Handbook* Chapters 8 and 34.

21. See *Handbook* Chapter 33.

22. This is the perspective of Katharine Craik in her valuable essay on *Complaints*, which highlights the 'deliberately minor' status of the poems and Spenser's evident desire to label them as apprentice work (Craik 2001: 70). Craik's characterization of the volume as Spenser's 'commentary on complaint' (72), as well as her recognition of some ways that complaint 'tends ironically to discredit its own voice' (77), anticipates key elements of my approach.

23. For a thorough comparison of Chaucer's and Spenser's poems, see Harris and Steffen (1978).

BIBLIOGRAPHY

Berger, H., Jr. (1988). *Revisionary Play: Studies in the Spenserian Dynamic*. Berkeley: University of California Press.

Bernard, J. D. (1989). *Ceremonies of Innocence: Pastoralism in the Poetry of Edmund Spenser*. Cambridge: Cambridge University Press.

Brink, J. R. (1991). 'Who Fashioned Edmund Spenser? The Textual History of *Complaints*'. SP 88: 153–68.

Brown, G. (2004). *Redefining Elizabethan Literature*. Cambridge: Cambridge University Press.

Brown, R. D. (1999). *'The New Poet': Novelty and Tradition in Spenser's Complaints*. Liverpool: Liverpool University Press.

Campana, J. (2005). 'On Not Defending Poetry: Spenser, Suffering, and the Energy of Affect'. *PMLA* 120: 33–48.

Cheney, P. (1993). *Spenser's Famous Flight: A Renaissance Idea of a Literary Career*. Toronto: University of Toronto Press.

—— (2003). 'Dido to Daphne: Early Modern Death in Spenser's Shorter Poems'. SSt 18: 143–63.

Craik, K. A. (2001). 'Spenser's *Complaints* and the New Poet'. HLQ 64: 63–79.

Crewe, J. (1986). *Hidden Designs: The Critical Profession and Renaissance Literature*. New York: Methuen.

Dubrow, H. (1986). 'A Mirror for Complaints: Shakespeare's *Lucrece* and Generic Tradition', in B. K. Lewalski (ed.), *Renaissance Genres: Essays in Theory, History, and Interpretation.* Cambridge, MA: Harvard University Press.

Ferguson, M. W. (1984). '"The Afflatus of Ruin": Meditations on Rome by Du Bellay, Spenser, and Stevens', in A. Patterson (ed.), *Roman Images: Selected Papers from the English Institute, 1982.* Baltimore: Johns Hopkins University Press.

Fowler, A. (1987). *Kinds of Literature: An Introduction to the Theory of Genres and Modes.* Cambridge, MA: Harvard University Press.

Harris, D., and Steffen, N. L. (1978). 'The Other Side of the Garden: An Interpretive Comparison of Chaucer's *Book of the Duchess* and Spenser's *Daphnaida*'. *JMRS* 8: 17–36.

Herron, T. (2006). 'Plucking the Perrot: *Muiopotmos* and Irish Politics', in J. B. Lethbridge (ed.), *Edmund Spenser: New and Renewed Directions.* Madison, NJ: Fairleigh Dickinson Press, 80–118.

Johnson, F. R. (1933). *A Critical Bibliography of the Works of Edmund Spenser Printed before 1700.* Baltimore: Johns Hopkins University Press.

Kerrigan, J. (1991). *Motives of Woe: Shakespeare and 'Female Complaint'.* Oxford: Oxford University Press.

Maclean, H. (1990). '*Complaints*'. *SE* 177–81.

Martin, E. E. (1987). 'Spenser, Chaucer, and the Rhetoric of Elegy'. *JMRS* 17: 83–109.

Montrose, L. A. (1996). 'Spenser's Domestic Domain', in M. de Grazia, M. Quilligan, and P. Stallybrass (eds), *Subject and Object in Renaissance Culture.* Cambridge: Cambridge University Press, 83–130.

Oram, W. A. (1981). '*Daphnaïda* and Spenser's Later Poetry'. *SSt* 2: 141–58.

—— (2005). 'Spenser in Search of an Audience: The Kathleen Williams Lecture for 2004'. *SSt* 20: 23–47.

Owens, J. (2002). *Enabling Engagements: Edmund Spenser and the Poetics of Patronage.* Montreal: McGill-Queen's University Press.

Patterson, L. (1992). 'Writing Amorous Wrongs: Chaucer and the Order of Complaint', in J. M. Dean and C. K. Zacher (eds), *The Idea of Medieval Literature: New Essays on Chaucer and Medieval Culture in Honor of Donald R. Howard.* Newark, DE: University of Delaware Press.

Peter, J. (1956). *Complaint and Satire in Early English Literature.* Oxford: Clarendon Press.

Peterson, R. S. (1998). 'Laurel Crown and Ape's Tail: New Light on Spenser's Career from Sir Thomas Tresham'. *SSt* 12: 1–35.

Prawer, S. S. (1976). *Karl Marx and World Literature.* Oxford: Clarendon Press.

Ramachandra, A. (2005). 'Clarion in the Bower of Bliss: Poetry and Politics in Spenser's "Muiopotmos"'. *SSt* 20: 77–106.

Ramazani, J. (1994). *Poetry of Mourning: The Modern Elegy from Hardy to Hearey.* Chicago: University of Chicago Press.

Rambuss, R. (1993). *Spenser's Secret Career.* Cambridge: Cambridge University Press.

Rasmussen, C. J. (1981). '"How Weak Be the Passions of Woefulness": Spenser's *Ruines of Time*'. *SSt* 2: 159–81.

Rasmussen, M. D. (1999). 'Spenser's Plaintive Muses'. *SSt* 13: 139–64.

—— (ed.) (2002). *Renaissance Literature and Its Formal Engagements.* New York: Palgrave.

Renwick, W. (ed.) (1928). *Complaints: Edmund Spenser.* London: Scholartis Press.

Sacks, P. J. (1985). *The English Elegy: Studies in the Genre from Spenser to Yeats.* Baltimore: Johns Hopkins University Press.

Schmitz, G. (1990). *The Fall of Women in Early English Narrative Verse.* Cambridge: Cambridge University Press.

Smith, H. (1952). *Elizabethan Poetry: A Study in Conventions, Meaning, and Expression*. Cambridge, MA: Harvard University Press.

Spargo, R. C. (2004). *The Ethics of Mourning: Grief and Responsibility in Elegiac Literature*. Baltimore: Johns Hopkins University Press.

Stein, H. (1934). *Studies in Spenser's Complaints*. New York: Oxford University Press.

Steinberg, G. (1998). 'Idolatrous Idylls: Protestant Iconoclasm, Spenser's *Daphnaïda*, and Chaucer's *Book of the Duchess*', in T. M. Krier (ed.), *Refiguring Chaucer in the Renaissance*. Gainesville: University Press of Florida, 128–43.

Van den Berg, K. T. (1978). '"The Counterfeit in Personation": Spenser's *Prosopopoia, or Mother Hubberds Tale*', in L. Martz and A. Williams (eds), *The Author in His Work: Essay on a Problem in Criticism*. New Haven, CT: Yale University Press, 85–102.

Vecchi, L. M. (1984). 'Spenser's *Complaints*: Is the Whole Equal to the Sum of Its Parts?', in F. G. Greco (ed.), *Spenser at Kalamazoo: 1984*. Clarion, PA: Clarion University, 127–38.

Weiss, A. (1999). 'Watermark Evidence and Inference: New Style Dates of Edmund Spenser's *Complaints* and *Daphnaida*'. *Studies in Bibliography: Papers of the Bibliographical Society of the University of Virginia*, 52: 129–54.

CHAPTER 13

COLIN CLOUTS COME HOME AGAINE, ASTROPHEL, AND THE DOLEFUL LAY OF CLORINDA (1595)

PATRICK CHENEY

1595 is the penultimate year of Spenser's publishing career. This year sees the publication of the marriage volume *Amoretti* and *Epithalamion*, and a less homogenous volume that contains Spenser's second pastoral, *Colin Clouts Come Home Againe*, his pastoral elegy on Sir Philip Sidney, *Astrophel*, and six other pastoral elegies on Sidney, including one that may (or may not) be by Spenser, *The Doleful Lay of Clorinda*.[1] The next year, 1596, will see the printing of the second installment of *The Faerie Queene*, of *Fowre Hymnes*, and of his last published poem, *Prothalamion*. Yet before 1595, Spenser had published still other works: his first pastoral, *The Shepheardes Calender* (1579), the first installment of *The Faerie Queene* (1590), *Complaints* (1591), and another elegy, *Daphnaïda* (1592). While the flurry of publications between 1590 and 1596 is dizzying, we can identify the 1595 pastoral volume under discussion here as one of four books published between the two installments of *The Faerie Queene*. The *Colin Clout* volume (as we might call it) is best understood as a multifaceted pastoral work that helps to span the two parts of Spenser's national epic. The dynamic of pastoral and epic derives from the literary career of Virgil, who published his *Eclogues* first and concluded with his *Aeneid*—a pastoral and an epic that he spanned through a third poem, the *Georgics*, about farm labor. Although the *Colin Clout* volume is not a georgic work, it plays a similar bridging role in the structure of Spenser's literary career. The precise nature of this bridge will be the subject of the present chapter.

As a book, the *Colin Clout* volume seems today a curious printing anomaly. It opens with a formal title page for only *Colin Clout*, followed by Spenser's 'Dedicatory Epistle' to Sir Walter Ralegh, succeeded by the 955-line poem itself. On the next leaf is a second but abbreviated title page, for *Astrophel* alone, which dedicates this poem to Frances Walsingham, formerly Sidney's wife, now re-married to the earl of Essex. The 216-line poem itself ends by announcing a 'vearse' (215) sung by Astrophel's sister, Clorinda, or Mary Sidney Herbert, Countess of Pembroke. Bearing neither title nor title page, this inset poem, now known as *The Doleful Lay of Clorinda*, is spoken in the grieving sister's voice, and carries on for 108 lines, perhaps to recall the 108 sonnets of Sidney's *Astrophil and Stella* (Fowler 1970: 174–80), ending with the announcement that Thestylis will sing the next song. Then, on the same page a new poem of 195 lines begins, 'The mourning Muse of Thestylis', written by Lodowick Bryskett. Without transition comes 'A pastorall Aeglogue upon the death of Sir Phillip Sidney Knight', a 162-line poem featuring two shepherd-speakers, 'Lycon' and 'Colin', who represent Bryskett and Spenser. Finally, come three more elegies on Sidney, each with a title but minus title pages, and all previously published in *The Phoenix Nest* (1593): 'An Elegie, or friends passion, for his Astrophill', at 234 lines, written by Matthew Roydon; 'An Epitaph upon the right Honourable sir Phillip Sidney knight', at 60 lines, by Ralegh; and 'Another of the same', at 40 lines, by either Edward Dyer or Fulke Greville. The number of lines in the seven Sidney elegies is important to mention because it matches the 955 lines of *Colin Clout*. As such, the volume divides into two parts, creating a diptych, the first printing a pastoral narrative celebrating the national authority of a living poet, Spenser; the second, a collective pastoral monument to a dead poet, Sidney. What links the two parts is a singular invention: that of the pastoral figure of the English national poet, past and present, in a professional genealogy that highlights the changing of the literary guard, from Sidney to Spenser. If the complete 1595 volume does form a bridge between the two installments of *The Faerie Queene*, we can expect the bridge to be about the figure of the English national poet himself: the author of a poem about the nation.[2]

Surprisingly, little criticism exists on the 1595 volume as a book.[3] Evidently, the modern penchant for *individuated authorship* as an oppositional principle to *collaborative authorship* has occluded an early modern principle that prints individuation comfortably within the space of collaboration (Cheney 2008: 142–5). More than any work in the Spenser canon, *Colin Clout* formalizes this principle, for it features a singular author working amicably among other authors. Yet Spenser critics attend to the two—or three—poems by Spenser himself, although they separate their analyses of individual poems. Most of the criticism focuses on *Colin Clout* (Burchmore 1977;

Dees 2001; Fairweather 2000; Kelsey 2003; Starke 1998; Van Es 2003; Warner 1997), often with *The Shepheardes Calender*, because these are Spenser's two major pastorals, both featuring his persona, the shepherd Colin (Cheney 2001; Hoffman 1977; Mallette 1979; Shore 1985). Criticism on *Astrophel* and *The Doleful Lay* tends to get separated out (Coren 2002; Jang 1999; Klein 1993; O'Connell 1971). One critic who looks at the complete book, Raphael Falco (1994: 52–123), foregrounds the seven Sidney elegies, but pays short shrift to *Colin Clout*.[4] Nonetheless, Falco pinpoints the historic significance of the volume to lie in its advertisement of the Sidney–Spenser relation as the literary genealogy inaugurating modern English literature—a genealogy that continues to organize literary histories today.

Recent editors of Spenser's 'shorter poems' (Spenser 1989, 1999) subscribe to modern practice by printing *Colin Clout*, *Astrophel*, and *The Doleful Lay* individually and then by commenting separately on them. Yet the effect has been to imagine these poems as individual works. Consequently, the time may be ripe for a holistic approach, one that examines the 1595 book as a book, that works from the early modern practice of seeing individuated authorship as part of a larger collaborative effort, and that aims to determine the volume's place both in the structure of Spenser's publishing career and in English literary history.[5]

This chapter suggests that the 1595 *Colin Clout* volume is historic as the first book in English literature to feature the national poet as the center of a national community of fellow poets and civic leaders, especially Ralegh and Queen Elizabeth, who were themselves poets.[6] In particular, the book depicts the English poet performing two vital roles as part of a national community: first, in *Colin Clout* Spenser presents his persona leading the nation because he has undergone a divinely inspired vision of purified erotic desire; and second, in *Astrophel* and *The Doleful Lay* he presents himself as a funeral poet helping the nation process its grief after he has undergone a professional vision of the soul's immortality, of the place of the national poet in eternity.[7] The two roles cohere in their wisdom about the sanctified character of poetic identity within a civic world of national achievement, as well as in their underlying project: 'Poetry serves as a consolation for loss.'[8]

COLIN CLOUTS COME HOME AGAINE

Until the latter half of the twentieth century, *Colin Clout* inspired only sporadic comment. In the early seventeenth century, the 'Spenserian poets' register its popularity, especially William Browne in *The Shepheards Pipe* (1614) and George Wither in *The Shepherds Hunting* (1615), both of whom advertise what we might call a *communal Spenser*.[9] In his *Observations on . . . Spencers Faery Queene* (1643), Sir Kenhelm Digby quotes *Colin Clout* (lines 612–14) to illustrate 'the influences of the superior substances . . . into the two differing parts of Man; to wit, of the Starres . . . into his body: and of the Angels...into his soul' (Cummings: 156). By 1709, however, Alexander Pope recognizes the importance of the *Calender* in the history of pastoral but fails to mention *Colin Clout* (Shore 1990: 173). Consequently, the poem is left largely in the hands of biographers. In his 1715 *Works*, John Hughes writes of Colin, 'we find him less a Shepherd than at first: He had then been drawn out of his Retirement,...and been engag'd in an Employment which brought him into a quite different Sett of Ideas' (Cummings: 272). Thus, as late as 1871, George L. Craik classifies *Colin Clout* as 'a poem of great beauty...in the highest degree interesting both from his bearing upon the personal history of Spenser himself, and from its numerous references to his contemporaries' (III, 201).[10]

Today, critics locate the poem's importance in its representation of a particular autobiographical history, which Richard McCabe calls 'autoreferential[ity]' (Spenser 1999: ix): Spenser's friendship with Ralegh in Ireland; their trip together to the court of Queen Elizabeth in 1589–90; and Spenser's return 'home' to Ireland.[11] In the epistle to Ralegh, Spenser calls his poem 'a simple pastorall', and says he has written it in a 'mean...stile' to convey a 'simple meaning', the nature of which he does not disclose, except to say that his pastoral fiction 'agree[s] ... with the truth in circumstance and matter'. Yet the terms of the dedication veil an epic significance to the pastoral allegory through a Virgilian career-discourse of *high* and *low*: 'Sir, that you may see that I am not alwaies ydle as yee thinke, though not greatly well occupied,...I make you present of this simple pastorall, unworthie of your higher conceipt for the meaness of the stile.' Here, the poet finesses his social predicament: as a lower ranking civil servant, Spenser writes a low-ranking poem to a 'higher' official on a topic of interest to them both, since during their 'late being in England' Ralegh showed Spenser 'singular favours', but also because the higher official can 'protect' the lower against 'the malice of evill mouthes'. In seeking Ralegh's patronage in terms of the Virgilian grid of pastoral and epic, the poet suggests how the lower form serves the higher goal of national literary 'truth'.

Since Spenser signs the dedication to Ralegh 'From my house of Kilcolman the 27. of December. 1591', we confront two complications. First, because Spenser lived at Kilcolman Castle, Cork, the nation is a new space linking Ireland with England. Thus, *Colin Clout* is important for etching the defining feature of Spenser's literary biography: he is an English national poet who writes in pastoral exile from Ireland (McCabe 1993). Second, Spenser wrote a draft of *Colin Clout* four years before publishing it. We do not know the cause of the delay, but several events alluded to occurred after 1591 (Shore 1990: 173). Notably, in 1592 Elizabeth banished Ralegh from court for marrying Elizabeth Throckmorton (Cheney 1993: 111–48). There is, then, both a curious temporal warp to the process of authorship and a complex spatial expansion of nationhood built into the book of *Colin Clout* and its fiction.

Moreover, the poem's genre 'remains remarkably difficult to specify' (McCabe 2006: 175).[12] Criticism distinguishes between two main versions of pastoral as a literary form. The *idealistic* version is a *pastoral of pleasure*, deriving from Schiller's *On Naïve and Sentimental Poetry* (1795–6), and it defines pastoral as a sentimental longing for the ideal and an escape from the actual (Poggioli 1975). In contrast, the *ideological* version is a '*pastoral of power*' (Montrose 1980), deriving from Putten-ham's *Arte of English Poesie* (1589), and it defines pastoral as an ideological practice of 'putting the complex into the simple' (Empson 1935: 22). Yet, from Virgil, Spenser would have understood the genre rather as a *pastoral of progression*, the inaugural form of a poet's epic career. In the *Calender*, what inaugurates his career is a distinct authorial experience: the poet solves his nation's problem of faith by undergoing an epiphany about the practical value of transcendence to the working of the nation (Cheney 2001: 84–5).

Unlike the *Calender*, however, *Colin Clout* is a relatively long narrative poem, one that expands Spenser's cultural model by featuring a balance of genders in the formation of British nationhood: Colin has moved from Kent to Ireland; and he interacts not simply with shepherds but with shepherdesses. Even so, the presence of a *second* pastoral within Spenser's Virgilian career is unusual among European authors (Cheney 2001: 81–3). Critics account for Spenser's second pastoral by seeing *Colin Clout* as a 'return' to the genre at the end of his career: whereas the *Calender* 'was conceived as a *prologue* to heroic poetry, Spenser's late pastorals are *alternatives* to it' (Alpers 1989: 797). In this view, Spenser returns to pastoral because he becomes disillusioned with epic values of national duty, retreating into the private space of transcendent artistic consciousness.

In form, however, *Colin Clout* looks less like Spenser's first pastoral than it does Elizabethan epyllia or minor epics, such as Shakespeare's *Venus and Adonis*.[13] In 1595, Michael Drayton identifies his epyllion, *Endymion and Phoebe*, as a companion poem to *Colin Clout* (Brooks-Davies 1994: 460): 'Colin . . . my Muse . . . rudely . . . presumes to sing by thee' (993–4). By re-classifying *Colin Clout* as a pastoral epyllion, we gain access to its fundamental bridging role in Spenser's literary career, for the 'minor epic was . . . the proving ground for . . . epic', a form 'above the pastoral . . . and below the epic, the transition between the two in the *gradus Vergilianus*' (Hulse 1981: 12). In this view, *Colin Clout* is not a return to pastoral but an instrument to the continuation of *The Faerie Queene*, and thus to Spenser's self-presentation as England's 'first laureate poet' (Helgerson 1983: 100).

The laureate poet's *gradus Vergilianus* structures the fiction of the poem itself, suggesting that Spenser gives his autoreferentiality the shape of a Virgilian career, which he had formalized in the 1590 *Faerie Queene* by announcing his turn from pastoral to epic (I, *Proem* 1). Accordingly, *Colin Clout* divides into three parts. In part one (1–55), Colin sings his songs in front of his 'peres, | The shepheard swains that did about him play' (5–6), to form what Hobbinol calls 'the shepheards nation' (17), and for whose benefit Hobbinol asks Colin 'to repeat | The passed fortunes, which to thee befell | In thy late voyage' (32–4). In the longer second part (56–907), Colin narrates his trip to Cynthia's court: his friendship with the Shepherd of the Ocean, Ralegh (56–177); their visit to Cynthia (177–907), including Colin's audience with his sover-eign (330–75), his catalogue of twelve her poets (376–455), his catalogue of twelve of her ladies (456–583), his satire of the court (680–730) and corresponding praise (731–70), and Colin's climactic Neoplatonic vision of love (775–906). In the briefer third part (908–55), Colin praises his own beloved, Rosalind, and blames himself for looking too high in loving her, after which he and the shepherds go home to 'rest' (955). This three-part pattern—progressing from the pastoral world of the shepherds to the epic world of the court and 'home againe'—depicts the 'formula of out-and-back' (MacCaffrey 1976: 366–7), which Spenser uses to represent his life as a British author with a Virgilian career.

The poem's fictional pattern proceeds through the formal pattern of its verse—so deftly handled it is practically invisible. Spenser deploys an unusual decasyllabic cross-rhymed quatrain, rhyming *abab*: his 'artful denial of . . . [the quatrain's] inherent tendency to impose its form on the poet's material constitutes an innovation almost of the order of the Spenserian stanza', which Spenser conceals by 'counterpointing grammatical and metrical divisions' (Shore 1990: 174). Spenser complicates this scheme further by blurring the boundaries between his nominal unit, the quatrain, and another, related unit, the tercet (or terza rima), a 3-line unit rhyming *aba*. Thus his opening eleven lines have the following rhyme scheme: *ababcbcdede*: 'This pattern might be variously described as a tercet preceding two quatrains, or as two quatrains and an intervening tercet' (Shore 1990: 174). The poet's ability to reveal and conceal his rhyme is among the most innovative in an innovative canon.

To open part one, Spenser introduces Colin as a Virgilian pastoral poet of desire renowned to the nation:

> The shepheards boy (best knowen by that name)
> That after Tityrus first sung his lay,
> Laies of sweet love, without rebuke or blame,
> Sate (as his custome was) upon a day,
> Charming his oaten pipe unto his peres.   (1–5)

By 'Tityrus', Spenser does not mean only Virgil but *Chaucer in comparison with Virgil*, as if to trace a typology of national poets.[14] The word 'after' means not only 'in the manner of' but also 'living after', so that the poem opens not simply with style and imitation but genealogy. Unlike Virgil and Chaucer, however, Spenser boldly wants his 'name' to be 'knowen' exclusively through his love poetry, and to be free of envy for doing so. Moreover, the word 'Charming' evokes Spenser's *magical* theory driving his erotic poetry (Cheney and Klemp 1984), emphasized through the effect of Colin's poetry on his auditors, who 'stand astonisht at his curious skill' (8).

Renaissance theories of poetry emphasize two aims famously articulated by Horace in the *Art of Poetry*: pleasure and instruction. In his *Defense of Poesy*, Sidney adds a third: moving the reader to virtuous action (Vickers 1999: 346). Yet Sidney also gestures to the magical effect of poetry ravishing the reader's soul.[15] Sidney and Spenser instill into English poetry an erotic poetics of ravishment, and in *Astrophel* Spenser attributes this magical poetics to Sidney himself:

> And many a Nymph both of the wood and brooke,
> Soone as his oaten pipe began to shrill:
> Both christall wells and shadie groves forsooke,
> To heare the charmes of his enchanting skill.   (43–6)

Spenser's word 'charmes' derives from the Latin *carmen*, meaning *song*. Throughout his poetry, Spenser uses magic as a metaphor for poetry, 'For pleasing wordes are like to Magick art' (*FQ* III.ii.15). Thus, in *The Teares of the Muses* Euterpe says that she and her sister Muses have 'Free libertie to chaunt charmes at will' (244). Similarly, Renaissance Neoplatonists identify Love as a magician, as Marsilio Ficino does in his commentary on Plato's *Symposium*, 'Because in love there is all the power of enchantment' (Jayne 1944: 199). In Book VI, canto x, of *The Faerie Queene*, Spenser will formalize the magical operation of erotic poetry, when Colin creates the Dance of the Graces in imitation of the Ptolemaic universe precisely to harness its power (Cheney and Klemp 1984).

In *Colin Clout*, Hobbinol attributes a magical effect to Colin's presence when he had left home, and later when he comes home again: 'Whilest thou wast hence, all dead in dole did lie: . . . | But now both woods and fields, and floods revive, | . . . That us late dead, hast made againe alive' (22–31). Colin possesses a magical connection to the land, so that all of nature ebbs and flows in proportion to his presence. The power to 'revive' what is 'dead' evokes Christ but also Orpheus, the legendary founder of poetry who uses his lyre to move stones, trees, and animals (Cain 1971). In *Colin Clout*, Spenser presents himself not simply as England's Virgil but also as the 'Bryttane Orpheus'.[16]

As the British Orpheus, Colin locates the feminine source of his inspiration in Queen Cynthia: 'Wake then my pipe, my sleepie Muse awake, | Till I have told her praises lasting long' (48–9). In an epiphany that constitutes the core experience of the Orphic poet's Virgilian career, Colin understands the beauty of his sovereign as divine in origin:

> And since I saw that Angels blessed eie,
> Her worlds bright sun, her heavens fairest light,
> My mind full of my thoughts satietie,
> Doth feed on sweet contentment of that sight.   (40–3)

Not just a convention, the poet's religious wisdom of an illuminated political consciousness empowers him to continue his national epic.

In part two of the poem, Colin records the contents of his 'song' (51), which begins with his meeting of 'The shepheard of the Ocean' (66). Spenser presents the meeting as an Elizabethan jam session, in which two artists play musical instruments and sing songs in an amicable display of reciprocal invention:

> aemuling my pipe, he tooke in hond
> My pipe before that aemuled of many,
> And plaid theron; (for well that skill he cond)
> Himselfe as skilfull in that art as any.
> He pip'd, I sung; and when he sung, I piped,
> By chaunge of turnes, each making other mery.   (72–7)

The doubly used word 'aemuling' means 'emulating, desiring to rival (a unique usage)' (Spenser 1999: 651). Ocean hears Colin's music, and emulates it as an act of friendly rivalry; in turn, Colin emulates Ocean, and the two reciprocate 'untill... both were weary' (79). Here Spenser does more than fictionalize the art of imitation, in which one poet models himself on another; he models the 'mery' temperament that should order that process in a civilized society.

When Cuddy asks Colin to 'tell what thou didst sing' (84), Spenser invites the reader to think about genre: 'Whether it were some hymne, or morall laie, | Or carol made to praise thy loved lasse' (86–7). The language evokes a hymn or divine poem, a didactic poem, or a love poem, yet Colin replies, 'Nor of my love, nor of my losse' (88), implying that the song he sang before Ocean was none of the three: 'But of my river Bregogs love I soong, | Which to the shiny Mulla he did beare' (92–3). In this poem about the land, Colin sings a national allegory of love—what Cuddy calls simply a 'lovely lay' (97), and Colin a 'tale' (100).

This last classification indicates that the tale of the Bregog and the Mulla is a narrative poem, and thus a miniature of *Colin Clout*. In particular, the tale resembles the Ovidian epyllion dominant in the mid-1590s: in their mutual love, Bregog and Mulla are blocked by Mulla's father, Old Mole, who has arranged another marriage for her, leading the lovers to elope, until 'a shepheards boy' (147) tells Mole, who seeks revenge on Bregog by turning him into a river. While mythologizing the Ralegh–Throckmorton affair (Spenser 1989: 523–4), the allegory also gestures to the way the poet speaks 'Under the foote of Mole' (57)—beneath his verse—to assert his freedom from Elizabethan power, chiefly Lord Burleigh (Kelsey 2003).

Colin does not record the Shepherd of the Ocean's song but describes its contents:

His song was all a lamentable lay,
Of great unkindnesse, and of usage hard,
Of Cynthia the Ladie of the sea,
Which from her presence faultlesse him debard.   (164–7)

Here Spenser alludes to Ralegh's own epyllion, the *Booke of the Ocean to Scinthia* (Oram 1989: 532). The symbolic interlock with Colin's song is ingenious: where he allegorizes Ralegh's affair with Elizabeth Throckmorton, Ocean complains of the Queen's wrath over this very event, calling for her 'pittie' (171). In the fiction, that is, the two poems have nothing to do with each other; symbolically, both fixate on the core idea driving the 1595 book: singing about loss within a community can make both self and other 'mery'.

Colin's ability to reciprocate Ralegh's poetry of loss amiably leads the courtier to take the shepherd to see Cynthia. The details of their voyage across the Irish Sea (195–261) celebrate Ralegh's role in the Queen's naval strength, followed by celebration of her land power: 'Both heaven and heavenly graces do much more | ... abound in that same land' (308–9). Colin extends his praise of 'Cynthias land' (289) to her person, dilating on the terms of his earlier epiphany in quintessential Spenserian verse:

I would her lyken to a crowne of lillies,
Upon a virgin brydes adorned head,
With Roses dight and Goolds and Daffadillies;
Or like the circlet of a Turtle true,

> In which all colours of the rainbow bee;
>
> .   .   .   .   .   .
>
> The image of the heavens in shape humane.   (337–51)

Colin's portrait emphasizes Cynthia's physical beauty and bounty, her regality and virginity, her fidelity and perfection. In the last line, he records his fundamental insight: the female's human 'shape' is an 'image' of the divine. Cynthia incarnates the godhead. Here Spenser solves the problem that had plagued Petrarch and his heirs, for whom the female serves rather as arch-impediment to the poet's union with the deity (Cheney 1993: 149–94). Colin's vision of the female sovereign as the minister of the deity qualifies him for the title of national poet.

Colin's audience with Cynthia suggests that Spenser read part of *The Faerie Queene* to Elizabeth:

> The shepheard of the Ocean (quoth he)
> Unto that Goddesse grace me first enhanced,
> And to mine oaten pipe enclin'd her eare,
> That she thenceforth therein gan take delight,
> And it desir'd at timely houres to heare.   (358–62)

Perhaps Spenser read Elizabeth the story of Timias and Belphoebe in III.v, which shows the huntress rescuing the squire from disgrace (Bednarz 1983: 69 n 23). At l. 175 of *Colin Clout*, Spenser raises the topic of *poetic instrumentality*, for Mariana says that Ocean's lamentable lay was so powerful Cynthia would 'move to take him to her grace againe'. Scholars believe that Spenser's 1596 continuation of the Timias–Belphoebe story in IV.vii–viii helped restore Ralegh to favor in 1597 (O'Connell 1977: 122), yet maybe *Colin Clout* was instrumental in ushering in this rare instance of poetic praxis.

When Alexis asks why Cynthia needs such a lowly poet when she 'hath so many shepheards in her fee' (370), Colin praises twelve of her poets. Colin names both William Alabaster (400), who had written an epic on the Queen, 'Eliseïs' (403), and Samuel Daniel (424), who had written the sonnet sequence *Delia* (416) and the epyllion *Complaint of Rosamond* (427). A few other poets are recognizable: not simply Astrophel as Sidney, but also Alcyon as Arthur Gorges, and Amyntas as Ferdinando Stanley, Lord Strange. Scholars identify Harpalus as George Turberville; Corydon as Abraham Fraunce or Edward Dyer; Palin as George Peele; Alcon as either Thomas Lodge or Thomas Watson; and 'old Palemon' (396) as Thomas Churchyard (on record as identifying himself here). Most evasive has been the identity of 'Aetion': 'A gentler shepheard may no where be found: | Whose Muse full of high thoughts invention, | Doth like himselfe Heroically sound' (444–7)—a description that may (or may not) evoke the name of Shakespeare. Such biographical speculation, however, occludes the real form that history here takes: Spenser is England's first modern poet to present himself as part of a larger national community of poets: 'All these...| ...do their Cynthia immortall make' (452–3).

When Lucinda rebukes Colin for neglecting Cynthia's 'Nymphs' (459), Spenser compliments twelve ladies of Elizabeth's court, most of whom we can identify: Urania, as Mary Sidney Herbert; Theana, Anne Russell, Countess of Warwick;

Marian, Margaret Russell, Countess of Cumberland; Mansilia, Helena, Countess of Northumberland; Galathea, Frances Howard, sister to Douglas Howard, whose death Spenser commemorated in 'Daphnaïda' (510); Neaera, Elizabeth Sheffield; Stella, Frances Walsingham; and 'Phyllis, Charillis, and sweet Amaryllis' (540), the three Spencer sisters, Elizabeth, Anne, and Alice (ancestors of the late Princess Diana), to whom Spenser claims kinship: a 'noble familie: | Of which I meanest boast my selfe to be' (537–8). In *Colin Clout*, Spenser presents himself as a poet of the court lady, attuned to the national value of the feminine.

Appropriately, the lass Aglaura encourages Colin to 'Finish the storie' (589), which he does through a bifold strategy that has long disturbed readers (Fairweather 2000: 303–4). First, he delivers a scathing satire of the court, indicting courtiers for violating human decency through *theatrical* character: 'each mans worth is measured by his weed' (711). Second, Colin offers a contradictory encomium to the court, centralized in the Queen's largesse: 'For Cynthia doth in sciences abound, | And gives to their professors stipends large' (745–6). Opposed to theatricality, Colin proffers 'spotlesse honestie, | And . . . profession of all learned arts' (753–4).

Colin's bifold depiction of the court leads Corylas to ask whether 'love' is 'professed there' (771–2), prompting Colin to identify *eros* as the virtuous courtier's central value: 'love most aboundeth there. | For all the walls and windows there are writ, | All full of love, and love, and love my deare, | And all their talke and studie is of it' (775–8). While Colin recognizes that some courtiers 'prophane' the 'mightie mysteries' of love (788), he claims that he and other 'poore shepheards . . . | . . . serve that God' with 'religion' (795–8)—an expression that catapults him into 'some celestiall rage | Of love', or Neoplatonic *furor*, a divine form of erotic inspiration that produces 'oracles . . . sage' (823–5). Cuddy's designation of Colin as 'Priest' of 'that God'—'So well thou wot'st the mysterie of his might, | As if his godhead thou didst present see' (832–4)—leads Colin 't'expresse his powre divine' (838) in a powerful Neoplatonic hymn of some sixty lines: Love creates the world out of chaos, leading all creatures 'each one his like to love, | And like himselfe desire for to beget' (863–4). The repetition of, and play on, the word 'like' underscores the similitude of desire, the masculine and feminine mutuality that Colin locates in Love's mother: 'Venus selfe doth soly couples seeme, | Both male and female through commixture joynd' (801–2). In this hermaphroditic model of companionate desire, Colin locates true 'grace' (881), the 'medicyn' to the fatal 'hurt' of Love's 'wound' (876–7). Because 'love is Lord of all the world by right' (883), the Neoplatonic mystogogue ends by admonishing 'all lovers' to 'honor' the erotic deity with 'chaste heart' (887–8). When Melissa praises Colin as 'deeply . . . divyn[ing] . . . | . . . love and beautie . . . with wondrous skill', she records the 'debt' that 'all wemen' owe to Colin's 'defen[se]' of their 'cause' (896–901).

In part three of the poem, Melissa's praise leads Lucid to introduce the topic of 'Faire Rosalind', who has been 'blamed' for being 'too cruell' to Colin (908–9). The *Calender* had ended with Colin bidding adieu to Rosalind after she had taken up with Menalcas. Sixteen years later, Colin is still separated from his beloved, but rather than blaming her, he now accepts blame. A 'simple swaine', he has 'lookt' too 'hie', while she remains true to herself: her 'loftie eye' (936–40), the center of her 'divine regard and heavenly hew' (933), does not look down. Like Cynthia, Rosalind incarnates the godhead. In his role as national poet of love, Colin demonstrates his ability to see the divinity of female beauty, and thus to use his poetry to seek feminine 'grace' (939). In the highest testament of this faith, Colin seals his laureate status by presenting himself as the 'simple trophe of her great conquest' (951).

If 'Rosalind' figures Spenser's second wife, Elizabeth Boyle (Burchmore 1977: 396), *Colin Clout* joins *Amoretti and Epithalamion* in bringing the poet's beloved into conjunction with his sovereign. Yet rather than 'displacing' the Queen in favor of his wife (Burchmore 1977: 405), Spenser likely sees the two as complementary (Warner 1997: 368–70). Rosalind may use her lofty eye to 'loath' Colin because he is a 'lowly thing' (938), but Spenser's career discourse identifies her as a virtual synecdoche for the bridge from low to high that this poem seeks to build (Edwards 1971: 63).

Accordingly, the poem concludes when Colin arises 'from [the] ground', followed by 'all the rest', who are 'All loth to part, but that the glooming skies | Warnd them to draw their bleating flocks to rest' (952–5). Anticipating Hamlet's final pun on 'rest'— 'The rest is silence'—Spenser's concluding rhyme speaks to the condition of national repose, the skies darkening around the poet and his community, as they perform their nurturing duty to their 'bleating flocks'. Refusing to soften the threat of loss, Spenser announces his preparation to jump the gap from pastoral to epic.[17]

ASTROPHEL

Astrophel, A Pastorall Elegy represents an interlocking yet different model of the national poet of community. Rather than celebrate the national poet of love against a poetics of loss, Spenser now presents himself as the national poet of loss in the genre of funeral elegy.[18]

Yet *Astrophel* has long been the most maligned poem in the Spenser canon. Between the late sixteenth and nineteenth centuries, almost no commentary exists. In 1715, Hughes mentions Spenser's '*Elegies on Sir Philip Sidney*', but 'leave[s]' them to 'the Reader's own Observation' (Cummings: 276). Nineteenth-century scholars routinely discuss the poem's date of composition, its connection with Sidney, and other biographical matters (*Variorum* VII, 484–5, 490). Most notorious is the judgment of Palgrave: 'None of Spenser's poems, I apprehend, so completely and so unexpectedly disappoints a reader as this' (*Variorum* VII, 487). What disappoints Palgrave is Spenser's 'failure' to include his 'lovely touches', 'his prevalent beauty and picturesqueness', and his 'expression of personal feeling' (*Variorum* VII, 487). As the cause of failure, Palgrave cites Spenser's 'patronage' relationship with Sidney (*Variorum* VII, 488)—evidently, a blot to Romantic ideas of spontaneous literary genius.

Toward the last quarter of the twentieth century, critics indicate why we might care about this poem: Spenser represents his relation to Sidney as the starting point of modern English literary history. Yet rather than offer a personalized portrait, Spenser displaces his eulogy through the classical myth of Adonis, Venus, and the boar. The principal source-texts are Bion's *Lament for Adonis* and especially Ronsard's epyllion *L'Adonis*, to a lesser extent Ovid's *Metamorphoses* (10.503–739), while two other classical poems help form the 'model for the Renaissance pastoral elegy' (Falco 1994: 59), Theocritus's Idyll 1 and Virgil's Eclogue 5 (*Variorum VII*, 486–7, 491–9; O'Connell 1971: 28–30). In particular, Spenser's debt to Ronsard may leave a trace of his interest in the Pléiade as a model for a national community of poets.[19] Yet the most neglected source, Moschus's *Lament for Bion*, includes three features important here:

1) *The formation of a community of poets*: Moschus puts himself in the company of seven classical elegists, from Hesiod to Theocritus (Edmonds 1928: 451–2);
2) *The advertisement of a literary genealogy*: Moschus sees himself as the 'inheritor' of Bion (Edmonds 1928: 453); and
3) *The building of a career-grid linking pastoral to epic*: Moschus offsets his pastoral elegy through reference to Homer's epics (Edmonds 1928: 451).

We probably also need to add as a source a contemporary work just published: Shakespeare's deeply erotic *Venus and Adonis* (1593), which Spenser may seek to chasten.[20]

Spenser's subtitle, 'A Pastorall Elegie', identifies the poem's genre: it is a pastoral in the elegiac mode, an elegy in the pastoral mode. Recently, critics have written extensively on this genre. G. W. Pigman III presents Spenser as 'a master of lament' who uses elegy to probe 'the moral problem of grief' (1985: 75), while Peter Sacks sees Spenser achieving the 'work of mourning precisely by resolving this question of the adequacy of language and its figures of consolation' (1985: 54). Dennis Kay follows up on both to see Spenser pursuing 'the consoling function of art', with *Astrophel* constituting 'an attempt to . . . teach the role artistic invention can play when human wit is challenged to make sense of premature and unexpected death' (1990: 48). More recently, Lynn Enterline shows how sixteenth-century elegists advance the 'movement from mourning to consolation' by offering 'the poem itself as a form of recompense for loss' (2007: 147).

In the *November* eclogue, *The Ruines of Time*, and *Daphnaïda*, Spenser applies the work of mourning to the nation as a whole (Cheney 2003). We need to view *Astrophel* within this career-long commitment to the role of the national funeral poet. Since Sidney had died in 1586, critics have wondered why Spenser and his colleagues would wait to publish their volume. We do not know the answer, but one possibility emerges: in *Astrophel*, Spenser is less concerned with the process of national mourning than he is with the national role of the funeral poet himself.

The poem begins with a three-stanza proem, written in a sixain stanza (like *Venus and Adonis*, or its models, *Januarye* and *December*), rhyming *ababcc*. While older critics often find the verse 'strangely pallid' and 'frigid' (*Variorum* VII, 483), Sir Sidney Lee disagrees: 'No sweeter imagery ever adorned an elegy than that to be met within Spenser's *Astrophel*' (*Variorum* VII, 483). Once we leave aside Romantic notions of *sincerity*, we can enjoy verse often stunning in its delicacy, as this on an event that never transpires: 'none is nigh, thine eylids up to close, | And kisse thy lips like faded leaves of rose' (137–8).

The proem is meta-poetry, about the poem itself. Spenser addresses 'Shepheards' that use 'pipes of oaten reed' to 'plaine' (complain) of their 'loves concealed smart', so that he may 'breed | Compassion' in the 'hart' of 'countrey lasses' (1–4). He asks his 'dolefull plaint' to be 'placed' among the shepherds' own songs to 'empierse' ladies' 'softened hearts' now that Astrophel has died (6–9). Thus, Spenser presents his poem as a pastoral complaint or elegy, designed to affect female emotion or interiority, in community with other grieving poets.

In the poem proper, Spenser adapts Sidney's biography to the Adonis myth: his birth, education, marriage, and career, followed by his death and funeral. Recurrently, Spenser presents Sidney as unusual because he jumps the gap of conceptual oppositions (Klein 1993: 42). Astrophel combines physical and moral beauty: 'He grew up fast in goodnesse and in grace, | And doubly faire wox both in mynd and face' (17–18). Astrophel also possesses military prowess and poetic virtuosity: 'For both in deeds and words he nourtred was, | Both wise and hardie' (71–2). Moreover, his 'skill' (85) in 'sports' (76) is 'matcht' with 'courage' (85), and he pursues a double goal: 'His mistress name, and his own fame to raise' (88). Even when he fights the boar, he does so 'Now with his sharp borespear, now with his blade' (108)—weapons of pastoral and epic. Thus, like Shakespeare's Adonis, Astrophel moves along the Virgilian career track: from the pastoral world of 'Shepheard[s]' (1) to the world of epic hunting, the fatal battle at Zutphen (Klein 1993: 46). Spenser presents Sidney as a poet-soldier who gave his life on 'forreine soyle' (the Netherlands) to defend his country from 'the brutish nation' of Spain (92–8) during a national process of fame.

As a funeral elegy, *Astrophel* naturally settles on a model of immortality. Critics label this model classical, because it imagines Sidney's fame as earthly renown, eschewing Christian glory. The key event is Astrophel's metamorphosis into a flower, which scholars cannot identify botanically (Oram 1989: 576). The reason is that Spenser invents the flower himself, after telling how Stella 'followed' Astrophel in death, 'To prove that death their hearts cannot divide, | Which living were in love so firmly tide' (178–80). When the 'Gods' see 'this paire of lovers trew', they 'Transform' both 'Into one flowre that is both red and blew' (181–4):

> It first growes red, and then to blew doth fade,
> Like Astrophel, which thereinto was made.
> And in the midst thereof a star appeares,
> As fairly formd as any star in skyes:
> Resembling Stella in her freshest yeares.   (185–9)

Spenser invents his Ovidian floral metamorphosis to express the principle of *faith in death*, in which the female remains 'firmly tide' to her lover after he dies by dying herself 'after him' (176). The perfect icon becomes a single flower of red turning blue (colors of passion and chastity) with a star of beauty shining in its center. Yet Spenser transposes the marital principle to a literary one, for Stella 'becomes symbolic of the ideals and inspiration behind Sidney's poetry', and the flower 'becomes a very delicate symbol for Sidney's poetry' itself (O'Connell 1971: 32).[21] For Spenser, in sum, Sidney has written an immortalizing poetry that nullifies death through marital faith.

Critics disagree about Spenser's attitude toward Sidney in *Astrophel*. Whereas most see Spenser using art to create consolation (Kay 1990; O'Connell 1971; Pigman 1985; Sacks 1985), some emphasize Spenser's criticism of the Sidneian ideal of poetic chivalry (Klein 1993: 43). Although Spenser does express detachment from Sidney's death-dealing heroism, he would seem to do so to perform the work of mourning as a vital part of his laureate career (Clarke 2000; Falco 1994).

THE DOLEFUL LAY OF CLORINDA

The transition from *Astrophel* to *The Doleful Lay* has long given readers pause. After Astrophel and Stella die, and the shepherds mourn 'that pitteous spectacle' (203), the poet describes how Astrophel's sister begins the process of grief; Clorinda

> began this dolefull lay,
> Which least I marre the sweetnesse of the vearse,
> In sort as she it sung, I will rehearse.   (214–16)

In the fiction, the narrator says he will 'rehearse' the 'dolefull lay' that Clorinda 'sung', the word 'rehearse' meaning *perform*. Yet we cannot tell whether this means that Spenser ventriloquizes the voice of Sidney's sister, or whether the Countess wrote the poem herself. While some Herbert scholars argue for the possibility of her authorship (Hannay 1998: II, 119–32), most Spenser editors argue for his authorship (Spenser 1989, 1999). Recently, Danielle Clarke grants authorship to Spenser but allows for a more capacious model that challenges the notion of individuated authorship with one based on collaboration: 'the *Colin Clout* volume suggests that the author figure is indeed a manipulable fiction or that the manipulation of these fictions of authorship works by indirection to instate the figure of Spenser as author' (2000: 452–3). No matter who wrote individual poems, the volume and the poem are Spenser's, even though 'the processes of verbal echoing, numerical patterning, and textual arrangement . . . suggest that we . . . rethink our notion of authorship, even with . . . a "self-crowned laureate" [such] as Spenser' (Clarke 2000: 467).

Written in a sixain stanza, *The Doleful Lay* complements its companion poem's classical model of immortality with a Christian one. The central question about 'that immortall spirit' (61) emerges at line 66: 'can so divine a thing be dead?' Clorinda answers, 'Ah no: it is not dead, ne can it die, | But lives for aie, in blisfull Paradise'

(67–8). In this way, the two-poem sequence—*Astrophel* with its earthly fame, *The Doleful Lay* with its heavenly salvation—re-produces the two-part movement of *November*, to anticipate, famously, Milton's *Lycidas* (1645):

> Lull him a sleep in Angelick delight;
> Whilest in sweet dreame to him presented bee
> Immortall beauties, which no eye may see.   (76–8)

Like *Astrophel*, *The Doleful Lay* concludes with a transition to the next part of the volume, the five concluding Sidney elegies, 'As everie one in order lov'd him best, | . . . | With dolefull layes unto the time addrest' (104–6):

> The which I here in order will rehearse,
> As fittest flowres to deck his mournfull hearse.   (107–8)

The elegies by Bryskett, Roydon, Ralegh, and Greville (or Dyer) then follow. While the question of authorship surrounding *The Doleful Lay* will no doubt continue, a related question emerges from Bryskett's second elegy, and we shall close with it.

AFTERWORD

A pastorall Aeglogue upon the death of Sir Phillip Sidney, a dialogue poem featuring 'Lycon' and 'Colin', closes with the initials 'L.B', prompting scholars to assign the elegy to Lodowick Bryskett. Yet in her 1990 article on '*Astrophel*' in *The Spenser Encyclopedia*, Katherine Duncan-Jones speculates that 'the poem may well be a collaboration between the two poets' (74). In 1986, Fred B. Tromly had followed the 'fullest discussion of Bryskett's authorship', a 1934 dissertation by Walter George Friedrich (384 n 1), but ended with an ambiguous statement: Byrskett 'presents his poem as an act of collaboration with a much greater poet' (388). Then, in 1998 Margaret Hannay cites Tromly and Duncan-Jones to suggest Bryskett's 'collaboration with Spenser' (I, 123), quoting lines 141–6:

> Behold my selfe with Colin, gentle swaine
> (Whose lerned Muse thou cherisht most whyleare)
> Where we thy name recording, seeke to ease
> The inward torment and tormenting paine,
> That thy departure to us both hath bred;
> Ne can ech others sorrow yet appease.   (141–6)

Thus Herbert's editors conclude that Bryskett 'wrote "A pastorall Aeglogue" for the occasion, probably with Spenser's help' (Hannay 1998: I, 124). Spenser scholars have never sufficiently debated this issue. The issue needs to be debated, because it could lead to the identification of 77 new lines of Spenserian verse.

Whoever wrote the poem, clearly Colin's voice differs from Lycon's, and it sounds distinctly Spenserian:

> Ye Nymphs and Nayades with golden heare,
> That oft have left your purest cristall springs
> To harken to his layes . . . (118–20)

Whether Spenser collaborated with Bryskett or not, *A pastorall Aeglogue* is probably the first poem outside the Spenser canon to present Colin singing in the authentic register of his creator. Perhaps, just as Spenser ventriloquizes Sidney's grieving sister, so Bryskett ventriloquizes Spenser, and both poetic acts 'rehearse' the act of 'aemuling' between Colin and the Shepherd of the Ocean earlier in the 1595 book. However scholars decide the issue, the *Colin Clout* volume remains historic for printing a fiction not simply by a community of English poets but also about the formation of an English community of poets for the nation: as the first poet to write a national epic, Edmund Spenser is England's laureate heir to Sir Philip Sidney, and together they preside over the inauguration of English literary history.

NOTES

1. Quotations from Spenser's shorter poems come from Spenser (1999); *The Faerie Queene*, from Hamilton (2001); and the non-Spenserian Sidney elegies from Spenser (1912).
2. Briefly, a national poet is a 'laureate' poet who writes poetry about the nation, and presents himself as doing so through the medium of print, in the European tradition of Virgil's *Aeneid*, even though he may not endorse the nation's contemporary leaders. See especially Helgerson (1992).
3. Only one quarto edition (1595), printed by William Ponsonby, exists, although two states survive (corrected and uncorrected). Meyer (1962) supplies a full list of textual variants.
4. For a review of scholarship, see McCabe (2006), 174–8.
5. The forthcoming Oxford Edition of the *Collected Works* of Edmund Spenser will print the complete 1595 book.
6. On Elizabeth as a 'poet', see Puttenham, *Arte of English Poesie*, in Vickers (1999), 213.
7. Cf. Kay (1990), who does not discuss *Colin Clout*: from 'the *Astrophel* volume', Spenser's followers 'derived a clear and practical sense of the nature of poetic community, . . . and the role and status of the laureate poet in relation to his fellows' (65–6).
8. Edwards (1971), 51, referring only to *Colin Clout*.
9. A 'communal Spenser' profitably joins the 'poetical Spenser' and the 'colonial Spenser' of modern scholarship (Rambuss 1996: 17). On a Spenserian 'model of the collective cultural production and historical agency' in William Browne and George Wither, see O'Callaghan (2000), 34.
10. Thanks to Dustin Stegner for this reference.
11. For the best overview, see Shore (1990); for the only book-length study, see Meyer (1969).
12. See Edwards (1971): 'it is a mélange of satire, love-complaint, panegyric, and autobiographical allegory' (60).
13. Hulse says he does not discuss the pastoral epyllion (1981: 12).
14. See Warton in *Variorum*, VII, 452; Renwick in *Variorum*, ibid.; Cheney (2002), 232–3.

15. See Lewis (1954): 'If poetry did not ravish, it is for him nothing' (346).

16. 'R.S.', *Commendatory Verse* 4.4, 1590 *FQ*, in Hamilton (2001), 723.

17. This formulation attempts to negotiate the triumphalist reading of Mallette (1979) and the more negative reading of Fairweather (2000: 301).

18. See McCabe (2005): 'The lament for Sidney is essentially a continuation of *Colin Clout*' (175).

19. Thanks to Anne Prescott for help with Ronsard.

20. Critics compare the Adonis myth in *Astrophel* with *FQ* III.i.34–8 (Spenser 1989: 566), without remembering that this is the version Shakespeare takes from Spenser (Cheney 2004: Chap. 3).

21. O'Connell's reading may help explain what has long troubled readers: not simply does Spenser identify 'Stella' as Frances Walsingham (rather than Penelope Devereaux, the 'Stella' of *Astrophil and Stella*), but he presents Sidney's still-living wife as *dying* in the fiction of the poem. Perhaps Spenser's obsession with (poetic) immortality is here at its most ingenious height.

BIBLIOGRAPHY

Alpers, P. (1989). 'Spenser's Late Pastorals'. *ELH* 56: 797–817.

Bednarz, J. P. (1984). 'Ralegh in Spenser's Historical Allegory'. *SSt* 4: 49–70.

Brooks-Davies, D. (ed.) (1994). *Silver Poets of the Sixteenth Century*. London: Dent; Rutland, VT: Tuttle.

Burchmore, D. (1977). 'The Image of the Centre in *Colin Clouts Come Home Againe*'. *RES* 28: 393–406.

Cain, Thomas H. (1971). 'Spenser and the Renaissance Orpheus'. *UTQ* 41: 24–47.

Cheney, P. (1993). *Spenser's Famous Flight: A Renaissance Idea of a Literary Career*. Toronto: University of Toronto Press.

—— (2001). 'Spenser's Pastorals: *The Shepheardes Calender* and *Colin Clouts Come Home Againe*', in A. Hadfield (ed.), *The Cambridge Companion to Spenser*. Cambridge: Cambridge University Press, 79–105.

—— (2002). '"Novells of his devise": Chaucerian and Virgilian Career Paths in Spenser's *Februarie* Eclogue', in P. Cheney and F. A. de Armas (eds), *European Literary Careers: The Author from Antiquity to the Renaissance*. Toronto: University of Toronto Press, 231–67.

—— (2003). 'From Dido to Daphne: Early Modern Death in Spenser's Shorter Poems'. *SSt* 18: 143–63.

—— (2004). *Shakespeare, National Poet-Playwright*. Cambridge: Cambridge University Press.

—— (2008). *Shakespeare's Literary Authorship*. Cambridge: Cambridge University Press.

—— and Klemp, P. J. (1984). 'Spenser's Dance of the Graces and the Ptolemaic Universe'. *Studia Neophilologica* 56: 27–33.

Clarke, D. (2000). '"In sort as she it sung": Spenser's "Doleful Lay" and the Construction of Female Authorship'. *Criticism* 42: 451–68.

Coren, Pamela (2002). 'Edmund Spenser, Mary Sidney, and the *Doleful Lay*'. *SEL* 42: 25–41.

Craik, G. L. (1871; 1971). *Spenser and His Poetry*. 3 vols. New York: AMS.

Dees, J. S. (2001). 'Colin Clout and the Shepherd of the Ocean'. *SSt* 15: 185–96.

Duncan-Jones, K. (1990). '*Astrophel*'. *SE*, 74–6.

Edmonds, J. M. (ed.) (1928). *The Greek Bucolic Poets*. Loeb Classical Library. Cambridge, MA: Harvard University Press; London: Heinemann.

Edwards, T. (1971). *Imagination and Power*. New York: Oxford University Press.

Empson, W. (1935; 1974). *Some Versions of Pastoral*. New York: New Directions.

Enterline, L. (2007). '"The Phoenix and the Turtle", Renaissance Elegies, and the Language of Grief', in P. Cheney, A. Hadfield, and G. A. Sullivan (eds), *Early Modern English Poetry*. New York: Oxford University Press, 147–59.

Fairweather, C. (2000). 'Inclusive and Exclusive Pastoral: Towards an Anatomy of Pastoral Modes'. *SP* 97: 276–307.

Falco, R. (1994). *Conceived Presences: Literary Genealogy in Renaissance England*. Amherst: University of Massachusetts Press.

Fowler, A. (1970). *Triumphal Forms: Structural Patterns in Elizabethan Poetry*. Cambridge: Cambridge University Press.

Friedrich, W. G. (1934). *The Astrophel Elegies: A Collection of Poems on the Death of Sir Philip Sidney (1595)*. Dissertation, Johns Hopkins University.

Hannay, Margaret, et al. (eds) (1998). The *Collected Works of Mary Sidney Herbert, Countess of Pembroke*, 2 vols. Oxford: Clarendon Press.

Helgerson, R. (1983). *Self-Crowned Laureates: Spenser, Jonson, Milton, and the Literary System*. Berkeley: University of California Press.

—— (1992). *Forms of Nationhood: The Elizabethan Writing of England*. Chicago: University of Chicago Press.

Hoffman, N. J. (1977). *Spenser's Pastorals: 'The Shepheardes Calender' and 'Colin Clout'*. Baltimore: Johns Hopkins University Press.

Hulse, C. (1981). *Metamorphic Verse: The Elizabethan Minor Epic*. Princeton, NJ: Princeton University Press.

Jang, H. (1999). 'Spenser's *Astrophel* and Clorinda'. *Medieval English Studies (Japan)* 7: 243–65.

Jayne, S. R. (ed.) (1944). *Marsilio Ficino's Commentary on Plato's 'Symposium'*. Columbia: University of Missouri Press.

Kay, D. (1990). *Melodious Tears: The English Funeral Elegy from Spenser to Milton*. Oxford: Clarendon Press.

Kelsey, L. (2003). 'Spenser, Ralegh, and the Language of Allegory'. *SSt* 17: 183–213.

Klein, L. M. (1993). 'Spenser's *Astrophel* and the Sidney Legend'. *Sidney Newsletter and Journal* 12: 42–55.

Lewis, C. S. (1954). *English Literature of the Sixteenth Century Excluding Drama*. Oxford: Oxford University Press.

McCabe, R. (1993). 'Edmund Spenser, Poet of Exile'. *Publications of the British Academy* 80: 73–103.

—— (2002). *Spenser's Monstrous Regiment: Elizabethan Ireland and the Poetics of Difference*. Oxford: Oxford University Press.

—— (2006). 'Shorter Verse Published 1590–95', in B. Van Es (ed.), *A Critical Companion to Spenser Studies*. Basingstoke: Palgrave Macmillan, 166–87.

MacCaffrey, I. G. (1976). *Spenser's Allegory: The Anatomy of Imagination*. Princeton, NJ: Princeton University Press.

Mallette, R. (1979). 'Spenser's Portrait of the Artist in *The Shepheardes Calender* and *Colin Clouts Come Home Againe*'. *SEL* 19: 19–41.

Meyer, S. (1962). 'Spenser's *Colin Clout*: The Poem and the Book'. *Papers of the Bibliographical Society of America* 56: 397–413.

—— (1969). *An Interpretation of Edmund Spenser's 'Colin Clout'*. Notre Dame, IN: Notre Dame University Press.

Montrose, L. (1980). '"Eliza, Queene of shepheardes", and the Pastoral of Power'. *ELR* 10: 153–82.

O'Callaghan, M. (2000). *'The Shepheards Nation': Jacobean Spenserians and Early Stuart Political Culture, 1612–1625*. Oxford: Oxford University Press.

O'Connell, M. (1971). '*Astrophel*: Spenser's Double Elegy'. *SEL* 11: 27–35.

—— (1977). *Mirror and Veil: The Historical Dimension of Spenser's 'Faerie Queene'*. Chapel Hill: University of North Carolina Press.

Pigman, G. W. III. (1985). *Grief and English Renaissance Elegy*. Cambridge: Cambridge University Press.

Poggioli, R. (1975). *The Oaten Flute: Essays on Pastoral Poetry and the Pastoral Ideal*. Cambridge, MA: Harvard University Press.

Rambuss, R. (1996). 'Spenser's Lives, Spenser's Careers', in J. H. Anderson, D. Cheney, and D. A. Richardson (eds), *Spenser's Life and the Subject of Biography*. Amherst: University of Massachusetts Press, 1–17.

Sacks, P. M. (1985). *The English Elegy: Studies in the Genre from Spenser to Yeats*. Baltimore: Johns Hopkins University Press.

Shore, D. R. (1985). *Spenser and the Poetics of Pastoral: A Study of the World of Colin Clout*. Kingston and Montreal: McGill-Queen's University Press.

—— (1990). 'Colin Clouts Come Home Againe'. *SE*, 173–7.

Starke, S. P. (1998). 'Briton Knight or Irish Bard? Spenser's Pastoral Persona and the Epic Project in *A View of the Present State of Ireland* and *Colin Clouts Come Home Againe*'. *SSt* 12: 133–50.

Tromly, F. B. (1986). 'Lodowick Bryskett's Elegies on Sidney in Spenser's *Astrophel* Volume'. *RES* 37: 384–8.

Van Es, B. (2002). *Spenser's Forms of History*. Oxford: Oxford University Press.

Vickers, B. (ed.) (1999). *English Renaissance Literary Criticism*. Oxford: Clarendon Press.

Warner, J. C. (1997). 'Poetry and Praise in *Colin Clouts Come Home Againe* (1595)'. *SP* 94: 368–81.

CHAPTER 14

....

AMORETTI AND *EPITHALAMION* (1595)

....

ROLAND GREENE

EDMUND Spenser's *Amoretti* and *Epithalamion* (published 1595) have not received their due from readers and critics. This is not to say that the two works are not often read and enjoyed, or that they are not in some ways among the most experimental and influential instances of their kinds. But it seems plausible to note, despite numerous recent studies, that the scholarship, as well as the impressions of educated readers, have delineated only poorly on what terms Spenser's achievement in these poems stands both among and apart from the comparable works by his contemporaries.[1] We have not attended to the poetics of the *Amoretti* and the *Epithalamion* with the kind of particularity that has been expended on that of *The Shepheardes Calender* or *The Faerie Queene*. While this unusual composite—an amatory sonnet sequence followed by a wedding song—participates in the convention that saw more than thirty sequences produced between 1582 and 1609, it establishes itself at a productive distance from the others (see Lever 1966). How and why the two works singly and together clear a space in late Elizabethan poetry is the topic of the present essay.

The *Amoretti* and the *Epithalamion* are closer to the poet's other works than is the case with the sonnet sequences of Philip Sidney and William Shakespeare. Readers and critics are accustomed to reading the *Calender*, *The Faerie Queene*, the shorter poems, and even the two works at hand within a fabric of intergeneric play and shared reference; they all pertain to a single Spenserian world populated by consubstantial figures—knights, Rosalinds, and Colin Clouts—as much as any of them belongs to its ostensible genre. Why is this so? First, despite all their traffic with convention, the *Amoretti* and the *Epithalamion* establish themselves in relation to an actual event, Spenser's marriage to Elizabeth Boyle of 11 June 1594, more than any other sequence of the period. (The marriage was Spenser's second: he had married Machabyas Chylde on 27 October 1579. See Hadfield 2008.)[2] When we speak of the logic and values of the *Amoretti* and the *Epithalamion*, we inevitably refer to this event, which is legible through many details of the poems. For other sonnet sequences we often make interpretive observations and then try to draw conclusions about their connection to a real person or happening, but for the *Amoretti*—the title is Italian for 'little loves', but I will refer to the entire sequence in the singular—it is the other way around: we start from the historical fact on which all interpretations must be based. Further, the two works inflect one another. Other sonnet sequences follow a teleological order, and some, like Samuel Daniel's *Delia* (1592), were first printed with a poem of another genre that puts the sequence in a different perspective. The *Amoretti* is unique, however, in representing a courtship that demonstrably leads to a marriage, while the wedding takes place not out of the reader's sight but immediately after the sequence, within the same volume of 1595. (Nearly all editors acknowledge the inseparability of these works by keeping them together, whether in modern editions of Spenser's works, anthologies of sixteenth-century poetry, or even general anthologies of English literature.) In the first edition, 'each sonnet and each stanza of the marriage song is given a page to itself, and the pages are tied together by an ornamental band running across the bottom throughout' (Nelson 1963: 84).

In the *Amoretti*, that pressure exerted by the poet's courtship and wedding in the real world, and the finitude imposed by the succeeding long poem, produce some striking effects for interpretation. In order of presentation, the first of these is a concern for the materiality of the poetic object. This is an explicit value of the *Amoretti* that reflects a preoccupation of Spenser's literary generation but overgoes it here for his immediate purposes. Several of Spenser's contemporaries see a renovated English poetry as newly attentive to all the elements of the poem—sounds, words, lines, gross form—in their auditory, visual, and experiential properties. In 1579, Spenser's *Shepheardes Calender* explored the notion of a socially, politically, and religiously engaged poetry that would emphasize these properties, producing a complex work that is material in both senses—that is, concerned with material reality of the present and aware of its own materiality. At about the same time, the theorist George Puttenham was writing his *Arte of English Poesie* (published 1589), in which many aspects of the poem—its ritual origins, its material body, its political effects—are represented as bound up together. Within fifteen years, Spenser will extend this attention to poetic materiality into the sonnet sequence and the epithalamion. What was in 1579 a perspective on poetry and politics that took outward forms seriously—that saw material bodies not as husks to be discarded in favor of inner meaning but as the dynamic means by which we approach that meaning— becomes by 1595 a serious intervention into the ideology around romantic love conceived by Francesco Petrarca (known in English as Francis Petrarch) in the fourteenth century and adapted by his poetic successors (see Chapter 33 below).[3]

Petrarch's *Canzoniere*, the model for the vernacular amatory lyric sequences of the sixteenth century, begins with an address to the reader drawing notice to the relation between the *rime sparse* (scattered rhymes) and the subjective events they relate:

> Voi ch' ascoltate in rime sparse il suono
> di quei sospiri ond'io nudriva 'l core
> in sul mio primo giovenile errore,
> quand' era in parte altr' uom da quel ch' i' sono,

(You who hear in scattered rhymes the sound of those sighs with which I nourished my heart during my first youthful error, when I was in part another man from what I am now) (Petrarch 1976: 36)

Even as this opening gesture calls attention to the verse itself, Petrarch's speaker emphasizes that his emotional travail not only precedes the poetry but validates it as virtual representation: here, prosodic sound is identical to his sighs, and the *vario stile* ('varied style') of the verses is really the alternation of his moods. In other words, experience precedes art, and art in turn conducts us toward virtual experience. While even the most beautiful forms, poetic or otherwise, are subject to the observation that concludes the sonnet, that 'quanto piace al mondo è breve sogno' ('whatever pleases in the world is a brief dream'), we are meant to understand that link between art and experience as indissoluble.

Now consider the first sonnet of the *Amoretti*:

> Happy ye leaues when as those lilly hands,
>   which hold my life in their dead doing might,
>   shall handle you and hold in loues soft bands,
>   lyke captives trembling at the victors sight.
> And happy lines, on which with starry light,
>   those lamping eyes will deigne sometimes to look
>   and reade the sorrowes of my dying spright,
>   written with teares in harts close bleeding book.
> And happy rymes bath'd in the sacred brooke,
>   of *Helicon* whence she deriued is,
>   when ye behold that Angels blessed looke,
>   my soules long lacked foode, my heauens blis.
> Leaues, lines, and rymes, seeke her to please alone,
>   whom if ye please, I care for other none.

In place of Petrarch's appeal to the reader, this speaker addresses the 'leaves, lines, and rymes' themselves, as though the essential character of the sequence lives there and not in some prior event or experience. The leaves or pages of the poem belong in the lady's hands, where she already holds the speaker's life: are the leaves a virtual representation of the best of his life? Do they distill all that he wants to retain of that life? Her hands as instruments of her stance toward him are benign and loving in lines 1 and 3, but ominous and potent in lines 2 and 4, implying that her treatment of 'you'—the leaves—may well determine how she understands 'my life' in its entirety. In the second quatrain, the 'happy lines' do not exactly represent 'sorrowes', but in being written with tears on the book of the heart, they are those sorrows in material form. And the 'rymes' of the final quatrain gain their franchise as poetry not from any intrinsic property of poeticity but from the validation of the lady's 'blessed looke'. The movement of the three quatrains goes from the physical codex to the visible page to the prosodic body of the poem—but as we approach the heart of his poetry from the outside in, the speaker emphasizes that there is no meaningful distance between his poems and a foregoing emotional history. What matters of his thoughts and feelings resides fully in these leaves, lines, and rhymes, and if they evoke pleasure, both the poem and the life are requited.

With this proem, Spenser puts his sequence at odds with the long history of Petrarchan poetry that emphasizes the emotional textures of unrequitedness as well as the poet's struggle to capture experience in lyric form. While its sonnets will often relate tensions between the lover and the lady—the second sonnet calls forth 'unquiet thought' in order to subdue it before the lady's presence, while a number of other poems tell of her pride (6, 27), 'disdaynfull scorne' (29), and cruelty (41)—the general tenor of their involvement implies not only a more than acquaintance but a kind of understanding, which of course ripens into marriage in the *Epithalamion*. Their disagreements are stylized, almost ritualized in their enactment of the stock situations between the Petrarchan lover and lady. At the same time, the sonnets of the *Amoretti* rarely conclude with the states of mental incompleteness, the jagged edges, that Petrarch famously introduces to European lyric and that many of the English sequences render progressively more theatrical (witness Sidney's *Astrophil and Stella* 71 and 72). In short, the *Amoretti* will be a fiction largely about requitedness, and its peculiar burden will be to sustain and develop such an approach across the tens of sonnets that became conventional to the genre in English after Thomas Watson's one hundred of the *Hekatompathia* (1582).

This is a distinctive program for an Elizabethan sonnet sequence, and it reveals not only a recognition of the conditions of Spenser's marriage in 1594 but in aesthetic terms perhaps a certain exhaustion of the conventions that had dominated the genre in recent years. Especially after the posthumous publication of Sidney's *Astrophil and Stella* in 1591, a sequence seen as the most thoroughgoing exploration of the possibilities of the genre to date, Spenser's emphasis on representing a more or less stable, reciprocal love might be best understood as a way of renewing the possibilities of the genre. In this way, the approach of the *Amoretti* seems opposite to—but is really cognate with—the kind of lyric fiction fashioned by William Shakespeare at about the same time, addressing his *Sonnets* (published 1609) to an equally unconventional theme, not one but two resistant lovers of opposite sexes.

Nonetheless, as much as Spenser may have written an unconventional amatory situation into his sonnet sequence, the nature of the genre demands some concession to its built-in discontinuities from sonnet to sonnet, its scale as a fiction about the self over time, and the top-heavy structure of the formal integer, the sonnet itself.[4] All of these factors conditioned the thematic character and emotional pitch of the run of sonnet sequences up to the *Amoretti*. How could they be fitted to a sequence about requitedness that culminates in a wedding? This is the problem, fictional and formal at once, the answer to which determined much of the nature of Spenser's sequence. What will be Spenser's concession, if not to unrequitedness in a thematic sense, then to other sorts of incompleteness, suspension, or even frustration? Most of his forerunners locate those properties within their fictions, as an effect of the ill-matched emotions of the principal figures of lover and lady, and allow the stylized imperfections of the genre—what Petrarch famously called its 'scattered' qualities—to reflect if not enhance those emotions. For these sequences, in other words, the unrequitedness or incompleteness is located squarely within the fiction itself. But Spenser offers an idealist account of romantic experience. Despite the occasional gestures toward a conventional antagonism between the lady and the speaker, such as sonnet 20, the developing mutuality between the two seems to render the relationship whole and complete. As the proem foresees, the 'leaves, lines and rymes' of the sequence are in their own way a model of completeness. Where Spenser plants a kernel of incompleteness or suspension is in the gaps between this poeticized amatory relationship and the larger world it must inhabit; between his love, for which the *Amoretti* develops a fit language, and everything outside—including readers, other sequences, society. Instead of representing a speaker and lady who can never fully understand one another, Spenser gives us a complex called the *Amoretti*—lover, lady, and sequence—we can never fully understand from our vantage as imperfect, often unrequited lovers.

   This tension between the inside and the outside of the *Amoretti* appears in many of the sonnets. To see how Spenser constructs each of these domains in relation to the other, one might look at two consecutive poems such as 15 and 16. Typical rather than unusual, these are not a pair in any overt sense, but represent the programmatic motions of Spenser's project. Sonnet 15 is often treated as one of the most topical poems in the *Amoretti*: it begins with the speaker's address to merchants of the sort who were exploring the possibility of East and West Indian trade in advance of the establishment of the East India Company in 1600:

> Ye tradefull Merchants that with weary toyle,
>   do seeke most pretious things to make your gain:
>   and both the Indias of their treasures spoile,
>   what needeth you to seeke so farre in vaine?

This quatrain introduces a statement of the lady's sufficiency in all the worldly criteria of material value. 'If Saphyres, loe her eies be Saphyres plaine'—and thus the speaker continues through a list of gems and other precious items including rubies, pearls, ivory, gold, and silver—in that slightly anticlimactic order. The procedure of the poem is to name things of value according to the public, commercial world, and confirm that the lady possesses a store of such riches in her own person. As the list accumulates, however, we obtain not at all a portrait of the lady but a checklist of elements confirmed as though from behind a screen; the conditional character of each clause—'if Rubies', 'if Pearles', 'if Yuorie'—seems to offer us each part (lips, teeth, forehead) provisionally, without assembling a comprehensible picture of the lady in her entirety. The incompleteness and even incoherence of the

descriptive convention called the *blason* (in English, the blazon) is well documented
for this period (Vickers 1981, 1985). But Spenser's blazon here is distinctive in that it
adduces the convention not as the man's imperfect attempt to itemize the lady's
perfections—a common approach that puts the blazon between a lover and a lady, a
rich tissue of misunderstanding—but as his canny effort to proclaim her value while
obscuring the details.[5] In other words, Spenser puts the blazon between the speaker
and the lady on one side and the world on the other; the blindnesses and ambiguities
of the convention are rendered tactical, a way of keeping inquiring eyes at a distance.
The concluding couplet, which in some ways makes a standard Neo-Platonic gesture,

> But that which fairest is, but few behold,
>   her mind adornd with vertues manifold

seems to promise that behind this blason is an even more layered and textured reality,
the mind, that defies any such conventional representation or system of value.[6]
The gulf between this pair and the world at large is rendered starkly, in terms that
first seem to promise some commerce but end up reinforcing only the lady's
incommensurability.

Sonnet 16 then recounts a more private encounter with another convention of
sixteenth-century love poetry:

> One day as I vnwarily did gaze
>   on those fayre eyes my loves immortall light:
>   the whiles my stonisht hart stood in amaze,
>   through sweet illusion of her lookes delight,
> I mote perceiue how in her glauncing sight,
>   legions of loues with little wings did fly:
>   darting their deadly arrows fyry bright,
>   at euery rash beholder passing by.

Adapted from the lyrics by Petrarch and others in which Love personified as Cupid
assaults the lover to cast him into a state of both dependence and unfulfillment, this
is Spenser's version of the *innamoramento*, the moment of falling in love. While most
of his contemporaries favor a direct, often martial struggle with Love, Spenser
envisions his 'loves' as the *putti* of Renaissance and Mannerist art—literally, *amoretti*.
This is hardly a semantically neutral choice: compared to a legion of tiny *putti*, a
powerful Cupid who interposes himself ambiguously between the lover and the lady
represents a different sort of Love, a serious antagonist. In fact, Spenser's reimagining
of the *innamoramento* raises several questions that go to the heart of the *Amoretti*.
Aside from the nature of personified Love, these questions include the location of
this episode in the sequence and its outcome. Petrarch's introduction of Love as
antagonist—'uom ch' a nocer luogo e tempo aspetta' (a man who waits for the time
and place to hurt)—famously occurs in the second poem of the *Canzoniere*, and for
many succeeding amatory sequences (notably *Astrophil and Stella*), that position
following the proem becomes almost standard, even when some resistance to conventional Petrarchism is registered. Now Spenser has already glanced at the

innamoramento in sonnet 8, when he extols the guidance received in part through the lady's eyes:

> Thrugh your bright beams doth not the blinded guest
> shoot out his darts to base affections wound:
> but Angels come to lead fraile mindes to rest
> in chast desires on heauenly beauty bound.   (5–8)

And sonnet 8 in turn appears among several others that celebrate 'those powrefull eies' (9.2) as beacons of virtue. When we arrive at sonnet 16, then, the *Amoretti* has established a discourse around the lady's eyes that makes the conventional *innamoramento* seem not only trite but fatally incomplete; the delay of the convention until this point is not only a rejection of its values but a humiliation of it as a signal episode in this amatory history. We must notice, of course, the turn that concludes sonnet 16:

> One of those archers closely I did spy,
> ayming his arrow at my very hart:
> when suddenly with twinkle of her eye,
> the Damzell broke his misintended dart.   (9–12)

The lady's thwarting of the *putto* archer means that her love cannot be understood as cupidinous in the received terms of amatory lyric; the *putto's* aim is 'misintended' because he believes this is one of his usual assignments—to infect a 'rash beholder'— when in fact he has no place here.

With the stock *innamoramento* downgraded to a quotidian event, and a frustrated one at that, the *Amoretti* returns our attention to the nature of the speaker's 'unquiet thought' in love. The sonnet concludes with this observation:

> Had she not so doon, sure I had bene slayne,
> yet as it was, I hardly scap't with paine.

The ambiguity is enticing: the last clause allows for a quantum of suffering that goes on between speaker and damsel, with little purchase from Petrarchism's conventional tropes. Again, Spenser locates such a convention not between the lovers but between them and us. We are reduced to wondering—as he addresses us in our language, using our figures—what their conventions within the closed society of the *Amoretti* might be, how they measure out their pain and pride, and how the snapshots of the sonnets accord with the phases of their life together on the inside. In other words, the position taken in sonnet 1—that the 'leaves, lines, and rymes' are sufficient in themselves, not a virtual experience that points us outside the *Amoretti*—is supplanted by our developing curiosity about this strangely anti-confessional sequence. We want to know what we are missing of the lovers' inner life.

A number of sonnets hint at the textures of that inner life. Sonnet 23 treats the lady's Penelope-like unweaving of the speaker's 'worke' (14) of wooing; the famously elliptical 35 considers how desire makes of him a Narcissus; and 60 laments that the duration of their involvement, one year, feels longer than the forty that preceded it. These decorous sonnets embrace their superficiality and removal from the facts of his life, a complex of 'leaves, lines, and rymes'. When the speaker announces at sonnet 62 that a new year is about to begin (not 1 January but 25 March or Lady Day, the day of the Annunciation) and proposes a corresponding new phase in their understanding, one feels—unlike in the *Canzoniere*, where the speaker is always counting the time—that something is about to happen (Dunlop 1969 1970). (That marking of time is one of several that furnish the sequence: the other milestones are New Year's Day (4), spring (19), Lent (22), Easter (68), and the second spring (80). See Prescott 1985.) And at 63, the climacteric number that marks the shift into a new phase of life, the speaker says

> I doe at length descry the happy shore,
>   in which I hope ere long for to arryue;   (5–6)

and with that achieves what is all but unheard of in the Elizabethan and later sequences, namely a self-determined division between two episodes of the fiction. Since the customary division of Petrarch's *Canzoniere* into the two sections *in vita* and *in morte*, which are bounded by Laura's death at poem 267, it was often a convention or even a superstition of the sonnet sequence to mark two such phases, often corresponding to the speaker's stages of awareness, to events, or to a religious conversion. Spenser's turn here in the *Amoretti* is a late instance, roughly contemporaneous with Shakespeare's —which (by the poet's design or not) parodies such turns by abruptly changing lovers at sonnet 127. Characteristically, Spenser's division both marks a shift toward the marriage and obscures the precise terms of that shift: from this point lover and lady are plainly proceeding toward the final resolution of the *Epithalamion*. These last twenty-seven sonnets occupy a period of moratorium within the fiction—a strange interval during which we can assess what we know and do not know. In other words, the poems are literally marking time until we can get to the threshold of the wedding and with it, the *Epithalamion*.

One of the most striking symptoms of this late phase in the sequence—in which the provision of sonnets as vessels filled with words is made especially manifest—is the repetition of sonnet 35 as sonnet 83, with the difference of only one word, in l. 6:

> My hungry eyes through greedy couetize,
>   still to behold the obiect of theyr paine:
>   with no contentment can themselves suffize,
>   but hauing pine and hauing not complaine.
> For lacking it they cannot lyfe sustayne,
>   and having it they gaze on it the more: (35. 1–6)
>
>   and seeing it, they gaze on it the more: (83. 6)

While the repeated sonnet has brought some readers to confusion, the effect is to remind us yet again of the poem's character as material object, this time in a way that makes a semantic shift—from 'having' to 'seeing'—into poetic artifice. This strategy witnesses, in part, the limits of artifice in a mature sonnet sequence. How might Spenser represent alteration or difference in a medium in which conventional manifestations of artifice, such as stanzaic forms, tropes, or rhymes, are fixed in place by precedent? How might he compel our attention afresh to the relation between form and fiction? (Recall that at a corresponding moment in the *Sonnets*, the transition at 126 between the last sonnet to the young man and the first to the dark lady, Shakespeare marks the boundary—and underscores his warning to the young man that in the end Nature will take him away—with a twelve-line sonnet, as though the young man were made to disappear from life and from the sequence two lines early.)

In fact, the repetition of sonnet 35 as 83 is a remarkable demonstration of the poetics of the *Amoretti*. Nothing could better embody Spenser's view that the sequence is a self-contained weave of words and figures, or better prompt our complementary (perhaps contradictory) inclination of many readers to wonder how its verbal weave refracts the events taking place in the other world to which we lack access, between the lovers. The sequence depends on the tension between these two positions. When we think of the shift from 'having' to 'seeing', we must notice that it reverses the movement of the amatory relation: when the speaker muses at 35 on 'having' the object of his desire, he does not have it; and when he reflects at 83 on merely 'seeing' it, he is closer to obtaining the lady through marriage than he has ever been. In other words, the repetition with a difference underscores his dawning awareness that the 'having' that once seemed to promise a kind of completeness is itself merely a 'seeing'. If the sonnets' positions were reversed, they would represent a naïve faith in romantic and erotic possession; but in this order, they comment ironically on the facts of his life. As the fulfillment of marriage approaches, he regards it with a mature Christian conviction that what once seemed an earthly grace is impoverished by comparison with an eternal salvation (Roche 1989: xiv). In a sense this is to change the stakes of the *Amoretti*, lifting the speaker's gaze just as the fiction is about to reach its promised conclusion. But in a more subtle fashion, Spenser also reminds us here that the kernel of incompleteness or suspension he planted between the poeticized relationship and the world—which always indicated that their love was not worldly in the usual Petrarchan sense—is matched by a corresponding incompleteness that keeps it from being spiritual. For all the poems' programmatic insistence ('leaves, lines, and rymes') that they tell a complete story, the developing sequence conveys and even encourages the notion that behind its conventions something remains inexpressible. As the poet recognizes, over time we wonder increasingly what that might be. At episodes of revelation and insight like these imperfectly mirrored sonnets, the nature of that inexpressibility widens, and the Petrarchan promise of a virtual experience through poetry seems ever further from reach. All we know without question is that the speaker sees here what he was not prepared to see earlier, and the repetition only emphasizes that shift of perspective.

Thus the *Amoretti* delivers its conclusion, in which the final sonnets such as 88 lament his condition in ways that equivocate between amatory and spiritual 'darkenesse'. Mysteriously, the last items in the sequence are four anacreontic poems of sixty lines that speak to a faith in the mythography of Cupid and romantic love in a way that has always been obsolete here. No one has offered a good explanation for what these poems are doing in the *Amoretti,* but the effect is undeniable, in that readers cannot miss the distinction between Spenser's sequence and what it has heretofore refused to give us. The fact that the *Amoretti* can end with these lines—that Cupid

> wounded hath my selfe
> with his sharpe dart of loue:
>
> .   .   .   .
>
> So now I languish till he please
> my pining anguish to appease

—cannot be explained in terms of the speaker's mind or mood, but must be seen as an irruption of an uncritical, anachronistic Petrarchism on the threshold of that mode's transformation into something new.

With that, we turn to the *Epithalamion,* one of the most successful wedding songs in any European vernacular (see Dubrow 1990; Greene 1957). It is customary to remark, after Thomas M. Greene, that Spenser adapts classical models such as Catullus 61, 62, and 64 by doing away with the disinterested speaker common to such poems, and making the bridegroom—presumably the speaker of the *Amoretti*—into the narrator of his own epithalamion. (The genre is also called epithalamium; in this discussion I will use Spenser's name for it.) And it is certainly true that, in much the same way that the *Amoretti* revises its models by allowing the lover to configure his relationship in words that are ritual and ceremonial rather than confessional, the *Epithalamion* manages a point of view on the event of the wedding that is both privileged and distant. Taken together, the *Amoretti* and *Epithalamion* might be seen as one of the period's most striking experiments in fictional point of view, alongside roughly contemporaneous narratives such as Christopher Marlowe's *Hero and Leander* (pub. 1598), Shakespeare's two poems *Venus and Adonis* (1593) and *The Rape of Lucrece* (1594), and Thomas Nashe's prose fiction *The Unfortunate Traveler* (1594).

The chief engine of the *Epithalamion* is its extraordinary stanza. It is eighteen or nineteen lines: stanzas 1, 2, 4, 5, 6, 10, 16, 21, and 23 include eighteen lines, while the rest consist of nineteen except for 15 (seventeen lines) and the envoy (seven lines). The metrical base is iambic pentameter, except for lines 6, 11, 16/17 (depending on whether an eighteen- or nineteen-line stanza), and 18, of which the first two are trimeters, the third a tetrameter, and the final one a hexameter (see Warkentin 1990). If the sonnet is a designedly unbalanced structure, this stanza is a solidly built artisanal edifice that can accommodate a range of attitudes and tones from the stately to the breathless. Where the sonnet embodies one major self-correction (starting at the ninth line) within a formally identical organization, this stanza involves subtler modulations in the short lines: not so much corrections as comments or adjustments, the three- and four-stress lines relieve the discursive pressure that can accumulate in a stanza of isochronous verses. At the same time, the final hexameter—which follows a semantic pattern, the first half involving the clause 'woods...answer' and the second 'echo...ring'—returns every stanza to a version of the same refrain.

The second stanza demonstrates what becomes possible:

> Early before the worlds light giuing lampe,
> His golden beame upon the hils doth spred,
> Hauing disperst the nights vnchearefull dampe,
> Doe ye awake, and with fresh lusty hed,
> Go to the bowre of my beloued loue,
> My truest turtle doue,
> Bid her awake; for Hymen is awake,
> And long since ready forth his maske to moue,
> With his bright Tead that flames with many a flake,
> And many a bachelor to waite on him,
> In theyr fresh garments trim.
> Bid her awake therefore and soone her dight,
> For lo the wished day is come at last,
> That shall for al the paynes and sorrowes past,
> Pay to her vsury of long delight:
> And whylest she doth her dight,
> Doe ye to her of ioy and solace sing,
> That all the woods may answer and your eccho ring.

Like many of the stanzas, this one begins with an allusion to the present moment in relation to time's passing, and with an imperative addressed to some element of the wedding party—here, the Muses who also serve as bridesmaids and ladies of the chamber to a bride who is for today, in Spenser's imagination, treated as royalty. When the first short line occurs, it qualifies the command to the 'learned sisters' with an intimate aside; just as the bridesmaids move from the public world to the privacy of the bedchamber, the transition from a long to a short line carries us from a general imperative to a personal endearment. The second short line, at 11, comes sooner than we might expect if we imagine the stanza as symmetrical, with relief from pentameter lines at the regular positions of lines 6, 12, and 18. Having the short lines at irregular places such as 11 and 16 undercuts the monumentality of Spenser's stanza; it gives these lines the character of asides or self-reflexive observations, as though the speaker cannot wait through the expected intervals to drop a comment or an epithet. (This is especially true in stanza 10, where his description of the lady's body is quickened by the unexpected appearance of a trimeter—'her paps lyke lyllies budded'—at line 10.) Like many of the poets born in the second half of the sixteenth century who tended to invest in ad hoc stanza forms—a procedure that runs at least from *The Shepheardes Calender* to George Herbert's *The Temple*—Spenser constructs here an adaptable vehicle that can accommodate his speaker's narrating the wedding from inside as well as outside, in a variety of stances and tones.

There are twenty-three of these stanzas and a six-line envoy in the *Epithalamion*, one for every hour in the notional day occupied by the poem. The first sixteen refrains are affirmative ('al the woods may answer and your eccho ring'), while the next seven evoke night and quiet ('the woods no more shal answere, nor your echo ring'), corresponding to the sixteen hours of daylight at the summer solstice in

England. The distinction between long and short lines is symbolic as well as func-
tional, for there are 365 pentameters and hexameters, the carriers of the poem's
public, ceremonial register. The *Amoretti* as well is a poem of patterns, in which
where something is said can matter as much as how or what is said; but because the
Epithalamion is organized around the unity of a single day, and because weddings are
patterned in ways that lives are not, its patterns are in the foreground within and
across stanzas. Even the 68 short lines—whether or not we accept A. Kent Hieatt's
rationalization that 68 is the sum of the seasons (four), months (12), and weeks (52)
in a year—are essential to the poem's way of patterning because they break the model
both programmatically and incidentally (Hieatt 1960, 1961).[7]

The process of the *Epithalamion* is to narrate the wedding day not only as an event
in itself but as an intersection of social and mythological significance, as though
Edmund Spenser's marriage to Elizabeth Boyle mattered equally to the townspeople,
distant merchants, and classical figures such as Hymen and Hesperus. Accordingly,
the poem follows the unfolding of the wedding day hour by hour, but also keeps an
eye on a larger context often present only by analogy or implication: the bridegroom
relates the important episodes, from the bride's awakening to the newly married
couple's retirement, but we hear almost as much of mythological events such as Jove's
conquest of the nymph Maia or the mundane 'labors' and 'delights' of the local
people who attend the ceremony—not to mention various angels and *putti* who
encircle the actors at times. This complex gaze endows what might otherwise seem an
ordinary middle-class wedding with unusual, even comical importance.

Moreover, Spenser's approach here raises a fundamental question about the
Epithalamion like those we asked about the *Amoretti*. Where the sonnet sequence
maintained a zone of privacy between the verbal textile of the poems and the inner
dealings of the lover and lady, prompting us to wonder whether we can ever see into
their relationship, the *Epithalamion* actually conceals the decisive moments of the
wedding day behind allusions, analogies, and cinematic shifts of perspective. In
stanza 13, for instance, bride and groom stand at the altar about to be joined in
matrimony, but the speaker's attention moves between the flush in her cheeks and the
expression in her eyes, as well as the literally invisible but mythological angels that
gather around her. When the next stanza begins, 'al is done' and the bride begins her
journey home, but we never hear the speech act that marries them or witness the
moment of fulfillment. The counterpart of this omission occurs at stanza 21, when
the couple retires to bed. The angels become 'an hundred little winged loves', or
amoretti, who obscure the bed, and the speaker mocks our interest in the consummation by confronting us: 'who is the same, which at my window peepes?' The direct
address is mitigated by his conjecture that the voyeur is Cynthia, goddess of the
moon, but the fact remains that we are figuratively peering into the window because
of what the poem omits or glosses over.

While in the *Amoretti*, then, we come to ask where and how the primary relationship takes place, in the *Epithalamion* we face the corresponding question of when and
how the events happen. We are provoked to wonder thusly not out of prurient
interest but out of philosophical speculation: is there such a thing as love and

marriage that can be recognized from without, as a discursive and social event? Both poems ostensibly celebrate love in its forms of *innamoramento*, courtship, and marriage, and on the surface they resemble other works of their genres. But the inescapable conclusion of the two poems taken in tandem is that what we conceive as the reality of this state is merely an array of external facts, much like how the two poems allocate and dispose words on a scaffolding—an immanent structure involving positions, patterns, and symmetries—that often matters as much as what the words say semantically. Love and marriage are not identical to those collections of words and facts, but exist in a private, inexpressible realm to which those signs can only refer. Other poets of sonnet sequences and epithalamia may think they write from within that state, but compared to this poet, they merely manipulate a vocabulary of conventions that witness their removal from it; they are further from requital than they know. As we learn to read the *Amoretti* and then the *Epithalamion* in these terms, seeing through the words and indeed the poems to a reality that exceeds their capacity, we learn something important about both poetry and experience—a lesson that is relevant to *The Faerie Queene* as well as to these poems. In Spenser's view, poetry cultivates habits of thought, not realities; poems prepare us to know the truth when we encounter it, but they are not true themselves. And the process of reading a poem—the virtual experience of 89 sonnets or 24 stanzas—raises the awareness that genuine experience resides somewhere else, in the complex negotiations of real people through their quotidian lives. As an allegorical poem such as Spenser's epic gestures toward abstract truths such as holiness and justice so that we will know them in practice, his sonnet sequence and wedding song point to the heart of amatory life so that we will find it for ourselves.

Notes

1. See De Neef (1982); Loewenstein (1987); MacArthur (1989); Gibbs (1990); Johnson (1990).
2. For autobiographical allusions in the sequence see Cheney (1984).
3. For the influence of Petrarch generally and on Spenser in particular see Forster (1969); Greene (1982); Dasenbrock (1985); Roche (1989); Klein (1992); Dubrow (1995).
4. For the form of the Spenserian sonnet, rhyming *ababbcbccdcdee* (as compared with the 'English' and 'Petrarchan' varieties) see Spiller (1992), 142–9; Philmus (1999); and Chapter 21 below.
5. See also Mazzola (1992).
6. For Platonic and Neo-Platonic influences see Casady (1941); Bieman (1988), 162–75; and Chapter 28 below.
7. For numerology see also Kaske (1978).

Bibliography

Alpers, Paul J. (ed.) (1969). *Edmund Spenser: A Critical Anthology.* Harmondsworth: Penguin Books.

Bieman, E. (1988). *Plato Baptized: Towards the Interpretation of Spenser's Mimetic Fictions.* Toronto: University of Toronto Press.

Casady, E. (1941). 'The Neo-Platonic Ladder in Spenser's *Amoretti*'. *PQ* 20: 284–95.

Cheney, D. (1984). 'Spenser's Fortieth Birthday and Related Fictions'. *SSt* 4: 3–31.

Dasenbrock, R. W. (1985). 'The Petrarchan Context of Spenser's *Amoretti*'. *PMLA* 100: 38–50.

DeNeef, L. (1982). *Spenser and the Motives of Metaphor.* Durham, NC: Duke University Press.

Dubrow, H. (1995). *Echoes of Desire: English Petrarchism and Its Counterdiscourses.* Ithaca, NY: Cornell University Press.

Dunlop, A. (1969). 'Calendar Symbolism in the *Amoretti*'. *N&Q* 214: 24–6.

—— (1970). 'The Unity of Spenser's *Amoretti*', in A. Fowler (ed.), *Silent Poetry: Essays in Numerological Analysis.* New York: Barnes and Noble, 153–69.

—— (1980). 'The Drama of *Amoretti*'. *SSt* 1: 107–20.

Forster, L. (1969). *The Icy Fire: Five Studies in European Petrarchism.* Cambridge: Cambridge University Press.

Gibbs, D. (1990). *Spenser's 'Amoretti': A Critical Study.* Aldershot: Scolar Press.

Greene, T. M. (1957). 'Spenser and the Epithalamic Convention'. *CL* 9: 215–28.

—— (1982). *The Light in Troy: Imitation and Discovery in Renaissance Poetry.* New Haven, CT/London: Yale University Press.

Hadfield, A. (2008). 'The Fair Rosalind'. *TLS* 12 December: 13–14.

Hieatt, A. K. (1960). *Short Time's Endless Monument.* New York: Columbia University Press.

—— (1961). 'The Daughters of Horus: Order in the Stanzas of *Epithalamion*', in W. Nelson (ed.), *Form and Convention in the Poetry of Edmund Spenser.* New York: Columbia University Press, 103–21.

Johnson, W. C. (1990). *Spenser's 'Amoretti': Analogies of Love.* Lewisburg, PA: Bucknell University Press.

Kaske, C. (1978). 'Spenser's *Amoretti* and *Epithalamion* of 1595: Structure, Genre, and Numerology'. *ELR* 8: 271–95.

Klein, J. L. (1992). '"Let us love, dear love, lyke as we ought": Protestant Marriage and the Revision of Petrarchan Loving in Spenser's *Amoretti*'. *SSt* 10: 109–38.

Lever, J. W. (1966). *The Elizabethan Love Sonnet.* London: Methuen.

Loewenstein, J. F. (1987). 'A Note on the Structure of Spenser's *Amoretti*: Viper Thoughts'. *SSt* 8: 311–23.

MacArthur, J. H. (1989). *Critical Context's of Sidney's 'Astrophil and Stella' and Spenser's 'Amoretti'.* Victoria, BC: English Literary Studies, University of Victoria.

Mazzola, E. (1992). 'Marrying Medusa: Spenser's *Epithalamion* and Renaissance Reconstructions of Female Privacy'. *Genre* 25: 193–210.

Nelson, W. (1963). *The Poetry of Edmund Spenser: A Study.* New York: Columbia University Press.

Petrarch, Francis (1976). *Petrarch's Lyric Poems*, ed. and trans. R. M. Durling. Cambridge: Harvard University Press.

Philmus, M. R. R. (1999). 'The Case of the Spenserian Sonnet: A Curious Re-creation'. *SSt* 13: 125–37.

Prescott, A. (1985). 'The Thirsty Deer and the Lord of Life: Some Contexts for *Amoretti* 67–70'. *SSt* 6: 33–76.

Puttenham, George (2007). *The Arte of English Poesy: A Critical Edition*, ed. F. Whigham and W. A. Rebhorn. Ithaca, NY: Cornell University Press.

Roche, T. P., Jr. (1989). *Petrarch and the English Sonnet Sequences*. New York: AMS Press.

Spiller, M. R. G. (1992). *The Development of the Sonnet: An Introduction*. London: Routledge.

Vickers, N. J. (1981). 'Diana Described: Scattered Woman and Scattered Rhyme'. *Critical Inquiry* 8: 265–79.

—— (1985). 'The Blazon of Sweet Beauty's Best': Shakespeare's *Lucrece*', in P. Parker and G. Hartman (eds), *Shakespeare and the Question of Theory*. New York: Methuen, 95–115.

Warkentin, G. (1990). 'Spenser at the Still Point: A Schematic Device in *Epithalamion*', in H. B. de Groot and A. Leggatt (eds), *Craft and Tradition: Essays in Honour of William Blissett*. Calgary: University of Calgary Press, 47–57.

CHAPTER 15

THE FAERIE QUEENE (1596)

ELIZABETH JANE BELLAMY

INTRODUCTION: A TALE OF TWO 'LODWICKS'

In 1595, Spenser journeyed from Ireland to England with Books IV–VI of *The Faerie Queene* in tow. The poet's clear-cut goals were to publish his manuscript with William Ponsonby and, he hoped, to be favorably received by the Queen. But the manuscript's incoherence and disunity could not match the clarity of Spenser's goals. What we now refer to as the 1596 *Faerie Queene* is alien to the tighter narrative structure of the 1590 *Faerie Queene*. Readers cannot be blamed if, on the most basic level of reader response, they no longer *feel* as if they are negotiating—recognizing, even—the narrative terrain mapped in the epic's first installment. To be sure, the 'Letter to Raleigh' is not always the most reliable guide for interpreting Spenser's epic; but at least the document provides some clues for how to enter into the poet's 'general intention' for the first three books. Readers of the 1596 *Faerie Queene*, however, are abandoned with nothing but memories of the prior installment's template to guide them through the 'darke conceits' that lead, without warning, to what will prove to be the epic's final books.

In the 1590 *Faerie Queene*, Arthur's heroic rescues of Redcrosse and Guyon succeed in placing the titular virtues embodied by these heroes in sharper relief. Although Redcrosse, Guyon, and Britomart get bogged down in aimless wandering, readers can still orient these protagonists (and themselves) in relationship to Spenser's tightly conceived definitions of Holiness, Temperance, and Chastity. But miraculous Arthurian rescues—and, consequently, textbook definitions of the titular virtues under scrutiny—are largely absent from the 1596 *Faerie Queene*. What, really, is Book IV's 'friendship'—and, in the final analysis, who are Cambel and Triamond, enmeshed in a pseudo-Chaucerian tale, to us? What is this virtue that Book V insists is 'justice', enforced more often by violence than tempered by equity or mercy? Is Book VI's 'courtesy' indeed a public virtue? Or must one risk life and limb in vulnerable, brigand-patrolled, pseudo-bowers in order to experience it, however fleetingly? In the 1590 *Faerie Queene*, the enemies of 'oneness' (or Una) are duplicitous (Duessa); and when the wedge or mirror of duplicity is destroyed, wholeness is once again restored. But the prevailing antagonists of the 1596 *Faerie Queene* are not subtle duplicity but rather outright chaos (Ate) or the Blatant Beast, the material reality of whose infections even the most disciplined allegory can never hope to heal. Finally, even death seems different in the 1596 *Faerie Queene*. One of Redcrosse's antagonists, Sansfoy, if nothing else, is allowed a version of a heroic death: choking in the dust where he has fallen, releasing his grudging ghost from his body, he is expunged from *The Faerie Queene*'s epic destiny—but not until his death rewards him with some traces of the dignity of the *Aeneid*'s Turnus, excised from the founding of Rome but a formidable warrior experiencing a sublime death. In Book V, by contrast, antagonists' bodies are smashed, decapitated, dismembered—barred from the battlefield of epic death.

Perhaps the only indisputable claim that can be made about the 1596 *Faerie Queene* is that it fails to conclude Spenser's grand plan for his epic, as first announced in the 'Letter to Raleigh'. To echo one of Spenser's privileged temporal topoi, *The Faerie Queene*'s second installment remains suspended 'in middest of the race' (I.vii.5)—i.e., the race to complete the author's projected, twelve-book dynastic epic history of Elizabethan empire. Decades ago, Josephine Waters Bennett (1942) cogently argued that *The Faerie Queene* always felt the weight of the later six books that would have 'completed' it. Bennett's overarching goal was to trace the 'evolution' of *The Faerie Queene*. But the ill-natured disappointment that particularly shadows the 1596 *Faerie Queene* forces readers to witness the devolution of the epic, its collapse before ever reaching closure. By the conclusion of Book VI, readers encounter not a Spenser happily anticipating *The Faerie Queene*'s future books, but rather a Spenser predicting that the existing books of *The Faerie Queene* will fall prey to the venomous Blatant Beast and to the same malicious misreadings that plagued such earlier poems as *Mother Hubberds Tale* and its angry portrait of William Cecil, Lord Burghley: 'Ne may this homely verse, of many meanest, | Hope to escape his [the Blatant Beast's] venomous despite, | More than my former writs' (VI.xii.41). Instead of moving toward epic closure, Spenser bitterly revisits earlier misreadings of his poetry.

All of which leads to a key question that frames this essay. Other than Queen Elizabeth, the epic's most prominent reader (although one is well reminded that James VI of Scotland was also a prominent—not to mention highly offended—reader of Book V's unfavorable portrait of his mother Mary, Queen of Scots), who did Spenser imagine as the reader most vigilant over the poem's wanton assault by the figures of Ate, Enuie, Detraction, and the Blatant Beast? In *Amoretti* 33,

Spenser, pondering *The Faerie Queene*'s incompletion, addresses a figure named 'lodwick':

> Great wrong I doe, I can it not deny,
>   to that most sacred Empresse my dear dred,
>   not finishing her Queene of faery,
>   that mote enlarge her living praises dead:
> But lodwick, this of grace to me aread:
>   doe ye not thinck th'accomplishment of it
>   sufficient worke for one mans simple head,
>   all were it as the rest but rudely writ.

This essay invites us to identify the principle reader of the 1596 *Faerie Queene* as a choice between two 'lodwicks', Spenser's friend and contemporary Lodowick Bryskett, and the ghost of Spenser's long deceased but much admired epic model, Ludovico Ariosto. These two 'lodwicks' lend further insight into why the 1596 installment failed to complete Spenser's grand epic design.

Editorial commentary has customarily identified the lodwick to whom *Amoretti* 33 is addressed as Spenser's friend Lodowick Bryskett, whom Spenser replaced as Clark of the Chancery for Faculties. But recently, Donald Cheney (2002/3) has suggested in passing that the lodwick in question might also be Ludovico Ariosto, author of the *Orlando Furioso* and one of the esteemed 'Poets historicall' whom Spenser singles out for praise in 'Letter to Ralegh'. This essay retains as its touchstones these two lodwicks, Ariosto as bearing the brunt of Spenser's faltering allegiances to dynastic epic, and Bryskett as a synecdoche for the consequences of the fact that Spenser composed much of his epic in colonized Ireland. To keep these two lodwicks in our sights is to open avenues for reassessing the 1596 *Faerie Queene* in light of two scholarly paradigms, the historical and the literary historical, that, over the past half century, have positioned the 'devolution' of *The Faerie Queene* at the center stage of the experience of reading the 1596 *Faerie Queene*.

If the lodwick in question is indeed identifiable as Spenser's epic predecessor Ariosto, praised in Book IV as 'that famous Tuscan penne' (iii.45), then we walk down the path of literary history, particularly the extent to which the 1596 *Faerie Queene* fails to fulfill Spenser's ambition, first announced in a 1580 letter to his friend Gabriel Harvey, that he intended to 'ouergo' his predecessor (*Prose*, 471). Neither the Dedicatory Sonnets nor (as mentioned earlier) the 'Letter to Raleigh' of the 1590 *Faerie Queene* accompanies the 1596 *Faerie Queene*. The latter document's absence can prompt speculation that Spenser's address, in his *Amoretti* 33, to lodwick [Ariosto] may be a confession that his commitment to the machinery of heroic narrative was beginning to wind down—that, in light of more pressing political events, he was losing interest in lingering over Ariostan 'Knights and Ladies gentle deeds' (I *Proem*, 1).

Between the two installments of *The Faerie Queene*, Spenser was highly productive, writing *Colin Clouts Come Home Againe*, the *Amoretti*, *Epithalamion*, *Fowre Hymnes*, and *Prothalamion*. Paul Alpers (1989) has compellingly argued that these lyric poems, had Spenser so desired, could have a found a place in the 1596 *Faerie Queene*. These poems are evidence of less a truancy than a loss of interest in upholding a founding premise of *The Faerie Queene*—that a knight must remain bound by, committed to, chivalry in the service of a monarch. Thus, the pastoral mode that dominates Book VI may, in fact, be Spenser's farewell to public service—and to Ariostan 'Knights and Ladies gentle deeds' that can no longer sustain his poetic voice.

But if the lodwick in question, as editorial commentary has commonly assumed, is indeed Spenser's friend Lodowick Bryskett, then this 'old' editorial interpretation ironically leads us to the threshold of, arguably, the most consolidated trend in Spenser studies over the past quarter century, i.e., the question of Spenser and/in Ireland. Nicholas Canny (2000) reminds readers that Bryskett, Clerk of the Council of Munster and member of the Grey faction, implicitly endorsed violence as a means of implementing reform in Ireland. Thus, the *Amoretti*'s lodwick is both one of *The Faerie Queene*'s approved and approving readers and a major proponent of Irish colonial repression. But the colonial repression that lodwick [Bryskett] endorsed is also the history that the unfinished 1596 *Faerie Queene* fails to contain within the master narrative of epic.

Book IV: Lost in Romances 'forepast'

In its broadest scope, Book IV is a haunted foreshadowing of Spenser's inability or unwillingness to finish his epic. The book 'concludes' with the postponement of Marinell and Florimell's impending wedding 'to another place . . . to be perfected' (IV.xii.35). A late nineteenth-century editorial perspective on the fits and starts of Book IV's narrative structure is Kate M. Warren's complaint, in her edition's introduction, that the book was 'a riot of formlessness', seemingly 'pieced together out of fragmentary stories and reflections that he [Spenser] had put by for working up in the future' (1899: ix–x). Decades later, Isabel MacCaffrey was far more inclined to grant Spenser a significant degree of narrative control over the book, observing that its 'abrupt lowering of the guillotine . . . is often attributed to weariness, but as with Shakespeare's "dotages", we may want to give the poet the benefit of the doubt' (1976: 331 n 14). But no benefit of the doubt can distract readers from the book's many narrative deferrals and intimations that Spenser would indeed leave *The Faerie Queene* inconclusive.

Coming into existence as, in effect, the cancellation of a conclusion (Scudamour and Amoret's blissful, hermaphroditic embrace that ends Book III in 1590), Book IV's legend of Friendship challenges the concept of narrative itself. Narrative threads from the 1590 *Faerie Queene* are resumed, re-entangled, and re-abandoned, questioning whether the storyline of epic romance can ever achieve closure. In this book, *The Faerie Queene*'s anticipated marriages end only in deferral. The marriage of royal spouses is the occasion traditionally impelling the narrative of dynastic epic to closure. But although Britomart is briefly reunited with her dynastic partner Artegall, she must renew her quest to rescue Amoret from the arms of Lust. Had Scudamour chosen to recognize Amoret standing before him, the prolonged story of their nightmarish wedding day might have achieved closure; but instead he relates to Blandamour and Paridell the story of how he seized Amoret from the temple of Venus. Scudamour's retrospective story cedes place, in turn, to the continuing (but, as mentioned before, never completed) story of Book III's Marinell and Florimell.

One effect of what Warren long ago referred to as Book IV's 'pieced together' texture is that the book's narratives present themselves as too long to recount. It was Spenser's announcement in Book IV's introduction to the river marriage of the Thames and Medway ('O what an endless worke haue I in hand', IV.xi.1) that prompted Jonathan Goldberg to entitle his study of *The Faerie Queene*'s narrative deferral, *Endlesse Worke* (1981). Goldberg argues for Book IV as an 'endlesse worke' within an endless work, demonstrating how Spenserian storytelling becomes a process of absorption into other narrative voices. One of the most prominent of Book IV's absorptive voices is Spenser's revered 'Dan *Chaucer*, well of English vndefyled' (IV.ii.32). The epic's readers have long noted how the book purports to finish Chaucer's *Squire's Tale* (via some wanderings into *The Knight's Tale*), an ending lost by 'wicked Time' (IV.ii.33). But Spenser's intermingling of his own Cambina and Triamond with a Chaucerian Cambel and Canacee marks the point at which Book IV becomes lost in Chaucerian supplement; and, at any given point, the reader comes to realize that Chaucer or Spenser or the Squire of Dames could all lay claim to owning the narrative.

The principal casualty of this loss of narrative control is the book's titular virtue of friendship. Book IV's purported guide to friendship begins optimistically enough. The book's subtitle, 'The Legend of Cambel and Telamond, or Friendship', promises a 'Telamond', a perfect world. The legend's focus on friendship offers salutary release from the intense dynastic design of Book III: the pressures of hierarchy, genealogy, ancestry, knowledge of 'name and nation' (I.x.67)—particularly as predetermined by family ties, either known or as yet unknown. Friendship has no genealogical destiny, no *telos*, no 'hard begin'. The titular heroes, Cambel and Triamond, are certainly bound by matrimony, with each marrying the other's sister. But their friendship— theoretically, at least—exemplifies how good will and companionship are unconstrained by the demands and duties of Book III's dynastic, kinship ties. For that matter, although Book IV cancels out Scudamour and Amoret's hermaphroditic embrace that concludes Book III, Spenser's examination of friendship at times succeeds in carving out intimate spaces for feminine friendship and desire, as evidenced when Spenser transports Amoret from Scudamour's embrace to Britomart's protection (Stephens 1998).

But the 'Telamond', or perfect world, promised in the book's subtitle is never achieved. (Indeed, Bennett's suggestion that the word 'Telamond' was almost certainly supplied by a printer or editor offers further evidence of Book IV's absorption by other margins or paratexts.) Cambel and Triamond's exemplary friendship is seemingly achievable only within the narrative bounds of myth. Moreover, through-out the book, friendship is all too easily parodied, such as the 'friendship' of the unscrupulous Paridell (a return-of-the-repressed from Book III) and the mediocre Blandamour.

The otherwise miraculous interchangeability of the -*mond* brothers also fails to achieve allegorical coherence. Decades ago, Neoplatonic readings of Book IV inter-preted Cambina's intervention as the fourth element, turning the combative triad of Cambel, Triamond, and Canacee into a tetrad harmonizing affection and friendship. And similarly, Cambina's resolution of their combat was allegorized as the Neopla-tonic dialectic of *discordia concors* (Fowler 1964; Roche 1964). But in the final analysis, the episode is without significance for the book as a whole, seemingly posing the question: which presiding 'lady' has more control over the course of friendship? Is it the harmonious peace-bringer Cambina? Or rather, is it the discordant hag Ate, 'most fit to trouble noble knights' (IV.i.9), stirring them to fury and rage? Readers cannot be blamed for focusing less on Cambel's and Triamond's friendship than on the violence of the duo's combat. Their joust paves the way not for an allegory of friendship-in-*chevalry* but rather for an allegory of male, homosocial desire. An unsettling alternative to earlier readings of the book's knightly combats as the dialectic of a *discordia concors* is to read Satyrane's tournament, another series of combats as pointless as they are violent, as nothing more than an organized aggres-sion over a pseudo-woman, the False Florimell, whom the combatants do not even desire (Cavanagh 1994; Silberman 1995).

At scattered moments throughout the *Orlando Furioso*, rape—or attempted rape—becomes the sado-comic subject of Ariosto's narrative (for example, the impotent hermit's and Ruggiero's attempted rapes of Angelica, and the orc's stalking of the vulnerable Olimpia). Ariosto manages to contain his romance subplots of sexual threat and imperiled female vulnerability within the generic constraints of epic. But in *Faerie Queene* IV, the rape and sexual aggression that plague so many of Book III's episodes continue unabated, further degrading Spenser's allegory of friendship. Timias attempts a chivalrous rescue of Amoret but instead wounds her. Readers are told that the -*mond* brothers were conceived from the decidedly fallen world of their father's rape of their mother Agape. Amoret's sadistic imprisonment in Book III by Busyrane deteriorates even further in Book IV into her imprisonment by Lust itself. Put another way, in Lust's cave the dominance of Busyrane's Petrarchan love-tropes becomes crudely literalized as male genitalia. Scudamour, *The Faerie Queene*'s paradigmatic knight of male aggression, tells the story of his seizure of Amoret from Venus's temple, with the goddess presiding over his reduction of Amoret to his 'spoyle'.

At one point, the poet, losing track of his narrative threads, confuses the identities of Scudamour and Blandamour (IV.iv.2–4); and, perhaps predictably, one canto later he confesses a writerly fatigue: 'my wearie team [is] nigh ouer spent' (IV.v.46), signaling a waning interest in the machinery of Iodwick [Ariosto's] heroic narrative. Readers become all the more aware that any number of Book IV's characters do not so much impel the narrative as cause it to trip over the nostalgic debris of earlier (forgotten?) romances. To be sure, the names of many of *The Faerie Queene*'s major characters derive from romance, such as Book II's Guyon, whose name echoes both Guy of Warwick and the protagonist of the continental romance *Huon of Bordeaux*. But when readers reach Book IV, these derivative names begin to lose their narrative and allegorical vitality. Even as the walls of Ate's cave are littered with 'ragged monuments of times forepast' (i.21), so also is Book IV's narrative littered with the 'ragged' names of romances 'forepast'. The Squire of Low Degree seems fashioned as less a character than the echo of the title of a fifteenth-century English romance. The names of Amyas and Aemylia seem listlessly copied from *Amis and Amiloun*, an old French tale of friendship. Book II's Claribell, Phedon's lady, resurfaces as Book IV's re-gendered Claribell, a knight defeated by Arthur. ('Claribell' is recycled yet again in Book VI as the name of Pastorella's mother.) And thus Book IV's Claribell joins the list of characters whose names have become empty ciphers of the exhaustion of Spenser's own self-plagiarizing romance imagination.

As further justification for noting Book IV's tendency to be swallowed up by other narratives, the 'Dan *Chaucer*' earlier serving as Spenser's privileged source for his tale of Cambel and Triamond suddenly cedes place to Ariosto, proclaimed, as mentioned earlier, 'that famous Tuscan penne'. To be sure, readers can at this juncture definitively identify lodwick as the author of the *Orlando Furioso*. But Spenser's investment in his once esteemed model of a 'Poet historicall' shows signs of weakening. At one point, Cambel and Triamond seal their friendship by drinking from Cambina's cup of nepenthe, the waters of love, 'The which [the *Orlando*'s] *Rinaldo* drunck in happie howre.' But Spenser misreads the nepenthe topos deployed by Ariosto's epic 'penne' (Kennedy 2000). Ariosto's nepenthe consists of two separate waters of love and hate: whereas Rinaldo drinks the waters of love that induce an intense desire for Angelica, she drinks the waters of hate that cause her to loathe Rinaldo. Hence, at best, Spenser's conciliatory nepenthe is a misreading of Ariosto's episode and, at worst, a hasty, pre-emptive foreclosure of the rich narrative possibilities generated by the dual waters of Ariosto's nepenthe. Earlier claiming to 'ouergo' his admired predecessor, Spenser not only ceases competing with Ariosto, but he also seems contented with careless *imitatio*.

Another of Spenser's nods in the direction of 'that famous Tuscan penne' can serve as the occasion for pondering the fact that the *Orlando* opens with a knight named Ferrau who, upon losing his helmet in a stream, resolves to win Orlando's (1.14). The ingenuity of Ariosto's romance narrative is such that Ferrau's quirky loss of his helmet and trivially petulant vow are eventually enfolded into the grander narrative of the epic clash between the forces of Charlemagne and Agramante. But the *Orlando*'s narrative ingenuity deteriorates amid Spenser's persistent echoes of the insignificant names of romances 'forepast'. Ariosto's Ferrau resurfaces as Book III's 'Ferraugh', who steals the False Florimell from Braggadocchio. By Book IV, Ferraugh's only reason for being is his drubbing by Blandamour; and in Satyrane's tournament, Blandamour is in turn defeated by a knight named 'Ferramont'. The *Ferr-* of both Ferraugh and Ferramont seemingly parodies the miraculous interchangeability of the *-mond* brothers: the poet implies that if the tournament is further prolonged, then

Ferra[mont], victor over Ferr[augh], can anticipate his own impending defeat by an as yet undisclosed, third *Ferr-* knight. And thus does Spenser's allegiance to 'that famous Tuscan penne' parody both the chivalry that lies at the heart of Ariostan combat and *The Faerie Queene*'s own earlier narrative.

Spenser's waning interest in the machinery of heroic narrative can be directly correlated with his growing preoccupation with New English colonial ventures in Ireland. Book V has customarily been viewed as the point at which the vexed question of Spenser in/and Ireland erupts to the surface of *The Faerie Queene*'s narrative. But Book IV shows early signs that *The Faerie Queene* will be unable to contain colonial politics within Spenser's larger allegory of fashioning a gentleman in 'vertuous and gentle discipline'. If we bear in mind that, as discussed in Spenser's *View*, 'Ferragh' is also an Irish battle cry (*Prose*, 103–5), then we are returned to *Amoretti* 33's lodwick as the more traditionally identified Lodowick Bryskett, both a reader of *The Faerie Queene* and, like Spenser, a civil servant in Ireland who endorsed colonial policies. The name of 'Ferraugh' may owe its origin less to the literary history of epic romance than to contemporary events in Ireland, specifically New English atrocities against 'Ferragh'-screaming foot soldiers. Thus, it may be more accurate to view the 'Fierce warres' alluded to at *The Faerie Queene*'s outset as springing not from Ariosto's 'Tuscan penne' but rather from Spenser's New English pen. Even Book IV's allegorical core of friendship is directly traceable to Ireland. When Cambel and Triamond's 'Fierce warres' are given a stanza-long comparison to the 'contrarie' tides swirling in the estuary of the Shannon River (IV.iii.27), Spenser illustrates the ease with which the purposefulness of his epic narrative can be distracted by glimpses of the Irish landscapes among which he wrote so much of *The Faerie Queene*.

The river marriage of the Thames and Medway is undeniably a triumph of Spenserian mythopoesis, hermetically sealed from historical contingency. But when Spenser notes the chorographic fact that 'Ne thence the Irish Rivers absent were' (xi.40), his mythopoesis also places readers at the threshold of the Irish question. The presence of such rivers as the 'baleful Oure' (xi.44) has the effect of probing the ambiguous history encoded by these rivers' presence. The Irish rivers flowing from the colonial margin have seemingly been forced to attend a river marriage at the imperial center, in the process exposing their reluctance to pay tribute to the Thames (Hadfield 1997; McCabe 2002; Van Es 2002). In sum, reassessments of the presence of these seemingly marginal Irish rivers suggest that in addition to Spenser's 'endlesse worke' of naming all the wedding guests at the marriage of the Thames and Medway, the poet has also begun undertaking the 'endlesse' task of trying to control how the history of these English and Irish rivers, flowing in regions with very different histories, will be conceived and judged by his readership.

On the banks of the aforementioned 'baleful Oure', Lord Grey, appointed the Queen's Lord Deputy in Ireland in 1580 and forced to return to England two years later to face an inquiry by the Privy Council, clashed with the O'Byrnes. Thus, the baleful Oure can be seen as the fourth book's most significant adumbration of Book V's entanglement in the Irish question, and in the trials and tribulations of Artegall, on his way to becoming less Britomart's dynastic spouse than an avatar of Lord Grey.

Artegall initially appears in Book IV as a moss-covered 'salvage knight', anticipating Faerie land's transformation from a dreamy romance backdrop of the search for a dynastic partner to a 'salvage' battlefield where Artegall/Lord Grey, operating *sans finesse*, seeks to police the colonial margin. And thus does Book IV's persistent reliance on the contingencies of narrative deferral now succumb to the pressures of a messy present that can be deferred no longer.

The Plunge into History: Book V's World 'grow[ing] daily wourse and wourse'

If portions of Book IV seemingly fade away into a hazy dream of romances 'forepast', Book V cannot awaken from a contemporary world of nightmarish violence, exerting a regressive, anti-prophetic pull on *The Faerie Queene*'s epic telos, and constituting *The Faerie Queene*'s most searing critique of Ariosto's 'Knights and Ladies gentle deedes'. Book IV's magic wands and cups of nepenthe are replaced by a bleak world of iron axes, iron-hooked chariot wheels, trapfalls, and dangerous bridges. Spenser's legend of justice is *The Faerie Queene*'s most violent book—not so much chivalric as punitive violence that seriously undermines the book's titular virtue of justice and its integrity as a document of moral and legal philosophy. Readers have long noted that Book V's punishments are as grisly as they are arbitrary: Sanglier decapitates his lady, whose head the iron man Talus then forces him to carry; Munera's hands and feet are ruthlessly chopped off by Talus; Pollente is brutally decapitated by Artegall, who elsewhere permits Talus to hurl the Egalitarian Giant off a rocky sea-cliff.

The book's decapitating, bone-crushing violence calls into question the moral efficacy of Artegall's and Talus's efforts to bring justice to Gloriana's realm. And, for that matter, the failure of the fiction to negotiate the demands of Elizabethan realpolitik not only sabotages attempts to reconcile justice with *The Faerie Queene*'s overall epic purpose, but also impedes literary interpretation itself. Early Spenser scholarship, working within the constraints of an older historical/biographical criticism, diligently identified a series of one-to-one correspondences between fictive and historical figures, relying on a biographical reductionism as the book's only hermeneutic pathway: Mercilla as Elizabeth; Duessa as Mary Queen of Scots; the Soldan's chariot as the Spanish Armada; Geryoneo as Spain's Philip II; Sir Burbon as Henri IV of France, etc. But, over time, these one-to-one correspondences, entangled within the book's raw proximities of justice and violence, its uneasy commingling of poetry and history, have stubbornly refused to cohere into a moral master narrative.

The era of the New Criticism witnessed valiant efforts to suffuse Book V with an aesthetic appeal. Iconographic analogies between, for example, the labors of Hercules and Artegall foregrounded the heroism of Spenser's knight of justice. Spenser's protagonist was portrayed as learning to renounce his pride and wrath to fashion himself worthy of rescuing Irena from Grantorto, or papal Catholic power. Presumably tracing an allegory of Artegall's moral development, the book was seen as the achievement of a New Critical thematic unity (Aptekar 1969; Dunseath 1968). But this new critical will to aesthetic and thematic coherence renders all the more impossible the task of integrating Book V's troubling collisions of justice and violence into *The Faerie Queene*'s overall program of fashioning a gentleman 'in vertuous and gentle discipline'.

Seeking to unite the generic aims of epic and the humanist conduct book, Spenser attempts to proffer justice as a 'public' virtue; but the book's exercising of justice often amounts to brute force. A memorable example is the fate of the Egalitarian Giant who, in debate with Artegall, 'all the world would weigh equallie' (ii.30). On the surface, we are tempted to side with Artegall against what can be perceived as the Giant's misguided efforts to restore a golden age based on equal distribution of property. But even though the Giant is the obvious target of Artegall's—and Spenser's—scorn, the knight of justice loses control of the debate as it unfolds. At one point, the knight, convinced that 'all change is perilous' (ii.36), claims that the Giant's redistributing the world's wealth will cause the stars to fall out of their orbits, an abrupt and illogical shift of the debate's subject matter from matters of state to cosmic phenomena. Thus, readers are prompted to review the giant's arguments not as spurious but as convincing. From this perspective, we come to understand that Artegall's objections to the Giant's distribution of wealth in no way accurately reflect the legal philosophy of sixteenth-century jurisprudence, as has often been assumed (Fowler 1995). The debate abruptly concludes neither in reconciliation nor the imposition of justice but rather a deterioration into Book V's signature brute force, as Artegall allows Talus to hurl the Giant over a sea-cliff to his death. In the final analysis, the episode becomes a virtual satire of one of humanism's most cherished goals, participation in principled, balanced, rational debate.

The most ominous threat to *The Faerie Queene*'s humanist agenda is the iron man Talus. Readers of Book V have the option of papering over Talus's persistent aggression by reading it through the legal philosophical lens of the *lex talionis*, a retributive justice legally inflicting pain in recompense for a hurt. But too often the book's exercise of justice is tantamount to Artegall's willingness to allow his iron henchman to do much of his punitive dirty work for him. So eerily robotic is Talus that he does not 'suffer sleepe to seaze | His eye-lids' (vi.26). Shunning hand-to-hand combat, Talus is neither an organic being nor, for that matter, a figure of allegory, but rather a war-machine utterly lacking the humanity that, by definition, underwrites humanism itself. Book V's inhuman(e) robotic terminator serves as less a realization of the *lex talionis* than as *The Faerie Queene*'s most serious undermining of Spenser's humanist project to 'fashion a gentleman'.

As if to compensate for Talus's brutality, Book V strives to allegorize 'That part of Iustice, which is Equity' (iii.4) as justice's more measured and benign counterpart, and a means of enfolding Gloriana/Elizabeth into the machinery of epic justice. Dispensed not with 'rigour' (i.7) but in accordance with the conscience of the magistrate, equity is presumably Spenser's salutary alternative to Artegall's iron-age justice. For example, Book V's allegory programs us to read Mercilla-as-Elizabeth's presiding over the trial of Duessa-as-Mary Queen of Scots (the latter continuing to reflect the anti-Catholicism of Book I's Duessa) as an example of law restrained by clemency. But the episode also encourages us to be as dubious about the moral efficacy of Spenser's equity as we are about his concept of justice. Though Duessa is on trial for treason and murder, the episode ends with the queen melting in hypocritical, 'piteous ruth' and shedding tears for the defendant (ix.45–50); and at this point, we are at liberty to examine the contradictions inherent in portraying mercy as the trial's guiding principle. The episode becomes entangled in its own irreconcilable efforts to portray Duessa's execution as a manifestation of Mercilla's clemency. This unstable surrogate for Elizabeth might more profitably be viewed as an embodiment of calculated evasiveness and moral casuistry, even poised to use slander, as embodied by the courtroom figure of Zele, to bolster the state's agenda (Burrow 1992; Gallagher 1991; Kaplan 1997). This ambiguous Mercilla discourages any inclination to recuperate this episode as Book V's successful union of clemency and justice under Gloriana's banner.

Readers searching elsewhere for a more satisfying allegory of equity could turn to Britomart's visit to Isis Church, particularly the iconography of the goddess Isis and her crocodile as one of *The Faerie Queene*'s great allegorical cores, equivalent to Book III's Gardens of Adonis. But crowding out any concerted effort at focusing on equity in Isis Church is the psycho-drama of Britomart's turbulent adolescent desires, whose irresolutions have been inherited from Book III. In Britomart's dream, the goddess's temple is assailed by a furious tempest and deadly, leaping flames that are eventually swallowed by a threatening crocodile approaching so close to Britomart that she 'soone enwombed grew' (vii.12). Thus, the dream amounts to less an allegory of equity than an 'erotic communion' (Gross 1985: 173). Its strangeness forces Isis's priests to smooth out its sexual violence, utterly mocking the somber practices of priestly exegesis. In the final analysis, Spenser's allegory of equity can be judged irrelevant, a tale of romance wandering of no significance to the pursuit of either justice or equity.

Britomart's erotic dream in Isis Church reminds us that the androgynous 'gender trouble' characterizing so many of her adventures in Books III and IV continues to haunt her appearances in Book V. The book of justice features yet another female warrior, Radigund, the provocative Amazon queen and, quite possibly, Britomart's alter ego. Spurned by her lover Bellodant, the enraged Radigund emasculates Artegall, clothing him in 'womans weedes, that is to manhood shame' (v.23). In an especially grisly combat, Radigund is eventually decapitated by Britomart, leaving readers divided over how to assess the combat's sadistic violence. Is Britomart's brutal defeat of Radigund to be interpreted as her usurpation of the latter's patriarchal authority? Or should we resist the temptation to maintain a distinction between Britomart the virtuous Amazon and Radigund the perverse Amazon (Cavanagh 1994; Schwartz 2000; Suzuki 1989)? Britomart's own ferocity suggests that she may share more significant parallels with Radigund than with the virtuous virgins Florimell and Amoret—or, for that matter, with her dynastic epic predecessor, Ariosto's female warrior Bradamante.

Another key consequence of the Radigund episode is its opening of the vexed question of Spenser in/and Ireland that haunts Book V. Britomart's defeat of Radigund can be read topically as allegorizing Spenser's agenda for subduing the Irish; and Artegall's humiliating imprisonment by the Amazon queen can be read as embodying Spenser's protest of Elizabeth's 'womanish' policies toward Ireland as partly to blame for its ongoing rebellion (Carroll 2001). And thus the episode's gender troubles, unresolved holdovers from Book III, lead directly to the Irish question that first raised its tentative head in Book IV.

Book V features the removal of the False Florimell's veil, a symbolic unveiling of duplicity itself (iii.17). The current scholarly focus on Ireland has likewise removed another veil—namely the veil obscuring the fact that so much of *The Faerie Queene* was written in Ireland by a civil servant on the fringes of Elizabeth's court. This historicizing trend, discouraging any attempt to interpret Book V morally or iconographically, has demonstrated just how thoroughly the legend of justice is imbricated in the complexities of Spenser's New English identity and its discontents. If we read through the lens of this identity, then historical fact's most significant incursion into the fictive world of epic is colonial Ireland; and the book's moral philosophy becomes, though not justifiable, certainly more visible and interpretable. Some ninety years ago, long before the current trend to trace *The Faerie Queene*'s deep roots in Ireland's 'salvage soyl', H. S. V. Jones claimed that Book V and Spenser's prose *View of the Present State of Ireland* should always be studied in tandem, for the legend of justice 'appears as a quite intelligible application of Spenser's moral philosophy' (1919: 13). With a sharper political edge, more recent criticism has argued that if Book V is indeed morally intelligible within an Irish context, then it is because the legend of justice serves as the dubious vindication of the *View*'s radical agenda, where Irenius insists on the necessity of violence to subdue Ireland.

What is perhaps most at stake in tracing Book V's parade of one-to-one correspondences between literary character and historical figure is the determination of Artegall's identity and a concomitant reassessment of the legitimacy of *The Faerie Queene*'s place within the literary history of dynastic epic. If readers focus solely on Artegall as a thinly veiled version of the Earl of Leicester, repelling incursions from Catholic Europe, then Book V's chief magistrate can easily be accommodated into the heroic machinery of (Protestant) epic: in such a scheme, Artegall is an exemplary epic protagonist, rescuing the lady Belge (the Protestant Netherlands) from Philip II's Spain.

But Artegall is, of course, more immediately identifiable as Arthur Grey de Wilton, appointed in 1580 as Lord Deputy of Ireland and participant in the massacre of some six hundred Spanish and Italian papal forces at Smerwick. If we unpack all the consequences of this identification, then the macrohistory of Elizabethan England as epic's latest version of *imperium sine fine* disintegrates into a sordid cross-section of New English microhistory, chronicling a not-so-heroic imperial dominance over a colonized margin. Is Artegall a Lord Grey, freeing Irena from Grantorto—i.e., *gran' torto* as the 'great wrong' of papal Catholic power? Or does it become the reader's burden to understand Grantorto as representing the *gran' torto* of New English atrocities against Irish 'rebels'? If we take the latter view, then Book V becomes the point at which a benign 'faerie queene' cedes place to a colonial Lord Deputy policing rebellion on England's borders. With colonial Ireland as their immediate frame of reference, readers are left with little incentive to return to earlier profferings of justice as a heroically 'public' virtue—little incentive to continue earlier readings of Book V as an epic allegory of the founding of a just and civil society. Significantly, the mythic, shape-shifting Proteus of Books III and IV transmutes, in Book V, into the topical, shape-shifting Malengine, whose entrapping fishnets and anti-chivalric 'legierde-mayne' are predictable backlashes against imperial violence. And, indeed, Malengine poses a thorny question for readers: who precisely *are* the malefactors in need of the imposition of justice? The refractory, colonized Irish? Or the New English colonizers who have forced the Irish into shifty guerilla tactics?

Reading the legend of justice with and against the grain of Spenser's New English identity currently possesses the most momentum in studies of Book V. But, interest-ingly, Willy Maley, though a key contributor to tracing *The Faerie Queene*'s roots in Ireland's 'salvage soyl' (1997), has also sounded a cautionary note about what he terms the worrisome 'critical commodification and fetishizing of Ireland' in recent Spenser studies: a sole focus on Ireland, argues Maley debating with Andrew Had-field, may simply be a refusal to read Spenser's epic closely (Hadfield and Maley 2000: 186). Maley seemingly implies that an at least partial return to close reading may be a salutary counter-impulse to the rising trend of reading Ireland *everywhere* in Book V.

Several recent returns to Book V have committed themselves less to reading Ireland 'everywhere' in *The Faerie Queene* than in renewing close contact with the capaciousness of Spenser's allegorical temper—even in a book as historically fraught as the legend of justice. Decades ago, Isabel Maccaffrey (1976) was among the first critics to occupy what has become the generally accepted view that *The Faerie Queene*'s allegory has, in Book V, deteriorated into a merely mechanical mode of expression, a loss of faith in allegory's potential to reflect the external world. But recent readings have sought to revitalize the allegorical aims of the book's 'darke conceits', arguing that throughout the book Spenser remains allegory's committed champion. Relevant here is the abrupt departure from the earth to the heavens of the goddess Astraea, the young Artegall's tutor in justice. To be sure, the Irish question can be read into her flight, signaling Elizabeth's abandonment of Ireland in the wake of failed efforts to replace Brehon with English law. Astraea flees because a colonized Ireland 'growes daily wourse and wourse'. But does this world growing worse necessarily refer to contemporary colonial events? Or rather, is Spenser adducing a more generic, discursive iron-age world more typical of apocalyptic allegory? To assess Spenser's anxiety about 'the state of present time' as not so much urgently, immediately topical as discursively mediated is to understand how Book V's allegory can be read as richly combining the hybrid topoi of biblical or apocalyptic prophecy (Borris 2000; Mallette 1997).

Astraea's abandonment of the earth is also a frequent topos of ancient history, again not always ineluctably leading to Spenser's contemporary Ireland, but rather to the many conceits of Spenserian allegory that keep ancient history and 'the state of present time' in productive tension with one another. Perhaps just as much as a book of justice, Book V is also a book of euhemerism, defined as an early phase of heroism when figures such as Hercules, Bacchus, and Theseus, hovering between the gods and mortals, customarily resorted to force to establish civil and just societies (Fletcher 1971). These euhemeristic gods-become-men, always already operating in a fallen world, had no other recourse than to found civilization by force, 'The club of Iustice dread' (V.i.2). Constrained by no moral code, their autochthonous, founding brutality, at least theoretically, was that which made morality possible. When read through the lens of Spenser's complex experiments with euhemerism's discursive roots in ancient myth, Astraea's departure becomes both an emblem of earthly decline and a necessary prelude to the establishment of justice, leading to the triumphs of Bacchus and Hercules as allegories of virtue (Van Es 2002).

However resolutely readers choose either to focus on or downplay Book V's Irish question, they find it impossible to exit the legend of justice without sensing Spenser's deep pessimism about the efficacy of epic poetry to promote the aims of Elizabeth's court. In the *Orlando Furioso*, the worst fate that could befall epic poets was to be slyly accused by Saint John, Astolfo's guide to the moon, of occasional exaggeration and pandering to patrons (Canto 35). But in *The Faerie Queene* V.ix, Arthur and Artegall encounter the alarming sight of the poet Bonfont (or is his name Malfont?), whose tongue has been nailed to a pole outside of Mercilla's palace (25–6). Bonfont/Malfont's punishment is among *The Faerie Queene*'s ominous signs that, particularly for poets, the world indeed 'growes daily wourse and wourse'. Is the poet a 'Bonfont', the poet of praise for his queen Mercilla? Or is he a 'Malfont', all too vulnerable to accusations of circulating slander at court? And when Bonfont/Malfont is disciplined and punished, can the consequences of England's struggles to subdue Ireland be far behind? The book concludes with the reviling of Artegall-as-Lord Grey as he is recalled to court by Gloriana–Elizabeth. We are well reminded here that in Book II, Guyon succeeds in stopping the 'bitter rayling' of Occasion by grasping her 'vngratious tong' and fastening it with an iron lock (iv.12). But Artegall, pursued by the hags Enuie and Detraction, is powerless to stop the malicious lies and calumnies that slander him for, from his perspective, doing his monarch's bidding; and, ultimately, he is powerless to stop the backbiting assaults of the Blatant Beast. Thus Book V leaves us with the growing impossibility that crusading knights and slander can ever coexist within the same narrative.

Book VI: The 'endless trace' of Epic Incompletion

Book VI, the legend of courtesy, begins with the poet's determination to restart the stalled engines of epic destiny: 'And when I gin to feel decay of might, | It [Faerie land] strength to me supplies, and chears my dulled spright' (VI Proem, 1). 'Dulled' by the sharp historical edges of Book V, Spenser seeks to tap into the aesthetic delights of Faerie land—and, specifically, to the virtue of courtesy—to restore his epic voice. Thus, one obvious starting point for erasing the nightmarish memories of Book V is to devote special attention to the motif of retirement that structures much of the sixth book's pastoral world. With its many woods, shades, dales, groves, and other protective cynosures, the legend of courtesy seemingly offers a welcome 'green world' retreat from Book V's violence and dismemberment, an opportunity for the poet to catch his breath, sift through current events once more, and retrieve what is most essential for his poetry. At the outset Spenser holds out the hope of courtesy's potential to reform what justice merely roots out and leaves brutally exposed.

But even in courtesy's green worlds, all is not well. J. C. Maxwell's stern judgment over a half-century ago that Spenser's handling of certain episodes in Book VI 'betrays a mind not fully engaged by what it is doing' (1952: 68) may be overstated. Nevertheless, signs of waning poetic energy are evident in Timias's trio of attackers, 'Despetto', 'Decetto', and 'Defetto', closer to the simple villains of a morality play than of complex allegory. Book IV's tiring struggle to invent new names for characters returns in one of the protagonists Calepine, who improbably echoes the name of the son of the fourteenth-century Turkish emperor Bajazeth. Nor is it an especially healthy sign of epic purposefulness that the name of literary history's first dynastic epic protagonist is weakly echoed in Book VI's 'Eneas', never more than a minor character and risibly mocking the scope of the *Aeneid*'s dynastic framework.

The legend of courtesy poses, without resolving, a number of nagging questions that continue to undermine *The Faerie Queene*'s epic integrity. For example, are the book's many episodes of pastoral *otium* to be viewed as convalescent and restorative, or are they signs of exhausted withdrawal? Why is the relatively minor figure of Pastorella allowed to discover her true parents (or why is Aladine allowed to be reunited with his father Aldus), while Arthur, no less than *The Faerie Queene*'s overarching hero of magnificence, must remain ignorant of his 'name and nation'? Does Book VI represent a salutary retreat into the realm of Faerie? Or can Spenser's genres of romance, allegory, and pastoral be read as steadily eroding, allowing history to intrude almost as disastrously into the narrative as it did in Book V? However optimistically or pessimistically readers choose to address these questions, it is a fact that the 'noisome breth' (viii.26) of Book IV's Sclaunder and the abusive revilings of Enuie and Detraction intensify, in Book VI, into the thousand tongues of the barking 'blatterings' of the Blatant Beast that succeeds in spreading its rancorous venom throughout Gloriana's realm.

The problems begin at the book's outset with Spenser's strangely inadequate definition of courtesy, its etymology enmeshed in circularity: 'Of Court it seemes, men Courtesie doe call.' There can be no doubt that Book VI offers textbook examples of *dis*courteous behavior, such as Maleffort's and Briana's collecting the hair and beards of those seeking entry onto the narrow bridge before Crudor's castle. But discourtesy's antithesis, trapped in tautology, does not so readily manifest itself. Perhaps the indefiniteness of Spenser's courtesy presents itself not as a weakness but as a strength, suggesting that within the book's pastoral retreats, courtesy is far more complex than a prescribed set of mannerly protocols. Viewed through such a lens, Spenser's courtesy reveals itself as contingent, pragmatic, flexible, deliberately refusing to assume the absoluteness of such often lonely virtues as temperance, and constituting an extended meditation on courtesy as a desire for community (Borris 1987; Chamberlain 2006; Teskey 2003). But it is also the case that such characters as Timias, the Hermit, Meliboe, Calepine, Serena, and the titular hero of courtesy Calidore himself end up inhabiting private spaces, non-intersecting worlds that scatter rather than consolidate epic *polis* (not to mention, render several of the book's characters all the more vulnerable to the Blatant Beast's entrapping attacks). In this dispersed world, Spenser himself seems hard pressed to showcase courtesy's virtues to the world at large. For that matter, as long as slander remains inherent in the human condition, the Blatant Beast is an antagonist that, almost by definition, cannot be eradicated. And thus does the legend of courtesy mark the final collapse of *The Faerie Queene*'s epic structure, the point at which 'the endlesse trace' (i.6) of the elusive Blatant Beast seals *The Faerie Queene*'s fate as an 'endlesse worke'.

Setting up a familiar opposition, Spenser observes that courtesy can be found not only at court but also far from court, growing on a 'lowly stalke' (VI Proem, 4). Courtesy is both Calidore's aristocratic 'gracious speech' (i.1) and the 'confused sound | Of senseless wordes' (iv.11) of the Salvage Man, curing Calepine's wounds with herbs and demonstrating, in Serena's words, a 'perfect gentle mynd', the triumph of nature over nurture. But this celebration of an innate, 'primitive' courtesy obscures more than clarifies. Not every wild man in Book VI can be counted on to possess the Salvage Man's 'gentle mynd'. The book's cannibals are also speechless, but they ogle the naked Serena, subjecting her not to shows of courtesy but rather to a sadistic voyeurism. When all is said and done, the cannibals' intention to rape Serena may be a sign that Spenser has become bored with, or is satirizing, his own trite oppositions of court and rural life.

Moreover, like Justice, courtesy proves to be yet another one of the 1596 *Faerie Queene*'s ambiguous 'public' virtues. Early in Book VI, after Calidore 'cleft his [Maleffort's] head asunder to his chin' (i.23), readers realize that courtesy, civility, and gentleness are incapable of warding off the kind of violence that consistently marred Books IV and V. Readers are well reminded that there is as much violence in Calidore's world as in Artegall's (Cheney 1966).

Spenser assures his readers there is 'none more courteous Knight, | Then *Calidore*, beloued ouer all' (i.2). There is no reason not to take Spenser's praise at face value; and to be sure, the gentle Calidore stands in obvious opposition to the uncivil knight Turpine, who refuses Calepine shelter. But Calidore, though conspicuously absent for much of the book (perhaps the most truant protagonist in epic literary history), also cultivates a bad habit of interrupting private dalliances, such as the lovemaking of Calepine and Serena, or Colin's fragile vision of the graces on Mount Acidale. Moreover, he defends the dubious reputations of Aladine and Priscilla, rendering his 'counter-cast of slight' (iii.16) a potential agent of slander; he boasts of his 'long aduentures' to Calepine while the Blatant Beast attacks Serena; he crassly offers money to Meliboe so that he can reside among the shepherds; he shamelessly patronizes the lowly shepherd Coridon, the point at which humanism's goal of courteous class distinctions deteriorates into condescension. Most seriously, his encounter with the Blatant Beast seems more an afterthought than the climax of epic *agon* (Neuse 1968).

Spenser's poetics, as we have seen, suffered mightily under Book V's crushing violence. Book VI, generically speaking, is a web of romance, allegory, and pastoral, representing a resurgence of his poetics that promises to hold together even if one generic strand collapses. But we can never finally be certain whether the layered richness of these genres enables or disables the poet's attempt to lend unity and coherence to Calidore's epic quest for the Blatant Beast.

First, a turn to the genre of romance. Mid-twentieth-century criticism customarily paid close attention to Book VI's many familiar romance motifs: foundlings, Wild Men, miraculous reunions of parents with children, benign hermits, 'lawlesse' brigands, etc. (K. Williams 1966; A. Williams 1967). These romance motifs were perceived as welcome escapes from chivalric narrative, where knights, having grown weary with the court, embrace the life of contemplation. At one point, for example, Calepine, searching for Serena, pointedly rejects Matilda's offer of a horse and arms (iv.39). But escape from the demands of chivalric heroism deteriorates into (inadvertent?) satires of romance, such as Calepine's rescue of a baby captured by a 'cruell Beare' (iv.17). When Calepine eventually turns the child over to the wardship of 'Sir Bruin', there is no apparent motive impelling Sir Bruin's adoption of this infant other than the poem's indulgence in romance circularity: because the guardian possesses the name 'Sir Bruin', he is thereby destined to be given a baby captured by a bear (Parker 1979).

We are equally unsure how to evaluate Book VI's epic allegory, specifically whether it represents a resurgence or a continued weakening of the allegory that barely survives Book V's plunge into history. The allegory of the confrontation between Arthur and Turpine is a particularly contested site. On the one hand, their confrontation can be read through the Christological lens of Spenser's Book I, with Turpine's former ally Eneas helping Arthur to outwit the villain, heroically delivering him to Arthur for punishment (Borris 2000). But on the other hand, perceptions linger that Book VI's allegory stalls out. When Arthur, awaiting a confrontation with Turpine, impulsively sheds his armor and falls asleep, are we expected to salvage an allegory here, such as Arthur's embrace of heavenly awareness? Or rather, is the slumbering Arthur a sign of Spenser's declining interest in allegorical coherence, effectively an attempt to 'sleep off the allegory' (Dolven 2002: 51), a 'nap' far less allegorically relevant than the disarmed Redcrosse sleeping by the nymph's fountain in Book I.vii?

The pastoral genre pervades Book VI; but in the final analysis, even this customarily restorative genre offers clues that the sixth book is as exposed to the turbulence of contemporary Elizabethan politics as Book V. What, for example, do we make of the old shepherd Meliboe, who counsels (a not-fully-comprehending) Calidore in what it means to live the pastoral life? One could argue that Meliboe, having rejected the court, clearly inhabits a world, if not of total pastoral innocence, then at least one of self-knowledge and self-acceptance. But not even this green world can escape the shadow of Spenser's worsening relations with his patron-queen. The fact remains that Meliboe's trajectory from court to presumed pastoral refuge ends in the shepherd's brutal murder by the brigands, potentially recognizable as Spenser's representation of Irish outlaw rebels. The genre of pastoral, then, may be Spenser's thinly disguised, autobiographical exposure of his disappointment at laboring in a 'salvage' nation far from court.

Even in the violent wake of the brigands' slaughter of Meliboe and his shepherd community, readers determined to recuperate Spenser's pastoral vision can always point to Canto x where Spenser's pastoral persona Colin pipes to the Graces on the secluded Mount Acidale. In this pastoral retreat, arguably the most important allegorical core of the entire *The Faerie Queene* (Lewis 1936; Tonkin 1972; K. Williams 1966), Spenser circles back to his earlier identity as *The Shepheardes Calendar*'s 'new Poete', holding out the promise that Book VI will, after all, conclude with the triumph of poetic imagination and career self-fashioning.

But in the final analysis, Calidore's blundering interruption of Colin's piping exposes the fragility of the shepherd's vision of the Graces, as well as Spenser's disillusionment with poetry itself (Miller 1979). If we choose to accept the challenge of inserting the Irish question of Book V into the book of courtesy, then we are well reminded that Spenser's Acidale has momentarily shifted the location of his epic from an unspecified 'faerie' land to a mappable Ireland. Thus Acidale revisits the Irish homeland of the 1595 *Colin Clouts Come Home Againe*, a poem highly ambivalent about whether Colin's poetry flourishes on a pastoral island paradise or deteriorates far from the epicenter of Elizabeth's court.

Calidore is forced to exit Acidale's pastoral retreat to renew his quest for the Blatant Beast, successfully muzzled but finally able to escape; and the necessity of his leave-taking can be exposed as the unfortunate inheritor of the unresolved tensions of Book IV, where Sclaunder's 'Pouring out streames of poison and of gall' (IV.viii.24) achieves its full potential in the Blatant Beast's venomous attack on Spenser's poetics. Even in the protective woods of Mount Acidale, *The Faerie Queene* can no more escape the Blatant Beast than any of his 'former writs'. Thus, Colin/Spenser is not the much-anticipated return of a poet once known as England's Virgil, but rather a dreaded return to Book V's Malfont, the 'bad' poet whose tongue has been nailed to a pole, his career ruined by court rumor and the waning support of a patron-queen. The epic begins with the poet's proud self-identification as 'Lo I the man', shedding shepherd's weeds to assume the role of epic poet. At the conclusion of the 1596 *The Faerie Queene*, however, this bold self-revelation cedes place to the tentative rhetorical question, 'Who knowes not *Colin Clout?*' The poet already implies the answer: he suspects that nobody knows Colin Clout, enshrouded within his own ironic self-deprecation.

CONCLUSION: EPIC CLOSURE AND HISTORY'S DISCONTENTS

My concluding remarks return to the question posed at the essay's outset: who is the 'lodwick' Spenser imagines as the reader most vigilant over the poem's destruction by the Blatant Beast? Is it the ghost of Spenser's esteemed dynastic epic predecessor Ludovico Ariosto? Or is it his friend Lodowick Bryskett, a synecdoche for the consequences of the fact that Spenser composed much of his epic in colonized Ireland? Or both?

An insignificant but no less intriguing episode the *Orlando* neglects to close out is Rinaldo's loss of his famous steed Baiardo, who runs away from his owner early in the epic's opening cantos (1.12) and, stolen by Gradasso in Canto 33, remains estranged from his rightful owner. Spenser apparently chooses to conclude Ariosto's dilatory tale of equine loss when Guyon, having lost his horse Brigadore in Book II, confronts the thief Braggadocchio in Book V (iii.34) and is tenderly reunited with his steed— perhaps the only truly 'equitable' outcome in the entire book of justice. But *The Faerie Queene*'s reunion of knight and steed that the *Orlando* failed to accomplish is almost comically trivial in light of Spenser's larger failure to close out the story of Elizabethan empire. The reunion of Guyon and Brigadore may, in fact, be the only surviving remnant of Spenser's earlier grand ambition to 'ouergo' his predecessor Ariosto.

Ariosto may have failed to reunite Rinaldo with his steed Baiardo, but he did offer an impressive blueprint for how to conclude a dynastic epic (and we are well reminded here that one of his goals was to complete his predecessor Boiardo's sprawling and incomplete epic romance, the *Orlando Innamorato*). In the final canto, the dynastic spouses Ruggiero and Bradamante, predecessors of *The Faerie Queene*'s Artegall and Britomart, solemnize their wedding vows in a pavilion given to Hector by his sister Cassandra. The pavilion, lavishly embroidered with images of the future glory of Ariosto's patron Ippolito, traces a historically and culturally laden path from Priam's Troy to Menelaus's Greece to Cleopatra's Egypt to Agrippa's Rome to Constantine's Byzantium and, finally, to Charlemagne's court. And thus does Ariosto afford his patron a virtuosic accommodation of the *fata Troiana* within a Ferrarese dynastic future.

Like Spenser, Ariosto also wearied of chivalric heroism, becoming increasingly aware of the effects of slander and envy at court. But unlike Spenser, Ariosto strategically quarantines these ills from his epic, confining their corrosiveness to his fragmented *Cinque Canti*, a cynical account of the civil wars, the 'calumnies, betrayals and death' (3.2) that eventually led to the dissolution of Charlemagne's empire from within (Sheers and Quint 1996). A narrative scrap of meat tossed to the hungry dog of history, the *Cinque Canti* is ripped apart by treachery, betrayal, *l'Invidia* ('fraud'), *Sospetto* ('suspicion'), Ganelon's *sciolse la crudel lingua* ('cruel tongue'), Desiderio's uniting of the Bohemians and Hungarians against Charlemagne, and forged letters slandering the *Orlando*'s hero Rinaldo. But none of these events occur until after the *Orlando* has safely secured the *translatio imperii* under the banner of epic dynasty.

Ariosto's Ferrarese epic successor Torquato Tasso, author of the *Gerusalemme Liberata*, also urged that epic poetry sequester itself from current events. At the heart of his epic aesthetics, as meticulously outlined in the 1587 *Discorsi Dell'arte Poetica*, is history—or, more accurately, the representation of a history whose details have receded from the memories of current readers. For Tasso, the subject matter of epic must be historical—not, however, the contemporary *de' nostri tempi* (the immediacy of whose current events resist poetic representation), but rather the history of *tempi remotissimi*. The history of more distant eras affords the most poetic freedom because, quite simply, memory cannot recall it. For Tasso, it is a weak, shadowy memory (*debole ed oscura memoria*) of past history that effectively opens up the aesthetic space for poetic creativity (*gran commodita di fingere*).

That Spenser was aware of the fragmented *Cinque Canti* and of Tasso's warning to keep epic poetry hermetically sealed from current events is evident in the 'Letter to Raleigh', where the poet announces that he has chosen the mythic Arthur as his epic protagonist, a legendary hero strategically positioned 'furthest from the daunger of envy, and suspition of present time'. But by Book VI, Arthur slumbers (perhaps receding into his mythic past) while the 'present time' (or the 'present state') of Ireland consumes Spenser's narrative. The 1596 *Faerie Queene*, offering readers no version of Cassandra's pavilion and leaving the epic as a whole without a conclusion, signals the end of the ambitions of dynastic epic, the Westerly translation of empire that, as Spenser had once promised his readers, would find its final resting place at Elizabeth's court. The venerable *fata Troiana*, the rise of a New Troy in a paradisal island nation in the Atlantic, is interrupted by the fate of Spenser's marginal Ireland, subdued by colonization but stubborn enough to halt the literary history of dynastic epic.

Perhaps Spenser encoded the fragmentation of Ariosto's 'five cantos' within his two 'Mutabilitie' cantos, *The Faerie Queene*'s 'final' cantos. But, echoing Book IV's voice of incompletion, that thought must be left to another place 'to be perfected'.

Bibliography

Alpers, P. (1989). 'Spenser's Late Pastorals'. *ELH* 56(4): 797–817.

Aptekar, J. (1969). *Icons of Justice: Iconography and Thematic Imagery in Book V of 'The Faerie Queene'*. New York: Columbia University Press.

Bennett, J. W. (1942). *The Evolution of 'The Faerie Queene'*. Chicago: Chicago University Press.

Borris, K. (1987). 'Fortune, Occasion, and the Allegory of the Quest in Book Six of *The Faerie Queene'. SSt* 7: 123–45.

—— (2000). *Allegory and Epic in English Renaissance Literature: Heroic Form in Sidney, Spenser, and Milton*. Cambridge: Cambridge University Press.

Burrow, C. (1992). *Epic Romance: Homer to Milton*. Oxford: Clarendon Press.

Canny, N. (2000). 'The Social and Political Thought of Spenser in His Maturity', in J. K. Morrison and M. Greenfield (eds), *Edmund Spenser: Essays on Culture and Allegory*. Aldershot: Ashgate, 107–22.

Carroll, C. (2001). *Circe's Cup: Cultural Transformation in Early Modern Ireland*. Notre Dame, IN: Notre Dame University Press.

Cavanagh, S. (1994). *Wanton Eyes and Chaste Desires: Female Sexuality in 'The Faerie Queene'*. Bloomington, IN: Indiana University Press.

Chamberlain, R. (2006). *Radical Spenser: Pastoral, Politics and the New Aestheticism*. Edinburgh: Edinburgh University Press.

Cheney, D. (1966). *Spenser's Image of Nature: Wild Man and Shepherd in 'The Faerie Queene'*. New Haven, CT: Yale University Press.

—— (2002/3). 'Spenser's Parody'. *Connotations* 12(1): 1–13.

Dolven, J. (2002). 'When to Stop Reading *The Faerie Queene*', in J. Lewin (ed.), *Never Again Would Birds' Song Be the Same: Essays on Early Modern and Modern Poetry in Honor of John Hollander*. New Haven, CT: Yale University Press.

Dunseath, T. K. (1968). *Spenser's Allegory of Justice in Book Five of* The Faerie Queene. Princeton, NJ: Princeton University Press.

Fletcher, A. (1971). *The Prophetic Moment: An Essay on Spenser*. Chicago: University of Chicago Press.

Fowler, A. (1964). *Spenser and the Numbers of Time*. London: Routledge and Kegan Paul.

Fowler, E. (1995). 'The Failure of Moral Philosophy in the Work of Edmund Spenser'. *Representations* 51: 47–76.

Gallagher, L. (1991). *Medusa's Gaze: Casuistry and Conscience in the Renaissance*. Palo Alto, CA: Stanford University Press.

Goldberg, J. (1981). *'Endlesse Worke': Spenser and the Structures of Discourse*. Baltimore: Johns Hopkins University Press.

Gross, K. (1985). *Spenserian Poetics: Idolatry, Iconoclasm, Magic*. Ithaca, NY: Cornell University Press.

Hadfield, A. (1997). *Edmund Spenser's Irish Experience: Wilde Fruit and Savage Soyl*. Oxford: Clarendon Press.

—— and Maley, W. (2000). 'A View of the Present State of Spenser Studies: Dialogue-Wise', in J. K. Morrison and M. Greenfield (eds), *Edmund Spenser: Essays on Culture and Allegory*. Aldershot: Ashgate, 183–95.

Jones, H. S. V. (1919). *Spenser's Defense of Lord Grey*. Urbana, IL: University of Illinois Press.

Kaplan, L. (1997). *The Culture of Slander in Early Modern England*. Cambridge: Cambridge University Press.

Kennedy, W. (1999). 'Spenser's Squire's Literary History', in P. Cheney and L. Silberman (eds), *Worldmaking Spenser: Explorations in the Early Modern Age*. Lexington, KY: University of Kentucky Press, 45–62.

Lewis, C. S. (1936). *The Allegory of Love: A Study in Medieval Tradition*. New York: Oxford University Press.

McCabe, R. (2002). *Spenser's Monstrous Regiment: Elizabethan Ireland and the Poetics of Difference*. New York: Oxford University Press.

MacCaffrey, I. G. (1976). *Spenser's Allegory: The Anatomy of Imagination*. Princeton, NJ: Princeton University Press.

Mallette, R. (1997). *Spenser and the Discourses of Reformation England*. Lincoln, NE: University of Nebraska Press.

Maxwell, J. C. (1952). 'The Truancy of Calidore', in W. R. Mueller and D. C. Allen (eds), *That Soueraine Light*. Baltimore: Johns Hopkins University Press.

Miller, D. L. (1979). 'Abandoning the Quest'. *ELH* 46(2): 173–92.

Neuse, R. (1968). 'Book VI as Conclusion to *The Faerie Queene*'. *ELH* 35: 329–53.

Parker, P. (1979). *Inescapable Romance: Studies in the Poetics of a Mode.* Princeton, NJ: Princeton University Press.

Roche, T. P., Jr. (1964). *The Kindly Flame: A Study of the Third and Fourth Books of Spenser's 'Faerie Queene'.* Princeton: Princeton University Press.

Sale, R. (1968). *Reading Spenser: An Introduction to* The Faerie Queene. New York: Random House.

Schwartz, K. (2000). *Tough Love: Amazon Encounters in the English Renaissance.* Durham, NC: Duke University Press.

Sheers, A., and Quint, D. (trans.) (1996). *Cinque Canti: Five Cantos.* Berkeley: University of California Press.

Silberman, L. (1995). *Transforming Desire: Erotic Knowledge in Books III and IV of* The Faerie Queene. Berkeley: University of California Press.

Spenser, Edmund (1897–1900). *The 'Faerie Queene',* vol. IV, ed. K. W. Warren. Westminster: Archibald Constable.

Suzuki, M. (1989). *Metamorphoses of Helen: Authority, Difference, and the Epic.* Ithaca, NY: Cornell University Press.

Teskey, G. (2003). ' "And therefore as a stranger give it welcome": Courtesy and Thinking'. *SSt* 18: 347–59.

Tonkin, H. (1972). *Spenser's Courteous Pastoral: Book Six of* The Faerie Queene. Oxford: Clarendon Press.

Van Es, B. (2002). *Spenser's Forms of History.* New York: Oxford University Press.

Williams, A. (1967). *Flower on a Lowly Stalk.* Lansing, MI: Michigan State University Press.

Williams, K. (1966). *Spenser's* The Faerie Queene: *The World of Glass.* London: Routledge and Kegan Paul.

CHAPTER 16

FOWRE HYMNES
AND
PROTHALAMION
(1596)

DAVID LEE MILLER

In memory of Richard Helgerson

1596 was a prolific year for Spenser. The six-book *Faerie Queene* appeared in January, followed by two more volumes in the fall: a set of divine hymns and a commissioned piece celebrating an aristocratic double marriage. These were the last works he would publish before his death in 1599.

Spenser had long since established himself as the first major poet in English to use print for the self-conscious fashioning of a literary career. *Fowre Hymnes* and *Prothalamion*, appearing soon after the second installment of *The Faerie Queene*, raise interesting questions about this project. Was the poet, in the closing lines of the epic, abandoning his laureate ambitions? Does *Fowre Hymnes* show him turning from worldly matters to heavenly contemplation, as *The Shepheardes Calendar* had long ago forecast? Does *Two Cantos of Mutabilitie* confirm this retreat, capping the national epic with a meditative hymn? Does *Prothalamion*, intruding the poet's disappointment into his celebration of aristocratic marriage, advertise his political disaffection, echoing the second part of *The Faerie Queene*? Or does it show him rediscovering his vocation, rededicating himself to England's destiny? Critics have answered these questions in different ways, and it is unlikely that a single narrative will become the consensus view.[1] More than one story is in play, and while readers are repeatedly asked to project a role and trajectory for their author, the character of the role and the outlines of the trajectory are held open. *Fowre Hymnes* and *Prothalamion* solicit this kind of speculation.

They do so because they show Spenser as a formal innovator, reminding us why later generations would send their verse to school with 'the poet's poet' (Alpers 1990): generic conventions, stanzas, figures of speech, images, rhythms, and sounds are all for him concrete ways of thinking. *Fowre Hymnes* and *Prothalamion* offer contrasting demonstrations of this gift, but as poetic thinking they also share a common ground in their veiled concern with mourning. This is in many ways a surprising discovery, since neither of the poems is an elegy.[2] But both contain elegiac motifs, and these are thrown into relief by Spenser's decision to republish a third poem—the pastoral elegy *Daphnaïda* (1591)—with the first edition of *Fowre Hymnes*.[3]

GENRE AND PRECEDENT IN *FOWRE HYMNES*

The dedication to *Fowre Hymnes* offers an account of the poems' origins that modern critics tend to dismiss. It seems odd that a poet would involve his patrons in what they, at least, must have recognized as a fiction (and an awkward one at that).[4] If one of the sisters to whom he dedicates the volume really had urged Spenser to 'call in' the earthly hymns because they were too passionate—and if he had really been willing to do so—it is hard to see why he would publish the offending verses along with the heavenly pair made 'in stead'.[5] But if the poems are, as most critics believe, mature compositions that make up an integrated series, then it is equally hard to see why Spenser should go out of his way to disavow the first two with an implausible story about the 'greener times' of his youth. The logic of this 'retractation' waffles from either/or to both/and as he first claims that the celestial hymns replace the earthly pair but then praises the Russell sisters as ornaments 'of all true loue and beautie, both in the one and the other kinde'.[6]

This curious dedication draws attention both to the fabrication of the poet's autobiography and to the structural problem of how the first, 'earthly' pair of hymns is related to the second, 'heavenly' pair. The gesture of renunciation appears again midway through the sequence (*HHL*, 8–22). In this context it registers not as a final judgment but as a perception, tied to its moment in the larger narrative. This larger narrative includes many statements that seem contradictory when placed side by side in the manner of the dedication, but it disposes them into a progression that renders *all* assertions provisional. The scheme for this progression comes from Petrarch's *Trionfi*. Critics studying the 'sources' of the hymns have focused heavily on the philosophical content of the poems (Neoplatonism) at the expense of their literary form, and perhaps for this reason the importance of the *Trionfi* as a generic model has not been fully appreciated. Petrarch's poetic sequence moves from earthly love, or 'Cupiditas', to Eternity. Each triumph conspicuously trumps its predecessor: Chastity prevails over Love, Death over Chastity, Fame over Death, Time over Fame, and Eternity over Time. Each victory also reverses its predecessor's terms, a pattern already apparent when the Roman emperors from whom Petrarch takes the form are displayed as captives in the first triumph.[7]

The reversals that define this progression are highlighted at its midpoint, when after her death Laura returns to the poet in a dream. He asks her *Dimmi pur, prego, s' tu se' morta o viva!* (II.22, 'Tell me, I pray, art thou in life or death?').[8] She answers *Viva son io e tu se' morto ancora | ... e sarai sempre infin che giunga | per levarti di terra l'ultima ora* (II.23–5, 'I am in life, and thou art still in death | ... as thou wilt be until there come | The hour that shall release thee from the earth'). Spenser adopts this reversal of terms while suppressing the event that anchors it for Petrarch.[9] Eliding Laura's death as a literal turning point, he absorbs it into the general mortality of all things. What was for Petrarch, then, an explicit work of mourning emerges in *Fowre Hymnes* as a program of idealization that labors to relinquish all earthly objects in favor of their divine counterparts.

By adding *Daphnaïda* after the close of *An Hymne of Heavenly Beautie*, Spenser in effect reintroduces the death he had elided. This is not the place for an extended discussion of Spenser's unconventional pastoral elegy, but it is worth noting that if the hymns present a work of mourning from which the specific event of death has been subtracted, the elegy presents a death for which all mourning is refused. Combining the poems in a single volume accentuates this contrast, highlighting just that aspect of the Petrarchan intertext which remains latent if the hymns are taken in isolation.

Spenser invokes Petrarch immediately by casting *An Hymne in Honour of Love* as a triumph. The speaker identifes himself as Cupid's captive, offering 'seruice' in hope of favor (*HL* 4–5). Petrarch's speaker had taken up a slightly different position: the *Trionfi* begin on the anniversary of his first glimpse of Laura, which is also the anniversary of her death, but when the grieving speaker falls asleep he enters a dream in which these events are still to come. At first he stands apart from Cupid's triumph, interviewing its captives like Dante's Pilgrim, instructed in his amazement by an unnamed guide. Then Laura appears, and suddenly the dreamer begins to speak *from within* the procession, describing his own suffering. This shift is important because of the way it qualifies his complaint: the description of Laura as *non curando di me né di mie pene, | di sue vertuti a de mie spoglie altera* (II. 122–3, 'careless of me and of my sufferings, | Proud of her power and my captivity') will be contradicted in the Triumph of Death when she confirms that she loved him chastely and sought his salvation. Spenser, locating his speaker among Love's captives from the start, assumes rather than narrates such shifts of perspective, much as he assumes the presence of death without making it an event, but both can be felt throughout his four-poem sequence.

Spenser also fuses the genre of the triumph with that of the sacred hymn.[10] In this form the provisional character of earthly perspectives appears as an artistic dilemma:

how can the mortal artist faithfully imitate a divine object? Sidney, always ready with a phrase, says the sacred poet attempts to 'imitate the inconceivable excellencies of God' (Kalstone 1970: 223). Spenser's strategy for imitating the inconceivable is broadly syncretic. Gathering pagan and Christian materials into a system of fourfold parallels, he creates a progression, situating revealed truth as the ultimate meaning foreshadowed by classical myth. At the same time, this structure inevitably suggests a kind of retroactive equivalence: since *all* human language and imagery fall short of a transcendent deity, even Christian imagery turns out, on close examination, to be the shadowy trace of an inconceivable origin.

    This is the mimetic impasse at the heart of the divine hymn. Spenser, fusing the forms of hymn and triumph, lets the triumph's impulse to narrative and the hymn's mimetic impasse deconstruct one another by turns throughout the sequence. His fourfold structure sets up clear markers of dialectical progression: the hymns move from effect (love) to cause (beauty), and then double this movement in ascending from earthly effects to heavenly causes. At the same time, these indications of progress are set within a common pattern to which each hymn returns: an opening invocation leads to a creation myth, a celebration of the deity, and a closing petition or prayer. Within this pattern, each hymn negotiates the mimetic impasse inherent in the form, and this impasse repeatedly prevents the dialectical progression that organizes the sequence from achieving closure.[11]

MIMETIC IMPASSE AND THE RHETORIC OF RETRACTATION: *AN HYMNE IN HONOUR OF LOVE*

Spenser's rhetorical strategies for negotiating this impasse may once again come from Petrarch, whose final triumph begins with an apocalypse in which verb tenses and all other temporal markers in human language are erased—but then falls back on just these linguistic features to explain that the triumph of Eternity has not yet occurred because it will take place only in Heaven. We come upon similar conundrums early in Spenser's first hymn when the speaker wonders

> who aliue can perfectly declare,
> The wondrous cradle of thine infancie?
> When thy great mother *Venus* first thee bare,
> Begot of Plentie and of Penurie,
> Though elder then thine own natiuitie;
> And yet a chyld, renewing still thy yeares;
> And yet the eldest of the heauenly Peares.   (*HL* 50–6)

These paradoxes look back to the Dedication, where the earthly hymns are chronologically prior—the eldest of the peers, or pairs—but are associated with youthful folly; and they look forward to the Christian mystery of a Son who is both eternal and begotten. They also establish equivocation ('Though ... and yet ... and yet') as the stylistic signature of retractation, the distinctive rhetoric of the mimetic impasse confronted by divine poetry.

Spenser has recourse to this rhetoric often in *Fowre Hymnes*. Before the creation, he says, Love 'through the world his way ... gan to take, | The world that was not till he did it make' (*HL* 74–5). Human lovers also navigate a world that doesn't exist until they create it:

> Thenceforth they playne, and make ful piteous mone
> Vnto the author of their balefull bane;
> The daies they waste, the nights they grieue and grone,
> Their liues they loath, and heauens light disdaine;
> No light but that, whose lampe doth yet remaine
> Fresh burning in the image of their eye,
> They deign to see, and seeing it still dye.   (*HL* 127–33)

These lovers are themselves the authors of their bane. They 'deign' and 'disdaine', choosing which light to see, projecting the image of 'tyrant Loue' (134) in order to portray themselves as victims. The speaker too is caught up in this dynamic of projection and disavowed responsibility, which generates the masochistic terms of the erotic triumph—the psychological and poetic 'world' through which Cupid's self-captivated captives move.

It is a world constituted by narcissism and idolatry. Retractation in *Fowre Hymnes* breaks with these illusions by undoing the closure they depend on. In its simplest form, the movement beyond captivity reimagines torment as the first stage in a narrative of redemption. The speaker explains this to Cupid, comically rationalizing his own distress by offering his captor a hopeful apology for erotic tyranny: 'ere thou doest them vnto grace restore, | Thou mayest well trie if they will euer swerue, | And mayest them make it better to deserue' (164–6). To survive this testing the lover must become a dialectician. Rather than disdain heaven's light in favor of his eye's image, he learns to refine that image (and with it his own mind) to reflect 'heauenly light' (190–9).

Having idealized his beloved, the lover re-enters narrative, imagining dauntless exploits through which to obtain the 'grace' he still lacks (244). But even that conquest leaves him unsatisfied: he wants not just to be loved but to be 'loued best; | And yet not best, but to be lou'd alone' (249–50). Here the fantasy that has served to purify his idolatry and motivate his valor goes badly astray. If projecting a narrative can contextualize the lover's suffering as redemptive, it can just as easily contextualize his success as emperiled. In retrospect, it seems significant that the models of heroic action are all lovers who ended badly: Leander, Aeneas 'in the Troiane fyre', Achilles, and Orpheus. In a compressed instance of retractation as stylistic signature, Spenser describes Orpheus 'daring to prouoke the yre | Of damned fiends, to get his loue *retyre*' (234–50, emphasis added), where 'retyre' means not only returned or brought back, but also withdrawn, departed, or removed.[12] The lover's progress from heroic success to anxious fear and finally loss of the beloved is here telescoped into the alternative senses of a single word.

Idealizing as Unmaking: *An Hymne in Honour of Beautie*

An Hymne in Honour of Beautie revises the first hymn's cosmogony: instead of the fledgling Cupid projecting a world to navigate, we have a 'workmaister' fashioning 'al things' according to 'A goodly Paterne' (*HB* 29–32). For a moment it seems there will be no revision of this master's works, for 'now so faire and seemely they appeare, | As nought may be amended any wheare' (34–5). But the speaker undercuts his assertion in the same breath that utters it: the central predication of the next stanza—'That wondrous Paterne . . . Is perfect Beautie which all men adore' (36, 40)—is woven through with counterstatements in subordinate clauses: 'wheresoere it bee . . . no man may it see', and therefore 'none the same may tell' (36, 38, 42). Eventually the speaker denies that the mystery he is describing has anything to do with 'proportion of the outward part' (75) or that it can reside in 'corrupted clay' (96). The shift from creation to undoing is completed when we learn that everything the workmaster makes 'Shall turne to dust' (98). Beauty will survive, but only because she 'Vnto her natiue planet shall retyre' (103)—a line that tellingly reinscribes the loss of Euridice from *An Hymne in Honour of Love*.

This shift from the act of creation to its undoing reappears when the hymn offers its program of idealizing beauty as a return from the corrupt body to the pristine soul. The 'more refyned forme' created by lovers who enroll in this program *reduces* 'the obiect of their eyes . . . to her first perfection', abstracting it from the body to purify it of natural frailty (211–17). This labor effectively reverses the act of making in which the soul fashions the body, and it therefore bears a suspicious resemblance to the work of death in lines 92–8, associating the culmination of the body's poesis with its complete undoing—the soul's return to 'her *first* perfection'. This link between idealization and death insinuates a certain provisionality, an incompleteness that haunts all acts of making in the hymns, whether the thing made is a world, a body, or a poem.

Because it withdraws from the beloved's presence in the world to her presence in the lover's mind, the discipline of 'pure regard' (212) may not finally escape from either the isolation of Narcissus or the wresting power of the sexual will:

> Thereof he fashions in his higher skill,
> An heauenly beautie to his fancies will,
> And it embracing in his mind entyre,
> The mirrour of his owne thought doth admyre.   (*HB* 221–4)

In the lines that follow, the stylistic signature of retractation asserts both the reality and the unreality of the image in which the lover 'setteth his felicitie, | Counting it fairer, then it is indeede, | And yet indeede her faireness doth exceede' (229–31).

DIVINE NARCISSISM AND THE DEATH OF GOD: *AN HYMNE OF HEAVENLY LOVE*

In *An Hymne of Heavenly Love*, this discipline of 'pure regard' is rewritten as a paradoxical seeing-what-cannot-be-seen. The hymn begins with the speaker's assertion that he'll be able to sing it *if* Love carries him to heaven, 'where I may see those admirable things... | Farre aboue feeble reach of earthly sight' (*HHL* 3–5). The conditional mood here leaves open the possibility that the heavenly hymn's seeing-what-cannot-be-seen will proceed as a singing-what-cannot-be-sung: praise of a deity 'Whose kingdomes throne no thought of earthly wight | Can comprehend, much lesse my trembling verse | With equall words can hope it to reherse' (40–2).

The unresolved problem of narcissism returns along with the mimetic impasse. The earthly hymns both defined love on the basis of sameness, with the result that difference could only be construed as corruption. This is what turns each of the four hymns, sooner or later, from its initial celebration of acts of embodiment to a wishful program for their undoing. *An Hymne of Heavenly Love* begins with this same tautology: 'It lou'd it selfe, because it selfe was faire; | ... and of it selfe begot | Like to it selfe his eldest sonne and heire' (29–31). Purely reflexive love begets a 'firstling... with equall honour crowned' (33–5) in an act of poesis untainted by imperfection.

This act of creation is the divine model the poet-speaker of the hymn cannot 'equall'—but neither can the Maker himself. He still 'loues to get | Things like himselfe', but 'His second broode' is 'not in power so great' (51–3). This inequality secures a degree of otherness that seems to diminish the spectre of Narcissus, but differing from perfection is risky. When it turns out that the Angels dislike their inferiority, their desire to be 'with equall honour crowned' appears as 'greedy bold ambition' (79), and the shift from creation to unmaking has begun: the rebel Angels are damned. Meanwhile the poet's own act of making undoes itself through a rhetoric of retractation that is by now familiar: the Maker, he says, gives his Angels 'the heauens illimitable hight, | Not this round heauen, which we from hence behold' (57–8); and in this heaven-not-heaven, 'they... caroll Hymnes of loue both day and night. | Both day and night is vnto them all one' (70–2). Place is not place and time is not time in this equivocal narrative.

Narrative thus emerges in *An Hymne of Heavenly Love* not, as in the first earthly hymn, to provide a way out of the human lover's entrapment, but to rescue the divine Maker from a similar isolation. Given his eternal perfection, though, narrative can emerge only through acts of making that depart from their model enough to produce *im*perfect beings—beings whose failures will generate the temporality in which narrative can unfold. From this dilemma emerges the human: 'Such he him made, that he resemble might | Himselfe, as mortall thing immortal could' (113–14). Love is still essentially narcissistic—'For loue doth loue the thing belou'd to see, | That like it selfe in louely shape may bee' (118–19)—but insofar as the human exists at all it does so because it also differs utterly, fashioned of 'clay, base, vile, and next to nought' (106).

And yet having revived and restated this conundrum, the hymn breaks with it decisively. Something happens to divine love: as it contemplates fallen humanity it ceases to be a purely reflexive desire for the same (stalked by the spectre of Narcissus), and in an unprecedented transformation, it extends to an object wrested so far from its origin that it lies 'like creature long accurst' (129). Rather than reforming this object to resemble its Maker, Love reforms *itself* in the image of its prostrate creature, descending 'like a most demisse | And abiect thrall' (136–7). In the wake of this reversal, the deep hostility toward creation and the body that has been latent in the motif of undoing rises to the surface in a violent image of destruction:

> And that most blessed bodie, which was borne
> Without all blemish or reprochefull blame,
> He freely gaue to be both rent and torne
> Of cruell hands, who with despightfull shame
> Reuyling him, that them most vile became,
> At length him nailed on a gallow tree,
> And slew the iust, by most vniust decree.   (148–54)

Through this sweeping reversal of roles the deity, having abjected himself in a movement of identification with his antithesis, manages 'To free his foes' (161). At this moment it would seem that the problems of captivity and freedom introduced in the earthly hymns have been definitively resolved.

This reversal transforms the mirroring that has bound like to like in all the hymns. The deity 'nought . . . ask'st in lieu of all this loue, | But loue' (176–7). This call for sameness, unlike the narcissistic 'regard' of *An Hymne in Honour of Beautie*, does not reject imperfection. Instead it imitates the deity's identification with all that is *not* himself, challenging us to love 'our brethren' despite differences in status or wealth (188–210). When mimesis takes as its object not the unknowable *being* of the divinity but his visible *act*, the very principle of imitation is transformed:

> Such mercy he by his most holy reede
> Vnto us taught, and to approue it trew,
> Ensampled it by his most righteous deede,
> Shewing vs mercie miserable crew,
> That we the like should to the wretches shew,
> And loue our brethren; thereby to approue,
> How much himselfe that loued vs, we loue.   (211–17)

The mirroring of language in these lines ('that loued vs, we loue') stands in stark contrast to that of 'Reuyling him, that them most vile became. | . . . And slew the iust, by most vniust decree' (152–4).

UNDOING THE DEATH OF GOD: *AN HYMNE OF HEAVENLY BEAUTIE*

After reaching this breakthrough, the hymn undoes it. We are enjoined to 'read through loue' (224), but in this reading we retrace the contemplative arc of the earthly hymns. It is therefore essentially an *unmaking* of the Incarnation. We are told to re-witness the Cruxifixion and re-experience the wound of love, 'Empierced . . . with pitifull remorse' (247), but this wounding does not lead to love of God's creatures; instead it leads back 'to th'author of thy weale' (256), and as it does the imperative mood gains urgency: 'Thou must him loue . . . | All other loues . . . | Thou must renounce, and vtterly displace' (261–4).

An Hymne of Heavenly Beautie also proceeds through a meditative discipline that undoes the creation by retracing it in reverse. The frame of the universe begins with the elements, rising from earth to fire and finally to the crystalline substance of the spheres, but that 'perfect end | of purest beautie' (46–7) does not complete an act of making. Instead it completes a contemplative return that abandons the creation in favor of its impeccable origin. Moving *against* the principle of likeness that governs the act of creation, the speaker denies comparison, urging us to turn our back on the universe and look at what we *cannot* see because the less we can see it, the more beautiful it must be.

The lines that describe this ascent play repeatedly on the near-homonyms 'faire' and 'farre', a pattern that builds to its climax at the threshold of the godhead:

> These thus in *faire* each other *farre* excelling,
> As to the Highest they approach more neare,
> Yet is that Highest *farre* beyond all *telling*,
> *Fairer* then all the rest which there appeare,
> Though all their beauties ioynd together were:
> How then can mortall tongue hope to expresse,
> The image of such endlesse *perfectnesse*?   (99–105, emphasis added)

In early modern use, 'perfect' still carries a strong sense of completion or of being finished, from its Latin root *perficere*. The paradox of 'endlesse perfectnesse', a flawless completeness that is never completed, thus distills the negative movement on which ascent is based. Such an object may be attained only through negation of everything that can 'there appeare'. The mimetic impasse here reaches degree zero, the vanishing point at which 'far' meets 'fair'. If heavenly beauty cannot be expressed by 'mortall tongue', a mimetic project can never go the distance. And yet the hymn continues, declaring what it has declared to be inexpressible with a tongue that has commanded itself to be silent.

To do so it must reverse the ascent it has just proposed, for God's 'essential parts' are displayed only in his 'vtmost parts' (107–8),

> As in a looking glasse, through which he may
> Be seene, of all his creatures vile and base,
> That are unable else to see his face,
> His glorious face which glistereth else so bright,
> That th'Angels selues can not endure his sight.   (115–19)

This takes us back to where the hymn started: 'Beginning then below, with th'easie vew, | Of this base world, subiect to fleshly eye' (23–4). The mirror in which the lover of the hymn to beauty embraced the image of his own mind now reappears as that in which the lover of heavenly beauty beholds divinity. The 'perfect speculation' (134) of this mirror introduces a combination of etymological puns so dense it seems to contain all the contradictions that have accumulated throughout the sequence. 'Speculation' is both the reflective property of the mirror (*speculum*) and the interpretive activity of the intellect: 'abstract or hypothetical reasoning on subjects of a deep, abstruse, or conjectural nature' (*OED* 6). But how can hypothesis and conjecture guarantee perfection? Luther warns that 'there is nothing more daunger-ous than to wander with curious speculations in heauen'.[13] Evidently the 'high flying mynd' (135) in its approach to God is no less subject to errant imaginings than the jealous lover of the first hymn.

The contemplative ascent in fact undoes itself. Imping the mind's wings with 'plumes of perfect speculation', we are told to fix our eyes on the sun 'like the natiue brood of Eagles kynd' (138). But no sooner have the wings of speculation landed us before the throne of the deity than we are warned *not* to look directly at his face, 'for feare, lest if he chaunce to looke on thee, | Thou turne to nought, and quite confounded be' (146–7). In other words, 'perfect speculation' can never be etymo-logically perfected—cannot reach the end of its narrative—because the final gaze is taboo. The goal of heavenly contemplation, if attained, would annihilate the con-templating mind.[14]

The hymn ends with a prayer from the speaker to his own soul, enjoining it to turn away from everything worldly in a final, decisive retractation. But 'the loue of God, which loathing brings | Of this vile world' (298–9) will do more than place the hymns to earthly love and beauty under erasure, for when it rejects the world once and for all as 'vile', this love is 'reuyling' the means of its own ascent, the substance of the heavenly hymns as well. Undoing the creation in this way is a human desire opposed to the motives of the Incarnation. Perhaps it is ironically appropriate, then, that when the speaker of the heavenly hymn expresses his contempt for the created world, he echoes his own description of the Roman soldiers who crucified Heavenly Love, 'Reuyling him, that them most vile became' (152).[15]

FORM AS THOUGHT

Fowre Hymnes is composed in a seven-line stanza known as rhyme-royal, formally less complex than the *Faerie Queene* stanza or the Spenserian sonnet but sharing with them a distinctive feature of its rhyme-scheme:

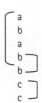

The second b-rhyme in this stanza occupies a pivotal position: it seems to conclude an opening quatrain, but turns out also to begin a couplet. Through this overlapping, the stanza compresses eight lines' worth of rhyming patterns (a quatrain and two couplets) into seven lines. The distinctive effect of this compression is one of delayed closure. As the quatrain seems to complete its pattern—

> Loue, that long since has to thy mighty powre,
> Perforce subdude my poore captiued hart,
> And raging now therein with restlesse stowre,
> Doest tyrannize in euerie weaker part;

—the verse comes to a rolling stop, accelerating again in the second line of the couplet:

> Does tyrranize in euerie weaker part;
> Faine would I seeke to ease my bitter smart . . .

The effect of closure then glides across several lines as the first couplet moves into the second:

> Faine would I seeke to ease my bitter smart,
> By any seruice I might do to thee,
> Or ought that else might to thee pleasing bee.   (*HL* 1–7)

Spenser employs such overlapping patterns in his sonnets, where the opening quatrain similarly modulates into a couplet (abab ➜ bb), which in turn modulates into a second quatrain that glides into a second couplet (bb ➜ bcbc ➜ cc) and then into a third quatrain (cc ➜ cdcd) before closing the pattern firmly with a couplet rhyme that does *not* emerge from the third quatrain:

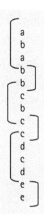

These overlapping patterns fold eighteen lines' worth of rhyming units into the sonnet's fourteen lines, and they offer a variety of ways to slow its movement or suggest a turning back. The *Faerie Queene* stanza likewise overlaps forms to create complex possibilities. It too opens with an 'abab' quatrain leading into a couplet and a second quatrain; unlike the sonnet, though, it closes by repeating the c-rhyme of the second quatrain, prolonging the effect of gliding to a close with the famous alexandrine in its final line:

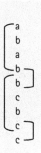

What these forms have in common is the tendency to treat patterns as overlapping rather than discrete, and the related tendency to develop extremely subtle effects based not on the abstract patterns themselves but on the ways in which syntax, phrasing, and rhythm allow the verse to *move through* the patterns. If the sense of delayed closure provides an apt formal analogy to the rhetoric of retractation, so too the delicate varying of movement across several lines of verse, and the light handling of the pauses, effectively conveys the provisional quality of statements always about to be revised.

Similar effects are created by the canzone of the *Prothalamion*. The opening quatrain follows a chiastic pattern (abba) rather than alternating rhymes, so that when it glides into a couplet after the end-stopped fourth line the effect is striking:

> Calme was the day, and through the trembling ayre,
> Sweete breathing *Zephyrus* did softly play
> A gentle spirit, that lightly did delay

> Hot *Titans* beames, which then did glister fayre:
> When I whom sullein care,
> Through discontent of my long fruitlesse stay

As the quatrain retroactively yields a pair of couplets, the trimeter line introduces a surprising variation, in contrast to which the following pentameter, concerned with the poet's 'long fruitless stay', seems that much longer. Across the stanza, patterns surface and subside without achieving dominance. Their interplay is varied in succeeding stanzas, which repeat the pattern established in the opening five lines but then follow with differing sequences of b- and c-rhymes. The overall effect is one of subtle variation within a consistent but complex and flexible pattern. The balance this stanza evokes between hesitation and tentative forward movement will turn out to be at the heart of its subject matter.

'LOUES COUPLEMENT' AND THE WORK
OF MOURNING

Prothalamion begins as its speaker walks away from the royal court, out toward the river Thames. Approaching the river, lost in his own concerns, he is greeted by a vision, first of river nymphs gathering flowers along the banks, and then of two shining swans, who are also brides traveling upstream with the tide to their destination at Essex House, where they will be formally betrothed to their grooms. Around this simple narrative Spenser weaves an extraordinary meditation.

On a first view, *Prothalamion* seems to contrast with *Fowre Hymnes* in almost every way. The hymns are not anchored in history or geography: they unfold in a mythic time and literary space defined by tradition, genre, and rhetoric. *Prothalamion* takes place on an afternoon in late September of 1596, along a particular stretch of the Thames between Greenwich and Essex House. *Fowre Hymnes* is preoccupied with the dynamics of ascent; its prevailing metaphor is winged flight. *Prothalamion* dwells in time and in the world; its prevailing metaphor is the river. And yet these very contrasts imply a connection, for *Prothalamion*'s ambivalent commitment to the world suggests a critique of the impulse central to the hymns, a critique that 'locates the genesis of assertions about eternity in the dream-like urge to abolish time'.[16] Acceptance of time implies acceptance of death, and so Spenser's marriage-song is deeply if implicitly elegiac.[17] In this sense it resolves the antithetical pairing of *Fowre Hymnes* with *Daphnaïda*: the unacknowledged mourning that keeps undoing acts of creation in the hymns, trying to forestall death by performing its work pre-emptively, comes into focus when juxtaposed to the stark refusal of all mourning in Spenser's experimental elegy. Following so closely on these poems, *Prothalamion* appears as a beautifully perfected work of mourning—one in which the lost love-object can finally be recognized as the poet himself.[18]

Prothalamion is an Ovidian poem, in which forms and personae metamorphose into one another like the rhyming patterns that emerge and recede in the progress of the eighteen-line stanza. But its Ovidian spirit is deeply internalized, identified so closely with the voice of the poet that metamorphosis—the central conceit, in which brides-to-be appear as swans—somehow feels less like a visionary flourish than like a condition of existence.[19] Words show a similar fluidity, 'Thames' murmuring *tempus* and 'times', 'brides' gliding into 'birds' and back, 'fowl' turning into 'foul', 'floor' into *flore* and Flora, 'loves couplement' irresistibly suggesting 'love's complement'. The actors and the setting also flow into one another. The flowers are natural objects but also flowers of rhetoric, 'the honour of the field' (74), and as such they link the poet to the place while foreshadowing his praise of Essex, 'Faire branch of Honor, flower of Cheualrie' (150). They are mythic flowers, too, associated with the rapes of Daphne and Proserpina and Chloris, who *became* Flora; so inevitably they are images of virginity about to be lost. Drawing these associations together, they wed the loss of intactness to a fluency of language and imagery that crosses the thresholds of identity.

The poem's other images also work to identify the actors with each other and with the place, combining intimations of loss with hints of cosmic harmony. Swans, like flowers, are a common sight along the river, but they are also a time-honored image of the poet and his song. When the betrothed virgins make their appearance, the metamorphosis identifies them as the creatures of his vision, and so, in a deep gliding movement of the imagination, hints at a universal marriage joining them and the poet to the natural world they all inhabit.

These identifications are most powerful when latent. The psychology of reluctant desire, which Spenser treats extensively in *The Faerie Queene*, surrounds the swans on the river as if it were not an internal state but an attribute of their environment.[20] In the opening lines the full complexity of their desire already is present in the setting and in the movements of the speaker's voice:

> Calme was the day, and through the trembling ayre,
> Sweete breathing *Zephyrus* did softly play
> A gentle spirit, that lightly did delay
> Hot *Titans* beames, which then did glister fayre:
> When I whom sullein care,
> Through discontent of my long fruitlesse stay
> In Princes Court, and expectation vayne
> Of idle hopes, which still do fly away,
> Like empty shaddowes, did afflict my brayne,
> Walkt forth . . .   (1–10)

In the unusual delicacy of its enjambments the verse dilates the connotations of 'play', 'delay', 'stay', and 'vayne'. It embodies varying combinations of reluctance with momentum, heat with tempering coolness, impatience with the wish to delay, the idleness of hope with the restless urge to walk forth.

This mingling of moods, at once internalizing the brides' ambivalence in the movement of the poet's voice and diffusing it 'through the trembling ayre' along the river, gives way to the poem's first, most subtle metamorphosis. A visionary scene unfolds easily from the natural landscape as flowers lead, through familiar associations, to maidens, maidens to bowers, and maiden's bowers to Paramours and bridal days, with the inevitable note of *carpe diem*. All this is at first a hypothetical consideration of what the flowers are 'fit' for, but in the second stanza these notional maidens are transformed into 'louely Daughters of the Flood' (21). The Naiads of the Thames turn back to pluck the blossoms they have emerged from with 'fine Fingers' that are themselves woven into the baskets they carry, 'Made of fine twigs entrayled curiously' (27, 25).[21] The poet's admiration of their handicraft reflects the quiet pleasure he takes in his own, the canzone that so curiously entrails rhymes and rhythms in weaving the scene.[22] The green hair of the nymphs, meanwhile, is unbound 'As each had bene a Bryde', but now the simile sounds conjectural rather than merely hypothetical; indeed, they gather flowers 'To deck their Bridegromes posies' (34) in anticipation of a real bridal day. By these delicate degrees, the subject matter and action of the poem take shape from its 'flowers', those that ornament the meadow and those that flourish in the language describing it.

As this vision unwinds, dark suggestions flicker at its edges like memories of a bad dream. The enjambment of ll. 2–3 suspends 'gentle spirit' in a kind of syntactic limbo: is it an appositive to 'Zephyrus' or the direct object of the verb play? If Zephyrus only *plays* 'A gentle spirit', is his 'play' recreation or impersonation? Is he there at all, 'breathing' the air, or is he merely nominal, a decorative naming of the breeze? These are not idle questions, for it was the god of the western wind who raped the maiden Chloris. Do Spenser's flowers have their roots in this mythology?[23] Proserpina was gathering 'the virgin Lillie' (32) when she was gathered by the god of the underworld. The subliminal presence of these rapes strengthens the sense of reluctance and adds resonance to the refrain, where '*Against* the Brydale day' means 'in anticipation of' and 'in preparation for', but also 'in opposition to'. The poet seems to empathize with this sense of imminent violation; his prayer itself runs softly and 'is not long'. And so if the light touch of the nymphs' 'fine Fingers' evokes an aesthetic self-regard, this refrain evokes by contrast a chastened Orpheus, one whose softened music no longer arrests the river in its tracks, asking it only to pause as his voice pauses, having learned the hard way that he cannot conquer death.[24]

These shadowy thoughts venture into daylight in the movement that discloses the bridal swans:

> Two fairer Birds I yet did neuer see:
> The snow which doth the top of *Pindus* strew,
> Did neuer whiter shew,
> Nor *Ioue* himself when he a Swan would be
> For loue of *Leda*, whiter did appeare:
> Yet *Leda* was they say as white as he,
> Yet not so white as these, nor nothing neare;
> So purely white they were,
> That euen the gentle streame, the which them bare,
> Seem'd foule to them, and bad his billowes spare

> To wet their silken feathers, least they might
> Soyle their fayre plumes with water not so fayre   (39–50)

As Jove's rape of Leda disrupts these lines with adversative clauses, the motif of retractation infiltrates the poem, marking one source of the hesitancy that pervades the opening lines. Purification calls forth the image of rape as its unacknowledged twin, refusing contact with its surroundings in resistance to an imagined contamination. This perception is associated with Narcissus, for the water might have seemed 'fowl' to the birds because it refects their images as 'Fowles so louely' (61), yet because they do not see themselves in their surroundings, the water seems 'foule' instead. This moment is antithetical to the sense of blending identities; yet even here the language blurs the thresholds it is trying to insist on. Like other subjective states in the poem, the fantasy of contamination is not localized: does 'Seem'd foule to them' mean in comparison to them, or in their eyes? The negations that dominate the passage begin with the poet's act of vision—'I yet did neuer see'—before extending into the nevers, nots, nors, and yets that hold contact and comparison at bay in the ensuing lines. The resistance is at once his and theirs.

The river shares this reluctance. He does not want to 'marre their beauties bright, | That shone *as* heauens light' (51–2, emphasis added). In the next stanza this simile will evolve into full-fledged surmise as the nymphs in their wonderment 'sure did deeme | Them heauenly borne' (61–2). Imagining the swans 'Angels or of Angels breede' (66), the nymphs personify the impulse to purification developed at length in *Fowre Hymnes*. Because they do, the speaker can recognize and reject their surmise, drawing his vision back down into a world of eroticized fertility:

> Yet were they bred of *Somers-heat* they say,
> In sweetest Season, when each Flower and weede
> The earth did fresh aray,
> So fresh they seem'd as day,
> Euen as their Brydale day, which was not long.   (67–71)

This turn, embedded in the name 'Somerset', freshens the world by absorbing the heat Zephir sought to 'delay'; as if in response, the refrain substitutes 'Euen' for 'Against', linking the season and the swans to their bridal day through a freshness 'that to the sense did fragrant odours yield' (75).

Accepting the beauty of a floral world, the narrator must accept its brevity: 'So fresh they seem'd as day . . . which was not long'. That which is soon to come will soon be past, and so the refrain tempers celebration with elegy. The simile comparing Thames to Peneus in the vale of Tempe revives the intimations of rape, for this was the landscape through which Apollo chased Daphne. But the chase has a different ending now: the waters 'appear through Lillies plenteous store, | Like a Brydes Chamber flore' (81–2). Two of the nymphs then crown the swans with garlands, a modestly triumphal gesture that lifts the scattered flowers off the bedroom floor, converting the sign of defloration into a crown.

These connotations are confirmed in the song 'one did sing' (87). Addressing the swans as 'the worlds faire ornament' (91), the singer marries them not just to their bridegrooms but to the world, for 'ornament' betokens not merely a decorative accessory but a universal harmony, hinting at a wedding of the cosmos.[25] Love's 'couplement' (95) is its 'complement', that which fulfills and perfects it. The verbs are optative, enclosing a wish for the future 'which is not long' (107) within a past 'which was not long' (89, 125). The seventh stanza expands this song into the world around it as first the other nymphs and then the 'neighbor ground' (112) echo the refrain; even the mute river pantomimes 'his glad affection' by 'making his streame run slow' (117–18), granting a wish the landscape has expressed. This expanding movement is completed as the other birds of the river are drawn into the procession, 'enranged well' (122) in another sign of natural harmony spreading through the scene.

Stanzas eight and nine move toward closure. The poem's 180 lines will bring the restless poet around 180 degrees, but the city to which he returns is not the court on which he turned his back. In place of 'idle hopes' the poet finds nurturing memories: 'mery London, my most kyndly Nurse, | That to me gave this Lifes first natiue sourse' (127–8). Contact with his source renews the speaker's sense of himself: in the next lines he goes from passive recipient to active agent, seizing and affirming a public identity: 'from another place *I take my name*, | An house of auncient fame' (130–1, emphasis added).[26] The speaker returns to this public world along with his brides-to-be, arriving where not only swans but 'bricky towres...on *Themmes* brode aged backe doe ryde' (132–3). This change of scene expands the poem's horizons and with them its sense of loss, which reaches back now to 'the Templer Knights' who occupied the Inner Temple at the Inns of Court (133–6). It also personalizes loss in the death of Leicester (137–9), returning the poet to his point of departure, his 'freendles case' at court (140). It signals an approaching conclusion, for the 'stately place' where Leicester once dwelt is the destination of the swans' progress, where 'Olde woes' are replaced by 'ioyes to tell' (142).

The ninth stanza turns expansive as the poet links the joys of the brides with the prospects of the nation. His praise of Essex echoes the praise of the swans, 'the worlds faire ornament, | And heauens glorie' expanding into 'Great *Englands* glory and the Worlds wide wonder' (91–2, 146). The optative mood returns in a series of parallel wishes for the confounding of enemies, the redounding of joys, and the blessing of Venus or Elisa. Spenser's pun on the brides' family name (Somerset/summer's heat) finds its complement in the happiness promised by Essex's surname (Devereux/ *devenir heureux*, 'to become happy', 153–4). The flowers cast before the swans, 'the honour of the field' (74), are recalled in the praise of Essex as 'Faire branch of Honor, Flower of Cheualrie' (150), and the 'Brydale day' itself expands to include Accession Day, which commemorated the Queen's 'marriage' to her kingdom (Norton 1944). The suggestion that on this day 'some braue muse may sing | To ages following' (159–60) is strikingly muted in contrast to the rest of the stanza. The confidence of the optative mood ('Which may your foes confound, | And make your ioyes redound', 105–6) gives way to a more diffident subjunctive: 'some braue muse' *may* sing, and if so it *may* be Spenser's, but the mood of *may* has altered subtly in the interim.

In this close the poet's betrothal to his *Faerie Queene*, the epic project that defined his career, remains equivocal. To a lesser extent, the same is true for the swans as they turn into brides. Essex 'descended' from 'high Towers' (166, 163) to greet them, and the poet compares him in descent not to the sun that has illuminated the procession but to the evening star. The bridegrooms in his train are like 'the twins of *Ioue*' (173), but this is an equivocal image. Visually it may suggest 'twins of *love*', but mythically it harks back to the rape of Leda just when that memory should be forgotten, and its glance at the destiny of the twins in the constellation Gemini, while invoking the brilliance of the night sky, does so like the image of Hesperus, intimating that this betrothal is an ending. The poet affirms 'their Loues delight' (176) in subdued tones, tempering celebration with elegy to the end.

The distinctively personal note of sadness in this poem has troubled critics over the centuries who are uneasy with its decorum, but the extraordinary fluidity which this sadness is absorbed into the scene and motives of celebration is precisely what defines the poem's achievement.[27] The swans in their progress upstream toward the city, serenaded by the poet's song, harbor another image latent in the refrain: that of Orpheus, singing his own swan song as his severed head floats down the river to the sea.[28] Spenser always knew how to hear it; in an early sonnet, known only from a fragment quoted by E. K. in *The Shepheardes Calender*, he says 'The siluer swan doth sing before her dying day | As shee that feeles the deepe delight that is in death' (*October*, gloss to 90).[29] Evoking this deep delight so pervasively without ever naming it is a remarkable piece of tact, one that rests on a fully perfected work of mourning for the poetic career and identity Spenser worked all his life to construct.

NOTES

I am grateful to Patrick Cheney for helpful comments on an earlier draft of this essay. *SSt* 24 (2009), which appeared after the present essay went to press, features illuminating work on *FH* by Ayesha Ramachandran, Richard McCabe, Kenneth Borris, Gordon Teskey, and Jon Quitslund.

1. On Spenser's conscious fashioning of a literary career, see especially Helgerson (1983), Cheney (1993), and Rambuss (1993).
2. The seminal analysis of mourning and its companion concept melancholy (or depression) is Freud (1955). Sacks (1985) uses this account of mourning as the basis for a theory of the English elegy.
3. Thanks to Cathy Blose of the University of Alabama for calling my attention to this publication history, which may have something to do with Ralegh's return to court and Arthur Gorges' petition for the wardship of his daughter Ambrosia. See Gibson (2004) and Sandison (1928) for details on the context of the elegy's initial publication and on the situation that prevailed in late 1596. For *Daphnaïda* see Chapter 12 above.
4. It also seems odd that he would address Anne Russell, widow of the first Earl of Warwick, as 'Marie Countesse of Warwicke'—not an embarrassment on the same scale as botching the sequence of dedicatory sonnets to *The Faerie Queene* in 1590, but still a curious oversight from a poet courting patronage among the surviving members of the Leicester faction.
5. I cite the text from Spenser (1999) throughout; the introduction and headnotes to individual poems in this edition are particularly astute.

6. On the peculiarities of the dedication, see Oates (1983) and Bieman (1988). I discuss 'retractation' in Miller (1988), 11–14, 88–92. See Ellrodt (1960), 14, on the conventional nature of such recantations.

7. Petrarch's more immediate source is the triumphal appearance of Beatrice at *Inferno* 29.

8. Neri et al. (1951), 524; English translation from Wilkins (1962), 61.

9. Spenser's strategic suppression of Laura's death exemplifies a form of intertextuality that recent criticism elaborates under the name 'transumption'. See especially Barkan (1991), 41–8.

10. On the hymn as literary genre, see Cheney (1993), 201–5; Welsford (1967), 37–8; and Rollinson (1969, 1971).

11. For further discussion of the dialectical structure governing *Fowre Hymnes*, see Miller (1988), 76–82.

12. Spenser's unusual use hovers between adjectival and adverbial. For the relevant verbal senses, see *OED* 'retire' (verb) senses 4 and 3a.

13. *Commentary on Galatians*, trans. Vautrollier (1575), cited in *OED* s.v. 'speculation', sense 5.

14. For a very different reading of how contemplation works in the hymns, see Rogers (1983), 184–202.

15. For a sharply contrasting reading of the hymns as representing 'a unified expression of a developing personality', see Oates (1983).

16. Berger (1965), 516. Berger is referring to a specific moment in the fourth stanza, but his comment applies to the poem as a whole. My account of *Prothalamion* is indebted throughout to this seminal essay.

17. See Greene (1957), Dubrow (1990). Spenser's *Prothalamion* is related to this genre but distinguished from it as etymologically 'toward' rather than 'upon' the wedding day.

18. Insofar as this 'poet himself' is not just a personal identity but a public role (as Cheney (1993) in particular urges), the sense of loss, too, must extend beyond the poet to the nationhood he has envisioned. On the sense of historical loss as fundamental to the antiquarian project of defining the origins of an English nation, see Escobedo (2004), Ch. 2.

19. *Prothalamion* perfectly exemplifies what Leonard Barkan observes about *The Faerie Queene* and the Renaissance more generally: 'what most essentially characterizes the Renaissance is a metamorphic aesthetics' in which 'the true connective tissue . . . is the poetic technique itself' (Barkan 1986: 242).

20. See Berger (1965), 514–16.

21. Compare the visual technique in Botticelli's *Primavera*, which hints at a merging of identities by letting Chloris's 'hands reach behind the flowers that decorate the garment of the new Flora' (Wind 1958: 115).

22. On the baskets as images of poetic form, see Fowler (1975), 65–6.

23. The 'goodly greenish locks' of his nymphs at l. 22 may mark them as daughters of Chloris, whose name derives from the Greek *khlōrós* pale green (cf. E. K., gloss to *Aprill* 122: 'Cloris the name of a Nymph, and signifieth greenesse'). For Ovid's version of the myth, see *Fasti* 5.193–214. For Neoplatonic interpretations of the myth, see Wind (1958). On the more general relation of flower imagery in the poem to 'myths of rough sexual capture', see Fowler (1975), 62–3.

24. See Hollander (1987); the quoted phrase appears on p. 18.

25. For ornament as 'cosmic image', see Fletcher (1964), 108–17.

26. The poet does not give his name directly, in contrast to his etymological play on 'Somerset' and 'Devereux' (see below).

27. Broadly speaking, this mingling of sadness and celebration corresponds to a characteristically Spenserian blurring of the difference between ending and beginning; see Miller (2003).

28. On the complexities of Orpheus as a humanist culture hero, see Cain (1971), esp. 42; Loewenstein (1986), 302.

29. Cf. the 'snowie Swan' of *The Ruines of Time*: 'There he most sweetly sung the prophecie | Of his owne death in dolefull Elegie' (590, 594–5). Andrea Alciato had declared the swan *insignia poetarum*, 'the badge of the poets', in his highly popular *Emblematum Libellus* (1534); in an amplification of Alciato's motto in his *Choice of Emblemes* (1586), Geffrey Whitney adds that the swan 'as it were by skill devine, with song foreshowes his ende' (Emblem 126). See Shire (1978), 175. Spenser may also be remembering Plato's fable that Orpheus chose to be reincarnated as a swan specifically because his soul remembers the Maenads with such fierce resentment: 'He saw one soul choosing the life of a swan; this had once been the soul of Orpheus, which so hated all womankind because of his death at their hands that it would not consent to be born of woman' (Cornford 1945: 620a). Thanks to Andrew Escobedo and Jon Quitslund for calling my attention to this passage.

BIBLIOGRAPHY

Alpers, P. (1990). 'poet's poet'. *SE*, 551.

Barkan, L. (1986). *The Gods Made Flesh: Metamorphosis and the Pursuit of Paganism*. New Haven, CT: Yale University Press.

—— (1991). *Transuming Passion: Ganymede and the Erotics of Humanism*. Palo Alto, CA: Stanford University Press.

Bellamy, J., et al. (eds) (2003). *Imagining Death in Spenser and Milton*. New York: Palgrave Macmillan.

Berger, H. Jr. (1965). 'Spenser's *Prothalamion*: An Interpretation', *Essays in Criticism* 15: 363–79; rpt. in A. C. Hamilton (ed.), *Essential Articles: Edmund Spenser*. Hamden: Archon, 1972, 509–23.

Bieman, E. (1988). *Plato Baptized: Towards the Interpretation of Spenser's Mimetic Fictions*. Toronto: University of Toronto Press.

Cain, T. (1971). 'Spenser and the Renaissance Orpheus', *UTQ* 41: 22–47.

Cheney, P. (1993). *Spenser's Famous Flight: A Renaissance Idea of a Literary Career*. Toronto: University of Toronto Press.

Cornford, F. M. (trans.) (1945). *The Republic of Plato*. New York: Oxford University Press.

Dubrow, H. (1990). 'epithalamium'. *SE*, 250–1.

Ellrodt, R. (1960). *Neoplatonism in the Poetry of Spenser*. Geneva: Librarie E. Droz; rpt. Folcroft, 1975.

Escobedo, A. (2004). *Nationalism and Historical Loss in Renaissance England: Foxe, Dee, Spenser, Milton*. Ithaca, NY: Cornell University Press.

Fletcher, A. (1964). *Allegory: The Theory of a Symbolic Mode*. Ithaca, NY: Cornell University Press.

Fowler, A. (1975). *Conceitful Thought*. Edinburgh: Edinburgh University Press.

Freud, S. (1955). 'Mourning and Melancholia', in *The Standard Edition of the Complete Psychological Works*, vol. XIV, trans. James Strachey. London: Hogarth, 239–58.

Garber, M. (ed.) (1987). *Cannibals, Witches, and Divorce: Estranging the Renaissance*. Baltimore: Johns Hopkins University Press.

Gibson, J. (2004). 'The Legal Context of Spenser's *Daphnaida*', *RES* NS 55(218): 24–44.

Greene, T. (1957). 'Spenser and the Epithalamic Convention'. *CL* 9: 215–28.

Helgerson, R. (1983). *Self-Crowned Laureates: Spenser, Jonson, Milton, and the Literary System.* Berkeley: University of California Press.

Hollander, J. (1987). 'Spenser's Undersong', in M. Garber (ed.), *Cannibals, Witches, and Divorce: Estranging the Renaissance.* Baltimore: Johns Hopkins University Press, 1–19.

Kalstone, D. (ed.) (1970). 'An Apology for Poetry', in *Sir Philip Sidney: Selected Poetry and Prose.* New York: Signet.

Loewenstein, J. (1986). 'Echo's Ring: Orpheus and Spenser's Career'. *ELR* 16: 287–302.

Miller, D. (1988). *The Poem's Two Bodies: The Poetics of the 1590* Faerie Queene. Princeton, NJ: Princeton University Press.

—— (2003). 'Death's Afterward', in J. Bellamy et al. (eds), *Imagining Death in Spenser and Milton.* New York: Palgrave Macmillan, 185–99.

Neri, F., et al. (eds) (1951). *Francesco Petrarca: Rime, Trionfi, e Poesie Latine.* Milan: Ricciardi.

Norton, D. (1944). 'Queen Elizabeth's "Brydale Day"'. *MLQ* 5: 149–54.

Oates, M. (1983). '*Fowre Hymnes*: Spenser's Retractations of Paradise'. *SSt* 4: 144–5.

Rambuss, R. (1993). *Spenser's Secret Career.* Cambridge: Cambridge University Press.

Rogers, W. (1983). '"Perfect Speculation" in Spenser's *Fowre Hymnes*', in *The Three Genres and the Interpretation of Lyric.* Princeton, NJ: Princeton University Press, 184–202.

Rollinson, P. (1969). 'The Renaissance of the Literary Hymn', *Renaissance Papers 1968*, ed. George Walton Williams. Southeastern Renaissance Conference, 11–20.

—— (1971). 'A Generic View of Spenser's *Four Hymnes*'. *SP* 68: 292–304.

Sacks, P. (1985). *The English Elegy: Studies in the Genre from Spenser to Yeats.* Baltimore: Johns Hopkins University Press.

Sandison, H. (1928). 'Arthur Gorges, Spenser's Alcyon and Ralegh's Friend'. *PMLA* 43(3): 645–74.

Shire, H. (1978). *A Preface to Spenser.* London: Longman.

Welsford, E. (1967). *Spenser: Fowre Hymnes, Epithalamion, a Study of Edmund Spenser's Doctrine of Love.* New York: Barnes and Noble.

Wilkins, E. (trans.) (1962). *The Triumphs of Petrarch.* Chicago: University of Chicago Press.

Wind, E. (1958). *Pagan Mysteries in the Renaissance.* New York: Norton; rev edn 1968.

CHAPTER 17

··

A VEWE OF THE PRESENTE STATE OF IRELAND (1596, 1633)

··

ELIZABETH FOWLER

First Appearances

··

A manuscript of nearly 70,000 words (now the Bodleian Library's Rawlinson B 478) entitled '*A vewe of the presente state of Ireland discoursed by waye of a dialogue between* Eudoxus *and* Irenius' was entered in the Stationer's Register on 14 April 1598 by Matthew Lownes, who would go on to publish many volumes of works by Edmund Spenser beginning in 1609. *A Vewe* was not, for reasons still unclear, printed during Spenser's lifetime, but the registered copy and some twenty-one other manuscript witnesses of the work survive. The number suggests a busy circulation. The witnesses date from between 1596 and the first third of the seventeenth century; none are in Spenser's own hand.[1] The circulation of *A Vewe* was much expanded by Sir James Ware's 1633 print publication in Dublin and London of a somewhat expurgated *A view of the state of Ireland, written dialogue-wise betweene Eudoxus and Irenaeus, by Edmund Spenser Esq. in the yeare 1596* in a volume that collected prose by Edmund Campion, Meredith Hanmer, and Henry Marleburrough, annotations by Ware, and a number of Spenser's poems. There are two title pages for the volume that carry the titles *The historie of Ireland* and *Tvvo histories of Ireland* (STC 25067a and 25067, respectively).

TOPICS AND ARGUMENTS

The dialogue is spoken between two characters; Eudoxus interviews Irenius, who has recently arrived from Ireland, as the first lines announce. (Most manuscripts agree in setting the dialogue rather vaguely in England by means of the deictics 'here' and 'there'.) Eudoxus wishes to know why Ireland has not yet been reformed and asks to have the causes in the faults of the government's previous 'plottes' (policies) revealed (43).[2] Irenius promises to recount the 'moste Capitall' evils that commonly occur 'bothe in the liefe and Condicions of private men And allsoe in the menage and [managing of] publike affaires and policye' (45). This division of ethic and politic recalls a similar division in Spenser's 'Letter to Ralegh', and announces an ambition to see the state of Ireland as one that requires a sense of everyday life as well as political history. Irenius agrees to cover three major topics: evils in the laws, evils in customs, and evils in religion; in sum, 'the abuses and inconveniences of that governmte' (146). The odd, old word 'inconveniences' means fundamental structural problems and unsuitabilities rather than minor irritations (see Anderson 2000 for a sense of the word's valence). These three topics make up the first part of the work. Irenius then turns to the second part of the dialogue (from 146), nearly as long as the first, which offers 'the meanes to Cure and redresse' those faults. Irenius does not fancy himself a designer of original policy recommendations, but rather a collector and reporter of overheard 'Consvltacions and accions of euerye wise gouernour and Counsellor whom I haue somtymes harde [heard] treate heareof' (230).

In early English systems of knowledge these three topics—laws, customs, and religion—correspond to three important *kinds of law*: prescriptive law, customary law, and ecclesiastical law. Much space is given to the first (45–75, 75–81), about the same to the second (81–136), but the third receives only a few pages (136–42). The second is the most difficult for modern scholars to see as a kind of law, yet local custom was considered to have the force of law. Local custom was in theory to be enforced by the common law courts unless it conflicted with the king's law.[3] The Gaelic system of Brehon law was occasionally backed by the king's courts in Ireland, and this was justified by treating it as customary law.[4] This rather anthropological view of law, that it arises through customs that, as Irenius says, 'followe the difference of nacions and people' (97), is part of an interesting attempt to produce a cultural analysis of the present political situation. Indeed *A Vewe* can be seen as primarily addressing the legal institutions or constitution of Ireland, the country's 'state' broadly and philosophically conceived, in addition to its present state understood as 'condition'. At the end of the conversation and the book, Eudoxus expresses the hope that on some future occasion he will be able to consult Irenius on the topic of Ireland's antiquities or authorities (the word varies in the manuscripts). The importance of this topic is evident already in *A Vewe*. While much martial history is mentioned by the speakers, they clearly believe that a material history of Ireland and its arts is an important companion topic to that of the description of its constitutional crisis. One imagines Spenser planning to delve more deeply into Gaelic sources and stories in a Yeatsian project of antiquarian and poetic interest. But the promised companion dialogue is not left to us, perhaps because Spenser was prevented by death. And though Spenser expresses his interest in Gaelic sources, he exhibits, as Richard McCabe suggests (2002), rather less engagement with them in *A Vewe* than we might have hoped.

The structure of the dialogue, then, is straightforward and easily indexed. The two men think English common law to be good in itself but ill-suited to the Irish people and situation. They bemoan the prevalence of the Irish 'Brehon law', which continued in practice as the late medieval submission of the Irish lords to the English Crown failed to solidify and expand the scope of English institutions with the passing of generations. Irenius describes Brehon law as vile (for instance, in that it allows for financial settlements rather than executions in the case of murder, 47) and as unjustly hierarchical (in that such settlements may benefit the head of the sept, or clan, more than the aggrieved parties, 48). The history of Irish submission to the English sword and its frequent unravelings is told in broad strokes by Irenius, who draws attention not only to military history but also to the system of Gaelic succession called *tanistry* as two means by which fealty to the Crown had been undermined. He explains how trial juries, the prosecution of accessories to felonies, wardship, land conveyancing, palatinate grants, distraint, and other cherished common law rights and actions have become corrupted in Ireland. Two statutes recognizing the ancient customs of 'Coigny and Liuery' (78) and of 'kincongishe' (80) are also described and decried.[5] Eudoxus delivers a provocative undersong of comparison between the conquests of England and those of Ireland that allows Irenius to distinguish the two. English law ought not, it seems, be established throughout the island, at least until its people are irrevocably transformed. This is a principle in marked contrast, for instance, to the later view of James's attorney general for Ireland, John Davies, expressed in his *A Discoverie of the True Causes Why Ireland was neuer entirely Subdued, nor brought vnder Obedience of the Crowne of England, Vntill the Beginning of His Maiesties happie Raigne* (London, 1612). Davies proposes there that people can be (and that many have been) made into good citizens of the Crown through their containment by and recourse to common law. For both Davies and Spenser's Irenius, the goal is the reform of the people to suit English institutions of government. Irenius declares that law should be suited to the disposition and manners of a people, or else produce a perhaps unintentional injustice (53–4). Tougher laws, he maintains, will only deplete the population without reforming it (69). This principle paradoxically goes on to justify martial law and the use of abrupt and brutal force throughout *A Vewe*.

Thus the customs of the Irish are interesting to Irenius from many angles: they must be taken account of to effect reform, they are crucial to an understanding of the disposition and manners of the people, and they have a legal history that must be reckoned part of any strong apprehension of the constitution. As does the theorist of poetics Philip Sidney in his *Defense of Poesy*, Irenius distinguishes his approach from that of a chronicler or historian (54). And indeed the history that appears in *A Vewe* is organized around an analysis of the state or present constitution of Ireland that preserves this double emphasis on institutions and what we would now call culture. In one of the most interesting passages in the dialogue, Irenius sketches a series of hypotheses about the customs of the Irish that might clarify their affiliation with other European peoples:

> with comparison of times likenes of manners and Customes Affinytie of wordes and names properties of natures and vses [practices, habits] resemblaunces of rightes and Ceremonies monimentes of Churches and Tombes and manie other like circumstances I doe gather a likelyhode of truethe, not certainlye affirminge anye thinge but by Conferringe of times nacions languages monimentes and such like I doe hunte out a probabilitye of things which I doe leaue vnto your Iudgement to beleeve or refuse. (84–5)

These arguments are sometimes taken to be trumped-up insults with the goal of discrediting any Irish claim to a historical tie with Catholic Spain, and indeed they do labor to sever the Spanish connection. Yet Irenius is far too curious and interested to make that a sufficient explanation, and methodologically (if not ideologically) his statement anticipates what we now call cultural studies.

The entire section on custom is fascinating, if occasionally repugnant, in its vivid accounts of contemporary life in Ireland. Irenius decries evil in both English and Irish customs, and is particularly interested in the reproduction and transmission of culture: nation or 'race' (which is malleable enough here to be contagious), cattle-keeping, language, grooming and dressing habits, marriage and fosterage, occupations (especially types of soldiers and bards), political assemblies and finance, and modes of property holding.

The pages on evils in religion (136–42) are vicious in their denunciation, but few. This is because, according to Eudoxus, it makes sense to achieve peace and quiet in civil matters before attempting reforms in ecclesiastical matters. The physician should come before the priest to attend to a greatly diseased person: so it is, says Irenius, in the state of a realm (139).[6] The old aphorism is odd and even threatening here, in that its priest follows the physician only to administer last rites, whereas Irenius apparently means to say more hopefully that efforts at conversion must wait for political stability. Many such images and metaphors and analogies are offered to the reader throughout the dialogue, and literary scholars especially have been intrigued by their logic and politics (e.g., Grennan 1982, McCabe 2001). Then, before Irenius turns to the second half of the dialogue and the litany of cures, he provides a somewhat hesitant coda bemoaning corruption in private men and, especially important and sensitive, in governors. The text seems aware of taking political risks, which it surely was, and unwilling to go beyond a certain degree of explicitness.

The second half of the dialogue (146–231) offers policy recommendations together with historical, philosophical, strategic, and financial justifications of them. There are references to recent events and to the policies of recent governors and the Crown. Most of this half of the dialogue is dedicated to Irenius's delivery of his 'plot', or strategic plan, offered for the consideration of present and future administrations. The distinctions among kinds of law that were crucial from the beginning largely disappear as the first half of the dialogue is left behind, and an essentially military strategy tries to integrate reforms to institutions, persons, and customs, often at the explicit expense of persons. Irenius takes an unabashedly tough military line here, with the uncomfortably familiar proposal that with a strong commander's free hand, enough troops, and plenty of money the war will be efficient and short-lived, saving lives and money in the long run. 'The ende will I assure me be verye shorte' (158);

And this I assure my selfe will demaunde no longe time but wilbe all finished in the space of one yeare, which howe small a thinge it is vnto the eternall quietnes which shall theareby be purchased to the realme and the greate good which shall growe to her maiestie shoulde me thinkes readelye drawe on her highnes to the vndertakinge of the enterprize. (174–5)

It is likely that this sadly perennial fantasy had, at the time, the capacity to both attract and outrage that it continues to have in the present.

As we are increasingly disabused of the expectation, raised by the first half of the dialogue, that a reform of Ireland must be a reform undertaken through law, Eudoxus stands in for the reader in the plaintive voicing of the question: 'Howe then doe ye thinke is the reformacion thereof to be begonne yf not by Lawes and Ordinaunces'? This is answered by Irenius in the bracing way that the logic of the whole will proceed: 'Even by the sworde. for all those evills muste firste be Cutt awaie by a stronge hande before anie good Cane be planted, like as the Corrupte braunches and vnholsome boughes are firste to be pruned and the foule mosse clensed and scraped awaye before the tree cane bringe forthe anye good fruite' (147–8). And such is the plan; the orchard of Ireland must be defoliated and replanted. After an initial call for the submission of all rebels is given proper time for response, those continuing in rebellion are to be reduced to starvation and waste. Once they are utterly subdued, another call for submission is to be issued. Those who refuse will starve; those who 'come in' to the English victors are to be separated from their septs (kinship and political clans) and dispersed to far parts of the country to become tenant farmers who will answer to English landlords. They will take on new trades and new surnames according to their qualities or occupations and relinquish the names of their people. Ultimately, they will blend with the communities of English, achieving:

an vnion of manners and Conformitye of mindes to bringe them to be one people, and to put awaie the dislikefull Conceite bothe of thone and thother which wilbe by no meanes better then by there enterminglinge of them, that neither all the Irishe maye dwell togeather, nor all the Englishe, but by translatinge of them and scatteringe them in smalle nombers amonge the Englishe, not onely to bringe them by dailye Conuersacion vnto better likinge of eache other but allsoe to make bothe of them lesse hable to hurte. (211–12)

Remember that though the tract is critical of the Old English communities, it has an interest in reforming them to suit the ideas of the new settlers Spenser may be counted among. An impression of even-handedness is gained from his position against both the 'Old English' and the 'mere Irish', but it is a polemical (rather than fair) position easily situated in the new colonial milieu (see Canny 2003).

An idealized agrarian, English-style commonwealth is aimed for, and the means of achieving it are shocking. Irenius defends his plan to bring the Irish to civility against an implicit charge of genocide, which he makes explicit just as it begins to haunt the reader's mind:

ffor by the sworde which I named I doe not meane The Cuttinge of all that nacion with the sworde, which farr be it from me that euer I shoulde thinke soe desperatlye or wishe soe vncharatablie: but by the sworde I meante the Royall power of the Prince which oughte to stretche it selfe forthe in her Chiefe strengthe to the redressinge and Cuttinge of all those evills which I before blamed, and not of the people which are evill: for evill people by good ordinaunces and government maye be made good/ but the evill that is of it selfe evill will never become good. (148)

Despite this sense of the moral malleability of the Queen's Irish subjects, and despite the promises of peace reached quickly which his name seems to signify, Irenius proposes a continuing presence for martial law in the position of the 'prouoste marshall', whose job it is to roam the countryside looking for loose persons ('Carrowes, Bardes Iesters or suche like') who have not found a place in the civil commonwealth, subjecting them (on the principle captured by the American felony sentencing policy 'three strikes and you're out', only this time it's two) to 'the bitternesse of marshall lawe', which we may presume to be death (219).[7] The independence of the 'prouoste marshall' will, Irenius hopes, protect the commonwealth from corrupting its sheriffs. We may recognize that the proliferation of legal jurisdictions here and elsewhere in his plan seems continually to bely Irenius' promise of peace.

But back to the means: to war. Irenius's plan requires the establishment of garrisons—forts with large numbers of troops—in strategic positions throughout the country. He prescribes locations, numbers of troops, and financial arrangements. After the country is settled, the garrisons and some remaining troops will be maintained by a tax on the inhabitants of the surrounding lands, lands which will have been divided up and named according to English landholding custom into hundreds, boroughs, shires, and counties. The plan combines force and nomination, testifying to the power of language. The English must sever by the sword all social ties that have threatened the administration and then reshape and remove survivors who will be given new names, new kinship networks, new obligations to new authorities, and new political geography.

As this schematic plan is unrolled by the dialogue, other topics are inserted frequently. These are important judgments of contemporary personages and events and have occupied scholars more closely than the plan itself, which is hypothetical and so, in the absence of its implementation, harder to assess. The virtues of some Lord Deputies are contrasted with the vices of others, and strategies are offered for success against the Crown's current enemies the Earl of Tyrone and Feagh Mac Hugh. The first interjection is a defense of Arthur Grey, fourteenth Baron Grey de Wilton, who suceeded Henry Sidney (father of the poet Philip) as the Crown's Lord Deputy in Ireland in 1580. Spenser arrived in Ireland with Grey as secretary to the new Lord Deputy and stayed on in other posts after Grey was removed from his post in 1582. Looking back on that intense period of war from a standpoint over a decade later, Irenius believes that Grey's strategies would have been effective had they been allowed to come to fruition. The defense is precipitated by the topic (indeed, the proposal) of famine and a now infamous description of the province of Munster's sufferings under Grey. As so often in the allegory of *The Faerie Queene*, a reversal of agency occurs and the horrific famine that fells the rebellion has been brought upon the people by themselves: 'in shorte space theare weare non allmoste lefte and a moste populous and plentifull Countrye sodenlye lefte voide of man or beaste, yeat sure in all that warr theare perished not manie by the sworde but all by the extreamitye of famine which they themselves had wroughte' (158). All this waste became mere waste, squandered, the two interlocutors agree, when Grey's tactics were decried as bloody and he was prevented from completing the reform at which he aimed. The people he had destined to be 'reformed subjects' were allowed to slip back into their state of rebellion by the Queen's pity and mercy, qualities which had been, Irenius claims, wrongly provoked by Grey's detractors.

It is against such detraction that Irenius then defends the Lord Deputy's execution in November 1580 of some six hundred Spanish and Italian troops and their followers (161–2). They were captured in the promontory fort Dún an Óir or Fort D'Oro at Ard na Caithne or Smerwick in the far West of Kerry, the territory of the rebel Earl of Desmond. After a successful siege, a quizzical Eudoxus reports, the late Grey was said to have acted especially cruelly either by promising life or by raising hope of it. Irenius seeks to verify his respondent defense of Grey with the claim, 'my selfe beinge then neare as anye', which scholars have sometimes taken both as evidence that Irenius stands for Spenser himself and also that Spenser was at Smerwick. That he was there is confirmed by an account of the incident in a letter from Grey to the Queen in Spenser's hand signed 'In campe at Smer{wic}k the xij of November 1580' (*SP* 63/78/29, Burlinson and Zurcher 2008: 22). By Irenius's account, still indignant some sixteen years after the event, it was appropriate that Grey denied his victims hope, refusing to allow them to leave their arms and escape with their lives (which they pled according to the custom of war and law of nations), on the charge that 'they weare not anie lawfull enemyes'. They carried, Irenius says, no commission from the Spanish king or the Pope. In fact, as Spenser knew, they had been sent by Pope Gregory XIII and one of the Spanish king's governors to assist in the rebellion of the Munster Geraldines, the Earl of Desmond and his followers.[8] Grey's letter to Walsingham of the same date says that commissions from the Pope were found in the fort (*SP* 63/78/30, Zurcher and Burlinson 2008: 25). As elsewhere, Irenius plays down the religious issue, arguing that the Irish rebels themselves were traitors, not lawful enemies, and thus the besieged soldiers were not entitled to negotiate terms. In the event, the Lord Deputy offered the surrendered troops the choice of submission; they unconditionally submitted, and Grey, according to John Hooker's account in Holin-shed's *Chronicles*, ordered Captains Walter Ralegh (like Spenser, then in his late twenties) and Humphrey MacWorth to see the soldiers were put to the sword and the followers hung. A few were interrogated, tortured, and hung (Burlinson and Zurcher 2008: 13; Quinn 1947: 33–4). It seems some of the captured were to be ransomed; Grey's letter says that six hundred were slain, but 'Those that I gaue lyfe vnto, I haue bestowed vpon the Capteines & gentlemen' (Burlinson and Zurcher 2008: xxvii, 19). Irenius argues that slaughter was necessary to prevent the Irish rebels from being emboldened by an act of mercy and thus taking comfort from the appearance of foreign aid; he cites too the importance of preventing the troops from joining with Desmond's forces. Grey was far from Dublin, lacked reinforce-ments, and had been badly defeated only a few months before at the battle of Glenmalure in the Wicklow Mountains south of Dublin. Elizabeth's government had long feared the possibility of a Spanish invasion of England through Ireland. Imperatives aside, it was surely a crushingly savage event, as were many others Spenser must have witnessed in his years in Ireland. Even today, skeletons reportedly continue to be uncovered by storms in the area, and there is more that archeologists might do (Lister 2004). The massacre became a motive for Grey's early recall to England after only two years of service; it became an infamous act of bad faith in Irish historiography, and in 1980 a monument to the slaughtered with a Gaelic inscription was erected on site in honor of the four hundredth anniversary of the killing.

A general policy, then, of achieving civility and lawfulness through brutality and actions reaching above and beyond the common law (not to mention the received canon law) is the theme and platform of *A Vewe*. The principle is paradoxical, and in my view quite unsupportable, but *A Vewe* is conscious of its costs, is aware of its contradictions, observes the form of moral reasoning, and seems passionately heart-felt and studiously thought through. It is a plan for converting the country from the rule of oppressive, warring regional Irish chieftains to the oppressive, warring, centralized rule of the English Crown. *A Vewe* insists on promoting a cultural transformation that evinces interest in the legacy of Gaelic Irish traditions while nonetheless proposing their extinction. Yet it is not a scheme primarily designed to steal the wealth of the country, advance purely partisan interests, or cater to the lowest common denominator of popular or elite feeling. Nor is it a short-term plan for victory that ignores the future or the larger aims not only of pacification but of the goods held by political philosophers to be worth attaining. It proposes what seems to be an unviable military project on the basis of faulty and dangerous moral reasoning. It is a remarkable project of thought, nevertheless, in that it opens up a range of topics and questions about government that remain unsettled and urgent in many parts of the globe. How can laws, customs, and religions be assessed and organized in a heterogeneous nation? How can a mixed population be fit to the institutional arrangements of government? How should law respond to that fit? What is the proper relation between constitutional justice and the goals of war?

KINDS, ANALOGUES, INFLUENCE

The form of the dialogue is crucial to this effect of opening up topics, as is the mismatch between the first half of the dialogue, concerned with kinds of law, and the second half with its military strategy and political institutions. The dialogue form holds together a text that is a mix of genres, disciplines, sources, and influences. In this sense it is unsurprising as an entry in Spenser's bibliography. It was a very common form: John Day cites over one hundred and twenty dialogues composed or published during Elizabeth's reign (1990: 217; see also Cox 1992). The mix of genres Spenser incorporates in the dialogue results in interesting difficulties for us. For instance, those who wish to treat it directly as a 'plat' or strategic plan run into trouble, because it is fictional and dialogic. On the other hand, its character as a polemical, policy-oriented scheme makes it difficult for those who wish to read it as humanist philosophical inquiry. My discussion of the topics of A Vewe may have made it seem more transparent than perhaps it truly is, because those topics are taken up in such a mixed form.

One dialogic 'kind' or genre we might compare to A Vewe is the philosophical dialogue on civility, one of the primary themes of A Vewe as well as The Faerie Queene. As an example, consider one in which Spenser appears as a character: A Discourse of Civill Life, written by his friend Lodowick Bryskett and published in 1606. Bryskett sets to Englishing Giovanni Battista Giraldi Cinthio's moral treatise Tre dialoghi della vita civile, restaging it (together with like bits by Alessandro Piccolomini and Stefano Guazzo) in a symposium near Dublin of philosophically minded friends who are named and easily traceable. The decades-long connection between Bryskett and Spenser can be traced to the Sidney circle, which had a primary influence on Spenser's work and career. Spenser's interest in moral philosophy is the shaping structure of The Faerie Queene, which is famously discussed by the inter-locutors, and here the dialogue form is similarly tied to the working out of an interface between ethics and 'civil life' or political society. An important question about the proper relation between the customs and characters of peoples and the shapes of their government drives and organizes much of A Vewe. In Bryskett's dialogue and its sources we find an intellectual context for that question as well as a way to connect the aims of A Vewe to those of The Faerie Queene.

Of course, tracts on Tudor colonial policy in Ireland and in the New World deserve careful scrutiny in conjunction with A Vewe, and have received some. As historians have long noticed, many English adventurers, like Walter Ralegh, sought lucrative positions in Ireland only to extend themselves next to the New World. And among those who stayed, many wrote. Spenser's was not the only humanist treatise to come out of the Munster Plantation, and, as Bradshaw (1988), Highley (1991), and others have shown, the others may be fruitfully compared with A Vewe. They are the dialogue Solon His Follie, or a Politique Discourse Touching the Reformation of Common-Weales Conquered, Declined or Corrupted, written in 1594 by Richard Beacon, the royal attorney for Munster during the time that Spenser was Clerk of the Council there, and a treatise by William Herbert, another undertaker in the plantation, a sometime official, and the cousin of the former (1551–2) Lord Deputy James Croft, entitled *Croftus, sive, de Hibernia Liber* (1591). The *Dialogue of Sylvanus and Peregrine* (1598) also bears mention here, though it is oriented more toward other provinces than Munster, especially because the interlocutors bear the names of Spenser's sons (see Maley 2003: 69–71; pp. 101–2 above). Works not quite so close to Spenser's in their composition but kin nonetheless include tracts by Philip Sidney, Robert Payne, John Derricke, Barnabe Rich, Fynes Moryson, and John Davies.

The legal structure and theme of the first half of Spenser's dialogue might remind us that the common lawyer Christopher St German composed a 1523 Latin *Dialogue* on the relation of kinds of law. The *Dialogue* was republished in English in 1531 as *Doctor and Student*. In that form it became a standard text for the education of lawyers for some two centuries. The conversation between a doctor of the canon law and a student of the common law probes parallels and differences in their areas of expertise, taking up questions like the status of divine law and the law of nature, the grounds of the law of England, the technical and institutional meanings of conscience, equity, reason, and the like. It's expository, but also exploratory and dialectic in what Frederick Pollock saw as a scholastic tradition of thought (1900: 432). Spenser's interest in comparison through the first half of *A Vewe* seems designed with this kind of jurisprudential thought as a model. He seems influenced as well by the works of the political theorist Jean Bodin, including the notion of universal history expressed in *Methodus ad facilem historiarum cognitionem* (1566).[9] That text too is concerned with the relations among kinds of law, types of government, and the histories of peoples, and it demonstrates methods of reasoning and evidence that were of interest to Spenser.[10] In this same vein, but sharing in a contagious humanist impulse toward antiquarianism and historiography, Spenser cites Johannes Boemus (*Mores, Leges, et Ritus Omnium Gentium*, 1541) and Olaus Magnus (*Historia de Gentibus Septentrionalibus*, 1555). They are all writers who consider legal history to be part of an anthropological project that forms a bridge between medieval natural law theory and the modern law of nations.

Indeed, *A Vewe* stands as an important example of the nascent discipline of anthropology (see Hodgen 1964). It draws on the twelfth-century Irish books of Gerald of Wales, as most writers on Ireland do, but also heavily on the Scottish history of George Buchanan and the English of William Camden and Raphael Holinshed: this comparatist interest in ethnography distinguishes it from chronicle (65) and its frankness about suffering from travel writing. It pays a newly precise attention to concerns that are still those of our contemporary field anthropologists: kinship structures, institutions of power and cultural production, habits of dress, sexuality, class structure, language, demography, race, the rituals of fosterage, marriage, mourning, and so forth. What we now rightly understand as the racism of the text is in part a product of this turn in discipline. The text articulates a vexed moral assessment of the consequences of this knowledge for scholars, politicians, and the military in a loud anticipation of what will later come to be the central issues of the discipline. On the other hand, this learning drives toward a plan of social engineering that is rightly, I think, condemned as immoral and that is easily seen to be in tension with Spenser's celebration, in *The Faerie Queene*, of the political virtues of friendship, justice, and courtesy.

A *Vewe* is an important text in part because it theorizes race and coloniality at the very beginnings of their modern forms. That it does this in a heavily comparatist framework that includes the earlier history of the subjection of England to colonial expansion from the Continent is perhaps a self-justifying gesture but also a scholarly collation of evidence necessary to develop a rigorous examination of the relation of forms of government to the characters of their citizenries. This is a topic that would come to grip the thinkers of the Enlightenment and, for instance, the participants in the debates behind the American constitution. That Spenser saw some form of 'race' as crucial to this discussion is, in sum, a mark of his modernity. At its heart, A *Vewe* is deeply worried about the question of the fit between culture and the political institutions of government. This requires a more sophisticated sense of the practice and reproduction of civility and citizenship than that developed by political philosophers who ignore anthropological and pedagogical questions entirely in favor of idealized and abstract notions of what shape a government must take in order to be just. Yet Spenser comes perilously close, in both A *Vewe* and *The Faerie Queene*, to advocating what we would term genocide (Fowler 1995).

A *Vewe* influenced English policy through such important conduits as Arthur Chichester, owner of a manuscript, who was appointed Lord Deputy in 1604, and Spenser's admirer John Davies, attorney-general for Ireland (d. 1626). The powerful statesman Thomas Egerton (d. 1617) indexed his copy in his own hand, commenting too in the margins. Other owners included the herald and sometime diplomat Henry St George (d. 1644) and the civil lawyer and government official William Trumbull (d. 1716). A *Vewe* was recommended as a guide for the governance of Ireland to both Oliver Cromwell and Thomas Wentworth (Lord Deputy 1632–40), and was highly regarded by John Milton. It evoked a record of complex response among Irish thinkers and writers that has been illuminated by Richard McCabe (2002). The dialogue is one of the most important pieces of political theory written in English before Thomas Hobbes's *Leviathan*, and it is particularly important because it addresses profound questions about the relations of government to the governed and of the common law to culture and customary law, not from the perspective of Westminster, the point of view that historians of political thought have best chronicled to date, but from the vexed standpoint of the colonial war in Ireland. Old English, Sythians, Anglo-Normans, Scots of several kinds, Irish of many admixtures, new colonists and undertakers, Protestants, Catholics, Continentally trained churchmen, the members of particular septs, regional and local peoples, townspeople, palatinate elites, bureaucratic careersmen, and military men of different kinds—the list goes on—all these swirled in Spenser's sense of human geography and its history. In recent years this standpoint on the margins of many cultures has begun to be appreciated generally for the central place it occupies in early modern events and thought.

AUTHORSHIP

It is important to note that a number of the extant manuscripts are subscribed by the initials 'E. S.', though there seem to be no manuscripts that contain Spenser's full name in the hand of their primary copyists (I have not yet held them all in my hands).[11] There is no record of early controversy about Spenser's authorship, and the native Dubliner James Ware, an accomplished historian as well as the text's first print editor, had no doubt about it. His own father came to Dublin in 1588 in the entourage of the Lord Deputy William FitzWilliam and lived there until his death in 1632. They were certainly in a position to know of, or even to know, Spenser. There has never been an ascription of *A Vewe* to any author other than Spenser. Questions about Spenser's authorship of *A Vewe* were raised by Jean Brink in a series of articles beginning in 1990; her skepticism has been countered by numerous scholars, most publicly the prolific Spenserians Andrew Hadfield (1991), Willy Maley (1997: 191), and Richard McCabe (1999). I add my own voice to theirs here, as elsewhere, on the basis of the reasoning and evidence presented.

Whatever one thinks of the appearance of the initials E.S., which are contemporary to the earliest manuscripts and strongly suggestive of our man if not fully definitive in themselves, it remains to be established which attribution of the text to the full name of Edmund Spenser is earliest. It is certainly false that there is none before Ware's. The Bodleian Library's MS Rawlinson B 478, the copy submitted to the Register in 1598, is inscribed twice by John Panton, who writes the title and '1596 by Ed: spenser gent.' at the beginning of the first page of the discourse. Panton was from 1594 at Lincoln's Inn (his overleaf signature includes 'Lincoln') as one of a group of Sir Thomas Egerton's men that included John Donne and John Davies, both of whom were, like Panton, secretaries to Egerton and, of course, learned readers of Spenser's poetry as well as men trained in the law (511–12 n).[12] So Panton moved in well-informed circles and likely would have known people who knew Spenser. In the Inn's Register he is written down as of co. Denbigh; a John Panton with property in Denbigh who left 'only three daughters' (thus was not Panton's father, but himself) was buried in Westminster Abbey in March of 1619, fourteen years before Ware's print edition appeared (Chester 1876: 115). Egerton himself (1540?–1617) owned and personally annotated another copy of *A Vewe*, now preserved in the Ellesmere papers at the Huntington Library. Panton's persuasive ascription of *A Vewe* to Edmund Spenser may date from quite near the text's entry in the Register; in fact, the signature on 1R, just above the title of the text, reads 'Io panton 1596'. Though Nicholas Canny has found that infrared light exposes us to uncertainty about the numeral 6, which may have been altered, the entire headnote strongly suggests that 'E. S.' was understood by his contemporaries to signify 'Edmund Spenser'. At the very least, it gives us a credible early attribution.

In addition to contemporary ascriptions, of course, there are other assessments of authorship. It can be by allusion: the 1598 *Dialogue of Sylvanus and Peregrine* echoes the topics and dialogue form of *A Vewe* while using the names of Spenser's sons for its interlocutors. Richard McCabe has drawn our attention to the fact that a 27 March 1657 letter from Oliver Cromwell to his deputy in Ireland describes a petition to him from Spenser's grandson William in which Edmund's writings 'touching the reduction of the Irish to civility' are blamed for bringing on him 'the odium of that nation' (2002: 284–5). This seems a clear echo by William of the opening lines of *A Vewe*, designed to appeal to Cromwell's knowledge of Spenser's authorship. A growing number of scholars have noted internal evidence in resonances between *A Vewe* and Spenser's poetry. Its patterns of allusion and imagery and lexicon are compatible with what we know of Spenser's learning and habits of style. The beginnings of our knowledge of its circulation suggest a pattern of reception by poets on the one hand and political strategists on the other (see, e.g., Maley 1993). The treatise has been examined as the product of the mentality of the 'New English' settler community by a number of historians, led by Nicholas Canny, and has been found to suit Spenser's place in his historical moment. In sum, according to standard criteria such as lack of contradictory evidence, history of attribution, style, content, reception, and historical context, the identification of Edmund Spenser as the author of *A Vewe* dates from near the composition of the text and remains quite secure. This is especially true in comparison with our suitably low thresholds for the attribution of other contemporary texts to their authors. Spenserians are to be grateful to Professor Brink nonetheless for her calls for closer textual investigations, long needed in the case of *A Vewe*.

EDITIONS

Demands for a proper scholarly edition of Spenser's prose dialogue begin at least as far back as 1805, when Sir Walter Scott proclaimed the importance of *A Vewe* (*Prose*, ix). Ware's 1633 edition served as the basis for many subsequent print versions and is thought to be based on a lost manuscript (*Prose*, 523). It was more than two centuries before another editor, Richard Morris, made use of manuscript sources; he based the useful 1869 Globe Edition on the British Library's Add. MS 22022, checked against Ware and Harley MSS 1932 and 7388 (Morris 1893: iv). Alexander Grosart's *Works* (1882–4) used Lambeth Palace Library MS 510. Twentieth-century editions that rely on more than one manuscript include W. L. Renwick's series (based on the Bodleian Library's Rawlinson B 478 and the Gonville and Caius MS, with eight other MSS consulted, in three editions: as part of the Oxford *Works*, 1930–2, in a separate *View*, 1934, and in a modern spelling version, 1970), as well as the monumental 1949 *Variorum* prose volume edited by Rudolf B. Gottfried. Gottfried worked with manuscript preparation by Ray Heffner that included a transcription of the Huntington Library's Ellesmere 7041 together with variants from fourteen other manuscripts and the Ware print edition. Andrew Zurcher's online transcription of Gonville and Caius

College manuscript 188/221 at http://www.english.cam.ac.uk/ceres/haphazard/vewe/veweindex.html now provides Spenserians with important access to the work; Risa S. Bear prepared an online version of Grosart's 1894 edtion, checked against Renwick, that is usefully searchable (http://www.uoregon.edu/~rbear/veue1.html). The 1809 reprint of Ware's *View* (1633) was the source for the convenient, affordable text edited by Andrew Hadfield and Willy Maley for Blackwell in 1997. Still, a full scholarly collation of the known manuscripts and the early print editions and a thorough annotation and indexing of the text await completion (and are now underway for Oxford University Press). Despite its astonishingly long and continuous print history, *A Vewe* has been relatively inaccessible to students and scholars who require significant literary and historical annotation to make sense of its numerous references to classical, Gaelic, medieval, and Renaissance sources, as well as contemporary events. The language itself is an easily mastered early modern English, but the allusions and specialized jargon come thick and fast.

CRITICAL HISTORY AND READINESS

The earliest uses of *A Vewe* are yet to be traced in the circulation of its manuscripts; work remains to be done on their early locations and ownership. In 1633, James Ware positioned the text within the historiography of Ireland by printing it together with antiquarian treatises by Edmund Campion and Meredith Hamner. Research is needed on the circulation of these early print copies as well as that of the manuscripts; it could provide an interesting piece of the larger history of English political strategy in Ireland and its other colonies. We have a late manuscript only recently discovered by Christopher Ridgway in the archives of Castle Howard. It's likely that *A Vewe* remained a 'brief' on Ireland for acting statesmen well into the last third of the seventeenth century, and it is possible that more early copies languish unknown in private collections. Where the *Variorum* editors knew fifteen, we now know of some twenty-two fragmentary or complete manuscripts. I would welcome further news from readers, especially regarding manuscripts in private hands.

Since the appearance of the *Variorum* an enormous amount has been added to our knowledge of sixteenth-century Irish history, so that many obscure references in *A Vewe* can now be clarified. The work of D. B. Quinn inspired an explosion in the investigation of early modern Ireland and the colonial administration there, and many important articles and books have followed his lead. One of the pivotal scholarly events of the 1980s was a series of articles in which Nicholas Canny and Ciarán Brady exchanged views on Spenser's work in the pages of *Past and Present*. Not only early modern historians of Ireland and England, but scholars working on colonial and post-colonial topics in other periods and regions (an ever larger group) have come to regard *A Vewe* as a document of high importance. Reviled and occasionally beloved by Irish (and Scottish) nationalists for centuries, it has a rich history of citation that would bear further study. *A Vewe* promises further to be an as yet unmined trove of early modern jurisprudential and political thought. Earlier historians of ideas neglected it, perhaps because it does not focus on England, Italy, or France. Instead, it attempts to consider an ideal polity under the conditions of a mixed cultural population, and is thus potentially more urgent and interesting to our own contemporary political thinking than the work of writers such as John Fortescue, Thomas More, Thomas Smith, or Thomas Hobbes.

Similarly, of course, *A Vewe* has been catapulted to the center of literary discussions of Spenser and of the English Renaissance. With the revival of historicism among Renaissance scholars at the end of the last century, *A Vewe* came to be required reading. If there were a reliable citation index in literary criticism, *A Vewe* would be seen, in the past twenty years, to have rocketed up the scale.[13] Students of the literature of colonial America and the trans-Atlantic early modern world have also come to see its importance as both a product of and precursor to ethnographic writing about the New World and to discussions of English policy in all its efforts of expansion (e.g., *Prose*, 86 n).

When in *Areopagitica* Milton writes that Spenser was a better teacher than Aquinas (1985: 729), he was referring to the scheme of ethics and political philosophy that structures *The Faerie Queene*. In *A vewe of the presente state of Ireland*, that philosophy is tested, brought into confrontation with a particular historical moment, and refashioned in the resulting heat. Having just published two installments of what many consider to be the most important English national epic, in *A Vewe* Spenser is at the height of his powers, his anxieties, and his ambitions for nation, historiography, and culture. He has the canon of political philosophy in mind in addition to the statute books, and frequently refers to such 'anciente Aucthours' (86) as Aristotle, Caesar, Cicero, and Virgil, as well as more recent theorists and historiographers such as Bodin, Machiavelli, Boemus, Erasmus, Camden, Holinshed, Buchanan, and Llwyd. In *A Vewe* the topics of constitutional, customary, and ecclesiastical law and policy are brought out from behind the 'dark conceit' of Spenser's allegory, and faced in an elegant, moving, sometimes chilling example of the Renaissance prose dialogue.

FUTURE DIRECTIONS

A Vewe begs further work in many directions. We would benefit from an informed assessment of it within the tradition of the Renaissance dialogue (English, Continental, classical) and from attention to its fictionality. Further work on its responsiveness to and interaction with Gaelic Irish history and literature is needed, as is further attention to its relations with its analogues from the colonial writers in English. Its pervasive allusions await clarification, as do its uses of specialized lexicons. It requires situating in the history of race, historiography, anthropology, jurisprudence, political philosophy, rhetoric, and military history. More collation with *The Faerie Queene* and Spenser's shorter poems will illuminate its place in Spenser's thought and literary production. Research into its circulation in manuscript and print promises to enrich our sense of the functions and uses of literature in social and political history. This is a text that will reward our interest and attention for many more centuries.

Notes

1. Internal evidence has led to scholarly consensus that *A Vewe* was composed in 1596 (*Prose*, 503–5). I'd like to express here my gratitude to Andrew Zurcher and Richard McCabe for their contributions to this work.
2. All quotations from *A Vewe* are cited by page number from *Prose*, unless otherwise specified. All material in square brackets is my addition.
3. The most well-known example of the common law's toleration of custom is perhaps *gavelkind*, where inheritance is divided equally among male heirs rather than according to primogeniture. This custom was practiced widely in England before the Norman Conquest and retained in Kent; it was also found in early modern Ireland and Wales.
4. An example can be seen in 'Ancient Pleadings' of Irish Chancery, Parcel A, Item 76. See K. W. Nicholls, 'Some Documents on Irish Law and Custom in the Sixteenth Century', *Analecta Hibernica* 26 (Dublin: Irish University Press for the Irish Manuscripts Commission, 1970): 103–43, and Margaret McGlynn, 'Equitable Jurisdiction in the Irish Chancery Court', (MPhil thesis presented to the National University of Ireland, University College, Dublin, May 1990).
5. '"Coyne (coign, coigny) and livery" was a phrase derived from the Irish word *coinnmheadh* or "guesting" and the English word "livery", meaning something handed out, in this case corn and straw for horses (as in the term "livery stables"). Together the words described a system of billeting used by Irish and Anglo-Irish lords in later medieval Ireland, whereby the lord's gallowglass and kern, his "chief" horses and their grooms, his huntsmen with their hounds, and his other employees were quartered on his tenants or subjects, exacting from their hosts not merely food and lodging but often the money for their wages also.' '"Kincogish" (Ir. *cin comocuis*, "the offence of a kinsman") is a term referring to the liability of a kinsman to pay compensation if an offender has evaded payment or has been unable to pay. Similarly, it was possible to distrain a kinsman if pressure could not be brought on a defendant directly. Because this principle by which kinsmen were contingently liable for each other's offences was strange to Anglo-Norman settlers, it was known by the Anglicized Irish term "kincogish".' S.v. 'coyne and livery', 'kincogish' in S. J. Connolly (ed.), *The Oxford Companion to Irish History.* Oxford University Press, 1998.
6. See the metaphor's appearance in the opening pages of the dialogue and Herbert (1591).
7. This is the one point upon which the ever judicious D. B. Quinn concludes that Spenser 'displayed wanton cruelty' (1990: 714).

8. In the 12 November letter to the Queen (*SP* 63/78/29, Burlinson and Zurcher 2008: 18), Grey reports (in Spenser's hand) his vehemently anti-Catholic response that their commissioning by evil commanders aggravated their wickedness.

9. On the pervasive legal and political thrust of Spenser's work, including connections between St German on equity and Spenser's experience in chancery as well as Spenser's engagement with Bodin (including his more frequently cited *Les Six livres de la République*, 1576), see the richly historical and theoretical Zurcher (2007).

10. See, for example, *Prose*, 278 n 12; see also Baker (2001), 51–9.

11. First print publications of Spenser's poetry seldom include an attribution to his full name; his earliest publications, in *A Theatre*, *The Shepheardes Calender*, and *Letters*, lack his name entirely; the title pages of the 1590 and 1591 printed works read 'by ED. SP.'. Nine of the seventeen dedicatory sonnets to *The Faerie Queene* are signed 'E. S.'; the others are unsigned.

12. John Donne succeeded Davies, joining Panton in Egerton's inner circle of secretaries (Knafla 2003: 44).

13. See the bibliographies by Willy Maley in various print locations and on the Spenser Home Page at http://www.english.cam.ac.uk/spenser/bibliography.htm for an authoritative, evolving list of works on *A Vewe*.

BIBLIOGRAPHY

Anderson, Judith (2000). '"Better a Mischief than an Inconvenience": The Saying Self in Spenser's View: Or, How Many Meanings Can Stand on the Head of a Proverb?', in Patrick Cheney and Lauren Silberman (eds), *Worldmaking Spenser: Explorations in the Early Modern Age*. Lexington: University Press of Kentucky, 219–33.

Baker, David J. (2001). 'Historical Contexts: Britain and Europe', in Andrew Hadfield (ed.), *The Cambridge Companion to Spenser*. Cambridge: Cambridge University Press, 37–59.

Beacon, Richard (1594). *Solon His Follie*, ed. Clare Carroll and Vincent Carey. Binghamton, NY: Medieval and Renaissance Texts, 1996.

Bradshaw, Brendan (1988). 'Robe and Sword in the Conquest of Ireland', in Claire Cross, David Loades, and J. J. Scarisbick (eds), *Law and Government Under the Tudors: Essays Presented to Sir Geoffrey Elton*. Cambridge: Cambridge University Press, 139–62.

Brady, Ciarán (1986). 'Spenser's Irish Crisis: Humanism and Experience in the 1590s'. *Past and Present* 111: 17–49.

Brink, Jean (1990). 'Constructing the *View of the Present State of Ireland*'. *SSt* 11: 203–30.

Bryskett, Lodowick (1606). *A Discourse of Civill Life*. London.

Buchanan, George (1582). *Rerum Scoticarum Historia*. Edinburgh.

Burlinson, Chrisopher, and Zurcher, Andrew (eds) (2008). *Edmund Spenser: Selected Letters and Other Papers*. Oxford: Oxford University Press.

Canny, Nicholas (1988). '"Spenser's Irish Crisis": A Comment'. *Past and Present* 120: 201–9.

—— (1983). 'Edmund Spenser and the Development of an Anglo-Irish Identity'. *YES: Colonial and Imperial Themes* 13: 1–19.

—— (2003). *Making Ireland British: 1580–1650*. Oxford: Oxford University Press.

Chester, Joseph Lemuel (ed.) (1876). *The Marriage, Baptismal, and Burial Registers of the Collegiate Church or Abbey of St. Peter, Westminster*, Publications of the Harleian Society, Vol. X. London: Mitchell and Hughes.

Cox, Virginia (1992). *The Renaissance Dialogue: Literary Dialogue in its Social and Political Contexts, Castiglione to Galileo*. Cambridge: Cambridge University Press.

Davies, John (1612). *A Discoverie of the True Causes Why Ireland was neuer entirely Subdued, nor brought vnder Obedience of the Crowne of England, Vntill the Beginning of His Maiesties happie Raigne*. London.

Day, John T. (1990). 'Dialogue, prose'. *SE*, 217.

Dean, Leonard F. (1942). 'Bodin's *Methodus* in England before 1625'. *SP* 39(2): 160–6.

Fowler, Elizabeth (1995). 'The Failure of Moral Philosophy in the Work of Edmund Spenser'. *Representations* 51: 57–86.

Grennan, Eamon (1982). 'Language and Politics: A Note on Some Metaphors in Spenser's *A View of the Present State of Ireland*'. *SSt* 3: 99–110.

Grosart, Alexander B. (ed.) (1882–4). *A Veue of the Present State of Ireland*. Vol. IX of *The Complete Works in Verse and Prose of Edmund Spenser*. London: Hazel, Watson, Viney.

Hadfield, Andrew (1991, printed 1998). 'Certainties and Uncertainties: By Way of Response to Jean Brink'. *SSt* 12: 197–202.

—— (2002). *Shakespeare, Spenser, and the Matter of Britain*. Basingstoke: Palgrave Macmillan.

—— and Maley, Willy (eds) (1997). *Edmund Spenser: A View of the State of Ireland*. Oxford: Blackwell.

Herbert, William (1591). *Croftus, sive, de Hibernia Liber*, ed. Arthur Keaveney and John A. Madden. Dublin: Irish Manuscripts Commission, 1992.

Highley, Christopher (1991). *Shakespeare, Spenser, and the Crisis in Ireland*. Cambridge: Cambridge University Press.

Hodgen, M. T. (1964). *Early Anthropology in the Sixteenth and Seventeenth Centuries*. Philadelphia: Pennsylvania University Press.

Knafla, Louis (2003). 'The Years with Sir Thomas Egerton', in David Colclough (ed.), *John Donne's Professional Lives*. Cambridge: D. S. Brewer, 37–71.

Lister, David (2004). 'Massacre victims from Raleigh's time return to haunt Irish shore'. *The Times*, April 13. [Online]. Available at: http://www.timesonline.co.uk/tol/news/uk/article822086.ece.

McCabe, Richard (1999). Review of Jean Brink. *RES* 50: 236–7.

—— (2001). 'Ireland: Policy, Poetics, Parody', in Andrew Hadfield (ed.), *The Cambridge Companion to Spenser*. Cambridge: Cambridge University Press, 60–78.

—— (2002). *Spenser's Monstrous Regiment: Elizabethan Ireland and the Poetics of Difference*. Oxford: Oxford University Press.

Maley, Willy (1993). 'How Milton and Some Contemporaries Read Spenser's View', in Brendan Bradshaw, Andrew Hadfield, and Willy Maley (eds), *Representing Ireland: Literature and the Origins of Conflict, 1534–1660*. Cambridge: Cambridge University Press, 191–208.

—— (1997). *Salvaging Spenser: Colonialism, Culture, and Identity*. New York: St. Martin's.

—— (2003). *Nation, State, and Empire in English Renaissance Literature*. New York: Palgrave Macmillan.

Milton, John (1985). *Areopagitica* in *Complete Poems and Major Prose*, ed. Merritt Y. Hughes. New York: Macmillan, 716–49.

Morris, Richard (ed.) (1893). *The Globe Edition: Complete Works of Edmund Spenser*. London: Macmillan.

Pollock, Frederick (1900). 'The History of the Law of Nature: A Preliminary Study', *Journal of the Society of Comparative Legislation* NS no. 3: 418–33.

Quinn, D. B. (1947). *Raleigh and the British Empire*. London: English Universities Press.

—— (1990). 'A Vewe of the Present State of Ireland'. *SE*, 713–15.

Renwick, W. L. (ed.) (1930–2). 'Volume 8', in *Works of Edmund Spenser*. Oxford: Basil Blackwell for Shakespeare Head Press.

—— (1934). *A View of the Present State of Ireland by Edmund Spenser*. London: Scholartis Press.

Zurcher, Andrew (2007). *Spenser's Legal Language: Law and Poetry in Early Modern England*. Cambridge: D. S. Brewer.

CHAPTER 18

TWO CANTOS OF MUTABILITIE (1609)

GORDON TESKEY

From the high ground of Arlo Hill perhaps more of Spenser's total work can be held in conspectus than from any other vantage point.

William Blissett

THE RELATION OF THE *MUTABILITIE* CANTOS TO *THE FAERIE QUEENE*

When Spenser died in mid-January 1599, probably in his forty-seventh year, *The Faerie Queene* was an incomplete epic allegorical poem of twelve intended books, six of which had appeared in two equal installments, three books in 1590 and three more in 1596, when the six books were published together under the title, *The Faerie Queene. Disposed into twelve bookes, Fashioning XII Morall vertues.* Six more books were expected to complete this poem, which is set in an imaginary British and Arthurian past called Fairy Land, and which proposes to offer an allegory of the twelve moral virtues. In 1596, at about forty-four years of age, Spenser was still young enough to believe he would do it. But Spenser died unexpectedly a little over two years later. His funeral was a public event, under the auspices of the Queen's favorite, the Earl of Essex, and he was buried in Westminster Abbey near Chaucer, the poets of the day casting their elegies into the grave, and the pens with which the elegies were written. England's great national epic was now left half-complete. Still, there was no reason not to expect materials from the promised second half of *The Faerie Queene* eventually to come to light.

And so they did in 1609, a decade after the poet's death, when the six completed books of *The Faerie Queene* were published in a large, folio edition edited, perhaps, by Spenser's scholarly friend at Cambridge, Gabriel Harvey. To these six books were added two more cantos and a two-stanza fragment, under the following head-note: '*Two Cantos of Mutabilitie*, which, both for Forme and Matter, appeare to be parcell of some following Booke of the *Faerie Queene*, under the Legend of *Constancie*. Never before imprinted'. The *Mutabilitie Cantos* were likely written in the twenty months between Spenser's return to Ireland, early in 1597, and the end of September 1598.

We do not know for sure that *constancy* is the virtue Spenser expected to treat of in these cantos, but if that is an editorial guess, it is a good one, assuming, as is eminently reasonable, that the text before us is 'parcell of some following Booke' intended to continue the Arthur-in-Fairy-Land narrative of the six preceding books. The assumption is eminently reasonable because in the course of the *Mutabilitie Cantos*, as he is about to tell his pastoral tale, Spenser actually refers to the larger epic poem to which these cantos belong, a poem of 'warres and knights' in which he is to intrude a story set among 'hilles and woods' (vi.37). It should also be said that the cantos of the *Mutabilitie Cantos* are identical in kind to the seventy-two cantos Spenser wrote in the first six books of *The Faerie Queene*: they are composed in the special, nine-line stanza invented by Spenser for *The Faerie Queene* as a whole; they are of about average length, fifty-five and fifty-nine stanzas, respectively; and they are both headed by the four-line 'arguments' in ballad measure that appear above all preceding cantos of *The Faerie Queene*. Following the two cantos is the fragment I referred to: two stanzas of an eighth canto bearing the heading, 'the viii canto, unperfite', where 'unperfite' means incomplete. To count everything up, we have 116 *Faerie Queene* stanzas plus two, four-line canto arguments, giving a total of 1,052 verses, all exactly conforming with the formal order of *The Faerie Queene* as a whole.

With their final line of apostrophic prayer, 'O that great Sabbaoth God, graunt me that Sabbaoths sight,' the two stanzas of the 'unperfite' canto, despite their fragmentary status, give what Frank Kermode called the *sense* of an ending. From this point of view, as Northrop Frye maintained in a classic article on *The Faerie Queene*, these two stanzas 'could not have been the opening stanzas of an eighth unfinished canto, as the rubric suggests'; and the *Mutabilitie Cantos* could never have been 'the core of a seventh book, unless that book was inconceivably different in its structure from the existing ones' (Frye 1963: 71). This intriguing possibility—that the *Mutabilitie Cantos* are, as Frye says on the same page, 'a single, beautifully shaped poem' not intended to be part of any future book of *The Faerie Queene*—can be no more than a possibility, a castle in the air, though castles in the air must not be thought always unwelcome in poetry. But let us be clear about the facts ranged against it, in addition to those cited in the preceding paragraph. Many cantos of *The Faerie Queene* open with one or two retrospective stanzas of this kind, and even that final line of prayer— without doubt it is a moving final line—is not definitively final. Nothing in these two stanzas that close *The Faerie Queene* as we have it is inconsistent with the poet's continuing on to finish the canto they open and to join it with others in a developing book of *The Faerie Queene* (Nelson 1963: 296). Had he lived, what else could Spenser have done? *The Faerie Queene* is a highly unpredictable poem and its most unpredictable event is its seventh book.

Even so, we should acknowledge striking differences between the *Mutabilitie Cantos* and the rest of *The Faerie Queene*. For one thing, although the *Mutabilitie Cantos* would have formed the 'allegorical core' of a Book of Constancy, they make a much longer 'core' episode than any comparable one in the preceding six books (Lewis 1938: 353). The themes, the intellectual framework, the physical setting, the tone, and the temporal orientation are all somewhat different from *The Faerie Queene*. For the themes, there is no mention of Prince Arthur, no mention of the Fairy Queen, no mention of the 'antique world' and no mention of any of the moral virtues. The intellectual problem actually addressed in the *Mutabilitie Cantos*— continuance-within-change—belongs to metaphysics, not ethics. For the physical setting, instead of taking us to Fairy Land, the action of the *Mutabilitie Cantos* unfolds in the heavens and then, unexpectedly, in the real landscape of Ireland, among named and identifiable places near the poet's home. No other scenes in *The Faerie Queene* are set explicitly in Ireland or any other identifiable landscape—or, for that matter, in the heavens. For the tone, the *Mutabilitie Cantos* indulge a lighter, more ironical mood than the high seriousness we are generally greeted with in *The Faerie Queene*. This is to be expected in the pastoral comedy of the Faunus episode, but the mood spills over into the mighty cosmic contest between Mutabilitie and Jove. The two distinct faces of the *Mutabilitie Cantos*, of low farce and high seriousness, seem to meld in the comparison of the stately goddess Diana to an angry 'huswife' who has caught a mouse in her dairy, 'and thousand deathes deviseth in her vengefull mind' (vi.48). The contagion of farce is caught by the other Olympians, who are thrown into panic by an eclipse of the moon and who gape at Mutabilitie, 'all astonied, like a sort of Steeres' (vi.28). Spenser's gods are closer to Homer's serio-comic Olympians than they are to Virgil's sober powers. This is not unprecedented in *The Faerie Queene*, as when Venus casts a jaundiced eye on the vaunted beauty of Diana's nymphs. In the *Mutabilitie Cantos*, however, the irony is not occasional but pervasive, affecting even the Goddess of Nature. Finally, for the poem's temporal orientation, instead of looking back, as Spenser does in the rest of *The Faerie Queene*, from a degenerate present to an idealized, antique world, the *Mutabilitie Cantos* look toward a future in which the cosmos will fall slowly into ruin, until it is burned at the Last Judgement.

To consider the *Mutabilitie Cantos* from what Roland Barthes called a 'writerly' point of view—in this case, from the perspective of the working writer in the midst of his labor—they are indubitably a part of the ongoing project of *The Faerie Queene*, disastrously halted by the poet's death in the prime of life. But for us the poet's death has become part of the meaning of this poem, and this death confirms what the broken structure of the *Mutabilitie Cantos* bears witness to mutely: the incompleteness of all our projects in this world. In another classic article, from which my epigraph is taken, William Blissett says the *Mutabilitie Cantos* may be 'now most patient of interpretation as a detached retrospective commentary on the poem as a whole, forming as they do a satisfactory conclusion to a foreshortened draft, a stopping place at which, after a seriatim reading, can be made a pleasing analysis of all' (Blissett 1964: 26). This complex description shows the inseparability of Spenser's work as a writer (note the phrases 'retrospective commentary' and 'foreshortened draft') from our work as readers (note the words 'interpretation' and 'now'). For Spenser as well as for us the *Mutabilitie Cantos* are not quite an ending and not quite a continuation. They are a 'stopping place'. There can, therefore, be no simple answer to the question of the relation of the *Mutabilitie Cantos* to *The Faerie Queene*, any more than there can be a simple answer to the practical question whether to refer to the *Mutabilitie Cantos* in the singular or the plural. Nor would we want simple answers to either question, for our uncertainty is not unrelated to the doubt raised in the *Mutabilitie Cantos* about the power of any *thing* in this world to escape change long enough to become an inviolable entity, as we commonly suppose great poems do. Like everything else, great poems decay, and the purpose of literary criticism is to slow that decay as much as possible by giving the poems new life in our minds. Time and change have made the fragmentary text of the *Mutabilitie Cantos* almost—not entirely, but almost—an independent poem, a peninsula attached to the continent of *The Faerie Queene*, and wearing away. Perhaps by now the peninsula is an island; perhaps not. It depends on water levels.

THE METAPHYSICAL THEME: CONTINUANCE WITHIN CHANGE

The metaphysical issues of identity, continuance, and change are raised in the *Mutabilitie Cantos* from a naturalistic point of view—Nature is the judge of them—with no reference, until the final stanza, to Christian hope or divine revelation. The main underlying question is this. Given that the world—'this wide great *Universe*' (vii.56)—is composed of things that are the *same* as themselves but that also *change* and alter, which of these two principles is the more fundamental: sameness (identity) or change, *mutability*? (*Mutability* is from L. *muto* 'to change', related to *moveo* 'to move', a point Spenser alludes to in the line 'all that moveth, doth mutation love', VII.vii.55.) A secondary question, although in Spenser's narrative it is the main point of contention between the protagonists, Jove and Mutabilitie, is whether a different kind of change exists in the heavens, above the sphere of the moon, from that kind of change—decay—which exists among us, in our world. Is change in the heavens a matter of recurrence, of things departing from themselves in order to return to themselves again, in perfection, a process reflected in the cyclical motions of the planets and even of the stars? That is the ancient, traditional view, as old as the Chaldean astronomers, which Jove upholds and Mutabilitie questions, arguing that there is no difference between the irreversible decay that rules in our world and the change that occurs in the heavens.

Mutabilitie argues her point by getting into motion. She ascends into the heavens and claims them for her own, violating the sphere of the moon, which marks the boundary between the two kinds of change. She doesn't win this argument and is 'put downe' (vii.59) at last, but that is not the poet's point. His point is rather to bring home to us the impermanence of everything in our own world beneath the heavens, where things wear down and pass away and, if they are living organisms, die. True, new life replaces old, like spawn in the river *Shure*, 'in which are thousand salmons bred' (vi.54). But Spenser's point is that the 'flowring pride' of our existence rests on an illusion. For we are not really persons, having stable identities; we are little turbulences in the underlying flow of continual change, like those salmon. We meet the enemy, Mutabilitie, and she is us.

This prospect leaves the poet filled with what Milan Kundera calls unbearable lightness, or what with more heaviness we may term ontological loathing, the feeling of not truly existing:

> Me seemes, that though she all unworthy were
> Of th'Heav'ns Rule; yet very sooth to say,
> In all things else she beares the greatest sway.
> Which makes me loath this state of life so tickle,
> And love of things so vaine to cast away;
> Whose flowring pride, so fading and so fickle,
> Short *Time* shall soon cut down with his consuming sickle.   (VII.viii.1)

In Aristotle's *Metaphysics*, an important text for the intellectual background of the *Mutabilitie Cantos* (as is *On the Heavens*), all things below the sphere of the moon have either independent being or freedom from change, but not both. Things enjoying freedom from change are the objects of mathematics; things enjoying independent being are the objects of physics. Although a triangular object decays, triangles do not. But mathematical objects such as triangles aren't quite real in the way physical objects are because they lack independent being. Physical objects have being but lack permanence; mathematical objects have permanence but lack being. Aristotle reasoned that there must be objects that lack neither permanence nor being and the planets seemed the likeliest visible instances of such objects, having independent being, as they certainly do, and seeming to be free from decay because they return to their original positions unchanged. Aristotle called this class of objects 'theological', not for theological reasons but simply because the planets are named after the gods. By the sixth century AD, reflection on such permanent objects, and also on first principles, such as time, space, motion, and substance, came to be called 'metaphysical', meaning both 'what comes after the study of nature, or *physis*' and 'what lies beyond or above nature, or *physis*'.

For Spenser there are two levels of nature, one above and one below the moon, called the superlunary and the sublunary realms. In the superlunary realm, objects, that is, planets and stars, change their positions with respect to one another, but they do not decay. In the sublunary realm, where we live, bodies die and objects (including dead bodies) wear down to nothing, to a scattering of salts. The moon was thought to be the boundary between the two realms because the side of the moon facing us undergoes visible change in its phases and has markings that suggest it decays. But the far side of the moon, which is turned away from us, was supposed to be pristine and unchanging, like a perfect pearl. The telescope—still a decade away from when Spenser wrote—would reveal what the naked eye might well infer: that craters on the edge of the visible orb of the moon continue into the shadowy region between the light and dark sides of the moon, and so very probably continue on the dark side. An inviolable boundary is crossed.

If Spenser was planning a Book of Constancy, that ethical virtue would have for its cosmic foundation the permanence of the heavenly bodies above the sphere of the moon. But recent scientific observations had thrown into question the dependability of the heavens as a model of constancy. In the final stanza of the *Mutabilitie Cantos*, therefore, the language of metaphysical speculation gives way to religious prophecy. To ensure the priority of permanence over change, of identity over non-identity, it is necessary to go outside metaphysics and natural philosophy to theology, in the Christian, not the Aristotelian sense: 'For, all that *moveth*, doth in *Change* delight; | But thenceforth all shall rest eternally | With Him' (viii. 2).

Canto Six: Mutabilitie's Assault on the Heavens and the Tale of Arlo Hill

In Canto six the goddess Mutabilitie, who is also called 'Change' and 'Alteration' (arguments to vi and vii), having wreaked havoc on earth, decides to seize the rule of the heavens. She climbs to the moon, threatens to force the goddess Cynthia from her chair (thus causing a lunar eclipse), and at the summons of Mercury ascends to Jove's heavenly palace, where she challenges him directly. Mutabilitie claims Jove has usurped her right to rule the heavens because she, Mutabilitie, is descended from Titan, the elder brother of Saturn, Jove's father. Jove reaches for his lightning bolt to strike her down, as he has done to other descendants of Titan who threatened his rule. But seeing Mutabilitie's beautiful face (for change is beautiful), Jove tries instead to seduce her to his party—and to his bed. Brusquely declining, Mutabilitie appeals to the judgement of the 'Father of the Gods and men by equall right, | To weet, the God of Nature' (vi.35). Jove is displeased but must comply. This means that Spenser sees the gods as nothing more than personifications of the powers of nature. But how firm are those powers?

The case is appointed to be tried on the summit of Arlo Hill, the highest peak in the Galtymore mountains to the northeast of Spenser's home: 'the highest head (in all mens sights) | Of my old father *Mole*' (vi.36). The unexpected local reference occasions an inset tale of the etiological kind (from *aitios* 'cause': a 'just so' story telling how something came to be as it is), accounting for why Arlo, which was once a *locus amoenus*, or earthly paradise, 'the best and fairest Hill | That was in all this holy-Islands hights', became 'the most unpleasant, and most ill', infested with wolves and thieves (vi.37). Because the tale relates to events in the deep past and is set not in Fairy Land but on local ground, and because the implicit subject of the tale is Queen Elizabeth's declining to supply enough troops to pacify Ireland, Spenser signals the change of register by asking the muse of history to aid Spenser's epic muse: Clio should lend Calliope her quill (vi.37).

Long ago, the goddess Diana loved to hunt on Arlo hill and to bathe in the stream Molanna, who was also one of her nymphs, after which the goddess would repose naked 'on the soft and downy grass . . . where none behold her may' (vi.42). Wishing to have sight of Diana naked, the wood god Faunus persuaded the nymph Molanna to hide him in a neighboring bush, having corrupted Molanna with apples and cherries, and with the promise that he will get her what she has long wished for: the love of the stream Fanchin. But when Molanna conceals Faunus and Faunus sees Diana naked, he foolishly betrays himself, laughing with pleasure and blurting out his admiration. He is haled forth and after more severe punishments are considered (they include gelding) he is covered in a deer-skin, and the hounds are set on him as goddess and nymphs chase him over hill and dale. His fate is happier than the hunter Actaeon's, who when he accidentally came upon Diana bathing was turned by the offended goddess into a stag, and devoured by his hounds. Faunus, however, proves faster than his pursuers, whereupon they return to poor Molanna, who was already 'shole' (vi.40), or stony and shallow, and overwhelm her with stones. But Faunus keeps his promise and persuades Fanchin to accept Molanna to his bed (the stream bed and the marriage bed are metaphorically conjoined), so that the two streams now flow together in Fanchin's deeper course. As for the offended Diana, she forsakes Arlo Hill, 'And all that Mountaine, which doth over-looke | The richest champian that may else be rid' (vi.54). That 'champian' (cf. French *campagne* 'countryside') is the plain on which the Munster Plantation was situated, in which Spenser lived at Kilcolman as one of the English 'undertakers' or colonists (Coughlan 1996: 320–1). At parting, Diana lays a heavy curse on the entire place: that it be infested ever after with wolves and thieves, 'Which too-too true', Spenser says with feeling, in the final line of the episode, 'that lands in-dwellers since have found' (vi.55).

CANTO SEVEN: THE TRIAL

Canto seven is occupied by the trial between Mutabilitie and Jove on the following question: who should rule the universe, Jove, as the principle of identity, or Mutabilitie, as the principle of change? Is each thing a *thing*, or is thingliness an illusion and all so-called 'things' merely disturbances, standing waves in an underlying flow? To judge this important question a mighty figure from late antiquity and the Middle Ages, the Goddess of Nature, is appealed to. She is introduced, in fully eight stanzas of spectacular beauty, enthroned among flowers that spring up joyously beneath her. But should this natural description of Nature seem insufficient, and it is anything but, Spenser refers us, with self-mocking erudition, to books: Chaucer's *Parliament of Fowls* and Alain de Lille's *De planctu naturae*. It is a wonder he did not add the common literary source for the figure of Nature, in the late Latin poet Claudian's *De consulatu Stilichonis*, without knowledge of which who can be well acquainted with nature?

From a legal if not from a poetic point of view, it is surprising Mutabilitie does not build her case on her good genealogical claim, 'From [her] great Grandsire *Titan*... Deriv'd by dew descent', which she mentions at the trial only in passing (vii.16; Burrow: 99). Jove is '*Saturnes* sonne', as Mutabilitie has pointedly called him (vi.34), and Saturn is the younger brother of Titan, from whom Mutabilitie is descended. But the judge is Nature, not an English magistrate, and good legal arguments do not impress her. Nature favors the young and the strong over those with good title but no courage to defend it. (Queen Elizabeth was of much the same mind, vis-à-vis the colonists of the Munster Plantation.) Dame Nature is there in the tsunami as much as the flower. In Nature's realm, where the seas can rise, carelessly effacing our property markers, possession is ten-tenths of the law.

Mutabilitie therefore builds her case on the less legally secure but more natural argument that she already occupies what she therefore has the right to possess, or at least she occupies *more* of it than Jove: 'I doe possesse the worlds most regiment' (vii.17). But does she? If she's right, she will win. For what Nature is judging is not whether Mutabilitie has a *right* to the heavens but whether Mutabilitie already occupies more of the heavens than Jove and should take the remainder by right of conquest. Mutabilitie's argument may be specious, however, that is, fair-appearing, being addressed to the eye, which reads surfaces, instead of to the mind, which penetrates below. It does not look good for Mutabilitie when she boasts to Nature that her argument 'Shall to your eyes appear *incontinent*', that is, immediately, without reflection, and when she enjoins Nature to 'judge...by verdit of thine eye', not by the verdict of her reason (vii.17, 27). In Book V, in the debate between Artegall and the giant with the scales, Spenser shows his contempt of arguments based on appearances. Artegall's response to the giant—'But in the mind the doome of right must bee' (V.ii.47)—is the perfect gloss for the *evidence* (a word that means 'bringing forth to sight') which Mutabilitie will present. For Spenser, seeing may be believing, but belief is often false. Judging is another matter altogether. Still, Mutabilitie makes a very strong case, as Nature will acknowledge when the outcome hangs in the balance.

EVIDENCE AT TRIAL: THE PAGEANT OF THE MONTHS, SEASONS, DAYS AND HOURS

Mutabilitie opens with a magnificent description of tumult in the earth and in the four elements below the sphere of the moon. 'All that . . . is ybredde', she says,

> How-ever fayre it flourish for a time,
> Yet see we soone decay; and, being dead,
> To turne again unto their earthly slime:
> Yet, out of their decay and mortall crime,
> We daily see new creatures to arize;
>
>   ·   ·   ·   ·   ·   ·   ·
>
> So turne they still about, and change in restlesse wise.   (VII.vii.18)

Passing from substance to temporality, Mutabilitie then asks that there be brought before the court 'the rest which doe the world in being hold' (vii.27), the 'times and seasons of the yeare that fall', followed by Day and Night, the Hours, or *Horae*, and lastly Life and Death—all the modes of temporality within which change unfolds. What follows in the next nineteen stanzas (28–46) is Spenser's last great pageant. As in all Spenserian pageants, the pleasure is as much in the succession of the figures as it is in the figures individually.

But the individual figures are delightful: *Spring* with his garment of flowers and leaves 'In which a thousand birds had built their bowres' (28); *Sommer* 'In a thin silken cassock, coloured greene', with a garland on his head and a bow and arrows in his hands (29); *Autumne* in yellow, 'Laden with fruits that made him laugh, full glad | That he had banist hunger' (30); and *Winter*, 'Chattering his teeth for cold', his breath making icicles in his beard and 'dull drops' falling from his purple nose, 'As from a limbeck' (31). After these figures have marched by 'in order' (32), the twelve months come in riding on the astrological signs. *Day* and *Night* follow, on white and black horses, with scepters on the tops of which the heavenly bodies are represented (44). The *Houres*, 'faire daughters of high *Jove*', come next. They are virgins of 'wondrous beauty, fit to kindle love', and from their station at Heaven's gate they divide the twenty-four hours of the day and night, each one waking and watching after the last (45). In the final stanza of the pageant *Life* and *Death* appear, *Death* with 'most grim and grisly visage', but 'Unbodied, unsoul'd, unheard, unseene' (46). *Life* comes before *Death* in the pageant. But still, *Life* is described last, as 'a faire young lusty boy . . . Deckt all with flowers, and wings of gold'.

Mutabilitie summarizes the meaning of this pageant: 'for, who sees not, that *Time* on all doth pray?' (47). We note that this argument is based on what we see. So far, that argument is directed at the 'lower world' below the sphere of the moon, but she will soon turn her eyes, and ours, to the heavens.

FURTHER EVIDENCE AT TRIAL: THE HEAVENS

Only now is Jove able to get a word in edgewise, countering that he and the gods are the true source of time, pouring it out like water from heaven. The gods therefore have authority over all things that are subject to time, including Mutabilitie herself:

> But, who is it (to me tell)
> That *Time* himself doth move and still compel
> To keepe his course? Is not that namely wee
> Which poure that vertue from our heavenly cell,
> That moves them all, and makes them changed be?
> So them we gods doe rule, and in them also thee.   (VII.vii.48)

This response is brushed aside by Mutabilitie as she carries her argument into the celestial regions. She alludes to recent, disturbing astronomical observations, especially of the planets and among them especially of Mars, the erratic movements of which would prove key, after Spenser's day, to discrediting the earth-centered Ptolemaic system:

> Now *Mars* that valiant man is changed most:
>   For, he some times so far runs out of square,
>   That he his way doth seem quite to have lost,
>   And cleane without his usuall sphere to fare;
>   That even these Star-gazers stonisht are
>   At sight thereof, and damne their lying bookes:
>   So likewise, grim Sir *Saturne* oft doth spare
>   His sterne aspect, and calme his crabbed lookes:
> So many turning cranks these have, so many crookes.   (vii.52)

Observed irregularities, or 'crookes', in the planetary motions, and 'turning cranks', or epicycles imposed upon the planets' orbits to 'save the appearances'—that is, to save the earth-centered, Ptolemaic system by adding complexity—pose a grave threat to the immortal status of the Olympian gods with whom those planets are identified.

Worse news is to follow. Many of the gods, not excluding Jove, have been born, and born on earth, too. After all, being born is as strong an argument against eternal existence as dying is. Mutabilitie puts the embarrassing question to Jove himself:

> Where were ye born? Some say in *Crete* by name,
> Others in *Thebes*, and others other-where;
> But wheresoever they comment the same,
> They all consent that ye begotten were,

And borne here in this world, ne other can appear.

Then ye are mortall borne, and thrall to me.   (vii.53–4)

At last, Mutabilitie carries her argument to the stars, which are fixed on their single, turning sphere, the 'starrie sky'. We might suppose that at least the stars are free from degenerative change, unlike the erring planets (the word *planet* is from a Greek verb meaning 'to wander'). But the stars and the astrological signs that they form also move, although they do so together, on their sphere:

> Onely the starrie skie doth still remaine:
> Yet do the Starres and Signes therein still move,
> And even it self is mov'd, as wizards saine.
> But all that moveth, doth mutation love:
> Therefore both you and them to me I subject prove.   (vii.55)

We notice that Mutabilitie has equated change-plus-decay, which occurs below the sphere of the moon, with simple change, or motion—the waving of grass in the wind, for example, or the movements of fish, which 'doe at randon range' (vii.21). Mutabilitie does so even where such motion, as is the case with the stars, does not entail decay. Formerly, it was thought that all the heavenly bodies above the sphere of the moon have both independent being and freedom from change, so that they move in their cycles without decay. Mutabilitie has shown that this is not so, so far as the planets are concerned. But she has not shown that the stars in their collective motion decay. If the stars are the highest things visible in the natural world, and if motion, in the Aristotelian–Ptolemaic system, is imparted to the other spheres from the perfect motion of the 'starrie sky', then all is not lost: there may still be a case for claiming that all things eventually return to themselves, just as the stars return eternally to their original places. The stars are the implicit model for Nature's judgement: everything is star-like, Nature will say. In the meantime, Mutabilitie makes her triumphant summary:

> Then since within this wide great *Universe*
> Nothing doth firme and permanent appeare,
> But all things tost and turned by transverse:
> What then should let, but I aloft should reare
> My Trophee, and from all the triumph beare?   (vii.56)

THE JUDGEMENT

After a period of reflection during which 'silence long ensewed' (vii.57), the Goddess of Nature pronounces judgement in favor of Jove: change is not the radical principal; identity is. All things are not subject to change; change is itself subject to those things as they use change to 'worke their owne perfection so by fate': 'Then over them Change doth not rule and raigne; | But they raigne over change, and doe their states maintaine' (vii.58). The stanza of judgement is followed by one in which the story is tied up briskly: Mutabilitie is 'put downe and whist', that is, reduced to her station below the sphere of the moon, and silenced at last; Jove is 'confirm'd in his imperiall see', that is, he is allowed to continue to rule the heavens; the assembly is 'dismist'; and Nature vanishes, 'whither no man wist' (vii.59), but not before delivering herself of an obscure prophecy: 'But time shall come that all shall changed bee, | And from thenceforth, none no more change shall see' (vii. 59). The first of these lines seems to predict a victory for Mutabilitie in the long run, despite her disappointment today: '*all* shall changed bee'. But the second line heralds Mutabilitie's annihilation.

In the two stanzas of the eighth canto 'unperfite', the poet draws back a little from this summing-up to reflect on its consequences for him. True, Mutabilitie is 'unworthy' to rule the heavens and has rightly been put down. Note that the poet says nothing about the justice of her claim: he says only that she is 'unworthy', however good her claim may be. He is judging morally and above all, as we shall see, aesthetically. But if the Titaness has been 'put down', she has been put down where he, Spenser, has to live, in a place where the fickleness of fate continues to bear 'the greatest sway' (viii.1). We saw that this recognition, which seems to controvert the judgement of Nature (*all* things 'raigne over change'), arouses in the poet a loathing of life and a desire to cast away his 'love of things so vaine'. Spenser does not say he wishes to cast away the things themselves, but rather his love of them. That would include his love of the hard-won Elizabeth Boyle and the young children he had with her. It is the temptation, one not unknown to middle age, to live without feeling, doing your duty, but without love. In the final stanza, the poet remembers Nature's obscure prophecy of a time when 'no more *Change* shall be', and he concludes with a prayer to the God of Hosts ('Him that is the God of Sabbaoth hight') to bring him at last to the sight of the apocalyptic day of rest, the 'Sabaoths sight'. Perhaps hope of that sight will give him the courage to love the good in life, however entangled it is with the bad, and however little time he has left in which to love.

THE RESCUE AND THE LOSS OF ALL THINGS

The final four stanzas of the *Mutabilitie Cantos* are among the best in *The Faerie Queene*, having the vast force of the epic behind them and achieving the rescue of all things, so that we may love them, or some of them, before acknowledging their ultimate loss. How will Spenser bring the immense aircraft trailing behind him down to earth, and land it? The four stanzas are the last two of the seventh canto and the two stanzas of the final, 'unperfite' canto. Despite the canto change dividing them, they describe together the catenary arc of Spenser's landing.

The first of these stanzas is Nature's judgement. The second stanza is divided between Nature's summary statement to Mutabilitie and the poet's summing up of the tale, between which, in the fourth and fifth lines, Nature delivers herself of the obscure prophecy mentioned above. The third stanza (viii.1) is the poet's reflection on his own disillusioned experience. The fourth stanza (viii.2), the last in the poem, seizes upon Nature's prophecy and leaps beyond the frame of the metaphysical debate as it has unfolded so far. The poet prays for the sight of eternity beyond change. This is the Apocalypse, and we should be clear that what the poet wishes to see will bring about the total destruction of the very world Nature has just saved—when, as Herbert says in his great poem 'Decay', all things burn.

In the stanza of judgement the rhymes in the first five lines, where the reasoning is a little more severe ('sayd', 'hate', 'wayd', 'estate', and 'dilate'), are sounded higher in the mouth than the deeper ones of the four lines with which the stanza draws to a close: 'againe', 'Change', 'raigne', and 'maintaine'. Medial rhymes are added as well, 'Change' in l. 8 and, in l. 9, 'raigne' and 'change'. Altogether, the rhymes ring like bells in a carillon on Easter Sunday, triumphantly affirming the victory of identity over change. All those brilliantly particularized figures we have been shown in the pageant of seasons and months are not perturbations in the long flux of change. They rule over change and, in despite of change, they remain what they are:

> I well consider all that ye have sayd,
> And find that all things stedfastnesse doe hate
> And changed be: yet being rightly wayd
> They are not changed from their first estate;
> But by their change their being doe dilate:
> And turning to themselves at length againe,
> Doe worke their own perfection so by fate:
> Then over them Change doth not rule and raigne;
> But they raigne over change, and doe their states maintaine.   (VII.vii.58)

We cannot help noticing—it is the most discreetly thrilling effect of this stanza—that it is by their own power that the things seem to hold their identity, as the active verbs imply: 'dilate', 'turne', 'worke', and 'raigne'. The system seems contained in itself, unaided by any invisible hand from the outside, unless it is 'fate' in l. 7. But in this context, 'fate' can mean nothing other than natural law, which belongs like everything else to the interior of the system.

Nature continues to speak in the first five lines of the stanza following her judgement, first to Mutabilitie and then to all present:

> Cease therefore daughter further to aspire,
> And thee content thus to be rul'd by me:
> For thy decay thou seekst by thy desire;
> But time shall come that all shall changed bee,
> And from thenceforth, none no more change shall see.   (vii.59)

The famous line, 'Thy decay thou seekst by thy desire', states the contradiction of Mutabilitie's wanting to establish herself as the universal rule. For Mutabilitie to wish to be the universal rule is to wish to be the opposite of what she is. It is to wish to be 'steadfastnes' instead. If change is permanent, then change is no longer change; and if permanence is change, then permanence is no longer permanent. Poetry seldom attains to such logical tightness. But there is more to it than logic. There is life in it, too, steering the verse in a different direction, one that will disturb the self-satisfaction with which we expose a contradiction in someone else's reasoning, oblivious to contradiction in our own. For is it not true that all living systems, in the very pursuit of what they desire (to capture energy and to reproduce themselves), seek their decay? As you read it, you should experience a moment of surprise when the phrase, 'thy decay thou seekst by thy desire', is turned on you, like a loaded gun. We are Mutabilitie too, and Nature is talking to us.

In the prophetic lines to follow a totally new concept of change is brought in. We have observed that the poem engages two kinds of change:

1) Superlunary change-as-circular-motion, or the eternal return of the same: This is the change that the stars seem still to have and that the planets no longer have.

2) Sublunary change-as-decay, the alteration of 'all things' into something else, without any hope of return: 'man dieth and wasteth away: yea, man giveth up the ghost, and where is he?' (Job 14: 10).

But the new kind of change now being referred to is sudden, total, and final: 'But time shall come that all shall changed bee, | And from that time none no more change shall see'. Note how the metronomic beauty of these lines imitates the precise divisions of time going forward. In the Book of Job, shortly after the passage just cited, Job asserts his faith that he will recover the very flesh that rots from his body and is eaten by worms: 'and though after my skin worms destroy this body, yet in my flesh shall I see God: whom I shall see for myself, and mine eyes shall behold, and not another' (Job 19: 26–7). It will be in my flesh, Job says, that I shall see God, and it will be with my own eyes, the ones I am looking through now, not with other eyes, spiritual eyes, that I shall see God. Job's inspired utterance is echoed in Saint Paul, who proclaims the mystery of which Job has had a prophetic intimation: 'Behold, I show you a mystery; we shall not all sleep, but we shall all be changed, in a moment, in the twinkling of an eye, at the last trump; for the trumpet shall sound, and the dead shall be raised incorruptible, and we shall be changed' (1 Cor. 15: 51–2). In stanzas 58 and 59 the word *change* is sounded seven times and rhymed with other words four times. It would have been impossible for Spenser's audience, it would be impossible for anyone who goes regularly to church, as Spenser's audience did, not to hear behind the insistent repetition of this word the most powerful statement of hope in the Bible: 'we shall be changed'. After this change, a change that *reverses* decay, 'none no more change shall see'.

Notwithstanding the good evidence against Jove, Nature confirms him as ruler of the heavens, for Nature, as we saw, favors the young and the strong, and Jove is both. Mutabilitie, having exaggerated her strength, is once again confined below the moon and 'whist', or silenced. In the last analysis, however, which we encounter in the third of these stanzas (viii.1), Nature's judgement may not appear to be entirely about power, for Spenser puts his thumb on the scales and slyly adds a reason for putting Mutabilitie down that is not metaphysical and not even moral: it is aesthetic. He doesn't like her tone of voice, which is grating, irascible, and discontented, a little like the Blatant Beast, and Spenser hears this noise coming at him from the future. It is bad enough here on earth, Spenser thinks, in the social world of London as much as in Ireland, and the poets, the satirists, are picking it up, for discontented melancholy was the literary fashion of the later 1590s and would provoke official and futile suppression in 1599. Reverberating profoundly in *Hamlet* (1600–1), its whining sound would continue on as the burden of the literature of the Jacobean period. Nor is the poet who published an entire volume entitled *Complaints* a stranger to its use, but he doesn't want this noise coming down on him from the heavens: 'Me seemes, that though she all unworthy were | Of the Heav'ns rule; yet very sooth to say, | In all things else she beares the greatest sway' (viii.1).

Let the heavens, at least, be our imaginary refuge from the noise of the future. Let the heavens ring with the music of the spheres while Jupiter is enthroned in his palace and the constellations move in state behind him. Still closer in, in our neighborhood, let Cynthia, the moon, reign unmolested by change, enthroned in her bright palace, 'All fairely deckt with heavens goodly story.' Let the stars attend Cynthia forever. And please do let her page, the evening star, be a guide for us as well as for her:

> *Vesper*, whom we the Evening-starre intend:
> That with his Torche, still twinkling like twilight,
> Her lightened all the way where she should wend,
> And joy to weary wand'ring travailers did lend.   (VII.vi.9)

Note the enriched meaning of 'travailers': those who travel; those who are in travail in this world, who struggle in pain to bring something forth.

If that is what our spirits need—for a glory to be settled on this world, in despite of all we know—it is for the poets to bring that glory to our sight. So Spenser appears to have concluded at the end of his own weary travail, when his Fairy Queen, Elizabeth Tudor, was old and also near the end of her travail in this world. The Queen had abandoned Arlo Hill and all the Munster Plantation it overlooks, including Spenser's estate at Kilcolman, leaving them to be overrun by wolfish outlaws, secure in the dense forests under Galtymore, by violent mobs and, at the end, by armies. It is true that to others it was Spenser and his fellow undertakers who stood among the wolves and the thieves. But Spenser was soon to join his 'weary wand'ring travailers' at night on a road leading into the dark, perhaps with a dead child, and with a burning house behind him. All things burn.

BIBLIOGRAPHY

Blissett, W. (1964). 'Spenser's Mutabilitie', in M. Maclure and F. W. Watt (eds), *Essays in English Literature from the Renaissance to the Victorian Age Presented to A. S. P. Woodhouse*. Toronto: University of Toronto Press, 26–42.

Burrow, C. (1996). *Edmund Spenser.* Plymouth: Northcote.

Coughlan, P. (1996). 'The Local Context of Mutabilitie's Plea', in A. Fogarty (guest ed.), *Spenser in Ireland: 'The Faerie Queene' 1596–1996. Irish University Review* Special Issue, 26. 2: 320–41.

Frye, N. (1961; rpt. 1963). 'The Structure of Imagery in *The Faerie Queene*', in *Fables of Identity: Studies in Poetic Mythology.* New York: Harcourt, Brace, 69–87.

Kermode, F. (1967). *The Sense of an Ending: Studies in the Theory of Fiction.* New York: Oxford University Press.

Lewis, C. S. (1938). *The Allegory of Love: A Study in Medieval Tradition.* Oxford: Oxford University Press.

Nelson, William (1963). *The Poetry of Edmund Spenser: A Study.* New York: Columbia University Press.

Zurcher, A. (2007). *Legal Language: Law and Poetry in Early Modern England.* Cambridge: I. S. Brewer.

....

CHAPTER 19

'LOST WORKS', SUPPOSITIOUS PIECES, AND CONTINUATIONS

....

JOSEPH L. BLACK

LISA CELOVSKY

THE lost works of classical writers haunted the Renaissance imagination. While many writings had of course been rediscovered, they remained tantalizingly in dialogue with works no longer or only partially extant. Consequently, the stray title, the orphaned fragment, and the rumoured book that may never in fact have existed were familiar and interpretable presences in the sixteenth century. Lost works suggested creative directions contemplated but abandoned, or taken but superseded, supplementary or alternative possibilities of genre, form, subject, approach, or audience. They also provided opportunities for attribution and reattribution as new evidence came available—or was supplied to fill the need. Textual absences inspired creative imagination, and throughout the Renaissance lost and incomplete works generated completions and continuations alongside the imitations and appropriations inspired by those that did survive.

A Renaissance poet aware of literary tradition may very well have encouraged a similar web of teasingly suggestive and generative possibilities around his own work. As several chapters of this *Handbook* make clear, Edmund Spenser was a highly self-conscious poet determined to shape his literary career in the public eye. Taking full advantage of the opportunities offered by print publication, Spenser, his friends, and his publisher employ paratextual apparatus (such as prefaces and glosses) in his poetry and the prose genre of the 'familiar' letter to situate his achievements so far and announce his ambitions for the future. In the process, they mention many writings that never made their way into print and appear not to have survived. These 'lost' works have been the subject of much speculation over the years. Did they exist in the first place? If so, why were they not published, and what happened to them? Moreover, like other writers thought to have written more than was publicly available, Spenser had additional works attributed to him both during his life and after his death, and his writings, apparently incomplete, furthermore inspired not only imitations but continuations. Like those of his classical predecessors, Spenser's lost works, attributed writings, and literary afterlives are interpretable. Some help us trace the evolution of his surviving writings, his creative aspirations, or even his personal connections. Others illuminate the career path that Spenser and his con-temporaries imagined as appropriate for the new poet they were presenting to the reading public, or show the ways Spenser was read and appropriated by the following generation of writers. Even if his lost works never existed, the titles, references, and quotations left by Spenser and his circle reveal a writer in dialogue with his peers, his patrons, and his literary ancestors, ambitiously creating an identity for Spenser as the heir and overgoer simultaneously of classical, Continental, and English literary traditions.

Lost Works: The Sources

Most evidence for Spenser's lost works appears in three sources, all printed in his lifetime: *The Shepheardes Calender* (1579), the Spenser–Harvey *Letters* (1580), and the preface by publisher William Ponsonby to Spenser's *Complaints* (1591).[1] Various ambiguities make it difficult to count precisely the number of works these sources collectively name or quote from. They total at least sixteen, and possibly up to twenty, not to mention various 'sondry others', 'other Pamphlets', and unnamed experiments in quantitative verse.[2] One of the named works comprises nine comedies and another seven psalms, which for some scholars raises the total to over thirty. However counted, the lost works constitute an exceptionally large group, even when compared with the records of other Renais-sance English poets and keeping in mind the natural losses expected for any writer working four centuries ago. Nevertheless, these three sources all carry the author-ity of Spenser's direct involvement or at least his probable complicity, suggesting that these works did exist or that Spenser and his associates wanted readers to think they existed.

The earliest references appear in *The Shepheardes Calender*. Their presence here helps to inaugurate a strategy employed by Spenser and his circle throughout his career—that of packaging his writings as components of larger, more ambitious literary and cultural projects. In his prefatory Epistle to Gabriel Harvey, E. K., the *Calender*'s possibly fictitious commentator, hopes that his editorial efforts will encourage Master Immerito 'to put forth divers other excellent works of his, which slepe in silence, as his Dreames, his Legendes, his Court of Cupide, and sondry others' (Spenser 1989: 19–20). Whether or not these poems were indeed ready to be awakened for public viewing, they link the 'new Poete' Immerito with the established master Chaucer. E. K. had opened the dedicatory epistle to Harvey with praise for Chaucer's 'excellencie and wonderfull skil in making', and Chaucer's works included, or were thought at the time to include, dream visions, legends, and a poem called *The Court of Love*. In a gloss to *November* 195, E. K. claims furthermore to have written a full commentary on *Dreames*. The gloss indicates that *Dreames* treats mythological subjects and may have included a story about Hebe (goddess of youth) staining the heavens with a cup of spilt nectar. More generally, E. K. suggests here that *Dreames*, like *The Shepheardes Calender*, is an accomplishment both worthy of and requiring explication. To write a commentary on a text not yet published was to argue for its status as instant classic. *Dreames*, E. K. promises, is both innovatively new and learnedly traditional, a fit companion for the ancient and medieval texts that had long enjoyed the prestige of commentary.

Spenser himself mentions *Dreames* in his correspondence with Harvey: along with *Dying Pellican*, another lost work, *Dreames* is now 'fully finished' and 'presentlye to bee imprinted'. In a postscript, Spenser adds that *Dreames* perhaps should 'come forth alone' because it has grown to the size of the *Calender* as a result of glosses added by E. K., 'running continually in manner of a Paraphrase'. In addition, the poem's 'Pictures' have been 'so singularly set forth, and purtrayed' that if '*Michel Angelo* were there, he could (I think) nor amende the best, nor reprehende the worst' (*Prose*, 17–18). These 'Pictures' may refer to actual illustrations, like those that accompanied the *Calender*, or to visual elements in the poem itself. In either case, Harvey in response reiterates Spenser's implicit desire to situate the work in an Italian as well as classical cultural context. At first, Harvey simply fans the flames of reader expectation: he will leave off dreaming of *Dreames* and the *Dying Pellican* until 'with these eyes [he sees] them forth indeed' (*Prose*, 459). In a later letter he continues his advance marketing by anticipating the poem's successful reception. Colin Clout, Harvey jokes, will be able to 'purchase great landes, and Lordshippes' with the money the *Calender* has already earned and that *Dreames* will bring him. But Harvey also whets public appetite for Immerito's promised work by praising *Dreames* for its 'singular extraordinarie veine and invention' and comparing his friend's achievement with the works of Lucian, Petrarch, Aretino, Pasquill, and 'all the most delicate, and fine conceited Grecians and Italians'. Spenser will be well satisfied, Harvey concludes, if '*Dreames* be but as well esteemed of in Englande, as *Petrarches Visions* be in Italy' (*Prose*, 471).

References to other lost works in *The Shepheardes Calender* likewise supplement Immerito's Chaucerian genealogy with his classical and Italian affiliations. In a gloss to a story about Cupid in the *March* eclogue, E. K. directs readers who would like to see more of 'Cupids colours and furniture' to read either Propertius (referring to Elegy 2.12) or 'Moschus his Idyllion of wandring love, being now most excellently translated into Latine by the singuler learned man Angelus Politianus: whych worke [E. K. has] seene amongst other of thys Poets [i.e., Spenser's] doings, very wel translated also into Englishe Rymes' (*March* (79)). This reference to a translation of the first Idyll of the ancient Greek lyricist Moschus, apparently based on the Latin version by Angelo Poliziano (first published in 1512), may be the *Court of Cupide* E. K. mentions in the dedication. But more likely it suggests a different work: Moschus's original poem says nothing about a 'court' and consists of a speech in which Venus describes her runaway son. The elegy by the Latin lyricist Propertius—an 'ekphrastic' description of an image of Cupid—is a similarly visual poem. Read in one light, the gloss exemplifies E. K.'s habits of pedantic allusion-hunting and name-dropping. But his references to Propertius and Moschus also emphasize Immerito's interest in classical traditions of iconographic or emblematic verse. A gloss in the *June* eclogue adds another lost work apparently written with these traditions in mind. Explaining a reference to the classical Graces, E. K. notes that 'thys same Poete [i.e., Spenser] in his Pageaunts sayth[:] An hundred Graces on her eyeledde satte' (*June* (25)). The line, E. K. adds, imitates one in a late classical poem by Musaeus about Hero and Leander; Spenser would later incorporate a revised version in *Amoretti* 40: 'when on each eyelid sweetly doe appeare | an hundred Graces as in shade to sit' (3–4). In its original context, though, the quoted line serves primarily to advertise *Pageaunts*, a title likely designed to remind E. K.'s readers of Petrarch's immensely popular and emblematic *Triumphs*.

The *Shepheardes Calender* is the source for two other lost works. In the *October* eclogue, E. K. glosses a reference to the swan's sweet song by quoting from a sonnet Immerito has elsewhere written: 'The silver swanne doth sing before her dying day | As shee that feeles the deepe delight that is in death' (*October* (90)). Finally, in that eclogue's prefatory argument, E. K. expresses his hope to publish the *English Poete*, a book that had 'lately come to [his] hands' and in which the author 'at large discourseth' on the sources of poetic inspiration. This work, he writes, complements the *October* eclogue, in that both depict poetry as 'no arte, but a divine gift and heavenly instinct not to bee gotten by laboure and learning, but adorned with both'. If it existed, *English Poete* would have been written shortly before (or possibly at about the same time as) Philip Sidney's *Defence of Poetry*, with which it apparently bears affinities. But if Spenser knew of Sidney's plans for the *Defence*, the reference may instead signal affiliation with the *Calender*'s dedicatee, suggesting that this 'new' English poet [i.e., Spenser] agrees with Sidney's ideas about the renovation of English poetry. The *English Poete* may even be a playfully oblique reference to Sidney's text, with Spenser and/or Harvey letting readers know (via the sometimes unreliable E. K.) that a contemporary has indeed written, or is in the process of writing, an English treatise on poetics.[3] In his *A Discourse of English Poetrie* (1586), William Webbe wishes he could have a sight of *English Poete*, presumably because he was pursuing a similar project without the benefit of a contemporary model (Sidney's *Defence* was not published until 1595). Webbe also pleads for the publication of Immerito's *Dreames*, *Legendes*, and *Court of Cupide* to 'satisfye the thirsty desires of many which desire nothing more' (D1ʳ). Webbe most likely reiterates E. K.'s references. However, if these other works had circulated in manuscript, Webbe may have known about them from other sources: he graduated from Cambridge the same year as Spenser, and was enough of a literary insider to name the *Calender*'s anonymous author as 'Master Sp.'.

The correspondence between Spenser and Harvey adds several lost works to those mentioned in the *Calender*. Spenser suggests that he may dedicate '*My Slomber*, and the other Pamphlets' to Edward Dyer, because these works may not suit the 'inclination and qualitie' of an unnamed alternative candidate, either Sidney or the Earl of Leicester (*Prose*, 6; *SE*, 432). *My Slomber* is likely the same work as *A Senights Slumber*, mentioned in the preface to *Complaints*, and is possibly the same as *Dreames*—though revelatory 'dream' visions and 'sleep'-related illusions constituted different literary traditions. Spenser also claims that he plans shortly to 'sette forth' a book entitled *Epithalamion Thamesis*. This poem, he explains, will draw on the geographical information in Raphael Holinshed's *Chronicles* (1577) to describe the ancestry of the Thames, 'all the Countery that he passeth thorough', his marriage, and his fluvial wedding guests. 'A worke beleeve me', Spenser assures his friend, 'of much labour' and cartographical research (*Prose*, 17). Harvey in response notes that this *Epithalamion* will provide a 'president, and patterne' for an up-and-coming 'brother' poet, one of whose projects may in time reach the 'length, bredth, and depth' of Spenser's river poem (*Prose*, 468–70). If he existed at all, this novice may be William Vallans, whose poem about the river Lee, *A Tale of Two Swannes* (1590, but probably composed about 1577), mentions *Epithalamion Thamesis*.[4] In his preface, Vallans wonders why the version he has seen in 'Latene verse' has been suppressed, and why the version in English, 'long since' promised, is 'not perfourmed' (A2ʳ).

Spenser also mentions his *Stemmata Dudleiana*, which includes 'sundry Apostrophes' addressed 'you knowe to whome', and reminds Harvey that it is not a work 'lightly' to be circulated; 'trust me', he adds in a moment of self-congratulation, 'I never dyd better' (*Prose*, 18). Apparently written in Latin, *Stemmata Dudleiana* may have been a genealogy of Spenser's patron, Robert Dudley, Earl of Leicester: Spenser suggests that the work follows Harvey's example, possibly indicating that the *Stemmata*, like Harvey's *Gratulationes* (1578), praised Leicester and proposed his marriage to Elizabeth (Orwen 1946). In response, Harvey claims that a week's 'pollishing and trimming' would suffice to finish either the *Stemmata* or another lost work, Spenser's 'nine Englishe *Commoedies*' (*Prose*, 459–60). In a later letter, Harvey notes that these works imitate Herodotus in being named after the nine Muses, and he likens them to Ludovico Ariosto's comedies for their 'finenesse of plausible Elocution' and 'rarenesse of Poeticall invention' (*Prose*, 471). The comparison of Spenser's elocution and invention with that found in some of the best known drama of the Italian Renaissance does not necessarily suggest—implausibly—that Spenser had written nine plays. Spenser (with Harvey following) may very well be drawing on the medieval use of 'comedy' for a narrative poem, particularly since Chaucer uses 'comedye' in this sense in the stanza of *Troilus and Criseyde* that begins 'Go litel bok' (V.1786), the line Spenser appropriates for the opening of *The Shepheardes Calender* ('To His Booke'). Spenser's 'commoedies' may therefore have been a series of shorter dramatic speeches, such as those in his *Teares of the Muses*.

The third major source for the lost works is the preface to Spenser's *Complaints* (1591). In 'The Printer to the *Gentle Reader*', Spenser's publisher William Ponsonby explains that the success of *The Faerie Queene* (1590) prompted him to try to 'get into [his] handes such smale Poemes of the same Authors; as [Ponsonby] heard were disperst abroad in sundrie hands, and not easie to bee come by, by [the author] himselfe; some of them having bene diverslie imbeziled and purloyned from him, since his departure over Sea'. While *Complaints* includes a thematically coherent selection of Spenser's works both old and new, Ponsonby asserts that the poet had also written

sundrie others, namelie *Ecclesiastes*, and *Canticum canticorum* translated, *A senights slumber*, *The hell of lovers, his Purgatorie*, being all dedicated to Ladies; so it may seeme he ment them all to one volume. Besides some other Pamphlets looselie scattered abroad: as *The dying Pellican, The howers of the Lord, The sacrifice of a sinner, The seven Psalmes, &c.* (Spenser 1989: 224)

As a group, these differ from other lost works in that most appear to treat devotional subjects. Three are biblical translations: Ecclesiastes, Canticles (the Song of Solomon, or Song of Songs), and the seven penitential psalms. The *Howers of the Lord* and *The Sacrifice of a Sinner* are self-evidently devotional, and in this context the *Dying Pellican*, also mentioned by Harvey alongside *Dreames*, suggests a treatment of the pelican in its traditional role as an emblem for Christ (because the bird was thought to feed its young with its own blood). As Ponsonby's preface is the only evidence for most of these works, their status as component parts of Spenser's literary self-fashioning is less secure than that of the works listed in the *Calender* or correspondence. But Spenser's probable involvement in the publication of *Complaints* lends some authority to Ponsonby's words: the two men certainly maintained a close working relationship, as Ponsonby had just published *The Faerie Queene* and would continue to publish Spenser's new books while Spenser lived. Furthermore, a manuscript commendatory sonnet dated 1588 (before the publication of *Complaints*) suggests that literary contemporaries thought Spenser had written devotional poetry. The poem discusses the forthcoming publication of *The Faerie Queene* and praises its author as a divinely inspired poet who writes of 'Heavens course' as well as the 'bloudy warrs of Men'. If readers doubt the judgment of the sonnet's anonymous author, he directs them to read Spenser's works, 'Then deeme, who may it be | That can each God in Heaven and Hell descrye' (Black 2001: 124). An inaccurate description of Spenser's publications so far or the forthcoming epic, these lines may describe one or more of the poems Ponsonby lists.

Evidence for two additional lost works appears in sources other than these three publications. In the *Vewe of the Presente State of Ireland* (1633), the speaker Irenius, often read as a figure for Spenser, notes his plans to produce a work on the *Antiquities of Ireland* (*Prose*, 81–2, 230–1). Finally, Spenser may have written additional instalments of *The Faerie Queene*. In the 'Letter to Ralegh' Spenser refers to the poem's 'first twelve bookes', and the title pages of the 1590 and 1596 editions both advertise the poem as 'disposed into twelve books'. In *Amoretti* 80 (1595), Spenser acknowledges that he has completed only the first six books, but indicates that he still considers the work but 'halfe fordonne'. The title page of the posthumous 1609 edition retains the promise of twelve books and prints the *Two Cantos of Mutabilitie* as Book VII, cantos 6 and 7 (plus two stanzas of an 'unperfite' canto 8). The packaging of this edition may suggest that Spenser's publisher thought, or at least hoped, that other parts of *The Faerie Queene* had been completed and would be discovered. These missing books of Spenser's epic have especially tantalized the imaginations of later writers and scholars.

READING THE LOST WORKS

What happened to the lost works? As Jack B. Oruch notes, 'For each item several possibilities exist: accidental disappearance, theft, deliberate suppression, incorporation into another work by a new title, or Spenser's failure to write what he and others spoke of as planned, in progress, or completed' (*SE*, 738). Some of the shorter poems Ponsonby described as 'disperst abroad in sundrie hands' or 'imbeziled and purloyned' from Spenser may never have been recovered from coterie circulation, whether authorized or unauthorized. In his *Epigrammatum libri quatuor* (1607), John Stradling claimed that some manuscripts had been consumed in a fire set by Irish rebels (G3^v). The final books of *The Faerie Queene* may likewise have been lost or destroyed: in 1633, Sir James Ware posited that the poem's conclusion was lost 'by the disorder and abuse' of a servant, 'whom [Spenser] had sent before him into England' (*Prose*, 531). Spenser himself encouraged such narratives of loss, dwelling on the vulnerability of 'good thoughts' to the ravages of 'wicked Time' in his continuation of Chaucer's unfinished *Squire's Tale*:

> O cursed Eld the cankerworme of writs,
> How may these rimes, so rude as doth appeare,
> Hope to endure, sith workes of heavenly wits
> Are quite devoured, and brought to nought by little bits?   (IV.ii.33)[5]

But 'cursed Eld' is not the only enemy to 'writs'. Spenser may have suppressed the *Stemmata Dudleiana*, for example, because it was dangerous to circulate pedigrees that advanced claims of royal blood (Bennett 1942: 92; Van Es 2002: 163). Finally, some of these lost works may never have been more than 'good thoughts' in the first place. The *Calender* and the correspondence are both self-consciously (not to mention self-promotingly) clever texts, full of coterie allusions to matters now opaque, and some of these references may have been the playful product of insider games or jokes.[6]

But of these various possibilities, scholarly attention has traditionally focused on the idea that revised versions of these lost works became embedded in the poetry Spenser eventually did publish. For example, *The Faerie Queene* may draw on the *Stemmata Dudleiana* in the genealogies of Artegall and Britomart, the *Court of Cupide* in the descriptions of Mirabella's trials or of Busirane's house, the *Epithalamion Thamesis* in the marriage of the Thames and Medway, the translation of Moschus in Venus's search for Cupid in Book III, canto 6, *My Slomber* and *Dreames* in the visions and dreams in Book I, or *Pageaunts* and *Legendes* in any number of places. *Stemmata Dudleiana* may have become the basis of *The Ruines of Time*, the *Epithalamion Thamesis* may have inspired aspects of *Prothalamion*, and *Dreames* may have been refashioned as the elegy for Douglas Howard in *Daphnaïda*, which recollects the dream vision of Chaucer's *Book of the Duchess*. The *Fowre Hymnes* (1596) may incorporate *The Hell of Lovers, his Purgatorie* and include the other works Ponsonby mentions as 'dedicated to Ladies' and suitable for gathering in one volume: the poems collected in *Fowre Hymns* focus on the philosophy of love and the book was dedicated to the Countesses of Warwick and Cumberland.[7] The published version of *The Faerie Queene* may even incorporate its 'lost' second half. Northrop Frye (1961: 110) notes that 'as one virtue is bound to involve others, Spenser's scheme was bound to foreshorten as he went on', so the extant six books may include passages and episodes Spenser initially envisioned as constituting additional books. A similar dynamic may be at work with many of these missing poems. Just as he revised for *Amoretti* the line about the eyelid-perching Graces originally intended for *Pageaunts* (quoted earlier), Spenser may have used other lost works where and when he saw opportunity and appropriateness.

Another way to understand the lost works is to see them as part of a self-consciously crafted campaign to promote Spenser as a 'prolific virtuoso writer in all genres, one who could supply much fine work to patron and public if only he were properly encouraged and rewarded' (*SE*, 738). But even beyond their possible role in generating publicity and patronage, the lost works serve to suggest important answers to implicit questions about the 'new Poete' at particular cultural and vocational moments. In what literary traditions and debates was it important that he intervene? What genealogies were claimed for him? What alliances did he forge, and in what literary communities did he participate? Whether or not they existed, the lost works reveal what Spenser and his circle assumed his ambitions, literary heritage, and networks should be. When English readers first encountered the anonymous Master Immerito he was a *tabula rasa*. Through their descriptions of his other writings, the *Calender*, the correspondence, and later the *Complaints* sought to 'create' him as a nationally significant figure.[8]

Several lost works, for example, signify interventions in ongoing debates about the literary resources of the English language, particularly the extent to which poetry in the vernacular should rely on classical principles. Should a fledgling poet employ the accentual-syllabic metre that would eventually become the norm for English verse, or the quantitative metres employed in Greek and Latin, which depend not on stress but on the quantity and duration of syllables? The question remained open in the 1570s and 1580s. Spenser informs Harvey that he lately prefers 'Englishe Versifying' (i.e., quantitative metre) and will employ it for *Epithalamion Thamesis* (*Prose*, 252). Spenser also plans to dedicate *My Slomber* to Edward Dyer, who, along with Sidney, had founded a 'faction' that promoted 'certaine Lawes and rules of Quantities of English sillables' (*Prose*, 17, 6). Spenser names this new literary club the Areopagus. Whether a real or imagined literary community, the Areopagus represents an English response to Continental academies such as the Pléiade in France, centres of artistic production and authority that promoted reliance on classical models.[9] These references thus align Spenser with major movements in Continental poetry as well as with influential English contemporaries. If Spenser had written these poems but then incorporated them in other works, he rewrote them in the accentual-syllabic verse increasingly recognized in the 1580s and 1590s as better suited to the expressive possibilities of poetry in English. Nonetheless, his experiments with quantitative poetry may have showed Spenser what English could and could not do relative to Latin, teaching him about the boundaries of play with word order, the potential for rhetorical variety within the verse line, and the poetic importance of each syllable (*Prose*, 479–83).

In general, these early discussions of lost works suggest that Spenser was experimenting with a variety of models and influences. If *Legendes* eventually evolved into the Legends of Holiness, Temperance, and Chastity, for instance, then the *Calender* envisions Spenser's career as moving not only along the Virgilian trajectory from pastoral to epic but also within a calendrical tradition, since 'legends' can describe hagiographic and martyrological texts associated with the calendar year (Chapman 2004). The topographical *Epithalamion*, the genealogical *Stemmata Dudleiana*, and the visionary *Dreames* (as well as the planned *Antiquities of Ireland*) anticipate Spenser's virtuoso use of the 'forms of history' available to him, such as the antiquarian, the chorographic, and the prophetic.[10]

But references to lost works in the *Calender* and correspondence also function more specifically to depict Spenser's culturally nationalist aims as they identify the classical, Continental, and English models Spenser sought to emulate and eventually to surpass. As mentioned earlier, the discussions of *Dreames* situate Spenser as Chaucer's heir and compare his powers of 'invention' favourably with those of classical Greek and Italian poets. The nine comedies demonstrate the new poet's range: he competes not only in the heavyweight class of epic, with his '*Elvish Queene*' seeking to 'overgo' Ariosto's *Orlando Furioso*, but he also measures up well against the Continental star in other literary weight classes, such as dramatic verse (*Prose*, 471). Moreover, the comedies indicate Spenser's shared commitment with Ariosto to marry classical sources with contemporary themes and vernacular expression. The reference to Petrarch's *Visions* in connection with *Dreames* likewise stresses Spenser's commitment to writing in the vernacular, as does the translation of Moschus: the new poet has remade a classical text into English just as Poliziano had translated it from Greek to Latin. Spenser's announced intervention in the epithalamic tradition similarly emphasizes his classical, Continental, and neo-Latin connections. At the same time, the influence of Holinshed on *Epithalamion Thamesis* places that work in the particularly English tradition of antiquarian river poems, linking Spenser with writers such as William Camden and John Leland. Many of the lost works thus elaborate on the picture of Master Immerito painted in the *Calender* as being 'yet both English, and also used of most excellent Authors and most famous Poetes' (Spenser 1989: 14). As a group, they consequently contribute to Spenser's self-characterization as a vernacular 'neoteric' poet—a writer who experiments with various 'lower' forms in ways that fruitfully inform his epic project, and who looks not only to the past for inspiration but also to the ideas and writers of the European present, employing them to reorient the past from a contemporary, international perspective.[11]

A decade after the publication of the *Calender* and correspondence, William Ponsonby announced what he, and perhaps Spenser, envisioned as the next career move of the 'new Poet' (Spenser 1989: 224). As a collection, *Complaints* represents the fruition of the verse experiments and Continental imitations mentioned a decade earlier in *The Shepheardes Calender* and correspondence (*SE*, 179–80). The volume also seems to have provided Spenser with a chance to recast earlier work. *Complaints* contains *Mother Hubberds Tale*, which the dedication contends was 'composed in . . . youth' and which originally engaged with events of the late 1570s, as well as reworked versions of Spenser's very first publications, the sonnets based on the work of Clément Marot and Joachim Du Bellay that had appeared in Jan Van der Noot's *A Theatre for Worldings* (1569). Other poems may also be based on earlier, apparently 'lost', work. The nine comedies named for the Muses may be connected in some way to the nine laments in *Teares of the Muses*; *My Slomber* and *Dreames* may be related to the three *Visions* that end the volume, or, in their shared use of the trope of sleep, to *Virgils Gnat* and *Mother Hubberds Tale*.[12]

But Ponsonby's preface implicitly addresses a more general question: with the publication of *Complaints* and the first three books of *The Faerie Queene*, what poetic avenues now opened? According to Spenser's publisher, the next step was not the second instalment of *The Faerie Queene* but shorter works that could be collected to similar 'grave and profitable' effect as *Complaints* (Spenser 1989: 222). These poems likely were, or were envisioned as, lyrics: popular devotional forms of the period included sonnets, hymns, and metrical psalms. Ponsonby's wistful catalogue of unavailable titles reflects Spenser's continued interest in the idea of poetry as divine gift, an idea established by his *English Poete*. Devotional poetry was regarded as a 'high' form that Spenser and his promoters may have thought worthy of the new poet's next efforts. After all, Sidney had praised poetry that imitated 'the inconceivable excellencies of God' as the pinnacle of poetic art, and Ponsonby's list echoes Sidney's examples: 'David in his Psalms; Solomon in his Song of Songs, in his Ecclesiastes, and Proverbs; Moses and Deborah in their Hymns; and the writer of Job' (Sidney 1989: 217). This potential move toward the explicitly devotional may reflect the influence of prominent Continental alternatives to the Virgilian career path, particularly that of the Augustinian turn from 'youthful, courtly, erotic poetry to aged, contemplative, divine poetry'.[13]

Spenser's association with metrical psalms has additional implications. There was a tradition of using psalm translation to convey an anti-court pose (Prescott 1991), a tradition consistent with the sceptical Spenser of the 1590s who critiqued the court in *Complaints* and *Colin Clout*. More generally, writing psalms would align Spenser not only with the Continental, Calvinist traditions established by Clément Marot and Theodore de Bèze but also with English ones, particularly the metrically and meta-phorically experimental verse translations of Philip Sidney and Mary Sidney Herbert, Countess of Pembroke.[14] More broadly, like other 'lost works', this reference may create and sustain Spenser's connections to Philip, who by the publication of Spenser's *Complaints* in 1591 had begun to assume posthumous mythical status as a literary and political hero, and to the Sidney family generally, a collective model of poetic skill and potentially a powerful source of patronage. Spenser began his civil career working for Leicester and Henry Sidney, and may have exchanged work in manuscript with Philip (see n. 3). *Complaints* itself is in some ways inspired by Philip and is unified by dedications and references to him and his Sidney and Dudley relatives (Lemmi 1930; *SE*, 180). These references anticipate and may have invited Mary Sidney Herbert's possible collaboration with Spenser on *Astrophel* and the *Doleful Lay of Clorinda* (1595).[15] If *Complaints* as a whole proclaims ties to the Sidneys and what they represent, the preface's depiction of Spenser's ambitions as religious lyricist suggests literary cross-fertilization and parallel career paths among Spenser, Sidney, and Pembroke. As the publisher of numerous works by Sidney, Pembroke, and Spenser in the 1590s, Ponsonby himself was a locus for a literary community that was both real in some respects and aspirational in others. He worked actively to foster this community, and perhaps encouraged Pembroke to release some of her brother's texts by publishing her own work as well as numerous dedications to her, including addresses by Spenser himself in *Complaints*, the 1590 *Faerie Queene*, *Colin Clout*, and *Astrophel*. Ponsonby's desire to publish Spenser's religious poetry as a collection corresponds to Fulke Greville's planned volume of Sidney's religious writings, and may even have been intended to invite Pembroke to provide him with the nearly or recently finished Sidneian *Psalmes* for publication. Ponsonby may also have hoped to loosen monopolies on publication of devotional works by whetting public appetite for those of so prominent a writer as Spenser.[16]

What happened to these apparent plans for a collection of devotional poems and biblical translations? In the sixteenth century, the devotional poem competed with the Petrarchan sonnet for primacy of lyric place (Dubrow 1995: 61–4; Hamlin 2005: 135). What may have been intended as a Sidney-inspired collection of psalms and other religious lyrics in 1591, shortly before the publication of *Astrophil and Stella*, may have become instead a sonnet sequence in the Petrarchan tradition once the popularity of Sidney's sonnets raised the prestige of what had been considered a 'low' form (Marotti 1982: 407–8). Perhaps torn between these two career options for an English poet, the devotional and the Petrarchan, Spenser chose to incorporate some of these intended religious works into *Amoretti and Epithalamion*, published by

Ponsonby in 1595. This collection rings with echoes of the Psalms and the Song of Solomon (mentioned in Ponsonby's preface to *Complaints*), follows the structure of the liturgical calendar, and marries earthly to spiritual love (cf. Kaske 2004: 38–46).

SUPPOSITIOUS WORKS

While uncertainties of attribution complicate the canon of many Renaissance writers, Spenser is associated with relatively few works of debated authorship. Three of these are discussed in more detail elsewhere in this *Handbook*. *A Vewe of the Presente State of Ireland*, written in 1596 and printed under Spenser's name in 1633, is widely accepted as Spenser's. A strong case has also been made for one of the three state papers known collectively as *A Brief Note of Ireland* (see Chapter 17 above). The one poem to spur discussion is the *Doleful Lay of Clorinda*, printed in *Astrophel*, the collection of elegies dedicated to Sidney and published with *Colin Clouts Come Home Again* (1595). The collection's poetic fiction ascribes the *Doleful Lay* to Astrophel's sister, suggesting that it was to be read as the voice of Mary Sidney Herbert; this attribution is still a matter of dispute.

The one remaining suppositious work is *Axiochus* (1592), a translation of a dialogue on death and immortality popular in the Renaissance and thought (incorrectly) to be by Plato.[17] The title page of the 1592 English version advertises itself as 'Translated out of Greeke by *Edw. Spenser*', a claim repeated in a prefatory note to the reader: 'translated out of Greeke, by that worthy Scholler and Poet, Maister *Edward Spenser*, whose studies have & do carry no mean commendation, because their deserts are of so great esteeme' (¶4r). The volume clearly intends readers to identify the translator as Edmund Spenser, the only well-known poet of that name. Because Spenser's publications had been either anonymous or had printed his name as 'Ed.', 'Edward' was a plausible error if the publisher, Cuthbert Burby, was unacquainted with Spenser. Scholars in favour of the attribution note that the original *Axiochus* was known among the Sidney circle—Philippe Duplessis de Mornay, a close friend of the Sidney family, had published a French translation in 1581—and argue for verbal parallels between the translation and both the prose in the *Vewe* and the poetry in *The Faerie Queene*. Supporting the attribution is the fact that the translation is not 'out of Greeke' but is based on a 1568 Latin version: Spenser's command of Greek is debated.

Scholars who question the attribution note that the translation is not mentioned in any contemporary discussion of Spenser's works (printed, manuscript, rumoured, or 'lost'), including the list compiled by Spenser's own regular publisher, Ponsonby; that many of the parallels are commonplace in Renaissance texts, and could also be the result of imitation rather than shared authorship; and that an attribution by somebody who apparently did not know Spenser carries little weight. In addition, the

1592 volume includes the text of a 'sweet speech' presented before the Queen at a tournament in January 1581, a speech Spenser could not have written since he was in Dublin at the time. Instead, this additional text is likely to be the work of poet and translator Anthony Munday, who is also the likely author of the book's dedication to London alderman Benedict Barnam. Since the dedication is for the translation, not the speech, the entire volume could very well be Munday's work. If so, was the use of Spenser's name an innocent publisher error, or was it instead a shady attempt to capitalize on Spenser's success? A similar question arises with *Brittain's Ida* (1628), a pirated edition of a Spenserian imitation by Phineas Fletcher published as 'Written by that Renowned Poët, Edmond Spencer'. With *Axiochus*, the 1592 volume was the first book Burby published, and he may have hoped the attribution would improve its chances in the literary marketplace. Munday, a man and a writer prone to impostures and impersonations, may even have been complicit in the strategy. Nonetheless, the *Axiochus* was attributed to Spenser in his lifetime and, as far as we know, was not disowned. It will be included in the new *Collected Works of Edmund Spenser*, where its presence will spur consideration of Spenser's engagements with Renaissance Platonic and humanist traditions.

CONTINUATIONS

The handful of suppositious works suggests that Spenser exercised an unusual degree of control over the circulation of his writings in manuscript and their publication in print. Only one poem (the *Doleful Lay*) has raised questions, and even in that case the doubts arise out of Spenser's own deliberate play with textual framing. But while Spenser left behind few works that *may* be his, many poets were inspired to create works that aspired to be *like* Spenser's. Beginning in his lifetime and for centuries to follow, Spenser was imitated, appropriated, and adapted for a wide range of creative purposes.[18] Spenser's literary influence is addressed elsewhere in this *Handbook* (see Chapter 36 below). However, this chapter concludes with the two major imitations that pushed imitation into the realm of continuation. In the decades following Spenser's death, Ralph Knevet and Samuel Sheppard extended Spenser's epic project through the reigns of James I and Charles I. Spenser's was still a contemporary voice to these writers: the *Vewe* was published in 1633, and hopes remained that other works would still come to light. Knevet and Sheppard wrote in dialogue with these hopes, continuing *The Faerie Queene* in a way they believed Spenser himself would have, were he witness to the reigns that followed Elizabeth's.

Ralph Knevet's *A Supplement of the Faery Queene*, written by 1635 but never published, continues Spenser's poem through three additional books.[19] Books VII and VIII offer the politically allegorical legends of Albanio or Prudence (James I) and Callimachus or Fortitude (Gustavus Adolphus II of Sweden, Protestant hero of the

Thirty Years' War); Book IX presents the more generally allegorical legend of Belcoeur or Liberality. Each book comprises twelve cantos, ranging in length from between 36 and 63 Spenserian stanzas, and imitates Spenser's diction, allegorical modes, characters, and chivalric epic-romance world. Throughout, Knevet deploys Spenserian strategies to engage with 'affaires both military and civill' (title page) of his own times. Even Book IX, which largely moves away from political commentary, offers an extended allegory of events in Ireland from the 1580s through the first decade of the seventeenth century (following Spenser's account in Book V, but perhaps also with awareness of the *Vewe*, published while Knevet was writing). Knevet's Arthur, like his Spenserian namesake, makes vigorously heroic appearances in all three books and unites their titular virtues in one person. He is a figure for Charles I, to whom Knevet dedicates the poem; Henrietta Maria assumes the role of the new Gloriana. With Albanio pursuing policies of peace even at the expense of his own daughter and Callimachus dying without achieving his quest, the *Supplement* registers a nostalgia for an Elizabethan militarism and pursuit of honour that Knevet assumes Spenser had celebrated and that Charles, Knevet hopes, will resurrect.

Knevet's monarchist Spenser became royalist in the civil wars of the 1640s, when political instability created a nostalgic desire among the King's supporters for a social order founded in calm obedience of royal rule. The anonymous *Faerie Leveller* (1648), for example, reprinted the episode in which Artegall and Talus defeat the Giant and scatter his 'rebellious mob' (V.ii.29–54). The pamphlet's preface argues that Spenser's tale was prophetical: in the context of the civil war, it claims, Artegall represented Charles I, Talus his forces, Munera Parliamentary taxation, and the socially and economically levelling giant Oliver Cromwell (King 1985). In a far more extended and creative appropriation, Samuel Sheppard revived Spenser as a literary authority for this royalist ideal in *The Faerie King*, an ambitious work of six books of six cantos each, written about 1650 but not published (Sheppard 1984). Unlike Knevet, Sheppard abandons Spenser's characters, diction, allegorical mode, epic-chivalric world, and even stanza form (he employs ottava rima). But he shares Knevet's sense of Spenser as the poet of strong, benevolent monarchy, an ideal against which Sheppard paints an ambivalent, anti-heroic evaluation of Charles I and the events that led to his execution. To Knevet and then to Sheppard, Spenser's Gloriana—at least, the Gloriana they read Spenser as unambiguously celebrating—remained the ideal against which her successors continued to falter. The scarcity of Spenserian continuations (as opposed to imitations and adaptations) suggests that Spenser's poetic successors recognized the danger that the same fate would await them, should they invite direct comparison.

NOTES

1. For surveys, see *Variorum*, VIII, 510–20; *SE*, 737–8. *SE* articles on *Complaints*, dreams, epithalamium, hymns, rivers, and visions have also proved useful in the preparation of this article.

2. Spenser 1989: 19–20; *Prose*, 6, 442–3. To these can be added the 'lewd layes' in praise of love Spenser himself mentions in *Heavenly Love* (8–9), published in *Fowre Hymnes* (1596).
3. For Sidney's possible connections with Spenser and Harvey, see Heninger (1987); *SE*, 656–7; Pask (1996), 83–112; Woudhuysen (1996), 219, 297; Brennan and Kinnamon (2003), 30, 58, 68.
4. See the article on Vallans in *NDNB*.
5. For a discussion of this passage, see Burrow (1996), 62–3. Spenser's continuation of Chaucer's tale occupies *FQ* IV.ii.31–IV.iii.52.
6. For the creation of Spenser's 'persona' in the correspondence, see Quitslund (1996).
7. For surveys of suggestions along these lines up to 1947, see *Variorum*, VIII, 510–20, 522, 526–8; *Prose*, 266–8. See also Bennett (1942), *passim*; *SE*, 737–8.
8. See Chapter 25 below.
9. On the Areopagus, see *Prose*, 479–80; *SE*, 55; Pask (1996), 98–104.
10. See Van Es (2002), 11–19, 58–66, 176–92.
11. For Spenser as neoteric poet, see Greene (2001). For surveys of Spenser's dialogue with his literary sources, see Chapters 26–34 below.
12. Spenser (1989), 224 n. See also *Variorum*, VIII, 511–12; *Prose*, 266–7.
13. See Cheney (1993), 5; see also 23–76, 195–224.
14. For the psalm tradition, see Hamlin (2004); and *Sidney Journal* 23(1–2) (2005), a special issue devoted to the subject. A new edition of the Sidney psalter is forthcoming, edited by Michael Brennan, Hannibal Hamlin, Margaret Hannay, and Noel Kinnamon.
15. See above Chapter 13.
16. See Woudhuysen (1996), 226, 416–17; Hannay (2002), 30, 34–5; Brennan (2002). For Ponsonby's connections with the Sidney circle (and other significant writers and socially prominent figures), publication choices, and support of Protestant causes, see Brennan (1983).
17. Printed in *Prose*, 19–38. For surveys of this debate, see *Prose*, 487–96; Erdman and Fogel (1966), 424–7; *SE*, 77.
18. For surveys, see *SE*, 395–403; Radcliffe (1996); Alpers (2001).
19. Edited in Lavender (1955); a new edition, by Christopher Burlinson and Andrew Zurcher, is in progress.

BIBLIOGRAPHY

Alpers, P. (2001). 'Spenser's Influence', in A. Hadfield (ed.), *The Cambridge Companion to Spenser*. Cambridge: Cambridge University Press: 252–71.
Bennett, J. W. (1942). *The Evolution of* The Faerie Queene. Chicago: University of Chicago Press.
Black, J. (2001). '"Pan is Hee": Commending *The Faerie Queene*'. *SSt* 15: 121–34.
Brennan, M. G. (1983). 'William Ponsonby: Elizabethan Stationer'. *Analytical and Enumerative Bibliography* 7: 91–110.
—— (2002). 'The Queen's Proposed Visit to Wilton House in 1599 and the "Sidney Psalms"'. *Sidney Journal* 20: 27–53.
—— and Noel J. Kinnamon (eds) (2003). *A Sidney Chronology 1554–1654*. Houndmills, Basingstoke: Palgrave Macmillan.
Burrow, C. (1996). *Edmund Spenser*. Plymouth: Northcote House.

Chapman, A. A. (2004). 'Legendary Spenser'. Unpublished conference paper. Abstract in *The Spenser Review* 35(3): 28.

Cheney, P. (1993). *Spenser's Famous Flight: A Renaissance Idea of a Literary Career*. Toronto: University of Toronto Press.

Dubrow, H. (1995). *Echoes of Desire: English Petrarchism and its Counterdiscourses*. Ithaca, NY: Cornell University Press.

Erdman, D. V., and Fogel, Ephim G. (1966). *Evidence for Authorship: Essays on Problems of Attribution*. Ithaca, NY: Cornell University Press.

Frye, N. (1961). 'The Structure of Imagery in *The Faerie Queene*'. *UTQ* 30: 109–27.

Greene, R. (2001). 'Spenser and Contemporary Vernacular Poetry', in A. Hadfield (ed.), *The Cambridge Companion to Spenser*. Cambridge: Cambridge University Press: 237–51.

Hamlin, H. (2004). *Psalm Culture and Early Modern English Literature*. Cambridge: Cambridge University Press.

—— (2005). '"The highest matter in the noblest forme": The Influence of the Sidney Psalms'. *Sidney Journal* 23: 133–57.

Hannay, M. P. (2002). 'The Countess of Pembroke's Agency in Print and Scribal Culture', in G. L. Justice and N. Tinker (eds), *Women's Writing and the Circulation of Ideas: Manuscript Publication in England, 1550–1800*. Cambridge: Cambridge University Press: 17–49.

Heninger, S. K., Jr. (1987). 'Spenser and Sidney at Leicester House'. *SSt* 8: 239–49.

Kaske, C. (2004). 'Spenser's *Amoretti and Epithalamion*: A Psalter of Love', in D. W. Doerksen and C. Hodgkins (eds), *Centered on the Word: Literature, Scripture, and the Tudor-Stuart Middle Way*. Newark: University of Delaware Press: 28–49.

King, J. N. (1985). '*The Faerie Leveller*: A 1648 Royalist Retelling of *The Faerie Queene*, V.ii.29–54'. *HLQ* 48: 297–308.

Lavender, A. (1955). 'An Edition of Ralph Knevett's *Supplement of the Faery Queene* (1635)', 2 vols. Unpublished PhD dissertation, New York University.

Lemmi, C. W. (1930). 'The Allegorical Meaning of Spenser's *Muiopotmos*'. *PMLA* 45: 732–48.

Marotti, A. F. (1982). '"Love is not Love": Elizabethan Sonnet Sequences and the Social Order'. *ELH* 49: 396–428.

Orwen, W. R. (1946). 'Spenser's "Stemmata Dudleiana"'. *N&Q* 190: 9–11.

Pask, K. (1996). *The Emergence of the English Author: Scripting the Life of the Poet in Early Modern England*. Cambridge: Cambridge University Press.

Prescott, A. L. (1991). 'Evil tongues at the court of Saul: the Renaissance David as a slandered courtier'. *JMRS* 21: 163–86.

Quitslund, J. A. (1996). 'Questionable Evidence in the Letters of 1580 between Gabriel Harvey and Edmund Spenser', in J. H. Anderson, D. Cheney, and D. A. Richardson (eds), *Spenser's Life and the Subject of Biography*. Amherst: University of Massachusetts Press: 81–98.

Radcliffe, D. H. (1996). *Edmund Spenser: A Reception History*. Columbia, SC: Camden House.

Sheppard, S. (1984). *The Faerie King (c. 1650)*, ed. P. J. Klemp. Salzburg Studies in English Literature, 107:2. Salzburg: Institut für Anglistik und Amerikanistik.

Sidney, P. (1989). *The Oxford Authors: Sir Philip Sidney*, ed. Katherine Duncan-Jones. Oxford: Oxford University Press.

Van Es, B. (2002). *Spenser's Forms of History*. Oxford: Oxford University Press.

Woudhuysen, H. R. (1996). *Sir Philip Sidney and the Circulation of Manuscripts 1558–1640*. Oxford: Clarendon Press.

PART III

POETIC CRAFT

....

CHAPTER 20

SPENSER'S LANGUAGE(S): LINGUISTIC THEORY AND POETIC DICTION

....

DOROTHY STEPHENS

ELIZABETHAN ENGLISH?

....

A poet's employment of unusual forms of language is more often admired than disliked by critics of modern and contemporary poetry, yet Spenserian scholars have often felt it necessary to defend Spenser by arguing either that he was a great poet despite his abuse of the language or that his abuse of the language has been greatly exaggerated. As early as 1754, Thomas Warton cut through what he believed was the prevalent notion that Spenser's language was compounded of archaisms, neologisms, and foreign imports, observing on the contrary that 'the ground-work and substance of his style is the language of his age' (Warton 1968: 133). This evaluation of Spenser's language as essentially Elizabethan vernacular was reinforced in the early decades of the twentieth century through painstaking textual analysis by Emma Field Pope (1926: 605–6), Bruce McElderry (1932: 168), and Herbert Sugden (1936: 9).

One might suppose the issue settled long ago, yet if Spenser's language is essentially Elizabethan, it is nonetheless noticeably different from Sidney's, Shakespeare's, or Jonson's—and anyone introducing college students to Spenser will find that for them, the issue is fresh and relevant. To readers conversant mostly with orthographically modern editions of Shakespeare's plays, Spenser's language can seem perverse, despite all teacherly assurances to the contrary (Pope 1926: 606). Understanding Spenser's language requires not simply a good glossary and an introduction to the basics of *u*'s and *v*'s, but an explanation of the philosophies and politics behind his word choices. Without these, it is almost impossible to connect his apparently erratic diction with the larger aims of his poetry.

To say that Spenser wrote in his country's vernacular is hardly to define his lexicon, much less his style, given that any vernacular is composed of many overlapping dialects and discourses. In addition, theorists across sixteenth-century Europe differed as to whether a poet writing in one major vernacular—such as English—was justified in borrowing from another—such as Italian. Furthermore, poets were expected to deploy vernacular vocabularies with skillful artifice rather than with naturalism. How much of this artifice should be the artist's own innovation, with the creation of new rules, and how much should result from the adroit following of pre-existing aesthetic rules, were open questions. Some linguists, indeed, believed that English was less in need of enrichment than of expurgation, with the latter activity directed toward un-English imports, archaisms, and overly rustic or overly pedantic words. In order to make sense of Spenser's diction, then, we must first look at the pre-existing theories upon which he drew.

PRE-EXISTING THEORETICAL FRAMEWORK

Imaginative literature—'poesy'—was defined partly by the idea that its diction should differ from that of other sorts of writing (Rubel 1941: 2), but the question was what should generate this difference and what patterns it should follow, if any. The use of English dialects had already been given a literary cast in the work of medieval writers such as the *Gawain* poet, Lydgate, Caxton, and Chaucer, as well as in the work of early Renaissance poets such as Skelton and Gascoigne, yet to some sixteenth-century English writers, the existing vernacular of their country seemed crude. These writers advocated a plentiful importation of terms from other languages, in order to polish the native tongue into the brilliance of classical Latin and Greek. They pointed out that the ancient Greeks and Romans had done the same thing with their own languages, engaging in linguistic commerce with surrounding peoples (Pope 1926: 582). In other words, the link between the desire to enrich English and the desire to make England a rich empire was not subtle. Other writers believed English already sufficient in itself; their brand of nationalism was constructed around a linguistic xenophobia (although, like xenophobes today, they could not do wholly without foreign imports themselves).

In deciding what words to borrow, a poet could refer to Aristotle for guidance, learning in *The Poetics* that although clarity was best served by using only ordinary and current words from a single vernacular, restricting oneself to such a vocabulary would result in banal verse. Composing with unusual words, on the other hand, would achieve the goal of elevated language, but overdoing it would result in barbarism. It was necessary, then, to choose carefully. Aristotle recommends that writers lengthen, contract, or otherwise modify existing words in order to achieve an elevated style while remaining clear (*Poetics*, xxii).[1] Turning to Horace, we read that the reason a poet is justified in coining words is that language resembles a tree whose new leaves replace the old, fallen ones. Poets who coin words help create new linguistic norms as the innovations enter common use (*Ars Poetica*, ll. 47–72). Tasso largely agrees with Aristotle, adding that suitably elevated language is what distinguishes the poet from the orator (1973: 124). Du Bellay and the *Pleiade*, other clear influences upon Spenser, advocate coining words as a method of enriching one's vernacular.

English theorists tended to be more conservative and parochial than those on the Continent, but moderates such as Peter Betham, Thomas More, and Thomas Wilson cautiously recommend innovation on the strict condition that it be allowed only when it enriches the expressive possibilities of English rather than putting perfectly adequate English words out of work (Betham 1544; More 1532; Wilson 1553; Rubel 1941: 7–8). Wilson emphasizes that simplicity and clarity must be the primary objectives (Wilson 1553; Pope 1926: 598).

From Aristotle onward, theorists largely agreed that language must observe decorum; that is, it must be appropriate for its subject matter and, in the case of dialogue, for its speaker (*Poetics*, xv). According to the rules of decorum, the overall pattern of poetic diction in courtly poems should differ from that in rustic poems, such as eclogues (Rubel 1941: 11). Alexander Barclay, who wrote the first vernacular eclogues in English in the early decades of the sixteenth century, observes, 'It were not fitting a heard or man rurall | To speake in termes gay and rhetoricall. | So teacheth Horace in arte of poetry, | That writers namely their reason should apply | Mete speeche appropring to euery personage, | After his estate, behauour, wit and age' (1928: 3). In other words, the rules of dialect could be interpreted to allow for the use of dialect, so long as it was appropriate to the literary situation. But in addition to using the dialects of their own vernaculars for the speech of shepherds, poets could decide whether to rehabilitate rural dialect words by inserting them into otherwise normative language. Thomas Wilson writes, '[E]ither we must make a difference of Englishe, and saie some is learned Englishe, and other some is rude Englishe, or the one is courte talke, the other is countrey speache, or els we must of necessitee, banishe all suche affected Rhetorique, and vse altogether one maner of language' (1553: 87[r]). Ronsard argues that the poet should judiciously adapt words from all dialects, even though that of the court is the most beautiful (1938: 1012–16).

In sixteenth-century England, Malory remained popular, but the idea that a Latinate, courtly language should predominate over the employment of dialect forms was prominent among the humanists. By the same token, most early Tudor theorists recommended against resurrecting archaic terms. Wilson, for example, writes scathingly, 'Some seke so farre for outlandishe Englishe, that thei forget altogether their mothers language. And I dare swere this, if some of their mothers were aliue, thei were not able to tell, what thei say; & yet these fine Englishe clerkes, wil saie thei speake in their mother tongue' (1553: 86^r). Yet poets writing in the courtly tradition often ignored this sort of recommendation in their admiration for Chaucer, whose works were becoming more available because of the printing press (Rubel 1941: 9, 14). Caxton calls him 'the worshipful fader & first foundeur & enbelissher of ornate eloquence in our englissh' (1928: 37). In the early decades of the sixteenth century, Chaucer seems to have been admired less for his embellishment of English than for making the vernacular more flexible, suiting his diction to his subject (Rubel 1941: 17). The very fact that so many poets took him as their model meant that by the time Spenser began writing, Chaucerian forms—or at least, any Chaucerian forms that had not been so thoroughly assimilated into ordinary speech as to have erased the awareness of their being Chaucerian—had become de rigueur poetic usage and were therefore beginning to be considered affected (Rubel 1941: 17–19; Davis 1933: 133). Wilson declares scornfully, 'The fine courtier wil talke nothyng but Chaucer' (1553: 86^v).

Chaucerian borrowings could serve a purpose more serious than fashion. An Augustinian idea developed by the Neoplatonists was that in Eden, there had been no difference between a word and its meaning, no possibility of slippage between speech and understanding. Italian, French, English, and even Latin were corruptions of the original, unified language, and although it was impossible in a postlapsarian world to recuperate that lost unity of signified and signifier—of God and creation— one could at least come nearer to a transcendental truth by chiseling away at the crude encrustations that these languages had acquired through the ages. To do so was to reveal at least some of the inner spirit of the language, the point where imperfect symbols came closest to Neoplatonic truth itself. Stephanie Jed has discussed the early Florentine humanists' desire to 'chastise' and 'chasten' their copies of ancient works, to correct the accumulated errors as a way of establishing the texts in legitimate lines of descent. In the process, the editors established Italy's right to claim itself the legitimate heir of republican Rome—which, according to Livy, had achieved the status of a republic after the male populace had become enraged over Tarquin's violation of the chaste Lucrece (Jed 1989: 24, 30). While Jed discusses the editing of ancient texts, the same theory can illuminate the editing of English vocabulary itself: by excising corruption, the humanists sought to claim for their country's vernacular a respectable place next to ancient Latin, but they wanted simultaneously to make their language pure, honest, and Edenically true. To some, the *addition* of dialect, archaisms, and foreign terms represented corruption, while to others, the *restoration* of older English forms—which might best be found in unfashionable dialects, medieval texts, or even foreign cognates in other Latinate languages—represented purification. For Spenser, Ireland posed a particular problem. While he opposed the appropriation of Gaelic terms as indicative of cultural degeneracy, insisting on maintaining the purity of the mother tongue in colonial situations (*Prose*, 119), words of Gaelic origin inevitably entered his own diction (Maley 2001).[2] McCabe comments,

One of the most surprising features of *A View of the Present State of Ireland*, considered as a dialogue, is the repeated necessity for Irenius to explain elements of his vocabulary to Eudoxus, an Englishman who has not been to Ireland. At the outset, for example, Eudoxus enquires, 'what is that which youe call the *Brehon* lawe it is a worde to us alltogeather unknowen' (*Prose*, 47). For a brief moment, the distinction between 'you' and 'us' locates Irenius with the Irish rather than the English, revealing him as someone whose association with Ireland has already begun to influence his vocabulary in such a way as to render comprehension difficult. 'Brehon' is an everyday component of the colonists' language, but is 'alltogeather unknowen' to Eudoxus…Almost imperceptibly, but surely, the language of the colonist, and by implication his political interests are beginning to diverge from those of his fellow countrymen. (2000b: 86)

Spenser's Diction: The Clinical Description

Archaisms

Whatever interpretation one places upon it, and whatever motivation one imagines for it, the most salient feature of Spenser's diction is its use of obsolete words and word-forms. Using the number of quotations given in the *OED* as his guide to the archaism or currency of any given word, McElderry calculates that there are 163 archaic words in *The Shepheardes Calender* and 154 additional archaisms in the other poems (1932: 153, 156). Blank agrees with McElderry's statistics but argues that in focusing on discrete words, McElderry ignored one important additional statistic: the number of times each word is used. Blank points out that counting occurrences rather than forms gives a total of almost twice the number of archaisms in *The Shepheardes Calender* as calculated by McElderry (Blank 1992: 76). Yet three hundred occurrences of archaic words in a poem of between 16,000 and 17,000 words (depending on whether one includes the arguments and emblems) is still not a tremendous number, and McElderry's original calculations may actually have been high in one respect: the *OED* tends to take its quotations chiefly from texts well known to its compilers. Words for which the *OED* gives only five or six quotations (few enough to earn them the designation of archaism in McElderry's scheme) may appear in other published or unpublished works of the period without having been noticed by the *OED* compilers. In some cases, these other appearances may be classifiable as non-normative dialect (which tends to preserve older forms); in others, not (see pp. 718–23 below).

   Yet the fact remains that E. K. (with the collusion or ventriloquism of the author) felt compelled to call attention to the archaism in *The Shepheardes Calender* and that reviewers of the period objected to what they perceived as archaisms in *The Faerie Queene*. Sugden's mode of quantifying Spenser's archaism may provide one answer to the question of why these poems written chiefly in Tudor English *feel* so persistently archaic: 'Out of the 55 stanzas in the first canto of [*FQ*] Book I, there are only 18 stanzas which do not contain some element of diction that would have sounded antiquated or strange to the ear of the Elizabethan reader' (1936: 11). In other words, a small but well-distributed sprinkling of archaisms keeps the presence of archaism on the reader's mind.

The list of verbs that may have been seen as archaic in Spenser's day includes, among others, 'awhaped', 'dight', 'behight', 'yold', 'alegge', 'vnderfong', the causative of 'do' ('doen him to die'), the enclitic auxiliary 'can' (meaning 'did', but perhaps erroneously associated with 'gan'), present-tense plurals with the '-en' ending (such as 'liggen'), and past participles with 'y-' prefixes ('yclept', 'ywrought'). Nouns include 'faytour', 'fon', 'newell' (meaning 'news'), 'flake' (meaning 'cinder' or 'flash'), and 'souenaunce'. Adjectives, adverbs, and conjunctions include 'forswonck', 'corbe', 'breme', 'alsoon', 'beforne', and 'enaunter'.

The fact that Spenser was not the only poet of his day enamored of the occasional Chaucerian throwback makes it especially difficult to tell which of his words would actually have been seen as archaic, which as 'poetic', which as simply a bit old-fashioned, and which as current but non-standard dialect. To complicate matters, words of 'Chaucerian' vintage were still in common use in Ireland among the Old English community (McCabe 2000b: 86). And in England words such as 'Holpen' and 'ween' were still in common use as recently as the time of More and Elyot. 'Couth', 'whilom', 'sith', 'ne', and 'rede' (in the sense of 'teach') all appear in the work of Sidney. Once more, our gut-level sense of sixteenth-century English may be unduly influenced by Shakespeare, who uses few of the words that we might be tempted to identify as archaic in Spenser. 'Yclept' appears only in an absurd letter written by the fantastical Armado, 'ween' appears once in the mouth of Shakespeare's Henry VIII (a character who is of an appropriate generation for slightly old-fashioned speech), and 'rede' appears only in an old proverb quoted by Ophelia.

This does not necessarily mean that these words were current in ordinary speech or writing, only that their literary use is not unique to Spenser. Yet the fact that Sidney and others felt impelled to criticize *The Shepheardes Calender* for its 'old rustic language' indicates that even if the archaic terms in that work were seldom unique to Spenser, their sheer concentration was by then felt to be either unusual or an example of an outmoded Chaucerian craze (Sidney 1973: 112).

Dialect

Words tend to become obsolete in urban centers long before they do in outlying areas, so it is impossible to draw a clean line between Spenser's archaisms and his uses of dialect. He never writes fully in dialect, in the sense of attempting to reproduce the speech pattern of a particular group of people, but he does scatter dialect words from northern areas of England throughout *The Shepheardes Calender*, and a handful of such words appear in *The Faerie Queene* (Draper 1919: 560; McElderry 1923: 149–50; Ingham 1992: 215). As Patricia Ingham points out, spellings often indicate pronunciations that differ from the cultural norm, as in 'gate' for 'goat' or 'han' for 'have' (1992: 215). Other candidates for dialect words in Spenser's poems include 'thilke', 'mickle', 'sicker' (meaning 'certain' or 'certainly'), 'garres', 'warre', and 'totty' (see pp. 718–23 below).

Foreign imports

Compared to most writers of his day, Spenser uses only a moderate number of Latinate terms, many of which have become thoroughly assimilated into English today: 'mutabilitie', 'alteration', 'indignant', 'pallid'. His borrowings from French (e.g. 'bel-accoyle', 'douceperes', and 'chevisaunce') chiefly come from the discourse of courtly love, which had become so firmly international as to hold only a faint flavor of the foreign in Elizabethan England (Pope 1926: 605, 613). His borrowings from Italian mainly take the form of proper names, freely adapted, though he also employs a very small number of other Italianate words, such as 'bascimano' (for 'bascio-mani'), 'canto', and 'capuccio'.

Coinages

'Blatant' is the most famous of Spenser's coinages, both because it is the most original and because it is such a common word today. (The Victorians who mainstreamed this word no longer used it as Spenser did when he Anglicized the Italian *blatero* and gave it overtones of the existing English verb 'bleat'—but because the Victorian definition, which is also our own, fits the Blatant Beast so well, modern readers are less likely to think of the word as antiquated while they read the poem.) Although 'blatant' is original and memorable, however, it is hardly the only coinage that bears study. Spenser often recombines or alters pre-existing linguistic elements to make new words. These alterations usually take one or more of the following forms.

First, he alters the meaning of an existing word—as when 'dernly', meaning 'secretly', becomes a synonym for 'dismally' or when 'frough', meaning 'crisp to the taste', becomes a synonym for 'stale'. These changes can give the poem extraordinary richness in the layerings of meaning—the most layered example perhaps being the various meanings of the word 'read'—and the fact that they also sometimes force the editors of the *OED* to make guesses as to meaning only gives the literary scholar more scope for interpretation.

Second, he uses existing words in new grammatical positions, as when 'compro-vincial' changes from a noun to an adjective, when 'fortune' becomes 'fortunize', or when Lydgate's 'dorrying do' ('daring to do', *Chronicles of Troy*, II.xvi) becomes the noun 'derring doe' ('intrepid feats').

Third, he shortens or lengthens existing words. Truncations include 'vaunce' for 'advance', 'bove' for 'above', 'gan' for 'began', and 'perlous' for 'perilous'. Adding prefixes and suffixes to existing words yields 'recomfortless', 'dispred', 'picturals', 'ioyaunce', and 'quietage'.

Fourth, he combines existing word elements into a new compound. Examples include the hyphenated epithet ('soft-sliding'), adjective + noun ('vndersong', 'jolly-head'), noun + adjective ('love-lavish'), adverb + past participle ('faire-forged'), adverb + infinitive ('to after-send'), double noun ('brayne-pan'), and combinations of the above.

Fifth, he gives quasi-medieval forms to Elizabethan words, generating pseudo-archaisms such as 'ygoe', 'frowie', 'adaw', and of course 'faerie'.

Other characteristics of Spenserian diction

In addition to the above innovations, Spenser's diction is distinguished by several other characteristics that he develops within ordinary Elizabethan English. The online resource WordHoard can help us compare Spenser's most frequently used words with those used most by Shakespeare, though a statistical comparison with other early modern writers is not yet feasible. Once we have culled out the words that both Spenser and Shakespeare employed with great frequency, normalized spellings, and adjusted for the larger total size of Shakespeare's vocabulary, we can see that some of the adjectives significantly more characteristic of Spenser than of Shakespeare are 'goodly', 'vain', 'sad', and 'cruel'. Spenser's characteristically frequent adverbs include 'forth', 'soon' (in Shakespeare, 'never' is by far more common), 'eke', and 'quite'. A characteristic Spenserian verb is 'seem'. His characteristic nouns include 'knight', 'self' (the latter surprisingly uncommon in Shakespeare), 'sight', 'ground', and 'paine'. Intriguingly enough, it is Shakespeare who uses both 'heaven' and 'time' proportionally more often.

Spenser is fond of adjectives ending in '-full', '-lesse', or '-y', frequently making these into transferred epithets ('senselesse ground', 'weary armour'). He magnificently ignores Ronsard's advice against piling up strings of adjectives (e.g. in 'Vile caitiue wretches, ragged, rude, deformd'), though his poetry generally avoids euphuistic hyper-ornamentation. He often uses multiple forms—not simply multiple spellings—of the same word, such as 'fone' and 'foes', 'enmoved' and 'amoved', or 'shright', 'schrieches', and 'shriekes'. These do not seem to be accidental on the author's part, given that multiple forms of one word frequently appear quite close together, even in the same line (Rubel 1941: 234–5). He uses alliterated oxymorons, perhaps influenced by Wyatt. In certain passages his vocabulary shows a marked Petrarchanism, derived from poets both English and foreign, but especially from Sidney. And finally, Spenser often revives the earlier literalism of words or word roots that had become metaphorical by the sixteenth century: 'implies' in Spenser's poetry means 'folds into itself', and 'inspyre' means 'inhale'. These words can function as

puns, but in each case it is the earlier, literal meaning that is foremost: '*Phœbus*... |
His blushing face in foggy cloud implyes' (I.vi.6).

Given the electronic tools now available, there is scope for more analysis of
differences among Spenser's poems—for example, in the frequencies of specific
words or specific categories of words. It is perhaps not earth-shattering to find that
in relation to each work's total word count, colors appear proportionally more often
in *The Faerie Queene*, the *Amoretti and Epithalamion*, and *Shepheardes Calender* than
in *Colin Clouts Come Home Againe*—or that 'un-' words (where the prefix indicates
negation) appear only three-fifths as often in the *Amoretti and Epithalamion* as in *The
Faerie Queene*, but statistics such as these can provide a foothold for useful interpretation. Craig Berry has given one elegant instance of such analysis, noting that the
word 'there' is significantly less likely to appear in *The Faerie Queene* than in the
shorter poems (Berry 2008). As Berry points out, this statistic is at first surprising,
given *The Faerie Queene*'s concern with location. However, the statistic makes more
sense once one considers that in *The Faerie Queene*, the reader is almost always 'here',
spatially and temporally in the present, whereas *Amoretti* concerns itself with the
'there' of a metaphysical place in which the speaker's metaphors exist, and *Colin
Clouts Come Home Againe* concerns itself with the 'there' of whichever home—
Ireland or England—the speaker is not in at any given moment. The linguistic
differences within Spenser's corpus may prove to be at least as telling as the linguistic
differences between his vocabulary and that of other authors.

LINGUISTIC LEGACY

It is just as well that the greatest legacies of great poets do not generally consist of
their additions to vocabulary lists. Fewer than thirty of Spenser's modifications to
English vocabulary survived into the nineteenth century, and most of those seem
antiquated today (Padelford 1941: 282). F. M. Padelford gave just eight Spenserian
neologisms that were still in use: 'blatant', 'creatress', 'daedal', 'equipage', 'lucid',
'pallid', 'penurious', and 'pupilage' (1941: 282). Of these, 'creatress' is decidedly on
its way out today, 'penurious' can rarely be found (though 'penury', which existed
before Spenser, is still in use), and 'blatant' has a different meaning from that
assigned to it by its inventor. Spenser used 'lucid' literally; it is now used exclusively
in the metaphorical senses. 'Equipage' may have existed as a noun meaning 'military
equipment' (in which sense it is still in use) before Spenser gave it the meaning
'retinue' and also made it into a verb. Only his noun made any real impression upon
the language, and it is archaic today. 'Pupilage' is still current, though hardly in
common use. 'Daedal' survives chiefly in corporate logos and web avatars. Padelford
does not mention 'derring doe', which actually does survive quite nicely with
Spenser's redefinition, though it is inevitably used with a consciously old-fashioned

air. Similarly, the spelling 'faerie' survives as a consciously poetic reference. 'Elfin' and 'analysis' are alive and well.

Poets who have used Spenser as a model include Drayton, William Browne, Wither, Davies, and Giles and Phineas Fletcher in the late sixteenth and early seventeenth centuries; Milton later in the seventeenth century; and Chatterton, Coleridge, Wordsworth, Keats, Shelley, Clare, and William Barnes among the Romantics. The early group, as Joan Grundy demonstrates, imitated some of Spenser's characteristic diction in phrases such as 'yon crawling Brier', 'His cheekes as snowie apples', 'seely Sheepe', and 'craggy rockes' (Grundy 1969: 186, 182).[3] In his contribution to *The Shepheards Pipe,* a poem containing eclogues by four poets, Davies experimented with a rustic vocabulary, clearly with *The Shepheardes Calender* in mind: 'But, well-away, thy nis the way to thriuen' (sig. G6^r). However, these early followers did not very often employ Spenser's archaisms, and even their use of his neologisms was relatively sparse. What interested them more than Spenser's diction were his metrical and tonal sweetness, and most of all they were taken by his use of shepherd-speakers to link himself to a poetic tradition (Grundy 1969: 94, 186).

The most important linguistic lesson Milton received from Spenser was about the usefulness of poetic misdirection, but Milton also absorbed bits of Spenser's vocabulary: 'adamantine chains' and 'devilish engines' are two direct quotations pointed out by Davis (1933: 156). He did not imitate Spenser's famously sweet style, nor did he have much use for Spenser's archaisms. He did initiate his career in a pastoral voice, but that is the subject for another sort of essay.

The English Romantics revived Spenser much as he had revived Chaucer—which is to say, with free interpretation of his plots, philosophies, and poetic forms. Though their pastoral politics differed greatly from his, they nonetheless admired his pairing of shepherd speakers with rustic dialects. Davis notes that Shelley's 'eyne', 'treen', 'griding', 'swink', 'crudded', and 'strook' are tributes to Spenser's archaism (1933: 157). It is only superficially ironic that Keats and Wordsworth use Spenserian neologisms—'undersong' and 'daedal'—in an elegiac mode; they are responding to Spenser's own sense of linguistic history, continuity, and loss.

THEORIES ABOUT SPENSER'S PURPOSES

Spenser's idiosyncratic modifications of Elizabethan English diction demonstrate that he followed neither the Continental linguists nor the English linguists slavishly, instead formulating his own blend of practices. Exactly what motivated Spenser's pattern of choices is still under debate—though, not surprisingly, recent theories tend to focus upon various political and ideological motives. Such has not always been the case. In the early decades of the twentieth century, Draper opined that when Spenser began his publishing career with *The Shepheardes Calender,* the inexperienced poet resorted to archaic words when their accents could get him out of metrical difficulties (1919: 560). Less than a decade later, Emma Field Pope speculated that the option of the old-fashioned '-en' verb ending was attractive to Spenser because of the flexibility it gave him metrically (1926: 608).

A desire for metrical flexibility, however, cannot explain the employment of archaisms for which there were contemporary analogues with the same number of syllables and the same pattern of stresses. What need had Spenser for not only the Chaucerian 'woxe' but also 'wexed', 'waxen', 'woxen', 'wexen', 'wext', 'waxe', and 'wexe'? Nor can we explain the employment of archaisms simply by positing the author's desire for other forms of flexibility, such as a greater choice among rhymes and alliterations. If convenience of choice were the only motivating factor, we could expect to find more plentiful examples of archaism in the early poetry, where the author might be presumed, as yet, to have developed less facility with meter, rhyme, and alliteration than in later decades. In general, this is true: *The Shepheardes Calender* contains more archaisms and dialect than does *The Faerie Queene*, and neither *Daphnaïda* nor *Astrophel* contains more than a few word choices that Spenser's contemporaries would have considered unusual in a poetic context. *Colin Clouts Come Home Againe* contains more archaisms than either of the above poems, but even here, as Veré Rubel argues, the rustic tone results more from orthography and syntax than from diction (1941: 258).

However, as Rubel also demonstrates, the thin scattering of archaic words in the 1569 versions of Spenser's translations of Petrarch and Du Bellay thickens into a markedly more frequent use of archaisms, compounds, and other experimental diction in the 1591 revisions of the same poems: the 1569 'villaines' becomes 'fone' in 1591; 'reache' becomes 'raught'; 'long was his beard' becomes 'side long beard'; 'fouled' becomes 'ray'; and so on (*VB*, 5, 7, 9, and 12; Rubel 1941: 222–3). Similarly, Andrew Zurcher demonstrates that Spenser systematically changed from using the word 'mought' to the older, more authentically Chaucerian 'mote' as his publishing career advanced (2006: 238).

Rubel deduces from this pattern that as Spenser's career advanced, he rejected 'an obviously mannered diction in favor of diction that was determined by decorum' and that his purpose was 'not to expand the language but to set the tone of his work' (1941: 271–2). Rubel concludes that *The Faerie Queene*'s setting in the distant past accounts for its greater use of archaisms than in, say, *Astrophel*. B. E. C. Davis argues that Spenser considered decorum throughout his career, beginning with his elevation of style and vocabulary 'when the shepherd turns courtier' in the *April* and *November* eclogues (1933: 134). The various shorter poems employ various vocabularies. This variation may be partly attributable to the fact that some of the poems are juvenilia while others are mature work; however, it is a reasonable hypothesis that the differences among the poems also represent the poet's desire to fit each literary genre and subject matter to an appropriate vocabulary. In *Mother Hubberds Tale*—a beast fable that parodies courtliness—we find a mixture of everyday Elizabethan speech and fashionable courtly terms. The same holds for *Colin Clouts Come Home Againe*, in which a lowly shepherd travels to court. In the *Epithalamion*, 'the resources of ornamental speech are squandered with all the prodigality proper to the choric ode', whereas the didactic *Hymnes* employ a sparer language (Davis 1933: 139). Padelford points out that the early poems, including the first three books of *The Faerie Queene*, contain more neologisms than the later poetry and use those neologisms more often (1941: 90). In addition, the first three books of *The Faerie Queene* employ a significantly larger vocabulary than do the final three books, leading Padelford to argue that Spenser was more interested in description while writing Books I–III (1941: 91). Other differences among the various poems are less clear: Davis asserts that the *Fowre Hymnes* use an unusually large number of abstract terms, but Davis did not have access to electronic search engines, and a session with WordHoard reveals that most of the words on Davis's list appear as frequently or more frequently in other Spenserian poems (Davis 1933: 139). Unsurprisingly, courtly terms appear more often in *The Faerie Queene*'s stories of knights errant than in any of the earlier work. Examples include 'aumayld', 'belamy', 'beauperes', 'checklaton', 'debonaire', 'feutre', 'gramercy', 'hacqueton', 'repleuie', 'seisin', and 'umbriere', all of which appear only in *The Faerie Queene*. However, Spenser fearlessly mixed this elevated diction with ordinary colloquialisms derived ultimately from Old English, such as 'algates', 'cleepe', 'groueling', 'halfendeale', 'leech-craft', and 'mucky' (Davis 1933: 138).

Because Spenser does not actually attempt to reproduce Chaucerian poetry or the speech of rural shepherds, we must still ask why he chose to sprinkle Elizabethan language with archaisms, dialect, foreign words, and neologisms. Was he following the program of the *Pleiade*, attempting to enrich his mother tongue? When, in the transparent guise of 'Immerito', Spenser writes to Gabriel Harvey that he wants to 'haue the kingdome of oure owne Language', he refers primarily to his belief that quantitative meter will work in English. He refers to diction only secondarily, insofar as certain English words must be modified to make their accents fit quantitative meter. The less-quoted sentence that precedes that famous declaration gestures more strongly toward a reason for Spenser's continued experimentation with archaisms, dialect, and neologisms long after he had dropped the experiments with quantitative meter: the '*lame Dogge*' of an English word put into a new accentual position 'is to be wonne with Custome, and rough words must be subdued with Vse' (*Prose*, 16). This statement suggests that Spenser was one of the many English writers who believed that English could be polished into a glory that would match that of classical Latin. More on the subject appears in E. K.'s editorial material for *The Shepheardes Calender*. Even if E. K. was not simply another transparent guise, Spenser surely colluded in generating E. K.'s editorial remarks—notwithstanding the comic ironies in those remarks—so it seems legitimate to examine what E. K. says for possible insights into Spenser's methodology and motivation. E. K. calls attention to the strangely 'auncient' words used by the author, 'of most men vnused, yet both English, and also vsed of most excellent Authors and most famous Poetes' (Spenser 1999: 25–6). He speculates that the author, 'Immerito', uses such words in the belief that they are appropriate in the mouths of shepherds, either because the roughness of these words will make the shepherds' verse more appropriately rustic or because people living in the country are more likely to use obsolete words. Importantly, E. K. adds that these old and dialect words give *grace* and *authority* to Spenser's poetry, especially given that Spenser uses them judiciously rather than stuffing them in everywhere. This latter argument is not necessarily in conflict with E. K.'s later statement that 'those rough and harsh termes enlumine and make more clearly to appeare the brightnesse of braue and glorious words' (Spenser 1999: 26–7). The fact that the older words are rougher and less glorious does not prevent their bringing an honestly home-grown grace to the work as a whole. This is an English version of the offhand manner of Castiglione's courtier, which brings grace to his equestrian exercises by making them seem more natural than practiced. Like Castiglione's *sprezzatura*, the poet's handling of these rough words will be more artful than appears immediately to the eye. E. K. declares that in his opinion, 'it is one special prayse, of many whych are dew to this Poete, that he hath laboured to restore, as to theyr rightfull heritage such good and naturall English words, as haue ben long time out of vse and almost cleane disherited' (Spenser 1999: 27). It is the poet's labor that will enable home-grown English words to stand up and claim their 'rightful heritage', and this very labor will also make the poet's own work a worthy heritage.

We must ask ourselves, however, whether an enriched and purified language constructs or conveys meaning in new ways—and if so, what those ways are. Davis has taken the position that Spenser's decorative language was art for art's sake, with a 'surface luster' that the poet meant 'to catch the eye and ear rather than to stir the mind' (1933: 155, 139). Writing in the 1930s, Davis was appreciative of this poetic quality, but more recent critics are unlikely to be satisfied with the admiration of luster as an isolated aesthetic phenomenon. Indeed, S. K. Heninger has gone to almost the opposite extreme, arguing that Spenser wanted his poetic language to be 'as transparent a medium as possible, calling no unnecessary attention to itself' (1987: 310). According to Heninger, metrical patterns were more important for Spenser than was language, since he could use earthly meter to adumbrate the perfection of cosmic forms such as those of the planetary spheres, the zodiac, or Pythagorean mathematical relationships (1987: 312). Language in Eden had been perfect, but in a postlapsarian world, language was an inevitable reminder of 'our fall from the grace of divine truth' (Heninger 1987: 313). For Spenser, language was valuable only to the extent that it was transparent, allowing the reader to look through it to truths beyond (Heninger 1987: 318).

It is difficult to conceive of a poet who either wrote or consented to the exuberant annotations of *The Shepheardes Calender* as being on a mission to make his language unobtrusive, and Zurcher must surely be right when he argues that Spenser 'took his diction, and the ability of his readers to assimilate and understand that diction in all its nuance, seriously' (Zurcher 2007: 4). However, various critics have made productive use of the idea that Spenser's poetry searches for a transcendent, and therefore inevitably elusive, conjunction of word and meaning. Åke Bergvall investigates some of the Augustinian roots of this search, specifically with respect to Book I of *The Faerie Queene* (Bergvall 1993, *passim*). Redcrosse's separation from Una indicates his loss of the Edenic state, in which there was no separation between a word and its meaning, and his subsequent attachment to Duessa indicates 'his bondage to the

*Du*plicity of postlapsarian language' (Bergvall 1993: 24). At the same time, postlapsarian words are our only means of approaching the Word, so Spenser invites us to join Redcrosse in his 'quest for the transcendental Sign' (1993: 37).

Other critics believe that Spenser valued human language despite its lack of transcendence, believing it a repository and guarantor of cultural values. McCabe points out that for E. K., at least, 'continuity of linguistic usage not merely reflects, but actively promotes, continuity of moral standards' (McCabe 2000a: 48). To the extent that Spenser agreed with E. K.'s glosses, then, he thought that preserving older strains of the English language could help preserve England's moral integrity.

There is ample evidence that for Spenser, language itself was ideological and political, over and beyond its efficacy in securing royal appointments for the writer. It is clear that he had a passionate set of ideas about what it meant to be—and to speak—English. To argue for the validation, preservation, purification, or sophistication of any particular forms of English was to take an ideological stance, even when the theory behind that stance was largely taken from the ancient Greeks and Romans (McCabe 2000b). Spenser's role as colonist doubtless exacerbated such anxieties, but even without discussing his desire to define England's linguistic heritage in contrast to that of Ireland, we can see that there is a problem with thinking of Spenser's use of archaisms as *simply* representing an attempt to purify the language. As Emma Field Pope points out, few archaic words appear in Spenser's poetry without doing so in one or more contemporary sixteenth-century forms, often in the same work and even in the same stanza (Pope 1926: 607). In most cases the number of times that a word appears in its contemporary form exceeds the number of times it appears in its antiquated form. 'Bren' appears twice; 'burnen' appears once; 'brent' appears fourteen times; 'ybrent' appears once; 'burn' appears thirty times (1926: 607).

Martha Craig has argued that Spenser's seemingly erratic use of archaisms and other non-standard word forms can be explained by looking more closely at how the Neoplatonists understood the process of etymologizing. In the sixteenth century, etymology was thought to reveal truth not by excavating a word's historically verifiable roots but by excavating its philosophically verifiable ones. The very fact that Spenser uses archaic forms in some places but not in others keeps the reader alert to the fact that the forms are significant; they must be analyzed rather than assumed. 'With archaism established as a mode of diction, Spenser is free to pick out archaic forms that are more suggestive of philosophic meaning' (Craig 1967: 451). Not even a language doctored in this way will reach perfection, but truth can be reached through the poet's and reader's continual comparison of 'the word, the definition, and the image' (Craig 1967: 453). As an example of Spenser's method, Craig argues that Spenser has Redcrosse ride through a veritable forest of puns on 'hero', 'errant', 'eros', 'arrogance', and so on (1967: 454).

Paula Blank offers a postmodern take on the ways that Spenser uses unusual words—in this case, dialect—to keep the reader off balance in *The Shepheardes Calender*. Blank argues that because Spenser 'deliberately manipulated orthography to give his diction an antique look' in *The Shepheardes Calender* but then used very little dialect in *The Faerie Queene*, it does not make sense to conclude that his purpose in using dialect was to enrich the English language (1992: 77). She argues that he took a risk in using northern English words because that area of the country was commonly either lampooned as being comically backward or vilified for harboring dangerous elements of society (82–3). Plain speech, rather than dialect, was the norm for literary shepherds, so in using dialect, Spenser risked being classified with the common balladeers rather than hailed as a poet laureate (84). Spenser was willing to take this risk in order to engineer a confrontation between the margins of power and the cultural center:

Colin composes his 'rurall musick' on pipes he has purposefully broken, not as an act of futility or resignation, but as a deliberate poetic strategy. . . . By insisting that his language is strange, too difficult for readers to understand without E. K.'s glosses, Spenser displaces the experience of desire onto his audience. . . . [By E. K.] we are told just enough to know that we do not know everything about the poem, and we become, in Colin's stead, unrequited suitors of a meaning that the poet will not completely divulge. (87–8)

Three critics have investigated the possibility that Spenser shaped aspects of his vocabulary less in imitation of Chaucer, the ancient Romans, or northern rustics than in response to more recent models. Thane Glenn argues that Spenser was thinking of John Foxe's *Actes and Monuments*, which had been published in 1570 but contained excerpts from centuries-old documents. According to Glenn, Foxe's collecting these documents into a Protestant martyrology caused their antiquated language to become associated with Foxe's project and therefore with 'the rhetorical values of true English Protestant heritage' (2006: 1). By evoking the flavor of this language, Spenser could align himself with those values. In a separate but compatible argument, Bart Van Es demonstrates that the language of *The Faerie Queene*, like that of E. K.'s glosses in *The Shepheardes Calender*, creates the effect of other writings that were generally recognized as prophetic. Without actually being so rash as to claim that he could prophesy the political future, which could get one into serious trouble, Spenser nevertheless develops a language that invests his epic with the ineffable power of prophecy (2000, *passim*). In a tour de force of linguistic analysis, Zurcher reveals that Spenser's precise and extensive legal terminology was inseparable from his invocations of precedent, his belief in the power of etymology, and his expectation that readers would devote a great deal of energy to layered readings (Zurcher 2007: 9–10). In Zurcher's formulation, Spenser's diction is hardly transparent; indeed; the difficulty of seeing into that language is one of its philosophical strengths: 'The artificiality and patterning of Spenser's diction . . . conspicuously place the language of Spenser's poetry in a paradoxical relation to meaning—the same relation obtaining between things and forms, images and truth, uses and laws' (11).

No matter which combination of these theories one chooses, one cannot ignore the textual evidence that for Spenser, the praise of English heroism, fashioning of courtly characters, resurrection of antiquated Chaucerisms, presentation at court of sturdy bits of dialect, and annexation of various Latin, Italian, French, and Celtic root-forms were all part of claiming 'the kingdome of oure owne Language' (*Prose*, 16). Spenser was not a nineteenth-century Romanticist looking to the rustics for superior sensibilities, nor was he a postmodern believer in the global village; his poetic diction was meant to acquire territory for the educated classes of his country and for himself as an aspiring laureate. To what extent he expected the monarch, nation, or other entities to be guarantors for the truth toward which his words reached is a matter for further debate, but his diction does not indicate a great faith in absolutes. After all, each of the heroes and heroines in *The Faerie Queene* is a word in search of a meaning: 'chastity' never comes to rest on any one definition—no matter how complex—nor does 'holiness', 'temperance', 'friendship', 'justice', or 'courtesy'. One might venture to say that if Spenser was fascinated by the idea of an Edenic time in which linguistic body and soul were one, he was also aware that in a post-Edenic world, the slippage between signifier and signified offered him a job. Words needed to be taught how to behave nobly—and if Castiglione was right about the courtier on horseback, even the inner soul could benefit from a good education.

Furthermore, although Spenser does seem to have been in search of an improved language that could point beyond itself to greater truths, his was not a poetics of pure transcendence. Calidore does not get to stay on Mount Acidale; Britomart longs for physical consummation of her love; and it is matter, rather than Neoplatonic form, that persists through time in the Garden of Adonis. Spenser's poetry delights not only in a dream of linguistic perfection but also in linguistic failures and duplicities— pronouns that bewilder, names that do not name, grand signposts to nowhere, bewitching veils, detours. Like Duessa's beauty, the lovely surfaces of the English language mislead us—and therefore that surface is endlessly fascinating.

Notes

1. All references are from Aristotle (1995).
2. For the linguistic aspects of the Irish colonial situation see Fogarty (1989); McCabe (1993); Neill (1994); Cronin (1996); Carey (1999); McCabe (2002), 177–96. More generally see Bliss (1979); Blank (1996); Miller (1997); Palmer (2001).
3. See Drayton, *The Shepheards Garland* 4.155; Giles Fletcher, *Christs Victorie, and Triumph* 2.11; Browne, *Britannia's Pastorals* 1.sig. B1^r and 2.sig. G1^v.

Bibliography

Aristotle (1995). *The Poetics*, ed. and trans. S. Halliwell. Loeb Classical Library. Cambridge, MA: Harvard University Press.

Barclay, A. (1928). *The Eclogues of Alexander Barclay*, ed. B. White. London: Oxford University Press for the Early English Text Society.

Bergvall, Å. (1993). 'The Theology of the Sign: St. Augustine and Spenser's Legend of Holiness'. *SEL* 33(1): 21–42.

Berry, C. (2008). 'The Shorter Poems and the WordHoard Spenser', Language and Langland Session, Spenser at Kalamazoo. International Congress on Medieval Studies. Western Michigan University, Kalamazoo. 10 May.

Betham, P. (1544). *The Preceptes of Warre*.

Blank, P. (1992). 'The Dialect of *The Shepheardes Calender*'. *SSt* 10: 71–94.

—— (1996). *Broken English: Dialects and the Politics of Language in Renaissance Writing*. London: Routledge.

Bliss, A. (1979). *Spoken English in Ireland 1600–1740*. Dublin: Cadenus Press.

Carey, V. (1999). '"Neither good English nor good Irish": Bi-lingualism and Identity Formation in Sixteenth-century Ireland', in Hiram Morgan (ed.), *Political Ideology in Ireland, 1541–1641*. Dublin: Four Courts Press, 45–61.

Caxton (1928). Prologue to *The Consolacion of Philosophie*, by Chaucer, in W. J. B. Crotch (ed.), *The Prologues and Epilogues of William Caxton*. London: Oxford University Press for the Early English Text Society.

Craig, M. (1967). 'The Secret Wit of Spenser's Language', in P. J. Alpers (ed.), *Elizabethan Poetry: Modern Essays in Criticism*. Oxford: Oxford University Press, 447–72.

Cronin, M. (1996). *Translating Ireland: Translation, Languages, Cultures*. Cork: Cork University Press.

Davis, B. E. C. (1933). 'Diction', in *Edmund Spenser: A Critical Study*. Cambridge: Cambridge University Press, 129–58.

Draper, J. W. (1919). 'The Glosses to Spenser's *Shepheardes Calender*'. *JEGP* 18: 556–74.

Fogarty, A. (1989). 'The Colonization of Language: Narrative Strategy in *A View of the Present State of Ireland* and *The Faerie Queene*, Book VI', in P. Coughlan (ed.), *Spenser and Ireland: An Interdisciplinary Perspective*. Cork: Cork University Press, 75–108.

Glenn, T. P. (2006). 'The Invented Language: John Foxe, Edmund Spenser, and the Rhetorical Development of English as a Genre of Heritage in the Sixteenth Century'. Dissertation, Temple University.

Grundy, J. (1969). *The Spenserian Poets: A Study in Elizabethan and Jacobean Poetry*. London: Edward Arnold.

Heninger, S. K., Jr. (1987). 'Words and Meter in Spenser and Scaliger'. *HLQ* 50(3): 309–22.

Horace (1989). *Epistles, Book II and Epistle to the Pisones (Ars Poetica)*, ed. N. Rudd. Cambridge: Cambridge University Press.

Ingham, P. (1992). 'Dialect', in *SE*, 215–16.

Jed, S. H. (1989). *Chaste Thinking: The Rape of Lucretia and the Birth of Humanism*. Bloomington: Indiana University Press.

Maley, W. (1994). 'Spenser's Irish English: Language and Identity in Early Modern Ireland'. *SP* 91: 417–31.

—— 'Spenser's Languages: Writing in the Ruins of English', in A. Hadfield (ed.), *The Cambridge Companion to Spenser*. Cambridge: Cambridge University Press, 162–79.

McCabe, R. A. (1993). 'Edmund Spenser, Poet of Exile'. *Publications of the British Academy* 80: 73–103.

—— (2000a). 'Annotating Anonymity, or Putting a Gloss on *The Shepheardes Calender*', in J. Bray, M. Handley, and A. C. Henry (eds), *Ma[r]king the Text: The Presentation of Meaning on the Literary Page*. Aldershot: Ashgate, 35–54.

—— (2000b). 'Translated States: Spenser and Linguistic Colonialism', in J. K. Morrison and M. Greenfield (eds), *Edmund Spenser: Essays on Culture and Allegory*. Aldershot: Ashgate, 67–88.

—— (2002). *Spenser's Monstrous Regiment: Elizabethan Ireland and the Poetics of Difference*. Oxford: Oxford University Press.

McElderry, B. R. (1932). 'Archaism and Innovation in Spenser's Poetic Diction'. *PMLA* 47(1): 144–70.

Miller, J. T. (1997). 'Mother Tongues: Language and Lactation in Early Modern Literature'. *ELR* 27: 177–96.

More, T. (1532). *The Confutacion of Tyndales Aunsvvere Made.*

Neill, M. (1994). 'Broken English and Broken Irish: Nation, Language and the Optic of Power in Shakespeare's Histories'. *SQ* 45: 1–32.

Padelford, F. M. (1941). 'Aspects of Spenser's Vocabulary', in B. Maxwell, W. D. Briggs, F. R. Johnson, and E. N. S. Thompson (eds), *Renaissance Studies in Honor of Hardin Craig*. Stanford: Stanford University Press. *PQ*, special issue 20(3) (1941): 279–83.

Palmer, P. (2001). *Language and Conquest in Early Modern Ireland: English Renaissance Literature and Elizabethan Imperial Expansion*. Cambridge: Cambridge University Press.

Pope, E. F. (1926). 'Renaissance Criticism and the Diction of *The Faerie Queene*'. *PMLA* 41(3): 575–619.

Ronsard (1938). Preface to *La Françiade*, in G. Cohen (ed.), *Œuvres complètes*, vol. 2. Paris: Bibliothèque Pléiade. (Original work published 1572.)

Rubel, V. L. (1941). *Poetic Diction in the English Renaissance from Skelton through Spenser*. New York: MLA.

Sidney, P. (1973). *A Defence of Poetry*, in K. Duncan-Jones and J. Van Dorsten (eds), *Miscellaneous Prose of Sir Philip Sidney*. Oxford: Clarendon Press, 59–121.

Sugden, H. W. (1936). 'The Grammar of Spenser's *Faerie Queene*'. *Language* 12(4): 9–228.

Tasso (1973). *Discorsi del Poema Eroico*, trans. and ed. M. Cavalchini and I. Samuel. Oxford: Clarendon Press.

Van Es, B. (2000). '"Priuie to his Counsell and Secret Meaning": Spenser and Political Prophecy'. *ELR* 30(1): 3–31.

Warton, T. (1968). *Observations on the Fairy Queen of Spenser*, vol. 1, 2nd edn. New York: Greenwood Press. (Original work published 1762.)

Wilson, T. (1553). *Arte of Rhetorique.*

WordHoard: An Application For The Close Reading And Scholarly Analysis Of Deeply Tagged Texts (2004–2006). Northwestern University. Available at http:wordhoard.northwestern.edu/userman/index.html.

Zurcher, A. (2006). 'Spenser's Studied Archaism: The Case of "Mote"'. *SSt* 21: 231–40.

—— (2007). *Spenser's Legal Language: Law and Poetry in Early Modern England*. Studies in Renaissance Literature. Woodbridge: D. S. Brewer.

CHAPTER 21

···

SPENSER'S
METRICS

···

JEFF DOLVEN

PERHAPS the most important thing that Spenser's letters to Gabriel Harvey have to teach us about his English metrics is the violence he was prepared to do to the word 'carpenter'. He grants that the middle syllable is 'shorte in speache': then as now, English speakers say cárpĕntĕr. But he and Harvey are trying to work out a new prosody, based upon the principles of Latin quantity, and those principles dictate that a vowel followed by two consonants be counted as long (the so-called 'rule by position'). The result will sound ugly at first, 'like a lame Gosling that draweth one legge after hir', but poets must have the courage of their quantitative convictions: 'it is to be wonne with Custome, and rough words must be subdued with Vse' (*Prose*, 16). The full extent of Spenser's sin against what George Gascoigne would call 'natural *Emphasis*' (Smith 1904: I, 49) is not entirely clear. Perhaps he intends the truly ungainly cărpéntĕr; or perhaps, as Seth Weiner suggests, the subtler accommodation of cárpéntĕr (1982: 20–1). Still we can say two things for certain. First, that Gabriel Harvey would have none of it: 'you shal neuer have my subscription of consent . . . to make your *Carpēnter*, our *carpĕnter*, an inche longer or bigger than God and his Englishe people haue made him' (*Prose*, 473–4). And second, whatever Spenser's reaction might have been to Harvey's chastisement—no letter in reply survives—he was willing, sometime in late 1579 and early 1580, to give the principles of his prosody the decisive upper hand, and count on them to wear away the resistance of the spoken language.

Again, the dispute in these letters is about the peculiar and, for Spenser, transient phenomenon of English quantitative verse; there will be more to say about his enthusiasm for 'refourmed Versifying' (Smith 1904: I, 87), but we have no record of his having tried it again. Nonetheless, his readiness to ride roughshod over 'carpenter' serves as a good introduction to the challenges for a modern reader of hearing his line. In the sixteenth century as much as today, ideas about how poetry *should* sound shaped how poetry *did* sound. This essay will venture an account of how Spenser meant his poetry to sound and how an astute reader of his time would have heard it, using the evidence implicit in his language and explicit in contemporary prosodic theory (such as it was). The achievements of recent theoretical linguistics in describing English meter will play only a background role, on the understanding that Spenser's idiosyncratic prosody will often override what the history of the pentameter line in aggregate can tell us—just as our own idiosyncrasies as readers can override that history and those principles, or at least defy their predictions. Such is the scandal of historical prosody. Sixteenth-century verse is particularly scandalous, making much more willful impositions on the language than twenty-first-century readers are used to. Eleanor Berry puts the matter well when she says that 'among the Elizabethan theorists . . . a view of metre as a *pattern artificially imposed on* the words, rather than as one realized by, and to be abstracted from, the natural pronunciation of the lines, was prevalent' (1981: 117). This business is ever a dialectical one for practicing poets, but if the dialectic favors natural emphasis over patterns of metrical expectation in our own moment, for the Elizabethans, the situation was reversed.

The analytic idiom here will therefore be that of traditional foot scansion, with only occasional reference to alternatives. There are costs to this choice: it is not obvious that Spenser is always thinking in terms of feet (particularly in *The Shepheardes Calender*), and the old repertory of iambs, trochees, etc., offers no notation for levels of stress beyond the two that Gascoigne calls 'grave' and 'light'. Those deficits will have to be supplied ad hoc. The principal advantage and best argument for foot scansion is just that this old system is closest to the way that Spenser's contemporaries talked and thought about the matter—and having said that, it is still not always so close. The influence of ideas of quantity, the classical reckoning of syllable length, is a complicating factor, and even more fundamental (and hardly unrelated) is the fact that the nature and authority of accent itself was a matter of widespread dispute among commentators.

Modern prosody uses 'accent' to refer to an emphasis given to individual syllables by some combination of increased volume, elevated pitch, greater length, and sharper articulation. ('Accent' typically describes the phenomenon in verse, 'stress' in ordinary language, though I will use them interchangeably here.) The description George Gascoigne offers in his 'Certayne Notes of Instruction' (1575) sounds close to our own: the 'grave' accent is 'drawne out or elevate, and maketh that sillable long whereupon it is placed; the light accent is depressed or snatched up, and maketh that sillable short upon the which it lighteth' (Smith 1904: I, 49).[1] He seems to be attending primarily to length and pitch, perhaps to volume, and his examples of scansion sort with what modern prosodists would offer. Later theorists like William Webbe (*A Discourse of English Poetrie*, 1586) and George Puttenham (*The Arte of English Poesie*, 1589) take up some of Gascoigne's language, but 'natural emphasis' competes and is sometimes confused with the idea that verse should be organized by quantity, whether the long and short syllables are determined naturally (as a sup-posed property of the words we speak) or artificially (by observing rules based on Latin), or by some vague compromise between the two. The nearest we can come to a consensus position is Sir Philip Sidney's ever-diplomatic summary: 'Now of versify-ing there are two sorts, the one Auncient, the other Moderne: the Auncient marked the quantitie of each silable, and according to that framed his verse; the moderne obseruing onely number (with some regarde of the accent)' (Smith 1904: I, 204). Spenser indeed has 'some regard of the accent': establishing the nature and extent of that regard will be the project here.

THE LINE OF *THE FAERIE QUEENE*

Spenser the metrist is at his most experimental near the beginning of his career: the verse forms in *The Shepheardes Calender* (1579) stage a running skirmish between the four- and the five-stress lines in English, between the old ballad and the new pentameter. By the time he published the first three books of *The Faerie Queene* (1590), however, he had made himself the most consistently regular pentameter poet—or great poet, at least—that the language has ever seen.[2] For just this reason, it will be easier to begin with that achieved norm and work backward, through the intervening shorter poems, and through the watershed of the *Letters* to Harvey, back to the radical contest of idioms sparked by his ambitious alter ego, Colin Clout. That mature norm is a string of five iambs. Gascoigne had somewhat reluctantly conceded the dominance of the iamb in English, that 'foot of two sillables, wherof the first is depressed or made short, and the second is elevate or made long' (Smith 1904: I, 50). Its dominance in *The Faerie Queene* is typically conspicuous in an unexceptional stanza from the end of Book I:

> And after to his Pallace he them bringes,
>   With shaumes, and trompets, and with Clarions sweet;
>   And all the way the ioyous people singes,
>   And with their garments strowes the paued street:
>   Whence mounting vp, they fynd purueyaunce meet
>   Of all, that royall Princes court became,
>   And all the floore was vnderneath their feet
>   Bespredd with costly scarlott of great name,
> On which they lowly sitt, and fitting purpose frame.   (I.xii.13)

The great majority of these lines scan as five iambs without resistance, and the expectations that such regularity creates—what John Hollander has called a 'metrical contract' (Hollander 1970)—will bias a responsive reader to regularize potential difficulties when they do arise. 'Clarions', for example, threatens to slip in an extra syllable ('with clárĭŏns swéet'), but -*ions* can readily be pronounced as a single, unstressed syllable by the technique of elision known as syncope. '[P]áuĕd' sustains the iambic movement when the -*ed* is sounded as a separate syllable, an option that Spenser exercises, like most poets of the period, whenever he wants. There may be a rhetorical temptation to read the eighth line as 'scárloŏtt ŏf gréat náme', giving spondaic punch to the last words, but again the regularity of the context encourages us to resist the temptation, and promote the 'of' instead: 'scárloŏtt óf gréat náme'.[3]

The reasoning here may seem circular: the norm is regular because most lines are regular, and most lines are regular because the norm is regular. Dialectical might be a better word, but either way there is no escaping this ongoing, practical adjustment of expectation to audition, informed (if not decided) by the authority of contemporary comment.[4] Gascoigne calls the various shifts by which a recalcitrant line may be subdued 'poeticall license', and he observes their variety with a characteristic wry pragmatism:

it maketh wordes longer, shorter, of mo syllables, of fewer, newer, older, truer, falser; and, to conclude, it turkeneth [changes] all things at pleasure, for example, *ydone* for *done*, *adowne* for *downe*, *orecome* for *ouercome*, *tane* for *taken*, *power* for *powre*, *heauen* for *heaun*, *thewes* for good partes or good qualities, and a numbre of other. (Smith 1904: I, 53–4)

Spenser avails himself of all of these devices, freely syncopating words or expanding them as the occasion demands. 'Heaven', for example, can be contracted to a single syllable, whether or not it is spelled with the second *e*: spelling is sometimes a clue to syllable count, but not an infallible one. He is just as ready to use synaloepha, eliding two vowels at a word boundary ('Th'eternall', 'th'other'). He plays with morphology to get the syllable count he needs ('daint' for 'dainty'). And such metrical flexibility is also a poetical advantage of his archaism, an advantage that, as Gascoigne shrewdly observes, keeps old words like 'thews' around in poems long after they have fallen out of everyday speech. 'Adown' and 'ydone' are both part of *The Faerie Queene*'s working lexicon, even though the poem remains more likely to use 'down' and 'done', as its author surely did in conversation.

Gascoigne, for all his licenses, is committed to natural emphasis—'such length or shortnesse, eleuation or depression of sillables, as is commonly pronounced or vsed' (Smith 1904: I, 49). Spenser's poetry too depends on an ordinary ear for ordinary speech, but he allows himself latitudes upon which Gascoigne would likely frown. With quicksand, for example: 'But by the way, there is a great Quícksánd', begins one of the stanzas on the way to the Bowre of Blisse, insisting on the iamb 'Quicksand' in that sensitive last foot (the most intolerant of inversion—or trochaic substitution— in a pentameter line). Five lines later, however, we find 'That quícksănd nígh wĭth wáter cóuerĕd', and the alexandrine concludes that 'Ĭt cálled wăs thĕ quíckesănd óf Vnthríftyhéd' (II.xii.18). The stanza as a whole prefers trochaic quícksănd two to one, and the general tendency of such compounds to carry the falling stress pattern of Germanic nouns makes the iamb quícksánd distinctly odd—but the first line insists upon it all the same. Nor is Spenser above reversing this operation with a noun of French derivation, like 'dúress'. French disyllables ordinarily carry a rising stress pattern, but not in Florimel's undersea complaint: 'Dŏ yóu bў dúress hím cŏmpéll thereto' (IV.xii.10). In both these cases, the choice is between displacing the stress most characteristic of the word, or preserving that stress and producing a line which would strain the iambic pentameter.[5] Partly to blame, it should be said, is the fact that there was some degree of uncertainty in the placement of primary stress in many words (especially disyllables of French or Latin origin) well into the seventeenth century (Dobson 1968: 446–9). Under the pressure of the poem's massive commitment to iambic movement, those words often buckle.

Such cases are frequent enough to deserve mention, but still rare. Much more common are cases where it is not word stress but rhetorical stress—the way in which the stress falls in a phrase or sentence—that seems to resist the iambic expectation for the line. A minor example: 'Which long time had been shut, and out of hand' (I.xii.3). The discomfort here arises from promoting 'long' and demoting 'time', when ordinary usage usually accords the stronger stress to the noun in a noun–adjective pair: 'long time'. The spoken vitality of Sidney's verse in *Astrophil and Stella* gives greater reign to such variations: '"But ah", Desire still cries, "give me some food"' (Sidney 1962: 201). Should Desire's demand be two iambs? A trochee and an iamb? A pyrrhic and a spondee? Or an ascending series of stresses, each greater than the last?[6] Whereas in Spenser, and *The Faerie Queene* especially, the contract with regularity is stronger. Even at the beginning of a line, where inversions are much more frequent in the period, we do well to be conservative. William Webbe seems to agree, offering the following scansion of a fourteener from Phaer's *Aeneid* in his *Discourse*: 'I that my slender pipe in verse was wont to sound' (Smith 1904: I, 273). Reading the line as though it were Sidney's, we might be inclined to stress Astrophil's all-important 'I', and allow an inversion. If it were Spenser's, then we would more likely say that Webbe has it right.

If this conformal pressure is so strong, then, when *should* we allow for metrical variation—for deviation from the steady chain of iambs? There are clear cases at the beginning of the line, for example, 'During which time, that he did there remaine' (V.xii.26), or 'Heaped together in rude rabblement' (I.xii.9). Even with these examples it is a case of the ear's tolerance—say 'During which time' enough, and the emphasis will start to sound natural—but the general frequency of such 'first inversions' in the period's verse encourages adopting them. Now and again present or past participles like 'during' or 'heaped' will crop up in the middle of the line with the suffix in what is ordinarily a stressed position: 'To fly about, playing their wanton toyes' (II.xii.60) or 'The ioyous birds shrouded in cheareful shade' (II.xii.71). In both these cases, the potentially offending word follows the line's caesura, and again custom grants particular permission for an inversion, for the second most likely place to find one is after such a break in syntax. There are also moments in *The Faerie Queene* where the collaboration of rhetorical pattern and metrical variation makes the latter unmistakable, for example, the parallelisms and inversions in Despaire's lulling seduction, 'Sleep after toyle, port after stormie seas, | Ease after warre, death after life doth greatly please' (I.ix.40). It is difficult to keep statistics for moments like these. Indeed, given the poem's constant global pressure to conformity, and the ad hoc character of resistance to it, keeping statistics on any of these phenomena is next to impossible. A rough census of the final cantos of each book suggests that inversions in the first position affect less than three percent of all lines. Internal variations are still scarcer. The basic counsel is, when in doubt, defer to the iamb.

This regularity is why Susanne Woods, proposing a distinction between mimetic and aesthetic metrists, places the Spenser of *The Faerie Queene* squarely in the latter camp. Mimetic metrists like Sidney write a line in which the scansion is constantly perturbed by rhetorical effects, always imitating what it is talking about. The aesthetic metrists adopt 'forms and rhythms which are themselves somehow pleasurable . . . but which do not directly imitate, represent, or promote either the effect of the speaking voice or the lexical meaning of the poem's statement' (Woods 1984: 15).[7] The distinction is somewhat rough and ready, and we will continue to see how Spenser can build pressure against metrical expectation when he wants to. But his ability to sustain his iambic movement with minimum variation is an achievement to which the poem as a whole aspires to tune our ears. That control is abetted by his careful management of the caesura, which gravitates to the spot after the fourth syllable, sometimes the sixth, generally near the middle of the line. Such placement—characteristic of Surrey and Gascoigne before him—allows Spenser to lodge complete phrases in each half of the line, which in turn minimizes the severity of his enjambments. The lesson of all this for interpretation is to be cautious of making too much of small disturbances of rhythm. The poem wants regularity, and as critics we should defy it only when we have strong local encouragement. Of course, sometimes the very impulse to regularity creates notable effects, like the fearful roar of chaos in the inversion of 'horror' at the end of the line, 'In hatefull darkenesse and in deepe horrore' (III.vi.36). And it is above all important to remember that these regularities are only crudely described by a scheme of alternating stressed and unstressed syllables, the scheme of scansion. The actual rhythm of any given line is a much more variable and subtle matter. Even where a reader decides, against some protest from the rhetoric or the syntax, to hold the line to its iambic promise, still a subtle voicing of a tricky passage—'Which knitting their rancke braunches part to part' (III.vi.44)—can suggest how 'rancke' barely consents to relinquish its accent, and how very thick and dense the branches are. Orchestrating greater or lesser strain against the meter's dictates is one hallmark of Spenser's virtuosity, even if, as a matter of scansion, the iamb almost always wins.

THE STANZA OF *THE FAERIE QUEENE*

If *The Faerie Queene*'s pentameter is unusually regular, the stanza—in its design and its execution—is anything but.[8] Its nine lines, eight pentameters and a final alexandrine rhymed ABABBCBCC, are Spenser's invention, though there are two obvious forbears. The first is the Italian ottava rima, eight decasyllables rhymed ABABABCC, used by Ariosto in his *Orlando Furioso* and by John Harington in his English translation of the poem (1591). From Ariosto, Spenser borrows (along with considerable narrative and thematic material) the rough dimensions of his stanza and perhaps a tendency to sententious closure in the final couplet, a closure native also to the English sonnet. His other obvious source is the rhyme royale stanza, seven lines of iambic pentameter rhymed ABABBCC and best known as the stanza of Chaucer's *Troilus*. From the rhyme royale, Spenser takes his first five lines and the mild surprise, after the alternating rhymes, of the ensuing couplets. The first structural innovation of his own stanza is to intensify that surprise, which somehow abides in *The Faerie Queene* over almost four thousand repetitions: the couplet surfaces, then subsides into alternating rhyme again to produce adjacent, linked quatrains, ABABBCBC.[9] A famous instance of this durably curious double-take occurs in the first stanza of the poem's first canto:

> A Gentle Knight was pricking on the plaine
>   Ycladd in mightie armes and siluer shielde,
>   Wherein old dints of deepe wounds did remaine,
>   The cruell markes of many' a bloudy fielde;
>   Yet armes till that time did he neuer wield: (I.i.1)

Second thoughts are not inevitable in that position: sometimes the fifth line is just an ordinary joint, at which the stanza bends to address a new topic; and sometimes the sentences sail right through it. But often, as in this stanza—where that 'yet' informs us, notwithstanding the dints in his armor, that our knight is innocent of combat—it changes everything.

The other cardinal oddity of the Spenserian stanza is the concluding alexandrine. Specifying its sources is trickier than tracing the stanza itself. The line was, and remains, a staple of French verse; its irregularity in an otherwise pentameter stanza may nod toward the more complicated shapes of *The Shepheardes Calender*.[10] But it also invokes the hexameter of classical epic, placing the whole stanza on a foundation of ancient dignity and authority. And then again, its strong propensity to locate the caesura in the middle of the line, after the sixth syllable, can break it into what are effectively two tetrameter lines, each closed by an unvoiced beat in the manner of some ballad stanzas: 'Yet nothing did he dread [ ], but ever was ydrad [ ]' (I.i.2). If you hear the line this way, its filiations are native, the ballad or the similarly timed hexameter in the so called 'poulter's measure' (couplets of alternating twelve- and fourteen-syllable lines). The poem's multiple lineages and allegiances—classical, European, native—are all inscribed here. And as various as these possible origins are the effects the alexandrine can achieve. Among the most characteristic is a kind of summary authority, often enhanced by the even-handed gravity of the medial caesura: 'If wind and tide doe change, [ ] their courses change anew' (IV.ix.26). The line can also function to provide some kind of provisional, narrative closure, rounding out a unit of action, as when Phaedria departs the scene on the way to the Bowre of Blisse: 'She turnd her bote about, and from them rowed quite' (II.xii.16). Caesurae after the fourth and eighth syllables occur from time to time, and a few alexandrines fall into three parts ('Whose sleepie head | she in her lap | did soft dispose' (II.xii.76)).

There are occasional lines that scatter their pauses wantonly, like the marvelous 'Birds, voyces, instruments, windes, waters, all agree' (70). Here the reader's labor in figuring out which words and syllables to accentuate, and which to (somewhat strenuously) suppress—'Bȋrds, vóyces, ȋnstrȗménts, wȋndes, wȃters, áll ăgrée'—calls the claim for concord into question. Or does it reinforce that concord, by drawing order from such resistant materials? Such nonce-allegorizations are always precarious, but they tempt particularly in this final line, which serves reliably as a bating place for the reader's mind.

As the alexandrine falls into various, significant parts, so does the stanza itself: carved up by that medial couplet, or by units of syntax that propose (sometimes against the rhyme scheme) alternative groupings. Arthur's speech after rescuing Redcrosse (I.viii.44), for example, has a three-part, almost syllogistic structure. The famous stanza describing the Castle of Alma is another striking demonstration of these resources: the sentences define units of two, three, and then four lines, a kind of pyramid, while the medial couplet splits the difference between masculine and feminine, and the alexandrine fixes the foundation:

> The frame thereof seemd partly circulare,
>   And part triangulare, O worke diuine;
>   Those two the first and last proportions are,
>   The one imperfect, mortall, foeminine;
>   Th'other immortall, perfect, masculine,
>   And twixt them both a quadrate was the base,
>   Proportioned equally by seuen and nine;
>   Nine was the circle set in heauens place,
> All which compacted made a goodly *Diapase*.   (II.ix.22)

Spenser made nearly four thousand of these stanzas, repairing to them, and to the regular iambic rhythms that they house, day after day over the nearly twenty years he worked on the poem. They must have come to serve him as a kind of architecture for thinking, both a reliable framework and a constant provocation, installing in every unit of verse both a second thought and an impulse to closure. The habits of mind played out across the poem's largest thematic and narrative structures—where associations temper or corroborate or undermine one another, where the story forever surges ahead, and the sententious narrator forever pulls up the reins—are all present with fractal potency in these nine lines.

SHORTER POEMS, 1580–99

Spenser seems to have begun writing *The Faerie Queene* as early as 1580, not long after *The Shepheardes Calender* went to the press. But he found time, at moments of repose from what the *Amoretti* call his 'long…race…Through Faery land' (80.1–2), to make a variety of other poems, published as the *Complaints* (1591), *Daphnaïda* (1591), *Colin Clovts Come Home Againe* (1595), *Amoretti and Epithalamion* (1595), *Fowre Hymnes* (1596), and *Prothalamion* (1596). Almost all are written in iambic pentameter. Attempts to describe a progression are complicated by questions about the history of composition and of revision: some of the poems in *Complaints*, for example, may have been written as early as 1569. Such attempts are also complicated, or perhaps just stymied, by the fact that there is not much change to be observed over those twenty years. The pentameter of the shorter poems from the 1580s forward is very much that of *The Faerie Queene*: formidably regular and (despite less of the epic's studied archaism) prone to exploit basically the same range of metrical license to maintain the hegemony of its iambs.

Spenser does, however, provide us with a benchmark for the achievement of that regularity when he revises his first published sonnets, the unrhymed translations of Du Bellay in *A Theatre for Worldlings* (1569), to make the rhymed *Visions of Bellay* in the *Complaints*. The first version, which Spenser must have prepared around the tender age of seventeen, is remarkably accomplished in its own right (see Chapter 8 above). The economy of its subsequent transformation—he conserves a remarkable percentage of the original language—is a testament to his stylistic consistency as well as to his gifts as a rhymer. Still, there are some telling metrical adjustments:

> It was the time when rest the gift of Gods
> Sweetly sliding into the eyes of men,
> Doth drowne in the forgetfulnesse of slepe,
> The carefull trauailles of the painefull day (*Sonets* 1: 1–4)

> It was the time, when rest soft sliding downe
> From heauens hight into mens heauy eyes,
> In the forgetfulnesse of sleepe doth drowne
> The carefull thoughts of mortall miseries (*VB* 1: 1–4)

The version of 1569 begins that second line with two trochees, and reading for local mimesis—was the young Spenser more tempted by such effects?—we might hear the downward slide they describe echoed in their falling rhythm. The later *Visions* rewrites the line to fix an iambic regularity. A subtler but perhaps still more telling alteration is to be found in the third line, where, *circa* 1569, the movement is sustained by the promotion of 'the'. In the *Visions*, the same is true again, but now the article has been shifted to bear the first stress in the line, a promotion that works only when the iambic expectation has considerable authority. The metrical contract has become notably stricter. One more example, from the end of the same poem:

> So I knowing the worldes vnstedfastnesse,
> Sith onely God surmountes the force of tyme,
> In God alone do stay my confidence. (*Sonets* 1: 12–14)

> So I that know this worlds inconstancies,
> Sith onely God surmounts all times decay,
> In God alone my confidence do stay. (*VB* 1: 12–14)

'Knowing' in 1569 is either an inversion in the second foot, or it must be pronounced with a stress on -*ing*, a distortion that the mature Spenser almost never allows in a disyllabic gerund. His revision—which is not compelled by the rhyme's new exigencies—shows a poet concerned to get himself out of what he has come to feel is an awkward spot.

This is not to say that Spenser's sonnets are altogether devoid of mimetic effects, any more than is *The Faerie Queene*. But again those effects are more often achieved by pressure against the iambic movement than by disruption of it. In the example from the *Visions* above, the near-equivalence of *rest, soft, slid-,* and *downe* in the first line—the iambs not inverted so much as blurred—has a lulling effect that might be taken as a more delicate rewriting of those trochees 'Sweetly sliding'. More patent variations in the stress pattern tend to arise, as with his epic, in predictable positions, and inversions of the first foot for emphasis are not uncommon in the *Amoretti*: 'Rúdelỳ thou wrongest my deare harts desire' (5:1), or 'Vénemoŭs toŭng tipt with vile adders sting' (86:1). (In the latter case there is some pressure towards an inversion of the third foot too, a sharp 'tipt' after the caesura.) First inversions will sometimes point up structural divisions, falling at the beginning of a new quatrain or the final couplet (e.g. sonnets 39 and 40). Still, they occur at the beginning of less than ten percent of lines, and are much rarer in the interior. By contrast, closer to twenty percent of lines in *Astrophil and Stella* are inverted in the first position, and we have but to audition a few (relatively dramatic) lines from Sidney's sequence to hear how much more locally expressive his meter can be:[11]

> Vértŭe, aŭaké, Béautĭe bŭt béautĭe ís,
> I may, I must, I can, I will, I do
> Leave following that, which it is gaine to misse.
> Let her go. Soft, but here she comes. Go to,
> Unkind, I loue you not: O me, that eye
> Doth make my heart give to my tongue the lie.   (Sidney 1962: 188)

As is often and justly said of Sidney, the rhythms respond to the pressure of strong emotion, foisting up the inversions in the first line and the barely contained chaos of the fourth. *Astrophil and Stella* as a sequence accustoms us to such brilliant disruptions. If our sensibilities are tuned to the *Amoretti*, however, they are apt to sound garish.

The other shorter poems of this period are cast in a wide variety of rhyme schemes: ottava rima, sixaines or ballade stanzas (rhymed ABABCC), rhyme royale, couplets, and alternating rhymes, more or less the repertory to be found in the miscellanies of the time, minus fourteeners and poulter's measure. The sonnets of the *Amoretti* are almost all in the distinctive and demanding form ABABBCBCCDCDEE. The only poems that mix different line lengths are the anacreontics that follow the *Amoretti*, and the great wedding songs, 'Epithalamion' and 'Prothalamion', which introduce short, trimeter lines into long, predominantly pentameter stanzas fashioned after the Italian *canzone*. 'Epithalamion'—whose twenty-four stanzas vary subtly in length and rhyme scheme—has three short lines in each, lines which serve as a kind of punctuation, leaving a pause where the missing feet would be. There is something of the hurry and wait of the wedding day about the resulting breaks in the pentameter's flow (see also Chapter 14 above). The same effect could be said to be at work in 'Prothalamion', where the stanza is more (but still not perfectly) fixed, and the short lines serve to break it into sonnet-like parts, two to separate the quatrains and then two more before the final couplet. The pentameter of these late poems partakes of the regularity of Spenser's mature style, but just as much of its rhythmic subtlety. In the seventh stanza of 'Epithalamion' the speaker asks Apollo to grant him a day's release from his duties of worship: 'But let this day let this one day be mine' (125). The phrase 'this day' falls differently across the iambs each time, so that 'this' is weak at first, and then—insisting upon the occasion, insisting that the god attend to the poem's present tense—it becomes 'this one day', and no other.[12]

LETTERS TO GABRIEL HARVEY

Back in 1580, however, all these accomplishments in English accentual syllabic verse would have been difficult to foresee: anyone reading Spenser's exchange of letters with his friend Gabriel Harvey, printed early that year in two parts, could be forgiven for assuming that he would never write anything like *The Faerie Queene*, much less begin the work that year. The letters treat a poetically fashionable subject, the composition of English verses in classical meters, or 'refourmed Versifying' (as the printer's title has it). Spenser writes of the new rules with the zeal of a convert. He tells Harvey, in the first letter, how

Master Sidney and Master Dyer . . . haue me, I thanke them, in some vse of familiarity, [and explains how] they haue proclaimed in their *areopagus* a generall surceasing and silence of balde Rymers . . . in steade whereof, they haue, by autho[ri]tie of their whole Senate, pre-scribed certaine Lawes and rules of Quantities of English sillables for English Verse, hauing had thereof already great practise, and drawen mee to their faction.

These sentences are charged with the excitement of membership in an avant-garde, albeit one seeking its principles in an ancient prosody. There had been experiments earlier in the century with English quantities, but Sidney's participation lent the project a new glamour, and at just this moment—the letter is dated 5 October 1579—Spenser must have imagined himself at the vanguard of a wholesale transformation of poetry in his native tongue. No more rhyme: from now on, he is 'more in loue with my Englishe Versifying' (*Prose*, 6).

What were these new old rules for making verses? The basic idea is clear enough. English verse written in rhyme, with a fixed number of syllables per line and (to quote Sidney again) 'some regard of the accent', struck many humanist-trained men as rough and crude by comparison with the resources of Latin. Latin builds its lines according to quantity, which the Elizabethans understood to be a matter of syllable length—actual duration in time, long or short. Schoolboys learned to determine these quantities by applying a few rules, the most prominent of which were the lengthening of diphthongs and the rule 'by position' (a syllable followed by a double consonant is long). The Latin hexameter that such rules structured, with its flexible substitution of spondees for dactyls, looked to them like a much more artistic framework than the English chain of iambs could ever be. The obvious solution to this inconvenience was to transpose the classical rules into English, and compose lines of equivalent flexibility and grace in their own tongue. The question was, how would such lines sound? Or at least, that is the modern question—for as Derek Attridge has pointed out, there is an antecedent question: how did Latin verse sound in the period? And scholars have more or less agreed with his conclusion that the rules of quantity were not actually audible in the Elizabethan speaking of Latin verse. Latin lines were sounded according to stress patterns picked up from listening to their teachers; quantity was 'an intellectual apprehension, not an aural one' (Attridge 1974: 76). In experimenting with English quantities, then, English poets had both to fix the old rules in their new application, and tune their ears to a most elusive music (see above pp. 185–7, 356–7).

The difficulty of hearing English quantities—and particularly, the problem of the distinction between quantity and accent—is the theme of the exchange with Harvey, even if that distinction can never be specified. The treatment of 'carpenter' is a test case. Spenser is prepared to allow the rule by position to lengthen that middle syllable, but Harvey reacts to the proposal with gleeful derision: 'you shall neuer haue my subscription or consent ... to make your *Carpēnter*, our *Carpĕnter*, an inche longer than God and his Englishe people haue made him. Is there no other Pollicie to pull downe Ryming and set vppe Versifying but you must ... forcibly vsurpe and tyrannize vppon a quiet companye of wordes ...?' (*Prose*, 473–4). As far as Harvey is concerned, setting up the laws of versifying above English custom is a species of tyranny, and his rebuke is fraught with political disapproval (Helgerson 1992: 1–18). In practice, Attridge observes, the verses the two men sent one another both make more or less the same compromises: accent (stress) and quantity (the rule-based calculation of syllable length) correspond more often than they do in Stanyhurst's unrepentantly quantitative *Aeneid*, but less than in Sidney's diplomatic efforts in *Arcadia* (Attridge 1974: 189). The real difference between them may be that Harvey holds vehemently to the fantasy of a pronunciation that will reconcile theory and present custom, while Spenser recognizes, properly, that one or the other has to give.

When Spenser writes his second letter, what gives is ordinary usage; or at least, he is determined that the new art should found a new usage, new habits distinctive to verse pronunciation: 'rough words must be subdued with Vse' (*Prose*, 16). As we have seen, this path is not the one his poetry takes. (One wakes in a cold sweat from the dream of a quantitative *Faerie Queene*.) But his fling with ancient prosody was not without influence on his later work, and to understand that influence, it is necessary to take the final step in this essay's backwards career, and consider *The Shepheardes Calender*.

THE SHEPHEARDES CALENDER

Metrically, the *Calender* is unlike anything else in Spenser's corpus. Its twelve months take an exceptionally wide sample of the then-fashionable repertory of forms, some simply adopted, others adapted: the sixaines of *Januarye* and *December*, the *canzone* stanzas of praise in *Aprill* and of elegy in *November*, the sestina in *August*, the unexpected rhyme schemes in *June* (ABABBABA) or in *October* (ABBABA). The choice of forms and of line lengths—which can change several times within a single eclogue—is more flexibly expressive than anywhere else in Spenser's works, and throughout there is an on-again, off-again romance with the four-beat line of the native ballad. A romance, or perhaps better, rivalry, for a contest between ballad and pentameter—played out across eclogues, within eclogues, and occasionally fought line by line—is as much the story of the poem as anything about Colin's career. Indeed, it *is* the story of Colin's career, his ambition and his nostalgia, his yearning toward epic and his allegiance to the rustic wellspring of his poetic energies.[13]

The best way to begin assessing that contest is to consider its poles, the pentameter and tetrameter in their purest instances. *Januarye* gives us Colin writing in excellent pentameter and high rhetorical melancholy. Seventy-eight lines show only three unequivocal inversions in the first foot, and none internally. There are moments where the patterning of phrases exerts a subtle pressure against the meter: 'All ás the thĕ Shéepe, sŭch wás the shĕpeheărds lóoke' (7), for example, tempts us to hear parallel inversions in the first foot and after the caesura. But more often, the phrasing and the iambs collaborate neatly, as with the chiasmus in the couplet, 'Thŏu wéake, Ĭ wanňe: thŏu leáne, Ĭ quite fŏrlórne: | Wĭth móurnĭng pyňe Ĭ, yóu wĭth pýnĭng móurn' (47–8). The situation is much the same in *December*, Colin's valedictory. This controlled pentameter is his favored mode of self-presentation, first and last.

But in the middle of the *Calender*, one finds such exercises as the boisterous back-and-forth between Willye and Perigot in *August*.

> *Perigot.*   It fell vpon a holly eue,
> *Willye.*   hey ho hollidaye,
> *Per.*   When holly fathers wont to shrieue:
> *Wil.*   Now gynneth this roundelay.   (53–6)

The lads' song exploits the strong isochrony of ballad lines, where the stress falls at more even time intervals than it does in pentameter—unstated off-beats keep the rhythm of the second line ('[ ] hey [ ] ho [ ] hollidaye'). For all practical purposes this pulse is instinctive in readers of English poetry, and Derek Attridge goes so far as to suggest that pentameter has developed as the sole sturdy alternative: 'it is the only simple metrical form of manageable length which escapes the elementary four-beat rhythm, with its insistence . . . and its close relationship with the world of ballad and song' (Attridge 1982: 124). This general claim has specific force in 1579, when iambic pentameter was still asserting itself as the line for an English high style. Poulter's measure and fourteeners had their advocates, like Phaer in his *Aeneid* or Golding in his *Metamorphoses*, but these poems actually hew very close to the ballad, their long lines tending to split into units of four beats. Colin casts his lot with pentameter as a way of leaving song behind. In so doing, he also leaves behind the jaunty bonhomie of Perigot and Willye's exchange, and commits himself to singing alone.

So these are the poles of the debate in *The Shepheardes Calender*. The eclogues where pentameter predominates—*June, October,* and the framing of *November*—are very like *Januarye* and *December*, and tend to record the words of Colin and his most self-conscious admirers. On the other side of the spectrum, closest to the song in *August*, are boyish exercises like the conversation between Willye and Thomalin in *March*, which is written in tetrameter tercets, gathered in rhyming units of AABCCB (often with an anapest or a feminine ending in the three-beat third line). The dispute in *Julye* between Thomalin and Morrell is cast in a strict ballad stanza, and then, nearest the middle of the *Calender*'s range, there is the tetrameter of *Februarie, Maye,* and *September*. *Februarie* is particularly rough and jaunty, an argument between the young Cuddie and the aging Thenot in lines that average nine syllables. Anapestic substitutions or double onsets (two unstressed syllables at the start) are the rule, and avoiding a chain of four iambs is the main rhythmic agenda.[14] *Maye* sounds a little smoother, though not because it is more iambic: here there are almost as many ten-syllable as nine-syllable lines (with the odd eleven), and the corresponding frequency of anapestic substitutions often approaches a triple rhythm. But these extra syllables can also have the effect of courting pentameter, and from time to time that courtship is consummated:

> The shepheards God so wel them guided,
> That of nought they were vnprouided,
> Butter enough, honye, milke, and whay,
> And their flockes fleeces, them to araye.
> But tract of time, and long prosperitie:
> That nource of vice, this of insolencie,
> Lulled the shepheards in such securitie,
> That not content with loyall obeysaunce,
> Some gan to gape for greedy governaunce   (113–21)

I have scanned these lines to suggest how they begin with a rough, nine-syllable shepherds' tetrameter, and how, when Piers begins to describe the insidious effects of worldly ambition, the syllable count goes up to ten and it becomes easiest to scan the lines iambically. The shift toward pentameter figures the bad pastors' desire to leave behind the pastoral, and the flocks there that depend upon them, for a higher style. The link with Colin's own poetic ambition is only implicit, but it is unsettling.

Such modulations are striking given the regularity and rhythmic predictability of Spenser's later verse, but they should not be confused with the mimetic responsiveness of Sidney's line. In the *Calender*, what is mostly at stake is a subtle competition among *kinds* of meter, between smoother and rougher versions of the iambic movement, and between the four- and the five-stress line; not so much local variation, that is, as contending norms. The competition may be most intimate and acute in *Aprill*. The eclogue begins with pentameter quatrains rhymed ABAB, and then offers up Colin's song to Eliza, in *canzone* stanzas rhymed ABABCCDDC with lines varying in length from pentameter (four lines) to dimeter (four lines), and a concluding tetrameter. The opening pentameter quatrains are strictly iambic, and so are the pentameter lines in the 'laye | Of fayre *Elisa*' (33–4), at least at the start. But as the song proceeds, those pentameters begin to waver, and by the time we get to the ninth stanza's middle couplet we have lines that are markedly awkward as pentameter, but that subside easily into the tetrameter of *Maye* (as the following scansion argues): 'Wănts nŏt ă foŭrth grăce, tŏ máke thĕ daŭnce éuĕn? | Lét thăt rowme tŏ my̆ Lády̆ bĕ ýeuĕn' (113–14). Intricate allegories may be constructed from the metrical ambivalence of the remaining long lines: the rustic flower catalogue falls into fours (140–1), while the last five-stress line restores a deferential, iambic propriety: 'Lét damĕ Ĕlĭza thánke y̆ou fór her sóng' (150). Such local phenomena may be arguable—calculatedly arguable, because metrically ambiguous—but it is clear enough across the poem that the ballad line exercises a stubborn pull on the pentameter. Colin's praise is an effort to represent and perhaps to fashion an Elizabeth whose debts and loyalties are native, and it cants toward song.

So which side is Colin on—four or five, home or abroad? The answer is both; or rather, four then, five now. The song in *Aprill* was written by the old Colin, a Colin who was still at ease in the country and in the company of shepherds, praising an Elizabeth who had not yet tested her subjects with the vivid prospect of a French marriage. The Colin of the *Calender*'s present tense—of that precarious year 1579— has become a poet of melancholy and incipient exile, who no longer trusts his own rusticity, who aspires to a solitary kind of greatness, and whose signature line has become the pentameter. The verse offers a metrical allegory of the whole poem's dilemma. The *Calender* is caught between the requirement to put away childish things—a requirement of ambition, and also of disappointment—and an abiding sense that the truest wellspring of an English poetry is still tended by a shepherdess. Five and four stand for those alternatives. Meter is a register for working through questions of personal growth, poetic career, and linguistic nationalism, and Spenser's skill in handling the strict forms makes possible the passages of ambiguity that figure something like a struggle for Colin's poetic soul.

But this metrical ambiguity is not an experiment that Spenser would attempt again. Why not? The answer may have something to do with that brief enthusiasm for quantitative verse, which seems to have taken hold of him in the months following the *Calender*'s publication. The letters to Harvey reveal a susceptibility to transports of strong judgment that finds expression throughout his poetry. Like most of those transports, this one did not last. Neither, however, did he go back to the up-for-grabs passages of the *Calender*, nor did he ever again allow the native seductions of the ballad line such free play. It may be that his commitment to such a regular iambic pentameter—the line he did so much to consolidate for English poetry ever after—was what was left over after his dalliance with reformed versifying. It was his own reformation, a magnificently consistent compromise between English rhythms and classical stature. Surrey had found that line first, in his *Aeneid*, but Spenser forged his version anew by staging a contest, in his twenty-eighth year, between the ballad and the *Areopagus*. He was loyal to the pentameter line that resulted to the end of his writing life.

Notes

1. Gascoigne also describes a third kind: 'the circumflexe accent is indifferent, sometimes short, sometimes long, sometimes depressed and sometimes elevate' (Smith 1904: I, 49). This is not, however, a third level of stress; rather a way of talking about words, especially monosyllables, where the accent is indeterminate and will be established only in context. He uses only grave and light for his scansions.
2. There is a useful survey of Spenser's meters given at the end of W. R. Renwick, *Edmund Spenser: An Essay on Renaissance Poetry* (1933: 189–91).
3. Moments such as these are occasions of frequent disagreement among metrists. Hearing '-ott of great name', Derek Attridge—whose system in *The Rhythms of English Poetry* avoids feet altogether—might describe the same moment as a 'stress-final pairing' (Attridge 1982: 175–86), taking the two unstressed syllables to be sufficiently light as to function as a 'double off-beat', with an unstated off-beat introduced between the two stressed syllables. David Keppel-Jones gives the same formation the classical label 'minor ionic' (Keppel-Jones 2001: 7). My scansion is again based on the assumption that Spenser's meter rides his sentences especially hard.
4. Dialectical in a strict sense: the thesis of the norm encounters the antithesis of the actual line; the synthesis is the adjusted norm, which in turn encounters the next actuality, and so on. As Thomas Cable puts it, 'It takes words to set up a linguistic beat, but the beat in turn modulates the words'; 'As often happens in historical metrics, both the phonology and the meter are uncertain. A degree of circularity, and of going back and forth, is always involved in reasoning through these matters' (Cable 2002: 125, 131).
5. Richard McCabe notes that Spenser's schoolmaster, Richard Mulcaster, gave a political cast to the adoption of loan words, speaking of the terms of their 'enfranchisement'— though Mulcaster aspired to more stable principles of orthography, for example, than his pupil ever did (McCabe 2002: 194).
6. For the last possibility, and an account of the system of four stress levels proposed by Jespersen and some other linguists, see Steele (1999), 31–6.
7. George Wright reaches essentially the same conclusion: 'Spenser's tens of thousands of iambic pentameter lines are notable for their regularity, fluency, and grace'; 'metrical variations are used conservatively' (Wright 1988: 61, 63). He allows a slightly greater incidence of inversions within the line, or of spondaic or pyrrhic substitutions, generally pointing to moments that I prefer to regard as moments of strain against the meter rather than metrical variation.
8. The classic treatment of the stanza is still William Empson's in *Seven Types of Ambiguity* (Empson 1966: 33–4). See also Woods (1984), 148–52, and Dolven (2004).
9. On the matter of the stanza's rhymes: it is a curious fact that the 1590 *Faerie Queene* has only one feminine rhyme (i.e., a two syllable rhyme, the second syllable weak, as 'soften' and 'often'), while the new books of 1596 have one hundred and sixty-three (Wilson-Okamura 2007).
10. On the influence of French (and Italian) verse on Spenser, see O. B. Hardison's *Prosody and Purpose in the English Renaissance*, which offers a very different approach to

understanding prosody of the period, emphasizing the importance of syllabic verse and 'the control of syntax and syntactical rhythms' (Hardison 1989: xii).

11. Such percentages can never be exact, not least because the prevailing metrical assumptions of the sequences might mean that the same line would be scanned differently in each: Sidney's 'Great expectation, weare a traine of shame' (Sidney 1962: 175) is probably best sounded with a first inversion in his sequence, but if it were transposed into Spenser's, with an initial iamb.

12. For the stanza and metrics of *Fowre Hymnes* see Chapter 16 above.

13. John Thompson's *The Founding of English Metre* gives a particularly thorough account of the *Calender*, and he also observes the difficulty of the eclogues *Februarie*, *Maye*, and *September*. He entertains the idea that their meter is a sixteenth-century reconstruction of Chaucer's line, without the benefit of sounding the final -*e*, but he concludes that 'a very powerful metrical pattern' of four beats presides and is 'to be maintained at no matter what expense to the language...the results are crudities in mis-using language, the decorum of shepherds—not new or shifting metrical patterns' (Thompson 1966: 93–4).

14. Susanne Woods argues that among the signs of Spenser's allegiance to a native tradition is the importance of the hemistich, or half line, defined by a strong medial caesura: in the 'rollicking four-stress nine and ten-syllable verse of "Februarie"' (Woods 1984: 141), but also in *The Faerie Queene*, even if the half lines there will always split the accents unevenly. For the half line see above pp. 214–15.

BIBLIOGRAPHY

Attridge, D. (1974). *Well-Weighed Syllables: Elizabethan Verse in Classical Metres*. London: Cambridge University Press.

—— (1982). *The Rhythms of English Poetry*. London: Longman.

Berry, E. (1981). 'The Reading and Uses of Elizabethan Prosodies'. *Language and Style* 14(2): 116–52.

Cable, T. (2002). 'Issues for a New History of English Prosody', in D. Minkova and R. Stockwell (eds), *Studies in the History of the English Language*. Berlin: Mouton de Gruyter, 125–51.

Dobson, E. (1967). *English Pronunciation 1500–1700*, 2nd edn. Oxford: Oxford University Press.

Dolven, J. (2004). 'The Method of Spenser's Stanza'. *SSt* 28: 17–25.

Empson, W. (1966). *Seven Types of Ambiguity*. New York: New Directions.

Hardison, O. B. (1989). *Prosody and Purpose in the English Renaissance*. Baltimore: Johns Hopkins University Press.

Helgerson, R. (1992). *Forms of Nationhood: The Elizabethan Writing of England*. Chicago: University of Chicago Press.

Hollander, J. (1970). 'Romantic Verse Form and the Metrical Contract', in H. Bloom (ed.), *Romanticism and Consciousness*. New York: W.W. Norton, 181–200.

Keppel-Jones, D. (2001). *The Strict Metrical Tradition: Variations in the Literary Iambic Pentameter from Sidney and Spenser to Matthew Arnold*. Montreal: McGill-Queen's University Press.

McCabe, R. (2002). *Spenser's Monstrous Regiment: Elizabethan Ireland and the Poetics of Difference*. Oxford: Oxford University Press.

Renwick, W. L. (1933). *Edmund Spenser: An Essay on Renaissance Poetry*. London: E. Arnold.

Sidney, P. (1962). *The Poems of Sir Philip Sidney*, ed. William Ringler. Oxford: Clarendon Press.

Smith, G. (1904). *Elizabethan Critical Essays*, 2 vols. Oxford: Oxford University Press.

Steele, T. (1999). *All the fun's in how you say a thing: An Explanation of Meter and Versification*. Athens: Ohio University Press.

Thompson, J. (1966). *The Founding of English Metre*. London: Routledge and Kegan Paul.

Weiner, S. (1982). 'Spenser's Study of English Syllables and its Completion by Thomas Campion'. *SSt* 3: 3–56.

Wilson-Okamura, D. (2007). 'The French Aesthetic of Spenser's Feminine Rhyme'. *MLQ* 68 (3): 345–62.

Woods, S. (1984). *Natural Emphasis: English Versification from Chaucer to Dryden*. San Marino: The Huntington Library.

Wright, G. (1988). *Shakespeare's Metrical Art*. Berkeley: University of California Press.

CHAPTER 22

··

SPENSER'S GENRES

··

COLIN BURROW

GENRE THEORY: ANCIENT, MODERN, AND EARLY MODERN

··

It is tempting to think of genres as a row of boxes—even prison cells, perhaps—into which unruly works of literature are placed by pedants like Polonius in *Hamlet*, with his 'tragedy, comedy, history, pastoral, pastoral-comical, historical-pastoral, tragical-historical, tragical-comical-historical-pastoral, scene individable or poem unlimited' (2.2.397–400). For the majority of modern theorists, though, genre is not a row of boxes but an interpretative tool: readers, they would argue, need genres as a way of provisionally placing works of fiction within a larger literary system, and as a means of beginning the process of interpretation (Fowler 1982; Frow 2005; Hirsch 1967). Texts give off signals which declare roughly what conventions they are following (a critical essay, a leading article in a newspaper, a post-colonial novel). They might then incorporate some features from other genres, or deliberately transform the conventions of the genre to which they appear to be contributing, or even construct an individual genre all of their own; but whether or not they do so, the attempt to identify a work as belonging to a particular genre is the way in which readers start to sound out what kind of text they have before them.

These present-day attitudes to genre provide a helpful way in to Spenser's dynamic juxtapositions of different literary kinds in his later works, as we shall see, but they have little in common with the complex body of thought about genre which the poet inherited. Spenser was influenced by classical genre theorists, who on the whole are straightforwardly taxonomic. They characteristically assume that genres cannot change, that texts can only belong to one genre, and that works of literature can be assigned to one of these unchanging categories on the basis of intrinsically distinct properties.[1] Aristotle, who established the most influential divisions of literature into different generic categories, makes distinctions between dramatic and narrative presentational modes and has often been thought to argue for a third group, of lyric or dithyrambic writing (although Genette 1992 would disagree). These kinds are then subdivided on the basis of the social status and actions of the principal characters: so, drama about high-born characters is tragedy, while narrative in verse about such figures is epic. Aristotle's *Poetics* was available in print from 1508 in Greek, and in Giorgio Valla's Latin translation from 1498.[2] Broadly similar theories about genre were also available to Medieval and Renaissance readers through Horace's *Ars Poetica*, a didactic poem generally believed in the Renaissance to versify Aristotelian principles. Horace is actually more tolerant than Aristotle of the idea that genres can be mixed, and he is also prone to identify genres with particular 'auctores', or generic originators, but he shares with his major predecessors the belief that each genre has its own decorum, which fitted particular kinds of content to particular metrical forms (Harrison 2007: 5).

Horace and Aristotle were influential in the sixteenth century, but attitudes towards genre in that period also owed a great deal to rhetorical writings from later antiquity. In the Alexandrian period rhetoricians had begun to build up prescriptive models of the kinds of speech which were appropriate to particular occasions. These were formalized and recorded in a pair of rhetorical treatises from the third century AD ascribed to a figure known as Menander the Orator ('Menander Rhetor'—who was in fact probably at least two people).[3] Menander provided an exhaustive list of generic labels for different kinds of speech, and Polonius would have loved him: a 'propemptikon' is a speech written to mark the departure of someone on a journey, an 'epibaterion' is a speech marking the return of a great man or ruler, while an 'epithalamion' of course celebrates a wedding. Menander's treatises were concerned with speeches of praise (panegyrics) rather than poems, and so might seem to us quite alien to literary criticism, but he and the tradition which he in part preserved had some influence on the ways in which lyrics were written and the ways in which they were classified in the later classical period. And Menander's treatises were first printed in the very volume in which Aristotle's *Poetics* was first made available to Renaissance readers. This volume was not called 'Greek Literary Criticism', but *Oratores Graeci* (1508), 'Greek Orators'. It is from this fusion of what we would think of as the literary critical and the rhetorical tradition that the idea of genres as a complex of classificatory boxes ultimately derives. Menander's multiplying generic categories, fused with some rather over-rigid misunderstandings of Aristotle's thoughts on literary kinds, entered the mainstream of vernacular and neo-Latin literary criticism through a number of influential Renaissance treatises, including most notably Julius Caesar Scaliger's *Poetices* (1561).

Spenser knew something of Aristotle and Scaliger, and probably something of Menander too. His understanding of what could be done with genres was, however, profoundly influenced by his reading in classical and Renaissance literature. Poets from the reign of the Emperor Augustus (notably Virgil, Ovid, and Horace) often did things with generic conventions which were strikingly at odds with the highly prescriptive views of classical literary theorists (Farrell 2003). Virgil's *Eclogues*, for example, is not just a book of ten poems about shepherds. Virgil marks his allegiances to the conventions of the eclogue tradition by frequent allusions to the Greek writers Theocritus and Bion, but he also brings into the genre traces of the vocabulary and idiom of didactic poetry, of contemporary politics, of erotic and funerary elegy. Virgil and his contemporaries aimed for what has recently been called 'generic enrichment'—that is, they continually probed, expanded, and hybridized generic categories (Harrison 2007). This, rather than a closed and static system of classification, was what Spenser found in the treatment of genres by the classical poets whom he read and emulated, and it left a profound mark on his own practice. Each of Spenser's contributions to a genre is driven not by the rigid taxonomies of classical theory, but by the dynamic, flexible, and transformative practice of classical poets. Spenser wrote eclogues which, as E. K. puts it, were 'Plaintiue', sometimes 'recreatiue', and sometimes 'Moral' (Spenser 1999: 32). These modal variations[4] in the treatment of pastoral were Spenser's equivalents, *mutatis mutandis*, of the way Virgil assimilated dozens of different genres into his eclogues. Pastoral poetry, that is, for Spenser allowed for a pattern of controlled shifts between a variety of elements: light-hearted singing contests, laments, didactic or encomiastic elements, all might jostle for position with satirical or topical material. Epic too—often treated even by classical theorists as a genre which comprehended all other genres—could incorporate passages of elegy, complaint, tragedy, topography, and a hundred subgenres and modes which even a Polonius would find it hard to list. It is because Spenser learnt more from the way classical poets treated genre than he did from the more rigid principles of classical theorists that modern genre theory can help in reading his verse: he expected his readers to recognize the ways in which he continually adapts and alters each of the major genres to which he made a contribution, and to attempt to identify genres and modal variations as they fly past.

GENRE AND PRINT

There are, however, a number of interconnected respects in which Spenser's treatments of genre were distinctively post-classical and also distinctly unlike modern genre theories. These are chiefly consequences of the fact that he was a poet who wrote for print. Print authors in the late sixteenth century enjoyed an unprecedented ability to mark their works as contributions to a specific genre. They could do this by titles, typography, prefaces, or other features of the printed book which Gerard Genette has termed 'paratexts' (Genette 1982: 94–103). Title pages and prefaces were for Spenser a way of declaring both the genre in which he was working and the novel ways in which he was doing so. His *Epithalamion* (1595), to take the most obvious example, was the first printed English marriage song to use this classical generic title on a title page. Spenser knew it, and wanted his readers to know it too.[5] His *Prothalamion or a Spousall Verse* (1596) presents and then gives a gloss for ('a Spousall Verse') a generic term which appears to have been entirely his invention.

Print could also enable what might be termed the 'eristic' use of generic markers. That is, printed poets were especially keen to mark their works as belonging to a particular genre when they had made significant modifications to that genre, or when they wanted their readers to think that they had gone significantly beyond the work of a predecessor. Spenser's sonnet sequence, the *Amoretti* (to which the *Epithalamion* is appended), is perhaps the clearest example of this competitive use of generic convention. By 1595 the content and structure of printed sonnet sequences were governed by fairly rigid generic expectations: they would usually dwell on unrequited or unrequitable love; they might gesture at attempts to transform love of a mistress into love of God, but their main sequence would be expected to end, as Sir Philip Sidney's *Astrophil and Stella* did, with the poet alone, locked in disappointment with only 'wailing eloquence' as his companion. After Samuel Daniel's *Delia* (1592), sequences might also be expected to be followed by a coda in a different genre, since *Delia* concludes with a seven-hundred-line complaint by Rosamond (the mistress of Henry II) about the sorrows of love. Spenser's *Amoretti* is a conscious performance in generic transformation: he establishes his own rhyme scheme for the sonnet (ababbcbccdcdee), breaks startlingly with convention by having his narrator aim at marriage, but then swerves back to the conventions of the sequence by having it end with his narrator apparently alone ('Lyke as the Culuer on the bared bough, | Sits mourning for the absence of her mate . . . So I alone now left disconsolate, | mourne to my selfe the absence of my loue' (89.1–6)). But after that point generic rules seem again to bend and break: the final sonnet is followed by a group of poems now generally called Anacreontics, or short love lyrics about the pains of desire, then the volume closes with the *Epithalamion*. The innovation of using the classical generic label for that poem would of course have struck its first readers; but they would have been amazed by the revolutionary way that the poem concludes the sonnet sequence with the marriage of the narrator, rather than his final disappointment. The new genre also transforms an old genre.

GENERIC CAREERS

Printed authors could use generic labels to declare their originality. They could also construct a distinct view of their own literary trajectory by contributing to particular genres at different periods in their careers.[6] In doing this they were assisted by one major difference of emphasis between classical and early modern discussions of genre. Writing about genre in the sixteenth century tended to be as much genealogical as taxonomic. That is, Renaissance literary criticism frequently linked the emergence and differentiation of individual genres to particular quasi-historical phases in the history of poetry. These were 'quasi-historical' rather than 'historical' because the stories told about the emergence of particular genres were often more or less self-consciously mythical. Book III of Scaliger's *Poetices* (first printed in 1561) presents the most detailed early modern taxonomy of the different poetic kinds, including (as we have seen) many subgenres drawn from the rhetorical works of Menander. Scaliger's first book, however, is devoted to discussing the genesis of individual literary genres: 'The earliest kind of poetry was of course the product of one of the earliest stages of life, either the pastoral stage, the hunting, or the agricultural' (Scaliger 1905: 21). Genres placed 'early' in these semi-mythical histories of poetry might be those most suitable for a young poet, who could then seek to replicate in his movement through the different kinds a small-scale version of the development of poetry.

This sounds like a simple matter. Pastoral, as Scaliger says, and as Virgil exemplified in his career, came first. In practice it was not so simple. Spenser knew of a wide variety of schemes for determining the origins and development of genres, and he drew on nearly all of them. He was clearly aware of the Virgilian model (which was sometimes, since the twelfth-century theorist John of Garland, set out in the form of a 'wheel') which progressed through pastoral to georgic, and thence to epic.[7] *The Shepheardes Calender* seems to establish a simple symmetry between early Spenser, early Virgil, and 'early' writing from the pastoral stage of human development. Spenser exaggerates this association by his willingness to lace his eclogues with the 'early' language of Chaucer, and the earliness of the poems is further emphasized by E. K.'s statement that the author of *The Shepheardes Calender* was 'following the example of the best and most auncient Poetes, which deuised this kind of wryting, being both so base for the matter, and homely for the manner, at the first to trye theyr habilities' (Spenser 1999: 29). Not all theorists, however, believed that pastoral was 'early': George Puttenham, the most influential English vernacular writer about genres, denied

that the eclogue should be the first and most ancient form of artificial poesy, being persuaded that the poet devised the eclogue long after the other dramatic poems, not of purpose to counterfeit or represent the rustical manner of loves and communication, but under the veil of homely persons and in rude speeches to insinuate and glance at greater matters. (Puttenham 2007: 127–8)

Spenser is unlikely to have read Puttenham's treatise before 1579, but he would have taken from Virgil's early (and frequently reprinted) commentator Servius the notion that eclogues could comment on politics as well as evoking the pastoral leisure of young men at their ease. Spenser thought of pastoral as a sophisticated form which could, under an appearance of youthful innocence, glance at the politics of church and state.

Spenser exploited uncertainties about the historical sequence and the relative levels of sophistication of different genres. He also presented his own career in multiple and conflicting ways. And these to a significant degree follow the uncertainties of

Renaissance genre theorists about the successive development of different literary kinds. Scaliger wavers over whether to present genres in historical order (which would place pastoral first) or according to the status of particular genres, in which case hymns would be given primary position. Puttenham thought that the primary impulse of poetry was religious worship, and that hymns therefore were early forms, and the neo-Latin poet Girolamo Vida declared in his *De Arte Poetica* of 1527:

> Iamque adeo in primis ne te non carminis unum
> Praetereat genus esse, licet celebranda reperti
> Ad sacra sint tantum versus, laudesve deorum
> Dicendas, ne religio sine honore jaceret.   (Vida 1976: I, 27–30)

Let us begin now: first, note that Song is not all of one genre. It is true that verses were devised in the beginning solely for the glorification of things sacred or for speaking the gods' praises, so that religion might not lack some particular mark of distinction.

Spenser responded directly not to one but to all of these varying theories about what kinds of verse were actually 'primary', in either chronology or significance, and this explains the curious way in which hymns in particular fit in to his poetic career. The *Fowre Hymnes* appeared in print relatively late (in 1596, only three years before his death and in the same year as the second instalment of *The Faerie Queene*), but they are prefixed by a note which describes the poet as 'Hauing in the greener times of my youth, composed these former two Hymnes in the praise of Loue and beautie' (Spenser 1999: 452).[8] This note suggests that hymns of love were an alternative Spenserian generic beginning, and implicitly places heavenly hymns at the culmination of his career.

   Even this is not the end of the story, since there is yet a third sort of generic origin to Spenser's poetic career. Vida suggests that young poets should begin, not with pastoral, but by experimenting with minor epic, and with genres which they could have found in a group of poems which from 1572 onwards was called the 'Appendix Virgiliana'. This was a collection of miscellaneous verses generally believed in the sixteenth century to include Virgil's juvenilia (Burrow 2008). Vida declares:

> Sed neque inexpertus rerum iam texere longas
> Audeat Iliadas. paullatim assuescat, & ante
> Incipiat graciles pastorum inflare cicutas.
> Iam poterit culicis numeris fera dicere fata,
> Aut quanta ediderit certamine fulmineus mus
> Funera in argutas, & amantes humida turmas,
> Ordirive dolos, & retia tenuis aranei.   (I, 459–65)

[A youngster], unskilled in matters [poetic], ought not to venture to compose long *Iliads*, but should gain experience little by little, making his debut by playing on the shepherds' slender pipes. Soon he will be able to tell in verse of the fearsome fates of a gnat, or of how in boundless battle the murderous mouse dealt death to the croaking troops of marsh-loving frogs, or weave a tale of the stratagems and webs of the subtle spider.

We might instinctively think of mock-heroic as a late and super-sophisticated genre, which preys on the conventions of epic and perhaps also revolts against them. This is a misconception. Early modern poets thought that Virgil's career (and probably Homer's too) began with what appear to us to be strange spin-offs from epic (which modern scholars have shown were in fact late pastiches of the Virgilian style): poems in epic style on sub-epic topics—battles between frogs and mice in the case of Homer, or about the death of a gnat in the case of Virgil. Spenser wove a tale of the stratagems of the subtle spider in *Muiopotmos*, of course, and also told in verse the fearsome fate of a gnat in *Virgil's Gnat*, his fairly literal translation of the *Culex*, one of the longer works from the 'Appendix Virgiliana'. Both these minor or mock epics appeared in the *Complaints* volume of 1591. Like the *Fowre Hymnes*, the *Gnat* is prefixed with a note that places it right at the start of Spenser's career: the poem was 'Long since dedicated To the most noble and excellent Lord, the Earle of Leicester, late deceased' (Spenser 1999: 210). The note creates blurred edges around Spenser's supposedly Virgilian generic career: he begins his official printed *oeuvre* with eclogues, but with the publication of the *Complaints* volume his readers would learn that he—like Virgil, or at any rate like the Virgil represented in early modern editions—also experimented as a young man with mock- or sub-heroic satirical narrative.

This association between the genres ascribed to the early Virgil and generic 'earliness' continued late into Spenser's career. His only other substantial allusion to a poem from the 'Appendix Virgiliana' occurs in Book III of *The Faerie Queene*, when Britomart falls in love with Artegall's image in a mirror (III.ii.30–51). This is described through a string of close allusions to the *Ciris*, a generically curious poem of uncertain date and uncertain authorship about Scylla's theft of a lock of hair from her father's head (see Virgil 1978). This poem was presented in most Renaissance editions as a piece of Virgilian juvenilia. Those allusions to an 'early', supposedly Virgilian, genre of erotic narrative poetry are artfully positioned within Britomart's story: they come just as an erotically innocent young girl transforms herself into a questing knight. Spenser's heroine begins her career in a world of mock-epic, in pseudo- or perhaps just early Virgilian genres, before she ventures on to higher kinds. Meanwhile Spenser's own generic career begins with pastoral. Or hymns. Or Virgilian juvenilia. Or all three.

EPIC?

It is very easy to stitch *The Faerie Queene* into Spenser's generic career. The poem declares itself to be an epic from its very first lines:

> Lo I the man, whose Muse whylome did maske,
>   As time her taught, in lowly Shephards weeds,
>   Am now enforst a farre vnfitter taske,
>   For trumpets sterne to chaunge mine Oaten reeds:
>   And sing of Knights and Ladies gentle deeds.   (1 Proem, 1)

No poem written in English before *The Faerie Queene* claimed so unequivocally to be an epic, and the audacity with which Spenser made his final and greatest declaration of generic novelty made a powerful impression on his first readers. But neither the poem—nor indeed its proem—is quite that simple. These lines are based on a prologue which was often printed with Virgil's *Aeneid* in the Renaissance, but which was even in that period widely suspected not to have been written by Virgil. The prologue, that is, declares *The Faerie Queene* to be following a pseudo-Virgilian just as much as a Virgilian path. It also hints at the ways in which sixteenth-century heroic poetry differed from its Augustan predecessors by promising to sing of 'Knights and Ladies' rather than of a Virgilian 'arms and the man'. This unmistakably locates the poem within the traditions of romance epic which flourished in Italy from the late fifteenth to the late sixteenth centuries. Matteo Maria Boiardo, Ludovico Ariosto, and Torquato Tasso had written long verse narratives with multiple heroes, in which love, self-parody, and (in Tasso) religion were major themes. Their work inspired extensive argument about the relative merits of heroic poems which had single heroes and predominantly martial and imperial content (for which the main model was Virgil's *Aeneid*) and those which tumbled together a glorious variety of love-smitten heroes and relished their chaotic and marvellous adventures (see Burrow 1993, Javitch 1991, and for the critical debate Weinberg 1961: 954–1073). *The Faerie Queene* is embedded in these debates, and would have struck its early readers as a thoroughly modern kind of epic, which combined Virgil's comprehensive grasp of different literary modes and kinds with the innovations of the Italian poets. Spenser's Italian predecessors tended to link different stylistic decorums (that is, different registers of language) and generic expectations with different characters, and very often would construct their narratives so that their heroes and heroines moved through a variety of different modes and literary landscapes, from the comically grotesque, through the courtly, to the aggressively Homeric (Burrow 1993). Spenser follows their example by drawing on a huge range of genres and modes in *The Faerie Queene*. He did so partly because he faced a conceptual and generic problem: *The Faerie Queene* at some point in its lengthy genesis may have aimed to fuse together the disparate erotic energies of the Italian tradition with the empire-building concerns of Virgil by presenting an epic narrative about the foundation and perpetuation of Gloriana's dynasty. Spenser's Queen Elizabeth, however, the dedicatee of the poem, remained unmarried, and by the time of the poem's publication was clearly set to remain so.

This simple fact has a radical effect on the generic form of *The Faerie Queene*. Spenser was always fascinated by generic hybridity. But by the time he wrote his epic that fascination was a necessity: he simply had to incorporate the delays, digressions, and erotic excurses of the romance form into his epic if he was not to write a work drastically unsuited to its unmarried dedicatee. The process of writing narrative fiction with multiple heroes also gave a new jolt of energy and unpredictability to his experiments with genre. Many characters in *The Faerie Queene* bring with them distinct generic conventions, and as a result when they appear the poem's mode begins to shift. Florimell, for instance, repeatedly evokes and enacts the conventions of mistresses in the Petrarchan tradition of love poetry; Braggadocchio, the braggart knight, seems to have stepped out of Ariosto via the *commedia dell' arte*. These correlations between individual characters and particular genres and modes are reinforced by Spenser's tendency to map social hierarchies onto their generic equivalents: Arthur tends to be represented in language rich in biblical allusions, and he tends to participate in actions—conquest, battles, liberation of heroes from captivity—which have epic associations. But because the poem contains so many characters and so many interlinked narrative threads these generically and socially distinct character types repeatedly encounter each other. This means that the poem continually tests both social and generic decorum. So, when the false knight Braggadocchio's sidekick Trompart meets Belphoebe for the first time, he shows his amazement by echoing the moment when Virgil's Aeneas meets his mother Venus in disguise:

> O Goddesse, (for such I thee take to bee)
> For nether doth thy face terrestriall shew,
> Nor voyce sound mortall . . .   (II.iii.33)

Aeneas's rapt 'o dea certe' ('oh surely you are a goddess', *Aeneid* 1.328) is pulled out of the lowbrow Trompart's mouth by the presence of one of the 'mirrours more then one' (3 Proem, 5) through which Spenser represents his queen. It seems as though the wonder generated by such figures can enable even characters who have their origins in comic and parodic kinds to speak in the voice of a higher genre. But the whole encounter between the virginal Belphoebe and characters who seem to have wandered into the poem out of comedy also brings overtones of parody to Spenser's engagement with epic (McCabe 2003), and we should remember here his belief that post-Virgilian mock and minor epics were in fact where Virgil's career began. Braggadocchio wonders at Belphoebe's beauty, and then, 'leaping light', attempts to embrace her while she is in the middle of a gracious speech. *The Faerie Queene* lets different genres encounter, unsettle, and even assault each other; and this feature of the poem is a major part of its literary-historical significance. Its delight in generic hybridity places it somewhere on the road towards the emergence of the novel, a form which forces dialogic relationships between different genres, and which gives a range of voices to distinct social classes (Bakhtin 1981: 3–40). But the poem is at best halfway down that road, since Spenser is always uneasy about the potential for bathos or contamination which can follow from encounters between generically and socially distinct characters. Belphoebe keeps her social, moral, and generic distance from the false knights: she is prevented even from addressing Trompart by the rustling in the bushes produced by his fearful overlord Braggadocchio, and she responds to Braggadocchio's assault by stopping her speech mid-sentence and pointing her 'Iauelin bright' at him. Silence and violence are very often the means by which Spenser maintains distance between characters from different generic origins. Such characters can meet in *The Faerie Queene*, but they cannot enter into a fully dialogic exchange.

Although *The Faerie Queene* does not quite allow dialogic interpenetration of genres, it is nonetheless drawn towards representing social and generic variety. Each book has a slightly different palate of genres and modes, and the extent to which each book explores coalescences between the different conventions on which it draws is related to its titular virtue. Book III shows Spenser at his most generically various, shifting from complaint, to dream allegory, to erotic idyll, to masque with extraordinary pace and fluidity. The unusual generic mutability of this particular book is not surprising. It is the book of Chastity, and that governing virtue necessarily brings in its train love, sexual desire, and erotic fear. As George Puttenham put it in *The Arte of English Poesie*, love brings a variety of moods which require a poet to be variable and inconstant:

Because love is of all other human affections the most puissant and passionate, and most general to all sorts and ages of men and women, so as whether it be of the young or old, wise or holy, or high estate or low... it requireth a form of poesy variable, inconstant, affected, curious, and most witty of any others, whereof the joys were to be uttered in one sort, the sorrows in another, and by the many forms of poesy, the many moods and pangs of lovers throughly to be discovered. (Puttenham 2007: 134)

The final section of Book III illustrates how love brings about lightning shifts in form and genre. In III.ix Britomart is among a group of knights reluctantly admitted to the castle of Malbecco. One of her companions is a knight called Paridell, who boasts of his descent from the Trojan hero Paris. At dinner he relates the prehistory of his race, and Britomart takes his story as a solemn epic parallel to her own dynastic history. Actually Paridell's narration is part of his attempt to seduce his hostess Hellenore. These two, Paridell and Helen-o'er again, replicants of the originals of the Trojan War, elope together, and are pursued by the jealous *senex amans* Malbecco. Throughout this sequence Spenser consistently links generic indicators with the wrong kind of narrative outcomes, and repeatedly twins epic and dynastic modes with incongruous elegiac and erotic doubles. Hybridity of genre becomes a necessary consequence of the increasing number of characters in the poem. So, for the heroically chaste Britomart, Paridell is an epic narrator of a glorious past, a new Aeneas. For Hellenore, however, he is an Ovidian master-seducer who secretly displays his knowledge of elegy and the arts of love. And that coincidence of distinct kinds within a single character in turn suggests a mischievous willingness on Spenser's part to hear a plurality of genres in his classical sources. In Book II of the *Aeneid* the hero Aeneas relates the fall of Troy in an epic narrative. Like Paridell's tale, however, this act of narration has erotic consequences, since it leads the Carthaginian queen Dido to fall in love with him. In the Malbecco episode Spenser replays this epic narrative in an erotic key in a way that ironically reflects both on Virgil's epic and on the generic tunnel-vision of his own characters. Britomart, caught up in her own dynastic epic pursuit of Artegall, naïvely fails to see the seduction which is masquerading as epic before her, while Paridell and Hellenore seem trashily reductive in their willingness to rewrite an epic history of a nation as an elaborate chat-up line.

Meanwhile genres multiply around them. Hellenore's husband Malbecco seems to belong to a different generic register altogether. He is the classic foolish old lover from medieval *fabliaux*, a character-type obsessed by material goods, and who traditionally has the sole aim of preventing his wife looking at any other man, and who inevitably has the fate of seeing himself (or not seeing himself, since such characters are often blind or blinded) cuckolded. His fate is his genre. But even Malbecco makes genres metamorphose around him. At the end of III.x, when he has suffered a particularly extreme version of the fate of old men in *fabliaux*, having seen his wife sleep with the satyrs and having lost all his gold as well, he is eventually transformed into an abstraction: he 'Forgot he was a man, and *Gelosy* is hight' (III.x.60). In Book III fixed and simple generic conventions are often aligned with single and limited points of view, and all kinds seem to be subjected to a law of transformation, whereby a genre is only inhabited for as much time as it takes a reader to recognize it, before it is supplanted by another. Moving from post- and near parodic epic, through love elegy, to *fabliau*, to metamorphic fiction, towards moralized allegory, the role of genre in Book III seems to be to give its readers a momentary chance mistakenly to think that they have found their bearings before another genre is introduced and warped in its turn. *The Faerie Queene* is reluctant to allow individual characters to enter into social and generic dialogue with those beneath them, but it does nonetheless repeatedly encourage its readers to experience a simultaneous multiplicity of genres, and to watch bewildered as those familiar reference-points seem no longer to hold.

Genre and Locus

It is tempting to see the generic fluidity of Book III of *The Faerie Queene* as the point towards which all of Spenser's career was tending. As we have seen, he probably learnt from his reading in classical and neo-Latin literature that many of the genres in which he principally operated were mixed, or open to modal modification—that pastoral could be written in a plaintive or in a 'recreative' key, and that epic could accommodate elements from any number of other genres. Here, though, we should recall that Renaissance literary criticism was inseparably linked with rhetorical traditions. Early modern students were trained to identify a variety of textual features as they read, which ranged from arguments, apothegms, and rhetorical figures through to elaborate ornaments such as 'chronographies', or descriptions of times of day (see pp. 425 ff below). These they were encouraged to record in notebooks in order to make use of them when composing their own works. Such 'commonplaces', as they were called, belong to a more fine-grained order of textual analysis than genres (see Beal 1993; Moss 1996): they could encompass topoi within a particular genre, such as descriptions of heavenly messengers within epic, or descriptions of 'beautiful places' (*loci amoeni*).[9] The fact that the Latin word *locus* and its Greek equivalent *topos* both mean 'place' is extremely significant: many topoi alluded to or transformed in *The Faerie Queene* are associated with particular types of location. Some of these have rich literary histories but no very clear generic affiliations—like the Cave of Sleep in I.i. 39–42 (Burrow 1999).

Others, such as Mammon's Cave in II.vii, fuse topographic description with allusions to particular kinds: Guyon's descent into the cave is a version of Aeneas's descent to the underworld in *Aeneid* 6. Places in *The Faerie Queene* are very often associated with actions and language appropriate to particular genres and their related modes. So the major generic topoi of romance (lustful knights, lost ladies, error, Errour herself, and errant heroes) are all found most often in forests (Saunders 1993), while castle interiors tend to be associated with erotic and elegiac modes.

As a result of these associations between place and topos, and between topos and genre, the way in which characters move through landscapes and places in the poem is part of its generic language. Sometimes the heroes seem to be led by the landscape itself into generically coded locations, which can be dangerous dead ends. So the Redcrosse knight is 'with pleasure forward led' (I.i.8) through a wood until he finds himself in Errour's lair, where he meets the ultimate adversary for an errant hero. Similarly, when Britomart leaves the Redcrosse knight in III.iv she seems just to drift, 'Following the guydaunce of her blinded guest [i.e. following Cupid], | Till that to the seacoast at length she her addrest' (III.iv.6). She ends up by the seashore partly for narrative convenience, since she must encounter and wound Marinell in order to set in motion a major strand of the narrative. But she is also driven by generic logic, since what she does by the sea is perform a love-complaint, a subgenre which in this period was strongly associated with a water-side locale.[10] A plaintive heroine must make the landscape around her turn to water.

This association between particular subgenres in *The Faerie Queene* and particular types of place plays a major part in the reading experience of the poem. The strange combination of episodic rigidity and generic fluidity with which the poem moves has frequently led critics to call it dream-like: as heroes move on to different places, so slightly different generic expectations suddenly seem to apply. There are times, indeed, when the narrative seems to be driven along by a kind of generic and locational drift, as though places are themselves determining what the heroes and heroines can do or say. On other occasions shifts of location are the deliberate results of actions by Spenser's heroes, and these are sometimes accompanied by violent generic modulations and transformations. The end of Book III—again the book which ranges most widely through kinds and modes—is particularly prone to map generic boundaries directly onto physical boundaries, and to associate a physical movement from one place to another either with a poetic movement from one set of generic conventions to another or with an explicit transformation of a genre into a slightly new form. In III.xi Britomart finds Scudamore locked out by a wall of flame from Busirane's castle. He is trapped within the conventional grieving solitude of a Petrarchan lover at the end of a sonnet sequence: 'Faire *Amorett* must dwell in wicked chaines, | And *Scudamore* here die with sorrowing' (III.xi.24), he complains. Britomart seeks to resolve this generic dead-end by bursting through the flames to rescue Amoret 'as a thonder bolt | Perceth the yielding ayre' (III.xi.25).

Britomart's passage through the wall of flame into Busirane's castle recalls in narrative form the generic transformation which occurs at the end of the *Amoretti*, when the narrator's solitary disappointment at the end of the sonnet sequence opens out into the new generic and emotional terrain of the *Epithalamion*. She breaks through space to show that she is also breaking through convention. Her violent entry into Busirane's castle also hints at a larger equation, which is rarely absent from *The Faerie Queene*, between purposive movement and generic transformation. We have seen that heroes can simply drift through a landscape and find themselves imprisoned by the related generic conventions; but they can also strike actively through one genre into another. This form of deliberate genre-busting is particularly associated with Britomart. Inside Busirane's castle she witnesses a new set of generic conventions as a series of court masques, which literalize the metaphors of Petrarchan love, unfold before her, and Amoret, with a knife in her breast, is displayed as a victim of sexual desire. These masque-like conventions again are linked to a locus, a courtly interior; and that locus again has a door, through which Britomart eventually slides to discover the enchanter Busirane himself 'Figuring straunge characters of his art' (III.xii.31). Deliberate shifts of location bring with them some of the most violent generic shifts in the poem. They can also mark transgressions of both genre and gender: Britomart, a female knight, having broken through a string of generic boundaries, goes on to defeat this demonically literal-minded male sonneteer, and 'maistered his might' (III.xii.32).

This leads on to a wider observation. Shifts of place and of genre or mode tend to be associated with releases of fictional energy in *The Faerie Queene*. This rule can also apply (and, as the poem progresses, it applies increasingly) to the shifts of genre and location presented as being brought about by the narrator rather than by the characters within the poem. The most dramatic of these occur in Book VI, when Spenser makes his return, very late in his career, to pastoral landscapes and topoi. The narrator turns his attention back to Calidore in VI.ix, as he ranges 'Through hils, through dales, throgh forests, and throgh plaines' (2), and thence to 'open fields', full of shepherds 'singing to their flockes'. The knight of Courtesy moves, physically, into the realm of pastoral, where he remains until 'he chaunst to come' (VI.x.5) into a classic *locus amoenus*, a hill within a plain bordered by a wood. There he witnesses the shepherd Colin Clout piping apace to the dance of the Graces, and celebrating his mistress. There is of course precedent in the epic tradition for the inclusion of extensive pastoral episodes: the descriptions of the Arcadian kingdom of Euander in Book VIII of the *Aeneid* suggest a pastoral prototype for Roman civilization. But Spenser's incorporation of pastoral into his epic is far rougher and more disturbing than anything in Virgil. By the later books of *The Faerie Queene* shifts of place and mode are often marked by indications that a hero is intruding into a space in which he does not properly belong. They are also frequently accompanied by signs that the narrator—who often intrudes to mark generic, temporal, and spatial transitions within the poem (see Alpers 1977; Durling 1965)—is becoming reluctant to carry through the ultimate objective of his panegyric epic and simply and only praise Queen Elizabeth. So Colin Clout's praise of his mistress breaks off with a stanza which could be in the poet's or the narrator's own voice:

> Sunne of the world, great glory of the sky,
>> That all the earth doest lighten with thy rayes,
>> Great *Gloriana*, greatest Maiesty,
>> Pardon thy shepheard, mongst so many layes,
>> As he hath sung of thee in all his dayes,
>> To make one minime of thy poore handmayd,
>> And vnderneath thy feete to place her prayse,
>> That when thy glory shall be farre displayd
> To future age of her this mention may be made.   (VI.x.28)

This stanza is representative of the later phases of *The Faerie Queene*, which are generally thought to manifest a growing detachment from the Queen and her court. This is marked by increasingly rough movements into generic environments which are apparently 'lower' than epic. *The Mutabilitie Cantos* include a similar shift of place and of genre, which is again described in a way that draws attention to the poem's movement away from epic praise. After describing Mutabilitie's assault on Jove, Spenser abruptly turns his attention to Ireland and to the reasons for its present ruin. This shift of place—from the high drama of the heavens to the rough pastoral of fauns and rural goddesses in Ireland—is clearly marked as a shift of genre:

> And, were it not ill fitting for this file,
>> To sing of hilles and woods, mongst warres and Knights,
>> I would abate the sternenesse of my stile,
>> Mongst these sterne stounds to mingle soft delights;
>> And tell how *Arlo* through *Dianaes* spights
>> (Beeing of old the best and fairest Hill
>> That was in all this holy-Islands hights)
>> Was made the most vnpleasant, and most ill.
> Meane while, ô *Clio*, lend *Calliope* thy quill.   (VII.vi.37)

Calliope (muse of epic) passes her quill to Clio (muse of history). This marks a shift at once of genre and of locus, to Spenser's own domain of Ireland, whose ruined state he ascribes to the vengeful actions of the goddess Diana in the Faunus episode that follows these lines. Passages which mark a shift of genre, away from epic and panegyric and towards pastoral, chorography (poems about landscapes), mythography, and history are increasingly associated in the later books of *The Faerie Queene* with a desire to have done with epic, and perhaps too to have done with praise of the Queen: a tale about a chaste goddess who destroys the landscape of the country in which Spenser lived is not the most obvious way to praise a virgin queen who was notable for her reluctance to fund the complete subjugation of Ireland.

   Spenser's later career is marked by an increasing willingness to switch abruptly and apparently indecorously between genres, and to say that he is doing so. *Colin Clouts Come Home Againe* (1596) is in this respect one of Spenser's late masterpieces. The poem declares a major generic innovation in its title, but it does so in a manner so homely and obscure that it has gone unnoticed for more than four centuries: it is, generically, a 'come home again', an English 'epibaterion' or celebration of a return home.[11] The main point of the poem, though, is that epibateria traditionally praised the landscape, customs, and government of the land to which the speaker had returned. Poor Colin Clout, exiled among the 'nightly bodrags' (raids) and wolves of Ireland, does the opposite. This 'simple pastoral', as Spenser ruefully calls the poem in its dedication to Ralegh, flashes through a multiplicity of genres and modes with extraordinary skill and speed. Pastoral epibaterion—a simple pastoral, a 'come home again'—expands to include the broken epithalamion of the river Bregog and the Mulla, a pair whose marriage is frustrated by the destruction of the groom. It also glancingly alludes to Ralegh's epic complaint about his unkind treatment by the Queen in *The Ocean to Cynthia*. Both of these allusions suggest that Colin's ability to create new genres by breaking old ones up is curiously enabled by the savage violence of the Irish landscape and by the reluctance of the Queen to reward her poets.

Shifting modes within a pastoral frame was of course nothing new in Spenser's career: complaint (lament for past times, for lost patronage, for dead poets) is the dominant mode of his shorter verse, and *The Shepheardes Calender*, from the very start of Spenser's career in print, had included both encomium and satire, as had most major contributions to the pastoral genre since Virgil. But *Colin Clout* makes these shifts of generic gear within a single poem and within a remarkably short space. The effect is violent and almost aggressive, and is frequently signposted as such: Colin's praise of Cynthia ends 'With that *Alexis* broke his tale asunder' (352), and repeatedly his audience is driven to silence as he exhausts one mode and needs to be prompted to move on to another. It is as though only a rough conjunction of genres, some old, some new, some transformed almost beyond recognition, will accommodate the poet's disappointment, and his wish to turn his full powers, finally, to praise of his own love, Rosalind (McCabe 1993). And here we might remember George Puttenham's reverse chronology for pastoral poetry, which he sees not as the first of the literary kinds but a late and sophisticated form which 'glances at' higher matters. *Colin Clout*, a poem from late in Spenser's career, artfully draws on all the kinds regarded by sixteenth-century theorists as 'young' genres: it has a mock-heroic voyage (201–89), sections of praise for Elizabeth (332–51, 590–615)—and most theorists placed panegyric of rulers 'early' in the chronological development of literary kinds—a rough satire on the court (660–770), and an inspired hymn to Cupid (824–94). All these 'early' genres are wrapped within the pastoral form, a kind associated with both early writing and sophisticated criticism. Spenser made the disrupted and disrupting pastoral—a form which jolts between genres while signalling at once its own awkwardness and its own novelty in doing so—the signature of his later career. This mode of writing suggested profound disillusionment with a simple laureate trajectory that culminated in epic. It also suggested an attempt to devolve poetry away from the need to praise a patron, towards a display of the poet's mastery in all kinds, and, increasingly, towards private concerns. Late Spenser goes beyond the aims of epic, beyond the aim of praising a queen or fashioning a gentleman, into a realm of generic inventiveness which no English poet, before or since, could match.

NOTES

1. Farrell (2003) explores disjunctions between theory and practice.
2. See Weinberg (1961), 349–714, esp. 635–714 on genre. A wider overview is in Halliwell (1986).
3. For a modern translation, see Menander (1981); for the application of Menander's genres to Roman poetry, see Cairns (1972).
4. I adopt the terminology of Fowler (1982), 56, 106: 'kind' is reserved for historically recognized genres (epic, pastoral), while 'modes' are adjectival modifications of these genres ('recreative', 'comic').
5. See 'Epithalamium' in *SE* for vernacular precedents which did not adopt the generic name. The anonymous 1588 translation of *Sixe Idillia* of Theocritus (a volume which in layout and lexis emulates *The Shepheardes Calender*) pre-empts Spenser by including 'Helens Epithalamion', but it is not an original poem.
6. On 'career criticism' see Helgerson (1979), Cheney (1993), Cheney and De Armas (2002).
7. For Virgil's wheel see Garland (1974), 38–41. On Spenser's vestigial engagement with georgic, see Sessions (1980).
8. On hymns in Spenser's generic career, see Cheney (1993), 195–224.
9. Many of these topoi have been used as foundations for comparative studies of epic poetry. See, e.g., Giamatti (1966) and Greene (1963).
10. See *TM*, 1–6; *TW*, Sonnet 8; Thomas Lodge's 'Glaucus and Scylla', ll. 1–2 in Clark (1994), 3; Shakespeare's 'A Lover's Complaint', ll. 38–9; and Kerrigan (1991), 41–3.
11. On the genre, see Menander (1981), 95; Scaliger (1581), 400–2.

BIBLIOGRAPHY

Alpers, P. (1977). 'Narration in the Faerie Queene'. *ELH* 44(1): 19–39.
Bakhtin, M. M. (1981). *The Dialogic Imagination: Four Essays*, trans. M. Holquist and C. Emerson. Austin: University of Texas Press.
Beal, P. (1993). 'Notions in Garrison: The Seventeenth-Century Commonplace Book', in W. S. Hill (ed.), *New Ways of Looking at Old Texts*. Binghamton, NY: Medieval and Renaissance Texts and Studies, 131–47.
Burrow, C. (1993). *Epic Romance: Homer to Milton*. Oxford: Clarendon Press.
—— (1999). '"Full of the Maker's Guile": Ovid on Imitating and on the Imitation of Ovid', in P. Hardie (ed.), *Ovidian Transformations: Essays on Ovid's Metamorphoses and Its Reception*. Cambridge: Cambridge University Press, 271–87.
—— (2008). 'English Renaissance Readers and the *Appendix Vergiliana*'. *Proceedings of the Virgil Society* 26: 1–16.
Cairns, F. (1972). *Generic Composition in Greek and Roman Poetry*. Edinburgh: Edinburgh University Press.
Cheney, P. (1993). *Spenser's Famous Flight: A Renaissance Idea of a Literary Career*. Toronto: University of Toronto Press.
—— and De Armas, F. A. (2002). *European Literary Careers: The Author from Antiquity to the Renaissance*. Toronto: University of Toronto Press.
Clark, S. (ed.) (1994). *Amorous Rites: Elizabethan Erotic Verse*. London: J. M. Dent.

Durling, R. M. (1965). *The Figure of the Poet in Renaissance Epic*. Cambridge, MA: Harvard University Press.

Farrell, J. (2003). 'Classical Genre in Theory and Practice'. *New Literary History* 34(3): 383–408.

Fowler, A. (1982). *Kinds of Literature: An Introduction to the Theory of Genres and Modes*. Oxford: Clarendon Press.

Frow, J. (2005). *Genre*. London: Routledge.

Garland, John of (1974). *The Parisiana Poetria*, ed. T. Lawler. New Haven, CT/London: Yale University Press.

Genette, G. (1982). *Palimpsestes*. Paris: Seuil.

—— (1992). *The Architext: An Introduction*, trans. J. E. Lewin. Berkeley/Oxford: University of California Press.

Giamatti, A. B. (1966). *The Earthly Paradise and the Renaissance Epic*. Princeton, NJ: Princeton University Press.

Greene, T. M. (1963). *The Descent from Heaven: A Study in Epic Continuity*. New Haven, CT/London: Yale University Press.

Halliwell, S. (1986). *Aristotle's Poetics*. London: Duckworth.

Harrison, S. J. (2007). *Generic Enrichment in Vergil and Horace*. Oxford: Oxford University Press.

Helgerson, R. (1979). 'The Elizabethan Laureate: Self-Presentation and the Literary System'. *ELH* 46: 193–220.

Hirsch, E. D. (1967). *Validity in Interpretation*. New Haven, CT/London: Yale University Press.

Javitch, D. (1991). *Proclaiming a Classic: The Canonization of Orlando Furioso*. Princeton, NJ: Princeton University Press.

Kerrigan, J. (1991). *Motives of Woe: Shakespeare and 'Female Complaint', a Critical Anthology*. Oxford: Clarendon Press.

McCabe, R. A. (1993). 'Edmund Spenser, Poet of Exile'. *Proceedings of the British Academy* 80: 73–103.

—— (2003). 'Parody, Sympathy and Self: A Response to Donald Cheney'. *Connotations* 13 (1/2): 5–22.

Menander (1981). *Menander Rhetor*, ed. D. A. Russell and N. G. Wilson. Oxford: Clarendon Press.

Moss, A. (1996). *Printed Commonplace-Books and the Structuring of Renaissance Thought*. Oxford: Clarendon Press.

Puttenham, G. (2007). *The Art of English Poesy: A Critical Edition*, ed. F. Whigham and W. A. Rebhorn. Ithaca, NY/London: Cornell University Press.

Saunders, C. J. (1993). *The Forest of Medieval Romance: Avernus, Broceliande, Arden*. Cambridge: D. S. Brewer.

Scaliger, J. C. (1581). *Poetices Libri Septem*. [Heidelberg]: Petrus Santandreanus.

—— (1905). *Select Translations from Scaliger's Poetics*, trans. F. M. Padelford. New Haven, CT: Yale University Press.

Sessions, W. A. (1980). 'Spenser's Georgics'. *ELR* 10: 202–38.

Vida, M. G. (1976). *The De Arte Poetica*, trans. R. G. Williams. New York: Columbia University Press.

Virgil (1978). *Ciris: A Poem Attributed to Vergil*, ed. R. O. A. M. Lyne. Cambridge: Cambridge University Press.

Weinberg, B. (1961). *A History of Literary Criticism in the Italian Renaissance*. Chicago: University of Chicago Press.

CHAPTER 23

SPENSER AND RHETORIC

PETER MACK

CLASSICAL RHETORIC

Rhetoric provided training in writing, reading, and public-speaking throughout Europe in the Hellenistic world, the Roman Empire, the later medieval period and the Renaissance. Aristotle (384–322 BC) defined rhetoric as 'the art of finding the available means of persuasion in each case' (Aristotle, 1355b26–7), while Quintilian (c.35–c.95 AD) called it 'the art of speaking well' (Quintilian, 2.15.38), giving that phrase a moral as well as a technical implication. These two famous definitions owe part of their longevity to the fact that they can be applied to different types of activity, for despite the popularity of classical texts in the Middle Ages and after, the teaching of rhetoric did in fact change quite considerably.

In this chapter I shall first describe the major texts and doctrines of classical and renaissance rhetoric, then consider the rhetoric which Spenser and his contemporary readers would have learned at school and university. Then I shall discuss the Ramist affiliations of Spenser's close friend Gabriel Harvey. Finally I shall examine ways in which approaches informed by rhetoric have been, and could be, used to interpret Spenser's works.

The major classical texts were Aristotle's *Rhetoric*, which introduced most of the major distinctions within the subject (see below) and gave a thorough account of the emotions which the orator might need to draw on; *Rhetorica ad Herennium*, which up to the end of the sixteenth century was generally believed to be by Cicero, and which surveys the whole subject and provides a particularly thorough account of the tropes and figures; Cicero's youthful *De inventione*, which concentrates on the outline of the oration and the arguments suited to the three types of oration; Cicero's mature *De oratore*, which reflects on the education of the orator and the ways in which the school doctrines are applied in practice; and Quintilian's *Institutio oratoria*, which provides a detailed consideration of all aspects of rhetoric and the training of the orator, comparing and reconciling previous opinions where possible. Spenser would almost certainly have known these four books, though, like his contemporaries he may have found it difficult to place Aristotle's Greek *Rhetoric*, which only circulated widely in Western Europe in the sixteenth century, within the longer established Latin Ciceronian tradition.

Rhetoricians taught three kinds of persuasion: through *logos*, words and arguments; *ethos*, the character of the speaker; and *pathos*, the arousal of emotions. Based on the situations in which a public speech might be given in a Greek city-state they identified three types of speech: judicial, a speech in a trial, addressed to judges or a jury; deliberative, the speech to a public assembly on a question of state policy such as law-making or debating alliances or wars; and the demonstrative, also called epideictic, the speech of praise or blame delivered on a social occasion, such as a wedding or a funeral. Where judicial and demonstrative oratory tended to focus on the past, deliberative oratory was mostly concerned with what would happen in the future. The ideal orator was supposed to master five skills: invention, finding the material (such as arguments, emotional appeals, proverbs) suited to persuading a particular audience; disposition, the arrangement of that material in an effective order; style, presenting the ideas in words, word patterns, and sentences which would delight and move their audience; memory, the techniques for memorizing and recalling a previously written speech; and delivery, the use of voice and gesture. These five skills and the parts of the oration, which follow, were used as the basis for organizing Latin textbooks of the whole of rhetoric, such as *Rhetorica ad Herennium* and Quintilian's *Institutio oratoria*. In practice most attention was given to invention and style. The style treatise recognized three levels of style (high, middle, and low) and gave labels, definitions, and examples of around 80 different tropes, figures of speech, and figures of thought.

According to Aristotle the oration should have four parts: the introduction or exordium, which should make the audience attentive, receptive, and well disposed, by explaining the importance of the subject and outlining the main points the speaker would make; the narration, in which the context would be set out and the case outlined; the argumentation, which would provide arguments supporting the speaker's view of the key questions raised by the case and refuting opposing arguments; and the conclusion, which would summarize the main points made and make an emotional appeal to the audience (Aristotle, 1414a30–b18). Later authorities advocated five- or six-part versions of this same structure by dividing the third section into confirmation (points supporting the speaker's view) and refutation (of opposing views) and by recognizing as a separate part the division, the moment at the end of the narration, in which speakers should explain what divides their views from their opponents' opinions and set out the main arguments they intended to prove in order to win the case. It will be noticed that this outline of an oral speech allows for a considerable degree of repetition of the main points, which suits the problems of addressing a large audience but would be less effective as part of a written, literary text.

Classical orators also wrote instructions for *Progymnasmata*, or writing exercises, which were used in medieval and Renaissance schools. Aphthonius's *Progymnasmata* gives lists of topics and labelled examples for fourteen forms of writing, including narrative, proverb, commonplace, comparison, speech for a character, and description. The *chreia*, 'a brief recollection of something said or done', for example, consists of a statement (e.g. 'hard times show you your true friends'), followed by eight sections: praise of the person speaking or action, explanation of what was said or done, argument from cause, contrary, comparison, example, opinion of the ancients, and epilogue (Aphthonius 1997). The *Progymnasmata* taught ways of elaborating material (such as moral axioms and narratives) found through reading and provided exercise in elements (such as comparisons, character speeches, and descriptions) which could be included in larger narrative works. Later Greek writers introduced some new aspects which were gradually absorbed into the Latin tradition in the later sixteenth century. Thus Menander Rhetor (*c.*300 AD) and (pseudo) Dionysius of Halicarnassus wrote treatises giving instructions for different types of epideictic speech, such as panegyrics, speeches for greeting princes, funeral orations, epithalamia, and praises of cities and countries (Russell and Wilson 1981). As epideictic became a more important part of practical rhetoric in the late Renaissance, these instructions came to be absorbed into mainstream rhetoric textbooks (Hardison 1962). Hermogenes of Tarsus (born *c.*160 AD) wrote a treatise on *Ideas of Style*, which showed how to write seven kinds of style (some of them subdivided), giving examples from Demosthenes. These descriptive types of style (e.g. clarity, grandeur, rapidity, sincerity, force) gave a more discriminating account of the ways in which diction, sentence structure, and figures combine to achieve a stylistic effect than was possible under the more traditional rubric of the three levels (Hermogenes 1987; Russell and Winterbottom 1972: 561–83). Hermogenes's texts became more widely available in the later sixteenth century, in Greek and in Latin translation. They had some currency in England because of the friendship between Roger Ascham (1515–68), author of *The Scholemaster* (1570), and Johann Sturm (1507–89), the Strasbourg school rector, who edited, translated, and promoted Hermogenes's works. Spenser may have read them at Cambridge.

RHETORIC IN THE RENAISSANCE

Renaissance rhetoric was greatly preoccupied with the recovery and dissemination of classical Latin rhetoric and with the absorption of ideas from Greek rhetoric, but the subject was also developed in new directions, notably through a new understanding of the relationship between rhetoric and logic, through Erasmus's work on *copia* and proverbs, through the new textbooks of the whole of rhetoric composed by Philipp, Melanchthon and Omer Talon, and through new manuals of letter-writing and of the tropes and figures.

Where Aristotle had recognized rhetoric and dialectic (for him the part of logic concerned with probabilistic reasoning; for others the whole of logic) as counterparts, and where Cicero had urged orators to master dialectic, providing a manual of the subject in his *Topica*, Rudolph Agricola (1444–85) placed the topics of invention at the heart of the process of writing. The topics are a list of headings (such as definition, cause, effect, circumstances, comparisons, similars, contraries, opinions of authorities) which you can apply to any subject assigned to you in order to find out more about it or recollect things about it which you might use to construct arguments. Agricola studied the nature of these topical relationships and gave examples from Cicero and from Roman literature of how they could be used in argument. He showed that the same principles would enable a writer to determine what to say in order to elicit particular emotions from an audience, making a link to Aristotle's work which had been neglected. Instead of repeating traditional teaching on the four-part oration, Agricola argued, with examples, that many different types of organization were possible and that the writer would have to consider his subject, his own position, and the audience he was trying to reach in order to devise a structure appropriate to each particular work. He showed how logic could be used to analyse the structure of a work and to understand how particular sections of a speech or a poem contributed to the impact the writer was trying to make on an audience (Agricola 1539; Mack 1993: 117–256). This work gave rise to the Renaissance genre of the dialectical commentary on Cicero's speeches, on poetry, especially Virgil, and on the Bible.

Erasmus's (*c*.1466–1536) *De copia*, which was printed 155 times between 1512 and 1580 (in addition to numerous editions of selections and epitomes), offers techniques for varying and expanding upon an existing text. *Copia* of words involves using the tropes (especially) and the figures to vary individual words or to add parallel expressions. This section culminates in a list of many different phrases one could employ for a given purpose, including 195 ways of phrasing the sentence 'your letters pleased me greatly' (Erasmus 1978: 295–354; 1988: 26–82). *Copia* of things involves using the topics of invention to generate additional material by looking into, for example, the parts, circumstances, causes, antecedents, and consequences of an event you need to describe. This section of the book also offers advice on the construction of descriptions and comparisons, and the use of maxims, fables, and examples (Erasmus 1978: 572–648; 1988: 197–269). Readers of *De copia* would learn both that every sentence involved a choice between many different ways of expressing an idea and a method of producing a densely amplified style. Erasmus's often enlarged and reprinted *Adagia* provided a list of Latin and Greek proverbs, with explanations of their meaning and derivation and examples of their use by classical writers and philosophers. This was intended both as an aid to reading classical texts and as a resource of 'sayings in popular use, remarkable for some shrewd and novel turn' for reuse in the readers' own compositions (Barker 2001: 5). Erasmus's introduction gives advice on the use of proverbs, while the longer essays (such as 'War is sweet for those who have not tried it') offer examples of elaborate persuasive writing on moral topics.

Renaissance writers also composed new textbooks of the whole of rhetoric and dialectic, notably a series of six works by Philipp Melanchthon (1497–1560), building on the need to coordinate the two subjects and also recognizing that some aspects of classical rhetoric (such as the division of all types of speech into three kinds) reflected the social conditions of the Greek city-state rather than the sixteenth century. With his close associate Omer Talon (c.1510–62), Peter Ramus (1515–72) inspired a new approach to both subjects. He believed that much of what was traditionally taught in Aristotelian logic (which continued to dominate many universities) was in fact metaphysics, so he reduced dialectic to the topics of invention (which he exemplified with quotations from classical speeches and poems), the forms of argumentation (especially the syllogism), and method, which dictated that a work of instruction should start with general principles and move by definition and division to individual instances. Since invention belonged to dialectic, rhetoric would be concerned with the tropes and figures (which Talon reduced to a smaller group, systematically organized) and with delivery (Bruyère 1984; Mack 1993: 334–55; Meerhoff 1986: 175–316; 2000). The purpose of this reduction, which meant that an overview of each subject could be presented on a single page, was to ensure that pupils learned the principal doctrines of both subjects very quickly so that they could move on to the real learning process which involved studying a Latin literary text in order to see how logic and rhetoric worked in practice. In Ramus's theory and practice, logic and rhetoric were always studied together and they always lead on to the understanding of both subjects in practice through the analysis of classical speeches and poems (Sharratt 1976). The literary examples which were such a strong feature of the manuals were intended to prepare for this practical way of learning the expressive use of language.

Ramus made it a part of his mission to produce logic and rhetoric texts in French; this required him and his associates (such as Antoine Fouquelin) to gather examples of logical arguments and structures and figures of rhetoric from contemporary French literature, notably from the poetry of the Pléiade. Some Italian-language manuals of the whole of rhetoric took a lead in absorbing Greek and poetic materials, but in general the vernacular texts were simply translations and adaptations of Latin works. It is highly significant that at this time authors and publishers found it worthwhile to print manuals of learned subjects in Italian, French, and English, but at the same time we must acknowledge that almost all the real innovation in both subjects came about through the Latin tradition. Twenty English language manuals of rhetoric and dialectic were published in the sixteenth century, reflecting several of the main types of Continental manual: textbooks of the whole of each subject (mainly based on Melanchthon or Ramus), letter-writing manuals (based on Erasmus or Hegendorff), manuals of tropes and figures (based on Mosellanus and Susenbrotus), and preaching manuals (based on Hemmingsen and Hyperius).

Of the twenty textbooks only four were printed more than twice in the sixteenth century: Thomas Wilson's *Rule of Reason* (based on Melanchthon and Agricola) and *Arte of Rhetoric* (based on the classical manuals, Melanchthon, and Erasmus), and two letter-writing manuals, William Fulwood's *Enemie of Idleness* and Angel Day's *The English Secretary* (Mack 2002: 76–84).

The provision of a style manual is an exception to the conclusion that only four of the English manuals were reprinted in significant numbers. Several different texts (notably the third book of Wilson's *Arte of Rhetoric*, the second part of Day, Sherry's *A Treatise of Schemes and Tropes*, Peacham's *Garden of Eloquence*, and Puttenham's *Arte of English Poesie*, which was printed only once) presented an account of the tropes and figures in English, with the result that in total there were 21 editions of the English style manual (Mack 2002: 84–102). These texts are generally based on each other and on *Rhetorica ad Herennium*, book IV, Melanchthon, Mosellanus's (1493–1524) *Tabulae de schematibus et tropibus* (82 sixteenth-century editions), and Susenbrotus's (d.1543) *Epitome troporum ac schematum* (29 editions). Identifying the tropes and figures was important because being able to give a particular form a name enabled readers to identify the way in which it was being used in a particular text, and observe the different uses to which writers put the same figure in different circumstances. Some textbooks offer advice on the effect of particular figures and on the way they should be used. Tropes (such as metaphor, metonymy, and irony) generally describe ways in which a writer can give particular words new or extended meanings. Figures include a wide range of linguistic forms and approaches, from patterns of words (such as anaphora and climax, for examples see below), aspects of grammar (zeugma and asyntedon), patterns of sentence construction (isocolon), to ways of emphasizing material (such as correctio), ways of signalling emotion (such as aposiopesis), and attitudes one might take to an audience (such as permissio and dubitatio). The tropes and figures constitute a categorization of the resources of language. Making an English version dignifies the language, by treating it in the same way as a classical language, and expands the readily available range of possibilities of writing. Composing such a manual requires a certain ingenuity in the adapting of Latin-based forms and the identification of suitable examples from English literature.

SPENSER'S RHETORICAL EDUCATION

Edmund Spenser attended Merchant Taylors' School, leaving in 1569 to go to Cambridge. We do not have direct evidence about the curriculum at Merchant Taylors' at this period but Tudor grammar school statutes generally specify a rather consistent syllabus: the elementary learning of Latin (and in a school like Merchant Taylors' also Greek), using the Lily-Colet grammar, books of moral sentences, Aesop's fables, and a set of schoolboy dialogues; the reading of a core curriculum of Latin texts (Terence,

Cicero's letters, *De officiis* and perhaps some of the orations, Virgil's *Eclogues* and *Aeneid*, Ovid's *Tristia* or *Metamorphoses*, Horace's *Epistles* and *Odes*, Sallust, or Caesar), though it's doubtful that they read many of these texts complete (perhaps 2–3 books of the *Aeneid* rather than the whole work, for example); and Latin composition exercises based on a letter-writing manual, Apthonius's *Progymnasmata*, Erasmus's *De copia*, and probably also a manual of tropes and figures (Mack 2002: 11–16). Records of sixteenth-century examinations at Merchant Taylors' suggest that the boys had read Homer in Greek and some of the psalms in Hebrew (Barker 1990).

This basic syllabus is rhetorical in the sense that rhetoric played a large part in the way that the texts were read, and in the sense that pupils' reading was intended to provide them with materials for their own writing, but it did not apparently include the study of one of the manuals of the whole of rhetoric. Teachers were expected to point out uses of rhetorical structures and figures and tropes (including allegory) when they read classical texts with their pupils. Several aspects of rhetoric were included in the instructions for writing in the *Progymnasmata*, the rules for generating abundant expression in *De copia*, and the manual of the tropes and figures, which was reinforced in the instruction to teachers to identify the ways in which writers used the figures when they were reading Latin texts with their pupils. The Latin letter-writing manuals, which went through hundreds of editions, provided short instructions (and copious examples) for writing letters in a variety of genres, for example letters of encouragement, recommendation, consolation, lamentation, request, and advice. These types suit the occasions of sixteenth-century writing better than the traditional three genres (judicial, deliberative, and epideictic). Erasmus's letter-writing manual also offers advice on thinking about the audience of a letter, and on composition issues such as formulae of greeting and farewell, use of examples, fables, and proverbs, techniques of argument, and amplification (Erasmus 1971, 1985; Chomarat 1981).

Pupils' composition exercises were closely related to the texts they were reading, for example close imitation of the simpler familiar letters of Cicero, or composition of letters related to the characters and situations of the books they were studying. School teachers like Sturm and Ascham were greatly preoccupied with the best methods of imitating classical texts. Almost everyone recognized Cicero as the Latin prose writer most worthy of imitation but controversies raged over whether one should restrict oneself to Cicero's vocabulary or whether the point was to approach one's own task in a way that reflected the techniques of invention and expression practised by Cicero. Some scholars also advocated the benefits of non-Ciceronian approaches, involving short, pithier sentences and the use of archaic or innovative vocabulary.

Grammar-school pupils learned a range of structures for texts (from the *Progymnasmata* and letter-writing manuals, rather than the four-part oration of the classical rhetoric manual); they learned to capture moral axioms, proverbs, and moral narratives from their reading for reuse in their own texts and they learned how to use them there; they learned about the tropes and figures, and about amplification.

Some of their writing exercises required an understanding of some of the topics of invention, such as cause, comparison, and contrary. Letter-writing taught them something about argument and narrative, and also about self-presentation (*ethos*) and anticipating the likely reaction of the recipient, seen as a type of audience. They also learned something about historiography and drawing moral and political lessons from history. Most of all they learned a craftsman's approach to some of the best texts ever written in Latin.

Recent research (which it must be admitted is based more on Oxford materials) suggests that Elizabethan university students pursued quite varied programmes of study and reading around a fairly well-defined core determined by university statute (Feingold 1997; McConica 1986: 1–68, 645–732). While he was a student at Pembroke Hall, Spenser would certainly have read Aristotle's *Logic*, *Physics*, and *Ethics* and a classical textbook of the whole of rhetoric, but he may also have read widely in geography, history, science, or modern foreign literature. It is highly likely that he continued and deepened his study of Greek. Under the guidance of Gabriel Harvey (see below), Spenser probably read Ramus's dialectic and Talon's rhetoric, but he probably did so alongside, or in preparation for, his study of Aristotle.

At Cambridge the first of the four years allocated for the BA was supposed to be given over to rhetoric and the texts were Quintilian, Hermogenes, or any of Cicero's works. The Cambridge booklists (derived from inventories of the possessions of members of the University who died while in residence) suggest that *Rhetorica ad Herennium* (50 entries out of 173 lists) and Cicero's orations (60 entries) were very frequently read. Quintilian (37) and Aristotle's *Rhetoric* (28) come behind them. Cicero's *De oratore* (19) and Hermogenes (16) appear in smaller but significant numbers. In logic the same lists include 89 people with copies of Aristotle's *Logic*, 45 with Rudolph Agricola's *De inventione dialectica*, 30 with Melanchthon, 18 with Caesarius, 17 with Ramus, and 12 with Seton's *Dialectica*, which was specifically composed and printed to be taught at Cambridge (Leedham-Green 1986; Mack 2002: 51–5) This selection of books suggests that logic was taught in a way which responded to Agricola's ideas about the importance of the topics and the connection between logic and the production and analysis of texts.

In order to obtain their degrees students were required to take part in disputations. These were question and brief answer debates on points of interpretation (of Aristotle or one of the other set texts) conducted in a highly formal way. The opponent makes arguments against the view the respondent is required to uphold. The respondent must summarize the argument and then either assent to it or deny it. The respondent must ensure that he neither contradicts himself, nor by implication denies the proposition that he is meant to be upholding, nor lets himself be reduced to confusion. In any of these cases he would lose the disputation. The respondent wins the disputation by maintaining his position intact for a specified period of time. Disputations reinforced the importance of acquiring logical skills, particularly in definition, in making distinctions between different meanings of a word and in seeing the logical implications of apparently unrelated propositions. There is some evidence of students giving orations (declamations) on ethical subjects in college and even of respondents making fairly long speeches adorned with classical references at the opening of the disputation, to outline their position before the disputation proper begins (Mack 2002: 58–66).

At Cambridge students read Latin textbooks on the whole of rhetoric and dialectic. Some of them may have used Wilson's English language manuals as an introduction or a crib (Mack 2002: 79). They would have had a good deal of practice in the logical and rhetorical interpretation of texts and would have applied their logical skills to the art of disputation.

GABRIEL HARVEY

Gabriel Harvey became a fellow of Pembroke Hall in 1570, when Spenser was a second year undergraduate (Stern 1979, 1990). They became friends for the rest of Spenser's life. In 1574 Harvey was appointed University Praelector in Rhetoric, with the task of giving several lectures a week to first-year students. He chose to give lectures on Cicero's speeches; on *Post reditum ad Quirites* in 1575 and *Post reditum in Senatu* in 1576 (Harvey 1945: 5–10). His inaugural lecture for the 1576 course, printed as *Ciceronianus*, demonstrates his allegiance to a strongly humanistic version of Ramism. The lecture announces his conversion, through reading Ramus's *Ciceronianus*, from an earlier phase in which he was commited to the exclusive and close imitation of Cicero to an understanding of the virtues of other classical writers. In a passage reminiscent of Erasmus's *Ciceronianus* Harvey asserts that true Ciceronianism consists not in copying Cicero's vocabulary and sentence structures but in observing Cicero's emphasis on invention and judgement, his cultivation of a broad encyclopaedic knowledge, and Quintilian's ideal of a good man, speaking well (Harvey 1945: 76–9). Harvey contrasts his former naive Ciceronian focus on *elocutio* with his new understanding of the importance of topical invention and logical organization. He urges his students to read Cicero with both rhetoric and dialectic in mind:

Remember that Homer calls words πτερόεντα, that is winged, since they easily fly away unless they are held balanced by the weight of subject-matter (*rerum*). Join dialectic and knowledge with rhetoric; join your mind with your tongue. Learn from Erasmus to glue together *copia* of words with *copia* of things; learn from Ramus to embrace philosophy joined with eloquence; learn from Homer's Phoenix to be not only authors of words but also doers of deeds (*rerum*). (Harvey 1945: 82)

From this viewpoint the most 'Ciceronian' thing may be not what Cicero himself writes but the practice of the best writers in every genre and on every subject. Harvey prefers his pupils to conduct a double analysis of their texts, focusing on invention, arrangement, and dialectic as well as on figures, delivery, and rhetoric. He divides rhetoric from dialectic on Ramist lines but he insists that his pupils must use both subjects to analyse Cicero's orations. Merely pointing out the figures, he says, is a petty kind of glory; what matters is to combine that with an understanding of how the topics of invention (such as causes, effects, subjects, and adjuncts) have been employed. Tellingly (and un-Ramistically) he includes the topics of deliberative and demonstrative oratory (the honourable, the useful, the pleasant) and self-presentation and emotional arousal (Harvey 1945: 85–9). Harvey's speech is closer to the Ramus we find in his commentaries on Cicero and Virgil than to the Ramus of the textbooks of rhetoric and dialectic (Mack 1998). Harvey shows that he has a wide knowledge of the other Renaissance commentators on Cicero, such as Sturm, Erythraeus, Latomus, and Manutius, though he states a strong preference for Ramus and Talon (Harvey 1945: 94–7).

Harvey's two-session inaugural lecture for 1575 was printed in 1577 as *Rhetor* (Harvey 1945: 5–6; Wilson 1945). The lectures are devoted to the role of talent, art, and practice in the development of the orator, a subject with clear links to the topic of Cicero's *De Oratore*. Harvey first insists on the importance of natural talent as the golden foundation of all oratory, particularly admiring the natural gifts of Aristotle and Cicero (Harvey 1577: A4^v, D1^r–2^r). But no one can become a great orator without a good teacher and the most fruitful teaching will be that which is clearest and briefest, the two-part (style and delivery) rhetorical work of Talon (Harvey 1577: D3^v, D4^v–E1^r). Harvey praises Rudolph Agricola, noting that he assigns invention to dialectic (Harvey 1577: H1^v–2^v). Talon may also be used as an introduction to the most important writers of the ancient rhetorical tradition: Cicero, Quintilian, Aristotle, and Hermogenes (Harvey 1577: H3^r).

In the second lecture, following Ramus, Harvey divides his account of practice into analysis, the reading of the great authors, and genesis, writing compositions of one's own (Harvey 1577: I1^v, K4^v–L1^r). Analysis involves naming the tropes and figures in speeches and other texts, and reading out the speeches of Cicero and Demosthenes so as to study delivery (Harvey 1577: M2^v–4^r). Genesis involves, first, imitation of Cicero and Demosthenes, varying their texts using the tropes and figures, and secondly, declamation, giving opposed speeches on themes related to the subjects of great orations. Harvey cites Johann Sturm's work on the practice of rhetoric in the university as a helpful example here (Harvey 1577: N2^r–3^r, O3^v–4^v). After the end of the speech Harvey adds lists of Greek, Roman, and modern authors to imitate, including some vernacular writers. He will say nothing at present about certain modern writers, naming Chaucer, More, Elyot, Ascham, and Jewell (Harvey 1577: P4^r–Q1^r).

Ramist rhetoric includes both a section on the different metres of Latin poetry and (like other rhetorics) an account of the trope of allegory. Quintilian defines allegory as saying one thing in words and a different or even a contrary thing in meaning. He regards it as an extended form of metaphor and shows that metaphors are helpful in presenting allegories (Quintilian 8.6.44–53). Talon goes further than Quintilian in treating allegory as a part of metaphor. Melanchthon says that allegory involves a similarity of thoughts rather than words, a sort of comparison between things which do not have to be named explicitly. Immediately after defining this trope he adds a discussion of the four ways of reading scripture, which includes discussion of allegorical reading of longer texts (Melanchthon 1846: 466–73). These are not features emphasized in Harvey's inaugural lectures but if Spenser followed the lecture course proper he may well have been prompted to further reflection on issues which would become central to his poetry.

Rhetoric in Spenser's Poetry

Rhetorical analysis of poetry plays an important role both in Spenser's immediate circle and in his first reception. E. K., who may well be a character invented by Spenser himself, is presented as a member of Spenser's coterie, able to ask him direct questions about the *dramatis personae* of *The Shepheardes Calender*, and sometimes having to report less than full answers (Spenser 1989: 19, 187). In the letter to Harvey, which prefaces *The Shepheardes Calender*, E. K. twice alludes to Cicero's *De Oratore* (Spenser 1989: 14, 15), and praises Spenser's skill in a way which recalls Harvey's emphasis on knowledge and invention alongside style.

[H]is wittinesse in devising, his pithinesse in uttering, his complaints of love so lovely, his discourses of pleasure so pleasantly, his pastorall rudenesse, his morall wisenesse, his dewe observing of Decorum everye where, in personages, in seasons, in matter, in speech, and generally in al seemely simplycitie of hondeling his matter and framing his words. (Spenser 1989: 13–14)

E. K.'s presentation of the poem is deliberately modelled on school editions of classical texts, with arguments for each poem and glosses which explain classical allusions and unusual vocabulary. A small proportion of the glosses point out Spenser's use of figures of rhetoric, for example paronomasia, comparison, metaphor, periphrasis, syncope, synecdoche, and icon.[1] E. K. is particularly fond of noting the figure epanorthosis or correctio, which he tends to take as indicating a questioning of an expression used, as in 'Why doe we longer live, (ah why live we so long)', rather than the apparent correction of one word or phrase and its replacement by another.[2] E. K. makes no comments on logical aspects of the poem and only a few on matters of structure (e.g. Spenser 1989: 29, 79, 210–12), which sets him against the programme outlined by Harvey.[3] There are many instances in which Spenser uses figures which might seem to call for comment (for instance, the uses of chiasmus in ll. 13–14 and 48 of *Januarie*) but E. K. makes none.

Abraham Fraunce (*c*.1558–1633), who was a member of the circle around Sir Philip Sidney, quotes examples from Spenser in his two Ramist works of 1588, *The Arcadian Rhetorike* and *The Lawiers Logike*. *The Arcadian Rhetorike* contains very brief precepts based on one of the later, short editions of Talon's *Rhetorica*, with examples for each of the figures from Homer, Virgil, Sidney, Tasso, Du Bartas, Boscan, and Garcilaso. One of Spenser's poems from the Harvey–Spenser correspondence ('Unhappie verse, the witnes of my unhappie state') is quoted as an example of the iambic form. Later Spenser's use of the sestina form is contrasted with Sidney's and a stanza (II.iv.35) from the as yet unpublished *Faerie Queene* is cited, both as examples of 'conceited verses', proceeding from figures of words (Fraunce 1588a: C4^r, D7^{r-v}, E3^r).

The *Lawiers Logike* contains a very large number of quotations (probably more than 100 in all, some of them quite long) from *The Shepheardes Calender*, primarily illustrating all the topics of invention, with in some cases several examples for each topic. Examples from Spenser also appear in the work's discussion of the proposition, the disjunctive proposition, and hypothetical syllogism ('Or Diggon her is, or I missay', *September*, 2; Fraunce 1588b: Cc4^v, Hh1^v), and the explicatory syllogism, where elements from *Maye*, 43–54, are rewritten as:

> He that plaieth while his stocke is unfed, can give no accompt to great God Pan.
>
> A good shepheard can geve accompt to great God Pan.
>
> Therefore a good shepheard playeth not while his stocke is unfed. (Fraunce 1588b: Ff2^v)

Spenser is not used as an example in Fraunce's discussion of method (the Ramist theory of the arrangement of sciences, speeches, and poems) but Fraunce does give a diagrammatic analysis of Virgil's second eclogue, on which Ramus and Freigius had also written commentaries (Fraunce 1588b: Kk4^r–Ll1^r).

FUTURE STUDY

How, finally, have modern critics of Spenser used his rhetorical inheritance and what might rhetorically informed approaches have to contribute to Spenser studies?

H. D. Rix, who wrote the only book-length study of rhetoric in Spenser's poetry, followed in the footsteps of E. K. and Fraunce in identifying passages where Spenser used particular tropes and figures. He provides a list of tropes and figures, giving definitions of each figure taken from Susenbrotus and Peacham, followed by examples from Spenser to illustrate each figure. So he gives 'Man into stones therewith he could transmew, | And stones to dust, and dust to nought at all' (I.vi.35) for climax, and 'So was he overcome, not overcome, | But to her yeelded of his owne accord' (V. v.17) for correctio (Rix 1940: 27, 38). He argues that Spenser's use of figures was dictated more by the type of writing he was engaged in than by any idea of development over time. He finds that Spenser is most likely to use figures intensively in elegaic passages, in the 'carefully contrived sonnets' of the *Amoretti* and in the *Epithalamion*, than in the narrative passages of *The Faerie Queene* (Rix 1940: 62). He analyses Spenser's use of figures in the complaint in *Januarie* and in Cymoent's lament (II.iv.36–9; Rix 1940: 64–6). He shows that the *Epithalamion* is much richer in figures than the *Prothalamion* (Rix 1940: 70) and how Spenser used figures like periphrasis, epitheton, antonomasia, and comparison to elevate the style of *The Faerie Queene* (Rix 1940: 70–3).

In similar vein, Sam Meyer provides a very detailed account of Spenser's use of tropes and figures in the final 100 lines of *Colin Clouts Come Home Again* (Meyer 1969: 12–14). He shows that Spenser employs figures in order to achieve *copia* of words, to amplify the style (especially through epitheton, periphrasis, sententia, and acclamatio) and to move the reader's emotions (especially through apostrophe, interrogatio, synathroismus, and anaphora) (Meyer 1969: 14–31). His analysis of the figures contributes further to his discussion of the tone and feeling of the poem, particularly in passages where Spenser invokes deeper emotions through his use of anaphora, occupatio, and sententia (Meyer 1969: 134–40). Brian Vickers analyses the use of paronomasia, asyntedon, polyptoton, isocolon, anadiplosis, and epiphonema in Despaire's speeches (I.ix.38–47; Vickers 1970: 157–60). There is more useful work to be done in analysing the way in which Spenser can use figures to alter the mood of a canto and to reinforce the reader's sense of his artistic control of his material.

Staying with *elocutio* there would be room for more study of the verbal markers and rhetorical functions of different kinds of style in Spenser. Readers rapidly become aware of differences in textual density between, for example, narrative, descriptive, and lyrical sections of *The Faerie Queene*. For example, a richly patterned lyrical stanza (II.vi.13) creates a transition to a mood of slothful sensual delight on Phaedria's island. Across his whole *oeuvre*, too, Spenser is notable for the range of different styles he can achieve and render decorous to their subject matter. Scholars have given a good deal of attention to Spenser's names—for example Perissa, excess (II.ii.35), and Cymochles, wavering (II.iv.41)—and especially to their Greek etymologies. Rhetorical approaches would offer a way of linking Spenser's practice to Renaissance ideas about paronomasia and etymology. The emphasis on moral sentences, narratives, and comparisons, which we find in grammar-school education and in such works of Erasmus as *Adagia*, *Parabola*, and *De copia*, would offer a contemporary way of approaching these important features of Spenser's thought and style.

Spenser's investment in descriptions of places could helpfully be investigated in the light of discussions of *topographia* in Erasmus's *De copia*, the *Progymnasmata*, and J. J. Scaliger's *Poetices libri septem*. Page Dubois has discussed Spenser's use of ecphrasis in the light of rhetorical ideas and the epic tradition (1982: 3–8, 74–86). Thomas H. Cain has suggested that the forms described in the *Progymnasmata* contributed to Colin Clout's praise of Elisa in *Aprill* (Spenser 1989: 68). Descriptions of places and marriage speeches are discussed in some detail in the classical treatises on epideictic rhetoric, principally those attributed to Menander Rhetor, which may be worth investigating as contributing sources for *Epithalamion* and *Prothalamion*. The new genres proposed by the letter-writing manuals, such as Erasmus's *De Conscribendis Epistolis*, may offer ways of understanding arguments and self-presentation in the speeches which are such an important feature of so many of Spenser's poems, but which are not generally long enough for ideas related to classical orations to be deployed usefully. Spenser writes apparently persuasive speeches which show the potential of rhetoric for deception, for example the speech of the egalitarian giant (V.ii.30–49) or Archimago's final attempt to prevent Redcrosse's marriage (I.xii.25–30).

Harvey's insistence that one should pay as much attention to the arguments and organization of a work as to its style suggests further topics for exploration. Dialogue and argument were important aspects of Spenser's poetry from the time of *The Shepheardes Calender* to some of the most effective episodes of *The Faerie Queene*. One could envisage a study of the development of Spenser's literary logic which also took in the argumentative form of the sonnets of *Amoretti*. Some of his debates and plot motifs depend on the kind of distinctions and reactions to individual words central to university training in disputation. When Una intervenes in Redcrosse's debate with Despair, for example, she insists that alongside God's justice there is always God's mercy, in which grace Redcrosse has a part (I.ix.53). Guyon's less than decisive answer to Mammon's third temptation (II.vii.19) opens him to the stronger testing of his wearisome journey through the Cave of Mammon.

More attention could be given to thinking about the way argument links episodes together. The sixth canto of Book III, for example, consists of three main episodes: Chrysogone's miraculous conception and the birth of Belphoebe and Amoret (III. vi.1–10, 26–7); Venus's search for Cupid and her dialogue with Diana (III.vi.11–28); and the description of the Gardens of Adonis (III.vi.29–52), where Venus takes refuge with her revivified lover and Amoret is educated. All three episodes are concerned with the relationship between love, generation, and corruption. Chrysogone's miraculous conception unites her offspring both to purity and to the Sun as the universal principle of life and fruitfulness. Venus's search presents Cupid's destructive and shaming power light-heartedly through the argument between Venus and Diana, which moves from tension and anger to compassion. The description of the Garden of Adonis presents a mythic solution to a philosophical problem, combining ideas from Plato and Aristotle to present both a conception of renewal through change and a recognition of the destructive power of time. Eternity through change depends both on love and on sinful and corruptible bodies; the Gardens offer a poetic way of holding these ideas in productive tension.

Central to a rhetorical approach to the larger structure of the poem is Spenser's claim, in tune with humanist theories, that the purpose of his poem was moral education, 'to fashion a gentleman or noble person in vertuous and gentle discipline'. Each book, even more than it is centred on an individual hero, is organized to display a virtue. The purpose of the whole work includes providing the knowledge required of a good citizen. The reader is invited to contemplate the different ways in which knowledge and moral teaching are put across. For example, Spenser famously conveys a great deal of his teaching through description of places. *The Faerie Queene* offers a particularly instructive laboratory for investigating the key rhetorical question of the relationship between narrative, other forms of exposition, and argument, in effective teaching. The reader is required to gather and compare different kinds of material in order to learn from the poem.

For example, the teaching of courtesy in Book VI is conducted through four main types of material. There are places where the book teaches openly, as when the hermit instructs Serena and Timias on the steps which they must take to avoid the corruption which engulfs them as a result of being wounded by the Blatant Beast (VI.vi.5–15) or when the poet compares natural and taught courtesy (VI.ii.2). More commonly we enjoy a narrative which either the narrator (typically at the start of a canto) or the hero then moralizes for us. For example, the terms of mercy which Calidore, after defeating Crudor, sets out for Briana give a sort of elementary primer in courtesy: avoid pride; realize that someone else's misfortune may later befall you and consequently act with sympathy; show special concern for women. The value of courteous attitudes is reinforced by narrative when Calidore's words and decisions are said to change Briana's disposition (VI.i.40–2, 45). Moral narrative and moral axiom were staples of grammar-school education and pupils were taught to make connections between them (Mack 2002: 32–6). A third kind of teaching is provided through character, as when Spenser reveals the inner treachery beneath Blandina's smooth words or comments on the innate courtesy of the salvage man who rescues Serena (VI.v.1–2; vi.41–4). The character of Mirabella in cantos 7 and 8 functions as a negative moral exemplum for women's behaviour towards their lovers.

Finally and most essentially Spenser teaches through poetic motifs. He presents Calidore's pastoral sojourn both as an investigation of inner happiness as the basis of courtesy, and as a dereliction of his duty to the Faerie Queene (VI.ix.18–31; x.1–3; xii.2). In canto 9 the pastoral world is presented as a place outside the day-to-day struggles of urban and court life where true values still reside, while at the end of canto 10 its contentment is shown to be utterly dependent on the security provided by armies and knights. Through opposition this corresponds to his portrayal of the court as both the nursery of courtesy and corrupt (VI.*Proem*, 5–7; i.1; ix.24–5; x.1–2). Within the pastoral section is the vision on Mount Acidale, where Spenser's persona Colin Clout explains to Calidore how the Graces (and among them love) dance at the centre of the concept of courtesy (VI.x.21–8). By the time he learns this, the knight of courtesy realizes that his intrusion has destroyed the vision, which cannot be reconstituted until the graces of their own will inspire another such vision (VI.x.18–20). Calidore is a model of courtesy who frequently (though unwillingly) breaks courtesy. Poetry confers moments whose power to convey harmonious understanding is entirely bound up with their evanescent nature.

Spenser's aim of conveying the ideals of his world while insisting on its realities requires an attentive reading which refuses premature conclusions and simplified lessons. He sets out moral precepts but then complicates them, asking us to compare the words, actions, and fates of different characters. The vision he portrays strikingly resembles Melanchthon's rhetorical reading of Virgil's *Aeneid*, which teaches through careful attention to the fiction, refusing easy lessons which distort the text in order to learn in more subtle, more realistic ways (Mack 2002: 20–4):

Knowledge of things feeds prudence; words nourish eloquence. So Virgil when he describes Aeneas creates a certain picture of a wise man, who among so many dangers overcomes everything that opposes him through reason and planning. But to this he also adds the Gods, rulers of favourable occurrences. For the poets saw that great things are achieved through reason, subject to the control and favour of the Fates. In the same way they conceive undeserved destinies in which someone dies in spite of the merit of their valour. For example Pallas here in Virgil. But there are others who are made excessively bold by fortune and favourable events, as Euryalus and Nisus were. In places like these the poets lament the misery of human kind. There are also places where bad things happen to those who deserve ill, for example those who abuse their fortune, as happens to the tyrant Mezentius. In the same way there are those who become insolent through good fortune, as in [*Aeneid* 10, 501 ff]. These things belong to justice. For the poets see that the final ends of robbers and tyrants are always cruel. But because Aeneas is imagined to be a ruler, so it should be seen that the poet gives him the arts of ruling a republic, the knowledge of war and justice [11, 126 ff], clemency . . . [11, 111 ff]. And the authority to suppress rebellions . . . [1, 151 ff]. Throughout, descriptions of emotions are added to the actions being carried out. In the same way there are descriptions of places and times, of diseases, of wounds and cures, all of which belong to natural science. There are also fables in the poems . . . The whole poem is devoted to the promotion of virtues in general. For it is the image of man as statesman and commander. (Melanchthon 1834: 22–3)

NOTES

1. Cf. the glosses to *Januarye* 61, *Februarie* 181, *March* 116, *Maye* 61, *Julye* 51, and *November* 178.
2. Cf. the glosses to *Januarye* 61, *June* 90, and *November* 73.
3. Cf the argument to *Januarye*; and glosses to *Aprill* 37, *December* 67, 73, 97–8, 151.

BIBLIOGRAPHY

In referring to Aristotle and Quintilian I have used standard paragraph numberings applicable to all editions of their works.

Aphthonius (1997). trans. Malcolm Heath at http://www.leeds.ac.uk/classics/resources/rhetoric/prog-aph.

Agricola, Rudolph (1539). *De Inventione Dialectica.* repr. Nieuwkoop: De Graaf (1967).

Barker, William (1990). *SE*, 468–9.

—— (2001). *The Adages of Erasmus.* Toronto: University of Toronto Press.

Bruyère, N. (1984). *Méthode et dialectique dans l'oeuvre de La Ramée.* Paris: Vrin.

Chomarat, J. (1981). *Grammaire et rhétorique chez Érasme,* 2 vols. Paris: Les Belles Lettres.

Dubois, P. (1982). *History, Rhetorical Description and the Epic: From Homer to Spenser.* Cambridge: D. S. Brewer.

Erasmus (1971). *De Conscribendis Epistolis,* in *Opera omnia* I-2. Amsterdam: North Holland.

—— (1978). *De copia,* trans. B. Knott, in *Collected Works of Erasmus,* vol. 24: 295–659. Toronto: University of Toronto Press.

—— (1985). *De Conscribendis Epistolis,* trans. C. Fantazzi, in *Collected Works of Erasmus,* vol. 25. Toronto: University of Toronto Press.

—— (1988). *De copia,* ed. B. Knott, in *Opera omnia,* I-6. Amsterdam: North Holland.

Feingold, M. (1997). 'The Humanities' and 'The Mathematical Sciences and the New Philosophy', in N. Tyacke (ed.), *The History of the University of Oxford*, vol. 4, *Seventeenth-Century Oxford*. Oxford: Oxford University Press, 211–448.

Hardison, O. B. (1962), *The Enduring Monument*. Chapel Hill: University of North Carolina Press.

Harvey, Gabriel (1945). *Ciceronianus*, ed. H. S. Wilson and C. A. Forbes. Lincoln, NE: University of Nebraska Press.

—— (1577). *Rhetor*. London: Binneman.

Hermogenes (1987). *On Types of Style*, trans C. Wooten. Chapel Hill: University of North Carolina Press.

Howell, W. S. (1956). *Logic and Rhetoric in England 1500–1700*. Princeton, NJ: Princeton University Press.

Leedham-Green, E. (1986). *Books in Cambridge Inventories*, 2 vols. Cambridge: Cambridge University Press.

Mack, P. (1998). 'Ramus Reading: The Commentaries on Cicero's *Consular Orations* and Vergil's *Eclogues* and *Georgics*'. *JWCI* 61 (1998): 111–41.

—— (1993). *Renaissance Argument: Valla and Agricola in the Traditions of Rhetoric and Dialectic*. Leiden: Brill.

—— (2002). *Elizabethan Rhetoric: Theory and Practice*. Cambridge: Cambridge University Press.

McConica, J. K. (1986). *The History of the University of Oxford*, vol. 3: *The Collegiate University*. Oxford: Oxford University Press.

Meerhoff, K. (2001). *Entre logique et littérature: Autour de Philippe Melanchthon*. Orleans: Paradigme.

—— (1986). *Rhétorique et poétique au 16ième siècle en France*. Leiden: Brill.

—— and Moisan, J-C. (2000) (eds). *Autour de Ramus*. Montreal: Nuit Blanche.

Melanchthon, Philipp (1834). 'Preface' to Virgil in *Opera omnia, Corpus Reformatorum*, II, 22–5. repr. New York: Johnson.

—— (1846). *Elementa Rhetorices*, in *Opera omnia, Corpus Reformatorum*, XIII, 413–506, repr. New York: Johnson.

Meyer, S. (1969). *An Interpretation of Edmund Spenser's 'Colin Clout'*. Cork: Cork University Press.

Rix, H. D. (1940). *Rhetoric in Spenser's Poetry*. State College, PA: University of Pennsylvania Press.

Russell, D. A., and Wilson, N. G. (1981) (eds). *Menander Rhetor*. Oxford: Oxford University Press.

—— and Winterbottom, M. (1972) (eds). *Ancient Literary Criticism*. Oxford: Oxford University Press.

Sharratt, P. (1976). 'Peter Ramus and the Reform of the University', in P. Sharratt (ed.), *French Renaissance Studies 1540–70*. Edinburgh: Edinburgh University Press, 4–20.

Stern, V. (1990). *SE*, 347–8.

—— (1979). *Gabriel Harvey*. Oxford: Oxford University Press.

Vasoli, C. (1968). *La dialettica e la retorica dell'Umanesimo*. Milan: Feltrinelli.

Vickers, B. (1970). *Classical Rhetoric in English Poetry*. London: Macmillan.

Wilson, H. S. (1945). 'Gabriel Harvey's Orations on Rhetoric'. *ELH* 12: 167–82.

CHAPTER 24

ALLEGORY, EMBLEM, AND SYMBOL

KENNETH BORRIS

COMPARABLE to Dante in his importance for allegory, Spenser creatively expanded its potential throughout his literary life. But the experimental vigor of his endeavor is too little acknowledged. While assimilating and building on medieval precedents, the poet's engagement with allegory subsumed diverse influences from the ancients to his own contemporaries in a unique new formulation. The consummate expression of Spenser's allegorical poetic, *The Faerie Queene* samples and redevelops myriad literary and other texts, forms, and discourses to manifest its own poetic world. Few books read like no others, and this poem's profound allegorism ensures it is one of them.

'SYMBOL', ALLEGORY, AND THE EMBLEMATIC COSMOS

Since Romantic 'allegoriphobia' has been discredited, we have become better sensitized to Spenser's particular mastery of poetic symbology. Coleridge claimed that allegory depends upon arbitrary correspondences, whereas symbol is intrinsically motivated or synechdochal, and hence 'abides as a living part in that Unity of which it is the representative' (1972: 30). Reconsidering this distinction, Paul de Man valorized allegory over symbol instead, because he found the former's presumed arbitrariness preferable to the mystifications entailed by symbol's appearances of essential aptness (1969: 191–2). Yet allegory and symbol resist any mutually exclusive distinctions that claim transhistorical validity, and any allegory involves images that may be considered in some sense symbolic. In view of such difficulties of definition, Jonathan Culler wonders if 'what we call "symbol" is only a special case of allegory' (1985: 54).[1] Coleridge's and de Man's distinctions between these terms are in any case inapplicable to early modern allegory, for its signs could evoke the ostensibly authentic or synechdochal motivation that they associate with symbol alone.

The 1590 *Faerie Queene* provides the *Oxford English Dictionary*'s first example of 'symbol' used in the sense 'something that stands for, represents, or denotes something else', especially 'a material object representing... something immaterial, abstract, as a being, idea, quality' (sb.[1] 2a). Ruddymane's bloodstain is thus 'a sacred Symbole' (II.ii.10). No doubt influential, this instance of that English usage would probably also have been early. The dictionary's examples for the diverse English senses of 'symbol' and its cognates are almost all post-Spenserian, except for the much older sense 'creed or summary of religious belief' (sb.[1] 1a). Throughout Europe, usage of the vernacular counterparts of 'symbol' would have been strongly influenced by their Greek and Latin roots. In early modernity, those were understood as complex words that somewhat converged with allegory, and their perceived range of senses differed greatly from the meanings of 'symbol' now. According to the renowned scholar Guillaume Budé in 1529, the corresponding Greek words may denote armed struggles; banquet offerings; interpretations, marks, or signs; tokens of friendship; fragments of wholes; similitudes; elements shared in common; or Pythagorean and other enigmas expressing hidden significance. On that account, Budé explains, '"symbolic" is said of what is allegorical and enigmatic (*allegorico et aenigmatico*)', and such expression characterizes mystical theology's guarded mediations of sacred insights (Drysdall 1994). Beginning in the fifteenth century, early modern usage of the Latin *symbolum* and *symbolus*[2] became informed by notions of hieroglyphs as natural and even revelatory signs.

As this and other cultural changes, such as the invention of printing with movable type, reinvigorated symbological thought, so the earlier 1500s introduced distinctive creations and redevelopments of varied symbolic forms. First published in 1531, Andrea Alciato's *Emblematum liber* initiated the vogue of the emblem book (Figure 24.1), and over 5,300 more were composed by 1700 (Daly 1998: 204). Though flexible in format, the sixteenth-century emblem became typified by an interactive tripartite structure consisting of a motto above a more or less enigmatic pictorial image, followed by an interpretation in verse or prose. Emblems themselves were seen to partake in allegorism, so that the early emblematist Guillaume de La Perrière refers to his '*sens allegoricque*'.[3] Spenser would have known Alciato's much-published text, and likely some version of Claude Mignault's commentary first printed in 1571. The latter's prefatory treatise explains the Latin roots of 'symbol' quite like Budé on the

Νΐφε κậὶ μέμνησ᾽ ἀπιsεῖ. ἄρθρα ταῦτα τῶρ
φρενῶρ. Sobriè viuendum : & non
temerè credendum.

Ne credas ne(Epicharmus ait) non sobrius esto,
   Hi nerui,humanæ membraq̃, mentis erun":
Ecce oculata manus credens id quod videt. Ecce
   Pulegium,antiquæ sobrietatis olus,
Quo turbam ostenso sedauerit Heraclitus,
   Mulxerit & tumida seditione grauem.

Fig. 24.1. *Be Moderate, Not Credulous*, from Andrea Alciato, *Emblemata* (Lyons: Guillaume Rouille, 1551), p. 22. Courtesy of the Thomas Fisher Rare Books Library, University of Toronto.

Greek, and relates the sense of enigmatic, learned content to Alciato's emblems. Having already translated interpretive epigrams for the pictures in Jacob Van der Noot's apocalyptic commentary *A Theatre of Worldlings* in 1569, Spenser further explored the possibilities of verbal-visual signification in *The Shepheardes Calender* (1579), where each eclogue significantly interacts with an initial illustration, and again in his unillustrated *Visions* sonnets in *Complaints* (1591).

Though scholars usually now reserve 'emblem' for contents of emblem books, in the later sixteenth century the term overlapped somewhat with a range of similar, more broadly 'emblematic' verbal-visual forms such as the *impresa*, device, rebus or enigma, commemorative medal, and illustrated proverb or beast fable. The *impresa*, for example, was a somewhat enigmatic pictorial image with a motto, devised for courtly personal expression (Figure 24.2). These correlative elements of early modern culture may be collectively termed 'emblematics'. Besides relating to emblems in particular, '*symbolum*' served to translate the vernacular terms for related verbal-visual forms such as *imprese* and devices (Fraunce 1991: 2–3). Significant visual images appeared ubiquitously in architecture, the decorative arts, personal dress, entertainments, and title pages of books (Figures 24.2, 24.3). Cross-currents of influence flowed freely between those depictions, the various symbolic forms, and the diverse verbal and visual means of mediating the conventions of imagistic signification, such as iconographical treatises, paintings, philosophical discourses, and literary texts.

For considerations of sixteenth-century literary allegory, then, particular emblem books and their contents are much less relevant than the verbal-visual habits of mind and representation more broadly characteristic of the culture (see Daly 1998: Chaps. 2–3). In one sense a digest of symbolic forms and materials including emblematics, Spenser's richly visualized *Faerie Queene* urges readers to 'behold' its represented sights, which are more interpretive than verisimilar (Manning 2002: 90). But the relations of his writings to emblem books tend to be elusive. Specific motifs or emblems in some of them may help explicate various Spenserian passages, yet have their own sources and intertexts, often non-emblematic, that the poet could have known independently. And Spenser characteristically appropriates symbolic norms for innovative adaptation, as in the case of his *Faerie Queene*'s unconventional Occasion (II.iv–v). Insofar as the emblem itself lacks intuitional and emotional content relative to symbol, as in one non-evaluative definition (Daly 1998: 108), Spenserian allegory, which involves readers in sympathetic characterizations and unfolding stories, is much more symbolic than emblematic.

Late sixteenth-century emblematics epitomize a common assumption, fundamental for much allegory of the time, that appropriate imagistic signifiers embody some essential truth. Supplementing the Bible, the natural world appeared a further revelation of its supposed Creator, replete with divinely authorized signs that verbal or visual compositions could evoke. This concept of 'nature's book' remained vigorous even in seventeenth-century scientific circles.

It had been reinforced by new hieroglyphic mentalities. One of the ancient texts rediscovered and disseminated in the humanist revival of antiquity was Horapollo's Greek explication of the Egyptian hieroglyphs. In that incorrect account, supported

LE
1IMPRESE HE-
ROICHE ET MO-
RALI RITROVATE DA
M. Gabriello Symeoni
Fiorentino,
Al gran Conestabile di Francia.

IMPRESA DELL'AVTORE.

ΕΥΔΟΚΙΑΣ.

Fig. 24.2. Author's Impresa, *With Body on Earth and Mind in the Heavens*, from Gabriele Simeoni, *Le imprese heroiche et morali*, title page; in Paolo Giovio, *Dialogo dell'imprese militari et amorose* (Lyons: Guillaume Rouille, 1574). Courtesy of the Thomas Fisher Rare Books Library, University of Toronto.

by some other ancient authorities and not superseded until the early nineteenth century, each hieroglyph is not a phonetic sign but rather an ideogrammatic representation of a word or concept, motivated by some intrinsic connection between the signifier and its signified. The hieroglyphs thus appeared to epitomize ancient wisdom through a primal imagistic means of representation more authentic than conventional verbal exchanges and alphabetic script. In one influential view favored by humanists with Platonic affinities, such pictographic techniques excel the regular discursive procedures of human language and reason by promoting an intuitive awareness akin to the direct, 'all at once' apprehension ascribed to the angels and God. In another view, comparable to Aristotelian sign theory, a hieroglyph's meaning depends on the signifier's relation to some supposedly intrinsic qualities of the natural object depicted. Hence the hieroglyph mediates the rational insights of natural philosophy, not an esoteric revelation, yet remains a natural rather than arbitrary or conventional sign. The syncretic tendencies of early modern thought ensured some intermingling of these views (Drysdall 1999: 116–19).

The distinctive new vogue for hieroglyphic signification complemented notions of 'the book of nature', promoted the development and currency of emblem books, and stimulated new interest in imagistic representation as well as the production of major iconographical handbooks. One of the first, largest, and most influential was Pierio Valeriano's so-called commentary on Horapollo first published in 1556, the *Hieroglyphica* (Figure 24.3). The Latin counterparts of the words 'hieroglyph' and 'symbol' became almost interchangeable in his usage; both also somewhat merged with 'emblem' in the period. The beliefs and aspirations to higher awareness that attended reception of the Egyptian hieroglyphs infused the phenomena of emblematics and verbal allegorical imagery.[4]

In this cultural milieu, many theorists of literature and the visual arts believed that the image could have unique epistemological power and impart essential truth (Gombrich 1972). Arguing for poetry's primacy among the disciplines of knowledge, except theology, Sir Philip Sidney's *Defence of Poetry* illustrates such assumptions. Whereas the philosopher presents 'wordish' descriptions of universals, and the historian relatively uninterpreted particulars, the poet, especially in heroic poetry or epic, surpasses both these competitors by focusing universals in particulars and thus producing lively images that move readers to admire the lineaments of virtue (1973: 85–92, 97–8). For Sidney, the poetics of the image afford means to bypass discursive reason to enable a more direct and compelling apprehension of truth (e.g., 85–7, 98). On account of philosophical idealism's former prestige, many theorists of both literature and the visual arts believed that the proper objects of mimesis were idealized conceptions of truth, good, and beauty surpassing their reflections in the phenomenal world.[5] Sidney himself assumes that poetic representation can manifest a 'golden world' beyond nature's brazen one. His fundamental premise is that the realm of 'right poetry' excels nature's possibilities because its heightened images informed by 'erected wit' better approximate truth and promote its pursuit (78–9).

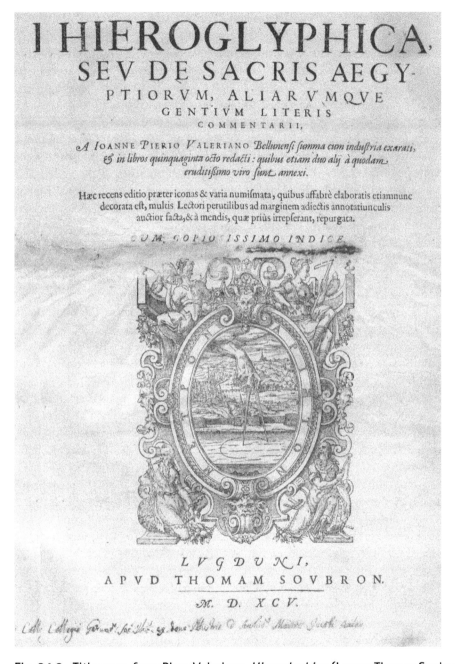

I HIEROGLYPHICA,
SEV DE SACRIS AEGY-
PTIORVM, ALIARVMQVE
GENTIVM LITERIS
COMMENTARII,

*A IOANNE PIERIO VALERIANO Bellunensi summa cum industria exarati,
& in libros quinquaginta octo redacti: quibus etiam duo alij à quodam
eruditissimo viro sunt annexi.*

Hæc recens editio præter iconas & varia numismata, quibus affabrè elaboratis etiamnunc
decorata est, multis Lectori perutilibus ad marginem adiectis annotatiunculis
auctior facta,& à mendis, quæ priùs irrepserant, repurgata.

CVM COPIOSISSIMO INDICE

LVGDVNI,
APVD THOMAM SOVBRON.

M. D. XCV.

Fig. 24.3. Title page, from Piero Valeriano, *Hieroglyphica* (Lyons: Thomas Soubron, 1595). Courtesy of the Centre for Reformation and Renaissance Studies, Toronto.

Similarly, when Torquato Tasso states in his *Discorsi del poema eroico* that the poet makes 'images in the fashion of a speaking painter', and that 'the poet's subject is rather the true than the false', Tasso insists that the poet should imitate intelligible rather than visible things, for it is the former that truly exist. 'Now to lead to the contemplation of divine things and thus awaken the mind with images, as the mystical theologian and the poet do, is a far nobler work than to instruct by demonstration.' Their imagistic sign-languages arise from the intellect, not from 'the divisible mind' or ratiocination (1973: 31–3). Sidney and Tasso share basic assumptions that apt poetic imagery epitomizes and reveals truth, awakens minds, and seeks to imitate philosophically idealist reality. Many other theorists of the verbal and visual arts thought likewise in the later sixteenth century, and the predominant concern to justify fiction in terms of some epitomized intrinsic truth strongly pressed Renaissance poetics in general towards allegorism.

Spenser's allegorical poetic developed in these cultural contexts for conceiving the nature, import, and value of imagistic signs. Early modern allegory functions much more according to Coleridge's and de Man's notions of symbol than their insufficiently historicized notions of allegory. For example, according to common early modern beliefs Una's significations of Truth and the Church (as the body of its rightful adherents) can be profoundly motivated and intrinsic. Not only did her representative role have precedents in what seemed to be God's Word, as in the formerly allegorized Song of Songs and the Protestants' Book of Revelation, but God had supposedly created humankind *in his image*, of which vestiges endured the Fall.[6] Besides the divine image Una's characterization would have entailed an immortal soul, and through both she could readily have appeared 'to abide as a living part of that Unity of which she is the representative', especially for monists.[7] Moreover, beauty and the virtues appeared to originate in God, and Una is exceptionally beautiful and good. Hence for many of Spenser's time, her relation to what she signifies would not have seemed arbitrary or merely conventional, and its provisional manifestation through her appealing depiction would have emotionally gratified desires for verified belief. Insofar as the perceived inscriptions of nature's book were to be read as insignia of God, the poet's allegorism was to clarify and heighten nature's. Una's lifted veil discloses not any particular countenance but a solar radiance like 'brightest skye' surpassing the poet's language (I.iii.4; vi.4; xii.23); that light positioned both in and beyond the text putatively orders and authenticates the allegory's signs, while yet transcending them. Much the same considerations apply to Gloriana herself insofar as she relates to divine glory through and beyond her topical referent, Elizabeth, said to be God's chosen proxy (compare I Proem, 4; II.ii.41). As Peter Daly observes, 'what is deemed intrinsic in one world-view may not be so in another' (1998: 104). From current agnostic and atheistic standpoints, de Man's critique of the mystifications of symbol as opposed to allegory would also apply to Spenser's and many other premodern allegories, if they are historically contextualized. The criterion of synechdochal intrinsicality that has often been claimed to differentiate symbol from allegory, as if the latter were simply 'continued metaphor', is actually relative, not necessarily definitive.

ALLEGORY/'SPEAKING OTHER'/*BRICOLAGE*

Literary allegory is especially characterized by some ongoing polysemous interplay of diverse senses, and so the mode is best distinguished from symbol by the formalization of that quality, not by suppositions of any necessary, transhistorical, and essential difference in the status of allegory's signs *versus* symbol's. Considered etymologically, 'allegory' (ἄλλος ἀγορεύω) denominates 'other speech' or polyphonic discourse that enables secretively coded public utterance (Whitman 1987: 263–8). Though allegory may be intermittent or relatively continuous, it is necessarily syntagmatic or extended and thus requires some implied or explicit narrative. And in adumbrating one or more patterns of alternate signification, it tends to be more or less programmatic, hence quasi-intentional. Texts that are structurally allegories, to some extent composed as such (like Spenser's *Legend of Holinesse*), are to be distinguished from ones imputed so, through interpretive allegorization. Allegorical interpretation in general may be termed 'allegoresis'. Depending on the extent to which an allegory explicitly structures a narrative, it assumes some position in a spectrum of possibilities ranging from 'simple' to 'complex' (Frye 1965: 12), and may shift somewhat across that range in successive passages. Whereas simpler allegory tends predominantly to use personified abstractions with identities name-tagged in the same language as the text (such as Contemplation, but not Orgoglio), complex allegories are relatively subliminal, mythic, and fraught with the suggestiveness commonly associated with symbol instead.[8]

Nevertheless, 'simple' and 'complex' are provisional, exploratory terms here. Even so-called simple or 'naive' allegories assymetrically involve ironies, local contradictions, ambivalences, and ambiguities. The conformation of the verbal and imagistic matter to its allegorical animus is never absolute. In any case, Spenser subsumes the techniques of simple allegory within his complex allegorical practice. The reception history of *The Faerie Queene*'s Errour and Despair, for example, evinces no simplicity, and the metamorphosis of Malbecco into Jealousy modulates allegorical registers to express the dehumanizing effects of that passion (III.x.55–60). The poet contextualizes his usages of personified abstractions within narratives involving a remarkable range of representative characterizations, and 'subcharacters' projecting psychic and other conditions or potentials of his protagonists.[9]

In definitions of verbal allegory, rhetorical approaches have long predominated, especially comparisons to continued or extended metaphor. Yet such descriptive shorthand is readily misleading. Allegory tends broadly to assimilate verbal discourse to a variety of tropes and schemes involving oblique reference or multiple meanings, such as not only metaphor and irony but also paronomasia, synecdoche, metonymy, sarcasm, hyperbole, enigma, and periphrasis. It can inscribe polyvalent puns or homonyms, as it were, throughout the whole scope of a text (Quilligan 1979), so much as to include not only single words and phrases but paragraphs, episodes, and the largest units of structure. Even pronouns become means of ambiguous double reference to merge characters and subcharacters in *The Faerie Queene* (see III.xii.37).

Literary allegory also rewards assessment as 'a game designed by the writer and played by the reader' (Teskey 1990: 16–22), especially in learned Renaissance iterations. Its characteristic 'play of senses' enables many anamorphic effects of playfulness and performance that facilitate the production of a tour de force such as *The Faerie Queene*. The poem's prestidigitations of ideas, images, narrative motifs, and intertexts of diverse types largely depend on allegory's expressive resources. Humanists such as Ficino, Erasmus, Sir Thomas More, and Alciato revelled in the intellectual recreations of textual play: conceitful displays of knowledge and wisdom facetiously intermeddled with paradoxical absurdities analogous to the fashionable visual *grottesche* (compare Figures 24.1 and 24.3). Around 1580 Spenser's Cambridge mentor Gabriel Harvey called early excerpts of *The Faerie Queene* '*Hobgoblin* runne away with the Garland from Apollo' (*Prose*, 472). Whereas some critics claim that allegory is authoritarian, it can free imaginative expression from public restrictions. And like parody it can readily become a means of 'authorized transgression' insofar as it solicits recognition of cultural codes and conventions while inviting their revaluation by resituating them in a fabulous context.

Though rhetorical approaches to verbal allegory often assume it is only a type of expression, it potentially affords a unique means of thought. It tends to foster experimental redefinition of the norms and limits of discourse, and readily becomes self-reflexive through meta-allegory. *The Faerie Queene* often addresses its own and other signifying practices, as in its representation of Error, Archimago, Gloriana, Malfont, Colin Clout, and the Graces. In relatively complex and capacious allegories, materials that are ordinarily heterogeneous become melded within the provisional affirmations of 'other speech', and are brought into unanticipated relationships in imaginative new ways. In a poem allegorizing philosophical and religious concepts such as Spenser's *Legend of Holinesse*, for instance, they are not just reported, sampled, or evoked, but narratively transfigured into lively images, through strategic redevelopment of literary and non-literary intertexts and generic precedents, so that these very diverse ingredients, including even satyrs, become newly interactive. Extensive complex allegories like Spenser's epitomize, rewrite, and rethink their cultures. Their reconfigured realities of the poetic imagination are literary thought experiments wherein readers may experience moral and interpretive challenges under to some extent controlled conditions (such as provision of poetic justice, or serendipitous outcomes). Yet in its probing of mysteries that manifests their abiding strangeness more than affording any answers, *The Faerie Queene* distinctively expresses and evokes the expanding efflorescences of exploratory thought.[10] Spenser's dynamic allegorism largely enables this epistemologically extraordinary poesis.

Since literary allegory is fundamentally a means of intermixing diverse discourses so that one or more appear in terms of another, historicized study of its formal aspects most fully reveals its operations, functions, and cultural significance.[11] Like parody and satire, it is best defined as a mode, for it appropriates 'host' forms and their conventional repertoires of themes and features, yet transforms them into vehicles of new significance. For example, when crossed with allegory, heroic poetry or pastoral become anamorphic, in that their respective generic properties are thus hybridized with sampled and stylized non-literary discourses. Among other possi-bilities, those may include autobiographical reflection, current politics and events, moral philosophy, or theology. Insofar as allegory involves the assemblage and coded, estheticized reconfiguration of cultural materials, it is somewhat akin to pastiche, cento, collage, montage, palimpsests, and the *bricolage* of Claude Lévi-Strauss. Recourse to textual allegoresis may arise from perception of a seemingly interrelated sequence of figurative correspondences, or from some perceived friction of elements: some incongruity, surplus in significance, or overdetermination of a narrative's features, for example, relative to the story's apparent needs. Una's association with some theological vocabulary and with imagery of the Book of Revelation leads us to look beyond the capacities of literal romantic-epic narrative in interpreting her story. Allegorical modulation of a host form invites interpretive reassessment of the whole field of cultural materials that the allegory incorporates, including the host's.

Over the history of its development allegory has accumulated a particular modal repertoire of diachronically variable options and characteristics. These include cer-tain fundamental metaphysical assumptions such as former beliefs in universal analogy and cosmic *discordia concors*; strategies of wordplay; polysemous discourse more or less implicitly conducted through figurative means; composite characteriza-tion involving subcharacters; personification; abstraction; omission of insignificant description; and a range of narrative motifs conducive to allegorism, such as journeys, quests, struggles, vulnerabilities, and encounters with monsters.[12] Com-parison with parody and satire further clarifies allegory's modal operations and cultural value, for these three modes all function as generic solvents or catalysts that enable new combinations and reactions of discursive resources. In short, by reinterpreting assimilated components and inducing new conditions of interchange between them, allegory can refresh and revitalize the expressive capacities of literary forms and structures. Allegory and allegoresis are harbingers, prototypes, and agents of literary change that accommodate genres and texts to shifts in cultural conditions: hence the allegorical reconfigurations of ancient pastoral and epic in the Christian era.

However, generalizations about allegory have a largely exploratory value, for its characteristics mercurially vary according to its host generic context and cultural circumstances. Renaissance allegory especially needs to be considered *in situ*, for not only did the metaphysical and religious assumptions of that time warrant distinctive notions of allegory's relations to reality, but the prestige of certain literary texts supported strong conceptions of genre and generic decorum through the educational system and otherwise. In the later sixteenth century, allegory appeared to have a very different scope, range of purposes, and literary history in lyric than in heroic poetry, considered an especially edifying encyclopedic form.[13] If allegory became ruinous in the unique context of seventeenth-century German *Trauerspiel* or 'mourning-play' (Benjamin 1972),[14] it otherwise long retained strong cultural linkages with personal and social edification ('building up'). Whenever the mode's relationships to particu-lar host forms became especially extensive, formalized, and hence codified, it developed particular genre-specific thematic and expressive repertoires. The literary genres most associated with allegory in Spenser's time were pastoral, where it was commonly designated a standard optional ingredient; and heroic poetry, which was often considered *allegorical by definition*.[15] 'Heroic poetry' here denotes epic's Renaissance conceptual expansion to include romantic, biblical, and other variants. Other contexts require more particular designations: 'epic' designates classical or classicizing exemplars and their former reception, for example, while 'romantic epic' denotes the sixteenth-century confluence of epic and chivalric romance.

Knowledge of the repertoires of Renaissance pastoral and heroic allegory clarifies the codes, conventions, and innovations of particular texts: their contextual norms of play, as it were (Borris 2000: Chap. 3). As Spenser's *Calender* indicates, early modern bucolic allegorism had certain conventional topics (such as ecclesiastical critiques, governance of the passions, a ruler's effect on national life), some common foundational tropes (care or abuse of sheep figured attitudes toward some social responsibility), and standard models (Virgilian precedents, Mantuanesque satire, the Parable of the Good Shepherd, among others). The particularly close relationship between sixteenth-century heroic allegory and moral philosophy readily accounts for Spenser's focus on allegorization of the virtues in *The Faerie Queene*.

Beyond the relevant literary exemplars and their documented former reception, study of allegory's pastoral and heroic variants involves some related cultural phenomena such as the visual symbolic forms already surveyed, mythography, and biblical interpretation. Insofar as mythography allegorized ancient myths, its former prestige supported literary allegory while authorizing mythic precedents, intertexts, and pretexts for the construction of allegorical fictions. Mythographical allegoresis was mainly euhemeristic, expounding a fable's historical applications; physical, explaining its reflections of the structure and operations of the universe; moral, addressing its expressions of inner orders and disorders of body and mind; or theological.[16] Ancient myth appeared to have encoded enlightened primal philosophy and theology in enigmatic tales, and poetry's apparent founders, such as Orpheus, Musaeus, Hesiod, and Homer, seemed exemplary fabulists of that kind. Poetry at best thus tended to imply allegorically veiled and vatic wisdom.[17] Spenser's significant appropriations of ancient myth in *The Faerie Queene* and other poems indicate this context's particular importance to his creativity.

Premodern biblical hermeneutics provided a further reservoir of intertexts and models for poetic allegorism. Beyond the 'literal' sense, Catholic biblical exegesis had distinguished three theologically oriented 'allegorical' senses. Events in the Old Testament, for example, could 'typologically' (or 'allegorically' as was said in one narrowed sense) prefigure their fulfillment in Christ and Christian beliefs; 'tropologically' demonstrate the moral processes of self-control (so that David's defeat of Goliath expresses mastery of the passions through grace and reason); and 'anagogically' anticipate eschatological transformations such as the projected afterlife (see pp. 490–5 below). Though claiming to reject usage of biblical allegoresis for doctrinal proofs, many Protestants nonetheless approved it for edification.[18] The traditional fourfold taxonomy has Spenserian investigative and descriptive value: Redcrosse's reception at liberated Eden impinges upon anagogy, for example, as does Pastorella's at Belgard (Borris 2006). Biblical contexts particularly relevant to Spenserian allegory include the parables and Song of Songs; from Protestant and Catholic viewpoints the Song allegorized Christ's relations with the soul and the Church, as in the Geneva Bible. For Protestants unlike Catholics, the Book of Revelation was a prophetic historical or quasi-typological allegory applicable to any situation entailing religious oppression, and that is a main basis of *The Faerie Queene*'s allegorism in Books I and V, and also in closing Book VI (Borris 1991; 2006: 161–2). These and other cultural factors helped ensure that, especially in the sphere of heroic poetry, the prestige of allegorism in literature remained compelling throughout Europe for decades after 1600, as it did in the visual arts.

LITERARY GENETICS OF SPENSERIAN ALLEGORY

Though in one sense *The Faerie Queene* presents an English national poet's retrospective summation of the inheritances and prospects of his country's culture, late-sixteenth-century humanism strongly conditioned Spenser's intertextual assimilations. Moreover, the norms of pastoral and heroic poetry, the primary generic vehicles for his allegorical poetic, encouraged writers to engage major precedents from the ancients onward, internationally. The *Calender*'s original commentator, E. K., immediately contextualizes the poem in that way (Spenser 1999: 29), and Spenser's polylingual comparatism intensifies in the encyclopedic context of heroic poetry.

For early modern poetics the most influential nondramatic poems of antiquity were Homer's *Iliad* and *Odyssey*, Virgil's *Eclogues* and *Aeneid*, and Ovid's *Metamorphoses*. They had elaborate traditions of allegoresis that forcefully continued long after Spenser's death, and allegory's recent critical rehabilitation has encouraged some classicists to find that it indeed somewhat structures these texts.[19] Besides supporting the dominant Horatian and Platonic assumptions that poetry should be socially and morally instructive, the former reception of Homer, Virgil, and Ovid shifted poetics in general towards allegory, while particularly linking it with pastoralism and, most of all, heroic poetry (Borris 2000: Chap. 1).

For Renaissance understandings of not only the latter genre but literary allegory in general, Homer has great importance. Having been long lost to Western culture, the *Iliad* and *Odyssey* only began to regain currency in the later fifteenth century, as did ancient commentaries allegorizing them. Throughout the sixteenth century and long after, Homer appeared 'the ocean of wisdom' or 'fount of knowledge' whose poems subsumed the learned disciplines, including theology, under allegory's 'living veil'. Well after the sixteenth century, the poetics, practice, and reception of heroic poetry revolved around this conception of Homer. Milton's poetic preparations certainly included study of the Homeric allegorists Heraclitus of Pontus and Eustathius (Borris 2000: 20).

Though Virgil's *Eclogues* and *Aeneid* and Ovid's *Metamorphoses* had been celebrated medieval exemplars of allegory, they nonetheless came to promote its renewal in the Renaissance as their reception was transformed by humanist concerns and responses to newly accessible ancient writings. Aside from Homer's poems and their commentaries, those textual recoveries included the great majority of Plato's dialogues, of which few had been known in the Middle Ages, and various discussions of poetics such as those of 'Longinus', Maximus of Tyre, Demetrius, Porphyry, and Aristotle. Virgil's following of Homeric models in the *Aeneid* became clear, as well as the debts of its ancient reception to the precedents of Homeric allegoresis. His practice appeared to confirm epic's special connections with allegorized moral and natural philosophy and theology, while supplementing those perceived Homeric emphases with dynastic reasons of state. Allegoresis of the *Metamorphoses* and ancient mythology burgeoned in commentaries, mythographical compendia, and the verbal and visual arts; such interpretation encompassed other ancient fictions such as Heliodorus's *Aethiopica* and Apuleius's *Golden Ass*. The fanciful episodic journeying of the *Odyssey* and the dazzling variations of the *Metamorphoses* would have encouraged Spenser's additive, interwoven, open-ended experiments in plot structure, as would Chaucer's *Canterbury Tales* and Ariosto's *Orlando Furioso*. The enhancement of narrative versatility increased scope for accommodating the allegorism and encyclopedic scope associated with heroic poetry.

Whereas Ariosto and Tasso had both downplayed the 'historically' figurative patriotic advocacy of Virgil's epic in their heroic poetry, Spenser fully exploits that precedent. Through the *Eclogues*, *Georgics*, and especially the *Aeneid*, Virgil elaborated a celebratory yet critical program of allusive reflection upon the Roman state, topically focused on the Augustan present, yet surveying Rome's origins, history, and prospects. His epic is thus quasi-typological: its representation of the past provides instructive archetypes for the present and future of the state, its rulers, and its people. These mutually complementary allusions may be considered 'complex allegory' because they constitute a pervasive, programmatic, analytic subtext. But it is not just 'historical' or even 'topical' because it addresses Roman potential—hence the future—as much as the past or present. From the *Calender* onward, Spenser transferred these motifs and techniques from Virgil, and somewhat also from Ovid's final heroically modulated books of the *Metamorphoses*, to England in its Elizabethan, Protestant, British, colonial, Continental, and transatlantic aspects. That is one main function of the *The Faerie Queene*'s allegorism.[20] Yet in seeking to look beyond the present and the limitations of particular states, even England, Spenser redefined Virgil's 'prophetic' dimension by assimilating biblical futurism as in the Book of Revelation. Spenser's Ovidianism further qualifies the Virgilian imperial model (Pugh 2005).

Among medieval poets, Chaucer probably influenced Spenserian allegorism most,[21] just as he appeared the founder of English poetic potential in the later 1500s. Chaucer's writings include personification allegories; beast fables comparable to Spenser's *Mother Hubberds Tale*; exempla; allegorical tableaux as in *The Parliament of Fowls*; the parabolic *Pardoner's Tale*; and didactic allegory of the soul's worldly travails in *The Tale of Melibee*. Yet since perceived benefit was the touchstone of hermeneutic validation in former allegoresis, and Chaucer's canon formerly included apocrypha such as *The Plowman's Tale*,[22] sixteenth-century perceptions of his allegorism would have had much more scope. Even now, some believe that *The Man of Law's Tale* and *Clerk's Tale* subtly allegorize much the same theme as *Melibee* (Rigby 1996: Chap. 3). Other recent studies of Chaucerian allegory trace intricate structural and allusive encodings of the Bible and biblical exegesis (Besserman 1998: Chap. 6). For Tudor Reformers, Chaucer appeared to anticipate their religious concerns, and his biblical engagements, attractive to Protestants, could well have influenced Spenser. Unlike many lesser poets, Chaucer would have instanced the possibilities of combining allegory with entertainment, complex characterizations, satire, and irony.

William Langland seemed another prototypical Reformer, and in *Piers Plowman* Spenser would have found a unique English precedent for compendious Christian narrative allegory with satiric and visionary aspects. Both his *Calender* and his *Faerie Queene* evince possible resonances of Langland's B-text (Anderson 1990: 425–6). John Lydgate and John Gower provided further native exemplars of socially purposeful narrative poetry that inwardly addresses conditions of the psyche and the state. Among the range of Middle English romances that Spenser may have read, some portray chivalric heroes in a quasi-hagiographical way, and impute providential meaning to English history (King 2000: Chaps. 3, 6). Though lacking allegory, these could have furnished not only a repertoire of narrative motifs particularly relevant to Book I, but also some native hints for Spenser's adaptations of ancient and contemporary allegorical heroic poetry to represent patrons of the virtues through quest narratives, and address the politics of English Protestantism.

Despite its Continental origins, the thirteenth-century *Roman de la Rose* begun by Guillaume de Lorris and expansively completed by Jean de Meun shared in Chaucerian Englishness because Chaucer was thought to have wholly translated a lengthy yet incomplete English version included in his printed collections. This paradigmatic allegory of erotic desire affected many representations of love and its challenges. Yet Spenser's allegorical technique strikingly differs from both Guillaume's and Jean's. Whereas Jean's continuation of the *Roman* largely consists of brilliant extended monologues, Spenser's *Calender* fully exploits the dialogism of pastoral, and his *Faerie Queene* transforms the imagistic and narrative resources of heroic poetry into means of dynamic allegorical expression. And by Spenser's time understandings of love had been substantially recast. For example, as Plato's dialogues exploring the significance of love and beauty were restored to Western culture in the later fifteenth century and increasingly disseminated, so eros had come to have apparent potential for yielding some genuine enlightenment. Spenser's allegories of love engage such notions from his *Calender* to his *Hymnes*, and most broadly in Books III and IV of *The Faerie Queene* (*October*, 91–6; III.ii.36; IV Proem, 3).

The labyrinths of Continental medieval romances would accommodate numerous further Spenserian intertextual excursions (P. Parker 1990: 609–18), as would various other literary forms of the Middle Ages, such as 'pilgrimage of life' allegories like Guillaume de Deguileville's. Petrarch's and Boccaccio's allegorical bucolics directly influenced Spenser's *Calender*, E. K. observes (Spenser 1999: 29). Along with later pastoralists such as Mantuan, whom E. K. also cites, they would have indicated how ancient pastoral allegorism could be adapted to ecclesiastical satire and Christian perspectives, beyond the precedents perceived in Virgil's Fourth or 'messianic' Eclogue. Petrarch's *Africa* could have helped clarify the options for allegorically reconciling Christianity with epic (Warner 2005: Chap. 1).

Whereas Spenser names, translates, or otherwise clearly appropriates a variety of other major poets, his relation to Dante seems relatively elusive. Yet Chaucer explicitly admired Dante; Spenser assiduously studied Italian literature; Harvey poetically appropriated Dante's Beatrice; the *Commedia* had been printed in many editions (the epithet *divina* only became normative later); London had a substantial Italian community; and Protestants had appropriated Dante's texts for anti-papal polemic.[23] The *Commedia*'s Spenserian quiescence may result from the disjunction of Dante's otherworldly settings with the romance-epic world, to which his narrative materials would not have been readily adaptable. The *Purgatorio* was incommensurate with Protestantism. And since the *Commedia*'s poetic status had become controversial, overt alignment with Dante could have seemed inappropriate. Not only had Dante's language and diction been attacked, but for some the *Commedia* grossly violated generic bounds. Was it a poem at all? If so, what genre? Though it was often designated a heroic poem, some said it would thus be 'a bad one'.[24]

The *Commedia* is nonetheless important for comparative study of Spenser's allegorism. Both he and Dante present fantastic allegorical journeys framed to test and refine readers' minds. *The Faerie Queene* has some intertextually complex Dantean resonances such as its originary wandering wood, and humanly bleeding tree (I.i.7–13; ii.28–33). But there may be more specific allusions, such as the stipulated descent of Spenser's invented monstrous giant Gerioneo from Geryon (V.xi.6–11). Drawing on Protestant apocalyptic historiography, that episode allegorically satirizes papal and Spanish power (Borris 1991: Chap. 3). Though Geryon derives from classical myth, Dante had redeveloped him for apocalyptic anti-papal satire in the *Commedia* (Friedman 1972), and no such other precedents are currently known.

Spenser's reconfiguration of romantic epic may itself seem somewhat broadly Dantean, for the extent of *The Faerie Queene*'s anagogy much overgoes even the sixteenth-century commentators' *Orlando Furioso* and *Gerusalemme Liberata*. More strongly than most premodern allegories, the *Commedia* and *Faerie Queene* both posit a transcendental vanishing point of their signification that tacitly defines their allegorical perspective: the Logos or One, as it were, beyond the multiplicities of the phenomenal world, ineffable in its sublime truth.[25] At some points *The Faerie Queene*'s elusive namesake, 'th' Idole of *her makers* great magnificence', appears much like divine Sapience in Spenser's *Hymne to Heauenly Beautie* (II.ii.41, my emphasis).[26] Gloriana's face and Arthur's shield are bedazzling unless veiled (I.vii.33–5; viii.19; II, Proem 5). Yet as in Book I's Contemplation episode, and perhaps in reaction to the *Paradiso*, Spenser defines the limits of his fiction, language, and imagery much more cautiously than Dante (I.x.53–61). Most often, Spenser obliquely intimates transcendental content *within* and *through* his realm of faery, as in Redcrosse's reception at liberated Eden, or the Graces' theophany upon Mount Acidale. Gloriana's elusiveness and the veilings of Una and Arthur's shield epitomize this general obliquity. Much has been written on Milton's notions and techniques of theological 'accommodation' (how to write about what cannot be written about), and though relatively unexplored in Spenser studies, such topics have no less importance for his poetry.

As with Homer, Virgil, Ovid, Ariosto, and Tasso, Dante's early modern reception is richly documented, and comparatively clarifies Spenser's allegorical techniques. In the critical controversies about the *Commedia*, for example, some said that its poetic diction should not have incorporated so many technical terms from the intellectual disciplines, for poetry should not seem like disputation. Instead, they argued, the conceptual dimensions of such poems should be more wholly allegorized, as in Homer's epics (Caesar 1989: 292–3). Despite the relevance of many technical terms to the *Faerie Queene*'s conceptual content, such as 'concupiscence' throughout Book II, Spenser eschews them, partly because they would rupture the quasi-verisimilar impressions of his fictive world. Hence the expression and recognition of ideas animating his allegory depend more on allusion, symbolic imagery, and wordplay unobtrusively evoking former philosophical and theological terms and concepts (Borris 2000: 101–6). We can also gain insight into Spenser's literary practice and milieu from the *Commedia*'s commentaries. Only 8 of its 36 sixteenth-century editions lacked any such expositions, and the commentary that predominated throughout that century, Cristoforo Landino's first published in 1481, privileged Neoplatonic allegoresis (D. Parker 1993: 108, 133–7). As in Landino's disquisition on the *Aeneid*, the *Commedia* thus allegorizes pursuit of the *summum bonum* through the course of life, a basic theme of much early modern heroic poetry, including *The Faerie Queene* (Borris 2000: Chap. 3).

Notwithstanding Spenser's attractions to Greco-Roman antiquity and native and other medieval models, much of his effort to reform English poetics reflects contemporary Continental literary values, writings, and vogues. Around 1580, when some portions of *The Faerie Queene* had already been drafted, Spenser's Rosalind and his friend Harvey were calling him '*Segnior Pegaso*', 'Italianate', and 'French'.[27] Erudite allegory, pastoral eclogues, and Italian romantic epics were all the height of literary fashion in late-sixteenth-century Europe. By transferring 'learnings threasures' and the Muses themselves from the Latinate Parnassus to the Italianate '*Parnasso*' in *The Faerie Queene* (VI Proem, 2), Spenser assigns Italy pre-eminence in current poetic and intellectual inspirations, while congratulating his own up-to-date literary and intellectual *italianismo* (cf. Chapter 33 below).

English sixteenth-century allegorical fictions prior to *The Shepheardes Calender* demonstrate the revolutionary genius of Spenser's poetic intervention. Though some say Spenser modeled *The Faerie Queene* or at least Book I on either or both of Stephen Hawes' clumsy conflations of allegory and romance, *The Example of Virtue* (1504?) and his optimistically titled *Pastime of Pleasure* (1509), romantic allegorism and the alleged parallels have many potential precedents (Edwards 1990: 348; P. Parker 1990: 609–18). None of Hawes's writings was published after 1555 until centuries later, and if Spenser had consulted the *Example* or *Pastime* and persevered, he would most have learned how not to write verse, narrative, and allegory. A more revealing though still turgid forerunner is Stephen Bateman's *Travayled Pylgrime* (1569), a versified chivalric allegory of pilgrimage involving anti-papist Tudor dynastic celebration (Prescott 1989). This unacknowledged adaptation of Olivier de La Marche's *Chevalier délibré* (1483) gives Elizabethan Protestant expression to an originally medieval narrative tradition wherein life is a pilgrimage involving parabolic prodigality. Further instancing that model's continued currency is William Goodyear's translation of Jean de Cartigny's allegorical romance *Le Voyage du chevalier errant* (1557), *The Wandering Knight* (1581). Spenser's depiction of Redcrosse combines heroico-romantic journeying with prodigally inflected pilgrimage, and that merger not only contextualizes the subsequent quests of virtue, but underwrites the conclusion of the 1596 *Faerie Queene* (Borris 2006).

By October of 1579, Spenser and Sidney had attained 'familiarity' in London, just as the latter was about to commence his *Defence of Poetry*, probably begun in 1580, and his incipiently heroic Arcadian romances (*Prose*, 6). Reflecting wide study of contemporary Continental literary criticism, the *Defence* advocates an allegorical poetic, as Sidney's own private secretary states in a summary prepared for Sidney himself, and the *Arcadias* reflect that theory (Borris 2000: Chap. 4). Though none of these Sidneian writings was printed until 1590, they had already circulated somewhat in manuscript; both *Arcadias* and Spenser's Book II feature a character named Pyrochles.

Whether vernacular or neo-Latin, the early modern Continental literature that affected Spenser's allegorism originated mainly in Italy and France. Francesco Colonna's strangely lovely *Hypnerotomachia Polyphilo* (1499) instances the enchantments of his era with esoteric verbal-visual symbolism. Spenser certainly studied the French Pléiade, and his own program for reshaping his nation's literature somewhat recalls theirs, which valorized erudite allegorism, allegoresis of ancient poetry including Homer's (following Jean Dorat), Platonizing content and poetic furor, and the emulation of Greek, Roman, and Italian models. For Spenser's *Faerie Queene*, already envisaged in his *Calender*, heroic precedents were most important, and Italy provided the most internationally renowned 'modern' exemplars and culture of literary assessment (Aguzzi 1959; Weinberg 1961). Though Spenser plundered those riches avidly enough to raid even Giangiorgio Trissino's relatively obscure *L'Italia Liberata dai Goti* (1547–8) when allegorizing Temperance, it was Ariosto's runaway success that he avowedly sought to 'ouergo'.[28] Aside from Homer and Virgil, the poets named in the 'Letter to Raleigh' are Ariosto and Torquato Tasso, who provide authoritative precedents for *The Faerie Queene*'s departures from ancient epic norms.

Ariosto and Tasso most illuminate Spenser's allegorism when we further study their early modern reception documented in commentaries, critical controversies, and treatises on poetics. Historicist approaches to Spenser's poetry should attend to such evidence of contemporary hermeneutic concerns and practices. Completed around 1532, Ariosto's *Orlando Furioso* exemplified how features of classical epic could be combined with chivalric romance to treat topics of love and war through multiple, relatively episodic actions involving allegory, fantastic invention, historical survey, and some quasi-Virgilian dynastic celebration. The medulla of Ariostan allegorism is the Logistilla-Alcina episode, where sensual desires tempt Ruggiero from adherence to reason. This adaptation of moral philosophy, theology, and Platonism to heroico-romantic expression epitomizes some main aims, themes, and techniques of sixteenth-century allegorical heroic poetry including Spenser's. Ariosto's commentators analyzed and codified them, as in Sir John Harington's account derived from Italian sources (1972: 558–78). Spenser's program of literary studies would likely have included the more substantial commentaries on the *Orlando Furioso*, such as Simone Fornari's two-part *Spositione* published in 1549–50 (Borris 2006: 156–8). Explicit critical models for allegorical heroic poetry were rapidly developing.

A leading early modern literary theorist as well as poet, Tasso increasingly favored allegorical poetics especially in heroic contexts. Most important for Spenser among Tasso's writings would have been his major romantic epic the *Gerusalemme Liberata* (1581), and most editions included the 'Letter to Raleigh''s clearest precedent, Tasso's explanatory 'Allegoria del poema'. There he analyzes the principles, themes, and conventions of allegorical heroic poetry, and how they apply to his poem, even explicating some imagery and wordplay (1981: 88–93). Although a surviving letter indicates that Tasso added much of his allegory relatively late in the poem's composition, the 'Allegoria' mediated the text to its public and reinforced the already strong linkages of allegory with heroic poetry in particular (Borris 2000: 41–6; see below p. 539). Rational control of the concupiscible and irascible appetites was fundamental in early modern moral philosophy, and Tasso's account of his allegorization of this conceptual scheme clarifies some main bases and innovations of Spenser's allegory of Temperance. Tasso's poem accumulated various commentaries involving allegoresis, and in 1586, John Wolfe, who was to print the 1590 *Faerie Queene*, published Scipione Gentili's in London. Though the *Gerusalemme Liberata* is more piously Christian, tonally serious, and classically unified in its action than the *Orlando Furioso*, Tasso published a still more earnest revision in 1593, the *Gerusalemme Conquistata*. Spenser mediates between Ariosto's romantic exuberance and Tasso's relative gravity.

The 'composite heroism' of *The Faerie Queene* is its central correlation with early modern allegoresis of Ariosto's and Tasso's heroic poems. As Spenser's 'Letter to Raleigh' states, he adumbrates Arthur's inclusive virtue through representatives of particular virtues, and they in turn have various subcharacters. This affords an allegorical unity of action subsumed in Arthur and his prospective union with Gloriana. Sixteenth-century commentators on Ariosto similarly condensed his *Orlando*'s diverse characters and multiple plots into broad allegorical or thematic structures. Tasso's *Allegoria* explains that his whole cast of protagonists constitutes a composite heroic persona concentrated in his general, Godfrey, who signifies the rational soul (Borris 2000: 84–8).

Yet however much Spenser drew generic insights, narrative materials, thematic content, symbolic conventions, and allegorical technique from Ariosto's and Tasso's precedents and reception, even translating Tasso at times,[29] he made them means of creative innovation. In Book V, for example, he based the climactic Arthurian Belge story on Ariosto's oppressed Olympia of the Low Countries, yet combined that narrative pretext with elements of England's recent military intervention there, the Book of Revelation, and Protestant historiography, so as to allegorize the relation of Justice to world history (Borris 1991: Chaps. 1–3). Spenser's complex allegorism characteristically evinces such resourceful *bricolage*, and he incorporates, as in this case, a much more diverse range of discourses, genres, and topics than even Ariosto. Insofar as heroic poetry was supposed to be encyclopedic, Spenser's romantic variant far overgoes its Italian precursors, even to the extent of recalling Ovid's mercurial inclusions, surveys, and modal epic samplings in the *Metamorphoses*. The Faerie *Queene*'s intensive allegorism enhances its scope by enabling the narrative to epitomize and coordinate diverse frames of reference at once. Aside from much expanding the historical and national content of Ariosto's and Tasso's heroic poems, the allegory of Spenser's Faery adds or augments various other ingredients including religious satire; erotic mysticism, drawing on Platonic theories of love and beauty; metaphysical speculation, as in the Garden of Adonis; and anagogy.

Spenser's resources of allegorical representation are themselves more varied than Ariosto's and Tasso's. Each book in *The Faerie Queene* has an allegorical repertoire and technique that are both correlative to those of its siblings and yet distinctive. Compared to its chief Italian precursors, *The Faerie Queene* includes more personified or 'demonsterative' abstractions, beginning with Errour. In that way it is comparable not only to medieval allegorical poetry, but also to the later ancient epics such as the *Aeneid*, where Virgil so uses Rumour and the fury Allecto, and to early modern visual allegories. While appearing, like Ariosto and Tasso, to avoid otherworldly matter such as Dante's in favor of a romance-epic *mise en scène*, Spenser much heightens that fictive world through faery idealization and allegory presenting avatars of ideals, such as Una, Belphoebe, and Alma.

As Virgil's relation to Homer is knowingly self-conscious and allusive, like James Joyce's, so likewise is Spenser's allegorism in relation to his precursors. In totality that aspect of his poetic genome would comprise not only further literary models and intertexts beyond the scope of this synopsis, but the manifold non-literary materials relevant to his allegories. Spenser's *Calender* and especially his *Faerie Queene* at once survey the past from antiquity onward in stylized, reinterpreted form, yet anticipate a cultural future they have changed through the enduring force and scope of their experimental reformulations. The poet's invention of the Spenserian stanza epitomizes these traits, and from the *Calender* onward he was distinctively drawn to open-formed, additive narrative structures that readily accommodated prolific variety and innovative play with readers' expectations of fictional patterns, meanings, and resolutions. So much remains to be understood about Spenser's landmark of allegorical fiction that even the basics of the faery queen's significance remain debatable. Glory in what sense or senses: simply regnant Elizabeth's, as some say, or also adumbrated 'grace and majesty diuine' (I Proem, 4)? Early modern allegory typically has a transcendental orientation, and Spenser's philosophical affinities are idealist. So in view of current interest in early modern material culture, recently introduced to Spenser studies (Burlinson 2006), what is the status of materiality in this poet's kind of allegorical mimesis? And how does Spenserian allegory develop? In the later twentieth century many critics assumed that *The Faerie Queene*'s investment in allegory declines, especially in Book VI; but more recent criticism argues it becomes more subtly complex and various. Do the *Mutability Cantos* inaugurate an altogether new and most critically self-reflexive phase of Spenser's allegorism? There he has been said to interrogate premodern allegory's metaphysical foundations and expose the processes of their construction and its hidden costs (Teskey 1990: 22; 1996: Chap. 8). Spenser strongly evokes such meditations on the directions of his allegorical poetic because his *Calender* and most of all his *Faerie Queene* promote reflection upon allegorism's operations, capacities, and transformations of the resources of thought and culture through its dark conceits. In doing so these poems continue to reshape our thinking.

NOTES

1. See further Whitman (2000).
2. Broadly synonymous terms in the Renaissance (e.g., Cooper 1565). On the elusive semantics, see Fraunce (1991), 2–3, 106.
3. La Perrière (1539), sig. B5^a. He added that phrase upon further reflection, for it does not appear in the first edition (also issued in 1539).
4. Compare La Perrière (1539), sig. A4^b–5^a. See Bath (1994), 51–2, 132–6; Russell (1995), 116–24; Daly (1998), 17–27.
5. Such as Fracastoro (1924), 60, 71. Idealized imitation also had quasi-Aristotelian versions that were less overtly Platonized. See Panofsky (1968); Steadman (1974). For applications to Spenser's allegory, see Borris (2009a).
6. *The Faerie Queene* refers to the divine image both directly (e.g., I.x.39, 42; IV.vi.17) and indirectly (e.g., IV.viii.30–3; VI Proem, 3).
7. Appropriating Coleridge's phrasing on symbol, quoted earlier. In other words, Una would have appeared to partake of the transcendental origins and prospects attributed to humanity. Cf. Redcrosse envisioning the New Jerusalem (I.x.55–61), Guyon anticipating 'heauenly Registers aboue the Sunne' where 'Saints' reside (II.i.32), and also the concept of the Church as members of Christ's body.
8. Compare Frye (1965), 12–15; Nohrnberg (1976), 93–4.
9. See Fletcher (1964), 35–8 on allegorical subcharacters (his term).
10. Teskey (2007); compare MacCaffrey (1976).
11. For further discussion of points in this paragraph and its successor, see Borris (2000), Ch. 2.
12. Drawing on Fowler (1982), 192.
13. Studies of the antecedents and development of early modern allegorical heroic poetry include Aguzzi (1959); Murrin (1980); Treip (1994); Borris (2000).
14. Whitman (2000), 295–9, summarizes and critiques Benjamin's approach.
15. As in the late sixteenth-century poetics of, e.g., Giovanni Viperano (1987: 71–3) and Tasso (1981: 88). See further Borris (2000), Ch. 1.

16. The standard studies of mythography in Renaissance culture are Seznec (1953), Wind (1968), and Allen (1970).
17. See Harington (1972), 3–7; Fraunce (1592), sig. B1^b–B2^a; and Conti (2006), 1: 1–3.
18. See Borris (2000), 39; cf. Pendergast (2006), 48–51.
19. On traditional allegoresis of these poems, see Allen (1970); Lamberton (1986); Clarke (1981); Warner (2005). On their recent allegoresis, see Laird (2003), 170.
20. See, e.g., McCabe (2002) and O'Connell (1990).
21. See Anderson (2008), Parts 1–2.
22. Miskimin (1975), Ch. 8. Krier's (1998) collection further surveys Renaissance Chaucer.
23. Harvey, *Letter-Book* (1884: 58). On Protestant appropriation, see Caesar (1989), 30–1, 273–6, 278–9. Sidney (1973), 74, 89, 121 cites Dante.
24. See Caesar (1989), 23–5, 32–5, 279–88; Weinberg (1961), 2: 819–911, 1106–12.
25. See Teskey's incisive account of Spenser's allegorism, (1990), 16–17.
26. See Fruen (1994), 56, 82 n 9, and Borris (2009b).
27. *Prose*, 466, 474; Harvey's *Letter-Book* (1884), 58, 65.
28. Quoting Harvey, *Prose*, 471. For an invaluable list of *The Faerie Queene*'s many proposed correlations with Italian poems, see Kostić (1969), 364–80. He marks those he doubts with an asterisk. The list evinces somewhat fewer correlations for the 1596 installment than for 1590, but still well over 150. The apparent decrease may just result from the 1590 text's predominance in Spenser scholarship to date.
29. See further, e.g., Kostić (1969), 364–80; Marinelli (1990), 56–7; Kennedy (1990), 363–5; Quint (1990), 678–9.

BIBLIOGRAPHY

Aguzzi, D. A. (1959). *Allegory in the Heroic Poetry of the Renaissance*. PhD dissertation, Columbia University.

Allen, D. C. (1970). *Mysteriously Meant: The Rediscovery of Pagan Symbolism and Allegorical Interpretation in the Renaissance*. Baltimore: Johns Hopkins University Press.

Anderson, J. H. (1990). 'Langland, William', in *SE*, 425–6.

—— (2008). *Reading the Allegorical Intertext: Chaucer, Spenser, Shakespeare, Milton*. New York: Fordham University Press.

Bath, M. (1994). *Speaking Pictures: English Emblem Books and Renaissance Culture*. London: Longman.

Benjamin, W. (1972). *Ursprung des deutschen Trauerspiels*. Frankfurt: Suhrkamp.

Besserman, L. (1998). *Chaucer's Biblical Poetics*. Norman: University of Oklahoma Press.

Borris, K. (1991). *Spenser's Poetics of Prophecy in* The Faerie Queene V. Victoria: University of Victoria Press.

—— (2000). *Allegory and Epic in English Renaissance Literature: Heroic Form in Sidney, Spenser, Milton*. Cambridge: Cambridge University Press.

—— (2006). 'Sub Rosa: Pastorella's Allegorical Homecoming and Closure in the 1596 *Faerie Queene*'. *SSt* 21: 133–80.

—— (2009a). 'Platonism and Spenser's Poetic: Idealized Imitation, Merlin's Mirror, and the Florimells'. *SSt* 24: 209–68.

—— (2009b). 'Reassessing Ellrodt: Critias and the *Fowre Hymnes* in *The Faerie Queene*'. *SSt* 24: 453–80.

Burlinson, C. (2006). *Allegory, Space and the Material World in the Writings of Edmund Spenser*. Cambridge: D. S. Brewer.

Caesar, M. (1989). *Dante: The Critical Heritage, 1314(?)–1870*. London: Routledge.

Clarke, H. W. (1981). *Homer's Readers: A Historical Introduction to the 'Iliad' and the 'Odyssey'*. Newark: University of Delaware Press.

Coleridge, Samuel Taylor (1972). *The Statesman's Manual, in Lay Sermons, Collected Works*, ed. R. J. White. Princeton, NJ: Princeton University Press, VI. 3–52.

Conti, Natale (2006). *Mythologiae*, trans. J. Mulryan and S. Brown, 2 vols. Tempe: ACMRS.

Cooper, Thomas (1565). *Thesaurus linguae Romanae et Britannicae*. London: Henry Wykes.

Culler, J. (1985). 'Changes in the Study of the Lyric', in C. Hošek and P. Parker (eds), *Lyric Poetry: Beyond New Criticism*. Ithaca, NY: Cornell University Press, 38–54.

Daly, P. M. (1998). *Literature in the Light of the Emblem*, 2nd rev edn. Toronto: University of Toronto Press.

De Man, P. (1969). 'The Rhetoric of Temporality', in C. S. Singleton (ed.), *Interpretation: Theory and Practice*. Baltimore: Johns Hopkins Press, 173–209.

Drysdall, D. L. (1999). 'Authorities for Symbolism in the Sixteenth Century', in P. M. Daly and J. Manning (eds), *Aspects of Renaissance and Baroque Symbol Theory 1500–1700*. New York: AMS, 111–24.

—— (1994). 'Budé on "symbolē, symbolon" (Text and Translation)'. *Emblematica* 8: 339–49.

Edwards, A. S. G. (1990). 'Hawes, Stephen', in *SE*, 348.

Fletcher, A. (1964). *Allegory: The Theory of a Symbolic Mode*. Ithaca, NY: Cornell University Press.

Fornari, Simone (1549–50). *La spositione sopra l'Orlando Furioso di Ludovico Ariosto*, 2 vols. Florence: Lorenzo Torrentino.

Fowler, A. (1982). *Kinds of Literature: An Introduction to the Theory of Genres and Modes*. Cambridge, MA: Harvard University Press.

Fracastoro, Girolamo (1924). *Naugerius*, trans. Ruth Kelso. Urbana: University of Illinois.

Fraunce, Abraham (1991). *Symbolicae philosophiae liber quartus et ultimus*, ed. J. Manning and trans. E. Haan. New York: AMS.

—— (1592). *The Third Part of the Countesse of Pembrokes Yuychurch*. London: Thomas Woodcocke.

Friedman, J. B. (1972). 'Antichrist and the Iconography of Dante's Geryon'. *JWCI* 35: 108–22.

Fruen, J. P. (1994). 'The Faery Queen Unveiled? Five Glimpses of Gloriana'. *SSt* 11: 53–88.

Frye, N. (1965) 'Allegory', in A. Preminger et al. (eds), *Encyclopedia of Poetry and Poetics*. Princeton, NJ: Princeton University Press.

Gentili, Scipione (1586). *Annotationi sopra la Gierusalemme Liberata di Torquato Tasso*. London: John Wolfe.

Gombrich, E. H. (1972). '*Icones Symbolicae*: Philosophies of Symbolism and their Bearing on Art', in *Symbolic Images: Studies in the Art of the Renaissance*. Oxford: Phaidon, 123–95.

Harington, Sir John (1972). 'A Preface, or Rather, A Briefe Apologie of Poetrie', and 'A Briefe and Summarie Allegorie', in Lodovico Ariosto, *Orlando Furioso*, ed. Robert McNulty. Oxford: Clarendon Press, 1–15, 558–78.

Harvey, Gabriel (1884). *Letter-Book*, ed. E. J. L. Scott. London: Camden Society.

Kennedy, W. J. (1990). 'Heroic Poem before Spenser', in *SE*, 363–5.

King, A. (2000). *'The Faerie Queene' and Middle English Romance: The Matter of Just Memory*. Oxford: Clarendon Press.

Kostić, V. (1969). *Spenser's Sources in Italian Poetry*. Belgrade: University of Belgrade Press.

Krier, T. M. (ed.) (1998). *Refiguring Chaucer in the Renaissance*. Gainesville: University Press of Florida.

Laird, A. (2003). 'Figures of Allegory from Homer to Latin Epic', in G. R. Boys-Stones (ed.), *Metaphor, Allegory, and the Classical Tradition: Ancient Thought and Modern Revisionism*. Oxford: Oxford University Press, 151–75.

Lamberton, R. (1986). *Homer the Theologian: Neoplatonist Allegorical Reading and the Growth of the Epic Tradition*. Berkeley: University of California Press.

La Perrière, Guillaume de (1539). *Le Theatre des bons engines*, 2nd rev edn. Paris: Denis Janot.

McCabe, R. A. (2002). *Spenser's Monstrous Regiment: Elizabethan Ireland and the Poetics of Difference*. Oxford: Oxford University Press.

MacCaffrey, I. G. (1976). *Spenser's Allegory: The Anatomy of Imagination*. Princeton, NJ: Princeton University Press.

Manning, J. (2002). *The Emblem*. London: Reaktion.

Marinelli, P. (1990). 'Ariosto, Lodovico', in *SE*, 56–7.

Mignault, Claude. (1577). *Syntagma de symbolis*. In Andrea Alciato, *Omnia emblematum*. Antwerp: Christoph Plantin, 29–43.

Miskimin, A. S. (1975). *The Renaissance Chaucer*. New Haven, CT: Yale University Press.

Murrin, M. (1980). *The Allegorical Epic: Essays in Its Rise and Decline*. Chicago: University of Chicago Press.

Nohrnberg, J. (1976). *The Analogy of 'The Faerie Queene'*. Princeton, NJ: Princeton University Press.

O'Connell, M. (1990). 'Allegory, Historical', in *SE*, 23–4.

Panofsky, E. (1968). *Idea: A Concept in Art Theory*, trans. J. J. S. Peake. Columbia: University of South Carolina Press.

Parker, D. (1993). *Commentary and Ideology: Dante in the Renaissance*. Durham: Duke University Press.

Parker, P. (1990). 'Romance', in *SE*, 609–18.

Pendergast, J. S. (2006). *Religion, Allegory, and Literacy in Early Modern England, 1560–1640: The Control of the Word*. Aldershot: Ashgate.

Prescott, A. L. (1989). 'Spenser's Chivalric Restoration: From Bateman's *Travayled Pylgrime* to the Redcrosse Knight'. *SP* 86: 166–97.

Pugh, S. (2005). *Spenser and Ovid*. Aldershot: Ashgate.

Quilligan, M. (1979). *The Language of Allegory: Defining the Genre*. Ithaca, NY: Cornell University Press.

Quint, D. (1990). 'Tasso, Torquato', in *SE*, 678–9.

Rigby, S. H. (1996). *Chaucer in Context: Society, Allegory, and Gender*. Manchester: Manchester University Press.

Russell, D. (1995). *Emblematic Structures in Renaissance French Culture*. Toronto: University of Toronto Press.

Seznec, J. (1953). *The Survival of the Pagan Gods: The Mythological Tradition and Its Place in Renaissance Humanism and Art*, trans. B. F. Sessions. New York: Pantheon-Bollingen.

Sidney, Sir Philip (1973). *A Defence of Poetry*, in *Miscellaneous Prose*, ed. Katherine Duncan-Jones and Jan Van Dorsten. Oxford: Clarendon Press, 73–121.

Steadman, J. M. (1974). *The Lamb and the Elephant: Ideal Imitation and the Context of Renaissance Allegory*. San Marino: Huntington Library.

Tasso, Torquato (1981). 'The Allegorie of the Poem', in *Godfrey of Bulloigne (Gerusalemme Liberata)*, trans. Edward Fairfax, ed. K. M. Lea and T. M. Gang. Oxford: Clarendon Press, 88–93.

—— (1973). *Discourses on the Heroic Poem*, trans. M. Cavalchini and I. Samuel. Oxford: Clarendon Press.

Teskey, G. (1990). 'Allegory', in *SE*, 16–22.

—— (1996). *Allegory and Violence*. Ithaca, NY: Cornell University Press.

—— (2007). 'Thinking Moments in *The Faerie Queene*'. *SSt* 22: 103–25.

Treip, M. A. (1994). *Allegorical Poetics and the Epic: The Renaissance Tradition to 'Paradise Lost'*. Lexington: University Press of Kentucky.

Viperano, Giovanni Antonio (1987). *On Poetry*, trans. P. Rollinson. Greenwood: Attic Press.

Warner, J. C. (2005). *The Augustinian Epic, Petrarch to Milton*. Ann Arbor: University of Michigan Press.

Weinberg, B. (1961). *A History of Literary Criticism in the Italian Renaissance*, 2 vols. Chicago: University of Chicago Press.

Whitman, J. (1987). *Allegory: The Dynamics of an Ancient and Medieval Technique*. Cambridge, MA: Harvard University Press.

—— (2000). 'Present Perspectives: The Late Middle Ages to the Modern World', in J. Whitman (ed.), *Interpretation and Allegory: Antiquity to the Modern Period*. Brill: Leiden, 260–314.

Wind, E. (1968). *Pagan Mysteries in the Renaissance*, 2nd rev edn. New York: Barnes and Noble.

CHAPTER 25

....

AUTHORIAL SELF-PRESENTATION

....

RICHARD A. McCABE

THE creation of an authorial 'persona' is arguably the principal means by which a poet negotiates his own 'canonicity', engaging in a dialogue with posterity through the contemporary reader. It involves not just the textual 'I' of the poetic speaker, but the paratextual 'I' of the dedicator, commentator, and explicator. The argument of this essay is that Spenser's various personae are sophisticated rhetorical devices designed to appropriate the readerly 'you' into an appreciative 'we'. Daniel's 1594 reference to 'our Spencer' testifies to the success of the endeavour (Cummings, 75), but Spenser was equally well equipped, as we shall see, to make aesthetic capital out of apparent rejection. To adopt such an approach to self-presentation is to restore it to the rhetorical category of 'ethos' or characterization, and particularly to the art of persuasion through characterization (see May 1998: 1–12). It is to recognize in the illusion of a professedly confessional or lyrical mode an ongoing process of adjustment to the ever-changing demands of genre, circumstance, and audience. We must not be too hasty in hailing 'the growth of a personal voice' in Spenser (Anderson 1976), lest we lose the element of 'persona' in the early modern sense of the 'personal'.

We need to begin, however, by asking what is meant by 'self-presentation'? What sort of 'self' is presented behind, or through, a 'persona' or mask? *The Faerie Queene* begins with the lines, 'Lo I the man, whose Muse whylome did maske, | As time her taught, in lowly Shephards weeds'. The act of moving from pastoral to epic is hereby presented not just as an act of changing 'masks' but of adopting a wholly new style of 'masquing', a new role for a new form of verbal 'play'. The author is presented as actor. And somewhere beneath all the camouflage, we are assured, is 'I the man'. But

AUTHORIAL SELF-PRESENTATION

which man? Is the 'I' that speaks in Spenser's numerous prefaces, proems, and dedications to be identified with the 'I' that speaks in the poems as narrator, lover, complainer, or visionary? What is the relationship of the paratextual to the textual 'I', of the self that writes to the self that is written?

The Spenserian canon is littered with references to the author's life: to his ancestry, his age, his marriage, his travels, his patrons, his friends, and his enemies (Anderson 1996; D. Cheney 1983; P. Cheney 1987; Helgerson 1978). Such references form part of a strategy which I have elsewhere termed auto-referential rather than auto-biographical, the distinction being that while it would be impossible to construct Spenser's biography from his writings, he makes it equally impossible to read them without some reference to his life (Spenser 1999: xvii). Glossing Hobbinol's invitation to Colin in the *June* eclogue of *The Shepheardes Calender*, for example, E. K. tells us that, 'This is no poetical fiction, but unfeynedly spoken of the Poete selfe, who for speciall occasion of private affayres (as I have bene partly of himselfe informed) and for his more preferment removing out of the Northparts came into the South, as Hobbinoll indeede advised him privately' (18).[1] What matters here is not whether this information is strictly true or false, but why we have been given it at all. What literary function does it perform, and what sort of hermeneutic is 'E. K.' trying to cultivate in the reader? Although the information he discloses is alleged to concern the author's 'preferment' and is twice designated as 'private', he is prepared to publish it to anyone who happens upon the *Calender*. A sophisticated rhetorical game is being played at this point. E. K. identifies Hobbinol as Gabriel Harvey and tells us that 'Colin' is the name 'under whose person the Authour selfe is shadowed' (Spenser 1999: 28). But for 'person' we must read 'persona', if for no other reason than that 'Colin Clout' was originally invented, as the same gloss informs us, by John Skelton. It is not only a 'poetical fiction', but another poet's fiction (Kinsman 1950).[2] And it is by no means coincidental, in terms of the author's 'preferment', that the other poet was commonly designated 'poet laureate' (Griffiths 2004).[3] The appropriation of the pseudonym anticipates that of the title.

In the sphere of the visual arts the early modern period saw the rise of the self-portrait, a development that has been convincingly related to 'the prevailing Renaissance ideology concerning the social status of art and artists'. Such self-portraits were 'created to mediate between the artistic self...and its Renaissance audience' (Woods-Marsden 1998: 1). The same is true, I would argue, of the poetic self-portrait. *The Shepheardes Calender* is an illustrated work, and its readers can 'see' Colin Clout in the woodcuts to *Januarye*, *Aprill*, *June*, *November*, and *December*. But what they see is a stylized figure in an emblematic landscape. When the *October* eclogue asks, 'O pierlesse Poesye, where is then thy place?' it links the ancient topos of self-presentation with Elizabethan topography, thereby establishing an association that persists through Spenser's career. Whether he is writing epic from the 'wastes' of Ireland, walking dejectedly along the banks of the Thames, or pondering the mutability of life on Arlo Hill, Spenser is always careful to locate, or dislocate, his persona. Such landscapes function as inscapes, charting the topography of the 'self' in all its variety. The Colin of *The Shepheardes Calender* is a denizen of Eliza's England; that of *Colin Clouts Come Home Againe* visits her court as a stranger from overseas. But even within the *Calender* Colin had appeared in multiple guises: as dejected lover, royal eulogist, despondent poet, pastoral friend, or noble elegist—moods and modes reflected in and through the visual and verbal landscapes of woodcut and verse. Such poses are as far from presenting a biography of the poet as are the accompanying illustrations from affording his portrait. But both have to do with the mediation of the 'artistic self', or the literary career. We tend to speak loosely of a persona such as 'Colin Clout' as constituting an 'alter ego' but without acknowledging the fundamental sense of 'alterity' in that expression: not just 'another self' but the self as 'other'. The *Calender*'s principal narrator, who calls himself 'Immerito', is at pains to distance himself from Colin despite the gloss that works to identify them. He introduces Colin in potentially disparaging terms: 'a shepeheards boye (no better doe him call)' (*Januarie*, 1). A problematical relationship is hereby established between the two figures from the outset: it is unclear whether the persona of Colin Clout is one of self-presentation, self-exploration, or self-parody. 'Colin' ends the *Calender* in dejection, 'Immerito' in exultation. In fact, if he is to proceed from pastoral to epic verse, Colin is the persona that Immerito must abandon— hence the shock of his recurrence in 1595 and 1596 after *December*'s sixfold 'adieu' (151–6). But the shock is part of a well-planned strategy. Simultaneously traditional and innovative, self and other, 'Colin' provided his creator with a powerful vehicle for mediating authorial anxieties to the reader in an aesthetically productive and suitably distanced manner. Even Colin's most apparently idiosyncratic gesture, the breaking of his pipes, is deeply rooted in pastoral convention (Kelsey and Peterson 2000). He speaks an ancient language of complaint but with a teasingly Elizabethan inflexion.

To speak in terms of a poetic 'career' raises the issue of teleology. The so-called Virgilian 'rota' or 'wheel' is sometimes seen to have presented Spenser with a template of movement from pastoral through georgic to epic poetry, and Spenser's initial choice of pastoral could certainly be seen in those terms (P. Cheney 1993). A desire to emulate Virgil might even generate the sort of 'anxiety of influence' (to use Harold Bloom's term) that necessitates professions of humility and self-deprecation in the very act of self-advertisement. But the idea, though attractive, is questionable. Sixteenth-century editions of Virgil contained a lot of material that defied categorization as pastoral, georgic, or epic, and to choose to emulate a classical poet in the *vernacular* was to open up a site of opportunity rather than anxiety (Kerrigan 1980: 287). The diverse authorial personae that Spenser proceeded to adopt suggest that he was not so much following the Virgilian rota as reinventing the authorial wheel. In the figure of 'Tityrus' he gestures not just towards Virgil but towards Chaucer, a conflation of classical and native traditions intended to produce a vernacular 'classic' identical to neither. And, by way of marking this achievement, he kindly provides in E. K. an editor prepared to treat a vernacular work as a classic (McCabe 1995).

THE NEW POET AND HIS EDITOR:
IMMERITO AND E. K.

....

Although the term 'self-presentation' was not used in the early modern period, the concept was familiar: 'Goe little booke: thy selfe present', says Immerito to *The Shepheardes Calender* (1579). He was employing an ancient trope in using the book as metonym for the author, conflating 'thou' and 'mee': 'when thou art past jeopardee, | Come tell me, what was sayd of mee'. Yet the adoption of anonymity would seem to be a very odd way to make one's name: 'But if that any aske thy name, | Say thou wert base begot with blame'. There was certainly some reason for caution. The political situation was dangerous. In so far as it touched upon the subject of the Queen's proposed marriage to the Duke of Alençon afterwards Anjou, the *Calender* courted considerable 'jeopardee'. Only a few months previously both the author and publisher of the notorious anti-Alençon diatribe, *The Discoverie of a Gaping Gulf whereinto England is likely to be Swallowed*, had lost their right hands for daring to oppose the Queen's marital intentions. The title page of the *The Shepheardes Calender* cultivates an aura of danger by dedicating the work to Philip Sidney, one of the principal opponents of the marriage, and by identifying the printer as Hugh Singleton, the printer of *The Discoverie* (McLane 1961). Its anonymous author appears on the literary scene as a potentially oppositional figure rather than a supporter of the establishment, as a prospective satirist as much as a future laureate.

But there was more to Spenser's anonymity than that. One of his greatest literary skills was the ability to translate political necessity into aesthetic advantage. The element of the covert had long been recognized as a principal component of pastoral poetry (Alexander 2004: 89). From the classical period onwards commentators on Virgil's *Eclogues* had detected an occluded element of opposition to Augustus beneath the veneer of praise, and E. K.'s first gloss to the *Calender* invokes the Virgilian exemplar when it informs us that 'Colin Cloute' is the pastoral pseudonym under which 'this Poete secretly shadoweth himself, as sometime did Virgil under the name of Tityrus'. Those familiar with Virgil, however, would notice a major discrepancy in this statement. Virgil's first eclogue takes the form of a dialogue between two very different speakers, Tityrus and Meliboeus. The former is the beneficiary of Augustus's patronage and speaks contentedly, the latter (through which it was commonly believed that Virgil voiced his opposition to Augustan policy) has been dispossessed of his lands and speaks disconsolately. The voice of Colin Clout, both in the *Calender* and throughout the wider Spenserian canon, is far more redolent of Meliboeus than Tityrus—and 'old Meliboe', a pastoral fugitive from the vanity of the court, is duly slaughtered by brigands in the sixth book of *The Faerie Queene*. It is as if Spenser has deliberately chosen to complete the story of Meliboeus's displacement that Virgil had begun to tell in the first eclogue, and to do so tragically. But in 1579 all of that lay in the future. More immediately, the Skeltonic associations of the name 'Colin Clout', together with the use of 'Colin' by the French poet Clément Marot, would have confirmed its oppositional associations for Spenser's first readers. Anonymity lent the frisson of the forbidden to Spenser's early verse; it withheld a name to create a reputation.

Because self-praise is traditionally regarded as no praise, one of the principal pitfalls of self-presentation is the likely imputation of conceit. In a wittily pre-emptive gesture Spenser allows E. K. to compare 'Immerito' to Narcissus who 'fell in love with his owne likenesse', thereby raising the issue of whether the creation of an alter ego serves to indulge or critique the 'self' (Spenser 1999: 127). The point is well taken since he also allows E. K. to compare Immerito to Theocritus, Virgil, Petrarch, Boccaccio, Mantuan, Marot, and Sannazarro, all the greatest 'names' in the Western pastoral tradition. Spenserian anonymity therefore involves two quite distinct forms of name-dropping. By means of illustrious association E. K. supplies his unnamed author with striking credentials and does the job so efficiently that his own identity has long been the subject of speculation. But it is far more profitable to discuss E. K.'s function than his identity, since the latter is clearly subordinate to the former. Spenser had learned a great deal from George Gascoigne, who skilfully wove webs of mystery around his work by generating a forest of initials and pseudonyms (Wilson 2006: 1–51). I have argued elsewhere that we need to locate *The Shepheardes Calender* in the context of a series of self-promotional publications that began in 1577 with Harvey's *Ciceronianus* and *Rhetor*, continued in 1578 with his *Smithus; vel Musarum Lachrymæ* and *Gratulationes Valdinenses*, and culminated with the publication of the *Calender* in 1579 and the Harvey–Spenser *Letters* in 1580 (McCabe 2007: 55–61). At this stage of their careers Harvey and Spenser would appear to have been working together, and the genesis of E. K. is most likely to be found in this collaboration.

As a literary editor E. K. has no existence outside the work on which he comments. Within it, however, he is given a distinct visual signature, a sort of printed voice articulated through a Roman typeface wholly distinct from the Gothic of Immerito's verse (McCabe 2000). But he remains as much a product of the *Calender* as its producer. In the Spenser–Harvey *Letters* of the following year where he is cited as a 'real' person, careful readers would notice that a couplet formerly attributed to him is asserted to have been 'translated . . . ex tempore' by Immerito (*Maye*, 69 gloss; *Prose*, 16). One should not be surprised. At critical moments in the *Calender* the two voices tend to merge, as when E. K. claims to draw upon his author's unpublished critical treatise 'the English Poete' to annotate *October*, thereby supplying Immerito's own vision of authorship to accompany the *Calender*'s principal discussion of literary patronage. Sometimes E. K. is privy to the author's 'secret meaning' but at other times conveniently not—with the predictable result that his denials of covert intention operate even more powerfully on the reader's imagination than his assertions.

As one would expect, E. K. represents himself merely as an interested third party, a friend of Harvey and confidant of Immerito, anxious that both of their works be drawn from manuscript circulation into print. It was a topos destined to recur through Spenser's career: William Ponsonby, the publisher of *Complaints*, asserts that the collection has been gathered together without the author's knowledge from scattered manuscripts, and Spenser alleges that manuscripts of the first pair of his *Fowre Hymnes* are circulating so widely that it is impossible to call them in. This was a singularly effective authorial strategy, lending to the act of printing the thrill of disclosing to a wider public materials formerly confined to a privileged readership. It also acted as a powerful prophylactic against the 'stigma' of print which consisted not in the fact of print per se—even the Queen was a published author—but in the implication of seeking one's livelihood through print, of being a mere tradesman in words. In promoting the publication of *The Shepheardes Calender*, E. K. gives us to understand that he has done signal service not just to his friend but to the nation. His dedicatory epistle to Harvey is in the nature of a literary manifesto, as revolutionary for its time as the 'Preface' to the *Lyrical Ballads*. It introduces its readers not to a new poet but to '*the* new poet' and that emphatically definite article informs all that follows. It is E. K. who contends that the use of archaism lends 'auctoritie' to Spenser's verse, a claim previously made by several leading Humanists for Petrarch (Kennedy 1995: 85–6). But as Petrarch's case suggests, 'auctoritie' is properly the prerogative of established poets, of those whose work has accumulated commentary over many generations. Indeed the power to generate such commentary was itself regarded as a hallmark of authority. E. K. functions to create 'auctoritie' *ab initio* by equipping the first edition of the *Calender* with the sort of commentary that attends the Classics, and by persistently suggesting that he is responding to comments generated in manuscript circulation. In this manner he fabricates a readerly pre-history for a brand new publication. Hence there is the suggestion in the gloss to *October* that 'some doubt' that Colin Clout and Cuddie are distinct characters. In such remarks, as in his lists of Immerito's yet unpublished poems, E. K. creates the illusion of a practised poet already well known and highly valued, but he also achieves something more important. By linking poetics to patriotism he raises the *Calender* to the sphere of public concern, using his prefatory epistles and gloss to present his unnamed author as a national figure in waiting, a Merito disguised as an Immerito. And his success is evident. By 1586 William Webbe was already invoking the 'authoritye' of 'Master Sp.' as 'the rightest English Poet, that ever I read', and one whose pastorals were 'inferiour to the workes neither of *Theocritus* in Greeke, nor *Virgill* in Latine' (Wells, I, 7). By 1588 we find Abraham Fraunce citing Spenser in *The Arcadian Rhetorike* as a stylistic authority alongside such writers as Horace, Virgil, Petrarch, Marot, and Tasso. In *The Lawiers Logike*, published the same year, Fraunce includes dozens of Spenserian quotations illustrative of various modes of logical argumentation (Koller 1940; Wells, I, 10–11). By 1589 Nashe was referring to 'divine Master *Spencer*' as the equal of any poet alive (Wells, I, 13). The *Calender* was destined to go through five editions during Spenser's lifetime. The second (1581), third (1586), fourth (1591), and fifth (1597) all appeared anonymously even though Webbe had identified the author. The question 'who knows not Colin Clout?' came to be so readily answered that anonymity became a badge of fame. There was no need to add Spenser's name to the title pages of the later editions of the *Calender* because 'Colin Clout' had been successfully developed from a pseudonym into a brand name.

The debate on patronage conducted between Piers and Cuddie in *October* is introduced by E. K.'s definition of poetry as 'no arte, but a divine gift and heavenly instinct not to bee gotten by labour and learning, but adorned with both, and poured into the witte by a certaine *enthousiasmos* and celestiall inspiration, as the Author hereof elswhere at large discourseth, in his booke called the English Poete' (Spenser 1999: 128). The statement is more significant than is generally recognized. Plato's allusion to inspiration as a form of divinely inspired 'madness' could be used to denigrate the poet as a mere instrument in the hands of the gods, lacking all sense of 'techne', or understanding of his art. But E. K.'s 'author' delicately balances inspiration with craft to emerge as a literary theorist in his own right, wholly distinguished from inferior 'rymers' by his capacity to join intellect to vision, an authorial stance that recurs throughout Spenser's canon and culminates in *Fowre Hymnes*. The impression was confirmed the following year in *Three Proper, and wittie, familiar Letters: lately passed between two Universitie men: touching the Earthquake in Aprill last, and our English Versifying*. 'Immerito' is there identified as a university graduate and, therefore, according to Sir Thomas Smith's classification, a 'gentleman' (Smith 1982: 72). His intellectual credentials are confirmed by his engagement with the technical problems of 'artificiall versifying' (the imposition of classical metres on vernacular verse); his gentility is confirmed by the familiarity he claims with Philip Sidney and other members of the 'Areopagus', which is presented as a sort of learned academy after the Italian and French modes (*Prose*, 6).

Yet the prefatory epistle to the *Letters* is addressed not, as one might expect, to 'the courteous reader' but to 'the courteous Buyer', and Harvey comments in some detail on the *Calender*'s commercial success and Immerito's future earning power (*Prose*, 470–1). This would appear to obviate the need for patronage that weighs so heavily upon Cuddie. Paradoxically, however, the more commercially viable an author such as Spenser became, the more imperative was the drive to dispel the stigma of commerce (of being a mere tradesman in words) by cultivating the status of 'laureate'. But the status of laureate, or any equivalent form of political patronage, potentially undermined the artistic freedom that lent the *Calender* its edge. Its 'moral' eclogues served notice that there can be no epic without critique—a message enforced in 1591 when the *Complaints* followed hard in the wake of *The Faerie Queene*. *October* links the concepts of authorship and patronage symbiotically through the metaphor of the 'gift'. The 'divine gift' of poetry is the 'gift' that poets confer on princes, and one that demands the gift of laureation. Yet properly speaking, as Harvey points out in the *Letters*, the laurel is 'the renowne of Prince, and Princely Poeta: | Th'one for Crowne, for Garland th'other thanketh *Apollo*' (*Prose*, 466). One laurel, but two distinct crowns, and therein lay the problem of conflicting 'authorities'. Immerito begins by sending his book perilously into the world; he ends by saying that it will last forever because it has secured 'a free passeporte' (Spenser 1999: 156). How 'free' only time would tell. The *Calender*'s concluding 'Embleme' cites both Horace and Ovid, a poet nurtured by Augustus and a poet he drove into exile. The reader is left to draw whatever conclusions seem appropriate.

INVENTING A NARRATIVE VOICE

Every aspect of the material layout of the 1590 edition of *The Faerie Queene* seems designed to enhance authorial prestige. The title page announces *The Faerie | Queene. | Disposed into twelve books, | Fashioning | XII. Morall vertues.* The impression created is that of a serious work of moral intent, or what Sidney would have called moral praxis, intended to 'fashion' virtue in its readers. The 'Letter to Ralegh' printed at the end of the volume reinforces this: the purpose of the work is 'to fashion a gentleman or noble person in virtuous and gentle discipline'. Not only is the author a gentleman himself but an authority on gentility, one who understands the relationship between true gentility and moral virtue. No author's name appears on the poem's title page. Rather, it is deliberately reserved for the verso where it appears as the signature to a dedication printed in monumental capitals: 'TO THE MOST MIGH- | TIE AND MAGNIFI- | CENT EMPRESSE ELI- | ZABETH, BY THE | GRACE OF GOD QUEENE | OF ENGLAND, FRANCE | AND IRELAND DE- | FENDER OF THE FAITH | &c. | Her most humble | Servant: | Ed. Spenser.' And then, without any further preface, the poem begins:

The first Booke of
the Faerie Queene.
Contayning
The Legend of the Knight
of the Red Crosse,
OR
Of Holinesse.

The visual effect created here is no less a vehicle of self-presentation than are the woodcuts to the *Calender*. Although there are no fewer than six commendatory verses (including tributes from Ralegh and Harvey) and, in the second state of the first edition, seventeen sonnets of dedication encompassing all of the major factions of the court and Privy Council, they are placed with the explanatory 'Letter to Ralegh' at the end of the volume. This has been variously explained as a sign of late composition or an accident of the printing house or some combination of both, of getting the matter 'back to front' (Zurcher 2005). But I would suggest that it is nothing of the sort. In fact the bibliographical evidence appears to suggest that most of the paratextual materials were always intended to follow the poem (Zurcher 2005– 6: 147). It is also worth noting that when the first three books were reprinted with important revisions in 1596 such paratextual material as was retained was again located at the back. Once might be attributed to a mistake in the printing house, twice suggests design.

The layout of the opening pages of the 1590 edition display a remarkable aesthetic economy, one might almost say a thematic economy. Emphasized in these pages, free of all clutter and distraction, are poem, queen, author, and authorial aspiration. The printing of the dedication on the verso of the title page allows it to act as a decryption of the poem's extraordinary title, translating Faerie into Tudor. Elizabeth's designation as 'Empresse' denotes the imperial ethos of epic, and suggests a coincidence of political and generic hierarchy. It hereby elevates the author, 'her most humble servant', even in the act of expressing his humility. Elizabeth's status as queen 'by the Grace of God' and 'Defender of the Faith' perfectly complements the *Legend of Holinesse* that begins on the facing page. As Drayton noted, the word 'legend' signifies 'things specially worthy to be read' and 'Master EDMUND SPENSER was the very first among us, who transferred the use of the word...from Prose to Verse...the Argument of his Bookes being of a kind of sacred Nature, as comprehending in them things as well Divine as Humane' (Cummings, 81). Such comments indicate that Spenser's authorial self-presentation was highly successful, that the 'sage and serious poet' of Milton's description was an important aspect of the persona the poet cultivated at this point in his career.[4] Then follows the proem to Book I:

> Lo I the man, whose Muse whylome did maske,
>   As time her taught, in lowly Shephards weeds,
>   Am now enforst a farre unfitter taske,
>   For trumpets sterne to change mine Oaten reeds:
>   And sing of Knights and Ladies gentle deeds,
>   Whose praises having slept in silence long,
>   Me, all too meane, the sacred Muse areeds
>   To blazon broade emongst her learned throng:
> Fierce warres and faithfull loves shall moralize my song.   (I Proem, 1)

The first four lines are obviously designed to echo the verses traditionally printed at the opening of Virgil's *Aeneid*, but Spenser has made them his own in a variety of ways. The use of the term 'maske' (absent in the pseudo-Virgilian verses) denotes the inherent variability of poetic personae while the elision of any reference to the *Georgics*, Virgil's agrarian poems, indicates that he intends to follow a rather different course. The only 'Georgic' that Spenser will produce is his legend of St George, a ploughman's son born of the earth as the etymology of his name indicates (Gregerson 2008). Virgil provides a point of comparison rather than a template. The concluding lines of the stanza seamlessly blend echoes of the opening of the *Aeneid* ('Arms and the man I sing') with echoes of the opening of Ariosto's *Orlando Furioso* ('Of ladies, cavaliers, of love and war, | Of courtesies and of brave deeds I sing'; Ariosto 1975: I, 117). This change in emphasis follows directly from Spenser's choice of dedicatee. Spenser is laureate not to an emperor but to an Empress and is very mindful throughout the poem of his female readership: the proems to Books I, II, and III contain addresses to the Queen, the third book centres on a female knight, and the narrator intervenes periodically to condemn the neglect of female 'atchievment' or to address 'faire Ladies' (III.vi.1). In Virgil the principal female character, Dido, is an impediment to epic valour; in Spenser women play a central role in its promotion. In Virgil the prophecy of Rome's imperial destiny is delivered to Aeneas; in Spenser the prophecy of England's imperial destiny is delivered to Britomart. Women are thus written back not just into history but into the history of reading.

Commenting on the role of the epic narrator, Robert Durling draws a useful contrast between the 'discursive narrator' encountered in Ariosto and the more classically self-effacing narrator favoured by Tasso. Throughout the *Gerusalemme Liberata*, he remarks 'most of the overt appearances of the "I" are directly patterned on passages in Homer and Virgil. They can roughly be classified as invocation, apostrophe, exclamation, and expression of diffidence' (Durling: 183). In the first instalment of *The Faerie Queene* Spenser steers a mid-course between these options. The speaker of the proem to Book I invokes the Muse and petitions the Queen to listen to 'the argument of my afflicted style' (4). The cantos that immediately follow are narrated in the third person but a more apparently personal voice intrudes at the opening of canto 3 with the narrator's expression of compassion for suffering beauty:

> I, whether lately through her brightnes blynd,
> Or through alleageance and fast fealty,
> Which I do owe unto all womankynd,
> Feele my hart perst with so great agony,
> When such I see, that all for pitty I could dy.   (I.iii.1)

For a moment it seems that the epic narrator has fallen into the style of an amorous sonneteer. He may 'lately' have been in love, and perhaps that is responsible. Or should we rather seek the cause in his extraordinary devotion to 'all womankynd'? In any case, he is so 'empassioned' that 'my frayle eies these lines with teares do weepe' (2). Look carefully and you may even see the stains on the paper. The speaker of the proem invites Elizabeth to 'heare' his story, but the narrator's reference to 'these lines' reveals the poem's 'speaking' voice as writerly and suggests that the narrator himself is part of someone else's narrative, that his passion for the fictitious Una is part of his author's wider fiction. It is no less significant for that, but it is significant in a different way. The 'self' that presents itself to us is intergeneric, exploiting the tension between lyric and heroic modes. Subject and object of its own narration, simultaneously omniscient and fallible, it rather explores authorial process than asserts authorial identity. Both its paratextual and textual expressions are rhetorical constructs, designed to do very different pieces of business. Aristotle asserted that 'Homer deserves praise for many qualities, but especially for realising, alone among epic poets, the place of the poet's own voice. For the poet should say as little as possible in his own voice, as it is not this that makes him a mimetic artist' (*Poetics*, 24). In response, Spenser engages in a form of self-mimesis: his authorial 'I' is one of self-representation rather than self-expression. The 'I' of the proems speaks of the poet's 'afflicted style' in traditional gestures of humility (I Proem, 4), but the narrator of the cantos as frequently calls attention to the significance of his own literary agency in the work. The twelfth canto of Book I opens and closes with an assertion of poetic achievement, a sense that both hero and author have laboured simultaneously towards the fulfilment of their respective quests. This is appropriate because both wish to please the 'Faerie Queene'. George's desire to 'winne him worshippe, and her grace to have' (I.i.3) is also the poet's. As George is transformed through heroic action from a 'clownishe younge man' into an honoured knight, the 'rustic' pastoral poet is transformed through heroic verse into an English laureate. And what is true for Book I is equally true of the first instalment of *The Faerie Queene* as a whole: 'Now cease your worke, and at your pleasure play; | Now cease your worke; to morrow is an holy day' (III.xii.47).

This tranquil farewell to subject, self, and reader—the last of its kind in the Spenser canon—is followed by 'A Letter of the Authors expounding his *whole intention in the course of this worke: which* for that it giveth great light to the Reader, for the better understanding is hereunto annexed' (Spenser 2001: 714). It is not misplaced, as is often claimed, but perfectly positioned, like the commentaries that follow the eclogues of the *Calender.* Here the author addresses Sir Walter Ralegh apparently in *propria persona,* but it is well to remember that even *propria persona* is a *persona* still. The letter 'expounds' certain aspects of the work but obfuscates others because its primary function is less to provide than to generate commentary—and the history of the poem's, and the epistle's, critical reception from 1590 to the present day testifies to its success. There then follow the commentary sonnets in which Ralegh and 'W. L.' hail Spenser as a laureate and Harvey celebrates the elevation of Colin Clout's concerns 'from Shepheardes unto kinges'. They are thus carefully positioned to undercut by pre-emption the studied 'humility' of the seventeen dedicatory sonnets that follow them. By encompassing, amongst many lesser circles of influence, both the Cecil and the Essex factions, these dedications directly associate the poem's interpretation of the past with the political present. They suggest that Spenser's vision of the nation transcends factional difference and that *The Faerie Queene* is not only a work of national significance but a potential catalyst for unity. Ideally the reader's response to Spenser's national vision will mirror Prince Arthur's reaction to the 'Briton Moniments': 'how much to her we owe, that all us gave, | That gave us all, what ever good we have' (II.x.69). And some of that gratitude should, in theory, pass to the poet.

Voicing Complaint

Yet it is ingratitude to poets that preoccupies Spenser's next publication, *Complaints* (1591). This is anything but what the reading public might have expected (Oram 2003).[5] The granting of a royal pension to Spenser in February 1591—a very rare occurrence in Elizabethan England and the closest thing to the granting of 'laureate status' that the Crown then afforded—could be seen to mark the high point in the poet's public career (Berry and Timings 1960). But the *Complaints* serve notice that the ideals of *The Faerie Queene* have not been realized in contemporary society. Instead Spenser adopts a plethora of satiric personae corrosive of the national unity envisaged in the epic. His emphasis, that is to say, shifts from political vision to political comment. And the shock is all the greater for the calculated manner in which the personae of Verlame and Mother Hubberd are allowed to slip, as the 'voice' of the fictive speaker modulates into a highly personalized attack on Lord Burghley and the Cecil family (*RT*, 216–17, 447–53; *MHT*, 1137–24). The calling-in of *Complaints* marks the moment at which the potentially oppositional cast of Spenser's work was recognized by the authorities as actual opposition. The work appears to brace itself for the onslaught by cultivating an ethos of unauthorized publication, but the very elaborate authorial dedications to the Countess of Pembroke and various members of the aristocratic Spencer family tell a different story of the volume's origins. Though addressed to particular patrons they speak beyond them to a wider public of the poet's 'dutie' to 'set . . . forth' his words of praise, a phrase then commonly associated with the medium of print. And in dedicating *The Teares of the Muses* to Alice Spencer, Lady Strange, Spenser initiates a wholly new phase in his self-presentation by claiming 'some private bands of affinitie, which it hath pleased your Ladiship to acknowledge' (Spenser 1999: 190). But those 'private bands' are now deliberately rendered public. Sir Thomas Smith allowed of 'gentility' through education, as we have seen, but he identified its primary root in 'gens' or family (Smith 1982: 7). And it is this form of 'gentility' that Spenser now advances. These are the *Complaints* not just of Spenser but of *one of the Spencers*. Lest the point be missed, the same kinship claim is repeated in the dedications to *Mother Hubberds Tale* and *Muiopotmos*—and was destined to be repeated some years later in *Colin Clouts Come Home Againe* (1595) and *Prothalamion* (1596). Precisely because Spenser has 'made' his name both in literature and society, anonymity can be dispelled and propriety asserted. Indeed we watch Spenser in the act of constructing his own canon as youthful poems published anonymously in Jan Van der Noot's *Theatre for Worldlings* are reclaimed to appear under his own name in *Complaints* (see Chapters 8 and 12 above).

REINVENTING COLIN CLOUT

Spenser's claims to noble kinship may have seemed all the more important in the wake of the controversy occasioned by the calling-in of *Complaints*. Among several witnesses from the period perhaps the most compelling is that of Sir Thomas Tresham, who aggravates Spenser's fall from grace by recalling his grander literary and social claims: 'He that writ this discourse', Tresham remarks,

is a Cantabrigian and of the blood of the Spencers. Yt is nott yett a yeare since he writt his booke in the prayse of the Quene . . . which was so well liked, that her maiestie gave him ane hundred marks pencion forthe of the Exchequer: and so clerklie was yt penned, that he beareth the name of a Poett Laurell. But nowe in medling with his apes tayle he is gott into Ireland; also in hazard to loose his forsayd annuall reward: and fynallie hereby proove himselfe a Poett Lorrell. (Peterson 1998: 8)

Here was a tale worth the telling: the lowly shepherd's boy elevated to gentility for his learning, adopted by the nobility for his talent, and crowned by the queen for his achievement, had risked the lot—and for what? Petulance or the 'libertas' so prized by the ancients? Would the public now see him as Laureate or Lorrell (fool), Virgil or Ovid? The episode certainly had its effect. Indicative of Spenser's response to the controversy is his reversion to the pastoral *persona* of Colin Clout, and not just in new pastoral poetry but even within epic itself. The latter is unprecedented in literary history: it is as if Virgil were to introduce Tityrus into the *Aeneid*.

As early as the eighteenth century commentators noticed a marked difference between the Colin of 1579 and that of the 1590s (Cummings, 272). The Colin of the *Calender* is characterized as an 'alienated' figure, never quite integrated into the pastoral community of which he formed part, but that sense of alienation is greatly exacerbated on his return and is to some extent heralded by the elegiac speaker of *Daphnaïda* (1591) who introduces himself as the world's 'most miserable man' (38). *Colin Clouts Come Home Againe* is therefore quite appropriately accompanied by *Astrophel*, a pastoral elegy for Philip Sidney and the lost, chivalric England he has come to represent. The Ovidian undertones of the poetry are now unmistakable. The Shepheard of the Ocean, alias Walter Ralegh to whom the poem is dedicated, takes a dim view of Colin's Irish domicile:

> He gan to cast great lyking to my lore,
> And great dislyking to my lucklesse lot:
> That banisht had my selfe, like wight forlore,
> Into that waste, where I was quite forgot . . .   (180–4)

This outlook is qualitatively different from earlier expressions of Colin's malaise. The Shepheard of the Ocean is concerned not with Colin's 'love' but with his 'lore' and the term 'banisht' evokes Tresham's allegation that Spenser had 'gott into Ireland' to escape the scandal of the *Complaints*. The Shepheard of the Ocean regards this strategy as a recipe for oblivion and urges Colin to visit Cynthia in his company. The resulting exposé of the Elizabethan court represents a major reversal of Spenserian policy. One of the most notable features of Colin's presentation in *The Shepheardes Calender* is his conspicuous absence from all of the eclogues that expressly attack contemporary society. In 1595, by contrast, it is directly through the persona of Colin Clout, 'under which name this Poete secretly shadoweth himselfe', that Spenser makes his most powerful onslaught on corruption. But this is quite a different Colin, no longer a lowly shepherd's boy but one who speaks disconcertingly out of character of 'the noble familie: Of which I meanest boast my selfe to be' (*CCH*: 537-8). By engineering the dramatic collision of 'meanest' and 'boast', Spenser captures the central paradox of his authorial self-representation, the persistent tension between self-abasement and self-assertion that depends for its resolution on the reader's recognition that the self-styled 'apprentice of the skill' is really its master (III Proem, 3).

Published the same year as *Colin Clout* and *Astrophel* was *Amoretti* and *Epithalamion*. The almost simultaneous appearance of these two very different volumes is particularly interesting because of the distance they both place between the author and his homeland. Ponsonby asserts that he has dedicated the *Amoretti* to Sir Robert Needham in Spenser's 'absence', a word heavy with Ovidian associations of displacement. Needham had just returned from service in Ireland and the manuscript is said to have come over in the same boat. Its author, however, has remained behind. This scenario would be familiar to all readers of Ovid's *Tristia* or *Epistolae ex Ponto* and the association is enforced in a commendatory sonnet by 'G:W. senior' (possibly the elder Geoffrey Witney) who laments the poet's 'stay' (an ambiguous word that can mean both sojourn and detainment) in 'forraine landes' and urges him to 'hie thee home', thereby anticipating an anxiety evident even in the title of *Colin Clouts Come Home Againe*. As there is no scope in this essay to follow every nuance of the speaker's self-dramatization from the miseries of unrequited love to the joy of the *Epithalamion*'s wedding day, I will concentrate on what he says of himself *as author*. In sonnets 33 and 80, for example, he goes out of his way to reflect upon *The Faerie Queene*'s state of incompletion. Addressing Lodowick Bryskett, his friend and fellow Irish colonist, he asserts,

> Great wrong I doe, I can it not deny,
>   to that most sacred Empresse my dear dred,
>   not finishing her Queene of faëry . . .   (33)

Love, as we have seen, is a traditional impediment to heroic endeavour and by implication love poetry is seen to impede heroic verse. Spenser had sought to reconcile the two by singing of both 'fierce warres' and 'faithfull loves' (I Proem, 1). In theory love and heroism should reinforce one another, and in sonnet 80 (which slyly reveals that the author has already written six books of *The Faerie Queene*, three more than had been printed) it is suggested that they will eventually do so. The problem, however, is that the object of the narrator's love is no longer 'that most sacred Empresse my dear dred' but someone else. There is an increasing sense that the poetry has moved beyond its alleged source of inspiration in terms of both person and place. In the *Epithalamion* the poet of dynastic epic breaks with all classical convention to celebrate his own wedding in royal style. And the poem is set on the lands of the Munster Plantation, the topography that constitutes Colin's 'home' in *Colin Clouts Come Home Againe* and later supplied the location for the *Mutabilitie Cantos*.[6] When an 'Orphic' note is struck in this landscape it sounds in an ominous key: 'So Orpheus did for his owne bride, | So I unto my selfe alone will sing' (16–17). Orpheus's epithalamion was the prologue to disaster and the legendary power of his verse could save neither his wife nor himself.[7]

GENTLE, FRIENDLESS, AND SUBLIME

Striking as they are, the publications of 1595 could scarcely have prepared Spenser's readers for the dazzling range of self-presentations that appeared the following year:

the self-defensive and sometimes caustic narrator of Books IV to VI of *The Faerie Queene*, the dejected speaker of *Prothalamion*, and the 'vatic' self-revisionist of *Fowre Hymnes*. The year's publications defy all attempts at categorization in terms of the Virgilian rota or any other classical template. Precedent functions now only as a marker of contrast as Spenser's poetics of self-presentation chart new generic territory.

Whether considered from the viewpoint of narrative, narrator, or genre, the second instalment of *The Faerie Queene* seems to be designed to shock. Gone is the blissfully tranquil ending of Book III which now concludes in frustrated deferral. Gone are the explanatory 'Letter to Raleigh' and all of the dedicatory sonnets that in 1590 created the effect of literary and political community. Only three of the commendatory sonnets are retained: Ralegh's two sonnets of literary praise and Hobbinol's 'To the learned Shepheard'. The re-deployment of the latter is particularly deft. By being made to conclude the First Part of the poem it serves to herald the intrusion of Colin Clout into the wider six-book structure of 1596. Its last lines urge Colin to turn from 'envy' and 'disdaine' to the queen: 'subject thy dome to her Empyring spright, | From when thy Muse, and all the world takes light'. As this is precisely what Spenser does in the proem to Book IV, the paratexts to Part Two are made to respond adversely to those of 1590:

> The rugged forhead that with grave foresight
> Welds kingdomes causes, and affaires of state,
> My looser rimes (I wote) doth sharply wite,
> For praising love, as I have done of late   (IV Proem, 1)

'To such therefore', the narrator concludes, 'I do not sing at all'. The imagined community of reception has shrunken dramatically. Readers familiar with the controversy surrounding *Mother Hubberds Tale* would readily identify the antagonist as Lord Burghley, but the question we need to ask is why they were invited to do so? It is not just a matter of political expediency, I would argue, but a daring aesthetic move. The attack on Burghley lends dramatic immediacy to Spenser's apostrophe to the Queen, who is now presented as the poem's ideal reader and the poet's preferred guardian. Spenser is re-defining his credentials by appealing above Burghley's head, and being seen to do so. Classical decorum demands a more detached storyteller, an 'I' that invokes the Muse and moves on. To inflect the text with the narrator's discontent at the reception of the narrative is to turn authorial agency into a thematic concern, an effect that Milton developed in *Paradise Lost* and Wordsworth carried to culmination in *The Prelude*. The speaker's celebration of heroic virtue is hereby infused with satire because we are given to understand that, for him at least, there is little friendship, justice, or courtesy in the world beyond the poem. Yet this is the world in which the poet must live. Colin's vision of the Graces is vulnerable to intrusion, just as Spenser's 'writs' are vulnerable to unjustified attack. As a result, the narrator of Books IV to VI seems far more self-conscious than the narrator of the first instalment.

The *Legend of Friendship* presents itself as a continuation of Chaucer's *Squire's Tale* and the narrator makes a very pointed entry into the narrative to assimilate Chaucerian 'authority' by invoking his predecessor's 'spirit':

> Ne dare I like, but through infusion sweete
> Of thine owne spirit, which doth in me survive,
> I follow here the footing of thy feete,
> That with thy meaning so I may the rather meete.   (IV.ii.34)

It was from the use of Chaucerian diction that the 'new' poet first drew 'auctoritie' and he returns to the same source to recover laureate status. Chaucer is further invoked in Book VI as 'that good Poet' (iii.1), but the horrendously violent episode of Bonfont and Malfont at Mercilla's court indicates just how politicized the terms 'bon' and 'mal' may become. Malfont was once known as Bonfont but has had his tongue 'nayld to a post' for spreading 'rayling rymnes' (V.ix.25–6). Since this is very much what Tresham alleges of Spenser himself, the episode gains a very urgent resonance. What justice can there be if Eliza's laureate suffers (even metaphorically) the fate of one who 'blasphemed' her? Who will shield poetry from the Blatant Beast? The proem to Book IV rests its hopes on the queen, but she is conspicuously displaced from the vision of the Graces on Mt Acidale. The discrepancy is both deliberate and dramatic: Spenser has engineered a direct conflict between the optimistic, paratextual 'I' of the proem and the despondent, textual 'I's of Colin Clout and the 'gentle poet' trapped in, and by, his own narration: 'ne may this homely verse, of many meanest, | Hope to escape his venomous despite, | More then my former writs' (VI.xii.41). Philip Sidney defined pastoral as the genre which 'sometime out of Melibeus mouth can shewe the miserie of people under hard Lords or ravening Souldiours. And again, by Titirus, what blessedness is desired to them that lye lowest from the goodnesse of them that sit highest' (Alexander 2004: 26). By introducing Meliboeus rather than Tityrus to the world of Colin Clout and then allowing him to be murdered, Spenser makes perhaps his sharpest comment on his perceived lack of countenance at court. The vision of the Graces is one of reciprocity, but it is precisely the lack of reciprocity that the poem laments: 'Therefore do you my rimes keep better measure, | And seeke to please, that now is counted wisemens threasure' (VI.xii.41). To have the narrator address his verse in such terms is to encapsulate in one couplet the despairing vision of *The Teares of the Muses*: the vision of a society unfit for epic, of a people 'which see not perfect things but in a glas: | Yet is that glas so gay, that it can blynd | The wisest sight, to thinke gold that is bras' (VI Proem, 5). Spenser had reached the point that Yeats would reach many centuries later in 'The Fisherman': 'All day I'd looked in the face | What I had hoped 'twould be | To write for my own race | And the reality' (9–12).

If 'home' is an ambivalent term for Colin Clout, the speaker of *Prothalamion* wants us to know that he really has returned 'home', 'to mery London my most kyndly Nurse, | That to me gave this Lifes first native sourse: | Though from another place I take my name, | An house of auncient fame' (128–31). This is one of the most explicitly biographical statements that Spenser allows any of his authorial personae to make: of gentle, if not noble, blood and London born—yet ultimately, and characteristically, from 'another place'. It would seem that even in his most apparently affirmative statements of belonging Spenser cannot resist adding a note of dislocation. His authorial identity is always just off the map, somewhere in a topography of loss. And the *Prothalamion*'s speaker is accordingly characterized as despondent and even 'freendles' (140). He walks along the banks of his native river, the Thames, like the exiled Psalmist by the waters of Babylon, in deep 'discontent' at 'my long fruitlesse stay | In Princes Court, and expectation vayne | Of idle hopes, which still doe fly away, | Like empty shaddowes' (6–9). Yet as he follows the swans upriver to Essex House, the former home of the Earl of Leicester 'where oft I gayned giftes of goodly grace' (138), the mood changes. Essex appears as 'radiant Hesper' to greet the swan-brides, and possibly also the swan-poet. As early as the *The Shepheardes Calender* 'Cuddie' had claimed that with the right patronage 'Colin' might 'mount as high, and sing as soote as Swanne' (*October*, 90). Three swans, not two, are seeking espousal in the *Prothalamion* and, as a 'spousal' rather than a wedding poem, it draws poetic power from the implicit hope that professional fulfilment may one day complement personal fulfilment. The poet might then have means 'to end his song'.

Just as *Prothalamium* attempts to reclaim elements of the past, the *Fowre Hymnes* attempt to rewrite, or at least recontextualize it. The dedication speaks of the first two hymns as erotic poems written in 'the greener times of my youth' and expresses a desire to 'reforme' them by way of 'retractation'. It is a gesture that Spenser had by now made central to his authorial persona. His boyhood contributions to Noot's *Theatre for Worldlings* had been re-formed by 'retractation' (recasting or re-handling) in his *Complaints*. The first instalment of *The Faerie Queene* had been re-formed by retractation in the second.[8] The Spenserian canon is hereby presented as endemically self-reflexive, as a self-generating creative process rather than a finished product, as an 'endlesse work'. The multiple echoes of language, image, theme, and convention from one poem, and indeed one form, to another serves to strengthen this impression. If the speaker of *Fowre Hymnes*, and particularly the last two, adopts a 'vatic' persona what he enjoys is not just vision but re-vision, the ability to see the potential in his early work for incorporation into mature structures.[9] We shall probably never know for certain whether the early hymns were circulating as widely in manuscript as Spenser claims, or even circulating at all, but the important point is that he presents them to the reader in that way. It is essential to his self-presentation at this stage of his life. If Burghley had castigated him as a 'loose' poet for 'praising love, as I have done of late' (IV Proem, 1), here was the perfect response, an author who could re-form the literary sins of his youth by re-fashioning them into something divine, an author who could rewrite himself (McCabe 2010).

THE MUTABLE SELF

The outcome of Spenser's publications in 1596 was not encouraging. When *The Faerie Queene* was banned in Scotland for denigrating the memory of Mary Queen of Scots, the English Ambassador assured James VI that, contrary to his suspicions, the poem had not been published with royal 'privilidge' (Carpenter, 41–2). It is seldom recognized just how damning that comment is: the great national epic did not speak for the nation's Queen or government. It represented one man's opinion and no more, the voice of a solitary singer. Whenever Spenser characterizes himself as singing 'alone' it is usually in a context of peril or disappointment that offsets the contrary implication of self-sufficiency. His authorial persona is obsessively self-reflexive precisely because it continuously exploits such perils and disappointments. It is forever in the process of narrating, a process that binds writer to reader in a state of mutual anticipation. The narrator concludes the fourth book of *The Faerie Queene*, for example, by leaving the work to be 'perfected' in yet 'another place' (xii.35). It is a testament to Matthew Lownes's appreciation of this aspect of the Spenserian aesthetic that he appended to his *Two Cantos of Mutabilitie* (1609) 'The VIII. Canto, unperfite'. 'Unperfite' splendidly conjures up the sense of final deferral that a dedicated Spenserian reader might appreciate and, from the publisher's viewpoint, transformed a fragment into a sort of consummation. The discovery of the *Cantos* allowed Lownes to represent himself as continuing Ponsonby's policy of rescuing Spenserian manuscripts from oblivion. According to the *Stationers' Registers*, Lownes had also intended to publish *A View of the Present State of Ireland* in 1598, possibly to the infringement of Ponsonby's financial interest in Spenser. Had the work appeared at that time the joint *personae* of Irenius and Eudoxus would certainly have altered contemporary perceptions of Spenser's authorial self-presentation at a crucial stage in the Nine Years' War. Irenius is more overtly a colonist than any of Spenser's other speakers and the choice of name would have disclosed the urgent political investment that had gone into the characterization of *The Faerie Queene*'s 'Irena'. By placing 'Irenius' (with its conflicting connotations of peace and ire) in a complex and often contradictory dialogue with 'Eudoxus' ('good learning'), Spenser reflects upon the difficult, and often unsuccessful, negotiation between politics and ethics attempted in *The Faerie Queene*.

Not only do the *Mutabilitie Cantos* serve as an epitome of Spenser's life-long strategy of deferral—to the sense in which all cantos of *The Faerie Queene* might be termed cantos of mutability—but the subject to which they themselves defer is identified in bold capitals as 'IRELAND', the 'other place' from which Spenser, while refusing to take his name, latterly took so much of his theme (vi.38). Since political mutability is identified as the curse of Irish government in *A View of the Present State of Ireland* (*Prose*, 163) the country provides the perfect topography for the Ovidian topos of the displaced author, a mere 'in-dweller' (vi.55) in lands not his own but also, and for that very reason, a creator of aetiological myths of appropriation. The narrator of Molanna's tale reminds us that her sister's story was made 'well knowne' by Colin Clout (vi.40). But the remark also calls attention to the mutability of the authorial persona itself. Just as each new addition to a poet's canon alters the configuration of the whole, each new inflexion of the authorial persona qualifies all previous inflexions through allusion, development, and contradiction. By alluding to Colin's tale of Mulla, the narrator of the Molanna episode reflects on both personae as well as on the relationship between them. The canon presents us with a process that provides no final product, not even a posthumous one. The 'Colin' who reappears in, say, the pastorals of William Browne is a figure still in development, as is Milton's 'sage and serious' Spenser, or the many Spensers of this *Handbook*. 'Trust me', says the narrator of *The Faerie Queene* to the reader (II.v.1), and up to a point we can. We can trust him to craft tantalizing comparisons and contrasts between his various identities in print, script, and life, exploiting the layers of fabrication and contradiction that inhere in all constructions of selfhood. We can trust him to exploit the limitless plurality of the first person singular.

NOTES

1. For similar issues in *CCH* see Meyer (1969), 142–71.
2. As E. K. points out, 'Colin' was also the persona of Clément Marot. See Patterson (1986).
3. For the concept of laureate in this period cf. Pask (1996), 10–36.
4. For a consideration of the role of the narrator/poet see Hinton (1974).
5. For the significance of *VG* in this context see Miller (1983), 210–12.
6. For issues of social class and colonial identity in the speaker's persona cf. Warley (2002).
7. For Spenser as Orpheus see Cain (1971); Loewenstein (1986); Heale (2003), 92–124.
8. For 'retractation' generally see Miller (1988), 11–14.
9. For the 'authority' of Spenser's visionary persona see Hyde (1983).

BIBLIOGRAPHY

Alexander, G. (ed.) (2004). *Sidney's 'The Defence of Poetry' and Selected Renaissance Literary Criticism*. London: Penguin Books.
Anderson, J. H. (1976). *The Growth of a Personal Voice: 'Piers Plowman' and 'The Faerie Queene'*. New Haven, CT: Yale University Press.
—— Cheney, D., and Richardson, D. A. (eds) (1996). *Spenser's Life and the Subject of Biography*. Amherst: University of Massachusetts Press.
Ariosto, Ludovico (1975). *Orlando Furioso*, trans. B. Reynolds, 2 vols. Penguin Books: Harmondsworth.
Berry, H., and Timings, E. K. (1960). 'Spenser's Pension'. *RES* 11: 254–9.
Cain, Thomas H. (1971). 'Spenser and the Renaissance Orpheus'. *UTQ* 41: 24–47.
Cheney, D. (1983). 'Spenser's Fortieth Birthday and Related Fictions'. *SSt* 4: 3–31.
Cheney, P. (1987). 'The Old Poet Presents Himself: *Prothalamion* as a Defence of Spenser's Career'. *SSt* 8: 211–38.
—— (1991). '"The Nightingale is Sovereigne of Song": The Bird as a Sign of the Virgilian Orphic Poet in *The Shepheardes Calender*'. *JMRS* 21: 29–57.
—— (1993). *Spenser's Famous Flight: A Renaissance Idea of a Literary Career*. Toronto: University of Toronto Press.
Durling, R. M. (1965). *The Figure of the Poet in Renaissance Epic*. Cambridge, MA: Harvard University Press.
Erickson, W. (ed.) (2005). *The 1590 Faerie Queene: Paratexts and Publishing*. Studies in the Literary Imagination 38(2).

Gregerson, L. (2008). 'Spenser's Georgic'. *SSt* 22: 185–201.

Griffiths, J. (2004). 'What's in a Name? The Transmission of "John Skelton, Laureate" in Manuscript and Print'. *HLQ* 67: 215–35.

—— (2006). *John Skelton and Poetic Authority: Establishing the Liberty to Speak*. Oxford: Clarendon Press.

Grossman, M. (1998). *The Story of All Things: Writing the Self in English Renaissance Narrative Poetry*. Durham, NC: Duke University Press.

Heale, E. (2003). *Authority and Authorship in Renaissance Verse: Chronicles of the Self*. Houndmills: Palgrave/St Martin's Press.

Helgerson, R. (1978). 'The New Poet Presents Himself: Spenser and the Idea of a Literary Career'. *PMLA* 93: 893–911.

—— (1983). *Self-Crowned Laureates: Spenser, Jonson, Milton and the Literary System*. Berkeley: University of California Press.

Hinton, S. (1974). 'The Poet and his Narrator: Spenser's Epic Voice'. *ELH* 41: 165–81.

Hyde, T. (1983). 'Vision, Poetry, and Authority in Spenser'. *ELR* 13: 127–45.

Kelsey, L., and Peterson, R. S. (2000). 'Rereading Colin's broken Pipe: Spenser and the Problem of Patronage'. *SSt* 14: 233–72.

Kennedy, W. J. (1995). *Authorizing Petrarch*. Ithaca, NY: Cornell University Press.

Kerrigan, W. (1980). 'The Articulation of the Ego in the English Renaissance', in J. H. Smith (ed.), *The Literary Freud: Mechanisms of Defense and the Poetic Will*. New Haven, CT: Yale University Press: 261–308.

Kinsman, R. S. (1950). 'Skelton's "Colyn Cloute": The Mask of "Vox Populi" ', in *Essays Critical and Historical Dedicated to Lily B. Campbell*. Berkeley: University of California Press: 17–23.

Koller, K. (1940). 'Abraham Fraunce and Edmund Spenser'. *ELH* 7: 108–20.

Loewenstein, J. (1986). 'Echo's Ring: Orpheus and Spenser's Career'. *ELR* 16: 287–302.

Masuch, M. (1997). *Origins of the Individual Self: Autobiography and Self-Identity in England, 1591–1797*. Stanford: Stanford University Press.

McCabe, R. A. (1995). ' "Little booke: thy selfe present": The Politics of Presentation in *The Shepheardes Calender*', in Howard Erskine-Hill and Richard A. McCabe (eds), *Presenting Poetry: Composition, Publication, Reception*. Cambridge: Cambridge University Press: 15–40.

—— (2000). 'Annotating Anonymity, or putting a gloss on *The Shepheardes Calender*', in J. Bray, M. Handley, and A. C. Henry (eds), *Ma[r]king the Text: The Presentation of Meaning on the Literary Page*. Aldershot: Ashgate: 35–54.

—— (2007). ' "Thine owne nations frend | And Patrone": The Rhetoric of Petition in Harvey and Spenser'. *SSt* 22: 47–72.

—— (2010). 'Spenser, Plato, and the Poetics of State'. *SSt* 24 (forthcoming).

McLane, P. E. (1961). *Spenser's 'Shepheardes Calender': A Study in Elizabethan Allegory*. Notre Dame: Notre Dame University Press.

May, J. M. (1988). *Trials of Character: The Eloquence of Ciceronian Ethos*. Chapel Hill: University of North Carolina Press.

Meyer, S. (1969). *An Interpretation of Edmund Spenser's 'Colin Clout'*. Notre Dame: Notre Dame University Press.

Miller, D. L. (1983). 'Spenser's Vocation, Spenser's Career'. *ELH* 50: 197–231.

—— (1988). *The Poem's Two Bodies: The Poetics of the 1590 'Faerie Queene'*. Princeton, NJ: Princeton University Press.

Montrose, L. A. (1979). ' "The perfect paterne of a Poete": the Poetics of Courtship in The Shepheardes Calender'. *TSLL* 21: 34–67.

Oram, W. A. (2003). 'Spenser's Audiences, 1589–91'. *SP* 100: 514–33.

Pask, K. (1996). *The Emergence of the English Author: Scripting the Life of the Poet in Early Modern England*. Cambridge: Cambridge University Press.

Patterson, A. (1986). 'Re-opening the Green Cabinet: Clément Marot and Edmund Spenser'. *ELR* 16: 44–70.

Peterson, R. S. (1998). 'Laurel Crown and Ape's Tail: New Light on Spenser's Career from Sir Thomas Tresham'. *SSt* 12: 1–35.

Pugh, S. (2005). *Spenser and Ovid*. Aldershot: Ashgate.

Quitslund, J. A. (1996). 'Questionable Evidence in the *Letters* of 1580 between Gabriel Harvey and Edmund Spenser', in J. H. Anderson, D. Cheney, and D. A. Richardson (eds), *Spenser's Life and the Subject of Biography*. Amherst: University of Massachusetts Press: 81–98.

Smith, Sir Thomas (1982). *De Republica Anglorum*, ed. Mary Dewar. Cambridge: Cambridge University Press.

Warley, C. (2002). '"So plenty me poore": Ireland, Capitalism, and Class in Spenser's Amoretti and Epithalamion'. *ELH* 69: 567–91.

Wilson, K. (2006). *Fictions of Authorship in Late Elizabethan Narratives*. Oxford: Clarendon Press.

Woods-Marsden, J. (1998). *Renaissance Self-Portraiture: The Visual Construction of Identity and the Social Status of the Artist*. New Haven, CT: Yale University Press.

Zurcher, A. (2005). 'Getting it Back to Front in 1590: Spenser's Dedications, Nashe's Insinuations, and Ralegh's Equivocations'. *Studies in the Literary Imagination* 38: 173–99.

—— (2005–6). 'Printing *The Faerie Queene* in 1590'. *Studies in Bibliography* 57: 115–50.

PART IV

SOURCES AND
INFLUENCES

....

CHAPTER 26

SPENSER AND THE BIBLE

....

CAROL V. KASKE

THIS essay will proceed from simple, empirical points to complex and speculative critical disputes. It will align critics around problems, noting new modes of intertextuality.[1]

VERSIONS OF THE BIBLE AVAILABLE TO SPENSER

....

There were many versions of the Bible available to Spenser in both Latin and English. Naseeb Shaheen has proved that he used the Vulgate and several English versions (1976). One of these was the Geneva Bible; it was the ordinary Bible of Elizabethan homes. It was mildly preferred by Spenser and is now preferred by scholars who lack the time to check his quotations in all of them. The first edition of the Geneva Bible (1560) remains definitive for the so-called Old Testament or Hebrew Bible. The Geneva is available electronically in Early English Books Online and several other databases. Everything in the 1560 edition was available to Spenser. Its New Testament glosses, however, are insufficient for Spenser studies because they do not include the many (mostly translations of glosses in the Latin Beza-Junius New Testament, see below) which were added by Laurence Tomson in 1576 (Daniell 2003: 351–7). Tomson's revision was first published separately and thereafter frequently substituted for the 1560 New Testament in complete Geneva Bibles, e.g. London 1584, 1587, and many others (Kaske 1990). Gerald T. Sheppard (1989) has published the 1602 edition of this New Testament, but unfortunately for us, as the introduction explains, 1602 includes still more notes, of an extremely Protestant tenor, added by Franciscus Junius in 1599, which Spenser could not have read. These notes are, however, mostly confined to Revelation, so that for practical purposes it is only on Revelation that the reader has to check an earlier edition. Those who know some Latin can read what came to be known as 'the Protestant Vulgate'—the glossed Junius-Tremellius Old Testament and the Beza New Testament, printed both together and separately. All versions published in the sixteenth century contained the Apocrypha. Harold Weatherby (1994) has argued convincingly for interest in and availability of Greek versions of Scripture (the Septuagint and Erasmus's New Testament).

What Parts of the Bible Spenser preferred and Where He Used Them

Spenser uses the Bible pervasively in the first book of *The Faerie Queene* and in the *Hymne of Heavenly Love* and the *Fowre Hymnes*, as well as sporadically throughout his poems, his letters, and the prose *Vewe of the Presente State of Ireland* (for more on this distribution, see Kaske 1990, 1999). The Bible does not appear in *Prothalamion*. Landrum (1926) tabulates borrowings in all Spenser's works including the *Vewe*; Shaheen (1976) replaces her on *The Faerie Queene*, and he is more rigorous.

When Spenser demonstrably uses the Bible, what parts does he turn to? 'Spenser alludes to Revelation more than any other book of the Bible', Landrum replies (1926: 517). According to Shaheen (1976: 181–2), Book I contains 42 out of the 60 citations of it in *The Faerie Queene*, and Book V contains most of the others. Revelation is therefore localized and thus cannot be treated as the key to Spenser's works. No one source is the key to this heteroglossic poem. Many references to Revelation are associated with Duessa in her role as Whore of Babylon (I.vii.16–18; viii.6, 14; Revelation 17–19: 3), a figure interpreted by Protestants of Spenser's day as the corrupt Church, and thus identified with the Roman Catholic Church. The commonly recognized contrast between her and the Woman Clothed with the Sun (Revelation 12), interpreted as the Whore's opposite number and allegorized as the true Protestant Church and partly reincarnated in Una, provided Protestants with a scriptural defense against the charge of having split the Church. Revelation also provided *Faerie Queene* I with a common and appealing plot—a good and a bad woman who compete for the hero's soul. This Protestant politico-religious reading of Revelation was a popular subject, one stressed by many commentaries on Revelation, of which an exceptional number existed in English, including the long commentary by Van der Noot in *A Theatre for Worldlings* (1569), where Spenser's first work was published (cf. Chapter 8 above). Revelation brings with it apocalypticism—the sense that current events are predestined and have been prophesied as signs that the world is about to end and that humanity is polarized into the sheep and the goats. Spenser does not pretend, as some people did, to know when the world will end, but he believes it will do so eventually (cf. VII.vii.59; viii. 2; Borris 1991: 80, 84).

Next to Revelation in number of clear borrowings come the Psalms (Landrum 1926: 517; Shaheen 1976: 181), the best known book of the Bible, perhaps even more so then than now, because at least one Psalm was included in every church service and they were also recommended for private and family devotions. The Book of Psalms also existed in more versions than any other book. A poet could choose to echo different translations in different places, as Shaheen has proved that Spenser did, especially in his treatment of Royal Psalm 110.3b (1976: 21–35).

Elizabethan literature also includes innumerable unofficial metrical paraphrases of the Psalter, on which see for example Rivkah Zim (1987). Most of one version was written by a woman—Mary Sidney, Countess of Pembroke, the sister of Sir Philip. Spenser for his part is said to have translated 'The seven Psalmes', or the seven 'Penitential Psalms' (6, 32, 38, 51, 102, 130, and 143), though his versions are no longer extant (cf. *Complaints*, 'The Printer to the Reader'). Translating and paraphrasing the Psalms must have directed attention to biblical poetics. Spenser borrows many of the images and some of the formal traits of the Psalms. Most pervasive is their semantic and syntactic parallelism: this device is also characteristic of *Thě Faerie Queene* as a whole, especially of the first three books; it is elegantly exemplified in Una's lament (I.vii.22–5).[2] A more problematic feature of the *content* of the Psalms which Spenser echoes is the affirmation that the monarch is divine and justified in waging war, on which last see Hamlin (2002).

More Favorites: The Apocrypha: Sapience, Una, and Gloriana

A further section of the Bible, labeled Apocrypha by Protestants, held a fascination for Spenser which seems Romanist to us because nowadays it is revered as canonical only by the Catholic and the Greek Orthodox denominations. Landrum finds 33 uses of the Apocrypha in Spenser's works (1926: 518). In his time, these books were not considered Romanist in that all Bibles contained them: English Protestant Bibles inserted most of them between the Old Testament and the New. Though the Geneva Bible cautions that they be 'not received by a common consent to be read and expounded publikely in the Church' (Apocrypha, 'The Argument'), the Church of England—following Melanchthon and the Catholics rather than the Geneva editors on this issue—recommended that they be read not for doctrine, it is true, but for morality (Article Six of the *Thirty-Nine Articles*, a document which could be found in most Books of Common Prayer before the 1970 revisions). The Church of England actually incorporated some of them into the official daily Scripture Lessons: Judith, Tobit, Wisdom of Solomon, Ecclesiasticus (now called Sirach), and Baruch once made up most of the Old-Testament lessons for Morning and Evening Prayer in October and November of the liturgical year (see the successive Lectionaries in the oldest Books of Common Prayer). The Apocrypha will repay further study.

An insufficiently recognized, striking, and extended use of the Apocrypha is the portrayal of Sapience in *An Hymne of Heavenly Beautie* (183–288; see Harvey 1990). Spenser's Sapience represents one of the three developed biblical characters in his works, the other two being Christ in the *Hymne of Heavenly Love* and Duessa as the Whore of Babylon in *Faerie Queene* I. Spenser's Sapience derives not only from the canonical Proverbs 1–9 (especially 9), but also from the Apocryphal Wisdom 6–9, Ecclesiasticus 1, 4, 6, 14–15, 24, and 51, and Baruch 3: 28–32. The character of Gloriana owes much to Sapience or Wisdom—both the book and the character. A. C. Hamilton notes that when Spenser calls Elizabeth a 'Mirrour of grace and majesty divine' (I Proem, 4), he is equating her with the similarly described Sapience in Wisdom 7: 26 (Spenser 2001: 30). Sapience 'reacheth from one ende to another mightily, and comely doth she order al things' (Wisdom 8: 1). Sapience's imperial attribute could justify the rule of a female monarch like Gloriana and her real-life counterpart, Queen Elizabeth (Fruen 1990: 66).

Una too resembles Sapience. Una says in what could be self-characterization, 'Wisedom warnes, while foot is in the gate | To stay the steppe' (I.i.13). She is a teacher to the Satyrs (I.vi) and frequently lectures Redcrosse. Una has sometimes been regarded as another surrogate for Queen Elizabeth; and Una like Gloriana is said to be 'borne of hevenly birth' (I.x.9), even though she has earthly parents as well as heavenly. Having earthly parents does not disqualify Una from being Wisdom; it only makes her a lower emanation in the same chain of being. One reason Spenser linked Elizabeth to Sapience by the attribute of heavenly birth is the presence of sacral monarchy in the Royal Psalms, as explained below. Linking her with Sapience functions as a scriptural counterweight to the Pauline strictures invoked by strict interpreters of St Paul and misogynists like John Knox who objected to having a female as the head or supreme governor of the Church—which office since Henry VIII had been a prerogative of the English Crown. We moderns have the opposite objection to Spenser's women: sexism. The standard defense of Spenser against this charge is that Book I also presents good women—Una and the female staff of the House of Holiness; but I must agree with feminist critics that this is only a baby step in the right direction because, as usually framed, it has Spenser just buying into Revelation's polarization of women into either Eves or Maries. Sapience has more agency than do Mary and Una's other biblical sources. Una's unappreciated and Elizabeth's seldom mentioned similarity to Sapience constitutes evidence that Spenser respects women for their minds and their leadership. True, the typical exegete allegorized Sapience as Christ, thus downplaying her gender; but the very existence of a feminine sign for Christ would have strengthened the claim of a woman to a

Christlike office. As Fruen has shown, Melanchthon and in a sense even Calvin equated the biblical Sapience not with Christ but with natural law and natural revelation—things which could be personified in a woman as well as in a monarch (Fruen 1990: 65–70). When her surrogates are linked with a quasi-divine personification, so is Queen Elizabeth herself. Thus Scripture and exegesis can sometimes serve the poet as a political tool. The biblical poet not only absorbs but on occasion attempts to manipulate his culture, making the influence reciprocal.

Another section of the Bible of predictable importance to Spenser is the Gospels, which are particularly pervasive in the *Hymne of Heavenly Love*. Three surprising allusions to them, surprising in view of their secular context, are the allusion to Peter's fall (V.vi.97); the association of the parthenogenesis of Belphoebe with that of Christ (III.vi.3, 27); and the associations of the goddess Nature with the transfigured Christ (VII.vii.7). On the first two, see Kaske (2008).

Straightforward, Oblique, and Eristic Uses

When Spenser demonstrably uses the Bible, how straightforwardly and respectfully does he use it? This question will dominate most of the rest of this essay. Spenser's reverential uses of the Bible range from a literal to an allegorical sense; from the straightforward to the oblique—allegorical, analogic, syncretic, parodic, or otherwise far-fetched; and from the political to the purely aesthetic. He quotes Scriptural phrases verbatim now and then, and quotation is the most direct use, unless it is ironical. The second most direct uses are translation and paraphrase, exhibiting the lowest degrees of creativity. Spenser is generally believed to be the translator of the four 'sonnets' paraphrased by his French source from Revelation that occur in *A Theatre for Worldlings*, and he is credited with translations, now lost, of some poetic books of the Bible.

Some of Spenser's imitations of the Bible are reverential, especially the passionately pious *Hymne of Heavenly Love* and parts of *Faerie Queene* I—works whose aim is clearly to enlist the Bible's allegedly salvific power as a means of grace to make the reader a better Christian (I.ix.19). The Bible in whole or in part is sometimes cited or portrayed explicitly, sometimes as a physical book, in Book I, the *Vewe*, the 'Letter to Raleigh', the *Shepheardes Calender*, and especially the glosses thereto (whether he authorized them or actually authored them), but nowhere else. In the 'Letter to Raleigh', for example, Spenser cites Ephesians 6: 11–17 to explain that Redcrosse's armor is 'the armour of a Christian man'. Redcrosse gives Arthur as a parting gift an actual copy of the Bible—'a booke, wherein his Saveours testament | Was writt . . . | A worke of wondrous grace, and hable soules to save' (I.ix.19).

A freer but still reverential imitation is illustrated in Artegall's re-enactment of the Judgment of Solomon (I Kings 3: 26–7; V.i.26–8). Two straightforward though remote imitations of plots and themes are those of David (played by both Redcrosse and Arthur) and Goliath (I Samuel 17: 38–49; I.vii.7–15; V.viii.2–25; Kaske 2008) and of the thirsty deer in Psalm 42 in *Amoretti* 67 (Prescott 1985). When the artist is imitating so complexly and at such a great distance as he is in *Amoretti* 67, he is exerting quite a bit of freedom.

Unlike the straightforward biblical allusion but equally respectful is the allusion whose relevance could not be fully understood without the tradition of biblical allegory—in other words one where Spenser has retained the clothing of allegory that the character or action wore or allegedly wore in the Bible. One example of this is allusion to the aforementioned Duessa as the Whore of Babylon in Revelation 17–19: 3. Without her Protestant symbolism as the false Roman Catholic Church (which occurs in *Faerie Queene* I alone; in *Faerie Queene* V she typifies Mary Queen of Scots), Redcrosse's fornication with her, meaning his starting to entertain Catholic ideas, would not be a sin so serious as to merit hell as it does: 'ever burning wrath before him laid, | By righteous sentence of th'Almighties law' (I.ix.50).

Another instance of filtering the Bible through allegorical exegesis is Redcrosse's unexpected announcement after the dragon-fight that he cannot marry Una right now but must first go back to Gloriana whom he has promised to serve for six years (xii.17–19, 41). Redcrosse then promises Una's father that he will come back in the mystic seventh year to consummate their marriage (I.xii.19). The episode recalls the biblical account of Leah and Rachel allegorized as typifying the active versus the contemplative lives (cf. Kaske 1975, 2008).

THE FOUR SENSES OF SCRIPTURE

The difference between allegory and typology leads us to the four senses of Scripture. The Bible, including both the Hebrew Bible and its Christian sequel, has until recently been credited with having a relevance to the lives of its individual readers or listeners. When relevance was hard to detect, it was read into the text, for example into picky specifications such as not plowing with 'an ox and an ass' (Deuteronomy 22: 10) or into cryptic, figurative prophecies like Ezekiel's vision of the wheels (Ezekiel 10); and this perceived relevance constitutes its allegory or symbolism. Kinds of relevance were classified into many 'senses' that a given passage might contain—senses which gradually and not without disagreement were narrowed down to one literal plus three 'allegorical'. One influential analysis in a long and complicated tradition is the medieval mnemonic jingle 'Littera gesta docet, quid credas allegoria, | Moralis quid agas, quo tendas anagogia'. Freely paraphrased, it means as follows: 'The literal sense teaches what has occurred; the allegorical sense, articles of faith [such as those found in the Creeds]; the tropological teaches the moral lesson of the passage; the anagogical teaches eschatology [the individual's final destiny and events and conditions during and after the end of the world]'. These senses are simply topics the Middle Ages considered important, just as today literature is made to seem 'relevant' by pointing out the topics of gender, class, and ethnicity. Under this thematic definition, the three 'spiritual senses' provide language with which to analyse and classify kinds of subject matter. The moral sense is almost ubiquitous both in the Bible and in secular literature, with the potential to turn every passage into a two-layer cake. Only rarely, however, are all three of these 'spiritual senses' found simultaneously, creating a four-layer cake, in a single passage. Sometimes, though, two levels may merge with each other. In an exhortation such as the Ten Commandments, the literal is the moral. In visions of the afterlife such as the bulk of the Book of Revelation, the literal is the anagogical. In Dante's *Commedia*, too, all the action after the first two cantos takes place in the afterlife—hell, Purgatory, and heaven—and so again the literal is the anagogical.[3]

Only the second, the so-called allegorical sense, raises problems of definition. 'Allegory' is apparently used in a special sense here, since all three extra or 'spiritual' senses can be and were called 'allegorical' as well. The second influential analysis of the senses of Scripture, too long and complicated to quote in its entirety, is by Thomas Aquinas in his *Summa Theologiae* I.1.10. Both sources are in agreement as to the literal, moral, and anagogical senses. About the second or allegorical sense, however, Aquinas says, 'So far as the things of the Old Law signify the things of the New Law [i.e., Christianity] there is the allegorical sense (Hebrews x.1)' (Aquinas 1945: I, 17). On this basis A. C. Charity off-handedly equates the jingle's definition of the second sense with typology: 'allegoria quid credas docet, the typological meaning, that is to say' (1966: 90). These expositors imply we should substitute into the jingle, '*typologia* quid credas docet'. But how can we reconcile Aquinas's statement that allegory relates the so-called 'Old Testament' to the New, with the jingle's definition that 'allegoria quid credas docet' ('allegory teaches what you should believe', i.e., 'matters of faith')? Aquinas adds, in effect, 'and how it is already prefigured in the Hebrew Bible'. These two dissimilar contents are yoked because in the Judaeo-Christian tradition, 'what you should believe' is not so much an abstract doctrine like 'there are three persons in God', as events, stories, a narrative: God created the world (Genesis 1–2); Adam and Eve ate the forbidden fruit and God cursed them (Genesis 3); 'God brought you out of the land of Egypt' (Exodus 3 to Psalms, *passim*); 'Christ Jesus came into the world to save sinners' (I Timothy 1: 15); and 'the end of all things is at hand' (I Peter 4: 7). These can be imitated by subsequent events in history. What Erich Auerbach says is generally true, that typology or figura is a connection between two historical events: '*figura* is something real and historical which announces something else that is also real and historical. The relation between the two events is revealed by an accord or similarity' (1984: 29).[4]

A simple example is where Jesus compared himself to Jonah and the whale, stating that the story was a prophecy which he was going to fulfill in his death and resurrection (Matthew 12: 40). Another is the parallel between the Holy Family's flight into Egypt and return therefrom and the Israelites' sojourn in Egypt and return to the Promised Land: 'This was done that the Scripture might be fulfilled': 'Out of

Egypt have I called my son' (Matthew 2: 12–15). This hermeneutic resulted in interpretations of the Hebrew Bible which came to be known in medieval exegesis and even in the New Testament itself as 'figures' or 'types', though the terminology is sometimes inconsistent. The epistles by or traditionally associated with St Paul himself devise Christian interpretations of Old Testament events and persons: of Hagar and her son Ishmael (Galatians 4: 21–31), of the rock that Moses smote to bring forth water (1 Corinthians 10: 4), and of the mysterious Melchizidek, King of Salem (Hebrews 5–7). In reading typologically, Christian exegetes tried to find Christian meanings (the *quid credas*) in parts of the Hebrew Bible in order not only to defend it by proving that it was not just a history of the nation of Israel but also to defend the New Testament by proving that it represented not a departure from but a fulfillment of the true, authentic Judaism. This typology is not only a defensive mode but also a discovery of recurring aesthetic patterns in that biblical history which was the subject of the literal sense. Though Aquinas denies the possibility (*Summa* I.1.10; Aquinas 1945: I, 16), literature sometimes imitates these implicit biblical analogies.

Though not mentioned in the two principal sources for the definition, there is also retrospective typology—chiefly involving re-enactments of the Fall of Man but also of the Exodus and the journey to the Promised Land. Retrospective typology is frequent and powerful in secular literature. When a literary character behaves badly or resists a series of graded temptations, comparing him or her to Adam or Eve lends an archetypal resonance and makes the sin or temptation more crucial.

In Spenser there are at least six widely recognized episodes that have clear typological overtones by virtue of analogies with key events in the Bible (Kaske 1990); for most of them, A. C. Hamilton's notes to Spenser (2001) identify the scriptural passages that are re-enacted. Arthur, Redcrosse, and Guyon replay events in the life of Christ, making them Christ figures or Christ figures manqué. Arthur's rescue of Redcrosse from Orgoglio's dungeon (I.viii.34–40, especially 'a deepe descent as dark as hell') re-enacts the credal Harrowing of Hell (Apostles' Creed: 'He descended into hell'). Redcrosse's rescue of the King and Queen of Eden from their prison by killing the Dragon (I.xi–xii) in a three-day battle re-enacts Christ's death (the dragon-fight), his Harrowing of Hell (referred to in *Amoretti* 68), and his resurrection after three days (I.xi.52). Redcrosse's betrothal to Una (xii) prefigures the Marriage of the Lamb to the New Jerusalem in Revelation 19–20. Guyon withstanding the temptations of Mammon and then being restored in some way by an angel (II.vii–viii.1–8) recapitulates Christ's temptations by Satan in the wilderness (Matthew 4: 1–11). Two re-enactments in different ways of the Fall of Man are, first, the exile of the King and Queen from Eden by the dragon ('Letter to Raleigh', I.vii.44) and, second, Mordant's drinking of Acrasia's wine in a garden and magically bequeathing it as a bloodstain (i.e., original sin) to his infant son Ruddymane (II.i.37–ii.4). Individual authors, both in the Bible and in secular literature, slant their typological re-enactments to emphasize different themes.

Another way besides allegory of using Scripture respectfully but independently is by exerting oneself to combine it with another text or discourse, as when Spenser boldly inserts between the expected heaven of 'happy soules' and the heaven of angels a mezzanine 'where those Idees on hie | Enraunged be, which Plato so admired' (*Hymne of Heavenly Beautie*). This project is called syncretism—yielding a viewpoint neither wholly religious nor wholly secular. It is common both in the Middle Ages and in the Renaissance. The prior text is called the subtext (Greene 1982: 38–51). Spenser creatively conflates both Duessa as the biblical Whore and Una as Sapience with the typical romance damsel in distress; he conflates Orgoglio as the typical oversized romance antagonist with the biblical Goliath (I.vii.7–15; viii.2–25; I Samuel 17: 38–49). The most creative choice is a subtext from a different culture, language, or outlook, for example a classical one. As Greene remarks, such cross-cultural combinations usually produce dialectical imitation, his favorite kind (1982: 51).

Another oblique and thus creative use of Scripture is the parodic (cf. Kaske 1990, 2008). Although the Bible retains its normative character and the irony is not at the expense of the sacred text but at the expense of the extra-biblical being who does not measure up and who may actually be twisting the scripture sophistically, the tone is not reverential but witty, comical, or cynical. Sophistry is displayed when Despaire quotes Scripture in I.ix.47 to make Redcrosse commit suicide and when Phaedria deviously misapplies 'consider the lilies of the field' (II.vi.15–16; cf. Matthew 6: 28–9) to authorize her frivolous idleness. In Spenser's social satire, *Mother Hubberd's Tale*, when the formal priest, recommending to the Fox and the Ape the easy life of errant Protestant clergy, says 'Ne is the paines so great, but beare ye may' (445), he is misapplying 'There hath no tentation taken you, but . . . ye may be able to beare it' (I Corinthians 10: 13). Some entire plots are parodic. The Giant with the scales (V.ii.37–8, 42–6) not only reflects Apocryphal villains but parodies almost blasphemously God's leveling of mountains and weighing of unquantifiable things (Isaiah 40: 4, 12; Wisdom 11: 21; Job 28: 25). Enjoyment of these ironies depends on the reader's recognition of the scriptural echo.

In the 1950s and 1960s criticism had to be apologetic and celebratory. 'Political' was a term of contempt and the motto was 'art for art's sake'. Critics heeded Pope's injunction to 'read each work of wit | With the same spirit that its author writ' (*Essay on Criticism* 2.233–4). Accordingly critics in the 1950s and 1960s talked as if they espoused—whether in truth or by an effort of historical imagination—that Christianity which medieval and Renaissance authors by and large believed. Then the learned world began to acknowledge the many flaws in biblical ethics—in the Hebrew Bible were, among others, militarism, the chosen-people concept, the idea that they who sin should suffer, and the divine right of kings. In part because of this, critics began to write from a standpoint outside the Bible, with an unflinching objectivity and even a zest for exposure and muckraking. And as for our chosen authors, either we try to prove that they do not believe their professed religion or, failing that, we unmask their vacillations and anxieties.

An aesthetic trend has led to a similar taste. One would think that biblical imitation would stifle creativity because the normativity of the text would seem to allow only a reverential, uncritical, unmediated imitation—scarcely more than a translation, one which aims to transfer to the new work some of the primary text's authority. Since complexity has long been valued over simplicity, negativity over celebration, and autonomy over reverence, Thomas M. Greene and G. W. Pigman privilege, in their cogent analyses of kinds of imitation in Renaissance theory and practice, the more adversarial kinds which they call 'dialectical' (Greene) and 'emulative' or 'eristic' (Pigman 180: 22–32). Greene seldom mentions any imitation of the Bible at all, never any by Spenser, although the reverential kind of 'sacramental imitation' that he discusses cries out for it. Instead he accuses Spenser of being historically naïve, revealing a tacit fear that the Bible's normativity precludes criticism and compels reverential and 'sacramental' imitation (1982: 38–9, 47, 57). Harry Berger (1998) boldly attacks the Bible for imposing limits on what its imitator can say. This oppression may be the reason for the phenomenon noted by Greenslade (1963), that few works whose plots and scenes come from the Bible attain the highest rank, the exception being *Paradise Lost*. Greenslade praises Spenser among others for finding his plots elsewhere, and he could have accorded the same praise even to the more pervasively religious Dante.

My first answer to Greene and Pigman is that complexity and a degree of authorial agency can be achieved without hostility to the Bible. As we have seen, imitations can be, in order of independence, allegorical, analogical, syncretic, or ironic. My second answer is that a contentious Christian author who is eristically inclined (i.e., inclined to disputation or controversy) such as Luther, Milton, or, on occasion, Spenser, can use the New Testament as a standpoint from which to express hostility to the Old Testament (see Perkins 2006).

In the *Vewe*, Spenser provides an example of a dialectic or eristic adaptation of a Scriptural passage and thus behaves as Greene wishes he would. It is owing to this option of reading eristically (through the eyes of Eudoxus) that we are now allowed to see the intolerance behind Irenius-Spenser's invocation of the biblical Whore of Babylon in ostensible exculpation of the Irish: 'In which Popes time and longe before it is certaine that religion was generallie | Corrupted with theire Popishe trumperie Therefore what other Coulde they learne then suche trashe as was taughte them And drinke of that Cupp of fornicacion with which the purple Harlott had then made all nacions drunken' (*Prose*, 137). Spenser foregrounds the intolerance by Eudoxus's objection and by Irenius's subsequent backpedaling to a position of greater tolerance.

Spenser's descriptions of the Mosaic Law and its origin are also what Greene calls dialectical (1982: 43–8) and Pigman eristic (1980: 22–32)—jaundiced and ambivalent. On the one hand, Spenser criticizes, relativizes, and historicizes the Old Testament in the light of the New along the lines of Christ's 'Antitheses' (e.g., 'Ye have heard that it hath been said, An eye for an eye and a tooth for a tooth, but I say unto you, resist not evil', Matthew 5: 38–9a) and of those epistles traditionally attributed to St Paul. The Ten Commandments given to Moses on Mount Sinai (Exodus 34: 1) are characterized by Spenser as what 'Paul' calls the 'letter' that 'killeth' (2 Corinthians 3: 6–7), namely, as the 'bitter doome of death and balefull mone' which is 'writ in stone | With bloudy letters by the hand of God' (I.x.53). At the same time, Spenser is still imitating straightforwardly 'Paul's' strictures on Mosaic law and those of Christ in the 'Antitheses' and a few other places. These strictures authorize such a skeptical treatment of the Hebrew Bible on the part of Christian authors and critics and make the Bible a self-contestatory work. Though this could lead to anti-Jewish sentiment, it need not do so because the Pauline strictures are not really about ethnicity but about two approaches to ethics: on the one hand, the grace-centered ethics operating through emotions of trust and love and pioneered by 'Paul', the Gospel of John, and the epistles associated with his name and, on the other, the old analytic ethics of the Hebrew Bible, the Epistle of James, and Roman Catholics centered on earning merit through efforts of will.

Moreover, a reader can also condemn both Testaments (though we are not talking about readers here), as in Berger's oppositional reading of them (1998). Spenser does so at one moment in the House of Holiness. Fidelia holds a 'sacred Booke, with blood ywritt'. All things considered, it seems to be the entire Bible. It is 'signd and seald with blood' (x.13), and out of it she teaches 'Of God, of grace, of justice, of free will' (x.19). So far so good, but Spenser says this Bible is capable of harming its readers. Fidelia's book contains 'darke things . . . hard to be understood' (x.13, 19; cf. 2 Peter 3: 15); and when Redcrosse hears them, he is filled with despair at his own unworthiness and wishes to die (x.21–9; cf. ix.50–1). Spenser seems to question as Catholics did the sufficiency of Bible-reading for salvation if an optimistic interpreter such as Speranza or Hope is not present (cf. McEachern 1996: 54); but whatever his political point here, he is not being entirely reverential towards his subtext the Bible.

Conspicuous Omission of the Bible

Another way of declaring one's independence from the Bible is to conspicuously avoid quoting or mentioning it at all—the zero-grade of biblical imitation. Some critics would say that because *The Faerie Queene* is one poem the biblical perspective should be added where it is not mentioned by reading allegorically or ironically, but I disagree. Nowadays, we accept that thematic unity may be loose and we welcome heteroglossia or a switch to a different discourse. This refusal makes for a secular discourse—classical or courtly-chivalric or merely ethical or prudential, giving an undoctored view of humanity as it is in itself—independent of God or the devil. Such a poem is *Prothalamion*, a poem celebrating a double betrothal. As I said, it is absent from Landrum's tabulations (538–44). The bulk of Spenser's romance-epic is secular discourse and should be read as such. The almost complete absence of Scripture from *Faerie Queene* III and IV means that, like Shakespeare, Spenser does not regard the Bible as containing the answer to every question—for example, the question dominating Britomart's quest: whom to marry.

TRENDS: PSYCHOLOGICAL AND POLITICAL

Two trends that show no signs of desuetude are psychological and political readings of the Bible and Spenser. Because older social formations frequently arouse distaste, these include many ironical, dialectic, and eristic imitations and many oppositional readings. Psychological critics of Spenser and the Bible are Berger (1998), McEachern (1995), and Krier (1998, 2000). I will concentrate on the political (see Chapter 41 below for psychological criticism). Besides the biblical sexism of which Berger complains, Spenser also endorses one biblical doctrine that moderns cannot discuss without some irony—the sacral nature of the monarch and his/her headship of the Church of England. Certain Psalms, which modern exegetes call the Royal Psalms, and frequent *obiter dicta* in other Psalms claim the king of Israel is sacred or divine. This caesaro-papism has alienated readers from the nineteenth century onwards. On three occasions, Spenser declares Elizabeth or one of her surrogates in the poem to be 'hevenly borne', 'of heavenly race', 'borne of heavenly birth'. All three instances echo that divine paternity attributed to the king of Israel in Royal Psalms 2: 7 and 89: 26–7, the former of which is used by Paul in a sermon in Acts 13: 33 to prove the divinity of Christ. The first occasion is when Spenser claims that Gloriana—the direct equivalent of Queen Elizabeth in the poem as the 'Letter to Raleigh' asserts—bestows 'glory' upon high achievers because she is 'hevenly borne, and heaven may justly vaunt' (I.x.59). Elkin Calhoun Wilson shows that Spenser and other Elizabethan writers spontaneously attributed to Elizabeth 'divine right' although she never dogmatized about it (1939: 224–6). That right was supported by these two Psalmic verses in particular. Some critics go further and interpret I.x.59 as saying that she has the right to bestow heavenly glory in heaven, as if she were responsible for souls and authorized, like the Roman Church, to canonize a saint. Eusebius, a widely read Greek Father, believed this about the emperor, delegating to him the spiritual as well as the temporal welfare of his subjects (Bergvall 1997).

Further endorsing the conceit of the monarch's divine paternity in Psalm 89: 26–7, speaking for the moment in the persona of God, the Psalmist proclaims: 'He shall cry unto me, Thou art my Father . . . Also I will make him my first borne.' The Geneva version glosses Psalm 89: 26–7 as follows: '[David's] excellent dignitie shall appeare herein that he shall be named the Sonne of God, and the first borne, wherein he is a figure of Christ' (gloss y). Moreover, this royal typology can be 'applied in a weak sense [*tenuiter*] to other sovereigns as types of him [Christ]' says the corresponding gloss in the Junius-Tremellius Latin Old Testament (see Bible 1585). Presumably this applies to any godly sovereign, male or female—though the 'female' part was hotly disputed. Spenser also echoes divine kingship in the notion that Eliza in the *Aprill* eclogue of *The Shepheardes Calender*—an even clearer Elizabeth figure, though in a more distanced mode, the pastoral—is 'O dea certe' and begotten by the god Pan.[5]

Spenser's third and less obvious Christological claim for Elizabeth is his statement that the birth of Belphoebe was 'of the wombe of Morning dew'. (Spenser declared Belphoebe to be another of Elizabeth's surrogates; see 'Letter to Raleigh' and III

Proem, 5.) The claim echoes the beautiful but mysterious verse 3b in Psalm 110—another Messianic Psalm which in some versions (not the Geneva) reads 'the deawe of thy birth, is of the wombe of the morning' (chiefly, the Psalter in the Book of Common Prayer, which reproduces Coverdale's version).[6] This verse in this version was traditionally interpreted as alluding to the virgin birth of Christ. Dew like rain symbolizes fertility; but because it materializes silently it is mysterious, like the virgin birth, and such parturition contrasts with ordinary births which are clamorous. Dewlike drops of water played a part in Chrysogone's conception of Belphoebe too (III.vi.6–8), and we can now see that these also derive from Psalm 103b, in conjunction, of course, with the scientific analogues for it which have already been recognized. These three deifications of Elizabeth—her heavenly paternity, her being 'o dea certe', and her being born of morning dew—must in turn have strengthened in the minds of Spenser's naïve readers her disputed claim to the Royal Supremacy over the Church of England to which Spenser must be alluding in this otherwise preposterous claim.[7] Royalism in general, and Royal Supremacy over the Church in particular, while archaic, are more acceptable to today's readers when the images are beautiful and the monarch is female. When poets 'go public', they do not always relinquish all of their autonomy: they participate in an alternating current of cultural energy, both being passively influenced by some important cultural text and also politicizing it and actively honoring it by alluding to it and thereby making it better known and more respected. This circularity differs from ordinary biblical allusion and ordinary intertextuality because of its religious and political charge.

BIBLICAL POETICS

An imitation both more and less direct than verbal and thematic imitation is biblical poetics. Two kinds of biblical poetics are adversarial enough to meet Greene's criteria—images *in bono* and *in malo* (in good and bad senses) and contradictory and self-correcting propositions. In addition to psalmic parallelism and the four senses, mentioned above, the repetition of images *in bono* and *in malo* is an element of biblical poetics which Spenser demonstrably employs throughout *The Faerie Queene* and the *Amoretti*—a biblical structure explored by patristic and medieval exegesis and recognized in the Renaissance. In *The Faerie Queene*, pious fasting is condemned when practiced by the legalistic Corceca (I.iii.14) but recommended in the House of Holiness and by the Hermit Contemplation in I.x.26.[8] In a work first published in 1963, Northrop Frye generalized about Spenser's contradictory pairs, calling them 'symbolic/demonic parodies' and the resulting structure 'dialectical' (1972). The good instance and the bad one are not always diametrically opposite as they are in the fasting example because they are sometimes in different areas of life, as with the good heraldic dragon on Arthur's helmet (I.vii.31) and that encountered by

St George (I.xii.8–14). Shifting evaluations of altars, pride, and a laurel leaf complicate the *Amoretti and Epithalamium* (*Amoretti* 27–8, 58–9, *Epithalamium* 162–4). These tergiversations, especially when they are in the same area of life, give the feeling of a progressive self-correction, yielding the Aristotelian conclusion that vice is to virtue as abuse is to the proper use of the same thing. Despite its biblical precedent, the strategy is versatile and adaptable to secular literature such as the later books of *The Faerie Queene* because tied not to religion or to allegory but to categories of good and evil, better and worse. It is more text-based than is allegory. The progressive self-correction is liberating to the author but it is a complex and an unsettling form of intertextuality for the reader because no one passage, not even a Bible-based one, can be trusted to give Spenser's last word about an image or practice; at the end of the poem the reader must construct a complex distinction to cover everything that was said, and some of those things may be contradictory, producing a situational ethics or even a suspension of judgment. The tenth canto of Book I contradicts Spenser's previous condemnations not only of fasting but of other religious practices. The resulting indeterminacy is meant to lead the reader towards suspension of judgment—a position called adiaphorism favored by a small group headed by the Queen that allowed a certain latitude regarding practices not explicitly and uniformly condemned by Scripture which could serve a good cause (as when Paul circumcised Timothy but not Titus, Acts 16: 3; Galatians 2: 3).[9]

Sometimes not only evaluations of images but whole propositions are contradicted, especially on two questions: do we obtain heaven by God's indefectible, irresistible grace springing ultimately from his predestination or by our own good works? And if we do so by works—winning merit, avoiding serious sin, and repenting when we fail to do so—are they performed through divine grace or through our own free will? Spenser, like the Bible, presents all these positions (on winning heaven by merit, see I.ix.53 versus I.x.41 and II.i.32; and on receiving heaven by grace, see I.x.1 versus I.vii.41, with II.i.33 in the middle). By contradicting the Bible or exposing its own self-contradictions—and thus in a sense deconstructing it—Spenser imitates the Bible ironically, dialectically, or even eristically.

COMPARABLE STUDIES

In literary appreciation, unity of theme versus breadth, inclusiveness, and objectivity constitutes a perennial conflict. The Bible is often expected to be unified in theme— interpreting the Councils that put it together as the voice of God. But to an unprejudiced observer, it presents a variety of outlooks—from the godless one of the Song of Songs, to Job's anguished questioning, to the works-centered Synoptic Gospels and James, to the occasionally doctrinaire Johannine Gospel and Epistles, and the Pauline Epistles. Kaske believes Spenser imitated this biblical pluralism, for instance in structuring his epic-romance in two contrasting halves (1999).

Kaske (1999) is one of three book-length studies of Spenser and the Bible that are text-centered, faithful to the history of theology, and heavily scriptural. They complement one another because each reading contains unique and relevant data and adopts a different critical perspective, with Kaske's in the middle. Darryl Gless (1994) is a dedicated study of Book I while John N. King (1990), like Kaske, takes the entire *Faerie Queene* as its province and also covers in more or less detail the shorter poems and the *Vewe*. Gless and King focus on English sources—namely, 'practical divinity' (Gless) and popular religious literature and visual art (King). Focusing on the more academic sources, Kaske alone attends to the many Latin Bibles (not only Romanist but Protestant) and to their commentaries—works which in the sixteenth century were written and reprinted overwhelmingly in Latin. Engaging the ongoing problem of thematic unity versus pluralism (on which see Kaske 1975), Kaske sees more Romanism in Spenser than does King owing to her use of Latin sources (especially of the conciliatory Melanchthon) and to her refusal to take *The Shepheardes Calender* as the key to Spenser's religious coloration in his other works. Kaske's and Gless's positions represent fairly new answers to the ongoing critical debate over the poem's thematic unity. They recuperate Spenser from attacks like that of Berger (1998) because if one views Spenser's thought as a monolith, one cannot ignore the occasional whiff of misogyny, but if one looks at subsequent books (such as Book III) pluralistically as starting anew from a non-biblical perspective, the taint is less pervasive. Partly because Spenser localizes his references to Scripture, Book I with its apocalypticism cannot be the key to the entire poem (though Revelation recurs briefly at the end of Book V and in the *Vewe*) and neither is the Bible as a whole. Kaske contends that Spenser is a disciplined pluralist; he offers an ideology in Book I (mostly scripturalist, though also stressing sacraments and sacramentals) which differs not only from that in Book II (infrequent scripture mostly syncretized with the predominant Aristotelian ethics), but also from that in the remaining books of this poem (broadly secular and humanistic in the Renaissance sense of that word). The same degrees of Christianity are found in the *Fowre Hymnes*, though not in the same order, namely, the *Hymne of Heavenly Love* (based mostly on the Bible and the Creeds), the *Hymne of Heavenly Beautie* (vaguely Christian but syncretized with Jewish and Platonic ideas), and the *Hymne of Love* and the *Hymne of Beautie* (secular and humanistic). (See Kaske 1973, 1999.)

Kaske falls between Gless and King in acceptance of Spenser's religious contradictions. Gless locates each pole of a contradiction, couched in sophisticated theological vocabulary, in the mind of an individual reader. His is a reader-response interpretation leading at times to indeterminacy (though at other times he claims for Spenser a consistent brand of Protestantism which he calls 'Reformed'). He shows mental agility in reading each Spenserian passage from both a Protestant and a Catholic point of view. This interpretation, being minimalist, is plausible; it is especially helpful in 'solving' the merit-versus-grace problem; it aims at both groups by showing that Spenser's use of 'mercy' in Canto 10 is deliberately equivocal. But Kaske is not quite so deconstructive as Gless in that she also attempts to see patterns in the contradictions and reasons for them within the literary context (such as adiaphorism); the virtue treated in the individual book; or the hero's current stage of religious development. Other books of a similar scope are Mallette (1997) and the scores of biblical citations within the polymathic documentation of Hankins (1971) and Nohrnberg (1976).

We have traced Spenser's 'footing' among the Scriptures. As a part-time biblical poet, Spenser excels not only in intense straightforward local imitations and rewritings of biblical images, doctrines, stories, and characters but also with respect to his far-flung structural patterns of typology and images *in bono* and *in malo*.

NOTES

1. For the sake of a balanced coverage, the present essay revisits topics found in my previous works, often in similar words. As my documentation reveals, the works that I echo pervasively are Kaske (1990), (1999), and (2009). I am of course incalculably indebted to the notes of A. C. Hamilton in Spenser (2001). *FQ* citations are from this edition and for the *Shorter Poems* from Spenser (1999). All citations are from these editions. Unless otherwise noted, biblical citations are taken from the Geneva Bible of 1594. I have modernized u-v-w and i-j-y. Unless otherwise noted, translations are my own.
2. For more on the role of the Psalms in Elizabethan literature and society, see Kaske (1990); (2004), 28–33; Zim (1987).
3. For a scholarly parallel-text translation with introduction and notes, see Hollander (2002).
4. Besides Aquinas on the four senses see also Hollander (2002), xxxi–xxxiii; Kaske (1990).
5. Cf. *April*, 50–4, 91–4; Thenot's emblem, and the last line of the gloss thereto, on which see King (1999) with bibliography and important corrections of other critics, e.g., 64 n 78.
6. For a fairly accurate conspectus of the versions of this verse, see Shaheen (1976), 193, Appendix C, Example 29.
7. For a sixteenth-century definition of the doctrine and refutations of its many critics see Rogers (1854), 334–5, Thirty-Nine Articles 37, Propositions 1–3; and Wells (1983), 30–1.
8. For lists of Spenserian examples, see Kaske (1990, 1994, 2008), and especially Kaske (1999), Appendix.
9. For more on adiaphorism and its roots, see Kaske (1999), 86–97; McEachern (1996), 61.

BIBLIOGRAPHY

Aquinas, St. Thomas. (1945). *Basic Writings of Saint Thomas Aquinas*, ed. Anton C. Pegis (from The English Dominican Translation). New York: Random House.

Auerbach, E. (1984). *Scenes from the Drama of European Literature*. Gloucester, MA: Peter Smith. First prt. 1959.

Berger, H. (1998). 'Displacing Autophobia in *Faerie Queene I*: Ethics, Gender, and Oppositional Reading in the Spenserian Text'. *ELR* 28(2): 163–182.

Bergvall, Å. (1997). 'Between Eusebius and Augustine: Una and the Cult of Elizabeth.' *ELR* 27 (1): 3–30.

[Bible]. (1585). *Testamenti veteris Biblia Sacra… Latini… ex Hebraeo facti.* Translated into Latin and edited with notes by Emmanuel Tremellius and Franciscus Junius. London: Henry Middleton.

—— (1594). *The Bible: That Is, The Holy Scriptures…* [Geneva version]. Tomson glosses will be found in almost any of the many editions between 1576 and 1598. London: Christopher Barker.

—— (1969). *The Geneva Bible (1560).* Facsimile. Lloyd E. Berry (ed.). Madison: University of Wisconsin Press.

—— (1989). *The Geneva Bible: The Annotated New Testament, 1602.* Facsimile. Gerald T. Sheppard et al. (eds). Contains Tomson and Junius glosses. Introductory essays by Sheppard and others. New York: Pilgrim Press.

Borris, K. (1991). *Spenser's Poetics of Prophecy in* The Faerie Queen *[sic] V.* Toronto: University of Victoria English Literary Studies, 52.

Charity, A. C. (1966). *Events and Their Afterlife: The Dialectics of Christian Typology in the Bible and Dante.* Cambridge: Cambridge University Press.

Daniell, D. (2003). *The Bible in English.* New Haven, CT: Yale University Press.

Dante, see Hollander.

Fruen, J. P. (1994). 'The *Faery Queen* Unveiled? Five Glimpses of Gloriana'. *SSt* 11: 53–88.

Frye, Northrop (1972—first pub. in *Fables of Identity*, 1963). 'The Structure of Imagery in *The Faerie Queene*'. Rpt in A. C. Hamilton (ed.), *Essential Articles for the Study of Edmund Spenser.* Hamden, CT: Archon Books: 153–69.

Gless, D. J. (1994). *Interpretation and Theology in Spenser.* Cambridge: Cambridge University Press.

Greene, T. M. (1982). *The Light in Troy: Imitation and Discovery in Renaissance Poetry.* New Haven, CT: Yale University Press.

Greenslade, S. L. (1963). 'Epilogue', in *The Cambridge History of the Bible.* Cambridge: Cambridge University Press. 3: 496–7.

Hamlin, H. (2002). 'Psalm Culture in the English Renaissance: Readings of Psalm 137 by Shakespeare, Spenser, Milton, and Others'. *RQ* 55(1): 224–57.

Hankins, J. E. (1971). *Source and Meaning in Spenser's Allegory: A Study of* The Faerie Queene. Oxford: Clarendon Press.

Harvey, E. R. (1990). 'Sapience', in A. C. Hamilton et al. (eds), *Spenser Encyclopedia.* Toronto: University of Toronto Press.

Hollander, Robert and Jean (eds and trans) (2002). *Inferno.* New York: Anchor Books (1st edn, hardback, 2000).

—— (2003). *Purgatorio.* New York: Doubleday.

—— (2007). *Paradiso.* New York: Doubleday.

Kaske, C. V. (1975). 'Spenser's Pluralistic Universe: The View from the Mount of Contemplation (*FQ*, I.x)', in R. C. Frushell and B. J. Vondersmith (eds), *Contemporary Thought on Edmund Spenser.* Carbondale: Southern Illinois University Press: 121–49, 230–3.

—— (1990). 'Bible', in *SE.*

—— (1994). 'The Audiences of *The Faerie Queene*: Iconoclasm and Related Issues in Books I, V, and VI'. *L&H* 3: 15–35.

—— (1999). *Spenser and Biblical Poetics.* Ithaca, NY: Cornell University Press.

—— (2004). 'Spenser's *Amoretti* and *Epithalamion*: A Psalter of Love', in D. W. Doerksen and C. Hodgkins (eds), *Centered on the Word: Literature, Scripture, and the Tudor-Stuart Middle Way.* Newark, DE: University of Delaware Press: 28–49.

Kaske, C. V. (2009). 'Edmund Spenser', in R. Lemon et al. (eds), *The Blackwell Companion to the Bible in English Literature*. Malden, MA: Wiley-Blackwell: 197–210.

King, J. N. (1990a). 'Queen Elizabeth I: Representations of the Virgin Queen'. *RQ* 43(1): 30–74.

—— (1990b). *Spenser's Poetry and the Reformation Tradition*. Princeton, NJ: Princeton University Press.

Krier, T. (1998). 'Generations of Blazons: Psychoanalysis and the Song of Songs in the *Amoretti*'. *TSLL* 40: 292–327.

—— (2000). 'Hosea and the Play of Identifications in *The Faerie Queene I*'. *Religion and Literature* 32(2): 105–22.

Landrum, G. W. (1926). 'Spenser's use of the Bible and His Alleged Puritanism'. *PMLA* 41(3) (Sept. 1926): 517–44.

McEachern, C. (1995). '"A whore at the first blush seemeth only a woman": John Bale's *Image of Both Churches* and the terms of religious difference in the early English Reformation'. *JMRS* 25(2): 245–69.

—— (1996). *The Poetics of English Nationhood, 1590–1612*. Cambridge: Cambridge University Press.

Mallette, R. (1997). *Spenser and the Discourses of Reformation England*. Lincoln, NE: University of Nebraska Press.

Nohrnberg, J. (1976). *The Analogy of* The Faerie Queene. Princeton: Princeton University Press.

Perkins, P. (2006). 'Spenser's Dragon and the Law'. *SSt* 21: 51–81.

Pigman, G. W. (1980). 'Versions of Imitation in the Renaissance'. *RQ* 23(1): 1–32.

Prescott, A. L. (1985) 'The Thirsty Deer and the Lord of Life: Some Contexts for *Amoretti* 67–70'. *SSt*, 6: 33–76.

Rogers, T. (1854). *The Catholic Doctrine of the Church of England: An Exposition of the Thirty-Nine Articles*. Cambridge: Parker Society.

Shaheen, N. (1976). *Biblical References in* The Faerie Queene. Memphis, TN: Memphis State University Press.

Weatherby, Harold (1994). *Mirrors of Celestial Grace: Patristic Theology in Spenser's Allegory*. Toronto: University of Toronto Press.

Wells, Robin Headlam (1983). *Spenser's* Faerie Queene *and the Cult of Elizabeth*. Totowa, NJ: Barnes and Noble.

Zim, R. (1987). *English Metrical Psalms: Poetry as Praise and Prayer 1535–1601*. Cambridge: Cambridge University Press.

....

CHAPTER 27

SPENSER AND CLASSICAL LITERATURE

SYRITHE PUGH

....

In the humanistic grammar schools of the sixteenth century, education centred on the acquisition of fluency in Latin through the study of classical poetry, drama, and prose. From an early age, boys were required to memorize, to translate into English and back into Latin, to vary, and to imitate passages from a wide array of Roman authors, including Cicero, Virgil, Ovid, Horace, Martial, Plautus, and Terence. At Merchant Taylors' Spenser would also have studied Homer and probably Hesiod (Baldwin 1944: I, 415–20). From our perspective such immersion in the literature of the distant past might seem likely to stifle creativity and independent thought—and a recent study has argued that it presented culture 'as something given, absolute, to be mastered, not questioned', fostering a 'docile attitude towards authority' both literary and political (Grafton and Jardine 1986: xii). But the express purpose of this training was to equip students with the rhetorical facility which would enable them to write and speak eloquently for themselves (Bushnell 1996). In fact its methods could be said to be far from reverential towards literary authority. Holding up literary texts as examples of stylistic excellence, it required students to take them apart and rework them. Students were encouraged to compile 'commonplace books', a personal store of passages and turns of phrase which struck them as particularly felicitous, culled from across their reading and arranged under headings, to be retrieved and reapplied in their own compositions. Their study of metrics involved them in practical consideration of the choices made by poets, and exploration of possible alternatives. Tasks such as producing metrical variations on chosen lines from Ovid's

Tristia must have made classical poetry seem not so much 'something given' as a work in progress, still malleable. As part of their rhetorical training, moreover, they were regularly required to argue on both sides of a given topic (*in utramque partem*), which must have encouraged a questioning and controversialist turn of mind (see Chapter 23 above). Among the topics suggested by Erasmus for this exercise was the preferability of monarchical or republican government. One might expect that an apt student so attuned to techniques both of imitation and controversy would go on to write poetry which used creative imitation at once to engage its classical models in debate and to enter into contemporary controversies—and this is precisely what Spenser did.

Alongside the humanists' rhetorical approach to the classics there also persisted an older tradition, which justified the study of poets like Virgil and Ovid and assimilated them to Christianity by reading their works as allegories encoding moral and religious truths (Murrin 1980). Though most strongly associated with the Middle Ages, such interpretations survived in commentaries reprinted alongside the text in sixteenth-century editions; Cristofero Landino published a highly influential allegorization of the *Aeneid* as late as 1480 (Murrin 1980: 27–50). The many fables of the *Metamorphoses* were the springboard for varied and often fantastical flights of allegorization; interpretations of the *Aeneid*, such as those by Bernardus Silvestris and Fulgentius, tended to be more consistent, reading Aeneas as the human soul progressing from ignorance and sin to wisdom. Handbooks like Conti's *Mythologiae* gathered together the diverse allegorical significations of each mythological figure. Again, though this approach might seem deadening to a modern reader, distorting the complex alterity of the classical text into a reflection of current dogma, it too could work as a creative spur, unfolding alternative possibilities within the source text for interpretation, development, and application. The anonymous fourteenth-century *Ovide moralisé* expands the *Metamorphoses* to six times the length of the original by the addition of allegorical interpretations—an exercise of creative ingenuity, no matter how perverse its readings may seem. The tradition paves the way for the form of Spenser's *Faerie Queene*, and means that this allegorical Christian epic would not have seemed to contemporary readers as strikingly different from the classical epics of Homer, Virgil, and Ovid as it does to us. But Spenser's view of his classical models is not governed by traditional allegorizations: rather he uses such material selectively and intermittently to enhance his own creative imitations.

Exiled Shepherds: Virgilian and Ovidian Career Models in Spenser

It is often asserted that Spenser not only modelled his most important works on Virgil's but also his career on Virgil's career, beginning with pastoral and progressing to national epic (Helgerson 1983). In the epistle prefacing *The Shepheardes Calender*, E. K. already draws this analogy:

the best and most auncient Poetes . . . deuised this kind of wryting, being both so base for the matter, and homely for the manner, at the first to trye theyr habilities: and as young birdes, that be newly crept out of the nest, by little first to proue theyr tender wyngs, before they make a greater flyght. So flew Theocritus, as you may perceiue he was all ready full fledged. So flew Virgile, as not yet well feeling his winges. (Spenser 1999: 29)

When the time for this 'greater flyght' arrives, *The Faerie Queene* duly opens by drawing attention to the author's generic progression:

> Lo I the man, whose Muse whylome did maske,
>   As time her taught, in lowly Shepheards weeds,
>   Am now enforst a farre vnfitter taske,
>   For trumpets sterne to chaunge mine Oaten reeds . . .

This translates the pseudo-Virgilian lines printed as the opening of the *Aeneid* in sixteenth-century editions:

> Ille ego qui quondam gracili modulatus avena
> carmen, et egressus silvis vicina coegi,
> ut quamvis avido parerent arva colono,
> gratum opus agricolis; at nunc horrentia Martis
> arma virumque cano . . .

[I am he who once tuned my song on a slender oaten reed, and then, leaving the woods for the neighbouring fields, I forced them to serve the farmer's highest hopes, and my work was pleasing to farmers. But now I sing of the bristling arms of Mars and the man . . .][1]

Spenser's contemporaries took the hint: Thomas Nashe refers in 1592 to 'Chaucer and Spenser, the Homer and Virgil of England', and Kenelm Digby describes Spenser as 'our English Virgil' in 1628.

By far the dominant strain in criticism of Virgil since the early commentators has been to see him as an unqualified supporter of, even propagandist for, the reign of Augustus, the first Roman emperor, who is generally believed to have patronized Virgil and to have commissioned the *Aeneid* (Hardie 1986). Voices within the *Eclogues* praise the emperor as a god and seem to promise a return of the Golden Age under his rule. The *Aeneid* presents an optimistic vision of Roman history shaped by divine destiny, and more explicitly predicts another Golden Age under the quasi-divine Augustus, whose piety and virtue is foreshadowed in his heroic ancestor Aeneas. Spenser's apparent identification with Virgil has been seen as evidence of a similar attitude towards Elizabeth, and there are undeniably elements in his poems which apply to her the most hyperbolic examples of Virgil's praise of Augustus. Merlin's prophecy to Britomart of her future descendants in Book III of *The Faerie Queene*, imitating Anchises's prophecy to Aeneas in Virgil's underworld, foretells of 'sacred peace' ending civil war, and the 'eternall vnion' of the nation, under 'a royall Virgin' (III.iii.49) descended 'out of the auncient Troian blood' (iii.22), drawing on the legend popularized by Geoffrey of Monmouth in which Britain is founded by Brute, a great-grandson of Aeneas. He thus performs for Elizabeth the same *translatio imperii* by which Virgil's *Aeneid* justifies Augustus's reign, tracing the origins of his authority to Troy and eliding his bloody suppression of rivals and overthrow of republican liberty. London is dubbed 'Troynovant' or 'New Troy' in *The Faerie Queene* (II.x.46).

But Spenser's engagement both with politics and with his classical models is more complex and ambiguous than this picture suggests. Confident of a readership intimately familiar with classical literature from their grammar school education, Spenser expects his reader not only to recognize his allusions to and imitations of classical poets, but to be alert to the ways in which he changes and combines them. His imitation of Virgil introduces pointed and systematic changes to his original, and is woven together with imitation of other models, classical and modern. Particularly prominent and pervasive is the presence of Ovid, a poet whose attitude towards political authority is oppositional at every turn. Moreover, Virgil is not himself so unambiguously Augustan a poet as the dominant tradition holds. The Augustan voice is important in his poems, but there are also competing voices, unanswered questions, and signs of ambivalence about, or even resistance to, the Augustan ideology they seem on the most obvious level to enshrine (Kallendorf 2007; Lyne 1987). When Spenser seems to be reacting against Virgil's Augustan voice, it is often by tuning into and amplifying these competing voices within Virgil's texts, and the same can be said of Ovid before him.

Tellingly, the only Virgilian poem which Spenser directly translates is the mock-heroic *Culex*, or *Virgils Gnat*. (The Renaissance ascription of *Culex* to Virgil is discredited today.) This appeared in his 1591 volume, *Complaints*, a varied collection of poems and translations ostensibly lamenting the universal 'vanitie' of mortal affairs, but in fact replete with specific complaints about the current state of England. The volume was in fact recalled, probably in reaction to the too obviously topical satire against Elizabeth's chief minister, Lord Burghley, in *Mother Hubberds Tale*, a poem whose conclusion chimes strikingly with the *Culex*. *Virgils Gnat* is a tale of punishment where reward was due, a tragic perversion of justice in the working of the patronage system: a gnat stings a sleeping shepherd to warn him of the approach of a serpent, and is killed by the shepherd before he realizes his danger. The ghost of the gnat then delivers a lengthy lament describing the horrors of the underworld, a comic reworking of *Aeneid* VI. Spenser's dedication presents the poem as a 'riddle' about the poet himself and his erstwhile patron the Earl of Leicester, addressed as the 'causer of my care' but what event he is referring to remains unknown (see Chapters 1 and 6 above). When the gnat's action is repeated at the end of *Mother Hubberds Tale* the meaning is more obvious: Mercury arouses the sleeping lion with a stinging rebuke for his 'sluggish' and 'senseles' inaction while his 'throne royall [is] with dishonour blent', an astonishingly frank swipe at Elizabeth herself, and a self-referential claim that the poet's biting satire is driven by fundamental loyalty. Virgil could furnish a model for sharp criticism of the monarch as well as for imperial praise.

Pastoral, the inaugurating genre of the Virgilian career, contains both these possibilities (Patterson 1987), and Spenser makes full use of its satirical potential in his first publication as sole author, *The Shepheardes Calender*. E. K.'s first gloss to *Januarye* informs us that in the shepherd Colin Clout 'this Poete secretly shadoweth himself, as sometime did Virgil vnder the name of Tityrus'. We are thus prompted to compare Spenser's opening eclogue with Virgil's, and to expect that Colin will echo the tone and views of Virgil's Tityrus. But Virgil's first eclogue is a dialogue between two shepherds with radically different perspectives on contemporary society. They are discussing the confiscation of their farms, clearly referring to a real and recent political event, the seizure of lands by Octavian to reward the troops who had brought him to power in the Civil Wars. Tityrus has journeyed to Rome and successfully petitioned a godlike youth, clearly Octavian, to be reinstated on his farm; now he reclines in the shade (*lentus in umbra*, 4), praising his benefactor as a god (6–7, 42–3). But the other speaker, Meliboeus, has had no such luck, and utters a bitter lament at his unjust treatment as he departs into exile. There is only one shepherd in Spenser's eclogue, and we quickly realize that he resembles the grieving Meliboeus rather than Tityrus (see pp. 465–6 above). Though Colin has made Tityrus's journey to 'the neighbour town', the result is not the benevolent patronage relationship Tityrus enjoys, but the suffering of unrequited love for the proud and scornful 'Rosalind', a deeply critical use of the widespread Petrarchan depiction of Elizabeth (Bates 1992). In place of the pleasant shade which protects Tityrus, Colin sees in the 'naked trees, whose shady leaues are lost' an image of his own ruined state. Like Meliboeus, who will 'sing no more songs' (*carmina nulla canam*, 77), Colin renounces his Muse and breaks his pipe, a gesture symbolic of protest at the failure of patronage in a tradition going back to classical poets (Kelsey and Peterson 2000).

The voice identified with the author's in the *Calender*, then, is not that of a grateful Tityrus deifying his ruler, but that of a disaffected Meliboeus complaining against injustice. When Colin reappears in *June*, he again plays the sorrowing exile, 'whom cruell fate, | And angry Gods pursue from coste to coste' (14–15). This time his complaint is counterpointed by a Tityrus-like Hobbinol, who urges Colin to come and share the delightful 'shade' of the 'dales' which he enjoys (2, 21). Colin now actively rejects such pleasures as 'weary wanton toyes', and calls on the shepherds to 'Beare witnesse' to Rosalind's 'wicked deede', the discontent of his persona taking on a more overtly satirical force (48, 108). Wide-ranging but necessarily oblique satire is the *Calender*'s dominant mode. It comments provocatively and from a strongly Protestant perspective on a range of topical issues, including 'popish' practices in the Church, economic abuses such as absenteeism, the punishment of Archbishop Grindal for his refusal to suppress 'prophesyings' at Elizabeth's command, and, persistently, the Queen's planned marriage to the French Catholic Duc d'Alençon (McCabe 1995).

The exception which proves the rule is Colin's 'laye | Of fayre *Elisa*' in the *Aprill* eclogue, which praises Elizabeth in the terms which Tityrus applied to Octavian in the Augustan voice of the first eclogue:

> Shee is my goddesse plaine,
> And I her shepherds swayne,
> Albee for swonck and for swatt I am.   (97–9)

Yet even within the 'laye' Colin expresses grave reservations about this form of praise, and he does so through allusion to another classical poet, Ovid. After an elaborate description of how Phoebus and Cynthia, gods of the sun and moon, are 'dasht' by comparison with the more resplendent Elisa (73–85), Colin continues:

> But I will not match her with *Latonaes* seede,
> Such follie great sorow to *Niobe* did breede.
>   Now she is a stone,
>   And makes dayly mone,
> Warning all other to take heede.   (86–90)

In Book VI of Ovid's *Metamorphoses*, Niobe is a queen who demands that her people worship her as a goddess, instead of Latona, the divine mother of Apollo and Diana (Phoebus and Cynthia). Her claim of superiority to the goddess is based on her boasted fruitfulness: she has fourteen children to Latona's two. Latona bids Apollo and Diana avenge her by killing Niobe's children and husband, and Niobe turns to stone through grief. Similar warning notes are sounded by E. K., who glosses the eclogue's earlier reference to Rosalind by referring to the poet Stesichorus, blinded 'by the vengeaunce of the Gods' for excessive praise of 'hys Idole' Himera. Though poets must voice their criticism of monarchs obliquely for fear of 'rebuke and Daunger' (*June* 69), yet Colin reminds us there is a higher authority and a stronger imperative which exert a control in the opposite direction, for to praise a mortal ruler as a god is to commit idolatry, and to risk bringing down the wrath of God himself on poet and ruler alike.

This allusion calls attention to the other great classical poet who exerts a shaping influence not only on Spenser's individual works but on his career and self-presentation (Pugh 2005). Unlike Virgil, whose moments of doubt about Augustus are only an undersong, subsumed in the larger celebratory narrative for which he was rewarded with the laurels of patronage, Ovid provided a model for sustained, though oblique, criticism of the abuse of centralized power. His provocative and racy elegies, particularly the mock-didactic treatise on seduction, the *Ars Amatoria* or 'Art of Love', defy the spirit, if not the letter, of the moral legislation by which Augustus attempted to police sexual behaviour. His epic *Metamorphoses* depicts a directionless world governed by the arbitrary whims, rapacious sexual desires, and vindictive cruelty of the gods to whom Virgil likens Augustus and attributes his destined rule. His *Fasti*, a poem on the origins of the festivals in the Roman calendar, uses Ovid's antiquarian knowledge and claims of divine inspiration to expose Augustus's insidious self-deification and manipulation of the state religion to consolidate his power. Ovid's career ends with two collections of verse epistles lamenting his exile, written in Tomis on the Black Sea, the frozen and war-torn region to which Augustus banished him in 8 AD, ostensibly as a tardy punishment for the *Ars*, written years before, but also, Ovid tells us, for a reason the emperor wishes kept secret (probably political).

Ovid is a real-life Meliboeus, victim and critic of imperial injustice, and together with his imitation of the Meliboean strain of Virgilian pastoral in his inaugural poem, Spenser weaves in imitation of Ovid too. The highly unusual calendrical structure of the *Fasti* makes it as clear a model for Spenser's *Calender* as Virgil's *Eclogues*, and it shares the *Calender*'s concerns over freedom of speech, the cultural deification of monarchs, and contemporary greed and corruption.

The year after the publication of the *Calender* Spenser was posted to Ireland, where he remained for the rest of his life, a coincidence which deepened his connection to the exiled poet. When he returns to the 'Virgilian' genre of pastoral in the 1595 *Colin Clouts Come Home Againe*, it is heavily inflected by Ovid. The pastoral setting is identified with Ireland, presented as a place of exile (182–3), and the ambivalent treatment of both Ireland (at once uncivil wilderness and haven for an idealized community of friends) and England (longed for as a centre of civility but rejected as corrupt) is strongly reminiscent of Ovid's exile poetry. Ovid's confidence in his own poetic powers and fame, despite the hostility of the emperor so vividly demonstrated in his permanent exile, affords Spenser a model for a poetic authority which bypasses Tityrean reliance on the monarch. His Irish 'exile', treated in Ovidian terms, becomes a symbol of disaffection and independence: the 'shepherds nation' of *Colin Clout* owe no allegiance to Cynthia, and follow the teachings of the vatic poet, 'Priest' of 'Love'.

Love is central to Spenser's ethics, politics, and philosophy, and Ovid's fame as a love poet also makes him an important source. The *Amoretti* and *Epithalamion*, normally read in relation to Petrarch and his imitators, are indebted to Ovid: the progress of Spenser's persona from the desire for sexual mastery at the beginning of the sequence to the vision of mutual love and service leading to marriage at the end is modelled on the transition in Ovid from the selfish and manipulative persona of the early *Amores* to the exile elegies, in which Ovid becomes the only poet before Spenser to write love poetry to his own wife. In Elizabethan England, where courtship and courtiership were inextricable, such varieties of love relationship had political implications, and the *Metamorphoses* contributes to *The Faerie Queene* a rich exploration of the psychology of desire and its intersections with power, as well as influencing its formal fluidity and multiplicity.

ALLEGORICAL EPIC ROMANCE: *THE FAERIE QUEENE* I–III

Virgilian, Ovidian, and other classical influences mingle in *The Faerie Queene* and *Mutabilitie Cantos*. As mentioned earlier, the proem to Book I begins by translating what Spenser believed to be the opening of the *Aeneid*. But the continuation of the stanza introduces strikingly non-Virgilian matter. Where Virgil sings of 'arms and the man', Spenser will 'sing of Knights *and Ladies* gentle deeds', of 'Fierce warres *and faithfull loues*'. Virgil's poem, at least in its overarching Augustan frame, is virulently antierotic, and even misogynistic. The major threats to Aeneas's quest to found a new homeland for the survivors of Troy in Italy come from females maddened by passion—the 'relentless anger of savage Juno' (I.4), the mad frenzy of sexual love in Dido (e.g. IV.101), the 'female anger' of 'mad' Amata (VII.345, 348). The first half of the poem is dominated by Aeneas's love affair with Dido, and his obedience to Jove's command that he must abandon her and resume his quest, suppressing any feeling of pity, functions at least on the surface as a confirmation of his piety, and an assertion of the importance of public duty over private desire, despite her tragic suicide. A positive view of 'Ladies gentle deeds' and 'faithfull loues' seems quite alien to imitation of Virgil.

In fact Spenser is following Ariosto, who expands on Virgil's 'arms and the man I sing' in the opening lines of his *Orlando Furioso*, an Italian epic romance published in 1516: *Le donne, i cavalier, l'arme, gli amori,* | *Le cortesie, l'audaci imprese io canto* ('I sing of ladies, knights, courtesies, and brave deeds'). The *Orlando Furioso* is an important influence on Spenser's poem, not only thematically, in this focus on love and chivalry, but also structurally, in the sophisticated way it sustains the many threads of its digressive and interlaced narrative—and this too is a departure from Virgil's predominantly linear structure, as Aeneas, once recovered from his single lapse with Dido, single-mindedly pursues his quest. In all of this both Ariosto and Spenser are indebted to the narrative drift, complex interweaving of fables, and amatory subject matter of Ovid's *Metamorphoses* (Javitch 1980, 1984; Pugh 2005). The rest of the proem indicates that love will in fact be Spenser's main emphasis, as he invokes Venus and Cupid to inspire his song, accompanied by Mars only in his disarmed Ovidian guise as Venus's lover, 'In loues and gentle iollities arraid, | After his murdrous spoyles and bloudie rage allayd' (3). This counter-Virgilian note points to what will be a systematic revision and rejection of the Augustan voice of the *Aeneid*, articulated largely through a turn to the opposing values of Ovid, but supported once again by imitation of counter-Virgilian moments within Virgil himself.

The first canto begins with a storm, which drives Una and Redcrosse to seek shelter in the Wandring Wood, and from here, after defeating the monster Errour in the cave at its centre, they progress to Archimago's house. Primed by the proem's quotation of the *Aeneid*, the reader will recognize this storm as reflecting the two storms early in the *Aeneid*: the first, in Book I, drives Aeneas ashore at Carthage, and the second, in Book IV, drives Aeneas and Dido, while out hunting, to take shelter in a cave, where they consummate their love. Spenser's wood, his cave, and the defeat of Errour, seem at first to transpose into allegory Aeneas's abandonment of Dido, and the negative view of their love affair which is the dominant voice in this section of the *Aeneid*. Yet a more literal imitation follows quickly, and overturns this view. At the beginning of canto ii, Redcrosse abandons Una, deceived by Archimago's slanderous and deceptive magic into believing her lustful and fickle. Archimago's deception seems to echo the denouncement of Dido as burning with lust and regardless of her reputation, first by Virgil's narrator and then by his strange personification of Fame, and Mercury's final warning to Aeneas *varium et mutabile semper femina* ('Woman is always fickle and changeful', IV.569–70). As Nahum Tate would do in his libretto for Purcell's *Dido and Aeneas* a century later, Spenser rewrites Virgil's divine command as the trick of a malicious enchanter. Since Una is explicitly labelled as the personification of Truth in the arguments to cantos ii and iii, there can be no doubt that, by imitating Aeneas and abandoning her, Spenser's knight of Holiness commits a disastrous fault.

Redcrosse immediately hooks up with Duessa, the embodiment of duplicity, who is later revealed as the Whore of Revelation 17.9 when she is decked out in gold and purple and set upon a seven-headed beast by Orgoglio (vii.16–18). The glosses to the Geneva Bible interpret this image as representing both the Roman Empire and the papacy which inherited its blasphemous pride, 'cruelty and tyranny'. So where Aeneas deserts Dido in favour of a destiny which leads to the Roman empire instituted by Augustus, Redcrosse similarly deserts Una for a Duessa who personifies imperial rule, as well as the papacy. Duessa leads Redcrosse to the House of Pride, ruled over by Lucifera, a female Satan and maiden queen who embodies the worldly pride of tyrannical monarchs who rule not 'with Law, but pollicie' (iv.12). During this episode, Duessa visits Hell, imitating Aeneas's descent to the underworld but with no suggestion of the prophecy underwriting Augustus's reign as divinely ordained which Aeneas receives there. Virgil's roll call of Aeneas's glorious descendants and future rulers of Rome, meanwhile, is largely reproduced in the list of the inmates of the dungeons of Lucifera's palace. The supernatural core of Virgil's Augustan ideology has been collapsed into bondage to Satan.

Spenser has succinctly reversed the ostensible values of Virgil's *Aeneid*, equating faithful love such as Aeneas failed to show to Dido with holiness and adherence to truth, and the worldly glory of empire to which Aeneas's *pietas* was bent, encapsulated in Anchises's underworld prophecy, with Satanic pride. Yet Virgil himself supplies Spenser with part of the means to do so. After Redcrosse has deserted Una, Errour seems in retrospect to take on a new significance, no longer embodying the threat posed to the heroic quest by amatory digression such as Dido represents to Aeneas, but rather anticipating the error Redcrosse will make in believing the slanderous aspersions cast on his lady love by Archimago, which we have likened to the denigration of Dido in the *Aeneid*. Now while it is true that Virgil's narrator participates in this denigration of Dido, Jove commands Aeneas to leave her because he has apparently learned of the affair, strangely, from the extremely denigratory and lubricious account spread by Fama. (Iarbas has heard it from Fama, and relays it in a prayer to Jove.) Fama, a monstrous personification of rumour, is described as sister to the rebellious Giants. With her many tongues 'she terrifies great cities, clinging to falsehood and corruption and pronouncing truth in equal measure' (IV.187–8), and in her report of Dido's 'shameless passion' (*turpi... cupidine*, 194) she mixes fact and slander equally (*pariter facta atque infecta canebat*, 190). Virgil is striking a deeply disturbing note when Jove's judgement of Aeneas's affair is presented as originating in the gossip (*sermone*, 189) of this impious monster, and when Spenser prefixes his imitation of Aeneas's abandonment of Dido with the monster Errour, similarly a quasi-literary purveyor of lies, he seems to be expanding on Virgil's hint.

Another Virgilian note of doubt informs the deception of Redcrosse. Archimago accomplishes his deception by means of a false dream fetched from the House of Morpheus 'Amid the bowels of the earth full steepe' (i.39). The episode imitates

Ovid's House of Somnus, from his story of the faithful love of Ceyx and Alcyone in Book XI of the *Metamorphoses*, but like the Ovidian episode itself it also looks back to Virgil's underworld and travesties the Augustan prophecy delivered there precisely by amplifying the most problematic crux of Virgil's text for critics, ancient and modern, who want the *Aeneid* to be unambiguously Augustan (Burrow 1999). Virgil's underworld episode is bracketed by two passages which disturbingly equate its contents with false dreams. In its entrance hall stands an elm thronged with 'empty dreams' (*somnia vana*, VI.283–4); at the end, there are said to be two exits from the underworld, described as 'two gates of Sleep' (*geminae Somni portae*, VI.893), one of horn, an exit for 'true shades' (*veris umbris*, VI.894), and one of ivory, through which 'false dreams' (*falsa insomnia*, VI.896) pass, and it is through this ivory gate that Aeneas passes, armed with Anchises's prophecy. Servius comments *vult enim intellegi falsa esse omnia quae dixit* ('for Virgil wants us to understand that everything he has said is false'), undermining at a stroke the whole basis of the *Aeneid*'s Augustan ideology. Spenser reproduces these twin gates in his House of Morpheus,

> Whose double gates [Archimago's sprite] findeth locked fast,
> The one fair fram'd of burnisht Yuory,
> The other all with siluer ouercast   (i.40)

At the end of his visit the sprite, like Aeneas, returns 'by the Yuorie dore' (44). Spenser's reversal of the Augustan values of the *Aeneid*, then, is conspicuously made to depend on Virgil's own implied distrust of those very values.

This rejection of the antieroticism of Virgil's Dido episode is quite at odds with the allegorizing tradition, which lauded Aeneas's abandonment of Dido as a triumph of reason over lust (Watkins 1995). But later in Book I Spenser deploys that tradition in the service of his own Christian alternative to the *Aeneid*'s worldly telos. Aeneas's descent to the underworld, where he learns of the destiny of his nation, had been allegorized by Bernard Silvestris as 'contemplation', his guide the Sibyl as 'divine counsel'. At the culmination of Redcrosse's visit to the House of Holiness in canto x, the 'godly aged Sire' Contemplation guides him to the top of a mountain, where he receives his vision of the New Hierusalem, and learns his true 'name and nation' as the English St George (x.48, 67). Spenser pits this Christianized Virgil against the original: the stuff of Anchises's prophecy is Rome as *urbs eterna*, but Redcrosse's vision of the heavenly city reveals to him the limitations of the earthly city Cleopolis, as religious faith is prioritized over political allegiance: 'this great Citty that does far surpas' (58). Good and bad Virgils are played off against one another.

Aeneas's entry into the underworld, past a host of personified evils which crowd the entrance, is more obviously the model for Guyon's descent into the cave of Mammon in Book II. Otherwise puzzling, for the knight of Temperance does not need to enter the cave and so seems to be seeking out temptation, the episode is more intelligible in the light of one of Bernard's allegorizations of Aeneas's descent: a 'wise person descends to mundane things through meditation . . . so that, having recognized their frailty, he may thoroughly turn from the rejected things to the invisible things and acknowledge more clearly in thought the Creator of creatures' (Bernard 1979: 32).

It is no coincidence that the clearest and most sustained example of this kind of allegorical reading of a classical text also occurs in Book II, whose secular virtue of Temperance, concerned with the control of the appetites, is most easily and plausibly read out of the classics by the moralizing commentaries. Guyon's voyage to the Bowre of Blisse at the beginning of canto xii is a reworking of Book XII of the *Odyssey* as moral allegory: Homer's Scylla and Charybdis become 'the Gulfe of Greedinesse' and 'Rock of Reproch', his Sirens the tempting mermaids past whom Guyon is guided by the Palmer's 'temperate advice' (xii.34). Acrasia herself is modelled on the Circe of Book X of the *Odyssey*, as well as earlier imitations in Italian romance, again in the spirit of moralizing allegory. She is referred to as 'Pleasure' in stanzas 1 and 48, and her victims' transformation reflects their bestial appetites: 'turned into figures hideous, | According to their mindes like monstruous' (xii.85). Gryll, who chooses to remain a hog rather than return to human form, is an addition from Plutarch's *Moralia.* The technique is that of the commentators and mythographers (compare Fulgentius 2.8–9 on the Sirens and Scylla, Whitney 82 on Circe), though even here there is evidence that Spenser is responding directly to Homer's text as well as to the mediating tradition (Demetriou 2006).

Book II resembles the *Aeneid* in many ways. Guyon's career is linear and purposeful; his battle with Pyrochles in canto v and Arthur's vengeful slaying of Cymochles and Pyrochles in canto viii recall Aeneas's slaying of Turnus at the end of Virgil's poem, like Guyon's destruction of the Bowre a startlingly wrathful conclusion. The suicide Amavia at the start of the book and Acrasia at the end both recall Dido: Guyon, Aeneas-like, suppresses his pity for the first and overcomes the temptation of the latter. The corrupt eroticism of the Bowre, meanwhile, is fraught with Ovidian allusions. But in Book III, as Spenser sets about recuperating true love from the threat of its perversions, the looser narrative form, strong heroines, and amatory subject matter of Ovid and of romance take over the poem.

As with Virgil in Book I, Spenser plays good and bad Ovids off against one another. The book is framed by the Ovidian tapestries of Malecasta and Busirane in cantos i and xi (Brown 1999: 39–56). Malecasta's tells the story of Venus and Adonis (*Metamorphoses* 10.519–739) in a way calculated to titillate her courtly guests. There is attractive tenderness in Venus's wooing and pathos in her grief (she uses her 'soft garment' to cover Adonis while he sleeps, and then to 'wipe away the gore' of his deadly wound), but also a more disturbing note:

> And whilst he bath'd, with her two crafty spyes,
> She secretly would search each daintie lim,
> And throw into the well sweet Rosemaryes,
> And fragrant violets . . .   (III.i.36)

Though softened by the pretty flower catalogue, Venus's secret spying—imported from another Ovidian tale, Salmacis and Hermaphroditus (*Metamorphoses* 4.285–380)—is disturbingly predatory, hinting at an underlying selfishness and exploitativeness, and recalling Acrasia 'greedily depasturing delight' as she sucks the spright of her sleeping lover through his eyes (II.xii.73). Ovid's Hermaphroditus is in fact raped by the nymph Salmacis. The viewers of the tapestry are drawn into this disturbing power relation, as their visual enjoyment of the work of art is reflected in Venus's voyeurism, a reification of physical beauty evidently to be continued in the knights' and ladies' treatment of each other as they make use of the chamber's 'many beds' (39). The combination of self-consciously illicit viewing and sexual aggression is again evident in Busirane's tapestries, which to celebrate the power of 'cruell *Cupid*' depict many tales of rape committed by gods in the form of beasts, most taken from the *Metamorphoses* (in fact closely coinciding with Arachne's tapestry in *Metamorphoses* VI). The effect of these tapestries is connected to the sinister coercion which Busirane tries to practice on his prisoner Amoret. Physical love is presented more openly as a violent threat, but another reference to secret spying implicates the viewer in a slightly different way. As Jove in the form of a swan approaches Leda to 'inuade' her,

> Shee slept, yet twixt her eielids closely spyde,
> How towards her he rusht, and smiled at his pryde.   (xi.32)

The viewer's (and reader's) visual enjoyment of the tapestries is now implicitly parallelled with a surreptitiously willing surrrender to violation, the viewer placed in the position of a victim invited to collude in what cannot be resisted. Britomart, Amoret, and we are effectively asked to assent to the most outrageous argument in Ovid's *Art of Love*, where the lover is advised that, if other methods fail to attract a mistress, he should use rape: 'You may use force: that force is welcome to girls. They often wish to have given reluctantly what nevertheless pleases them' (I.673–4). Busirane's selective reading of Ovid reflects, and tries to propagate, a perverse view of sexual love as necessarily founded in compulsion and antagonism—a view which seems to have inspired Scudamour when he dragged the unwilling Amoret from the Temple of Venus (as he recounts at IV.x.57), and which prevents the couple from coming together in the kind of free and mutual love advocated by Britomart at III.i.25 and by Arthur at IV.ix.37.

Before she can pursue and achieve such an harmonious relationship herself, Britomart must learn to distinguish her natural and virtuous desire for Artegall from such perversions: the conversation with her nurse recounted in canto ii (an episode modelled on the pseudo-Virgilian *Ciris* and also on its likely source in Ovid's Myrrha episode) differentiates her from Myrrha, Biblis, Pasiphae, and Narcissus, all tales of perverse desire familiar from Ovid. At the centre of Book III the account of the birth and upbringing of the twins Belphoebe and Amoret argues that true love and virginity are equally chaste, drawing heavily on classical myth and especially on Ovid. Their mother, Chrysogone, is miraculously impregnated by 'sunbeames' while sleeping after bathing, a story inspired by Danae, visited by Jove in the form of a shower of gold in the *Metamorphoses*, and the *Fasti*'s Silvia, unwittingly made pregnant with Romulus and Remus by Mars as she slept. A simile comparing the spontaneous generation from the mud of Nile is drawn from Ovid's account of earth's regeneration after the flood in Book I of the *Metamorphoses*, an early hint that the sexuality to be celebrated in this episode is the principle sustaining creation itself.

Spenser then describes how Venus and Diana, classical goddesses of sexual love and virginity respectively, searching for Venus's truant son Cupid (a tale inspired by Venus's lament over her runaway son in a Greek idyll by Moschus) instead find Chrysogone, who has now given birth in her sleep. Each takes one of the baby girls to foster, Belphoebe among Diana's nymphs in the woods, Amoret in Venus's 'ioyous Paradize' (vi.29), the Garden of Adonis.

A complex poetic image of the cycles of nature, the Garden of Adonis is philosophically elusive and even inconsistent. The 'endlesse progeny' (30) which grow there before being 'sent forth to liue in mortall state' (32), returning after death to be replanted in the Garden for a thousand years, and so on, seem at first to be souls awaiting bodies, recalling Anchises's lecture on metempsychosis, or the reincarnation of the soul, in Virgil's underworld (*Aeneid* VI.713–51); Spenser's formulation in stanzas 37 and 38 is clearly based on the core of Pythagoras's speech about metempsychosis in Ovid (*Metamorphoses* XV.252–8). But this doctrine would be impossible to square with Christianity, and sometimes the 'progeny' seem instead to be bodies awaiting souls (35). But the description gradually stabilizes around the idea of the continuity of life through sexual reproduction, giving a mystical aura to what might otherwise seem a mundane matter. At the centre of the Garden, in the central stanza of the 1590 Book III, stands 'a stately Mount' (an anatomical allegory of the *mons Veneris*), where grows 'euery sort of flowre, | To which sad louers were transformde of yore' (45). A vast array of tales from the *Metamorphoses* is implicitly evoked, though Spenser mentions only a few examples, preparing the way for a reworking of the Ovidian tale which was the subject of Malecasta's tapestry. Lapped in these flowers, Venus and Adonis enjoy perpetual lovemaking, by which Adonis becomes 'the Father of all formes...that liuing giues to all', and transcends his own death through reproduction: 'All be he subject to mortalitie,' Adonis

> is eterne in mutabilitie,
> And by succesion made perpetuall,
> Transformed oft, and chaunged diuerslie.   (47)

The extraordinary image combines the two main themes of Ovid's *Metamorphoses*—change and sexual love—into a newly beneficent whole, linked to the Christian idea of divine providence sustaining creation through the invocation of God's command 'That bad them to increase and multiply'(34).

UNDOING EPIC: *THE FAERIE QUEENE* IV–VI AND THE MUTABILITIE CANTOS

The last three books of *The Faerie Queene* offer a darker perspective on contemporary society, and this is accompanied by a shift in the poem's relationship to classical

literature. Book V opens with a gloomy reference to the myth of the declining ages—
drawing on the *Metamorphoses* and Hesiod's *Works and Days*, and wittily capping
Ovid's account by adding a final 'stonie' age generated from Ovid's own tale of
Pyrrha and Deucalion—and announces that he must draw matter for his poem
about virtue from the lost Golden Age, and not from 'present dayes, which are
corrupted sore' (V Proem, 3). Yet in fact of all the books of the poem Book V is the
most topical, and its account of its virtue the furthest from idealization and the
closest to fallen reality, ending with Artegall's recall before he can properly accomplish his reform of Irena's realm, reflecting Spenser's dissatisfaction with Elizabeth's
policy in Ireland. A similar note of pessimistic topicality is struck at the end of Book
VI, when the poem breaks off under attack from its own monster, the Blatant Beast,
which has escaped the bands imposed on it by Calidore and startlingly resurfaced 'in
Britaine land' and in the present tense: 'So now he raungeth through the world
againe' (VI.xii.39–40). The density of allusions to Virgil and Ovid which characterized the 1590 *Faerie Queene* falls off sharply in these books, in keeping perhaps with
the starker presentation of contemporary society, but at the same time Spenser
retreats deeper into the literary past, returning to the origins of epic to revise the
genre's preoccupation with violence and complicity with power.

The arch-enemy of Friendship, the foundation of all social bonds and the virtue of
Book IV, is 'Ate, mother of debate, | And all dissention' (i.19). Her house contains
memorials of the great cities she has ruined, including 'Rome that raigned long' (22),
Virgil's *urbs eterna* now placed firmly in the past tense. For Troy, there is the golden
apple which Eris (or Strife), mother of Ate according to Hesiod's *Theogony* but often
conflated with her in the Renaissance, threw among the goddesses at the wedding of
Peleus and Thetis, causing the beauty contest between Venus, Juno, and Minerva (the
apple is to be awarded to the fairest), settled by the Judgement of Paris: Paris's reward
for choosing Venus is Helen, whose abduction causes the Trojan War, subject of
Homer's *Iliad* (the story is told for instance by the second-century mythographer
Hyginus, *Fabulae* 92). This myth is therefore the origin of the genre in which Spenser
is working, and he uses it in Book IV to subject traditional epic values to ethical
scrutiny and ridicule. Ate sows dissention over who is to possess the false Florimel
(the imitation of the beautiful Florimel created by the witch in Book III), a discord
culminating in the 'Turneyment for beauties prise' (vii.3), which goes comically awry
in cantos iv and v. The prize for the beauty contest is the *cestus* given by Venus to the
true Florimel: imbued with 'the vertue of chast loue' (v.3), it will not fasten around
the waist of the beautiful but unchaste false Florimel, to whom it is awarded, but only
around Amoret's. The episode parodies the high valuation of physical beauty in the
Judgement of Paris, but Spenser is also drawing on an alternative version of Helen's
story, originating in Stesichorus and preserved by Plato and Euripides, according to
which the real Helen sojourned in Egypt while her phantom double was abducted by
Paris (Nohrnberg 1976: 114–19). The Trojan War was thus utterly pointless. Spenser's
tourney, a parody of that war, is won by Britomart, who to the amazement of the
other knights rejects the prize of the false Florimel, preferring Amoret's virtue before
empty beauty. Both the means and the goals of epic strife are reduced to absurdity, as

masculine martial prowess is revealed as thrall to the vanity of the senses rather than serving virtue.

The pastoral interlude towards the end of the poem also functions to undo epic in several ways. Firstly, it reverses the Virgilian progression from pastoral to epic: Spenser himself enters the poem in his old pastoral guise as Colin Clout, in a community presided over by the shepherd Melibee, who presents a critical perspective on the vain pride and ambition of court life again reminiscent of Virgil's disaffected Meliboeus. Secondly, when Calidore abandons his quest to sojourn among the shepherds he re-enacts an early part of the Trojan myth *in reverse*. Priam's son Paris had been exposed as a baby because of a prophecy that he would cause Troy's destruction, but survived and was brought up as a shepherd on Mount Ida, marrying the nymph Oenone; in adulthood he is recognized and reinstated as a prince of Troy, abandoning the shepherd's life and Oenone to pursue Helen (Hyginus, *Fabulae* 91; Ovid, *Heroides* V, XVI). As Calidore exchanges his 'bright armes' and 'spear' for 'shepheards weed' and 'hook' he is compared to 'Phrygian Paris by *Plexippus* brooke, | When he the loue of fayre *Oenone* sought' (VI.ix.36). We have returned to a time before the first stirrings of epic, both in mythology and in the poet's career. Finally, the climax of Book VI, the vision on Mount Acidale in canto x, reworks the opening of Hesiod's epic *Theogony*, the greatest account of poetic inspiration in classical literature, but redirects its subject matter onto private love, as if in an attempt to deflect the entire epic tradition at its origin from its concern with violent struggle and power. The vision of the dancing Graces, their 'many feet fast thumping th'hollow ground' (x.10), which answers the piping of the shepherd Colin echoes Hesiod's description of his meeting with the dancing Muses, who taught him fine singing as he tended his sheep on Mount Helicon: 'the dark earth rang round them as they sang, and from their dancing feet came a lovely *estampie*' (*Theogony* 1–115).[2] Yet where Hesiod's song is of strife and the exchange of power among the gods, Colin's vision is centred on his private love, presented as a fourth Grace: it is quite unconnected to his powerful dedicatee Elizabeth and to the epic quests of the poem. As he does elsewhere for the Muses, Spenser follows Hesiod here in the names and parentage of the Graces (*Theogony* 907–11): they are begot by Jove on Eurynome. But Spenser adds that this happened as Jove returned from the wedding of Peleus and Thetis. An implicit connection is forged with the mythical origins of the Trojan War, yet the apple of Discord goes unmentioned, as if we are tracing from this foundational moment a parallel possible development of poetry, into which Strife, war, and empire never entered.

Jove's defeats of the Titans and Giants, which comprise an important part of the *Theogony*'s subject matter, became in Horace and Virgil the central myth justifying the rule of the earthly Jove, Augustus (Hardie 1986), and in Book II Spenser compares his chronicle of Briton kings, leading up to Elizabeth's rule, to the 'triumphes of *Phlegraean Jove*' (II.x.3). But in the *Mutabilitie Cantos* he recasts the Titanomachy as a legal debate between his Titaness Mutabilitie and the Olympians, judged by divine Providence in the person of Nature, and set in Ireland, the scene of Spenser's Ovidian 'exile'. Now it is dependent on justice rather than force, the outcome is ambivalent:

Mutabilitie's hereditary claim to the usurping Jove's throne is not upheld; yet although the narrator says that Jove is 'confirm'd in his imperiall see' Nature's judgement says nothing about Jove, looking instead to the Apocalypse, when God's kingdom will supercede all such disputes (VII.vii.59; Fowler 1995). Along the way, the Olympians and the earthly rulers they reflect are depicted with Ovidian scepticism and irreverence. Jove resembles the passion-driven, blustering, and tyrannical god of the *Metamorphoses*, and Ovid's story of Actaeon, with its critical view of Diana, is brought to bear on Elizabeth in the Faunus episode of canto vi (Montrose 2002: 920). Ovid's goddess 'seemed to some more violent than just' (*Metamorphoses* III.253–4). The personal injustice and violence are muted in Spenser: where Ovid's Actaeon glimpsed the naked goddess by accident, Faunus's deliberate spying is more culpable; and though Diana's 'vengefull mind' devises 'thousand deaths' for him, she cannot contravene the law protecting 'the Wood-gods breed, which must for euer liue' (50) and must merely 'punish him in sport' (51). But her frustrated 'indignation' over-flows onto the landscape. She abandons Ireland with a curse condemning it to the depredations of wolves and thieves, 'Which too-too true that lands in-dwellers since haue found' (55). The cruelty of Ovid's Diana is given a newly political application, holding Elizabeth's mismanagement responsible for all Ireland's ills. The attitude to authority Spenser derives from his immersion in classical literature, and articulates through its imitation, is far from docile.

NOTES

1. All translations are my own unless otherwise stated.
2. Hesiod (1988). *Theogony and Works and Days*, trans. M. L. West. Oxford: Oxford University Press.

BIBLIOGRAPHY

Baldwin, T. W. (1944). *William Shakespeare's Small Latine and Lesse Greeke*, 2 vols. Urbana: University of Illinois Press.

Bates, C. (1992). *The Rhetoric of Courtship in Elizabethan Language and Literature*. Cambridge: Cambridge University Press.

Bernard Silvestris (1979). *Commentary on the First Six Books of Virgil's 'Aeneid'*, trans. E. G. Schreiber and T. E. Maresca. Lincoln, NE: University of Nebraska Press.

Brown, S. A. (1999). *The Metamorphosis of Ovid: From Chaucer to Virginia Woolf*. London: Duckworth.

Burrow, C. (1999). '"Full of the Maker's Guile": Ovid on Imitating and on the Imitation of Ovid', in P. Hardie, A. Barchiesi, and S. Hinds (eds), *Ovidian Transformations: Essays on the* Metamorphoses *and its Reception*. Cambridge: Cambridge Philological Society, 271–87.

Bushnell, R. W. (1996). *A Culture of Teaching: Early Modern Humanism in Theory and Practice.* Ithaca, NY: Cornell University Press.

Demetriou, T. (2006). '"Essentially Circe": Spenser, Homer, and the Homeric Tradition'. *Translation and Literature* 15: 151–76.

Fowler, E. (1995). 'The Failure of Moral Philosophy in the Work of Edmund Spenser'. *Representations* 51: 47–76.

Fulgentius (1971). *Fulgentius the Mythographer,* trans. L. G. Whitbread. Columbus: Ohio State University Press.

Grafton, A., and Jardine, L. (1986). *From Humanism to the Humanities: Education and the Liberal Arts in Fifteenth- and Sixteenth-Century Europe.* Cambridge, MA: Harvard University Press.

Hardie, P. (1986). *Virgil's Aeneid: Cosmos and Imperium.* Oxford: Clarendon Press.

Helgerson, R. (1983). *Self-Crowned Laureates: Spenser, Jonson, Milton, and the Literary System.* Berkeley: University of California Press.

Javitch, D. (1980). '*Cantus Interruptus* in the *Orlando Furioso*'. *MNL* 95: 66–80.

—— (1984). 'The *Orlando Furioso* and Ovid's Revision of the *Aeneid*'. *MLN* 99: 1023–36.

Kallendorf, C. (2007). *The Other Virgil: Pessimistic Readings of the Aeneid in Early Modern Culture.* Oxford: Oxford University Press.

Kelsey, L., and Peterson, R. S. (2000). 'Rereading Colin's Broken Pipe: Spenser and the Problem of Patronage'. *SSt* 14: 233–72.

Lyne, R. O. A. M. (1987). *Further Voices in Virgil's Aeneid.* Oxford: Oxford University Press.

McCabe, R. A. (1995). '"Little booke, thy selfe present": The Politics of Presentation in *The Shepheardes Calender*', in H. Erskine-Hill and R. A. McCabe (eds), *Presenting Poetry: Composition, Publication, Reception.* Cambridge: Cambridge University Press.

Montrose, L. A. (2002). 'Spenser and the Elizabethan Political Imaginary'. *ELH* 69: 907–46.

Murrin, M. (1980). *The Allegorical Epic: Essays in its Rise and Decline.* Chicago: University of Chicago Press.

Nohrnberg, J. (1976). *The Analogy of* The Faerie Queene. Princeton, NJ: Princeton University Press.

Patterson, A. (1987). *Pastoral and Ideology: Virgil to Valéry.* Berkeley: University of California Press.

Pugh, S. (2005). *Spenser and Ovid.* Aldershot: Ashgate.

Servius Grammaticus (1902–27). *Servii Grammatici qui feruntur in Vergilii Carmina,* ed. G. Thilo and H. Hagen. Leipzig: Teubner.

Watkins, J. (1995). *The Specter of Dido: Spenser and Virgilian Epic.* New Haven, CT: Yale University Press.

Whitney, Geffrey (1586). *A Choice of Emblemes and Other Devices.* Leiden: Christopher Plantin.

CHAPTER 28

SPENSER AND CLASSICAL PHILOSOPHY

ANDREW ESCOBEDO

SPENSER assumed that poetry and philosophy shared the goals of teaching virtue and fashioning just citizens within a just society. Yet, like Sidney, he would have imagined that they went about these goals differently: philosophy teaches categorically, by thesis and explanation, whereas poetry teaches affectively, by delighting and illustrating.[1] Certainly, the two disciplines borrow tricks from one another, yet their history reveals distinct ways of doing business. Philosophy asks for logical consistency, and philosophers since Socrates have grounded their disagreements with each other on the accusation of self-contradiction. Poetry, on the other hand, succeeds or fails based on its effort to *make* something for us, whether that something be an imitation of a person or event, an illustration of a virtue, or the arousal of a feeling. When a work of philosophy contradicts itself, we usually perceive it as a problem to be solved. When a poem contradicts itself, that contradiction may be meaningful in itself, a feature of the landscape of ideas the poet has fashioned for us.

The differing templates of philosophy and poetry, ostensibly imposing 'the impossibility of pinning any poet, whose very wrigglings are the manifestation of his life as a poet, to a philosophy' (Roche 1964: 118), has often dissuaded critics from looking for coherent philosophical ideas in Spenser's poems. Scholars have likewise voiced doubt that Spenser's Plato, Aristotle, Cicero, and Seneca bore any resemblance to our own, since he read them through the lens of centuries of reinterpretation. Rosemond Tuve, for example, has demonstrated the degree to which Aristotle's conception of the virtues underwent profound transformation during the medieval period, splitting into multiple theological and literary strands that Spenser could have used in place of the Greek philosopher (1966: 57–143). Robert Ellrodt (1960) has done the same with Plato. Contextualizing scholarship of this sort is essential, but none of it gives us any reason to doubt that Spenser read Aristotle, that he understood him, or that he could discern the difference between Greco-Roman philosophical ideas and Christian ones. Marsilio Ficino, the great Renaissance Christian apologist for Plato, saw quite plainly that 'the secret of the Christian Trinity is never to be found in the books of Plato. He has formulations that superficially resemble those for the dogma, but their true meaning is otherwise' (Allen 1984: 556). Likewise, Tudor English writers used Aristotelian ideas about ethics with the full knowledge that some of their Protestant colleagues condemned Aristotle's notion of habituated virtue for failing to coincide with the doctrine of human depravity.

Spenser saw both overlap and difference between classical philosophy and Christian theology, and in the comments below I note both. I have confined the scope of my inquiry to classical writers, not to deny the importance of medieval and Renaissance elaborations to Spenser, but rather to accommodate in the space available some of the complexity of the classical texts, a complexity that Spenser appreciates and sometimes imports into his poetry.[2] Spenser's interest in the philosophers was not identical to ours—he did not care whether the *Timaeus* was a product of Plato's middle or late period—but we can nonetheless grant, without denying his poetic wrigglings, that he recognized the presence of 'problems' within the philosophical works he read, and that in his poetry he uses these problems to help shape the contours of his fictional landscape. This essay focuses on three such problems— *eudaimonia*, *akrasia*, and mutability—that stem from questions that most readers would agree are central to Spenser's art: Should we be happy? Why do we lose control over ourselves? What does change mean?

EUDAIMONIA

Classical philosophers all agreed that the virtuous person was a happy person. The proper goal of human activity, according to Plato, Aristotle, and others, was *eudaimonia*, translated variously as 'happiness', 'flourishing', and 'well being'. The root *daimōn* suggests the associated ideas of guiding inner voice, fate, and divinity, helping to explain Aristotle's insistence that *eudaimonia* is 'among the most godlike things; for that which is the prize and end of virtue seems to be the best thing in the world, and something godlike and blessed' (*Nic. Ethics* I.9.1099b15).[3] (The idea of fate still lingers in the English word 'happily'.) For Aristotle, *eudaimonia* consisted of the possession of a virtuous character predisposed to practice, and actively practicing, virtuous behavior. For Plato, it consisted of attaining a knowledge of virtue that produced a harmonious state of soul happier (*eudaimonesteros*) than that possessed by the unjust man (*Republic* 361d3).[4] Although more suspicious of pleasure than his Greek predecessors, the Stoic philosopher Seneca agreed in *De Vita Beata* that 'pleasure should be . . . the companion of a right and proper desire. . . . To live happily is the same thing as to live in accordance to Nature' (VIII.1–2).[5] Even Epicurus and his followers, who made virtue a means to pleasure rather than an end in itself, never questioned the basic link between happiness and the virtuous life: as the epicurean Manlius Torquatus noted in Cicero's *De Finibus*, 'no one can live pleasantly without living wisely, honorably and justly, and no one wisely, honorably, and justly without living pleasantly' (I.18.57).[6]

Corresponding to this association between happiness and virtue was the philosophical confidence that the virtuous man was immune to injury. In striking contrast to the depiction of moral life in Greek tragedy, Socrates declared famously in the *Apology* that 'nothing can harm a good man either in life or after death' (41c). This was not to say that the good man could not experience misfortune, but that his attitude toward external goods would be such that their loss could not seriously upset his *eudaimonia*. For Plato, Socrates's statement meant that virtue entailed a proper understanding of happiness, such that one valued lasting and unchanging things, such as the Forms, over transient and mutable ones. Later Roman philosophers tended to emphasize the themes of endurance and freedom from chance. Cicero insisted in the *Tusculan Disputations* that virtue alone was sufficient 'to make us high-souled and in fact never appalled by any event and always undefeated' (V.18.53),[7] and Seneca likewise argued in *Of Constancy* that virtue is 'so steeled against the blows of chance that she cannot be bent, much less broken. Facing instruments of torture she holds her gaze unflinching, her expression changes not at all' (V.4).

The automatic association between happiness and virtue has a distinctly odd ring in modern ears. Our philosophers, starting most notably with Kant, have taught us that virtue is a duty, one that may require us to sacrifice our happiness for the sake of the good. Of course, we find it natural to say (or hope) that the virtuous and the wicked get their just deserts, and that good people will end up with more friends, wealth, peace of mind, and security than bad people: a sort of work ethic of sacrificing now for gain in the future. But this is not what the ancient philosophers had in mind as *eudaimonia*: for them, by and large, the knowledge and practice of virtue produces happiness in itself. Virtue is the essential ingredient of happiness, not an instrument for gaining it (Ackrill 1974). The association between happiness and virtue also fits rather uneasily within a Renaissance Christian sensibility. Certainly, some Christian writers insisted that giving up vice would make people happier, but salvation, not happiness, is the goal of Christian virtue. In other cases, unhappiness, discomfort, and privation are the surest signs that one is practicing Christian virtue.

In *The Faerie Queene*, Spenser undertakes a literary analysis of six virtues, and the nature of virtue is one of the poem's primary philosophical concerns. To what degree does Spenser imagine the virtuous man to be a happy man and the unvirtuous unhappy? His villains are frequently self-defeating agents whose wicked efforts to secure gain yield frustration and dissatisfaction, or worse. Analogously, Spenser sometimes describes virtue in terms of happiness. He mentions that the unjust Athenians condemned '[w]ise Socrates' to drink hemlock, 'who thereof quaffing glad | Pourd out his life' (II.vii.52)—the inclusion of 'glad' seems to make the eudaimonic point that virtuous people are happier to die than unjust people are to live. The narrator also tells us that temperate people enjoy 'the goodly peace of staied mindes' (II.v.1). Sir Guyon describes his preference of chivalry over wealth as 'another happines, another end' (II.vii.33), and Scudamour reads at the castle of Venus that 'Blessed the man that well can use his blis' (IV.x.8). These two latter examples of virtuous happiness are susceptible, in context, to ironic readings, but the question at issue is not whether Spenser's heroes always succeed in practicing virtue (they don't), but whether, when they do succeed, this success produces happiness.

Much of *The Faerie Queene* does not align happiness with virtue, and this marks the poem's distance from the philosophical notion of *eudaimonia*. This distance derives both from Spenser's brand of Reformation devotionality and from his pessimistic sense of the sway of mutability in earthly life. The *Legend of Holinesse* perhaps best exemplifies this, since holiness is a virtue that one does not so much practice as one receives from God. The classical philosophers would probably be puzzled by Spenser's inclusion of it with the other virtues. Even if Spenser followed Thomistic Aristotelianism in designating holiness as the virtue of religious action (Morgan 1986), the poet nonetheless overwhelmingly emphasizes the *failure* of the knight of Holiness to practice this virtue. The Redcrosse knight is by and large an unhappy hero, beginning his quest 'too solemne sad' (I.i.2) and almost succumbing to Despaire in canto 9. Yet, as the knight's continuing hopelessness in the House of Holiness (I.x.21–2, 25) and in the dragon-fight (I.x.28) suggests, despair is not merely the opposite of holiness, but rather also part of its structure: despair registers our moral awareness that we are unworthy before the Law, particularly in Lutheran theology. As Susan Snyder has put it, 'Where Augustine and Bernard warn the Christian, "You may despair," Luther thunders, "You must!"' (1965: 25). Certainly, there is joy in Grace, but we cannot practice Grace, we can only receive it. The happiness that Redcrosse knight feels at his betrothal at the end of Book I—'Thrise happy man the knight himself did hold' (I.xii.40)—significantly occurs within a pointed allegory of end time, when there will no longer be the need to exercise virtue. Furthermore, the legend of Holiness postpones even this happy ending, deferring the marriage of Una and Redcrosse knight for six years. The other titular heroes of the poem are not as sad as Redcrosse knight, but as often as not Spenser represents their practice of virtue as a sacrifice, not an acquisition, of happiness.

The exception to this rule may be Prince Arthur. Certainly, he expresses his share of unhappiness. He endures the 'fresh bleeding wound' (I.ix.7) of his love for Gloriana, and he gives up his frustrating chase of Florimell '[w]ith heavy looke and lumpish pace' (III.iv.61). Yet Arthur also represents Spenser's sense of the happiness that virtue can ideally bestow in this life; he is one of the poem's few *eudaimones*. Part of this happiness stems from his allegorical duties as divine Grace, but in his workaday labors his cheer derives from a certain attitude toward virtue. Declining any reward from the grateful Belge, he comments, 'What other meed then need me to requite, | But that which yeeldeth vertues meed alway? | That is the virtue selfe, which her reward doth pay' (V.xi.17). The assertion that virtue is its own reward is proverbial, but it speaks to Arthur's cheerful self-sufficiency. He has what the other heroes still lack, a figure 'perfected in the twelve private morall vertues, as Aristotle hath devised', as Spenser reports in the 'Letter to Ralegh'. If the Arthur of the actual poem falls short of perfected virtue, Spenser's letter nonetheless implies a special moral status for the British prince. Although this letter tells us that Arthur represents Aristotelian magnificence, Spenser may, as many critics have contended, actually have in mind Aristotle's notion of magnanimity (Grk. *megalopsychia*) from the *Nichomachean Ethics*, for this virtue 'is a sort of crown of the virtues; for it makes them greater, and it is not found without them' (IV.3.1124a1), and it is concerned above all with honour, reminding us of Arthur's squire Timias.[8] Although Arthur possesses too much Christian humility to represent a fully Aristotelian *megalopsychia*, Spenser sometimes describes Arthur's magnanimity as bound up with his virtue and with a certain freedom from injury. Standing over the defeated Pyrocles, Arthur offers the villain a chance to reform himself:

> But full of princely bounty and great mind,
>   The Conquerour nought cared him to slay,
>   But casting wronges and all revenge behind,
>   More glory thought to give life, then decay.   (II.viii.51)

If Arthur is not always able to stand above injury through his great-mindedness, he is nonetheless more likely to do it than any other hero in the poem. His sense of bounty and his happiness are part of his virtue. He brings Una back from her despair 'with cheerfull words' (I.vii.52), and he releases the captive Poena 'for more joy' (IV.ix.13), persuading her to reform her wicked ways 'through his well wonted grace' (14).

   Another reason to suspect that Spenser has a vaguely Aristotelian *megalopsychia* in mind is that Arthur's *eudaimonia* is closest to Aristotle's version of happiness. Since Aristotle concedes the value of external goods (wealth, safety, health, etc.) to a greater extent than does Plato or the Stoics, he is more ready than they to acknowledge the degree to which misfortune interferes with the happiness of even virtuous men. Hence, in the *Nichomachean Ethics* he qualifies the Socratic confidence that the virtuous man's indifference to external goods immunizes him from misfortune:

Now many events happen by chance, and ... if they turn out ill they crush and maim happiness, for they both bring pain with them and hinder many activities. Yet even in these nobility [*kalon*] shines through, when a man bears with resignation many great misfortunes, not through insensibility to pain but through nobility and greatness of soul [*megalopsychia*]. (I.10.1100b22–32)

In the midst of setbacks, the virtuous man has a *kalon*, an inner beauty made outwardly visible, that Aristotle links to *megalopsychia*. This is a state of character that derives happiness from the practice of virtue without denying the power of chance.

Part of the point of *kalon*, for Aristotle, is that it allows other people to see one's virtue and allows one to see the virtue of others. *Kalon* works both ways for Spenser's Arthur, who is an agent of happiness for others and magnanimously self-sufficient himself. He is sometimes able to find beauty in the trials of misfortune, discerning 'great magnanimity' in Guyon's lifeless face (II.viii.23). Even as he concedes that 'bliss may not abide in state of mortall men' (I.viii.44), he nonetheless urges the recently imprisoned Redcrosse knight to keep trying: 'Henceforth, Sir Knight, take to you wonted strength, | And maister these mishaps with patient might' (I.viii.45). Modern readers tend to prefer the melancholy concession to chance over the exhortation to patient might. Yet Spenser intends his readers to admire both. After his ordeal in Orgoglio's dungeon Redcrosse knight has become a 'chearelesse man' (I.viii.43), and Arthur is trying to help him regain some of his cheer. If Arthur represents divine Grace here, then that Grace has arrived regardless of any merit or demerit on Redcrosse knight's part. This would indicate Spenser's sense of the limits of human virtue. Yet Arthur in fact urges Redcrosse knight to practice virtue, to 'maister' fortune, and that the patience he recommends is a 'patient might' suggests the *kalon* and *megalopsychia* described by Aristotle. It is almost as if Arthur is urging Redcrosse knight to try to be happy.

AKRASIA

Virtue is above all a kind of orderliness. Plato's notion of temperance in the *Republic* was harmony among the parts of the city and, by analogy, of the soul, and his notion of justice specified the importance that each part actively work to maintain this harmony (430e–5b). Cicero, following Plato's scheme of the four cardinal virtues (wisdom, courage, temperance, justice) in *De Finibus*, upgrades temperance to the ringleader position: 'there follows a fourth kind, possessed of equal beauty, and indeed combining in itself the other three. This is the principle of order and of restraint' (II.14.47). Aristotle's notion of virtue as a mean, in which the good is a kind of target set between two vicious extremes, likewise expresses a sense of harmony, following 'the dictates of the right rule' (*Nic. Ethics* IV.1.1138b19).

Since the orderliness and symmetry of virtue was so clear, the philosophical concept of *akrasia* (translated variously as incontinence, lack of control, and power-lessness) posed a basic question: why do people who know better nonetheless do bad things? The philosophers answered that the orderliness of the soul was imperiled when people allowed its irrational or appetitive parts to overreach their function. Indulging one's passions, in particular, risked psychic disorder. Yet they disagreed about what counted as indulgence. Aristotle characteristically treated the proper expression of passion as a mean. Too much anger is inappropriate, but so is too little, depending on the context (*Nic. Ethics* II.7.1108a4–19). If someone kills your child, you should be angry about it and use that anger to motivate you into action. The Stoics, by contrast, argued that the passions by their nature were excessive and inimical to virtue. Seneca admonished in *De Ira* that the passions 'await no man's gesture and are not possessed, but possess' (1.17.1).

In this matter, at least, Spenser is Aristotelian: his heroes get angry, and usually he represents their anger as amplifying their just might. Affect helps humans appropriately nuance their response to a given situation. The apt contrast is Talus, Spenser's robotic figure of executive Justice, who may enjoy the advantage of never falling for a pretty face, but his violence is terrifying precisely because he almost never becomes angry (see also Wolfe 2004: 203–35). Spenser likewise insists on the value of erotic passion, criticizing those who condemn love and affection as 'Stoicke censours' (IV Proem, 3). Lucan's approving account of Cato, who on his wedding night refuses 'to renew the former relations with his wife: that iron nature was proof even against wedded love' (1928: 2.278–9), holds no attraction for our poet.

Yet if Spenser dislikes the Stoic version of *apatheia*, he finds the Stoic depiction of rage, lust, and sloth congenial to his own sense that the passions in excess are terrifying. Seneca provided a famously detailed portrait of the angry man at the beginning of *De Ira*:

But you have only to behold the aspect of those possessed by anger to know that they are insane. For ... the marks of a madman are unmistakable—a bold and threatening mien, a gloomy brow, a fierce expression ... his eyes blaze and sparkle, his whole face is crimson with the blood that surges from the lowest depths of his heart, his lips quiver, his teeth are clenched, his hair bristles and stands on end, his breathing is forced and harsh, his joints crack from writhing, he groans and bellows. (I.1.3–4)

Without insisting on direct derivation, we can see echoes of this portrait in Spenser's Wrath, whose 'eies did hurle forth sparcles fiery red | ... | Trembling through hasty rage, when choler in him sweld. | His ruffin raiment all was staind with blood, | Which he had spilt, and all to rags yrent, | Through unadvized rashness woxen wood' (I.iv.33–4). Spenser likewise recalls Seneca's angry man in his Furor, 'a mad man', who drags by the hair the furious Phaon, 'Whom sore he bett, and gor'd with many a wownd, | That cheeks with teares, and sides with blood did all abownd' (II.iv.3). These examples at least concede Seneca's insistence that we don't use the passions; the passions use us. Wrath, Furor, and Phaon signal their lack of virtue generally, and their intemperance specifically, with a wild disorderliness and failure to stay within bounds.

Yet what process of moral psychology allows a provoking occasion or tempting object to lead one to such excesses? According to the Aristotelian template in the *Nicomachean Ethics*, there are four characteristic ways of responding to temptation, listed here in descending order of virtuousness: temperance (*sōphrosyne*), continence (*enkrateia*), incontinence (*akrasia*), and intemperance (*akolasia*). The temperate man has so habituated himself to following reason that when provoked by a tempting object he feels no inclination to pursue it. The continent man, not quite so adept in managing his appetite, feels the inclination but manages to overcome it with the rational knowledge that he ought not to choose it. The intemperate man, the worst case, has so habituated himself to following appetite that he no longer hears the promptings of reason: he succumbs to temptation with scarcely a second thought (*Nic. Ethics* VII). Temperance, continence, and intemperance, so understood, are easy cases to explain because they conform well to the influential Platonic notion that a person who knows the good does not choose the bad. As Plato insists in the *Meno*, wrongdoers 'don't desire evil but what they think is good, though in fact it is evil; those who through ignorance mistake bad things for good obviously desire the good' (77e). Plugging this notion back into the Aristotelian template, we can say that both temperate and continent men know the good and so refrain (with varying degrees of alacrity) from choosing the bad, whereas the intemperate man is ignorant of the good and so follows the promptings of appetite to choose the bad.

This leaves us with the difficult case of the incontinent man, or *akrates*. The incontinent man, according to Aristotle, pursues temptation knowing that its object is bad. The akratic's reason is not absent, merely ineffective, and he therefore knowingly chooses against his self-interest. But why would anybody do this? We could suppose that one's appetite for the tempting object was unusually strong, but then why not assume in such a case that a correspondingly strong knowledge of the good was lacking? Yet Aristotle wants to contest the Socratic assumption that knowledge is sufficient for virtue, a position that makes the akratic case non-existent: 'Socrates . . . held that there is no such thing as incontinence. . . . Now this view plainly contradicts the observed facts' (VII.2.1145b26–8).

Aristotle's account of *akrasia* is complex and at times quite perplexing (Price 2006), yet two aspects of his exposition are especially relevant to Spenser. The first is his notion that the akratic agent fails to link a particular premise about the tempting object to a universal premise about appropriate behavior concerning this object. Aristotle's favorite example is something sweet to the taste. The general premise might be (1) 'Potential gluttons should not taste pleasant things', while the particular premise might be (2) 'I am a potential glutton, sweet things are pleasant to the taste, and this cake is sweet.' In a temperate or continent state, the agent concludes (3) 'I will not eat this', and acts on her conclusion by refraining. In *akrasia*, however, appetitive desire disjoins the particular premise from the universal such that only the seductive part of the particular premise remains. This can happen, according to Aristotle, because there is nothing unreasonable per se about the premise that sweet things are pleasant to the taste: 'it is an opinion opposed not in itself but only incidentally . . . to correct reasoning' (VII.3.1147b1). This appears to be a problem inherent in the valuing of external goods, like sweets, in relation to larger ethical considerations. Another aspect of Aristotle's exposition is his suggestion that at the moment of akratic failure the agent has the universal premise in her mind as a kind of idle recitation, 'like the drunkard saying the verses of Empedocles', or as an imperfectly understood script, 'in the manner of those who are reciting' (VII.3.1147b10 and 1147a24). Aristotle here attempts to describe a state of mind that possesses the promptings of reason but possesses them emptily or merely formally. The akratic knows what she should do, but at the moment of crisis doesn't *really* know it.

Before considering how Spenser represents the unsuccessful response to temptation, let us start with the successful response. Although 'temperance' had been the
common English translation of Aristotle's *sōphrosyne*, by the late sixteenth century
'temperance' also translated *enkrateia* (continence), and this is the concept that
Spenser has in mind for his heroes (Weatherby 1996). Rarely do they ignore temptation or provocation without a second thought. Allegorically speaking, the figures of
virtuous restraint often have a hard time defeating the figures of appetitive license:
Guyon restrains Furor with difficulty (II.iv.6–15), and Arthur faces his most challenging battles with Pyrocles, Cymocles, and Maleger (II.viii and xi). Literally
speaking, the heroes bring their concupiscent and irascible passions under control
only with significant effort. Seeing the naked wrestling women in the Bowre of Blisse,
Guyon experiences intense desire, until the censure of his Palmer helps him abstain
(II.xii.68–9). Arthur is close to wrathfully killing the defeated Druon, Claribell,
Blandamour, and Paridell until, touched by the merciful entreaties of Scudamour
and Britomart, 'he gan himselfe advise | To stay his hand' (IV.ix.35). Artegall restrains
his urgent passion for Britomart with dramatic effort:

> Besides her modest countenance he saw
> So goodly grave, and full of princely aw,
> That it his ranging fancie did refraine,
> And looser thoughts to lawfull bounds withdraw;
> Whereby the passion grew more fierce and faine,
> Like to a stubborne steede whom strong hand would restraine.   (IV.vi.33)

'Lawfull bounds' recalls the orderly and bounded nature of temperance in classical
philosophical discourse, although the last two lines of the stanza suggest that
Artegall barely hangs on to his *enkrateia*. Spenser's metaphor of the 'stubborne
steede' may owe something to Plato's description in the *Phaedrus* of the increasingly violent efforts of the appetitive soul, upon seeing a beautiful person, to resist
the tempering force of the rational soul, a scenario metaphorized in this dialogue
as the struggle of a willful horse to resist the governing bridle of the rational
charioteer:

At that sight the driver's memory goes back to that form of beauty, and he sees her once again
enthroned by the side of temperance upon her holy seat; then in awe and reverence he falls
upon his back, and therewith is compelled to pull the reins so violently that he brings both
steeds down on their haunches, the good one willing and unresistant, but the wanton sore
against his will. . . . Once again [the wanton horse] tries to force them to advance . . . with head
down and tail stretched out he takes the bit between his teeth and shamelessly plunges on. But
the driver . . . jerks back the bit in the mouth of the wanton horse with an even stronger pull,
bespatters his railing tongue and his jaws with blood, and forcing him down on legs and
haunches delivers him over to anguish. (254b–e)

Even when Spenser appears to go to Plato rather than Aristotle for a depiction of
temperance, he is drawn to a dialogue that dramatizes the conflict between two
opposing impulses of the soul. No calm Socratic abstention in his poem: Spenser's
heroes often have to struggle to maintain their spiritual harmony.

So much for the successful response to temptation in *The Faerie Queene*. Turning to the unsuccessful, readers can find numerous examples of *akolasia*, or hardened intemperance, in the villains of the story. Braggadoccio, ravished by Belphoebe's beauty, immediately '[g]an burne in filthy lust, and leaping light, | Thought in his bastard armes her to embrace' (II.iii.42). Likewise, Paridell has so cultivated the habit of casual love that it is second nature for him, such that the first thrill of lust does not even ache anymore: 'But nothing new to him was that same pain, | Ne paine at all; for he so ofte had tryde | The power thereof, and lov'd so oft in vaine, | That thing of course he counted, love to entertaine' (III.ix.29). These figures follow the promptings of appetite without a second thought, and in terms of moral psychology, at least, they are not especially complicated. Yet what about Aristotle's difficult case; does Spenser give us examples of akratic behavior in the specifically Aristotelian sense?

Not many direct examples, but Aristotle's notion of *akrasia* does nonetheless seem to have fired Spenser's imagination. After Guyon offers three scornful stanzas about the wickedness of wealth, Mammon sarcastically asks, 'And why then . . . | Are mortall men so fond and undiscreet, | So evill thing to seeke unto their ayd?' (II.vii.14). What Mammon asks in mockery Aristotle asks sincerely: why do people often hanker after things that they know will end up hurting them? Guyon's (Platonic) answer is that such people lack knowledge: 'But would they thinke' (II.vii.15) how little nature needs for self-sufficiency, they would despise wealth. Yet when Mammon then offers to show him his treasure, Guyon does not outright refuse but rather states that he needs assurance of the treasure's legitimate origin. This complicates his earlier insistence that the drive to acquire wealth simply derives from ignorance: he now implicitly concedes that wealth is an external good that people must value in proper relation to other ethical considerations. According to Aristotle, as we have seen, the valuing of external goods is one of the difficulties facing the akratic agent. Guyon does not succumb directly to the temptations of the Cave of Mammon, although his faint at the end of the episode raises again the issue of the external goods necessary for human success.

We can also find examples of Aristotle's suggestion that the akratic agent possesses knowledge of the good only as a kind of script for recitation. As Redcrosse knight begins to succumb to the persuasions of Despaire, his counterarguments become increasingly wooden, and at a certain point we cannot be sure which one asks 'Who then can strive with strong necessitie, | That holds the world in his still changing state?' (I.ix.42). Redcrosse knight's desire to be free of sin and misery—not an innately impious desire, cautiously understood—detaches itself from the larger premise that suicide is a sin. He knows that the larger premise is true, but he can only express it in terms that lend themselves to Despair's script. Some commentators have likened *akrasia* to the contradictory state of self-deception, in which we blind ourselves with open eyes, and this would apply to Redcrosse knight's experience as he raises the dagger to kill himself.

The notion of self-deception might also allow us to recognize an akratic 'style' in some of Spenser's hardened, acolasic villains. Cymochles, although clearly habituated to lust and sloth, has a curiously circuitous response to the naked women trying to seduce him in the Bowre of Blisse:

> Sometimes he falsely faines himselfe to sleepe,
> Whiles through their lids his wanton eies do peepe,
> To steale a snatch of amorous conceipt,
> Whereby close fire into his heart does creepe:
> So, he them deceives, deceivd in his deceipt,
> Made dronke with drugs of deare voluptuous receipt.   (II.v.34)

A bit like Aristotle's inebriate reciting Empedocles, Cymochles follows a seduction script that feigns unawareness in order that he might more erotically observe women who are already doing their best to appear erotic in his presence. Lust works best for him when he partly deceives himself about its mechanism. Self-deception might also illuminate an aspect of Acrasia herself, the intemperate center of the *Legend of Temperance* of whom we see very little directly. In one of the few stanzas devoted to her description, Spenser describes the manner in which she hangs over the sleeping Verdant:

> And oft inclining downe with kisses light,
> For feare of waking him, his lips bedewd,
> And through his humid eyes did sucke his spright,
> Quite molten into lust and pleasure lewd;
> Wherewith she sighed soft, as if his case she rewd.   (II.xii.73)

The odd mixture of tenderness, malevolence, and sympathy in these lines suggests a moral psychology not quite in control of its own evil intentions. The akratic makes ethical decisions in the subjunctive mood of 'as if'.

MUTABILITY

Much as the philosophers agreed that the virtuous soul was an orderly soul, so they agreed that the orderly nature of the cosmos signified its goodness. The Stoic Balbus argued that the regular movement of the stars revealed the workings of divine intelligence rather than chance, 'for chance loves variation and abhors regularity' (II.16.43),[9] and even the empirically minded Aristotle conceded that the constant rotations of the heavens implied an unmoved mover (*Physics* VIII). If the universe was basically good and regularity a sign of its goodness, then why did mutability appear to play such a large role?

One of the most profound and influential classical responses to this question came from Plato's *Timaeus*, which describes the creation of the universe by a divine maker. The dialogue accounts for the mutability of this universe in terms of the necessary gap between creator and creation: 'Now the nature of the ideal being was everlasting, but to bestow this attribute in its fullness upon a creature was impossible' (37d). Thus, the distinction between original and copy—as Timaeus discusses earlier in the dialogue (27d–31b)—always withholds perfect constancy from physical things. Further impeding perfection was the innate recalcitrance of substance. The maker could not create any universe he desired, but rather had to comply with inherent structures of physical being: 'the creation of the world is the combined work of necessity [anankē] and mind [nous]. Mind, the ruling power, persuaded necessity to bring the greater part of created things to perfection' (48a). But only the greater part: certain necessary aspects of physical reality, such as sensations, 'create a great and mighty movement . . . stirring up and violently shaking the courses of the soul, they completely stopped the revolution of the same by their opposing currents' (43d). The material world innately eschews perfect constancy.

The tension between the perfection-seeking Mind and the perfection-limiting Necessity stems in part from Timaeus's two differing accounts of the universe's origin. In the first (28c–29c), the maker looks to an ideal pattern [paradeigma] and imitates this pattern when creating the physical universe; in the second (30a), the maker confronts an already existing chaos and fashions it into a cosmos, bringing order out of an originary disorder [ataxia]. The divergent origins, ideal pattern, and primordial disorder, adumbrate the oscillation between perfection and imperfection in Timaeus's account of the physical universe. The maker produces a world that has worsened compared to its ideal pattern and yet improved compared to its pre-cosmic chaos. The world is ontologically removed from its perfect model, but it nonetheless evinces the ordering intelligence imposed on its original raw material, such that Timaeus ends the dialogue by urging that flawed humans, 'by learning the harmonies and revolutions of the universe, should correct the courses of the head which were corrupted at our birth . . . renewing our original nature' (90d). In the *Timaeus*, material things both lead away from and back to the ideal (Lovejoy 1961: 24–66).

Spenser appears to have found this sense of the bi-directionality of mutability congenial to his poetic dispositions. He alternately imagines earthly change as a devastating tragedy and as the working out of a design that will return the world to perfection. Spenser even rehearses the divergent creation accounts from the *Timaeus* in his *Fowre Hymes*. The *Hymne in Honour of Love* describes how the god of Love fashioned the world '[o]ut of great Chaos ugly prison' (58), 'tempering' (85) the warring elements and placing them in 'order' (87).[10] Creation is a process, and the hymn goes on to consider the processes by which love inspires people to produce offspring, encourages them to seek virtue, and forces them to endure a purgatory of suffering that (sometimes) leads to paradise. By contrast, the *Hymne in Honour of Beautie* describes how the maker consulted '[a] goodly Paterne, to whose perfect mould | He fashioned them as comely as he could' (32–3), an ideal pattern of which 'as every earthly thing partakes, | Or more or lesse by influence divine, | So it more faire accordingly it makes' (43–5). Creation is product, and the hymn goes on to consider the degree to which this product approaches or falls short of its pattern. The failure to coincide sometimes occurs, Spenser tells us, through the stubbornness of 'substance' (144) that 'will not yield unto her formes direction' (146).

Substance and form reference another avenue by which the philosophers sought to account for mutability. Aristotle speculated that change occurs when matter (*hylē*), lacking the imprint of a given form (*morphē*), is made to take on this form (*Physics*: I.7). In this hylomorphic account, as it is sometimes called, form rather than matter determines the identity of things: 'by form I mean the essence of each thing, and its primary substance' (*Metaphysics* VII.7.1032b1). In the *Generation of Animals*, Aristotle infamously genders his distinction between active form (masculine) and passive matter (feminine), arguing for the natural superiority of men over women (732a10). Aristotle partly derives this account, including its gendering, from Plato, although Plato's version is more tentative. What Aristotle calls 'matter' Plato calls the 'receptacle [*hypodochē*] . . . of all generation' in the *Timaeus* (49b), and he later refers to it as 'space' [*chōra*] (52a), using the figure as a kind of conceptual passage between intangible, immutable Forms and three-dimensional, mutable things. On the one hand, the receptacle must be entirely malleable and passive to allow the Forms to express themselves in the material world as things—they are the 'father' and the receptacle is the 'mother' (50d)—and so in a sense the receptacle is mutability itself. Yet, on the other hand, the receptacle's ubiquity makes it a principle of continuity: 'it is eternal, and admits not of destruction and provides a home for all created things' (52b). The superiority of forms (lower case) over matter is thus not quite so certain in Plato. Aristotle, for example, insisted in the *Metaphysics* that a golden statue ought properly to be called by its form (statue), not its matter (gold) (VII.7.1033a7). Yet Plato had already used this example in reverse: if someone fashions and refashions gold into various geometric shapes, an observer would do best to say, '"That is gold", and not to call the triangle or any other figures which are formed in the gold "these", as though they had existence, since they are in process of change while he is making the assertion' (*Timaeus* 50b).

Spenser's Garden of Adonis canto reveals the influence of many philosophical traditions (Quitslund 2001: 184–266), but it relies in a basic sense on Aristotle's strong hierarchy between masculine form and feminine matter. It begins, after all, with the masculine Titan shooting his beams upon, and impregnating, the naked body of the sleeping Chrysogone (III.vi.7), an event likened to the spontaneous generation of animals, '[i]nformed in the mud, on which the Sunne hath shynd' (III.vi.8). Since both Plato and Aristotle make use of the example of gold matter, it is tempting to see Chrysogone's name ('golden-born') as a nod toward this philosophical question. In any case, Spenser carries the gender tension into his account of the Garden itself, with the 'stately Mount' (III.vi.43) protecting itself against 'Phoebus beams' and 'Aeolus sharp blast' (III.vi.44). Yet Spenser's representation of substance, emerging from a primordial Chaos (36), relies on Plato to complicate Aristotle's gender hierarchy:

> All things from thence doe their first being fetch
>   And borrow matter, whereof they are made,
>   Which whenas forme and feature it does ketch,
>   Becomes a body and doth then invade
>   The state of life, out of the grisly shade.
>   That substance is eterne, and bideth so,
>   Ne when the life decayes, and forme does fade,
>   Doth it consume, and into nothing goe,
> But changed is, and often altred to and froe.   (III.vi.37)

Form is the fragile principle here: it must borrow matter and it fades with the passing of life. Matter, by contrast, although originating problematically from 'the grisly shade', confirms the Platonic verdict that the receptacle is eternal in its malleability. Spenser's matter is also less inertly passive than Aristotle's: notice the middle-voice quality of 'ketch' (3), somewhere between 'seize' and 'receive'. Like the receptacle, Spenser's chaos-born substance functions as a kind of threshold between universal and particular and between death and life.

By the time we reach Adonis, who, Phoebus-like, is 'the Father of all formes', the provenance of form has been significantly revised, since Adonis 'is eterne in mutabilitie, | And by succession made perpetuall' (III.vi.47). This sounds much like Spenser's earlier account of substance, and some commentators have been inclined to read Spenser's 'formes' here as actually referring to matter, but that is unlikely: Adonis is still 'subject to mortalitie' (47). Instead, Spenser suggests an uneasy reconciliation between masculine and feminine: form seems to have 'borrowed' matter's malleability as a means to assert continuity, but in doing so must abandon its traditionally dominant status. With what we might call hermaphroditic hylomorphism, Spenser uses Adonis to register the tragedy of change in Adonis's mortality and simultaneously to reinterpret this change as continuity. As such, Adonis looks forward to Spenser's most famous hermaphrodite, Dame Nature.

Spenser structures the Mutability Cantos to a large degree along the lines of the tension between his two contradictory attitudes toward mutability (tragic decay and vital growth). Mutability 'did pervert' (VII.vi.5) the original conditions of nature in a gesture that recalls the fall from Eden, but she is also the happy means by which the things of the world, according to Dame Nature, 'worke their owne perfection so by fate' (VII.vii.58). In defense of the positive interpretation, Spenser has the titanness Mutability present a case for the supremacy of change that simultaneously presents a case for orderly continuity: the elements, seasons, and months follow each other with smooth regularity. Yet there is also a deliberate wildness in Spenser's depiction of these figures of worldly alteration. His Winter, for example, 'cloathed all in frize, | Chattering his teeth for cold that did him chill' (VII.vii.31), comes right out of Lucretius—'Hiemps sequitur crepitans hanc dentibus algu' (V.747)—and Spenser's procession of the seasons generally approximates the analogous procession in *De Rerum Natura* (5.737–50).[11] At this point in his exposition, significantly, Lucretius is arguing for the possibility that the moon is destroyed and reformed at the shift from one lunar cycle to the next, reflecting the larger Epicurean view of the universe composed by the random collision of atoms yet nonetheless maintaining a fixed ratio between destruction and creation. Such a prospect of a boundless, godless, eternal, violent, and self-sustaining cosmos, Lucretius concedes, causes one to react with both 'divina voluptas | . . . atque horror' (3.28–9), and this description, despite Lucretius's atheism, captures an important dimension of Spenser's dual attitude toward mutability (Esolen 1990).

Sometimes Spenser feels the *horror* more than the *voluptas*, and on occasion he acts abruptly to arrest the play of mutability. Dame Nature significantly follows her account of developmental change with an assertion of apocalyptic ending, 'from thenceforth, none no more change shall see' (VII.vii.59), and it is the idea of apocalypse, not of developmental change, that comforts the poet in the following stanzas (VII.viii.1–2). The forensic and juridical context of the *Mutabilitie Cantos*, as well as the apocalyptic language, recall the scenario of the *Legend of Justice*, and it is appropriate to conclude this discussion of mutability by considering its interpretation under the aspect of justice. The *Legend of Justice* is, among other things, an effort to contend with the social consequences brought about by the cosmic effects of mutability, which has caused the world to 'runne quite out of square' (V Proem, 1). Much as Dame Nature is a judge, Artegall's practice of justice relies centrally on his capacity to judge between true and false, an activity that imposes clarity and eschews ambiguity. Among his various activities in the first half of Book V, Artegall exposes finally the ongoing deceptions of the False Florimell and Braggadocchio (V.iii), he adjudicates the consequences of chance in the maritime dispute between Bracidas and Amidas (V.iv), and, with a touch of apocalyptic finality, he abruptly destroys the Egalitarian Giant when the Giant refuses to grant Artegall's account of mutability as divine design (V.ii). Why does Spenser inflect his version of justice as a particular kind of response to change and deviation?

One of Spenser's philosophical sources may be partly responsible. Plutarch's *Isis and Osiris*, which Spenser relies on in the Isis Church episode (V.vii), is an account of the philosophical and scientific truths reputedly allegorized by myths about the Egyptian gods. These truths include, among other things, the heterogeneity and ambiguity of earthly life: 'Nature brings, in this life of ours, many experiences in which both evil and good are commingled . . . our life is complex, and so is the world' (369C).[12] Indeed, the most prominent mythic event in Plutarch's treatise involves the dismembering of Osiris by Typhon, as well as Isis's efforts to reassemble her husband/brother; at the end of the search Osiris still lacks his penis, in compensation for which Isis fashions the phallus (357F–358B). We are reminded, obviously, of Britomart's efforts to restore Artegall's manhood upon his humiliation by Radigund (V.vii). Plutarch goes on to offer a fully Platonic interpretation of this myth, aligning Osiris's soul with the Forms, Isis with the receptacle, Osiris's body with transient forms impressed on the receptacle, their son Horus with the natural world, and Typhon with the force of disorder (372E–373A). After Osiris has been reassembled, Typhon seeks a juridical means to defeat Horus, the figure of orderly nature:

Therefore it is said that he is brought to trial by Typhon on the charge of illegitimacy, as not being pure nor uncontaminated like his father, reason unalloyed and unaffected of itself, but contaminated in his substance because of the corporeal element. He prevails, however, and wins the case when Hermes, that is to say Reason, testifies and points out that Nature, by undergoing changes in form with reference to the perceptible, duly brings about the creation of the world. (373B)

We have here, strikingly, many of the conceptual ingredients in the trial of Mutability, including the charges of illegitimacy against a god, the plaintiff's strict division between purity and mixture, and a judgment about creative change.

If Spenser postpones this Plutarchan accommodation of worldly change until the *Mutabilitie Cantos*, then in the *Legend of Justice* he dramatizes the apocalyptic effort to minimize change through an absolute culling of the false from the true. Dame Nature's response to mutability, like that of the hermaphroditic Adonis, is both/and. Artegall's is either/or. This does not mean that Spenser disapproves of Artegall's style of virtue: justice is, among other things, the strict imposition of the letter of law.[13] But it may mean that Plutarch's account of justice and mutability inclined Spenser to use the equity figure of Britomart—who like Isis wanders to restore her lover—to point out the inability of justice alone to negotiate the complexity of moral life. Equity is in fact the Aristotelian quality that complements the strict letter of the law with an attention to the vagaries of context (*Nic. Ethics* V.10). Much as Spenser supplements Dame Nature's account of vital change with apocalyptic closure, so he supplements Artegall's strict restraint of change with a principle of accommodation. Nonetheless, the fear of change and the inclination to arrest it governs Book V, and the legend of Justice aggressively looks forward to the defeat of the litigious titanness. Athegall's weapon, purloined from Jove's storehouse, is the Chrysaor, the 'golden sword' that the thunder god used to put down the rebellious titans (V.i.9). If the golden substance, like Chrysogone's name, is another slight nod toward Plato and Aristotle's examples of hylomorphic change, Artegall's sword is masculine form, not feminine matter.

NOTES

1. This is essentially the distinction of Sir Philip Sidney and others, although we have no reason to suspect that Spenser shared Sidney's misgivings about the 'sullen gravity' (1985: 23) of moral philosophers.
2. For the Platonic and Neo-Platonic influence on Spenser see Ellrodt (1960), Welsford (1967), Bieman (1988), Quitslund (2001) and the essays collected in *SSt* 24 (2009). For that of Aristotle and scholastic philosophy see Morgan (1986) and Horton (1990). For the development of Renaissance Neo-Platonism see Allen (1981, 1984). For early modern philosophy generally see Schmitt and Skinner (1988).
3. English quotations of Aristotle come from *The Basic Works of Aristotle*, ed. and trans. R. McKeon, New York: Random House, 1941. Original Greek quotations come from *The Nicomachean Ethics*, trans. H. Rackham, Cambridge, MA: Harvard University Press, 1934.
4. English quotations of Plato come from *The Collected Dialogues of Plato*, ed. E. Hamilton and H. Cairns, Princeton, NJ: Princeton University Press, 1961. Original Greek quotations come from *Platonis Opera*, vol. 2, ed. J. Burnet, Oxford: Oxford University Press.
5. All quotations of Seneca come from *Moral Essays*, ed. and trans. J. W. Basore, 2 vols, Cambridge, MA: Harvard University Press, 2001.
6. Cicero, *De Finibus Bonorum et Malorum*, trans. H. Rackham, New York: Macmillan, 1914.
7. Cicero, *Tusculan Disputations*, trans. J. E. King, Cambridge, MA: Harvard University Press, 1971.

8. For an argument that Arthur represents instead a specifically medieval notion of *magnificentia*, bearing little relation to Aristotle, see Tuve (1966), 57–143. For a counterargument that aligns magnificence and magnanimity closely, see McCabe (1993).
9. Cicero, *De Natura Deorum*, trans. H. Rackham, Cambridge, MA: Harvard University Press, 1951.
10. All quotations of Spenser's shorter poems are from Spenser (1989).
11. *De Rerum Natura*, trans. W. H. D. Rouse and M. F. Smith, Cambridge, MA: Harvard University Press, 1975.
12. Plutarch, *Isis and Osiris. Moralia*, trans. F. C. Babbitt, Cambridge, MA: Harvard University Press, 1993.
13. Fowler (1995) offers a differing conclusion about Spenser's philosophical view of the pursuit of justice in Book V.

BIBLIOGRAPHY

Ackrill, J. L. (1974). 'Aristotle on *Eudaimonia*'. *Proceedings of the British Academy* 60: 339–59.
Allen, M. J. B. (1981). *Marsilio Ficino and the Phaedran Charioteer*. Berkeley: University of California Press.
—— (1984). 'Marsilio Ficino on Plato, the Neoplatonists and the Christian Doctrine of the Trinity'. *RQ* 37(4): 555–84.
Bieman, E. (1988). *Plato Baptized: Towards the Interpretation of Spenser's Mimetic Fictions*. Toronto: University of Toronto Press.
Ellrodt, R. (1960). *Neoplatonism in the Poetry of Spenser*. Geneva: Droz.
Esolen, A. (1990). 'Spenserian Chaos: Lucretius in *The Faerie Queene*'. *SSt* 11: 31–52.
Fowler, E. (1995). 'The Failure of Moral Philosophy in the Work of Edmund Spenser'. *Representations* 51: 47–76.
Horton, R. A. (1990). 'Aristotle and his commentators'. *SE*.
Lovejoy, A. O. (1961). *The Great Chain of Being: A Study in the History of an Idea*. Cambridge, MA: Harvard University Press.
Lucan (1928). *Pharsalia*, trans. J. D. Duff. Cambridge, MA: Harvard University Press.
McCabe, R. A. (1993). 'Prince Arthur's "Vertuous and Gentle Discipline"', in Eiléan Ní Cuilleanáin and J. D. Pheifer (eds), *Noble and Joyous Histories: English Romances, 1375–1650*. Dublin: Irish Academic Press: 221–44.
Morgan, G. (1986). 'Holiness as the First of Spenser's Aristotelian Moral Virtues'. *MLN* 81: 817–37.
Price, A. W. (2006). 'Acrasia and Self-Control', in Richard Kraut (ed.), *The Blackwell Guide to Aristotle's Nicomachean Ethics*. Oxford: Blackwell: 234–54.
Quitslund, J. A. (2001). *Spenser's Supreme Fiction: Platonic Natural Philosophy and* The Faerie Queene. Toronto: University of Toronto Press.
Roche, T. P. (1964). *The Kindly Flame: A Study of the Third and Fourth Books of Spenser's* Faerie Queene. Princeton, NJ: Princeton University Press.
Schmitt, C. B., and Skinner, Q. (eds) (1988). *The Cambridge History of Renaissance Philosophy*. Cambridge: Cambridge University Press.
Sidney, Philip (1985). *An Apology for Poetry*, ed. F. G. Robinon. New York: Macmillan.

Snyder, S. (1965). 'The Left Hand of God: Despair in Medieval and Renaissance Tradition'. *SR* 12: 18–59.

Tuve, R. (1966). *Allegorical Imagery*. Princeton, NJ: Princeton University Press.

Weatherby, H. L. (1996). 'Spenser's Legend of Ἐγκράτεια'. *SP* 93(2): 207–17.

Welsford, E. (1967). *Spenser: Fowre Hymnes, Epithalamion*. Oxford: Basil Blackwell.

Wolfe, J. (2004). *Humanism, Machinery, and Renaissance Literature*. Cambridge: Cambridge University Press.

....

CHAPTER 29

SPENSER AND HISTORY

....

BART VAN ES

IN the second stanza of what he has promised will be an epic poem, Spenser turns to
the sources of his narrative:

> Helpe then, O holy virgin chiefe of nyne,
>   Thy weaker Nouice to performe thy will,
>   Lay forth out of thine euerlasting scryne
>   The antique rolles, which there lye hidden still,
>   Of Faerie knights and fayrest *Tanaquill*,
>   Whom that most noble Briton Prince so long
>   Sought through the world, and suffered so much ill,
>   That I must rue his vndeserued wrong:
> O help thou my weake wit, and sharpen my dull tong.   (I Proem, 2)

The first proem of *The Faerie Queene* offers little certainty on the subject of
'Spenser and History'. Though the Briton Prince and the Roman Tanaquill are
loosely historical, they come from different eras and here rub shoulders with 'Faerie
knights'. The 'holy virgin chiefe of nyne' could be a muse of either history or poetry:
the object of the poet's appeal for inspiration remains provocatively unnamed.
Turning to the back of the 1590 volume, we find in any case that the choice between
Clio and Calliope would constitute no judgement on the poem's content. In the
'Letter to Ralegh' appended to the first edition, Spenser distinguishes the epic poet
from the historian only through the *sequence* of his narrative. Placing himself in the
tradition of 'antique Poets historicall' such as Homer, Virgil, and Ariosto, the poet
observes that:

The Methode of a Poet historical is not such, as of an Historiographer. For an Historiographer discourseth of affayres orderley as they were donne, accounting as well the times as the actions, but a Poet thrusteth into the middest, euen where it most concerneth him, and there recoursing to the thinges forepaste, and the diuining of things to come, maketh a pleasing Analysis of all. (Spenser 2001: 716)

Both the proem and the 'Letter' addressing the first-time reader of *The Faerie Queene* make only an ambiguous claim for historicity.

To an uninitiated audience in the 1590s, this introductory matter might logically suggest that the subject of Spenser's poem would be a conflict or a quest from the legendary past. That, certainly, was the conventional source for work with aspiration towards epic. Homer's *Iliad* was quasi-historic; Virgil's *Aeneid* concerned Rome's mythic origins; Ariosto's *Orlando Furioso* was set in Europe in the age of Charlemagne; Tasso's *Gerusalemme Liberata* celebrated the First Crusade. These poems were Spenser's principal models, and though they employed a great deal of creative license they did retain some grounding in plausible truth for an early modern audience. The role of Poet Historical was most self-consciously adopted by Tasso, whose 'Allegoria del poema' was an important influence on the 'Letter to Ralegh' itself (see above p. 455). The Italian poet was wedded to a certain level of realism, although this could coexist with invention, episodes of magic, and under-lying structures of allegory. In *Discorsi dell'arte poetica*, Tasso had stated that 'material taken from chronicles is much the better, since the epic poet must try for verisimilitude in every part of his poem' (Rhu 1993: 100). Some grounding in early written accounts was essential, for without it the heroic poem could not hope to move to pity or emulation. Distant legend, specifically the time of King Arthur, was an ideal midpoint: it left room for poetic invention without stretching the reader's credulity too far. That material feels close to the 'antique rolles' of Book I's proem. Spenser's claim in the 'Letter to Ralegh' that he 'chose the historye of king Arthure, as most fitte for the excellency of his person, being made famous by many mens former workes, and also furthest from the daunger of enuy, and suspition of present time' again suggests that the legendary exploits of sixth-century Britain will be his principal theme.

The practice of *The Faerie Queene*, however, is something very different. Even in the 'Letter to Ralegh' the story that Spenser goes on to describe is that of a feast at the Court of Faerie involving dwarves and enchantments, a story evidently drawn from romance and fairy tale. Spenser, in fact, connects Arthur with the very material that English defenders of his historicity (such as John Leland) had tried so hard to scratch away. Any reader of *The Faerie Queene* (encountering giants, dragons, monsters, and a host of purely allegorical characters such as Despaire or Impatience) might be bemused by the description of this as an historical poem. In the nineteenth century Samuel Taylor Coleridge stated that it fell in 'the domains neither of history or geography', that it was 'ignorant of all artificial boundary, all material obstacles' but was 'truly in land of Faerie, that is, of mental space' (Coleridge 1936: 36). In the light of this judgement, Spenser's claim to be a 'poet historical' such as Homer, Virgil, Ariosto, or Tasso looks decidedly weak.

We might think, then, that Spenser offers a poetics closer to that of Sir Philip Sidney, whose *Defence of Poesy* defines the poet's essential art as that of 'feigning notable images' (Sidney 1989: 219). Sidney sets the poet in opposition to the historian. The poet 'nothing affirms, and therefore never lieth' (235). There are connections here with Manzzoni's *Difesa della Comedia di Dante*. In contradistinction to Tasso and in defence of Dante's allegory in the *Divina Commedia*, Manzzoni argued that poetry was essentially fantastical. For him, as for Sidney, the poet is concerned with creating images ('idoli') that transcend the real or historical world. Reading the first canto of *The Faerie Queene* (with Redcrosse's journey into a Dantean wood and his battle with the Dantean monster Errour) we might reasonably conclude that Spenser is, at heart, a 'maker' according to Sidney's model.

As we read further into the *Legend of Holinesse*, however, an historical element does slowly re-emerge. When Redcrosse is tricked into abandoning his companion Una (or Truth) he soon finds himself attracted to a new paramour. She is 'a goodly Lady clad in scarlot red, | Purfled with gold and pearle of rich assay' who claims to be 'sole daughter of an Emperour, | He that the wide West vnder his rule has, | And high hath set his throne, where *Tiberis* doth pas.' (I.ii.13; 22). It quickly becomes clear that this is Duessa or Falsehood, but her appearance and lineage also invite us to see her as something more. Later, when Redcrosse is physically imprisoned, she takes on still more regalia, including a 'triple crowne set on her head full hye' (I.vii.16). By this point in the narrative we can confidently identify Duessa with the Church of Rome. Redcrosse, revealed as St George the patron saint of England, can in turn be recognized as his nation's representative.

The romance story of Redcrosse and Duessa can be decoded as history. In John Foxe's *Actes and Monuments* (popularly known as the *Book of Martyrs*) the Protestant nation had found a new religious heritage. In this account the true faith had been present in England from the earliest stages. Only gradually had Papal Rome courted and entrapped the nation, finally reducing England to a spiritual captivity. With the Reformation under the Tudors, England had returned to Truth. The capture of Redcrosse and his eventual return to Una fits easily with this story. Spenser's early readers were certainly receptive to this mode of historical allegory. John Dixon, whose extensive annotations survive, wrote next to the defeat of the Dragon in Canto xi: 'Antichristian religion overthrown and the maintainer thereof, Queen Mary, by death victored' (Hough 1964: 8). At the same time, Dixon was also happy to gloss a moral narrative: Una, for example, is labelled both as 'Eliza' and 'Holynesse'.

For parts of Book I we might say that Spenser reverses the constituent parts of Tasso's theory. The Italian argued that a poet should write what looks like history, but that this history should have an allegorical core (in *Gerusalemme Liberata* the story of the battle for the Holy Land is also an allegory of the soul's journey towards salvation). Spenser, in contrast, writes a surface moral allegory (involving opponents such as Guile and Lust) that has history hiding beneath. This model for Spenser's compositional framework is sometimes helpful, particularly in parts of Book I and Book V. Elsewhere, however, episodes of direct correspondence are much more fragmentary. Even Book I does not offer easy parallels. John Dixon identified Redcrosse at an early stage as 'Lord Leicester' but that linkage cannot be carried to other parts of the poem. As Michael O'Connell observed, sustained historical allegory does not fit with the realities of a reader's experience: 'none of the various historical allegories fastened upon Book I, for instance, can actually be kept in mind while one is reading the poem attentively' (O'Connell 1977: 12).

For readers of *The Faerie Queene*, then, visions of coherence between history and moral allegory tend to be momentary. This has profound implications for the place of history in Spenser's poem and takes us back to the 'Letter to Ralegh''s primary definition of the work as a 'dark conceit'. For the fact that the historical presence is fragmentary does not make it less important. It was C. S. Lewis who wrote that although the world of *The Faerie Queene* was not 'like life', the experience of reading it was 'like living' (Lewis 1936: 360). In the same way, although not much of the poem is strictly historical, the experience of reading it does resemble the poet's sense of existence through time. Low-church Protestantism laid particular stress on history as a recognizably authored and ordered process. God existed outside time and evidence of His Providential control could be found in regular divisions between epochs and in patterns of recurrence from one age to the next. John Foxe, for example, thought of the persecution of Protestants under Mary as a predestined and meaningful repetition of the sufferings of the early Church. Thomas Blundeville's *True Order of Wryting and Reading Hystories*, from a less polemical perspective, also stressed the importance of an ultimate order to history: though God 'suffreth the wicked for the most part to live in prosperitie, and the good in adversitie: yet we maye see by the many notable examples, . . . that nothing is done by chaunce, but all things by his foresight, counsell, and diuine providence' (F3^{a-b}). Patterns were not easily discovered. True certainty was God's alone, yet the search for coherence was the mark of a lively faith. In this sense the fragmentary and cloudy presence of history in *The Faerie Queene* does approximate Spenser's sense of the temporal condition of mankind.

There are moments in the poem at which fleeting visions of coherence are made present to the protagonists. Angus Fletcher defined such episodes as 'prophetic': critical junctures at which the 'prophetic order of history is revealed' (Fletcher 1971: 45). In Canto x Redcrosse is led up to a high hill by the figure Contemplation. This place, we are told, is like that ascended by Moses to receive the Ten Commandments or by Christ when he went to pray. From it, we can see Jerusalem and thus an eventual outcome to all human history. It is here that Redcrosse is finally given details of his own place in this wider picture:

> To yonder same *Hierusalem* doe bend,
> Where is for thee ordained a blessed end:
> For thou emongst those Saints, whom thou doest see,
> Shalt be a Saint and thine own nations frend
> And Patrone: thou Saint *George* shalt called bee,
> *Saint George* of mery England, the sign of victoree.   (I.x.61)

At the same time the knight is told of his place in a more localized story:

> thou springst from ancient race
> Of *Saxon* kinges, that haue with mightie hand
> And many bloody battailes fought in place
> High reard their royall throne in *Britans* land.   (I.x.65)

From the perspective of Contemplation there is a connection between the grand divine narrative and the details of individual actions. His mountain is a 'type' of Mount Sinai or Mount of Olives. The latter was connected biblically with the ending of the world. Yet when Redcrosse first returns to earthly duties he finds himself 'dazed' by his vision. In a phrase that connects with the 'Letter to Ralegh' he observes how 'darke are earthly thinges compard to things diuine' (I.x.67).

On the Mount of Contemplation Redcrosse is afforded a perspective that connects his personal religious election with national history. This makes him eager to abandon knightly toil for a spiritual pilgrimage. Contemplation is clear, however, that his duty must remain that of service to the English race. This insistence on a more quotidian political destiny is a repeated message of the poem; that destiny can only be a version of the final end.

The moment on the Mount of Contemplation affords both reader and knight a glimpse of a narrative that extends beyond that of poem proper. There are several such instances dispersed across the first instalment of Spenser's work. In Book II.x the knights Arthur and Guyon read the British chronicle from the reign of King Brutus to the time of Uther Pendragon (stopping just short of Arthur himself) and also a fairy history that ends on a shadowy version of the Tudor dynasty. Twice in Book III the knight Britomart is also presented with such a narrative: Paridell, in Canto ix, tells the nation's past; Merlin, in Canto iii, tells of its future. Such moments involve national celebration, moral instruction, and a vision of the order that shapes historical events. In Book III.iii Britomart's 'prophetic moment' is cast in the future tense (although for *The Faerie Queene*'s readers it is history, stretching from just after the death of King Arthur up to the reign of Elizabeth herself). This prophecy is the moment at which Spenser comes closest to the conventional position of poet historical. His choice of canto number (III.iii), in fact, involves a deliberate 'over-going' of Ariosto, whose Merlin gave an equivalent prophecy in Canto iii of *Orlando Furioso*.

The prophetic history of Book III responds to a long tradition of poets historical. Following the narrative strategy established by Virgil, action is set in a period of the historical or quasi-historical past during which a struggle for national identity takes place. This portion of *The Faerie Queene* is the only part that specifies a recognizable point of British history and geography, being set in '*Deheubarth* that now South-wales is hight, | What time king *Ryence* raign'd' (III.ii.18). It is from this point that the poet's prophetic history can project forward to the present. This is what happens in Book VI of the *Aeneid*, in which Aeneas descends to the underworld and hears the story of his descendants' future up to the reign of Caesar Augustus, thus discovering the ultimate purpose behind his quest. That shift toward the poet's present-day ruler is matched by Spenser in Merlin's cave, where the prophecy ends on a Royal Virgin who 'shall | Stretch her white rod ouer the *Belgicke* shore' (III.iii.49).

The history that Britomart hears is dynastic. It tells the story of the royal line that she will establish through her marriage with Artegall. As Andrew Fichter (1982) has observed, in the post-classical West the notion of the noble bloodline became increasingly important for the epic tradition. Given the Tudors' Welsh (and therefore theoretically Briton) origins, it was commonplace for the family to trace its origins to Arthurian roots. For the Tudor dynasty, as for the Protestant Church, it was thus possible to re-claim a fairly recent emergence as a mystical *return*. Monmouth's prophecies of Merlin described the fall but also the eventual reappearance of the Briton line. Henry VII, in naming his first son Arthur, had attempted to effect this kind of symmetry. It is thus dynastic triumph, as much as national history, that Spenser celebrates when he has Merlin declare 'So shall the Briton blood their crowne agayn reclame' (III.iii.48).

The promise of the Arthurian epoch, however, was one of more than simply racial return. As was made clear by Edwin Greenlaw, who was the first scholar to recover this backdrop to Spenser's poem, 'the prophecy was interpreted mystically; in the Tudors, Arthur reigned again' (Greenlaw 1932: 57). In Monmouth's account Arthur's rule was a time of extraordinary foreign conquests. If Virgil could envisage Rome as a new Troy (thus establishing the motif of *translatio imperii*) it was also possible for Spenser to represent the 'empire' of Elizabethan England as a comparable recovery. Later in the *Legend of Chastity* that comparison is made explicit when Britomart meets Paridell and the two knights trade stories of imperial destiny. Paridell, a descendant of Paris, tells the story of Troy's destruction and the eventual founding of a new city in Latium. In response, Britomart remembers how 'a third kingdom yet is to arise, | Out of he *Troians* scattered ofspring, | That in all glory and great enterprise, | Both first and second *Troy* shall dare to equalise' (III.ix.44). Whether this is Arthur's or Elizabeth's kingdom is not quite certain. Given the historical doubts about the former's achievements and the uncertainty about Elizabeth's prospects, that ambiguity is useful. Yet the mood of Merlin's conclusion on a Queen who shall 'the great Castle smite so sore with all, | That it shall make him shake, and shortly learn to fall' (III.iii.49) remains one of martial triumph.

This aspect of Spenser's imperial vision connects to a more widespread tendency, both in *The Faerie Queene* and in Elizabethan politics, to present current concerns under an archaic covering. Arthur Ferguson has spoken of an 'Indian Summer of English chivalry' in which a feudal class whose military and social power had waned drew more fervently than ever on the knightly symbolism of a bygone age. Great aristocrats such as Spenser's patron the Earl of Leicester conducted jousting contests, commissioned pageants, and even waged war in a spirit of medieval errantry. Ferguson writes of Spenser's recruitment of chivalry as 'a vehicle for moral instruction in a protestant and Erastian England' (Ferguson 1960: 97). Yet, as New Historicists such Richard McCoy (1989), Richard Helgerson (1992: 57–9), and Susan Frye (1993) have pointed out, the martial independence of the medieval knight was also potentially at odds with current political reality. Medieval kings did not exercise the close managerial control of Tudor monarchs. Elizabeth could be angered by those who claimed privileges (including ancient heraldic privileges) that conflicted with her own. Thus, when Spenser (in Book V) represents Leicester's actions in the Low Countries as if they were great Arthurian victories, his polemical purpose does not necessarily match with that of the Queen.

As far as imperial achievement is concerned, Spenser's historical project is more contentious than Virgil's. The religious aspect of his poem, in contrast, gives him greater ambition. In the *Aeneid*, as Fichter points out, it is impossible for the pagan author to extend beyond the vision of an imperial triumph. The Christian dynastic poet, however, can feel confident about a universal order to history. The promised end thus becomes not merely a momentary celebration at the arrival (and dynastic return) of the ruler to whom the work is addressed. That moment is also analogous (though not equivalent) to the final end of history itself. Merlin's conclusion tips fractionally beyond the reign of Spenser's sovereign:

> But yet the end is not. There *Merlin* stayd,
>   As ouercomen of the spirites powre,
>   Or other ghastly spectacle dismayd,
>   That secretly he saw, yet note discourse.   (III.iii.50)

The poet's words here echo Christ's on the ending of time itself, 'but the end is not yet' (Matthew 24: 6). As with the vision offered to Redcrosse, divine history is placed in tandem with the national and personal. Although Britomart soon re-enters a world of internecine conflict (in which her own intended husband is to die through treachery), she does so convinced of an underlying order to those affairs.

What is true for Redcrosse on the Mount of Contemplation or Britomart in Merlin's cave also applies to the reader of *The Faerie Queene* in general. History is present in the poem through fragmentary episodes of allegory, analogy, allusion, and chronicle. But it is also present in more pervasive themes and structures that darkly suggest progress and return, however disorderly its individual elements may appear. The poem's projected twelve books, for example, suggest the hours on a clock or (as in *The Shepheardes Calender*) the months of the year: they are both circular and forward moving. The 'Letter to Ralegh' adds to this ambiguous feeling of circularity by telling us that 'the Faery Queene kept her Annuall feaste xii. dayes, vppon which xii. dayes, the occasions of the xii. seuerall aduentures hapned' (Spenser 2001: 717). In the poem itself it would seem that the adventures are annual and consecutive, though this too is problematic given Arthur's ageless presence across the books. Annual and diurnal cycles are conflated, giving a mystical sense of their connectedness. Renaissance historians and theologians were deeply concerned with such structures. Richard McCabe states that 'the poem is designed as a great paradigm of the pattern of providential history' (McCabe 1989: 16). St Augustine had conceived of history itself as a divine 'week' matching up with the days of Creation. As it stands, Spenser's seven-book poem, ending with an 'vnperfite' prayer on the Final Judgement, does provisionally suggest that structure.

In the words of McCabe, who has done more than anyone to set out the complexities of *The Faerie Queene*'s engagement with providential history, the Poet Historical 'is committed to the view that life has a meaning, that the events in human history however perplexing or even calamitous lead mankind to a preordained end in the light of which all preceding phenomena become explicable' (McCabe 1989: 16). This is true. Yet the realities of early modern England's engagement with history were not simply those of a steady religious faith. The Reformation and Renaissance brought a crisis to medieval ideas of historiography. England's history had been written largely by monks in defence of kings who served papal authority. The *Actes and Monuments* sought to produce an alternative history, but to make his case Foxe had to rely on Catholic accounts of the prosecution of heretics, who were now reclaimed as martyrs for a suppressed Protestant church. Much official history was thus profoundly open to doubt.

New historical methods put further strain on the old chronicles. Geoffrey of Monmouth's *Historia regum Britanniae* (*c.*1137) had provided a history of Britain from the first slaying of its native giants over 700 years before Christ. This narrative was repeated in all national chronicles, including those of Holinshed (1577, 1587). Yet its authenticity was increasingly open to question. Scholars concerned with documentary evidence, anachronism, and the nature of early societies could see that there was little evidence for Monmouth's story. The *Historia* had always been the object of scepticism but, as Arthur Ferguson and Daniel Woolf have shown, as the sixteenth century progressed, the whole notion of coherent monarchical government before and immediately after the Roman invasion became progressively less tenable (Ferguson 1979: 104–13; Woolf 1990: 95–117). As a result, in the words of Andrew Escobedo, English nationhood in the Renaissance was 'linked to a perception of historical loss, the sense that the past was incommensurate with and possibly lost to the present' (2004: 3).

It is this kind of apocryphal history that we find in Book II of Spenser's poem, where the knights Guyon and Artegall enter the castle of Alma to discover 'an auncient booke, hight *Briton moniments*, | That of this lands first conquest did deuize' (II.ix.59). In the ensuing canto Spenser provides 'A chronicle of Briton Kings, From Brute to Vthers rayne', taking us from the first peopling of the island to the reign of Prince Arthur himself. Its scope is near identical to that of Monmouth's *Historia*. Coming in the tenth canto, just like Redcrosse's vision of Jerusalem, it aught to constitute an equivalent 'prophetic moment': the point where Arthur comes to recognize his place in history. Critics have certainly found providential design in the canto's placement and contents. The chronicle, according to Leath Mills (1976) and others, contains numerological patterns showing order behind an apparently random succession of good and bad kings. Such numbers were a key part of the providential decoding of Renaissance scholars. Jean Bodin's *Methodus*, for example, identified the importance of the numbers nine and seven throughout time (Bodin 1945: xx). McCabe stresses the moral lessons of the history and argues that, when seen alongside the accompanying faerie chronicle, it reveals that 'there is "linear" progress after all' (McCabe 1989: 112).

Spenser certainly treated the British history with care. Carrie Anna Harper showed that he compiled the chronicle by drawing on a variety of sources, including manuscripts. He did not simply pick up the first available version of the story that came to hand. Yet whether the 'chronicle' in Canto x is the same thing as the 'Briton moniments' that Arthur discovers in Canto ix is not quite certain. Those 'moniments', we are told, 'of this lands first conquest did deuize, | And old diuision into Regiments, | Till it reduced was to one mans gouernements' (II.ix.60). That picture of an island first made up of numerous competing kingdoms matches the kind of narrative that antiquarians were proposing for pre-Roman history and which could be found in Book V of Lucretius's *De Rerum Natura*. 'Moniments' can denote documents and physical remains: they constitute the sort of material evidence through which real history could be retrieved. The 'chronicle' in Canto ix, however, gives simply a smooth Monmouth-like succession of rulers in which Britain is governed by one man (the mythical Brutus) from the start. When Arthur, with a pun on 'Brute' and 'British', declares 'How brutish is it not to vnderstand, | How much to her we owe, that all vs gaue' that claim is not without irony (II.x.69). The Briton Moniments, it is worth remembering, are found only in the mind of an allegorical body (the person-shaped Castle of Alma). Connections with the 'antique rolles' that lie 'hidden still' in the first proem are difficult to resist.

The chink of light between the 'moniments' and the 'chronicle' is important. Spenser, in *The Faerie Queene* and beyond, could be regretful about the loss of records, but also playfully ironic. His antiquarian elegy, *The Ruines of Time*, complains of the failure to immortalize achievements in British history, while also mocking those ambitions to immortality. There is gentle comedy in the poem, for example, as the spirit of the ancient city of Verulamium is placed on banks of the river Thames to bewail her disappearance. In the recently published *Britannia* (1586) Camden had argued with particular vehemence against those misled 'by a corrupt place in *Gildas*' to believe 'that the river *Tamis* sometimes had his course and channel this way' (222). Thus, as Verlane laments the loss of 'the christall *Thamis*' from her city and at the same time offers high praise for '*Cambden* the nourice of antiquitie' (169) she reveals a conspicuous failure to read his work. In such episodes Spenser distinguishes himself from previous humanist poets, such as Joachim Du Bellay, whose antiquarian verse he had translated as *The Ruines of Rome*. Du Bellay's poem had pondered the spectacular remnants of the imperial city. By choosing a Roman town for which there were *famously* no surviving ruins, the English poet chose to 'overgo' his Continental predecessor with a certain knowing perversity.

Appropriately enough, in *The Ruines of Time* Spenser eulogized Camden using the same narrative form that the antiquarian had adopted for the *Britannia*. Instead of a chronicle structure (moving chronologically from one year to the next) the *Britannia* used chorography. This mode (literally 'earth writing') involved the description of regions and places as a way of approaching their past. In Camden's hands it had some connections with modern archaeology, although he worked largely with documents rather than travelling himself. By writing in this way Camden was able systematically to explore evidence of ruins, local customs, and myths that provided stories of the past. It was by means of this mode that he rejected, albeit tentatively, the legends of King Arthur's supposed imperial reign. At the same time, Camden also used it to anthologize historical poetry, which often celebrated such mythical tales.

Camden deployed chorography to set out a new story of the nation's past. Spenser was interested in these discoveries. Yet, like Camden, he also used chorography to explore and expand the mythology of place. In his early years he may have written a full chorographical poem, *Epithalamion Thamesis*, but, if so, it has not survived. Book IV of *The Faerie Queene*, however, concludes with a chorographic river pageant that may have drawn its material from this earlier work. Its method of tying history to place by means of a network of rivers is closely related to Camden's approach: alongside Harrison's 'Description of Britaine' in Holinshed's *Chronicles*, the *Britannia* was an important source. Each river described has its history. For example:

> Next these came Tyne, along whose stony bancke
>   That Romaine Monarch built a brasen wall,
>   Which mote the feebled Britons strongly flancke
>   Against the Picts, that swarmed ouer all.   (IV.xi.36)

Such accounts of a divided island were not easily accommodated into chronicle, but Harrison's 'Description' and Camden's *Britannia* provided a different perspective on the past. Not least, they provided what John Kerrigan (2008) calls an 'archipelagic' rather than simply English nation.

For Spenser, as an inhabitant of Ireland, this was particularly important. In his pageant he made a point of including the Irish rivers alongside English ones. In the *Britannia*, however, the Irish section had been an awkward presence. Because it had not been colonized by the Romans, Ireland did not have the same kind of antiquity that Camden had uncovered in the main section of his book. Instead, the island was characterized by a more recent violent history and a Gaelic mythology inaccessible to the English mind. Spenser was aware of this disjunction and as a member of a strident and embattled colonial minority he put it to polemical use. The Irish rivers come last and cast a pall over the conclusion of the catalogue. The poet tells us he 'Cannot recount, nor tell their hidden race, | Nor read the saluage cuntreis, thorough which they pace' (IV.xi.40). He delivers unheard of tales of Irish giants and concludes on the 'baleful Oure, late staind with English blood' (IV.xi.44). With this final river 'Oure' he punningly transports the reader from ancient myth to recent political history, thus exploiting the unique temporal capacities of chorography (Van Es 2003: 213–17).

The impact of Ireland on Spenser's historical understanding was not restricted to topographical poetry. In fact, his most sustained and systematic historiographic thinking is found in *A View of the Present State of Ireland*, his prose dialogue promoting the violent repression of the island's native and resistant Catholic inhabitants. Revealingly, the *View* was first printed in 1633 as part of a gathering of historical writers (cf. Chapter 17 above). An early manuscript copy also presented it as an antiquarian tract. Though the object of the *View* was to promote a brutal policy, its historical foundations go deep. Much of the tract is spent describing and ethnographically tracing Irish customs. Accounts of past conquests are central to this work. Not only is Spenser's 'diagnosis' based upon Ireland's supposed history, his 'cure' is also founded on what he claims is historical precedent. It is unsurprising that the final words of his tract should read 'gathered of the Antiquities of Ireland' (*Prose*, 231).

The argument of the *View* (voiced by its principal speaker, Irenius) is that Ireland is an uncivilized country that requires a violent reformation. Specifically, it is claimed that the Ireland of the sixteenth century is in a state comparable to that of Britain when it was split into competing local kingdoms. As I have noted, this was a central insight of the new antiquarian thinking. Irenius proposes dividing Ireland into shires on an English model, stating that this law was made 'by a Saxon kinge at what time Englande was verie like to Irelande as it now standes' (*Prose*, 202). Repeatedly, Irenius claims historical backing for his programme. A proposal for supporting English soldiers in Ireland through a local tax is termed a 'Romescot' because 'this was the Course which the Romaines observed in the Conquest of Englande' (*Prose*, 180). The *View*'s programme is based on an acknowledgement of England's early state as a factional territory. It accepts and makes use of the thinking of Camden and other antiquaries.

Throughout the *View* Irenius makes statements about native Irish customs and language, attempting to align these with the characteristics of the ancient Scythians. McCabe notes that 'Spenser modelled his investigation of Irish origins upon Herodotus's methodology, praising the manner in which the Greek historian discovered Homer's race by analysing his accounts of religious rituals' (McCabe 2002: 148). Irenius claims that 'by the same reasone maie as I reasonablie Conclude that the Irishe are discended from the *Scythyans* for that they vse even to this daie some of the same ceremonies which the *Scythyans* auncientlye used' (*Prose*, 107). Spenser's primary source was Joannes Boemus's *Omnium Gentium Mores, Leges, et Ritus* (1520), which McCabe describes as one of the earliest attempts at comparative ethnography. Bodin's *Methodus*, in addition, stressed the importance of language as a way of discovering the origins of peoples (Bodin 1945: 337). It is with this logic that Irenius connects the Irish battle cry 'Ferrah Ferragh' to a Scythian root. As he works, Spenser cites numerous scholarly sources (Camden and Buchanan stand alongside Lucian and Herodotus). In this sense his tract participates in an 'advanced' debate about the nature of early societies (Van Es 2002: 94).

As is clear from the study of Spenser alongside Gaelic writing, however, Spenser's attempts to trace current Irish customs to ancient cultures are deeply flawed. Early philological methods were simply not equal to the demands placed upon them. Spenser's partial selection from an inchoate body of tracts and chronicles was also an unreliable basis for genuine ethnography. In McCabe's analysis, race remains relevant to Spenser's thinking despite the *View*'s acknowledgement that 'theare is no nacion now in Christendome nor muche farther but is mingled and Compounded with others' (92). Even in the *View*, McCabe argues, Spenser resists the erasure of racial difference between British and Irish, thereby attempting to maintain the dynastic ambitions set out in *The Faerie Queene*. As Irenius reveals his reliance on ancient Irish chronicles while admitting that the Scythians never 'had Letteres amongst them', we find that 'the whole structure of the argument teeters on the verge of collapse' (McCabe 2002: 149).

It can be difficult to reconcile the idealized image of Spenser as a philosopher of providential order with his practice as a colonial polemicist. In the same way, the poet's role as a champion of national heroic achievement may appear at odds with the scepticism of the antiquarian. Yet the intellectual climate of early modern England did not demand absolute consistency: under the interlocking pressures of faith and ideology an amalgamation of competing approaches could still be held in place. In any case, the borders between the literary and the historical were not the same as those of modern scholarship. One subject where this applies is that of Spenser's giants. For although such fairytale figures might look uncomplicatedly 'fantastical' to today's readers, they were a staple feature of early history in the Elizabethan age. The first inhabitants of Albion in the chronicle of Book II, Canto x, are the most striking instance:

> far in land a saluage nation dwelt,
> Of hideous Giaunts, and halfe beastly men,
> That neuer tasted grace, nor goodnes felt,
> But like wild beastes lurking in loathsome den,
> And flying fast as Roebucke through the fen,
> All naked without shame, or care of cold,
> By hunting and by spoiling liueden;
> Of stature huge, and eke of corage bold,
> That sonnes of men amazd their sternesse to behold.   (II.x.7)

Though these early inhabitants featured routinely in suspect medieval chronicles, their status was, in fact, regarded as less doubtful (Ferguson: 106–13). The 'Description of Britain' in Holinshed's *Chronicles* of 1587 endorsed the reality of giants, not as a matter of patriotic faith but as a reasoned probability. The Bible contained accounts of early giants and there were good reasons to associate them with lust, tyranny, and the unjustified possession of land. In Cooper's *Epitome of Chronicles* (1559) giants after the Flood are traced from Nimrod, who was also the first tyrant. Their offspring were connected to a variety of wild peoples including the Scythians (Cooper: f. 12^a–13^b). Long after Spenser's death the addressee of *The Faerie Queene*'s prefatory 'Letter', Sir Walter Ralegh, could still argue vigorously for the physical reality of early giants 'without all allegorical construction' (Van Es 2002: 130).

This matrix of biblical and racial associations was politically useful to Spenser. It rested on history of the most open and expressive kind. In creating giants, St Augustine explained, God had produced a kind of living allegory, combining moral and bodily excess. Throughout Spenser's poetry, giants appear as an ethical, imperial, and religious 'other': they are part of a consistent portrayal of wildness as a rebellion from God. In the *Ruines of Rome* that city is founded on the slain bodies of the 'old Giants' (48). The unruly Goths who rise against her are characterized as the 'new Giant brood' (149) and as 'the children of the earth' (155). In *A Theatre for Worldlings'* sonnet 11 'great Typhæus sister' represented Papal tyranny. In *The Faerie Queene* giants are common adversaries of Spenser's heroes and include a tyrannical figure 'like to a Giant for his monstrous hight' (V.xii.15) who is used to characterize Irish rebellion in Spenser's day. None of these figures are strictly historical, but they do gain purchase from their connection to an historical type.

That historical basis, as well as having biblical grounding, depended on a belief that behind classical myth there lay a foundation in ancient history. That assumption was widespread in the early modern period and is today known as 'euhemerism' after its first practitioner, Euhemerus of Messene (*fl.* 311–298 BC) (Ferguson 1993: 23–4). In the Legend of Justice Spenser himself sets out the logic of this embedded historical truth in the fictions of an earlier time. Describing the Egyptian god Osiris, he tells us that:

> Well therefore did the antique world inuent,
>   That Iustice was a God of soueraine grace,
>   And alters vnto him, and temples lent,
>   And heauenly honours in the highest place;
>   Calling him great *Osyris*, of the race
>   Of th'old Ægyptian Kings, that whylome were;
>   With fayned colours shading a true case:
>   For that *Osyris*, whilest he liued here,
> The iustest man aliue, and truest did appeare.   (V.vii.2)

Spenser here depicts history itself as writing a kind of poetry—'With fayned colours shading a true case'. This kind of thinking was applied to many mythical heroes, including Hercules, who in Cooper's *Epitome of Chronicles* was depicted as Osiris's son (f. 21[b]). The euhemeristic perspective further complicates the poet's engagement with a simultaneous literal and allegorical history. In Book V, for example, we see Arthur save Belge from the monstrous tyrant Gerioneo. That act (by an ancient British hero) is modelled on one of Hercules's labours and is also a representation of Elizabethan foreign policy. Spenser thus pairs his moral allegory of justice with at least three strands of narrative, each of which has some claim to a connection with history.

With giants and mythological reference more widely we come to see how closely the 'fantastical' and the 'historical' interrelate in the work of the Poet Historical. Despite elements of tension, it is this connectivity that must lie at the heart of any assessment of 'Spenser and History'. The concluding *Two Cantos of Mutabilitie*, which at first sight appear free of historical connections, may be said to embody this multiform connection. With their pageant of the seasons, months, and hours and concluding meditation on the Apocalypse, the Cantos contain Spenser's most sustained meditation on the structure of time. We see patterns of repetition, but also of regression and advance. As with *The Faerie Queene*'s opening appeal to the 'antique rolles' that contain the records of King Arthur, so Mutabilitie's 'antique race and linage ancient' are found 'registred of old, | In *Faery* Land mongst records permanent' (VII.vi.2). Spenser, confirming a wider pattern in his poem, conflates the world of classical myth with that of faerie, thereby extending as well as containing its historical referents. As Isabel Rathborne suggested, Fairyland is in part a 'land of fame' in which generations of heroes and villains overlap (Rathborne 1937: vii). An episode such as Mutabilitie's challenge to Jove and heaven is an exemplary instance of this way of working with the past. Though distinct, the Titans' war with Jove was often associated with the rebellion of the giants. Euhemeristically this was, in turn, identified with the building of Babel (for which the biblical giant Nimrod was held responsible). These associations all play a part in Spenser's depiction of events in Book VII.

Nor does Spenser restrict himself to ancient biblical and mythical history. By setting the bulk of the action in a specific location in Ireland he gives it a contemporary political resonance. The debate that Spenser sets up applies as much to the current Irish as to the ancient giants' rebellion. Though the associations are not pressed, the defeat of Mutabilitie implies an imperial vision in which even the claims about Scythian barbarism and the rights of conquest in *A View of the Present State of Ireland* play a part. As Nature delivers her verdict she encapsulates a vision of time in which cycles move forward providentially towards ultimate apocalypse. Given her location, even England's violent repression of a native population might be a 'type' of that event:

> Cease therefore daughter further to aspire,
>   And thee content thus to be rul'd by me:
>   For thy decay thou seekst by thy desire;
>   But time shall come that all shall changed bee,
>   And from thenceforth, none no more change shall see.
>   So was the *Titaness* put down and whist,
>   And *Ioue* confirm'd in his imperiall see.   (VII.vii.59)

Combining fiction with ancient, local, universal, political, and prophetic narrative, the Cantos provide as good a point as any through which to encapsulate the place of history in Spenser's work. They are gentle in their celebration of providential rhythms and they end with an uncertain prayer. Yet they are also vested in an ideology of Protestant imperialism.

BIBLIOGRAPHY

Blundeville, T. (1574). *The True Order of Wryting and Reading Histories*. London.
Bodin, J. (1945) *Method for the Easy Comprehension of History*, trans. B. Reynolds. New York: Columbia University Press.
Coleridge, S. T. (1936). *Miscellaneous Criticism*, ed. T. M. Raysor. London: Constable.
Escobedo, A. (2004). *Nationalism and Historical Loss in Renaissance England: Foxe, Dee, Spenser, Milton*. Ithaca, NY: Cornell University Press.
Ferguson, A. B. (1960). *The Indian Summer of English Chivalry: Studies in the Decline and Transformation of Chivalric Idealism*. Durham, NC: Duke University Press.
—— (1979). *Clio Unbound: Perception of the Social and Cultural Past in Renaissance England*. Durham, NC: Duke University Press.

Ferguson, A. B. (1993). *Utter Antiquity: Perceptions of Prehistory in Renaissance England.* Durham, NC: Duke University Press.

Fichter, A. (1982). *Poets Historical, Dynastic Epic in the Renaissance.* New Haven, CT: Yale University Press.

Fletcher, A. (1971). *The Prophetic Moment: An Essay on Spenser.* Chicago: Chicago University Press.

Frye, S. (1993). *Elizabeth I: The Competition for Representation.* Oxford: Oxford University Press.

Greenlaw, E. (1932). *Studies in Spenser's Historical Allegory.* Baltimore: Johns Hopkins University Press.

Harper, C. A. (1910). *The Sources of the British Chronicle History in Spenser's* Faerie Queene. Philadelphia: John Winston.

Helgerson, R. (1992). *Forms of Nationhood: The Elizabethan Writing of England.* Chicago: University of Chicago Press.

Hough, G. (1964). *The First Commentary on* The Faerie Queene, *Being an Analysis of the Annotations in Lord Bessborough's Copy of the First Edition of* The Faerie Queene. Privately Published.

Kerrigan, J. (2008). *Archipelagic English.* Oxford: Oxford University Press.

Lewis, C. S. (1936) *The Allegory of Love.* Oxford: Oxford University Press.

McCabe, R. A. (1989). *The Pillars of Eternity: Time and Providence in* The Faerie Queene. Dublin: Irish Academic Press.

—— (2002). *Spenser's Monstrous Regiment: Elizabethan Ireland and the Poetics of Difference.* Oxford: Oxford University Press.

McCoy, R. (1989). *The Rites of Knighthood: The Literature and Politics of Elizabethan Chivalry.* Berkeley, CA: University of California Press.

Mills, J. L. (1976). 'Spenser and the Numbers of History: A Note on the British and Elfin Chronicles in *The Faerie Queene'. PQ* 55: 281–7.

O'Connell, M. (1977). *Mirror and Veil: The Historical Dimension of Spenser's* The Faerie Queene. Chapel Hill, NC: University of Carolina Press.

Rathborne, I. E. (1937). *The Meaning of Spenser's Fairyland.* New York: Columbia University Press.

Rhu, L. F. (1993). *The Genesis of Tasso's Narrative Theory: English Translations of the Early Poetics and a Comparative Study of their Significance.* Detroit: Wayne State.

Sidney, Philip (1989). *Works,* ed. K. Duncan-Jones. Oxford: Oxford University Press.

Van Es, B. (2002). *Spenser's Forms of History.* Oxford: Oxford University Press.

—— (2003). '"The Streame and Currant of Time": Land, Myth, and History in the Works of Spenser'. *SSt* 18: 209–29.

Woolf, D. R. (1990). *The Idea of History in Early Stuart England.* Toronto: Toronto University Press.

CHAPTER 30

....

SPENSER, CHAUCER, AND MEDIEVAL ROMANCE

....

ANDREW KING

SPENSER'S creative response to both the legacy of Chaucer and also to the tradition of native medieval romance is a profound and engaging feature of his work—one that deserves to be set alongside more studied aspects, such as his absorption and transformation of classical models.[1] What characterizes Spenser's response to both Chaucer and medieval native romance above all is a sense of strategy. A number of Spenser's texts provoke the reader into moments of recognition, where s/he must negotiate the significance of the work's signalled relationship with earlier native literature. More than just borrowing, Spenser's response to Chaucer and native medieval romance involves complex manipulations of the authority and meaning of the earlier literature, impacting on the authority of his own works. What is perhaps most interesting is how Spenser's handling of both Chaucer's legacy and the tradition of native medieval romance achieves synthesis, since the two traditions represented an intrinsic opposition.

SPENSER AND CHAUCER:
THE SHEPHEARDES CALENDER

From the outset of his writing career, Spenser is acutely conscious of shaping the presumed trajectory of his literary achievement in relation to Chaucer's legacy (see Chapter 25 above).[2] Indeed, Spenser's concern not merely with individual works but with the narrative of a poet's career, coupled with intermingled anxiety and hope regarding his future literary reputation, are very Chaucerian elements. Chaucerian works and passages such as *Chaucers Wordes unto Adam, his Owne Scriveyn* and the envoi to *Troilus and Criseyde* (V.1786–99) represent one means by which Chaucer sought to establish his own authority: an insistence that the precise words of his texts be adhered to within a scribal culture.[3] More subtle and ironic but nevertheless effective is Chaucer's construction of himself as a character within a number of his own works, such as the amanuensis pilgrim or the bookish 'Geffrey' of *The House of Fame*. Whilst Spenser certainly pays homage to the first of these 'Chaucers'—the 'Dan *Chaucer*, well of English vndefyled' (IV.ii.32) who is Spenser's master and figure of authority—he also imitates Chaucer in the second strategy, constructing his own fictionalized self in the figure of Colin Clout. Spenser's self-reflexiveness is a pre-eminently Chaucerian gesture, and his self-representation in *The Shepheardes Calender* as Immerito involves an irony as deliberate as Chaucer's claim in *The General Prologue* (I.725–36) that he is merely the recorder of other people's words.[4]

Chaucer's apprenticeship poetry, in which he constructs his fictional self-representation, is his dream-visions, and Spenser may indeed have first written dream poetry, imitative of his master.[5] However, Spenser follows the classical and Virgilian model of authorship with *The Shepheardes Calender*, locating his early poetic ambition within the pastoral world (Cheney 1993; Cooper 1977; Helgerson 1983). Astonishingly, this move does not diminish the presence of Chaucer and his legacy in Spenser's works. Though Chaucer wrote no (surviving) pastoral poetry, Spenser rewrites Chaucer into a Virgilian framework: Chaucer becomes 'Tityrus the God of shepheards, comparing hym to the worthines of the Roman Tityrus Virgile' (Spenser 1999: 25). Colin then represents this reformed classical Chaucer, 'Tityrus', as his poetic master, 'Who taught me homely, as I can, to make' (*June*, 82). He constructs himself as responsive to Chaucer's genius, hoping to be the recipient of 'some little drops . . . | Of that the spring was in his learned hedde' (*June*, 93–4). But Colin's seemingly passive gesture masks Spenser's manipulations of Chaucer's legacy in relation to his own projected literary career. Making Chaucer Virgilian here and elsewhere[6] not only elevates the medieval poet; it also provides a more noble pedigree for his Elizabethan heir.

Spenser's reshaping of Chaucer's legacy and meaning—in a sense, precisely what Chaucer feared—continues according to the Virgilian model. *Troilus and Criseyde*, the imposed Virgilian paradigm suggests, is not so much Chaucer's 'litel . . . tragedye' (V.1786) but his great epic. Chaucer's influential envoy to the poem invites this perception of its ambition:

> Go, litel bok, go, litel myn tragedye . . .
> But litel book, no makyng thow n'envie,
> But subgit be to alle poesye;
> And kis the steppes where as thow seest pace
> Virgile, Ovide, Omer, Lucan, and Stace.   (V.1786–2)

When Chaucer accepts that *Troilus* must 'subgit be to alle poesye' (V.1790), he intends those works that have come before—the tradition of classical epic. What of course he does not envisage is that his poem must be 'subgit' to future 'poesye'. But Spenser performs that subjection of *Troilus* in *The Shepheardes Calender* in the rendering of Chaucer's legacy into the subject of his own literary ancestry—even as he pays homage. The envoy to *The Shepheardes Calender* signals a particularly subtle relationship with *Troilus*:

> Go lyttle Calender, thou hast a free passeporte,
> Goe but a lowly gate emongste the meaner sorte.
> Dare not to match thy pype with Tityrus hys style,
>   Nor with the Pilgrim that the Ploughman playde a whyle:
> But followe them farre off, and their high steppes adore.   ('Envoy', 7–11)

Immerito emerges as less able to follow Chaucer—'followe them farre off'—compared to the Chaucerian narrator's humble but nevertheless more approximate pursuit of the classics: 'kis the steppes where as thow seest pace' (V.1791). Nonetheless, Spenser's adaptation of the Chaucerian passage signals his use of Chaucer as subject. And the particular matter which he is adapting here is appropriately the ambition for literary fame. But significantly Spenser does not just end with Chaucer's envoy; he also starts *The Shepheardes Calender* with it:

> Goe little booke: thy selfe present,
> As child whose parent is vnkent . . .   ('To His Booke', 1–2)

The Shepheardes Calender appears like a foundling child of uncertain origin, though the verbal reminiscence contained in 'Go little booke' hints at Chaucerian ancestry, if not parentage. Like the token ring or blanket (or handbag) typically left with the foundling child, designating his noble origins, so here the Chaucerian echo is a sign that this creature too is of distinguished birth.

From 'To his Booke' and E. K.'s opening discussion of 'the olde famous Poete Chaucer . . . the Loadestarre of our Language' (25), through the reactions within the collection to the 'English Tityrus', and to the closing Chaucerian envoy, *The Shepheardes Calender* is creatively obsessed with Chaucer's authority and legacy. No wonder the work of the 'new Poete' seems paradoxically old, with archaic diction and the sort of critical apparatus that would have accompanied much older and established texts (Heninger 1988). The strong sense that readers of 1579 must have had of encountering an older work means that the poet may only be 'new' in relation to their acquaintance with him. In all other ways, the poet appears antique—rooted in past literary traditions, or else reflecting contemporary presentations of older texts (A. King 2000: 2–5). Both old and new, *The Shepheardes Calender* demands its readers to rethink their collective literary past—to recognize in Chaucer a kind of national literary heritage that they might not have presumed to possess. And this redefinition of the old is the basis for launching the new. The 'new Poete' arrives with useful anachronism, giving us in the English Tityrus new ways to think about old texts, and in the glossed and archaic *Shepheardes Calender* old ways to think about new texts.

THE CANTERBURY TALES AND THE FAERIE QUEENE: STRUCTURE, MEMORY, AND RESPONSE

Creative anachronism, suggesting both the antiquity and the novelty of a work, is also central to *The Faerie Queene*. Through that anachronism, the text establishes its authority in a number of subtle rhetorical gestures directed towards the reader. One major aspect of *The Faerie Queene* that seems at once old and new (so new that Spenser must explain it in a public letter) is the overall structure of the work (A. King 2001). The essential characteristic of the work's structure, at least as it is described in the 'Letter to Ralegh', is schematicism:

I deuise that the Faery Queene kept her Annuall feaste xii. dayes, vppon which xii. seuerall dayes, the occasions of the xii. seuerall aduentures hapned, which being vndertaken by xii. seuerall knights, are in these xii books seuerally handled and discoursed. (Spenser 2001: 717)

This kind of structure, where the sections called Books are intended to represent the relatively self-contained narrative adventures of single knights, demonstrating their respective virtues, is very different from the continuous (even if interlaced) narrative models that Spenser found in classical epic and Italian romance-epic. Its structural qualities seem easily reminiscent of medieval scholastic culture, with its schematized, narrative-enhanced guides to virtues and vices; Gower's *Confessio Amantis* would be a late example, like *The Faerie Queene* assimilating this encyclopedic, manual tradition into vernacular literature. Given the established importance of Chaucer's works for Spenser, it is also interesting to think of *The Canterbury Tales* as a structural model for *The Faerie Queene*.[7] The assignment of one knight per Book resonates with each tale having a strong attachment to its pilgrim narrator. Of course Spenser's schematic structure breaks down, particularly in Book IV; and even in Book V the characters and concerns of Books III and IV are still seeking resolution. Content exerts intensifying pressures on form in the poem's second half, yet those aberrations also have a counterpart in the structural model of *The Canterbury Tales*. Not only do the tales have obvious points of thematic intersection, but also moments when other pilgrims interrupt the progress of a story (such as the Pardoner's intrusion into the Wife of Bath's narrative-driven Prologue at III.163–86), and even one instance where one of the pilgrims appears as a fictionalized element within the narrative world of a tale: Justinus, advising Januarie against marriage in *The Merchant's Tale*, refers to the views of 'The Wyf of Bathe' (IV.1685). Playful violations of the decorum of fictional layers and of structural demarcations also occur in *The Faerie Queene*. For example, Colin Clout, central character of *The Shepheardes Calender*, appears in Book VI, suggesting that Calidore has wandered into a different kind of narrative world (McCabe 2002: 233). Both *The Canterbury Tales* and *The Faerie Queene* announce their intention to fulfil a certain kind of schematic structure—four tales per pilgrim, one knight per Book—yet both display a richness of narrative content that challenges the tendency of its formal structure towards partition and containment.

In the case of both *The Canterbury Tales* and *The Faerie Queene*, the schematized structure struggling to contain its content and uphold essential demarcation directs the reader to what seems to be both behind and ongoing within that structure: the act of memory. The Spenserian narrator describes his epic as 'matter of iust memory' (II Proem, 1). In a more ironic sense, *The Canterbury Tales* also appears to be matter of just memory. Indeed the narrator lays emphasis on 'just', in one possible sense of 'only'. He will 'reherce as ny as evere he kan | Everich a word' (I.732–3); he must remember what he heard rather than 'fynde wordes newe' (I.736). When it comes to his own tale, he recalls something he 'lerned longe agoon' (VII.709); it is, he protests when interrupted, 'the best rym I kan' (II.928). If his memory here offers limited choice, at least his recollection of the other tales seems more assured. However, the anxiety concerning the task of memory revealed in *The Faerie Queene* (e.g. IV.xi.10) also emerges, less consciously, in *The Canterbury Tales*; certain passages in the tales seem to reveal the palimpsest of a different assigned speaker, such as a cleric for *The Merchant's Tale* (IV.1251, 1322) or a woman for *The Shipman's Tale* (VII.11–19). Of course this is likely to be Chaucer's own unsettled reworking of his material; but in relation to the experience of reading *The Canterbury Tales*, such passages seem to be moments of faulty memory, something like 'canker holes' that mar the books of memory in Eumnestes's library in *The Faerie Queene* (II.ix.57). Chaucer the pilgrim has seemingly misremembered, and the reader too might feel his/her anxiety reflected in, even intensified by, these moments of confusion.

Furthermore, the inability of both works to reach closure offers the reader the experience of memory's failure, part of the human fallibility of both works. A Chaucerian aspect of *The Faerie Queene* which Spenser presumably did not intend but which is nevertheless part of the reading experience of the poem is that it is unfinished.[8] A number of Chaucer's pilgrims fail to tell a story: the Yeoman, the Haberdasher, the Carpenter, the Weaver, the Dyer, the Tapestry-Weaver, and the Ploughman.[9] And none tells the proposed amount of four tales: 'tales tweye | To Caunterbury-ward . . . | And homward . . . othere two' (*General Prologue*, 792–4). Not only are numerous narrative strands obviously incomplete at the end of Book VI of *The Faerie Queene*, but perhaps more interestingly the work has signalled in various places what seem to be projected Books and their possibly titular heroes or certainly major characters. Just as some of Chaucer's pilgrims are presented in *The General Prologue* but remain mute within the story-telling, so in *The Faerie Queene* briefly mentioned characters such as Sophy (II.ix.6) and Peridure (III.viii.28) seem to claim major future narrative space within the poem, yet fail to possess it. The publication of a Spenserian fragment—both remembered and dismembered—ten years after Spenser's death is the final, unforeseen Chaucerian gesture in this writer's work: a fragment or half-recalled tale of a larger work, to set alongside *The Squire's Tale*, *The Cook's Tale*, and other incomplete parts of *The Canterbury Tales*. Matthew Lownes, the publisher of the *Two Cantos of Mutabilitie* (1609), figuratively fulfils the role of Anamnestes, assistant to Eumnestes (II.ix.58). He presents the fragment as 'parcell of some following Booke of the *Faerie Queene*' (Spenser 2001: 691). Its midpoint canto numbers vi–viii along with the condition of the last canto as 'vnperfite' resonate with the broken fragments of *The Canterbury Tales*, the places where linking passages fail or where tales break off incomplete. In the 1561 edition of Chaucer's *Workes*, the abrupt ending of *The Squire's Tale* is followed by an expanded version of Lownes's descriptor 'vnperfite': 'There can be founde no more of this foresaid tale, which hathe ben sought in diuers places' (fol. xxvii.ʳ).

COMPLETING *THE SQUIRE'S TALE*

Spenser's completion of *The Squire's Tale* in Book IV of *The Faerie Queene* offers a particularly insightful and focused instance of the intertextual relations between his work and *The Canterbury Tales*. When *The Squire's Tale* breaks off, a number of generative plot devices remain unrealized: the flying steed, the mirror, and the healing sword. For this reason alone, the tale invites completion.[10] However, it presents such an ambiguous model of literary worthiness that any poet taking it up must develop a carefully strategic response, defining precisely the significance of his undertaking. One possible reaction to the tale's incompleteness would see the Franklin tactfully halting a story that promises to expand into a vast and shapeless narrative sprawl. The Squire's clear enthusiasm for his seminal, generative material is offset by his own admission that he is an inexperienced Phaeton at the reins, playing with narrative fire. He confesses that his language is 'insufficient' (V.37) and that he lacks the requisite knowledge for his tale (V.246, 283–90, 301). What the subject matter really needs is 'a rethor excellent' with 'colours' (V.38–9). That wish, aligned with the Franklin's subtle emphasis on the probable future fruition of the Squire's ability (V.679), sets up Spenser as that future 'rethor'—the squire who has now grown into his knightly father's greatness. The Chaucerian Squire's echoes of *The Knight's Tale*,[11] aligned with the fact that Spenser's continuation of *The Squire's Tale* begins with an echo of the first line of *The Knight's Tale*,[12] encourages the reader to see the father–son analogy extending to the narrative of the two writers, where the younger 'squire', Spenser, is now ready to collect his spurs. And the generational analogy—Knight to Squire, and Chaucer to Spenser—extends into the royal aegis pertaining to the two books: just as Spenser's *Faerie Queene* is dedicated to Elizabeth, so the 1561 Chaucer *Workes* retains William Thynne's dedicatory prologue to her father, Henry VIII, as well as an image of Henry surmounting a genealogical tree on the title page to *The Canterbury Tales*.[13]

However, the interpretation of *The Squire's Tale* as interrupted because fundamentally flawed undercuts the value of the tale as a source for future narratives. So the other view emerges—the one that Spenser's continuation advances explicitly—that 'wicked Time' has 'defaste' Chaucer's work 'And robd the world of threasure endlesse deare' (IV.ii.33). Thus Spenser's work is built on a sure foundation.[14] But of course he can really have it both ways. In the legend of Cambel and Triamond the Spenserian narrator can brag that Chaucer's spirit 'doth in me suruive' (IV.ii.34). Just as the Squire will grow into the Knight, so Spenser now 'is' Chaucer. The theme of metempsychosis in the continuation, as Cheney points out, enhances the sense in which Chaucer's genius has passed into his foster poetic son, Spenser (Cheney 1985: 154). So interlocked is *The Faerie Queene* with *The Canterbury Tales*, that if we seek the conclusion of Chaucer's tale—'which hathe ben sought in diuers places'—then we can 'find' it in Spenser's poem. Both what was great but lost has been found, and what was youthful and unruly has attained its maturity.

GENERIC CONTESTATION: *THE MERCHANT'S TALE* AND PARIDELL

The Canterbury Tales is not only a story collection; it is also a story contest. Given the different social classes and moral conditions of the speakers, the story-telling contest frequently entails competition at other levels too. That kind of struggle, in which the ideological or political is figured in the literary and generic, may not seem so apparent in Spenser's work. However, the 1596 *Faerie Queene* in particular increasingly resembles a story-contest, where certain modes or genres, such as pastoral and fabliau, threaten to reverse the direction of the poem towards epic celebration. That this tendency of the poem towards multiple generic voices, competing for mastery and ideological definition of the overall poem, has its roots in *The Canterbury Tales* is best illustrated in the Malbecco episode. Paridell's seduction of Hellenore, Malbecco's wife, in Book III of *The Faerie Queene* is strongly intertextual with Chaucerian fabliau, in particular *The Merchant's Tale*.[15] The old jealous Malbecco and his young, promiscuous wife Hellenore represent a classic fabliau marriage of the January–May type. Spenser invites his readers to see an explicit connection with *The Merchant's Tale*, not just through similarities of plot but through direct textual links. For example, in *The Merchant's Tale* the squire Damian is instructed by letter from May to arrange an encounter:

> Ther lakketh noght oonly but day and place
> When that she myghte unto his lust suffise,
> For it shall be right as he wole devyse.   (IV.1998–2000)

In Spenser's reworking of this passage, Hellenore is given a more active, sexually aggressive role:

> Nought wants but time and place, which shortly shee
> Deuized hath, and to her louer told.
> It pleased well.   (III.x.11)[16]

Furthermore, the Spenserian narrator's introduction to the Malbecco episode— 'Then listen Lordings, if ye list to weet...' (III.ix.3)—recalls the opening of *Sir Thopas*: 'Listeth, lordes, in good entent...' (VII.712). This invocation of *Sir Thopas*, which is a parody of the popular native romance tradition, directs the implied audience towards the notion of parody. Paridell, the key figure in this Spenserian episode, is (as his name hints) a figure associated with parody. He is the illegitimate son of Paris (III.ix.36), and his actions in this scene help to create a parodic or bastardized version of crucial events in the Trojan war—with Hellenore, or 'Helen-whore', as a 'second *Helene*' (III.x.13). Like Troy, Malbecco's treasury burns (III.x.12–13), and he plays the roles of both Priam and Menelaus.

This parody of the story of Troy is particularly challenging to the seriousness of the poem at this point, justifying the notion of the story-contest. The fall of Troy is the foundational episode for an idealized, providential account of the origins of Britain—the British History derived from Geoffrey of Monmouth's *Historia Regum Britanniae*.[17] The Malbecco episode is the context for the recital of the first part of that epic narrative, from the fall of Troy to the arrival of Brutus in Britain. But parody, made more effective through the intertextuality of the scene, threatens to undermine this foundation. Paridell's account of the sack of Troy is used as a seduction technique for Hellenore; her willingness to listen and be sexually attracted makes her a parody of Dido, enraptured by Aeneas's account of the city's fall.[18] Both the rape of Helen and the fatal attraction of Dido (events that surround the fall of Troy) combine in Hellenore. Yet for all this mnemonic stimulus Paridell—at once Paris and Aeneas—forgets the most significant part of his narrative: that out of the fall of Troy came not only Rome but also the foundation of Britain. Britomart has to supply the deficiency:

> But a third kingdom yet is to arise,
> Out of the *Troians* scattered ofspring,
> That in all glory and great enterprise,
> Both first and second *Troy* shall dare to equalise.   (III.ix.44)

Britomart is enforcing a narrative that provides the basis for seeing her world in terms of epic, providential romance; she is fighting to maintain the fit between her chivalric behaviour and her environment. Paridell's omission, however, and the subsequent shaping of his experience into a fabliau-like episode, threatens to steer *The Faerie Queene* in a different direction. Without the Trojan foundation of Britain, the genealogical theme, crucial to romance epic, would be invalidated. Britomart would be a Quixotic figure, wearing armour but stranded in the wrong kind of literary landscape. Within this context of generic contestation, Paridell brings the same anarchic and destructive energy as Chaucer's Miller. He becomes one of a number of competing voices that challenge the poem's ambition towards definition as an epic romance version of the British and Elizabethan experience.

THE FAERIE QUEENE AND MIDDLE ENGLISH ROMANCE: SIR THOPAS, SIR BEVIS OF HAMPTON, AND GUY OF WARWICK

Spenser's response to Chaucer's legacy is a far more complicated gesture than simply establishing his own authority based on reference to an illustrious literary past. Rather, aspects of *The Canterbury Tales* in particular become embedded in *The Faerie Queene* as crucial hermeneutical devices; the incorporation of elements of *The Squire's Tale* or *The Merchant's Tale* highlight *The Faerie Queene*'s heuristic struggle towards definition as epic romance. And of course these elements can be threatening rather than supportive in that process. Indeed, what is most striking in Spenser's response to Chaucer is his tendency to employ Chaucerian elements that cannot fail to have an ironic presence in his work. The underlying of *Sir Thopas* in Arthur's dream of Gloriana is perhaps the most provocative instance.[19] Arthur's dream of an elf queen is the structural keystone of the entire poem: his search for her unites all the Books and promises to be the climax of the work as a whole. However, this project seems jeopardized from the start given that it rests on so unstable ground as *Sir Thopas*, Chaucer's devastating parody of Middle English popular verse romance. Spenser's response to Chaucer here is both strategic and competitive. Chaucer's aim in *Sir Thopas* was to signify his own literary achievement by highlighting the putative absurdities of the native romance tradition; the irony, of course, is that the character Chaucer offers this tale as 'the best rym that I kan' (VII.928). But Spenser wants to create space both for assimilating Chaucer's advancements and, crucially, for drawing upon the native verse romances that Chaucer's text derided. His response is something of a master class in Chaucerian irony: he implicitly takes *Sir Thopas* seriously, just as he has taken *The Squire's Tale* seriously. He chooses to ignore the distinction readers usually make between Chaucer the author and Chaucer the pilgrim-narrator. Since *Sir Thopas* is the tale of 'Chaucer' himself amongst the pilgrims, it is quite rightly given the place of honour in *The Faerie Queene*, as the lynchpin for the whole poem. And the fact that the irony is so delicately poised here adumbrates the increasing difficulty of *The Faerie Queene* in its later stages to reach closure. Spenser's poem is based on a 'misreading' of Chaucer, and that misreading allows into *The*

Faerie Queene the native popular romances that Harry Bailey, judge of the tales, would exclude from the Canterbury story collection.

Spenser's 'story collection', however, has emphatically made room for that material, and attention now shifts to his engagement with medieval native romance in *The Faerie Queene*. Focus is on the most popular Middle English verse romances that continued to be read and redacted in both manuscript and print well into the sixteenth century: romances such as *Sir Bevis of Hampton, Guy of Warwick, Sir Eglamour of Artois, Octavian, Sir Tryamour, Sir Isumbras, Sir Degare*, and others.[20] Two major challenges faced Spenser in incorporating this particular literary tradition into his epic poem, and one of these has already been expressed by Chaucer. The first is the perceived literary inferiority of these works, especially according to reading tastes from *c*.1570 onwards; and the other is the potentially 'papist' taint of pre-Reformation texts which frequently stray into areas of pious indoctrination and quasi-hagiographical narrative motifs (Adams 1959–60; Cooper 2004: 36–9; A. King 2008: 176–7). Both of these difficulties are brilliantly negotiated in Book I of *The Faerie Queene*.

Book I draws upon some of the best known Middle English romances in a number of ways, relating to language, generic hybridization, narrative patterns, and thematic interest. One borrowing in particular, though, seems especially calculated to provoke a critical response in readers: Redcrosse's climactic encounter with the dragon draws upon one of the most popular of all Middle English romances, *Sir Bevis of Hampton*.[21] In fighting the dragon, Bevis twice falls accidentally into a miraculous healing well. On his third attempt he slays the dragon. Spenser echoes a number of details from this scene in his description of Redcrosse's encounter with the dragon, as Thomas Warton first observed.[22] Most obviously, Bevis's two falls into the miraculous well are replicated in Redcrosse's single immersion into the Well of Life, followed by his falling against the Tree of Life, which also has 'as from a well, | A streame of trickling Balme' (I.xi.48).

Yet the early modern reader's perception of this borrowing—a calculated rhetorical effect elicited by the text—must have entailed surprise and even shock. The scene in *Bevis* is unrepentantly pre-Reformation. The well is not symbolic of baptism or symbolic in any sense, but is simply a magic, holy well—a well whose waters will physically cure with every encounter. The purely physical efficacy of Bevis's well, deriving its miraculous powers from the bathing of a virgin, is anathema to Protestant, specifically Calvinist, understanding. Calvin denies that baptismal water offers any intrinsic or physical cure, that such 'water contains in itself the power to cleanse, regenerate, and renew' (Calvin 1960: II, 1304). In Spenser's reworking, though, this physical well becomes symbolic—the Well of Life from Revelation, emblematic of a grace freely given to the individual by God and in no way acquired or merited.

The interesting thing, though, is that even as the reader moves from physical sign to transformed meaning, s/he must be surprised to note that the physical sign derives from a popular old native romance of dubious literary and moral value. Spenser's rhetorical strategy is rooted in the response to medieval culture in John Foxe's foundational *Actes and Monuments*, or *Book of Martyrs* (first published in England,

1563). The nature of that response is not iconoclastic, but rather aims towards a redefinition of certain native, pre-Reformation figures and works as offering in latent or disfigured form the elements of essential truth. Crucially for Foxe, the English Reformed Church is not a new creation, but the resuscitation of the True Church, conferred by Christ on Peter, but obscured over the centuries through human error and neglect (Foxe 1837–41: I, xix–xx). The Roman Church, writes Foxe, deviated from the True Church and became a false simulacrum—arrogating to itself the authority of the True Church but failing to provide a suitable vessel for that divine entity. Meanwhile, the True Church still existed, though it remained largely invisible. Like Una, whose brilliance, covered by a black stole, cannot be seen by Redcrosse (I.i.4), the obscurity of the Church was not a lack of presence intrinsic to the Church itself but rather registered the failure of vision of those around it. But, for Foxe, there were some whose eyes were not dimmed. Medieval writers such as Chaucer, Langland, Wyclif, and others, who seemed to expose the illegitimacy of the Roman Church, saw the radiance of the True Church, however obscured it must have seemed. Foxe's interpretation allowed a resuscitation of these pre-Reformation writers as something like harbingers of the recovery of the True Church; at the same time, Foxe's theory of the Reformed Church as the True Church rather than a new body gains authority through these 'prophetic' voices (J. King 1982: 66, 68).

It is into this context that we need to place Spenser's reception of Middle English romance. Just as, in Foxe's scheme, Chaucer's or Langland's works can only be perfectly understood with post-Reformation hindsight, so too a text like *Bevis* seems to finally have come into its own meaning in Spenser's handling. Of course Spenser's manipulation here involves a far more radical reconfiguration of the received text's meaning, compared to Foxe's reception of Chaucer. But that is part of the strategic complexity of Spenser's text, its ability to provoke an 'eureka' moment in the reader. *Bevis*, with its healing well not quite properly understood as baptismal in that text, was gesturing towards this Spenserian moment, though its meaning was veiled and corrupted. This strategy allows Spenser to recover a body of medieval native literature that otherwise might be unacceptable to his readers. And in the process *The Faerie Queene* acquires the authority that comes with already well-established roots. Like Foxe's Church, *The Faerie Queene* is not a new poem, but the recovery of something much older. It is the place where prophecies are fulfilled, and meanings achieved. Redcrosse is not an entirely new hero, but rather the correctly understood version of a hero of long-standing reputation and popular esteem in the nation's collective consciousness.[23]

That reader's experience of encountering in the 'new' text simply a new way of thinking about an old text pertains not merely to the episode of the dragon-fight. Indeed, the whole of the narrative structure of Book I is rooted in two of the most popular and influential story patterns in native romance: the displaced youth, and the slandered lady. The narrative of the displaced youth is evidenced not only in *Bevis*, but also throughout the medieval English romance tradition: in *King Horn*, *Havelok*, narratives of Arthur, the figure of Florent in *Octavian*, *Sir Triamour*, *Sir Torent of Portyngale*, *Sir Degare*, *Sir Perceval*, and *Lybeaus Desconus*, amongst others

(Cooper 2004: 324–53; A. King 2000: 145–53; Rovang 1996: 23–38). The essential narrative focuses on a youth (usually male) who is of special birth: aristocratic, royal, or even of some supernatural or divine descent. In infancy, the youth is displaced from his proper upbringing and from one or both parents, and he is reared in a degenerate context, usually ignorant of his true origins and patrimony. The place of rearing stands in extreme contrast to his natural context, so it may be economically impoverished, a wilderness setting, or even pagan lands. The story type admits variations, but in general the youth will feel in this exile the ineluctable promptings of his true nature; even though he is probably ignorant of his true identity, he will feel an irrepressible attraction towards kingship, chivalry, wizardry, or whatever is his proper patrilinear identity. In some instances, the exile and deprived upbringing may impede the youth's expression of his true nature, making his early efforts at his paternally derived identity, such as chivalry or even Christian faith and manners, clumsy; or in other examples the youth may instinctively know, for example, the proper handling of horse and spear without any previous training. In either case the youth progresses towards achieving the identity and context that are his birthright and should have been in his possession all along. The paradoxical dynamic of the story is that even as the youth seems to earn a special identity from which he was removed in infancy, these stories always carry an intrinsic insistence on the importance of birth.

On a literal level the story of Redcrosse clearly evokes this popular romance narrative. Like Lybeaus Desconus, Redcrosse arrives at the court as a rustic figure who has been displaced from his proper context. Redcrosse, who has been raised by a ploughman, does not realize that he is a changeling and is in fact derived 'from ancient race | Of *Saxon* kinges' (I.x.65–6). His desire to 'winne him worshippe... | Which of all earthly thinges he most did craue' (I.i.3) clearly did not come from his ploughman foster-father. His initial efforts at chivalry are inept—his 'angry steede' (I.i.1) recognizes a bad rider, and he is nearly defeated by the monster Error—yet he must be goaded by some memory of his true identity to seek such adventures in the first place. His exile has had a detrimental, but not irrevocable, effect on his royal identity. Just as Bevis gradually, through a process of trial and error, overcomes displacement and exile to regain his identity as a Christian, English earl, so too Redcrosse eventually proves himself to be St George and royal. But that idea of 'proves' is misleading: both King Edgar in recognizing Bevis and Contemplation in naming St George clearly uphold the heroes' identities on the basis of their birth and not through any individual merits on their part.

But as an act of recuperative memory, Spenser's recollection of the displaced youth story in the figure of Redcrosse is more than an imitation of its literal, surface narrative. What is remarkable in Spenser's handling of the displaced youth story is his realization that this very old and familiar tale provides a striking narrative vehicle for the Calvinist account of human transgression, history, and salvation. For Calvin, all humanity are displaced youths, removed from their proper context and proximity with their true father—the heavenly father, God. The exile that Bevis suffers in pagan lands becomes in Book I properly understood as the exile from Eden or heaven. Bevis's loss of patrimony is reconceived through Redcrosse as every human subject's loss of the pre-lapsarian association with God. Calvin emphasizes the depravity of humans as a consequence of the Fall and our inability to effect any good action through our own strength (Calvin 1960: II, 726–7). The ineptitude and clumsiness of the displaced youth as he seeks to overcome exile lead in Spenser's Calvinist revision of the narrative to the effects of the Fall and Original Sin on the human will to achieve good. Florent's clumsy handling of borrowed armour, which is 'sutty, blakk and unclene' in *Octavian* (85), prior to fighting a giant, leads to Redcrosse's armour, 'wherein old dints of deepe woundes . . . remaine' (I.i.1); it is not so much the armour that is borrowed but rather the dints, emblematic of an inherited condition of sinfulness. The crucial and most ingenious element in this analogy is the significance of noble or special birth in the displaced youth narratives; this translates into God's Predestination and Election of the individual for salvation—a fact determined before the individual's birth and, like aristocratic or kingly birthright, entirely outside of the individual's control. Una reminds Redcrosse that he has been 'chosen' (I.ix.53), just as Bevis was born to or 'chosen' for (rather than choosing) the earldom of South-ampton. No matter how assiduous his efforts, Bevis could never become earl without the gift of birth; and so Redcrosse could never achieve the overcoming of exile from his heavenly home without the gift of Election—a gift that similarly comes from his 'Father'.

The relationships between the Calvinist paradigm of Fall and salvation and the displaced youth narrative has another level of complexity, however, since it is precisely the chivalric ethos in the literal narrative that is the manifestation of the sinfully proud, self-sufficient mindset of Redcrosse. What is inimical to Calvinist holiness is a sense that the human individual can do anything to repair his/her spiritual condition, marred through Original Sin. In Spenser's adaptation of the story to this set of ideas, the romance hero's desire 'to proue his puissance in battell braue' (I.i.3) becomes the very obstacle to his recovery. His chivalric derring-do is emblematic of pride, of a presumed self-sufficiency that relates not simply to romance adventures but extends to his personal salvation. Indeed, the very fact that Book I is so patently an old fashioned, archaic sounding chivalric romance—a book that, as Elizabethan readers, we might have read in childhood—entails an extraordinary crisis. Like the later examples of Rafe in *The Knight of the Burning Pestle* or indeed Don Quixote, Redcrosse seems to be generating this kind of landscape around him. It is a naive, puerile landscape that we are seeing through his eyes, scripted as it is by his mindset. The chivalric romance world in Book I is in fact an attitude that both Redcrosse and the reader must reject, if we are to achieve the understanding of holiness as a realization of complete dependence on the grace of God.[24] Spenser's translation of the story to the Calvinist paradigm involves us in that sense of finally discovering what this old story always tried to tell us, but was muffled in doing so. And once we have acquired its meaning, we realize that the earlier versions were, because of their failed intentions, dangerously misleading. Like the House of Pride, the glittering surface of romance narrative is something that must eventually be repudiated once its falseness or inadequacy is perceived.

Una also offers a character whose experiences are central to a number of the most popular and influential Middle English romances: the slandered lady, deriving from the 'Constance-Florence' legends.[25] As with the displaced youth, so here the reader is manoeuvred into recognition that a familiar story is only now fully revealed in its true meaning. The basic narrative involves a virtuous lady who is slandered to her husband, by either a jealous mother-in-law or a rejected courtier. Examples are in *Sir Eglamour, Octavian, Sir Torent, The Earl of Tolous*, and Chaucer's *Man of Law's Tale*. In *Octavian*, the mother-in-law engineers a visual deceit by putting a naked squire into bed with the sleeping Florence, and then brings her son into the room. Archimago's creation of a false Una and squire—'miscreated' sprites (I.ii.3)—offers Redcrosse a comparable ocular deception, and the familiar motif gains new significance in a narrative world in which the visual is generally misleading or meretricious. Una's association with the 'woman clothed with the sun' (Revelation 12: 1), glossed in the Geneva Bible (1560) as 'ye Church which is compassed about with Iesus Christ',[26] intensifies the sense in which this familiar romance narrative achieves in Spenser's handling its full and proper meaning. And the necessity in those earlier stories for the husband figure to understand the wife's truthfulness and seek out her forgiveness becomes an apt vehicle for the Knight of Holiness's need to have faith in Una, the principle of unity.

Along with *Bevis of Hampton*, the other Middle English verse romance that achieved the same level of popularity, dissemination, and influence, extending into the early modern period, is *Guy of Warwick*.[27] Spenser invites recognition of the palimpsest of *Guy of Warwick* in Book II, the legend of *Guyon*. For one, in both medieval manuscripts and the sixteenth-century printed editions of *Guy of Warwick*, Guy's name frequently takes the form 'Guyon', usually to achieve a rhyme. Furthermore, the essential narrative of *Guy of Warwick* is mirrored in Spenser's text. *Guy* offers a diptych structure: in the first half, the relatively low-born Guy battles enemies and monsters throughout Europe to win the hand of Felice, daughter of the Earl of Warwick; in the second half, Guy abandons Felice in pursuit of the higher love of God. Again, he battles pagan armies and monsters, though this time in the name of Christianity rather than for personal aggrandizement. Crucially, in the first part he is equipped like a knight, but in the second half he deliberately exchanges his knightly sword, armour, and horse for a pilgrim's staff, clothes, and reliance on his own two feet. This transformation from knight to pilgrim is mirrored in Spenser's text by Guyon being accompanied by a pilgrim. Indeed, a broadside ballad, *A pleasant song of the Valiant Deeds of Chivalry, atchieued by the Noble Knight, Sir Guy of Warwick* (1592),[28] presents in visual terms the bipartite nature of Guy's career. Its single page contains two woodcut images of Guy: as a young knight in full chivalric mode; and as an old palmer barefoot and with pilgrim's staff. Though later than the publication of Book II, this easily derived sense of the bipartite career of Guy seems to be conveyed at the very start of Book II, in which Guyon rides into view with his accompanying pilgrim. Like the woodcut accompanying the ballad, Spenser collapses the narrative chronology and progression of the medieval Guy into a single, simultaneous moment: in effect, both the young Sir Guy seeking chivalric renown and the older, penitent pilgrim Guy appear together at the start of Book II. The function of the allegory, to make the pilgrim an extension of part of the faculties available to Guyon, indicates a particular tension: unlike the progress in *Guy of Warwick* from knight to pilgrim, with no backward glances, Book II promises a more dynamic struggle between chivalric impulse for worldly fame and secular love set against the restraining wisdom of an ascetic cast of mind. The tension and temptations that Guyon feels in Mammon's Cave or the Bowre of Blisse, and his ability to overcome them, come precisely from the collapsing together of the two ends of the spectrum of the medieval Guy's career. Guy of Warwick feels no temptation to worldly things in the second part, and little or no inclination to heavenly joys in the first part. But the simultaneity of Spenser's Guyon will ensure precisely this tension, enacting for the reader a potentially more insightful, because realistic and accessible, image of temptation truly felt yet overcome—in short, temperance.

When Guyon's horse is stolen, he resembles even more closely the peregrinatory Guy of Warwick of that work's second half. The medieval Guy is an appropriate antecedent for Spenser's Knight of Temperance because Guy represents above all a renunciation of worldly success, riches, and love. More than that, the medieval text entails a subtle and effective critique of chivalry, and the resonances of that in Spenser's text are particularly interesting following on from the interrogation of the chivalric ethos contained in Book I of *The Faerie Queene*. Braggadocchio is one figure in Book II who highlights an anxiety regarding chivalry, one which inevitably extends to the writer's employment of the chivalric romance mode: a concern that its outward trappings, which contain strong recognition elements, can be easily adopted whilst the moral core remains hollow. Braggadocchio, significantly a thief of the eponymous emblem of chivalry, the horse, is the 'scorne of knighthood and trew cheualrye, | To thinke without desert of gentle deed, | And noble worth to be aduanced hye' (II.iii.10). Guy of Warwick gives insight into how a Braggadocchio might come to be. Early in the narrative, Guy, still untested, seeks and attains knighthood so that he can ask for Felice's hand. Felice points out that without 'doughty deedes' (sig.D.ii.ʳ) his knighthood means nothing:

> Nor no better arte thou a plight,
> Saue onely thou hast the order of a knight.   (sigs. D.ii.ʳ⁻ᵛ)[29]

Similarly Pyrochles's violent rages in Book II resonate with losses of temper in Guy's early career, such as his slaying of Earl Florentyn's son. A potential fault of the chivalric ethos is its propensity towards unbridled displays of violence, putatively based on honour or dignity. It is a tendency that must be resisted not simply by the character, but (texts such as *Guy of Warwick* and Book II suggest) by the reader, whose relationship to romance must remain vigilant and awake to its moral dimension.

CONCLUSION: AT KILCOLMAN

Spenser's strategic situating of his career in relation to Chaucer's extended beyond that career, and the task of course fell to others: his burial in Westminster Abbey in proximity to Chaucer's tomb was a symbolic act that sealed his authority as England's great laureate, even as it involved the appropriation of that authority for new politics and cultural patterns. But Spenser also *lived* with the physical Middle Ages and the popular monuments of romance before this final resting place. Kilcolman castle is, of course, a startlingly appropriate place to write a poem largely set in a medieval romance, chivalric world. It is more than tempting to think of this ruin in terms of buildings within *The Faerie Queene*: Alma's castle, Malbecco's castle, the House of Pride. And like all good romance worlds, Spenser's had its dark side: close to Kilcolman castle is a cave that seems to be part natural, and part medieval quarry.[30] Caves in *The Faerie Queene* are inevitably dangerous sites—the caves of Error, Despair, Mammon, and Lust—and Spenser's personal 'romance' landscape at Kilcolman replicated the fragility of the poem's romance world. Although we cannot recover its origins fully, his engagement with the Middle Ages was arguably one of the most personal, subjective strands in his creativity.

It is impossible within the scope of this chapter to deal with the full range of Spenser's response to Chaucer and Middle English romance.[31] What the chapter has sought to describe is a framework that defines the strategic nature of Spenser's response. Chaucer is at once central and, in his indictment of Middle English verse romance, 'misread'. Spenser achieves a coalescence of two very different textual traditions. Chaucer's authority and poetic brilliance are an empowering inheritance for the 'new Poet' as well as for the epic poet of *The Faerie Queene*. But with regards to Middle English verse romance, the resuscitation of an increasingly misunderstood, obscured, yet 'prophetic' literature—so the construction of Spenser's response runs—is an equally vital coup in Spenser's poetics. Like Una, or the Woman Clothed with the Sun, or the True Church, or the displaced youth, texts like *Bevis* and *Guy* are brought out of the wilderness, cleansed, and attired in radiant new vestments. At the same time, they seem to speak to Spenser's readers with authority from the past, fully justifying the present.

NOTES

I am pleased to acknowledge financial support for research from the College of Arts, Celtic Studies, and Social Sciences of University College, Cork. I am grateful to Professor Helen Cooper and Dr Matthew Woodcock, as well of course to this volume's editor, for helpful reactions to this work.
1. See further Anderson (1998), Berry (1998), Cooper (2004), Hieatt (1998), Higgins (1990),
   A. King (2000), and Rovang (1996).

2. The text of Chaucer that Spenser is most likely to have used is *The Workes of Geffrey Chaucer* (1561), printed by John Kingston for John Wight. See Burrow (1990) and Hieatt (1975).
3. *Chaucers Wordes* occupies an interesting position in the 1561 *Workes*: it is the last text (fol. ccciv.^v), providing something of an epitaph or envoy for the entire volume. In the context of a *printed* collection, this final plea against future scribal corruption is of course particularly arresting. The poem is followed by 'Et sic est finis' and the colophon 'Thus endeth the workes of Geffray Chaucer'.
4. Citations from Spenser's works are from Spenser (1999) and Spenser (2001). Citations to Chaucer's works are from Chaucer (1987); citations from the 1561 *Workes* of Chaucer will be specifically highlighted.
5. E. K.'s 'Epistle' to Gabriel Harvey prefacing *SC* refers to 'diuers other excellent works of his [Spenser's], which slepe in silence, as his Dreames, his Legendes, his Court of Cupide, and sondry others' (Spenser 1999: 30).
6. See also in *SC*: *Februarie*, 92–9; *December*, 4; 'Envoy', 9. See also *CCH*, 2.
7. Parkes (1991), 64–5, argues that the structure of *The Canterbury Tales*, especially as presented by the Ellesmere scribe, reflects the influence of scholastic *compilatio*.
8. *The Canterbury Tales* in the 1561 edition does not include Chaucer's retraction. Following *The Parson's Tale*, it simply says 'Here endeth the Parsons tale' and 'Thus endeth the booke of Canterburie tales' (fol. cxiii.^v). Clearly the edition seeks to disguise somewhat the unfinished quality of the work, yet it is apparent that the promised amount of stories has not been delivered.
9. However, the 1561 edition does have the (non-Chaucerian) *Plowmannes Tale* (fol. xc.^r–xcvii.^r). The editor/printer has ingratiated the tale by adjusting the first line of *The Parson's Prologue* (X.1), substituting 'Ploweman' for 'Maunciple'.
10. In addition to Spenser, John Lane also offered a completion (1615, rev. 1630). It remains unpublished. See Cooper (2004), 415. On Spenser's completion in general, see Berry (1998); Cheney (1985); Goldberg (1981), 31–72, 114–19; and Hieatt (1998).
11. Cf. *Knight's Tale*, 1.1761 and *Squire's Tale*, V.479; *Knight's Tale*, I.3042 and *Squire's Tale*, V. 593.
12. Cf. *Knight's Tale*, I.859 and *FQ*, IV.ii.32.
13. See sig. ♠.ii.^r–A[sic].iii.^r, sig. ✠.i.^r.
14. The 1561 edition, with its editorial colophon noted earlier, obviously supports this view of the tale as lost rather than deliberately interrupted.
15. For a more detailed treatment of the episode in a wider context, see A. King (2003).
16. Another textual link is January's blindness (IV.2069–71) and Malbecco's blindness in one eye (III.x.15).
17. *FQ* relates the complete British History, largely from Geoffrey of Monmouth and Holinshed, in three parts: from the fall of Troy to the arrival of Brutus in Britain (III.ix.33–51); from Brutus to Uther Pendragon (II.x.5–68); from the post-Arthurian period to Elizabeth (III.iii.26–50).
18. Cf. *Aeneid*, IV.1–5 and *FQ*, III.ix.52.
19. Thopas is also mentioned at III.vii.48 with the slaying of Ollyphant, in the 1590 text only.
20. On Spenser's creative handling of the native romance tradition, and the wider context of early modern reading of medieval romance, see Cooper (2004) and A. King (2000).
21. *Bevis* survives in eight manuscripts from the medieval period and was printed at least nine times in the sixteenth century. It continued to be printed in its substantially medieval text and as a relic of medieval and early modern reading (rather than a scholarly edition) until 1711. See further Fellows (1996). For a fuller discussion of Spenser's use of *Bevis* in Book I, see A. King (2000), 126–59.

22. Warton (1762), I, 46–54 (cf. *Variorum* I, 66–75). See A. King (2000), 130–2, for a full citation of the dragon-fight from Thomas East's print of *Bevis* from c.1585, the closest surviving print in date to *FQ*.

23. See further McCabe (1989), 118–27.

24. On the inherent contradiction between the theology of election and the expectations of romance narrative, see further McCabe (1989), 170–84.

25. See further: Cooper (2004), 269–323; A. King (2000), 78–90, 153–9; and Severs (1967), 120–32.

26. Una is connected to the woman clothed with the sun through her 'sunshyny face' (I.xii.23) and her persecution by a dragon (cf. Rev. 12: 3–6). See further: J. King (1989), 203–4 and Fig. 64; (1990), 119, 122.

27. See further: Cooper (2004), 31–3; Richmond (1996); and Wiggins and Field (2007).

28. See facsimile in Richmond (1996), Pl. 21.

29. Citations are to Copland's print of c.1565, the Harvard College Library copy on EEBO.

30. The quarry is surely the source of the castle's stone. I have explored this cave inwards to approximately 20 metres. It runs back in the direction of the castle, and the main passage appears to be carved out of a naturally occurring fissure in the rock. There is a tradition that the passage connects to the castle and that Spenser and his family made their escape this way when Kilcolman was sacked: Johnson (1990), 421–2.

31. Amongst other areas for further investigation are the character of Tristram in *FQ*, VI.ii; the intertextuality of *The Parliament of Fowls* and *TCM*; and the revision of *The Book of the Duchess* in *Daph*.

Bibliography

Adams, R. P. (1959–60). '"Bold bawdry and open manslaughter": The English New Humanist Attack on Medieval Romance'. *HLQ* 23: 33–48.

Anderson, J. (1998). 'Narrative Reflections: Re-envisaging the Poet in *The Canterbury Tales* and *The Faerie Queene*', in T. Krier (ed.), *Refiguring Chaucer in the Renaissance*. Gainseville: University Press of Florida: 87–105.

Barron, W. R. J. (1987). *English Medieval Romance*. Harlow: Longman.

Berry, C. (1998). '"Sundrie Doubts": Vulnerable Understanding and Dubious Origins in Spenser's Continuation of the *Squire's Tale*', in T. Krier (ed.), *Refiguring Chaucer in the Renaissance*. Gainseville: University Press of Florida: 106–27.

[Bevis] (1885, 1886, 1894). *The Romance of Sir Beues of Hampton*, Eugene Kölbing (ed.). London: EETS ES 46, 48, 65.

Burrow, J. A. (1990). 'Chaucer, Geoffrey', in *SE*, 144–8.

Calvin, J. (1960). *Institutes of the Christian Religion*, ed. J. T. McNeil, trans. F. L. Battles, 2 vols. Philadelphia: Westminster Press.

Carruthers, M. J. (1990). *The Book of Memory*. Cambridge: Cambridge University Press.

Chaucer, Geoffrey (1561). *The Workes of Geffrey Chaucer*. London: printed by John Kingston for John Wight.

—— (1987). *The Riverside Chaucer*, ed. L. D. Benson. Boston: Houghton Mifflin.

Cheney, P. (1985). 'Spenser's Completion of *The Squire's Tale*: Love, Magic, and Heroic Action in the Legend of Cambell and Triamond'. *JMRS* 15: 135–55.

—— (1993). *Spenser's Famous Flight: A Renaissance Idea of a Literary Career*. Toronto: University of Toronto Press.

Cooper, H. (1977). *Pastoral: Mediaeval into Renaissance*. Cambridge: D. S. Brewer.

—— (1983). *The Structure of* The Canterbury Tales. London: Duckworth.

—— (2004). *The English Romance in Time: Transforming Motifs from Geoffrey of Monmouth to the Death of Shakespeare*. Oxford: Oxford University Press.

Fellows, J. (1993). 'St George as Romance Hero'. *Reading Medieval Studies* 19: 27–54.

—— (1996). '"Bevis redivivus": The Printed Editions of Sir Bevis of Hampton', in J. Fellows et al. (eds), *Romance Reading on the Book: Essays on Medieval Narrative Presented to Maldwyn Mills*. Cardiff: University of Wales Press.

Foxe, J. (1837–41). *The Acts and Monuments of John Foxe*, ed. G. Townsend, 8 vols. London: Seeley and Burnside.

Gillespie, A. (2006). *Print Culture and the Medieval Author: Chaucer, Lydgate, and their Books, 1473–1557*. Oxford: Oxford University Press.

[Guy] (1875, 1876). *The Romance of Guy of Warwick: The Second or 15th-Century Version*, ed. J. Zupitza. London: EETS ES 25, 26.

Helgerson, R. (1983). *Self-Crowned Laureates: Spenser, Jonson, Milton, and the Literary System*. Berkeley: University of California Press.

Heninger, S. K., Jr. (1988). 'The Typographical Layout of Spenser's *Shepheardes Calender*', in K. J. Höltgen et al. (eds), *Word and Visual Imagination: Studies in the Interaction of English Literature and the Visual Arts*. Erlangen: Universitätsbund Erlangen-Nürnberg: 33–71.

Hieatt, A. K. (1975). *Chaucer, Spenser, Milton: Mythopoeic Continuities and Transformations*. Montreal: McGill-Queen's University Press.

—— (1998). 'Room of One's Own for Decisions: Chaucer and *The Faerie Queene*', in T. Krier (ed.), *Refiguring Chaucer in the Renaissance*. Gainseville: University Press of Florida: 147–64.

Higgins, A. (1990). 'Spenser Reading Chaucer: Another Look at the *Faerie Queene* Allusions'. *JEGP* 89: 17–36.

Jacobs, N. (1982). '*Sir Degaré, Lay le Freine, Beves of Hamtoun*, and the "Auchinleck bookshop"'. *N&Q* 29: 294–301.

—— (1984). 'The Second Revision of *Sir Degarre*: The Egerton Fragment and its Congeners'. *Neuphililogische Mitteilungen* 85: 95–107.

Johnson, D. N. (1990). 'Kilcolman Castle', in *SE*, 421–2.

King, A. (2000). The Faerie Queene *and Middle English Romance: The Matter of Just Memory*. Oxford: Oxford University Press.

—— (2001). '"Well Grounded, Finely Framed, and Strongly Trussed Up Together": The "Medieval" Structure of *The Faerie Queene*'. *RES* 52: 22–58.

—— (2003). 'Lines of Authority: The Genealogical Theme in *The Faerie Queene*'. *SSt* 18: 59–77.

—— (2007). '*Guy of Warwick* and *The Faerie Queene*, Book II: Chivalry Through the Ages', in A. Wiggins and R. Field (eds), *Guy of Warwick: Icon and Ancestor*. Cambridge: D. S. Brewer: 169–84.

—— (2008). '*Sir Bevis of Hampton*: Renaissance Influence and Reception', in J. Fellows and I. Djordjević (eds), *Sir Bevis of Hampton in Literary Tradition*. Cambridge: D. S. Brewer: 176–91.

King, J. (1982). *English Reformation Literature: The Tudor Origins of the Protestant Tradition*. Princeton, NJ: Princeton University Press.

—— (1989). *Tudor Royal Iconongraphy*. Princeton, NJ: Princeton University Press.

King, J. (1990). *Spenser's Poetry and the Reformation Tradition.* Princeton, NJ: Princeton University Press.

Krier, T. (ed.) (1998). *Refiguring Chaucer in the Renaissance.* Gainseville: University Press of Florida.

McCabe, R. A. (1995). '"Little booke: they self present": The Politics of Presentation in *The Shepheardes Calender*', in H. Erskine-Hill and R. A. McCabe (eds), *Presenting Poetry: Composition, Publication, Reception.* Cambridge: Cambridge University Press, 15–40.

—— (2002). *Spenser's Monstrous Regiment: Elizabethan Ireland and the Poetics of Difference.* Oxford: Oxford University Press.

Meale, C. (ed.) (1994). *Readings in Medieval English Romance.* Cambridge: D. S. Brewer.

Mehl, D. (1968). *The Middle English Romances of the Thirteenth and Fourteenth Centuries.* London: Routledge and Kegan Paul.

Mills, M., Fellows, J., and C. Meale (eds) (1991). *Romance in Medieval England.* Cambridge: D. S. Brewer.

Parkes, M. B. (1991). 'The Influence of the Concepts of *Ordinatio* and *Compilatio* on the Development of the Book', in *Scribes, Scripts, and Readers.* London: Hambledon: 35–70.

Richmond, V. B. (1996). *The Legend of Guy of Warwick.* New York/London: Garland.

Rovang, P. R. (1996). *Refashioning 'Knights and Ladies Gentle Deeds': The Intertextuality of Spenser's Faerie Queene and Malory's Morte Darthur.* Madison, WI/London: Fairleigh Dickinson Press.

Severs, J. B. (ed.) (1967). *A Manual of the Writings in Middle English, 1050–1500: Fascicule I,* 'Romances'. New Haven, CT: Yale University Press.

Shakespeare, W. (2005). *The Complete Works,* ed. S. Wells and G. Taylor, 2nd edn. Oxford: Oxford University Press.

Warton, T. (1762). *Observations on the Fairy Queen of Spenser,* 2nd edn, 2 vols. London: Dodsley.

Wiggins, A., and Field, R. (eds) (2007). *Guy of Warwick: Icon and Ancestor.* Cambridge: D. S. Brewer.

Yates, F. A. (1966). *The Art of Memory.* Chicago: University of Chicago Press.

CHAPTER 31

SPENSER AND NEO-LATIN LITERATURE

LEE PIEPHO

WHILE Edmund Spenser's debut as 'Immeritô' was *The Shepheardes Calender* (1579) it is important to recognize that his other long poem printed around the same time—'*Ad ornatissimum virum*' (1580)—was in Latin, not English. For Spenser moved in a bilingual world, a world in which, partly because of him, the balance between English and Latin was shifting, but also one in which Latin as a living language put him in touch not only with the culture of ancient Rome but with recent Neo-Latin writers in Britain and Continental Europe.

In the later sixteenth century Latin still expressed and contributed to the cohesion of what Peter Burke has described as the 'imagined community' of *res publica litterarum*, the republic of letters (Burke 2004: 7, 44). A transnational fellowship, this community, initiated by Petrarch and Italian *quattrocento* humanists, had created by Spenser's time, as J. W. Binns (1990), and Joseph Ijsewijn and Dirk Sacré (1990–8), have shown, a body of Neo-Latin texts that rivaled in breadth and interest the ancient Roman literature that inspired it. Entrance into this literary world came through training in the grammar schools. And it was here that the young Spenser encountered a Neo-Latin text that he was to rely heavily on in his *Shepheardes Calender*.

SPENSER'S *SEPTEMBER* AND MANTUAN'S NINTH ECLOGUE

Among the works listed in the curriculum as being taught at the Merchant Taylors' School when Spenser entered we find, in addition to the plays of Terence, Cicero's letters and *De Officiis* (his treatise on moral duties), and the poetry of Horace, Ovid, and Virgil, the *Adulescentia*, ten Latin eclogues by the fifteenth-century Italian humanist Baptista Mantuanus (commonly known in England as 'Mantuan'). The story of why this solitary Neo-Latin text wound up on Merchant Taylors' curriculum tells us a great deal about how Spenser received and used Mantuan's poems in his collection of eclogues.

Famously pronounced by Desiderius Erasmus as the 'Christian Virgil', Mantuan's poetry was quickly embraced by tutors and schoolmasters because of its treatment of moral questions within a Judeo-Christian cultural context at a level stylistically superior to early Christian poets like Sedulius and Proba (Piepho 2001: 9–32). In Protestant England an additional reason ensured that his *Adulescentia* in particular would be taught in the schools (Piepho 2001: 94–101). Under a traditional allegorical veil in which *pastores* become shepherds of men's souls, the ninth eclogue in his collection mounts a towering attack on corruption within the papal Curia at Rome. A prominent advocate of reform within the Church in the generation before Luther, Mantuan and his 'Eclogue IX' were accordingly picked up early by English Protestant polemicists like John Bale. That Mantuan was Catholic and in religious orders (he was a prominent spokesman for the Carmelites) made him an especially effective witness against papal corruption. As the anonymous English Protestant author of *The Abuses of the Romish Church Anatomized* put it, 'lest [my critics] should say, that these testimonies have been devised by men of our profession, to disgrace them and theirs, let us hear what *Mantuan*, one of their own sect saith of them' (Anon. 1623: sig. B2^r).

Thus it came about that the young Spenser studied Mantuan's eclogues as a scholar at the Merchant Taylors' School. That he was aware of how familiar 'Eclogue IX' was to his readers through its use by schoolmasters is evident from his striking deployment of the poem in *September*. *Julye*, the other moral eclogue in Spenser's collection that draws on Mantuan's *Adulescentia*, is typical in using specific passages from the Italian writer's poems. In *September*, by contrast, Spenser self-consciously invoked Mantuan's ninth eclogue as an overall allusive frame for his narrative.

In the allegorized setting of 'Eclogue IX' the shepherd Candidus recounts how he has driven his flock to Rome in the expectation of gain only to find it a wasteland populated by sleek herds that devour the grasses and wolves that prey on his sheep. Diggon Davie replaces Candidus in Spenser's *September*, returned from an allegorized Rome with stories of abuses of the Church and what the eclogue's argument describes as 'the loose living of Popish prelates'. Given that Mantuan's poem had been picked out for use in the schools because of its catalogue of charges of corruption within the papal Curia, Spenser expects his readers to pay attention to Diggon's parallel set of charges. For England's Protestant Reformation was old enough that it was beginning to accumulate its own set of abuses. At the beginning Spenser creates a *trompe l'oeil* in which Diggon's accusations (the pride of prelates, oppression of the lower clergy, the sloth, covetousness, and ignorance of the priests) can be understood as applying to both the papal Curia and the English Church. But when he recounts charges that prelates seek 'to deck her Dame, and enrich her heyre' (115), Spenser is clearly referring to the English clergy, whom the Reformation had freed to marry and contemporary writers condemned for giving too much to their wives and children. And Diggon's next charge is even closer to home. A group of critics, he claims, say that the troubles in the English Church begin at the Court. There one can find greedy courtiers who, as he puts it, lick the fat from prelates' beards:

> For bigge Bulles of *Basan* brace hem about,
> That with theyr hornes butten the more stoute:
> But the leane soules treaden vnder foote.
> And to seeke redresse mought little boote:
> For liker bene they to pluck away more,
> Then ought of the gotten good to restore.   (124–9)

Diggon is referring here to the depletion of church properties and revenues, most notoriously by means of the Exchange Act passed during the first years of Elizabeth's reign. Paul McLane believes that his accusation applies only to lesser figures at the Court who lived off appropriations and legal chicanery (McLane 1961: 138). But Diggon's charge has an enigmatic openness that allows it to travel into more dangerous waters. What, for example, of Spenser's patron, the Earl of Leicester, who procured 'one of the most inequitable of the long leases granted by a bishop via the queen' (Heal 1980: 213)? And indeed, what of Elizabeth herself, under whom the Act was passed and who was notorious for translating her bishops frequently so as to enjoy a steady income of first fruits and taxes?

Spenser intensifies the specificity and gravity of Diggon's charge by two further modulations based on Mantuan's eclogue. The first derives from his use of the biblical imagery with which Diggon shapes his accusation. The 'bigge Bulles of *Basan*' whom he condemns are meant to remind Spenser's readers of the sleek herds in Mantuan's 'Eclogue IX'. In using the image the Italian poet was connecting them with the 'cattell' of Ezekiel 34: 20–2 and the he-goats of Matthew 25: 32–3, a link intended to suggest that anagogically they will be judged and condemned at the end of time. Spenser is in comparison far more pessimistic, steadfastly refusing to open out the potential of Diggon's image towards the anagogical end suggested by its biblical context.

His second modulation on 'Eclogue IX' is directed at the Queen, for Spenser and his readers knew that Mantuan had provided a place for her in his poem. After cataloguing the Curia's iniquities Candidus in Mantuan's eclogue concludes by proclaiming that there is a shepherd in Rome who has the power to protect the flocks and drive away the wolves. Like modern editors, the commentary Spenser used identifies this protector as Falcone de' Sinibaldi, apostolic treasurer under Innocent VIII, whom Mantuan hoped would reform the papal Curia. Contemporary Neo-Latin pastoral gave Spenser ample precedent for introducing Elizabeth into this position (in Thomas Drant's *Apomaxis* she appears to scold the Pope for attempting to assert his authority in England and Giles Fletcher the Elder represents her as defending the English Church against the incursions of the Marian bishop Edward Bonner (Piepho 2001: 120, 111)). That he refused at the end of his poem to put her in the place Mantuan had provided must have struck his readers as the strongest indictment he could make of her as the putative protector of the Protestant church in England.

Spenser's *October*, Mantuan's Fifth Eclogue, and the Organization of the *Adulescentia* and *Shepheardes Calender*

Public concerns drew Spenser, like English Protestant polemicists and educators, to Mantuan's ninth eclogue. His other major use of a poem from the *Adulescentia* is more private and reflective of Spenser's professional interests at the beginning of his literary career. This involves his use of Mantuan's 'Eclogue V' in *October*, his contemplation on various identities open to the poet and the audience and the estimation accorded to his work.

Mantuan's fifth eclogue deals with the relation between the poet and his patron, an old topic in pastoral poetry (Theocritus, Calpurnius, Petrarch, and Boccaccio had all written on it). Despite these possible sources, Mantuan drew much of his literary material outside pastoral, from the seventh satire of Juvenal, whose bitterness is often echoed in the characterization and overall tone of Mantuan's eclogue. In a landscape of impending winter the shepherd-poet Candidus complains to his patron, Silvanus, that in exchange for his verses he has been repaid only 'with empty praise and meaningless words'. When he was young, youthful enthusiasm was satisfaction enough. But now Candidus has grown old and needs Silvanus's material support. The eclogue concludes with yet another empty promise of reward from Silvanus, which prompts Candidus to curse him, wishing that like Midas he might gild everything he touches 'since in your eyes excellence is cheaper than gold'.

In adapting Mantuan's poem Spenser most immediately changed the nature and relationship of the speakers in *October*. Piers is not miserly and dishonest like Silvanus but a sympathetic and supportive friend to the shepherd-poet Cuddie in Spenser's poem. The effect is to mute Mantuan's satiric force, changing *October* from a bitter argument into a dialogue between two companions vexed by the poet's role and plight in an unsupportive world.

At the beginning of the poem Cuddie is closer to Mantuan's Candidus and the lines often echo 'Eclogue V'. Like him, Cuddie has withdrawn from his fellow shepherds and no longer sings his songs (1–12; cf. V.1–5, 21–2, 28–9, 31, 35–7), and like Candidus he complains to Piers of the 'sclender prise' he has received for his verses (13–18; cf. V.55–7). In contrast to Spenser's *September, October* is by no means self-conscious in its use of Mantuan's eclogue. Quite the opposite, following a common practice learned in grammar school,[1] Spenser is utilizing it as a springboard for inspiration. The difference is underlined in E. K.'s annotation. Lest the reader miss the relation of *September* to Mantuan's ninth eclogue E. K. guides him to it by noting that lines 76ff are 'translated out of Mantuane'. In contrast, his general note to *October* hides Spenser's indebtedness, stressing instead tenuous links with Theocritus's sixteenth idyll. This difference is evident in lines 19ff where, having used Mantuan's poem as a stimulus, Spenser lets Piers take off in a different direction.

Lines 37ff return, however, to the concerns of Mantuan's eclogue. Like Silvanus Piers urges Cuddie to 'sing of bloody Mars' and turn his attentions 'to those, that weld the awful crowne' (37–42; cf. V.126–8). But, like Mantuan's Candidus, Cuddie will have none of this. 'Romish Tityrus' (Virgil) had Maecenas to support him (55–60; cf. V.86–8), but 'Mecœnas is yclad in claye,| And great Augustus,' Virgil's other patron, 'long ygoe is dead' (61–2; cf. V.121). The 'worthies' whose heroic deeds inspired great poetry are all gone (63–4; cf. V.157–9) and now poets are forced to sing of 'mens follies' and 'rolle . . . in rymes of rybaudrye' (67–72; cf. V.153–9 and 73–6; cf. V.148–52).

At this point Spenser's poem breaks utterly from the gloomy line of argument developed in Mantuan's eclogue. Make 'winges of thine aspyring wit', Piers counsels; leave princes' courts to 'fly back to heaven', a poetic ascent (he insists) that love and the contemplation of earthly beauty will encourage. Editors mistakenly note (*Variorum* 7: 386) that from here on Spenser never returns to Mantuan's poem.[2] In this regard Cuddie's response to Piers's insistence on love's ability to inspire the poet is especially interesting. Echoing Mantuan's Candidus, Cuddie declares that poetic inspiration demands a mind free from conflicting claims on its attentions (100–2; cf. V.18–20). In Mantuan's poem these are the daily cares of the shepherd's life. For Cuddie they are the effects of love's tyranny: 'where he rules, all power he doth expell.' Towards the end of *October* Spenser in effect returns to the complaint recurrently voiced in Mantuan's eclogue. And within the overall design of *The Shepheardes Calender* Cuddie's insistence on love's harmfulness to the poet has its point. If anyone can achieve the 'famous flight' Piers advocates, it will in Cuddie's judgment be Colin Clout. But at the end of *The Shepheardes Calender* we find Colin in *December* lapsed into a self-pitying paralysis, enthralled and ultimately destroyed rather than exalted by love. If Colin, for all the poetic gifts displayed in his *November* elegy, is incapable of Piers's ascent, who is?

The question is worth asking because it is connected with one final response Spenser made to the *Adulescentia*, a response that involves two interlocking aspects in the organization of Mantuan's collection of eclogues (Mantuanus 1989: xxxv; Piepho 1985: 578–9). The commonly repeated notion that Spenser's innovation within the eclogue tradition was combining the calendar form with the eclogue-book (cf. e.g., Cheney 1989: 138) is based on the fact that neither of the two major ancient models for eclogue books, Theocritus's idylls and Virgil's bucolics, has a seasonal organization. Spenser would have known, however, that the precedent for such an organizational principle lay in Mantuan's *Adulescentia*. The first three poems in his collection all have a springtime setting. His fifth eclogue is suffused with the impending physical hardships of late autumn, and the sixth announces that winter has arrived in earnest. Mantuan's eighth and ninth eclogues bring us back to late spring and summer. And, balancing the first eclogue's vernal setting, 'Eclogue X' returns us to a wintry scene. Having recognized this seasonal underpinning, Spenser's genius came from modelling the form of his collection on the *Kalender of Shepherdes*, a widely reprinted, vernacular compilation more appropriate to the generic expectations of his English pastorals.[3]

But while the cycle of the seasons influenced the form, it is by no means the thematic link that binds together either Mantuan's or Spenser's collection of poems. And it is here that, in comparison with the *Adulescentia*, the significance of the discordance between the English poet's *October* and *December* eclogues is most evident. Complementing its seasonal movements Mantuan's poems have a clearly marked out tropological organization, moving thematically from considerations of this world to concerns with the spiritual life. As its title—*Adulescentia*, literally 'Youth'—suggests, the beginning of his collection deals with topics (erotic love, marriage, the nature of women) that would have touched the lives of young readers. Mantuan's seventh eclogue is pivotal, depicting a mystically based conversion experience that leads Pollux (alluding to its Pauline model) into religious orders. From here the collection turns outward spiritually, devotion to the Virgin being substituted for erotic love and the papal Curia as well as Mantuan's Carmelite order being scrutinized for the secular world's corruptions. Within this overall movement the subtitles of the last four poems—written 'when the author [was] aspiring to enter religious orders' and 'after his entry into religious orders'—increasingly make clear the values of an implied author who has gone beyond youth and stands behind the collection as a whole. Especially with regard to erotic love a certain toleration is allowed (love is okay for simple shepherds, so long as it ends in marriage). But Mantuan's fifth eclogue initiates a tendency in the later poems to dramatize absolute oppositions of right and wrong. Candidus may be embittered but his denunciation of the miserliness and vulgarity of Silvanus and other patrons is allowed to stand unchallenged. Likewise in 'Eclogue IX' he is ferocious and absolute in his condemnation of the papal Curia's waywardness.

The conversion of Mantuan's one-sided argument in 'Eclogue V' to a dialogue between colleagues in Spenser's *October* coupled with the validity of Cuddie's skepticism regarding love's power to inspire Colin's poetry suggest that *The Shepheardes Calender* will not have the *Adulescentia*'s absolute oppositions or the close identification of characters like Candidus with the author implied in the eclogues. An influential argument has been advanced that, having exhausted the possibilities of the pastoral genre, Spenser rises above the seasonal concerns of Colin, Piers, and Cuddie to emerge in the opening lines of *The Faerie Queene* with a Virgilian transition into the world of epic (Hamilton 1956: 181–2). Certainly, in *October* he created poetry not out of one voice but from the interplay between opposing views about poetry and the poetic profession (Spenser 1999: 560). But, in assembling his *Shepheardes Calender* Spenser may finally have been less certain where his poetic gifts would lead him (Helgerson 1983: 69). And one reader has even contended that, in contrast to the authorial identity discernible at the end of Mantuan's collection, Spenser sent forth a text with a nameless author, a text that invokes 'an exchange in which the poet is always already depleted by the one to whom the text, for whom the text is written' (Goldberg 1986: 66).

Spenser and the Poetry of Georgius Sabinus and Petrus Lotichius

If Mantuan's *Adulescentia* is a text that helped train Spenser for entrance into the *res publica litterarum*, two other texts give us a rare glimpse of his engagement with this international literary community. These are collections of poetry and prose by two German Neo-Latin writers, Georgius Sabinus and Petrus Lotichius, copies of which have recently been discovered to have been in Spenser's private library (Piepho 2002: 77–86).

Less well known today than Ariosto, Du Bellay, and other vernacular poets who influenced Spenser's poetry, during the sixteenth century Sabinus and Lotichius were counted among Continental Europe's finest writers. Spenser's copy of Lotichius's poems and letters was printed in 1576, and it seems likely that he acquired it, bound with Sabinus's poetry and prose, at Cambridge or soon afterwards during a time of poetic apprenticeship when he would have been interested in the foremost poets of the preceding half-century.

Ironically, evidence of Spenser's most immediate engagement with the two writers' verse comes from a prefatory letter and two poems that he transcribed into his copy from another edition of Lotichius's works (see Piepho 2003: 123–9). One of the poems singles out the German poet as being '*Venator Vates*' because his eclogues deal with the lives of hunters, not shepherds. Hunting eclogues are comparatively rare in pastoral poetry (Leonard Grant, in his survey of 1965, found only nine of them), and Lotichius's variation on the genre no doubt drew the attention of a young poet like Spenser interested in making his own innovations in pastoral verse.

The second poem he copied out touches on a general theme in Spenser's work. In it Lotichius's elegies are introduced with a *recusatio*, stressing that they vanquish 'lascivious' readers and are intended only for 'chaste bosoms'. Early in Spenser's career Harvey was to insist that love and the poetry of love are only the toys of youth, a charge this poem responds to and one which was to animate the English poet's repeated distinctions between love and lust in *The Faerie Queene* and elsewhere in his verse.

Two themes in the prefatory letter doubtless drew Spenser to transcribe it. A slightly awkward encomium by Lotichius's pupil stresses the great learning that has gone into his tutor's poems, which 'have taken their fill from abstruse and hidden wellsprings and been severed from the understanding and judgment of the un-tutored'. Like Harvey, Spenser was drawn to an ideal of the *doctus poeta* and would have responded to this representation of the learned poet. So too the letter praises the man who was to become Lotichius's patron, Erasmus Neustetter, for being 'conspic-uous in your praise of letters and liberal studies' and in particular for not shrinking 'from the study of poets, by whom minds are trained in the path of virtue and rendered more apt in every kind of enthusiasm'. All in all an attractive picture of the poet and patron, one which Spenser perhaps copied out with the expectation of adapting it in some future bid for patronage. In its outlines it sketches a humanist ideal of patronage and commitment to *bonae litterae* that stretch back to the time of Petrarch, one that was to be tested and modified in Spenser's various appeals for patronage to Elizabeth and members of her court.

Unlike the poets of ancient Rome, the poetry of Sabinus and Lotichius put the young Spenser in touch with the politics and culture of contemporary Continental Europe. Moreover, unlike Mantuan, they were Protestants (Sabinus was Philip Melanchthon's son-in-law) and their poems are filled with allusions to seminal events in Protestant histories of the times. Lotichius writes a harrowing and (typic-ally) personal account (*Elegia* III.4) of the siege and overthrow of Magdeburg, a Protestant stronghold he fought to defend during the religious wars in Germany. And Sabinus has a remarkable elegy (*Elegia* V.1) on the sack of Rome in 1527, an event that like many Protestant writers he viewed as a chastisement of Clement VII's political machinations.

More than Lotichius, Sabinus is associated with the powerful and the famous in Continental Europe, and a collection of letters at the end of his works opens up this world. A commendatory letter by Pietro Bembo and a letter congratulating him on his marriage initiate a lively correspondence between Sabinus and the distinguished Italian humanist. There are the usual letters to and from Continental European nobility. The most remarkable one, given pride of place in Sabinus's collection, is from Charles V in which the most powerful man in Europe praises the German poet and his works for their intelligence and great learning.

From the standpoint of Spenser's *Shepheardes Calender* both collections are most significant for the eclogues in them (in Lotichius's case a rich, complicated eclogue book composed during the last years of his life). Spenser's Latin models have sometimes been limited to Mantuan's *Adulescentia* and Virgil's bucolics (cf., e.g., Cullen 1970: 2–4) but, as Grant's (1965) survey made clear, by Spenser's time the number of Neo-Latin pastoral poems was vast, and Lotichius's and Sabinus's ec-logues broaden our understanding of the options open to him, revealing choices that Spenser modified or turned away from in his collection.

A choice he made differently involves his attacks on abuses of the Church in *September* and his other 'moral' eclogues. Mantuan's ninth eclogue would lead us to believe that this was a common strain in sixteenth-century Latin pastoral. So it is a surprise to discover that there is no ecclesiastical satire in Sabinus's and Lotichius's eclogues. Nor is this uncommon in Continental Neo-Latin pastoral. Grant lists very few eclogues dealing with abuses of the Church, most of them from the early part of the century. To a German or Italian reader Spenser's *September* might therefore seem old-fashioned. But much the same can be said about a good deal of English Neo-Latin literature in the later sixteenth century (Piepho 2001: 106–13, 120). English literature was still a long way from accepting Samuel Johnson's condemnation of pastoral poetry in which priests in poetic disguise fall to attacking errors within the Church (Johnson 1969: 204–5).

An option Spenser modified in comparison to the eclogues of Sabinus and Lotichius involves his inscription of the expectations of an epithalamium within his *April* eclogue. Readers familiar with pastoral through Virgil and Mantuan would find this development surprising. But epithalamia appear early in humanistic Latin pastorals (two early fifteenth-century ones were written for the marriages of the humanistically trained Ginevra and Isotta Nogarola), and pastoral epithalamia included in Sabinus's and Lotichius's collections show how completely integrated this post-classical development had become within the genre by the middle of the sixteenth century. In introducing it into his eclogue Spenser's striking variation was to make the bridegroom not a man but England herself, thereby aligning himself with a faction at the Court resisting Elizabeth's proposed marriage to the French Catholic Duc D'Alençon (Johnson 1990: 141–4). His use of epithalamic conventions in *April* can seem elliptical, but the presence of pastoral epithalamia in Sabinus's and Lotichius's collections provides a context that makes it more easily discernible.

Moreover, comparison with the epithalamium in Lotichius's eclogue book re-affirms a distinctive choice Spenser made in the overall design of his *Shepheardes Calender*. Lotichius's eclogue concludes his collection with a pervasive emphasis on continuity and peace to counterbalance the suffering and death he depicts in much of the rest of his collection. Spenser's *April* portrays Elisa as the embodiment of music, a harmony capable of both ordering the state and inspiring Colin's song. But these are not to be the concluding strains of *The Shepheardes Calender*. As was apparent in comparison to the organization of Mantuan's *Adulescentia*, there will be no strong closure in Spenser's collection, nothing like the resolution of tensions Lotichius's epithalamium sets forth at the end of his eclogue book.

Spenser's 'Ad ornatissimum virum' and Lotichius's Elegies

Among the Latin works by Spenser mentioned in his correspondence with Gabriel Harvey the only survival is 'Ad ornatissimum virum', a poem appended to his first letter.[4] In many ways it is a strange work. Most immediately, Spenser is oddly double about the status and nature of his trip. It will be an important voyage made by a young man of talent to advance his own career. But it has not yet been undertaken. Nor will it be pleasant, Spenser speaking of it in terms of unwished-for hardships: travels to 'foul Babylon' (*Babylona turpem*), almost certainly Rome, and more fancifully to the 'mountainous Pyrenees'.

To understand what he is doing, it seems to me helpful to consider his poem's genre expectations in relation to the *hodoeporicon*, the travel poem, and specifically in comparison to the genre's appearance in an elegy by Lotichius. Both Sabinus and Lotichius wrote *hodoeporica*,[5] but while Sabinus's '*Hodoeporicon itineris Italici*' is better known, Lotichius's most striking one—*Elegia* III.1, roughly titled 'On His Unhappy Return from France, Since All Things Burned There with Civil War'—is more complicated and likely to have impressed the young Spenser.

Although Lotichius's poem is the account of a specific journey, much of his adult life was consumed in traveling, most of it in a kind of exile. Having fought in the religious wars, he left Germany, spending several years as a tutor in France. By 1554 he sensed, however, that France was about to be torn apart by the same conflicts that had devastated Germany and resolved to return to his beloved, much missed homeland. *Elegia* III.1 is a record of the journey home. Except that he never gets there. Coming into Heidelberg he discovers that the area has been decimated by enemy troops and is unsafe to enter. In an unknown realm, he concludes bitterly, he must now seek a *patriam novam*, a new homeland. And sure enough in succeeding elegies we find him like Sabinus traveling in Italy. But as the poems make clear, it is an Italy of art and culture, an Italy of the imagination, with only the wan hope expressed at the end of the book that Lotichius can return to a kind of Tibullian contentment in the land from which he has been exiled.

In '*Ad ornatissimum virum*' Spenser would seem to have adapted an unresolved central tension that, opened up in Lotichius's first poem, pervades his third book of elegies. On the one hand Lotichius is living a humanist's dream.[6] But on the other hand he has been separated from the homeland he loves and which he took up the responsibility of defending. Spenser's poem displays a similarly unresolved tension. On one side are adult responsibilities and the need to reconcile virtue with love and pleasure. In this regard Gabriel Harvey in his poem plays Cato, reproving what one of his letters describes as 'this yonkerly, and [woomanish] humor'. Against this, Spenser follows Horace, who in one of his epistles (II.17) uses Aristippus to symbolize a balanced philosophy which refuses to regard pleasure as an evil in itself.[7] And against the opening criticism of love attributed to Harvey Spenser directs the Horatian dictum of mixing *utile dulci*—what is useful with what delights—to the goal of finally winning his mistress in marriage. His journey is in this regard an extension of his good sense and adult responsibility. It is the sensible thing to do for a talented young man who doesn't want to hide his light under a bushel. And it is a weighty mission that will take him to unpleasant and potentially dangerous places. But Spenser's journey has another aspect. His hyperbolic suggestion that he will traverse 'the desolate Caucasus (*inhospita Caucasa*)' suggests it best. The phrase has been linked with Horace's defense, in his famous ode 'Integer vitae', of love's power to overcome all dangers and hardships (Spenser 1999: 579). But the underlying motif is closer to the lovelorn Gallus's wanderings in Virgil's tenth eclogue when, denied his mistress, the famous Roman love poet roams Maenalus's heights and braves the snows of Thrace (*Eclogues* X.55, 66). For Spenser's love interest and, more important, his interest in writing about it have not disappeared but been sublimated. Like Ulysses he will wander encountering new loves but, because he is separated from Harvey, denied the means of writing about them. Like Lotichius, his journey is unfulfilled (because in Spenser's case not yet undertaken), and it will take him to a land of passion and imagination; but it is also a journey counterbalanced against adult responsibilities that Harvey would put upon him.

All this, of course, isn't literally true. Like Cuddie and Colin Clout and the image Spenser presented in his letters, the poem embodies an early attempt to fashion a poetic persona for himself. At the same time, with the various unpublished works he and Harvey discuss, '*Ad ornatissimum virum*' is self-promotional. Together with his elaborate itinerary, they are all intended to suggest that he 'has pen—will travel' (Quitslund 1996: 92). That one of his first poetical works was in Latin rather than English testifies to the fact that the literary milieu Spenser entered as a young man remained heavily Latinate. If he ultimately set out to use English to make a nation of his own, the books in his library and the poetry he published at the beginning of his literary career suggest that he also recognized the role Neo-Latin literature continued to play in British high culture.

NOTES

1. Cf., e.g., Shakespeare's use of the same practice in his sixtieth sonnet with a passage from Ovid's *Metamorphoses* (XV.178–84).
2. Piers's generous offer of a kid to support Cuddie at the conclusion of *October* is, for example, clearly based on Silvanus's miserly response at the end of Mantuan's eclogue.
3. For the influence of Ovid's *Fasti* on *SC* see Chapter 27 above.
4. The other Latin work he refers to is '*Stemmata Dudleiana*'. Its purpose, indeed whether it was written in verse or prose, remain unknown. There is information on Spenser's Latin poetry in *SE*, 435, 737–8, but a good, full discussion remains a desideratum of Spenser studies. For the Spenser–Harvey *Letters* cf. Chapter 10 above.
5. As a genre *hodeoporica* had their roots in ancient literature but were largely a Neo-Latin affair, most extensively developed by writers in Germany: on Sabinus and Lotichius, see Wiegand (1984), 71–91, 203–20.
6. From Italy he writes that: 'Now I am as rich in leisure as I always wished to be. I attend the lectures of the learned doctors [at the University of Padua] with great pleasure, as well as lectures by [the Paduan humanist Francesco] Robortello on history and Aristotle' (quoted in Zon 1983: 287). (Robortello's most important work was a commentary on Aristotle's *Poetics*.) And in a poem to Sabinus in the third book he speaks of having visited Petrarch's grave and viewed a plane tree brought by Pietro Bembo from Enna's fair fields.

7. In the complicated intertextuality of his poem Spenser seems in citing Aristippus to be placing himself in relation to Harvey's use of Aristippus in *Castilio, sive Aulicus*, a Latin poem on the successful courtier that Harvey had recently dedicated to Sir Philip Sidney.

BIBLIOGRAPHY

Anon. (1623). *The Abuses of the Romish Church Anatomized*. London: Augustine Mathewes for John Grismand.

Binns, J. W. (1990). *Intellectual Culture in Elizabethan and Jacobean England: The Latin Writings of the Age*. Leeds: Francis Cairns.

Burke, P. (2004). *Languages and Communities*. Cambridge: Cambridge University Press.

Cheney, D. (1989). 'The Circular Argument of *The Shepheardes Calender*', in G. M. Logan and G. Teskey (eds), *Unfolded Tales: Essays on Renaissance Romance*. Ithaca, NY: Cornell University Press.

Cullen, P. (1970). *Spenser, Marvell, and Renaissance Pastoral*. Cambridge, MA: Harvard University Press.

Goldberg, J. (1986). *Voice Terminal Echo: Postmodernism and English Renaissance Texts*. London: Methuen.

Grant, W. L. (1965). *Neo-Latin Literature and the Pastoral*. Chapel Hill: University of North Carolina Press.

Hamilton, A. C. 'The Argument of Spenser's *Shepheardes Calender*'. ELH 23: 171–82.

Heal, F. (1980). *Of Prelates and Princes: A Study of the Economic and Social Position of the Tudor Episcopate*. Cambridge: Cambridge University Press.

Helgerson, R. (1983). *Self-Crowned Laureates: Spenser, Jonson, Milton and the Literary System*. Berkeley/Los Angeles: University of California Press.

Ijsewijn, J., and Sacré, D. (1990–8). *Companion to Neo-Latin Studies*, 2 vols, 2nd edn. Leuven: Leuven University Press.

Johnson, L. S. (1990). *'The Shepheardes Calender': An Introduction*. University Park: Penn State University Press.

Johnson, Samuel (1969). *Works*, vol. III: *The Rambler*, ed. W. Jackson Bate and A. B. Strauss. New Haven, CT: Yale University Press.

McLane, P. (1961). *Spenser's* Shepheardes Calender: *A Study in Elizabethan Allegory*. South Bend: University of Notre Dame Press.

Mantuanus, Baptista (1989). *Adulescentia: The Eclogues of Mantuan*, ed. and trans. L. Piepho. New York: Garland.

Piepho, L. (1985). 'The Organization of Mantuan's *Adulescentia* and Spenser's *Shepheardes Calendar*: A Comparison'. *Acta Conventus Neo-Latini Bononensis*. Binghamton, NY: Medieval and Renaissance Texts and Studies: 577–82.

—— (2001). *Holofernes' Mantuan: Italian Humanism in Early Modern England*. Bern/New York: Peter Lang.

—— (2002). '*The Shepheardes Calender* and Neo-Latin Pastoral: A Book Newly Discovered to Have Been Owned By Edmund Spenser'. *SSt* 16: 77–86.

—— (2003). 'Edmund Spenser and Neo-Latin Literature: An Autograph Manuscript on Petrus Lotichius and His Poetry'. *SP* 100: 123–34.

Quitslund, J. (1996). 'Questionable Evidence in the Letters of 1580 between Gabriel Harvey and Edmund Spenser', in J. Anderson et al. (eds), *Spenser's Life and the Subject of Biography*. Amherst: University of Massachusetts Press.

Wiegand, H. (1984). *Hodoeporica: Studien zur neulateinischen Reisedichtung des deutschen Kulturraums im 16. Jahrhundert.* Baden-Baden: Valentin Koerner.

Zon, S. (1983). *Petrus Lotichius Secundus: Neo-Latin Poet.* Bern/New York: Peter Lang.

CHAPTER 32

....

SPENSER AND SIXTEENTH-CENTURY POETICS

....

ELIZABETH HEALE

THE NEW POET

....

The Shepheardes Calender boldly announces the advent of a new and ambitious poet, but it is also concerned with the question of what that role might be and the kind of poetry it entails. The *Calender* presents its verse ambitiously with woodcuts and critical commentary by the unidentified E. K. that recall Renaissance editions of Virgil's eclogues (Luborsky 1990: 654). Eclogues were, as E. K. reminds the reader, commonly regarded in the Renaissance as the first stage in an aspiring poetic career: 'the best and most auncient Poetes ... deuised this kind of wryting ... at the first to trye theyr habilities: and as young birdes, that be newly crept out of the nest, by little first to proue theyr tender wyngs, before they make a greater flyght. So flew Theocritus ... So flew Virgile' ('Epistle', 144–50).[1] Startlingly for so promotional a volume, the new poet is not named. Spenser appears only as 'Immerito'. This veiling of authorial identity may be primarily motivated by potentially dangerous allusions to the Anjou marriage negotiations (McCabe 1995: 47). However, Spenser may also have been wary of attacks and even of censorship as a writer of verse. English vernacular rhyming poems were not universally admired in 1579.

Attacks on English poetry as unlearned and immoral increased in the 1570s (Herman 1996: 46–51). Earlier in the same year, an outspoken attack by Stephen Gosson,

The School of Abuse, was printed, possibly at the instigation of the London authorities, and dedicated, like the *Calender*, to Sidney (Rae 1967: 19). Spenser refers to
Gosson dismissively in correspondence with Gabriel Harvey (*Prose*, 6). Potentially
more serious, because weightier, was Roger Ascham's attack on vernacular rhyming
verse, in *The Scholemaster* (1570), as 'lewd and rude rymes' that 'make great shew of
blossomes and buddes, [but] in whom is neither roote of learning nor frute of
wisedome at all' (Smith 1904: I, 31). Most worrying may have been George Gascoigne's experience. Gascoigne's collection of verse, *A Hundreth Sundrie Flowres*
(1573), seems to have provoked criticism and even censorship. When he reissued the
poems in a reformed edition as *The Posies* in 1575, he prefaced it with an apologetic
epistle, 'To the reverende Divines', members of the Court of High Commission who
had the power of censorship and who had, apparently 'thought requysite that all
ydle Bookes or wanton Pamphlettes shoulde bee forbidden' (Gascoigne 2000: 360).
Despite Gascoigne's apology, copies of *The Posies* were recalled in 1576 (Prouty 1942:
79; Gascoigne 2000: liii). E. K. refers to Gascoigne in a gloss on the name Philomele,
the nightingale/poet whose tongue was cut out in a bid to silence her (*November*,
141). I shall suggest below that Gascoigne and the image of Philomele figure
significantly in Spenser's imagination throughout his career.

There were a number of defences of poetry written in the early 1580s, following
Gosson's attack. Thomas Lodge's answer to Gosson was refused a licence and was
printed privately in 1579 (Rae 1967: 21). Most of the defences cite classical or biblical
champions of verse, and theorize about what verse should be and do, but they agree
in finding contemporaneous verse sadly wanting. Sidney's *Apologie for Poetry*, probably written in the period 1581–3, praises the 'delightful teaching' of 'right poets', but
scorns most current practitioners as 'base men with servile wits...who think it
enough if they can be rewarded of the printer' (Sidney 1965: 102–3, 132). Even the
poet of the *Calender* comes in for faint praise (Sidney 1965: 133). William Webbe, in
A Discourse of English Poetrie (1586), quotes E. K. extensively to attack the current
shortcomings of English verse, and regrets that even the best of them, among whom
he counts the poet of the *Calender*, do not put more effort into reformed classical
versification. This view was apparently supported by letters between Spenser and
Gabriel Harvey published in 1580 as *Three Proper and wittie familiar Letters*, and
Two other very commendable Letters, that discuss and experiment with classical
versification.

The *Calender*, with its acclaim for the 'new Poete', enters a hotly fought debate
about the status and legitimacy of poetry. E. K.'s 'Epistle' is a manifesto for an
ambitious vernacular verse that positions itself in a classical and international
tradition of ambitious poetic careers, those of Virgil, Petrarch, and 'diuers other
excellent both Italian and French Poetes' (149–53). Nevertheless, while the 'Epistle'
condemns the 'base regard and bastard iudgement' (104–5) evident in much contemporaneous verse, it is concerned, in some detail, to correct and develop the native
tradition rather than to reject it altogether. E. K. praises the 'good and naturall
English words, as haue ben long time out of vse and almost cleare disherited'
('Epistle', 80–1), and condemns those who attempt to patch up its 'holes with peces

and rags of other languages, borrowing here of the french, there of the Italian, euery where of the Latine, ... So now they haue made our English tongue, a gallimaufray or hodgepodge of al other speches' ('Epistle', 85–91). What is needed is poetry that assimilates prestigious classical and Continental models into a native English tradition, rather than one that scorns the native or attempts to disguise it with a display of foreign affectation (Hadfield 1994: 175).

In its concern to improve English verse, the 'Epistle' seems closer in spirit to the censored Gascoigne, rather than those defenders of poetry who scorned the native sixteenth-century tradition. Glossing *November*, E. K. rather patronizingly described Gascoigne as 'a wittie gentleman, and the very chefe or our late rymers, who and if some partes of learning wanted not ... no doubt would haue attayned to the excellencye of those famous Poets' (*November*, 141). Nevertheless E. K.'s 'Epistle' echoes Gascoigne's comments on English verse in his epistle 'To the reuerend diuines':

I have alwayes bene of opinion, that it is not unpossible eyther in Poemes or in Prose too write both compendiously, and perfectly in our Englishe tongue. And therefore although I chalenge not unto my selfe the name of an English Poet, yet may the Reader finde oute in my wrytings, that I have more faulted in keeping the olde English wordes (*quamvis iam obsoleta*) than in borowing of other languages. (Gascoigne 2000: 360–1)

Spenser and Gascoigne's commitment to a native English vocabulary contrasts strikingly with Sidney's dismissal of Spenser's 'old rustic language' in the *Apologie* (Sidney 1965: 133). Sidney, like George Puttenham in *The Arte of English Poesie* (1589), prefers to restrict English to 'the dialect in use at the royal court' (King 1990: 29). It is not only his concern with language that links Spenser's poetics to Gascoigne's. Despite his apparent enthusiasm for classical versification in the letters exchanged with Harvey, Spenser seems in the *Calender* to share Gascoigne's concern with developing an English prosody based on 'natural *Emphasis* or sound' (Gascoigne 2000: 456).

While Spenser in the *Calender* seems in some respects more attuned to Gascoigne's poetics than Sidney's or Webbe's, Gascoigne, in E. K.'s words, falls short of that 'excellencye of those famous Poets' to which the new poet aspires. True poetry, according to E. K. is more than a matter of vocabulary:

Now for the knitting of sentences, whych they call the ioynts and members therof, and for al the compasse of the speach, it is round without roughnesse, and learned wythout hardnes, such indeede as may be perceiued of the leaste, vnderstoode of the moste, but iudged onely of the learned. For what in most English wryters vseth to be loose, and as it were vngyrt, in this Authour is well grounded, finely framed, and strongly trussed vp together. In regard wherof, I scorne and spue out the rakehellye route of our ragged rymers (for so themselues vse to hunt the letter) which without learning boste, without iudgement iangle, without reason rage and fome. ('Epistle', 112–23)

E. K. attacks merely superficial effects, whether the imported 'hodgepodge' of foreign words, or meaningless alliteration. It is a lack of structure, coherence, and discrimination that E. K. finds wanting in the writing of mid-century poets. Sidney seems to have E. K.'s attack in mind when, excepting Chaucer, the *Calender*, and a few other examples, he finds English verse lacking in 'poetical sinews': 'a confused mass of words, with a tingling sound of rhyme, barely accompanied with reason' (Sidney 1965: 133).

The *Calender* is a self-conscious manifesto for its author and his verse, and its sense of competitiveness with the English vernacular past and its need to differentiate the new poet from less ambitious versifiers (the 'rakehelly . . . rymers') is everywhere evident. Nevertheless the *Calender* is closely concerned with both the verse and the poetic ambitions of its immediate predecessors. The achievements of Spenser's poetry are well-nigh inconceivable without the explosion of mid-century printings of Tudor verse that imitated and were influenced by *Tottel's Miscellany* which went through seven editions before 1579. The *Miscellany* brought to a print reading public the highly experimental and innovative verse of Sir Thomas Wyatt and the Earl of Surrey, who introduced into English sophisticated new verse forms, such as the sonnet and blank verse, as well as imitating and translating classical and Continental genres and models. Like other single-author collections of verse that follow in Tottel's footsteps, such as Googe's *Eclogues, Songs and Sonets* (1563) and Gascoigne's *A Hundreth Sundrie Flowres* (1573), the *Calender* presents a varied display of the poet's work designed to show off the skills and abilities of the new poet across a range of genres and metrical forms.

The eclogue is a genre in which poetic excellence and the competition to out-perform rivals are recurring and traditional themes, and it is appropriate that Spenser uses it to issue implicit challenges to the poets he feels he overgoes. In the *Julye* eclogue, partly based on Mantuan's eighth eclogue, Spenser's use of fourteeners invites comparison with George Turbervile's use of the same popular mid-century verse form to translate Mantuan in 1567. Ascham had scorned vernacular poets who 'can easely recken vp fourten sillabes, and easilie stumble on euery Ryme' (Smith 1904: I, 31). Spenser elegantly shows how caesurae, enjambement, and syllables of different lengths can transform the monotony too often characteristic of the form:

> There is the caue, where *Phebe* layed,
>   the shepheard long to dreame.
> Whilome there vsed shepheards all
>   to feede theyr flocks at will,
> Till by his foly one did fall,
>   that all the rest did spill. (63–8)

The hunting of the letter by E. K.'s 'ragged rymers' is replaced by a subtle use of internal and end rhymes in 66–8, creating the 'will | Till . . . fall | . . . all . . . spill' narrative sequence (64–8). Spenser's reference, not in the original, to virginal Pheobe's lapse in her erotic dream of the shepherd Endymion, adumbrating the fall, introduces an allusion with potential political resonance in the context of the Anjou marriage proposals in 1579. Spenser's 'well grounded, finely framed, and strongly trussed vp' lines are designed to be 'iudged only of the learned' ('Epistle', 118–19, 116).

The *Julye* eclogue's fourteeners also implicitly challenge comparison with those of Barnabe Googe, a writer of eclogues more significant for the *Calender* than Turbervile (King 1990: 15). Googe's eclogues in *Eclogues, Songs and Sonets* (1563) draw, like Spenser's, on a number of classical and Continental sources, including Virgil and Mantuan. Googe was an important participant in a mid-century movement by Protestant poets to counter the association of verse with amorous and courting topics. Another participant was John Hall, who wrote moralizing versions of courtly verse, particularly Wyatt's, in *The Court of Virtue* (1565) (King 1982: 225–6). *Eclogues, Songs and Sonets* ends with a long dream allegory, 'Cupido Conquered', in which the forces of Cupid are defeated by Diana. A major theme of his eclogues is illicit love and its dire consequences, against which old Amintas warns in Eclogue 1: 'Of griefs, the greatest grief, no doubt, | is to be Venus' thrall' (Googe 1989: 48). In Eclogue 4, the ghost of a lover warns other young shepherds:

> 'With fond affection I did flame
>   which now I most repent,
> 'But all too late, alas, I wail,
>   sith hope of grace is spent.
> 'The fickle fading form and face
>   that once so much I sought,
> 'Hath made me lose the skies above,
>   and me to hell hath brought.   (ll.73–80)

Old Thenot in Spenser's *Februarie* eclogue echoes both Amintas's views and his aphoristic plain style:

> For Youngth is a bubble blown vp with breath,
> Whose witt is weakenesse, whose wage is death,
> Whose way is wildernesse, whose ynne Penaunce.   (*Februarie*, 87–9)

Spenser is, like Googe, interested in moralizing the theme of love, setting young men's appetites in the context of Christian teaching on virtue, but his juxtaposition of viewpoints in the *Calender* complicates the moral teaching, signalling a new, more sophisticated Protestant poetics which eschews, in the words of the 'Letter to Ralegh' prefixed to the 1590 *Faerie Queene*, precepts 'deliuered plainly . . . or sermoned at large'.[2]

The *Calender*'s debt to another tradition of Protestant poetics is signalled by the name Colin Clout with its allusion to John Skelton's anti-ecclesiastical satirical persona in his poem *Collyn Clout* written in 1523, but reprinted in an edition of Skelton's *Workes* in 1568. Skelton's Collyn is a spokesman for the people, who voices an attack on the abuses within the hierarchy of what, in his pre-Reformation day, was the Roman Catholic Church. Skelton's satire, and his rough plain style, had been eagerly appropriated after the Reformation for Protestant attacks on Roman Catholicism (King 1982: 255). That Spenser was a close reader of Skelton's poem is suggested by the way in which, in the *September* eclogue, Diggon adopts the same self-protective technique of reporting and denying other men's criticisms: 'They sayne . . . | Other sayne, but how truely I note | . . . Some sticke not to say '(108–13) (Kinsman

1990: 661). The new poet of the *Calender* acknowledges the importance to him of the tradition of Reformist polemical literature with which Skelton's Collyn Clout became associated. In the 'Epilogue' Spenser names another example of the genre, *The Plowman's Tale*, thought to have been written by Chaucer (Tityrus), as one of the models to which he would aspire were he not inhibited by modesty: '*Dare not to match thy pype with Tityrus hys style,* | *Nor with the Pilgrim that the Ploughman playde a whyle.*'

The *Calender*, then, alludes, in its style and its topics, to native traditions of reformist sixteenth-century poetics both as part of its engagement with an ongoing debate about Protestantism's compatibility with the feigning arts of poetry, and in its effort to forge a new sophisticated English poetics. In so doing, he assimilates the classical and Continental model of the eclogue to a plain-speaking vernacular verse of moral reflection and satire. The result is a poetry that, while appearing to be humble, in fact makes ambitious claims, and intervenes boldly on highly controversial religious, social, and, more covertly, political matters. Interestingly, Colin Clout is not used for religious criticism in the *Calender*. Instead, he shadows the person of the author himself ('Epistle', 133–4), the composer of the magnificent tour de force poems of *Aprill, June,* and *November,* but also the poet of love, silenced by the pains of love.

The place of love in the *Calender* is highly problematic. E. K. identifies some of the eclogues as 'recreatiue, such as al those be, which conceiue matter of loue' (Spenser 1999: 32). Amorous poetry was, however, the focus of Protestant attacks on verse. Gascoigne identifies 'my doings at the common infection of love' as the reason for the reverend divines' disapproval of his verse (Gascoigne 2000: 366). Colin's preoccupation with love leaves him hanging up his pipe on a tree in the *December* eclogue, just when the ambitious new poet should be moving on to greater themes; love seems to impede the Virgilian career of national celebration and exhortation to virtue. Cuddie's judgement in the *October* eclogue apparently confirms such prejudices as those of the 'reuerende Divines': Colin, 'were he not with loue so ill bedight, | Would mount as high, and sing as soote as Swanne' (89–90).

On the other hand, the firm identification of the new poet with the poet of love, Colin Clout, suggests that Spenser is not so readily abandoning love as a fit subject for the best verse. Cuddie's proposed subjects of imperial and heroic celebration fail in the *October* eclogue, and it is love that, according to Piers, teaches Colin to

> climbe so hie,
> And lyftes him vp out of the loathsome myre:
> Such immortall mirrhor, as he doth admire,
> Would rayse ones mynd aboue the starry skie.   (91–4)

It is not, perhaps, love that marginalizes Colin in the *Calender*, but his inability to find in it a source of poetic inspiration. Colin's impasse may be understood as a dilemma in the face of doubts about both private amorous verse, 'dapper ditties... | To feede youthes fancie' (*October*, 13–14), and celebratory public verse. McLane suggested that the object of Colin's love, Rosalind, may be a figure for Elizabeth I

(1961: 27–46). If so, Colin's lovesickness may be understood both as part of the *Calender's* troubled negotiation of a Reformist suspicion of love poetry and as part of the new poet's ambivalence about Elizabeth as an inspiring subject for an ambitious Virgilian poetics.

COLIN CLOUT AND AN INSPIRED POETRY OF LOVE

Elizabeth is explicitly celebrated by Colin in the *Aprill* eclogue, and implicitly praised and mourned in the *November* eclogue that elegizes Dido. Both poems seem to allude to the proposed Anjou marriage, opposed by Spenser's patron, Leicester, and the dedicatee of the *Calender*, Sidney (Hadfield 1994: 177–86; McLane 1961). In the *November* eclogue, the name Dido recalls 'the Virgilian queen who destroyed herself through infatuation with a foreign prince' (McCabe 1995: 33) and the poem can be read as an elegy for the queen who will be lost if she marries a foreign Catholic prince. In the *Aprill* eclogue, 'fayre *Elisa*, Queene of shepheardes all' (*Aprill*, 34) is praised insistently for her virginity. The *Aprill* eclogue, with its politically pointed praise of Elizabeth, may once again invoke the spectre of Gascoigne, as an object of competition, but also as a figure of warning.

Spenser's rapturous praise of Elisa in *Aprill* sets her in a mythological landscape in which she appears as both a nymph and a royal Queen:

> See, where she sits vpon the grassie greene,
>   (O seemely sight)
> Ycald in Scarlot like a mayden Queene,
>   And Ermines white.
> Vpon her head a Cremosin coronet,
> With Damaske roses and Daffadillies set . . .   (*Aprill*, 55–60)

This figuring of the virginal Elisa, attended as she is by 'Ladyes of the lake' (*Aprill*, 120), may well have recalled *The Princely Pleasures at Kenelworth Castle* published in 1576, in which Gascoigne described Elizabeth's entertainment by Leicester in an Arthurian and mythological landscape. Elizabeth was attended by a 'lady of the lake', and celebrated iconically by Gascoigne as Diana's nymph, Zabeta who appears as both an idealized virgin and as a royal queen. Diana urges Elizabeth to remain her virgin follower even though she is now a queen:

> And be content for all your statelie grace,
> Stil to remaine a maiden alwaies meeke.
> *Zabeta* mine (now Queene of high renowne)
> You know how wel I loved you alwaies.   (Gascoigne 1910: II, 117)

In Gascoigne's interlude, Diana's arguments for virginity are trumped by Iris, the emissary of Juno, who claims that Zabeta is destined for marriage; the entertainment was, after all, written to promote Leicester's withering hopes, in 1575, of marrying Elizabeth himself. Nevertheless, Gascoigne's mythological and pastoral image of the virgin queen Zabeta may have provided a model for Spenser's own image of Elizabeth, devised to address the rather different royal marriage politics of the Leicester faction in 1579. If so, Spenser's interlacing of the pastoral and the royal in an intricate and varied verse form can be seen as effortlessly out-competing Gascoigne's rather plodding verse. It is possible that the Kenilworth celebrations may also have acted as a warning to Spenser of the potential dangers of poetic advice to the Queen on the matter of marriage, however obliquely expressed (Norbrook 1984: 84–9). Elizabeth almost certainly censored Gascoigne's part of the entertainment, including the scenes with Zabeta, which were not performed at Kenilworth. Frye goes so far as to speculate that his role in the celebrations explains 'why Gascoigne remained downwardly mobile' (1993: 63), although there is no evidence to suggest that Gascoigne suffered personally from the Queen's displeasure (Austen 2008: 118, 126, 131–2).

The *November* eclogue likens Colin's song to that of the nightingale Philomele (25 and 141). E. K.'s gloss (141) refers us to Gascoigne's poems, *The complaynt of Phylomene* and *The Steele Glas*, printed in 1576. In both poems Gascoigne identifies himself with Philomene, who in *The Steele Glas* is allegorized as Satyra, a figure of plain speaking. Satyra describes how first her sister, 'Poesys', has been seduced by courtly 'vayne Delight' and carried off to court, and then how 'Vayne Delight' turns his attention to Satyra, rapes her, and cuts out her tongue (Gascoigne 1910: II, 143–6). Gascoigne/Philomene/Satyra finds himself/herself marginalized and alienated:

> And thus I sing, in corner closely cowcht
> Like Philomene, *since that the stately cowrts,*
> *Are now no place, for such poore byrds as I.*   (II, 146)

Gascoigne's allegory has powerful resonance in Spenser's verse which is ambivalent from the *Calender* onwards about the role of the poet: that of a Virgilian celebrator of the nation and its queen, deserving of royal patronage, or an unpalatable truth-speaker, forced into an oppositional role. In the *October* eclogue, Piers urges the poet Cuddie to high poetic endeavours in terms that anticipate the programme of *The Faerie Queene*:

> may thy Muse display her fluttryng wing,
> And stretch her selfe at large from East to West:
> Whither thou list in fayre *Elisa* rest,
> Or if thee please in bigger notes to sing,
> Aduaunce the worthy whome shee loueth best.   (43–7)

Cuddie replies that lack of support makes such poetry impossible:

> But ah *Mecœnas* is yclad in claye,
> And great *Augustus* long ygoe is dead:
> And all the worthies liggen wrapt in leade,
> That matter made for Poets on to play . . .   (61–4)

Cuddie can find neither the powerful patronage he needs, nor the worthy models he requires for inspired verse.

Instead of finding support for inspired verse, Cuddie complains that if 'any buddes of Poesie, | Yet of the old stocke gan to shoote agayne' then it 'mens follies mote be forst to fayne, | And rolle with rest in rymes of rybaudrye' (73–6). Cuddie seems here to be attacking the popularity of courtly amorous verse. Only such rhymes, like Gascoigne's seduced 'Poesye', find favour with patrons. What has been described as the 'anti-laureate' verse of Sir Thomas Wyatt, printed in the influential *Tottel's Miscellany*, was much imitated in mid-century miscellanies. Such verse presents itself as a gambit in courtly play, cynical about love, and hiding its very considerable skill and art under gestures of courtly *sprezzatura* (Meyer-Lee 2007: 220–30). Helgerson designates such verse 'amateur', in opposition to a laureate poetics (1983: 25–35).

In the 'Argument' to the *October* eclogue, E. K. offers a very different idea of poetry. It is 'rather no arte, but a diuine gift and heauenly instinct not to bee gotten by laboure and learning, but adorned with both: and poured into the witte by a certaine ἐνθοσιασμός. and celestiall inspiration, as the Author hereof elswhere at large discourseth, in his booke called the English Poete' (Spenser 1999: 128). E. K.'s words, while they allude to Plato's account of inspired poetic frenzy in the Phaedrus, also place Spenser in an English 'laureate' tradition that is very different from that of such 'courtly makers' as Wyatt (Puttenham 1936: 60). This tradition had been articulated, in terms suggestive for Spenser, by Skelton (Hadfield 1994: 171). In *The Garlande of Laurel*, Skelton is ambivalent about the poet's role and his means of winning the laurel. He might gain fame by praising powerful patrons, but in so doing he becomes vulnerable to the accusation of writing mere flattery. On the other hand to speak the truth is to risk banishment, like Ovid (XXI, 78–84).[3] In his final poem, *A Replycacion*, Skelton asserts an inspired authority, that of the divinely inspired vates, independent of state patronage:

> there is a spyrituall,
> And a mysteriall,
> And a mysticall
> Effecte energiall,
> As Grekes do it call,
> Of suche an industry
> And suche a pregnancy,
> Of hevenly inspyracion
> In laureate creacyon,
> Of poetes commendacion,
> That of divyne myseracion
> God maketh his habytacion
> In poetes whiche excelles,
> And sojourns with them and dwelles.   (XXIV, 365–78)

Spenser is both 'a natural conclusion' and a new beginning in a tradition of 'laureate poetics' that stretches back through Skelton to the fifteenth century (Meyer-Lee 2007: 220).

Spenser returns to the theme of poetic inspiration, the relation of poetry and love, and the vexed issue of the poetry of patronage, when he returns to the figure of Colin Clout in *Colin Clouts Come Home Againe* (1595). As has often been noted, 'home' in this poem is ambiguous (Hadfield 1994: 188–90; McCabe 1993: 89–94). In the first part of the poem, Colin is excited to be returning from banishment in the 'waste, where I was quite forgot' (183) to the English Court in the company of 'the shepheard of the Ocean' (66), Spenser's patron, Sir Walter Ralegh. The Court, however, proves an alien place, and Colin willingly returns to 'the shepheardes nation' in the countryside of Ireland. Ireland may lack the 'happie peace and plenteous store' (310) of England, but its remoteness from the Court and courtly culture guarantees its moral superiority.

Central to the contrast between the Irish pastoral and the English Court are different kinds of love poems and different ideas about the role of poetry in relation to love. Before leaving for the English Court, Colin listens to the 'lamentable lay' of the Shepherd of the Ocean, mourning his estrangement from his Mistress the Queen:

> Of great vnkindnesse, and of vsage hard,
> Of *Cynthia* the Ladie of the sea,
> Which from her presence faultlesse him debard.
> And euer and anon with singulfs rife,
> He cryed out, to make his vndersong
> Ah my loues queene, and goddesse of my life,
> Who shall me pittie, when thou doest me wrong?   (164–71)

Colin listens sympathetically, but his own song about Bregog's illicit love and its terrible punishment acts as a sceptical commentary on the outcome of Ralegh's amorous courting of Elizabeth, especially from the perspective of 1595 after Ralegh's disgrace in 1592. As in the Belphoebe/Timias narrative in Books III and IV of *The Faerie Queene*, another figuring of Ralegh's political courting of Elizabeth, the false amorousness that the Queen encouraged among her favourites is presented as unrewarding and unequal, productive of sterility and endless complaint (Pugh 2005: 152–3).

It is not just Elizabeth's personal cult of love that is criticized, but a general vogue for superficial amorousness:

> For all the walls and windows there are writ,
> All full of loue, and loue, and loue my deare,
> And all their talke and studie is of it.
> Ne any there doth braue or valiant seeme,
> Vnlesse that some gay Mistresse badge he beares:
> Ne any one himselfe doth ought esteeme,
> Vnlesse he swim in loue vp to the eares.   (776–82)

The 'ydle name' of love serves 'But as a complement for courting vaine' (789–90). It is this false and insincere cult of Petrarchism that drives Colin from the English Court, despite his hopeful depiction of Elizabeth, no doubt with his authors' pension of 1591 in mind, as a patron of learning: 'For *Cynthia* doth in sciences abound, | And giues to their professors stipends large' (745–6).

In verse quite different from the 'lamentable lays' of the Shepherd of the Ocean and the false Petrarchism of the versifying courtiers, Colin, inspired by the 'celestiall rage | Of loue' (823–4), displays his vatic powers:

> loue is Lord of all the world by right,
> And rules the creatures by his powrfull saw:
> All being made the vassalls of his might,
> Through secret sence which therto doth them draw.
> Thus ought all louers of their lord to deeme:
> And with chaste heart to honor him alway:
> But who so else doth otherwise esteeme,
> Are outlawes, and his lore do disobay.
> For their desire is base, and doth not merit,
> The name of loue, but of disloyall lust . . .   (883–92)

Love, rightly understood, and rightly celebrated in verse, becomes the theme that differentiates the true vatic poet from the courtly makers, whether the virtuous but doleful Ralegh or the degenerate Petrarchists. Colin's 'celestiall rage' is close kin to the 'celestiall inspiration' that E. K. attributed to the perfect poet in the 'Argument' to the *October* eclogue. Piers's tentative identification of love as the source of inspiration (*October*, 91–4) was dismissed by Cuddie, for whom love is a tyrant. In the poems of the 1590s, however, Spenser explores a new and very distinctive poetics of love that offers the possibility of a poetry of national significance which remains independent of monarchical patronage, rescuing the poetry of love from its entrapment by the 'political Petrarchism' of the Court (Pugh 2005: 172), and answering the Reformist critics who accused love poetry of being 'a provoker of vyces' (Gascoigne 2000: 360).

A Reformed Poetry of Love

Surveying the current state of verse in the early 1590s in *The Teares of the Muses*, Spenser returns to many of the same themes as the *Calender*, but in more harshly critical terms. Terpsichore complains that poets lack learning and ambition, and worse, use their rhymes to corrupt their hearers:

> The noble hearts to pleasures they allure,
> And tell their Prince that learning is but vaine,
> Faire Ladies loues they spot with thoughts impure,
> And gentle mindes with lewd delights distaine:
> Clerks they to loathly idlenes entice,
> And fill their bookes with discipline of vice.   (331–6)

Erato takes up Terpsichore's complaint, but blames patrons of verse as well as versifiers:

> For neither you nor we shall anie more
> Finde entertainment, or in Court or Schoole:
> For that which was accounted heretofore
> The learneds meed, is now lent to the foole;
> He sings of loue, and maketh louing layes,
> And they him heare, and they him highly prayse.   (409–14)

As in the *Calender* and in *Colin Clout*, Spenser remains ambivalent about the role of Elizabeth who is both implicated in the courtly Petrarchism he despises, but who remains, nevertheless, a potential patron of more ambitious verse, supporting, Polyhymnia claims, 'with rich bountie and deare cherishment, |...the praise of noble Poësie' (573–4).

The conflict between praise of an idealized Elizabeth as patron of worthy deeds, and attacks on a dangerous courtly culture of erotic verse over which she presides, recurs throughout Spenser's Virgilian undertaking, the 1590 *Faerie Queene*. Particularly in Book III, the Book of Chastity, Ovidian verse and elaborate cults of love are associated with courts and dangerous games of seduction. Malecasta rules a court that passes its idle hours in elaborate ritualized games of love; the ethos of this court is figured by the Ovidian tapestries of the seduction of Adonis that decorate its walls (III.i.34–8). In canto 9, the degenerate Paridell seduces Hellenore with a seductive language of eye glances and spilled wine derived from Ovid's *Art of Love*. The contrast between Paridell's seductive use of verse and Britomart's enthusiasm for heroic narrative is made clear in their very different responses to the Troy story. Most dangerous are the ornate halls of the House of Busyrane dominated by versions of Arachne's tapestries, with their subversion of all order (III.ix.28–46). They surround an altar on which is placed an idolatrous statue of a cruel and destructive Cupid (III.xi.42–9). In an inner room of this sumptuous House, a courtly masque presents love as a sinister and destructive courtly game that traps the bride, Amoret, before her marriage to Scudamore can be consummated (III.xii.3–22).

The Teares of the Muses contrasts such a degenerate poetics of love, bewailed by Terpsichore and Erato, with the divine verse of poets inspired by Urania's 'heauenlie light of knowledge' (488) that lifts the poet to 'looke into the Christall firmament' and view 'Th'eternall Makers maiestie' (506, 512). Nevertheless, Erato describes another possibility, an inspired poetry of love. Rightly understood, she says, love is the 'schoolmaster of my skill' (385), a 'celestiall fire' (391) derived from 'th'Almighties bosome, where he nests; | From thence infused into mortall brests' (389–90). Erato, like Colin in *Colin Clout*, enunciates a poetics of love that seeks to wrest the theme from a lewd and fashionable amorous verse associated with the Court, in order to create a new and ambitious love poetry. Erato's description of the unmistakably Christian origins of the 'celestiall fire' of love develops, but goes far beyond, the effort to create a Protestant Christian poetics already evident in the 1560s in the poetry of Barnabe Googe. This ambitious, reforming agenda shapes *Amoretti and Epithalamion* (1595) and *Fowre Hymnes* (1596).

Where in the *Calender*, the passing of time left the complaining Colin in *December* in the same or a worse state as we found him in *Januarye*, in *Amoretti and*

Epithalamion the complaints of the Petrarchan lover are gradually disciplined and educated through the Christian year to bring about a new understanding of love and its power (King 1990: 163; Pugh 2005: 159–69). Inspired by love, and educated by his chaste mistress, the lover moves from an idolatrous love of his lady in the first Lent sonnet (xxii) to an understanding of love as part of a Christian paradigm in the second Easter sonnet: 'So let vs loue, deare loue, lyke as we ought, | loue is the lesson which the Lord vs taught' (lxviii). Instead of ending, as Sidney's *Astrophil and Stella* sequence does, in the typical Petrarchan impasse of unrequited desire, Spenser's lover, a version of the poet himself, learns to reconcile his desire with virtue, leading to the sequence's culmination in *Epithalamion* which celebrates Spenser's marriage to the bride he has wooed throughout the sonnet sequence. The culmination of the sequence in the longer *Epithalamion* may be seen as a deliberate reworking of Daniel's sonnet sequence *Delia*, which was followed by the longer *Complaint of Rosamond* when printed in 1592, creating, Wall suggests, a pattern for subsequent editions of sonnet sequences (1994: 253). Colin rebuked Daniel in *Colin Clout* for wasting his time 'In loues soft laies and looser thoughts delight' (420–3). *Amoretti and Epithalamion* shows how the truly ambitious poet writes love poetry that combines the profane and the Christian.

In *Amoretti* (xxxiii and lxxx), Spenser tells his monarch that her praises must wait while he celebrates his private courtship and marriage. But *Amoretti and Epithalamion* is more than a volume with private significance. In it Spenser transforms his courtship and marriage into an exemplary model of Christian civility. Taking place in Ireland, to Spenser that most unruly and disordered place, his poetry of Protestant Christian courtship and marriage provides a pattern of the civilizing effects of an ordered and godly love (Heale 2003: 92–124). It is from the courtly margins that Spenser offers a new poetry of national significance, one that bypasses the Court and its virgin queen to address a print readership of citizens, through a new Christian poetry of love that is both celestial and erotic (Pugh 2005: 153, 172–7).

Spenser's interest in a poetics that reconciles erotic and Christian love in a vatic poetry is further developed in *Fowre Hymnes* printed in 1596. The hymn was considered an even more elevated form than the epic (Cheney 1993: 201). Spenser refers to the first two hymns, in honour of love and beauty, in the familiar apologetic formula used by Gascoigne; they are 'lewd layes' written 'in th'heat of youth' (*HHL*, 8 and 10). However, the relationship between profane and divine love in all four hymns is not resolvable into simple models of opposition or renunciation; it is, in McCabe's words, 'not so much an ascent from Eros to Agape as a discovery that, properly considered, Eros is Agape' (Spenser 1999: 706). In *Fowre Hymnes*, profane love, if truly understood, always has divine origins and is able to lift the lover 'vpon thy golden wings, | From this base world vnto thy heauens hight' (*HHL*, 1–2).

While *Fowre Hymnes* can be seen as another attempt by Spenser to forge a new ambitious Protestant poetics (Cheney 1993), Colin Clout's final appearance in Book VI of *The Faerie Queene*, printed in the same year, suggests the persistence of doubts and conflicts about the Virgilian role of the poet as public teacher and celebrator of his monarch. Colin is again found far from the court, in the pastoral countryside. This is where Gloriana's knight, Calidore, charged with pursuing the Blatant Beast, has retired to find respite from the 'shadowes vaine | Of courtly fauour' (VI.x.2). Who would blame him, asks the narrator:

> For who had tasted once (as oft did he)
> The happy peace which there [in the country] doth ouerflow,
> And prou'd the perfect pleasures, which doe grow
> Amongst poore hyndes, in hils, in woods, in dales,
> Would neuer more delight in painted show
> Of such false blisse, as there [at court] is set for stales
> T'entrap vnwary fooles in their eternall bales.   (VI.x.3)

In this pastoral retreat, Calidore stumbles on Colin and the ravishing vision that his piping has produced: a circle of maidens dance around the three Graces who in turn enclose 'a countrey lasse' (25), Colin's own love. The reader of the *Calender* realizes that the vision reproduces a similar dance in the *April* eclogue, but this time there is no Elisa (Hadfield 1994: 191–2). Unlike the *Aprill* eclogue, this vision is for Colin's personal pleasure alone. Calidore's sudden appearance interrupts the dance and its figures disappear. The vision, it seems, cannot be summoned at will, nor can it be shared with even so courteous an agent of the court as Calidore.

Colin's last appearance echoes his first; he breaks his pipes, a gesture of frustration and pessimism. In the *Calender*, Colin's poetry of love seemed marginalized and in conflict with the idea of vatic ambition. In *Colin Clout*, Spenser used Colin to assert a new poetics of vatic inspiration, through a Christian understanding of love that bypassed the court, and Elizabeth as an object of praise. Colin's last appearance, however, seems to present the poet's dilemma as being as acute as ever. Colin's alternate vision of love seems to have no role in the world of *The Faerie Queene*, and is vulnerable to misinterpretation (Hadfield 1994: 192–3). At the end of Book VI, the Blatant Beast attacks, in particular, 'the gentle Poets rime' (xii.40):

> Ne may this homely verse, of many meanest,
> Hope to escape his venemous despite,
> More then my former writs, all were they clearest
> From blamefull blot, and free from all that wite,
> With which some wicked tongues did it backbite ...   (xii.41)

At the end of his career, in warning how the Blatant Beast 'raungeth through the world againe' (xii.40), Spenser seems once more to remember Gascoigne who warned that 'the line, of that false caytife king | (Which ravished fayre Phylomene ...) /And then cut out her trustie tong for hate.../ Lives yet':

> *Whose greedy lust, unbridled from their brest,*
> *Hath raunged long about the world so wyde,*
> *To finde a pray for their wide open mouthes*   (Gascoigne 1910: II, 144)

Seen from the perspective of Book VI, the poet's career, so ambitiously but hesitantly envisaged in the *Calender* ('Epistle', 149) as following the 'greater flyght' of Virgil, turns out instead to have much in common with that of Gascoigne, subject to the powerful displeasure of those with little understanding of, or sympathy for, verse, and only intermittently successful in catching the eye of the Queen whose laureate poet he ought rightly to be. Colin's broken pipes, however, should be held in balance with Edmund Spenser's creation, through his new poetics of Christian love and instruction, of an 'endlesse moniment' of verse, despite 'hasty accidents' and an uncetain Cynthia.

NOTES

1. All quotations from Spenser's *Shorter Poems* are from Spenser (1999). E. K.'s 'Epistle' to *SC* is cited by line numbers from this edition.
2. Quotations from *The Faerie Queene* are from Spenser (2001).
3. All quotations are from Skelton (1983).

BIBLIOGRAPHY

Austen, G. (2008). *George Gascoigne.* Woodbridge, Suffolk: D. S. Brewer.

Cheney, P. (1993). *Spenser's Famous Flight: A Renaissance Idea of a Literary Career.* Toronto: Toronto University Press.

Frye, S. (1993). *Elizabeth I. The Competition for Representation.* Oxford: Oxford University Press.

Gascoigne, George (1910). *The Complete Works of George Gascoigne*, ed. J. W. Cunliffe, 2 vols. Cambridge: Cambridge University Press.

—— (2000). *George Gascoigne. A Hundreth Sundrie Flowres*, ed. G. W. Pigman II. Oxford: Clarendon Press.

Googe, Barnabe (1989). *Barnabe Googe, Eclogues, Epitaphs and Sonnets*, ed. J. M. Kennedy. Toronto: University of Toronto Press.

Hadfield, A. (1994). *Literature, Politics and National Identity. Reformation to Renaissance.* Cambridge: Cambridge University Press.

Heale, E. (2003). *Authorship and Autobiography in Renaissance Verse: Chronicles of the Self.* Basingstoke, Hants: Palgrave Macmillan.

Helgerson, R. (1983). *Self-Crowned Laureates: Spenser, Jonson, Milton and the Literary System.* Berkeley: University of California Press.

Herman, P. C. (1996). *Squitter-Wits and Muse-Haters: Sidney, Spenser, Milton and Renaissance Anti-Poetic Sentiment.* Detroit, MI: Wayne State University Press.

King, J. N. (1982). *English Reformation Literature: The Tudor Origins of the Protestant Tradition.* Princeton, NJ: Princeton University Press.

—— (1990). *Spenser's Poetry and the Reformation Tradition.* Princeton, NJ: Princeton University Press.

Kinsman, R. S. (1990) 'Skelton, John', in *SE*.

Luborsky, R. S. (1990). '*The Shepheardes Calender*, Printing and Illustration of', in *SE*.

McCabe, R. A. (1993). 'Edmund Spenser: Poet of Exile', British Academy Chatterton Lecture on Poetry, in '1991 Lectures and Memoirs'. *Proceedings of the British Academy* 80: 73–103.

—— (1995). '"Little booke: thy selfe present": The Politics of Presentation in *The Shepheardes Calender*', in Howard Erskine-Hill and Richard A. McCabe (eds), *Presenting Poetry. Competition, Publication, Reception. Essays in Honour of Ian Jack*. Cambridge: Cambridge University Press: 15–40.

—— (2002). *Spenser's Monstrous Regiment. Elizabethan Ireland and the Poetics of Difference.* Oxford: Oxford University Press.

McLane, P. E. (1961). *Spenser's Shepheardes Calender. A Study in Elizabethan Allegory.* Notre Dame, IN: University of Notre Dame Press.

Meyer-Lee, R. J. (2007). *Poets and Power from Chaucer to Wyatt.* Cambridge: Cambridge University Press.

Norbrook, D. (1984). *Poetry and Politics in the English Renaissance.* London: Routledge and Kegan Paul.

Prouty, C. T. (1942). *George Gascoigne. Elizabethan Courtier, Soldier and Poet.* New York: Columbia University Press.

Pugh, S. (2005). *Spenser and Ovid.* Aldershot: Ashgate.

Puttenham, George (1936). *The Arte of English Poesie by George Puttenham*, ed. G. D. Willcock and A. Walker. Cambridge: Cambridge University Press.

Rae, W. D. (1967). *Thomas Lodge.* New York: Twayne.

Sidney, Sir Philip (1965). *Sir Philip Sidney: An Apology for Poetry*, ed. G. Shepherd. London: Nelson.

Skelton, John (1983). *John Skelton: The Complete English Poems*, ed. J. Scattergood. New Haven, CT: Yale University Press.

Smith, G. G. (ed.) (1904). *Elizabethan Critical Essays*, 2 vols. Oxford: Clarendon Press.

Wall, W. (1994). *The Imprint of Gender. Authorship and Publication in the English Renaissance.* Ithaca, NY: Cornell University Press.

CHAPTER 33

SPENSER AND ITALIAN LITERATURE

JASON LAWRENCE

SPENSER'S KNOWLEDGE OF ITALIAN

Spenser's profound relationship with Italian literature is manifest from his earliest printed poetry, even if initially his engagement with it seems to have been mediated through French verse. The *Epigrams* printed in Van der Noot's collection in 1569 are a close rendition of Clement Marot's *Le Chant des visions de Petrarque* (1533), the French poet's translation of Petrarch's *canzone* 'Standomi un giorno solo a la fenestra'. Spenser's original English version follows Marot rather than Petrarch directly,[1] suggesting that Spenser was unable to read Italian when he first worked on the translation, presumably as a pupil at the Merchant Taylors' School before he went up to Pembroke Hall in 1569. This raises important questions about when (and how) Spenser learnt the Italian language, and the subsequent depth of his knowledge of Italian literature, as evidenced in much of his later work. The *Epigrams* were revised and expanded for inclusion in the *Complaints* in 1591 with the new title *The Visions of Petrarch; formerly translated*, although there are still no clear traces of the Petrarchan original in the poem. The new title echoes that of Marot's earlier translation, and also seems to recall deliberately the first of many late-sixteenth-century English texts which consider Spenser's work in relation to European vernacular traditions, and Italian literature specifically.

In the spring of 1580 Gabriel Harvey, Spenser's friend and mentor at Cambridge, addresses 'A Gallant Familiar Letter' to the poet, in which he praises his as yet unprinted *Dreames*:

I dare saye you wylle holde your selfe reasonably wel satisfied, if youre *Dreames* be but as well esteemed of in Englande, as *Petrarches Visions* be in Italy. (*Prose*, 471)

Spenser's poem never reached print, thus denying it the native literary reputation that Harvey here imagines for it in terms of the fame of Petrarch's *Trionfi* in Italy, but the very comparison suggests that both the writer and recipient of the letter are familiar with Petrarch's vernacular poetry, and also that this knowledge of Italian literature is being signalled to any potential reader of the letter when it is printed later in the same year. The references to Italian writers in the letter do not, of course, prove a direct familiarity with the Italian language on Spenser's part at this point, but we do know that Harvey himself had started to learn the language in the years immediately preceding his correspondence with Spenser. Marginal annotations in Latin in his copy of John Florio's Italian-English language-learning manual *Florio his First Fruites* (1578) made soon after its publication reveal the scholar's frustrations at the progress of his Italian studies:

Why can Axiophilus (Harvey) not speak it with the same dexterity? In three days he learnt the principles of Roman law; why cannot he therefore pick up Italian, which is half Latin, in two or three days?...Florio, how often have you instantaneously created blossoming Italians? Florio and [William] Thomas in close connection will intensely inspire me with their language. This shall I learn. Where there is love, there does the eye fasten itself.[2]

Harvey's initial endeavours to learn Italian by means of Florio's manual and William Thomas's *Principal Rules of the Italian Grammar* (1550) are later augmented by the efforts of a private tutor. The 1580 letter to Spenser mentions an unnamed 'Italian maister', who has set Harvey and his younger brother John a 'hollydayes exercise' translating passages from Latin and Italian into English verse;[3] the Italian example used is Petrarch's sonnet 187 from the *Canzoniere*, the poem recently quoted in Italian in the gloss to the *October* eclogue of *The Shepheardes Calender*, as Harvey notes. If Spenser himself (possibly with Harvey's assistance?) were responsible for the commentary supposedly written by 'E. K.', then this might again suggest a direct knowledge of Petrarch's Italian poetry by the end of the 1570s. Whether Spenser started to learn the language at university in the first half of the decade or at the same time as Harvey is probably impossible to determine precisely, but Harvey is sent a copy of Jerome Turler's *The Traveiler* (1575) 'ex dono Edmundi Spenserii, Episcopi Roffensis Secretarii' in 1578, demonstrating their developing mutual interest in Italy and Italian history towards the end of the decade.[4] It is certainly tempting to speculate that scholar and poet were striving to learn the language simultaneously towards the end of the decade, possibly employing the same methods and sources, and that the commentary in *The Shepheardes Calender* and frequent comparisons to Italian authors in their published correspondence show the first fruits of a deepening (and direct) engagement with Italian literature.

Spenser had certainly developed a sound reading knowledge of Italian by the early years of the following decade, as evidenced in his enduring friendship with Lodowick Bryskett in Ireland. Bryskett, born in England to Italian parents, reveals in *A Discourse of Civill Life*, not printed until 1606 but recounting events from the early 1580s, both that Spenser had offered to help him learn to read Greek and that he had asked the poet to look over a (private) translation of his from Italian into English made 'for mine exercise in both languages'. In the prefatory dialogue Spenser's character tells the other interlocutors that he has read Bryskett's translation from Cinthio, and suggests that it be read aloud, both because of its relevance to the topic under discussion and as 'the translation (may) happily fare the better by some mending it may receiue in the perusing, as all writings else may do by the often examination of the same' (Bryskett 1606: 27–8). Spenser's perusal of the translation and his subtle suggestion that it might be improved on a further reading seem to confirm both his ability to read Italian fluently and his knowledge of at least this particular Italian work by the early years of his professional life in Ireland.[5] It is certainly possible, as Josephine Bennett conjectured in the 1940s, that Bryskett acted as a conduit to Italian materials, as in the case of Cinthio's dialogue, for Spenser during this period.[6] If Harvey's letter of 1580 suggests at least some prior knowledge of Petrarch's vernacular poetry and, more famously, Ariosto's *Orlando Furioso* (1532) on Spenser's part, the poet's familiarity with the most recent of the three most significant Italian influences on his work must date directly from the period of his acquaintance with Bryskett in Ireland; Tasso's epic poem *La Gerusalemme Liberata* is only printed in its entirety for the first time in 1581, notably after the first mention of an existing draft of 'the *Elvish Queene*' in Harvey's letter.

SPENSER AND ARIOSTO

This early allusion to the nascent *Faerie Queene* considers it specifically in relation to Ariosto's epic masterpiece (even if Harvey himself is doubtful about any affinity between the poems, suggesting that Spenser's *Nine Comoedies* are more similar to Ariosto's plays 'for the finenesse of plausible Elocution, or the rareness of Poetical Invention' than are the two epics), and every critical discussion of Spenser's relationship with Italian literature for over a century now has, of course, examined the poet's professed desire 'to emulate, and hope to ouergo' the *Orlando Furioso* in his own epic poem. An investigation into Spenser's techniques of *imitatio* and *aemulatio* in relation to his principal Italian models, particularly Petrarch, Ariosto, and Tasso, will constitute the main focus of this essay, after a brief discussion of the extent and depth of his knowledge of what is certainly the poet's 'most frequently and continuously utilized source' from Italian literature (Durling 1965: 211). For more than a hundred years critics have demonstrated widely divergent views on the exact nature of Spenser's allusions to and borrowings from Ariosto (and possibly his Italian commentators), prompting Peter Wiggins to describe theirs as 'one of the most ambivalent literary relationships of the sixteenth century'; there has, however, been very little disagreement about the profound impact that the poem had on Spenser, and the evidence of his impressive knowledge of it, resulting in 'what appears, at moments, to be an ability to recall any passage of the *Orlando Furioso* at will' (Wiggins 1988: 77; 1991: 268). Paul Alpers suggests that 'the opening canto of *Orlando Furioso . . .* is one Spenser must have known almost by heart' given the frequency of his borrowings from it (1967: 198), primarily (but not exclusively) in Book III of *The Faerie Queene*, and certainly the poet seems to have had a copy of the poem readily available to him when translating or working closely from the Italian. For example, Britomart's 'mightie speare' is derived directly from Astolfo's enchanted lance, which he lends to the heroine Bradamante, to the extent that Spenser chooses a rare English usage for 'saddle' in maintaining his proximity to the original:

> For neuer wight so fast in sell could sit
> But him perforce vnto the ground it bore.   (III.iii.60)

> quella lancia d'or, ch'al primo tratto
> quanti ne tocca de la sella caccia.   (VIII.xvii.5–6)

[that golden lance, which at the first strike throws whosoever it touches from the saddle][7]

There has also been much (often frustrating) critical speculation about the extent of Spenser's knowledge of the commentaries and allegories frequently printed in and alongside sixteenth-century Italian editions of the poem, but there is firm evidence of his use of the extratextual materials from some later editions. The principal source for the episode at Malbecco's castle in Book III, canto ix, is the Rocca di Tristano episode in canto XXXII of *Orlando Furioso*, but in Malbecco's striking conversion into the abstraction Jealousy in the following canto Spenser is also recalling Ariosto's account of the tyrant's transformation into the immortal Sospetto in the second of the *Cinque Canti* (1545),[8] originally conceived as a sequel to the *Furioso* but never completed by the poet, although often printed at the end in posthumous editions of the epic. There is even evidence that Spenser paid attention to textual variants in the different versions of the poem, again sometimes recorded in the later editions. Spenser transposes the opening of Ariosto's praise of the Este dynasty in canto III to his own chronicle account of *Briton Moniments* at the start of Book II, canto x, unusually translating the first two stanzas quite closely here, as well as returning to the episode in his revelation of Britomart's 'famous Progenie' in Book III. His allusions to the 'Sunne' and '*Phoebus*' at II.x.2–3 echo the original and revised versions of Ariosto's canto exordium respectively: the forty-canto versions of 1516 and 1521 apostrophize the sun ('non vedi, o Sole, che illumini la terra'), whereas the definitive version of 1532 addresses Phoebus directly in invoking 'quel profetico lume' to aid the poet's panegyric task ('non vedi, o Febo, che'l gran mondo lustri, | più gloriosa stirpe' (III.ii.3–4)).

If the depth of Spenser's knowledge of the Italian poem has never really been questioned, there has been far less consensus about how he responds to Ariosto's complex shifts of *tone*, and particularly the ironic 'sorriso' that underpins so many of the key episodes. There is still some critical disagreement about the extent to which Spenser either misses Ariosto's irony altogether or rather wilfully chooses to ignore it in his imitations from the Italian. Peter Marinelli blames the many posthumous moral and allegorical interpretations of the poem in Italy, which 'failed signally to show how it established its meaning and values through laughter', for Spenser's apparent blindness to Ariosto's ironic humour. Alpers, however, argues that this critical insistence on the idea that Spenser relied predominantly on an allegorized *Orlando Furioso* for his imitations of it leads to a serious misreading of *The Faerie Queene*, which offers instead 'a full and intelligent response to the poem itself'.[9] According to C. P. Brand, Spenser's reading of the poem *was* responsive to the humour and irony of the original, even occasionally echoing it in his:

He is not impervious to the humour of the *Furioso*. On the contrary, a fair number of the derivations from Ariosto are from particularly amusing episodes in the *Furioso*, and I see no reason to doubt that Spenser smiled or laughed at them very much as we do. (. . .) It is quite clear to us that Spenser understood and appreciated Ariosto's humour and that he was not averse to reproducing it in his own poem.[10]

In general, however, critics have emphasized rather how Spenser tends to transmute such amusing episodes from Ariosto into a more serious key. Thus, Fiordispina's unrequitable (but genuine) passion for Bradamante, of whose real gender she is unaware, in canto XXV is recast into Malecasta's lust-enflamed response to Britomart in her armour at the start of Book III (with the opportunistic consummation of this desire with Bradamante's twin brother Ricciardetto in the Italian naturally removed). For Wiggins, such drastic re-workings are almost a travesty of the original, constituting 'dismissive allusions' to and a conscious repudiation of Ariosto, by which the English poet 'presents himself as transforming a mere lascivious tale, an Italian toy, into a moral lesson of transcendent import' (1988: 82–3). Certainly Malecasta is a more obviously negative character than her Italian equivalent and, as such, presents the first threat to the champion of chastity in Book III, but it is equally significant that Spenser returns to and echoes Fiordispina's lament to Love in the following canto, where he treats Britomart's painful revelation of her love for Artegall to Glauce in a 'benign and comic manner', which is analogous to the Italian though obviously transferred to the principal (and positive) character in this case (Alpers 1967: 183). This use of a single episode or character from the source in more than one situation in *The Faerie Queene* is a marked feature of Spenser's borrowings from Ariosto.

His treatment in Book III of Ariosto's scornful Angelica, the object of the eponymous hero's love (as well as that of many other knights) and cause of his madness, is similarly multidimensional. The pagan princess's fleeting first appearance in the poem, where she is chased by Ferraù and Rinaldo, is echoed in the multiple pursuit of the faithful Florimell in the opening canto, who later in the Book is almost raped by an old man, as is Ariosto's character; more daringly, however, Spenser also associates the wanton Angelica with another of his female characters in the Book, the militantly virginal Belphoebe, who the poet declares to be one of the figures representing Queen Elizabeth in the poem. Belphoebe's discovery and subsequent healing of the wounded Timias in canto v is modelled closely on Angelica's nursing of the foot-soldier Medoro in canto XIX, where both women feel 'insolita pietade in mezzo al petto ... che le fe' il duro cor tenero e molle' (XIX.xx.5–7) ('an unaccustomed sense of pity in the breast ... which made her hard heart soft and tender'):

> But when shee better him beheld, shee grew
> Full of soft passion and vnwonted smart:
> The point of pitty peerced through her tender hart.   (III.v.30)

After the successful cure with herbs in each case, however, the episodes progress along very different paths, with the alteration again signalled by Spenser's transference of a memorable passage from the Italian to a different character and thus context in the English version. As Medoro's wound heals in the original, Angelica is wounded by Love ('Il giovine si sana: ella languisce | di nuova febbre', XIX.xxix.3–4), whereas in Spenser it is Timias whose heart is pierced by his nurse even as he recovers externally:

> Still as his wound did gather, and grow hole,
> So still his hart woxe sore, and health decayd: (III.v.43)

Angelica's newly felt love leads to almost immediate physical consummation with Medoro (and the apparent loss of her virginity, though Ariosto's narrator is sceptical), and thus to Orlando's eventual insanity, but Timias's feelings can lead only to amorous frustration in view of the poem's strong emphasis on Belphoebe's virginity. This, for Wiggins, is another 'glaring case of allusion as quotation-out-of-context' by means of which Spenser 'moves in and manipulates the *Orlando Furioso*, distinguishing himself from Ariosto and trumpeting his corrections of the predecessor's work' in relation to the more pronounced moral purpose of his own poem (1988: 78–9). For Colin Burrow, though, this episode and the following canto provide a more positive illustration of how exactly Spenser was striving to 'ouergo' Ariosto: in his reading the inevitably frustrated erotic desire of Timias at the end of canto v is redirected immediately towards the natural and fecund Garden of Adonis, which 'concludes and consummates Timias's love for Belphoebe in a suitably displaced, temporally distant, and tactful form' and 'replaces the erotic climax of *Orlando Furioso* by a generative metamorphosis transformed' (Burrow 1993: 119–20; see also Rhu 1993).

If Spenser's re-working of Ariosto in the Belphoebe–Timias episode is a cynical one in Wiggins's interpretation, the same critic argues that in fact such polemical and 'dismissive allusions mask imitations woven into and shaping some of his best poetry', distinguishing between conspicuous allusion as the clearest manifestation of Spenser's professed desire to emulate the Italian poem, and a more subtle level of what he describes as 'dissimulative' imitation, which instead 'pays homage to Ariosto'. In this instance the 'masked' allusion is to the moment in canto XXXIII where the Ethiopian emperor Senapo, 'Ariosto's central symbol of deluded humanity', mistakes the English knight Astolfo for a God or an angel, just as the confused Timias does Belphoebe: 'Angell, or Goddesse doe I call thee right?' (III.v.35) (Wiggins 1988: 82–4). It is certainly possible that Spenser is alluding to two different episodes from the *Furioso* simultaneously here (in contrast to his more habitual practice of using a single episode from the Italian on more than one occasion), but the principal problem with such a reading lies in the level of expectation placed upon the sixteenth-century reader of *both* poems in determining the exact relationship(s) between the imitative text and its original subtext. In the terms of Thomas Greene's influential analysis, the mark of a 'genuine imitation' in Renaissance poetry lies in the way that 'the relationship to the subtext is deliberately and lucidly written into the poem as a visible and acknowledged construct' which can be discerned by a 'knowledgeable contemporary reader' (Greene 1982: 31, 49). Wiggins, however, has to distinguish between the kind of reader who would have been able to recognize only the allusion to (and drastic re-working of) the Angelica and Medoro story in the Belphoebe–Timias episode and the 'far from average English reader of Spenser's time', who was 'almost as avid an admirer of the *Orlando Furioso* as Spenser himself was and could, therefore, have been expected by Spenser to perceive his imitation [of the Senapo episode], not as an example of defeat by an overwhelming predecessor, but as an act of homage to a greatly respected kindred spirit' (Wiggins 1991: 273–4). There is unfortunately no contemporary evidence to confirm any such careful readings of Spenser's imitations from Ariosto (although his simultaneous borrowings from Tasso *were* detected and even imitated almost immediately). Perhaps more significantly, the most advanced levels of imitation in Greene's model (the heuristic and the dialectical) must always demonstrate the poet's deliberate effort to distance himself from his acknowledged subtext as a 'declaration of conditional independence', as in Burrow's reading of the episode, rather than merely pay homage to it, as in Wiggins's reading, at the most basic level of reproductive or sacramental imitation (Greene 1982: 41);[11] the former is certainly more characteristic of Spenser's considered approach to Ariosto, and indeed his other principal Italian sources. It suggests that ultimately his 'hope to ouergo' *Orlando Furioso* in *The Faerie Queene* is successful in these specific terms, whatever Harvey's initial reservations about the relationship between the Italian poem and the draft of Spenser's that he read and referred to in 1580.

Spenser does not simply allude to and adapt individual episodes from the Italian, however; he is also responsive to Ariosto's structural principles, particularly the interwoven and frequently deferred storylines, which often break off prematurely only to be resumed some cantos later, a technique memorably described by Javitch (1980) as the *cantus interruptus*. A development from this technique is apparent in Spenser's three-part non-chronological account of British chronicle history up to the reign of Elizabeth (Book II.x, then Book III.iii and ix), which takes its cue from the vision of Bradamante's ancestors revealed to the heroine by Melissa in Merlin's cave in canto III of *Orlando Furioso*. When considered together, the three parts reveal a more detailed and complex history than Ariosto offers, and they also complicate the frequent speculation concerning the possible order of composition of *The Faerie*

Queene. The English poet's careful use of the same sequence from Ariosto in two distinct books problematizes Burrow's contention, following the work of Bennett and Owen, that Books I and II were written later than Book III 'after Spenser had drunk Tasso into his system' (Burrow 1993: 121). The bulk of Book II, with its significant structural and verbal borrowings from the Rinaldo and Armida episode in Tasso's epic (cantos XIV–XVI), must certainly have been written after Spenser had read *La Gerusalemme Liberata*, first printed in 1581, but the allusions to Ariosto in the linked chronicles of both Books II and III suggest a less rigid demarcation in the development of Spenser's response to his Italian sources.

The critical desire to see the interlaced and continually deferred narratives in the third and fourth books of *The Faerie Queene* as characteristically Ariostan, in contrast to the more linear narratives of the opening two books, which have frequently been said to derive from the theory and practice of Tasso, leads to a misrepresentation of the overall impact of Italian epic on Spenser's poem.[12] The frequency with which Spenser turns to *both* Ariosto and Tasso throughout Books I–III of *The Faerie Queene*, the first instalment of the poem as it is printed in 1590, demonstrates their pervasive influence on his poetic imagination.[13] Unsurprisingly, therefore, critical accounts of Spenser's relationship to his Italian sources have focused almost exclusively on the first instalment of *The Faerie Queene*. Thus, despite the contention that Books III *and* IV are the most consistently Ariostan, analysis has been restricted largely to the former. The relationship between the two books has always caused critical problems, given that Book IV continues (and eventually resolves) many of the narratives of the preceding book, but is only printed for the first time some six years after the first instalment.[14] In terms of Italian material specifically, there is a noticeable diminution in what Spenser borrows from Ariosto (and indeed Tasso) in the fourth book, despite the one direct reference to the Italian poet in *The Faerie Queene*:[15]

> Much more of price and of more gratious powre
>   Is this, then that same water of Ardenne,
>   The which *Rinaldo* drunck in happie howre,
>   Described by that famous Tuscane penne:
>   For that had might to change the hearts of men
>   Fro loue to hate, a change of euill choise:
>   But this doth hatred make in loue to brenne,
>   And heauy heart with comfort doth reioyce.   (IV.iii.45)

Spenser substitutes the water from Ariosto's magic fountain with the Nepenthe that Cambina, whose name of course indicates change, uses to achieve concord between the warring Cambello and Triamond. The alteration also marks a significant shift away from the substance of Italian epic itself in the new books printed in the second edition: Craig Berry suggests that by Book IV 'the river of Italian romantic epic is an impure source' for Spenser, drawing attention to the grammatical uncertainty of the 'that' in l. 5, which could refer to either the water of the fountain or the Tuscan pen which describes it (1998: 122). In this book the poet chooses instead to allude to a native poetic tradition in figuring himself as the literary heir to 'Dan *Chaucer*'

(IV.ii.32), in his desire to offer a conclusion to the story of Cambello and Canacee from the unfinished *Squire's Tale* (see pp. 476–7, 558–9 above) The 'ample spirit' (II. x.1) that Spenser has borrowed so conspicuously from Ariosto in Books II and III is now replaced by that of his great English predecessor 'through infusion sweete | Of thine owne spirit which doth in me survive' (IV.ii.34). This turning away from Ariosto as a persistent source for specific episodes in Book IV is characteristic of the second volume of *The Faerie Queene* as a whole, where Spenser borrows from Italian epic far less frequently than in the first three books. This is certainly the most obvious explanation for the sustained critical focus on the first edition of the poem in relation to both Ariosto and Tasso, although it is one that, perhaps surprisingly, has rarely been proffered.

SPENSER AND TASSO

There is an exception in this general movement away from Italian epic in the second volume, however, in Calidore's retreat amongst the shepherds in Book VI, canto ix, where Spenser, for the second time in his poem, makes extensive use of Tasso's *La Gerusalemme Liberata*, focusing on the episode of *Erminia fra i pastori* from canto VII. The earlier example of sustained attention to Tasso's poem in the first edition of *The Faerie Queene* is the account of Guyon's arrival at Acrasia's Bowre of Blisse and rescue of Verdant in the final canto of Book II, modelled closely on Carlo and Ubaldo's recovery of Rinaldo from Armida's island in cantos XIV to XVI. This episode has been described by Donald Cheney as 'Spenser's most famous single borrowing from the *Gerusalemme Liberata*', a judgment borne out by the extensive body of criticism on it, which tended to focus initially on Spenser's proximity to Tasso but latterly has emphasized rather his subtle adjustments to the Rinaldo and Armida sequence (1966: 93).[16] In both of these extended passages of engagement with Tasso's poem Spenser in a number of places translates almost directly from the Italian, something he does only rarely in his imitations of Ariosto. This perhaps helps to explain why readers and critics at first noticed only the similarities in the renderings, leading to suggestions of a close affinity between the two poets based on Tasso's 'deeper influence' on Spenser's poetic imagination than even Ariosto had;[17] these borrowings and translations focused on self-contained episodes in Tasso might, however, indicate that the recently printed epic in fact had a less pervasive impact on *The Faerie Queene* than Ariosto's, despite the structural prominence given to the Italian-influenced episodes in Books II and VI, respectively.

The apparent verbal proximity to Tasso's Italian in the Acrasia episode is, however, like so much else in the Bowre, deliberately illusory and misleading. If, at a first comparative glance, readers are struck by the clear similarities between Tasso's 'due donzellette garrule e lascive' playing in the fountain (XV.58–60) and Spenser's 'two naked Damzelles' (II.xii.63–8), and also Tasso's *canto della rosa* (XVI.14–15) and Spenser's 'louely lay' (II.xii.74–5), a closer examination elucidates the significant alterations that Spenser makes, almost all of which cast a negative moral light on the material being imitated. Anne Lake Prescott has detected a rare note of 'wry self-mockery' in Spenser's rendering of the celebrated song of seduction, where 'the closeness of the translation suits an episode that comments negatively on imitation' itself, but the added suggestion that the listener 'mayst loued be with equall crime' at the end of the English version gives a very different resonance to the final *carpe diem* plea than in the original, however close they are until that point (Prescott 2006: 112). Similarly Robert Durling has demonstrated effectively how Spenser subtly alters the aesthetic sensuality of Tasso's naked sirens to emphasize both the 'direct sexual provocation' of his own wrestling bathers and the 'signes of kindled lust' (II.xii.68) in Guyon's voyeuristic response to them before he is sternly rebuked by the Palmer (1954: 338–40). After this the knight rescues Verdant and summarily razes the Bowre to the ground 'with rigour pittilesse' (II.xii.83), whereas in Tasso it is Armida herself who causes the enchanted garden to disappear, in anger at her abandonment by Rinaldo. For John Watkins such strong changes of emphasis are the defining characteristic of the English poet's moral response to the tempting eroticism of this particular Italian source:

Episodes like the Bower of Bliss inculcate Virgilian self-denial on both a fictional and a metafictional level. Spenser not only applauds Guyon's resistance to Acrasia but upholds his own resistance to Tassean romance as a lesson in temperance. (Watkins 1995: 4)

Spenser's sustained response to Tasso in these imitations was detected almost immediately by alert readers of the two poems in the late sixteenth and early seventeenth centuries, pre-dating the first critical attention to his borrowings by almost three hundred years. This again suggests that the poet's contemporaries frequently considered Spenser's work in relation to his European vernacular models as well as classical and native sources, an approach which Roland Greene has recently encouraged modern critics to (re-)adopt:

As the borders between the national literatures become more permeable, perhaps it will become possible to see Spenser's work as a nexus of international models and an instance of how—from Petrarchism to pastoral and to epic—those elements that seem most characteristic of Elizabethan literature are often most indebted to the contemporary vernaculars. (Greene 2001: 249)

Edward Fairfax's *Godfrey of Bulloigne*, for example, the first complete translation of Tasso's poem into English verse printed in 1600, demonstrates in its clear verbal echoes from Spenser in the renderings of Tasso's cantos VII and XV–XVI the translator's familiarity with both principal imitations from the Italian in the recently printed English epic poem, providing for David Quint 'another example in Renaissance letters of how the imitation of an earlier literary work could affect the subsequent history of its translation' (1990: 679).[18] The allusions to Tasso in Calidore's pastoral retreat are also noted in the early seventeenth century by William

Drummond in marginal annotations in his copies of *The Faerie Queene* and *Godfrey of Bulloigne*, which were both read in 1610, according to the poet's manuscript reading lists. Drummond also read Tasso and Ariosto's epic in Italian in the same year (along with Harington's translation of *Orlando Furioso*, using the English versions as parallel texts to aid his understanding of the originals), and, most strikingly if apparently incongruously, he also refers to Spenser's poem as one of the 'Italian bookes red by me' that year (Lawrence 2005a: 47–9). This suggests that Drummond came to the English poem through the lens of the two Italian epic poets specifically mentioned in the 'Letter to Ralegh', and his careful bilingual parallel readings would make him the almost ideal contemporary reader of *The Faerie Queene* in terms of the comparative approaches of both Wiggins and Greene. Like many later readers, however, Drummond seems to have been drawn rather to the similarities than the alterations in Spenser's re-workings of Tasso, commenting alongside stanza 20 in canto ix of Book VI that 'all this is Tor. Tassos can. 7.1 [*sic*] Gier. of Erminia che poco é il desiderio e poco é il nostro bisogno, onde la vita si conservi'.[19]

Tasso's old shepherd is indeed the immediate source for much of Meliboe's speech on the advantages of the pastoral world over life at court (VI.ix.20–5), and certain aspects of Calidore's response also follow Erminia's quite closely, but Spenser makes significant adjustments to the episode in Tasso in order to highlight his titular knight's growing uncertainty about fulfilling his epic quest (the capture of the Blatant Beast), towards the end of what became the last completed book of *The Faerie Queene*. Calidore, like Erminia, is deeply affected by the shepherd's 'sensefull words (which) empierst his hart so neare' (rendering perfectly Tasso's 'saggio parlar, ch'al cor le scende', VII.14.3), but additionally by a 'double rauishment', the physical beauty of Meliboe's supposed daughter Pastorella (VI.ix.26), which replaces Tasso's emphasis on the calming effect of these words on Erminia's own storms of passion ('le procelle... de' sensi'), caused by her love for the enemy knight Tancredi. Alpers argues that this change adds a 'pastoral erotics' to the episode, in which the knight of Courtesy chooses, at least temporarily, to privilege his own private emotions over the demands of his royally ordained public duty (1989: 802). Spenser does not ignore Tasso's metaphorical storm, however, but instead turns it into the key image in emphasizing Calidore's strong desire to remain far from the court world in this attractive pastoral retreat:

> Giue leaue awhyle, good father, in this shore
> To rest my barcke, which hath bene beaten late
> With stormes of fortune and tempestuous fate,
> In seas of troubles and of toylesome paine.   (VI.ix.31)

Calidore figures himself as a storm-beaten ship longing for repose in the sanctuary of port, a striking if familiar image, which in this instance echoes quite closely Tasso's poetic self-description in the dedication of his epic poem to his patron, 'magnanimo Alfonso, il qual ritogli | al furor di fortuna e guidi in porto | me peregrino errante' ('magnanimous Alfonso, who rescued me, a wandering traveller, from the storms of fortune and guided me into the port' (I.4.1–3)).[20] Spenser, however, noticeably transfers the words from Tasso's figure of the poet, where they are part of a generous compliment to the Duke of Ferrara for enabling the poet to complete his epic task, to the book's principal character in a pastoral context, where they are addressed instead to the old shepherd who can provide this rest, and conspicuously *not* to his own dedicatee, Queen Elizabeth, an ardent admirer of Tasso's poem,[21] who would have been able to detect the apparent slight in this altered allusion. Spenser's isolated re-working of Tasso's episode in Calidore's pastoral interlude in Book VI hints that the perceptible uncertainty about the successful completion of an epic task in this instance extends beyond the titular knight to the figure of the poet himself.

Spenser's use of Italian materials in his later poetry seems to mirror this movement away from sustained epic endeavour. His indebtedness to both Ariosto and Tasso is, as already suggested, considerably reduced in the second volume of *The Faerie Queene*, and, at the same time (or so the poet would have us believe in *Amoretti* LXXX), Spenser switches his attention to a sequence of love sonnets, printed in 1595. It is significant that this change of focus is registered, at least partly, by a concomitant shift in the *type* of Italian sources that the poet chooses to draw upon. Many of the *Amoretti* are both generically, and specifically, Petrarchan, and Spenser's use of Petrarch is frequently filtered through his knowledge of later Italian and French sonneteers, including prominently the lyric poems of Tasso.[22]

SPENSER AND PETRARCH

Spenser's work is first associated with Petrarch's Italian poetry in Harvey's letter of 1580, and then again strikingly in Sir Walter Ralegh's dedicatory sonnet, 'A Vision vpon this conceipt of the *Faery Queene*', printed in the first edition of 1590:

> All suddeinly I saw the Faery Queene:
> At whose approach the soule of *Petrarke* wept,
> And from thenceforth those graces were not seene.
> For they this Queene attended, in whose steed
> Obliuion laid him downe on *Lauras* herse: (6–10)

In this conceit, the appearance of Spenser's eponymous character effectively consigns Petrarch's beloved Laura to poetic oblivion, suggesting that the English poet in his work has both assimilated and superseded the Italian poet's vernacular lyrical achievements. In fact Spenser rarely imitates Petrarch directly in the epic poem,[23] as he does Ariosto and Tasso, but this sense of competition in relation to Petrarch (and his followers) is a marked characteristic of the European sonnet tradition, which features equally strongly in Spenser's later sonnet sequence. Again, it is one of the dedicatory sonnets (by Geoffrey Whitney Senior) which encourages readers to

approach Spenser's 'learned' work in a pan-European context, specifically as an
English challenge to the poet's foreign predecessors and contemporaries:

> Then, hie thee home, that art our perfect guide,
> and with thy wit illustrate Englands fame,
> dawnting thereby our neighboures auncient pride,
> that do for poesie challendge cheefest name.
> So we that live and ages that succeede,
> With great applause thy learned works shall reede.   (9–14)

The immediate neighbours here may be the sixteenth-century French poets who had
already assimilated the Italian sonnet into French verse (and with whom the poet also
engages directly in *Amoretti* and elsewhere: Du Bellay, Ronsard, and Desportes), but
the principal object of this challenge in Spenser's sequence is certainly Petrarch
himself. Prescott argues that Petrarch's *Canzoniere* provides specific 'models for
both imitation and avoidance' in the *Amoretti*, and suggests that it is Spenser's
careful re-workings of these most celebrated sonnet sources that are the defining
element in his response to Petrarch's foreboding presence in contemporary European
love poetry:

More interesting than discerning this or that source . . . is watching Spenser evoke Petrarchan
motifs that he exploits to signal his ability to go beyond all those blocked and failed
Continental lovers. (Prescott 2006: 109)

This poetic exploitation is structural as well as thematic, even if, unlike most
Italian and French imitators, Spenser chooses not to follow the precise Petrarchan
forms in devising his own unique version of the English sonnet: the single most
significant alteration to the Petrarchan model in *Amoretti* is in the very nature of the
relationship between the poet and his beloved, which progresses gradually from the
habitual situation of unrequited love at the start towards reciprocity and mutual love
in the final third of the sequence, replacing Petrarch's increasingly spiritual and
contemplative *in morte* sequence with a more positive worldly outcome. The separation of the lovers in the final *Amoretti* sonnets, and particularly the image of the dove
in the last one, may seem to cast some uncertainty on this resolution, but the printing
of the autobiographical *Epithalamion* in the same volume suggests that it is only a
brief absence before marriage ensues. The comparison to the mourning bird has its
origin in Petrarch's 'Vago augelletto' (353), which, as William Kennedy has noted, was
often printed as the final sonnet in sixteenth-century editions of the *Canzoniere*
(Kennedy 1994: 273); Spenser, however, replaces the unremittingly sombre tone in the
Italian poet's final consideration of his terminal separation from Laura with some
hope of comfort at the beloved's eventual return ('Dark is my day, whyles her fayre
light I mis', LXXXIX, 13).

The addition of new hope also characterizes another significant thematic and
structural re-working of one of the most familiar Petrarchan topoi in Spenser's
sequence: the image of the lover as a stricken ship lost at sea without the guidance
of the beloved. Sonnet 189, 'Passa la nave mia colma d'oblio', is certainly the best

known and most sustained use of the image in Petrarch's sequence, but it recurs frequently (on at least another six occasions);[24] Spenser seems to have sensed its wider thematic importance by alluding to and developing Petrarch's image on three separate occasions in his own sequence. On the first occasion the memorable image of the beloved's eyes as guiding stars, hidden from view in the mist and rain, from sonnet 189 becomes the controlling conceit for the octave of sonnet XXXIIII, but even here there is the possibility that 'my *Helice* the lodestar of my lyfe | will shine again' (10–11), in comparison to the unrelieved despair in Petrarch's concluding lines. In the second allusion Spenser stresses, in contrast to the uncertain guidance of the male figures in both his earlier sonnet and the Petrarchan original, the steadiness of the female pilot who 'like a steddy ship, doth strongly part | the raging waves and keepes her course aright' (LIX, 5–6), which enables the final positive transformation of the Italian image in sonnet LXIII, where the poet's 'silly barke' 'After long stormes and tempests sad assay' eventually glimpses 'the happy shore' of its destination. This 'drama of affective transformation' of Petrarch's image is another significant marker in the movement towards reciprocity in the relationship between poet and beloved in the final third of the sequence (Kennedy 1994: 197).

In other sonnets Spenser demonstrates a keen awareness of earlier re-workings of familiar Petrarchan images and motifs; the octave of the final sonnet, for example, also echoes Tasso's madrigal 'O vaga tortorella' (1586), which itself borrows the image of the mourning dove from Petrarch. Another Spenserian adaptation of a celebrated Petrarchan image, in which the poet figures the beloved as a wild deer (in sonnet 190 and canzone 323), also uses one of Tasso's lyrics as an intermediary to positive effect at an important juncture in the sequence (just before the pivotal Easter sonnet). Tasso's sonnet 'Al signor Cesare Pavesi' (1583), in which Petrarch's unattainable 'fera gentil' instead turns and approaches her male observer, is a rare light-hearted moment on the poet's part, inspired by the uncanny similarity of the dedicatee's name to a line in 'Una candida cerva', where the inscription on the doe's collar reads 'Libera farmi al mio Cesare parve' ('It has pleased my Caesar to make me free') (190, 11). In Tasso's poem the deer willingly submits to the possession of another Cesare, in a concluding fantasy of erotic fulfilment:

> Pavesi, s'or tal gioia al cor v'inspira,
> Che sarà poi quando più volte il viso
> D'amor vi baci di pietate ardente?   (12–14)

[Pavesi, if now she gives such joy to your heart, what will happen later when, burning with compassion, she will often and lovingly kiss your face?][25]

Spenser's version similarly has the 'gentle deare' approaching a weary male observer, but his emphasis in the ensuing relationship between them is markedly different:

> There she beholding me with mylder looke,
> sought not to fly, but fearelesse still did bide:
> till I in hand her yet halfe trembling tooke,
> and with her owne goodwill hir fyrmely tyde.   (LXVII, 9–12)

Spenser here transforms, via Tasso's contemporary rendering, Petrarch's symbolic visions of Laura's impending death, already familiar from his own early and recently reprinted version of Marot's translation of Petrarch's canzone, into another striking symbol of the burgeoning reciprocal relationship between male poet and female beloved which distinguishes this unique English sonnet sequence.

Spenser's re-workings of Petrarch in his *Amoretti*, which manage skilfully to emphasize simultaneously a proximity to and distance from their Italian sources, are entirely consistent with the methods used earlier to approach and signal his complex interaction with the principal Italian models for romantic epic poetry. In each case Spenser set out deliberately to fashion distinctive English versions of these imposing Italian forms that both emulated and then surpassed their originals. For at least one contemporary Italophile poet, Samuel Daniel, driven by a similar desire to demonstrate to the Countess of Pembroke 'how far Thames doth out-go | The Musike of declined Italie' (78–9) in English verse of the mid-1590s, Spenser's ongoing poetic project was an entirely successful one, even if, linguistically, the rest of Europe was not yet capable of appreciating the extent of his vernacular achievement:

> Wherby great *Sydney* and our *Spencer* might,
> With those *Po*-singers being equalled,
> Enchaunt the world with such a sweete delight,
> That their eternall Songs (for euer read)
> May shew what great *Elizaes* reigne hath bred.   (*Cleopatra* (1594), 89–93)

Notes

1. For example, Spenser's hind 'So faire as mought the greatest God delite' (5) in the first vision is taken from the French 'Bische à Main dextre | Belle pour plaire au souverain des Dieux' (4–5) rather than Petrarch's less specific but more striking 'fera... | con fronte umana da far arder Giove' (4–5) ('a wild creature... with a human face such as to enamour Jove'). See further Chapter 8 above.

2. 'Cur non Axiophilus eadem iam iamque dexteritate? Triduo ille J. C. Cur non ego biduo, aut triduo Italus semilatinus?... Florio quot fecit ex tempore florentes Italos? Me Florio et Tomaso contesti inspirabunt, nobis linguis flagrantem. Hoc age. Ubi amor, ibi oculus' (Stern 1979: 156–7).

3. For language-learning translation exercises from Italian poetry, particularly Petrarch, see Lawrence (2005a), 30–46.

4. Turler's book is a guide to foreign travel in general, and a description of the Kingdom of Naples specifically, similar in kind to William Thomas's *Historie of Italie* (1561), which Harvey also owned and annotated heavily.

5. Bryskett's account of the conversations with his friends, supposedly occurring on three consecutive days in the spring of 1582, alludes to events as late as the summer of 1584.

6. 'We know that this Italian was interested in his native literature and in poetry and that he communicated with relatives in Italy and probably had in his library in Ireland some of the important Italian books of the day. We cannot estimate the degree to which he stimulated and directed Spenser's reading' (Bennett 1942: 249).

7. See also *Orlando Furioso*, XXIII.xv.7–8.
8. George Gascoigne translates these stanzas on Suspicion from *Cinque Canti* into prose in his *Adventures of Master F. J.* (1573).
9. Marinelli (1990), 527; Alpers (1967), 160–1. The most widely known of the commentaries is Simone Fornari's *La Spositione . . . sopra L'Orlando Furioso* (1549–50).
10. Brand (1973), 106. Brand finds examples of this Ariostan irony in the poet's apology at the start of III.ix for the 'odious argument' of Hellenore that he is about to recount, and in the handling of the Squire of Dames' vain search for a chaste woman, modelled on Giocondo's quest in Ariosto's notorious canto XXVIII.
11. See Greene (1982), 38–46, for an explanation of the four distinct levels of imitation.
12. 'In particular, the tight structure of Books I, II and V of *FQ*—all of them focusing on a single quest undertaken by a single hero—imitates the unified linear structure devised by Tasso in the *Gerusalemme Liberata*, rather than the multivarious, interwoven structure of the *Orlando Furioso*' (cf. Fox 1997: 141).
13. For Spenser's voluminous borrowings see Neil Dodge (1897), Gilbert (1919), Koeppel (1889), Blanchard (1925), and Castelli (1936).
14. See, for example, Goldberg (1981).
15. See Neil Dodge (1897), 202, and Gilbert (1919), 231, for borrowings from Ariosto in Book IV; see Koeppel (1889), 356–8, Blanchard (1925), 214–17, and Castelli (1936), 32, for borrowings from Tasso.
16. See also Lewis (1936), 324–40; Durling (1954); Greenblatt (1980), 157–92; Kates (1983), 136–44 and appendix; Fox (1997), 162–74.
17. Neil Dodge (1897), 195–6. See also Brand (1965), 230–3.
18. For Fairfax's specific echoes of Spenser, see Scarsi (2007), 127–30 and 142–50.
19. See Fowler and Leslie (1981). Drummond actually quotes the first two lines of canto VII, stanza 11.
20. See Lawrence (2005b), 268–70.
21. See Castelvetro's letter to Tassoni of June 1584, printed in Solerti (1895), ii, 204–5.
22. For the sources of *Amoretti* see Scott (1929), 159–77 and 319–20, and Kostic (1969), 38–75.
23. The most striking exception is Britomart's love lament on the sea shore at III.iv.8–10, which is an expanded paraphrase, with the genders reversed, of Petrarch's celebrated sonnet 189. See Wofford (1987), 31–48.
24. See *Canzoniere* 151, 177, 180, 234, 235, and 268.
25. Translation by Barbara Spackman in Dasenbrock (1991), 231.

Bibliography

Alpers, P. J. (1967). *The Poetry of the Faerie Queene*. Princeton: Princeton University Press.
—— (1989). 'Spenser's late pastorals'. *ELH* 56: 797–817.
Bennett, J. W. (1942). *The Evolution of* The Faerie Queene. Chicago: University of Chicago Press.
Berry, C. A. (1998). '"Sundrie doubts": Vulnerable Understanding and Dubious Origins in Spenser's Continuation of the Squire's Tale', in Theresa M. Krier (ed.), *Refiguring Chaucer in the Renaissance*. Gainesville: University of Florida Press: 106–27.
Blanchard, H. H. (1925). 'Imitations from Tasso in the *Faerie Queene*'. *SP* 22: 198–221.
—— (1925). 'Spenser and Boiardo'. *PMLA* 40: 828–51.

Brand, C. P. (1965). *Torquato Tasso: A Study of the Poet and of his Contribution to English Literature*. Cambridge: Cambridge University Press.

——(1973). 'Tasso, Spenser, and the *Orlando Furioso*', in J. A. Molinaro (ed.). *Petrarch to Pirandello: Studies in Italian Literature in Honour of Beatrice Corrigan*. Toronto: University of Toronto Press: 95–110.

Bryskett, Lodowick (1606). *A Discourse of Civill Life*. London.

Burrow, C. (1993). *Epic Romance: Homer to Milton*. Oxford: Clarendon Press.

Castelli, A. (1936). *La Gerusalemme Liberata nella Inghilterra di Spenser*. Milan.

Cheney, D. (1966). *Spenser's Image of Nature: Wild Man and Shepherd in the* Faerie Queene. New Haven, CT: Yale University Press.

Dasenbrock, R. W. (1991). *Imitating the Italians: Wyatt, Spenser, Synge, Pound, Joyce*. Baltimore/London: Johns Hopkins University Press.

Durling, R. M. (1954). 'The Bower of Bliss and Armida's Palace'. *CL* 6: 335–47.

——(1965). *The Figure of the Poet in Renaissance Epic*. Cambridge/London: Harvard University Press.

Fowler, A., and Leslie, M. (1981). 'Drummond's copy of *The Faerie Queene*'. *TLS* July 17: 821–2.

Fox, A. (1997). *The English Renaissance: Identity and Representation in Elizabethan England*. Oxford: Blackwell.

Gilbert, A. H. (1919). 'Spenser's Imitations from Ariosto: supplementary'. *PMLA* 34: 225–32.

Goldberg, J. (1981). *'Endlesse Worke': Spenser and the Structures of Discourse*. Baltimore: Johns Hopkins University Press.

Greenblatt, S. J. (1980). 'To Fashion a Gentleman: Spenser and the Destruction of the Bower of Bliss', in *Renaissance Self-Fashioning: From More to Shakespeare*. Chicago: University of Chicago Press.

Greene, R. (2001). 'Spenser and Contemporary Vernacular Poetry', in A. Hadfield (ed.), *The Cambridge Companion to Spenser*. Cambridge: Cambridge University Press: 237–51.

Greene, T. M. (1982). *The Light in Troy: Imitation and Discovery in Renaissance Poetry*. New Haven, CT/London: Yale University Press.

Javitch, D. (1980). '*Cantus interruptus* in the *Orlando Furioso*'. *MLN* 95: 66–80.

Kates, J. A. (1983). *Tasso and Milton: The Problem of Christian Epic*. Lewisburg: Bucknell University Press.

Kennedy, W. J. (1994). *Authorizing Petrarch*. Ithaca, NY/London: Cornell University Press.

Koeppel, E. (1889). 'Die englische Tasso-Übersetzungen des 16. Jahrhunderts'. *Anglia* 11: 341–62.

Kostic, V. (1969). *Spenser's Sources in Italian Poetry*. Belgrade.

Lawrence, J. (2005a). *'Who the Devil taught thee so much Italian?': Italian Language Learning and Literary Imitation in Early Modern England*. Manchester: Manchester University Press.

——(2005b). '*Calidore fra i pastori*: Spenser's return to Tasso in *The Faerie Queene*, Book VI'. *SSt* 20: 265–76.

Lewis, C. S. (1936). *The Allegory of Love*. Oxford: Oxford University Press.

Neil Dodge, R. E. (1897). 'Spenser's Imitations from Ariosto'. *PMLA* 12: 151–204.

Prescott, A. L. (2006). 'Sources', in Bart Van Es (ed.), *A Critical Companion to Spenser Studies*. Basingstoke: Palgrave, 98–115.

Owen, W. J. B. (1953). 'The Structure of *The Faerie Queene*'. *PMLA* 68: 1079–1100.

Rhu, L. F. (1993). 'Romancing Eliza: The Political Decorum of Ariostan Imitation in *The Faerie Queene*'. *Renaissance Papers* 31–9.

Scarsi, S. (2007). 'Translating Women: Female Figures in the Elizabethan Translations of Three Italian Renaissance Epic Poems'. Unpublished PhD dissertation, University of Hull.

Scott, J. G. (1929). *Les sonnets élisabéthains*. Paris: Honoré Champion.

Solerti, A. (1895). *La Vita di Torquato Tasso*. Turin and Rome.

Stern, V. F. (1979). *Gabriel Harvey: A Study of his Life, Marginalia, and Library*. Oxford: Clarendon Press.

Watkins, J. (1995). *The Specter of Dido: Spenser and Virgilian Epic*. New Haven, CT: Yale University Press.

Wiggins, P. D. (1988). 'Spenser's Anxiety'. *MLN* 103: 75–86.

——(1991). 'Spenser's Use of Ariosto: Imitation and Allusion in Book I of *The Faerie Queene*'. *RQ* 44: 257–79.

Wofford, S. L. (1987). 'Britomart's Petrarchan Lament: Allegory and Narrative in *The Faerie Queene* III, iv'. *CL* 39: 28–57.

CHAPTER 34

....

SPENSER AND FRENCH LITERATURE

....

ANNE LAKE PRESCOTT

THE attitude of most educated Elizabethans towards France is pithily summed up in Philip Sidney's characterization of that nation as England's 'sweet enemy'.[1] If on the one hand the French had fought the English, off and on, for many centuries, and if after the Reformation a Catholic France was a threat to England's by now Protestant majority—not least if a more persecutory France were to ally itself with Spain and Spain were to gain a foothold in Ireland—then on the other hand the English could look to the French for chic fashions, a dynamic and magnificent court culture, elegant literature, and humanist learning that frequently offered vernacular versions of Greek and Latin texts that many in England could read only with effort. Italians had all this, of course, but the French were closer, and France, unlike Italy, was a politically if not culturally unified nation under a single dynasty with which the English had to deal diplomatically, economically, and militarily. Some, like Sidney, had close friends in the French Protestant community, but many friendships crossed confessional lines, as did English interest in French literature. This latter point bears stressing, for Spenser was not alone in admiring, appropriating, and otherwise exploiting Catholic as well as Protestant French writers.

Spenser would have agreed, then, that France was a sweet enemy—sweeter than Spain, less of an enemy than the Papacy, and with a culture in his eyes more legible and more impressive than that of the native Irish.[2] His earliest extant poetry translates a brief sonnet sequence by Joachim Du Bellay, his *Shepheardes Calender* (1579) adapts two poems by Clément Marot; the *Complaints* (1591) turn again to Du

Bellay and praise Guillaume Salluste, Sieur du Bartas; *Amoretti* borrows from Philippe Desportes as well as, possibly, from Queen Marguerite de Navarre and Pierre de Ronsard; and it has been argued that the *Fowre Hymnes* exploit Ficino by way of a French translation. Spenser's debt to French letters is extensive. And yet, if he enjoyed the sweetness of French poetry he also responded, whether with dismay or half-cynical resignation, to the often-bloody history of France. Sidney himself had been in Paris on 24 August 1572, St Bartholomew's day, when thousands of French Protestants were massacred at the order, it was then widely believed, of Catherine de Medici and her sons under pressure from the Duc de Guise and his family. Those in Elizabeth's government with whom Spenser most sympathized both admired French culture and viewed its ruling family with opinions varying over the years from disgusted fear to acceptance of the need for alliances with one or another of them.

Despite the two nations' religious differences, two French princes, first the duc d'Anjou, future Henri III, and then the duc d'Alençon, later the duc d'Anjou, would with perhaps minimal personal desire woo Elizabeth. The thought of a French Catholic prince consort dismayed many in England, not least the Earl of Leicester, his nephew Sidney (who wrote the queen a semi-public letter on the matter), and Spenser himself. It is possible that the *Aprill* eclogue in *The Shepheardes Calender* is an attempt to persuade the Queen that she was already married to England, and the animal fable in *Mother Hubberds Tale* certainly satirizes William Cecil and Jean de Simier, the negotiator on behalf of the French monarchy.[3] The marriage negotiations failed, but the diplomatic situation itself would become more complicated. During the French religious wars the English supported the Protestant Henri de Navarre, but sometimes Elizabeth's counsellors courted the king, Henri III, when both governments found it useful to ally themselves against the violently Catholic and pro-Spanish 'Holy League', a quasi-revolutionary faction headed by the militant Henri, Duc de Guise (this stage of the tumults in France, in which Guise's supporters and their Spanish allies for a time occupied Paris, has sometimes been called 'the war of the three Henries'). Anjou himself, however repellent many in England had found him as a possible husband for Elizabeth, at times looked like an ally during the revolt of the Low Countries against Spain. After the duke died in 1584—of syphilis, ran the rumour—the childless Henri III declared Navarre his heir, a declaration that made the English all the more willing, if with some distaste, to be on intermittently good terms with the French king no matter how much he was held in contempt by many in his own nation. That contempt reached England in force, thanks to his enemies' propaganda campaign condemning the king as a cross-dressing, heretical, nun-abusing, and demonic sodomite. At least, thought Elizabeth's advisers, he was not as bad as the Guise.

On 1 August 1589 a Jacobin monk, Jacques Clément, many said at the urging of Pope Sixtus V and almost certainly encouraged by members of the League, assassinated the king. Some saw in this regicide a crude justice, for the king himself had, that past December, arranged for the murder of the Duc de Guise and his brother, a cardinal. Spenser's first three books of *The Faerie Queene*, in other words, were published after Europe and England had been rocked by the assassinations of major political figures (William of Orange, Guise, Henri III) as well as attempts on Elizabeth, the execution of Mary Stuart, and the defeat of the Armada. After Henri III's assassination the English government supported Navarre's military and political campaign to secure his throne, but when in July of 1593 Henri announced his conversion to Catholicism (although not, so far as the evidence shows, actually saying 'Paris is worth a mass') Elizabeth reacted with a carefully calculated temper tantrum in the form of a blisteringly reproachful letter and Spenser reacted with an allegory expressing both dismay and the same political realism that characterized England's continuing support for the beleaguered Henri IV.[4] Whatever the cost to strict Justice, Spenser suggests in *Faerie Queene* V.xi–xii, Elizabeth had no choice in such a dangerous and unpredictable world but to support a moderate Catholic monarch who seemed unlikely to persecute Protestants vigorously or to support international attempts to subdue Protestant England. In the terms of Spenser's allegory, Sir Artegall, with some contempt and only after scolding him for throwing away his shield of faith, helps Sir Burbon (Henri de Navarre was the first king of France from the House of Bourbon) to win the lukewarm maiden Flourdelis while his iron servant Talus makes short work of the Guise-led rabble.[5] Henri officially married Fleurdelis, so to speak, at his coronation in 1595, after Spenser had finished Book V but before it was published the next year.

Much of Spenser's poetry, then, gains resonance when we remember the degree to which throughout his career as a poet France had witnessed devastating violence and political drama. This is all the more the case because for some years England had seen a flood of sometimes government-inspired pamphlet literature defending Navarre, attacking the Guise and their supporters, or simply giving the news from across the Channel. Just before Spenser published Books I–III of *The Faerie Queene* the flood had become a tsunami, some of which revived and even intensified the anti-Catholic and anti-papal language and metaphors of Henrician and Edwardian propaganda. We do not know whether Spenser finished work on Books IV–VI just before or just after the assassination of Henri III, but he almost certainly wrote them shortly after the publication of many such pamphlets. One, for example, figures the Pope as a whore impregnated by Satan and giving birth to the League; another mocks the powerful sister of the Duc de Guise, Catherine, Princesse de Montpensier, an enchantress who plays the incestuous sister to Brother Jacques Clément, who has offered her own 'meat' to starving Parisians, and who has learned Latin by French-kissing all the monks in town.[6] The Duessa who is executed in Book V (in the white space between cantos ix and x), now more clearly a figure for Mary Stuart, owes something not only to the 'Mistress Missa' of early anti-Catholic polemic by the likes of John Bale but to more recent images of the Pope-loving and Spanish-allied League. After all, Mary was a Guise on her mother's side and hence allied to the family that first killed Henri III and then tried to prevent Sir Burbon's union with Fleurdelis.

Spenser's most visible interest in French poetry began early, when he was asked, perhaps by his schoolmaster Richard Mulcaster, to translate a set of sonnets by Joachim Du Bellay (*c.*1522–60) for an English version of the Flemish poet Jan Van der Noot's anti-Catholic polemic, *A Theatre for Voluptuous Worldlings* (1569).[7]

Du Bellay was himself a Catholic, if a moderate who could satirize the Church corruption he witnessed when living in Rome as secretary to his richer cousin, the cardinal and diplomat Jean Du Bellay. Nevertheless, the fifteen sonnets of his *Songe* (1558) lament the fall of Rome in ways that with a little nudging can be made to seem to threaten the modern Papacy, as well as to prophesy the looming French religious civil wars. Van der Noot's commentary reads Du Bellay's sonnets, four of which he has exchanged for Apocalyptic poems presumably of his own devising, as anti-papal allegory, but young Spenser may well have been equally drawn to Du Bellay's powerful images of mutability, to his vision of collapsing architecture, spoiled land-scapes, blasted trees, ruined arches, and barbarian invasion. At some point he reworked his translations (adding those of the four sonnets that Van der Noot had omitted) for his 1591 *Complaints*, where they appear as *The Visions of Bellay*. All in this world, warns the first sonnet, is 'flying vanitee', and only God offers a 'stay' against 'this worlds inconstancies' (see Chapter 8 above).

In his *Complaints* Spenser also published the *Ruines of Rome*, a translation of Du Bellay's haunting sonnet sequence *Les Antiquitez de Rome*, to which his *Songe* is a sort of appendix. These poems are likewise a lament for self-destructive greatness, for worldly pride punished by the heavens, for barbarian invasions made possible by imprudence, and above all for the predations of a Time armed with scythe and teeth. More such depredations, and with evidence that Spenser was still thinking of Du Bellay, continue in *The Ruines of Time*, with its weeping city-spectre and its sorrow over the dead Sidney. The concluding sonnet praises Du Bellay as the 'first garland of free poesie'. The 'garland' implies that the French poet not only deserves laurels but is also in some sense himself a garland encircling the head of Poesie.

Such praise, Spenser may have thought, particularly suited one who had composed the first French Petrarchan sonnet sequence, *Olive* (1548), an olive wreath, in effect, and one with calendrical and liturgical allusions that even more precisely than Petrarch's *Rime* anticipate those of Spenser's *Amoretti*.[8] That the garland is of 'free' Poesie may suggest some sense that in his hands poetry had risen above an older style of mere cleverness and courtier subservience. Whatever the older accomplishments by the 'brave wits' of which France had been so 'fruitful', the Pléiade (that constella-tion of self-consciously elegant, classically learned, revisionary poets for which Du Bellay had provided a manifesto, the 1549 *Defence et illustration de la langue fran-çoyse*), had, in its own view, breathed fresh spirit into French culture and helped liberate it from its mistaken sense of inferiority to Rome. Richard Mulcaster, the headmaster and writer at the Merchant Taylors' School who was probably responsi-ble for getting Spenser to translate the poems for *A Theatre for Worldlings*, was evidently impressed by the *Defence*, for its arguments resemble those in his *Elemen-tarie* (1582).

There were to be no more translations of Du Bellay in Spenser's works, but the time-felled oak in 'Ruines' 28, itself from a tree in Lucan's *Civil Wars* that represents Pompey, has a cousin in the *Februarie* eclogue of the *Calender* and, if one may judge by her phrasing, Spenser's Clio in *The Teares of the Muses* laments mutability (after all, as the Muse of History she has a professional interest in such matters) with

phrasing familiar from the *Antiquitez*. More importantly, throughout his career
Spenser was moved by what one could call the discourse of ruination, incorporating
it not only into his *Ruines of Time* and some stanzas of *The Faerie Queene* but into the
very end of his epic as we have it: the image of all things firmly stayed upon the pillars
of Eternity (VII.viii) reverses the earthquake that ruins the pillared and jewelled
palace/temple of 'Visions of Bellay', 2. Even the illustration in *A Theatre for Worldlings*
of a still intact building looks something like what Spenser might have imagined
as a Sabbaoth Sight.[9] What he learned from Du Bellay, moreover, was not merely
how to lament Time's cruelty, for the *Antiquitez* and *Songe*, whatever their grief
over collapsed empire and lost grandeur, also imply not only a *translatio imperii*, a
translation of empire from Rome to France and England, but also an enlarged space
(a 'room' that in early modern English rhymed with 'Rome') for modern poets such
as Du Bellay and Spenser. Rome is dead, and although Virgil lives he may now have
some French and English company, especially for those who can write epics, although
this was an ambition that Du Bellay rather flashily insists, in the *recusatio* that helps
begin his sonnet sequence *Les Regrets*, he did not harbour. For Spenser, furthermore,
as for other Elizabethans, there is comfort to be had in the thought that if pagan
Rome had fallen so might papal Rome, and then the 'pillars of Eternitie' would all the
sooner support a New Jerusalem, a restored Temple, in defiance of the Pope, Spain,
and other persecutory forces that opposed the Reformation and the Gospel. Translation of empire remains, though, a deeply ambiguous matter for so thoughtful a
Christian writer as Spenser. If papal Rome will face ruin in its turn, if *imperium* and
letters can be translated to England, what then? As Du Bellay himself says in his
Songe, and whatever the old Virgilian claims for empire (possibly more ironic
than Augustus or the Renaissance quite realized), there is nothing steadfast in the
City of Man.[10]

It is possible, however, that for Spenser Du Bellay was not only the poet of ruins
and author of love lyrics, not only one who had suffered what felt like an Ovidian
exile (albeit paradoxically, in Rome itself) and who like Spenser had employment
that kept him far from his birthplace, but also one who at the end of his too short
career had turned to verse satire not unlike the cynical poetry becoming fashionable just as Spenser was publishing the second half of *The Faerie Queene*. Du
Bellay's *Poète courtisan*, printed in 1559 after he had returned to France, offers
pseudo-advice on how to be a successful courtier poet. It has some verbal overlap
with the very end of Book VI, and no wonder, for the *Legend of Courtesie*
demonstrates considerable unease concerning the slippery art of courtiership—
the hero Sir Calidore's very name, in one etymology, recalls 'callidus', or cunning.
The sonnets in Du Bellay's *Regrets* include biting satire, some of it anti-court, but
his *Poète courtisan* is a venture into the sort of verse satire, albeit less Juvenalian,
that John Marston and Joseph Hall were to write in the 1590s. Perhaps, one can
speculate, the conclusion of Spenser's epic as it was published in 1596 hints that the
author was becoming interested in the same genre in which a younger generation
was demonstrating its prodigality by implicitly cocking a snook at elders such as
himself.

He is no Aristotle, says Du Bellay, for 'the court is my author, my example, and my guide'. And he will be brief, for long works bore courtiers. Be gallant—don't bite your nails, beat the table, dream, or have a brain boiling with thoughts. (If this sounds like the opening of Sidney's *Astrophil and Stella* that is because both poets are sacking Rome—look in thy heart and see what Horace writes in *Satire* I.x, where we see a poet 'Oft in the pangs of labour scratch his head, | And bite his nails, and bite them, till they bleed'.) Let the Court, mother of good wits, continues Du Bellay, be your Virgil and Homer. Sing the weddings and festivals of great lords (as indeed Spenser did in his *Prothalamion*). Get your verses into the royal chamber—but please no hard words and neologisms. Do not seem envious whatever you feel and avoid appearing to slander. Be wise ('saige'), content with the judgment of those whom you please ('plaire') and who can advance you with valuable ('riches') rewards. 'Seeke to please', as Spenser puts it, for that 'now is counted wisemens threasure'—treasure that recalls the counting-house of the Secretary of the Treasury, the censorious William Cecil of the furrowed brow who disapproves of love poetry in the proem to *Faerie Queene* IV.[11] For both Spenser and Du Bellay the laurel leaves of free poesie are starting to curl into satire's poison ivy.[12]

Some years after his introduction to Du Bellay's poetry Spenser found an earlier French poet who would inspire him to imitation if not to praise: Clément Marot (1496–1544), chief poet at the court of François Ier. Many contemporaries admired Marot, although he was entangled in an entertaining but undignified slanging match with another poet, François Sagon, and although he sometimes got into trouble with religious and political authorities. Once he was jailed for reasons that remain unclear, and on occasion he fled France to escape prosecution and persecution for his heterodox opinions, although his exact beliefs are still debated.[13] Marot's adroit verse translations, in varied meters, of about a third of the psalms into French were at first meant for the court, where they were for a time popular, but soon they came to seem heretical, whether because they were in the vernacular or because of their author's doctrinal unreliability. Eventually an expanded version was published, at Geneva with those by Theodore Beza; the completed translation became the immensely influential and widely imitated Huguenot Psalter, chief model for the versions by Philip and Mary Sidney, among many others.[14]

Spenser was not the first English poet hoping to establish an English pastoral tradition to rival or at least to domesticate that of Theocritus and Virgil, but he was the most ambitious, and so it is not surprising that he exploited Marot's pastorals, for Marot was the first in France to write true pastoral eclogue in the vernacular (and also the first to write a traditional elegy and epithalamion). Spenser was doubtless amused, in this regard, to note Marot's semi-serious denials and more serious claims to be France's 'Maro', its Virgil, for Virgil's eclogues had seen the start of a career eventuating in an epic. In his preface to the *Calender* Spenser's commentator E. K., whoever he was, gives Marot grudging credit. He explains that the 'most auncient Poetes, which devised this kind of wryting', did so in order to 'prove theyr tender wyngs, before they make a greater flyght'. Theocritus did so, says E. K., and so did Virgil, Mantuan, Petrarch, and Boccaccio. And 'So Marot, Sanazarus, and also divers other excellent both Italian and French Poetes, whose foting this Author every where followeth, yet so as few, but they be wel sented can trace him out' (Spenser 1999: 29). Now this new poet (Spenser) is flying before his wing feathers are fully grown.

E. K. knows his pastoral tradition, but Marot does not fit the pattern: so far as we know he never did attempt an epic and the pastoral that Spenser adapts for the *December* eclogue was written late in his career. In E. K.'s Virgilian terms, Marot flew all his life with mere fledgling down. One can make a case that he did tentatively edge away from conceiving his role as that of a court poet to a conception of poetry as inspired, but the inspiration he imagined was more Davidic than Neoplatonic.[15] In the shape of his career and in his claims for himself as a poet, whatever his friendly access to a ruler who was himself a prolific poet, he remained the Maro of the Eclogues, not the *vates* Maro who could (with whatever shimmers of irony or shades of melancholy) celebrate a dynasty or empire like Ronsard or even the Creation like Guillaume du Bartas. That may be one reason why E. K. also puts distance between the would-be Virgilian Spenser and the not-quite-Maro French pastoralist. Commenting on the name Colin in his notes to *Januarie*, E. K. rightly mentions Skelton but adds that 'indeede the word Colin is Frenche, and used of the French poete Marot (if he be worthy of the name of a Poete) in a certaine Æglogue'.

By 'a certaine Æglogue' E. K. means Marot's 1531 elegy for Louise de Savoie, the formidable mother of king François Ier who ruled the nation while her humiliated son, captured at the battle of Pavia by the forces of Emperor Charles V, suffered imprisonment in Spain.[16] Spenser adapts it loosely for his *November* eclogue. Here the deceased is 'Dido', usually read—with a variety of explanations and puzzlements—as the still very much living Elizabeth. That Dido's other name was 'Elissa' may help explain her presence in *November*, and praising a queen under her name, whatever one might think of its suitability (Dido was a clever and ingenious leader of her people, but not a wise lover), had precedent. E. K. identifies Spenser's source as the eclogue by Marot, and then adds, 'But farre passing his reache'. Hardly generous.[17] The following *December* eclogue imitates Marot's 1539 'Eglogue de Marot au Roy, soubs les noms de Pan & Robin' ('Eclogue from Marot to the king under the names Pan and Robin'), written when the poet was back in France after a period of exile but not in full confidence of his safety.[18] In this late pastoral the shepherd Robin begs Pan, god of pastoral poetry but also king of France perhaps with a touch of God himself, for protection. The protection is for both shepherd and sheep. It has been plausibly argued that the shelter Robin needs is not just against the poverty and weaknesses of age but also against those trying to silence Marot for his evangelical beliefs, and that his 'flock' represents persecuted lovers of the Gospel. When the king responded by giving his poet a house, the gesture may have been made with a deliberate and ironic literalism.[19] The verses themselves are as touching as they are charming: the poet remembers his sunlit spring of youth when first learning his art, but now he is getting old in the winter of his years, and the wolves prowl and he has no shelter. The eclogue, which Spenser follows only intermittently, gains even more poignancy when we remember that Marot was famous for translating the psalms of David—who likewise had to flee an angry king—and is now addressing a king who was himself often called a David.[20] Marot's circumstances do not parallel Spenser's, for whatever the latter's ties to the Leicester group at court he was hardly in danger of persecution for his religion. But the sense of threat, of confusion over just what a poet should be or do, may make Marot's eclogue all the more relevant to the *Calender*, with its moping Colin Clout, rejected by his beloved, even if not explicitly by his queen, and uncertain about poetry's place.

This question of 'place' may further explain E. K.'s hesitant, even dismissive, treatment of Marot. His role as a beleaguered psalmist might have played some part in Spenser's decision to adapt two of his eclogues, and it has been argued that it did so. It is also true, though, that Marot's reputation in England was inflected by what seemed to some a certain imprudent clownishness, for while a number in England knew of Marot's misadventures as well as of his position as the king's good servant (if God's first), the few extant allusions to his suffering are surprisingly unsympathetic.[21] Marot could write with fierce passion when he wished to but he was also willing to indulge in broadly comic self-mockery that would have sat uneasily with Virgilian longings; it is not surprising that he would eventually figure as the protagonist of a Dutch jest book that shows him, on the title page of one edition, with coxcomb and bells.[22] To put it unfairly, he was to the *vates* Ronsard as Skelton was to what Spenser might become, or so E. K. might have thought. Whatever his accomplishments as a court poet on easy terms with his king, whatever the protection of the powerful Marguerite de Navarre, he was not a true poet whose verses would deserve the 'place' in princes palaces longingly imagined in the *October* eclogue for 'peerlesse poesie'. It is possible, then, that E. K. (and hence Spenser?) is responding to a shift in French culture towards a more resplendent conception of poetry's cultural situation, one in which highly ambitious poets such as Ronsard, however witty, appeared to take themselves more seriously than had Marot and his generation, at least when not following David.

Spenser never again named Marot in print, but he did not forget him. Two of the four little poems that follow his *Amoretti* in 1595, serving as a palate cleanser between the melancholy last few sonnets and the triumph of the *Epithalamion*, paraphrase epigrams first printed in Marot's 1538 *Œuvres*.[23] The second poem, 'As Diane hunted on a day', imitates 'L'Enfant Amour', Marot's brief report that Cupid and Diana have changed weapons. How does the poet know? Because Love often chases beasts ('Bestes') and Diana wounds the truly manly ('hommes de vertu').[24] Spenser changes the men of virtue, presumably made chaste by a shot from the Virgin Goddess into some part of their anatomy, to 'my loves hart', which—along with possible gender-bending wordplay on hart/heart—explains his lady's refusals. Marot's poem seems vaguely public, with its virtuous men, whereas Spenser's paraphrase turns the poem to a love complaint complimenting the still virginal Elizabeth Boyle. Neither poet says why we need a myth to explain why beasts are oversexed, but the sly suggestion is that we do need an explanation for male virtue and female recalcitrance. The third poem, 'I saw in secret to my dame', closely follows 'Amour trouva celle qui m'est amere', in which Cupid greets his mother, then realizes that the lady in question is in fact the poet's own beloved, and then reddens with shame. Do not blush, says the poet to the abashed little god, for many who see more clearly than you ('plus cler voyans') have thus erred.[25] Spenser's English has to omit the punning rhyme on 'amere' [bitter] and 'mere' [mother], but the poet also drops Marot's concluding witticism about Cupid's eyesight, either because he has missed the joke or because he finds it illogical that a blind god can even think he sees his mother.

Many editors and critics call these poem's 'Anacreontics', for the publication in 1554 of Henri Estienne's great edition of the poems he ascribed to the Greek poet Anacreon had accelerated a French fashion for elegant brief lyrics, epigrams, epitaphs, odes, or odelettes, many on wine, love, Cupid, roses, and so forth in Anacreon's style. Marot's epigrams on occasion anticipate the fashion, but of course he published them before Estienne's anthology saw print. Spenser, then, has chosen poems to imitate that evoke a manner still chic in France but he has reached to the years before Estienne and the Pléiade. Perhaps that is why, even aside from authorial ego, the pose of a lover, and the potential look of the page, he gives no credit to Marot. Or perhaps, just as Marot had received only a backhanded compliment in 1579, so now his name would only dull the glitter of an ostensibly recent elegance from across the Channel. Fashion could travel slowly across that strait, of course, and in fact by 1595 French elegance had acquired yet another new look. But as a model of prestige, fame, and epic hopes, the likes of Pierre de Ronsard (1524–85) had more glamour. French literature had moved on since Marot's day, and Spenser probably wanted to move with it.

Spenser never mentions Ronsard in his extant works (in fact he names few modern vernacular poets of any nationality), but there is clear evidence that he read him. True, Ronsard had written bitterly and at length against Protestantism and was himself in minor orders. It is also true that he served a dynasty that Spenser had ample cause to dislike. His career, however, ranging from reviving the Pindaric ode and writing love sonnets of exquisite beauty, to imitating the philosophic Homeric hymns, to attempting an epic, to supplying the words for court masques and to addressing the great in verse epistles, offered Spenser an almost intimidating model. Ronsard even literally had a 'place' in a prince's palace, for he had for a while lived in the Louvre. As so often, English literary taste did not correlate with ideological conviction. Even the *Calender*'s appearance, for all its anxiety about a French match, may owe something to a glance across the Channel to French fashion, for the *mise en page* of its text and notes, has been compared not only to the look of classical and Italian Renaissance texts but also to that of the 1553 edition of Ronsard's *Amours de Cassandre*, a canonizing and laurels-awarding performance by the learned humanist Marc-Antoine Muret.[26] The little story of a wounded Cupid in the *Calender*'s *March* eclogue, moreover, seems to be from Ronsard's 'Un enfant dedans un bocage' in the *Nouvelle Continuation des Amours* (1556). The later elegy for the Protestant hero Sidney, *Astrophel*, moreover, although derived ultimately from Bion's great lament for Adonis, seems to have reached Spenser by way of Ronsard's own 'Adonis' (1563).[27]

More significantly, although without leaving any evidence behind, Spenser must have read Ronsard with some fellow feeling along with, one suspects, some envy.

Ronsard, widely thought the 'prince of poets', may sport laurels in Muret's edition of his *Amours*, but he himself could show a sometimes defensive and sometimes defiant inability or unwillingness to finish his epic, the *Franciade*, sometimes alluding to it with rueful excuses, including the perhaps incautious explanation that he was insufficiently supported by the great. The topic recurs in his love poetry: if Ronsard cannot finish the story of how young Francus led his band of Trojans to found France, at least he can write about ladies with names such as Cassandra and Hélène and thus work a little epic into his Petrarchan sonnets. Both he and Spenser had a precedent for their witty unease in Ovid's excuse (*Amores* I.1) that one day Cupid flew by and laughingly stole a foot from his dactylic hexameter couplets, leaving him to hobble in elegiacs; hence he must abandon the epic for the amatory, although later in the collection he also claims—in a conceit with a long future—that Eros is a warrior.[28] *Amoretti*, too, sends sidelong glances at the epic that the lover is not writing, and like Ronsard Spenser plays with garlands, leaves, and laurels: 'The bay (quoth she) is of the victours borne' (*Amoretti* 28), and although this fact is common knowledge, the lady may also have been reading Ronsard's 1578 *Sonnets et Madrigals pour Astrée* xi: 'Le Laurier est aux victoires duisant'. In both cases the lady speaks of laurels when her poet, some might say, should be earning them by getting back to work.

The unfinished but published epic, although there is no evidence that Spenser borrowed from it, must have formed part of his view of, and perhaps mental rivalry with, Ronsard, for *La Franciade* deals, as does *The Faerie Queene* in many regards, with the movement of empire and with the legends concerning the Trojan origins of several modern dynasties. Like Du Bellay, but with an epic inflection, both poets treat with varying degrees of enthusiasm and skepticism the movement of empire that in a synergy of biblical and classical thought was assumed to have moved the focus of rightful power from ancient Western Asia to Rome and thence to . . . ? The answer depended in large part on nationality, for the Holy Roman Empire claimed to be Rome's heir, members of the Habsburg dynasty even encouraging genealogists to locate ancient Trojan ancestors as well as some biblical ones. Du Bellay's discourse of Roman ruination implicitly, and Ronsard's and Spenser's epic discourse explicitly, were each tied in one way or another to genealogy, with the added complexity for Spenser of the presence in England of structures ruined not by Time or ancient civil war and conquest but by the despoiling of the monasteries that attended Henry VIII's own claims to Roman *imperium*. Even the Guise family, when arguing that it had a better claim to the French throne than did the Valois dynasty, liked to claim descent not only from ancient Gallic and Frankish kings but from the heroes of Troy. The quasi-genealogical *translatio* of both studies and empire had thus spread from its Middle Eastern and then Roman roots into an entire tree of related European languages and competing imperial claims. And among those making those claims in epic form were Ronsard and Spenser.

What else might Spenser have gleaned from reading in French literature, or hearing about it and such other aspects of French culture as Henri III's *Académie du Palais* with its links to Platonism and the encyclopaedia of learning?[29] At the end of the *Ruines of Rome* Spenser praises Du Bartas's 'muse'—probably the muse of astronomy who in 'Uranie', a poem published in the French poet's *Muse Chrestienne* (1574), appears to Du Bartas and urges him to write poetry based on the Bible and thus become famous and admired by kings. Spenser never wrote biblical poetry himself, but perhaps he found in Du Bartas's extraordinarily influential *Sepmaines* a sense of the not always well-behaved heavens' wheeling splendour and the fluid, mutable—and legible—earthly Creation. For example, Du Bartas compares the material world to a courtesan receiving the imprint of many form-giving lovers, not unlike Spenser's Venus with her Adonis (III.vi), the latter not a multiplicity of partners, to be sure, although Venus certainly had them, but at least playing the father of all forms to her *materia*. Or, as Ronsard says when grieving over the felled forest of Gastine, 'La matiere demeure, et la forme se perd' ('Matter remains, and [or although] form is lost').[30]

What of other French writers? *Amoretti* 15 adapts a sonnet by the fashionable and much-translated Philippe Desportes (*Diane* I.32), although Spenser typically adds a compliment to the beloved's mind. The basic pattern of St George's adventures in *The Faerie Queene* Book I follows one first imagined by Bernard of Clairvaux but most notably set out in verse by the Burgundian poet Olivier de la Marche; the sequence (a rider on a restive horse experiences error, pride, despair, and recovery in a curative house) probably came to Spenser, however, if indeed it did come, by way of Steven Batman's *Travayled Pylgrime* (Prescott 1989).[31] Marguerite de Navarre? Her *Heptaméron* was well known to England's educated, whether in the translations by William Painter or simply by reputation, and it is in her *Chansons spirituelles* that one finds the closest parallel to Spenser's *Amoretti* 67, the sonnet in which the hunted deer voluntarily gives itself up. In both sequences, furthermore, the following poem is on the Passion or Easter and the next on spring; there is probably more to be done on these two sets of lyrics and their liturgical allusions.[32] Perhaps Spenser not only exploited the translation of Ficino by the French secretary to the Duc d'Anjou, Guy Le Fèvre de la Boderie, for his *Fowre Hymnes* but also noticed in Le Fèvre's long Neoplatonic *Galliade* (1578) a close parallel to the Redcrosse knight's ascent up the Hill of Contemplation.[33] I can find no trace of French drama in Spenser's extant work, nor any sign of Rabelais, although Spenser would have enjoyed him, and it would be interesting to compare Montaigne on cannibals to Serena's rescue from hungry satyrs in *Faerie Queene* VI. Did Spenser consult French scholarship such as Jean de Sponde's annotations on Homer? Or the encyclopedic Pierre de la Primaudaye's much-read writings on psychology and cosmology? Did he know that Jean Salmon Macrin had preceded him in escaping the Petrarchan dilemma by writing love lyrics and an epithalamion to a future wife? The answer in some of these cases could well be yes, but we cannot truly tell. Aside from the dubious entertainment value of tracing poetic conceits uphill to some verbal rivulet of a source, and aside from the powerful impact on Spenser's imagination of poets we do know that he read with intense scrutiny, there remains the mere fact of an energetic and glittering literary culture, one he must often have found enviable and engaging, lying so close to England and Ireland and yet so often separated from him by the memory of ancient—and the threat of present—conflict. 'Sweet enemy' indeed.

Notes

1. *Astrophil and Stella* 41. For a general view of Spenser's sources see Prescott (2006) and the relevant articles in *SE*.

2. On Spenser and France, in addition to the works mentioned here, see Brown (1999), especially Ch. 2. I have doubts about some of Brown's generalizations, but his is a valuable study.

3. Spenser's dismay over the projected Alençon match has attracted notice, although too often we ignore the complexities that made such a courtship seem to Cecil and others a possible help against Spain rather than a capitulation to French Catholicism. For recent comments, and citation of useful earlier work, see Nohrnberg (2007), and on *Aprill* see especially Johnson (1981).

4. Sir Robert Sidney, e.g., advised Elizabeth in 1595 to support Henri for fear of losing him to Spanish domination; see Prescott (2000a), 205–6.

5. *FQ* V.xi–xii. 'Guise' inevitably suggests 'guise' and 'disguise'; Spenser's Guizor and his brothers, sons of the crafty Dolon (V.vi), must recall the Guise family, if not Henri himself.

6. *A Letter Written by a Catholic Gentleman* [i.e., a 'politique' supporter of Navarre] *to the Lady Jane Clement, the haulting Princesse of the League* (1590); *A True and Perfecte Description of a Straunge Monstar* [sic] *borne in the City of Rome in Italy, in the Yeare of our Salvation. 1585* . . . (1590).

7. Smith (1994) gives the French originals and Spenser's translations, although with readings of Du Bellay that may make him too anti-Papist and with criticisms of Spenser privileging literal accuracy. Helgerson (2006) offers an eloquent and meticulous modern translation. Spenser's relation to Du Bellay has received considerable scrutiny; see in addition to works cited below, fine essays by Ferguson (1984), Stapleton (1990), Coldiron (2002), and Melehy (2003). Recent scholarship has tended to give Spenser higher marks than those he received in the past century; the danger, one now largely avoided, is to minimize Du Bellay's ambivalence towards ancient Rome.

8. Prescott (1996); Spenser's liturgical patterning in *Amoretti*, though, is far more elaborate, and from what I can determine more tied to a particular year, in this case 1594.

9. Prescott (1996). By this time, though, Spenser may have been thinking less of Du Bellay himself than recycling images he had so deeply interiorized that traces of the *Antiquitez* are less intertextual than intratextual.

10. The ambiguities of a perpetually sliding *imperium* are explored by Helfer (2007), arguing against a more triumphalist reading of Spenser and proto-British imperialism.

11. Miller (1996) also notes Spenser's 'references to rating, measuring, and counting' (170).

12. This present essay cannot explore all passages in which Spenser recalls Du Bellay, consciously or not; for one significant moment, though, see Brown (1999), 144, 154–7 (citing earlier scholarship as well) on *TM* and Du Bellay's 1550 'Musagnoeomachie', an imagined battle between the Muses and the powers of Ignorance, including older French poets lacking the Pléiade's dramatic claims to Parnassian inspiration. To this Brown adds as an influence Ronsard's great Pindaric 'Ode à Michel de L'Hospital', an encyclopedic vision of poetry's powers which expresses a jubilant confidence of which Spenser's discouraged Muses can only dream.

13. The degree to which Marot was ever fully Lutheran remains disputed, in part because religious distinctions were still fluid. To call him a 'Protestant', as is sometimes done by Spenser scholars, defines him too sharply, whatever his growing sympathy for Lutheran ideas. On his probable moderation and our own ignorance see, e.g., Ahmed (2005).

14. Literature on the Marot–Beza translations is too huge to describe here, but for a good edition of Marot's psalms see Defaux (1995), and for some English reactions see Prescott (1978).

15. Preisig (2004) traces this evolution, distinguishing between prophetic and poetic inspiration in ways important for Marot's relation to secular power. For more on Marot's frightening, sometimes pleasantly 'complicit' relation to his versifying king see Bamforth (1997); the other essays in this large collection are also valuable.

16. Marot (1964), 321–37; extensive notes explain the context.

17. E. K. translates Colin's appended emblem, 'La mort n'y mord', as 'death biteth not', giving it a persuasive religious meaning (although it would also suit a claim to poetic immortality), but he does not mention that the motto was Marot's. Older French writers saw Dido as a clever ruler and chaste wife. Marot's father, Jehan, had called Anne of Brittary France's 'other Dido, a second Minerva' (J. Marot 1999: 145).

18. Marot (1964), 343–53; the notes give literary sources for Marot's (and thus Spenser's) conceit that a life is like the turning seasons, but the analogy was in any case familiar from one genre of illustrations (the other is the labors of the months) that any literate reader would have found in printed books of hours.

19. Preisig (2004), 133–5, who adds an appendix on the once common Maro/Marot pun.

20. Reamer (1969) usefully sets *December* against Marot's text to show that only a minority of the lines corresponds. Reamer underestimates Marot's anguish and the particularity of his admittedly idealized autobiography when he says that Robin is 'traditional' and Colin is 'individual' (n. 17). Marot's praise of François may be 'sycophantic' but as Spenser must have known the poet's sycophancy covers a daring plea for help against real enemies in a time of gathering clouds. Marot's eclogue is more than a plea for money.

21. On the relevance to Spenser of Marot's religion see Patterson (1986). On the surprising lack of sympathy in English comments, however, see Prescott (1978, 1991).

22. Scollen-Jimack (1989) reprints the title page; John Skelton, too, became a jestbook protagonist as taste changed and broad self-mockery gave way to a drier irony.

23. Mystifyingly, the entry for 'Anacreon' in *SE* omits to mention that two of the four 'Anacreontics' closely follow Marot.

24. Marot (2007), 448; a note mentions the fashion for poems on exchanged weaponry.

25. Marot (2007), 466; the editor notes Marot's wordplay with 'amere' and 'mere', typical of the 'grand rhétoriqueur' style of an older generation.

26. Adams (1954); Rémy Belleau did an edition in 1560 of the second book of *Amours*, likewise with commentary and attractively varied fonts.

27. On these parallels see Prescott (1978) and notes citing previous scholarship.

28. For more parallels see Prescott (2000b).

29. News of French 'academies' and Ronsard's connections to them could have come to Spenser by way of Sidney, perhaps, or from his acquaintance Daniel Rogers, whose Latin verses tell of hearing Ronsard recite his verse. See Prescott (1978) for some references.

30. The famous last line of Elegie XXIV (Ronsard 1994: II, 408). For Earth as the courtesan Lais see the second 'day' (l. 227) of Du Bartas's *Premiere Sepmaine* in Sylvester (1979).

31. Batman (or Bateman) had connections with the Sidneys. The illustrations of a mounted knight guided by Reason strikingly suggest Guyon and his Palmer. Batman, though, uses a Spanish translation of the French original.

32. Prescott (1985) and Marguerite (2001), 96–100 (the French poem Christianizes a cheerfully indecent poem that plays on venison and 'venir'—'to come'). Marguerite's Easter (or more precisely Good Friday) poem is spoken by a dying pelican, Christ the crucified bridegroom. Could a translation of this possibly be the lost 'Dying Pelican' to which the printer Ponsonby alludes in his preface to *Complaints*? Marguerite was widely known in England both as a writer and as an important figure at the court of François Ier.

33. On Spenser and Le Fèvre's Ficino (but not Contemplation's hill), see Ellrodt (1960); on the Hill see Prescott (2009).

BIBLIOGRAPHY

Adams, M. (1954). 'Ronsard and Spenser: The Commentary'. *Renaissance Papers* 24–9.

Ahmed, E. (2005). *Clément Marot: The Mirror of the Prince.* Charlottesville, J VA: Rookwood Press.

Bamforth, S. (1997). 'Clément Marot, François Ier et les Muses', in *Clément Marot: 'Prince des poëtes françois' 1496–1596: Actes du Colloque international de Cahors en Quercy 21–25 Mai 1996.* Paris: Champion, 225–35.

Brown, R. D. (1999). *'The New Poet': Novelty and Tradition in Spenser's 'Complaints'.* Liverpool: Liverpool University Press.

Coldiron, A. E. B. (2002). 'How Spenser Excavates Du Bellay's *Antiquitez*: or, The Role of the Poet, Lyric Historiography, and the English Sonnet'. *JEGP* 101(1): 41–67.

Du Bellay, J. (1994). *'Antiquitez de Rome' translated by Edmund Spenser as 'Ruines of Rome',* ed. M. C. Smith. Binghamton, NY: Medieval and Renaissance Texts and Studies.

—— (2006). *The Regrets,* with *The Antiquities of Rome, Three Latin Elegies,* and *The Defense and Enrichment of the French Language.* A Bilingual Edition, ed. and trans. R. Helgerson. Philadelphia: University of Pennsylvania Press.

Ellrodt, R. (1960). *Neoplatonism in the Poetry of Spenser.* Geneva: Droz.

Ferguson, M. (1984). '"The Afflatus of Ruin": Meditations on Rome by Du Bellay, Spenser, and Stevens', in A. Patterson (ed.), *Roman Images: Selected Papers from the English Institute.* Baltimore, MD: Johns Hopkins University Press.

Helfer, R. (2007). 'Remembering Sidney, Remembering Spenser: The Art of Memory and *The Ruines of Time'. SSt* 22: 127–51.

Johnson, L. S. (1981). 'Elizabeth, Bride and Queen: A Study of Spenser's April Eclogue and the Metaphors of English Protestantism'. *SSt* 2: 75–91.

Marguerite de Navarre (2001). *Chansons spirituelles,* in *Œuvres Complètes* IX, ed. M. Clément. Paris: Champion.

Marot, Clément (1964). *Œuvres Lyriques,* ed. C. A. Mayer. London: Athlone Press.

—— (1995). *Cinquante pseaumes de David mis en françoys selon la vérité hébraïque,* ed. G. Defaux. Paris: Champion.

—— (2007). *Œuvres Complètes* I, ed. F. Rigolot. Paris: Flammarion.

Marot, Jehan (1999). *Les Deux Recueils,* ed. G. Defaux and T. Mantovani. Geneva: Droz.

Melehy, H. (2003). 'Spenser and Du Bellay: Translation, Imitation, Ruin'. *CLS* 40(4): 415–38.

Miller, D. L. (1996). 'The Earl of Cork's Lute', in J. Anderson, D. Cheney, and D. A. Richardson (eds), *Spenser's Live and the Subject of Biography.* Amherst, MA: University of Massachusetts Press, 146–71.

Nohrnberg, J. (2007). 'Alençon's Dream/Dido's Tomb'. *SSt* 22: 73–102.

Patterson, A. (1986). 'Re-Opening the Green Cabinet: Clément Marot and Edmund Spenser'. *ELR* 16(1): 44–70.

Prescott, A. L. (1978). *French Poets and the English Renaissance: Studies in Fame and Transformation.* New Haven, CT: Yale University Press.

—— (1986). 'The Thirsty Deer and the Lord of Life: Some Contexts for *Amoretti* 67–70'. *SSt* 6: 33–76.

—— (1989). 'From *The Travayled Pilgrime* to The Redcrosse Knight: Spenser's Chivalric Restorations'. *SP* 86: 166–97.

—— (1991). 'Musical Strains: Marot's Double Role as Psalmist and Courtier', in M. R. Logan and P. L. Rudnytsky (eds), *Contending Kingdoms: Historical, Psychological and Feminist Approaches to the Literature of Sixteenth-Century England and France.* Detroit, MI: Wayne State University Press, 42–68.

Prescott, A. L. (1996). 'Spenser (Re)Reading Du Bellay: Chronology and Literary Response', in J. Anderson, D. Cheney, and D. Richardson (eds), *Spenser's Life and the Subject of Biography*. Amherst, MA: University of Massachusetts Press, 131–45.

—— (2000a). 'Foreign Policy in Fairyland: Henri IV and Spenser's Burbon'. *SSt* 14: 189–214.

—— (2000b). 'The Laurel and the Myrtle: Spenser and Ronsard', in P. Cheney and L. Silberman (eds), *Worldmaking Spenser*. Lexington, KY: University Press of Kentucky, 63–78.

—— (2006). 'Sources', in Bart van Es (ed.), *A Critical Companion to Spenser Studies*. Houndmills, Basingstoke, Hampshire: Palgrave Macmillan, 98–115.

—— (2009), 'Hills of Contemplation and Signifying Circles: Spenser and Guy Le Fèvre de la Boderie'. *SSt* 24: 155–83.

Preisig, F. (2004). *Clément Marot et les métamorphoses de l'auteur à l'aube de la Renaissance*. Geneva: Droz.

Reamer, O. J. (1969). 'Spenser's Debt to Marot—Re-examined'. *Literature and Language* 10(4): 504–27.

Ronsard, P. de (1993). *Œuvres Complètes*, ed. J. Céard, D. Ménager, and M. Simonin, 2 vols. Paris: Gallimard.

Scollen-Jimack, C. (1989). 'Clément Marot: Protestant Humanist or Court Jester?' *RS* 3(2): 134–46.

Stapleton, M. L. (1990). 'Spenser, the *Antiquitez de Rome*, and the Development of the English Sonnet Form'. *CLS* 27: 259–74.

Sylvester, J. (trans.) (1979). Guillaume de Saluste, Sieur du Bartas, *The Divine Weeks and Works*, ed. Susan Snyder, 2 vols. Oxford: Clarendon Press.

PART V

RECEPTION

CHAPTER 35

....

SPENSER'S TEXTUAL HISTORY

....

JOSEPH LOEWENSTEIN

CALENDER, CALENDARIUM, AND CANON: ATTRIBUTION AND EDITING
....

IN *Ida* Vale (who knowes not *Ida* Vale?)
When harmelesse *Troy* yet felt not *Graecian* spite:
A hundred Shepheards woon'd
> (*Brittain's Ida*)

Odd as it may perhaps seem, H. J. Todd's variorum edition of *The works of Edmund Spenser... with the principal illustrations of various commentators* (1805), includes a list of professed imitations of Spenser, of which there had been many in the previous two centuries. Textual criticism, commentary, and imitation had been inextricably combined since, say, Thomas Warton, whose *Observations on the Faerie Queene* of 1754 locates Spenser in his classical and Italian and native literary traditions, meticulously identifies his irregularities and solecisms, points out the oddities of his syntax and the inconsistencies in his allegory, and everywhere displays that fervent enthusiasm for the poet which distinguished the mid-eighteenth century, probably the moment of greatest literary engagement with Spenser, and almost certainly the moment at which imitations are most abundant. Warton had written several such imitations, thus instancing—as do John Upton, Gilbert West, and so many others—the steady traffic between imitation and criticism that characterizes Spenserian literary culture at mid-century. But imitation solicits not only criticism but also edition: Upton had offered a *New Canto of the Fairy Queen* with commentary in 1747, eleven years before publishing his great edition of Spenser's epic. Todd's list of imitations, and particularly Upton's *New Canto*, reminds us how blurred the edges of the Spenser canon have been since its blurred inception.

One must use the possessive advisedly to say that 'Spenser's' first publication is a set of translations published in Jan Van der Noot's *Theatre for Voluptuous Worldlings*. The prose portion of the *Theatre*, a polemical commentary on those poems, is itself a translation from the Dutch and, while Van der Noot attributes the poems to Petrarch and Du Bellay, he himself claims to 'haue out of the Brabants speache, turned them into the Englishe tongue' (F3-F3v), whereas in fact 'he' had translated from the French in which Du Bellay had written his sequence, and from the French into which Marot had translated Petrarch's 'Canzone of Visions'.[1] Todd is the first of Spenser's editors to reclaim Petrarch's, Du Bellay's, and Van der Noot's poems as Spenser's.

Of course, the tangle of Early Modern attributive gestures, and the fact that Spenser's name is unmentioned in the *Theatre*, were quite banal in 1569. And while it is one of an editor's first duties to firm up what counts as Spenser's (or Virgil's, or Shakespeare's), the editorial usage of 'Spenser's' remained imprecise. Like the *Theatre*, 'Spenser's' next published work is also a collection of poems accompanied by illustrations and learned commentary, although in this instance the poems are attributed, not to Van der Noot, but to 'Immeritô', yet even this attributive gesture is confounded by the title page, by which the book is signed over to someone else:

THE

Shepheardes Calender

Conteyning tvvelue Æglogues proportionable

to the twelue monethes.

Entitled

TO THE NOBLE AND VERTV

ous Gentleman most worthy of all titles

both of learning and cheualrie M.

Philip Sidney.

The commentary by E. K.; the woodcut illustrations anonymously produced (the woodcuts passing from printer to printer in successive editions of the *Calender*); the book, Immeritô's, but deeded over to Philip Sidney; and all of it, in a different sense, Spenser's—and all of it therefore printed in 1611 as part of an omnibus folio volume, not a Complete Works, but plainly aspiring to be so:

THE

FAERIE QVEEN:

THE

Shepheards Calendar:

Together

WITH THE OTHER

Works of England's Arch-Poët,

EDM. SPENCER:

¶ *Collected into one Volume, and*

carefully corrected.

'Arch-poet' might seem to individuate, to consolidate the stiffening attributive habits of the 1590s, which saw the publication of the work of Ed. Sp. (*Daphnaida* and *Complaints*, 1591), Edw. Spenser, (*Axiochus*, 1592), Ed. Spencer (*Colin Clouts Come Home Againe*, 1595), Edmunde Spenser (*Amoretti and Epithalamion*, 1595), and Edm. Spenser (*Fowre Hymnes* and *Prothalamion*, 1596). But however much the *Works of England's Arch-Poët* may build on this attributive drift, it must also make room for Immeritô, for the title page of Matthew Lownes's 1611 folio *Calender* keeps Spenser in reserve and again entitles the eclogues to Sidney.[2] One might regard this as a matter of mere editorial inertia: each of the editions of the *Calender* since 1581 seems to have been set directly from its predecessor. (Indeed, the folio *Calender* shares the distinguishing defect of its predecessor of 1596, the absence of one stanza at lines 89–96 of *June*.) But it would be more accurate to speak of this folio as preserving, within a burgeoning authorial literary culture, Spenser's persistent self-representation as a member of bibliographical collectives.

Collaboration sustains and unsettles the Spenser 'canon': after the *Theatre* and the *Calender* comes the *Three proper, and wittie, familiar letters: lately passed betvveene two universitie men* (and the *Two Other, very commendable Letters, of the same mens writing*)—the Spenser–Harvey correspondence published anonymously in 1581. And it is not merely a matter of juvenilia: in 1595, *Colin Clouts Come Home Againe* again gives us a Spenser whose poetical character, whose hand and voice, is distinctively indistinct, at least in the second half of the volume. There the pastoral singer of *Astrophel* solicits anthology, first 'rehearsing' the *Dolefull Lay of Clorinda* and then,

> When she ended had, another swaine
> Of gentle wit and daintie sweet device:
>
> .   .   .   .
>
> Hight *Thestylis*, began his mournfull tourne,
> And made the *Muses* in his song to mourne

Mary Sidney may have written Clorinda's lay and Lodowick Bryskett may well have written Thestylis's complaint—some editors have thought so, though some attribute them to Spenser—and most ascribe the ensuing *Pastorall Æglogue* to Bryskett (since the first edition prints 'L. B.' beneath the eclogue). The conclusion of the *Dolefull Lay of Clorinda* is somewhat more non-committal, announcing only an anonymous suite of mourners—'And after him full many other moe'—who will follow Thestylis, with the *Pastorall Æglogue, An Elegie, or Friends Passion, An Epitaph vpon the right Honourable sir Phillip Sidney,* and *An other of the same.* Once editors made 'Spenser' the organizing principle of their labors, they have had to confront the difficulty of individuating this representation of communal mourning. The title page of the 1611 folio certainly seems to sponsor such arch-poetic individuation, and Lownes had already performed an important act of specifically Spenserian recovery, having published, in 1609, the first edition of *The Faerie Queene* to include the *Two Cantos of Mutabilitie*. Yet however important the attributive drift between 1579 and 1611 might be, it hardly issued in seismic transformation: Lownes includes both of the Sidneian agglomerations, the *Calender* and *Colin Clouts Come Home Againe*, in the 1611 folio, so that Edm. Spencer's umbrella extends to cover the affiliations and solidarities that had been so important to the work of Immeritô.

Not everything could squeeze under this umbrella. Excepting prefatory epistles and the commentary of E. K., the folio collects only verse. The pseudo-Platonic dialogue, *Axiochus*, 'translated out of Greeke, by that worthy Scholler and Poet, Maister *Edward Spenser*' was excluded, as was other less explicitly attributed prose—the anonymous Spenser–Harvey correspondence and *A Vewe of the Present State of Ireland*, not yet printed and attributed in the early manuscripts, when attributed at all, only to an 'E.S.' The verse satire, *Mother Hubberd's Tale*, was also excluded: perhaps Lownes—or someone connected with the edition—wished to avoid offending Robert Cecil whose father seems to have been one of Spenser's objects of satire. Indeed, Lownes—or someone connected with the edition—went so far as to touch up *The Ruines of Time*, rendering blandly impersonal several lines (447–54) that, when first printed in 1591, might have been thought to point quite sharply at William Cecil. The wariness over the Cecils seems to have lifted with Sir Robert's death in May of 1612, after which Lownes reissued *Mother Hubberd's Tale*. But except for the scruple over this work and the omissions of the Spenser–Harvey correspondence and of any portion of Van der Noot's *Theatre*, the 1611 folio was inclusive and generously undiscriminating, gathering up the *Calender* and all the Spenserian volumes of the 1590s. It recovers fifteen of the seventeen dedicatory sonnets that had appeared in the final pages of the *First Part of the Faerie Queene*, but that had dropped out of the 1596 and 1609 editions of the poem. Its *Shepheardes Calender* preserves the composite character of its ancestral quartos, retaining the woodcuts, the editorial contribution of E. K., the collected poems of Immeritô, and, as has already been observed, even the title page entitling the *Calender* to Sidney. This folio *Calender* was reprinted in 1617, but this second folio version is perhaps the last edition to capture the sense of the *Calender* as a complex coherence, an art book produced by a consortium under Sidneian sponsorship.

Subsequent editors reshaped it: in 1653, for example, the *Calender* is printed without its woodcuts and E. K.'s monthly glosses have been combined, simplified, and shifted to the final pages of the volume—which is to say that Sidney's and Immeritô's book has been substantially Spenserianized. Yet the newly Spenserian *Calender* retained its capacity to bind other works to it. This same edition of 1653 is actually two editions in one, with one title page faced by a second:

The
SHEPHERDS
Calendar,
CONTAINING
TWELVE ÆGLOGUES
Proportionable to the
TWELVE MONTHS.
BY
EDMUND SPENSER
Prince of English POETS.

CALENDARIUM
Pastorale,
SIVE
ÆGLOGÆ DUODECIM,
TOTIDEM
Anni Mensibus accommodatæ
Anglicè olim Scriptæ
AB
EDMUNDO SPENSERO
Nunc autem
Eleganti Latino carmine donatæ
A
THEODORO BATHURST

This format—English to the left and Latin translation on facing page—persists across the volume. The *Calender* may have shed its illustrations and much of its original editorial apparatus, but Bathurst's Latin translation of the *Calender* would adhere to Spenser's pastoral sequence for centuries: the next folio edition of Spenser's *Works* will print Bathurst's Latin and the 1653 glossary on its last pages.

The title of Jonathan Edwin's 1679 folio, *The works of that famous English poet, Mr. Edmond Spenser... Whereunto is added An Account of his Life; With other new Additions Never before in Print*, announces it as a work of augmentation. Yet if it absorbs the *Calender/Calendarium* of 1653, along with its glossary, it constitutes the *Calendarium* and glossary as a mere appendix; indeed, in many copies, it is separated from the bulk of the volume, by a page advertising Edwin's other offerings.[3] But other 'new Additions' (all of which, despite the claims of the title page, had appeared before in print) are more fully absorbed, taken up into the folio before this bibliographical membrane. Edwin reprints substantial selections from the Spenser–Harvey correspondence, and he supplements the poetic canon of the previous folio with *Britains Ida*, an erotic poem '*Written by that Renowned Poët, Edmond Spencer*', according to the title page of the first edition, of 1628.

It's worth considering at this juncture why Spenser's canon was so frequently animated by the spirit of the additional. Completeness is a scholarly virtue and addition an economic one, at least insofar as one can charge more for the more lavishly additional forms of completeness. But addition was also prompted by the open-endedness of Spenser's canon, and especially by the manifest inconclusiveness of *The Faerie Queene*, for which the posthumously published *Two Cantos of Mutabilitie* was the glaring sign. And that bright inconclusion, refashioned as puzzled and yearning in the final stanzas of the *Two Cantos of Mutabilitie*, had been further illuminated in 1633 with yet another posthumous publication, *A Vewe of the State of Ireland*, which James Ware adjoined to *Two histories of Ireland. The one written by Edmund Campion, the other by Meredith Hanmer*. In his preface to the *Vewe*, Ware reported that although Spenser 'finished the later part of that excellent poem of his

Faery Queene' in Cork, that 'later part' 'was soone after unfortunately lost by the disorder and abuse of his servant, whom he had sent before him into England'. Whether or not Ware's account was accurate, it joined with the *Two Cantos of Mutabilitie* to evoke a powerful sense of the deficiency of the Spenser canon.

That sense of deficiency is perhaps answered by posthumous supplementation of Spenser's canon, of which *Two Cantos of Mutabilitie*, *Brittain's Ida*, and the *Vewe* are the most important instances: 'it must be a Worke of Spencers, of whom it were pitty that any thing should bee lost,' writes Walkley (with commercial disingenuousness) of *Brittain's Ida*. Hughes registered doubts about the Spenserian pedigree of *Britains Ida* as early as 1715; Warton suggested its resemblance in theme and manner to that of Phineas Fletcher's *The Purple Isle* in 1762; and by 1926, the accumulated work of Grosart, Boas, and Seaton had finally effected the reassignment of *Brittain's Ida* to Fletcher.[4] Other decanonizations have also been undertaken: in his Boston edition of Spenser's *Works* (1855), Francis Child betrayed doubts concerning Spenser's authorship of the *Ruins of Rome*; four years later, Gilfillan and Clarke removed the translations from their edition. Jean Brink (1990: 203–28) has recently assayed the decanonization of the *Vewe*, alleging that Ware is the first to make the attribution (as Walkley was the first to attribute *Brittain's Ida* to Spenser), whereas the previous manuscripts identify the author only as an 'E.S.'.[5] Modern Spenserians have countered Brink with a fervor the remarkable intensity of which may partly derive from the nagging sense that Spenser's canon remains constitutively in need. That need has been variously answered—first, in 1609 and 1611, by *Two Cantos of Mutabilitie* and the *Calender* (fully attributed for the first time in 1611, if never in doubt); by the *Vewe* in 1633, by Bathurst's *Calendarium* in 1653, and, in 1679, by the selections from the Spenser–Harvey correspondence that were 'added' to Edwin's folio. Just as the open incompletion of *The Canterbury Tales* had rendered Chaucer especially available as author of the sharply critical *Plowman's Tale*, so the inconclusiveness of *The Faerie Queene* assists in giving dissident authority, however facetiously, to a work of 1648, *The Faerie Leveller: or, King Charles his Leveller descried and deciphered in Queene Elizabeths dayes. By her Poet Laureat* Edmond Spenser, *in his unparaleld Poeme, entituled, The Faerie Queene.*

Beginning with Hughes's six-volume illustrated edition of 1715, editors make increasingly explicit efforts to distinguish Spenser's hand from those of his associates and imitators. Hughes broaches the practice: he prints *Brittain's Ida*, though he expresses his reservations about Spenser's authorship; he reproduces *Colin Clouts Come Home Againe* in its entirety, but ascribes the last four elegies to others; and, in a gesture of resolute exclusion, he banishes E. K.'s commentary from his edition of the *Calender*, substituting for it 'A GLOSSARY Explaining the Old and Obscure Words'. When we speak of Hughes as having inaugurated the modern editorial tradition, we refer at least partly to this, his nervous winnowing of the canon. But this sorting of Spenser from non-Spenser, of Immeritô from E. K., finds its proper context in a burgeoning culture of Spenserianizing, the origins of which may be traced back through *Spencer Redivivus*, a paraphrase of Book I in (fairly energetic) heroic couplets from 1687; through *The Faerie Leveller* and the distinctively adapted Spenserian voice of Milton's 1645 *Poems*; and, earlier, to the imitations of Giles and Phineas Fletcher and the other Spenserian poets of whom Michelle O'Callaghan (2000) has written with such penetration (see Chapter 36 below).

HUGHES, CHURCH, AND THE FORMATION OF EDITORIAL PRINCIPLE

The textual situation at the uncontested center of the Spenser canon is relatively uncomplicated. We have a great number of secretarial letters in Spenser's hand, yet although manuscript copies of his work did circulate during his lifetime, no literary autographs survive. Several versions of the eighth sonnet of the *Amoretti* survive in manuscripts written before the printing of that work, and a handwritten copy of the first sonnet of the *Amoretti* may also precede its print publication (Cummings 1964: 125–35; Gollancz 1907–8: 99–105).[6] Spenser is a *printed* poet: we have remarkably few manuscript witnesses of his poems and there is no reason to believe that the trivial adjustments between first and subsequent early editions are based on recourse to contemporary manuscript authority.

By Hughes's day, the *Calender* had been printed many times, but (barring new discoveries by Patrick Cheney, who is collating the early editions) each of the early editions seems to have been set from the prior one.[7] *Daphnaïda*, first printed in 1591, was reprinted almost mechanically in 1596 as an adjunct to *Fowre Hymnes* (see Chapter 16 above), and this second edition appears to have served as copy text for the folio version of 1611. *Complaints* (which includes revisions of most of the poems in Noot's *Theatre*, revisions so substantial as arguably to constitute complex imitations of the earlier poems), *Amoretti and Epithalamion, Colin Clouts Come Home Againe, Fowre Hymnes*, and *Prothalamion* were all printed only once in Spenser's lifetime and received (albeit not rigorously challenged) opinion has it that Spenser had arranged to be in London and had attended personally to at least some stages of the printing of each of all these texts save *Complaints*. With the exception of the *Two Cantos of Mutabilitie*, the folio editions of the 1610s (and the undated copy of *Mother Hubberd's Tale* probably printed in 1627 or 1628) were all set from printed copy. As F. R. Johnson demonstrated (1933: 33–48), most copies of those folios come down to us as composites, with some parts of the copies printed early in the decade and other parts printed later.

The situation of *The Faerie Queene* is somewhat more complicated, and we are fortunate to be able to consult the meticulous analyses of Johnson, of Hiroshi Yamashita, Masatsugu Matsuo, Toshiyuki Suzuki, and Haruo Sato (1993), and, more recently, of Andrew Zurcher (2004–5: 115–50). The first installment of *The Faerie Queene* was printed in 1590 and Yamashita and his collaborators distinguish three compositors setting the text, each of whose work is distinguished by differentiated habits of departure from and submission to Spenser's orthography—or at least to those spelling habits manifest in the surviving non-literary autograph manuscripts (Smith 1958). The very fact that it is possible to distinguish compositors on the basis of such variation reminds us that we assess the 'secret wit' of Spenserian orthography from at least one remove.[8] The Yamashita team did not attempt to characterize the manuscript copy from which the compositors worked. It may have been autograph or it may have been a scribal copy and, if the latter, we are placed at yet a second remove from the secrets of authorial wit. Zurcher describes Spenser's involvement in the printing of the work, an involvement that may occasionally have restored some textual features that had been lost during copying and the setting of type, but even this involvement was not deep or systematic enough to give us 'an author's printed book'. Although some pains were taken with the printing, albeit late in the production process, the back matter of the book includes a list of 110 'Faults Escaped in the Print', and this compilation is by no means exhaustive.[9] The second edition (1596) of this part of The Faerie Queene includes a stanza (I.xi.3) not found in the first edition; internal evidence suggests, albeit not conclusively, that the stanza was mistakenly omitted in the first edition, not composed for insertion in the second.

The second edition of this part of the poem is more strikingly distinguished from the first by the removal of the dedicatory sonnets, by changes to the wording of the dedication to Queen Elizabeth and, above all, by the new ending that Spenser composed for Book III, deferring the reunion of Amoret and Scudamour. On the evidence of the distribution of currently surviving copies, we may surmise that a great many copies of the first edition were still unsold by 1596 and that these continued to be sold unaltered, although now paired—awkwardly, with respect to the narrative continuity of the poem—with the new Second Part of the Faerie Queene (Johnson 1933: 19; Spenser 2001: 21–2). The two editions differ in innumerable subtler ways, although few of the differences are securely traceable to authorial intervention. Although 1596 takes over most of the punctuation of 1590, it substantially augments it, offering a good deal more syntactic sorting than is offered by the 1590 pointing (which had devoted a higher proportion of its punctuation to marking rhythmic units).[10] The 1596 edition is hardly meticulous. Its version of The First Part was set page-for-page from 1590 and although it corrects scores of errors of punctuation in the first edition and dozens of other obvious errors, it repairs only a few more than half the errors noted on the 1590 errata sheet. Many defects in 1590—mispaginations, incomplete lines, imperfect rhymes, and narrative confusions—carry over without adjustment; the extent of these flaws led Evans (1965) to suspect that, in this case, Spenser did not come to London to supervise the printing.[11]

As noted above, the Two Cantos of Mutabilitie were not printed until 1609, when they were appended to a reprint of the 1596 edition of the first six books of The Faerie Queene. The compositors of this edition somewhat tamed the irregularities of fairyland by adding stanza numbers; they also freely adjusted the spelling and punctuation of their copy text, yielding a text more thoroughly oriented to syntactic punctuation, more 'modern' in its orthography and capitalization, and in which the low-level textual features of the two parts of the poem are more homogeneous. The edition introduces some substantive variants as well, although whether they derive from Spenser's own corrections to the prior editions or from others' editorial will is impossible to assess. Manifest errors in 1596 are often corrected without recourse to superior readings in 1590, which suggests either that whoever was responsible for such corrections was unaware of the differences between the 1590 and 1596 texts or that copies of 1590 were unavailable.

It may be worth stopping at this juncture to assess the evidence of Spenser's investment in print culture, to characterize his bibliographic ego, but the evidence suggests the unemphatic nature of those investments. Ushered into print as a translator, he fashions for himself a print persona of comic reserve, the pseudony-mous and self-deprecating Immeritô, a persona that he and Harvey somewhat comically reconstitute as the 'Signior Immeritô' of their serious, learned, and some-times flamboyantly mannered correspondence (see Chapter 25 above). The poems of Immeritô are reprinted with some frequency, but the reprintings do not involve expansions, refashionings, or textual improvements: Spenser is apparently content to let Harrison do with Immeritô as he wishes. He writes an epic for print and, when enough of it is ready to make up a printed book, tends to its publication, turning the book over to a publisher well-known to his patrons and their literary circle, fussing over its dedicatory poems, and attending, but irregularly and irresolutely, to the quality of its text. His work coheres, but not necessarily along an axis of print: when *The Faerie Queene* recurs to Spenser's earlier work—and it does so with great ceremony—the persona it revives is not Immeritô, a maker of books, but Colin Clout, an Orphic singer of songs. After the *Calender* and the first installment of *The Faerie Queene*, what other verse we have by Spenser comes down to us in printed books, but there is no evidence that Spenser paid close attention to their format or to the fidelity of their texts to the copy transmitted to the printers. These books have something to say about unfaithful transmission, about false and falsified writing, but other infidelities—false report, distraction, and other errors of the will—outweigh the errantry of the letter. We are speaking, then, of a bibliographic ego less highly developed than those of, say, Jonson or Wither or, arguably, Gascoigne or Donne. Spenser is *in* print, *by means of* print, but not remarkably *for* or *of* it.

To return to his textual history, in print or manuscript, and to that of the less securely attributed texts, all but the *Vewe* have straightforward stemmas and, by the time Hughes undertook his edition, a relatively uncomplicated publication history. Before Hughes, the *Theatre* had had only a single edition, and few of its formes had been altered during printing. The Spenser–Harvey correspondence, also lightly adjusted during its first printing, had not been reprinted in its entirety, though Edwin had presented four of the five letters in the opening pages of the 1679 folio in sharply abridged versions that mute some of the letters' pretentious waggishness. Edwin had reprinted *Brittain's Ida* from the 1628 edition, modernizing its spelling, but preserving its pointing and more than a few obvious misprints; he had reprinted Ware's edition of *A Vewe of the Present State of Ireland* with very few adjustments.

But the stemma of the *Vewe* is remarkably complex, for, besides Ware's edition, twenty-two early manuscript witnesses of the text also survive. (Rudolf Gottfried's extraordinary achievement in working out the relationship among the manuscripts is marred by the fact that five of the extant copies only came to light after he prepared the textual analysis for his edition of the *Vewe* for the Hopkins *Variorum*; see *Prose*, 506–24.) Lownes apparently intended to print the *Vewe* in the form it takes in one of the surviving manuscripts, Bodleian MS Rawlinson B. 478, for he registered it for publication in 1598, but Lownes's undertaking never reached fruition; Ray Heffner has argued (1942: 507–15) that a later manuscript, Bodleian MS Gough Ireland 2, was also prepared with an eye to print publication. Ware claims to have based his text on a now-lost manuscript belonging to Archbishop James Ussher that seems to have been closely related to Gough. But Ware was a busy editor: he had more than one manuscript at his disposal and he drew on at least two of them for his edition. Compared to that of the other witnesses his text is an outlier, altering place names and supplying details absent in other copies: the variations are less likely to be traceable to his copy text than to his own editorial effort. Moreover, Gottfried noted that Ware's text is less aggressive toward the Old English than are the other witnesses at a variety of junctures, and it seems likely that Ware is responsible for this softening. Spot-checking suggests that Edwin transmitted Ware's version of the *Vewe* with only the most trivial adjustments in punctuation; Ware's text remained the canonical version of the *Vewe* until 1869, when Richard Morris published a considerably more anti-Irish text based on British Library Additional MS 22022, a copy probably made in the first decade of the seventeenth century. For his variorum edition of 1805, Todd consulted five of the surviving manuscripts, and he shows himself to have been aware of the existence of still others, but he remains loyal to Ware as a base text.

This sort of comparative evaluation of differing witnesses, however casual, had begun almost a century earlier, with Hughes's edition of 1715. Published by subscription and quickly reprinted in a trade edition, Hughes's edition was advertised as offering a text 'fully corrected' by a collation of the early witnesses. In fact, he relies almost entirely on the folio recensions—he consults several, including Edwin's edition of 1679—although he does not ignore the sixteenth-century texts, for he apparently draws on one of the first three quartos of the *Calender* to correct readings in the folio that provided his base text. He makes a great stir over having included the text of the original conclusion to Book III of *The Faerie Queene*, yet he based his text of the rest of *The First Part*, not on the Elizabethan quartos, but on the 1609 Folio, and his *Second Part* seems to follow the folio of 1612–13.

Hughes's Spenser was received with considerable censure. Dr. Johnson (1905: II, 162) had little use for the edition and was dismissive, perhaps not surprisingly, of Hughes's lexicographic skills. John Jortin's *Remarks on Spenser's Poems*, published anonymously in 1734, includes stringent aspersions on Hughes's edition, which Jortin compares to the 1679 folio to Hughes's disadvantage. He seems to have contemplated doing his own edition, but, suffering some failure of resolve, he offers the *Remarks* as a 'rough draught of a Commentary'. Jortin seems to have been especially impressed, and daunted, by the collational zeal of such editors of Shakespeare as Theobald, whose edition had appeared in 1733, and this provides a standard against which not only Hughes's, but his own imagined efforts, are found wanting: 'much more might be done, particularly towards settling the text, by a careful collation of Editions, and by comparing the Author with himself; but that required more time and application than I was willing to bestow, and more copies than I had by me' (1734: 168–9).[12]

Although early eighteenth-century literary culture was steeped in Spenser, no editor of any scholarly ambition stepped forward to polish Jortin's 'rough draught'. In the years following Jortin's *Remarks* Spenser was anthologized—in Cooper's *Historical and Poetic Medley* (1738) and Thomas Hayward's *The British Muse* (1738)—and excerpted—quite heavily in Dodsley's *Preceptor* of 1748; extract and selection, imitation and parody maintain Spenser's literary presence until the middle of the century, when Tonson finally reissued Hughes's *Works*. Hastily prepared, this second Hughes was distinguished, possibly in belated response to Jortin's call for more careful collation, by adjustments that bring the text of *The First Part of the Faerie Queene* closer to the 1590 quarto—and appreciably closer at the conclusion of *The First Part*, where the revised ending of 1596 was simply dropped without comment.[13] But even as the revised Hughes moved through the press, Upton was rousing himself to replace it, or at least its *Faerie Queene*.[14] As has already been observed, Upton had published his own imitation of *The Faerie Queene* in 1747 and had gone on to publish an edition of three plays of Ben Jonson in 1749. Two years later, he issued a 39-page *Letter Concerning a New Edition of Spenser's Faerie Queene*.[15] Intensifying the tradition of disdain for Hughes's scholarship and judgment, the *Letter* contains some brilliant analytic achievements, a few of them springing from comparison of the seventeenth-century folios with the sixteenth-century quartos on which they were based.

Upton's *Letter* and the revised Hughes are not the only signs of mid-century editorial interest. William Kent, Thomas Edwards, John Sympson, and Robert Thyer all mooted editions of *The Faerie Queene* around mid-century. Kent was the most serious of these, but when he died in 1748, it fell to Thomas Birch to complete his edition, with some help from Edwards. Birch concentrates his energies almost entirely on providing 'a just Representation of the genuine Text, not hitherto given in any single Edition', although he is quite aware that an interested reader might wish for something more: 'Nothing therefore now remains for the Honour of our Poet, and the Satisfaction of the Public, but that the Learned and Ingenious unite their Labours towards such a Commentary upon his admirable Poem, as Mr. JORTIN has oblig'd the World with a Specimen of in his *Remarks*' (1751: I, xxxvii). Birch's 1751 edition comprises three volumes, the first of which includes not only a biography, but also a detailed collation of the 1590 and 1596 versions of Part 1 of *The Faerie Queene* followed by a similar collation of the 1596 and 1609 versions of Part 2.

Birch's edition is distinguished not only by this unprecedented (if uneven) collational effort, but also by his decision to use 1590 as the base text for *The First Part of the Faerie Queene*, corrected in deference to the 1590 'Faults Escaped', a decision that most subsequent editors have followed. Birch thus initiates the withdrawal of allegiance from later, often more regular editions, a development that would unfold slowly: not until John Payne Collier's 1862 *Works* would an editor rely primarily on the first quarto of the *Calender* for his text; not until 1869 would Richard Morris declare himself, in the Globe edition, 'simply content to reprint the earliest known editions of Spenser's various poems, correcting here and there some few errors that have crept into them, by a careful collation with subsequent editions, most of which were published in the lifetime of the poet' (iii). Morris is Birch's heir, and more fastidious than his ancestor: despite Birch's collational ambitions, his text is both carelessly proofread and inconsistent, marred by such unsystematic selections from among variant readings and by such well-meaning 'improvements' to received diction and word order as characterize much eighteenth-century editorial labor. Although he attests to the accretion of errors and deplores the failure of earlier editors of *The Faerie Queene* to adopt the corrections of the 'Faults Escaped', he often adopts readings from the later folios (including Edwin's); if he usually accepts Jortin's textual arguments, he also accepts dubious conjectures derived from Hughes.

This flurry of activity in 1750–51 was answered and augmented in 1758. Tonson brought out yet another reprint, this time in octavo, the text of which shows Birch's influence, since it brings Hughes' text into even closer conformity to the 1590 quarto and picks up the corrections indicated in the 1590 'Faults Escaped'. But there were two new Spensers in that year, both annotated: Upton's two-volume *Faerie Queene* and Church's in 4 volumes. Both editions take cues from contemporary editions of Shakespeare, taking unprecedented pains to note variation among editions and to assess their origins. Upton's edition extends the collational efforts found in Birch's, for he collates two copies of both of the early quartos of *The Faerie Queene*, carefully recording such variants as could be uncovered by means of this rudimentary turn of attention to intra-editional variation. He offers rudimentary sketches of the origins of misreadings, imagining an illegible autograph copy text and proposing, in several instances, errors deriving from eye-skip. And he plainly means for his edition to be a watershed, reviewing and characterizing the texts of all previous editions, although as it turns out Church does a slightly better job of assessing the work of earlier editors. Although Upton dismisses the 1596 edition of *The First Part of the Faerie Queene* as careless, he adopts its readings freely in *The First Part*, as he does those of the folios throughout. (He is especially taken with the heavy marking of elision in the folio, and claims that the folio here preserves a feature of Spenser's text that the earlier editions failed to transmit.) Only lightly constrained in his selection from various readings, Upton also generally emends without compunction, changing readings that arguably make sense but that offend his sense of taste—as when he 'corrects' instances of identical rhyme. Upton's commentary on *The Faerie Queene* may be the most judicious and most comprehensive to be found in any edition prior to Hamilton's of 1977 (although Upton is somewhat neglectful of Spenser's debts to medieval romance); it is certainly the eighteenth century's most important critical work on Spenser. But the eclecticism of Upton's text makes it less estimable than his commentary.

Church's text is appreciably better, by modern standards, if only because it hews more closely to its copy-texts, 1590 for *The First Part of the Faerie Queene* and 1596 for the Second Part, albeit with occasional emendations, largely authorized by readings from one or another of the seventeenth-century folios. Moreover, Church's textual scholarship is also more impressively encompassing than Upton's. He is alert to the bibliographical challenge of the variant states of the final gatherings in the 1590 *Faerie Queene* and he offers a much more thorough review of prior editions than Upton's, substantially clarifying previous understandings of the history of the Lownes folios of the 1610s. Aware, no doubt, of the competition from Upton, whose pre-eminence as a commentator must have been obvious, Church stakes his edition's claim on the fastidiousness of its textual work: the record of variants he has accumulated appears as a running apparatus, as constant reminder to his reader of the scholarly *bona fides* of the edition. But perhaps his most important contribution to the editorial tradition is his resolute engagement with the problem of Spenser's orthography and pointing.

Hughes had been the first to drag the problem of spelling into the light. If his approach to copy text had been irresolute, pulled in one direction by a reliance on the folio texts, but veering in another in his recourse to Elizabethan readings in the *Calender* and by his decision to reprint the original conclusion of Book III, he betrays an even more divided mind in his handling of spelling and punctuation. He insists on the importance of preserving Spenser's spellings 'to keep the exact Sense, which wou'd sometimes be chang'd by the Variation of a Syllable or a Letter', yet he also notes 'that *Spenser* himself is irregular in this, and often writes the same Word differently, especially at the end of a line' and 'in this, the old Editions are not every where follow'd; but when the Sense is render'd obscure by such Alterations the Words are restor'd to their proper Orthography.' In other words, Hughes follows the 'original' orthography (of the early folios)—except when he doesn't. Modern smoothness generally wins out: he adjusts the use of *u* and *v* to conform to contemporary practice, he updates the punctuation, and he imposes much heavier capitalization.

Todd especially censures the ill-judged 'modern orthography' of Hughes's text in his variorum of 1805, expressing a textual conservatism that had been championed recently by such editors as Malone, who had, in 1790, entertained the value of publishing an 'unaltered' reprint of the Shakespeare First Folio. Eighteenth-century editors of Shakespeare had modernized their texts without compunction; but mid-eighteenth-century readers of Spenser, alerted by Warton to Spenser's medieval sources and to the 'gothic' complexity of his design, were sharply aware that the lexical difficulties of Spenser's texts were more than an accident of the passage of time. This awareness especially shapes Church's approach to Spenser's text. He preserves the rough and antique orthographic character of his copy, taking Hughes especially to task for modernizing the early editions. Yet although he criticizes the more systematic punctuation that was imported into the folio text and thence into subsequent editions, he himself intervenes busily in repunctuating his own text. Such repunctuation is one of the hallmarks of eighteenth-century editing, a quietly desperate attempt to mitigate the strange mixed motives of Early Modern pointing for an age in which systematic syntactic pointing was becoming a powerful norm. It has remained obligatory among many of Spenser's most conservative editors, of whom Morris (1869) and R. E. Neil Dodge (1908) are the most noteworthy.

PRODUCING SPENSER'S AUDIENCES

Upton died before producing his planned edition of the minor poems, the *Vewe*, and *Axiochus* ('not taken notice of by any Editor of any part of his works' [1758: ix], he observed, firm in his allegiance to additional completeness); that projected edition, paired with his *Faerie Queene*, might easily have supplanted Hughes's *Works*. Instead, Hughes's edition remained unrivaled and, despite the criticism that it had sustained and would continue to suffer, Hughes's *Works* went through almost a dozen editions in the second half of the eighteenth-century, its completeness complementing the mid-century surge of *Faerie Queene* editions and the sustained output of anthologies and imitations to which I've already referred.[16] Frushell links this groundswell in Spenser publication to the development of a minor movement for 'practical' educational reform, especially at dissenting academies (1999, especially Chapter 1); the proposed new curriculum was now to include English literature, in which the triumvirate of Shakespeare, Spenser, and Milton was to figure prominently. Extracts from these three provide the core for Dodsley's influential (and steadily reprinted and enlarged) *Preceptor: Containing a General Course of Education*, an anthology first published in two volumes in 1748. This dedication of Spenser to pedagogical use seeps into editorial practice with Upton's edition, for he not only glosses the unfamiliar words in Spenser's epic, but, by devising a glossary that can also serve as a concordance and index, renders *The Faerie Queene lexically* navigable. Upton's is a schoolmaster's edition.

Todd's, on the other hand, is an archivist's, his commentaries not so much composed as compiled. In the spirit of accumulation, Todd is the first editor since Edwin to include E. K.'s arguments and commentary on the *Calender*. He is inclusive *and* discriminating, printing *Brittain's Ida* (while excluding it from the canon), the *Dolefull Lay of Clorinda* (ascribed to Mary Herbert), the *Mourning Muse of Thestylis* and *A Pastorall Aeglogue* (Lodowick Bryskett), and *An Elegie or Friends Passion* (Matthew Roydon), although his discriminations are sometimes a bit capricious: *Axiochus* is not included; the Spenser–Harvey correspondence is only excerpted; and the poems of the *Theatre* are discussed but not printed. The sense of caprice is compounded by the mere fact of all the supplementary material for which Todd makes room: Hughes's essay on allegorical poetry; Spence's essay on Spenserian allegory; long selections from Warton, Upton, and Hurd, together with lists of prior editions, criticism, and imitations. That said, Todd does much to bring the density and texture of his commentary on the *Calender* up to the level to which Upton had brought *The Faerie Queene*, though he is less successful in his commentary on the other works. With a text even more conservative than that of its predecessors, and with its heap of commentary, Todd's edition initiates a process that would be substantially advanced three more times, with the Hopkins *Variorum* of 1932–47 and the Longman editions of 1977 and 2001, an archaizing and monumentalizing process that confirms Spenser's difficulty by the strenuousness of its efforts to mitigate that difficulty.

Todd's textual work is of mixed character. Dismissive of Hughes, he relies heavily on Church and Upton for *The Faerie Queene* (though he treats their critical commentary with considerable skepticism); he unwisely follows Upton in the latter's mistaken assessment of the early folios. His text of the *Calender* is eclectic: modern commentators have identified Q5 and F as Todd's base text, whereas he draws on several editions, though not at all from the first two quartos. It is slightly easier to ascertain Todd's base text for the other poems in the corpus, but no principle regulates his choice: his *Daphnaida* is based on one of the early folios, but he adopts some readings from the second quarto; *Colin Clouts Come Home Againe* is based on the quarto, with readings from one of the folios; he claims to have adopted the quarto as the copy text for *Fowre Hymnes* but departs from it frequently, drawing on the folio and on his own quickened emendational ingenuity.

Todd's unwieldy eight-volume edition was not always gratefully received. George Hillard, the editor of the first American edition of Spenser's works (1839), pronounced Todd's apparatus 'learned rubbish' and Wordsworth anticipated Hillard's assessment in a letter to Walter Scott (7 November, 1805): three parts of four of the 'Notes' are 'absolute trash'. Sadly for Todd, Scott was recruited to review the edition and he was also ungenerous, though he was more disappointed with Todd's omissions than with his lavish inclusions. Not surprisingly, Scott wanted the kind of rich commentary on topicalities that would bind Spenser's poems to their Elizabethan moment, and, in this respect, Todd compared unfavorably with Upton. Not reprinted until 1852, Todd's edition suffered even fiercer criticism from Collier. Collier correctly observed that, in whatever low esteem critics and editors had held Todd's notes, they had deferred to the authority of his text—this was certainly true of Child's Boston edition of 1855—and he demonstrated that, in at least a few instances, they had allowed Todd to mislead them.[17] But it is an index of how slowly systematic editorial principle coalesced that in his own edition of 1862, Collier is himself so deeply, and sometimes so incautiously, indebted to Todd.

Of course, Collier's bad faith is legendary: his claim to have compared all of Spenser's early texts through the Edwin folio of 1679 cannot be credited, but that lapse is hardly as egregious as his references to annotations by Drayton in a copy of a 1611 folio of Spenser's works, annotations that were among the first of Collier's forgeries.[18]

That Collier refers to these annotations without ceremony throughout his edition measures the utility of the forgery, the ease with which 'Drayton's copy' answered to relentless editorial need. 'Drayton's' notes not only give early-seventeenth-century warrant to emendations that Collier wished to make and illumine dark topical references that Collier has discerned, they also indulgently confirm that passages which Collier finds difficult were always felt to be so, that they are not the shameful sites of the failures of the editor's scholarship or imaginative sympathy. The fabrication indicates (and somewhat relieves) the nineteenth-century editor's shortness of intellectual breath: the sense that editing is inescapably capricious, that the scholarly audience was so ungenerous that extraordinary persuasions were necessary if one were to aspire to convince, and that Elizabethan culture, long an object of nostalgia, was now felt to be the locus of irreducible alienations. Like all competent forgers, Collier draws on an extraordinary fund of information, but the forgery itself betrays what Collier experiences as the inadequacy of that information.[19]

Although Todd curbed the taste for the densely annotated edition, Spenser's works were in no way neglected by the book trade. Hillard's *Works* had its fifth edition in 1857; by 1875 Child's was also on its fifth edition. Carpenter's *Reference Guide to Edmund Spenser* (1923) records two dozen nineteenth-century editions, a list that Radcliffe deems far from complete (1996: 111), but most of these editors were careful not to overwhelm their readers with learned commentary. Hillard's adopts a populist hostility to Todd's erudition and keeps his annotations to a minimum; Collier's annotations are light, learned, but engaging; Morris's much-reprinted Globe edition is without annotations—and sometimes without documentation of its unusually few emendations.

Only Child's and A. B. Grosart's editions (1855 and 1882–4 respectively) hazard displays of erudition even remotely comparable to Todd's, and in both, the annotations are comparatively light, and Child is careful to apologize to those readers 'who are annoyed by marginal notes of any kind' (1: iv). Child's edition was well-received and frequently reprinted, although it probably cannot be regarded as a popular edition: Joann Krieg is no doubt correct in suggesting that Child's was a niche market, the American university audience (*SE*, 28). Indeed, it may be that Child's edition, rather more than Todd's is responsible for transforming Spenser from the poet's poet of the eighteenth-century to the scholar's poet of our own era. Grosart's edition, which takes its place among editions of most of the major figures and many of the minor figures of Elizabethan and Jacobean literature, is very different from Child's—save insofar as they share an almost obsessive concern with Spenser's family. He and the scholars whose contributions he solicited for his Spenser Society edition offer no glosses or interpretive assistance as the poems unfold, packing all of their historical (especially genealogical) and critical (especially philological) work into introductions and appendices. His text proper rests—critically and as a matter of page layout—on the fullest collational apparatus that had been offered to date.

Grosart was a whirlwind of earnest and imprecise productivity: his collations are flawed and he never produced the tenth volume in which he was to provide a good deal of the textual information upon which many of his editorial decisions rested. 'Some may regard our painstaking in so laboriously and anxiously presenting the "Various Readings," spellings, pointings, etc....as "Love's Labour Lost," and un-called for,' Grosart reflects in his prefatory note to the *Calender*, and the motive he claims may seem slightly startling. 'Unless I very much mistake, the genuine and capable student of Spenser will rejoice to be put on a level with the fortunate owners (few, very few), of the rare and costly original and early editions', and this conception of editing as an instrument of democratic access shifts without transition to another fervent address to access: 'nor will they [the genuine and capable student] readily accept the lazy conclusion that "Various Readings" and various spellings and the like were mere printers' changes, independent of the Author.' This turns out to be a profession of faith: 'I for one trow not. Contrariwise, on all important points—and many are important—I hold that Spenser, and other of our great Poets, must have seen carefully and nicely to the printing of their books' (II.8)—hence Grosart's adoption of the last quarto for the text of his *Calender* and of the edition of 1596 for his text of *The First Part of the Faerie Queene*. Grosart imagines himself, that is, to be offering very nearly direct access to the Author, unobstructed by printer or wealthy bibliophile, to the capable student.

The explicitness of Child's and Grosart's concern with their audience bears attention. Since Church, who claimed to have framed his annotations 'principally to help the common *English* Reader', a great many editors strove to extend Spenser's readership.[20] These editions respond not only to a tradition of redaction especially solicitous of the unlearned, a tradition that begins with Bicknell's *Prince Arthur, an Allegorical Romance* (1779) in prose, but also to a vein of popularizing criticism that begins with a series of essays by John Wilson that spread across five issues of *Blackwood's Magazine* from 1833 to 1834. Deriding Todd's variorum even as he plundered it, Wilson devoted most of his treatment of Spenser to a redaction of *The Legend of Holinesse* built up out of quotations and an energetic, almost rollicking, running commentary. Wilson's warm effort had a number of imitators: despite the animosity between the two men, one can trace Wilson's influence in Leigh Hunt's *Imagination and Fancy* (1844), in which Hunt undertakes an extended commentary on *The Faerie Queene*, quoting at length as he goes (see Chapter 36 below). Hunt's is followed by other book-length popularizing texts: John Hart makes a similar popularizing effort in his *Essay on the Life and Writings of Edmund Spenser, with A Special Exposition of The Faerie Queene* (1847), quoting at length and offering a moral commentary. George L. Craik quotes more generously in *Spenser and His Poetry* (1845), a work of a full three volumes. He cuts only about a third of *The Faerie Queene*, but fills in the gaps thus produced with utterly inefficient prose summaries: no pages are saved, though the burden of archaized verse is somewhat alleviated.

Combining text and commentary, these publications self-consciously repurpose Spenser for a kind of early Victorian Open University. But Wilson's essays are followed more immediately by a related but perhaps even more interesting undertaking, for his handling of Book I of *The Faerie Queene* for *Blackwood's* may very well have inspired *Holiness; or The Legend of St. George*, a prose rendering by 'A Mother' which appeared the year after the conclusion of the *Blackwood's* series. *Holiness* is by no means the first effort to target Spenser to children. By mid-century, many editions and redactions are meant to carry Spenser into the schoolroom. G. W. Kitchin's edition (1867) commends Spenser to the teacher for four reasons: because Spenser will purify and ennoble the young person's taste and 'exercise his imagination'; because the teacher will find in Spenser's poetry 'plentiful texts on which to hang historical instruction' concerning the Elizabethan period, a period especially 'likely to arouse a boy's sympathies and interests'; because the peculiarities of Spenser's language are especially adaptable to instruction in history of the language; and because 'clear and vivid description of human qualities' can occasion many 'lessons of religious and moral truth'.

Kitchin will be followed by Towry's *Spenser for Children* (1885), Maclehose's *Tales from Spenser* (1892), Macleod's *Stories from the Faerie Queene* (1897), and, to close out the century, Thomson's *Tales from the Faerie Queene* (1900), the latter as scholastic an undertaking as Kitchin's. If Book I was singled out and recast for youthful readers in 1836 as *Holiness*, the heyday of such treatments came later, with Royde-Smith's *Una and the Red Cross Knight* (1905) and C. D. Wilson's *The Faerie Queene, Book I, Rewritten in Simple Language* (1906). Mary Litchfield performs a similar, if perhaps more interesting simplification by cutting and pasting to produce the continuous biographical narrative of *Spenser's Britomart* (1896); Litchfield's textbook may be said to anticipate the great modern classroom edition of Maclean (1968; the third edition of 1993 co-edited with Prescott) which selects sparingly from across Spenser's corpus, but carefully leaves Books I and III intact.[21]

Maclean's edition, part of a series of Norton Critical Editions that had been inaugurated in 1961, lodges Spenser solidly in a university curriculum. Its purpose is 'to render the text reasonably accessible to modern readers who are unfamiliar with Spenser's poetry'. Glosses abound, quotation marks stabilize and personalize utterance, and footnotes dispel mysteries before they can envelop the reader—identifying sources and, in *The Faerie Queene*, naming characters long before Spenser's narrator does so. 'It is the editor's hope that readers new to the poetry of Spenser may find these remarks useful as a bridge between the poems and the critical essays included in this volume': useful, that is, as access not only to unfamiliar poems, but to a culture of academic criticism. Many other editions mirrored Maclean's undertaking. Three years earlier, Kellogg and Steele had edited a similar selection—Bks. I and II of *The Faerie Queene* (with 1590 as their base text), *Two Cantos of Mutabilitie*, and a few of the other poems—boldly modernizing the orthography. Only Roche and O'Donnell's *Faerie Queene* of 1978, more lightly annotated than the others, and with its annotations and textual apparatus both tucked into the concluding pages of the volume, holds back from claiming special suitability for classroom use.

One can account in a variety of ways for the abundance of editions in the 1960s and 70s, which would eventually be supplemented by editions of the shorter poems by William Oram *et al.* in 1989 and Richard McCabe in 1999. The expansion of American universities provided a market and the startling growth of academic scholarly interest in Spenser during the central third of the twentieth century provided a cadre of faculty both eager to teach Spenser's works and capable of annotating them. The well-spring of that scholarly interest was, arguably, Johns Hopkins, which Edwin Greenlaw had established as a center of Spenser scholarship upon his arrival in 1925: under his editorship, *Modern Language Notes* became the leading journal for studies in Spenser; he trained a number of distinguished Spenserians in his graduate seminars; and, before he died in 1931, he assembled a team to edit a modern variorum edition of Spenser's complete works.[22]

From the present historical vantage, the Hopkins *Variorum* (1932–49) is a remarkably disappointing work. Greenlaw was especially interested in establishing the historical references of Spenser's poems, but beyond this he seemed to have encouraged his editors to a nearly inscrutable neutrality. Especially useful in its collection of opposing arguments concerning already-recognized critical and textual cruces, the commentary to the *Variorum* samples widely from three centuries of criticism and annotation, but samples so thinly that the non-specialist reader who consults the edition can hardly feel oriented to Spenser's poetry or to the literary culture from which it springs: the teacherly helpfulness of the next generations' editions is plainly compensatory, an attempt to make up for the most conspicuous inadequacy of the *Variorum*.

The *Variorum* editors concentrated primarily on providing a carefully-edited text, yet their textual work is uneven. As has already been observed, the handling of the stemma for the *Vewe* marks an important advance on earlier treatments; the critical bibliography that Johnson prepared as a foundation for the edition and published in 1933 is an even more remarkable achievement. The textual work on the *Calender* and *Complaints* is systematic and convincing, but largely because the editors could rely, in these particular cases, on De Selincourt's especially careful work on the *Calender* for his 1910 Oxford edition of the *Minor Poems* and on Stein's *Studies in Spenser's 'Complaints'* of 1934. For *The First Part of the Faerie Queene*, the editors follow the Oxford edition (and Grosart) in adopting 1596 as their copy text, declaring that edition to have been 'very probably under the author's supervision'. Then comes the necessary back-pedaling, the supervision reduced to 'an incidental revision' and not a 'correction of *1590* line by line'; finally, we are left to negotiate something like the Wandering Wood, a small thicket of negation—'It was not a new printing in the author's absence of a finished work, such as the later editions of the *Shepheardes Calender*' (Grosart 1882–4: I, 516). One may be excused for uncertainty over what is being claimed.

THE OXFORD EDITION AND THE FUTURE OF SPENSER'S TEXTS

Grosart's confidence in the immediacy of Early Modern authors in Early Modern printed books suffered persistent and increasingly systematic erosion in the ensuing century. By the time Charlton Hinman wrote his stunning analysis of *The Printing and Proof-Reading of the First Folio of Shakespeare* in 1963—stunning in many senses—bibliography had achieved remarkably detailed accounts of the industrial and mechanical processes that transformed a manuscript into a marketable printed book. The author had receded as the maker of the printed page and a sizable proportion of the scholarly community had come to regard predications like 'Shakespeare published' as deeply metaphorical. Deeply metaphorical, but explicably so: thanks to the work of the so-called New Bibliographers, serious editors of Early Modern printed books could no longer propose to reconstruct authorial manuscripts, yet they had also developed a calculus for generating, from the details of multiple copies of printed books, what seemed a plausible range of the manuscript features from which those details derived.

From these developments, most bibliographical work on Spenser's printed works was insulated. Johnson's *Critical Bibliography* is responsive to the New Bibliography, but the other members of the *Variorum* team were content to take their textual cues from J. C. Smith and Ernest De Selincourt, the editors of the Oxford *Poetical Works* of 1909–10. And, in the light of then contemporary textual scholarship on the mediation of authorial manuscripts to Early Modern printed books, Smith's 1909 edition of *The Faerie Queene* seems quaint in its rehearsal of Grosart's authorial pieties. '1596 was produced under Spenser's eye and by his authority. That authority must be held to cover both volumes, not the second only.' And the priestly accents of Smith's next sentence indicate that the truth of these principles is founded on faith: 'Behind this we cannot go' (xvi).[23] Ernest De Selincourt, whose 1910 edition of the Minor Poems was attached to Smith's *Faerie Queene* to make the Oxford edition of the *Poetical Works*, is far more cautious in his assessment of textual data and he is patient in arguing for his tentative conclusions. Responding to the recent turn to systematic assessment of stop-press correction among other textual critics of printed books, he makes some effort to identify corrected and uncorrected states of his copy text of *Complaints* and expresses some genial exasperation at earlier editors who tax *other* editors with carelessness, when the source of their differences is simply that they were consulting different copies.[24] Yet his own intra-editional collations are hardly systematic: although De Selincourt examined 6 copies of the 1591 *Complaints*, he compared only 2 copies of *The Shepheardes Calender* Q1, and seems to have based his edition of the other Minor Poems on single copies of each early edition. Smith's attention to intra-editional variation is similarly unsteady. In preparing his edition of *The Faerie Queene*, he collated 3 copies of 1590, 3 copies of 1596 *First Part* (adopted as his copy text), 5 copies of 1596 *Second Part*, 5 copies of 1609 (only 3 for the *Second Part*), 2 of 1611 (*First Part*), one of 1612 (*Second Part*), and 3 of 1613 (*Second Part*). But Smith's disclaimer leaves one in doubt as to his procedure: most of these, he tells us, were 'not collated *verbatim*' and were only 'examined for variants'. Presumably he was relying on the (very imperfect collations) of earlier editors. Disappointingly, Padelford's edition of *The Faerie Queene* for the Hopkins *Variorum* is even less attentive to these matters: he collates two copies of 1590 and 2 copies of 1596 (one from a photostat copy), supplementing these with spot-checking for (previously identified) variants in seven other copies by librarians at the holding repositories.

The prestige of the Oxford and Hopkins editions had the lamentable effect of suggesting to subsequent scholars and editors that Spenser's texts needed no further attention. While the study of the transmission of the texts of Renaissance drama advanced, inquiry into the nature of Spenser's texts—the copy texts from which they were printed, the paper on which they were printed, the procedures of the composition and proofreading—was stunted. The superiority of 1596 as a copy text for *The Faerie Queene* was accepted and, although he offered annotations of unprecedented breadth and imaginative depth, Hamilton was content to reproduce the Oxford text for his Longman *Faerie Queene* of 1977, and the editors of the 1989 Yale edition of the Shorter Poems incautiously declared that 'a near-complete list of variants is available in the *Variorum Minor Poems*' (781). In the concluding paragraphs of his article on 'Critical Bibliography' for *The Spenser Encyclopedia* (1990), William Proctor Williams is rueful: 'for all of the *Variorum*'s virtues, textually it marks no advance,' 'despite the many editions of Spenser, only two works'—*Prothalamion* and *Complaints*—'have ever been examined in the detail we have come to expect as the usual standard for a critical edition' (93); in conversation he was less measured, 'textual scholarship on Spenser is stuck somewhere near the end of the eighteenth century'.

Williams offered that damning assessment in quite excusable ignorance of the exhaustive analyses that had been performed by the team of Yamashita, Matsuo, Suzuki, and Sato and had issued in their *Concordance to the 1590 Faerie Queene* (1990) and *Textual Companion to the Faerie Queene, 1590* (1993). Here were systematic studies of orthography, punctuation, and rhyme, as well as compositorial analyses, a rich documentary thickening of the description that could be offered of the transmission of the text of *The Faerie Queene*, all of which tended to unsettle the Grosart–Smith–Padelford orthodoxy that 1596 most closely represented the texture of Spenserian autograph. 'Clearly, the 1590 text has preserved more of the generally accepted Spenserian characteristics,' as Yamashita and Suzuki would put the matter in their textual introduction to the second Longman's edition (2001): they had convinced Hamilton, who had turned the preparation of the text over to them. As in Birch's mid-eighteenth-century edition, the first three books of the new Longman *Faerie Queene* are based on the quarto of 1590. It may be worth remarking that their case for choosing the 1590 text is complicated—not only because it contains more 'Spenserian characteristics', but because it was, they argue, more widely read during the 1590s and early 1600s (Spenser 2001: 21–2). Of course, the sway of the 1590 edition of the First Part was brief, since the early folios are based on the 1596 version. That Yamashita and Suzuki adduce this argument is revealing however, since it discloses a competiton for our attention between the Spenser whose writing is imperfectly registered in print and the 'Spenser' whose circulation in print—as the author of *The Faerie Queene*, *Fowre Hymnes*, and *Brittain's Ida*—invites us to imagine the writing Spenser.

Despite the considerable achievement of Yamashita, Suzuki, and their colleagues, Williams's summary judgment in *The Spenser Encyclopedia*—'Although much work has been devoted to the text of Spenser, much remains to be done' (93)—can still stand, or can stand with minor adjustment: much is being done. The WordHoard digital project has provided a powerful new tool for advancing the sort of philological inquiry that Child had initiated and that Greenlaw had promoted through his editorship of *MLN*, and Stan Dubinsky has renewed the study of Spenser's syntax. A new Oxford edition of the *Collected Works* is currently in preparation, as part of which Elizabeth Fowler and Nicholas Canny are preparing an edition of the *Vewe* that will take systematic account of all the surviving witnesses. Christopher Burlinson and Andrew Zurcher's edition of Spenser's diplomatic correspondence has already appeared (2009). It is fitting to end here, with a new and deeply problematic addition to the Spenser canon—problematic because, although they survive in autograph, they have never before entered into the 'Spenser' canon; problematic because, although they were written by Spenser, they circulated as the writings of others; because, although they were *written* by Spenser, they *were* the writings of others. Unlike *Brittain's Ida*. Not unlike the poems for the *Theatre for Voluptuous Worldlings*. Unlike, but not very unlike, E. K.'s commentary on the *Calender.*

Notes

1. For more on the non-English versions of *TW*, see Chapter 8 above.
2. After the 1579 edition of the *Calender*, Hugh Singleton had assigned the right to publish the *Calender* to John Harrison, who maintained the bibliographical presence of Immeritô (and Spenser's anonymity) across four more editions—in 1581, 1586, 1591, and 1597.
3. Such discrimination is half-hearted, however: in other copies Edwin's advertisement has been cut out from its gathering (Kkkk) and bound in at the end of the volume, after the *Calender* and glossary (Aaaaa).
4. See Boas's letter to the *TLS* of 29 March 1926.
5. In Chapter 17 above (pp. 325–6) Elizabeth Fowler argues that the earliest attribution to Spenser, in the Rawlinson manuscript, substantially antedates Ware.
6. In his dedicatory epistle to *Fowre Hymnes* Spenser claims, perhaps disingenuously, that the first two hymns had already had wide circulation before they were printed, although none of these early manuscript copies have survived.
7. The stanza that dropped out of the *June* eclogue in the fifth quarto edition left a gap not corrected until the 1653 edition.
8. This is not to suggest that the fact of a compositorial filter disables Martha Craig's great general argument for the network of puns produced by 'Spenserian' orthography, but that individual instances of those claims need to be tested individually (1967).
9. Though many of these 'faults' are transmissional errors—compositorial or scribal lapses—some of the corrections suggest themselves as authorial second thoughts. Yamashita's team identified 83 obvious misprints and half as many possible ones not caught in the Faults Escaped. In some cases, such as the correction to 'Pyrochles' of the first instance in which 1590 prints 'Pyrrhocles', we might suppose that a single listing in the 'Faults Escaped' was meant to signal a correction that was to operate on all instances. As for stop-press correction, David L. Miller estimated (in a private communication) no more than 160, an average of a correction for every 115 type-lines.
10. Although there is a relatively consistent drift to the refashioning of the first part of *FQ*, the entire 1596 edition is not submitted to a fully coherent 'house style'. Frank B. Evans (1965: 49–67) shows that a pair of compositors set the first part of the edition and that one member of the pair was replaced for the second half of the edition.
11. Evans's assessment is at odds with Jewel Wurtsbaugh's (1936: 65–6 n.).
12. For a good example of Jortin's proposed method of 'comparing the Author with himself', see his discussion of Spenser's use of the verb 'to tine' (1734: 63).
13. Hughes had died in 1720; the editor who revised his edition has not been identified.
14. Upton eventually anticipated a *Complete Works*: in the first pages of his *Faerie Queene*, but also, in a volume to follow, the minor poems, the *Vewe*, and, in the interests of completeness, *Axiochus*, 'not taken notice of by any Editor of any part of his works' (1758: ix).

15. This 'letter' was addressed to Gilbert West, whose imitations of Spenser (*A Canto of the Fairy Queen*, 1739, and *Education*, 1751) Dodsley had published. For West see Chapter 36 below (pp. 670–1).

16. For a survey of the leading anthologies, see Wurtsbaugh (1936: 139).

17. De Selincourt deplores Child's having followed Todd in editing the *Calender* from Q3, and supposes it 'highly probable that he printed from his own corrected copy of Todd' (1910: 508).

18. In the preface to his 1858 edition of Shakespeare's *Works*, Collier announced his fortunate acquisition of this copy, and the discovery of several other important sixteenth- and seventeenth-century books that, he offers, 'near the end of the last century...had probably come out of an old Roman Catholic library in Berkshire' and 'were now scattered over the neighbourhood of Reading and Newbury' (x).

19. For Collier's protestations concerning his scrupulous avoidance of plagiarism *and* of unwarranted speculation, see his preface, 1: xii and n.

20. They are followed by Lilian Winstanley's *Fowre Hymnes* of 1907: 'This edition of Spenser's *Fowre Hymnes* is intended mainly for the use of students and, since it has not been possible to assume in all cases a knowledge of the original languages, the writer has employed Jowett's translations of the *Phaedrus* and *Symposium* and has made either translations or summaries of the passages quoted from Ficino's *Commentarium in Convivium* and Bruno's *De gl'Heroici Furori*' (v).

21. Litchfield's undertaking was surely influenced by Jameson's (1832), Clarke's (1850), and Dowden's 'Heroines of Spenser' (1888), his first foray into Spenser criticism, soon to be followed by his contribution to the Grosart's edition, 'Spenser, The Poet and Teacher'.

22. The Hopkins *Variorum* is not, of course, *sui generis*; for a sensitive account of the late-nineteenth-century efflorescence in scholarship on which the *Variorum* builds, albeit one that slightly scants the alternation between edition and critical scholarship, see Radcliffe (1996), particularly Chap. 4.

23. Smith's edition is steadily marred by hunches cast as certainties and probabilities cast as truth: 'What is certain is that toward the close of 1595 Spenser followed Needham to London with the manuscript of the second part of the *F.Q.*' (xiv); 'The view that these cantos [i.e., *TCM*] are spurious is unworthy of serious discussion' (xv).

24. The turn to consider variations within editions as systematically as possible begins with Dodge's edition of 1908. Dodge adopted as copy-texts British Library copies of the first editions of Spenser's works and then collated his printed proofs with such alternate copies of those editions as he could locate in American repositories. (He could not locate American copies of the *SC*, *Daphnaïda*, the *Amoretti* and *Epithalamion*, the *Prothalamion*, and a few other miscellaneous poems; for the *SC*, he collated his proofs against Sommers's photographic facsimile edition.)

BIBLIOGRAPHY

Anon. (1648). *The Faerie Leveller: or, King Charles his Leveller descried and deciphered in Queene Elizabeths dayes. By her Poet Laureat* Edmond Spenser, *in his unparaleld Poeme, entituled, The Faerie Queene*. London.

Anon. (1687). *Spencer Redivivus Containing the first book of the Fairy queen*. London: T. Chapman.

Bathurst, Theodore (trans.) (1653). *The Shepherds Calendar / Calendarium pastorale, sive Æglogæ duodecim*. By Edmund Spenser. Londini [London]: M. Meighen, T. Collins and G. Bedell.

Bicknell, Alexander (1779). *Prince Arthur: an allegorical romance. The story from Spenser*, 2 vols. London: G. Riley.

Birch, Thomas, and Kent, William (eds) (1751). *The faerie queene*. By Edmund Spenser, 3 vols. London: J. Brindley.

Boas, F. S. (1926). 'Song & Drama'. *TLS* 1271 (29 March): 394.

Brink, J. R. (1994). 'Constructing the *View of the Present State of Ireland*'. *SSt* 11: 203–28.

Burlinson, C., and Zurcher, A. (eds) (2009). *Edmund Spenser: Selected Letters and Other Papers*. Oxford: Oxford University Press.

Carpenter, F. I. (1923). *A Reference Guide to Edmund Spenser*. Chicago: University of Chicago Press.

Child, Francis James (ed.) (1855). *The Poetical Works of Edmund Spenser*, 5 vols. Boston: Little, Brown.

Church, Ralph (1758). *The Faerie Queene*, 4 vols. London: William Faden.

Clarke, Mary Victoria Cowden (1850). *The girlhood of Shakespeare's heroines*. London.

Cooper, E. (1738). *The historical and poetical medley*. London: T. Davies.

Collier, John Payne (1858). *Shakespeare's comedies, histories, tragedies, and poems*, 6 vols. London: Whittaker.

—— (ed.) (1862). *The Works of Edmund Spenser*, 5 vols. London: Bell and Daldy.

Craig, M. (1967). 'The Secret Wit of Spenser's Language', in P. Alpers (ed.), *Elizabethan Poetry: Modern Essays in Criticism*. New York: Oxford University Press: 447–72.

Craik, George Lillie (1845). *Spenser, and his Poetry*, 3 vols. London: Charles Knight.

Cummings, L. (1964). 'Spenser's *Amoretti* VIII: New Manuscript Versions'. *SEL* 4(1): 125–35.

De Selincourt, Ernest (ed.) (1910). *The Poetical Works of Edmund Spenser*, 3 vols. Oxford: Clarendon Press.

Dodge, R. E. Neil (ed.) (1908). *The Complete Poetical Works of Edmund Spenser*. Boston: Cambridge Edition of the Poets.

Dodsley, R. (1748). *The Preceptor: Containing a General Course of Education*, 2 vols. London: R. Dodsley.

Dowden, E. (1888). *Transcripts and studies*. London: K. Paul, Trench.

Edwin, Jonathan (ed.) (1679). *The works of that famous English poet, Mr. Edmond Spenser*. London: J. Edwin.

Evans, F. B. (1965). 'The Printing of Spenser's *Faerie Queene* in 1596'. *Studies in Bibliography* 18: 49–67.

Fletcher, Phineas (1633). *The purple island, or The Isle of Man*. Cambridge: Universitie of Cambridge.

Frushell, R. C. (1999). *Edmund Spenser in the Early Eighteenth Century: Education, Imitation, and the Making of a Literary Model*. Pittsburgh: Duquesne University Press.

Gilfillan, George, and Clarke, Charles Cowden (eds) (1859). *The Poetical Works of Edmund Spenser*, 5 vols. Edinburgh: J. Nichol.

Gollancz, I. (1907–8). 'Spenseriana'. *Proceedings of the British Academy* 99–105.

Greenlaw, Edwin, Osgood, Charles Grosvenor, and Padelford, Frederick Morgan (eds) (1932–47). *The Works of Edmund Spenser: A Variorum Edition*, 10 vols. Baltimore: Johns Hopkins University Press.

Grosart, A. B. (ed.) (1882–4). *The Complete Works in Verse and Prose of Edmund Spenser*, 8 vols. London.

Hart, John S. (1847). *An Essay on the Life and Writings of Edmund Spenser, with a special exposition of the Fairy Queen*. New York: Wiley and Putnam.

Hayward, Thomas (1738). *The British Muse*. London: F. Cogan.

Heffner, R. (1942). 'Spenser's *View of Ireland*: Some Observations'. *MLQ* 3: 507–15.

Hillard, George (ed.) (1839). *The Poetical Works of Edmund Spenser*, 5 vols. Boston: Little and Brown.

Hinman, C. J. K. (1963). *The Printing and Proof-Reading of the First Folio of Shakespeare*. Oxford: Clarendon Press.

Hughes, John (ed.) (1715). *The works of Mr. Edmund Spenser*, 6 vols. London: Hughes.

Hunt, Leigh (1844). *Imagination and fancy*. London.

Jameson, Anna (1832). *Shakespeare's Heroines*. New York: Dutton.

Johnson, F. R. (1933). *A Critical Bibliography of the Works of Edmund Spenser Printed Before 1700*. Baltimore: Johns Hopkins University Press.

Johnson, Samuel (1905). *Lives of the English Poets*, ed. G. B. Hill, 3 vols. Clarendon Press: Oxford.

Jortin, John (1734). *Remarks on Spenser's poems*. London: J. Whiston.

Kellogg, Robert, and Steele, Oliver (eds) (1965). *Books I and II of the Faerie Queene: the Mutability Cantos, and Selections from the Minor Poetry*. By Edmund Spenser. New York: Odyssey Press.

Kitchin, George William (ed.) (1867). *The Faery Queen*. By Edmund Spenser. Oxford: Clarendon, 1867.

Krieg, J. (1990). 'America to 1900, influence and reputation', in *SE*.

Litchfield, Mary E. (1896). *Spenser's Britomart, from books 3, 4, and 5 of the Faery Queene*. By Edmund Spenser. Boston: Ginn & Co.

Lownes, Matthew (ed.) (1611). *The Faerie Queen: The Shepheards Calendar: Together with the other Works of England's Arch-Poët, EDM. SPENSER: Collected into one Volume, and carefully corrected*. By Edmund Spenser. London: M. Lownes.

—— (ed.) (1617). *The Faerie Queen: The Shepheards Calendar: Together with the other Works of England's Arch-Poët, EDM. SPENSER: Collected into one Volume, and carefully corrected*. By Edmund Spenser. London: M. Lownes.

McCabe, Richard A. (ed.) (1999). *Edmund Spenser: The Shorter Poems*. London: Penguin.

Maclean, H. (ed.) (1968). *Edmund Spenser's Poetry: Authoritative Texts (and) Criticism*. New York: Norton.

—— and Prescott, A. L. (eds) (1993). *Edmund Spenser's Poetry: Authoritative Texts (and) Criticism*, 3rd edn. New York: Norton.

MacLehose, Sophia H. (1889). *Tales from Spenser: chosen from the Faerie Queene*. Glasgow: James MacLehose & Sons.

Macleod, Mary (1897). *Stories from the Faerie Queene*. London.

Malone, Edmond (ed.) (1790). *The Plays and Poems of William Shakespeare*, 10 vols. London: J. Rivington and Sons, L. Davis, B. White and Son, T. Longman.

Milton, John (1645). *Poems of Mr. John Milton*. London: H. Moseley.

Morris, R. (ed.) (1869). *The Globe Edition. Complete Works of Edmund Spenser. With a Memoir by J. W. Hales*. London: Macmillan and Co.

Mother, A. (pseud.) (1836). *Holiness; or the legend of St George: a tale from Spencer's Fairie Queene*. Boston.

O'Callaghan, M. (2000). *The 'shepheards nation': Jacobean Spenserians and Early Stuart Political Culture, 1612–1625*. Oxford: Clarendon.

Oram, William A. et al. (eds) (1989). *The Yale Edition of the Shorter Poems of Edmund Spenser*. New Haven: Yale.

Radcliffe, D. H. (1996). *Edmund Spenser: A Reception History*. Columbia, SC: Camden House.

Roche, Thomas P. (ed.) (1978). *The Faerie Queen*. By Edmund Spenser. Harmondsworth: Penguin.

Royde-Smith, Naomi Gwladys (1905). *Una and the Red Cross Knight and other tales from Spenser's Faery Queene*. London.

Smith, J. C. (ed.) (1909). *Spenser's Faerie Queene*. Oxford: Clarendon.

Smith, R. M. (1958). 'Spenser's Scholarly Script and "right Writing"', in D. C. Allen (ed.), *Studies in Honor of T. W. Baldwin*. Urbana: University of Illinois Press.

Spence, Joseph (1747). *Polymetis*, 10 vols. London: R. Dodsley.

Spenser, Edmund (1595). *Amoretti and Epithalamion*. London: W. Ponsonby.

—— (1592). *Axiochus*. London: C. Burbie.

—— (1595). *Colin Clouts Come Come Againe*. London: W. Ponsonby.

—— (1591). *Complaints*. London: W. Ponsonby.

—— (1591). *Daphnaïda*. London: W. Ponsonby.

—— (1590). *The Faerie Queene*. London: W. Ponsonby.

—— (1596). *The Faerie Queene*. London: W. Ponsonby.

—— (1609). *The Faerie Queene*. London: M. Lownes.

—— (1596). *Fowre Hymnes*. London: W. Ponsonby.

—— (1612). *Mother Hubberd's Tale*. London: M. Lownes.

—— (1596). *Prothalamion*. London: W. Ponsonby.

—— (1579). *The Shepheardes Calender*. London: H. Singleton.

—— (1580). *Three proper, and wittie, familiar letters: lately passed betweene two universitie men. Two other, very commendable letters, of the same mens writing*. London: H. Bynneman.

—— (1633). *A vewe of the State of Ireland*, ed. James Ware. Dublin: Society of Stationers.

——. *A vewe of the State of Ireland*. Gough Ireland 2 MS. Bodleian, Oxford.

——. *A vewe of the State of Ireland*. Rawlinson B. 478 MS. Bodleian, Oxford.

——. *A vewe of the State of Ireland*. Additional MS 22022. British Library, London.

Stein, H. (1934). *Studies in Spenser's 'Complaints'*. New York: Oxford University Press.

Theobald, Lewis (ed.) (1733). *The Works*. By William Shakespeare. London: A. Bettesworth, C. Hitch, J. Tonson, F. Clay, W. Feales, and R. Wellington.

Thomson, Clara L. (1902). *Tales from the Faerie Queene*. Shaldon: E. E. Speight.

Todd, H. J. (ed.) (1805). *The works of Edmund Spenser in eight volumes, with the principal illustrations of various commentators; to which are added, notes, some account of the life of Spenser, and a glossarial and other indexes by the Rev. Henry John Todd*, 8 vols. London: F.C. & J. Rivington.

—— (ed.) (1852). *The Works of Edmund Spenser*. London.

Tonson, R. (pub.) (1750). *The Fairy Queen*, 2 vols. London: R. Tonson.

—— (pub.) (1758). *The Works Spenser*, ed. John Hughes, 6 vols. London: R. Tonson.

Towry M. H. (1885). *Spenser for Children*. London: Chatto and Windus.

Upton, John (1747). *A New Canto of Spencer's Fairy Queen*. London: G. Hawkins.

—— (ed.) (1758). *Spenser's Faerie Queene*, 2 vols. London: J. and R. Tonson.

Van der Noot, Jan (1569). *A Theatre wherein be represented as wel the miseries & calamities that follow the Voluptuous Worldlings*. London: Henry Bynneman.

Walkley, Thomas (ed.) (1628). *Brittain's Ida*. [By Phineas Fletcher]. London: T. Walkley.

Warton, Thomas (1754). *Observations on the Faerie Queene of Spenser*. London: printed for R. and J. Dodsley; and J. Fletcher.

—— (1762). *Observations on the Faerie Queene of Spenser*. London: printed for R. and J. Dodsley; and J. Fletcher.

West, Gilbert (1739). *A Canto of the Fairy Queen. Written by Spenser. Never before published*. London: G. Hawkins.

—— (1751). *Education: A Poem*. London: R. Dodsley.

Wilson, Calvin Dill (1906). *The Faerie Queene, First Book, Rewritten in Simple Language*. Chicago.

Wilson, J. (1833). 'Spenser I'. *Blackwood's Edinburgh Magazine* 34, Nov: 824–56.

—— (1834). 'Spenser II'. *Blackwood's Edinburgh Magazine* 36, Sep: 408–30.

—— (1834). 'Spenser III, *The Faerie Queene*, The Legend of Redcrosse Knight'. *Blackwood's Edinburgh Magazine* 36, Nov: 681–714.

—— (1834). 'Spenser IV, *The Faerie Queene*, The Legend of Redcrosse Knight'. *Blackwood's Edinburgh Magazine* 36, Dec: 715–37.

—— (1835). 'Spenser V, *The Faerie Queene*, The Legend of Redcrosse Knight'. *Blackwood's Edinburgh Magazine* 37, Jan: 49–71.

—— (1835). 'Spenser VI, *The Faerie Queene*, The Legend of Redcrosse Knight'. *Blackwood's Edinburgh Magazine* 37, Mar: 540–56.

—— (1835) 'Spenser VII, The Legend of Redcrosse Knight'. *Blackwood's Edinburgh Magazine* 37, Apr: 659–76.

Winstanley, L. (1907). *Fowre Hymnes*. Cambridge: Cambridge University Press.

Wordsworth, William (1907). *Letters of the Wordsworth Family*, 3 vols. Boston: Ginn.

Wurtsbaugh, J. (1936). *Two Centuries of Spenserian Scholarship, 1609–1805*. Baltimore: Johns Hopkins University Press.

Yamashita, Hiroshi, et al. (eds.) (1990). *A Comprehensive Concordance to The Faerie Queene, 1590*. Tokyo: Kenyusha.

—— (eds) (1993). *A Textual Companion to The Faerie Queene, 1590*. Tokyo: Kenyusha.

Zurcher, A. (2004–5). 'Printing *The Faerie Queene* in 1590'. *Studies in Bibliography* 57: 115–50.

CHAPTER 36

....

SPENSER'S LITERARY INFLUENCE

....

MICHELLE O'CALLAGHAN

Milton was the Poetical Son of *Spencer* . . . *Spencer* more than once insinuates, that the Soul of *Chaucer* was transfus'd into his Body; and that he was begotten by him Two hundred years after his Decease. *Milton* has acknowledg'd to me, that *Spencer* was his Original.

(Dryden 1956–2000: VII, 25).[1]

John Dryden, in the 'Preface' to his *Fables* (1700), written just over a century after Spenser's death, named Spenser the founding father of a distinctly English literary tradition. Dryden points to Spenser's own hand in delineating the lines of descent. It is Spenser who began to elevate vernacular poets, most notably Chaucer, to take their place alongside classical authors as models of influence. Spenser, Dryden recognized, was a key figure in the formation of the English literary canon. He was one of the first authors to harness the resources of print to forge an identity as a public, national poet and, just as importantly, to ensure his own posterity. As Dennis Kay noted, it was Spenser who 'invented Spenserian poetry' (Kay 1990: 65–6). Part of the reason why subsequent generations of poets found Spenser such a congenial literary father was that he formulated a model of literary influence that was open and communal. This is particularly noticeable in *Astrophel*, Spenser's collection of elegies for Sir Philip Sidney, published together with *Colin Clouts Come Home Againe* in 1595. Taken together, they delineate the contours of a Spenserian tradition for later poets. In the case of *Astrophel,* Spenser acted as poet-editor, the organizing intelligence behind the volume, who initiates and gives voice to the community gathered in its pages. It lies in the power of the Spenserian poet to shape and sustain the memory of powerful poetic forebears, epitomized by Sidney. In Spenser's hands, the figure of the shepherd-poet and his responsive echoing song produces an author function able to bring into being and sustain a native literary tradition. When Spenser invented Spenserian poetry, he also invented a model of literary influence that crucially is dependent on the agency of poetic communities. Spenser's position as the 'Prince of Poets' was ensured in his own life-time. William Smith's dedication of his *Chloris* (1596) to Spenser, through its conscious echoing of Spenser's dedication of *Shepheardes Calender* to Sidney, as Richard McCabe notes, imagines the 'empowerment of poetical "gifts" by the poetically gifted, the "secret comfort" of illustrious precedent' (McCabe 2008: 47).

THE JACOBEAN SPENSERIANS

The first decade of the seventeenth century was decisive in terms of establishing Spenser's legacy. 1609 saw the publication of the first folio edition of *The Faerie Queene,* which introduced a new, as yet unpublished work to the public, the *Two Cantos of Mutabilitie.* Two years later, in 1611, Spenser's collected *Works* were published, making available the full Spenser corpus, and giving added impetus to the Spenserian revival. In 1628, a new work was attributed to Spenser—*Brittain's Ida.* This erotic epyllion, probably the work of Phineas Fletcher, initiates a tradition of 'discovering' supposedly lost or unpublished works that continues throughout the seventeenth century, and reaches its height in the eighteenth century (see Chapter 35 above).

The works of Richard Niccols, the first avowedly Spenserian poet, testify to the lively generic variety of the Spenserian canon in the early seventeenth century. Niccols's first known work was *Epicedium* (1603), a Spenserian funeral elegy for Elizabeth I; he would later write an elegy for Prince Henry, *The Three Sister's Teares* (1613). The deaths of Elizabeth and Henry sparked revivals that gave a distinctive tone to Jacobean Spenserianism. The 1603 elegies mark the point when Elizabeth's memory is entwined with that of her poet laureate. Henry Chettle, in his *England's Mourning Garment,* called for the renewal of Spenser's memory to enshrine and perpetuate Elizabeth's legacy. Spenserian elegies for Prince Henry are distinguished by their political, often apocalyptic tone (Kay 1990: 125–43). Subsequent Spenserian poetry on national themes assumes an elegiac cast in which lament modulates into complaint. Niccols's next publication, *The Cuckow* (1607), rewrites the Bowre of Blisse through the Chaucerian beast fable (Niccols 1992: 5–9, 236–40). Like other Spenserians, Niccols was attracted by the political possibilities of the Bowre of Blisse, and turned the allegory into a complaint against the luxurious ease of the Jacobean peace, which had emasculated the formerly puissant nation gloriously represented by the Eliza-bethan age. His *The Beggar's Ape* recast *Mother Hubberds Tale*, which had been republished in 1612/13, into a satire directed at prominent Jacobean courtiers. Spenser was read as a political poet in the years following Prince Henry's death. His Protest-ant allegories were revived to denounce Spain and popery, while his *Complaints* gave shape to laments for the decline of a military culture and bitter satires denouncing court corruption (Norbrook 2002: 173–98).

'Colin', the pastoral author function Spenser had fashioned across a series of poems—*The Shepheardes Calender*, Book 6 of *The Faerie Queene*, *Astrophel*, and *Colin Clouts Come Home Againe*—proved attractive to this first generation because it authorized an expansive pastoralism. These poets favour the 'Colin' of *Colin Clouts Come Home Againe*, who tells a story of neglect and exile, and finds a new home outside corrupt courts among the 'shepheards nation' (*CCH*, 17). The story of Spenser's persecution at the hands of William Cecil, Lord Burleigh, and his son, Sir Robert Cecil, circulated soon after his death. William Browne, in Book II of his *Britannia's Pastorals*, cast Cecil as Avarice whose malice has 'rob'd our *Colin* of his Monument' (Browne 1616: II, 27; O'Callaghan 2000: 113). When Drayton revised *The Shepheardes Garland* (1593) in 1606, he rewrote Roland's love lament into a complaint against court corruption (Tylus 1990: 184–6). Browne's *Shepheards Pipe* (1614) simi-larly gives Spenserian pastoral an anti-court cast. The volume was a collaborative effort and includes eclogues by Christopher Brooke, George Wither, and John Davies of Hereford. The cause that unites these men is Wither's unjust imprisonment. Wither published his sequel, *Shepherds Hunting* (1615), the next year in which his visitors in his 'country' exile are his friends from *Shepheards Pipe*. Phineas Fletcher's *Piscatorie Eclogues*, begun around 1604, but not published until 1633, transforms Cambridge into a pastoral world, and laments his own and his father's failure to secure a permanent college fellowship, which he attributes to 'envy' and ecclesiastical corruption (Bou-chard 2000: 22–3, 101). What is remarkable about this first generation of Spenserians is the way they realize the communal aspects of Spenser's *Shepheardes Calender* and fashion themselves as distinctive print communities (O'Callaghan 2000: 11–18, 27–41).

The Fletchers like Spenser were Cambridge men. They are part of a distinct school of Cambridge Spenserianism notable for reading Spenser predominantly as a Prot-estant, visionary poet. Giles Fletcher placed Spenser alongside the Huguenot poet, Du Bartas, when identifying a tradition for his own biblical epic, *Christ's Victorie, and Triumph* (1610) (Hunter 1977: 19). The Cambridge connection is illuminating because it draws attention to the role of educational institutions in the consolidation of traditions—Wordsworth will later write in his *Prelude* of his discovery of Spenser and an English literary tradition at Cambridge. Milton's *Lycidas*, his elegy for a fellow Cambridge student, which brings together the pastoral and the piscatory, appeared just four years after Fletcher's *Piscatorie Eclogues* was printed at Cambridge.

Given the times were not perceived to be conducive to stories of 'fierce warres' (I Proem, 1), alternative national themes were explored when composing long public poems. Drayton's *Poly-Olbion* turns to the land itself, and draws on Spenser's English and Irish river poems for his expansive chorographical poetic. Browne's pastoral epic, *Britannia's Pastorals* (1613; 1616), revives the Protestant apocalypticism of *The Faerie Queene* to tell the story of Aletheia-Truth and to celebrate the nation's deliverance from the Gunpowder Plot. This event also inspired Phineas Fletcher's violently anti-Catholic *The Locusts, or Apollyonists* (1627), an avowedly Spenserian political poem evident in its variation on the Spenserian stanza, as well as its vision of Hell and depiction of Sin, an amalgam of Errour and Duessa. His *Purple Island* (1633) amplifies and politicizes Spenser's allegory of the body in Book II of *The Faerie Queene* to produce a twelve canto prophetic poem that looks forward to the providential regeneration of the body politic under James I (Sawday 1995: 175).

Spenser was still a lively presence for these poets and they read his works eclectically and experimentally. It is this generation that is responsible for enshrining Spenser's reputation both as the founding father of a Protestant and English epic tradition and as the original English pastoral poet, the 'famous Shepheard Collin' (Basse 1893: 170).

MILTON AND THE LATER SEVENTEENTH CENTURY

Milton dominates the story of Spenser's influence in the second half of the seventeenth century. The young Milton was introduced to Spenser when a schoolboy by Alexander Gill, the High Master of St Paul's School. Gill's deep admiration for Spenser is evident in the poet's frequent appearance in the examples for *Logonomia Anglica* (1619), his pedagogical work on English grammar and rhetoric (Frushell 1999: 20, 25). Gill had written of 'our Spenser' that 'he is more correct in beautifying his language, and as he is more fertile of neatly expressed general truths, so he is more serious, and as he is richer in the variety of his invention, so he is the more useful in his conception of any topic' (Gill 1621: 124–5; Cummings: 144).

Milton followed his schoolmaster's advice in his early vernacular poetry, perhaps most famously in 'Il Penseroso'. Spenser offered Milton a distinctively English literary storehouse. Milton gives his language in 'On the Morning of Christ's Nativity' (*c*.1629) a distinctly Spenserian timbre, evident in the 'wont' of the second stanza which echoes Spenser's 'wonned' in the *Februarie* eclogue of his *Shepheardes Calender* (Milton 1931–40: I, 1). There are 'inventions' drawn from *The Faerie Queene*, but it is the pastoralism of the poem, the depiction of 'mighty *Pan*' and the 'Shepherds on the Lawn' (Milton 1931–40: I, 4–5) that most clearly announces the debt to Spenser. The diction of Milton's 1634 masque *Comus* is even more overtly Spenserian. Many of the masque's characters, speeches, and its broader theme of chastity are adapted from John Fletcher's Spenserian pastoral tragicomedy, *The Faithful Shepherdess* (Finkelpearl 1987: 285–88). Milton departs from the reified chastity of Fletcher's drama, and returns to Spenser, reading canto xii of *The Legend of Chastity* in conjunction with

The Legend of Temperance to show how '*Heavn hath timely trid*' the '*faith*', '*patience*', and '*truth*' of the Lady and her brothers (Milton 1931–40: I, 121).

Milton's *Lycidas* could be said to perfect the Spenserian pastoral elegy. What Humphrey Moseley said of Milton's *Poems* (1645) as a whole, was especially the case with *Lycidas*. Introducing Milton, the heir to '*our famous* Spencer', he noted that Spenser's '*poems in these English ones are as rarely imitated, as sweetly excell'd*' (Milton 1931–40: I, 415). Just as Spenser's *Astrophel* had initiated a Spenserian elegiac poetics, Milton's pastoral elegy presents itself as the culmination of this tradition. Milton realizes the political value of the pastoral elegy for imagining beleaguered communities. Yet, whereas the Spenserian poet gains consolation from his community, the resounding weight given to 'Pastures new' (Milton 1931–40: I, 83) in the closing lines of *Lycidas* marks a conscious break with tradition and looks forward to the solitary, visionary poet of *Paradise Lost*.

To an extent, Milton's response to Spenser can be understood within a tradition of Cambridge Spenserianism. Like Henry More, the Cambridge Platonist and Spenserian, he admired Spenser for his '*divine Morality*' (More 1647: A2v). Milton's indebtedness to Phineas Fletcher's *Locusts, or Apollyonists* for his depiction of Sin in *Paradise Lost* and Giles Fletcher's *Christ's Victorie and Triumph* for his Satan in *Paradise Regained* have been recorded (Hunter 1977: 313). That said, Milton understood the rhetorical subtlety of Spenser's use of language to 'fashion a gentleman' in ways that earlier Spenserians did not. By far the most productive critical approach to understanding Milton's response to Spenser has been Maureen Quilligan's focus on Milton's reflection on his position as a reader of Spenser. Milton famously described the Spenserian reader in *Areopagitica* when writing of his distaste for 'a fugitive and cloister'd vertue... that never sallies out and sees her adversary':

Which was the reason why our sage and serious Poet *Spencer*, whom I dare be known to think a better teacher than *Scotus* or *Aquinas*, describing true temperance under the person of *Guion*, brings him in with his palmer through the cave of Mammon, and the bowr of earthly blisse that he might see and know, and yet abstain. (Milton 1931–40: IV, 311; Quilligan 1983: 14–15)

Milton's sensitivity to Spenser's fashioning of the temperate reader was already evident in the tried and tested virtue of *Comus*. Earlier Spenserians had recast the Bowre of Blisse into contemporary political allegories that warned of the papist threat or national decline. It was Milton who comprehended the political and ethical significance of its rhetorical strategies. The active, disciplined Spenserian reader provided Milton with a means of understanding and imagining the dialectic between free will and obedience in *Paradise Lost*.

Writers turned to Spenser's allegory during the English Revolution to make sense of the tumultuous times. Milton interpreted the ecclesiastical satire of the May Eclogue in his *Animadversions upon The Remonstrants Defence* (1641) in terms of the corruption of 'our Prelates, ... Those our admired *Spencer* inveighs against, not without some presage of these reforming times' (Milton 1931–40: III, 165–6). Eighteen years later, this reading was revived by the Quaker Henry Stubbe, although by 1659 the 'false Shepheard *Palinode*' was no longer a Laudian prelate but 'our *Presbyteriall*

Ministers' (Stubbe 1659: 175). *The Faerie Queene* received similar treatment. An excerpt from the second canto of Book 5, *The Legend of Justice*, was published in mid 1648 under the title *The Faerie Leveller*, with a preface 'explaining' the allegory. Charles I was cast as Artegall, Talus, his army, and the Giant Leveller was Cromwell (Hulse 1988: 339–41). In the early 1650s, the Royalist newspaper writer, Samuel Sheppard rewrote Spenser's epic into an historical romance in order to come to terms with the fall of Charles I. Sheppard read his Spenser alongside Shakespeare. Prince Ariodant, loosely representing Charles I, following his father's murder by his uncle, must, like Hamlet, decide on the course of action to take. He makes the wrong choices due to a complex of reasons: youth, the influence of evil counsellors, and personal failings (Sheppard 1984: v–vii, xxiii–iv).

Spenser's allegory proved attractive to writers with different political allegiances throughout the seventeenth and first half of the eighteenth centuries because its flexibility enabled them to respond to changing national concerns, from civil war to education. Spenser's allegory did not find favour with all. William Davenant, in his *Discourse upon Gondibert* (1650), recognized Spenser's place in the canon of 'Heroick Poets' but objected to his language, stanza, and allegory, because it resembles 'a continuance of extraordinary Dreams' (Davenant 1650: II, 13). The 'feverishness' he identifies in Spenser's allegory suggests Davenant's political and religious discomfort with the visionary, prophetic responses to Spenser during the English civil wars. Later eighteenth century poets would attempt to tame Spenser's style through Neoclassicism or parody it through irreverent burlesques.

EIGHTEENTH-CENTURY SPENSERIANISM

In the eighteenth century, Spenser took his place alongside Shakespeare and Milton in the pantheon of British poets, native geniuses 'as great . . . as ever were produced in *Rome* or *Athens*' (Felton 1753: 234). After Milton, Spenser was the most imitated English poet in the eighteenth century (Frushell 1999: 2). He continued to be criticized for his style, yet this seems to have encouraged would-be imitators in their attempt to revise and reform his imperfections (Kucich 1991: 14–17). Given that Spenser was the first English poet to model his career on the Virgilian pattern, he played a key part in the canonization of English Literature in the eighteenth century, and not surprisingly pastoral and epic dominate Spenserian imitations.

Spenser had established the formal pastoral eclogue as a classical English form. When Ambrose Philips and Alexander Pope in the early 1700s imitated *The Shepheardes Calender* in their *Pastorals*, the very different views on what his legacy should be, views that structure responses to Spenser in the first part of the eighteenth century, were made strikingly clear. Both sets of pastoral eclogues were published in 1709 in the popular series, *Poetical Miscellanies*, edited first by Dryden, then Jacob Tonson, and now in its sixth part. Philips's *Pastorals* head the volume, and his preface explicitly claims to revive pastoral for a new generation. Theocritus, Virgil, and Spenser are cited as founding models, yet it is Spenser's native influence that is most apparent (Tonson 1709: B2v). His *Pastorals* use Spenserian diction, English rustic names, and his songs have a native rustic air. Pope's *Pastorals*, which close the collection, also follow in Spenser's footsteps, but the effect is very different:

> First in these Fields I try the Sylvan Strains,
> Nor blush to sport on *Windsor's* blissful Plains:
> Fair *Thames* flow gently from thy sacred Spring,
> While on thy Banks *Sicilian* Muses sing . . .   (Tonson 1709: 723)

Pope has harmonized Virgil and Spenser in his 'Sylvan Strains', and like Spenser before him, he has transplanted Arcadia onto English soil. Unlike Philips, Pope's Spenser is cultivated rather than rustic. Pope rejects the roughness of Spenserian diction, and refines other poetic markers of English rusticity according to Neoclassical principles. This 'singing contest' between Philips and Pope started an argument between the Ancients and the Moderns over the nature of not just pastoral, but English poetry more generally. The dispute, as David Hill Radcliffe points out, had a political aspect given that those who emphasized Spenser's Britishness and defended his diction in terms of native primitivism tended to be Whigs (1996: 37–41).

In the early 1700s, writers continued to recognize that Spenser was the foremost English model for public, political poetry. Once again, ideological differences inform the way Spenser was read. Matthew Prior's 1706 *An Ode, humbly inscrib'd to the Queen*, married the Horatian ode with a variant on the Spenserian stanza to celebrate the success of Malborough at the battle of Ramillies. For Prior, the Englishness of Spenser's style could not be separated from the military glory identified with the Elizabethan golden age. Queen Anne is Elizabeth revived, the 'Fairest Model of Imperial Sway!' (Prior 1706: 2). Whigs criticized 'An Ode', yet this did not prevent them from putting Spenser to political uses. Samuel Croxall's *An Original Canto of Spencer: Design'd as Part of his Fairy Queen, but never Printed* (1714 [1713]) 'discovered' a new episode in the story of Britomart and Artegall. Like Prior, Croxall invoked Spenserian martialism to praise Queen Anne, under the guise of Britomart, and Malborough, the faithful Talus. His satire was directed at the Tory prime minister, Robert Harley, depicted as the villainous enchanter, Archimago, who holds Britomart in thrall with the aid of his fawning curs. This Whig reading transformed Una, divine Truth, into 'Faire Liberty, bright Goddess, Heavenly-born, | So high esteem'd by ev'ry living Wight' (Croxall 1714: 7; Radcliffe 1996: 32). In 1739, Gilbert West printed another 'unpublished' *Canto of the Fairy Queen*. It is a political satire on very similar lines to Croxall's, except that West's Archimago is Robert Walpole, and he is far more critical of the monarchy, satirizing the courts of George II and Queen Caroline (Gerrard 1994: 178).

The fashion for continuations and 'discoveries' of unpublished cantos resulted from the unique, incomplete status of *The Faerie Queene*. Spenser's unfinished epic was thought to be particularly open to revisions and rewritings. A number of the eighteenth-century 'discoveries' were burlesques that disclosed the comic and satiric potential of Spenserian grotesque, particularly monstrous figures such as Errour (Kucich 1991: 23–5). Pope's *The Alley. An Imitation of Spenser* (1727) draws on Errour, and other monstrous Spenserian figures, in his depiction of Obloquy and her companions, Slander, Envy, and Malice, to give Spenser's noble river, '*Thamis*', mock-heroic treatment in a manner reminiscent of Jonson's wonderfully vulgar 'On the Famous Voyage' (Pope 1961–69: 6:43). The stanza Pope originally chose for the motto for his *Dunciad*, although later discarded (Pope 1961–69: 5:9), suggests he was well aware of the comic, burlesque potential of Spenser: 'As gentle Shepheard in sweet even-tide... | A cloud of combrous gnattes do him molest' (I.i.23). Pope recognizes the complex mock-heroic incongruity involved in Spenser's use of this somewhat clownish extended simile to describe Redcrosse's encounter with Errour's 'cursed spawne'.

William Shenstone's *The Schoolmistress* was first written in 1737 as a mocking parody of the Spenserian style. He revised the poem over a number of years, adding new stanzas, and removing the playful scatology. A later version published in 1742 suggests not only how Shenstone responded to the readerly qualities of Spenser's poem, but also to changing literary tastes. He had started out 'trifling and laughing' at Spenser, particularly his 'ridiculous' language, but now was 'really in love with him', discovering in his poetry '*a peculiar* Tenderness *of* Sentiment' (Shenstone 1770: III, 55; 1742: Advertisement). Such tenderness manifests itself in the nostalgic remembrance of an English country childhood—Shenstone's village schoolboy returns as a 'mute, inglorious Milton' in Thomas Gray's *Elegy in a Country Churchyard* (1751). Shenstone's moralism is resoundingly nationalistic in the final version, and produces a modernized and distinctly British mode of Spenserian pastoral (Radcliffe 1996: 55).

Spenser continued to be admired for his 'divine Morality'. Gilbert West's *Education, a Poem* (1751) used Spenserian allegory to promote educational reform. In the first canto, West turned the 'Bowre of Blisse' into an elaborate formal, artificial garden, complete with topiaries manicured with 'preposterous Skill' (West 1751: 15), and made it home to false Education. From the aristocracy to the lower orders, Britain has given itself over to 'the low Services of brutal Sense', 'by false Taste of Pleasure led astray' (West 1751: 35–6). West had been inspired by James Thomson's *The Castle of Indolence* (1748), and its depiction of the overthrow of the 'false Inchanter' Indolence by the Knight of Arts and Industry (Thomson 1748: 25). Thomson's reading of the Spenserian bowers of Phaedria and Acrasia is more complex than West's. His 'House of Indolence' picks up on a strand of Spenserianism, evident in the playful eroticism of *Brittain's Ida* (1628), which gave an appreciative, almost Marlovian reading of Spenser's bowers. There is a tension in Thomson's poem between the didacticism of his allegory, which rejects the moral irresponsibility of Indolence, and the dreamlike, almost visionary qualities of his enchanter's aesthetic. *The Castle of Indolence* became 'the most popular mid-eighteenth century Spenserian poem among the Romantics' because it recognized in Spenser this unresolved tension between the moral responsibility demanded of poetry and the sensual and imaginative qualities of poetic illusion (Kucich 1991: 56–60).

Thomson's openness to Spenser's enchanting pictorial richness arose out of the key part played by the *The Faerie Queene* in defining a Gothic as opposed to Neoclassical aesthetic. One consequence of the argument that *The Faerie Queene* was seriously flawed when judged against Neoclassical principles, was the view that its beauties lay elsewhere, in an alternative Gothic poetic. In the words of John Hughes, the important eighteenth-century editor of Spenser's *Works*: 'The chief Merit of this Poem consists in that surprising Vein of fabulous Invention, which runs thro it, and enriches it every where with Imagery and Descriptions more than we meet in any other modern Poem' (Spenser 1750: I, xlii). When James Beattie produced his imitation of Spenser in *The Minstrel; or, The Progress of Genius*, unlike earlier poets, he rejected Spenser's allegory and instead concentrated his attention on the Spenserian stanza, because 'it pleases my ear, and seems, from its Gothic structure and original, to bear some relation to the subject and spirit of the poem' (Beattie 1775: I, vii). Although the young 'genius', Edwin, eventually submits himself to the guidance of Reason in the second canto, the impression is given that true poetic inspiration is to be found in the 'sublimely sweet, serenely gay' songs of childhood and nature: 'O let your spirit still my bosom sooth, | Inspire my dreams, and my wild wanderings guide' (Beattie 1775: I, 22). Gothic Spenser, a poet of fairy and fancy, is given a particular association with the visionary dream world that influences his reception in Romantic poetry.

ROMANTIC SPENSERIANISM

The Romantic writers are credited with a revisionary reading of Spenser so powerful that it dominates the subsequent history of Spenser's influence. Just as Milton had comprehended the rhetorical strategies of the Spenserian text in a way that no previous writer had, the Romantics recognized Spenser's potential for modern visionary poetics. A visionary reading of Spenser goes back to the seventeenth century. The fundamental difference is that earlier writers shared Spenser's nationalistic religious politics and the Romantic poets did not. Modernizing Spenser in revolutionary times necessitated a radical reading that responded creatively to the contradictions it disclosed in Spenser's poetic. When Wordsworth, for example, revolutionized Spenser's political allegory in his *Salisbury Plain* poems, he did not simply reject Spenser's neo-chivalric aristocratic politics, rather they return in the form of negative, violent historical forces that energize his visionary landscape.

The revisionary character of Romantic Spenserianism is evident in its response to earlier eighteenth-century imitations. Many came to Spenser through the works of Beattie, Shenstone, Thomson, and others. Shelley did not begin reading Spenser until early 1813; his earlier political poems written in Spenserian stanzas, *Henry and Louisa* (1809) and *Queen Mab* (1812) follow the didacticism of eighteenth-century Spenserian imitations, yet, in doing so, critique their patriotic religious and political values from within (Kucich 1991: 246–56). Blake's illustrations to Thomas Gray's *Poems* (1790) open a window onto this revisionary process of transmission. By giving his illustration to Canto 3, verse 3 of *The Bard*, (beginning 'The verse adorn again | Fierce War, and faithful Love, | And Truth severe, by fairy Fiction drest'), the title 'Spenser Creating His Fairies', Blake did not simply draw attention to Gray's indebtedness to Spenser, but through his visualization of the creative process, criticized the oppressive character of blind tradition. Spenser is depicted as the father-creator who sends his fairy child forth into the deadly world of his allegory, his 'Truth severe'. The illustration is disturbing because it demands simultaneous apprehension of 'gentle' Spenser nurturing his Gothic fairy vision and the cruelty of his allegory with its vision of Truth. Blake criticizes Gray's imitation of Spenser in *The Bard* because it is not transformative and therefore cannot liberate the visionary, imaginative qualities of Spenser's 'fairy Fiction' (Gleckner 1985: 12–17, 26).

Romantic writers shared Blake's sense of Spenser as the gentle father-author who nurtures and sustains subsequent generations. Romantic Spenserianism should be viewed in the context of a wider revival of poetry of the first literary 'golden age'. This generation was highly conscious of bringing about a second Renaissance, which raised the inevitable question of whether it was possible to overgo the literary giants, Shakespeare and Milton (Kucich 1991: 66–9). Spenser did not induce such anxieties of influence, possibly because, with *Astrophel*, he had already invented a Spenserian tradition that was communal in impulse. Wordsworth in Book III of *The Prelude* relates his youthful immersion in a thoroughly British literary canon, beginning with Chaucer, then 'that gentle Bard':

> Sweet Spenser, moving through his clouded Heaven
> With the Moon's beauty and the Moon's soft pace,
> I call him Brother, Englishman, and Friend!

Sublime, 'awful', and solitary Milton follows, 'our blind Poet, who, in his later day, | Stood almost single' (Wordsworth 1985: 68–9).

Companionable Spenser provided writers with a medium for imagining and consolidating literary fellowships. Coleridge adopted the pen-name Satyrane in correspondence during the period that Wordsworth was writing his Spenserian 'Stanzas Written in My Pocket Copy of *The Castle of Indolence*', a poetic account of their companionship. The poem relates how the 'noticeable Man, with large dark eyes', usually identified with Wordsworth, 'would entice that other man to hear | His music, and to view his imagery' (Wordsworth 1983: 582–3). Since friendship is conflated with literary influence and the transmission of literary traditions—Coleridge reads Wordsworth, while Wordsworth imitates Thomson imitating Spenser—creative processes, including imitation, are imagined through the forms of companionship and consanguity. Hunt coined the term 'Spenserianizing' to describe this type of playful and companionable referencing of Spenser. For a younger poet like Keats, as Kucich points out, appreciation of Spenser allowed him to make a 'vicarious claim' to membership of circles of older poets—Coleridge, Lamb, Southey, Byron, Hazlitt, and especially

Hunt. Hence, Keats entered the literary scene proclaiming his Spenserianism with the Hunt-inspired 'Imitation of Spenser' (Kucich 1991: 147–8).

To explain the gentle temperament of their companionable Spenser, the Romantics revived the early seventeenth-century story of his victimization. One of the causes of the 'melancholy grace' infusing Spenser's poetry, according to Coleridge, was that he was 'saddened by the unjust persecution of Burleigh' (Coleridge 1983: I, 36) Spenser could thus be viewed as a poet particularly sensitive to the plight of the oppressed, although as Blake pointed out such a 'gentle' Spenser struggled with the 'Truth severe' of his allegory. Wordsworth, in his 1815 preface to his *Poems*, returned to the visionary qualities of Spenser's allegory, which, 'by a superior effort of genius . . . give the universality and permanence of abstractions to his human beings, by means of attributes and emblems that belong to the highest moral truths and the purest sensations' (Wordsworth 1989: 638–9). His *Salisbury Plains* poems, redrafted over a number of years, turned Una and Redcrosse into 'human beings', the Female Vagrant and her male fellow-traveller, and literalized their spiritual trials in the physical suffering of the destitute. Truth-telling becomes a demand for social justice and condemnation of war and the hardships it visits on ordinary people. An early version, dating from around 1793–4, ends in a prophetic strain, calling on the 'Heroes of Truth' to 'pursue your march, uptear | Th'Oppressor's dungeon from its deepest base' (Wordsworth 1975: 38).

While the Romantics were in sympathy with persecuted Spenser, they found his aristocratic politics less attractive. The fate of the 'democratic' Giant in Book 5 was particularly troubling. Wordsworth identified Artegall and Talus with brutal oppression in *Salisbury Plains* (1793–4), 'Must Law with iron scourge | Still torture crimes that grew a monstrous band' (Wordsworth 1975: 37), which sits uneasily with his other Spenser, a poet of sympathy and pathos. In his final months, Keats attempted to correct Spenser's flawed political vision in a single Spenserian stanza that has the Giant, now named 'Typographus', redeemed from 'his brutishness' by education, encounter 'Artegall and Talus grim'—'one he struck stone-blind, the other's eyes wox dim' (Keats 1970: 743). Shelley's response was to champion the oppositional voices in Spenser. He returned repeatedly to Mutabilitie in his lyrics of 1816, 'Mutability' and 'On Death', and *The Revolt of Islam*, because her 'dissonant strings' provided him with a figure for comprehending violent and eternal historical change, revolution and counter-revolution: 'Nought may endure but Mutability' ('Mutability', Shelley 1971: 523). The closing cantos of *The Revolt of Islam* read the Cave of Proteus through the mutability myth in its image of the 'vast stream, a long and labyrinthine maze' and 'Tumultuous floods' (Shelley 1971: 154–5). Shelley wrote *The Revolt of Islam* while staying with Byron in 1816 when Byron was working on his *Childe Harold's Pilgrimage* (1812–18). Both poets redeem the voice of Mutabilitie to imagine the regeneration of society and the collective psyche following climactic political upheaval (Kucich 1991: 124–6, 267–73).

The Romantic response to Spenser was not univocal. Whereas Wordsworth sought to revive the visionary aspect of his allegory, Hunt sidelined allegory to concentrate on the gorgeous surface of Spenser's pictures. Hunt explained Charles Lamb's verdict that Spenser was 'the most poetical of poets' by arguing that 'there was an indolence and . . . a sensuality in his temperament, resembling that of a man addicted to lying on the grass and weaving dreams of pleasure, which disposed him to content himself, if not with the surface of what he beheld, yet with the beauty of its forms and the vivacity of its colours' (Hunt 1956: 420). Keats was strongly influenced by Hunt's indolent and sensual Spenser. Radcliffe has said of *The Eve of St. Agnes* that 'the seduction described in the narrative appears to be a figure for Keats's own desire to be possessed by Spenser's descriptive gorgeousness' (Radcliffe 1996: 91). This may be so, yet Keats, unlike Hunt, was also highly attuned to the dangers lurking within Spenser's bowers; his poem in Spenserian fashion docs not fail to leave warning signs that its 'woofèd phantasies' (Keats 1970: 472) may be fatally debilitating (Kucich 1991: 202–5).

   This tender and sensual Spenser was a particularly feminized version of the poet. Spenser was valued for his female figures. Una was particularly popular—she is Wordsworth's model for his patiently suffering and abandoned heroine, Emily, in *The White Doe of Rylstone*. Other Romantics found Duessa and Acrasia more attractive. In poets' responses to these enchantresses it is possible to trace anxieties about the influence of a feminine and effeminizing Spenser. Addiction to the enchanting world of fairy is the subject of Keats's 'La Belle Dame Sans Mercy' (1819), which was, in turn, heavily influenced by Coleridge's 'Christabel'. Keats's wild 'fairy's child' (Keats 1970: 503), with her siren song, is not simply influenced by Spenser's enchantresses but becomes a figure for assessing the seductive power of the Spenserian tradition as Keats receives it. The charms of Phaedria's bower and the Bowre of Blisse, when read through Thomson's *Castle of Indolence*, Patricia Parker has explained, are 'the charms of the tradition of romancing itself' (Parker 1972: 380). Keats's knight is consumed by his vision and fancy. The danger is that 'lying on the grass and weaving dreams of pleasure' may become so addictive that it is not possible to rouse oneself, and the poet is held back from higher poetic pursuits, typically identified with sublime Milton, who soared 'Above the Aonian mount' (*Paradise Lost*, I, 15; Parker 1972: 383). In their conversations with Spenser, the Romantic poets composed complex narratives of literary influence which ranged from Wordsworth's 'Brother, Englishman, and Friend' to the more troublingly and potentially disabling Spenser described by Coleridge, whose mind was so 'constitutionally tender, delicate, and, in comparison with his three great compeers, I had almost said, *effeminate*' (Coleridge 1983: I, 36).

SPENSER AND THE VICTORIANS

The death of Keats in 1821 and Shelley in 1822 marked the revival of a conservative reading of Spenser. Wordsworth's earlier republican 'Brother, Englishman, and Friend' was recast in Christian and patriotic guise (Radcliffe 1996: 97). Romantic

Spenserianism nonetheless continued to influence responses to Spenser throughout the nineteenth century. Tennyson was hailed by Hunt as the worthy successor to Keats and Wordsworth (Hunt 1956: 526–7). The gorgeousness of Spenser's pictures admired so fervently by Hunt continues in the fleshliness of Victorian paintings of episodes from *The Faerie Queene*, for example, William Etty's *Britomart Redeems Faire Amoret* (1833) or Joseph Pitt's sculpture of *Sir Calepine Rescuing Serena* (1852). Ruskin also admired Spenser's pictorialism, yet unlike Hunt he insisted that its proper interpretive context was the morality of Christian allegory. For Ruskin, Spenser was the great Renaissance poet, 'who exactly marks the junction of mediaeval and classical feeling', precisely because of his allegory, whose 'completeness' of vision surpassed even Dante (*Stones of Venice*, II, 318, 383). One particular reading of Spenser that crystallizes in the nineteenth century is his association with childhood and the youthful imagination. Prose versions of *The Faerie Queene* written specifically for children began to appear in the late eighteenth century, reaching the height of their popularity in the nineteenth (see Chapters 19 and 35 above).

Tennyson reputedly said that Spenser 'was not much known or admired by him' (*SE*, 683). His 'The Lotos-Eaters' and 'The Lady of Shalott' could not have been written without Spenser, even so, it is possible that Tennyson came to Spenser only through eighteenth-century and Romantic Spenserianism, although the specificity of his borrowings suggest otherwise. Behind the 'mirror clear' in which the 'Shadows of the world appear' (Tennyson 1969: I, 390–1), including the Lady of Shalott's fateful vision of Sir Lancelot, is the mirror in which Britomart beholds her future, Artegall. The broader influence of the Spenserian tradition is evident in the bower of the fairy Lady, whose world of shade and shadows must be left behind. 'The Lotos-Eaters', written partly in Spenserian stanzas, is Tennyson's most explicit engagement with Spenserianism. Tennyson places himself in a long line of poets who responded to Spenser's Phaedria and her siren song, and brings it to a close. Her enchanting song is now sung by the mariners, a transference that intensifies the sense of aesthetic and moral unease with their repudiation of manly industrious imperial pursuits for the illusory promise of stasis and repose; Phaedria's song has become deathly, 'a doleful song', 'a lamentation and an ancient tale of wrong' (Tennyson 1969: I, 476).

Elizabeth Barrett Browning read Spenser extensively, and from a young age (*SE*, 116). *A Vision of Poets* is thoroughly Spenserian: it is prefaced by an echo poem from Book II of Browne's *Britannia's Pastorals*, and the poet's guide, 'a lady riding slow | Upon a palfrey white as snow' (Browning 1994: 163), is a version of Spenser's Una. Spenser appears in the vision as a poet of sensual indolence:

> And Spenser drooped his dreaming head
> (With languid sleep-smile you had said
> From his own verse engendered)   (Browning 1994: 167)

Barrett Browning reads Spenser as a specifically feminine poet; he is wittily cast as the archetypal love poet alongside Petrarch in 'Lady Geraldine's Courtship', in which the hero, Bertram, 'Read[s] the pastoral parts of Spenser' (Browning 1994: 222) to woo his Geraldine. Barrett Browning's 'languid' Spenser, like that of Keats, may have been influenced by Mary Tighe's reading of Spenser in her *Psyche; or, the Legend of Love* (1806). Writing from the perspective of Psyche, Tighe equated the sensuality of Spenserianism with a distinctly feminine poetic, to the extent that when the poem was republished posthumously in 1811, the preface so fully identified Tighe with her Spenserian subject that the tender and 'suffering' Psyche was proffered as a figure for the female author (Tighe 1811: iii).

Christina Rossetti's *Goblin Market* (1862) is a similarly suggestive response to Spenserianism and the world of fairy by a woman writer. Rossetti was familiar enough with Spenser for A. B. Grosart to commission her in 1876 to identify the Italian sources in *The Faerie Queene* for his edition of the *Works* (1882–4)—this work was not completed due to ill health (Rossetti 1999: II, 89). *Goblin Market* is an allegory of temptation, fallenness, and redemption. In its engagement with a concept of sapience as taste, we can see the influence of a Miltonic reading of Spenser. Lizzie, like Milton's Guyon, 'sallies out and sees her adversary', exposing herself to Keatsian goblin fruits so that she might 'see and know, and yet abstain' (Milton 1931–40: IV, 311). The difference is that in Rossetti's re-reading we do not have a story of manly temperance but rather a potent tale of sisterhood.

One path increasingly taken by those rewriting *The Faerie Queene* in the nineteenth century was that of children's literature. From Cowley, who claimed to have read all of *The Faerie Queene* before he was twelve 'and was thus made a poet' (Cummings: 86), to Keats, whose youthful reading of Spenser similarly 'awakened his genius', Spenser was seen as a poet particularly suitable for youthful imaginations (Kucich 1991: 5; Radcliffe 1994: 123). Between 1829 and 1929, twenty-six adaptations of *The Faerie Queene* written specifically for children were published (*SE*, 289–91). One of the earliest is a Spenserian imitation by Lucy Peacock, *The Adventure of the Six Princesses of Babylon, in their Travels to the Temple of Virtue: An Allegory* (1785), which was dedicated to Princess Mary and aimed at a youthful female readership. Her next Spenserian imitation, *The Knight of the Rose. An Allegorical Narrative: Including Histories, Adventures, &c. Designed for the Amusement and Moral Instruction of Youth* (1793), based on Book II, has a male protagonist. While Peacock acknowledged the difficulties posed by allegory, she concluded that 'for that class of [youthful] readers, the author cannot think that moral truths will make the less impression, for being addressed so strongly to the imagination' (Peacock 1793: A2ᵛ). Now deemed suitable for fashioning young readers in gentle discipline and Christian virtues, Spenserian allegory took on new directions in prose redactions for children.

SPENSER AND IRELAND

If we want to trace a continuous line of Spenser's influence from the seventeenth into the twentieth century and beyond, then we need to turn our attention away from

England to Ireland. Spenser and the Elizabethans continue to be a significant political presence in Irish culture. On the one hand, Spenser has been embraced as the father of an Anglo-Irish literary tradition, and, on the other, repudiated as the murderous representative of English rule. Spenser's *A View of the Present State of Ireland* remains the most influential statement of the premise 'that only a conquered Ireland can be truly civilized', and set the terms for English treatises and policy on Ireland throughout the seventeenth century and beyond (Rankin 2005: 3, 67). When unrest in Ireland became a pressing problem for the English at the turn of the nineteenth century, there was renewed interest in Spenser's *View*: Henry Todd reprinted this 'excellent and profound' treatise in his 1805 edition of Spenser's *Works*, and it was included in the 1809 Dublin edition (Kucich 1991: 93).

Sir James Ware's 1633 edition of *A View*, by incorporating Spenser's 'Irish' poetry— the Irish topographies from Book IV of *The Faerie Queene* and *Mutabilitie Cantos* and the poems addressed to the Earls of Ormond and Cork, Lord Grey and Sir John Norris—presented Spenser both as an historian of Ireland and, significantly, as an Anglo-Irish poet (McCabe 2002: 278). His place at the head of an Anglo-Irish literary tradition was well-established by the late seventeenth century. A 'Mr. Adams', in his Spenserian *A Pastoral, Written at Dublin, in May 1683*, posed the question of Spenser's successor in a specifically Irish literary context: 'Who to these Groves shall foreign Numbers bring? | Where once great *Spencer* did triumphant reign' (Tate 1685: 45). What was required was an Irish heroic poetry capable of celebrating its national heroes, the Earls of Ossory, Arran, Ormond, and particularly Armagh: 'And all the ecchoing Plains, th'attentive Woods | Of *Armagh* sing, of *Armagh* all the Floods' (Tate 1685: 48). Other writers were less appreciative of Spenser's legacy in Ireland. Seathrún Céitinn was highly critical of *A View* when it was first published in 1633, and drew attention to Spenser's profound ignorance of Gaelic culture. Céitinn mockingly turned Spenser into a type of Archimago; rather than history, *A View* was a web of invention, made up of 'poetic romances with sweet-sounding words to deceive the reader' (McCabe 2002: 279). Spenser also had his critics in England. Thomas Edwards's sonnet, 'On the Cantos of Spenser's Fairy Queen, Lost in the Passage from Ireland', first published in 1748, sympathizes with 'Ill-starr'd *Hibernia*!' and imagines it is 'well . . . appaid' by the loss of Spenser's epic poem of Irish conquest, and 'No longer now with idle sorrow mourn | Thy plunder'd wealth, or liberties restrain'd', since 'Severe revenge on Britain in thy turn, | . . . thy treacherous waves obtain'd, | Which sunk one half of Spenser's deathless fame' (Dodsley 1748: II, 331).

When W. B. Yeats sought to enter the Dublin literary establishment in the late nineteenth century he turned, like Keats before him, to Spenser to make himself into a poet and announce his arrival on the literary scene. One of his earliest university poems was a Spenserian imitation, 'Sir Roland'. *The Island of Statues* (1885), his first published work, was a Spenserian pastoral tragicomedy that is given epic, visionary scope. For Yeats, Spenser was the archetypal English Renaissance poet who could enable this 'new Poete' to orchestrate his own Irish Renaissance and assume his place at the head of the Irish Literary Revival (Gardiner 2001: 48–56). Yeats's selected edition, *The Poems of Spenser* (1906), is a complex reappraisal of Romantic readings of Spenser in an Irish context. Part of his solution to the problem of Spenser's politics was to produce a variant on persecuted Spenser. Yeats's Spenser is ideologically enslaved to the Elizabethan state; a victim of its imperialism which has left him deaf and blind to Irish bardic culture: 'Spenser, the first poet struck with remorse, the first poet who gave his heart to the State, saw nothing but disorder, where the mouths that have spoken all the fables of the poets had not yet become silent' (Yeats 1906: xxxiii–xxxiv). What Yeats occludes is that it was Spenser in his *View* who demanded these voices be silenced. There is an unresolved tension in Yeats's appropriation of Spenser. Although part of Spenser's appeal was the precedent he offered as a national political poet, in order to reclaim him for an Irish literary canon the Spenserian poet 'must sit apart' from the world 'in contemplative indolence playing with fragile things' (Yeats 1906: xli).

The creative dialogue between the Northern Irish Renaissance and the Troubles in the 1960s and 1970s provided the context for a reassessment of Spenser's legacy. J. G. Farrell named the principal Anglo-Irish character of his novel, *Troubles* (1970), Edward Spencer. John Montague, an Ulster Catholic, returned to an Elizabethan Spenser in order to negotiate his own place in a divided Ireland and redefine an Irish tradition (Gardiner 2001: 121–5). His major work, *The Rough Field* (1972), set up a dialogue between Elizabethan and contemporary Ireland. It is illustrated with wood-cuts from John Derricke's *A Discoverie of Woodkarne* (1581), which as Montague explained, 'depicts the life of the Irish in Ulster and Sir Henry Sidney's campaigns against them' (Montague 1989: 87), and extracts from Elizabethan tracts on Ireland, including Spenser's *View*. Montague aligns his own voice with bardic culture, relating in his preface that he 'saw the poem as taking over where the last bard of the O'Neills left off' (Montague 1989: vii)—the clan responsible for Spenser's expulsion from Kilcolman. Montague reappropriates powerful figures and symbols of Irish culture— the bards, and Irish mantles in 'The Great Cloak' (1978)—from the colonizing discourses of Spenserian civility. The *Dead Kingdom* (1984) where, as he told David Gardiner in an interview, he 'finally had it out with Spenser' (Gardiner 2001: 184), includes the poem 'Gone' in which he writes of his Irish goddess-muse, Mutabilitie:

> Chiding Spenser, I yet sing
> of the goddess Mutability,
> dark Lady of Process,
> our devouring Queen.   (Montague 1984: 19)

Mutabilitie, a potent counter-voice for the Romantic poets, is reclaimed by this generation of Irish writers and returned to her Irish home in Galtymore, which Spenser named Arlo Hill in the *Mutabilitie Cantos*.

Frank McGuinness's play, *Mutabilitie* (1997), was performed in November 1998 when the Belfast Agreement was being negotiated (Murray 2002: 168). This Irish history play is set on the eve of Spenser's flight from Kilcolman. McGuinness presents us with a 'gentle' yet brutalized Spenser, reminiscent of Yeats's image of Spenser as the 'hysterical patient' who 'drew a complicated web of inhuman logic out of the bowels of an insufficient premise' (Yeats 1906: xix). McGuinness's Spenser's mind is 'broken' by the contradictions which constitute the colonial subject—in scene six, it is Spenser who sets fire to his castle (McGuinness 1997: 98). The counter-voice in the play is File, a bard, whose anachronistic femininity amplifies her oppositional status. Her song is one of 'mutabilitie', death, and violence, which ultimately must also be rejected. Into this milieu, McGuinness introduces Shakespeare, who at first holds out the possibility of an alternative model of Irish theatre—as William says 'I am with the loser'—but is ultimately rejected because the promise he offers is illusory and 'fearful' (McGuinness 1997: 93). The hope for reconciliation between English and Irish, North and South, Protestant and Catholic resides with Spenser's lost child, sacrificed by his father for his colonial ideals, who escapes the fire and remains in Ireland nurtured by an Irish bardic culture. Like Shelley before him, McGuinness finds in Mutabilitie a figure that simultaneously dramatizes political conflict and prophetically imagines its 'resolution outside of time' (Murray 2002: 171).

Following Yeats, poets have constantly returned to the question of whether Spenser is redeemable for Irish poetry as part of a wider debate about the future of Ireland. Montague in his essay, 'In the Irish Grain' prefacing his 1974 Faber Book of Irish Verse, like Yeats, implied that only a suffering Spenser might be acceptable: 'From Spenser to Hopkins, a succession of English poets have suffered in Ireland, but we have only an oblique claim on them, although I thought of including the passage on the rivers from The Faerie Queene to challenge any narrow definitions of Irish poetry' (Montague 1974: 27). Brendan Kennelly, a Munster poet, for his sonnet sequence, Cromwell (1983) gave Spenser a wittily crude, 'barbarous' voice that jars in burlesque fashion with the lyricism of the sonnets, and so works against any easy assimilation of Spenser's literary inheritance. If 'Yeats is of the lineage of Spenser', as Jon Stallworthy notes, then 'Seamus Heaney claims descent from those who burnt Spenser's castle' in his poems 'Exposure' and 'Bog Oak' (Stallworthy 1982: 159). That said, Heaney's recent introduction to his verse translation of Beowulf suggest a rapprochement, even perhaps sympathy with Spenser as a means of imagining a different future for Ireland and British literature:

every time I read the lovely interlude that tells of the minstrel singing in Heorot just before the first attacks of Grendel, I cannot help thinking of Edmund Spenser in Kilcolman Castle, reading the early cantos of The Faerie Queene to Sir Walter Raleigh, just before the Irish would burn down the castle and drive Spenser out of Munster back to the Elizabethan court. Putting a bawn into Beowulf seems one way for an Irish poet to come to terms with that complex history of conquest and colony, absorption and resistance, integrity and antagonism, a history that has to be clearly acknowledged by all concerned in order to render it ever more 'willable forward / again and again and again'. (Heaney 2002: xxxviii)

The school of contemporary Cork poets, influenced by Montague, similarly draw attention to Spenser's acts of linguistic colonization in his 'Irish' poetry. Seán Dunne's poem, 'Doneraile Court', published in The Sheltered Nest (1992), resists Spenser's linguistic possession of the land, his poetic renaming of the lands around his estate, by recasting the refrain to his seminal Anglo-Irish poem, Epithalamion: 'No woods can answer and no echoes ring' (Gardiner 2001: 206–8).

These recent literary and dramatic negotiations of Spenser are significant because they coincide with critical interest in an Irish and colonial Spenser which is part of a wider intellectual and political reassessment of Britain's colonial legacy. For contemporary Irish writers and critics, Spenser and the late sixteenth century are still very much alive in the political topography of Ireland. As Gardiner points out, this new generation of Irish poets embraces the idea that 'Spenser wrote in a time when language wielded real power' (Gardiner 2001: 197). It serves to remind us that the relevance of Spenser, from the Jacobeans to the Romantics and to twentieth-century Irish writers, is recognized when the dangerous and fruitful proximity of art and politics is understood.

NOTE

1. I thank John Holmes for his comments on sections of this essay, and Stephen Matthews and David Norbrook for their advice on contemporary Irish 'Spenserians'.

BIBLIOGRAPHY

Basse, William (1893). *Poetical Works*, ed. R. W. Bond. London.

Beattie, James (1775). *The Minstrel; or, The Progress of Genius. A Poem in Two Books*. Dublin.

Bouchard, G. M. (2000). *Colin's Campus: Cambridge Life and the English Eclogue*. London: Associated University Presses.

Browne, William (1616). *Britannia's Pastorals. The second Booke*. London.

Browning, Elizabeth Barrett (1994). *The Works of Elizabeth Barrett Browning*, introd. K. Hill. Ware: Wordsworth Editions.

Coleridge, Samuel Taylor (1983). *Biographia Literaria*, ed. J. Engell and W. Jackson Bate, 2 vols. London: Routledge and Kegan Paul.

Croxall, Samuel (1714 [1713]). *An Original Canto of Spencer: Design'd as Part of his Fairy Queen, but never Printed. Now made Publick, by Nestor Ironside*. London.

Davenant, William (1650). *A Discourse upon Gondibert*.

Dodsley, R. (ed.) (1748). *Collection of Poems by Several Hands, In Three Volumes*, 2nd edn. London.

Dryden, John (1956–2000). *The Works of John Dryden*, ed. V. A. Dearing, 20 vols. Berkeley: University of California Press.

Felton, H. (1753). *A Dissertation on Reading the Classics, and Forming a Just Style*, 5th edn, 2 vols. London.

Finkelpearl, P. J. (1987). 'John Fletcher as Spenserian Playwright: *The Faithful Shepherdess* and *The Island Princess*'. *SEL* 27: 285–302.

Frushell, R. C. (1999). *Edmund Spenser in the Early Eighteenth Century: Education, Imitation, and the Making of a Literary Model*. Pittsburgh: Duquesne University Press.

Gardiner, D. (2001). *'Befitting Emblems of Adversity': A Modern Irish View of Edmund Spenser from W. B. Yeats to the Present*. Omaha, NE: Creighton University Press.

Gerrard, C. (1994). *The Patriot Opposition to Walpole: Politics, Poetry, and National Myth, 1725–42.* Oxford: Clarendon Press.

Gill, Alexander (1621). *Logonomia Anglica*, 2nd edn. London.

Gleckner, R. F. (1985). *Blake and Spenser.* Baltimore: Johns Hopkins University Press.

Heaney, Seamus (2002). *Beowulf: a verse translation*, ed. D. Donoghue. New York/London: Norton.

Hulse, C. (1988). 'Spenser, Bacon, and the Myth of Power', in H. Dubrow and R. Strier (eds), *The Historical Renaissance: New Essays on Tudor and Stuart Literature.* Chicago: University of Chicago Press: 315–46.

Hunt, Leigh (1956). *Leigh Hunt's Literary Criticism*, ed. L. H. Houtchens and C. W. Houtchens. New York: Columbia University Press.

Hunter, W. B. (ed.) (1977). *The English Spenserians: The Poetry of Giles Fletcher, George Wither, Michael Drayton, Phineas Fletcher and Henry More.* Salt Lake City: University of Utah Press.

Kay, D. (1990). *Melodious Tears: The English Funeral Elegy from Spenser to Milton.* Oxford: Clarendon Press.

Keats, John (1970). *The Poems of John Keats*, ed. M. Allott. London/New York: Longman.

Kucich, G. (1991). *Keats, Shelley, and Romantic Spenserianism.* Philadelphia: Pennsylvania University Press.

McCabe, R. A. (2002). *Spenser's Monstrous Regiment: Elizabethan Ireland and the Poetics of Difference.* Oxford: Oxford University Press.

—— (2008). 'Rhyme and Reason: Poetics, Patronage and Secrecy in Elizabethan and Jacobean Ireland', in D. Womersley and R. A. McCabe (eds), *Literary Milieux: Essays in Text and Context, Presented to Howard Erskine-Hill.* Newark: Delaware University Press: 30–51.

McGuinness, Frank (1997). *Mutabilitie.* London: Faber and Faber.

Milton, John (1931–40). *The Works of John Milton*, ed. F. A. Patterson et al., 18 vols. New York: Columbia University Press.

Montague, John (1974). *The Faber Book of Irish Verse.* London: Faber & Faber.

—— (1984). *The Dead Kingdom.* Portlaoise: Dolmen Press.

—— (1989). *The Rough Field, 1961–71.* Loughcrew, Odcastle: The Gallery Press.

More, Henry (1647). *Philosophical Poems.* Cambridge.

Murray, C. (2002). 'Of *Mutabilitie*', in H. Lojek (ed.), *The Theatre of Frank McGuinness: Stages of Mutability.* Dublin: Carysfort Press.

Niccols, Richard (1992). *Selected Poems*, ed. G. Pursglove. Lewiston, NY: Edwin Mellen Press.

Norbrook, D. G. E. (2002). *Poetry and Politics in the English Renaissance*, 2nd edn. Oxford: Oxford University Press.

O'Callaghan, M. (2000). *The 'shepheards nation': Jacobean Spenserians and Early Stuart Political Culture, 1612–25.* Oxford: Clarendon Press.

Parker, P. (1973). 'The Progress of Phaedria's Bower: Spenser to Coleridge'. *ELH* 40: 372–97.

Peacock, Lucy (1793). *The Knight of the Rose. An Allegorical Narrative: Including Histories, Adventures, &c. Designed for the Amusement and Moral Instruction of Youth.* London.

Pope, Alexander (1961–9). *The Poems of Alexander Pope*, ed. J. Butt et al., 11 vols. London: Methuen; New Haven, CT: Yale University Press.

Prior, Matthew (1706). *An Ode, Humbly Inscrib'd to the Queen. On the Late Glorious Success of her Majesty's Arms. Written in Imitation of Spencer's Stile.* London.

Quilligan, M. (1983). *Milton's Spenser: The Politics of Reading.* Ithaca, NY: Cornell University Press.

Radcliffe, D. H. (1996). *Edmund Spenser: A Reception History.* Columbia: Camden House.

Rankin, D. (2005). *Between Spenser and Swift: English Writing in Seventeenth-Century Ireland.* Cambridge: Cambridge University Press.

Rossetti, Christina (1999). *The Letters of Christina Rossetti*, ed. A. H. Harrison, 4 vols. Charlottesville: University Press of Virginia.

Sawday, J. (1995). *The Body Emblazoned: Dissection and the Human Body in Renaissance Culture*. London: Routledge.

Shelley, Percy Bysshe (1971). *Complete Poetical Works*, ed. T. Hutchinson, corrected by G. M. Matthews. Oxford: Oxford University Press.

Shenstone, William (1742). *The School-Mistress, A Poem in Imitation of Spenser*. London.

—— (1770). *The Works in Verse and Prose of William Sherstone*, 3 vols. Edindurgh.

Sheppard, Samuel (1984). *The Faerie King (c. 1650)*, ed. P. J. Klemp. Salzburg: Salzburg Studies in English Literature.

Spenser, E. (pseud.) (1648). *The Faerie Leveller: or, King Charles his Leveller described and deciphered in Queene Elizabeths dayes*. London.

Spenser, Edmund (1750). *The Works of Spenser. In six volumes*, ed. J. Hughes. London.

Stallworthy, J. (1982). 'The Poet as Archaeologist: W. B. Yeats and Seamus Heaney'. *RES* 33: 158–74.

Stubbe, Henry (1659). *A Light Shining out of Darknes*, 2nd edn. London. Wing S6057.

Tate, Nahum (1685). *Poems by Several Hands, and on Several Occasions Collected by N. Tate*. London.

Tennyson, Arthur Lord (1969). *Poems of Tennyson*, ed. C. Ricks, 3 vols. London: Longman.

Thomson, James (1748). *The Castle of Indolence. An Allegorical Poem. Written in Imitation of Spenser*. London.

Tighe, Mary (1811). *Psyche, with Other Poems*, 3rd edn. London.

Tonson, J. (ed.) (1709). *Poetical Miscellanies: The Sixth Part. Containing a Collection of Original Poems, With Several New Translations. By the most Eminent Hands*. London.

Tylus, J. (1990). 'Jacobean Poetry and Lyric Disappointment', in E. D. Harvey and K. E. Maus (eds), *Soliciting Interpretation: Literary Theory and Seventeenth-Century English Poetry*. Chicago: University of Chicago Press: 174–98.

West, Gilbert (1751). *Education, a Poem: in Two Cantos. Written in Imitation of the Style and Manner of Spenser's Fairy Queen*. London.

Wordsworth, William (1975). *The Salisbury Plain Poems*, ed. S. Gill. Ithaca, NY: Cornell University Press; Hassocks: The Harvester Press.

—— (1983). *Poems, in Two Volumes, and Other Poems, 1800–1807*, ed. J. Curtis. Ithaca, NY: Cornell University Press.

—— (1985). *The Fourteen-Book Prelude*, ed. W. J. B. Owen. Ithaca, NY/London: Cornell University Press.

—— (1989). *Shorter Poems, 1807–1820*, ed. C. H. Ketcham. Ithaca, NY/London: Cornell University Press.

Yeats, W. B. (ed.) (1906). *The Poems of Spenser Selected and with an Introduction by W.B. Yeats*. Edinburgh.

CHAPTER 37

SPENSER AND THE VISUAL ARTS

CLAIRE PRESTON

IT did not take E. K.'s tantalizing reference to Spenser's 'pictures' in *The Shepheardes Calender* to suggest the pictorial quality of his work to readers of the last four centuries (Spenser 1999: 26). From almost the beginning of his career, Spenser seems consciously to have referred his poetic images to the concretely painterly and plastic; and he was consistently recognized and applauded even in his own day for the rich, apparently 'visual' character of his poetry. His earliest published work— the anonymous translations of the visionary sonnets and epigrams in Van der Noot's *A Theatre for Voluptuous Worldlings* (1569)—blends poetic vision with the accompanying woodcuts which followed etchings already published in the Dutch and French editions (Bath 1998). His first major work, *The Shepheardes Calender* (1579), has been described as the first poem in English to be accompanied by a 'programmatic set of illustrations designed as an integral part of a printed artefact'; and both works have been likened to emblem-books and almanacs, genres to which they have only an incomplete likeness (Friedland 1956: 107; Heninger 1998: 33). The importance of the visual arts in Spenser is witnessed by the persistence of lavishly illustrated editions of *The Faerie Queene*, as well as some of his other poems, as late as the mid-twentieth century, and by the large body of opinion and scholarship which has devoted itself to discussions of Spenser's pictorial technique, identifications of specific pictorial referents and artistic styles behind certain Spenserian images, and speculation as to the kind of pictorial material which would have been available to him in England. All these interpretive strands firmly locate Spenser within the realm of the literary-pictorial. The nature of Spenser's relationship to the visual arts, what precisely is meant by Spenser's 'pictorialism', and the contingency of all the other matters of the Spenserian visual on such a definition, is the subject of the following remarks.

SPENSER AND LITERARY PICTORIALISM

The Renaissance obsession with (partly misapprehended) notions and debates inherited from ancient writers—*ut pictura poesis* (the Horatian dictum that was interpreted as 'let poems be like pictures'), the *paragone* or debate between the arts, the Neo-platonic enthusiasm for hieroglyphical and supposedly denotative language, and the use of ekphrasis (or vivid description) and associated rhetorical figures—proved irresistible to the English poetic imagination between 1550 and the middle of the seventeenth century. There is much modern writing on an obsession which virtually ensured that the poets would attempt to imbue their work with visual attributes.[1] Although the full details of Renaissance visual-verbal relations can only be alluded to here, it is important to recognize its two most important features: first, that Sidney's remarkable intervention in the *Defence of Poetry*, where he audaciously claims the traditional superiorities of art-forms appealing to sight (the noblest of the senses) for the poet and poetic 'speaking pictures of virtues, vices, and what else', ensured that his protégés and successors like Spenser championed poetic technique which seemed to raise the verbal to the summit of moral and didactic efficacy previously associated with the visual arts; and second, that in a climate of rising uneasiness with mimesis or representation—an uneasiness that had already manifested itself in a powerful iconophobia and the destruction of images—the power of the poet to reserve the visual to a rhetorical rather than a sensory category which was all but unassailable (because merely conceptual) proved highly attractive, even to godly poets who themselves might well have disapproved of the plastic arts in the flesh, so to speak. Spenser calls his poetic pictures 'colour showes' (III Proem, 3), and Renaissance literary pictorialism, as he practised it, was a tool of immense affective power which safely conveys the reader through the otherwise dangerous delights of the eye.

Even before there can be said to be anything like a Spenser 'industry', readers noticed the pictorial quality of his writing; his work, especially *The Faerie Queene* and especially from the eighteenth century onwards, was generally regarded as a kind of verbal picture-gallery. It is hardly surprising that this should be the case: a brief list of the pictorial elements in the poetry include descriptions of art-objects (pictures, emblems, heraldic devices, tapestries, architecture, costume, jewels, sculpture, and ornamental landscapes with grottoes and fountains), episodes set in and dependent on the displays of such objects (for example, the tapestries and bas reliefs in the house of Busirane and in Castle Joyous in *Faerie Queene* III; the chamber of Phantastes, 'dispainted' with 'infinite shapes' in the Castle of Alma; and the minutely rendered artifice of the Bowre of Blisse in *Faerie Queene* II); and the frequency of deictic signals such as 'there you might see', 'the sight whereof' (*TW*), and 'painted', 'portrayed', and 'enwoven' (*FQ*), which invite the mind to inspect verbal images as if they were present to the eye, together with verbs of display ('show', 'portray/pour-traict', 'figure', 'shadow', 'picture', 'image'—a lexical habit Spenser shares with Sidney). Indeed, words alluding to controlled and guided sight (as distinct from the sense of vision more generally) appear in five Spenser titles (*A Theatre for Worldlings*, *Visions of the Worlds Vanitie*, *The Visions of Bellay*, *The Visions of Petrarch*, and even *A Vewe of the Present State of Ireland*). It is impossible, therefore, to resist the 'pictorial' as a primary feature of his work.[2]

The ontological distinction between the pictorial and the merely descriptive is, however, vexed; and the difficulty is inherent in an uncritical acceptance of the metaphor *ut pictura poesis*, an acceptance often entertained by the Renaissance poets but not one that they could easily sustain in practice.[3] The problem is, of course, whether words can in any sense be deployed to render the processes of visual perception. As John Bender states the case, 'how can poems . . . seem like pictures at all?' (Bender 1972: 24). Bender himself has proposed three categories of Spenserian pictorialism—focusing, framing, and scanning—which go some way to identifying certain features of Spenser's technique. In each, descriptive material works narrative-ly, either to suspend, intensify, or spatially regulate our 'view' of events in *The Faerie Queene* and some of the minor poems. Such pictorial interventions are, it is essential to understand, not ornaments subsidiary to meaning and to narrative progression but the very stuff of meaning itself. Whether or not one agrees with Bender's precise division of poetic material into such categories, to understand Spenser's art in this way helps to dispel the much older view of his allegory as consisting of abstract ideas tricked out with convenient, supporting images.

Thus, when Spenser tells us of a tapestry

> Wouen with gold and silke so close and nere,
> That the rich metall lurked priuily,
> As faining to be hid from enuious eye   (III.xi.28),

he is introducing an artefact whose subject-matter will have bearing on the episode in which it is displayed; but he is also making that artefact (with its snake-like gold lurking in the weft to suggest the sins of lust which are depicted) function as a craft-generated embodiment of his theme. When he then announces that 'in those Tapets weren fashioned | Many faire pourtraicts', he engages in the practice which most obviously marks out his pictorialism: he proposes an imagined art-object or other item within the narrative of the poem as available for our close inspection. Such ekphrastic events happen many times in *The Faerie Queene*, when either (or both) character or reader is directed to attend to described physical details, details which are often the pictorial subject itself but also sometimes consist instead of a catalogue of the technical skills which have produced it.[4] The lines describing the weaving of gold into the body of Busirane's tapestry, the rendering of the hierarchies of space that produce the illusion of perspective in Redcrosse's vision of the new Jerusalem (I.x.55–9), or the arming of Clarion in *Muiopotmos* (57–96), for example, are as pictorially prominent as the blow-by-blow enumeration of 'curious imageree' such as the porch and the fountain in Acrasia's highly artful Bowre of Blisse, 'rare deuices' so cunningly fashioned that anyone not 'well auis'd' 'would surely deeme it to be . . . trew' (II.xii.61). Add to this his remarks which praise the virtuosity of such renditions—the story of the oak and the briar in the February eclogue of *The Shepheardes Calender* which is told 'so lively and so feelingly, as if the thing were set forth in some picture before our eyes', or the claim that the poetic image 'passeth Painter farre | In picturing the parts of beautie daint' (III Proem, 2)—and we are enveloped in the illusions of the painted word.

In poetic pictorialism 'acts of perception . . . must precede acts of interpretation' (Kamholtz 1980: 59), and the necessity of such acts are constantly drawn to our notice by Spenser, who deploys ekphrastic description to halt narrative in favour of inspection, and frequently places internal viewers of visual information before our eyes so that the perception and its interpretive act are mediated by sensibilities other than our own. At other times we are invited to oversee such moments with superior analytic ability, to observe characters' misapprehensions of, and bewilderment by, the visual and the pictorial. In each case, such moments are transmitted by elaborate visual catalogues. We find a simple Spenserian pictorial moment in a description of a bull bitten by a gadfly in the second poem in *Visions of the Worlds Vanitie*:

> In Summers day, when *Phoebus* fairly shone,
> I saw a Bull as white as driven snowe,
> With gilden hornes embowed like the Moone,
> In a fresh flowring meadow lying lowe:
>   Up to his eares the verdant grasse did growe,
>   And the gay floures did offer to be eaten;
>   But he with fatnes so did overflowe,
>   That he all wallowed in the weedes down beaten
>   Ne car'd with them his daintie lips to sweeten.

This picture is not a rendition of some standard art subject, and specifically it is not framed as an artefact: Spenser tells us, as so often in his vision-poems, that he 'saw' this scene. And although the bull becomes, in this description, a symbol or a *donnée* of complacency, the carefully described, familiar attitudes of bovine contentment ('up to his ears' in grass and sleekly fat) are ones we recognize not from Ovid or from tapestries but from experience; description *makes* experiential memory pictorial and compels us to inspect, approve, and actively interpret it. When the 'breeze', his antagonist, bites the bull, displeasure erases all the richly depicted satisfaction of the earlier lines. Rather as the motto of an emblem organizes our perception of accompanying image, Spenser's conclusion, 'so by the small the great is oft diseased', frames the word-picture of the bull and the insect and pictorializes it.

The indication of active looking ('I saw') in the previous example is only rudimentary compared to much more elaborate scenes of inspection and framing that we find when Spenserian characters encounter visual significance, as for example when Britomart studies (and quite fails to make anything of) the tapestries and carvings of Busirane; or when she and Redcrosse find themselves in Malecasta's festal hall in Castle Joyeous. There, spectacular 'clothes of Arras and of Toure' show the tale of Venus and Adonis. 'Living wit,' Spenser remarks, 'cannot display' this chamber adequately, but after five intensely descriptive stanzas which belie that claim, he concludes with Adonis transfigured into an anemone '[w]hich in that cloth was wrought, as if it lively grew' (III.i.38). This scene is carefully imagined in order to show the reaction of the two knights: Redcrosse is utterly seduced by its sensual attractions; for Britomart, however, 'they all but shadowes beene' (III.i.45). The vigour with which the poem urges our attention in such scenes is connected to the presence of imagined artefacts such as pictures, tapestries, goblets, statues, and the like. For example, Spenser's frequent rendition of tapestries is likely to be prompted not only by his familiarity with real tapestries, but also by the way in which tapestries are produced in discrete panels—in the case of those in Castle Joyeous, four panels which show the phases of the story—and allow him naturally to frame and pace the pattern of inspection and interpretation.

SPENSER'S VISUAL CULTURE

In a letter to Gabriel Harvey Spenser described the woodcuts for his unpublished 'Dreames' as 'pictures so singularly set forth, and portrayed, as if *Michael Angelo* were there, he could (I think) nor amende the best, nor reprehende the worst' (*Prose*, 18). It is hard to judge this remark: either Spenser had not seen any Michelangelo and must be forgiven for so bathetic and fanciful a comparison; or he *had*, and we must reluctantly allow that even Homer sometimes nods.

The difficulty with much of the critical attention to word–image relations in Spenser is that his plausible pictorial renditions of items like pictures and tapestries have appealed to scholars and critics who have repeatedly tried, without success, to discover their referents in the plastic arts. Titian, Rubens, Rosa, Claude, Caracci, Correggio, Rembrandt, Raphael, Michaelangelo, Sassetta, Giulio Romano, Guido Reni, Poussin, Lorraine, Albano, Veronese, Dürer, Giorgione, Caravaggio, Bosch, El Greco, Tintoretto, Mantegna, Botticelli, Uccello—there is hardly an artist of note in the period 1300–1600 who has not been 'found' in Spenser (see Gottfried 1952).

Like the arguments about whether Keats was referring to, or had even seen, the Portland Vase in the British Museum when he wrote his 'Ode on a Grecian Urn', the numerous attempts to show that Spenser's word-pictures are 'like' certain painters or certain pictures, or 'like' Renaissance triumphs, or to prove that he had or had not seen good perspectival paintings from the continent, or to demonstrate that certain well-known tapestry subjects were readily available to him in the northern latitudes of the British Isles when the most advanced fine art of Italy and France was not, are energetic and interesting but ultimately of only peripheral concern (Gent 1981; Hard 1930; Hard 1940; Kamholtz 1980).

Although there is no debate about the relative rarity in Elizabethan England of examples of the more astonishing technical advances in painting—of elaborated central perspective and of *chiaroscuro* in particular—it is harder to determine what if any such artefacts Spenser would have seen through his connexions with the court and especially through grandees such as Leicester and the Countess of Pembroke, among others, who possessed collections of pictures, sculptures, tapestries, and illuminated manuscripts. Lucy Gent has taken great care in analysing the precise nature of English painting and English exposure to continental work, and concludes that, aside from the simple fact that the English, until the late-sixteenth century, lacked even the vocabulary to discuss and describe the latest technical innovations, English artists regarded drawing and draughtsmanship as tools associated with geometry and measurement, and painting itself not as the manipulation of light and shadow, mass, and vista, but rather as outlines filled in with colour as inherited from medieval illumination. The deployment of central perspective, of associated techniques of shading, and the rendition of light as developed by the Italian masters, were unknown to English painters. Mainly, those who attempted to discuss the art of painting did so with reference to treatises and other descriptions rather than to actual works of art (Gent 1981: 8, 17, 25). The Spenserian technical notion of *pictura* is thus likely limited by the sorts of art works he had seen (or had perhaps heard of), and is hard to define; as Joseph B. Dallett puts it succinctly: 'even faced with the very tapestries, illuminated manuscripts, and emblems he must have "seen", one cannot reconstruct how he saw them' (Dallett 1960: 98).

That he *was* influenced by visual artefacts of some kind seems incontrovertible, since it is difficult to imagine a poet unfamiliar with or unmoved by the visual referring to it so consistently and minutely. If parody is a mode available only to those with knowledge of the original, Colin Clout, who parodies the decorated chambers of the Elizabethan aristocrat when he describes his view of the court, must be speaking from Spenser's own experience:

> For all the walls and windows there are writ,
> All full of love, and love, and love my deare,
> And all their talke and studie is of it.   (*CCH*, 776–8)

And indeed, the fashion for 'wall-histories'—tapestries, or, in more elevated settings, painted or frescoed chapters in series from mythological or historical sources— would likely have been very familiar to Spenser: it is not merely the comfortably-off classes who used hangings as a form of insulation as well as of decoration, but also the great households which displayed spectacular collections of them. Henry VIII's sensationally beautiful tapestries of Bible stories were used to decorate Westminster Abbey for Elizabeth's coronation; and Spenser is virtually certain in 1579–80 to have been in some kind of service at Leicester House and thus to have known Robert Dudley's collection, which contained various 'histories' of the gods (Hard 1930: 170–7). The episodic structure of such hangings would have offered the poet a ready-made spatial framework, both of representation and of the act of reading it, for some of the pictorially notable episodes in *The Faerie Queene* referred to above (Hard 1930: 165). The easy availability of illuminated manuscripts—many of these owned by aristocratic owners with connexions to Spenser—with their punctuating capitals and borders, provided a highly conventionalized rhythm of word–image relations which may have shaped not only the epic but also some of the minor works (Tuve 1940: 149–50).[5] The developing conventions of printed book-illustration, too, are possible influences on the poetry, influences which will be discussed in the final section of this essay. The many romantic claims of Spenser's likeness to specific painters are impossible to judge since they rely heavily on personal impressions; but such claims do require us to think about whether the poet had access at all to even one or two specimens of the perspectivally rich art of the continent. Spenser's characters have been judged to inhabit 'both the older and newer ideas of space' (Kamholtz 1980: 59); to have demonstrated his familiarity with the 'newer [i.e., perspectival] space' in E. K.'s epistle to Harvey in *The Shepheardes Calender*, with his references to 'exquisite pictures' which 'shadow the rude thickets and craggy clifts, that by the baseness of such parts, more excellency may accrew to the principall' (Spenser 1999: 26)—a description thought to describe *chiaroscuro* (Hard 1940: 121); but also to have had little or no exposure to perspective art, which did not become familiar in England until the 1590s (Gottfried 1952: 208; Gent 1981: 25).

Such judgements are partly historical, but rest partly on what Panofsky called 'neo-gothic' space—the shallow-field, discontinuous, non-perspectival English arts of the period, primarily portraits but secondarily the craft arts such as stained glass, manuscript illumination, and woodcut book illustrations—which may work very well for the visual arts themselves, but which depends on an unreliable and merely speculative analogy between the visual artefact and vividly rendered poetic descriptions which are purely imaginative. Judith Dundas summarily lays to rest such fretful divisions and analogies: '[Spenserian] pictures are composed not to be optically convincing but to be imaginatively real' (Dundas 1981: 82). Spenser knew that no verbal description can make visual experience as precise as pictorial representation can, and whatever his local visual influences may have been, we must accept that they are transmuted into something unavailable to the eye and therefore remote from any specific source or style.

Book Illustrations

Illustrations in Spenser's lifetime

All of the illustrations of Spenser discussed below are, as one expects of such work, inspired by and designed to accompany the existing text. The reverse, however, is the case for *A Theatre for Worldlings* (1569), a set of six visionary epigrams and fourteen sonnets each accompanied by a woodcut (see Chapter 8 above). Spenser was commissioned to translate these existing poems by Jan Van der Noot (themselves translations of Petrarch and Du Bellay) which had already appeared in Dutch and French editions in 1568; those two earlier editions had copperplate engravings, probably by Lucas de Heere, although they have been misattributed to Gheeraerts the Elder (Bath 1988: 73; Friedland 1956: 110–12); an unknown artist made cheaper woodcuts for the English edition—engraving was to remain unreasonably expensive in England until the seventeenth century (cf. Corbett and Lightbown 1979; Hind 1935: 1952–64)—all but one of which is clearly related to the engraved version (Bath 1988; Friedland 1956: 1956).[6] Each woodcut, representing the 'vision' of the poem, codes its space to refer to the poem's temporal sequence, so that the phoenix at first viewed by the poet in all its splendour within a flowering wood stands within the frame next to the later version of itself which strikes its breast and dies by the dead tree and the dried-up spring which caused its 'great despite' (*TW*, epigram 5). This bifurcation of the picture is dictated by the Dutch and French versions of the poem and replicated by Spenser in his translation, where the situation changes from life to death, soundness to decay, wholeness to ruin. The *Theatre* is in fact an extensive prose tract on *vanitas*, in which the poems and pictures are only a small part: 'to sette,' as Van der Noot says, 'the vanitie and inconstancie of worldly and transitory things, the livelier before your eyes, I have broughte in here twentie sightes or visions [the poems themselves], & caused them to be graven, to the ende that al men may see with their eyes, which I go aboute to express by writing, to the delight and pleasure of the eye and eares, according unto the saying of Horace' (*TW*, 12–13). Although these are not technically emblems, the immediate relationship of the explanatory poem to the illustrating picture is strongly reminiscent of the standard emblem, and even supplies, in most of the poems, the missing motto which would complete the resemblance: the phoenix epigram, showing the transitory quality of life and the equivalently transitory phoenix, observes, 'Eche thing at length we see | Doth passe away' (Figure 37.1). Further emblematic commentary on each poem appears in the 'declaration' which comprises the bulk of the volume.

Much more complexly verbal-visual is *The Shepheardes Calender*, Spenser's first major poem, and the only one of his original works to have been supplied with a full set of integrated illustrations. The *Calender* is of special interest because of the clearly non-conventional, and even symbiotic, relation of the pictures to the poems, a relationship which may be the result of an unusual degree of direct authorial design in the pictures. Each of the twelve sections consists of a woodcut (with the

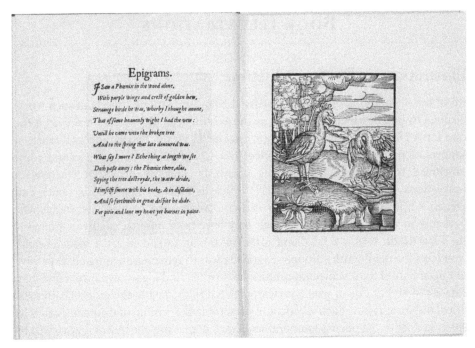

Fig. 37.1. Epigram 5 (anonymous woodcut), (Jan Van der Noot, *A Theatre for Voluptuous Worldlings* (1569)). Reproduced by kind permission of the Syndics of Cambridge University Library.

appropriate sign of the zodiac within it), a brief 'argument', the eclogue itself, an emblematic adage, and the extensive glosses of E. K. The work is, in other words, an exercise in the paratextual, and the woodcuts, like the glosses and arguments, have to be judged in some such relation to the eclogues. The *Calender* has been likened to popular almanacs of the day, many of which also featured woodcuts, and to calendrical illuminated manuscripts. The careful mutuality of text and picture is also reminiscent, as in *A Theatre for Worldlings*, of emblem-book structure. There is, as well, a likeness to collections of Aesop, where the key moment in the fable is also presented visually in a woodcut scene (Heninger 1988: 33). But no one of these models fully represents Spenser's *Calender*.

Illustrated books were reliable sellers, and English printers were eager to promote them for commercial ends; however, the *Calender* seems additionally to have been an exercise in *picta poesis*, a synthesis of word and image which signals Spenser's highly developed verbal pictorialism in *The Faerie Queene* and later works.[7] The major themes of the eclogues are labour, love, and poetry, and in portraying the first of these the woodcuts clearly develop the conventions of earlier calendrical illustrations when they allude to traditional georgic and pastoral tasks associated with each month; but it is only the last, poetry itself, which is universally illustrated with piping or declaiming shepherds, actual pipes (of various types, including pan pipes, shawms, and cornettos) either whole or broken, and the garland of laurels in *November*. The woodcuts were probably executed by three different artists, and thus other decisions about focus and detail are varied. The monthly task is sometimes relegated to the background, as in *August* (making the sheaves), and sometimes foregrounded, as in *Februarie* (wood-chopping), but in either case it often refers to explicit cues in the eclogue. The day is hot, we learn from the *August* eclogue, the 'Bellibone' (who is pictured) is referred to as a harvest queen, and is placed in front of the gathered haystacks in the field. Willye's detailed ekphrasis of the elaborate carved mazer which he offers as a prize for the singing contest is realized in the woodcut, lying on the ground in front of the competitors (Figure 37.2). In *Februarie* the figure of Cuddie chopping a tree is directly related to Thenot's folktale of the oak and the briar (Luborsky 1990: 654). Some of the cuts assist in exemplifying the name of the month: the *March* woodcut, for example, shows Cupid caught in Thomalin's birding net, an allusion to the original entrapment of Cupid's parents, Venus and Mars (for whom the month is named) by Vulcan, albeit a jocular one, since Thomalin not only fails to catch Cupid but is shot in the heel by the god of love. Like the cuts in *A Theatre*, this *March* illustration contains a temporal progression which follows Thomalin's narrative by showing, on the right, Cupid sitting complacently under a

Fig. 37.2. *August* eclogue (anonymous woodcut), (Edmund Spenser, *The Shepheardes Calender* (1579)). Reproduced by kind permission of the Syndics of Cambridge University Library.

Fig. 37.3. *November* eclogue (anonymous woodcut), (Edmund Spenser, *The Shep-heardes Calender* (1579)). Reproduced by kind permission of the Syndics of Cambridge University Library.

tree and the stealthy figure of the shepherd with his net creeping forward, and on the left the entangled Cupid, with Tomalin and Willye, his interlocutor, conversing in the foreground. The inconsistency here is that Thomalin says he went to shoot birds, not to snare them, and yet the woodcut shows him with a net draped over his arm, a detail possibly inserted by the craftsman to make the analogy with Venus and Mars more clear.

Other cuts seem to explicate simultaneously details of the poem and more general associations for each month. The *Maye* woodcut depicts the celebratory procession which brings home the May Queen Flora and her King on a litter. The *November* cut shows in the background the funeral procession of Dido, lamented in the poem by Colin, and in the foreground the forlorn sheep hang their heads 'as they would learne to weepe'. The leafless branches of the tree and shrub add to the general scene of 'dreriment', as described in the dirge. This grim scene is punctuated only by the upraised hand of Thenot, who offers a crown of bays to the piping Colin (Figure 37.3). It is, of course, Colin, Spenser's *alter ego*, who calls upon his muse (Melpomene, in this eclogue, the 'mournefulst Muse of nyne' [53]), and Colin who is enjoined to 'honor *Pan* with hymnes of higher vaine' (8). The crown of bays, in other words, refers back to the *October* eclogue, where Cuddie identifies Colin as an epic poet-in-waiting who will like Virgil leave his 'Oten reede' (8), and forward to Colin's decision in the *December* eclogue to hang his pipe upon a tree and forsake his flock, a decision which according to the argument refers to Colin's mortality, but which is glossed by Immeritô as the intention to follow Virgil and Chaucer 'farre off, and their high steppes adore' (Spenser 1999: 156). The *December* cut does not include the pipe on the branch that later illustrators were careful to show, although a broken pipe lies on the ground beside Colin, an emblem of his forsaking of the pastoral mode for the epic.[8] At a less elevated level, the woodcut artists seem peculiarly attuned to the ovine, and the sheep in the cold months are all very convincingly huddled, downcast, and weatherbeaten, whereas those of *Maye*, *June*, and *Julye* are remarkably active and happily foraging all over the landscape.

Typically such illustrations would have been organized by the printer rather than the poet, and the pictures would more than likely have relied to some extent on stock images and associations. These woodcuts do not rely much on convention, and attend with unusual precision to the unique matter of the eclogues. The conclusion must be that these pictures were commissioned if not by Spenser himself then by someone who knew the poem well, and this is supported by the fact that Hugh Singleton, the printer, was in jail during part of 1579, and was not therefore in a position to give detailed instructions which followed Spenser's ideas or could refer backward and forward to other illustrations (Luborsky 1990: 655).

In its early editions, *The Faerie Queene* attracted only the handsome woodcut of St George killing the dragon which appeared between Books I and II of the 1590 and 1596 editions. Unlike the cuts for *The Shepheardes Calender*, it is a purely conventional image which surely stands for Spenser's Redcrosse, with his Christological, Pauline, political, patriotic, and chivalric resonances. More will be said about later representations of Redcrosse below.

Post-Elizabethan book illustrations

It was not until the eighteenth century, when the fashion for the gothic mined Spenser for inspiration, that illustrations of the *The Faerie Queene* and the construction of landscapes and garden features based on it became frequent (Hadfield 1994: 1–4). Pope, Collins, and Thompson, among many others, were enthusiastic Spenserians who in turn influenced the Romantic poets and Romantic artists. The first illustrated edition was issued by Tonson and Hughes in 1715, and included nine engravings by Louis du Guernier which attempt to summarize the whole of a book of the poem within individual engravings. The first extensively illustrated edition, however, was that edited by Thomas Birch in 1751 with thirty-two engravings by William Kent, the renowned architect and designer of gardens and interiors. For the next one hundred and fifty years this remained the most comprehensively illustrated Spenser.

As a landscape designer, Kent claimed to have taken all his horticultural ideas from Spenser. He built a grotto for Queen Caroline based on the description of Merlin's cave, and at Stowe a hermitage based on Archimago's cell as well as a temple frescoed with the story of Malbecco and the satyrs (Hadfield 1994: 3–4). However distinguished in architecture and landscape design, he was no draughtsman, and the illustrations for the Birch edition of the poem were not much admired by the arbiters of the day (Hogarth and Walpole cruelly disparaged them); Kent did not in any case live to complete the series. Nevertheless, although it is true that he has an imperfect command of perspective and is given to stilted figures in somewhat histrionic poses, he has a good eye for Spenser's architectural details, which are often (and not surprisingly) the best-rendered elements in his pictures, and also for occasional gothic notes which, even if not wholly Spenserian, heighten the sense of local grotesquerie. The vernacular styles of the witch's hut (III.vii) (Kent 1751: plate 23) and of the old woman's house (I.iii.13) (Kent 1751: plate 5) (Figure 37.4) contrast

Fig. 37.4. William Kent (engraving), the old woman's house (Edmund Spenser, *The Faerie Queene* (1751)). Reproduced by kind permission of the Syndics of Cambridge University Library.

The Redcroſs Knight Introduced to the House of Pride by Dueſsa.

Fig. 37.5. William Kent (engraving), the House of Pride (Edmund Spenser, *The Faerie Queene* (1751)). Reproduced by kind permission of the Syndics of Cambridge University Library.

convincingly with the stylistically jumbled splendours of the House of Pride (I. iv) (Kent 1751: plate 7) (Figure 37.5); and Error (I.i) (Kent 1751: plate 1) is a tour de force of revolting reptilian detail, even though the vomited books and papers specified by Spenser do not figure in Error's spew. Likewise, the atmospheric rendition of Britomart consulting a Merlin surrounded by books of spells and a cloud of demons, serpents, and flying dogs (III.iii) (Kent 1751: plate 21) (Figure 37.6), and of Arthur being shown his destiny and his genealogy by Timon and Merlin in the moonlight (Figure 37.7), are arresting. In this last picture, Kent inserts in the background a visionary figure of Queen Elizabeth hovering in the sky over an English village. Elizabeth features in Merlin's imparted information to Arthur, but she is not *pictured* by Spenser in the scene. As a rule, however, Kent sticks closely to Spenser's visual details. He is also inclined to classicize his figures when he not gothicizing them.

Fig. 37.6. William Kent (engraving), Britomart and Merlin (Edmund Spenser, *The Faerie Queene* (1751)). Reproduced by kind permission of the Syndics of Cambridge University Library.

Nineteenth- and twentieth-century book illustrations

Many illustrations of Spenser's works followed Kent's, and those of the nineteenth century are, unlike Kent's eighteenth-century blend of the neo-classical and the gothic, very obviously responding to the perceived 'medieval' quality of Spenser's archaisms with imitations of manuscript illumination, calligraphy, and pre-modern *mise en page*. The editions of Spenser's works published by John Aiken in 1802 and 1810 contain ten interesting engravings designed by Thomas Stothard; and another edition of 1819 published by Suttaby, Evance, and Fox includes four designs by Richard Westfall. In this period Routledge first published its parlour edition of Spenser with illustrations by Edward Corbould, an edition that sold well for the next four decades. But the best and most abundant examples of Spenserian illustration are of the 1890s and the turn of the century by Arthur J. Gaskin (1896), Louis Fairfax-Muckley (1897), Walter Crane (1894–8), and Jessie M. King (1906); and half a century later, Agnes Miller Parker and John Austen (1953) were still working within the Arts and Crafts style of Crane. All these later Victorians were doubtless also

Prince Arthur educated by Timon & Merlin —

Fig. 37.7. William Kent (engraving), Arthur and Merlin (Edmund Spenser, *The Faerie Queene* (1751)). Reproduced by kind permission of the Syndics of Cambridge University Library.

influenced by Tennysonian medievalism and the Arthurian revival, and by the Pre-Raphaelite school.

Fairfax-Muckley's design for *The Faerie Queene* is in the style of William Morris, but the woodcut illustrations themselves are perceptibly stylized in the manner of Aubrey Beardsley. The lay-out is self-consciously medieval-looking, with the simple and boldly designed woodcuts framed in heavily trellised borders serving as the title-pages and as frontispieces for each of the books, uncial black-letter font with the occasional red letter, and lozenges at the head of each canto, some merely decorative and general, others reproducing specific characters or events. Most interesting are freestanding full-page and double-page illustrations of certain episodes such as the battle between Cambel and Priamond/Diamond/Triamond for Canacee (IV.iii) which is interrupted by the arrival of Cambina wielding her serpent-whips in her lion-drawn chariot (Figure 37.8). These details are set in a precisely drawn tilting ground complete with crowds in the background observing the fight. Radegund (V.v) is stunningly presented as an olympian valkyrie; the monster Geryoneo (V.xi) has his claw-like hands (Figure 37.9); and the three Graces (VI.x) appear in a 'September Morn' style which spares no blushes.

Fig. 37.8. Louis Fairfax-Muckley (woodcut), Cambel and the Mond brothers (Edmund Spenser, *The Faerie Queene* (1897)). Reproduced by kind permission of the Syndics of Cambridge University Library.

The Kelmscott Press's *Shepheardes Calender* (1896) was illustrated by Arthur J. Gaskin (Figure 37.10), and the influence of Morris can be detected at the same time in Walter Crane's splendid and voluminous Arts and Crafts-inspired illustrations for editions of *The Faerie Queene* (1894–6) and *The Shepheardes Calender* (1898). Like

Canto xi

PRINCE Arthure overcomes the great
Gerioneo in fight:
Doth slay the Monster, and restore
Belgè unto her right.

i

IT often fals, in course of common life,
That right long time is overborne of wrong
Through avarice, or powre, or guile, or strife,
That weakens her, and makes her party strong;
But Justice, though her dome she doe prolong,
Yet at the last she will her owne cause right:

Fig. 37.9. Louis Fairfax-Muckley (woodcut), Geryoneo (Edmund Spenser, *The Faerie Queene* (1897)). Reproduced by kind permission of the Syndics of Cambridge University Library.

Fairfax-Muckley's, Crane's work probably also owes something to Howard Pyle and the style of the Brandywine School. His *Shepheardes Calender* reproduces the format of a woodcut for each eclogue, and these appear to be inspired by but not especially faithful to the originals of 1579. Crane's technique is very delicate compared with Fairfax-Muckley's, and highly detailed, so that the relative ages of competing shepherds is clearly marked (and Colin in the *Januarye* vignette has the brooding good looks and improbably trim moustache of an Edwardian blade) (Figure 37.11); Rosalind, the uncooperative Bellibone of the *August* eclogue, is markedly scornful of an obviously plaintive Perigot/Colin (Figure 37.12); *November*'s funeral of Dido shows mourners and the Graces scattering bays on the coverlet of the bier; and in the *December* vignette Colin actually has hung his pipe on a branch as he threatens in the poem, rather

Fig. 37.10. Arthur J. Gaskin (woodcut), *Januarie* eclogue (Edmund Spenser, *The Shepheardes Calender* (1896)). Reproduced by kind permission of the Syndics of Cambridge University Library.

Fig. 37.11. Walter Crane (woodcut), *Januarie* eclogue (Edmund Spenser, *The Shepheardes Calender* (1898)). Reproduced by kind permission of the Syndics of Cambridge University Library.

than merely broken it on the ground as in the 1579 woodcut. In addition to these woodcuts, peopled and trellised borders frame each page of verse. This effort to medievalize Spenser is of a piece not only with what may have been an undifferentiated historical sense promoted initially by the various archaisms of *The Faerie Queene* itself, but also with the ethos and social preoccupations of the Arts and Crafts movement.

Crane was a collaborator of Morris's at the Kelmscott Press, and his *Faerie Queene* is not only supreme in such antique effects, but also in brilliant solutions to the problem of the Spenserian pictorial. The wealth of illustrations—full-page scenes, portraits of individual characters, borders and other ornamentation—is too abundant to do justice to in brief. An indication of Crane's sensitivity to the material, however, is the picture of Britomart in the House of Busirane (Figure 37.13). The episode in *The Faerie Queene* III.xii is an extended ekphrasis in which we see Britomart 'reading' the depicted loves of the gods and the heroes, rehearsed ever more brutally in 'thousand monstrous formes' which strike the reader forcibly but which have little effect on Britomart herself, who is impatient with such show and wishes to act decisively. In other words, the ekphrastic complexity of this scene is compounded by the presence of an interior reader whose experience is not only different from ours, but for whom the pictures unfold temporally as she reads them both sequentially and spatially within the design of the entire work of art (they are organized in groups based on each of the male gods) and detects their relation to one another within each panel and within each room. For all these reasons—the massive and highly detailed work itself, its setting, the competing reactions to it—it is difficult to portray the scene easily (Preston 2007: 126–9). Crane's solution is to foreground Britomart (as the primary reader of the pictures) forcing her way through the fiery barricade which guards Busirane's castle. Instead of placing the tapestries and painting within this scene, the picture of the active Britomart is framed by borders depicting the gods and their erotic adventures, so that the sense of encounter with the pictures on the wall is translated into a typographical convention which offers sufficient and convincing detail, feels simultaneous within the *mise en page* with Britomart herself, and surrounds her much as the walls of the room do. The poem's extra-narratorial delivery of the loves of the gods is replicated in the placement of this material in an extra-pictorial relation to Britomart: as border-art, it does not inhabit the same ontological or conceptual universe as she. Elsewhere, other almost peripheral details are worked in by Crane which show that he is alive to Spenser's allusions—for example, Busirane is portrayed with a pharaonic headdress which correctly connects him with Busiris, an Egyptian tyrant and adulterer (Figure 37.14).

There is a somewhat unfortunate history, especially in the twentieth century, of saccharin Spenserian illustrations; thankfully, these are mainly obscure. Fortunately, too, Jessie M. King's delicate pink-washed line-drawings for W. B. Yeats's *Poems of Spenser* (1906), presenting characters as diaphanous Art Nouveau figures with trailing garments and elongated anatomies which recall Arthur Rackham, Kay Nielsen,

Fig. 37.12. Walter Crane (woodcut), *August* eclogue (Edmund Spenser, *The Shepheardes Calender* (1898)). Reproduced by kind permission of the Syndics of Cambridge University Library.

Fig. 37.13. Walter Crane (woodcut), Britomart and the tapestries of Busirane (Edmund Spenser, *The Faerie Queene* (1894–6)). Reproduced by kind permission of the Syndics of Cambridge University Library.

Fig. 37.14. Walter Crane (woodcut), Busirane (Edmund Spenser, *The Faerie Queene* (1894–6)). Reproduced by kind permission of the Syndics of Cambridge University Library.

and Gustav Klimt, just avoid the cloying. In contrast to those of her contemporaries, her pictures are less like compositions than like punctuating atmospheric interventions or, occasionally, borders; they are not in any sense narrative, and make almost no attempt to replicate any details from the verse. They are strewn with flowers (picked out in red and pink), languorous Pre-Raphaelite tresses abound, and they have none of the bold energy and swagger of Fairfax-Muckley or Crane. King's are rather 'impressions' of Spenser than illustrations.

A brief word should be said about children's illustrated versions of *The Faerie Queene* in this period. These are naturally much abridged and condensed versions of certain episodes of the poem, but among the best are H. J Ford's spirited pictures for Andrew Lang's *The Red Romance Book* (1905) (Hosington and Shaver 1990). Ford's seven-headed serpent and Una's convincingly lifelike

Fig. 37.15. H. J. Ford (watercolour), the seven-headed serpent (Andrew Lang, *The Red Romance Book* (1905)). Reproduced by kind permission of the Syndics of Cambridge University Library.

lion and lamb must have made Spenser come alive to young and old readers alike (Figure 37.15).

The last major illustrated Spenser, *The Faerie Queene* by Agnes Miller Parker and John Austen (1953), was clearly influenced by Fairfax-Muckley and Crane, and although Austen's decorations are somewhat affected (and he had the misfortune to be interrupted by the Blitz, as well as paralysed in one arm), the engravings by Miller Parker, who completed the commission, are strong and muscular in the manner of her nineteenth-century predecessors although even more anachronistic in the post-war period (Farmer 1990a: 391).

PAINTINGS

There have been so many paintings of Spenserian subjects in the past three centuries that only a very brief and selective overview is possible here; rather than attempt an exhaustive list of works (for which see Farmer 1990a), the following discussion concerns a few representative works.[9] Spenser's pictorial popularity coincides with

Fig. 37.16. George Stubbs, *Isabella Saltonstall as Una* (1782), reproduced by kind permission of The Fitzwilliam Museum, Cambridge.

the rise of 'history' subjects among late-eighteenth-century painters, who chose vignettes or series of vignettes from important narrative works—the *Odyssey*, the Bible, the *Divine Comedy*, Virgil, Ariosto, Shakespeare, and Milton; for them Spenser was a natural extension of this predilection.

Fuseli, Reynolds, Stubbs, Copley, and Romney are among the many important painters who produced works based on *The Faerie Queene* in the eighteenth century. In George Stubbs's *Isabella Saltonstall as Una* (1782) (Figure 37.16), the subject is presented in an emblematic space rather than as part of a narrative progression or as an obviously specific moment in the poem. In her simple, chronologically unplaceable white dress and veil, and with the black stole that shows she 'inly mourned' (I.i.4.6), Una's startlingly white figure against the surrounding gloom of the forest works upon the eye as Spenser indicates: 'Her angels face | As the great eye of heaven shyned bright, | And made a sunshine in the shadie place.' (I.ii.4.6–9). Her companions are the white ass and a very fine lion (whom she does not in fact meet until later in the poem), but Stubbs omits the milk-white lamb. The three figures stand out against the neutral forest background; and the lion in particular is reminiscent of Stubbs's much better-known pictures of wild animals, but the medium here (fired enamel on an oval porcelain disc), the domestic genre (an identified portrait of a lady), and the subject (the contemplative, static figure in her glowing raiment) are as far from his usual sporting subjects, horses and dogs,

Fig. 37.17. Henry Fuseli, *Prince Arthur's Dream of the Fairy Queen* (c.1785–8), reproduced by permission of the Kunstmuseum, Basel.

as can be, and evoke instead a decorative devotional scene of a much earlier period. The picture clearly refers to its narrative context but resists narrative movement.

Henry Fuseli's characteristic supernaturalism in *Prince Arthur's Dream of the Fairy Queen* (c.1785–8) (Figure 37.17), although contemporary with Stubbs's Una, offers a completely different idea of the poem. In contrast to Stubbs's almost naïve austerity, Fuseli's evocation of magic and motion catches the evanescent quality of the poem's eponym. With diaphanous neoclassical draperies outlining her baroque *contraposto* form, her elaborately dressed hair, and the improbably intricate sash which seems to float in her slip-stream, she is a vision of transient energy, clearly moving past and certainly not lingering with the sleeping figure of Arthur. Her almost casual gesture of benediction or of spell-casting is echoed by the hand and arm of the angelic figure in her wake, and the painting's restrained palette emphasizes the circle of cloudy, diffused light which surrounds her against the shadowy form of the prince drowsing heavily on his helmet. Although Arthur says of this vision,

Fig. 37.18. John Singleton Copley, *The Red Cross Knight with Fidelia and Speranza* (1793), reproduced by kind permission of the National Gallery, Washington, D.C.

> Most goodly glee and lovely blandishment
> She to me made, and bade me love her deare,
> For dearely sure her love was to me bent . . .   (I.ix.14)

Fuseli's version shows a fairy queen too momentary and elusive to sustain such confidence, and points rather to the delusion of dreams rather than to any predictive or visionary security.

John Singleton Copley's *The Red Cross Knight with Fidelia and Speranza* (1793) (Figure 37.18) is in the historical style this American artist himself helped to popularize in England in the 1780s, although this is the only purely literary example in his *oeuvre*. An odd mixture of medieval detail (Redcrosse's armour), late-eighteenth-century ladies' fashions (the dress, headgear, and coiffures of the two women), and Fidelia's distinctive halo and communion cup extracted from counter-reformation religious painting, the work is a digest of Copley's artistic practices and experience as fashionable portraitist, Grand Tourist in Italy, and narrative specialist. The painted details are rigorously faithful to the illustrated verses (I.x.12–14): Speranza leans on an anchor, her expression is, as described, more pensive than Fidelia's, and her eyes are

Fig. 37.19. William Blake, *The Characters of The Faerie Queene* (c.1825), reproduced by kind permission of the Syndics of Cambridge University Library.

cast up toward heaven as Spenser specifies. Although it is striking and technically
accomplished, the painting literally depicts Spenser's idea but it lacks the haunting
stillness of Stubbs or the magical grace of Fuseli.

In the nineteenth century the single most elaborate and coherent contribution to
the Spenser genre was Blake's *Characters in Spenser's 'Faerie Queene'*, executed and
still hanging at Petworth (Gleckner 1985: 158–262) (Figure 37.19). This large and
imperfectly explicated tempera shows a triumphal procession of twenty-four
mounted and ambulant figures together with divine personages and abstractions
hovering in the sky between visions of heavenly cities. It is thought to have been a
companion-piece to his earlier *Chaucer's Canterbury Pilgrims*, which exhibits analogous spatial and gestural organization. The well-known idiosyncrasies of Blake's
iconography make any brief or precise analysis difficult, but broadly speaking the
arrangement of the major figures from each of the first five books is spatially
significant, with a notably unwarriorlike Britomart seated centrally on a palfrey,
Redcrosse and Una leading, and Archimago and Duessa with the Blatant Beast in
captivity following at the rear. The significant 'middest' place in the triumph,
interestingly, is assigned to Britomart in a period when the female character most
often depicted was Una.

J. M. W. Turner produced at least two Spenserian works, including the atmospheric *Cave of Despair* (Tate Britain); Charles Eastlake also painted the Cave of Despair
episode in 1829 (Soane Museum); and William Etty produced several Spenserian
works, including the rescue of Amoret from the House of Busirane (1833) (Tate
Britain). Prince Albert commissioned William Leitch's *The Birth of Belphoebe and
Amoret* in the 1850s as a birthday present for Queen Victoria (Royal Collection); and
a series of nine paintings of Spenser's heroines for a house in Kensington Palace
Gardens was made by Alfred Stevens starting in 1855 (Courtauld Institute). The
Queen herself appeared on a celebrated gold five pound piece of 1839, designed by
William Wyon, as Una accompanied by her lion. A *Triumph of the Red Cross Knight*,

commissioned from G. F. Watt for the new Parliament building in 1854, was destroyed by fire, although we have other smaller Spenserian works by Watt. William Bell Scott (*Una and the Lion* [National Gallery of Scotland]), Landseer (*Una*, now lost), and Burne-Jones (*The Masque of Cupid* [private collection]) are three of many others in the second half of the century who participated in the Spenser boom; and it was, indeed, a boom: the Zodiac Windows at Betteshanger House, Kent, by Thomas Erat Harrison (1880s) are based on the months from the *Mutabilitie Cantos*; and Frederick Shields, the Pre-Raphaelite painter, designed six enormous windows depicting the adventures of Britomart, that excellent female role-model, for the Cheltenham Ladies College in the 1880s. Figurines were commercially produced, and at least two horse-racing trophies, including the Ascot Cup of 1852, bore scenes of Red Cross and Una on them.

Without question, however, the most enthusiastic of Spenser's artistic imitators in this period was F. R. Pickersgill, with at least twelve works. The Victorian painters responded as enthusiastically and as variously as Tennyson and other poets did to the matter of the mid-century Arthurian Revival; it is little wonder, then, that *The Faerie Queene*, itself a product of the Elizabethan Arthurian revival, should have suggested itself to them as a source of material. Pickersgill, however, is unusual in producing at least two very distinct, strongly narrative, Spenserian styles. *Amoret, Aemylia, and Prince Arthur in the Cottage of Sclaunder* (1845) (Figure 37.20) highlights the huddled

Fig. 37.20. F. R. Pickersgill, *Amoret, Aemylia, and Prince Arthur in the Cottage of Sclaunder* (1845), reproduced by kind permission of Tate Britain.

women in soft rose and cream garments, as if their virtue were illuminating the comfortless gloom of the dreary cottage. The discontented hag Sclaunder is, like the faithful Arthur on the other side of the composition, just visible in the murky atmosphere (even though, in the poem, she is allotted most of Spenser's descriptive detail). The work has elements of a sentimental Victorian domestic scene, Aemylia comforting Amoret who leans gracefully on her shoulder; and yet the cold squalor of the place, with its 'chearelesse hunger' and 'cancred malice', is about as domestic as a cave. In engravings of this work, moreover, the huge cold fireplace (which is almost lost in the shadow of the painting) is clearly visible behind the figures. The genre-painting quality of this picture is quite unlike Pickersgill's *Contest of Beauty for the Girdle of Florimell: Britomartis Unveiling Amoret* (1853), where the studied medieval-ism of the Pre-Raphaelites is very striking. Quite apart from the lush period detail in dress and armour, the staged look of the composition is heightened: the girdle on a cushion is foregrounded in the centre; the only standing figures are Amoret with Britomart theatrically discovering her among the competing ladies and their para-mours lounging on benches; the whole is framed and anchored by a pair of antique columns, and *putti* on beams of light form Amoret's entourage. This pageant-like arrangement has much in common with Blake's earlier *Faerie Queene* procession, and predicts the statuesque, ceremonial manner of Edward Burne-Jones a few years later.

In the first half of the twentieth century, perhaps surprisingly in the age of Modernism, Spenser continued to inspire pictures, although he has more often appeared as the source of book illustrations. The 1902 Royal Academy's annual competition was on the subject of 'The Masque of Cupid', and the walls of the Baltimore Free Library's reading room were covered in a mural of 1800 square feet by Lee Woodward Ziegler in seventeen sections in the 1930s (Farmer 1990b: 31).

Even allowing for the likelihood that the successive taste for the gothic, for the chivalric, for romance narrative, and for the generally medieval in the form of the Arts and Crafts and Pre-Raphaelite movements, would suggest Spenser as a natural subject for illustration, it is the poetry itself, and Spenser's commitment to and arsenal of literary pictorial techniques characteristic of the most ambitious Renais-sance writing, which has invited readers and artists alike to imagine his scenes, characters, and events so richly and persistently.

NOTES

1. See Bender (1972), Dundas (1985), (1993), Fletcher (1917), Gent (1981), Krieger (1992), Lee (1940), Leslie (1985), Preston (2007), Steiner (1988), and Mitchell (1986).
2. Gottfried by contrast concludes that 'the pictorial interest . . . is actually a minor ingredient of Spenser's art' (Gottfried 1952: 212).
3. On the history of *ut pictura poesis*, see Lee (1940).

4. On Spenser's ekphrasis see Bender (1972) and Preston (2007); for a history of ekphrasis and word–image relations see Krieger (1992).

5. Tuve suggests that manuscript illustrations even conventionalized the figures who received pictorial treatment, so much so that habitual descriptive details became hardened, rather as emblem figures did, in the cultural consciousness of poets like Spenser. See also Sonn (1959), 161.

6. It was always assumed that the woodcuts were made after the engravings, but Michael Bath suggests the reverse, that the woodcutter was following a set of watercolour pictures now held in Glasgow University Library (see Bath 1988: 76–8).

7. Heninger has suggested that the whole paratextual layout of the eclogues, including the cuts, was designed in direct imitation of Sanazzaro's *Arcadia* and thereby as an express compliment to Sidney (Heninger 1988: 34 ff).

8. For further discussion of the symbolism of Colin's broken or abandoned pipes, see Kelsey and Peterson (2000).

9. Farmer (1990b) contains reproductions of many of the works mentioned below.

BIBLIOGRAPHY

Bath, M. (1988). 'Verse Form and Pictorial Space in Van der Noodt's *Theatre for Worldlings*', in Karl Josef Holtgen, Peter M. Daly, and Wolfgang Lottes (eds), *Word and Visual Imagination: Studies in the Interaction of English Literature and the Visual Arts*. Erlangen: Univ.-Bibliothek Erlangen-Nurnberg: 73–106.

Bender, J. (1972). *Spenser and Literary Pictorialism*. Princeton, NJ: Princeton University Press.

Corbett, M., and Lightbown, R. W. (1979). *The Comely Frontispiece: The Emblematic Title-Page in England, 1550–1660*. London: Routledge, Kegan Paul.

Crane, Walter (illus.) (1894–6). *Illustrations and Ornamentation from the Faerie Queene*. Rprt Mineola, NY: Dover, 1999.

—— (illus.) (1898). *The Shepheardes Calender*. London/New York: Harper & Bros.

Dallett, J. B. (1960). 'Ideas of Sight in *The Faerie Queene*'. *ELR* 27(2): 87–121.

Dundas, J. (1968). 'The Rhetorical Basis of Spenser's Imagery'. *SEL* 8(1): 59–75.

—— (1981). 'Fairyland and the Vanishing Point'. *Journal of Aesthetics and Art Criticism* 40(1): 82.

—— (1985). *The Spider and the Bee: The Artistry of Spenser's* Faerie Queene. Urbana: University of Illinois Press.

—— (1993). *Pencils Rhetorique: Renaissance Poets and the Arts of Painting*. Newark/London/Toronto: University of Delaware Press and Associated University Presses.

Fairfax-Muckley, L. (illus.) (1897). *The Faerie Queene*, 2 vols. London: J. M. Dent.

Farmer, N. K. (1984). *Poets and the Visual Arts in Renaissance England*. Austin: University of Texas Press.

—— (1990a). 'Illustrators', in *SE*, 388–92.

—— (1990b). '"A Moniment Forever More": *The Faerie Queene* and British Art, 1770–1950'. *Princeton University Library Chronicle* 52(1): 25–78.

Fletcher, J. B. (1917). 'The Painter of the Poets'. *SP* 14: 153–66.

Ford, H. J. (illus.) (1905). *The Red Romance Book*, ed. Andrew Lang. London: Longmans, Green.

716   CLAIRE PRESTON

Friedland, L. S. (1956). 'The Illustrations in *The Theatre for* Worldlings'. *HLQ* 19(2): 107–20.

Gaskin, A. J. (illus.) (1896). Edmund Spenser, *The Faerie Queene*. Hammersmith: Kelmscott Press.

Gent. L. (1981). *Pictures and Poetry 1560–1620: Relations between Literature and the Visual Arts in the English Renaissance*. Leamington Spa: James Hall.

Gilman, E. B. (1986). *Iconoclasm and Poetry in the English Reformation: Down Went Dagon*. Chicago: University of Chicago Press.

Glazier, L. (1955). 'The Nature of Spenser's Imagery'. *MLQ* 16: 300–10.

Gleckner, R. F. (1985). *Blake and Spenser*. Baltimore: Johns Hopkins University Press.

Gottfried, R. (1952). 'The Pictorial Element in Spenser's Poetry'. *ELH* 19(3): 203–13.

Hadfield, Andrew (1994). 'William Kent's Illustrations of *The Faerie Queene*'. *SSt* 14: 1–81.

Hard, F. (1930). '"Clothes of Arras and of Toure"'. *SP* 27: 162–85.

—— (1940). 'E.K.'s Reference to Painting: Some Seventeenth Century Adaptations'. *ELH* 7(2): 121–9.

Heninger, S. K., Jr. (1988). 'The Typographical Layout of Spenser's *Shepheardes Calender*', in K. J. Holtgen, P. M. Daly, and W. Lottes (eds), *Word and Visual Imagination: Studies in the Interaction of English Literature and the Visual Arts*. Erlangen: Univ.-Bibliothek Erlangen-Nurnberg, 33–71.

Hind, A. M. (1952–64). *Introduction to a history of woodcut*. 2 Vols. New York: Dover.

Hosington, B. M., and Shaver, A. (1990). '*The Faerie Queene*, Children's Versions', in *SE*, 289–91.

Kamholtz, Jonathan Z. (1980). 'Spenser and Perspective'. *Journal of Aesthetics and Art Criticism* 39(1): 59–66.

Kelsey, L., and Peterson, R. S. (2000). 'Rereading Colin's Broken Pipe: Spenser and the Problem of Patronage'. *SSt* 14: 233–72.

Kent, William (illus.) (1751). *The Faerie Queene*, ed. Thomas Birch, 3 vols. London: J. Brindley and S. Wright.

King, Jessie M. (illus) (1906). *Poems of Spenser*, ed. W. B. Yeats. Edinburgh: T. C. and E. C. Jack.

Krieger, M. (1992). *Ekphrasis: The Illusion of the Natural Sign*. Baltimore: Johns Hopkins University Press.

Lee, R. W. (1940). '*Ut Pictura Poesis*: The Humanistic Theory of Painting'. *Art Bulletin* 22(4): 197–269.

Leslie, M. (1985). 'The Dialogue Between Bodies and Souls: Pictures and Poesy in the English Renaissance'. *Word and Image* 1: 16–30.

Luborsky, R. S. (1990). '*The Shepehardes Calender*, Printing and Illustration of', in *SE*, 654–5.

Miller Parker, Agnes, and Austen, John (illus.) (1953). *The Faerie Queene*. Oxford: Limited Editions Club.

Mitchell, W. J. T. (1986). *Iconology: Image, Text, Ideology*. Chicago: University of Chicago Press.

Praz, M. (1970). *Mnemosyne: The Parallel between Literature and the Visual Arts*. London: Oxford University Press.

Preston, C. (2007). 'Ekphrasis: Painting in Words', in S. Adamson, G. Alexander, and K. Ettenhuber (eds), *Renaissance Rhetorical Figures*. Cambridge: Cambridge University Press: 115–32.

Sonn, C. R. (1959). 'Spenser's Imagery'. *ELH* 26(2): 156–70.

Steiner, W. (1988). *Pictures of Romance: Form against Context in Painting and Literature.* Chicago: University of Chicago Press.

Tuve, R. (1940). 'Spenser and Some Pictorial Conventions, with Particular Reference to Illuminated Manuscripts'. *SP* 37: 149–76.

—— (1947). *Elizabethan and Metaphysical Imagery.* Chicago: University of Chicago Press.

Watkins, W. B. C. (1950). *Shakespeare and Spenser.* Princeton, NJ: Princeton University Press.

CHAPTER 38

THE FORMALIST TRADITION

DAVID SCOTT WILSON-OKAMURA

THE word *formalist* was coined, apparently, by Sir Francis Bacon as a term of abuse for faux intellectuals: those laborious hair-splitters who 'do nothing or little very solemnly' (1996: 390).[1] History, though, has been on the side of the formalists. Critics have been writing about Spenser for more than four centuries, and for the first three of those centuries, most critics wrote about subjects which today would be classified as formalist. For example, what is the best plan for an epic poem? or the best kind of verse? Someone, of course, has always been doing research on Spenser's biography, or trying to identify the real-life originals of Prince Arthur, Sir Calidore, and Sir Artegall. But the recurring issues in Spenser criticism—the ones that critics have come back to, not just decade after decade, but century after century—have historically been questions about form. In particular, what is the effect of Spenser's dialect and archaic diction? What is the nature of his stanza? And what, if anything, confers unity on his *Faerie Queene*?

DIALECT AND ARCHAIC DICTION

The oldest controversy about Spenser, which is also the earliest complaint, concerns his use of northern dialect (such as *kirk* 'church', *queme* 'please', *wimble* 'quick'), obsolete words (such as *whilom* 'once', *eke* 'stretch', *chaffar* 'trade') and archaic forms of familiar words (such as *holpen* 'helped', *bren* 'burn', *glitterand* 'glittering'). For several decades before Spenser was born, poets and speechmakers had been using these and similar terms to make their language either more lapidary or more exotic, so that it was reported during Edward VI's reign that 'The fine courtier wil talke nothing but *Chaucer*' (Wilson 1553: 148). This trend was transnational and lasted the whole length of the sixteenth century (see pp. 371–3 above). But when Spenser did it, readers noticed. Why seemed it so particular with him?

A detailed account of Spenser's dialect and diction is given in Chapter 20 above; what concerns us here is the controversy they provoked. In Spenser's complete works there are about 50 dialect words, which would not be a lot except that most of them are in one poem, *The Shepheardes Calender* (Draper 1919; McElderry 1932). There are also, in the complete works, about 350 words which, to contemporary ears, would have sounded old-fashioned. Many of these, such as *clepe* 'call', *guerdon* 'reward', and *swinck* 'toil', Spenser got directly from 'Dan *Chaucer*, well of English vndefyled' (IV. ii.32). To other words he gave a Chaucerian flavor by adding a prefix: *y-*, for example, to make a past participle (*yplast* 'placed' and *ydrad* 'dreaded'; cf. Chaucer's *yclad*, which Spenser also used) or *to-* for completeness (*to rent* 'torn apart' and *to worne* 'worn out'; cf. *tobroken* 'broken up' in Chaucer).[2] Excluding translations, the only poems which Spenser does not archaize are his *Fowre Hymnes*. His epic is brimful of old words and old forms, as are his *Complaints* and even his love poems (Kuin 1998: 52–4). But the greatest concentration of such words is in *The Shepheardes Calender*, and this was the chief source of controversy.

Half of all the archaisms that Spenser would ever use are already found in *The Shepheardes Calender*, including sixty such words which he decided never to use again. Apparently this called for an explanation, because the poem's official commentator, E. K., devotes approximately sixty percent of his notes to explaining hard or unfamiliar words, especially archaisms and northern dialect. In *Maye*, for example, when Palinode complains 'That shepheardes so witen ech others life, | And layen her faults the world beforne' (159–60), *witen* is glossed as 'blame' and *her* is explained as the pronominal adjective 'theyr, as useth Chaucer'. In this case, the gloss cites a precedent, Chaucer, but most of E. K.'s glosses do not, and when they do it is not always the author of *Troilus*. In *Februarie* 4, for example, he glosses *gride* as 'perced: an olde word much vsed of Lidgate, but not found (that I know of) in Chaucer.'

Someone is showing off. But the notes are defensive, as well as ostentatious. They expect the archaisms to be controversial, and in his preface E. K. offers an artistic theory of archaism which anticipates criticism. First, although the 'auncient' words in this 'new Poete' may sound foreign, they are in fact 'English, and also vsed of most excellent Authors', such as Chaucer, Lydgate, and Gower. Second, the poems of *The Shepheardes Calender* are spoken by shepherds, whose speech, being 'rustical', is not only 'rough'-sounding but conservative, preserving 'such olde and obsolete wordes [as] are most vsed of country folke'. Third, Cicero, Livy, and Sallust would sometimes use 'an auncient worde' in order to 'maketh the style seeme graue, and as it were reuerend: no otherwise then we honour and reuerence gray heares for a certain religious regard, which we haue of old age.' Fourth, the use of old words produces a kind of chiaroscuro effect, which E. K. likens first to 'rude thickets and craggy clifts' in the background of a painting, which please us by their 'naturall rudenesse' and their 'disorderly order'; next, to 'a dischorde in Musick [which sometimes] maketh a comely concordaunce'; and then, to a beauty spot on 'a wel shaped body.' Finally, says E. K., modern English does not have a large enough vocabulary. Some authors have added to the lexicon by borrowing words from foreign tongues, but this produces a 'hodgepodge'; a better solution, which the still-anonymous author of *The Shepheardes Calender* has adopted, is to restore by using them 'good and naturall English words' from the age of Chaucer and Gower (Spenser 1999: 26–7).

Over the long term, the strategy worked: of the obsolete words which Spenser tried to revive, approximately one quarter were adopted by other writers and achieved some kind of currency (McElderry 1932: 169). But in the short term, readers complained, including some of Spenser's fellow poets. The first of these was Spenser's would-be patron, Sir Philip Sidney (1554–86). In *An Apologie for Poetrie* (*c.*1583), Sidney praised the *Calender* as having 'much Poetrie'; but he could not endorse 'its old rustick language ... sith neyther *Theocritus* in Greeke, *Virgill* in Latine, nor *Sanazar* in Italian did affect it' (Smith 1904: I, 196). In fact, there was ancient precedent both for Spenser's archaisms and for his use of dialect. Virgil, it was known, had put archaisms in the mouth of his shepherds because, as Castiglione explained, country speech preserves old usages.[3] Theocritus, it was also known, made his goatherds use 'rustick language'—Doric rather than Attic Greek—because as country-folk they would be expected to have country accents and use country forms of speech.[4] Rustic features were also notable in Mantuan (1447–1516), whose Latin eclogues were a standard text in Elizabethan classrooms (Cooper 1977: 132).

Sidney's objections, though mistaken as scholarship, were influential as criticism. In 1598, when Spenser was still alive, the satirist Everard Guilpin reported,

> Some blame deep Spenser for his grandam words,
> Others protest that in them he records
> His masterpiece of cunning, giving praise
> And gravity to his profound-pricked lays.   (Alpers 1969: 52)

Guilpin sides, evidently, with Spenser's defenders, but the blamers soon outnumber him. In a manuscript treatise titled 'The Model of Poesy' (*c.*1600), William Scott quotes repeatedly from Sidney's *Apologie* and echoes its censure of Spenser 'for his affecting old words and phrases' (Wells 2003: 14). Edmund Bolton, in his manuscript *Hypercritica* (*c.*1618), argues that Spenser's epic and pastoral are inferior to his hymns, because the former do not savor of 'practick *English*', any more than do '*Jeff. Chaucer, Lydgate, Pierce Ploughman,* or *Laureat Skelton*' (Cummings: 292).

In 1638, Sir Kenelm Digby justifies the archaisms, because they express Spenser's meaning 'more lively and more concisely ... and whensoever he useth them, he doth so polish their native rudeness as, retaining the majesty of antiquity, they want nothing of the elegance of our freshest speech' (Alpers 1969: 58). This is overshadowed, however, by Ben Jonson's complaint in *Timber* (1640) that '*Spencer*, in affecting the Ancients [i.e., Chaucer and Gower], writ no Language' (1925–52: VIII, 618).

Jonson knows about the archaisms in Virgil; what he protests, rather, is the fabrication of a mongrel language that is not the language of living men, and not the language of Chaucer either. 'Yet', Jonson continues, 'I would have him [Spenser] read for his matter; but as *Virgil* read *Ennius*.' What seems like a concession is really the unkindest cut of all. Ennius was famous in the Renaissance as the author of Latin literature, but his crude meter and uncouth diction were equally notorious. Virgil, when he was found reading Ennius, reportedly 'answered that he was gathering gold from the manure of Ennius. For indeed that poet had outstanding maxims hidden beneath words not very refined' (Ziolkowski and Putnam 2008: 364).

By 1650, the complaint about Spenser's 'obsolete language' was so common as to be called 'the most vulgar accusation that is lay'd to his charge'; but that did not stop Sir William Davenant (1606–1668) from echoing the inculpation, or giving what he calls 'the vulgar excuse; which is, That the unlucky choise of his *Stanza*, hath by repetition of Rime brought him to the necessity of many exploded words' (Cummings 1971: 187, 189). After 1650, poets who imitated Spenser generally did so sans archaism (and minus the rhyming stanza). In 1687 an anonymous 'Person of Quality', probably Edward Howard, published a *rifaciamento* of book one, with couplets in place of stanzas and omitting those 'words and expressions, which time and use had well nigh exploded' even when Spenser wrote them and which 'so much obscure the glory of his thoughts' (Bradner 1938: 324).

Even Dryden (who names '*Virgil* in *Latine*, and *Spencer* in *English*' as his 'Masters') can be heard objecting to Spenser's 'obsolete language', although it is excusable (he adds), because the sense 'is still intelligible, at least after a little practice' (Alpers 1969: 74). But he is speaking only of *The Faerie Queene*; for in his remarks on *The Shepheardes Calender*, Dryden praises Spenser, as one who 'being master of our northern dialect and skilled in Chaucer's English, has so exactly imitated the Doric of Theocritus that his love is a perfect image of that passion which God infused into both sexes, before it was corrupted with the knowledge of arts and the ceremonies of what we call good manners' (Alpers 1969: 75). In pastoral, then, archaism has a classical pedigree and is warranted by decorum.

The other Augustans are less persuasible. Pope concedes that 'Doric had its beauty and propriety in the time of Theocritus; it was used in part of Greece and frequent in the mouths of many of the greatest persons'; but this is not, he maintains, an adequate defense of Spenser, whose 'old English and country phrases . . . were either entirely obsolete or spoken only by people of the lowest condition' (Alpers 1969: 76). John Gay, Pope's fellow Scriblerian, revives the objection that Spenser's language is a hothouse hybrid, 'such as is neither spoken by the country Maiden nor the courtly Dame; nay, not only such as in the present Times is not uttered, but was never uttered in Times past; and, if I judge aright, will never be uttered in Times future' (Radcliffe 1996: 42). The last word in this rich vein of abuse is uttered by Dr. Johnson in 1750, when he denounces the 'obsolete terms and rustic words' of *The Shepheardes Calender* (which some 'very learnedly call Doric') as 'a mangled dialect which no human being ever could have spoken', a gross example of 'studied barbarity' (Turnage 1970: 563).

Then, after Johnson, the critics stop complaining. Beginning in the second half of the eighteenth century, there is a new interest in folk poetry, as evidenced by Bishop Percy's *Reliques of Ancient English Poetry* (1765) and Sir Walter Scott's *Minstrelsy of the Scottish Border* (1802). Dialect, which had long been an object of scorn, becomes now an object of study, a medium for new poetry (Robert Burns) and for new fiction (Scott's Waverley novels). What is more, the archaisms—which Spenser cultivated for special effect—are starting to blur now with the rest of language. By the end of the nineteenth century, all of Spenser, not just the archaizing bits, sounds old-fashioned.

Beginning with Sidney and ending with Samuel Johnson, the question about archaism and dialect is critical: do they embellish Spenser's poetry, or disfigure it? After Johnson, the critical question is replaced by scholarly ones. Can Spenser's dialect words be localized? Which words in Spenser would have seemed archaic to his original audience? Finally, what did contemporary (meaning, sixteenth-century) theory have to say about archaism and dialect?

In the nineteenth century, research on Spenser's dialect is spurred on by interest in his biography. Where did Spenser live after he received his M.A. from Cambridge (1576) and before he took employment with the Bishop of Rochester (1578)? Also, who was the girl 'Rosalind', glossed by E. K. as 'a feigned name, which beyng wel ordered, wil bewray the very name of [the author's] love and mistresse, whom by that name he coloureth'? Spenser grew up in the south of England, but *The Shepheardes Calender* has about forty dialect words that were, as E. K. says, 'Northernly spoken'. Might this have been where he met Rosalind? Several attempts were made to localize the dialect further, to Yorkshire or east Lancashire, but the data could not sustain this level of precision (*Variorum* 7: 312–15, 616). It is possible even, that Spenser learned his northernisms in London, where he attended the Merchant Taylors' School. The headmaster there, Richard Mulcaster (1531/2–1611), was from Carlisle and some of the teachers that he hired for the school were known to have been 'Northren men borne', who did not 'pronounce so well as those that be brought vp in the schole of the south partes of the Realme' (Millican 1939: 212).

With Spenser's archaisms, the picture is clearer. Using the *OED* and glossaries of hard words from the sixteenth century, it is possible to distinguish what seems archaic today from what was actually archaic when Spenser was writing (McElderry 1932; Gans 1979). For example, the adjective *eke* 'also', which sounds archaic to us, was apparently not archaic to Spenser's contemporaries. However, the verb *eke* 'stretch', which writers now use every day ('Stocks eke out gains as gold hits a 24-year high'), was not part of most writers' vocabulary in the sixteenth century, and would have seemed old-fashioned (McElderry 1932: 148, 158). This is an area where there is still room for more research. Using a searchable text of the *OED* and other databases, we shall probably find more words like the adjective *eke*, which seem archaic to us but which turn out, when we learn more about Elizabethan writers other than Spenser, not to have been peculiar. Meanwhile, our best tools for studying Spenser's language are Osgood's *Concordance* (1915), online resources such as WordHoard, and dictionaries, including of course the *OED*, but also Latin and other foreign language lexicons that were being published in Spenser's lifetime (Anderson 1996).

Already we know more than, say, Pope or Samuel Johnson about the theory of archaism and dialect that was current in the sixteenth century. Writers have always discussed literary theory, but the history of literary theory was not a subject much looked into until the end of the nineteenth century. Since then, we have learned several things that should modify how we evaluate Spenser's archaisms and his use of northern dialect. First, it has been noticed that most of Spenser's dialect words are concentrated in the 'morall' (viz., satirical) eclogues of *The Shepheardes Calender*; this is significant because, in Elizabethan literary theory, satire was supposed to use 'rough and bitter speaches' (Ingham 1971). Second, the proper use of archaic diction was a topic that was being discussed all over Europe in the sixteenth century, not just in England (Renwick 1922; Pope 1926; Zitner 1966). Finally, Renaissance theorists do not seem to have classified archaism as 'Gothic' or 'medieval'; it was defended, rather, by humanists as an act of recovery, in the same way that editing an ancient text was recovery, or writing a more classical prose style: they were, all three of them, opportunities for restoration, even reformation (Kostic 1959; Major 2002).

THE SPENSERIAN STANZA

The stanza which Spenser used for *The Faerie Queene*, a staff of nine verses rhyming *ababbcbcc* and tipped with twelve syllables in the last line, was apparently his own invention (see also Chapter 21 above). Many poets have used it since, for narrative, elegy, philosophy, even for versified science. But there was a long spell of two centuries when almost nobody used it for anything.

This is unexpected. *The Faerie Queene*, like *The Shepheardes Calender*, was an instant classic, with quotations appearing even before publication and full-blown imitations as early as 1596. But while Spenser had many admirers, only two of them, Richard Barnfield (1574–1620) and Gervase Markham (1568?–1637), adopted his stanza while the inventor was still alive.[5] Following Spenser's death in 1599, John Davies of Hereford (1564/5–1618) wrote several poems in Spenserian stanzas, including the long *Microcosmus* (1603).[6] But within a decade or two, stanzas would go out of fashion altogether. In 1619, Ben Jonson confided to William Drummond that 'Spencers stanzaes pleased him not'; also that, for epic poetry, rhyming couplets were 'the bravest sort of Verses . . . and that crosse Rimes and Stanzaes . . . were all forced' (1925–52: I, 132). By the time of the Civil War, Jonson's low opinion—of Spenser's stanza and of stanzas per se—was general all over England. Davenant, as we saw already, blamed the stanza for Spenser's archaisms, because (as his sponsor, Thomas Hobbes, explained) it encourages padding: 'forcing a man sometimes for the stoping of a chink to say something he never did think' (Spingarn 1909: II, 57). Dryden, too, thought Spenser's 'choice of so long a Stanza' an 'unhappy' one, but again (as in

Jonson) the prejudice is general: 'no kind of Staff', he goes on to say, 'is proper for an Heroick Poem; as being all too lirical' (1956–2000: V, 332).

The story of how stanzas became associated with lyric, and couplets with heroic poetry has never been fully told.[7] Surprisingly, the phrase *heroic couplet* is not recorded in the *OED* before 1828. Still some things are clear. Prior to, say, 1748 (when James Thomson used it for *The Castle of Indolence*), the Spenserian stanza was something that poets avoided and critics apologized for, when they were not attacking it outright. Among critics, the lone exception seems to have been Milton's nephew and biographer Edward Phillips (Wurtsbaugh 1936: 25–6). The change, though, when it did come, came first in poetry not in criticism. In 1771, James Beattie published a long poem in Spenserian stanzas, *The Minstrel: Or, the Progress of Genius*. Byron read it, and adopted its stanza for his first great success in publishing, *Childe Harold's Pilgrimage: A Romaunt* (1812–1818); only later did he read the *The Faerie Queene* itself. *Harold* made Byron famous and was the first poem in Spenserian stanzas to have a European, not just an English, readership. After *Harold*, the deluge: in the first two hundred years after Spenser died, there were only about one hundred poems in Spenserian stanzas; but in the three-decade period between 1800 and 1830, there were three hundred such poems, including Keats's *Eve of St. Agnes* (1820) and Shelley's elegy for Keats, *Adonais* (1821) (Radcliffe 1996: 77–88). Tennyson's 'Lotos-Eaters' (1832) is a late example of the same, Byron-fueled enthusiasm.

As above, in poetry, so below, in literary criticism. In his notebooks and margin-alia, Coleridge ebulliates over the Spenserian stanza as 'that wonderwork of metrical Skill and Genius! that nearest approach to a perfect Whole, as bringing the greatest possible variety into compleat Unity by the never interrupted interdependence of the parts' (1951: 158), 'a perfect whole . . . to which nothing can be added, and from which nothing can be removed' (1969–: 12/3, 910). It was Coleridge who, with William Hazlitt, established our modern notion of Spenser's prosody as primarily musical. Spenser's verse, said Coleridge in conversation, 'is like the beloved one singing to you in twilight' (1969–: 14/2, 464). On one occasion, Coleridge was said to have read Spenser in 'his finest and most musical manner'; on another, to have recited Spenser 'with such an excess [of 'intonation'] that it almost amounted to a song' (1969–: 5/1, 286, 476). Hazlitt had reservations about Spenser's stanza, but preached a similar doctrine about his versification, commending it as 'the most smooth and the most sounding in the language. It is a labyrinth of sweet sounds . . . that would cloy by their very sweetness, but that the ear is constantly relieved and enchanted by their continued variety of modulation—dwelling on the pauses of the action, or flowing on in a fuller tide of harmony with the movement of the sentiment. . . . Spenser was the poet of our waking dreams; and he has invented not only a language, but a music of his own for them' (Alpers 1969: 138).

Between them, the critics and especially the poets of the late eighteenth and early nineteenth century rehabilitated Spenser's stanza and launched his reputation for musicality. Since then, scholarship on Spenser's prosody has largely revolved around two questions. Where did the Spenserian stanza come from? And what is the effect, in the stanza's final line, of those two extra syllables?

After more than a hundred years of active inquiry, the origin question is still unsettled. Hazlitt assumed, like most critics before him, that Spenser's rhyme scheme (ababbabcc) was a modification of *ottava rima* (abababcc), because that was the meter of the Italian poems, *Orlando Furioso* and *Gerusalemme Liberata*, which he was manifestly imitating.[8] Madrigals and *terza rima* have also been suggested as possible influences (Pope 1926; Corse 1972). But the tendency, for the last hundred years, has been to look for sources closer to home, in English poets and English prosody. In Tudor poetry, there were precedents in Tottel's *Miscellany* (1557) and in *Mirrour for Magistrates* (1559).[9] Rhyme royal (ababbcc), as practiced by Chaucer and much loved of the Elizabethans, has also been proposed as a likely source, and is one that Spenser would have known well (Maynard 1934). An even closer analogue, the Monk's Tale stanza (ababbcbc), has until now been dismissed as 'unusual'. However, Steven May and William Ringler's comprehensive index of Elizabethan verse forms shows that the Monk's Tale stanza was, in fact, extremely popular (2004: 3:2156–7); this is another area where new tools have the potential to upset old conclusions.

A Spenserian stanza can be organized in one of several ways: pausing at the end of lines, at the couplet in the middle, or not pausing at all until the alexandrine.[10] On the effect of that last and longer pause, there have been two schools of thought. Does the alexandrine at the end of each stanza function as a brake on the narrative, impeding the flow of storytelling, or as a breather, refreshing the reader for further exertions? 'The danger' of any stanza, as George Saintsbury explained, 'is its tendency to *isolation*, its apparent suitableness rather to lyric than to narrative.... But the Spenserian', he argued, 'has nothing of this. Despite its great bulk and the consequent facilities which it offers for the vignetting of definite pictures and incidents within a single stanza, the long Alexandrine at the close seems to launch it on towards its successor *ripæ ulterioris amore*, or rather with the desire of fresh striking out in the unbroken though wave-swept sea of poetry. Each is a great stroke by a mighty swimmer: it furthers the progress for the next as well as itself.'[11] This sounds encouraging, but not everyone has agreed. According to John Hughes, who published an edition of Spenser's complete works in 1715, 'The same Measure, closed always by a full Stop, in the same Place, by which every Stanza is made as it were a distinct Paragraph, grows tiresom by continual Repetition, and frequently breaks the Sense, when it ought to be carry'd on without Interruption' (Mueller 1959: 27). The complaint is echoed more recently by O. B. Hardison, who claims, 'the Alexandrine acts as terminal punctuation every nine lines. The stanzas tend to segment the narrative into arbitrary chunks' (1989: 217).

The effect is particularly noticeable when *The Faerie Queene* is read alongside of other stanzaic poems from the same period, such as *Orlando Furioso* and *Gerusalemme Liberata* (Greene 1963: 327), and raises a question for further research: why did Spenser employ stanzas in the first place? Richard Helgerson has suggested a political explanation (1992: 19–62), but the question needs to be studied in a broader, international context. Why were all of the great epics of the sixteenth century, not just *The Faerie Queene*, written in stanzas instead of blank verse?

UNITY

The unity of *The Faerie Queene* is both the most controversial issue of the last four hundred years, and the only major topic in formal criticism that was not remarked by Spenser's contemporaries. In Italy, there had been a long-running quarrel about *Orlando Furioso* (1516), whether the episodes of the story were connected causally, according to the laws of nature and human psychology, or casually, by chance and whim (Weinberg 1961: I, 564–634; II, 954–1073). One of the quarrelers, Giraldi Cinzio, argued that (for modern readers) several heroes are more pleasing than one, and this may have encouraged Spenser to disperse his virtues among multiple knights (McCabe 1993: 225). In England, however, critics seem not to have worried about multiple plots or multiple heroes; what occasioned their handwringing was Ariosto's lack of morality.

The debate over Ariosto's unity, which occupied critics in Italy for most of the 1500s, traveled more slowly than the poem itself and did not arrive on English shores until the Restoration. Even then it came indirectly, by way of France, where Charles II's court had wintered in exile and where rules for writing everything—from epics to alexandrines—were being codified with cool exactitude and reforming fervor. In new poetry, the rules were a creative force. But in criticism *The Faerie Queene* (and Shakespeare too) came to be seen as 'irregular', in the old, etymological sense of unruly, unscientific, a product of fancy rather than art, achieving greatness by fits and starts, but not guided by any principles, and so not capable of *sustained* greatness over the course of a long poem. This would be the received wisdom on Spenser for approximately one hundred years, beginning with Davenant (1650) and ending with Richard Hurd's *Letters on Chivalry and Romance* (1762).[12] The chief exhibit in the charge of artlessness was Spenser's plot, which in spite of having a plan (twelve books for twelve moral virtues) did not have the kind of coordinated variety which Aristotle admired in nature and legislated for poetry. For Aristotle, the books of an epic (like the organs of a body) should not compete with each other, but subordinate their splendor to something larger and more glorious, which is the climax of the whole poem, as the head is crown over the whole body. *The Faerie Queene*, being unfinished, was at a disadvantage here—but even with a climax, explained Dryden, it would still have lacked unity because its author 'aims at the accomplishment of no one action; he raises up a hero for every one of his adventures; and endows each of them with some particular moral virtue, which renders them all equal, without subordination or preference' (Alpers 1969: 73).

Prince Arthur, continued Dryden, provides *The Faerie Queene* with a degree of continuity; but that is not the same as unity. Bishop Hurd, writing at the end of this period, suggested that *The Faerie Queene* is like a Gothic garden, where alleys radiate from a common center, and that its 'unity... consists in the relation of its several adventures to one common *original*, the appointment of the Fairy Queen, and to one common *end*, the completion of the Fairy Queen's injunctions.' For Hurd, this was too schematic; he could see the logic of it, but he preferred a style of poetry—and of gardening—in which symmetry is palpable but unobtrusive, and in which wholeness is expressed by all of the elements, not just the endpoints (Alpers 1969: 115–16).

Hurd was not satisfied, and yet after Hurd the question of unity moved into the background. It was still discussed by critics in the nineteenth century,[13] but it was no longer an obstacle to enjoyment. What absorbed the attention of Romantic critics was the texture of Spenser's poetry more than its structure. They commented, as we have seen, on its musicality and they likened its stories either to episodes in a dream or paintings in a gallery.[14] Almost two hundred years later, scholars are still writing about Spenser's technique of word-painting (Bender 1972; Krier 1990; see Chapter 37 above), but this was different. In the nineteenth century, gallery walls would be crowded with paintings from floor to ceiling and canvases were sorted, if at all, by size rather than subject. Conceived as a gallery, then, *The Faerie Queene* was not a structured sequence of stories so much as what Keats called 'a little Region [for the Lovers of Poetry] to wander in where they may pick and choose, and in which the images are so numerous that many are forgotten and found new in a second Reading: which may be food for a Week's stroll in the Summer' (1970: 27). According to Leigh Hunt, Keats's friend and sponsor, 'we never took any interest in [Spenser's] narratives; nor should we have cared to read him continuously' if not for the prospect of 'new and unexpected beauties' (Evett 1965: 47).

Discussion of unity resumed in the 1930s and 1940s, when scholars began to speculate about the layers or stages of *The Faerie Queene*'s composition (Spens 1934; Bennett 1942). Since then critics have continued to pose two questions. What is the structuring principle of Spenser's epic as a whole? And is it complete?

A few scholars have rejected the concept of structure altogether, arguing that large-scale unity is not to be looked for in a poem that was composed episodically over a twenty-year period, and that exhibits inconsistencies of plot, language, and characterization (Bennett 1942; Alpers 1967). For C. S. Lewis, the structure of Spenser's epic—the sequence of its events—was less important than its tone: 'In reading him we are reminded not of falling in love but of being in love' (1954: 391). But the heart has its reasons too: perceptions are structured, no less than syllogisms. As Isabel Maccaffrey (1976) argued, what organizes the poem may not be ethics so much as epistemology.

When deconstruction was in vogue, readers were urged to embrace disorder as programmatic (Goldberg 1981). Others before and since have labored at saving the appearances (Horton 1978: 194). It has been suggested, for example, that each book of *The Faerie Queene*, including *Two Cantos of Mutabilitie*, corresponds with a number, a day of the week, and that day's planetary god (Fowler 1964). Whether this particular scheme is valid (Nelson 1965), numbers and especially calendars do provide structure in Spenser's shorter poems, including, of course, *The Shepheardes Calender*, but also *Amoretti* and *Epithalamion* (Hieatt 1960; Kaske 1978), and they might have done so again in a twelve-book *Faerie Queene* (Tuve 1935). The effect of Spenser's multiple storylines has been compared with that of fugue in music or interlace in tapestry (Lewis 1966: 133–5; Horton 1978: 139–84). Recurring images, such as mountains, towers, and wells, are also traceable, not just within single episodes but from book to book; this was a standard technique in biblical exegesis and, when applied to *The Faerie Queene*, reveals another level of structural coherence (Kaske 1999).

Granted a structure of some sort, what are the strands of Spenser's story converging on or toward? The plot is punctuated by what have been called 'temples', episodes of revelation and recognition; but most of it is 'labyrinth', wandering (Fletcher 1971: 11–56). How was it supposed to end? Does the programme outlined in Spenser's 'Letter to Ralegh', for twelve books on private moral virtues, describe an advanced stage in the poem's evolution (Spens 1934; Bennett 1942)? Or, as later critics have thought, an early one which Spenser abandoned: because the meaning of his poem was already complete in six books (Frye 1961; Nohrnberg 1976); because the instinct of his poem, or of romance as a genre, is to resist completion (Parker 1979; Goldberg 1981; cf. Wilson-Okamura 2008); because Spenser despaired of his audience (Neuse 1968; Miller 1979); or changed his mind about the queen (Caine 1978: 155–85; Oram 2003)?

Even unfinished, *The Faerie Queene* is already very long and few have wished it longer.[15] Since the 1960s, many critics have been content to read book six as Spenser's farewell to poetry and *Mutabilitie* as his summation, epilogue, or encore. Book six, though, is far from conclusive (Stewart 1984) and Spenser, when he died, was hardly an old man (Lethbridge 2006). Until the twentieth century, it was assumed that Spenser did write additional books after book six, which fire consumed or a servant mislaid (see pp. 129, 355 above). What would those lost (or just unwritten) books have looked like? Attempts have been made to reconstruct their contents, especially of those books which would have concerned public virtues (Kuin 2002; Wilson-Okamura 2009). More than the impulse to complete a pattern, it is the quality of Spenser's posthumous writing that invites speculation. As Lewis argued, 'His verse [in *Two Cantos of Mutabilitie*] has never been more musical, his language never so strong and so sweet. Such poetry, coming at the very end of the six books, serves to remind us that the existing *Faerie Queene* is unfinished, and that the poet broke off, perhaps, with many of his greatest triumphs still ahead. Our loss is incalculable; at least as great as that we sustained by the early death of Keats' (1936: 357).

NOTES

1. For the term's subsequent history see Thompson (1971) and Strier (2002).
2. The *-en* suffix, which Spenser sometimes used to form plural nouns (*eyen* 'eyes'), plural verbs (*breathen* 'breathe'), and past participles (*broughten* 'brought'), was literary but still current. Cf. *brethren* 'brothers' in the King James' Bible (1611) and *bounden* 'bound' in Cranmer's liturgy (1549).
3. Castiglione, *The Courtier* bk. 1, chs. 31 and 35. For Virgil, see Servius (1887), III, 30 on *Eclogues* 3.1 and Ziolkowski and Putnam (2008), 194.
4. Guglielmo Moizio, *Virgilius a calumniis vindicatus* (1575), in Jacobus Pontanus, *Symbolarum libri XVIJ Virgilij* (Augsburg: J. Prætorius, 1599), facs. rept., 3 vols. (New York: Garland, 1976), I, 27. The same view was held by Trissino (1564); see Pope (1926), 588.
5. Morton (1907), 643–4; May and Ringler (2004), EV 11690, 16595.

6. May and Ringler (2004), EV 7989, 20301, 25901, 31597.
7. But see Saintsbury (1923), 2.193–4, 339, 342, 351–2, 440–1; and Piper (1969).
8. Alpers (1969), 137. But see Coleridge (1969–), 12/3: 910.
9. Bradner (1928); Morton (1907), 641–3.
10. Empson (1930), 33–4, 207–8; Dolven (2004).
11. Saintsbury (1923), I, 366–7; more recently Gross (1983); Krier (2006).
12. Alpers (1969), 63, 73, 75, 90–2, 101–2, 114–16; Evett (1965), 9–10, 18–24, 35; Radcliffe (1996), 22–8, 55, 56, 63, 65.
13. E.g., Radcliffe (1996), 115, 121, 144, 145.
14. For dreams, see Alpers (1969), 138, 148–50; Evett (1965), 72–5, 76–9, 127–31, 165. For paintings, Alpers (1969), 135, 158–9; Evett (1965), 43, 46–7, 125–6, 182.
15. Evett (1965), 3, 5, 43, 148–9, 199–200; Alpers (1969), 119.

BIBLIOGRAPHY

Alpers, P. J. (1967). *The Poetry of 'The Faerie Queene'.* Princeton, NJ: Princeton University Press.
—— (ed.) (1969). *Edmund Spenser: A Critical Anthology.* Harmondsworth: Penguin.
Anderson, J. H. (1996). *Words that Matter: Linguistic Perception in Renaissance England.* Palo Alto, CA: Stanford University Press.
Bacon, Francis (1996). *Francis Bacon*, ed. B. Vickers. Oxford: Oxford University Press.
Bender, J. B. (1972). *Spenser and Literary Pictorialism.* Princeton, NJ: Princeton University Press.
Bennett, J. W. (1942). *The Evolution of* The Faerie Queene. Chicago: University of Chicago Press.
Bradner, L. (1928). 'Forerunners of the Spenserian Stanza'. *RES* 4: 207–8.
—— (1938). 'The Authorship of *Spencer Redivivus'. RES* 14: 323–6.
Cain, T. H. (1978). *Praise in 'The Faerie Queene'.* Lincoln: University of Nebraska Press.
Coleridge, Samuel Taylor (1951). *Inquiring Spirit: A New Presentation of Coleridge from His Published and Unpublished Prose Writings*, ed. K. Coburn. New York: Pantheon.
—— (1969–). *The Collected Works of Samuel Taylor Coleridge*, 16 vols. Princeton, NJ: Princeton University Press.
Cooper, H. (1977). *Pastoral: Mediaeval into Renaissance.* Ipswich: Brewer.
Corse, L. E. (1972). '"A straunge kinde of harmony": The Influence of Lyric Poetry and Music on Prosodic Techniques in the Spenserian Stanza'. PhD dissertation, North Texas State University.
Dolven, J. (2004). 'The Method of Spenser's Stanza'. *SSt* 19: 17–25.
Draper, J. W. (1919). 'The Glosses to Spenser's *Shepheardes Calender'. JEGP* 18: 556–74.
Dryden, John (1956–2000). *The Works of John Dryden*, ed. E. N. Hooker et al., 20 vols. Berkeley/Los Angeles: University of California Press.
Empson, W. (1930). *Seven Types of Ambiguity*, 3rd edn. Rept. New York: New Directions, 1966.
Evett, D. (1965). 'Nineteenth-Century Criticism of Spenser', PhD dissertation, Harvard University.
Fletcher, A. (1971). *The Prophetic Moment: An Essay on Spenser.* Chicago: University of Chicago Press.
Fowler, A. (1964). *Spenser and the Numbers of Time.* London: Routledge and Kegan Paul.

Frye, N. (1961). 'The Structure of Imagery in *The Faerie Queene*'. *UTQ* 30: 109–27.

Gans, N. A. (1979). 'Archaism and Neologism in Spenser's Diction'. *MP* 76: 377–9.

Goldberg, J. (1981). *Endlesse Worke: Spenser and the Structures of Discourse*. Baltimore: Johns Hopkins University Press.

Greene, T. M. (1963). *The Descent from Heaven: A Study in Epic Continuity*. New Haven, CT: Yale University Press.

Gross, K. (1983). '"Each Heav'nly Close": Mythologies and Metrics in Spenser and the Early Poetry of Milton'. *PMLA* 98: 21–36.

Hardison, O. B. (1989). *Prosody and Purpose in the English Renaissance*. Baltimore: Johns Hopkins University Press.

Helgerson, R. (1992). *Forms of Nationhood: The Elizabethan Writing of England*. Chicago: University of Chicago Press.

Hieatt, A. K. (1960). *Short Time's Endless Monument: The Symbolism of the Numbers in Edmund Spenser's 'Epithalamion'*. New York: Columbia University Press.

Horton, R. A. (1978). *The Unity of 'The Faerie Queene'*. Athens: University of Georgia Press.

Ingham, P. (1971). 'Spenser's Use of Dialect'. *ELN* 8(3): 164–8.

Jonson, B. (1925–52). *Ben Jonson*, ed. C. H. Herford, P. Simpson, E. Simpson, 11 vols. Oxford: Clarendon Press.

Kaske, C. V. (1978). 'Spenser's *Amoretti and Epithalamion* of 1595: Structure, Genre, and Numerology'. *ELR* 8: 271–95.

——— (1999). *Spenser and Biblical Poetics*. Ithaca, NY: Cornell University Press.

Keats, John (1970, corr. 1975). *Letters of John Keats*, ed. R. Gittings. Oxford: Oxford University Press.

Kostic, V. (1959). 'Spenser and the Bembian Linguistic Theory', *English Miscellany* 10: 43–60.

Krier, T. M. (1990). *Gazing on Secret Sights: Spenser, Classical Imitation, and the Decorums of Vision*. Ithaca, NY: Cornell University Press.

——— (2006). 'Time Lords: Rhythm and Interval in Spenser's Stanzaic Narrative'. *SSt* 21: 1–19.

Kuin, R. (1998). *Chamber Music: Elizabethan Sonnet-Sequences and the Pleasure of Criticism*. Toronto: University of Toronto Press.

——— (2002). 'The Double Helix: Private and Public in *The Faerie Queene*'. *SSt* 16: 1–22.

Lavender, A. (1955). 'An Edition of Ralph Knevett's *Supplement of the Faery Queene* (1635)'. PhD dissertation, New York University.

Lethbridge, J. B. (2006). 'Spenser's Last Days: Ireland, Career, Mutability, Allegory', in J. B. Lethbridge (ed.), *Edmund Spenser: New and Renewed Directions*. Madison: Fairleigh Dickinson University Press: 302–36.

Lewis, C. S. (1936). *The Allegory of Love*. Oxford: Oxford University Press.

——— (1954). *English Literature in the Sixteenth Century, Excluding Drama*. New York: Oxford University Press.

——— (1966). *Studies in Medieval and Renaissance Literature*. Cambridge: Cambridge University Press.

Long, P. W. (1917). 'Spenser's Visit to the North of England'. *MLN* 32: 58–9.

McCabe, R. A. (1993). 'Prince Arthur's "Vertuous and Gentle Discipline"', in E. Ní. Chuilleanáin and J. D. Pheifer (eds), *Noble and Joyous Histories: English Romances, 1375–1650*. Dublin: Irish University Press: 221–43.

MacCaffrey, I. G. (1976). *Spenser's Allegory: The Anatomy of Imagination*. Princeton, NJ: Princeton University Press.

McElderry, B. R., Jr. (1932). 'Archaism and Innovation in Spenser's Poetic Diction'. *PMLA* 47: 144–70.

May, S. W., and Ringler, W. A. (2004). *Elizabethan Poetry: A Bibliography and First-line Index of English Verse, 1559–1603*, 3 vols. New York: Thoemmes Continuum.

Major, J. (2002). 'Purity, Translation and Dialectical Rhetoric in Spenser's "Well of English Undefyled"'. PhD dissertation, University of Oregon.

Maynard, T. (1934). *The Connection between the Ballade, Chaucer's Modification of It, Rime Royal, and the Spenserian Stanza*. Washington, DC: Catholic University of America.

Miller, D. L. (1979). 'Abandoning the Quest'. *ELH* 46: 173–92.

Millican, C. B. (1939). 'The Northern Dialect of *The Shepheardes Calender*'. *ELH* 6: 211–13.

Mills, J. L. (1967). 'Spenser's Castle of Alma and the Number 22: A Note on Symbolic Stanza Placement'. *N&Q* 14: 456–7.

Morton, E. P. (1907). 'The Spenserian Stanza before 1700'. *MP* 4: 639–54.

Mueller, W. R. (1959). *Spenser's Critics: Changing Currents in Literary Taste*. Syracuse: Syracuse University Press.

Nelson, W. (1965). Review of Fowler 1964. *Renaissance News* 18(1): 52–7.

Neuse, R. (1968). 'Book VI as Conclusion to *The Faerie Queene*'. *ELH* 35: 329–53.

Nohrnberg, J. (1976). *The Analogy of* The Faerie Queene. Princeton, NJ: Princeton University Press.

Oram, W. A. (2003). 'Spenser's Audiences, 1589–91'. *SP* 100: 514–33.

Parker, P. (1979). *Inescapable Romance: Studies in the Poetics of a Mode*. Princeton, NJ: Princeton University Press.

Piper, W. B. (1969). *The Heroic Couplet*. Cleveland: Case Western Reserve University Press.

Pope, E. F. (1926). 'Renaissance Criticism and the Diction of *The Faerie Queene*'. *PMLA* 41: 575–619.

—— (1926). 'The Critical Background of the Spenserian Stanza'. *MP* 24: 31–53.

Radcliffe, D. H. (1996). *Edmund Spenser: A Reception History*. Columbia, SC: Camden.

Renwick, W. L. (1922). 'The Critical Origins of Spenser's Diction'. *MLR* 17: 1–16.

Saintsbury, G. (1923). *A History of English Prosody from the Twelfth Century to the Present Day*, 2nd edn, 3 vols. London: Macmillan.

Servius (1887). *Servii Grammatici qui feruntur in Vergilii carmina commentarii*, ed. G. Thilo and H. Hagen, 3 vols. Leipzig: Teubner.

Smith, G. G. (ed.) (1904). *Elizabethan Critical Essays*, 2 vols. London: Oxford University Press.

Spens, Janet (1934). *Spenser's* Faerie Queene: *An Interpretation*. London: Arnold.

Spingarn, J. E. (ed.) (1909). *Critical Essays of the Seventeenth Century*, 3 vols. Oxford: Clarendon Press.

Stewart, S. (1984). 'Sir Calidore and Closure'. *SEL* 24: 69–86.

Strier, R. (2002). 'How Formalism Became a Dirty Word, and Why We Can't Do Without It', in M. D. Rasmussen (ed.), *Renaissance Literature and Its Formal Engagements*. New York: Palgrave: 207–15.

Thompson, E. M. (1971). *Russian Formalism and Anglo-American New Criticism*. The Hague: Mouton.

Turnage, M. (1970). 'Samuel Johnson's Criticism of the Works of Edmund Spenser'. *SEL* 10: 557–67.

Tuve, R. (1935). 'Spenser and the *Zodiake of Life*'. *JEGP* 34: 1–19.

Weinberg, B. (1961). *A History of Literary Criticism in the Italian Renaissance*, 2 vols. Chicago: University of Chicago Press.

Wells, S. (2003). 'By the Placing of His Words'. *TLS* 5243 (26 Sept.): 14–15.

Wilson, T. (1553; 1908). *The Arte of Rhetorique*, ed. G. H. Mair. Oxford: Oxford University Press.

Wilson-Okamura, D. S. (2009). 'Belphoebe and Gloriana'. *ELR* 39: 47–73.

Wilson-Okamura, D. S. (2008). 'Errors about Ovid and Romance'. *SSt* 23: 215–34.

Wurtsbaugh, J. (1936). *Two Centuries of Spenser Scholarship (1609–1805)*. Baltimore: Johns Hopkins University Press.

Ziolkowski, J., and Putnam, M. C. J. (eds) (2008). *The Virgilian Tradition: The First Fifteen Hundred Years*. New Haven, CT: Yale University Press.

Zitner, S. P. (1966). 'Spenser's Diction and Classical Precedent'. *PQ* 45: 360–71.

CHAPTER 39

THE HISTORICIST TRADITION IN SPENSER STUDIES

JOHN D. STAINES

'THE poet's poet' is perhaps the most common critical cliché about Spenser, uttered by some in admiring tones, by others in dismissive ones.[1] But Spenser is also a historian's poet, deeply engaged in the political, religious, and cultural battles of his age. That Spenser is simultaneously a poet's poet and a historian's poet is for many readers a fruitful paradox that opens up the richness of his literary achievement. For others, it is a mere contradiction, an irritation to be pushed to the side as an irrelevant distraction from the serious business of literary interpretation. It has also led in part to Spenser's curious place in the academy: He plays a central role in graduate curricula, producing dissertations and scholarship surpassed in early-modern English studies only by Milton and, of course, the Shakespeare industry, yet his 'difficulty', defined in large part by his historical difference, has limited his popularity not only with the common reader but increasingly with undergraduates and non-specialists. A consideration of the historicist tradition in Spenser criticism thus raises enduring theoretical concerns about both poetry and criticism, as well as anxieties about the literary canon, the academic profession, and Spenser's place in them. For many, the most surprising revelation might be that these are not new concerns produced by the critical movements of recent decades but questions raised from the very beginning by the challenges of Spenser's poetic project.

Spenser, whose mind and imagination were always a fertile mix of confidence and anxiety, introduces these problems himself in the first critical commentaries on his poems, E.K.'s glosses to *The Shepheardes Calender* and the 'Letter to Ralegh' appended to the 1590 *Faerie Queene*. E.K's historical and political commentary can range from the specific to the vague and misleading, a useful strategy that invites the reader into the process of determining meaning while also providing a degree of political cover for the poet when presenting his 'Satyrical bitternesse' (Spenser 1989: 23). *The Shepheardes Calender* itself mixes passing topical allusions with some more elaborate political allegories, just as *The Faerie Queene* does on a much larger scale. The 'Letter to Ralegh' directly encourages the reader to approach *The Faerie Queene* as a historical poem, though in taking on the title of a 'Poet historical' (Spenser 2001: 716), Spenser is actually attempting to place some distance between his work and the present political situation, choosing Arthurian legend, he says as being 'furthest from the daunger of enuy, and suspition of present time' (715). He distinguishes the *poet historical* from the *historiographer*: 'For an Historiographer discourseth of affayres orderly as they were donne, accounting as well the times as the actions, but a Poet thrusteth into the middest, euen where it most concerneth him, and there recoursing to the thinges forepaste, and diuining of things to come, maketh a pleasing Analysis of all' (716–17). The distinction is something of an ancient and Renaissance commonplace, but Spenser's unique vision shows in how he turns traditional commentaries on the poet launching *in medias res* into a vision of the poet as seeing history in past, present, and future all at once. The historical includes the present and the prophetic, and the poet is not just one who teaches by pleasing, as Horace might say, but one who gives 'a pleasing Analysis', a philosopher, not just a teacher. It is the poet's analytical work that distinguishes him from the historiographer who tells only 'affayres orderly as they were done'. The challenge of historicist criticism has thus always been to work out a dialogue between the historiographer's accounts of things as they were with the poem's other perspectives on time. Indeed, the 'Letter to Ralegh' can be misread to give added weight to the topical, as when Dryden extrapolates from it, and from his sense of the function of satire, the notion that 'the original of every knight was then living in the court of Queen Elizabeth, and [Spenser] attributed to each of them that virtue which he thought most conspicuous in them' (Cummings: 203). Dryden's comment in the 'Discourse on the Origin and Progress of Satire' occurs as he is censuring Spenser for including multiple plots and heroes instead of following neo-classical unities, and it is not clear how seriously he means for us to take his assertion about the historical originals being identifiable at Elizabeth's court. As wrongheaded as such a totalizing approach might seem to us, less extreme variants of it underlie much historicist criticism. The 'Letter to Ralegh' itself does try to draw attention away from such topical readings, which can breed 'gealous opinions and misconstructions', by setting forth the 'general intention and meaning' of the poem (Spenser 2001: 714), and yet it simultaneously tells us to read specific characters as allegories for Queen Elizabeth and her place in British history. The result is a push and pull between the specific and the general.

As Michael O'Connell has demonstrated, Spenser derives much of this sense of the epic's relationship to history and contemporary events from his engagement with Virgil's *Aeneid*, filtered through Italian commentaries on Virgillian epic and the Italian epic-romances of Ariosto and Tasso (1977: 16–37).[2] Servius's fourth-century commentary, the only complete one to survive antiquity, is the main authority for Renaissance readers and critics of Virgil, dominating the scholarly apparatus in most printed editions. Servius has a strong sense that an epic needs to engage history while submerging it in the poetry: history appears in the *Aeneid* '*per transitum* [in passing]' and cannot appear openly 'because of the laws of poetic art'. He goes so far as to deny that Lucan's Roman epic *De Bello Civili* [*On the Civil War*] is really poetry since it is too much of a retelling of historical events: 'Therefore Lucan does not belong among the poets because he is thought to have composed history, not a poem' (quoted in O'Connell 1977: 27). Servius's judgment would shape medieval and Renaissance discussions of both Lucan and the epic in general. For instance, Tasso's *Discourses on the Heroic Poem* dismisses Lucan for following the chronology of events, like a historian, rather than employing poetic invention (Quint 1993: 134). This distinction between the poet and the historian of course makes its way into Spenser's 'Letter to Ralegh', as well as contemporary works of literary criticism like Philip Sidney's *Apology for Poetry*. Ironically, when later critics condemn Book V for failing as poetry since it follows history too closely, they are echoing the criticisms of Lucan that shaped Spenser's sense of his project. Servius and his followers prefer for a poet to show the presence of history through passing allusions, which, as O'Connell suggests, can create typologies (Aeneas as Augustus, Gloriana as Elizabeth) that shed light on present concerns without building up complete historical allegories, if by 'historical allegory' we mean extended representations of history that are developed systematically and consistently (1977: 30–1). Servius's commentary thus has an effect not just on the poet in his method of composition but on his audience in their methods of reading: history appears in transitory, flexible allusions whose consistency lies not in specific allegorical referents but in the ethical, moral, and political vision underlying them all as a group.

Spenser's sense of the role of the poet historical reflects not only his readings in epic and epic theory but his sense of what 'history' itself means. A historicist reading that attempts to pin down the meaning of any moment in the text by tying an allegorical figure to a specific historical moment runs up against the problem of the multiple time scales of past, present, and future that operate simultaneously in his poetry. Moreover, the modern distinction between the facts of history and the fictions of myth and legend was just coming into being through the work of antiquarians and historiographers such as William Camden. Although in using Arthurian material, Spenser steps into an area of contemporary historiographical debate about the historical reality of the legend, he doesn't take a position. At times he uses the chronicles and legends as historical sources; at others he seems to treat them skeptically as poetic fictions. Bart Van Es's suggestive study of Spenser's approaches to history sees him experimenting in a number of discrete forms: history as chronicle of the nation's past, as chorography of the nation's landscape, as antiquarian research into the nation's cultural practices, as euhemeristic decoding of pagan myth and uncovering of universal history, as analogy to the nation's present situation, as prophecy for the nation's future (Van Es 2002; see also Helgerson 1992). Spenser's approach to history is thus eclectic, and he can work in a variety of forms in sequence or even at the same time. Readers understandably respond to the aspect of

Spenser's historical fiction that resonates most strongly with their poetic, intellectual, political, and historical interests. Some of these forms of history can seem to many readers not to be 'history' at all, which is frequently defined in critical discourse as political history or the history of Spenser's present time.

CONTEMPORARY RESPONSES TO THE HISTORICAL ALLEGORY

In John Dixon's marginalia, written around 1597 in his copy of the 1590 *Faerie Queene*, we can see the ways that a common reader responds directly to the historical allegory. Reading from the perspective of a patriotic, Protestant English gentleman, Dixon frequently wants to identify characters with specific real-world heroes and villains. His comments can be read as a cipher—and he even puts some of his identifications in his own cipher, as if to keep the secret to himself—and these identifications often say more about his views than we might feel they say about Spenser's, as when he identifies the Redcrosse knight with Leicester (Hough 1964: 2). He does not actually explore that allusion any further; it is more an association with him than a developed allegory, which is true of many of his notes. He has moreover no trouble shifting his historical referents. Duessa can be simply falsehood, or she can become a specific queen. He associates her with Mary Tudor in a commentary on the argument to I.xii, 'Though false Duessa it to barre / Her false sleightes doe imploy' (Hough 1964: 9), while a little later in the same canto, he identifies Duessa's challenge to the marriage of Redcross and Una as 'A fiction of a Challinge by Q[ueen]: of: s[cots]: that the religion by hir maintained to be the truth' (10). Dixon shows a willingness to play with the allegory, to let himself find a variety of applications and associations. His general thesis, again reflecting his personal views more than (perhaps) Spenser's, is that the allegory of the marriage of Una and Redcross is an allegory of Elizabeth's securing of the Protestant religion, and his comments on the final stanzas identify the wedding day with 'The day of the Crownation of o[ur] bleesed princess Eliza[beth]' (11).

We can see in these examples a desire to read the historical allegory both as a *roman à clef* and as something more open. In the quirkiness of Dixon's identifications, we can also see the way the 'darke conceit' invites a reader to participate in applying the allegorical concepts to his or her own particular view of a particular real-world situation (Spenser 2001: 714). Readers, indeed, will feel free to apply Spenser's allegory even to situations that did not arise until after it was written but on which the poem can offer perspective. Readers may want to identify a specific person or event as being Spenser's intended allegorical referent, yet the multiple possibilities also encourages them to enter into dialogues with the text and with each other. The poet himself can claim, seriously or disingenuously, that some readings are 'misconstructions', but readers nonetheless scan the text to understand Spenser's original intent and its continuing applications. King James VI of Scotland is perhaps the most famous example of such a reader and the one that posed the most danger to Spenser during his lifetime. In 1596 the English ambassador in Edinburgh reported James's anger over Duessa's trial and 'some dishonorable effects (as the k[ing] demeth thereof) against himself and his mother deceassed. He alledged that this booke was passed with previledge of her ma[jes]t[y']s Commission[er]s for the veiwe and allowance of all wrytinges to be receaued into Printe. But therin I haue (I think) satisfyed him that it is not given out w[i]th such p[ri]viledge: yet he still desyreth that Edward Spencer [sic] for his faulte, may be dewly tryed & punished' (Wells, I, 45). James could clearly see in the transparent representation of his mother's trial and execution a rejection of her claim to the throne, and he might also have seen in Spenser's decision to represent the trial of a monarch a hint of George Buchanan's republican defenses of his mother's overthrow by the Scottish people, works he had done much to suppress and argue against. But James was surely most concerned about how other readers at the English court, especially Elizabeth, were reading and applying Spenser's dark conceit. Were they reading the rejection of Mary's claim to the succession as a rejection of James's claim? The dispute over whether the government let the book be printed with 'privilege' is precisely about that issue, and in the assertion that it was not, James received his assurance that Spenser was not speaking for Elizabeth and her court (see pp. 478–9 above). The need for Spenser's punishment to serve as a sign or allegory of Elizabeth's position thus became superfluous, which may account for why the issue was eventually dropped, with Spenser receiving no punishment and his book no direct official censorship.[3] That Spenser understood the dangers of historical and political allusions, whether intended or not, shows in his choice to preface Duessa's trial with the allegory of the punishment of the poet Bon Font / Malfont.[4]

Spenser's intention, of course, is not irrelevant to many readers, and even James felt the need to insist on Spenser's punishment, despite receiving what he most wanted, a diplomatic assurance of his succession rights. Indeed, much of the historicist tradition is intertwined with Spenser's biography and the ways his life can shed light on the meanings of his poem. Since Spenser explicitly makes his life the subject of his poetry and prose and since his political career has left a significant trace in the historical record, biography has played a larger role in Spenser criticism than in just about any other Elizabethan writer. (Shakespeare, who has left few documentary records and whose references to himself in his poems and plays are few and enigmatic, is the obvious contrast.) Indeed historicist critics from the start have sought biographical and archival methods for fixing and defining Spenser's intentions, even as the meaning of any given allegorical referent seems multiple and otherwise far from simple. Ben Jonson, for instance, tells William Drummond of Hawthornden of the existence of a key to Spenser's historical allegory: 'That in that paper Sir W. Raughly had of the Allegories of the Fayrie Queene, by the Blating Beast the Puritans were understood...' (Cummings 1971: 136). This comment reflects certain tendencies in the historicist tradition. First, it assumes the referent in the historical allegory to be a single, identifiable contemporary figure or group ('the Puritans'). Second, for support, it encourages readers to search into the archives for 'that paper', some outside, material documentation to back up the interpretation. The citation of contemporary witnesses, Walter Ralegh, Jonson, even Spenser himself, serves the same legitimizing function. The problems in this story, however, soon become clear. An attack upon 'the Puritans' sounds more like Jonson's opinions in 1619 than Spenser's in 1596. The existence of 'that paper'—a key to unlock Spenser's allegorical intent—is a bit too perfect, an obvious reimagining of the 'Letter' of 1590, missing from the 1596 edition, as some secret document that would show what Spenser had hidden under the veil of his dark conceit, presumably for safety's sake. The slippery passive voice in that sentence—'by the Blating Beast the Puritans were understood'—obscures the agency behind this understanding. Jonson, or perhaps Drummond, is the one who understands the allegory this way, though the passive voice silently makes Spenser complicit in the understanding. Indeed, the eccentricities in Jonson's and Dixon's attempts to fix the meaning of the historical allegory reveal the openness of historical allegory, despite its initial impressions of fixed certainty: readers bring their historical and political perspectives to bear upon the reading experience, shaping their responses to historical allegory as much as to any other aspect of the allegory or story. An allegory like that of the Blatant Beast speaks to the broader issue of slander and libel as a political weapon, and readers can apply it to incidents past, present, and future. Although Spenser may have had specific slanderers in mind as he wrote various episodes, determining that specific intent is usually, though perhaps not always, difficult if not impossible. Nonetheless, the existence of the dark conceit encourages readers to enter into games of figuring out 'exactly' who or what the poet is referring to. The Ralegh family copy of the 1617 *Works* contains marginal glosses of both kinds: Sir Walter's wife Elizabeth Throckmorton wrote notes for her son Carew detailing specific places that (she claimed) refer to her and his father, while other comments, apparently in Walter's hand, seem to show him applying the moral allegory to his personal experience, pondering '*Ambition*', '*Night*', and '*Despair*' while imprisoned awaiting execution (Oakeschott 1971: 1–21). Identifying specific allusions alongside the general allegory is clearly part of the pleasure of reading the poem, drawing Ralegh and his family to reread and reflect upon it decades after the events to which it alludes.

James Ware's 1633 publication of Spenser's *View of the Present State of Ireland* arrived in time to shape how Spenser would be read during the Civil War. The manuscript had circulated in the 1590s, but a projected printing in 1598 had never come about. Although no firm evidence of direct censorship has come to light, it is clear that such a publication might have embarrassed the government or inflamed the simmering conflict in Ireland (see pp. 314–15 above). Three decades later, the text, though in many ways outdated, retained an ability to generate controversy. Ware did not produce a scholarly edition of Spenser's work, but adapted the text for inclusion in his *Historie of Ireland* (1633). His revisions not only reflected the current situation and his own views on it but amounted to expurgation of some of Spenser's most cruel and bigoted comments about the Old English, Roman Catholics, and the Irish people in general. This version would remain the standard print edition until the publication of editions drawn from the manuscripts during the Victorian period. Even in the altered form, the dialogue was soon provoking responses from both English and Irish readers, and its prescriptions for the pacification of Ireland would echo, directly or indirectly, in future accounts of the conflict. Milton, for instance, read Ware's edition and quotes from it in his commonplace book, recognizing Spenser as an authority on political and military affairs (Milton 1953–82: I, 465, 496). The publication of *A View* also served as a reminder that Spenser saw himself as a poet of Britain, a vision all the more relevant as the Civil War ranged across and among the three kingdoms, England, Scotland, and Ireland. He was no mere celebrator of royal majesty but a civil servant offering what was often unwelcome advice. He could thus be a model for a loyal servant of the crown, or an iconoclastic republican.[5]

There was thus no one 'Spenser' when the Civil War broke out and divided a national culture along religious and political lines.[6] Milton and other republicans saw in Spenser an iconoclastic reformer. One version of this Spenser appears in *Areopagitica* as 'our sage and serious Poet *Spencer*, whom I dare be known to think a better teacher then *Scotus* or *Aquinas*', a stern, wise, even calm teacher of the virtues through the experience of poetry (Milton 1953–82: II, 516). Milton also recognizes in Spenser's writings a defense of a reformation that comes not only through a Palmer of gentle reason but through men and women of violent force. Indeed, as Willy Maley has argued, radicals like Milton saw continuity between reason and violence, reformation and colonialism, all parts of the same program (Maley 1993: 191–208). Milton will thus invoke Spenser as a poet of apocalyptic violence, as in *Eikonoklastes* when he calls upon his Talus to help him smash the king's image:

If there were a man of iron, such as *Talus*, by our Poet *Spencer*, is fain'd to be the page of Justice, who with his iron flaile could doe all this, and expeditiously, without those deceitfull formes and circumstances of Law, worse then ceremonies in Religion; I say God send it don, whether by one *Talus*, or by a thousand. (Milton 1953–82: III, 390)

Milton turns to Spenser to imagine a violent disciplinary agent of reform, enlisting him in the republican cause. This is the same Spenser who informs Milton's own pamphlet on the wars in Ireland, *Observations upon the Articles of Peace with the Irish Rebels*, with its advocating of harsh military measures against the Irish, especially the Catholic population.

Curiously, in the same year that Milton imagines Spenser's Talus as a leveler throwing down a king and the laws in favor of divine justice, a royalist reader of Spenser produces a pamphlet, *The Faerie Leveller: Or, King Charles his Leveller described and deciphered in Queene Elizabeths dayes*, that reprints the episode of the egalitarian giant and his destruction by Talus to argue against the social and political leveling efforts of Parliament. A key to the cipher makes specific identifications, identifying, for example, Artegall with King Charles and 'The Gyant Leveller' with Cromwell (*Faerie Leveller* 1648: 4). Both the republican and the royalist can decipher Spenser's historical allegory into divergent allegories of their times. That Spenser could serve both republicans and royalists is a function of both the cultural divide opened by Charles's execution and Spenser's own equivocal portraits of royal power. Indeed, these two versions of Spenser's politics—Spenser the radical republican and Spenser the conservative royalist—remain with us to this day as readers and critics respond to the allegory through the double lens of past history and current events (see Hadfield 1998; 2003b; Wilson-Okamura 2003).

RESTORATION AND EIGHTEENTH-CENTURY COMMENTARIES AND EDITIONS: SPENSER AND LITERARY HISTORY

The next century saw efforts to establish a national literary tradition for England, with Spenser as one of its major pillars.[7] Spenser could be a national poet in a literary tradition largely washed clean of its writers' political engagements, a view shaped in part by Dryden's comments in *Fables Ancient and Modern* of 1700:

Milton was the Poetical son of Spencer . . . ; for we have our Lineal Descents and Clans as well as other Families: Spencer more than once insinuates, that the Soul of Chaucer was transfus'd into his Body, and that he was begotten by him Two hundred years after his Decease. Milton has acknowledg'd to me, that Spencer was his Original. (Dryden 1958: IV, 1445)

Dryden's obsession with origins and patriarchal lineages among poets envisions literary history as a lineal progress or transmigration of souls. Just how each poet reads or misreads the earlier generation is less important than the tradition itself, and the existence of an established tradition defined by critics tends to obscure the specific ways any given poet responds to his or her social and political world. Spenser's distinctive originality—to use the word *original* quite differently from Dryden—is lost in favor of looking for his origins in a continuous and stable tradition. The poet's original and specific responses to his time, though, are the subject of historicist criticism and where it diverges from literary history.[8]

In the eighteenth century, the first critical editions of Spenser's work began to appear. Those early editions continued the process of securing a place for Spenser in English literary history envisioned as a chain of inheritance: Chaucer, Spenser, Shakespeare, Milton. To a lesser degree, they began to piece together parts of the historical and political allegory that were becoming more obscure with the passage of time. These editors struggled with Spenser's historical difference, at pains to explain his irregularity and refusal to follow the rules and standards of taste that the eighteenth century wanted to claim as universal. In part because of the success of these editions in securing his place in the canon, Spenser, despite his archaic style and method, was read as a model for political and historical allegory, most brilliantly in the case of Pope's satires like *The Rape of the Lock* and *The Dunciad*.

These critics and editors focus on how to evaluate Spenser's achievement, rather than on how to interpret his poems, and when they do historicist work, it is largely to deal with the problem of how to value a poet after the passage of time has led to radical shifts in language and taste. Reading Spenser gives an acute sense of historical change despite the attempt to create a national narrative of cultural and literary continuity. For example, in 1715, the editor John Hughes defends Spenser and allegorical poetry on the grounds of national heritage:

[Chaucer and Spenser] seem to have taken deep Root, like old *British* Oaks, and to flourish in defiance of all the Injuries of Time and Weather. The former is indeed much more obsolete in his Stile than the latter; but it is owing to an extraordinary native Strength in both, that they have been able thus far to survive amidst the Changes of our Tongue, and seem rather likely, among the Curious at least, to preserve the Knowledg of our Antient Language, than to be in danger of being destroy'd with it, and bury'd under its Ruins. (Hughes 1715: I, xxvi)

Hughes picks up on one of Spenser's great historical themes, the ruins of language and culture, turning his anxiety over loss into a celebration of his enduring achievement as representative of English national character. Hughes does not want a dead monument, however, and his primary concern is that Spenser be read despite his distance in time and culture. He modernizes the spelling and provides 'A Glossary Explaining the Old and Obscure Words' (I, cxv–cxl). He gives a cogent explanation of the allegorical method, recognizing the shift in taste away from allegory before remarking on the return of moral allegory, even Spenserian allegory, in some of Addison's writings (see pp. 646–8 above).[9]

John Upton's edition of 1758 is the first to attempt to give a detailed accounting of Spenser's historical allusions and their bearing on the interpretation of his work. His notes would be the starting point for all subsequent research into Spenser's historical allegory, the basis for much of the work of the *Variorum* edition, even if many of his identifications fail to stand up to scrutiny.[10] Upton does not attempt a systematic account of the historical allegory, noting that 'as times and circumstances altered during the first planning of the poem, and the publishing of it, so the poet was obliged in this particular scheme to alter likewise, and to complicate and perplex the allusions' (Upton 1758: I, xxxi). For Upton, then, the historical allusions are local and ever-shifting in meaning across the poem (see p. 647 above). He says he provides a variety of allusions for the reader so that 'if the reader, with proper knowledge of the history of Queen Elizabeth's reign, delights in such mysterious researches, he may easily, with these hints given pursue them further' (I, xxxii). The historical allusions are a sort of pleasant game for the modern reader interested in the history. It would be up to other readers to develop the allusions into fuller accounts of the historical allegory.

VICTORIAN SPENSER: THE IMPERIAL TRADITION

By the beginning of Victoria's reign, the national canon, first glimpsed in E.K.'s glosses and then developed by Dryden and others through the 18th century, had become firmly entrenched. As the foremost poet with a distinctively imperial vision, Spenser found enthusiastic readers as the British Empire reached its height. Indeed, Spenser's strategy of rooting his fully modern epic-romance in a neo-Gothic style was one shared by Victorians as they built their modern industrial empire. The Gothic fantasies of the Westminster Parliament (1836–70) or the St Pancras train station (1866–73) recall the ways Spenser simultaneously declared himself a 'new Poet' while tying his project to a native English vernacular. In Victorian hands, such medievalism asserted a continuity of tradition between the modern and the ancient, forming a conservative defense against modern novelty in its rejection of the classical style then associated with republican France. Spenser likewise used his native Gothic style to distance himself and the English tradition from the Catholic culture of France and Spain, though this analogy can have the anachronistic effect of making Spenser look more conservative and monarchist than he was. It was while reading an English historian who had used Spenser's *View* as an authority on Irish customs and institutions that Karl Marx jotted down his immortal jab, 'Elizabeth's arse-kissing poet' (*SE*, 457), which is a mirror, albeit distorted, of the Victorian understanding of him.

Alexander Grosart's eight-volume edition of Spenser's poetical works (1882–84) is a monument to the national tradition (see pp. 652–3 above). Grosart begins the work with a dedicatory sonnet to the current poet laureate, Alfred, Lord Tennyson:

> The works of Spenser in thy hands I place,
>   As from his hands they came; at last set free
>   From touch profane—worthy of him and thee,—
> Thee Tennyson, true child of that high race,
> A singer born!— Methinks 'tis meet to grace
>   This loving labour so; that men may see
>   Thro' what a luminous continuity
> Our English muse still lifts her awful face.
> *His* the rich vision of the 'Faerie Queene',
>   'Eclogues', and marriage-lay; *Thine*, matchless songs,
> 'Arthur', 'The Book of Memory'; and I ween
>   The later voice the first full note prolongs:—
> Happy our England that from age to age
> Keeps bright her grand poetic heritage.   (Grosart 1882–84: I,iii)

While carefully restoring the text to Spenser's original spelling and usage, against the eighteenth-century tendency to modernize him, Grosart's historicism builds a 'continuity' between Spenser and Tennyson's Arthurian projects. Much as Spenser's grounding of religious reform in a (supposed) native tradition serves to obscure radical change and discontinuities, so Victorian Arthuriana hides the disruptions of industrialization under the continuities of an age-old heritage. Locomotives can hide under the skin of a Gothic cathedral, as can modern religious and political views. This Victorian Spenser, moreover, is like Tennyson a conservative servant of monarchy and empire, making it impossible to sense in him any potential republican sympathies.

Grosart devotes the full first volume of his edition to a thorough biography, one of the first lives to benefit from the project, begun in 1838, to centralize the British archives in the Public Record Office (for Spenser's Victorian editors see Chapter 35 above). Over the next decades, access would be made increasingly free to the public in a building specifically designed for both storage and research. The massive scholarly effort of cataloguing the contents of the state papers had begun by the 1850s. Those calendars, which would take decades to produce, are the tools that have made modern historicist research possible. For the first time, Spenser's poetry and his *View* could be put in the context of his work for Lord Grey in the conquest of Ireland, giving new energy to historicist accounts of Spenser, one that is still generating new knowledge and new interpretations. Grosart begins the process of reconciling the poet and the government servant in his biography, giving only the second publication of *A View* drawn from a manuscript copy since Ware's highly altered edition of 1633. This shift in editorial practice—the first edition of a manuscript, in Richard Morris's *Complete Works* of 1869, was followed by Grosart's, W. L. Renwick's (1928–34), and the *Variorum*'s—resulted from the new access to archives, the Victorian interest in antiquarianism, and finally the growing professionalization of research practices. *A View* and the archives, however, proved to be a challenge to the triumphal vision of the rise of empire that Grosart in particular wanted to proclaim.

Grosart's biography celebrates Spenser as 'one of England's, one of the race's great Poets and Singers' (I, 252). He is a national poet, though in Grosart's expansion from England to 'the race'—the white, Anglo-Saxon race—and in the participation in the editorial project of an American scholar like Harvard's Francis James Child, we can see the birth of a trans-Atlantic approach to Spenser, one produced not by a shared nation-state but by interrelated institutions of language, culture, and education. Writing at a moment of historical change, Grosart sees historical continuity not just in the work of poetry but the work of empire. For example, he draws analogies between Elizabethan wars in Ireland and Victorian imperial wars, as when he explains that 'Historically the new "Rebellion" [i.e., Tyrone's in Ireland] broke forth as did the Mutiny in India' (I, 227). Indeed, the style of his account of the sinister spread of the Irish rebellion surely owes as much to reports that came out of India in 1857 as to the State Papers of the 1590s. He then mounts a touchy and testy defense of Spenser and English imperialism:

The 'Sepoy Revolt' was thus put down. The Civil War of the Southern States was thus put down by the free North. It is sentimentalism, not sentiment; it is to read backward England's 'rights' of conquest and possession; it is to canonize a crew of the falsest, basest, most treacherous of men; it is to misdirect sympathy; for one moment to concede that Elizabeth and her statesmen had any choice but to 'subdue Ireland'. One even at this late day is touched by the allegiance of the 'common people' to their 'chiefs', by their unbought service in face of all hazards, by their ignorant yet consistent adherence to 'the old religion', by their love for their homesteads and hearths; but none the less must the historic verdict be that to 'subdue' Ireland was a necessity for England and the best thing for Ireland. (I, 234)

Grosart writes this as the Irish campaign for Home Rule was gaining traction—the first Home Rule bill would appear, and fail, in Parliament in 1886—itself an outgrowth of the Catholic Emancipation movement of the opening decades of the century. His assertion that history is on the side of imperial violence—of the ultimate good of using Talus's pitiless sword 'to reforme that ragged common-weale' (V. xii.26)—makes a conservative stand against the challenges to an empire then at its height. The Irish, though, were getting the chance to give their own 'historic verdict' on the empire, while Grosart's use of an analogy to the American Civil War and the use of violence against slavery is another reminder that his audience is no longer comprised solely of subjects of the British Empire.

That Grosart feels it necessary to declare that the empire was 'the best thing' not only for England but for the peoples subdued by it is a sign of the stubborn resistance that would finally wear it down. Spenser's reputation has suffered as attitudes towards empire have shifted, a revaluation made more poignant by our new ability to see in the archives just how implicated he was in the bloody colonization of Ireland. Indeed, Grosart's attack on 'sentimentalism' surely takes aim at R. W. Church's 1879 biography, the first archivally-based life of Spenser to appreciate the 'decisive influence' of Spenser's move to Ireland and of 'the fierce and narrow interests of a cruel and unsuccessful struggle for colonization' (Church 1879: 53). Church gave the nineteenth century's most complete and scholarly account of Spenser's life and career, one that is acutely aware of the historical distance between the Elizbethan and the modern. His assessment of A View—'But there does not appear a trace of consideration for what the Irish might feel or desire or resent . . . of English cruelty, of English injustice, of English rapacity, of English prejudice, he is profoundly unconscious' (174)—is the sort of modern liberal viewpoint that drives the imperialist Grosart to fits of invective. It is also very much the direction that historicist criticism would take, with Grosart's confidence in the good of empire becoming as embarrassing to modern readers as some of Spenser's comments on the Irish have become chilling. At the same time, the growing political, economic, and cultural power of the English-speaking former colony across the Atlantic would provide a new place for Spenser studies, one that would use Spenser and English literary history to build American links to the English liberal tradition (Radcliffe 1996: 154–66).

THE EARLY TWENTIETH CENTURY AND THE RISE OF ACADEMIC HISTORICISM

With the rise of the research university in the late nineteenth and early twentieth centuries, scholarship became a profession, and interpretation became a means to a career based on the continued production of new knowledge. The critic became less an evaluator of poetry than an interpreter, and Spenser's complex poetry was immediately recognized as a prime candidate for detailed exegesis. While the first professional critics turned to Spenser out of philological and linguistic interest—his experiments in archaic speech proving fertile ground for those interested in the history of language—the richness of historical allusion in Spenser made him especially suited for the sort of 'scientific' research prized by the modern university. A trip to the archives became a prime route to the Ph.D. and thus the profession. What marks so many of these earliest works of academic historicism is a naïve faith in the ability of the archives to provide a key to the entire work. Documents uncovered in the British Museum or the State Papers would serve the same function as the lost paper on the allegories of *The Faerie Queene* that Jonson claims Ralegh once possessed. Most of these works are long since forgotten, though they often reflect great creative energy, like Lilian Winstanley's elaborate, if misguided, reading of Book I as an allegory of the coming of the Reformation to England under Henry VIII (Winstanley 1915).

Edwin Greenlaw set the standard for the first stage of academic historicism, and his thorough research and attention to the nuances of allegory make his contributions indispensable. In the essays collected in *Studies in Spenser's Historical Allegory*, Greenlaw parodies the academic historicism of his time for turning *The Faerie Queene* into 'a sustained or allegorical transcript of Tudor history' (Greenlaw 1932: 59). He sees the trend plaguing all areas of Renaissance studies, reducing the literature of Spenser, Shakespeare, and others not just to mere 'documentary stuff for literary historians' but 'a crossword puzzle' (59). That one of the best-known practitioners of historicism should make such a lament over bad historicism, one still made in various forms today, is a sober warning to us of the hazards of the method. As a way out of this methodological trap, Greenlaw usefully distinguishes between topical allusion and continued allegory (see especially 80–103). Topical allusions form a part of the texture of the poem, but they do not need to be developed across the entire work. They are moreover unlikely to be poetic re-creations of secret papers now discoverable in the state archives but unknown to Spenser and most of his contemporary readers. Allegory, by contrast, 'is simple, makes its presence known, has a general rather than a minute application' (97). Thus Duessa might be a specific topical reference to Mary Queen of Scots in Book V, Canto Nine, but there and elsewhere she serves as a more general allegory for the seductions of false religion. Analyses of topical allusions tend to be most persuasive in discussions of small portions of the poem, a canto or even a stanza; moving beyond the confines of a brief episode, the allegory combines a variety of topical allusions that are in aggregate not historically consistent with each other. Artegall might at times enact events from Lord Grey's career, but trying to map the man's career back onto Artegall's entire series of adventures is a foolish impossibility. To move to the larger scale involves what is essentially an inductive move from the local to the general, pulling together a variety of historical examples to develop a broader moral vision. This does not imply, as some would have it, that the general moral allegory has no political or historical content. As Greenlaw explains, Spenser's allegorical method is marked by 'the blending of moral allegory with political intent' (87). The allegory encourages readers to apply the moral to the political, a process that we can see in the commentaries and responses of early readers like Dixon and Milton.

Greenlaw's version of historicism does have certain blindspots that distinguish it from what would, a half-century later, be known by the contrasting term, 'the new historicism'. First, in practice, observing Greenlaw's distinction between topical allusions and continued allegory allows the critic to harmonize the various local incidents and episodes into political universals and Renaissance commonplaces. Greenlaw prefers coherence and simplicity in the allegory over conflict, contradiction, and dissent, as in E. M. W. Tillyard's influential *Elizabethan World Picture* (1944), where literature serves as examples of views (supposedly) common to the age. Greenlaw, for instance, reads the allegory of Mercilla's court as a 'brilliant apology for the execution of Mary', part of his general tendency to see the poem as 'an allegory that unifies and interprets' (Greenlaw 1932: 165, 166). The dissenting voices in the allegory of Duessa's trial and its oblique criticism's of Elizabeth's policies are kept out of his portrait as distractions from the poem's (assumed) intention of celebrating Elizabeth and the British imperial destiny.[11] Greenlaw presents *The Faerie Queene* as 'an interpretation of Elizabethan political idealism without parallel elsewhere'. Spenser 'saw beyond the welter of court intrigue and petty politics the glorious vision of an imperial England' (165). Topical allusion is reduced to 'court intrigue and petty politics', while moral and political allegory is associated with 'the glorious vision of an imperial England'. This particular chapter, 'Spenser and the "Party and Progress"' was originally published in 1912 as 'Spenser and British Imperialism' in a form that does not acknowledge the political conflicts and tensions that even a high Victorian imperialist like Grosart had to confront. Even in the revised version of 1932, the American Greenlaw seems unaware of the imperial retreat already underway in Ireland, India, and elsewhere. Writing in service of the imperial project seems to him an obvious, idealistic good. His Spenser has envisioned the glorious empire that others, with their petty politics, would bring into being.

The *Variorum Edition* is the great monument to that first age of academic historicism. Greenlaw and his team of scholars pulled together the range of past commentaries on the allegories and allusions, adding their own research, particularly into historical and political allusion. The edition shows how thoroughly the new research university had transformed the understanding of sixteenth-century English poetry. The *Variorum* made possible many new readings of Spenser, historicist and formalist, even if not all the historicists would follow Greenlaw's advice on historical allegory.[12] In its intimidating heft, however, the *Variorum* has the unfortunate effect of turning Spenser into a poet whose historical difference requires the guidance of the specialist.

HISTORICISM DURING THE NEW CRITICISM

Greenlaw's emphasis on the moral allegory is linked to a preference for the study of the history of ideas over political history. The historical detail of the *Variorum* is the means of leading to the truths of philosophy and morality as expressed in the poetry. This prejudice would become stronger once the New Criticism replaced philological and historicist approaches as the dominant research and teaching paradigm in the university, particularly in the United States. The New Critics did not ignore history, as some historicists charge, but they generally reduced historical data to tools for interpreting the poem itself, with questions of the poet's intentions and his or her responses to the contemporary world pushed aside as far as possible (see Strier 2002). The New Critic's valuing of ambiguity and irony did, however, have the salutary effect of checking the temptation to read Spenser's historical allegory as a transcript of history, even if the complementary thrust of New Criticism as reading the poem objectively in isolation from the poet's subjective intentions pushed historicism and biography to the edges of critical interest.

We can see these trends in one of the best analyses from this era to take on the otherwise neglected Book V, Jane Aptekar's *Icons of Justice: Iconography and Thematic Imagery in Book V of 'The Faerie Queene'.* Building on the important work of Rosemond Tuve (1947; 1966), Aptekar offers a rich and detailed account of *The Legend of Justice* in the context of contemporary emblem books and iconography. She shows the impact of new formalist understandings of allegory when she criticizes attempts like Tillyard's to flatten out Spenser's views into a stable world picture, allowing instead for a moral allegory that is 'frequently ironic, paradoxical, and aware of contrarieties' (Aptekar 1969: 2). Aptekar is still doing historicist research, showing many of the images and ideas that a Renaissance reader would have brought with him or her to a reading of Spenser, yet she is very sensitive, even defensive, about the historicity of her work and of *The Faerie Queene* itself. 'It will be observed that this study gives very little attention to . . . the question of the Legend's relationship to history', she writes, limiting 'history' to just political events (7). She then asserts, 'Spenser was more interested in what (for him) *is* than in what men were doing or should do: he was writing a philosophical not a political poem' (8). For a work so thoroughly invested in the history of ideas, this is a curiously ahistorical understanding of Renaissance humanism, asserting an absolute preference for the *vita contemplativa* over the *vita activa*, whereas Spenser's epic explores both approaches, showing philosophy in action. Her defensiveness reflects an attempt to evade the complaint of readers like A. C. Hamilton who dismiss Book V as a place where Spenser's poetry fails since he lets 'fact press down upon the fiction' (Hamilton 1961: 173), 'saving' Book V from critical oblivion by leaving aside its messy engagement with politics and history and examining its place in a history of representation that stands outside and above the particularities and contingencies of historical events. Nonetheless, Aptekar's account of the iconographies of justice and politics actually has a lot to say about Renaissance philosophies of what men and women 'should do' politically, just as Spenser does.

In another approach to the challenge of historical fact in Spenser's poetry, Angus Fletcher's account of Book V recreates Greenlaw's distinction between topical allusion and allegory as an essential part of Spenser's prophetic method: 'allusions to current happenings tend to go *through* their historical particularity, till they reach a level of transcendent meaning' (Fletcher 1971: 42). An allusion to one moment in time becomes a prophecy transcending time. Michael O'Connell develops Fletcher's suggestions into an account of history in the full poem, going so far as to reject the usefulness of the term 'historical allegory' for how Spenser represents contemporary events in the poem—with the exception of the always troublesome Book V. There, in the Legend of Justice, Spenser feels the need 'to confront history more fully and insistently than he had done earlier', with the result that the allegory becomes something closer to the transcript of history that so many critics find stifling (O'Connell 1977: 13); however, elsewhere O'Connell sees Spenser transcending the historical moment in a prophetic mode learned from Virgil. In O'Connell's account, the prophetic is not an evasion of history and politics but a way that the moral allegory meditates on and responds to urgent contemporary questions about the political exercise of power.

THE NEW HISTORICISM, CULTURAL MATERIALISM, AND THE POLITICAL CRITICISM OF THE LATE TWENTIETH CENTURY

The return of political history to the study of Spenser's allegory would come through the political engagement of academic critics during the late 1970s and 1980s. Spenser's politics, of course, have always raised opposition, and even a conservative, Anglo-Irish historicist of the traditional school, C. S. Lewis, would remark of Book V that Spenser 'becomes a bad poet because he is, in certain respects, a bad man. . . . Spenser was the instrument of a detestable policy in Ireland, and in his fifth book the wickedness he had shared begins to corrupt his imagination' (Lewis 1936: 348–9). Lewis's assessment of the 'bad man', however, would reek of a sentimental liberal humanism to a new generation of political critics who were using the poet's frequently unpalatable political views to criticize the political structures and institutions of modern capitalism. These movements have gone by the names of the new historicism and cultural materialism, though these are catch-all terms for an interest in cross-disciplinary work, influenced variously (and not consistently) by approaches drawn from anthropology, linguistics, psychoanalysis, and economics, and in particular structuralism and post-structuralism. They share a refusal to distinguish between text and context—perhaps their sharpest methodological difference with traditional academic historicism. They also avoid the problem of intention in historical allegory by thinking in terms of discourses, seeing meaning produced not by a single intelligence but by larger systems of language and culture.

Stephen Greenblatt's brilliant reading of the destruction of the Bowre of Blisse as an act of regenerative violence, of a tragic but necessary renunciation of pleasure and beauty required by the processes of creating civility and fashioning a gentleman, is usually taken as the point of origin of the new historicism in Spenser studies (Greenblatt 1980: 157–92). What makes Greenblatt's historicism 'new' and different are several moves that characterize much of the historicism of the 1980s and 1990s. First, he argues that in Spenser ' "civility"—civilization— ... is achieved only through renunciation and the constant exercise of power', a formulation that equates Spenser's 'civility' with Freud's 'civilization' before melding it into Foucault's conception of the inescapable presence of power (Greenblatt 1980: 173). Such an account of power would resonate throughout the 1980s, finding their strongest development in the work of Jonathan Goldberg (1981; 1983). Second, Greenblatt portrays Spenser's attitudes towards civility and power as being shaped by and shaping the colonial experience. Greenblatt's passionate indictment of colonial policy and his refusal to excuse Spenser's role in it, moreover, reflect the great shift that has occurred since Greenlaw wrote so admiringly of Spenser's patriotic service to the ideal of a British Empire. Third, providing a model that would be used by numerous imitators, Greenblatt makes many of his links through analogies built largely by the force of his rhetoric: '*In just this way*, Europeans destroyed Indian culture ...' or 'In the *Inventarium monumentorum superstitionis* of 1566, for example, *we may hear* repeated echoes of Guyon's acts ...' (183, 188, my emphasis). These early efforts at a historicist revival were not notable for their deep research into the archives but for the persuasiveness (or, in less skillful hands, lack of persuasiveness) of such analogies.

Among the most important of the new historicist responses to Greenblatt's account of Spenser have been Louis Montrose's investigations into Spenser's relationship to Elizabeth. Montrose has a similar interest in Elizabethan ideology, but he sees power more as a give-and-take exchange between subject and authority. This conception of power would set historicist research off in a quite different direction from that first posited by Greenblatt and Goldberg. Where Greenblatt claims, '*The Faerie Queene* is ... wholly wedded to the autocratic ruler of the English state' (Greenblatt 1980: 174), Montrose responds that 'Spenser's relationship to royal authority is more equivocal, and the ideological situation more complicated' (Montrose 1986: 329). Montrose's theoretical sense of how power operates accords well with recent trends in Elizabethan historiography, and the work of historians has helped him and others to deepen our appreciation of the complexities of Spenser's oppositional stance (Montrose 2002). Although Elizabeth had some pretensions to absolute authority, she was never an 'autocratic ruler' but one who had to negotiate with powerful male figures who frequently opposed her policies and resented her usurping of male authority; the nobility and gentry saw England not as an absolute monarchy but even, arguably, as a 'monarchical republic' (Collinson 1987; 1994). This discontent became stronger after Elizabeth and her Protestant regime survived the crises of 1586–1588, so that historians now speak of that time as the start of the 'second reign of Elizabeth' (Guy 1995). At this time Spenser appears to have allied himself with those who were dissatisfied with Elizabeth and her policies. Thus Book V's historical allegory centers on many of the crisis moments that marked the start of that time of disillusionment and dissent: the trial and execution of Mary Queen of Scots, the Spanish Armada, the campaigns in Ireland and the Netherlands. The equivocal nature of Spenser's praise of Elizabeth, particularly in Book V, has long been recognized as an interpretive problem (Cain 1978), and recent historicist readings of Spenser have generally followed Montrose's lead, emphasizing the poem's complicated interweaving of praise and blame, loyalty and opposition. David Norbrook (1984; 2002), John King (1982; 1990a), and Kenneth Borris (1991) have been particularly effective at showing how Spenser's prophetic mode belongs to a Reformation tradition which he adapts to serve the religious and political programs of his patrons and allies at court.

The new historicist refusal to distinguish between text and context—'The Historicity of Texts and the Textuality of History' (Montrose 1986: 305)—and its response to the postmodern 'death of the author' did not end an interest in Spenser's biography but renewed a fascination with his attempts to fashion himself into a national poet. Richard Helgerson has led the way by examining Spenser's writing as a function of a developing discourse of the 'laureate system', an idea of the author developed in relation to the cultural history of the nation (Helgerson 1983). Richard Rambuss looks at the importance of Spenser's role as a secretary, the keeper of secrets, in shaping allegory (Rambuss 1993), while Patrick Cheney shows the centrality of Reformation discourses to shaping Spenser's idea of his career (Cheney 1993).[13] Studies of Spenser's life thus situate him and his work within a larger culture in turmoil and transition, and historicists have proven increasingly willing and able to dig deeply into the archives to re-create it more fully than a mere isolated analogy or anecdote can.

Given Spenser's celebration of empire and his direct involvement in the colonization of Ireland, the historicist revival has inevitably intersected with the political and intellectual ferment created in the aftermath of the British Empire's collapse. Book V and A View have thus been read with a new attention that has made them central to understandings of Spenser's larger cultural and political project. Irish readers raised in the Irish Republic or in the Northern Ireland of the Troubles have brought new political and cultural sensibilities to Spenser, while readers looking from the perspective of the ruins of the British Empire or the rise of American imperialism have turned to Spenser to ask questions about the origin and development of empire. Fitting Spenser's own concept of a poet historical, postcolonial historicism uses him to create a historical narrative of empire, one that is both retrospective and prophetic. Historians of Ireland like Nicholas Canny have read Spenser closely and, in Canny's case, argued that his Irish writings had real consequence in shaping English colonial policy (Canny 2001), while a range of literary critics have fleshed out Greenblatt's suggestion that Ireland 'pervades' the entire Faerie Queene (Greenblatt 1980: 186) to revolutionize understandings of Spenser as an English, Irish, and British poet. Spenser has been approached as a creator of English and British national identity (Hadfield 1994; Escobedo 2004), while Richard McCabe (2002), by digging into Irish-language poetry and sources, has given voice to the Irish perspective that Spenser often sought to efface as he rewrote Ireland into Britain. Such recovery work, however, faces the great difficulty of the scattered and fragmentary nature of the archives: the Irish Public Record Office, with most of the records of the English governance of Ireland, was destroyed in 1922 at the opening of the Irish Civil War.[14]

McCabe (2002), Christopher Highley (1997: 110–33), and Clare Carroll (1990) have also adeptly knitted postcolonial questions about Spenser and Ireland into the other major project of postmodern criticism, understanding concepts of gender. Indeed, perhaps the greatest innovation of the new historicism has been to argue for the importance of gender construction to Spenser's poetry. Many traditional historicist critics were aware of the tensions produced by Elizabeth's position as a woman governing a male-dominated system. James E. Phillips (1941; 1942; 1964) still gives a fine account of sixteenth-century anti-feminist attacks upon the regiment of women, and Frances Yates (1975) remains the indispensable starting point for considerations of how Elizabeth and her court represented her authority as a woman ruler (though now supplemented by King 1989, 1990b). However, the revolution in woman's political and social power in the late twentieth century has reshaped how these questions are addressed. Such historicist readings place Spenser's writings in the context of the early-modern rethinkings of gender identity and sexuality. They have suggested ways that Spenser's approach to gender is shaped by factors like Protestantism's re-conception of marriage and, above all, the anomaly of wealthy, politically powerful men answering to an assertive queen regnant despite the rules and structures of the patriarchal system. The historians Anne L. McLaren (1999) and Kristin Walton (2007) provide such feminist perspectives on the problem of female sovereignty in the sixteenth century, while Spenser critics like Robin Headlam Wells (1983), Pamela Benson (1985), and Montrose (1980; 1983; 1986; 2002) have complicated the ways we understand Spenser's representations of sexual and political power (see Chapter 40 below).

NEW DIRECTIONS: HISTORICISM, FORMALISM, HISTORICAL FORMALISM

Two decades of political battles and institutional change in the academy have left English departments struggling to identify what it is that we do. The cultural turn has made the discipline of English interdisciplinary, which has left many to wonder just what distinguishes this field from any other. In complaints about dissertations and books being all history and no poetry, boring historical documents and not living literature, we can hear echoes of Greenlaw's attacks upon the flawed historicism of a century ago. Historicism has always had to wrestle with the temptation to reduce literature to mere history, to crossword puzzles for antiquarian scholars. Such crude allegorizing can be too easily lampooned, discrediting the entire historicist enterprise. Even more worrisome than making a scholar look ridiculous, however, is the fear that historicism might make Spenser seem irrelevant, the subject of antiquarian interest only. Renaissance antiquarians, however, were fully aware that their research addressed contemporary political, social, and religious disputes. This must be the guiding purpose of historicist criticism: to make Spenser live by exploring the social, cultural, political, and literary questions he poses which resonate most strongly in our historical moment.

If, at the start of a new century, we seem to be at a moment of change, where the new historicism meets a new formalism, it is worth noting that neither formalism nor historicism mean the same thing that they did fifty years ago. If the new formalism is a historical formalism—a term used by Helgerson to describe his method (Helgerson 1992: 7) and defined more recently by Douglas Bruster as 'a critical genre dedicated to examining the social, cultural, and historical aspects of literary form, and the function of form for those who produce and consume literary texts' (Bruster 2002: 44)—then it is very much the sort of criticism that the best historicists have always tried to produce. Spenser criticism has by necessity integrated form and history since that merger is central to Spenser's poetic designs. It is imperative that we remember that research into the past is a means to understanding the present and future. In doing so, we honor and continue Spenser's ambitious cultural project.

NOTES

1. Richard McCabe provided welcome guidance in shaping the final version of this essay. I am also grateful to the generations of Spenserians who have created what we can now call historicist scholarship.
2. Also essential for understanding the place of history in the epics of Virgil, Lucan, and their Renaissance imitators (though not primarily Spenser) is Quint (1993).
3. On this episode, see Phillips (1964), 201–5; Goldberg (1983), 1–17; Hadfield (2003a), (2004), 122–36; McCabe (1987); Staines (2009), 117–43.
4. Provocative historicist readings of this episode as a commentary upon allegory, authority, and intention include Goldberg (1983), 1–17, and Miller (1996), 162–71.
5. On the early reception of A View, see McCabe (2002), 270–87; Maley (1993), 191–208.
6. David Norbrook has given the seminal study of the interplay between poetry and Reformation politics in the century before the English Civil War, with Spenser and reactions to him playing a central role (1984; 2002). On the cultural divide produced by the Civil War more generally, see Norbrook (1999).
7. Radcliffe (1996) sketches Spenser's literary reputation over time.

8. For historicist criticisms of this sort of ahistorical literary history, see Patterson (1993), 35–56; Staines (2002).
9. For another eighteenth-century defense of Spenser's allegory in historical context, see Warton (1969), II, 87–113.
10. See Greenlaw's demolition of Upton's argument that Guyon is Essex, which overlooks the fact that Essex was just a boy when Spenser wrote Book II (Greenlaw 1932: 63).
11. For alternative readings, see Staines (2009), 117–43; Hadfield (2003a; 2004).
12. See, for instance, McLane (1961).
13. Also useful on aspects of Spenser's life are the essays in Anderson, Cheney, and Richardson (1996). On Spenser and the Reformation, John King gives essential perspectives (1982; 1989; 1990a, b).
14. See Hadfield (1997), Maley (1997), and Chapter 42 below.

BIBLIOGRAPHY

Anderson, J. H., Cheney, D., and Richardson, D. A. (eds) (1996). *Spenser's Life and the Subject of Biography*. Amherst: University of Massachusetts Press.

Aptekar, J. (1969). *Icons of Justice: Iconography and Thematic Imagery in Book V of* The Faerie Queene. New York: Columbia University Press.

Benson, P. J. (1985). 'Rule, Virginia: Protestant Theories of Female Regiment in *The Faerie Queene*'. ELR 15: 277–92.

Borris, K. (1991). *Spenser's Poetics of Prophecy in* The Faerie Queene V. English Literary Studies Monograph Series, 52. Victoria, BC: University of Victoria Press.

Bruster, D. (2002). 'Shakespeare and the Composite Text', in M. D. Rasmussen (ed.), *Renaissance Literature and Its Formal Engagements*. Basingstoke: Palgrave-Macmillan: 43–66.

Cain, T. H. (1978). *Praise in* The Faerie Queene. Lincoln: University of Nebraska Press.

Canny, N. (2001). *Making Ireland British, 1580–1650*. Oxford: Oxford University Press.

Carroll, C. (1990). 'The Construction of Gender and the Cultural and Political Other in *The Faerie Queene* 5 and *A View of the Present State of Ireland*: The Critics, the Context, and the Case of Radigund'. *Criticism* 22: 163–91.

Cheney, P. (1993). *Spenser's Famous Flight: A Renaissance Idea of a Literary Career*. Toronto: University of Toronto Press.

Church, R. W. (1879). *Spenser*. London and New York.

Collinson, P. (1987). 'The Monarchical Republic of Queen Elizabeth I'. *Bulletin of the John Rylands University Library of Manchester* 69: 394–424.

—— (1994). 'The Elizabethan Exclusion Crisis and the Elizabethan Polity'. *Proceedings of the British Academy* 84: 51–92.

Dryden, J. (1958). *The Poems*, ed. John Kinsley, 4 vols. Oxford: Oxford University Press.

Escobedo, A. (2004). *Nationalism and Historical Loss in Renaissance England: Foxe, Dee, Spenser, Milton*. Ithaca, NY: Cornell University Press.

The Faerie Leveller: Or, King Charles his Leveller described and deciphered in Queene Elizabeths dayes. (1648). London.

Fletcher, A. (1971). *The Prophetic Moment: An Essay on Spenser*. Chicago: University of Chicago Press.

Goldberg, J. (1981). *Endlesse Worke: Spenser and the Structures of Discourse*. Baltimore: Johns Hopkins University Press.

Goldberg, J. (1983). *James I and the Politics of Literature*. Baltimore: Johns Hopkins University Press.

Greenblatt, S. (1980). *Renaissance Self-Fashioning: From More to Shakespeare*. Chicago: University of Chicago Press.

Greenlaw, E. (1912). 'Spenser and British Imperialism'. *MP* 9: 347–70.

—— (1932). *Studies in Spenser's Historical Allegory*. Baltimore: Johns Hopkins University Press.

Grosart, A. B. (ed.) (1882–84). *The Complete Works in Verse and Prose of Edmund Spenser*, 10 vols. London.

Guy, J. (1995). 'Introduction: The Second Reign of Elizabeth I?', in J. Guy (ed.), *The Reign of Elizabeth I: Court and Culture in the Last Decade*. Cambridge: Cambridge University Press: 1–19.

Hadfield, A. (1994). *Literature, Politics, and National Identity: Reformation to Renaissance*. Cambridge: Cambridge University Press.

—— (1997). *Spenser's Irish Experience: Wilde Fruit and Salvage Soyl*. Cambridge: Cambridge University Press.

—— (1998). 'Was Spenser a Republican?' *English* 47: 169–82.

—— (2003a). 'Duessa's Trial and Elizabeth's Error: Judging Elizabeth in Spenser's *Fairie Queene*', in S. Doran and T. S. Freeman (eds), *The Myth of Elizabeth*. Basingstoke: Palgrave-Macmillan.

—— (2003b). 'Was Spenser Really a Republican After All? A Reply to David Scott Wilson-Okamura'. *SSt* 17: 275–90.

—— (2004). *Shakespeare, Spenser, and the Matter of Britain*. Basingstoke: Palgrave Macmillan.

Hamilton, A. C. (1961). *The Structure of Allegory in* The Faerie Queene. Oxford: Oxford-Clarendon.

Headlam Wells, R. (1983). *Spenser's* Faerie Queene *and the Cult of Elizabeth*. London and Canberra: Croom Helm; Totowa, NJ: Barnes and Noble Books.

Helgerson, R. (1983). *Self-Crowned Laureates: Spenser, Jonson, Milton, and the Literary System*. Berkeley: University of California Press.

—— (1992). *Forms of Nationhood: The Elizabethan Writing of England*. Chicago: University of Chicago Press.

Highley, C. (1997). *Shakespeare, Spenser, and the Crisis in Ireland*. Cambridge: Cambridge University Press.

Hough, G. (1964). *The First Commentary on* The Faerie Queene. Privately printed.

Hughes, J. (ed.) (1715). *The Works of Mr. Edmund Spenser*, 6 vols. London.

King, J. N. (1982). *English Reformation Literature: The Tudor Origins of the Protestant Tradition*. Princeton, NJ: Princeton University Press.

—— (1989). *Tudor Royal Iconography: Literature and Art in an Age of Religious Crisis*. Princeton, NJ: Princeton University Press.

—— (1990a). *Spenser's Poetry and the Reformation Tradition*. Princeton, NJ: Princeton University Press.

—— (1990b). 'Queen Elizabeth: Representations of the Virgin Queen'. *RQ* 43: 30–74.

Lewis, C. S. (1936). *The Allegory of Love*. Oxford: Oxford University Press.

McCabe, R. A. (1987). 'The Masks of Duessa: Spenser, Mary Queen of Scots, and James VI'. *ELR* 17: 224–42.

—— (2002). *Spenser's Monstrous Regiment: Elizabethan Ireland and the Poetics of Difference*. Oxford: Oxford University Press.

McLane, P. E. (1961). *Spenser's 'Shepheardes Calender': A Study in Elizabethan Allegory*. Notre Dame, IN: University of Notre Dame Press.

McLaren, A. N. (1999). *Political Culture in the Reign of Elizabeth I: Queen and Commonwealth 1558–1585*. Cambridge: Cambridge University Press.

Maley, W. (1993). 'How Milton and Some Contemporaries Read Spenser's *View*', in B. Bradshaw, A. Hadfield, and W. Maley (eds), *Representing Ireland: Literature and the Origins of Conflict, 1534–1660*. Cambridge: Cambridge University Press: 191–208.

—— (1997). *Salvaging Spenser: Colonialism, Culture, and Identity*. Basingstoke: Macmillan.

Miller, D. L. (1996). 'The Earl of Cork's Lute', in J. H. Anderson, D. Cheney, and D. A. Richardson (eds), *Spenser's Life and the Subject of Biography*. Amherst: University of Massachusetts Press: 146–71.

Milton, John (1953–82). *Complete Prose Works of John Milton*, ed. D. M. Wolfe. New Haven, CT: Yale University Press.

Montrose, L. A. (1980). '"Eliza, Queen of Shepheardes", and the Pastoral of Power'. *ELR* 10: 153–82.

—— (1983). 'Of Gentlemen and Shepherds: The Politics of Elizabethan Pastoral'. *ELH* 50: 415–59.

—— (1986). 'The Elizabethan Subject and the Spenserian Text', in P. Parker and D. Quint (eds), *Literary Theory/Renaissance Texts*. Baltimore: Johns Hopkins University Press: 303–40.

—— (2002). 'Spenser and the Elizabethan Political Imaginary'. *ELH* 69: 907–46.

Morris, R. (ed.) (1869). *The Complete Works of Edmund Spenser*. London.

Norbrook, D. (1984). *Poetry and Politics in the English Renaissance*. London: Routledge and Kegan Paul.

—— (1999). *Writing the English Republic: Poetry, Rhetoric, and Politics, 1627–1660*. Cambridge: Cambridge University Press.

—— (2002). *Poetry and Politics in the English Renaissance*, rev edn. Oxford: Oxford University Press.

Oakeschott, W. (1971). 'Carew Ralegh's Copy of Spenser'. *The Library* 5th ser., 26: 1–21.

O'Connell, M. (1977). *Mirror and Veil: The Historical Dimension of Spenser's* Faerie Queene. Chapel Hill: University of North Carolina Press.

Patterson, A. (1993). *Reading between the Lines*. Madison: University of Wisconsin Press.

Phillips, J. E. (1941). 'The Background of Spenser's Attitude toward Women Rulers'. *HLQ* 5: 5–32.

—— (1942). 'The Woman Ruler in Spenser's *Faerie Queene*'. *HLQ* 5: 211–34.

—— (1964). *Images of a Queen: Mary Stuart in Sixteenth-Century Literature*. Berkeley and Los Angeles: University of California Press.

Quint, D. (1993). *Epic and Empire: Politics and Generic Form from Virgil to Milton*. Princeton, NJ: Princeton University Press.

Radcliffe, D. H. (1996). *Edmund Spenser: A Reception History*. Columbia, SC: Camden House.

Rambuss, R. (1993). *Spenser's Secret Career*. Cambridge: Cambridge University Press.

Renwick, W. L. (ed.) (1928–34). *The Complete Works of Spenser*. London: Scolartis Press.

Staines, J. D. (2002). 'Charles's Grandmother, Milton's Spenser, and the Rhetoric of Revolution'. *Milton Studies* 41: 139–71.

—— (2009). *The Tragic Histories of Mary Queen of Scots 1580–1660: Rhetoric, Passions, and Political Literature*. Aldershot: Ashgate.

Strier, R. (2002). 'Afterword: How Formalism Became a Dirty Word, and Why We Can't Do Without It', in M. D. Rasmussen (ed.), *Renaissance Literature and Its Formal Engagements*. Basingstoke: Palgrave Macmillan: 207–15.

Tillyard, E. M. W. (1944). *The Elizabethan World Picture*. New York: Macmillan.

Tuve, R. (1947). *Elizabethan and Metaphysical Imagery: Renaissance Poetry and Twentieth-Century Critics*. Chicago: University of Chicago Press.

Tuve, R. (1966). *Allegorical Imagery: Some Medieval Books and Their Posterity*. Princeton, NJ: Princeton University Press.

Upton, J. (ed.) (1758). *The Faery Queene Disposed into Twelves Books Fashioning Twelve Moral Vertues*, 2 vols. London.

Van Es, B. (2002). *Spenser's Forms of History*. Oxford: Oxford University Press.

Walton, K. P. (2007). *Catholic Queen, Protestant Patriarchy: Mary, Queen of Scots, and the Politics of Gender and Religion*. Basingstoke: Palgrave Macmillan.

Ware, J. (ed.) (1633). *The Historie of Ireland, collected by three learned authors*. Dublin.

Warton, T. (1969). *Observations on the 'Fairy Queen' of Spenser*, 2 vols. London, 1762. Repr., New York: Haskell House.

Wilson-Okamura, D. S. (2003). 'Republicanism, Nostalgia, and the Crowd'. *SSt* 17: 253–73.

Winstanley, L. (ed.) (1915). *The Faerie Queene, Book I*. Cambridge: Cambridge University Press.

Yates, F. (1975). *Astraea: The Imperial Theme in the Sixteenth Century*. London and Boston: Routledge and Kegan Paul.

CHAPTER 40

SPENSER AND GENDER STUDIES

THERESA KRIER

INTIMACY AND INTIMACIES: THE NINETEENTH AND THE TWENTY-FIRST CENTURIES

It is no surprise to say that Spenser is a poet of erotic intimacies, unfolding through them philosophical, historical, political, and aesthetic thought that addresses every period's gender concerns. This fact has long invited complex critical responses. Early in the nineteenth century, William Hazlitt contrasted Milton's purity with Spenser's more disconcerting orientation to intimacies: 'Spenser . . . is very apt to pry into mysteries which do not belong to the Muses. . . . Spenser has an eye to the consequences [of describing beautiful objects], and steeps everything in pleasure, often not of the purest kind' (Hazlitt 1816: 110). The nineteenth and early twentieth centuries were keenly aware of their own excruciation before such Spenserian intimacies; one might reflect, after reading scholarship from Hazlitt to G. Wilson Knight, that readers are vigilant about the experience of intimacies brought so perilously close in the verse. Further, the logic of vigilant touchiness about this aspect of the poetry gives rise to another aspect of nineteenth-century work on gender, namely its ardent idealizations of the feminine. This idealization functions in part to distance the feminine and its perils. Thus in Edward Dowden's rapturous 1879 paean to the ideal of the feminine, 'Heroines of Spencer', we read 'behind each woman [in *The Faerie Queene*] made to worship or to love rises a sacred presence—womanhood itself. Her beauty of face and limb is but a manifestation of the invisible beauty, and this is of one kin with the divine wisdom and the divine love' (Dowden 1879: 771; see also Kinney 2002). His first exemplar is Una—radiant, tender, wise, patient, compassionate, long-suffering, courageous, unflinching, un-complaining, loyal, grave, vulnerable, an Arnoldian heroine who 'sees life steadily and sees it whole' (775).

But erotic *intimacies* in Spenser's work make up only one aspect of his broader achievement as a major poet of *intimacy*. Spenser's work seeks the quick of affect, pain, ineffable corporeal and psychic processes. He is a poet of unnerving openness to streams of experience both subtle and gross, and his work challenges readerly capacities for nearness to the flux of phenomena—a nearness that we alternately desire and flee in our professional reading traditions. Openness of this kind may disconcert any reader of Spenser, just as his interest in erotic intimacies may do; our professional ways of registering the latter often speak to our scholarly and critical traditions' relationship to the former, as I suggest in what follows.

Hazlitt's remarks about Spenserian mysteries refer to the representation of erotic intimacies, but they also get at something of what I mean by intimacy. Hazlitt's verb 'steeps' ('Spenser steeps everything in pleasure') participates in the well-known critical trope of Spenserian fluidity, which had begun during Spenser's lifetime as a way to praise his mellifluousness, then became a way to articulate the effect of dissolving intimacy that his versification has on readers. Thus James Russell Lowell's remarks on Spenser, first printed in 1875, register a benign curiosity about how near one can get to one's own sensations, and for how long, without drowning, or becoming something other than human.[1] Lowell says of Spenser's verse:

He loves to prolong emotion, and lingers in his honeyed sensations like a bee in the translucent cup of a lily. . . . He is the most fluent of our poets. Sensation passing through emotion into revery is a prime quality of his manner. And to read him puts one in the condition of revery, a state of mind in which our thoughts and feelings float motionless, as one sees fish do in a gentle stream, with just enough vibration of their fins to keep themselves from going down with the current, while their bodies yield indolently to all its soothing curves. (Lowell 1904: II, 300)

The question of how near to or far from Spenserian intimacy readers might venture fuels every approach discussed in the present essay. Spenser's work is enrolled in sharp debates within and about feminist critique, the history of sexuality, and queer studies, as well as in more irenic and archivally devoted studies on the ecology of the passions and the lived experience of late-Elizabethan people. Recently, Spenser has become less a poet of idealisms focused around clear, heterosexual gender identity, more a poet of multiple registers of sexual desire, complex gender identity, corporeal experience, and forms of aliveness besides the human. New approaches seek to articulate mobile and expanding fields of experience (for example, of women, of Irish people, of erotic affect), often by means of immersion in the current that Lowell describes, with its vitalizing risks to the reader.

EPITHALAMIC SPENSER: FROM 1930

Readers of Spenser in the middle third of the twentieth century inclined to celebrate and unfold a Spenserian ideal of heterosexual union, giving the scholarship an epithalamic tone; the work on Spenser closely joined similarly celebratory work on the Shakespeare of the high romantic and festive comedies, with Spenser as the great mythographic and metaphysical parallel to Shakespeare. C. S. Lewis (1936 and 1967), Thomas Roche (1964), A. C. Hamilton (1961), Isabel MacCaffrey (1976), and James Nohrnberg (1976) offered rich readings in Spenser's development of ancient mythic figures, often juxtaposing metaphysical binaries of male and female, or hermaphroditic figures who combine these two great sexes, or of Venus and Diana who, after Virgil, often contain or disguise aspects of each other within themselves, or Diana in more Amazonian guise.[2] Like contemporaneous scholars of Shakespeare, Spenserians unfolded the dense resonances of mythological and archetypal patterns, tracing the poet's transformative engagements not only with (hetero)sexuality in relation to desire but also with sexuality in relation to the pervasive theme of generation, elaborating narratives with implicitly comic plots. Behind them stands the work on comic and tragic rhythms of philosopher of aesthetics Susanne Langer (*Feeling and Form*, 1953) and the mythic and romantic modes of Northrop Frye (*Anatomy of Criticism*, 1957—a book that began, as Frye notes, as a book on *The Faerie Queene*). They draw literary work into the orbit of the philosopher Ernst Cassirer and work on the visual arts by Edgar Wind, Irwin Panofsky, and others associated with the Warburg School, explicating the capacious symbolic and mythographic systems of the European Renaissance.

Scholars in this tradition, taking marital union as telos, enjoy Spenser's expansive eroto-cosmic scope in the odes and hymns. They attend to female characters in *The Faerie Queene*, mapping the iconography of Renaissance symbolic languages onto mid-twentieth-century psychologies of developmental maturation. They take seriously the romance mode's commitment to affective experience. They turn to the epithalamic and the symbolic as a labor of recognizing and responding to the Renaissance syntax of the passions. When Roche describes the Ariostan plot structure of *Faerie Queene* III and IV as profound, it is so because 'it opens out the multiple possibilities inherent in the virtue and defies definition' (Roche 1964: 211). He thus looks backward to the long tradition of reading for the virtue of love and the nature of heroism in *The Faerie Queene*, and forward to critics forty years later, who certainly ratify Roche's 'multiple possibilities' but who seek to read for increasingly diverse experiences of the passions, affect, embodiment, and consciousness traced by the poem.

When critics of the middle part of the twentieth century turn to female characters, it is less often to Una, whose purity spoke to nineteenth-century readers, and more often to Britomart, who crosses the threshold of a male/female binary as she makes room for her spacious heroic self; who has much in common with Shakespearean heroines of the late 1590s; who, like those heroines, will emerge to a gendered identity heterosexual and procreative, but strengthened by her engagements with masculine roles. In the early twenty-first century, as we will see, neither Una nor Britomart looks quite as they did in 1975, on account of intervening work in feminist critique and the new historicism, with their attention to yet another of Spenser's female protagonists, Belphoebe, and behind her, Queen Elizabeth I.

FEMINISMS: FROM 1980

To take Britomart as enacting a comic and benign teleological drive to festive wedding now seems incomplete. This view, though it remains unsurpassed in its iconographic richness and its relevance to Elizabethan social structures, now seems to under-emphasize crucial disruptive details with which Spenser curves that plot. Working from developmental and heterosexual assumptions about the notion of gender identity now seems to under-emphasize certain bodily experiences and intimacies in which Britomart finds herself, and seems too limited an understanding of the history of sexuality. Before scholarship had the tools to put new questions about gender identity and desire, it needed to undergo a fierce influx of critique from feminist theory and poetics. To feminism we owe not only transformative theory (see Bellamy 2006), but also the explicit opening of literary criticism to its readers' political commitments and emotions. Opposition, anger, skepticism, resistance became affective and cognitive sites of generative reading strategies. These would pave new paths for analysis of narrative and poetry, and raise the stakes of interpretative positions.

One project of the new feminist mode of critique straightforwardly attacked misogyny—in the poems, in early modern cultures, in twentieth-century academic traditions. Sheila Cavanagh's *Wanton Eyes and Chaste Desires* puts the baldest, boldest, most devastatingly clear case: 'In Spenser's epic, women, however virtuous, generally evoke suspicion. Female sexuality remains intertwined with images of danger, actual or potential. Women and wickedness often seem synonymous. . . . this thread of suspicion winds through the entire poem' (Cavanagh 1994: 1–2); 'women merely circulate through the text, serving as receptacles for male fantasies and tender for the kinship market' (108). Her argument sustains a constant skepticism about the gender-biased cultural work done by narrative, narrators, characters, tropes, and literary-critical work: 'these [allegorical and metaphorical aspects] do not erase the metacommunications about women being presented' (3).

In the same year, Susan Frye's provocative and controversial essay on rape in Spenser appeared in *Signs*. 'I identify Spenser,' she says, 'as a central popularizer, aestheticizer, and enforcer of marriage through the threat of rape' (Frye 1994: 52). She discusses 'the degree to which Spenser is implicated in his own violence by appraising his relation both to the narrator who relates the rape of Amoret and to the poet-magician and rapist, Busirane'. Claire McEachern too brings arguments against Spenserian misogyny and its binarisms, through her analysis of the gendering of Reformation debates. Her sweeping discussions of Reformation polemics intentionally glide between the representations within Reformation culture broadly and representations within the poem, and between poet and titular hero: 'Spenser's confusions—sartorial, sexual, semiotic, and sumptuary—do not belong only to the province of literary play. What is endemic to *The Faerie Queene* was a perennial problem for Reformation culture, and the confusion that bedevils Redcrosse plagued other Reformation warriors as well' (1996: 44).

The broad force of arguments fueled by anger about representation cannot be abandoned. Yet those made in the 1990s, despite their clarity about the inimical rhetorical effects of the misogyny saturating cultural representations, often fail to offer sufficiently complex social, readerly, or narrative dynamic by which these effects come about. Indeed they share the misogynist's formal impulse to aggregate masses of such representations. Harry Berger, among others, argues against this approach, particularly in studies of Reformation discourse, by turning from representation to narrative process—and just plain mischief—as Spenser's weapons in *targeting* Reformation misogyny, especially in *The Faerie Queene* I (see below; see also Gregerson 1995; Mallette 1997; Krier 2000). From his vantage point, it is a problem that such rhetorical indictments of cultural misogyny preclude a precisely literary sense of language, in which they could, in David Lee Miller's words, 'describe the text as staging and exploring the disjunctions' that they identify (D. L. Miller 2006: 163; see also Maley 2003: 284).

Other discourses do yield productive analysis of period misogyny when brought into play with poetic narrative. Recent Spenser scholarship participates in studies of long-standing medical and philosophical propositions about the physiology of gender, and the multifarious ways that these propositions give form to male anxieties about the feminine. Thomas Laqueur (1992) delineates two masterplots to be found in pre-modern reproductive anatomy, a two-sex model and a one-sex model; this powerful account, along with the influential work of Gail Kern Paster and Michael Schoenfeldt, has shaped renewed attention to the humoral body. Gordon Teskey argues that the logic of allegory violently subjects a feminized, disorderly matter to a fantasized and dematerialized abstraction identified with the masculine. Elizabeth Harvey studies Helkiah Crooke's 1615 *Microcosmographia*, heavily indebted to Spenser, to argue that Spenser's elision of generative organs in the House of Alma manifests this allegorical logic, which is 'a refusal not just to expose the inner workings of sexuality but also to reveal the material version of generation that sustains allegory's capture of the material'. Both allegory and anatomy thus 'displace anxieties about the abjected, mortal, and material body onto a feminine principle' (Harvey 2003: 299, 312; see also Greenblatt 1980; Schoenfeldt 1999). David Lee Miller discusses Spenser's relation to the period's 'nausea of fertility' through Lacanian theory: 'one begins increasingly to wonder whether the underlying scene of horror [here, in relation to Errour] may not be that of the womb itself as it haunts the Renaissance male unconscious' (D. L. Miller 1988: 241, 252; see also Goldberg 1975).[3]

BEAT THE BINARY

As I said, arguments about misogynistic representation as a given in Spenser's work provoke others to investigate gender ideology with an eye to narrative dynamics, narrator role, figuration, allegory, and relationship of reader to narrator. Linda Gregerson sums up the cumulative effect of such studies when she argues that the representations of misogyny in the poem function to *critique* their cultural logic: 'Again and again in *The Faerie Queene*, Spenser lays bare the oppositional dynamics of Petrarchan sexuality.... Spenser did not build the House of Busirane to stand for a rare aberration in heterosexual love as his culture had encoded it: his critique is far more sweeping; his poem is full to bursting with chronic abuse' (Gregerson 2001: 182–3). Already in 1978, Madelon Gohlke had put forward a brilliant argument that the hero of *Faerie Queene* II, Sir Guyon, far from representing the virtue of temperance in the face of demonic and highly feminized temptations, represents a tension between the allegorical structure of the virtue and the narrative of a hero who suffers its pathology. For Gohlke, Guyon is alienated from his own affective life, from 'the ordinary human capacity for pleasure and compassion' (Gohlke 1978: 138), trapped by his genre and its represented and paranoid world; she argues for 'an ironic relationship between the moral allegory and the fiction'. Gohlke's great essay marks a breakthrough in thinking about gender in Spenser by thinking through its dynamics in a complex weave of narrative, allegory, and genre.[4] For it is the seductive Acrasia, who has long drawn to herself vast amounts of commentary about the undermining wickedness of the fatal temptress and her Bowre of Blisse, who crystallizes Guyon's purgative rage and his failure to acknowledge his own affective and bodily life, as well as others' pain. In this response of denial of his own embodiment and rage against the feminine, Guyon bears some similarity to the Redcrosse Knight of Janet Adelman, who resists 'monstrous enmeshment in this hideous—and hideously female—world', who projects his own disavowal of male sexual desire onto feminine figures, until late in his career when he grounds his very virtue of holiness in the material reality of the generative body and of his own origin from the earth (Adelman 2005: 20).

Harry Berger, Jr. has been the most spirited and visible proponent of Spenser as a poet who targets the misogynistic discourses and traditions saturating his culture: 'the misogynist and gynephobic representation of woman may be a target rather than a donnée of *The Faerie Queene*' (Berger 2003: 89). Berger builds strong arguments for Spenser's ironic critique of his discourses. Thus, for example, the Ovidian tree catalogue in *Faerie Queene* I.i, along with its Orphic context in Ovid, suggests 'the underlying continuity of a tradition of male discourse that embraces pagan and Christian, Catholic and Protestant, in a single structure of self-protective and self-justifying antifeminism' (Berger 2004: 206; see also D. L. Miller 2006).

Berger posits a Spenser whose skepticism about gender matters would have startled readers a century before. Other feminist critics in the 1980s and 1990s argued, like Berger, for reading through specifically literary categories like figure, topos, plot, genre, imitation—though they incline to hear other tones than the irony of Berger's Spenser. All attend to the gendered binary of the hybrid genre of romance-epic, with epic understood as masculine, linear, teleological, resistant to passion and affect, and romance understood as feminine, errant and dilatory, entertaining the possibility of yielding to passion.[5] Taken as a whole, they focus less on a comic telos than on the tragic incommensurability of epic and romance. Patricia Parker's 'Suspended Instruments: Lyric and Power in the Bower of Bliss' (1987a) and *Literary Fat Ladies: Rhetoric, Gender, Property* (1987b) pursue a wide range of references to the anxieties of a masculinized epic ethos and a feminized romance ethos, indicating the richness of such a binary without indicating any way out of it. Subsequent books on the romance-epic genre argue for narrative's power to transcend its own apparent impasses.[6] As Dorothy Stephens says, 'there are other narrative positions possible besides ventriloquism on the one hand and subversion on the other' (Stephens 1998: 32), or between the hard-worked opposition between containment and subversion. How does this happen?

An explicit focus on narrative mobility as distinct from representation of objects informs work by Lauren Silberman (1995) and Dorothy Stephens (1998). Silberman argues for a Spenser who discovers his commitment to risk and improvisation in narrative as in ethics, simultaneously discovering the limits of certitude. For Silberman, the catalogue of rivers attendant at the marriage of the Thames and the Medway in *Faerie Queene* IV 'both imposes and subverts linear order since the object of sequential reference is a system of flux' (1995: 131). By this point in the book 'multiple unfoldings of a greater plenitude provide an alternative to the castrating economy of absence and presence' (136), an economy that elsewhere tyrannizes the book's violent knights, competing damsels, and their genres (see also Silberman 1986). Stephens's book argues for narrative's provisional nature. For her, the interface between social and aesthetic is to be found in the multiplying nature of narrative representation, narrative voice, and reader situation. Thus she wonders, for example, not only 'What does [Amoret's] story mean for female or male readers who do not desire the particular sort of closure that [her lover] Scudamour . . . desires?' but even more 'why should we believe that the poem expects us to desire this particular closure?' (1998: 27). The pleasures of narrative in these two studies have become risky, which is to say that pleasure itself becomes deeper, larger, darker or more ruthless than criticism earlier in the twentieth century had posited.

Opposing views about the capacities of the literary, like those represented on the one hand by Cavanagh and Frye, and on the other by Stephens, Berger, or Gohlke, occur also in feminist critique of Petrarchan lyric and its heirs, a vigorous line of scholarship that emerged in the 1980s, spurred by Nancy Vickers's influential argument about Petrarchan blazon and its inclination to inventory, itemize, dismember the Petrarchan mistress (Vickers 1981). The idea of the blazon of the sonnet mistress serves as site of debates about the ways that the discourses of lyric traditions commodify and exchange women, silence women writers, control women's agency and sexuality, and mystify masculine desire as normative

(Dubrow 1995; Bell 1998). Scholars took feminist critique of Petrarchism to the *Amoretti*, sometimes arguing that Spenser subjects the woman addressed in the sequence to these Petrarchan abuses, sometimes arguing that Spenser represents the speaker himself subjected by and wrestling away from what Joseph Loewenstein urbanely sums up as 'the discourse of what might be called 'vulgar Petrarchism' (Loewenstein 1987: 315).

THE SPENSERIAN QUEEN

Misogyny was one of two great, generative topics of feminist work on Spenser in the 1980s. Queen Elizabeth I was a second. Fueled by the energies of the new historicism and its fascination with the Queen as avatar of the powerful woman in relation to equally fascinated but subjected, anxious, ambitious courtiers and poets, critics like Louis Montrose and Maureen Quilligan forged influential studies on the shaping fantasies inspired by Elizabeth and on the role of Spenser's female audience, taken in the first instance as Queen Elizabeth herself, as a kind of Prime Reader postulated within the poem. Analyses of misogyny were now joined by analyses of the construction of gendered subjectivities and subject positions, as shaped by gender politics in the Elizabethan decades, and by the unstable mix of desire and dread as masculine responses to feminine power and authority.[7] While Una had been a favorite figure of commentary for late 19th-century readers, and Britomart for mid-20th-century readers, it was Belphoebe who crystallized much of the combined dearness and dread evoked by new historicism's Queen Elizabeth, who entangled her courtiers in dramas of submission and domination. Later, as the twentieth century ended, critics understood Spenser to be critical of his queen, resistant to and disenchanted with her or his culture's idealized representations of her and her court (Bates 1992; Tylus 1993; McLaren 1999; Owens 2002; McCabe 2002).

Early in the 1980s, Jonathan Goldberg had articulated his sense of these representations in terms of tense relationships between Queen and author, author or text and reader (who is sometimes Queen), in a brilliant book on the anxieties of being fashioned as a subject when mastered by an Other, indeed fashioned *by the desire* of the Other (1981). Goldberg's recurring drama of subjectivity is the sexual politics of anxious male submission to the annihilating desire of a powerful woman: 'Elizabeth, like Venus in the text, is a figure of desire who demands that those who desire her remain unsatisfied. Nonetheless, she demands their desire' (152). Maureen Quilligan's influential book *Milton's Spenser* (1983) took Spenser to be writing 'in service' to conflicting interests of his culture's sexual politics; she sounds confident in knowing what Spenser's genre is and what Spenser's ideological interests are in writing epic. Thus 'Queen Elizabeth's unique and anomalous existence poses special problems for

Spenser's Protestant epic—and in these problems we see how her unique sexual status causes him great trouble because he writes in service of a specific social program' (1983: 177). A few years later, Louis Montrose tightly wove into a mutually constitutive circuit the Queen, her culture, her representations, and her subjects: 'The cultural work of the subject/poet, his informing power, contributes to the legitimation and implementation of the social and political order within which he himself is subjected' (Montrose 1986: 320).

Montrose's work on Spenser's Queen focuses on representations in all its familiar New-Historicist senses; Goldberg is fascinated with a politico-erotic drama of subjectivity revolving around the Queen. Quilligan's book too takes up the salience of the Queen in *The Faerie Queene*, but because her questions concern the Queen as reader, her discussion opens onto issues concerning women readers more broadly. She and others have developed a strong vein within the 20th-century project of recovering early modern women writers, a vein exploring Spenser's influence on other early modern writers like Mary Wroth and Aemilia Lanyer. This work focuses less on representation in its new historicist senses than on narrative technique. Thus Susanne Woods argues that Spenser's technique of effecting 'solutions from the margins of a story's action', a technique that aims to remind the reader of authorial consciousness, is used by Lanyer when she 'negotiates...male-centered narrative to make women central to the meaning of the story' in *Salve Deus Rex Judaeorum* (Woods 2000: 102–3). Mary Ellen Lamb examines the narrative implications of Spenser's engagement with disreputable traditions of old wives' tales and fairy tales: Spenser risks the fusion of epic with fairy tale and 'reveals the gendered conflicts at the core of its own narrative act', among them the effeminizing effects of fiction. On the other hand, 'it could be said that the use of classical narratives in *The Faerie Queene* displaced or appropriated childhood fictions to redeem fiction itself for masculinity' (Lamb 2000: 82, 86; see also J. Miller 2000; Hackett 2000; McManus 2002). We might think of Spenser's listening to such tales by hearkening to the lines from 'The Informant', Eiléan Ní Chuilleanáin's poem about a young man listening to an old Irish woman recounting a tale: 'She is sitting with tea at her elbow | And her own fairy-cakes, baked that morning | For the young man who listens now to the tape | Of her voice changing, telling the story' (Ní Chuilleanáin 1991: 36).

The figure of Queen Elizabeth has also played a part in ongoing analysis of masculine subject formation in Spenser's work. Elizabeth Jane Bellamy's psychoanalytic studies of Elizabeth and of romance-epic argue for 'gender as trauma' (Bellamy 1992: 203). David Lee Miller's Lacanian reading of *The Faerie Queene* (1988) speak to the anxieties and the pathos of early modern masculine subjectivity as it seeks wholeness, as do analyses of chivalric group identity and homosociality in Spenser (see also Silberman 1995; Gregerson 1995; Krier 2001). Lisa Celovsky grounds her analysis of the anxiety of masculine identity in distinctions between youth and manhood: 'once they anticipate their mature roles, Artegall, Scudamour, Timias, and Marinell cannot recover unconflicted youthful status; nor can they fully advance to adult status without continuing to feel youthful impulses'. Timias and Marinell, for instance, end their roles in Book III 'without status ... vulnerable and insecure ... cut off from any 'normal' masculine existence, whether youthful or mature' (Celovsky 2005: 226). Utilizing recent theorizing on masochism, Joseph Campana argues that Spenser aims for a 'rescue of masculinity' in *Faerie Queene* III such that suffering itself offers a resolution to the dilemma of masculinity. Thus, for instance, in Britomart 'Spenser generates a subject struggling to experience states of painful affect that vitalize and activate her at the level of the body and thus grant her the possibility of agency and expression' (Campana 2007).

The history of sexuality and queer studies, driven as fields by Foucault's influence, bring to Spenser's work and to early modern work generally their powerful debates expanding and complicating terms and categories involving sexuality, gender, desire, social identity, and embodiment (see Bellamy 2006). Models of Spenserian gender binaries came in the later 1990s to compete with or yield to the lability of gender identity, or to subtle fields of desire and identity. A theoretical distinction between sexual acts and sexual identities provoked historians to seek those other ways of defining the self and defining desire. Elaborations of the masculine homosocial and the homoerotic historicized through the influence of humanism, movingly fuels analysis of Spenserian fictional chivalric combats, real-life political and professional alliances, friendships, education (Goldberg 1992, 1994; Guy-Bray 2002; Highley 1997; Rambuss 1993). The poetry's female homosocial and homoerotic bonds, certainly more elusive than masculine bonds, have yielded remarkable studies. The remarks on narrative from Dorothy Stephens already cited first appeared in an influential essay discussing the relationship of Britomart and Amoret, and arguing that some of the poem's 'narrative voices seem on the point of acknowledging that ... socially marginal alliances [among women] provide the poem with an energy found nowhere else' (Stephens 1991: 534; see also Sedinger 2000). Kathryn Schwarz's study of Amazons as figures of female masculinity uses queer theory to shift the terms in which we have taken Britomart as fusing clear female and male identities. Schwarz resists this clarity or this reification of identity: '[Britomart's] performance links homosociality to heterosexuality through the continuity of eroticism, suggesting that both systems of desire and the bodies within them may be vulnerable to mutual substitution. ... Transitions, whether from homosocial to heterosexual bonds or from chivalric to domestic narratives, are replaced by an economy of distributed—and implicitly redistributable—roles' (Schwarz 2000: 148). Schwarz thus shifts her critical terms from representation to narrative temporal form, from a modernist valorizing of objects (representations) to distributings, displacings, sojourning. Schwarz also works the notion of voice and multiple voices in the poetry, as do Berger and E. D. Harvey (1992). To swerve thus from representation to narrative process is also to open paths through the impasses to which new historicist work like Montrose's, and feminist critique like Cavanagh's, both of which rely heavily on the notion of representation, otherwise lead us.

'LIKE A BOY IN A STORY FACED WITH A SMALL LOCKED DOOR. | WHO IS THAT HE CAN HEAR PANTING ON THE OTHER SIDE?' SPENSER, IRELAND, AND GENDER

The last decade and a half's ferociously vigorous work on Spenser and Ireland welcomes the critical anger informing feminist studies in the 1980s, finding itself at home with powerful, straightforward indictments of misogyny and debate about how to do justice, as we say, to the aesthetic dynamics of a work while also summoning justice for oppressed groups by rectifying the misrepresentations of history—including misrepresentations within the aesthetic forms of poems, treatises, letters, and dialogues. As Ní Chuilleanáin says just before discussing Spenser's *View*, 'History has been particularly alive for me as for many Irish people. . . . like others who share my linguistic background, I am aware always of the presence of the past and of the strangeness, the un-typical edge on the way I read history. We read with anger, anger forced through the narrow passages created by minority languages and small audiences' (Ní Chuilleanáin 1995: 571).[8]

A tormented sense of gender, linked with torment about the vulnerable human body, haunts Spenser's Ireland work, as in the passage from *A View of the Present State of Ireland* in which Irenius attests to seeing the foster mother of Murrogh O'Brien, at his execution, 'take vp his heade whilste he was quartered and sucked vp all the blodd rvnninge theareout Sayinge that the earthe was not worthie to drinke it and theare-with allso steped her face, and breast and torne heare Cryinge and shrikinge out moste terrible' (*Prose*, 112; on this passage see Hadfield 1997; Craig 2001). The extremity of the foster mother's anguish, whether we take it as elided or as figured through the dense weave of blood, milk, dismemberment, and chthonic maternity, pervades the *View* and the 1596 *Faerie Queene*. It joins many passages from elsewhere in the treatise and also in the poetry on embodied suffering, and makes clear that embodiment and the suffering of experience must fuel further studies on the gender politics of Spenser's Irish writing. Christopher Highley argues that the New English in Ireland functioned as a homosocial community far from Queen Elizabeth's court (Highley 1997). Claire Carroll documents representations of the feminized land and culture of Ireland: 'Both Old and New English early modern writers used the metaphor of "Circe's cup" to conjure up the bewitching, sexually seductive, and morally debilitating influence that they attributed to Irish culture' (Carroll 1992: 1; see also Coughlan 1989; Carroll 1996; Bowman 2003; Myers 2007). The sense in which Queen Elizabeth I can be said to govern Spenser's politico-poetic concerns, especially in his later work with its increasing disenchantment about court service, gains renewed salience in studies of anxieties on the part of military and political English-men about the Queen's management of her Irish policy (Craig 2001; McCabe 2002). Thus McCabe argues that 'the experience of writing from Ireland intensified

Spenser's sense of alienation from female sovereignty' (McCabe 2002: 3), a position argued throughout his book *Spenser's Monstrous Regiment*. McCabe suggests that these anxieties about the Queen's governance are also about change, aging, and death, as in the *Mutabilitie Cantos*: 'Cynthia [and by extension Elizabeth] is not just exposed by Mutability, she is exposed as Mutability' (McCabe 2002: 259). Such anxieties about feminine rule and the broader gender binarisms into which they drive Irenius, Artegall, Colin Clout, Spenser himself, and our own work suggest an impasse not only in early modern English culture but also in our own excruciated thinking about sixteenth-century Ireland and England. Somehow the very act of struggling with these gender structures can allow scholarship still to hold real Irish culture and real Irish people away from ourselves.

UNDISTANCING

Work on many fronts thus seeks to give ear to others' voices and experiences. Spenser's work lends itself to such negotiations with intimacy and distance, and it is worth thinking why this is so. David Lee Miller designates a narrative structure subtending *The Faerie Queene* by the name 'epistemological romance'.

> Its power derives from a consolidation of knowledge with masculine desire. This consolidation is what enables Truth to appear in a poem like Spenser's as a romance heroine. Viewed as a structure of desire, epistemological romance begins in the loss or denial of bodily presence, analogous to the philosophical denigration of material being. (Miller 1988: 95)

Spenser's narrative continually examines the pathos of dwelling without access to intimacy. The search for access to sheer presence, raying out in dozens of tales, can make Spenser's work sound less like a celebration of narrative flux and more like a hell-realm of binary presence and absence, masculine/feminine, plenitude/lack, sadism/masochism, from which there can be no exit. It is surely true that all of Spenser's work, verse and prose alike, examines the pathos of dwelling without intimacy, far away from or closed off from other humans, from communities of non-human others, from objects of desire, from others' pain, from one's own corporeal experience. But Miller's sense of epistemological romance as rooted in loss or denial of bodily presence just as surely describes leanings within scholarly traditions. Perhaps those traditions keep us from perceiving some form of presence that the poetry does proffer—keep us from the combination of nearness and openness that is intimacy.

These days readers are pursuing notions about gender, sexuality, intimacies, and intimacy suggesting that Spenser's work is larger than the dramas of subjects and subject-positions that have typically been so productive in gender studies. Sufferers of epistemological romance are now situated in relation to other forms and processes of life; current readers aim to articulate how the poem generates closeness to these processes, without giving up critique and the distantiation of discursive strategies. Recent approaches bespeak not an attempt to master a text but to stand alongside it and listen to it, or—as in recent studies of the passions—to mark how texts elicit and shape readerly attention, care, sympathy, fellow-feeling. Such projects remain rooted in critical gender studies, bringing those fields back to the notion of intimacy. We might briefly return to James Russell Lowell's wonderful description of a reader immersed like a fish in the eddies of Spenserian stanzas, risking or enjoying a liminal condition between being human and dissolving into water itself. Spenser risks this condition on behalf of his readers, in order to open them to intimacy of this kind, to critique the epistemological-romance ideologies of his characters, even to offer them access to rather than estrangement from the world. Roger Kuin and Anne Lake Prescott harbor hopes that we may 'create for our activity a space of hitherto unimagined freedom,' through a 'complex exercise of *undistancing*', which could emerge into 'a new simplicity' (Prescott and Kuin 2003: 92).

Recent studies of embodiment and gender turn this point into a specific group of concerns about the centrality of lived experience to Spenser. As Garrett Sullivan observes, 'If Shakespeare is a poet of subjectivity, Spenser tends to approach the question of what it is to be human from the perspective of the vitality of *all* forms of life' (Sullivan 2007: 283). Sullivan's own favorite example is Verdant in the Bowre of Blisse, whose somatic experience 'suggests his ineradicable affinity with other forms of vitality, with vegetable life' (284); as Sullivan and Mary Floyd-Wilson suggest elsewhere, 'The Bower of Bliss episode is particularly well suited to recent critical analysis of the relationship between body and environment' and bodily habitus (2007: 2; see also Paster 2007). Verdant once appeared in scholarship to focus the dangers of the erotic passions to masculine heroic subjectivity; now he focuses scholarship's attention on *The Faerie Queene*'s openness to states of aliveness and deathliness. It is not accidental that such work so often turns to *The Faerie Queene* II, a key work for testing the stakes of embodiment, affect, vitality, and deathliness (see, among many others, Campana 2005).

I end by citing Eiléan Ní Chuilleanáin once more, in her remarks about O'Brien's foster-mother in Spenser's *View*. Her words suggest both poetic and scholarly yearning—in Bell Hook's sense (1999), a yearning for knowledge projects that promote justice—for the vitally unfamiliar voices of Early Modern people:

That demented hag speaks for a culture of intimate bonds, of bodily and verbal affections that we know closely with our tongues because we know the language and the poetic shapes, the keening formulae and the bardic idiom of praise, which gave them expression. Never mind for the moment the incompleteness of our knowledge: its exclusiveness prints it sharply. As an undergraduate in Cork I remember trying to capture the closeness of that moment to me, its refusal to recede into the merely past... In the early modern period, languages keep their sharp edges, their strangeness to one another... I want the alien to go on keeping its distance. (Ní Chuilleanáin 1995: 571, 573)

Notes

1. These are questions that Tennyson had put, with more anxiety, in his 1832 'The Lotos-Eaters', composed in Spenserian stanzas. A century later, G. Wilson Knight is dismayed by 'the baggy, bulgy, loose effect, the fluidity . . . [and] an immorality of technique which . . . is . . . all but decadent' (Knight 1939: 14).
2. See also Greene (1957), Williams (1966), Aptekar (1969), Hieatt (1975), Davies (1986), Watkins (1995), and Quitslund (2001).
3. On issues of maternity and the reproductive body see also Goldberg (1975), Nohrnberg (1976), Quilligan (1983), Hadfield (1988), D. Miller (1988), Bellamy (1992), Silberman (1995), Krier (2001), and Gough (1999).
4. For a recent alternative view, see Tilmouth, whose careful study of early modern writers in relation to moral philosophy concludes that Spenser's commitment to the pre-rational poetic image of psychomachia is questioned nowhere in the poem (2007: 37).
5. See also the influential remarks of Bakhtin (1981), 16.
6. See Wofford (1988, 1992); Suzuki (1989); Krier (1990); Bellamy (1992); Silberman (1995); and Stephens (1998).
7. See Yates (1975); Goldberg (1981); Quilligan (1983); Wells (1983); Woods (1985); Benson (1985, 1992); Montrose (1986, 2002); Berry (1989); Eggert (2000a); Frye (1993); Bellamy (1987); Anderson (1982); Miller (1988); Walker (1998); McCabe (2002).
8. The lines in the subtitle to this section occur in Ní Chuilleanáin's poem 'Gloss/Clos/Glas' (2001: 46).

Bibliography

Adelman, J. (2005). 'Revaluing the Body in *The Faerie Queene* I'. *The Spenser Review* 36(1): 15–25.

Anderson, J. (1982). ' "In liuing colours and right hew": The Queen of Spenser's Central Books', in M. Mack and G. Lord (eds), *Poetic Traditions of the English Renaissance*. New Haven, CT: Yale University Press: 47–66.

Bakhtin, M. M. (1981). *The Dialogic Imagination: Four Essays*, ed. M. Holquist, trans. C. Emerson and M. Holquist. Austin: University of Texas Press.

Bell, I. (1998). *Elizabethan Women and the Poetry of Courtship*. Cambridge: Cambridge University Press.

Bellamy, E. J. (1992). *Translations of Power: Narcissism and the Unconscious in Epic History*. Ithaca, NY: Cornell University Press.

—— (2006). 'Gender', in B. Van Es (ed.), *A Critical Companion to Spenser Studies*. Houndmills/New York: Palgrave Macmillan: 76–97.

Benson, P. (1992). *The Invention of the Renaissance Woman: The Challenge of Female Independence in the Literature and Thought of Italy and England*. University Park, PA: Pennsylvania State University Press.

Berger, H., Jr. (2003). 'Wring Out the Old: Squeezing the Text, 1951–2001'. *SSt* 18: 81–121.

—— (2004). 'Sexual and Religious Politics in Book I of Spenser's *Faerie Queene*'. *ELR* 34(2): 201–42.

Berry, P. (1989). *Of Chastity and Power: Elizabethan Literature and the Unmarried Queen*. London: Routledge.

Bowman, M. R. (2003). 'Distressing Irena: Gender, Conquest, and Justice in Book V of *The Faerie Queene*'. *SSt* 17: 151–82.

Campana, J. (2005). 'On Not Defending Poetry: Spenser, Suffering, and the Energy of Affect'. *PMLA* 120(1): 33–48.

—— (n.d.). 'Suffering romance: Edmund Spenser and the Pain of Reformation'. Work in progress.

Carroll, C. (1996). 'The Construction of Gender and the Cultural and Political Other in *The Faerie Queene* 5 and *A View of the Present State of Ireland*: The Critics, the Context, and the Case of Radegund'. *Criticism* 32: 163–91.

—— (2002). *Circe's Cup: Cultural Transformations in Early Modern Ireland*. Cork: Cork University Press.

Cavanagh, S. (1994). *Wanton Eyes and Chaste Desire: Female Sexuality in* The Faerie Queene. Bloomington, IN: Indiana University Press.

Craig, J. (2001). 'Monstrous Regiment: Spenser's Ireland and Spenser's Queen'. *TSLL* 43(1): 1–28.

Dowden, E. (1879). 'Heroines of Spencer'. *Littell's Living Age* 28 June: 771–82.

Eggert, K. (2000a). *Showing Like a Queen: Female Authority and Literary Experiment in Spenser, Shakespeare, and Milton*. Philadelphia: University of Pennsylvania Press.

—— (2000b). 'Spenser's Ravishment: Rape and Rapture in *The Faerie Queene*'. *Representations* 70: 1–26.

Fitzpatrick, J. (2000). *Irish Demons: English Writings on Ireland, the Irish and Gender by Spenser and his Contemporaries*. Lanham, MD/Oxford: University Press of America.

Frye, S. (1993). *Elizabeth I: The Competition for Representation*. Oxford: Oxford University Press.

—— (1994). 'Of Chastity and Violence: Elizabeth I and Edmund Spenser in the House of Busirane'. *Signs* 20(1): 49–78.

Gohlke, M. S. (1978). 'Embattled Allegory: Book II of *The Faerie Queene*'. *ELR* 8: 123–40.

Goldberg, J. (1975). 'The Mothers of Book III of *The Faerie Queene*'. *TSLL* 17: 5–26.

—— (1981). *Endlesse Worke: Spenser and the Structures of Discourse*. Baltimore: Johns Hopkins University Press.

—— (1992). *Sodometries: Renaissance Texts, Modern Sexualities*. Palo Alto, CA: Stanford University Press.

—— (1994). *Queering the Renaissance*. Durham, NC/London: Duke University Press.

Greenblatt, S. (1980). *Renaissance Self-Fashioning: From More to Shakespeare*. Chicago: University of Chicago Press.

Greene, T. (1957). 'Spenser and the Epithalamic Convention'. *Comparative Literature* 9: 215–28.

Gregerson, L. (1995). *The Reformation of the Subject: Spenser, Milton, and the English Protestant Epic*. Cambridge: Cambridge University Press.

Guy-Bray, S. (2002). *Homoerotic Space: The Poetics of Loss in Renaissance Literature*. Toronto: University of Toronto Press.

Hackett, H. (2000). *Women and Romantic Fiction in the English Renaissance*. Cambridge: Cambridge University Press.

Hadfield, A. (1997). *Edmund Spenser's Irish Experience: Wilde Fruit and Salvage Soyl*. Oxford: Clarendon Press.

Harvey, E. D. (1992). *Ventriloquized Voices: Feminist Theory and English Renaissance Texts*. New York/London: Routledge.

—— (2003). 'Sensational Bodies, Consenting Organs: Helkiah Crooke's Incorporations of Spenser'. *SSt* 18: 295–314.

—— (2004). 'Pleasure's Oblivion: Displacements of Generation in Spenser's *Faerie Queene*', in C. Ivic and G. Williams (eds), *Forgetting in Early Modern English Literature and Culture: Lethe's Legacies*. London/New York: Routledge, 53–64.

Hazlitt, William (1816). 'On the Character of Milton's Eve', in P. P. Howe (ed.), *The Complete Works of William Hazlitt*, 21 vols. London: Dent, 1930–4: IV, 105–11.

Highley, C. (1997). *Shakespeare, Spenser, and the Crisis in Ireland.* Cambridge: Cambridge University Press.

Hooks, B. (1999). *Yearning: Race, Gender, and Cultural Politics.* Cambridge MA: South End Press.

Kinney, C. (2002). 'What s/he ought to have been': Romancing Truth in *Spencer Redivivus*'. *SSt* 16: 125–38.

Knight, G. W. (1939). 'The Spenserian Fluidity', in *The Burning Oracle: Essays on the Poetry of Action.* Oxford: Oxford University Press.

Krier, T. (1990). *Gazing on Secret Sights: Spenser, Classical Imitation, and the Decorums of Vision.* Ithaca, NY: Cornell University Press.

—— (2000). 'Hosea and the Play of Identifications in *The Faerie Queene* I'. *Religion and Literature* 32(2): 105–22.

—— (2001). *Birth Passages: Maternity and Nostalgia, Antiquity to Shakespeare.* Ithaca, NY: Cornell University Press.

Kuin, R., and Prescott, A. L. (2003). '"After the First Death, There Is No Other": Spenser, Milton, and (Our) Death', in E. J. Bellamy, P. Cheney, and M. Schoenfeldt (eds), *Imagining Death in Spenser and Milton.* New York/London: Palgrave Macmillan: 78–94.

Lamb, M. E. (2000). 'Gloriana, Acrasia, and the House of Busirane: Gendered Fictions in *The Faerie Queene* as Fairy Tale', in P. Cheney and L. Silberman (eds), *Worldmaking Spenser: Explorations in the Early Modern Age.* Lexington: University Press of Kentucky: 81–100.

Laqueur, T. (1992). *Making Sex: Body and Gender from the Greeks to Freud.* Cambridge, MA: Harvard University Press.

Lewis, C. S. (1938). *The Allegory of Love: A Study in Medieval Tradition.* Oxford: Oxford University Press.

—— (1967). *Spenser Images of Life.* Cambridge: Cambridge University Press.

Loewenstein, J. (1986). 'Echo's Ring: Orpheus and Spenser's Career'. *ELR* 16(2): 287–302.

—— (1990). 'A Note on the Structure of Spenser's *Amoretti*: Viper Thoughts'. *SSt* 8: 311–23.

Lowell, J. R. (1904). *Among My Books*, first and second series, 3 vols. New York: Houghton Mifflin.

McCabe, R. A. (2002). *Spenser's Monstrous Regiment: Elizabethan Ireland and the Poetics of Difference.* Oxford: Oxford University Press.

MacCaffrey, I. (1976). *Spenser's Allegory: The Anatomy of Imagination.* Princeton, NJ: Princeton University Press.

McEachern, C. (1996). *The Poetics of English Nationhood, 1590–1612.* Cambridge: Cambridge University Press.

McLaren, A. N. (1999). *Political Culture in the Reign of Elizabeth I: Queen and Commonwealth 1558–1585.* Cambridge: Cambridge University Press.

McManus, C. (2002). *Spenser's* Faerie Queene *and the Reading of Women.* Newark: University of Delaware Press.

Maley, W. (1997). *Salvaging Spenser: Colonialism, Culture and Identity.* London: Macmillan; New York: St. Martin's Press.

Mallette, R. (1997). *Spenser and the Discourses of Reformation England.* Lincoln: University of Nebraska Press.

Miller, D. L. (1988). *The Poem's Two Bodies: The Poetics of the 1590* Faerie Queene. Princeton, NJ: Princeton University Press.

—— (2006). '*The Faerie Queene* (1590)', in B. Van Es (ed.), *A Critical Companion to Spenser Studies.* Houndmills/New York: Palgrave Macmillan: 139–65.

Miller, J. (2000). 'Lady Mary Wroth in the House of Busirane', in P. Cheney and L. Silberman (eds), *Worldmaking Spenser: Explorations in the Early Modern Age.* Lexington: University Press of Kentucky: 115–24.

Montrose, L. (1986). 'The Elizabethan Subject and the Spenserian Text', in P. Parker and D. Quint (eds), *Literary Theory/Renaissance Texts.* Baltimore: Johns Hopkins University Press: 303–40.

—— (2002). 'Spenser and the Elizabethan Political Imaginary'. *ELH* 69: 907–46.

Myers, B. P. (2007). 'Pro-War and *Prothalamion*: Queen, Colony, and Somatic Metaphor among Spenser's "Knights of the Maidenhead"'. *ELR* 37(2): 215–49.

Ní Chuilleanáin, E. (1991). *The Magdalene Sermon and Earlier Poems.* Loughcrew: The Gallery Press.

—— (1995). 'Acts and Monuments of an Unelected Nation: The Cailleach Writes about the Renaissance'. *The Southern Review* 31(3): 570–80.

—— (2001). *The Girl Who Married the Reindeer.* Loughcrew: The Gallery Press.

Nohrnberg, J. (1976). *The Analogy of* The Faerie Queene. Princeton, NJ: Princeton University Press.

Owens, J. (2000). 'The Poetics of Accommodation in Spenser's *Epithalamion*'. *SEL* 40(1): 41–62.

Parker, P. (1979). *Inescapable Romance: Studies in the Poetics of a Mode.* Princeton, NJ: Princeton University Press.

—— (1987a). 'Suspended Instruments: Lyric and Power in the Bower of Bliss', in M. Garber (ed.), *Cannibals, Witches and Divorce: Estranging the Renaissance.* Selected Papers from the English Institute, 1985 NS II. Baltimore: Johns Hopkins University Press, 21–39.

—— (1987b). *Literary Fat Ladies: Rhetoric, Gender, Property.* London/New York: Methuen: 8–35 and 54–66.

Paster, G. K. (2007). 'Becoming the Landscape: The Ecology of the Passions in the *Legend of Temperance*', in G. Sullivan, Jr. and M. Floyd-Wilson (eds), *Environment and Embodiment in Early Modern England.* Houndmills/New York: Palgrave Macmillan: 137–52.

Quilligan, M. (1983). *Milton's Spenser: The Politics of Reading.* Ithaca, NY: Cornell University Press.

Quitslund, J. (2001). *Spenser's Supreme Fiction: Platonic Natural Philosophy and* The Faerie Queene. Toronto: University of Toronto Press.

Rambuss, R. (1993). *Spenser's Secret Career.* Cambridge: Cambridge University Press.

Roche, T. P. (1964). *The Kindly Flame: A Study of the Third and Fourth Books of Spenser's* Faerie Queene. Princeton, NJ: Princeton University Press.

Schoenfeldt, M. (1999). *Bodies and Selves in Early Modern England: Physiology and Inwardness in Spenser, Shakespeare, Herbert, and Milton.* Cambridge: Cambridge University Press.

Schwarz, K. (2000). *Tough Love: Amazon Encounters in the English Renaissance.* Durham, NC: Duke University Press.

Sedinger, T. (2000). 'Women's Friendship and the Refusal of Lesbian Desire in *The Faerie Queene*'. *Criticism* 42(1): 91–113.

Silberman, L. (1986). 'Singing Unsung Heroines: Androgynous Discourse in Book 3 of *The Faerie Queene*', in M. W. Ferguson, M. Quilligan, and N. J. Vickers (eds), *Rewriting the Renaissance: The Discourse of Sexual Difference in Early Modern Europe.* Chicago: University of Chicago Press: 258–71.

—— (1995). *Transforming Desire: Erotic Knowledge in Books 3 and 4 of* The Faerie Queene. Berkeley: University of California Press.

Stephens, D. (1991). 'Into Other Arms: Amoret's Evasion'. *ELH* 58(3): 523–44.

Stephens, D. (1998). *The Limits of Eroticism in Post-Petrarchan Narrative: Conditional Pleasure from Spenser to Marvell.* Cambridge: Cambridge University Press.

Stewart, A. (1997). *Close Readers: Humanism and Sodomy in Early Modern England.* Princeton, NJ: Princeton University Press.

Sullivan, G., Jr., and Floyd-Wilson, M. (2007). 'Introduction: Inhabiting the Body, Inhabiting the World', in G. Sullivan, Jr. and M. Floyd-Wilson (eds), *Environment and Embodiment in Early Modern England.* Houndmills/New York: Palgrave Macmillan: 1–13.

—— (2007). 'Afterword'. *SSt* 22: 281–7.

Suzuki, M. (1989). *The Metamorphoses of Helen: Authority, Difference, and the Epic.* Ithaca, NY: Cornell University Press.

Teskey, G. (1996). *Allegory and Violence.* Ithaca, NY: Cornell University Press.

Tilmouth, C. (2007). *Passion's Triumph over Reason: A History of the Moral Imagination from Spenser to Rochester.* Oxford: Oxford University Press.

Traub, V. (2002). *The Renaissance of Lesbianism in Early Modern England.* Cambridge: Cambridge University Press.

Vickers, N. (1981). 'Diana Described: Scattered Woman, Scattered Rhyme'. *Critical Inquiry* 8: 265–79.

Walker, J. (1998). *Medusa's Mirrors: Spenser, Shakespeare, Milton and the Metamorphosis of the Female Self.* Newark: University of Delaware Press.

Watkins, J. (1995). *The Specter of Dido: Spenser and Virgilian Epic.* New Haven, CT: Yale University Press.

Wells, R. H. (1983). *Spenser's* Faerie Queene *and the Cult of Elizabeth.* London and Canberra: Croom Helm.

Wofford, S. (1988). 'Gendering Allegory: Spenser's Bold Reader and the Emergence of Character in *The Faerie Queene* III'. *Criticism* 30: 1–21.

—— (1992). *The Choice of Achilles: The Ideology of Figure in the Epic.* Palo Alto, CA: Stanford University Press.

Woods, S. (2000). 'Women at the Margins in Spenser and Lanyer', in P. Cheney and L. Silberman (eds), *Worldmaking Spenser: Explorations in the Early Modern Age.* Lexington: University Press of Kentucky: 101–14.

CHAPTER 41

PSYCHOANALYTICAL CRITICISM

ELIZABETH D. HARVEY

RENAISSANCE literature and psychoanalytic theory would seem, on the face of it, to be natural allies. Jacob Burckhardt famously designated the Renaissance as the birth of human self-consciousness (1958: 143 ff), and Sigmund Freud made the unconscious foundational to his late nineteenth-century invention of psychoanalysis. The potential analogies and points of contact between these two 'epistemic moments' suggest tantalizing possibilities for understanding the development of subjectivity and the operations of the psyche (Bellamy 1992: 1–2). Yet although traditional psychoanalytic theory offers potent strategies for literary interpretation, perhaps especially in the methods Freud devised for dream interpretation, many readers of Renaissance literature have regarded psychoanalysis as a fundamentally anachronistic or belated theory. Stephen Greenblatt influentially articulated this idea in his controversial essay, 'Psychoanalysis and Renaissance Culture', objecting to psychoanalysis in terms that shaped the fortunes of psychoanalytic criticism as an interpretive strategy for understanding Renaissance literature (Greenblatt 1986). Greenblatt's fundamental disagreement with psychoanalysis is that it is based on a stable, continuous concept of the self that supposedly precedes and therefore enables psychoanalytic insight. Since he finds no evidence that this proprietary self existed in the Renaissance, he concludes that the hermeneutical enterprise of psychoanalysis rests on a foundation that is at once fictitious and erroneous. More representative of the period's emergent conception of personal identity, according to Greenblatt, is Thomas Hobbes's definition of the 'Naturall Person' as 'Feigned or Artificiall', a theatrical or masked impersonation that is fashioned rather than pre-socially constituted (221–3). Imposing a psychoanalytic model on early modern culture, Greenblatt argues, obscures the complex historical and cultural forces in the Renaissance that began to produce the idea of 'continuous selfhood' (Greenblatt 1986: 214), and privileges sexuality and a particular conformation of the *fin de siècle* European bourgeois family that effaces early modern beliefs about the body and kinship structure. Psychoanalysis can be redeemed as a method, proclaims Greenblatt, 'only when it historicizes its own procedures' (1986: 221).

In the appendix to his essay, Greenblatt turned from Renaissance drama in general to Spenser's *Faerie Queene*, identifying the poem, among other non-dramatic works, as an agent in the pre-psychoanalytic fashioning of the proprietary self. He suggests that Spenser's interest in 'psychic experience' is less an exploration of a character's inner life than it is a projection of that interiority onto a landscape. Spenser's mapping of the psyche is imaged, according to Greenblatt, in social terms; the inner self is 'conceived as a dangerous, factionalized social world, a world of vigilance, intrigue, extreme violence, and brief, fragile moments of intense beauty—just such a world as Spenser the colonial administrator inhabited in Ireland' (1986: 223). This interpretation reveals the strong new historicist and culturally situated aspect of Greenblatt's approach, a method that is apparent in his earlier analysis of *The Faerie Queene* in *Renaissance Self-Fashioning*, which draws on psychoanalysis even as it renders the insights of the psyche subservient to the political and social imperatives of early modern culture. In his interpretation of the Bowre of Blisse episode, Greenblatt cites Freud's assertion in *Civilization and Its Discontents* that all civilization is 'built upon a renunciation of instinct' (Greenblatt 1980: 173). The Bowre must be destroyed precisely because its pleasures threaten the civility upon which the social fabric relies. The integrity of the self and the social body depend on the dialectic between desire (epitomized by Acrasia) and the disciplining of that desire (imaged in early modern terms by the virtue of Temperance). Greenblatt reads the Bowre of Blisse as an allegory of the colonial encounter between European and native cultures; the seductiveness of the Edenic New World is always desired but must be continually destroyed, renounced, or tempered so that the social institutions of power can sustain themselves. This structure of desire and repression, a 'complex technology of control' originates in the Renaissance and, claims Greenblatt, undergirds and shapes Freud's theory of repression (1980: 174). While he does suggest that Lacanian theory may hold promise, particularly with respect to its privileging of language and its conception of identity as alterity, Greenblatt's critique is ultimately limited by the narrowness of its definition of psychoanalysis as Freudian ego psychology.

The immediate legacy of Greenblatt's essay was to marginalize psychoanalytic approaches to Renaissance literature. But it also inaugurated a critical debate about the relationship between historicism and psychoanalytic theory that intensified critical reflexiveness about method (Mazzio and Trevor 2000; Marshall 2002; Schiesari 1991; Walker 1998). *Renaissance Self-Fashioning*, which develops Burckhardt's focus on the birth of individualism through Greenblatt's elaboration of a cultural poetics, kindled renewed interest in subjectivity, the anatomy of the human subject, the social forces that mold it, its relationship to the body, and especially the much-debated question of whether, and at what point in history, the subject came to possess 'interiority'. These became pressing topics of literary analysis in the 1980s and 1990s. In his study, *Bodies and Selves in Early Modern England* (1999), Michael Schoenfeldt explored the concept of 'inwardness' in Book II of *The Faerie Queene*, charting the early modern subject's 'capacity to order a physiological self and the inner and outer beauty of that self' (1999: 41), a process of self-government epitomized by the virtue of temperance. Although Schoenfeldt traverses some of the same territory as Freud—the relation among physiological urgencies, emotion and desire, and ethical or social codes of behavior—he distinguishes his method from a traditional psychoanalytic approach. When Freud insisted in *The Ego and the Id* that the 'ego was first and foremost a bodily ego' (1984: 364), he joined physiology and psychology in a linkage that foregrounded the biological basis of subjectivity. Schoenfeldt also sees subjectivity as intimately sutured to physiology, in keeping with the Galenic model that prevailed in early modern culture. According to Galen, bodies were constituted by a delicate balance among the four humors, which were expressed as temperament (1999: 56–7). The emotions or passions arose from the body (1999: 49–51) and assumed a life of their own, and as '[p]hysiological double agents' could threaten the fragile stability of the self. Schoenfeldt reads the Castle of Alma and the Bowre of Blisse as episodes that inculcate the self-control necessary to maintain the integrity of the subject. He distinguishes his historicized, Foucauldian account of early modern psychology from the Freudian psychoanalytic interpretation of the Castle of Alma furnished by David Miller in *The Poem's Two Bodies* (1988). Schoenfeldt contends that interpreting Spenser's exclusion of the genitals from the Castle as an instance of Freudian repression, as Miller does, imposes a transhistorical theory that privileges sexuality in disproportionate ways (see also E. D. Harvey 2002, 2004). He argues for a historically inflected understanding of erotic desire, one that recognizes, with Michel Foucault, the primacy of alimentation and digestion as fundamental to health. In the Castle of Alma, 'the stomach rather than the genitals is at the narrative and conceptual centre of the well-ordered self' (Schoenfeldt 1999: 62–3).

THE ROOTS OF PSYCHOANALYSIS: EARLY MODERN FACULTY PSYCHOLOGY AND THE PASSIONS

'Psychology', the study of the psyche, came into English, the *OED* tells us, in 1654. It was aligned with a study of the soul (psyche), a branch of learning going back at least to Pythagoras and Plato, when it was a division of philosophy. Scholars and philosophers continued to debate the nature of the soul throughout the Middle Ages, of course, influenced especially by Plato's *Timaeus* and *Republic* and by Aristotle's *De anima* and *Nicomachean Ethics*. In the Renaissance, the study of the soul joined the discourses of anatomy in the encyclopedic tradition, religious controversy, philosophy, and natural philosophy. Spenser's depiction of the Castle of Alma provided an enduring poetic and architectural representation of the soul's dwelling. Spenser's first psychological critic was Kenelm Digby in his *Observations on the 22.Stanza of the 9ᵗʰ Canto of the 2d. Book of Spencers Faery Queen* (1644). Digby attempts to parse the geometrical intricacy of the stanza in which Spenser describes the ligature of the body and the soul. As Schoenfeldt notes, the material aspects of this union include the Paracelsian elementals of Salt, Sulphur, and Mercurie, as well as the Aristotelian/ Galenic elements of earth, air, water, and fire and the four humors that derive from them (1999: 56). The soul, for Digby, was the divine principle that God breathed into man (1644: 7). The joining of corruptible matter with the immortal soul was depicted by Spenser and glossed by Digby as gendered: just as the female is imperfect and 'receives perfection from the masculine', so by analogy does the body of man derive coherence from the soul. The body only 'administers' the organs, but it is the soul that gives intelligence and meaning to their operations (Digby 1644: 14–5). This explanation is plausible, though limited, but as Schoenfeldt notes, it does not even begin to account for the strange aspects of gender in the Castle: that the soul for Digby is masculine, but Alma is represented as female; that the castle is ambiguously sexed; or that the genitals are omitted from the allegorical body (Schoenfeldt 1999: 57).

Digby cannot define what 'ligament' ties the physiological to the psychic, but medical discourse identified spirits as crucial intermediaries; they originate in the body, a froth or heat that is concocted by the blood, and then become incorporeal. The vital spirits generated by the heart give rise to the passions of joy, grief, anger, and fear, and are also carried to the brain, converting there into the animal spirits that engage the five senses and the inward wits (E. R. Harvey, 1990: 566). Ruth Harvey provides a detailed analysis of the medical tradition upon which Spenser's representation of the brain's function in the Castle of Alma depends (1975). The three counselors who advise Alma and preside over their respective ventricles are *phantasia, cogitatio,* and *memoria,* the 'inward wits' (E. R. Harvey 1975: 2), faculties that in later psychoanalytic theory become invested with new significance. James Broaddus draws on the matrix of Renaissance psychology and medical discourse, Helkiah Crooke and Thomas Wright in particular, to explain Guyon's faint at the end of the seventh canto of Book II (65–6). He contends that Spenser's psychology is entangled with physiology; just as the soul and the spirits are coextensive with breath, so is the heart the productive site of the passions that must be managed by temperance (Broaddus 2004). Tracing the tripartite representation of the soul from Plato's *Timaeus* through Neoplatonism, St Augustine, and the Chartrean school to Ficino and Castiglione, Robert Reid seeks to redress the critical accounts that depict Spenser's psychology as predominately Aristotelian (1981; 1982). He notes that most critics adopt Aristotle's empirical revision of the Platonic tripartite scheme, whereas, as Kenelm Digby recognized early on, psychology in the Castle of Alma is an intricate synthesis of Platonic and Aristotelian paradigms (Reid 1982: 364).

Recent scholarship has sought to unearth the foundations of psychoanalytic theory through its exploration of the soul, the passions, the senses, and the cognitive faculties in early modern faculty psychology and medicine (Paster 2007; Trevor 2004; E. D. Harvey 2002, 2003, 2004, 2007). Psychoanalysis is twinned with cognition and consciousness in the historical phenomenological work of Bruce Smith. In his interpretation of the turret in Alma's Castle, Smith charts the transition from theories of the psyche or soul to theories of consciousness (2009: 94–7). Although there is no simple correlation between Spenser's three ventricles and Freud's tripartite psyche (id, ego, superego) or Lacan's three psychic registers (imaginary, symbolic, Real), there is a suggestive linguistic development between the ideas of conscience and consciousness. As Smith says, 'consciousness' came into circulation as a word and a concept in the seventeenth century. Before that, there was 'conscience', a word preceded by 'inwit', which is etymologically cognate with conscience and designates the 'faculty of common sense that fuses sensations and distributes them through the body via *spiritus*' (Smith 2009: 34). The crucial aspect of conscience, then, is an inward knowledge, a cognitive process that becomes a state of being, a quality of consciousness (Smith 1999: 35).

In his study of early modern melancholy, Douglas Trevor explores the relationship among the passions, Spenser's career as a courtier and a poet, and the representations of sadness that populate *The Shepheardes Calender* and *The Faerie Queene*. Readers have long recognized a quality of disappointment that saturates Spenser's writing, but this 'bitterness' is balanced by an equally pervasive sense of promise and expectation, what Harry Berger, Jr. terms 'paradisal expectations' (Berger 1988: 278). Spenser's optimism, according to Trevor, is Neoplatonic, a philosophical proclivity that privileges the spiritual over the mundane. It is this quality of transcendence that permeates Spenser's sadness. Trevor distinguishes Spenser from other sixteenth- and seventeenth-century writers, who understood their sadness as an imbalance of the humors that typically expressed itself as scholarly melancholy. Whereas this Galenic surplus of black bile implied a materialist conception of subjectivity, Spenser's Neoplatonic sorrow was spiritual and redemptive. The ambition to become a national poet required Spenser to present himself as learned but without the psychological encumbrance of a temperamental handicap. His fashioning of a poetic persona in *The Shepheardes Calender* and the first edition of *The Faerie Queene* reveals the poet's desire to display his 'knowledge of current intellectual debates' without adopting the pose of the melancholy scholar (2004: 40). Trevor's interpretation of Spenser's literary career and poetry is a historicized exploration of the emotional life of an early modern subject. Influenced by Lacanian theory, Trevor works against both essentialist and new historicist notions of the Renaissance subject, arguing that the self participates in its 'own circumscription' and 'even its own erasure at times' (2004: 3).

The early modern subject's passional existence often serves to demarcate, or sometimes blur, the boundary between inside and outside. Norbert Elias asserted that the firmly 'bounded' individual, *homo clausus*, was an invention of the Renaissance (Hillman 2007: 7). Elias's sociological and historical interpretation of the development of civilization itself depends upon Freudian models (*Civilization and Its Discontents* in particular), and it is therefore not surprising to note the clear analogies between the early modern emergence of *homo clausus* and psychoanalytic paradigms that describe the development of coherent, boundaried identity. The border between self and world and between the exterior and interior of the body is the contested territory of subjectivity, and it is an especially rich domain for studies of Spenser's poetry. This is the province of allegory, but it is also an area that is beginning to be charted in the new ecological criticism, particularly as it unfolds from humoral criticism of the body (Paster 2007; Schoenfeldt 1999). Gail Kern Paster maps this terrain in her study of the passions and landscape in Book II of *The Faerie Queene*, where she examines metaphorical and analogical comparisons between weather systems and human emotion. Winds and tempests are linked not only by the correspondence between macrocosm and microcosm, but also because the universe was animated by desire, and this pervasive emotion was visible in the doctrine of signatures, a system of correspondences that recognized echoes of shape or colour as expressive of divine design—thus goldenrod could be used to treat jaundice because both were yellow; pulmonaria was an effective treatment for lung disease because its leaves were shaped like the lobe of the lung (Paster 2007: 139–40). Whereas Schoenfeldt and Trevor read the early modern passions as controllable and relatively governable by the subject, Paster suggests that the saturation of the landscape by emotion dissolves the boundaries of the human subject. In her account, the human and the world are reciprocally engaged in ways that challenge the primacy of a psychoanalytic model organized into such enduring and foundational dualities as subject–object and body–world (2007: 150).

Garrett Sullivan contends that whereas Shakespeare is a 'poet of subjectivity' who provides rich insight into the nature of the human, Spenser's approach to the representation of subjectivity is more elusive (2007b: 282). Spenser understands humanity's essence not just in relation to individual subjects but also as a function of 'the vitality of *all* forms of life' (Sullivan 2007: 283). In other words, Spenser defamiliarizes the human by representing it as disturbingly contiguous with animal and vegetable life. Sullivan's point may begin to explain why critics of the last two decades have preferred drama to *The Faerie Queene* for studying the historical emergence of human subjectivity. Those critics who do examine Spenserian subjectivity return repeatedly to Book II, the part of *The Faerie Queene* that, alongside Book III's focus on the erotic, is most obviously cognate with psychoanalysis. Not only do Guyon's adventures instantiate the forms of social, emotional, and instinctual restraint that produce the subject, but Book II also furnishes allegorical representations of the mind's interior, most obviously in the Castle of Alma. Yet, as Sullivan reveals, the most unsettling visions of subjectivity in the poem are depicted through such altered states of mind as dreams, swoons, or bodily transformations (Grill's metamorphosis, for instance). Graham Hough long ago compared the structure of *The Faerie Queene* to the organization of a dream, noting the parallel between allegory and Freud's interpretation of dreams with their manifest and latent content (Hough 1962: 131). Characters who faint or sleep in the poem seem self-reflexively to figure the poem's affiliation with dreams and the contents of the mind. As Sullivan remarks, these moments also register the borders between different states of consciousness, between human and animal, and between life and death (2007). Verdant's post-coital slumber is a perfect example of a fluid subjectivity that hovers at 'the intersection of the animal, vegetable, and human' (Sullivan 2007: 284). Rather than investigating the emotional and ethical restraints that secure the human subject within the confines of a bounded subjectivity, as critics such as Greenblatt and Schoenfeldt do in their different ways, Sullivan, Paster, and Floyd-Wilson follow John Sutton's model of distributed cognition to explore a dispersed subject (Sutton 2007). Paster augments cognitive processes through her attention to the passions, and Sullivan focuses on memory and such states of altered consciousness as sleep and dreaming. Sullivan and Floyd-Wilson argue that in the Bowre of Blisse, bodies and the environment do not merely mirror one another, they interpenetrate (2007: 2), and it is this intermingling and dissolution of borders that simultaneously draws on and interrogates the categories of the subject and the unconscious or the imaginary.

PSYCHOANALYSIS, ALLEGORY, AND ROMANCE

Coleridge designated the 'land of Faery' as 'mental space' (quoted in McFarland 1990: 171), an idea that that Janet Spens elaborated as 'the inner experience of each of us' (quoted in Provost 1975: 34). When Spenser speaks of *The Fairie Queene* in the 'Letter to Raleigh' as a 'continued Allegory, or darke conceit', he sowed the seeds for critical considerations of allegory and romance that acknowledge the psychological or psychoanalytic dimensions of the poem. Graham Hough detailed Spenserian allegory's affiliations with Freudian theory in the narrative's 'loosely associative, half-unconscious methods like those of the dream', in the mechanisms of condensation—where one element of an allegorical representation can refer simultaneously to a historical, moral, or psychic framework—and to splitting, where a single character can be divided into separate figures (Hough 1965: 131–7). Hough's account ran counter to the position of a number of influential Spenserian critics who resisted psychoanalytic interpretations of allegory, often on the grounds that allegorical figures are not to be equated in any simple way with human characters. Isabel MacCaffrey provided a representative voice. She asserted that 'although allegory makes visible various sorts of invisibility', 'not all of it is psychic' (1976: 178). She acknowledges that Spenser figures a psychic life 'flowing beneath ordinary consciousness', but cautions that to 'say that all of the poem's places are also "places of the soul"' 'simplifies allegory unduly because it blurs some of the statements he wants to make about the relations between psychic and non-psychic (but invisible) reality' (1976: 184; see also Tuve 1966; Roche 1964). Despite the resistance to psychoanalytic approaches, however, there has also been a prevalent recognition that psychoanalysis and Spenserian thought share certain affinities. Angus Fletcher identified the correlates between myth and dream, and he catalogued psychoanalytic analogues in allegory—daemonic agency, cosmic imagery, magical causality, ritualized action, and ambivalent thematic structure—noting the complex ways that feeling is expressed symbolically in both (1962: 279–303). The essence of allegory, from *allos* (Greek, 'other') and *agoreuo* ('to speak in the marketplace'), is its capacity to articulate in a range of significations (see Chapter 24 above). This polysemy, what Maureen Quilligan calls 'verbal ambidextrousness' (1979: 26), cultivates in the reader a radical self-consciousness about meaning and interpretation. Quilligan's argument, that narrative structure in allegory is generated from wordplay (1979: 22), foregrounds the linguistic nature of the allegorical mode. If, as Fletcher suggests, all allegorical language is encoded (1964: 3), then the wordplay and etymological punning that feature so pervasively in *The Faerie Queene* also links its process of signification to the covert operations of the psyche that Freud named parapraxes, mistaken actions, puns, slips of the tongue. Quilligan describes Spenser's repetition of the word 'error' and its cognates in Book I, as a kind of witty etymological punning that simultaneously structures the narrative and engages the reader 'subliminally' (Quilligan 1979: 34. See also Craig 1967).

Northrop Frye's studies of romance in *The Anatomy of Criticism* and *The Secular Scripture* influentially defined the genre's alignment with myth and the archetypal structures that subtend Jungian and Freudian psychoanalysis. Frye's taxonomy lists the motifs and images of romance that also undergird many cultures: patterns of ascent and descent, magical or animistic landscapes (labyrinths, caves, gardens, woods), seasonal change (spring as rebirth, the fertility of the land), animals with symbolic import (dragons, speaking birds, sea monsters), objects invested with special power (shields, swords, belts, lances), threshold symbols (gates, doors), bodily transformations (trees, rocks, animals), signs or portents (dreams, oracles, prophecies), counterfeit doubles, and figures invested with special significance (enchanters, witches, giants, dwarfs, guides, faeries) (Frye 1976; Parker 1990). Frye drew frequent parallels between the work of myth, the nature of romance, and the structure of dreams. Descent themes, he speculated, often center on 'parental figures buried in a world of amnesia or suppressed memory' (1976: 81). He suggests that romance appears to replace the world of waking consciousness with a dream world, and he argues that the states of dreaming and waking in romance are always important (1976: 38), because defensive strategies are frequently employed as a mechanism to strengthen the 'barrier between the waking consciousness and other parts of the mind' (1976: 41). Frye aligns this process with 'kidnapped romance', a term that defines the constant pressure to contain the 'romantic thrust of sexuality and wish fulfillment' as the contest among the Freudian id, ego, and superego (1976: 41). In his discussion of the symbol, Frye invokes Freud's description of the operations of condensation and displacement in dream imagery: 'Like the dream image, [the social symbol] is a mirror of our own identity: it looms up out of a mass of vanished and submerged impressions, and it speaks to us from a context of silence. Like the dream image, again, it bypasses all mental conflict' (1986: 329).

The fertility and critical elasticity of Frye's approach licensed subsequent critics to explore the nexus of myth and psychoanalysis. James Nohrnberg's erudite encyclopedic study of mythological resonances and classical and continental intertexts, *The*

Analogy of 'The Faerie Queene', is fluently conversant with the structures of developmental psychoanalysis. His analysis of Maleger, for instance, draws as much on Augustine and Robert Burton as it does on Freud's discussion of mourning and melancholia (1976: 320–3). Nohrnberg suggests that one way to understand Britomart's figuration as the *Venus armata* is through Freud's concepts of fetishism and penis envy; the 'stays and gussets' of female clothing serve as a substitute for the phallus, and Britomart's armor becomes a bid for equality (1976: 460). Although Nohrnberg's references to sublimation, primal scenes, and transference are present, his approach is catholic, for they share company with a vast range of alternative explanatory strategies. Patricia Parker's important study, *Inescapable Romance*, descends in a critical genealogical line from the Frygian matrix. Supplementing more traditional studies of romance with psychoanalytic, structuralist, and deconstructive theory, she characterizes romance, citing Fredric Jameson, as necessitating 'the projection of an Other, a *projet* which comes to an end when that Other reveals his identity or "name"' (quoted in Parker 1979: 4). In her account, romance is a liminal or threshold space; it involves the 'dilation' of a space in order to 'defer' closure (1979: 5). Standing behind her glossing of these terms in relation to Neoplatonic theories of emanation and Patristic doctrine is Derrida's coinage of 'différance', a conjunction of 'to differ' and 'to defer'. The same process of endless postponement that governs the Derridean explication of signification in language also shapes the interminable structure of romance. Just as Maureen Quilligan understood wordplay as having a generative force in allegory, for Parker 'etymological complexes', such as Spenser's 'error', have the capacity to reproduce meaning in romance. This phenomenon, Parker argues, is grounded in the propagative capacity of the female body, a linkage she anatomizes in fuller depth in *Literary Fat Ladies* (1987b). She explores the figuration of the 'suspended instruments' in the Bowre of Blisse, a term that refers not only to Verdant's 'warlike arms' hanging in the tree, and not only to the sexual castration that this scene figures, but also to the instruments of lyric expression (1987a: 53–7). Parker associates Verdant's suspended instruments with Colin Clout's breaking of his pipe in *The Shepheardes Calender* and with Spenser's position as a male subject in Elizabethan England. The Bowre is an overwhelmingly female space, a place of suffocating maternal power, and Parker uses feminist and psychoanalytic theory to explore Spenser's subjection and the virility of his poetic voice under the rule of a powerful female monarch.

Harry Berger, Jr. borrows Frye's term, 'kidnapped romance' (Berger 1989) to rethink his own critical position on eroticism and psychological complexity in Book III of *The Faerie Queene*. Whereas traditional commentary has focused on 'psychomachian simplicities', and where psychological strategies of interpretation often founder on the vexed problem of character, Berger determines that the best approach is '*metapsychological*' (1989: 239–40). By this he means to focus on the 'roles, positions, and interactions inscribed in an ensemble of traditional discourses' rather than on the 'players or agents'. What happens to these characters becomes less significant than what happens 'in' and 'through' them, for the attention is now refocused from individual psyches to 'their positions in the discourses that traverse and "subject" them' (1989: 241). Berger seeks to read allegory in Lacanian terms, moving from Fletcher's important cataloguing of allegory's attributes, particularly 'the tendency for allegories to function as "mirrors of ideology,"' to understanding allegories as 'distorting mirrors that target the ideological implications of the discourses they represent' (1989: 241–2). Berger's metapsychological interpretation of chastity in Book III reveals the complexity of the virtue. No longer a 'single-valued structure', chastity's ambivalence locates its meaning from within the structures of desire. This is an emergent virtue, connected to the roots of gender formation, and it is also profoundly situated in language. If, as Lacan famously said, the unconscious is structured like a language, then redirecting attention to the language and discursive structures of Spenser's poem rather than the characters can give us access to the psychological drama that is the interplay of discourses. Spenser's relationship to the 'discursive regimes' of the literary culture he inhabited was one of submission and resistance (1989: 243). The 'kidnapped' discourses of desire in Book III include Ovidian intertexts and Petrarchan lyric, and by means of such devices as the use of a narratorial voice, Spenser encourages his readers to pay attention to the elements of mimicry, allusion, parody, and wordplay, to enter the 'maze' of interpenetrating discourses (Berger 1989: 250–6).

LACAN'S LEGACY

The radical instability of language and discursive structures in *The Faerie Queene* may help explain why critics have recognized strong affinities between Spenser's poem and Lacanian thought. In *Endlesse Worke*, a provocative engagement with structure and discourse in *The Faerie Queene*, Jonathan Goldberg acknowledges structuralism and Roland Barthes as central influences. Jacques Lacan, who appears only in footnotes, is an equally potent theoretical presence, however, perhaps most visibly in the concepts of 'lack' and 'misrecognition'. Goldberg begins with an ending that is not an ending: the cancellation and rewriting of the conclusion to Book III in the 1596 edition of *The Faerie Queene*. Drawing attention to Britomart's stance as spectator, where she 'halfe' envies the bliss of the embracing Amoret and Scudamour, and to the restoration of Amoret's riven heart to a 'perfect hole', Goldberg notes the homonymic destabilization of meaning that is also an inscription of loss (1981: 1–5). Where the reader might anticipate the satisfactions of narrative conclusion or textual and semantic stability, Goldberg's reading substitutes the Lacanian, deconstructive, and Barthesian pleasures that are characterized by a lack of closure, ambiguous meaning, wounded bodies, deferred consummations, and disappearing characters. His central chapter, 'Other Voices, Other Texts', is an intertextual study of Chaucer's unfinished *Squire's Tale* and Spenser's absorption of the broken text into his narrative in Book IV. Far from a Bloomian and Freudian agonistic, Oedipal struggle for poetic authority, Goldberg's analysis charts a textual interpenetration, a study of lost voices, and of other voices (1981: 31–5), a poetics of alienation, of misrecognition, of desire, and of lack.

David Lee Miller's historicist and Lacanian treatment of the 1590 *Faerie Queene* in *The Poem's Two Bodies* is also underwritten by the idea of anticipated but deferred wholeness (1988: 4). Because he focuses on identity and bodies—Kantorowicz's double monarchical corpus is the immediate referent for his title—Miller employs psychoanalysis as the 'natural' discourse for mediating between historicist and formalist modes of criticism. His central theoretical text is Lacan's 'The Mirror Stage As Formative of the Function of the I', the foundational description of the child's emergence into the illusory wholeness of subjectivity. In this critique of Freudian ego psychology, Lacan emphasizes the primacy of the linguistic, the imaginary nature of completeness, and the recognition that the self is created through—and in relation to—reflected images of others. 'The Mirror Stage' articulates for Miller 'the dynamics of castration and socialization with a theory of mirroring' (1988: 7), a specular logic that encodes Lacan's recognition of symbolic castration as the condition for entry into language and the register of the law. Spenser's project of writing empire through his celebration of Elizabeth I is inextricable from his own poetic vocation and his ambition to assume the Virgilian role of poet laureate (1988: 26). Miller's analysis persuasively shows how the rhetorical inscription of idealized sovereignty in Spenser's poem mirrors the inherently tropological legal and political texts of the period. The ideal body of the monarch is as much a mirage as the infant's complete body is in Lacan's mirror; wholeness is always deferred and can be glimpsed only in pieces through the refracted and deferred images of Spenserian allegory and the idealized visions of authority generated by Tudor ideology.

The figure of the mirror structures Linda Gregerson's *The Reformation of the Subject* in an analogous way. Gregerson examines Spenser's poem in the context of iconoclastic controversy in Reformation England, analyzing the poem's 'generative instability', in relation to Lacanian theory (1995: 4). She focuses on authorial disruptions and such moments of self-reflection as Britomart's gazing in the magic mirror to investigate how the subject is 'formed and *re*formed in cognitive, erotic, and civic realms' (1995: 7). In *Translations of Power*, Elizabeth J. Bellamy explores dynastic epic and subjecthood through Freudian and Lacanian psychoanalysis. Where Miller joins Lacanian narratives of psychogenesis with historicist readings of political ideology in mutually illuminating reciprocity, Bellamy interrogates new historicism's tendency to understand the subject's embeddedness within networks of social power. She argues that new historicist critics traced the dispersal of the subject within ideological structures, but its collective efforts at destabilizing a unified bourgeois self have taken place 'entirely on the level of consciousness', thus prematurely 'foreclosing' on the operations of the unconscious (1992: 5–13). Bellamy sees her book as cognate with the Frankfurt School project of historicizing Freud and understanding neurosis in relation to historical processes (1992: 37). The concepts of Marxist alienation, Althusserian interpellation, and Lacanian misrecognition problematize the relationship between ideology and the psyche, suggests Bellamy, thus revealing the imaginary or unconscious dimensions of ideology.

While the Freudian unconscious is imaged as a deep archeological layer, the Lacanian unconscious emerges only at the moment the subject enters the Symbolic. It is therefore always a 'recursive' structure, structured by lack and *méconnaissance*. Bellamy sees the unconscious as the site of resistance within the sociocultural, and she aims to map the intersection of the subject and social structure in narratives positioned at the interface of the literary and the political. Dynastic epic for Bellamy is necessarily about 'the gap between history and its representation' (1992: 25), for it depends on a political unconscious in which the vision of a providential future is motivated by desire and shaped as aesthetic form (1992: 26). Most revealing for her purposes is the hybridity of a poem like *The Faerie Queene* epic, which incorporates the errancy and deferred structure of romance into the architecture of epic. Bellamy, echoing Frye's psychoanalytic theorization of romance, suggests that romance, with its quest structure of desire, dream-like quality, and its liminal suspensions of identity, is the locus of the unconscious (1992: 28). If the ego's primal narrative is narcissistic, a kind of romance about the founding and fundamental misrecognition of the self, then by analogy, the exile from Troy in epic is the narcissistic origin of the *translatio imperii* (1992: 31). Troynovant in Spenser's poem becomes in Bellamy's account the intersection of psyche and history. But it is also a city not seen, a function of desire (1992: 191, 195). Her focus is prophecy, the projection into a dynastic future, and its counterparts, memory and narratives of origin. Arthur and Britomart, embodiments of the promised Tudor destiny, are the disoriented questers. The border between Fairie and Briton is, however, an enigmatic threshold that creates the 'alienation of the subject and the deferral of empire' (1992: 193). Bellamy glosses this boundary in relation to Lacan's concept of the *vel*, a point of alienation that occurs somewhere between the self and the other, or between Briton and Faerie, and it is this *vel*, she asserts, that constitutes *The Faerie Queene*'s unconscious (1992: 194).

BODY AND PSYCHE: SEXUALITY, GENDER, PSYCHOANALYSIS

Given Spenser's complex, perhaps even fraught, relationship to his powerful virgin queen and given the natural kinship between body criticism and psychoanalysis, it is not surprising that gender studies should offer a supportive theoretical framework for psychoanalytic approaches. One of the most influential parts of David Lee Miller's Lacanian analysis is his analysis of gender and sexuality in *The Faerie Queene*. In 'Alma Nought', Miller considers the 'epicene' body of Alma's castle, which, he asserts, re-inscribes Arthur's castration because Spenser's representation 'avoids' the genitals

(Miller 1988: 168). Where Schoenfeldt sees the erasure of the genitals as confirming his own emphasis on Galenic digestion, Miller understands this bodily eclipse as a proto-Lacanian moment about lack and negative metonymy (1988: 180). Reading the omission in Freudian and Lacanian terms allows Miller to recognize Spenser's elaborate erotic and scatological wordplay and to provide a reading of the encounters in the parlor of the heart that centers on shame, blushing, the blank arras as Freud's mystic writing pad, and displacements of desire. He glosses the concept of 'sublimation' as simultaneously historical—particularly with respect to the Aristotelian and Platonic psyches, as Kenelm Digby's seventeenth-century interpretation suggested—and psychoanalytically resonant (1988: 169–83). Miller's account of human reproduction of the *Amoretti* and the Garden of Adonis is similarly eclectically compelling, invoking Ficinian and Plotinian theories of generation and Freudian and Lacanian ideas of castration and anaclitic attachment (in which erotic choices are based on early infantile prototypes).

Harry Berger's important treatment of eroticism in Book III (1971) inaugurated a tradition of psychoanalytic commentary that continues to shape understandings of Spenserian sexuality. Bellamy's is one of the most sustained Lacanian readings; she focuses on the reproductive imperatives of imperial dynasty, the anxieties about genealogical continuity and gendered subjects that inflected the reign of Spenser's ageing queen, and the strange ambivalences about sexual difference, incest, and sodomy that trouble Spenser's representation of the virtue of chastity (1992: 196–9; see also Quilligan 2005). Bellamy's analysis of the spaces of feminine enclosure (marine caves, bowers, mews) evokes the psychoanalytic imaginary, what Julia Kristeva named the chora, that undifferentiated world of maternal union, a fusion that is simultaneously feared and desired (Bellamy 1992: 199–203; 2004; see also Krier 2001, 2003a, b). In *Birth Passages*, Theresa Krier provides a powerful antidote to Lacanian and Freudian studies of female sexuality and maternity, most of which privilege lack, mourning, and loss. She draws on the British psychoanalytic tradition—D. W. Winnicott and Melanie Klein—and the writings of the Belgian psychoanalyst, philosopher, and linguist Luce Irigaray in order to explore the psychic topography of this dark maternal space. Inspired by the celebrations and praise of the maternal, evocatively captured in Irigaray's lyrical utopian writings, Krier maps the prehistory of psychoanalytic thought and uses its insights to reread the maternal energies that subtend the great creation texts of Western literature, beginning with Lucretius and culminating in Spenser and Shakespeare. Like Irigaray, Krier argues that Lacanian psychoanalysis's emphasis on the past and 'misrecognition' sentences the subject to a past without a future. Krier focuses instead on the transformative potential of maternal discourse (2001: xv), an approach that informs her treatment of erotic union in Spenser's *Amoretti*. Her reading of Spenser's blazons evokes an Irigarayan elemental physics that makes persuasive sense of Spenser's imaging of the air, the earth's fecundity, and of the larger place of the mother in the sonnet sequence. Krier's analysis of Book IV of *The Faerie Queene* traverses some of the same poetic territory that Goldberg does in *Endless Worke*, but the emphases are very different. Krier traces the allure of the chthonic mother, a death drive that is imaged as a nostalgia for the maternal, but when she turns to the Lucretian intertextual echoes in Spenser's hymn to Venus, she argues that the salvific potential of nature's maternal vitalism redeems the poetic process.

Although not explicitly psychoanalytic in approach, the topic of Krier's 1990 *Gazing on Secret Sights* forecast the preoccupation with vision and the gaze that became a prominent feature of psychoanalytic studies of sexuality. Julia Walker's study of interiority concentrates on the trope of the mirror and the gaze (1998). Taking Britomart as a mirror of Elizabeth I, she tracks Spenserian specular encounters and recognition scenes, examining the complex interplay between the characterological and metaphorical mirrors that simultaneously reveal the private interiority of the female self and also displace that image onto a public surface (1998). Bellamy explores the trauma of Britomart's encounter with her reflected image in her father's closet in a more explicitly Lacanian register (1992: 203). Poised on the threshold of sexual maturity, Britomart's confrontation with herself in this womb-like space would seem to enact the stage of primary narcissism, for she seeks her reflection 'in vaine'. Britomart initially avoids the psychic trauma of differentiation, claims Bellamy, at least until self-consciousness appears. Rather than seeing the image of Artegall, her future lover, Britomart's 'mirror stage' becomes for Bellamy an instance of Lacanian *méconnaissance*, a demonstration of the way sexuality is constituted by the 'trauma' of splitting from maternal homeostasis (1992: 208). Kathryn Schwarz's study of the Amazon in Renaissance literature also offers a Lacanian reading of Britomart's specular encounter. Schwarz's analysis explains Glauce's catalogue of monstrous sexuality as positioning Britomart's triangulated desire between 'mutually affirming masculinity' (Narcissus) and heterosexuality: Britomart 'is connected to Artegall mimetically through allegory and armor and teleologically through her determination to marry him and have his child' (2000: 141). Schwarz compares Britomart's prosthetic masculinity and its troubling of gender identity to the early modern ambivalent fascination with the Amazon and to Spenser's depiction of the hermaphrodite in Scudamour and Amoret's embrace. Britomart is implicated in the lovers' union through her passionate gaze—'halfe enuying their blesse'—a phrase powerfully evocative of psychoanalytic theories of gender and subjectivity (2000a; see also Silberman 1987; Cavanagh 1994). Schwarz contends that the figure of the hermaphrodite stages 'another return to the mirror stage, in which appetite reforms identity and detaches desire from any embodied condition of difference' (Schwarz 2000: 144–5). Critical fascination with the gaze opens Spenser's text not only to the relationship between early modern and psychoanalytic theories of gender and sexuality but also to the pervasive questions about subjectivity that undergird the history of identity from the Renaissance to Freud and his successors. These difficult questions—about the nature of the human; about how the self is constituted by the body, the passions, the soul, consciousness, and language; and about how identity is formed in relationship, in kinship, and in the social and political world—shape our understanding of our subjectivity. They problematize our readings of the past, our assessments of psychoanalytic theory, and they trouble and enrich our understanding of Spenser's powerful poetic depictions of the human subject.

BIBLIOGRAPHY

Bellamy, E. J. (1989). 'Reading Desire Backwards: Belatedness and Spenser's Arthur'. *SAQ* 18(4): 789–809.

—— (1992). *Translations of Power: Narcissism and the Unconscious in Epic History.* Ithaca, NY: Cornell University Press.

—— (1997). 'Waiting for Hymen: Literary History as "Symptom" in Spenser and Milton'. *ELH* 64: 391–414.

—— (2004). 'Spenser's Coastal Unconscious', in E. D. Harvey and T. Krier (eds), *Luce Irigaray and Premodern Culture: Thresholds of History.* London: Routledge: 88–104.

Berger, H., Jr. (1971). 'Busirane and the War between the Sexes: An Interpretation of *The Faerie Queene* III.xi–xii'. *ELR* 1: 99–121.

—— (1988). *Revisionary Play: Studies in the Spenserian Dynamics.* Berkeley: University of California Press.

—— (1989). 'Kidnapped Romance: Discourse in *The Faerie Queene*', in G. Logan and G. Teskey (eds), *Unfolded Tales: Essays in Renaissance Romance.* Ithaca, NY: Cornell University Press: 208–56.

—— (1994). 'Actaeon at the Hinder Gate: The Stag Party in Spenser's Garden of Adonis', in V. Finucci and R. Schwartz (eds), *Desire in the Renaissance: Psychoanalysis and Literature.* Princeton, NJ: Princeton University Press: 91–119.

Broaddus, J. W. (2004). 'Renaissance Psychology and the Defense of Alma's Castle'. *SSt* 19: 135–57.

Burckhardt, J. (1958). *The Civilization of the Renaissance in Italy.* New York: Harper and Row.

Cavanagh, S. (1994). *Wanton Eyes and Chaste Desires: Female Sexuality in* The Faerie Queene. Bloomington: Indiana University Press.

Craig, M. (1967). 'The Secret Wit of Spenser's Language', in P. Alpers (ed.), *Elizabethan Poetry: Modern Essays in Criticism.* New York: Oxford University Press: 447–72.

Digby, K. (1644). *Observations on the 22.Stanza of the 9th Canto of the 2d. Book of Spencers Faery Queen.* London.

Fletcher, A. (1962). *Allegory: The Theory of a Symbolic Mode.* Ithaca, NY: Cornell University Press.

Freud, S. (1984). *The Ego and The Id* in *On Metapsychology: The Theory of Psychoanalysis*, ed. J. Strachey. London/New York: Penguin Books.

Frye, N. (1976). 'The Secular Scripture: A Study of the Structure of Romance', in J. Adamson and J. Wilson (eds), *The Secular Scripture and Other Writings on Critical Theory, 1976–1991.* Toronto: University of Toronto Press: 3–124.

—— (1986). 'The Symbol as a Medium of Exchange', in J. Adamson and J. Wilson (eds), *The Secular Scripture and Other Writings on Critical Theory, 1976–1991.* Toronto: University of Toronto Press: 327–41.

Goldberg, J. (1981). *Endlesse Worke: Spenser and the Structures of Discourse.* Baltimore: Johns Hopkins University Press.

—— (1992). *Sodometries: Renaissance Texts, Modern Sexualities.* Palo Alto, CA: Stanford University Press.

Greenblatt, S. (1980). *Renaissance Self-Fashioning: From More to Shakespeare.* Chicago: University of Chicago Press.

—— (1986). 'Psychoanalysis and Renaissance Culture', in P. Parker and D. Quint (eds), *Literary Theory/Renaissance Texts.* Baltimore/London: Johns Hopkins University Press: 210–24.

Gregerson, L. (1995). *The Reformation of the Subject: Spenser, Milton, and the English Protestant Epic.* Cambridge: Cambridge University Press.

Harvey, E. D. (1992). *Ventriloquized Voices: Feminist Theory and English Renaissance Texts*. New York/London: Routledge.

—— (2002). 'The Touching Organ: Allegory, Anatomy, and the Renaissance Skin Envelope', in E. D. Harvey (ed.), *Sensible Flesh: On Touch in Early Modern Culture*. Philadelphia: University of Pennsylvania Press: 81–102.

—— (2003). 'Sensational Bodies, Consenting Organs: Helkiah Crooke's Incorporation of Spenser'. *SSt* 18: 295–314.

—— (2004). 'Pleasure's Oblivion: Displacements of Generation in Spenser's *Faerie Queene*', in C. Ivic and G. Williams (eds), *Forgetting in Early Modern English Literature and Culture: Lethe's Legacies*. London/New York: Routledge: 53–64.

—— (2007). 'Nomadic Souls: Pythagoras, Spenser, Donne'. *SSt* 22: 257–79.

Harvey, E. R. (1975). *The Inward Wits: Psychological Theory in the Middle Ages and the Renaissance*. London: Warburg Institute.

—— (1990). 'Psychology', in A. C. Hamilton et al. (eds), *The Spenser Encyclopedia*. Toronto: University of Toronto Press: 565–8.

Hillman, D. (2007). *Shakespeare's Entrails: Belief, Scepticism and the Interior of the Body*. Houndmills/New York: Palgrave Macmillan.

Hough, G. (1962). *A Preface to* The Faerie Queene. London: Duckworth.

Krier, T. (1990). *Gazing on Secret Sights: Spenser, Classical Imitation, and the Decorums of Vision*. Ithaca, NY: Cornell University Press.

—— (2001). *Birth Passages: Maternity and Nostalgia, Antiquity to Shakespeare*. Ithaca, NY: Cornell University Press.

—— (2003a). 'Daemonic Allegory: The Elements in Late Spenser, Late Shakespeare, and Irigaray'. *SSt* 18: 315–42.

—— (2003b). 'Mother's Sorrow, Mother's Joy: Mourning Birth in Edmund Spenser's Garden of Adonis', in J. C. Vaught and L. D. Bruckner (eds), *Grief and Gender 700–1700*. New York: Palgrave Macmillan: 133–48.

Lehnhof, K. R. (2006) 'Incest and Empire in *The Faerie Queene*'. *ELH* 73(1): 215–43.

MacCaffrey, I. (1976). *Spenser's Allegory: The Anatomy of Imagination*. Princeton, NJ: Princeton University Press.

McFarland, T. (1990). 'Coleridge, Samuel Taylor', in *SE*, 170–2.

Marshall, C. (2002). *The Shattering of the Self: Violence, Subjectivity, and Early Modern Texts*. Baltimore: Johns Hopkins University Press.

Mazzio, C., and Trevor, D. (2000). 'Dreams of History', in C. Mazzio and D. Trevor (eds), *Historicism, Psychoanalysis, and Early Modern Culture*. New York/London: Routledge: 1–18.

Mikics, D. (1994). *The Limits of Moralizing: Pathos and Subjectivity in Spenser and Milton*. London/Toronto: Associated University Press.

Miller, D. L. (1988). *The Poem's Two Bodies: The Poetics of the 1590* Faerie Queene. Princeton, NJ: Princeton University Press.

Nohrnberg, J. (1976). *The Analogy of* The Faerie Queene. Princeton, NJ: Princeton University Press.

Park, K., and Kessler, E. (1988). 'The Concept of Psychology', in C. B. Schmitt et al. (eds), *The Cambridge History of Renaissance Philosophy*. Cambridge: Cambridge University Press: 455–63.

Parker, P. (1979). *Inescapable Romance: Studies in the Poetics of a Mode*. Princeton, NJ: Princeton University Press.

—— (1987a). 'Suspended Instruments: Lyric and Power in the Bower of Bliss', in M. Garber (ed.), *Cannibals, Witches, and Divorce: Estranging the Renaissance*. Baltimore: Johns Hopkins University Press: 21–39.

—— (1987b). *Literary Fat Ladies: Rhetoric, Gender, Property.* New York/London: Methuen.

—— (1990). 'Romance', in *SE*, 609–18.

Paster, G. K. (2007). 'Becoming the Landscape: The Ecology of the Passions in the *Legend of Temperance*', in G. Sullivan, Jr., and M. Floyd-Wilson (eds), *Environment and Embodiment in Early Modern England.* Houndmills/New York: Palgrave Macmillan: 137–52.

Provost, F. (1975). 'Treatments of Theme and Allegory in Twentieth-Century Criticism of *The Faerie Queene*', in R. C. Frushell and B. J. Vondersmith (eds), *Contemporary Thought on Edmund Spenser.* Carbondale: Southern Illinois University Press: 1–40.

Quilligan, M. (1979). *The Language of Allegory: Defining the Genre.* Ithaca, NY: Cornell University Press.

—— (2005). *Incest and Agency in Elizabeth's England.* Philadelphia: University of Pennsylvania Press.

Reid, R. L. (1981). 'Alma's Castle and the Symbolization of Reason in *The Faerie Queene*'. *JEGP* 80(4): 512–27.

—— (1982). 'Spenserian Psychology and the Structure of Allegory in Books 1 and 2 of *The Faerie Queene*'. *MP* 79(4): 359–75.

Roche, T. P. (1964). *The Kindly Flame: A Study of the Third and Fourth Books of Spenser's* Faerie Queene. Princeton, NJ: Princeton University Press.

Schiesari, J. (1991). 'The Gendering of Melancholia: Torquato Tasso and Isabella di Morra', in M. Migiel and J. Sciesari (eds), *Refiguring Woman: Perspectives on Gender and the Italian Renaissance.* Ithaca, NY/London: Cornell University Press: 233–62.

Schoenfeldt, M. (1999). *Bodies and Selves in Early Modern England: Physiology and Inwardness in Spenser, Shakespeare, Herbert, and Milton.* Cambridge: Cambridge University Press.

Schwarz, K. (2000). *Tough Love: Amazon Encounters in the English Renaissance.* Durham, NC: Duke University Press.

—— (2000a). 'Breaking the Mirror Stage', in C. Mazzio and D. Trevor (eds), *Historicism, Psychoanalysis, and Early Modern Culture.* New York/London: Routledge: 272–98.

Sedinger, T. (2000). 'Women's Friendship and the Refusal of Lesbian Desire in *The Faerie Queene*'. *Criticism* 42(1): 91–113.

Silberman, L. (1987). 'The Hermaphrodite and the Metamorphosis of Spenserian Allegory'. *ELR* 17(2): 207–23.

Smith, B. R. (2009). *The Key of Green: Passion and Perception in Renaissance Culture.* Chicago: University of Chicago Press.

Sullivan, G., Jr., and Floyd-Wilson, M. (2007). 'Introduction: Inhabiting the Body, Inhabiting the World', in G. Sullivan, Jr. and M. Floyd-Wilson (eds), *Environment and Embodiment in Early Modern England.* Houndmills/New York: Palgrave Macmillan: 1–13.

—————— (2007). 'Afterword'. *SSt* 22: 281–7.

Sutton, J. (2007). 'Spongy Brains and Material Memories', in G. Sullivan, Jr. and M. Floyd-Wilson (eds), *Environment and Embodiment in Early Modern England.* Houndmills/New York: Palgrave Macmillan: 14–34.

Tuve, R. (1966). *Allegorical Imagery: Some Medieval Books and Their Posterity.* Princeton, NJ: Princeton University Press.

Walker, J. M. (1998). *Medusa's Mirrors: Spenser, Shakespeare, Milton, and the Metamorphosis of the Female Self.* London/Toronto: Associated University Press.

CHAPTER 42

···

POSTCOLONIAL
SPENSER

···

ANDREW HADFIELD

SPENSER has a lot to answer for. According to Edward Said,

> The idea of English racial superiority became ingrained; so humane a poet and gentleman as Edmund Spenser in his *View of the Present State of Ireland* (1596) was boldly proposing that since the Irish were barbarian Scythians, most of them should be exterminated . . . Since Spenser's . . . tract on Ireland, a whole tradition of British and European thought has considered the Irish to be a separate and inferior race, usually unregenerately barbarian, often delinquent and primitive. (Said 1993: 268, 284)

Said's comments represent a widely held perception of Spenser outside the confines of the academy—and often within it too. Spenser occupies a particular position as an especially wicked writer, because he, more than any of his illustrious contemporaries, actually was a colonist. Accordingly, he is a particularly apt subject for postcolonial criticism. Said's two statements also express the peculiar bewilderment that Spenser's canon inspires which has led to an ambiguous, often confused attitude to his work and legacy. On the one hand Said argues that Spenser's work reflects an ideological hegemony that has developed from the need to justify the English presence in Ireland, something that has become 'ingrained' as part of the grubby intellectual furniture. On the other, Spenser can be seen as the originator of a discourse, a pre-eminent English poet whose writings were read and recycled and whose attitudes helped to expedite centuries of colonial rule in Ireland.

Said's comments also express a certain wistful regret and surprise that so cultured and civilized an author could have expressed himself in such vile and disturbing terms. In doing so he is building on the comments of W. B. Yeats, one of the key authors who inform Said's conception of postcolonial literature, and C. S. Lewis, probably the greatest of all Spenser critics. Both were Irish, Yeats an Anglo-Irish Protestant aristocrat from Dublin, Lewis the son of a well-off Welsh solicitor who had emigrated to Belfast and a mother from an Anglo-Norman family which had settled in Ireland in the twelfth century. There is a rather neat irony in Spenser's reputation being salvaged by members of the race he savaged so brutally in *A Vewe*, in which the Anglo-Normans who have become Irish ('degenerated') are seen as the principal cause of Ireland's decay (Maley 2003), especially given the assaults on Spenser's character and writing elsewhere. Other critics concerned with Spenser's relationship with Ireland, have a very different approach to his life and work. For John Arden Spenser was an architect of 'genocide'; for Tom Paulin he was an advocate of 'a policy of extermination' (Arden 1979; Paulin 1984: 22), both casting Spenser as a proto-Nazi.

Yeats's introduction to his edition of Spenser's selected poems confronts this problem directly. For Yeats, there are two Spensers, one good and one bad:

When Spenser wrote of Ireland he wrote as an official, and out of the thoughts and emotions that had been organized by the State. He was the first of many Englishmen to see nothing but what he desired to see. Could he have gone there as a poet merely, he might have found among its poets more wonderful imaginations than even those islands of Phaedra and Acrasia. He would have found among wandering story-tellers, not indeed his own power of rich, sustained description, for that belongs to lettered ease, but certainly all the kingdom of Faery, still unfaded, of which his own poetry was often but a troubled image. (Yeats 1961: 372)

Yeats creates a fantasy relationship: the experience of the imagined Spenser mirrors what he saw as his own productive encounter with Anglophone culture, transforming Spenser into his counterpart and equal, each staring back at the other from opposite sides of St George's Channel. Instead of dull, lifeless allegory Spenser concentrates on life-enhancing symbolism, leaving behind the weary, morally and intellectually bankrupt drudgery of colonial administration for the inspiring life of art and poetry. Yeats's manoeuvre is brilliant, and it enables him to fashion the Spenser he wants to read: tolerant, aristocratic, and imaginative, Said's humane poet and gentleman. Lewis performs a similar feat of deliberately selective memory, excising the passages of Spenser's work that he cannot bear to read. Lewis acknowledges what he sees as Spenser's flaws and limitations. Discussing the actions of Talus, the iron man, on the Salvage Island (Ireland), the critic turns away in disgust, arguing that they are 'something I shall not attempt to excuse . . . Spenser was the instrument of a detestable policy in Ireland, and in his fifth book the wickedness he had shared begins to corrupt his imagination' (Lewis 1963: 349). While Yeats is able to reclaim Spenser as a symbolic poet, Lewis reads him as one who helps the reader 'grow in mental health', as long as the violent and aggressive sections are conveniently excised (Lewis 1963: 359).

The assumption that Spenser's work can be neatly divided like this is, of course, problematic. As numerous studies have pointed out, the comments on Ireland cannot easily be confined to Book Five, but recur throughout *The Faerie Queene* and other works, often occurring at important narrative cruces (Herron 2007;

McCabe 2002). More significant, perhaps, is the assumption that what appears to be gentle and humane, or wishes to represent itself as such, should be read that way. Taking the Renaissance at face value is a perilous and invariably naïve assumption (Mignolo 1997). There is often a confusion between an early modern conception of humanism and a more recent understanding of the term. Humanism in the sixteenth century meant a commitment to the humanities, the study of the classics as a means of education, not a desire for secularization. Serious debates took place about the extent to which classical knowledge could be used, whether it was always subordinate to Christian revelation, or whether it impeded rather than enhanced sacred thought and writing. But signalling a commitment to the study of the humanities did not mean that the adherent was necessarily a pacifist (Kraye 1996). Even Erasmus, author of the most famous adage against war in this period, 'Dulce bellum inexpertis' ('war is sweet to the ignorant'), was not a straightforward pacifist as we understand the term. He counselled princes against belligerence, and was especially critical of bogus reasons for promoting war, but was principally concerned to protect the church, by a defensive war if necessary (Hadfield 1997: 54–9). Advocating civilized human values does not mean that the author is opposed to the violent means of implementing them. Indeed, this can be seen as the central point of *A Vewe*, which adopts one of the favourite humanist literary forms, the dialogue (Coughlan 1989). The rational, but ignorant Eudoxus (meaning, 'good doctrine'?) is horrified by the measures that the experienced Irenius ('man of anger', 'man of Ireland', or even 'man of peace/eire-nic'?), who has just returned to England from Ireland, advocates as the only way of transforming Ireland from its lawless state. Irenius points out that English law does not and cannot function in Ireland and that the only way to establish order is to send over a huge army to defeat the rebels using any means possible, including mass killings, a scorched earth policy, and enforced starvation (Brady 1986). Horrific measures can hardly be welcomed, as *A Vewe* implicitly and explicitly acknowledges. But sometimes they are the logical conclusion of the right way of thinking and the proper direction of policy.

Spenser's apparent frustration in his work is that the necessary policies have been ignored in Ireland, a position that allies him with many other New English voices who were similarly strident in their demands that the English crown take sterner action to protect their legitimate interests, and to preserve English rule in Ireland. In doing so Spenser effectively became a key spokesperson for the colonists throughout the seventeenth century and beyond (Canny 1975; Hadfield 1997). Spenser makes the same point in a number of his writings published in the 1590s after he had acquired his estate at Kilcolman, notably in *Colin Clouts Come Home Againe*, in which the besieged shepherds do not even realize that there is a land over the ocean, a sign of how cut off they have become from the crown's legitimate power. A related point is made in the *Amoretti* and *Epithalamion*, in which the happiness of the courting couple and newly weds takes place against the background of their perilous existence as colonists in Ireland, an indictment of the crown's lack of commitment to its English subjects in Ireland (Fleming 2001; Wilson 1995: Chap. 3). A small incident in *The Faerie Queene*, one that has rarely been noted by critics even though it occurs in a much analysed canto, makes the same case. Immediately after they have defeated and destroyed Malengin, the shape-shifting Jesuit/Irish rebel, Artegall and Talus come to the court of Mercilla and enter the queen's court:

> they passing in
> Went vp the hall, that was a large wyde roome,
> All full of people making troublous din,
> And wondrous noyse, as if that there were some,
> Which vnto them was dealing righteous doome.
> By whom they passing, through the thickest preasse,
> The marshall of the hall to them did come;
> His name hight *Order*, who commaunding peace,
> Them guyded through the throng, that did their clamors ceasse.
>
> They ceast their clamors vpon them to gaze;
> Whom seeing all in armour bright as day,
> Straunge there to see, it did them much amaze,
> And with vnwonted terror halfe affray.
> For neuer saw they there the like array,
> Ne euer was the name of warre there spoken,
> But ioyous peace and quietnesse alway,
> Dealing iust iudgements, that mote not be broken
> For any brybes, or threates of any to be wroken.   (V.ix.23–4)

The pointed sarcasm of the verses is clear, even before we consider that they occur immediately before the knights witness the disturbing figure of the poet Bonfont with his tongue nailed to a post and his name changed to Malfont (25–6). All is not well at the court of Mercilla and it should come as no surprise to us when she gives way to pity and has to be forced by her subjects, notably Zele, on one level an allegorical representation of Spenser's patron, Arthur, Lord Grey de Wilton, to execute the dangerous Duessa (Mary Queen of Scots) (McCabe 1987; 1989: 39–47). Here, the focus is Ireland; or, rather, the lack of interest in and understanding of Ireland in England. The fine courtiers cannot comprehend what knights are or what they do and are horrified at what they see as a rude intrusion, the armour of Artegall and Talus disturbing them. Instead, they deal justice—the verb may well be appropriate, given the subsequent description of bribes—but without ever having to confront the problem of military conflict, something they never discuss. Spenser shows that the court thinks it can govern the queen's dominions, but that it has absolutely no idea what happens within them. A dangerous war was taking place in Ireland which threatened the security of the whole realm, as the previous episode with Malengin demonstrates, yet the courtiers are entirely ignorant of such matters and imagine that they can exist without even thinking about military conflict and security. Like Eudoxus, they do not realize how serious the situation in Ireland has become, the unwelcome presence of the knights reminding the reader at least that the current place for the Knight of Justice should be the battlefield not the court. As a result, the allegorical figures that we do witness at court, Awe and Order, stand as empty ciphers, deprived of their proper significance.

Spenser establishes an opposition between the desires and needs of the colonists in Ireland and the metropolitan authorities who fail to comprehend the reality of life in the 'contact zone' (Pratt 1992). The problem is one that any reader of postcolonial literature and fiction will understand: the colonists, cut off from the motherland will start to change their identity and, as a result, become caught between their masters and the natives (Hall 1996; Young 1990: 119–26). Spenser's hostility towards the English court, shows that he knows that he has changed identity, as the poem *Colin Clouts Come Home Againe* acknowledges, questioning where the poet's home really is (the dedication to Raleigh accepts this as Ireland) and recognizing that the process of trading places transforms the self. The shepherds of *The Shepheardes Calender* have been transplanted and now think and act like the New English, defending their hard won pastoral spaces from the hostile, indigenous Irish. A useful comparison might be made between Spenser's anger and the situation represented in *The Day of the Jackal*, although that is not a postcolonial novel as such, having been written by an Englishman, Frederick Forsythe, about France (Forsythe 1971). In Forsythe's novel it is the French colonists and ex-soldiers from Algeria, the pieds-noirs, who wish to assassinate President De Gaulle, feeling that he has sold them out by not pursuing the war in Algeria to its proper conclusion and granting the former colony independence instead of crushing resistance. Spenser does not, of course, go this far, but, like the pieds-noirs, it could be claimed that his true loyalty is to his fellow colonists rather than the capital.

The great achievement of Edward Said's *Culture and Imperialism* was to complicate a facile understanding of the colonial and the postcolonial. Said demonstrated that there was more continuity between writing that was classified as colonial and therefore assumed to be monolithic, with a straightforward dichotomy between civilized colonizers and savage natives, and the postcolonial, with its attendant concepts of hybridity and mimicry, than most commentators had realized, showing that concepts of postcolonial criticism had an application to work produced during the period of European colonialism. Said demonstrates how Rudyard Kipling, the most vociferous apologist for the British Empire, had a more comprehensive and developed sense of Indian life than many liberal writers who had more obvious sympathies for Indian independence, such as E. M. Forster (Said 1993: 159–96, 241–8). Kipling was actually the more hybrid writer.

Said did not push his analysis back to the origins of modern empire. If he had done so he would not only have had more doubts about Spenser's sense of identity and allegiance, but would have recognized that from the start there was opposition to and nervousness about the imperial project. One of the key imperial texts, Thomas Harriot's *A Briefe and True Report of the New Found Land of Virginia* (1588, 1590), produced in a splendid edition with John White's drawings of the natives as part of Theodor De Bry's attempt to tell the story of the first sustained contact with the Americas to Europeans, is addressed 'To the Adventurers, Favorers and Welwillers of the Enterprise for the Inhabiting and planting in Virginia.' Harriot acknowledges on the opening page that 'There haue bin diuers and variable reportes with some slanderous and shamefull speeches bruited abroad by many that returned from thence ... Which reports have not done a little wrong to many that otherwise would have also favoured & adventured in the action, to the honour and benefite of our nation' (Hariot 1972: 5; Sloan 2007). Colonial discourse never was a straightforward, coherent discourse that distinguished between the colonizer and the colonized. Jeffrey Knapp has made a powerful case that Spenser, like many of his countrymen, was particularly nervous about the prospect of colonial expansion and felt that the establishment of an empire could well be a means of dissipating and undermining a coherent conception of Englishness (Knapp 1992: Chap. 3). The problem was that, whatever the disadvantages and the undesirable nature of expansion, staying the same was probably not an option. As Richard Hakluyt argued, a little, insular Protestant England would be swamped by the ever expanding Catholic Empire of the Spanish who had already colonized vast areas of the New World and made themselves the most powerful nation in Europe in the process (Hadfield 1998: Chap. 2). In the proem to *Faerie Queene* II Spenser refers directly to the Americas:

> Many great Regions are discouered,
> Which to late age were neuer mentioned.
> Who euer heard of th'Indian *Peru?*
> Or who in ventrous vessel measured
> The *Amazons* huge riuer now found trew?
> Or fruitfullest *Virginia* who did euer vew?
>
> Yet all these were, when no man did them know;
> Yet haue from wisest ages hidden beene:
> And later times things more vnknowne shall show.
> Why then should witlesse man so much misweene
> That nothing is, but that which he hath seene?
> What if within the Moones faire shining spheare?
> What if in euery other starre vnseene
> Of other worldes he happily should heare?
> He wonder would much more: yet such to some appeare.
>
> Of Faerie lond yet if he more inquire,
> By certaine signes here set in sundry place
> He may it find[.]   (II Proem, 2–4)

Spenser makes a comparison between the recently discovered lands in the New World and his own fictional landscape, Faerieland. The movement of the verse is particularly interesting because it is so uncertain. Reading the first two stanzas cited here would lead the reader to imagine that Spenser is about to acknowledge that what was once thought to be fictional is actually real, that this is a normal process, and we shall find that heaven and earth are full of stranger things than we have ever imagined. But, in fact, the next stanza moves us in the opposite direction. What we do get is a characteristically cheeky argument that Faerieland is actually real; or, at least, as real as Peru, Virginia, the Amazon, and the Moon. After all, we know that it refers to real events and has a purchase on the world outside the poem, not least because the 'Letter to Raleigh' tells us so. The effect is to make us think about the power of fiction, and in doing so, to see the essence of the poem and the truths it tells us as more important than an external reality which is tied to facts rather than imaginative truths, precisely what Sir Philip Sidney had argued in his *Defence of Poesy* (Sidney 2002: 111). Having raised the issue, the poem actually moves us away from any interest in overseas colonization. The reference to the Americas, which we might have expected would turn the subject to the question of imperial ambition, 'leads to an appeal not to colonize the New World but to believe in the existence of Fairyland' (Knapp 1992: 106).

The point can be taken too far. Spenser was either a friend of Sir Walter Raleigh's at this moment, or eager for the patronage of his powerful neighbour on the Munster Plantation. Accordingly, he carefully placed references in *The Faerie Queene* to Raleigh's plans to establish colonies in, and bring back substantial wealth from, the Americas, as well as to Raleigh's devotion to the queen and sorrow at his exile from court (Kelsey 2003; McCabe 2007). Spenser's work has indeed been linked to a larger imperial project and Nicholas Canny has suggested, controversially, that *A Vewe* was later used as a colonial handbook (Canny 2001: Chap. 1; McLeod 1999: Chap. 2; Scanlan 1999: Chap. 3). However, it would be hard to argue that Spenser's real focus was not on Ireland and the need to secure English rule in Ireland in the face of what he saw as the lack of concerted effort on the part of the crown and court. Even at his most shocking and brutal, Spenser has been seen by some commentators to acknowledge a bond between colonizer and colonized, most significantly in the famous passage describing the effects of the Munster famine in *A Vewe*:

Out of euerie Corner of the woods and glinnes they Came Crepinge forthe vppon theire handes for theire Legges Coulde not beare them, they loked like Anotomies of deathe, they spake like ghostes Cryinge out of theire graues, they did eate the dead Carrions, happie wheare they Coulde finde them, Yea, and one another sone after, in so muche as the verye carkasses they spared not to scrape out of theire graves. And, if they founde a plotte of water Cresses or Shamarocks, theare they flocked as to a feaste for the time, yeat not able longe to Continve thearewithall, that in shorte space theare were non allmoste lefte and a most populous and plentifull Countrey sodenlye lefte voide of man or beaste, yeat sure in all that warr theare perished not manie by the sworde but all by the extreamitye of famine which they themselves had wroughte. (*Prose*, 158)

The passage has excited much comment, hardly surprisingly as it draws attention to itself as a rhetorical tour de force justifying what seems to be beyond explanation and defence. For Jonathan Dollimore and Alan Sinfield the description shows Spenser expressing 'compunction at the effects of English policy', and the comments demonstrate that the 'human cost of imperial ambition protruded through even its ideological justifications' (Dollimore and Sinfield 1985: 226; Coughlan 1989: 55). This might seem an obvious reading of so terrifying a passage which dwells on each painful detail and draws attention to the destructive impact of English policy in Ireland. Spenser also justified the behaviour of Lord Grey when he massacred the prisoners who had surrendered at Smerwick on the grounds that they were rebels, not a lawful army, and so could not expect the treatment that would have been afforded legitimate prisoners of war, a decision that, as *A Vewe* recognizes, was controversial at the time (Spenser 1997: 159–62; McCabe 1989: 85–7). Clearly, criticism of excessive brutality in Ireland did take place.

Nevertheless, there is a danger that we might be reading Spenser with a post-potato famine perspective, given the terrible guilt which that event inspired and continues to generate, as well as its crucial role in defining Ireland as a postcolonial nation.[1] A contrary argument can be made. Spenser's dialogue is designed to lead the reader away from assumptions that seem to make sense and to show them that the reality of experience in Ireland will make them question everything they imagine to be true. Here, the reader is forced to confront the unpalatable truth that, as the last phrase indicates, it is the Irish who are to blame for their fate, not the English. Ireland has degenerated so far that only unimaginable horrors can save it from itself. The Irish have transformed themselves into the most savage of all creatures, the cannibals, who were recently being rediscovered in the New World, eating each other and so becoming 'anatomies of death' (Hulme 1986). Spenser makes great play on the pun savage/salvage throughout his works, a trope that comes into play here even though it is not actually articulated (Hadfield 1997). The passage demonstrates that Irish rebels against English law are savages who cannot be salvaged and only those who learn from this terrible spectacle can be saved.

Whichever way we read this section of A Vewe indicates that English colonial discourse that represented Ireland was not unified. If we assume that Spenser feels pity for the Irish then he is implicitly criticizing the excesses of military policy and acknowledging the terrible cost of occupation. If, on the contrary, we assume that Spenser is supporting the action taken, he is working against the reader and assuming that he or she probably feels that such actions cannot be justified. The power of the description of the Munster famine then rests on its counter-intuitive brilliance and desire to confront the reader with the horrible things that must be done to maintain stability and order. Spenser is laying bare what actually goes on as a means of justifying the extremity and severity of English rule in Ireland. As Mr. 'Whisky' Sisoda points out in Salman Rushdie's The Satanic Verses, 'The trouble with the Engenlish is that their hiss history happened overseas, so they dodo don't know what it means' (Rushdie 1988: 343). Spenser gives his English readers a sharp lesson in history, showing them the arts required to maintain the kingdom and daring them to dissent. The words of Albert Memmi are equally relevant here:

One should not be too surprised by the fact that institutions depending, after all, on a liberal central government can be so different from those in the mother country. This totalitarian aspect which even democratic regimes take on in their colonies is contradictory in appearance only. Being represented among the colonized by colonialists, they can have no other. (Memmi 1965: 63)

Government, law, legal status and rights simply cannot be the same in England and Ireland, as Irenius argues when he claims that laws must be made to fit the people and that they cannot stand as universal codes and benchmarks (Spenser 1997: 29–30).

The description has played an important role in the contemporary Anglo-Irish literary landscape, having been read and refigured in a variety of ways by contemporary writers. Surveying the Irish countryside in 'Bog Oak' Seamus Heaney ends his poem

> Perhaps I just make out
> Edmund Spenser,
> dreaming sunlight,
> encroached upon by
>
> geniuses who creep
> 'out of every corner
> of the woodes and glennes'
> towards watercress and carrion.   (Heaney 1990: 19–20)

Heaney seems to be rethinking and refiguring Yeats's response to Spenser, pursuing similar lines but casting the Englishman in a harsher light. Yeats argued that if Spenser had looked at Ireland more carefully he would have seen the symbolic beauty that defined the country and could have cast away his colonial spectacles. Heaney, who appears to be thinking not simply of the Munster famine description but another one later when Irenius explains the military singularity of Ireland, is less convinced:

[I]t is not with Ireland as it is with other countries, where the warres flame most in summer, and the helmets glister brightest in the fairest sunshine: But in Ireland the winter yeeldeth best services, for then the trees are bare and naked, which use both to cloath and house the kerne; the ground is cold and wet, which useth to be his bedding; the aire is sharp and bitter, to blowe through his naked sides and legges. (Spenser 1997: 98)

Heaney's poem suggests that he has read Spenser very carefully and has responded to the lyrical nature of the descriptions. For Spenser, as Patricia Coughlan has shown, wars that flame brightly in summer happen elsewhere, 'the shining moment of chivalric clarity is quickly past, and the inhuman plan of hunting down the kerns like their cattle takes place' (Coughlan 1989: 54). Heaney imagines Spenser 'dreaming sunlight' and missing the reality of the Irish countryside, with its cold and dearth, around him, locked in his own imaginative world. For Yeats there was a purpose to the symbolic world he saw in Spenser, one he could share with the English poet. For Heaney, Spenser seems oblivious and myopic, his very English imaginative world having no place in Ireland. Spenser sees dying Irish rebels creeping out of the woods when, in reality, they are geniuses, talented and individual in their own right, and, symbolically, figures who keep the Irish tradition alive. Spenser's words are turned against their author, a familiar postcolonial ruse (Ashcroft, Griffiths, and Tiffin 1989).

The passage is also reproduced almost verbatim in Frank McGuinness's play about the Nine Years War, *Mutabilitie*, based on Spenser's life in Ireland. Spenser is cast as a straightforward colonial servant and apologist, committed to civilizing the barbarous Irish. In dialogue with his wife in the first act, Spenser expresses a brittle confidence in the success of his mission and defends its necessity. When Elizabeth argues that the starving Irish must hate the English, Edmund replies:

They are civilized. I have succeeded in that. Perhaps in that alone, but I have succeeded. From that I draw strength. Say you are right, say the castle is surrounded and we must flee. These you would be rid of may be the saving of us in London. They are proof we may succeed in this accursed island . . . Our duties in this country are manifold. We are here at the behest of our sovereign. We must win this people to England's law, to England's custom, to her religion. If we fail, then we abandon this lost people to the devil. This conquest does not depend on the sword or the scabbard but on our souls, and if we keep faith with the almighty God whose destiny we praise and follow, then we shall win the Irish to our cause. (McGuinness 1997: 10; see Mikami 2002: 108–26)

Here, McGuinness equates Spenser and his character Irenius; or, rather, a particular version of Irenius. In describing Ireland as 'this accursed island' a pun is made monolithic, so that the explanation in the dialogue (excised from the published edition) that Ireland used to be called '*Banno* or *sacra Insula* takinge *sacra* for accursed' (*Prose*, 145) is taken at face value as if the word did not have the potential for change. Spenser is also cast as a Protestant proselytizer, which, given that McGuinness stated in an interview that 'the play is a metaphor for 1998' (Mikami 2002: 113) suggests that *Mutabilitie* stands as an allegory of postcolonial Ireland.

McGuinness, like Heaney, reads Spenser in terms of the Yeatsian paradigm. And, like Heaney, adds his own particular twist. If Spenser is the myopic English colonial servant, he is balanced on the Irish side by the File, the chief bardic poet, who, as Queen Maeve points out, is his mirror image:

Your English master, Edmund, he is no different to you. He serves his queen as you served your king. He writes exalted verses to her as she sits in glory upon her throne. That is his dignity. You have no such dignity any more. You worship a king grown old before his time, foraging for sustenance in a forest, in danger of forgetting his own name. You are no longer his poet. You are his spy, as is Edmund the queen's spy. (McGuinness 1997: 31)

Spenser is Karl Marx's 'arse-kissing poet', for all his sophistication, a hired court lackey in the service of the crown, like his Irish counterpart (Hadfield 1997: 69). McGuinness has turned Yeats's attack on English culture to a dying Irish culture, attempting to exorcise the sentimental myth of the 'hidden Ireland' in order to move forward. If Spenser had been able to visit Ireland as a poet and not as a colonial official, he would have seen a mirror image of himself, not much different from the ideological version he accepted and recycled.

Mutabilitie shows two similar worlds locked in conflict, a Manichean vision that needs to be overcome. The answer lies in drama rather than poetry, an imaginative response to the world, rather than a vision imposed upon it that obliterates its difference. McGuinness imports Shakespeare into the play and he stages a pastiche version of *A Vewe* in Act Three, taking the role of Eudoxus who is by no stretch of the imagination an interlocutor that Edmund can intimidate into submission. William explains the power of drama to Spenser: 'I have paraded before the people those thoughts, those images, those words, those hearts, those minds, that until the time of the reformation lay concealed in the corrupt cloisters and confined courts of kings— let those see who would see, hear who would hear. I let the lives I create burn in brilliant, everlasting fire' (McGuinness 1997: 52). Spenser and the File represent the old, colonial world with its irreconcilable differences and aggressive power relations; Shakespeare speaks for the new spirit of postcolonial reconciliation and exploration of the identity of the 'other.' Drama is a more amenable and democratic form than poetry for this world, which is why we should look back to Shakespeare not Spenser. But all is not lost. The play ends with Spenser's castle burned down and a child left wandering, clearly a version of the 'little child new born' who Ben Jonson thought had perished in the fire (*Prose*, 198–9). The child is adopted by the Irish, including the File, who agree to foster him/her as one of their own, the curtain coming down as the characters share a joke and a meal: '*Child*: I am hungry. I could eat a horse, Hugh. *Annas*: Our bill of fare does not stretch to horse, but there are berries and meat and sweet herbs and water to drink' (McGuinness 1997: 101). The creative lies that the playwright tells point the audience towards a more hopeful future.

How should we understand Spenser's role and identity? Was he simply a colonial servant, something that infects his verse more than those Irishmen, Yeats and Lewis, were prepared to accept? Or can he be seen as part of a hybrid Irish tradition, suggesting that the colonial and the postcolonial are not as far apart as many might think? Did Spenser take Irish culture seriously? Assessments of how much he actually knew and responded to Irish culture differ. Richard McCabe argues that when Spenser claimed he had the Irish bards translated for him, he was disguising his knowledge of Irish, and his interaction with Irish culture so that he would not attract unwelcome attention as a 'degenerate' English settler (McCabe 2002: Chap. 2). Patricia Palmer, on the other hand, argues that the words and phrases of Irish found in the writings of English colonists show no real interaction with native language and culture, something that would have been possible, given the experts available in Ireland at the time. Linguistic colonialism was too strong a force to counteract as colonists tried to force the Irish to become English. Spenser shows a bit more understanding than many but not much: 'though a wordsmith's curiosity may have drawn him to pick over Irish words more closely than did others . . . his interest was forensic and superficial . . . his handling of Irish words indicates no more than a shallow acquaintance' (Palmer 2001: 79). Without being able to reconstruct the culture of south-west Munster in the 1590s it is hard to judge with any certainty, especially if we bear in mind McCabe's point that Spenser would have had good reason to disguise the extent of his knowledge of Irish. We might also wonder how easy it was for English settlers to live in Ireland without considerable interaction with the natives, given the need for servants and the corroborating evidence that colonial enterprises in sixteenth-century Ireland were always under suspicion because, however draconian government warnings that colonists and natives were not to mix, the practical realities of life invariably made such injunctions redundant (Hadfield: 2005). Conversely, one might ask just how much Irish such interaction actually demanded.

Specialists who debate such matters often see Spenser as an ambivalent and complex figure with an uncertain identity and problematic relationship to Irish culture. More widely he is read in terms of the Yeats/Lewis paradigm, paradoxically enough, *especially* in a context sensitive to the nuances of postcolonial thinking. In his survey of Irish literature Declan Kiberd perceives Spenser within these familiar paradigms: 'The sheer ferocity of Spenser's writings on the Irish resistance—a ferocity quite at odds with the gentle charm of his poetry—can only be explained as arising from a radical ambivalence. He wished to convert the Irish to civil ways, but in order to do that found that it might be necessary to exterminate many of them' (Kiberd 1996: 11). This is an ambivalence that is not really an ambivalence, certainly not compared to the unstable and challenging modes of identity and thought that are discovered in the postcolonial 'contact zone' (Bhabha 1994; Bart Moore-Gilbert 1997). Spenser is cast in terms of the same dichotomy and his poetry given routine praise as if it were harmless and anodyne.

A selection of Spenser's work is included in the definitive *Field Day Anthology of Irish Writing*, where exactly the same descriptions are given and judgements are made. Spenser, it is stated, 'set some of the most important passages in his poetry in Ireland and, although he had the typical humanist's condescending attitude to native culture, he was genuinely interested in the country and its people. However, Spenser was also a colonial administrator with the attitude of mind necessary for the task' (Deane 1991: I, 171). We have the good and bad Spenser, the poet and the colonial official. The selections from Spenser again make reference to him as a nature poet: 'he chose to set important episodes of his major poetic work, *The Faerie Queene*, in Ireland. In doing so, he became the first English poet to make use of the Irish landscape and of Irish mythology' (Deane 1991: I, 225). The latter statement is true, but it masks and distorts a far more complex relationship between the writer and his sense of place, one that in its ambiguity, dislocation, and problematic understanding of identity, is actually far closer to the postcolonial culture against which Spenser is invariably defined.

Note

1. Morash (1995); Hadfield and McVeigh (1994), 251–65; King (1995); Young (2001), 299–307; Eagleton, Jameson, and Said (1990).

Bibliography

Arden, J. (1979). 'Rug-Headed Irish Kerns and British Poets'. *The New Statesman*, 13 July: 56–7.
Ashcroft, B., Griffiths, G., and Tiffin, H. (eds) (1989). *The Empire Writes Back: Theory and Practice in Post-Colonial Literatures*. London: Routledge.
Bhabha, H. K. (1994). *The Location of Culture*. London: Routledge.
Brady, C. (1986). 'Spenser's Irish Crisis: Humanism and Experience in the 1590s'. *Past and Present* 120: 17–49.

Canny, N. (1983). 'Edmund Spenser and the Development of an Anglo-Irish Identity'. *YES* 13: 1–19.

—— (2001). *Making Ireland British, 1580–1650*. Oxford: Oxford University Press.

Coughlan, P. (1989). '"Some secret scourge which shall by her come unto England": Ireland and Incivility in Spenser', in P. Coughlan (ed.), *Spenser and Ireland: An Interdisciplinary Perspective*. Cork: Cork University Press: 46–74.

Deane, S., et al (eds) (1991). *The Field Day Anthology of Irish Writing*. Derry: Field Day.

Dollimore, J., and Sinfield, A. (1985). 'History and Ideology: The Instance of *Henry V*', in J. Drakakis (ed.), *Alternative Shakespeares*. London: Routledge: 206–27.

Eagleton, T., Jameson, F., and Said, E. (1990). *Colonialism, Nationalism and Literature*. Minneapolis: University of Minesota Press.

Fleming, J. (2001). 'A *View* from the Bridge: Ireland and Violence in Spenser's *Amoretti*'. *SSt* 15: 135–64.

Forsythe, Frederick (1971). *The Day of the Jackal*. London: Viking.

Hadfield, A. (1997). *Spenser's Irish Experience: Wilde Fruyt and Salvage Soyl*. Oxford: Clarendon Press.

—— (2005). 'Irish Colonies and the Americas, 1560–1610', in R. Appelbaum and J. W. Sweet (eds), *Envisioning an English Empire: Jamestown and the Making of the North Atlantic World*. Philadelphia: University of Pennsylvania Press: 172–91.

—— and McVeigh, J. (eds) (1994). *Strangers to that Land: British Perceptions of Ireland from the Reformation to the Famine*. Gerald's Cross: Colin Smythe.

Hall, S. (1996). 'When was "the post-colonial"? Thinking at the Limit', in I. Chambers and L. Curti (eds), *The Post-Colonial Question: Common Skies, Divided Horizons*. London: Routledge.

Hariot, Thomas (1972). *A Briefe and True Report of the New Found Land of Virginia*. New York: Dover.

Heaney, Seamus (1990). *New and Selected Poems, 1966–1987*. London: Faber.

Herron, T. (2007). *Spenser's Irish Work: Poetry, Plantation and Colonial Reformation*. Aldershot: Ashgate.

Hume, P. (1986). *Colonial Encounters: Europe and the Native Caribbean, 1492–1797*. London: Routledge.

Kelsey, L. (2003). 'Spenser, Ralegh, and the Language of Allegory'. *SSt* 17: 183–213.

Kiberd, D. (1996). *Inventing Ireland: The Literature of the Modern Nation*. London: Vintage.

King, S. H. (1995). '"Pictures Drawn from Memory": William Carleton's Experience of Famine'. *The Irish Review* 17–18: 80–9.

Knapp, J. (1992). *An Empire Nowhere: England, America, Literature from* Utopia *to* The Tempest. Berkeley: University of California Press.

Kraye, J. (ed.) (1996). *The Cambridge Companion to Renaissance Humanism*. Cambridge: Cambridge University Press.

Lewis, C. S. (1963). *The Allegory of Love: A Study in Medieval Tradition*. Oxford: Oxford University Press.

McCabe, R. A. (1987). 'The Masks of Duessa: Spenser, Mary Queen of Scots, and James VI'. *ELR* 17: 224–42.

—— (1989). 'The Fate of Irena: Spenser and Political Violence', in P. Coughlan (ed.), *Spenser and Ireland: An Interdisciplinary Perspective*. Cork: Cork University Press: 109–25.

—— (2002). *Spenser's Monstrous Regiment: Elizabethan Ireland and the Poetics of Difference*. Oxford: Oxford University Press.

—— (2007). '"Thine owne nations frend / And Patrone": The Rhetoric of Petition in Harvey and Spenser'. *SSt* 22: 47–72.

McGuinness, Frank (1997). *Mutabilitie.* London: Faber.

McLeod, B. (1999). *The Geography of Empire in English Literature, 1580–1745.* Cambridge: Cambridge University Press.

Maley, W. (2003). '"This ripping of auncestors": The Ethnographic Present in Spenser's *A View of the Present State of Ireland*', in P. Berry and M. Tudeau-Clayton (eds), *Textures of Renaissance Knowledge.* Manchester: Manchester University Press: 117–34.

Memmi, A. (1965). *The Colonizer and the Colonized,* trans. Howard Greenfield. New York: Orion.

Mignolo, W. (1997). *The Darker Side of the Renaissance: Literacy, Territoriality, and Colonization.* Ann Arbor: University of Michigan Press.

Mikami, H. (2002). *Frank McGuinness and His Theatre of Paradox.* Gerrards Cross: Colin Smythe.

Moore-Gilbert, B. (1997). *Postcolonial Theory: Contexts, Practices, Politics.* London: Verso.

Morash, C. (1995). *Writing the Irish Famine.* Oxford: Clarendon Press.

Palmer, P. (2001). *Language and Conquest in Early Modern Ireland: English Renaissance Literature and Elizabethan Imperial Expansion.* Cambridge: Cambridge University Press.

Paulin, T. (1984). *Ireland and the English Crisis.* Newcastle: Bloodaxe.

Pratt, M. L. (1992). *Imperial Eyes: Travel Writing and Transculturation.* London: Routledge.

Rushdie, Salman (1988). *The Satanic Verses.* London: Viking.

Said, E. W. (1993). *Culture and Imperialism.* London: Vintage.

Scanlan, T. (1999). *Colonial Writing and the New World, 1583–1671.* Cambridge: Cambridge University Press.

Sidney, Sir Philip (2002). *An Apology for Poetry (Or The Defence of Poesy),* ed. G. Shepherd, rev. Robert Maslen. Manchester: Manchester University Press.

Sloan, K. (ed.) (2007). *A New World: England's First View of America.* London: British Museum.

Wilson, S. (1995). *Cultural Materialism: Theory and Practice.* Oxford: Blackwell.

Yeats, William Butler (1961). *Essays and Introductions.* London: Macmillan.

Young, R. (1990). *White Mythologies: Writing History and the West.* London: Routledge.

—— (2001). *Postcolonialism: An Historical Introduction.* Oxford: Blackwell.

INDEX

Achilles 297

Adelman, Janet 762

admonition controversy 35–8, 40–2, 117

Aesop 425, 692

Agricola, Rudolph 423, 425, 427, 429

Agrippa, Vipsanius Marcus 289

Aiken, John 698

Alabaster, William 7, 245

Albert, Prince Consort 712

Alciato, Andrea 438, 439, 446

Alcyon 245

Alençon, Duke of *see* Anjou

Alexandrines 304, 388, 390, 391–2, 725, 726

Allday, John 119

allegory 2, 6, 9, 132, 199, 203–9, 213, 227, 244, 271–2, 276–90, 429–30, 437, 445–57, 490–2, 498, 504, 539–42, 667–77, 736–40, 761–2, 782

Allen, M. J. B. 521

Alpers, Paul J. 170, 172, 173, 241, 273–4, 294, 415, 605, 606, 720, 721, 724, 726, 727

Althorp 25, 114, 126, 220

Althusser, Louis 785–6

Amis and Amiloun 277

anadiplosis 432

Anderson, Judith H. 139, 140, 179–80, 462, 463, 722

Andrewes, Lancelot 15, 128, 130

Anglican Church 31–45, 55, 119, 131, 133, 239, 381, 429, 487–8, 496–7, 540–1, 545, 562–3

Anglo, Sydney 51, 52

Anjou, Duke of 61, 93, 180, 465, 507, 581, 589, 592, 621

Anne, Queen of England 670

antonomasia 432

Aphthonius 422, 426, 432

apocalypse 40, 149, 150, 152, 154, 156, 283, 344–5, 440, 452, 487, 499, 518, 533–5, 550–1, 623, 665, 667, 739

Apocrypha 486, 487, 488

Apollo 20, 129, 178, 308, 395, 446, 468, 508

Apostles' Creed 492

Aptekar, Jane 280, 747–8, 770

Apuleius 450

Aquinas, Saint Thomas 328

Arachne 229, 514, 597

Aragnoll 229

archaism 42, 168, 367–81, 388, 393, 426, 467, 543, 555–6, 565, 652–3, 698, 700, 704, 712, 718–23, 745

Arden, John 793

Areopagus 22, 128, 135, 142*n*, 185–7, 357, 395, 400, 468

Ariadne 224

Ariosto, Ludovico 4, 289, 290, 357, 410, 411, 450, 453, 454–6, 470–1, 510, 539, 542, 579, 604–13, 709, 726, 734

 Faerie Queene and 273, 276–9, 284, 289–90, 391

Aristotle/ Aristotelianism 51, 56, 110, 116, 337, 338, 369, 404, 420–1, 423–4, 427–30, 433, 450, 471, 520–1, 524–33, 722, 723, 726, 777, 778

Arminianism 45

Arthur, Thomas 78

Ascham, Margaret 113

Ascham, Roger 113, 422, 426, 429, 589

astrology 341–3

astronomy 118, 243, 337, 342, 629–30

Attridge, Derek 185, 397, 396, 401n

Aubrey, John 128

Auerbach, Erich 491

Augustine of Hippo, Saint 544, 549, 778, 783

Augustus Caesar 404–5, 465, 468, 505, 507, 508, 517, 542, 577

authorial persona 125–6, 216, 128–30, 136, 192–3, 241, 432, 462–82, 508–9, 579, 586, 639

Austen, John 698, 708

Aylmer, John, Bishop of London 131

Babel 551

Bacchus 284

Bacon, Sir Francis 718

Bagenall, Sir Nicholas 79

Bajazeth 285

Bakhtin, M. M. 411, 770

Balbus 530

Bale, John 574

ballad stanza 248–9, 250, 394

Baltinglass, James Eustace, 3rd Viscount 20

Barclay, Alexander 369

Barclay, William 162

bards, Gaelic 317, 319, 673, 679–80, 769, 801, 802

Barnam, Benedict 361

Barnes, John 79

Barnes, William 376
Barnfield, Richard 723
Barthes, Roland 35, 192–3, 784
Baruch 488
Bateman, Stephen 454
Bath, Michael 154–5
Bathe, Thomas 88
Batman, Steven 630
Beacon, Richard 22, 52, 101, 322, 323
Beale, Robert 66, 67, 70, 84
Bear, Risa S. 327
Beardsley, Aubrey 699
Beattie, James 671, 724
Bellamy, Elizabeth Jane 765
Bellehachius, Ogerius 119
Bembo, Pietro 580
Bender, John B. 155, 686, 727
Benjamin, Walter 447
Bennett, H. S. 118, 121
Bennett, Josephine Waters 272, 275, 355, 616*n*,
        727, 728
Benson, Pamela J. 751
Berger, Harry, Jr. 171–2, 226, 234*n*, 311*n*, 494, 495,
        496, 499, 761, 762–3, 766, 779, 783–4, 787
Bergeron, David 182, 183
Bergvall, Åke 379–80
Bergvall, H. 496
Bernard of Clairvaux, Saint 630
Bernard, John D. 160
Bernardus Silvestris 504, 512
Berry, Craig 375, 609
Berry, Eleanor 386
Betham, Peter 369
Bèze, Théodore de 359, 485, 486, 625
Bhabba, Homi K. 803
Bicknell, Alexander 653
Binns, J. W. 574
Bion 248, 405, 628
Birch, Thomas 130, 647–8, 657, 695–6
Blake, William 673, 674, 712*i*, 712, 714
Blanche of Castille 232
Bland, Mark 117, 119–20, 121
Blank, Paula 371, 380–1
blazon 210, 213, 214, 261, 763, 787
Blayney, P. W. M. 115, 116, 121
Blissett, William 333, 336
Bloom, Harold 464
Blount, Edward 27, 119
Blundeville, Thomas 541
Boas, F. S. 642
Boccaccio, Giovanni 1, 2–3, 5, 116, 452, 466, 576
Bodin, Jean 53, 54–5, 323, 329*n*, 330, 548
Boemus, Johannes 323, 548
Boiardo, Matteo Maria 289, 410
Bolton, Edmund 720
Bonner, Edward, Bishop of London 576

Book of Common Prayer 31, 33–4, 37, 425, 488, 497
Book of Homilies 31–2, 33, 34
Borris, Kenneth 283, 286, 287, 449, 450, 455,
        487, 750
Boscan, Juan 431
Boswell, James 126
Bowes, Robert 25
Boyle, Alexander 26
Boyle, Elizabeth see Spenser, Elizabeth
Boyle, George 26
Boyle, Joan 24
Boyle, Richard, 1st Earl of Cork 24
Bradbrook, Muriel 137
Bradshaw, Brendan 88, 322
Brady, Ciaran 137, 327, 794
Brady, Hugh, Bishop of Meath 75
Brand, C. P. 606, 617*n*
Bray, Alan 184
Brehon law 283, 315, 316, 371
Brett, Jerome 90
Brigden, Susan 149
Brink, Jean R. 14, 15, 27, 112, 121, 140, 142, 325,
        326, 642
Broaddus, James W. 778
Bromley (Kent) 110
Brooke, Christopher 666
Brown, Richard Danson 222, 631*n*
Brown, William 239
Browne, Sir Valentine 96, 97, 100
Browne, William 376, 480, 666–7, 676
Browning, Elizabeth Barrett 676–7
Bruno, Giordano 659*n*
Bruster, Douglas 752
Brutus 542, 546, 560, 569*n*
Bryskett, Lodowick 142, 238, 276, 322, 475,
        614, 616*n*
    ES and 21, 65, 70, 74, 113, 132, 238, 251–2,
        271–4, 278, 289, 475, 604, 639, 650
Buchanan, George 323, 548, 737
Budé, Guillaume 438 440
Bullinger, Heinrich 119
Burby, Cuthbert 120, 360, 361
Burchmore, David W. 238, 247
Burckhardt, Jacob 775
Burghley, Lord see Cecil, William
Burke, Peter 574
Burne-Jones, Sir Edward Coley 713, 714
Burns, Robert 722
Burrow, Colin 139, 140, 281, 340, 512, 607–9
Burton, Robert 783
Butler, Edward 78, 82
Butler, Thomas, 10th Earl of Ormond 75–6, 79,
        80, 88, 90, 93–4, 95, 99, 102, 113, 678
Bynneman, Henry 16, 116, 117
Byron, George Gordon, Lord 673, 674, 724
Byzantium 289

Cable, Thomas 400
Caesarius, Johann 427
Cain, Thomas H. 243, 432, 728, 750
Calliope 109, 339, 416, 538
Calpurnius Siculus 576
Calvinism 38, 40, 43–4, 45n, 134, 205, 359, 489, 562, 564–5
Cambridge University 15–16, 40, 56–7, 110, 117, 135
Camden, William 27, 127, 129, 139, 186, 323, 358, 546–8, 735
Campana, Joseph 180–3, 232, 766, 769
Campion, Edmund 314, 327
Campion, Thomas 185
Canny, Nicholas 92, 98, 99, 101, 274, 325, 326, 327, 657, 750, 794, 798
career criticism 137–9, 237–55, 406–13, 464
Carew, Sir Peter 89–90, 94
Carey, Lady Elizabeth 113, 114
Carey, Sir George 114
Carey, Henry, 1st Lord Hunsdon 113
Caroline, Queen Consort to George II 670, 696
Carpenter, F. I. 142, 479, 652
Carroll, Clare 282, 751, 767
Cartigny, Jean de 454
Cartwright, Thomas 117
Cassandra 289, 290, 629
Castiglione, Baldassare 116, 379, 778
Castle Howard 327
Cateau-Cambrésis, treaty of 16
Catullus 223, 224, 265
Cavanagh, Sheila 276, 281, 760–1, 763, 766, 788
Caxton, William 368, 370
Cecil, Sir Robert, 1st Earl of Salisbury 640, 666
Cecil, William, Lord Burghley 5, 25, 45n, 56, 61, 66, 69–70, 75, 79, 88, 109, 113, 625
     ES and 127, 131, 133, 136, 221, 272, 473, 476, 621, 640, 666
Céitinn, Seathrún [Geoffrey Keating] 678
censorship 2, 5, 9, 58–61, 76, 169, 212, 473–5, 478, 586–8, 593, 736–9
Ceres 190
Chaloner, John 70
Chamberlain, Richard 172–3, 286
Chapman, George 120
Charity, A. C. 491
Charlemagne 289
Charles I, King of England 361, 362, 669, 740
Charles II, King of England 128, 726
Charles V, Holy Roman Emperor 580, 626
chastity 23, 44–5, 201–2, 204–6, 283, 295, 495–8, 543
Chatterton, Thomas 376
Chaucer, Geoffrey 223, 242, 368, 370, 372, 376–7, 381, 450, 452, 725, 741, 784
     ES and 193, 340, 351, 407, 429, 451, 464, 664, 673, 719, 720

works 39, 168, 173–4, 228, 232, 275, 354–6, 391, 450–1, 476–8, 591, 642
     Squire's Tale 355, 476, 558–9
Cheney, Donald 139, 273, 463, 578, 610
Cheney, Patrick 137, 138, 139, 171, 219–20, 232, 273, 286, 463, 464, 554, 559, 598, 750
Chettle, Henry 665
Chichester, Sir Arthur, Lord Deputy of Ireland 324
Child, Francis J. 132, 133, 134, 642, 651, 652, 657, 743
children's literature 676, 677, 704–5
Chloris 306, 307, 665
Church of England see Anglican Church
Church, Ralph 130, 131, 132, 134, 648–9, 653, 744
Churchyard, Thomas 21, 179, 194n, 245
Chylde, Maccabaeus see Spenser, Maccabaeus
Chylde, Robert 19
Cicero, Marcus Tullius 42, 51, 116, 420–1, 423, 426–30, 503, 522, 525, 574, 719
Cinthio, Giovanni Battista Giraldi 322, 726
ciphers 70–1, 76, 736, 739–40
civility 215, 286, 319, 321–2, 324, 326, 509, 598, 679, 749, 776
Clare, John 376
Clarion 229, 687
Clarke, Mary Victoria Cowden 642
Clarke, Danielle 250
Claudian 340
Clegg, Cyndia Susan 116
Clément, Jacques 621
Clement VII, Pope 580
Cleopatra 289
Clifford, Ann, Countess of Dorset 27, 125
Clifford, George, 3rd Earl of Cumberland 113
Clifford, Lady Margaret, Countess of Cumberland 114
Clio 109, 339, 416, 538, 623
Coke, Sir Edward 186
Coldiron, A. E. B. 631n
Coldock, Francis 119
Coldock, Joan 119
Coleridge, Samuel Taylor 376, 438–9, 444, 457n, 539, 673, 674, 675, 724, 781
Colet, John 425
Colin Clout 19, 22, 108, 138, 155, 256, 351, 381, 446, 768, 783, 796
     as authorial persona 387, 397–9, 434, 462–72, 473–5, 476–8, 479–80, 507, 554, 583, 590–2, 626–7, 632n, 639, 645, 666, 694–5, 783
     in CCH 6, 107, 112, 237–47, 417, 464, 473–5, 509, 595–6, 639, 666, 689
     in FQ 5–6, 286–8, 415–16, 446, 476–8, 517, 557, 598–600, 666
     in SC 6, 8, 108–10, 155, 160–77, 193, 194n, 225, 432, 462–72, 507–8, 517, 557, 577, 578, 581, 592–3, 597, 666, 694, 701, 783

Collier, John Payne 132, 133, 648, 651–2, 659*n*
Collins, William 695
Collinson, Patrick 37, 38, 39, 45, 749
colonialism 4, 20, 22–3, 26–7, 9, 40, 86–105, 134–8,
        140, 480*n*, 322, 324, 327–8, 340, 370–1,
        380, 549, 679–81, 739, 744, 749, 792–5,
        798–9, 802–3
Colonna, Francesco 454
Compton, Lord Henry 114
Constantine, Emperor of Rome 289
contemplation 42, 201, 205, 286, 311, 452–3, 542
Conti, Natale 504
Cooper, Elizabeth 647
Cooper, Helen 554, 562, 564
Cooper, Thomas 549, 550
Cope, Edward 26
Copley, John Singleton 495, 709, 711*i*, 711–12
Corbould, Edward 698
Coren, Pamela 239
correctio 425, 430, 431
Coughlan, Patricia 339, 767, 794, 798, 800
courtesy 44, 45, 73, 76, 175, 272, 284–8, 324, 415,
        434, 476, 612
Coverdale, Miles 15, 497
Cowley, Abraham 677
Cowley, Robert 88
Cowley, Walter 88
Cox, Virginia 322
Coyne and livery 329
Craig, Martha 380, 782
Craik, George Lillie 132, 142, 240, 653
Crane, Walter 698, 700–1, 703–4, 705–7*i*, 708
Cranmer, Thomas, Archbishop of
        Canterbury 33–4
Creede, Thomas 118, 120
Crete 342
Crewe, Jonathan 219, 221
Croft, Sir James 74, 323
Cromwell, Oliver 324, 326, 362, 669
Cromwell, Thomas 88, 138
Crooke, Helkiah 761, 778
Croxall, Samuel 670
Cuddie 108, 109, 165, 166, 167, 168, 169, 174, 398,
        467, 468, 478, 576, 577, 578, 583, 591,
        593–4, 596, 693, 695,
Cullen, Patrick 168, 170, 171, 580
Culler, Jonathan 438

Dallet, Joseph B. 689
Daly, P. M. 438, 440, 444
Daniel, Samuel 24, 222, 245, 257, 406, 462, 598, 616
Daniell, David 485
Dante Alighieri 1, 24, 25, 218, 237, 246, 248, 294–5,
        305, 356, 377, 438, 452–3, 456, 474, 491,
        494, 540
Daphne 232, 306, 308

Darcy, Sir William 88
Davenant, Sir William 669, 721, 723, 726
Davies, John 316, 323, 324, 325, 377–8, 379, 666, 723
Davies, Richard, Bishop of St David's 157
Davis, B. E. C. 370, 376, 377, 378, 379
Day, Angel 67, 181–2, 425
Day, John 116
De Bry, Theodor 796
De Gaulle, Charles 796
De Lille, Alain 340
De Man, Paul 438, 444
de Mornay, Philippe 120
De Sélincourt, Ernest 135, 136, 655, 656, 659*n*
de Vere, Edward, 17th Earl of Oxford 112
Deane, Seamus 803
death 191, 249–50, 295, 299–302, 338, 341, 674,
        691, 692
Dees, Jerome S. 239
Deguileville, Guillaume de 452
Demetrius 450
Demosthenes 422, 429
Denny, Sir Edward 97, 99
Derricke, John 323, 679
Derrida, Jacques 181, 783
Desmond, Earl of see FitzGerald, Gerald fitz James
Desportes, Philippe 614, 621, 630
Devereux, Penelope 253
Devereux, Robert, 2nd Earl of Essex 25, 27, 55–6,
        62*n*, 66, 90, 92, 94, 113, 115, 133, 238,
        253, 309, 334
dialect 165, 168, 368–74, 377–81, 588, 718–23
Dido 163, 166, 167, 172, 211, 412, 470, 510–13, 560,
        595, 626, 632*n*, 694, 701
Digby, Sir Kenhelm 239–40, 505, 720, 778, 787
Dillon, Sir Lucas 78, 80
Dillon, Nathaniel 74
Dionysius of Halicarnassus 422
Dixon, John 540, 541, 736, 738
Dodge, R. E. Neil 649, 659*n*
Dodsley, Robert 647, 650, 678
Dollimore, Jonathan 798
Dolven, Jeff 173, 287
Donne, John 65, 325, 329*n*, 645
Dorat, Jean 454
Douai, English seminary 34
Dove, Richard 163
Dowden, Edward 757–8
dragons 151, 200, 492
Drant, Thomas 20, 185, 576
Draper, J. W. 373, 376–7, 719
Drayton, Michael 186, 241, 376, 470, 651, 666
Drummond, William 611–12, 723, 737, 738
Drury, Sir William 18
Dryden, Erasmus 16
Dryden, George 27
Dryden, John 128, 664, 721, 723–4, 726, 734, 740–2

Drysdall, D. L. 438, 442
Du Bartas, Guillaume 431, 626, 629–30, 666
Du Bellay, Joachim 150, 152, 153, 224, 229–30, 369,
    377, 393, 546, 579, 614, 629, 638
Dubinsky, Stan 657
Dublin 40, 90, 91, 99
Dubois, Page 432
Dubrow, Heather 265, 311n, 359, 764
Dudley, Robert, Earl of Leicester 93, 282, 353,
    543–4
  and Elizabeth I 180, 592–3, 621
  and patronage of ES 16, 18–19, 40, 109, 111, 117,
    125–6, 128, 130–1, 133, 180, 353, 359, 409,
    506, 575, 592, 627, 689–90
  and poetry of ES 114, 220, 224, 227–8, 282, 309,
    541, 543–4, 736
Duncan-Jones, Katherine 251
Dundas, Judith 690
Dunne, Seán 680
Dunseath, T. K. 280
Durling, R. M. 415, 471, 611
Dyer, Sir Edward 19, 128, 132, 184, 185, 238, 245, 251,
    353, 357, 604

earthquake (in 1579) 178, 179, 194
East, Thomas 118
East India Company 260
Eastlake, Charles 712
Ecclesiasticus (Sirach) 488
ecological criticism 780
Edmondes, Sir Clement 120
Edward VI, King of England 31, 33, 34, 719
Edwards, A. S. G. 454
Edwin, Jonathan 642, 645, 646, 648, 650, 651
Effin, prebendary of 22
Egerton, Sir Thomas 324, 325
Egypt 289, 491, 550
eighteenth-century criticism (Spenserian) 126,
    129–31, 740–1
E.K. 2, 162–3, 173–4, 175n, 310, 352–3, 358, 371,
    378–9, 407, 430, 431, 463, 465–8
Elias, Norbert 779–80
Elizabeth I, Queen of England 30–1, 59, 172, 240,
    340, 361, 410, 444, 496, 622, 741
  and Catholicism 34, 149, 172, 321, 507, 581, 592,
    621–2, 631n
  and Church of England 31–5, 41, 119, 239
  and ES 75, 77, 80, 81, 82, 107, 127–9, 133–4,
    149–51, 163, 575, 580, 764–6
  and FQ 112, 245, 272, 279, 284, 415–16, 444, 469,
    470, 488, 489, 542, 543, 544, 737
  government 52, 53, 55–60, 70, 88, 282, 516, 518
  proposed marriages 93, 180, 399–400, 465, 507,
    581, 589, 592, 621
Ellrodt, Robert 521
Elyot, Sir Thomas 56–7, 372

emblems 4, 154, 178, 199, 212, 224–5, 227, 230, 284,
    312, 351, 354, 437–44, 448–56, 567, 632n,
    684–5, 687, 691, 747
Empson, William 241, 400n
Ennius 721
Enterline, Lynn 248
epanorthosis 430
Epicurus 522
epiphonema 432
Erasmus, Desiderius 31, 66, 79, 116, 181–2, 423–8,
    432, 446, 486, 504, 794
Erastianism 35
Erythraeus, Valentinus 429
Essex, Earl of see Devereux, Robert
Este, Ippolito d' 289
Estienne, Henri 628
Etty, William 676, 712
eudaimonia 521–5
Eudoxus 2, 20, 314–21, 371, 479, 494, 794, 795, 801
euhemerism 284, 297, 475, 550
Euripides 516
Europa 229
Eusebius 496
Eustace, James, 3rd Viscount Baltinglass 20
Eustace family 87–8
Eustathius 450
Euterpe 226, 243

Fairfax, Edward 611
Fairfax-Muckley, Louis 698–701, 700–1i, 707, 708
Fairy Land 212, 333–5, 339, 550–1, 798
Falco, Raphael 239, 248, 250
Fame 25, 107, 132, 133, 135, 138, 141, 155, 249, 251,
    295, 309, 467, 477, 509, 510, 550–1, 554,
    555, 567, 594, 603, 614, 628, 678
Farrell, J. G. 679
Faunt, Nicholas 66, 67, 84
Feingold, Mordechai 427
Fenton, Geoffrey 21, 75, 92
Ferguson, Arthur B. 543, 545, 549, 550, 631n
Ferguson, Margaret W. 225
Ficher, Andrew 543, 544
Ficino, Marsilio 243, 446, 521, 621, 630, 659n,
    778, 787
Field, Richard 120
Finglass, Patrick 88
FitzGerald, Gerald, 11th Earl of Kildare 87
FitzGerald, Gerald fitz James, 14th Earl of
    Desmond 22, 24, 69, 78, 87–9, 924,
    95, 98–9, 100, 320
FitzGerald, Sir John 90
FitzGerald, Thomas, 10th Earl of Kildare 77,
    87, 89, 95
FitzMaurice, James 69
Fitzwilliam, Sir William, Lord Deputy of
    Ireland 90–1, 320, 325

Fletcher, Angus 284, 541, 728, 748, 781–2, 784
Fletcher, Giles 376, 576, 643, 666, 668
Fletcher, John 667
Fletcher, Phineas 361, 376, 642, 643, 665, 666–8
Florio, John 21, 24, 27, 603
Floyd-Wilson, Mary 769, 781
Ford, H. J. 707–8, 708*i*
formalist criticism 8–9, 221–3, 718–32, 746–8, 751–2, 785
Fornari, Simone 455
Forster, E. M. 796
Forsythe, Frederick 796
Fortescue, Sir John 53, 58
Foucault, Michel 192–3, 749, 766, 777
Fouquelin, Antoine 424
Fowler, Alastair 276, 403, 727
Fowler, Elizabeth 280, 360, 518, 657, 658*n*
Foxe, John 32, 39–40, 381, 540–1, 545, 562–3
Fracastoro, Girolamo 457*n*
France 15, 16, 34, 357, 378, 625, 626
Fraunce, Abraham 24, 120, 245, 430, 431, 440, 467
Freckleton, Ferdinando 24
Frederick, Elector Palatine 150–1
Freigius, Johann Thomas 431
French language/ literature 153–5, 158, 163, 370, 381, 388, 391, 424, 614, 602–4
Friedrich, Walter George 251
friendship 130, 133, 138, 141, 178–87, 188–94, 272, 274–8, 476–7, 516
Fruen, J. P. 488, 489
Frushell, Richard C. 141*n*, 650, 667, 669
Frye, Northrop 334–5, 356, 445, 497, 728, 759, 782, 783
Frye, Susan 543–4, 593, 760–1, 763
Fulgentius 504, 513
Fulke, William 34
Fuller, Thomas 127
Fulwood, William 72–3, 425
Fuseli, Henry 709, 710*i*, 710–12

Galbraith, S. K. 120, 121
Galen 777
Galtymore Mountains 339
Ganelon 289
Garcilaso de la Vega 431
Garnier, Robert 120
Garrett, Lord 75
Gascoigne, George 368, 385–8, 390, 400*n*, 466, 587–94, 596, 598–9, 645
Gaskin, Arthur J. 698, 700, 702
gavelkind 329*n*
Gay, John 721
Gemini 310
gender 57–8, 119, 229, 242, 265, 276, 281, 306, 308, 310, 471, 757–74
Genette, Gerard 404, 405
genre 403–17

complaint 108–9, 114, 155–6, 165–6, 218, 219–33, 354–60, 406, 409, 412, 417, 464, 472–4, 623, 665–6
elegy 166, 172, 223, 232, 237, 247–51, 294–5, 305–10, 405, 581–3, 625–6, 665–8
epibaterion 416–17
epic 284–90, 409–13, 509–18
epithalamion 138, 141, 178, 256–7, 259, 263, 265–8, 353, 356–9, 375, 377–8, 394–5, 405–6, 417, 431–2, 474–5, 498, 547, 581, 597–8, 680, 759–60
hodoeporicon 582
hymn 244, 246, 293–305, 408–9, 486–9, 499, 531, 597–8
love poetry 242, 244, 261, 410–12, 475, 509, 592–600, 625, 629, 676, 719
pastoral 160–75, 407–9, 413, 415–17
propemptikon 405
prothalamion 305–10, 406
romance 274–9, 509–15, 553–8, 672–5, 781–4
satire 39, 41, 133, 166, 168, 222, 228, 241, 246, 417, 446–8, 451–2, 506–7, 591, 624–5, 640, 666, 734
visions 58, 220–30, 353, 356–8, 393–4, 554, 685–8
Gent, Lucy 689–90
Gentili, Alberico 51
Gentili, Scipione 455
Gentillet, Innocent 51
Geoffrey of Monmouth 211, 506, 543, 545, 559, 560
George, Saint 216, 217, 470, 471, 497–8, 512, 540, 541, 564, 630, 653, 695
George II, King of England 670
Gerald of Wales 323
Germany 217
Gheeraerts, Marcus, the Elder 155, 691
Gilbert, Sir Humphrey 17, 90
Gildas 546
Gilfillan, George 642
Gill, Alexander 667
Gilman, E. B. 46
Ginzburg, Carlo 187
Giovio, Gabriele 441
Giovio, Paolo 441
Giraldi, Giambattista 113
Glenmalure (Wicklow) 20, 321
Glenn, Thane P. 381
Gless, Darryl J. 43, 44, 45, 49, 62*n*, 499–500
Goebel, J. 95
Gohlke, Madelon S. 762, 763
Goldberg, Jonathan 59, 138–9, 182–4, 275, 579, 727, 728, 749, 764, 766, 784
Golding, Arthur 179, 194*n* 397–8
Goliath 448, 490, 493
Gollancz, Israel 142, 643
Gombrich, E. H. 442
Goodyear, William 454
Googe, Barnaby 21, 162, 589, 590, 597

Gorges, Sir Arthur 218, 231, 232, 245, 310*n*
Gorges, Sir Thomas 114
Gormanston, Lord 79
Gosson, Stephen 586–7
gothic movement 186, 649, 672–3, 690, 695–8, 714, 723, 726, 742
Gottfried, Rudolph B. 326, 646, 688, 690
Gower, John 451, 556, 719, 720
Grant, W. Leonard 579, 580, 581
Gray, Thomas 671, 673
Greece 163, 186–7, 289, 368, 404, 422, 424, 425, 487
Greenblatt, Steven 46, 137, 749–51, 761, 775–6, 781
Greene, Robert 119
Greene, Roland 171, 611, 612
Greene, Thomas M. 265, 311*n*, 493, 494, 497, 608, 725, 770
Greenlaw, Edwin A. 125, 543, 646, 654, 657, 745–6, 751, 753*n*
Greenslade, S. L. 494
Gregerson, Linda 46, 470, 761, 762, 765, 785
Gregory XIII, Pope 320
Greville, Fulke 119, 128, 175, 238, 251, 359
Grey, Arthur, Baron de Wilton, Lord Deputy of Ireland 2, 7, 14, 17, 20–1, 25, 65–85, 88, 102, 111–13, 127, 133, 138, 278–9, 282–3, 284, 320–1, 330, 678, 743, 798–9
Grindal, Edmund, Archbishop of Canterbury 15, 39, 41, 61, 131, 169, 507
Grosart, Alexander B. 132–4, 142, 152, 155, 157, 326, 642, 652–3, 655–7, 677, 742–4
Grundy, Joan 376
Guazzo, Stefano 322
Guernier, Louis du 695
Guillén, Claudio 181
Guilpin, Everard 720
Guise, Henri Duc de 621, 622, 629
Gustavus Adolphus II, King of Sweden 361–2

Haddon, Walter 17
Hadfield, Andrew 23–4, 26, 48, 53–4, 58, 62*n*, 101, 137, 139–42, 257, 278, 283, 325, 327, 588, 592–9, 695–6, 767, 740, 751
Hagar 492
Hakluyt, Richard 16, 797
Hales, J. W. 132, 133, 134
Hall, John 590
Hall, Joseph, Bishop of Norwich 4, 624
Hamer, Douglas 13, 16, 17, 26, 142
Hamilton, A. C. 166, 171, 488, 492, 579, 656–7, 747, 759
Hamilton, Hans 77
Hamner, Meredith 22, 314, 327
Hankins, John Erskine 500
Hannay, Margaret P. 250, 251
Hap Hazard estate 77
Harding, Thomas 34

Hardison, O. B. 400–1, 422, 725
Harley, Robert 670
Harper, Carrie Anna 546
Harrington, Sir John 24, 391, 455, 612, 658*n*
Harriot, Thomas 796–7
Harrison, John II (the younger) 117, 118, 120
Harrison, Thomas E. 713
Harrison, William 547
Hart, John S. 132, 133, 653
Harvey, Elizabeth D. 761, 766, 777
Harvey, Gabriel 14, 16, 17–22, 50, 51, 54, 60, 108, 110, 111, 112, 114, 116, 117, 128, 132, 134, 135, 138, 140–1, 155, 165, 169, 175–6*n*, 178–97, 273, 334, 350, 351–4, 357, 378, 385, 387, 395–400, 420, 427, 430–1, 433, 446, 452, 453, 463, 466–7, 468, 469, 472, 579, 580, 587, 588, 603–4, 608, 613, 616*n*, 639, 640, 641, 642, 645, 650, 688, 690
  'Ad Ornatissimum Virum' 581–3
  Letters (Spenser-Harvey) 20, 116, 117, 178–99, 468, 587, 639
  and Ramus 428–30
  'Sonnet to Harvey' 22
  see also Hobbinoll
Harvey, John 603
Hatton, Sir Christopher 97, 112, 116
Hawes, Stephen 453–4
Hayward, Thomas 647
Hazlitt, William 673, 724, 725, 757, 758
Heaney, Seamus 680, 800, 801
Hebe 351
Hector 289
Heere, Lucas de 691
Heffner, Ray 14, 15, 24, 26, 27, 326, 646
Hegendorff, Christoph 424
Helgerson, Richard 126, 138, 171, 186–7, 219, 241, 252*n*, 293, 396, 463, 505, 543–4, 554, 594, 579, 631*n*, 725, 735, 750, 752
Heliodorus 450
Hemmingsen, Niels 424
Heninger, S. K., Jr. 117, 379, 555, 684, 692, 715*n*
Henley, Pauline 135, 136
Henri III, King of France 621, 622, 629
Henri IV, King of France (Henri de Navarre) 621, 622
Henrietta Maria, Queen Consort to Charles I 362
Henry IV, King of England 279
Henry VII, King of England 543
Henry VIII, King of England 170, 690
Henry, Prince 665
Heraclitus of Pontus 450
Herbert, George 266
Herbert, James 101, 323
Herbert, John 66
Herbert, Sir William 22, 99, 101–2, 103*n*, 323, 325, 345
Hercules 279, 284, 550

Hermogenes of Tarsus 422, 427, 429
Herodotus 353, 548
Hesiod 448, 503, 516, 517
Hesperus 267, 310, 478
Hieatt, A. Kent 267, 727
Highley, Christopher 322, 751, 766
Hillard, George 651, 652
Hind, Arthur M. 691
Hinman, C. J. K. 655
historicist criticism 135, 137, 172, 219, 221–3, 241,
        279–80, 543–4, 733–56, 760–1
Hobbes, Thomas 324, 723, 775
Hobbinoll 108, 110, 163, 165, 169, 193, 194*n*,
        241, 243, 463, 476, 507
    see also Harvey, Gabriel
Hoffman, Nancy Jo 171, 172, 239
Hogarth, William 696
holiness 23, 39, 42–5, 200–1, 203, 205, 209, 211, 271,
        357, 445, 446, 469, 470, 488, 495, 497, 512,
        523, 540, 653
    see also Anglican Church; Bible; Roman
        Catholicism
Holinshed, Raphael 116, 178, 321, 323, 353, 358, 545,
        547, 549
Holland, Philemon 120
Holland *see* Netherlands
Hollander, John 387
Holy Roman Empire 88
Homer 1, 27, 174, 211, 409, 426, 428, 431, 448–50,
        453, 454, 456, 471, 503–16, 539
homoeroticism 182, 193, 766
homosexuality 182
homosocial relationships 138, 182, 183, 188, 193,
        276, 765, 766, 767
Hooker, John 321
Hooker, Richard 34, 33, 186
Horace 369, 404, 426, 449, 467–8, 503, 517, 574,
        583, 625, 691, 734
Hough, Graham 540, 736, 780, 781
Howard, Charles 113
Howard, Douglas 218, 231, 356
Howard, Edward 721
Howard, Henry, Earl of Surrey 589
Huguenots 16
Hughes, John 129, 130, 240, 247, 642, 646–51, 695,
        725, 741
Hume, Anthea 45
Hunt, Leigh 653, 673–5, 676, 727
Huon of Bordeaux 277
Hurd, Richard, Bishop of Worcester 726–7
Hutson, Lorna 193
Hyperius, Andreas 424
Hypocrisy 41, 136

Idolatry 32, 297
Idrone, barony of 89–90
illustration, of books 9, 154–5, 163–5, 219, 220, 230,
        351, 440, 463–4, 624, 638, 642, 679, 684–714

Ijsewijn, Joseph 574
Immeritô 19, 108, 111, 138, 160, 162–3, 166, 168–9,
        170, 171, 173, 174, 179, 180, 188, 191–2,
        351–2, 356, 358, 378, 464, 465–8, 554, 555,
        573, 586, 638–40, 642, 645, 658*n*, 695
India 260
Ingham, Patricia 373, 723
Ireland 14, 16–26, 37, 52, 55, 86–105, 125, 129, 131,
        134, 137–8, 240, 271, 273, 274, 278, 282–4,
        288, 289, 290, 314–32, 355–6, 357, 360, 416,
        463, 469, 473–5, 479, 509, 547–8, 551,
        792–803
Irenius 2, 3, 5, 9, 18, 20, 52, 282, 314–21, 354–5,
        371, 479, 494, 548–9, 767, 768, 794,
        799–801
Irish language 88, 370–1, 380, 381, 382
Irigaray, Luce 787
Italian language and literature 152, 163, 320, 353,
        370, 381, 390–1, 394, 399, 424, 602–19
    see also Ariosto, Dante, Ficino, Petrarch, Tasso

Jacob de Voragine 216
James, Saint 495, 498
James VI and I, King of Scotland, King of
        England 25–6, 59, 61, 272, 361, 478, 737
Jameson, Fredric 5, 783
Janus 167, 168
Jardine, Lisa 17, 503
Javitch, Daniel 410, 510
Jean de Sponde 630
Jed, Stephanie H. 370
Jenkins, Raymond 22
Jenyson, Thomas 69, 75, 76
Jesuits 38, 133, 795
Jewel, John, Bishop of Salisbury 34, 429
John, Saint 284, 495
John of Garland 407
Johnson, F. R. 121, 643–4, 655, 656
Johnson, Lynn Stanley 166, 171, 173, 581
Johnson, Samuel 126, 141*n*, 646, 721, 722
Johnston, Robert 127
Jonah 491
Jones, H. S. V. 282
Jones, William 21, 25
Jonson, Ben 27, 127, 129–32, 134, 645, 647, 671,
        720–1, 723, 737–8, 802
Jortin, John 646–7, 648, 658*n*
Jowett, Bejamin 659*n*
Joyce, James 456
Judith 488
Judson, Alexander C. 27, 107, 110, 130, 135–7, 140
Julius Caesar 426
Jung, Carl Gustav 782
Junius, Franciscus 485, 486, 496
justice 44–5, 48, 53–4, 60, 268, 272, 279–86, 289, 324,
        382, 433, 456, 476–7, 506–8, 517–18, 525–6,
        534–5, 550, 621–2, 739, 747–8, 767, 795
Juvenal 576

Kant, Immanuel 522
Kaplan, L. 281
Kaske, Carol V. 360, 489, 490, 727, 728
Kay, Dennis 248, 250, 664, 665
Keating, Geoffrey see Céitinn, Seathrún
Keats, John 376, 673–4, 675, 677, 678, 689, 724,
    727, 728
Kellogg, Robert 654
Kelsey, Lin 109, 239, 244, 464, 507, 798
Kennedy, William J. 1, 277, 467, 614, 615
Kennelly, Brendan 680
Kent, county of 18–19, 20, 24, 27, 37–8, 110, 131
Kent, William 647, 695–9i
Keppel-Jones, David 200
Kermode, Frank 334
Kerrigan, John 547
Kiberd, Declan 803
kincogish 316, 329
King, Andrew 168, 172, 451, 564, 598
King, Jessie M. 698, 704–7
King, John N. 45, 46, 150, 499, 563, 590,
    750, 751
Kinsman, R. S. 463, 590–1
Kipling, Rudyard 796
Kirk(e), Edward 17, 175 see also E. K.
Kitchin, George William 653–4
Klein, L. M. 239, 249, 250, 787
Klemp, P. J. 242, 243
Klimt, Gustav 707
Klingelhöfer, Eric 13
Klotz, E. L. 118
Knapp, Jeffrey 137, 797, 798
Knevet, Ralph 361–2
Knights Templar 309
Knox, John 58, 119, 488
Koller, Katherine 467
Krieg, Joann 652
Krier, Theresa M. 496, 787–8
Kristeva, Julia 787
Kucich, G. 669, 671, 673–4, 675, 677, 678
Kuin, Roger 719, 728, 769
Kundera, Milan 337
Kyd, Thomas 15

La Marche, Olivier de 454
La Perrière, Guillaume de 438
La Primaudaye, Pierre de 630
Lacan, Jacques 779, 784–6, 787, 788
Lamb, Charles 673, 674
Lamb, Mary Ellen 765
Landino, Cristoforo 453, 504
Landrum, G. W. 486–7, 495
Landseer, Sir Edwin Henry 713
Lane, John 27, 569n
Lane, Robert 162
Lang, Andrew 707–8

Langer, Susanne 759
Langland, William 451, 468, 492, 563
language 37, 163, 183–4, 187, 317, 367–82
    see also Irish language
Lanyer, Amelia 765
Laqueur, Thomas 761
Latin prosody 185–7, 356–7, 385, 395–6
Latomus, Bartholomew 429
Laura 263, 295, 311n, 613, 614, 615
    see also Petrarch
laureation 4, 126–8, 132, 138–9, 179, 188, 198, 219,
    221, 241, 247, 250, 252, 293, 381–2, 417,
    463, 468, 470, 472, 474, 477, 568, 594,
    665–6, 750, 785
Law 53, 55, 94–5, 102, 187, 281, 283, 315–25, 328,
    489–91, 494, 523, 548, 739, 794, 799, 801
    see also Brehon law
Lawrence, Jason 153, 612
Leander 297
Leda 310
Lee, Sir Sidney 249
Le Fèvre de la Boderie, Guy 630
Legouis, Emile 136
Leicester, Earl of see Robert Dudley, Earl of
    Leicester
Leitch, William 712
Leland, John 358, 539
Lévi-Strauss, Claude 447
Lewis, C. S. 46, 109, 136, 288, 335, 541, 727, 728, 748,
    759, 792–3, 802–3
Lille, Alain de 340
Lily, William 425
Limerick 22, 26, 92
Lister, David 321
Litchfield, Mary E. 654, 659n
Livy 17, 370, 719
Lodge, Thomas 15, 245, 587
Loewenstein, Joseph 119, 121, 138, 153, 155, 232, 764
Loftus, Adam, Archbishop of Armagh 75
London 14, 15, 16, 17, 18, 19, 24, 25, 26, 27, 37, 47–8,
    62n, 68, 70, 77, 80, 110, 111, 115, 116, 118,
    119, 309, 314, 316, 347, 361, 452, 454, 455,
    477, 506, 587, 643, 644, 659n, 722
Longinus 450
Lorde, Alice 19
Lorris, Guillaume de 451
Lotichius, Petrus 580, 581–3
Louise de Savoie 626
love 162, 165–6, 180–3, 187–93, 241–7, 256–68,
    294–302, 305–10, 344, 406, 410–13, 451,
    474–5, 508–15, 531, 577–9, 582–3, 590–600,
    606–7, 613–16, 627–30, 757–9, 762–3
Lowell, James Russell 758, 769
Lownes, Humphrey 120
Lownes, Matthew 7, 26, 117, 120, 314, 479, 639,
    640, 646, 649

Luborsky, Ruth S. 175*n*, 586, 693, 695
Lucan 174, 623, 735
Lucian 548
Lucretius 533, 546, 787
Luther, Martin 302, 494, 523, 631*n*
Lydgate, John 368, 373, 451, 719

McCabe, Richard A. 18, 28, 46, 61, 137–8, 169–70,
     188, 192, 240, 316, 324, 325, 326, 371,
     380, 400, 544–5, 548–9, 654, 751,
     767–8, 802
MacCaffrey, Isabel G. 171, 242, 274, 283, 727,
     759, 781
MacCarthy-Morrogh, Michael 92, 95–100
McCoy, Richard 543–4
MacDonalds of Rathlin Island 90
McEachern, Claire 495, 496, 761
McElderry, B. R. 367, 373, 719, 720, 722
McGuinness, Frank 679–80, 800–2
Machiavelli, Niccolò 49–54, 120
McKenzie, D. F. 116, 117–18, 121
McKeon, Michael 67
McKerrow, R. B. 118, 121
McLane, Paul E. 20, 149, 465, 575, 591
McLaren, A. N. 56, 58, 59–60, 751, 764
Maclean, Hugh 222
MacLehose, Sophia H. 654
Macleod, Mary 654
Macrin, Jean Salmon 630
MacWorth, Humphrey 321
Magennis, Hugh 79
magic 135, 242–3, 492, 510, 539, 562, 609, 708–9,
     781–2, 785
Magnusson, Lynne 181
Magrath, Meiler, Archbishop of Cashel 80
Malby, Sir Nicholas 75, 80
Maley, Willy 101, 140–1, 283, 323, 325–7, 371, 739,
     761, 793
Mallette, Richard 46, 239, 283, 500, 761
Malone, Edmond 142, 649
Malory, Sir Thomas 369
Malta 217
Manlius Torquatus 522
Mantua 448
Mantuan, Giovan Battista Spagnoli 19, 162, 167–8,
     174, 452, 466, 720, 574–81, 589, 590
Manutius, Aldus 429
Manzzoni, Alessandro 540
Marguerite de Navarre, Queen 621, 630
Marinelli, Peter 606
Markham, Gervase 723
Marleburrough, Henry 314
Marlowe, Christopher 24, 165, 265
Marot, Clément 150–2, 154–5, 162, 174, 230, 358–9,
     465–7, 602, 616, 620, 625–8, 631*n*,
     632*n*, 638

marriage 24–5, 178, 192, 207, 237, 256–68, 274–5,
     278, 293, 305–10, 353, 356, 405–6,
     490, 492, 523, 586, 589, 592, 598, 736,
     742, 760
Mars 342
Marston, John 624
Martial 503
Martin, Ellen E. 232
Marxism 133, 139, 140, 226, 742, 785–6, 801
Mary I, Queen of England 31, 32, 39, 54, 93,
     541, 737
Mary Stuart, Queen of Scots 5, 22, 25, 34, 58, 59,
     60, 279, 281, 478, 490, 622, 750
Masten, Jeffrey 182, 183, 195*n*
Matsuo, Masatsugu 643–5, 657
Matthew, John 26
Maximus of Tyre 450
Maxwell, J. C. 285
May, Steven 725
Medea 219
Medici, Catherine de 621
Medway, River 178, 275, 278, 356, 763
Melanchthon, Philipp 423, 424, 425, 427, 429–30,
     434–5, 489
melancholy 127, 134, 310, 347
Melchizidek, King of Salem 492
Memmi, Albert 799
Menander Rhetor 404, 407, 422, 432
Menelaus 289
Merchant Taylors' Company/School 14, 15, 30–1,
     40, 132, 142, 425, 622, 623, 722
metre 9, 132, 153–4, 167, 173, 185, 213–14, 305, 356–7,
     385–402, 429, 468, 503–4
     see also Latin prosody
Meun, Jean de 451
Meyer, Sam 432
Michelangelo Buonarroti 351, 688
Middleton, Henry 119
Mignault, Claude 438, 440
Miller, David Lee 121, 138, 140, 171, 288, 631*n*, 658*n*,
     728, 761, 762–3, 765, 768, 777, 785, 786–7
Millican, C. B. 18, 722
Mills, J. Leath 545
Milton, John 25, 132, 134, 138, 190–1, 209, 223, 232,
     251, 328, 376, 449–50, 453, 470, 476, 480,
     494, 643, 650, 664, 666–9, 672, 673, 675,
     677, 724, 739, 740, 746, 757
Minerva 229, 516
Mirror for Magistrates 222, 224
Mohl, Ruth 139
Moliere, Jean-Baptiste Poquelin 39
monarchism 53–9, 60, 61, 274–5, 284, 362, 385, 387,
     422, 496–7, 509, 544, 545, 749
Montague, John 679, 680
Montrose, Louis Adrian 166, 172, 219, 233*n*, 241,
     518, 749–50, 751, 764–6

Moore-Gilbert, Bart 803
More, Henry 668
More, Sir Thomas 249, 369, 372, 446
Morgan, Hiram 14, 52, 88, 90, 94
Mornay, Philippe Duplessis de 360
Morris, Richard 646, 648, 649, 652, 743
Morris, William 699–700, 704
Moryson, Fynes 323
Moschus 248, 352, 357, 515
Moseley, Humphrey 668
Mosellanus, Petrus 424, 425, 435
Moses 492, 494, 541
Mulcaster, Richard 15, 109–10, 400, 622, 623, 722
Mulla 244, 417, 479
Munday, Anthony 361
Muret, Marc-Antoine 628
Musaeus 352, 448

Nagel, David and Ellin 19
Narcissism 170, 262–3, 297, 298–301, 308, 466, 514,
        786, 788
narratology 199–214, 216, 226, 271, 274–8, 294,
        297–300, 391–2, 409–15, 421–2, 431–4,
        445–7, 450–6, 469–72, 542, 556–67, 609,
        686–7, 760–6, 768, 781–2, 784–6
Nashe, Thomas 24, 110, 219, 265, 467, 505
Needham, Sir Robert 114, 475, 659n
Neo-Latin literature 153, 358, 404–5, 408, 413, 454,
        573–84
Neo-Platonism 171, 241–2, 243, 246, 261, 268n, 276,
        294–5, 370, 380, 453, 535n, 626, 630, 685,
        778–9, 783
Netherlands 150–2, 154, 155, 157–8, 282
Neusetter, Erasmus 580
New World, discovery of 181, 322
Ni Chuilleanáin, Eiléan 765, 767, 769
Niccols, Richard 665–6
Nielsen, Kay 704
Nimrod 551
Nogarola, Ginevra and Isotta 581
Nohrnberg, James 500, 516, 728, 759, 782–3
Norbrook, David G. 40, 46, 151, 163, 169, 172, 666,
        750, 752n
Norris, Sir Henry 16, 18, 19
Norris, Sir John (Black Jack) 21, 65, 68, 83, 99,
        113, 678
Norris, Sir Thomas 17, 26, 65, 68, 77, 83
Norton, William, printer 119
Nowell, Alexander, Dean of St Paul's 15, 16
Nowell, Robert 15, 16, 17, 110
Nugent, John 82

O'Brien, Murrogh 18, 20, 767
O'Byrne, Feagh MacHugh 320; O'Byrne clan 20,
        68, 278
O'Callaghan, Michelle 643, 666

O'Connell, Michael 541, 734, 735, 748
O'Connor clan 89, 94
Octavian see Augustus Caesar
O'Donnell, C. Patrick 654
O'Donnell, Sir Hugh 78
Olaus Magnus 323
Olivier de la Marche 630
Olympus 342–3
O'More clan 89, 94
O'Neill, Sir Brian MacPhelim 90
O'Neill, Hugh, Earl of Tyrone 26, 68, 79, 131, 320
O'Neill, Shane 94
O'Neill, Turlough Luineach 68
Oram, William A. 107, 112, 121, 139, 140, 218, 221–2,
        226, 232, 244, 249, 472, 654, 728
Ormond, see Butler, Thomas, 10th Earl of Ormond
Orpheus 297, 310, 312, 448
Oruch, Jack B. 355
Orwin, Thomas 120
Osgood, Charles Grosvenor 722
ottava rima 390–1, 394
Oure, River 278
Ovid 116, 169, 223, 224, 229, 244, 248, 397–8, 404–5,
        426, 436, 449, 450, 453, 456, 468, 475,
        503–4, 516, 518, 574, 629
Owens, Judith 121, 222, 764
Oxford 427

Padelford, F. M. 375, 378, 656, 657
Page, William, publisher 117
Painter, William 630
Palgrave, Francis Turner 247
Palmer, Patricia 802
Panofsky, Erwin 690, 759
Panton, John 325
paronomasia 430, 432, 445
paratexts 1, 7, 68, 121n, 141, 163, 175, 216n, 275, 350,
        405–6, 469, 476, 691, 716n
Parker, Agnes Miller 698, 708
Parker, Matthew, Archbishop of Canterbury 116
Parker, Patricia 287, 451, 454, 675, 728, 763, 782, 783
Parnassus 453
parody 6, 210, 464, 493
Paster, Gail Kern 761, 769, 779, 780, 781
patronage 25, 55–6, 107–15, 119, 215–16, 465–6, 468,
        478, 575–6, 580, 595, 697
Patterson, Annabel 167, 169, 171, 172, 506
Paul, Saint 346, 488, 492, 494–5, 496, 498–9
Paulin, Tom 793
Payne, Robert 101, 323
Peacham, Henry 24, 425, 431
Peacock, Lucy 677
Peele, George 24, 245
Pelham, Mary 20
Pelham, William 19–20
Pembroke, Countess of see Sidney, Mary

Pembroke College (Cambridge) 40, 110, 128
Penshurst (Kent) 131
Percy, Henry, 9th Earl of Northumberland 112
Percy, Thomas 722
periphrasis 430, 432, 445
permissio 425
Perrot, Sir John 21
personation 205–9
Peter, Saint 489
Peterson, R. S. 109, 139, 233*n*, 464, 473, 507
Petrarch, Francesco 150–1, 162, 215–16, 257–63,
    294–5, 298, 374, 377, 452, 467, 509, 587,
    602–4, 613–16, 623, 638
  ES and 16, 40, 110, 116, 152–5, 223–33, 248, 312,
    356, 546–7, 686, 691
Phaer, Thomas 389, 397
Philip II, King of Spain 39, 92, 279
Philips, Ambrose 669, 670
Phillips, Edward 127
Phillips, James E. 751
Piccolomini, Alessandro 322
Pickersgill, F. R. 713*i*, 713–14
Pigman, G. W. III 248, 250, 494
Pitt, Joseph 676
Pius V, Pope 149
Plato 6, 41, 131, 243, 268*n*, 312, 361, 433, 468,
    499–51, 516, 521–33, 535*n*, 629
  and allegory 442, 449, 450, 451, 454–6, 455
  and psychoanalytical criticism 777, 778
Platonic love 456, 499
Platonic philosophy 521–33, 535*n*
  see also Neo-Platonism
Plautus 503
Pléiade 357, 378, 424
Plotinus 787
Plutarch 116, 120, 534
Pocock, J. G. A. 61–2
poet laureateship see laureation
Pole, Reginald, Cardinal 51
Poliziano, Angelo 352, 357–8
Pollock, Frederick 323
Ponet, John 54
Ponsonby, William, publisher 23–4, 27, 114–20,
    217–36, 350, 354–6, 358–60, 466–7,
    475, 479
Pope, Alexander 78, 240, 493, 669, 670, 671, 695,
    721, 723, 725, 740
Pope, Emma Field 367, 368, 369, 373,
    377, 380
Popham, Sir John 97
Porphyry 450
Portugal 217
Pre-Raphaelites 697–703, 713–14
Prescott, Anne Lake 263, 359, 454, 490, 611, 630,
    654, 769
Priam 289, 517, 560

Prior, Matthew 670
Privy Council 26, 59–60, 77, 81–3, 96–8, 278
prophecy 36, 39, 204, 215, 283, 338, 344–5, 381, 470,
    490–1, 505–6, 511–12, 517, 542–4, 623, 735,
    748, 786
Provost, F. 142
Psalms 224, 354, 487, 488, 490, 491, 496, 497,
    500n
psychoanalytical criticism 42, 310*n*, 323, 496–7,
    749, 765, 775–88, 794, 798
Ptolemy 243, 342
publishers, of ES 115–21, 637–63
  see also Lownes, Matthew; Ponsonby,
    William
Pugh, Syrithe 450, 595, 596, 598
Purcell, Henry 510
Puttenham, George 241, 257, 386, 407, 408, 412,
    417, 425, 588, 594
Pyle, Howard 701
Pythagoras 379, 515, 777

Quilligan, Maureen 445, 668, 764–5, 782, 783,
    787
Quinn, D. B. 88, 90, 95, 321, 327, 329
Quint, David 289, 611, 735
Quintilian 421, 420, 427, 428, 429
Quitslund, Jon A. 142*n*, 180, 188, 532, 583

Rackham, Arthur 704
Radcliffe, David Hill 132, 142, 670, 671, 675, 677,
    721, 724, 744
Radcliffe, Thomas, 3rd Earl of Sussex 89, 94
Rae, W. D. 587
Rahe, P. 51
Raleigh, Carew 738
Raleigh, Sir Walter 16, 23, 41–2, 244, 322, 489, 496,
    538–9, 541, 544, 549, 737–8
  and ES 24, 111–16, 126, 130, 135, 239, 249, 245,
    417, 595
  and Faerie Queene 24, 112, 130, 199, 200, 202,
    204, 216*n*, 271, 272, 273, 290, 355, 469
  and Ireland 20–2, 92, 321, 798
  as poet 120, 251, 424, 455–6, 469, 472, 476, 613
Rambuss, Richard 14, 67, 126, 139, 140, 221, 252*n*,
    750, 766
Ramus, Peter 424, 427–31
Rasmussen, Carl J. 151, 152, 224
Rathborne, Isabel E. 550–1
Rathlin Island 90
Reid, Robert L. 778
Renwick, William L. 137, 218, 221, 233*n*, 326, 327,
    723, 743
republicanism 18, 48–54, 55–62, 435, 504, 573, 675,
    737, 739–40, 742, 749
retractation 294, 296–9, 302, 304, 308, 310*n*,
    358, 478

Revelation, book of 40, 42, 43, 44, 119, 150, 151, 152, 154, 156, 230, 440, 444, 447, 449, 450, 456, 486, 511, 562, 566, 794,
Reynoldes, Timothy 74
Reynolds, Sir Joshua 709
rhetoric 210–11, 216, 389, 420–36, 396, 454, 466–7
rhyme royal 303
Rich, Barnaby 21, 323
Richardson, David A. 139
Richlin, Amy 182
Ridgway, Christopher 327
Rinaldo 289
Ringler, William 725
Rix, H. D. 431–2
Robortello, Francesco 583n
Roche, Maurice, 6th Viscount Fermoy 22, 23, 24, 77
Roche, Richard 23
Roche, Thomas P. Jr. 264, 276, 521, 654, 759, 781
Roche, William 23
Rogers, Daniel 19
Roman Catholicism 31–5, 37–9, 52, 54, 88, 93, 123–4, 134, 136, 138, 149–51, 165, 172, 200, 280, 282, 317, 330n, 448–9, 457–8, 486–8, 490, 495, 507, 545, 547–8, 574, 581, 592, 620–2, 631n, 679–80, 739, 742, 744, 797
Roman de la Rose 451
Rome, ancient 50, 151, 154, 224, 230, 272, 289, 539, 543, 546, 549, 623–4, 625, 629
    see also Du Bellay, Joachim
Romney, George 709
Ronsard, Pierre de 248, 614, 621, 626, 628–9, 631n
Rosalind 128
Rosamond 245
Rossetti, Christina 677
Rouille, Guillaume 439, 441
Royde-Smith, Naomi Gwladys 654
Roydon, Matthew 238, 251, 650
Rubel, Veré L. 368, 370, 374, 377
Ruggiero 289
Rushdie, Salman 799
Ruskin, John 676
Russell, Anne, Countess of Warwick 114, 245, 294, 310n, 356
Russell, Francis, 2nd Earl of Bedford 114

Sabinus, Georgius 580, 582
Sacks, Peter M. 248, 250, 310n
Sackville, Thomas, Baron Buckhurst 113
Sacré, Dirk 574
Sagon, François 625
Said, Edward W. 792, 793, 796
St George, Henry 324
St German, Christopher 323, 330
Saintleger (St Leger), Sir Warham 78, 82, 90, 91, 92, 96, 99

Saintsbury, George 725
Salluste, Guillaume 426, 612, 719
San Giuseppi, Sebastiano di 20
Sannazaro, Jacopo 117, 466
Sansovino, Francesco 66, 117
Sapience 452, 487–9, 493
Sato, Haruo 643–5, 657
Satterthwaite, Alfred W. 150, 152
Saturn 338, 340, 342
Savonarola, Girolamo 151
Saxons 211
Scaliger, Julius Caesar 404, 407, 408, 432
Schiller, Johann C. F. von 240
Schleiner, Louise 175–6
Schoenfeldt, Michael 761, 777, 778, 780, 781, 787
Schwartz, Kathryn 281, 766, 788
Scotland 5, 61, 90, 134, 478
Scott, Sir Walter 326, 651, 722
Scott, William Bell 713, 720
Scylla 409
Scythians 548–9, 551
Seckerstone, Roger 24
Sedulius 574
Seneca 522, 526
Septuagint 486
Servatius Rogerus 182
Servius 3, 407, 512, 734–5
Seton, John 427
Seven Deadly Sins 213
sexuality 45, 138, 179–84, 514, 751, 757–63, 766, 767, 775–6, 782, 786–8
Shaheen, Naseeb 485, 486–7
Shakespeare, William 27, 133, 186, 440, 448, 451, 456, 457, 495, 650, 669, 673
    and critical theory 374, 726, 737, 759, 780
    ES and 223, 245, 249, 256, 259, 263, 264, 278, 372, 374
    poems 241, 248–9, 259, 264–5, 265
Shannon, Laurie 182
Shelley, Percy Bysshe 376, 672–3, 674, 680, 724
Shenstone, William 671, 672
Shepherd, Simon 133, 139, 140
Sheppard, Samuel 361, 362, 669
Sherry, Richard 425
Shields, Thomas Frederick 713
Shore, David R. 171, 239, 240, 242
Short, Peter 120
Shropp, James 23
Sidney, Sir Henry, Lord Deputy of Ireland 18, 69, 90–1, 94, 102n, 128, 320, 679
Sidney, Mary, Countess of Pembroke 111, 113, 114, 119, 221, 225, 238, 245, 250, 251, 359, 487, 625, 639, 650, 689
Sidney, Sir Philip 3, 5, 40, 119, 120, 132, 161, 247, 250, 256, 296, 323, 358–9, 372, 387, 396,

Sidney, Sir Philip *(cont.)*
    430–1, 454, 467, 477, 520, 588–9, 620–1,
    625, 631*n*
  and Elizabeth I 65, 117, 592
  and ES 18, 19, 108, 111, 113, 119, 120, 128–9, 130–1,
    180, 184, 468–9
  Defence of Poesy 25, 108, 163, 185, 242, 317, 352–3,
    540, 587, 684, 720, 735, 798
Silberman, Lauren 276, 763, 765, 788
Simeoni, Gabriele 441
Simier, Jean de 621
Sinai, Mount 494
Sinfield, Alan 798
Singleton, Hugh 117, 161, 162, 465, 658*n*, 695
Sirach (Ecclesiasticus) 488
Sixtus V, Pope 621
Skelton, John 368, 463, 483, 590, 591, 594, 720, 626
Smerwick 20, 68, 69, 77, 134, 282, 320, 798
Smith, Bruce R. 171, 779
Smith, J. C. 656, 657, 659*n*
Smith, Sir Thomas 17–18, 56–62, 60, 90, 94, 466,
    468, 473
Smith, Thomas, Jr. 17
Smith, William 665
Snackenborg, Helena, Marquise of
    Northampton 114
Snyder, Susan 44, 523
Socrates 522, 527
Solomon 488, 489–90
Somerset, Edward, 4th Earl of Worcester 25, 115
sonnets
  dedicatory 21, 22, 25, 111–13, 114, 120, 273, 469,
    472, 476, 640, 644
  Spenserian 258–9, 268*n*, 303–4
  see also *Amoretti*; *Ruines of Rome*; *Ruines of
    Time*; *Visions of Bellay*; *Visions of
    Petrarch*; *Visions of the Worlds Vanitie*
Southey, Robert 673
Spain 20, 35, 38, 279, 317, 320, 321
Spens, Janet 727, 728, 781
Spenser, Alice, Lady Strange 114, 473
Spenser, Anne, Lady Compton and
    Mounteagle 114
Spenser, Edmund, life
  early life/ education
    birth and early life 13–15, 16–17, 83, 140
    forbears 14–15, 211, 407
    parents/ siblings 14, 26
      see also Spenser entries
    Merchant Taylors' School 14–16, 109, 132, 331,
      425–7
    Pembroke College (Cambridge) 16–18, 30–1,
      40, 110, 117–18, 135, 142, 427–8
  marriages/ children
    Maccabaeus Chylde (first wife) 13, 19, 24,
      135, 257

  Elizabeth Boyle (second wife) 14, 24, 27, 132,
    138, 142, 247, 344
  children
    Katherine (son of ES and Chylde) 19
    Peregrine (son of ES and Boyle) 24, 26
    Sylvanus (son of ES and Chylde) 19, 23
  grandchildren
    Spenser, William (ES's grandson)
      137–8, 326
    Spenser, Katherine (ES's grand-daughter) 19
    Spenser, Hugolin (ES's great-grandson) 129
  in Ireland
    early connections 17–22
    assistant to Lodowick Bryskett 21, 65, 70,
      74, 113
    planter in Munster 22–3, 26, 27, 86–105
    sheriff of Cork 26, 102
  employment and patronage
    William Cecil, Lord Burghley *see* Cecil, William
    Robert Dudley, Earl of Leicester *see* Dudley,
      Robert
    Lord Grey de Wilton 20–1, 25, 65–75, 102,
      111–13, 320, 743
      see also Grey, Arthur
    Sir Henry Norris 16–17, 18, 26
    Sir John Norris 21
    Sir Henry Sidney 18, 69, 111, 128, 132, 320, 358
      see also Sidney, Sir Henry
    Mary Sidney, Countess of Pembroke 111–14,
      119, 221, 238, 250–1
      see also *Doleful Lay of Clorinda*; Sidney, Mary
    Sir Philip Sidney 18, 19, 108, 111, 113, 119, 120,
      128–9, 130–1, 180, 184, 468–9
      see also *Astrophel*; Sidney, Sir Philip
    John Young, Bishop of Rochester 18, 40, 110,
      135, 722
  pension 22, 24, 27, 37–8, 112, 127, 674
  politics 48–65, 86–105, 538–52, 792–805
  religious outlook 35–47, 485–500
  death
    death and funeral 27, 115, 127, 333–4, 336, 568
    memorial monument 27–8, 107, 125, 131
    memorial elegies 27, 334
  biographers 125–45
Spenser, Edmund, works
  Amoretti 13, 14, 24, 114, 116, 120, 134, 237, 247,
    256–65, 267, 272–4, 278, 353, 355, 356, 359,
    377, 392, 393, 394, 431, 433, 474–5, 490,
    492, 497–8
  Anacreontics 394, 406, 628
  Astrophel 7, 25, 237–9, 242, 245–53, 259, 261,
    359–60, 377, 389, 394, 406, 474, 598,
    625, 664
  Axiochus 120, 360, 361
  Colin Clouts Come Home Againe 24, 25, 108, 112,
    114, 120, 135, 138, 174, 237–47, 252, 273–4,

288, 351, 359, 360, 375, 377, 393, 416–17,
   432, 463–5, 467, 472–80, 689
   see also Colin Clout
Complaints 5, 23–4, 48, 109, 114, 117, 120, 150,
   155, 156, 216–36, 237, 245, 347, 350,
   353–4, 356, 358–60, 393, 409, 440, 466,
   468, 472–3
Daphnaïda 24, 117, 120, 219, 231–3
Dolefull Lay of Clorinda 237, 238, 239, 250–1,
   359, 360, 361
Faerie Queene 5, 19, 21, 61, 113, 114, 130, 137, 157,
   178–80, 185, 198–217, 252*n*, 271–92, 304,
   306, 309, 319, 322, 333–4, 339–40, 354–62,
   372, 373, 375, 377–82, 387–93, 396, 397,
   408–16, 437–61, 449–57, 462, 465,
   469–70, 472, 475–6, 479, 486–8, 538–52
   Book 1 (Holiness) 23, 39, 42–5, 200–1, 203,
      205, 209, 211, 271, 357, 445, 446, 469, 470,
      488, 495, 497, 512, 523, 540, 653,
   Book 2 (Temperance) 23, 44–5, 190, 200, 201,
      204, 209, 210, 271, 286, 357, 382, 454, 455,
      512, 513, 525–30, 567, 611, 668, 677, 762
   Book 3 (Chastity) 23, 44–5, 201–2, 204–6,
      209, 210–11, 271, 283, 295, 357, 412–13,
      495–8, 543, 597, 606, 667–8, 784
   Book 4 (Friendship) 4, 44, 157, 178–9, 193,
      274–9, 283, 284, 285, 324, 476–7, 516
   Book 5 (Justice) 5, 44–5, 59, 60, 279–85, 287,
      288, 456, 550, 526, 534–5, 622, 669, 739,
      747, 748, 795
   Book 6 (Courtesy) 44, 284–8
   characters 205–9
   Acrasia 8, 201–2, 205, 210, 213, 492, 513,
      525–30, 610–11, 671, 675, 687, 762,
      776, 793
   Adonis 118, 157, 210, 213, 241, 248–9, 253*n*,
      265, 281, 382, 433, 456, 513, 515, 532, 533,
      535, 597, 607, 626, 630, 688, 787
   Agape 276, 598
   Aladine 285, 286
   Aldus 285
   Alma 2, 208, 392, 456, 545, 546, 686, 761,
      777–80, 786
   Amoret 202, 205, 212, 275–6, 281, 414–15,
      433, 514–15, 597, 644, 676, 712, 713*i*, 714,
      760, 766, 784
   Archimago 42, 43, 200, 201, 203–4, 205,
      209–10, 433, 446, 510–12, 566, 670, 678,
      696, 712
   Artegall, Sir 48, 58, 60, 208, 212, 275,
      278–84, 286, 289, 340, 356, 362, 409, 412,
      489, 514, 516, 528, 534–5, 543, 545, 606,
      622, 669, 670, 674, 676, 739, 745, 765,
      788, 795
   Arthur 2, 6, 9, 43–4, 58, 60, 200–9, 211–12,
      214–15, 232, 271–2, 277, 284, 285, 287, 290,

392, 411, 452–6, 472, 489–90, 492, 497,
   545–6, 550, 513–14, 523–5, 528, 542, 545–7,
   550, 697, 699*i*, 710*i*, 710–11, 713*i*, 714, 718,
   726, 734, 786, 787
Astraea 150, 226, 228, 283–4
Ate 272, 276, 277, 516
Belge 282, 456, 523, 550
Bellodant 281
Belphoebe 7, 201, 206, 210, 212, 213, 214,
   215, 245, 411, 433, 456, 489, 496–7, 514,
   515, 529, 595, 607–8, 712, 760, 764
Blandamour 275–7, 528
Blatant Beast 5, 131, 207, 272, 284–9, 347,
   373, 434, 477, 516, 599, 612, 712, 738
Bonfont 2, 59, 284, 477, 737, 795
Braggadocchio 201, 210, 214–15, 277, 289,
   411, 529, 567
Bregog 244, 417, 595
Briana 285, 434
Brigadore 289
Britomart 2, 45, 199–204, 205, 208, 211, 212,
   215, 271, 275, 281–2, 289, 356, 382, 409,
   412, 414–15, 470, 495, 505, 514, 516, 528,
   534–5, 542–4, 560–1, 597, 605, 606, 654,
   670, 676, 688, 697, 698*i*, 704, 706*i*,
   712–14, 759–60, 764, 766, 783–6, 788
Bruin 287
Burbon, 279, 622
Busirane 2, 205, 213, 356, 414–15, 513–14,
   686–8, 704, 706–7*i*, 712, 761, 762
Calepine 285–7, 676
Calidore, Sir 5, 175, 286–8, 382, 415, 434,
   516, 517, 557, 599, 610, 611–13, 624
Cambel 272, 275–8, 559, 609, 610, 699, 700*i*
Cambina 275–6, 277, 609, 699
Canacee 275, 276, 610, 699
Care 157
Chrysogone 433, 497, 514, 515, 532, 535
Claribell 277, 528
Contemplation 201, 202, 205, 211, 445, 452,
   497, 512, 541–2, 544, 564, 630
Corceca 497
Coridon 287
Crudor 285, 434
Cupid 169, 261, 264–5, 295, 297, 298, 352–3,
   356, 414, 417, 433, 510, 514, 515, 597, 627–9,
   693–4
Cymochles 432, 513, 528–30
Cynthia 6–7, 241, 243–7, 267, 338, 347, 417,
   474, 508, 509, 595, 600, 768
Despair 42, 43, 45, 200, 206, 207, 209, 210,
   389, 432, 433, 445, 493, 523, 529, 568,
   712, 738
Detraction 272, 284, 285
Diana 214, 335, 339, 416, 433, 508, 515, 518,
   590, 592–3, 627, 759

Spenser, Edmund, works (*cont.*)

Duessa 38, 39, 42–3, 58–61, 157, 209–10, 272, 279, 281, 379, 382, 486, 488, 490, 493, 511, 540, 622, 667, 675, 712, 736–7, 745, 746, 795

'Egalitarian' Giant 279, 280, 534

Enuie 162, 272, 284, 285

Errour 202–3, 231, 414, 445, 456, 510–11, 540, 667, 671, 761

Ferraugh 277–8

Ferramont 277–8

Fidelia 495, 711–12*i*

Florimell 43, 199, 201–2, 232, 274–7, 281–2, 410–11, 523, 606

Florimell, False 208, 210, 276, 277, 282, 516–17, 534

Geryoneo 279, 550, 699, 701*i*

Graces 5, 6, 163, 175, 243, 243, 288, 352, 356, 415, 434, 446, 453, 476, 477, 517, 599, 699, 701

Gloriana 4, 7, 8, 38, 109, 215–16, 279, 280, 281, 284, 285, 362, 410, 416, 444, 446, 452, 453, 455, 487–90, 496, 523, 561, 599, 735

Grantorto 280, 282

Guyon, Sir 2, 8, 44, 45, 138, 200–1, 203–4, 207–10, 271, 277, 284, 289, 414, 433, 492, 512–13, 523, 525, 528–9, 542, 545, 566–7, 610–12, 677, 749, 762, 778, 780

Hellenore 206, 211, 412, 559–60, 597

Irena 280, 282, 479, 516

Isis 281, 534–5

Jove/ Jupiter 228, 229, 267, 308, 335, 337–42, 343–4, 346, 347, 416, 510–11, 514, 517–18, 535, 551

Kirkrapine 39

Malbecco 206–8, 209, 215, 412–13, 445, 559–60, 568, 605, 696

Malecasta 203, 209, 210, 513, 515, 597, 606, 688

Maleffort 285, 286

Maleger 209, 528, 783

Malengin 283

Malfont 2, 59, 284, 288, 446, 477, 737, 795

Mammon 203, 209, 414, 433, 492, 529, 567, 568

Marinell 199, 202, 212, 274, 275, 414, 765–6

Matilda 287

Meliboe 5, 286, 287–8, 465, 477, 507–8, 517, 612

Mercilla 7, 58–60, 279, 281, 284, 477, 746, 795

Mercury 228, 338

Merlin 7, 204–5, 211, 215, 505–6, 542–4, 608, 696–9, 698*i*, 699*i*

Molanna 339, 479

Mordant 492

Mutabilitie see *Two Cantos of Mutabilitie*

Nature 264, 335–6, 339–47, 489, 517–8, 522, 533–5, 551

Occasion 284, 440

Orgoglio 39, 151, 445, 492, 493, 511, 525

Osiris 534, 550

Palmer 200, 201, 205, 206, 208, 513, 528, 611, 739

Paridell 202, 207, 211, 275, 276, 412, 528, 529, 542, 543, 559–61, 597

Pastorella 131, 277, 285, 448, 612

Perissa 432

Phaedria 210, 391, 432, 493, 671, 675, 676, 793

Phantastes 208, 686

Pollente 279

Priamond 699

Priscilla 286

Proserpina 306, 307

Proteus 283, 674

Pyrocles 524, 528

Radigund 281–2, 534, 699

Redcrosse Knight 40, 42–5, 200–5, 208–12, 231, 271–2, 278, 287, 379–80, 414, 433, 448–9, 453, 454, 489–90, 492–3, 495, 510, 511, 512, 523, 525, 529, 540–2, 544, 545, 562–6, 630, 671, 674, 687, 688, 695, 711*i*, 712, 761

Ruddymane 438, 492

Ryence 542

Salvage Man 286

Satyrane 212, 276, 277, 673

Sclaunder 285, 288, 713–14*i*

Scudamour 157, 200–2, 274–6, 514, 523, 528, 644, 763, 765, 784, 788

Serena 286–7, 434, 630, 676

Soldan 279

Syluanus 214

Talus 5, 48, 279–80, 362, 526, 622, 669, 670, 674, 739, 744, 793, 795

Tanaquill 538

Telamond 275

Timias 208, 245, 276, 285, 286, 434, 524, 595, 607–8, 765, 766

Titan/ Titans 305, 306, 338, 340, 344, 517, 532, 551

Triamond 272, 275–8, 559, 609, 699

Turpine 286–7

Una 38–40, 42–3, 200–1, 203, 205, 208–9, 211, 272, 379, 433, 444, 447, 453, 456–7, 471, 486–8, 490, 492–3, 510–11, 523–4, 540, 563, 565–6, 568, 615, 654, 670, 674, 675, 676, 707, 709–10*i*, 712*i*, 713, 732, 758–60, 764

Zele 59, 281, 795

places

Acidale, Mount 5, 175, 286, 288, 382, 434, 453, 477, 517

Adonis, Garden of 157, 210, 213, 253, 281, 382, 433, 456, 515, 532, 607, 787
Alma, Castle of 2, 208, 392, 545–6, 568, 686, 761, 777–80, 786
Arlo Hill 333, 339, 347, 416, 463, 679
Belgard 449
Bowre of Blisse 45, 138, 210, 388, 528, 529–30, 567, 610, 668, 675, 686–7, 749, 763, 769, 776–7, 781, 783
House of Holiness 39, 44, 488, 495, 497, 512, 523
House of Pride 213, 511, 565–6, 568, 697i
Isis Church 281, 534–5
Jerusalem, Heavenly 200, 205, 541, 545, 624, 687
Mammon, cave of 203, 213, 414, 433, 492, 512, 529, 567, 668
Venus, temple of 275, 276, 281
continuations 670–2
  A Supplement of the Faery Queene (Knevet) 361–2
  Faerie King 362
  Faerie Leveller 362, 642, 669, 739–80
Epithalamion 13, 24, 41, 114, 116, 120, 134, 138, 141, 232, 237, 247, 256–7, 259, 263, 265–70, 273–4, 359, 375, 377–8, 393, 394–5, 404–6, 431–2, 474–5, 498
Fowre Hymnes 25, 114, 205, 237, 273–4, 293–302, 316, 323–7, 356, 378, 393, 408, 409, 451–2, 467–8, 476, 478, 486, 488–9, 493, 499
Latin Poems 153, 243, 353, 357, 367, 368, 370, 381, 387, 574–85
  Ad Ornatissimum Virum 22, 188–92, 193, 573, 581–3
Letters (Three Proper... Two Very Commendable...) 20, 116, 117, 178–99, 468, 587, 639
lost works 178, 349–64, 479
Muiopotmos, or the Fate of the Butterflie 114, 220, 228–9, 234, 409
Prosopopoia. Or Mother Hubberds Tale 7, 22, 60–1, 127, 136, 139, 228, 229, 272, 358, 377, 451, 476, 493
Prothalamion 15, 25, 109, 115, 120, 138, 232, 273, 293–4, 304–10, 356, 393–5, 406, 432, 473, 476–8, 486, 495, 625, 643, 657
Ruines of Rome 150, 229–30, 546, 549, 623, 629
Ruines of Time 114, 156, 223–5, 226–8, 231, 232, 233, 248, 312, 356, 546–7
Shepheardes Calender 1, 2, 5, 14, 19, 24, 37–41, 56, 108–11, 117–18, 125, 128, 131–2, 136, 138–9, 149, 155, 160–80, 192, 219–20, 226, 239–41, 246, 266, 330, 352–3, 371–81, 386–7, 391–2, 397–400, 407, 417, 430–1, 433, 440, 448, 451, 456, 457, 463–6, 468, 474, 478, 489, 500n, 544, 638–9, 684, 687, 690–5, 694i, 700–1, 702–3i, 705i,

Januarye 18, 108–9, 155, 193, 194, 226, 248, 397, 431
Februarie 165, 168, 170, 173, 174
March 165, 167, 169, 173
Aprill 163–5, 164, 167, 170, 172, 397, 399, 432
Maye 22, 99, 163, 165, 166–7, 172, 173
June 165–6, 167, 169, 172, 397, 463
July 22, 166, 167, 169, 173
August 166, 167, 397, 693, 693i, 701, 705i
September 166, 169, 172, 173
October 6, 109, 131, 166, 168–9, 173, 174, 397, 467, 468
November 131, 155, 163, 166, 167, 168, 171, 172, 173, 251, 397
December 162, 166, 167, 169, 171, 173, 174, 175, 248, 397, 404
see also in the main body of the index Colin Clout; Cuddie;E.K.;Hobbinol;Immeritô
'Sonnet to Harvey' 22
'Sonnet to Nennio' 21, 25
Two Cantos of Mutabilitie 7, 23, 120, 233, 290, 293, 333–48, 355, 416, 475, 479, 509, 517–18, 534–5, 550–1, 640–4, 654, 665, 674, 678–80, 713, 727, 728, 768
Teares of the Muses 5, 225–7, 228, 232, 243, 266, 354, 358, 477
Theatre for Worldlings 7, 16, 110, 116, 149–58, 393, 440, 473, 478, 486, 489, 549, 622–4, 638, 684, 686, 691–2, 692i
Vewe of the Present State of Irelande 2, 7, 18, 20, 25–6, 52, 54–5, 120, 129, 134, 136–8, 314–32, 354–5, 360, 361, 479, 486, 547–8
Virgil's Gnat 1, 114, 125, 150, 220, 227–8, 358, 408–9, 506, 671
Visions of Bellay 155, 229, 230, 393–4
Visions of Petrarch 155, 229, 230, 351, 352, 357
Visions of the Worlds Vanitie 227, 229, 230, 440, 686, 687
works attributed to Spenser 360–1
  Brittain's Ida, 361, 637, 641, 642, 645, 650, 657, 658
  attribution generally 637–43
Spenser, Elizabeth (mother of ES) 26
Spenser, Elizabeth (née Boyle, second wife of ES) 13, 14, 24, 27, 132, 138, 142, 247, 257, 267
Spenser, Hamlet 13, 27
Spenser, Hugolin (great-grandson of ES) 129
Spenser, James, Master of Ordnance in Ireland 14, 17, 20, 21
Spenser, John (brother of ES) 14, 17, 20
Spenser, John (father of ES?) 14
Spenser, Sir John (of Althorp) 25, 114, 126, 220
Spenser, Katherine (grand-daughter of ES) 19
Spenser, Maccabaeus (née Chylde, first wife of ES) 19, 24, 135, 257
Spenser, Peregrine (son of ES) 24, 26
Spenser, Sarah (sister of ES, later Travers) 22, 145

Spenser, Sylvanus (son of ES) 19, 23
Spenser, William (grandson of ES) 137–8, 326
Statius 174
Stallworthy, Jon 680
Stanley, Ferdinando, Lord Strange 114, 245
Stanley, William, Lord Mounteagle 114
stanza (Spenserian) 213–15, 242, 258–9, 303–5, 362,
    390–2, 456, 667, 670, 672–6, 723–5
Stationers' Company 106, 115, 117, 119, 479
Steele, Oliver 654
Stein, Harold 221, 222, 655
Steinberg, Glenn 232
Stella 253 see also Devereux, Penelope
Stephens, Dorothy A. 275, 763, 766
Stevens, Alfred 712
Stevens, Forrest Tyler 182
Stewart, Alan 67, 193
Stibarus, Erhardus 79
Stone, Nicholas 27
Stonyhurst 396
Stothard, Thomas 698
Stradling, John 355
Strathmann, E. A. 24
Strawbridge, Hugh 23
Stubbe, Henry 668–9
Stubbes, John 117, 172, 465
Stubbs, George 709*i*, 709–10, 712
Stump, Donald V. 139, 140
Sturm, Johann 422, 426, 429
Sugden, Herbert 367, 372
Sullivan, Garrett, Jr. 769, 780–1
Supremacy, Act of 31
Surrey see Howard, Henry, Earl of
Susenbrotus, Johann 424, 425, 431
Sussex see Radcliffe, Thomas, Earl of
Sutton, John 781
Suzuki, M. 281
Suzuki, Toshiyuki 121, 643–5, 657
Sympson, John 647
synaloepha 388
syncope 214, 388, 430
syncretism 30, 493
synecdoche 430, 445
Synoptic Gospels 498
Syrinx 170

Talon, Omer 423, 424, 427, 429, 430
Tanistry 316
Targoff, Ramie 36–7
Tasso, Torquato 4, 290, 410, 431, 444, 450,
    452–6, 467, 471, 539–40, 604, 609–13,
    734, 735
Tate, Nahum 510
temperance 23, 44–5, 190, 200, 201, 204, 209,
    210, 271, 286, 357, 382, 454, 455, 512, 513,
    525–30, 567, 611, 668, 677, 762

Ten Commandments 491, 494, 541
Tennyson, Alfred Lord 699, 713, 724, 742,
    767, 770*n*
Terence 425, 503, 574
Terpsichore 226
Teskey, Gordon 121, 286, 446, 457, 761
textual criticism (Spenserian) 637–59
Thames, River 178, 223, 225, 275, 278, 305, 306, 307,
    308, 353, 356, 357, 358, 463, 478, 546, 547,
    616, 670, 763
    'Epithalamion Thamesis' 178, 353, 356, 357,
      358, 547
Thebes 342
Theobald, Lewis 646–7
Theocritus 3, 232, 248, 405, 418*n*, 467, 576, 577,
    625, 670, 720
Theseus 284
Thomas Aquinas, Saint 328
Thomas, William 603
Thompson, John 401
Thomson, Clara L. 654
Thomson, James 671–2, 673, 675, 695, 724
Throckmorton, Elizabeth 244, 738
Thyer, Robert 647
Thynne, William 559
Tighe, Mary 677
Tillyard, E. M. W. 746
Tilmouth, Christopher 770*n*
Time 163, 169, 199, 202–3, 213, 275, 277, 283, 295,
    341–2, 538–52
Timings, E. K. 24, 27, 112, 472
Titus 498
Tobit 488
Todd, H. J. 132, 133, 134, 142, 464, 637, 638, 649,
    650–1, 652, 678
Tomson, Laurence 485–6
Tonson, publishing house 647, 669–70
Tottel, Richard 589, 725
Tours (France) 16
Towry, M. H. 654
Travers, John 22
Tremellius, Immanuel 486, 496
Tresham, Sir Thomas 473, 474, 477
Trevor, Douglas 776, 779, 780
Trinity College, Dublin 40
Trissino, Giangiorgio 454
Trollope, Anthony 39
Tromly, Fred B. 251
Troy 174, 211, 289, 290, 373, 412, 506, 510, 516, 517,
    543, 560, 569*n*, 597, 629, 637, 786
    see also Homer; Virgil
Troynovant 290, 506, 786
Trumball, William 324
Tudor dynasty 211, 543, 735, 748, 786
Turberville, George 17, 162, 167, 245, 589, 590
Turler, Jerome 18–19, 603, 616*n*

Turner, J. M. W. 713
Tuve, Rosemond 520, 690, 715n, 727, 747, 781
twentieth-century criticism (Spenserian) 135–9, 279–80, 696–705, 744–8, 765, 776–91
Tynte, Robert 24
Tyrone, see O'Neill, Hugh, Earl of

Uniformity, Act of 31–3, 37, 45
Upton, John 130, 131, 637–8, 648, 649, 650, 651, 658n, 741, 746
Ussher, James, Archbishop of Armagh 646
Uther Pendragon 542

Valeriano, Ionne Pierio 442, 443
Valla, Giorgio 404
Vallans, William 353
Valois dynasty 629
Van den Berg, Kent T. 228
Van der Noot, Jan 156, 157, 358, 473, 602
Van Dorsten, J. A. 110, 150, 153
Van Es, Bart 155, 239, 278, 284, 355, 735
Variorum Edition (Johns Hopkins University Press) 1, 7–8, 188, 194n, 247–9, 326–7, 577, 740–1, 743, 746–7
Varisco, Giovanni 117
Vecchi, Linda M. 222
Vestiarian controversy 35, 38
Vickers, Sir Brian 242, 432
Vickers, Nancy J. 261, 763
Victoria, Queen of England 712
Victorian criticism (Spenserian) 132–4, 741–4
Vida, Girolamo 408
Vincent, Henry 27
Vindiciae Contra Tyrannos 51, 53–4
Virgil 1, 3, 138, 211, 241, 448, 574, 670
    Aeneid 6, 24, 165, 198, 211, 241, 242, 249, 285, 297, 396, 397, 399, 410, 411, 412, 414, 415, 426, 434–5, 449, 450, 451, 453, 456, 470, 539, 542, 544
    Culex and Virgil's gnat 1, 114, 125, 150, 220, 227–8, 358, 408–9, 506, 671
    Eclogues 1, 5, 24, 165, 172, 174, 238, 248, 407, 426, 431, 450, 452, 454, 465, 467, 470, 580, 581, 583
    influence on ES 220, 223, 232, 404–5, 423, 426, 429, 431, 453, 503, 504–5, 542, 544, 587, 590, 734
visual arts 684–714
    see also illustration; woodcuts

Waldegrave, Robert 118
Wales 211, 542
Walker, Julia M. 776, 788
Walker, Thomas 27
Walkley, Thomas 642
Waller, Gary 139, 140

Wallop, Sir Henry 20, 70, 75, 76, 92
Walpole, Sir Robert 670, 696
Walsingham, Frances, Countess of Essex 238, 253, 320
Walsingham, Sir Francis 25, 56, 66, 68–72, 78, 75, 79–83, 109, 113, 119, 220
Walton, Kristin P. 751
Warde, Ralph 27
Ware, Sir James 7, 120, 129, 314, 325, 326, 327, 355, 641–2, 645, 646, 678, 738–9
Warren, Kate M. 274
Warton, Thomas 8, 367, 562, 637, 642, 649, 650
Warwick, Countess of, see Russell, Anne
Waterhouse, Edward 75, 82
Waterson, Simon 120
Watkins, John 512, 611
Watson, Thomas 245, 259, 269
Watt, G. F. 713
Watts, Thomas 15
Weatherby, Harold 486, 528
Webbe, William 163, 170, 352–3, 386, 467, 587, 588
Weinberg, Bernard 410, 454, 72
Weiner, Seth 385
Wells, Robin Headlam 751
Wentworth, Sir Thomas 324
West, Gilbert 637, 670, 671
Westfall, Richard 698
Westminster Abbey 125
White, Nicholas 76
Whitgift, John, Archbishop of Canterbury 40, 93, 117
Whitney, Geoffrey 114, 312n, 513, 613–14, 475
Whore of Babylon 42, 156, 486, 488, 511
Wiggins, Peter D. 605, 607, 608, 612
William of Occam 151
William of Orange 622
Williams, William Proctor 657
Wilson, Calvin Dill 654
Wilson, Elkin Calhoun 496
Wilson, John 653
Wilson, Richard 27
Wilson, Thomas 65, 369–70, 425, 428, 719
Wilson Knight, G. 757, 770n
Wilson-Okamura, D. S. 400n, 728, 740
Wind, Edgar 759
Windet, John 118, 120
Winnicott, D. W. 787
Winstanley, Lilian 659n, 745
Wither, George 239, 376, 645, 666
Wolfe, John 118, 120, 455, 526
Wolsey, Thomas, Cardinal 88
Wood, John 17
woodcuts 16, 109, 117, 149, 154–5, 163–5i, 219, 230, 463–4, 469, 566–7, 638, 640, 679, 684, 688, 690–5, 699–707
Woods, Susanne 390, 401, 765

Woods-Marsden, Joanna 463
Woolf, Daniel 545
Worcester, Earl of *see* Somerset, Edward
Worden, Blair 48, 62&*n*, 93, 150
Wordsworth, William 132, 376, 651, 666, 672–5
Wotton, James 16
Wright, Thomas 778
Wroth, Mary 765
Wyatt, Sir Thomas 206, 374, 589, 590, 594
Wyclif, John 563
Wyon, William 712

Yamashita, Hiroshi 121, 643–4, 657
Yates, Frances 751

Yeats, William Butler 135, 136, 477, 678–9, 680,
    704, 792–3, 801, 802–3
Yellow Ford, Battle of 26
Youghal 112
Young, John, Bishop of Rochester 18, 40, 110,
    135, 722

Ziegler, Lee Woodward 714
Zim, Rivkah 487
Zurcher, Andrew 7, 14, 121, 320, 321,
    326–7, 377, 379, 381, 469, 643,
    644, 657
Zutphen, battle of 249
Zephir 308

Lightning Source UK Ltd.
Milton Keynes UK
UKHW030620120719
346031UK00003B/6/P